ISBN 978-0-428-70363-9
PIBN 10315466

Biographies and Portraits

...OF THE...

# Progressive Men of Iowa

Leaders in Business, Politics and the Professions

TOGETHER WITH
AN ORIGINAL AND AUTHENTIC

## History of the State

...BY..

Ex-Lieutenant-Governor B. F. Gue

Des Moines
Conaway & Shaw, Publishers
1899

PRESS OF
CONAWAY & SHAW
DES MOINES

# PREFACE

ITHIN the memory of the pioneer residents still living in Iowa, our home-land was in as wild and primitive a condition as are now the uttermost parts of Africa. Not a white or civilized human being had ever settled down to subdue its acres and call it home. It was inhabited by copper-colored savages without history and with meagre tradition.

In the short span of seventy years Iowa has been made the greatest in material productions of all the states of the great union, as it is one of the fairest in natural beauty.

All this has been accomplished by an industrious people, who have just reason for pride, not only in their material accomplishments, but in the fact that they have carried forward the state as well in all those elements—education, arts, sciences, moral and religious training—which go to make up the fully-developed, rounded, manly character.

Yet with all this—while we have accumulated much historical and biographical material—we have been somewhat careless and regardless in the matter of its crystallization into an authentic and consecutive history.

The pioneers who have made this history are rapidly passing away, and with them all opportunity to winnow out the chaff of error and fiction from the genuine, first history of Iowa.

With the humble desire to rescue and record the essentials of this history, the publishers have directed the preparation of this work.

Their object was to be secured in two ways: First, through the labor to this end, of many years, on the part of ex-Lieut.-Gov. B. F. Gue. He is conceded by all familiar with Iowa to be best fitted to prepare such history. A pioneer editor, a legislator, and man of affairs in the crystallization of the elements into a state, he early became a collector of the materials for Iowa history.

The publishers have reason to congratulate themselves and their patrons upon securing his first systematic and comprehensive work. It is necessarily condensed, yet it is the most pretentious and extended, if not the only, history of Iowa yet completed and offered to the public.

Governor Gue has material gathered for many volumes, and purposes, *Deo volente*, the publication, later, of a more exhaustive work.

On this account, and for the further reason that some of the pirates of letters have been waiting for the publication of this volume, to prepare from it school "histories of Iowa," to be issued by school-book publishers, the whole has been copyrighted, and all infringements will be exposed and punished.

The second essential of this pioneer history of Iowa was to be secured in perhaps quite as interesting and valuable a form, by gathering and recording the personal reminiscences, the biographies of the pioneers and of the progressive men who are now making Iowa history.

We have not sought these to swell the pride of men, but to leave in the public and private libraries of Iowa records of the state makers.

Iowans are a thrifty people. Where history or pedigree has a commercial value we are keen to procure and preserve it.

On a preliminary survey it was found that the people who left the older states and communities and homes to rough it in the west, were so engrossed with exciting contests, cares and duties that they largely lost sight of family lines and lineage. Many of the progressive men of Iowa found, on examination, that they had fuller pedigrees of some of their domestic animals—going back dozens of generations to the old continent—than they could gather of their own children.

The desire to re-awaken an interest among our people in the re-establishment of their lines of family ancestry, and to put such genealogies as can be secured, in permanent record form, for the benefit of succeeding generations, is the second essential motive of this work.

Our success has been gratifying beyond our most ambitious hopes.

There is no human product beyond criticism, but we feel that the two volumes here presented maintain a high standard.

The second volume will immediately follow the first.

Every person of state-wide acquaintance will find herein a large percentage of familiar names and faces. It is not beyond the range of possibility that,—exalted as some of our citizens are in national fame and personal character,—the differentiation of the coming years may bring into equal prominence some of the faces included in this work, who are now less conspicuous. Who can tell? There are none better than Iowa's sons.

The labor involved in these volumes has been beyond all expectation or calculation, requiring the full time of many persons for more than two years. Trusting the result may be regarded as commensurate with the effort and cost, we beg the pleasure of subscribing ourselves,      Your friends,

                                        F. R. CONAWAY,
                                        A. B. SHAW.

# INDEX

# HISTORICAL SKETCH OF IOWA.

BY EX-LIEUT.-GOVERNOR B. F. GUE.

## CHAPTER I.

*Early Explorers of the Mississippi Valley—De Soto's Expedition, 1539-1543; Claude Allonez, 1669—Father Jacques Marquette and Louis Joliet Discover Iowa in 1673; Hennepin and La Salle, 1680-1682.*

Bounded on the east and west by the two greatest rivers of the North American continent, Iowa and her people are closely identified with the interests and history of the great Mississippi valley. The mighty river which flows along our eastern shore drains the most fertile agricultural region in the world.

The great river was discovered by the expedition fitted out by Governor Hernando De Soto, of Spain, who had won fame under Pizarro in his conquest of Peru. De Soto was a favorite of Charles V, and easily procured from the Spanish monarch a grant of eastern Florida and the appointment as governor of Cuba. He was authorized to explore the unknown country of the far west.

When it became known that De Soto was fitting out an expedition to explore and conquer a region supposed to be rich in gold mines, men of wealth, soldiers of fortune, young and ambitious cavaliers and nobles of high rank flocked to his standard. Visions of wealth and position in the new country dazzled their imagination and they hastened to join the great expedition. De Soto and many of his enthusiastic followers invested their entire fortunes in the alluring enterprise.

Nine hundred and fifty picked men were chosen from the thousands who volunteered, and he embarked his army on ten vessels and sailed for Cuba to complete his preparations. Here he swelled his ranks to 1,000 infantry and 350 cavalry. Priests, miners and artisans joined him; live stock and implements for founding colonies; chains, fetters and bloodhounds were provided for the enslavement of the Indians; coats of mail, helmets and breast-plates shielded his soldiers for battle with the natives; and the best arms and equipments for all were provided.

The expedition embarked from Havana on the 12th of May, 1539, gaily as a pleasure party, little dreaming of the awaiting fate. It was a roving band of gallant freebooters in quest of plunder and fortune; an army rendered cruel and ferocious

by avarice, ready to march to any point with slaughter where they might suppose an Indian village was stored with gold. They plunged into the wild forests and trackless swamps of eastern Florida.

For a year they were wandering among the fierce Seminoles, fighting, plundering, destroying. Their captives craftily led them through dismal, tangled forests into impassable swamps, where the stealthy warriors harassed them day and night. The Seminoles fiercely defended their homes against the cruel invaders. But still the freebooters pressed on until they reached the Cherokee country of Georgia, leaving a bloody trail and burning villages in their path. On the Alabama river the Indians had gathered a large army to make a stand against the destroyers of their homes, and a desperate battle took place. The Spanish lost heavily in killed and wounded and the Indians burned most of their baggage.

They still pushed on into Mississippi, where they met savage resistance, losing in battle many men and horses and most of their armor and clothing. Everywhere they robbed and slaughtered the natives and mutilated them with the fierce bloodhounds.

In April, 1541, they had reached a large Indian village called Chisca, on the banks of a majestic river, the largest by far they had ever seen. They stood upon its low banks and gazed out upon its turbid waters sweeping southward with resistless power, bearing upon its bosom great trees uprooted by its mighty current. Its great width and depth were barriers to their further progress. They camped upon its shore and named it the "Rio Grande."

Their ranks were decimated by battles, sickness and death from exposure. They were but a forlorn remnant of the grand expedition that two years before had started out to conquer and plunder the Indian country. Their search for gold had been in vain. Their long line of march was marked by graves of those who had perished on the way. Exhausted by suffering, harassed by hostile Indians, thousands of miles from home or help, their spirits were broken and they would gladly have turned back.

But De Soto had invested all he possessed in the enterprise, his fortune and fame, and nothing but gold and the establishment of a Spanish colony could save him. He could not consent to abandon all and barely escape broken in fortune, reputation and health. He stood on the bank of the mighty river, late into the night, trying to solve the desperate problem before him. There was one more possible chance to find the gold fields west of the Rio Grande. In the morning his stern command was issued to his artisans to build boats to convey his depleted army across the river.

From descriptions they gave of the country it is supposed that his place of crossing was near the northwest corner of the state of Mississippi. Here were embarked on the waters of the greatest river of the continent the first boats of white men that ever sailed on the Mississippi. The fame of De Soto will live in history as its discoverer.

All his dreams of wealth, power and fame vanished as he led his men westward still, to the plains of Kansas, in the vain search. When every hope had vanished and half of his army had perished, in despair he turned back. He would plant a colony on the great river and send a few of his trusted officers in vessels, to be built, down to the sea, and on to Cuba for supplies and reinforcements, while he remained to select the site for a city and colony.

Arriving at the Mississippi again, the building of the brigantines was begun. The Indians gathered about and harassed them night and day. Disease was rapidly depleting their ranks, and De Soto was at last stricken down with fever.

In delirium he talked wildly of his accumulated disappointments and disasters until death forever closed his lips. The survivors gathered sadly about the cold form of their stern leader while the priests chanted over his remains a requiem—the first ever heard on the banks of the Mississippi. To conceal his death from the hostile Indians, his comrades made an excavation in a green oak log, enclosed the body in it, at midnight rowed out into the middle of the great river and sunk the rude coffin beneath the murky waters. As long as the waters of the great river wash the Iowa shore, the tragic romance of the discoverer of the mighty Mississippi will be read with interest by the generations as they come and go.

The ambitious schemes and cruel march of the remorseless Spaniard came to naught, and a terrible retribution quickly overtook him and defeated all of his plans. But his name is linked with the great river of the continent forever, in a way that he never could foresee.

After months of wandering, suffering and despair

among the trackless forests and over wild prairies, De Soto's surviving comrades were reduced in numbers to 350. These finally constructed seven boats and on the 2d of July, 1543, they embarked and sailed down the Mississippi, where no white man had ever sailed before. After unparalleled suffering, in which 100 more perished, the remnant at last reached a Mexican settlement. Of the 1,300 who sailed five years before, with wild visions of wealth and glory, but 250 survived to reach their homes. The thousands of Indians slaughtered, and villages desolated, the unsurpassed cruelties which marked their bloody march, had all been fearfully avenged, when these ragged, woe-begone, half demented wrecks of men reached the shores of Spain to recount the horrors of the five years wanderings.

## II.

The next white men who saw the Mississippi river were some French gold seekers from a colony that had been planted in Florida in 1565, but no settlement was attempted in the region of the Mississippi.

More than 130 years elapsed after the discovery of the Mississippi river by De Soto before an effort was made by any white man to explore the valley. The French had gradually been extending a chain of settlements along the St. Lawrence river, and westward around the Great Lakes.

The pioneers in these westward movements were Jesuit priests, who led the way into remote regions among the most warlike tribes of Indians. In 1669 Father Claude Allonez, a French missionary, penetrated the great forests through Canada to the shore of Lake Superior, and learned from some members of a remote western tribe of Indians that there was a great river in the far west called, by the Indians, Mis-sis-se-pe or "Great River." They said that no white man had ever been seen in that region. The valley of this great river was described as divided into dense forests and vast meadows covered with tall grass. The Indian name, Mis-sis, signified meadow, and the word se-pe means river; hence Mis sis-se-pe, as some early French writers spell it, signifies "River of the Meadows." It was first supposed that the "Great River" flowed westward towards the Pacific ocean, and would afford the long sought for direct and short route to India and China.

The nations of western Europe had, since the discovery of America, expected to find a direct water route to China, and it was believed it would now be found through the great river of which the Indians had often spoken.

In the Jesuit Revelations given by Father Claude Dablon in 1670-71, in speaking of the Illini Indians, he says:

"These people were the first to trade with the French at Green Bay. They live in the midst of

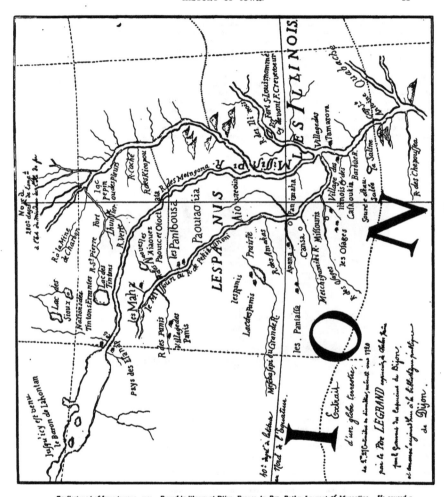

Earliest map of Iowa terrene—1720. Found in library at Dijon, France, by Rev. Father Laurent, of Muscatine. He caused a copy to be preserved in the Iowa Historical Department. A line drawn horizontally, above the words "Paoute et Otoctata," from the Missouri to the Mississippi, and another, parallel, below the words "Aio vreoiis," includes, approximately, the land forming Iowa. It will be seen that they had a magnified idea of the Des Moines river (R. des Moingona), making it the main stream, and heading it in great northern lakes.

a beautiful country, away south towards a great river named Mis-sis-sep-pe. It takes its rise far in the north, flowing towards the south, discharges itself in the sea. That the great country through which it flows is prairie without trees. It is beyond this river that the Illini's live, and from which are detached the Mes-co-tins—which signifies a land bare of trees."

It does not seem to have been suspected by any of the early French writers or explorers that this was the great river—Rio Grande—discovered by De Soto more than a hundred years before.

Father Jacques Marquette, a French Jesuit, who was then a missionary among the Huron Indians, had in 1669 determined to explore the far west to

missionary, for many years, built up little churches among them, learned their language and endeared himself to the natives by his kindness to them during a long period of friendly intercourse. An intelligent and experienced trader of Quebec, Louis Joliet, was selected by M. Talon to accompany Marquette. Five other Frenchmen were chosen to make up the party, and on the 13th of May, 1673, they embarked from Michlimacinac, in two birch canoes on the voyage of exploration.

They sailed on Green Bay to the mouth of the Fox river, and ascending that stream some distance they found a village of Miami and Kickapoo Indians. This was the extreme western limit of explorations made by the French, and Marquette here engaged

*The first spot in Iowa seen by Joliet and Marquette, near McGregor.*

the great river and had secured the co-operation of M. Talon, the French intendent, to aid him in fitting out an exploring expedition. Father Marquette, who was a man of great intelligence and energy, in order to prepare himself for the enterprise, had selected as a companion, a young Illini Indian to aid him in learning the language of that tribe, so that he might be able to converse with the nation supposed to inhabit a large portion of the country contiguous to the great river.

It was not until 1673 that the expedition was ready to embark upon its perilous enterprise. Father Marquette had traveled thousands of miles among the Indians, far in advance of white settlements. He had lived and labored among them as a

some Miami guides to pilot them to the Wisconsin river. The guides then returned home and left the fearless explorers to find their way through the unknown region into which they had now entered.

Floating down the Wisconsin for many days they finally emerged into the great river they had sought for. It was a majestic stream, the western shore of which arose in high, abrupt bluffs, covered with forests. It was on the 17th day of June, 1673, when they looked out upon the rugged shores of the Iowa of the future.

They were its discoverers, as no white man had ever before seen the upper Mississippi river and shores. They floated out on the broad bosom of the great river of the continent and drifted along with its mighty current that swept the eastern shore of Iowa.

The point first seen was a few miles below McGregor, in the present county of Clayton. They landed some miles down the river and ascended the Iowa bluffs to get a view of the new country they had discovered. Forests shut off the western outlook, but over on the Wisconsin side, they could see miles of beautiful meadow land, stretching out toward a high range of hills in the distance. Prairie du Chien has since been built on this broad prairie. Some glimpses could be seen of a vast expanse of rolling prairie, that extended westward beyond the bluffs by the vast stretches of bottom-lands on which herds of deer, elk and buffalo were grazing. But not a human being had yet been seen.

They passed over the rapids of the beautiful Rock Island, by the long, low, prairie of Muscatine island, down by the flint hills of Burlington, and, on the 25th of June landed on the west shore of the river, where they discovered footprints in the sand. Leaving the boats in care of the men, the two leaders followed a path leading westward, and kept on for five or six miles, when they reached an Indian village. It stood on the banks of another river, much smaller than the Mississippi, the water

*A bend in the Mississippi, south of Lansing—A raft on its way down the river.*

bluffs. The air was laden with the perfume of wild vegetation, and gentle breezes were sweeping over the landscape, the most beautiful the voyagers had ever looked upon. The silence of a vast uninhabited region pervaded the whole country around. Not a human being nor an animal was in sight, and the only sound that reached their ears was the ripple of the waters of the great river below, and the rustle of the breeze among the leaves of forest trees.

Iowa was at that time as wild and unexplored as central Africa. For many days the voyagers floated down the current of the great river, passing by the bluffs of Dubuque, looking off over the wide-spreading prairies of the Illinois side; gliding along of which was clear and rapid. The banks were low, shaded by forest trees.

The Indians of the village seemed greatly astonished, as they approached, for it is presumable they had never before seen a white man. Soon, however, they made signs of friendship, and offered the Frenchmen the pipe of peace. They were found to be a band of the Illini tribe, and had two other villages a few miles distant. Marquette was able to converse with them, and learned that the river near their villages was called the Mon-in-go-na. He explained to them the object of their voyage, and his pleasure in meeting the natives of this beautiful country. The Indians gave them a cordial welcome and they were invited to a feast which had been prepared for them. They had fish, corn meal pudding and roast buffalo meat.

Marquette and Joliet were so charmed with the beauty of the country that they remained five days with the hospitable Indians, who devoted their time to entertaining their stranger guests. When they could not be prevailed upon to stay longer, more than 600 of the Indians accompanied the explorers to their canoes and regretfully bade them goodbye as they pushed their frail boats out into the swift current of the great river.

The exact location of the point on the Mississippi shore, where Marquette and his party landed to visit these Indians, is not certainly known, but from the brief description given, nearly all writers

prairie, woodland and unbridged creeks and rivers. The race who possessed the land had but few wants, which were generously supplied by the wild game and fruit that abounded on land, and the fish that swarmed in rivers and lakes. It was a paradise for the red men, who had for unnumbered generations lived and died undisturbed by civilization.

When Father Marquette took his departure, the Illini chief presented him with a pipe of peace, the sacred calumet ornamented with brilliant feathers, which, suspended from his neck, was to be a safeguard among the strange tribes that he might encounter on his voyage down the great river. The next day they passed the mouth of the Des

*A Crow Indian's grave.*

agree that it must have been near where Montrose now stands, in Lee county, near the head of the lower rapids. The report which Joliet wrote of their voyage was most unfortunately lost by the capsizing of his canoe while on his return to Quebec, and all that he said of Iowa and this most interesting expedition was destroyed.

It was more than 200 years ago that this first glimpse of Iowa was given to the world. No plow had ever turned a furrow on its virgin soil; the sound of firearms had never echoed among its groves and valleys. Its vast, natural meadows were covered with a carpet of waving grass, intermingled with myriads of brilliant wild flowers, radiant in the glow of a July sunlight. Nature here ruled supreme over the broad expanse of

Moines river, named by the Indians the Mon-in-go-na, signifying "the road."

They sailed by the mouth of an immense, muddy river, which they named the Pe-ki-ta-no-ni [Missouri] and passed the mouth of the Ohio, called by the Indians the "Beautiful River."

Day after day they floated down the great river, which had now broadened to double the size it was where they first entered upon it. Its shores now became low and swampy, and in places it was many miles in width, where it spread its mighty volume of water out over the lowlands through which it flowed. Dense canebrakes shut them in at times; the heat became very oppressive and the swarms of insects intolerable.

Reaching latitude 33°, they came upon an Indian village of the fierce Michigames, whose traditions told them of the barbarities inflicted upon their ancestors by De Soto's army more than 130 years before. When Marquette's little party of seven approached, in their two canoes, the natives, armed, advanced upon them in their war canoes, brandishing their weapons. The brave Marquette, unawed by the threatened danger, coolly approached them, holding aloft the sacred calumet. Seeing the token of peace, the chief restrained his warriors, extended to the strangers the hand of friendship, and invited them to the village, where they were treated with cordial hospitality for several days.

Again, embarking with a fresh supply of food, they descended to the village of Ak-an-sea, beyond the limits of the Algonquin dialect. Here, by means of an interpreter, they learned from the Indians the course of the river below, and the distance to the sea. They were near the mouth of the Arkansas river, and learned that the great river, upon which they had sailed more than 1,100 miles, emptied into the Gulf of Mexico.

During their long voyage Marquette and Joliet had each made sketches of the course of the river and its tributaries, and from these were afterwards engraved the first maps of the Mississippi and its branches from the mouth of the Wisconsin to the Arkansas. As the survivors of De Soto's party had sailed from here to its mouth, the whole course of the river from Wisconsin to its termination in the Gulf had now been explored.

From here they turned back and, beneath the burning sun of the far south, began the hard labor of rowing against the current on the return voyage. They finally reached the mouth of the Illinois river, ascended it, and crossed over to the Chicago, and into Lake Michigan.

The news of their great voyage, the vast region explored, filled all of New France with rejoicings, as, by right of discovery, all of the vast region embraced in the Mississippi valley, north of the Arkansas, belonged to France.

Thus, Iowa from this time became a part of the French dominion of America. Marquette had found the Indians then occupying what has since become the states of Wisconsin, Iowa, Illinois, Kentucky, Missouri, Tennessee and Arkansas, to be similar in all respects to the tribes along the St. Lawrence and the great lakes. The Algonquin tongue, which was spoken along the St. Lawrence and over to the Des Moines, was most widely diffused. At this time, 1673, Illinois contained but five or six Indian villages, and Marquette only found one village in traversing the entire river boundary of eastern Iowa.

It is not creditable that Iowa has done nothing to commemorate the memory of Father Marquette, who planned, organized and conducted the daring, and, at that time, most perilous enterprise which discovered our beautiful land, explored its eastern shores, first made known to the world its existence, and discovered the upper Mississippi river. We have towns, counties and rivers named for Indians, Mexican battlefields, and ordinary men, but seem to have forgotten or ignored the great explorer who discovered our magnificent domain 115 years before the first white man settled within its limits, — Father Marquette.

Louis Hennepin was the next to lead an exploring expedition from the mouth of the Illinois river up the Mississippi along the eastern shore of Iowa, in 1680. He ascended the great river to St. Anthony's Falls, thus first exploring that portion of the Iowa shore above McGregor.

La Salle, another French explorer, finished the exploration of the lower Mississippi to its mouth in 1682.

De Soto, its first discoverer, named the Mississippi river the "Rio Grande;" Marquette, the discoverer of the upper Mississippi, named it the "Conception;" Hennepin called it the "Colbert;" La Salle named it the "Great River," while the Indians had given it the name Mis-sis-se-pe. Posterity has united in preserving, with a slight change in orthography, the original Indian name.

In 1702 Lesueur, with a party, ascended the Mississippi, sailing along the entire eastern border of Iowa and up the St. Peter's river, where he erected a fort and formally took possession of the vast region now embraced in the states of Iowa, Minnesota and the Dakotas.

The great war between England and France, which prevailed from 1756 to 1763, gave England all of the vast French possessions in America east of the Mississippi river, except a portion of Louisiana, but Iowa still remained in the French possessions. It is one portion of the United States which never passed under the government of Great Britain. Soon after the close of the seven years' war between England and France, the king of the latter country, by secret treaty, ceded all of the remainder of the French possessions in America to Spain, and Iowa passed under the dominion of the Spanish government.

During the eighty years that the territory embraced in Iowa had belonged to France, no permanent settlement had been made within its limits. French hunters and trappers had explored its rivers in search of furs and game, and had given names to some of them, but no other mark of their occupation remained.

## CHAPTER II.

*Origin of the Prairies—Professor Hall—The Mound Builders—Iowa Indian Tribes: Mascoutines, Iowas, Sac and Foxes, Winnebagoes, Pottawattamies, Dakotas.*

Prairie is a French word signifying meadow, and was the name first applied to the great treeless plains of North America by the French, who were the discoverers of the prairie region of the upper Mississippi valley. East of Ohio prairies are unknown, and as we go westward they increase in number and size until western Indiana is reached, from whence they broaden out and possess almost the entire country from there to the Rocky mountains. Iowa was formerly a vast prairie with the exception of the region bordering on some of its rivers and creeks and in the northeastern portion of the state. The soil of the prairies varies as much in quality, color and formation, as in the forest regions. In Indiana, Michigan and Illinois, the prairies are inclined to be quite level, the surface soil, black vegetable mold. In Iowa, Kansas, Nebraska and the Dakotas, the surface is generally rolling and in some sections decidedly hilly. Large bodies of broken land in places extend back from the water courses, originally covered with hazel brush and scattering trees called "barrens."

While Iowa was largely prairie in early days, almost every variety of surface soil is found, showing conclusively that it is not the peculiar soil formation that causes forests to grow in some portions and vast treeless prairies to prevail in other localities. Professor Hall, who made a geological survey of a portion of the state before much of its surface was disturbed by the plow, in discussing the various theories of the origin of the prairies, arrives at the following conclusions: "If we go into the thickly wooded regions of northern Michigan and examine those portions of the surface which have not been invaded by forests, we observe that the beds of ancient lakes which have been filled by the slowest possible accumulations of detrital matter and are now dry, remain as natural prairies and are not trespassed on by the surrounding woods. We can conceive of no other reason for this than the extreme fineness of the soil which occupies the basins, and which is the natural result of the slow and quiet mode in which they have been filled up. We find these natural meadows covered with a most luxuriant crop of grass. Applying these facts to the case of the prairies of larger dimensions further south, we infer on what seems to be reasonable grounds that the whole region now occupied by the prairies of the northwest was once an immense lake into whose basin a sediment

of almost impalpable fineness gradually accumulated; that this basin was drained by the elevation of the whole region, but at first so slowly that the finer particles of the superficial deposits were not washed away but allowed to remain where they were originally deposited. After the more elevated portions of the former basin had been laid bare, the drainage became concentrated in comparatively narrow channels, the current thus produced acquired sufficient velocity to wear down through the finer materials in the surface, washing away portions of it altogether, and mixing the rest so effectually with the underlying drift materials as to give rise to the different character of soil in the valleys from that of the elevated lands. This valley soil containing a larger proportion of coarse materials than that of the upland, seems to have been adapted to the growth of forest vegetation. In consequence of this we find such localities covered with an abundant growth of timber. We sometimes meet with ridges of coarse material, apparently of drift deposits, on which from some cause there has never been an accumulation of fine sediment. In such localities we invariably find a growth of timber. This is the origin of the groves scattered over the prairies, for whose isolated position and peculiar circumstances of growth we are unable to account in any other way." Other writers hold that the prairie region was once submerged and attribute the drainage to slow upheavals of the land, which in time caused the water to find its way to the ocean, wearing great channels through the soil and rocks, thus forming the valleys that are now found along the water courses, not only of the great rivers, but of creeks which were but arms of the great rivers when this vast inland sea was expelled towards the ocean.

During some of these periods, glaciers from the north helped to grind down the higher points of land and as the glaciers melted they deposited foreign bits of rock, pebbles and even some great granite boulders, from northern geological formations, over most of the surface of the state. Geologists tell us this glacial grinding down did not cover all the surface but left untouched a small area in northeastern Iowa, covering Allamakee county and portions of Winneshiek, Clayton and Dubuque. Here may be seen almost the only markedly varied and romantic scenery of the state, termed by some the "Switzerland of Iowa."

It is probable the long continuance of the treeless condition of portions of the bed of the vast inland sea has, in recent ages, been owing to the fires set out by the Indians, which have annually swept over the great plains and destroyed tree growth. There can be no doubt that the conditions of the soil for several hundred years have been such that trees would have encroached and grown up on the prairies if not destroyed by fires. How old the prairies are; how many thousand years ago the great inland sea was drained, can only be conjectured. But that a race of people lived here before the Indians appeared, is now generally conceded. The work of that race is found in many parts of Iowa in the earth mounds and defenses that were made by them, and the skulls and human

## MOUND BUILDERS

were dispossessed of Iowa, by the Indians, at a remote age. Where the Indians came from is not known. But it is supposed, by some writers, that the fierce Dakotas crossed the Rocky mountains in great numbers and gradually exterminated the less warlike Mound Builders, many generations before Iowa was discovered by Marquette and Joliet. When Iowa was first explored by the whites, the Dakotas were found in possession of Minnesota and northern Iowa, while the Algonquins occupied southern Iowa and northern Missouri. The Algonquins were divided into tribes known as Illinois, Sauks, Foxes, Chippeways, Ottawas and Pottawatamies. The tribes of the Dakota family found in

*Oneota Bluff, near New Albin. (The crest is four hundred and twenty feet above grade of railway at the base. On the very highest crest there is a row of prehistoric mounds.)*

bones found preserved in the mounds. There is evidence that the great prairies have been in many places covered with a growth of forest since the mound builders disappeared. There are along the Des Moines and other rivers, earthworks made by the mound builders upon which immense trees have grown and large forests have appeared.

## IOWA INDIAN TRIBES.

When the whites first began to look with longing eyes upon the Indian country west of the Mississippi river, which afterwards became known as Iowa, it was peopled by many powerful tribes of Indians. It is generally believed that the earliest known inhabitants of Iowa and the west, called the

the upper Mississippi valley were the Iowas, Omahas, Winnebagoes, Osages, Sissetons, Missouris and Otoes.

## THE MASCOUTINES.

This tribe, which was first mentioned by Father Allonez in 1670, as found in the valley of the Wisconsin river, afterwards moved over into Iowa. They were on friendly terms with Illini Indians, and were occupying a portion of Iowa west of Muscatine island, where they located after being driven out of Wisconsin by hostile tribes. The Mascoutines built a village on Muscatine Island, which was a level prairie, embracing about 20,000 acres. They were a fierce, warlike tribe and fought frequent battles with the Sacs and Foxes, long before Iowa was explored by white men. A long time ago a large party of Sacs and Foxes was descending the

Mississippi in a fleet of canoes, and when near the mouth of the Iowa river they were attacked by the Mascoutines. A desperate conflict ensued, lasting all day, when, the Sacs and Foxes, being outnumbered, were compelled to turn back. The Mascoutines took to their canoes and assailed the retreating enemy by land and water and nearly exterminated them. But one-quarter of the Sacs and Foxes escaped slaughter. After living many years near where Muscatine now stands, the tribe became weakened by wars and finally merged with some other nation. Long before the first white settlers came to Iowa the Mascoutines had disappeared.

### THE IOWAS.

The Iowa Indians were first mentioned in 1690, when they were found in the vicinity of the Great Lakes. Many years later they moved west of the

Sioux and Osages. In about 1810 the smallpox ravaged their villages and swept off more than 300 of them. Twelve years later 200 more of them perished by the same disease. In 1819 they were attacked by a large band of Sioux warriors, vanquished and many of their best warriors slain, and a large number of their women carried into captivity. Ma-has-ka was one of their most noted chiefs when they lived in Iowa

The last great battle between the Iowas and Sacs and Foxes was fought near the old town of Iowaville, in about the year 1824. The Iowas had assembled in great numbers to have a horse race on the river bottom. The Sac and Fox chiefs, Pash-e-pa-ho and young Black Hawk, led their warriors in the battle. They secreted their warriors in the dense forest and when the unarmed Iowas were in the midst of their exciting sport, their enemies rushed

*"The Switzerland of Iowa" (northeast). The waterfall of the Devil's Den, four miles south of Waukon. The water issues from a cavern in the face of a bluff.*

Mississippi river and established their villages along the valley of the Iowa river, giving to that stream its name. They were first called by the early explorers, the Ayouways; in later years, the Ioways and, finally the name was written Iowas, with accent on the I. Antoine Le Claire, the well known half-breed of French and Indian parentage, defines the meaning of the word Iowa to be, "this is the place." The Iowas moved from the Great Lakes in about the year 1693 to the mouth of the Rock river, and afterwards over to the Iowa. From there they went to the Des Moines valley and built villages in the limits of the counties of Davis, Wapello and Van Buren. Many years later they made a long journey through western Iowa, up the Missouri valley into Dakota, extending their hunting excursions over to the Little Sioux and Okoboji and Spirit lakes. They had frequent wars with the

upon them with terrific war-whoop. The Iowa warriors made a dash for the village where their arms had been left. But there they encountered young Black Hawk, with his band, burning the village and slaughtering the people. After a desperate struggle the Iowas who survived the massacre were compelled to surrender. By this disaster the power of the Iowas was broken and the renown of the once powerful tribe departed. They moved from place to place for many years. In 1838 the Iowas sold their Iowa lands to the United States and settled west of the Missouri river. In 1891 they surrendered their tribal organization and accepted lands in severalty.

### SACS AND FOXES.

The Sacs called themselves Sau-kies, signifying "man with a red badge." Red was the favorite color used in adorning their persons. The Indian name of the Foxes was Mus-qua-kies, signifying "man with a yellow badge." These two tribes which were nearly related, in early times occupied the country near the mouth of the St. Lawrence river. In 1680 the Foxes were found near Green Bay, and in 1689, Sauk villages were found on the Fox river. The two tribes united while in that region, and together moved west into the valley of the Mississippi river. The united tribes now numbered about three thousand. In 1780 they are found in the vicinity of the lead mines of Galena and Dubuque. When Lieutenant Pike ascended the Mississippi in 1805, he found four Sac villages between the mouth of the Des Moines river and the mouth of the Turkey river. At this time the two tribes had about 1,100 warriors. The Sac village on the Rock river was one of the oldest in the upper Mississippi valley.

500 of his tribe held the village and lands on Rock river. In 1831, when Black Hawk and his band returned from a hunting excursion, they found their cabins had been seized and occupied by white men, who claimed their lands. Black Hawk drove the intruders off and restored the cabins to their owners. Governor Reynolds called upon General Gaines to expel the Indians, which he did with an army of 1,600 soldiers, driving the Indians over into Iowa. Black Hawk, with his band, returned in the spring to put in corn, to raise a crop for his people. Then began the Black Hawk war, which resulted in the slaughter of most of Black Hawk's band, men, women and children, and the capture of the old chief. Keokuk, who had consented to surrender their lands to the whites, now succeeded Black Hawk as chief.

On the 21st of September, 1832, Gen. Winfield

*Cascades in gorge at Pinney's Spring, six miles southeast of Waukon.*

Black Hawk, in his autobiography, states that it was built in 1731 and was named Saukenuk. This was by far the largest village of the Sacs and in 1825 had a population of not less than 8,000. In November, 1804, William H. Harrison, governor of Indiana Territory, negotiated a treaty with five Sac and Fox chiefs in which they were induced to agree to cede to the United States, 51,000,000 acres of their lands, embracing a region on the east side of the Mississippi, from St. Louis to the Wisconsin river. Black Hawk never agreed to this sale and repudiated the treaty, claiming the five chiefs had no authority to thus dispose of their lands In 1816, when the United States began to erect a fort on Rock Island, Black Hawk protested against it, but Keokuk, another chief, gave his consent and agreed to surrender all claim to the lands and move over to the west side of the river. But Black Hawk and

Scott and Governor Reynolds negotiated a treaty with the Sacs, Foxes and Winnebagoes by which there was ceded to the United States 6,000,000 acres of land on the west side of the Mississippi river, known as the "Black Hawk Purchase." The treaty was made on the ground where the city of Davenport now stands. The purchase embraced a strip of country north from the Missouri state line to the mouth of the Upper Iowa river, and extending west of the Mississippi, an average width of about fifty miles. There was reserved to the Sac and Foxes within the limits of the grant, 400 square miles of land along the Iowa river, including Keokuk's village. This tract was called "Keokuk's Reserve," and was occupied by the Indians until 1836, when it was sold to the United States. The Sacs and Foxes then moved to a reservation on the Des Moines river, where an agency was established for them on the site where Agency City stands. Here, Keokuk, Wapello and Appanoose, chiefs of the united tribes, each had a large farm. These farms were on what is known as Keokuk Prairie. Appanoose's farm included a portion of the ground upon which Ottumwa has been built. In October, 1842, another treaty was made with the Sac and Fox Indians in which they conveyed all of their

the Pottawattamies who first returned to the Iowa river. In 1859, Maw-me-wah-ne-kap, a Fox chief, with a number of his tribe, joined Johnny Green's band and all lived peaceably, cultivating some land, hunting and fishing for several years. In 1866 a special agent was appointed by the government, who paid them a share of the annuities due their tribe. Two thousand dollars of this money

BLACK HAWK.
*From an old colored lithograph in McKenney's and Hall's "History of the Indian Tribes," in the Historical Department of Iowa.*

remaining lands in Iowa to the United States. They vacated the last of them on the 11th of October, 1845, and moved to a reservation in Kansas. The Musquakies of Tama county are a remnant of the Foxes and Pottawattamies, who returned from Kansas about the year 1850. They were so much attached to Iowa that they persisted in staying. Che-me-use, or, "Johnny Green," was the chief of

was used to purchase lands in Tama county, and additions have been made to their farms from time to time until they have several thousand acres. In 1880 the band numbered 335 people. Their personal property was valued at $20,000. Their buildings are poor, resembling in style those of the wild tribes. The illustrations show their old chief, Ma-tau-E-qua, and their "wickiups."

### THE WINNEBAGOES.

This tribe belongs to the Dakota group and was known to the French as early as 1669. In 1766 they were living in the Rock river country. These and the Iowas are the only tribes of the Dakota nation known to have migrated to the east side of the Mississippi river. Meeting the Algonquin tribes of Pottawattamies, Chippeways, Sacs, Foxes, Mascoutines, and Ottawas, they finally formed an alliance south, with whom they were friendly. Their hunting grounds were along the Turkey, Wapsipinicon, and Cedar rivers. In October, 1846, they were induced to cede their Iowa lands to the government in exchange for a tract in Minnesota, north of the St. Peters river, to which they soon after removed. One of their most noted chiefs was Wee-no-shiek or Winneshiek, as it is now written. In the Winnebago war, in 1827, young Winneshiek took an active part. He was captured by Colonel Dodge, but

*POWESHIEK.*
*A chief of the Musquakies and a friend of Keokuk.*

with them which continued for more than 150 years. They joined the Pottawattamies in the massacre at Fort Dearborn in 1812, and with Black Hawk's band were allies of the British during that war. They were also allies of Black Hawk in his war in 1832, and at its close were required to leave their lands in Wisconsin and Illinois, and remove to Iowa, on what were called the neutral lands. Here they found themselves between the hostile Sioux on the north, and the Sacs and Foxes on the refused to surrender, and had to be forcibly disarmed. He fought bravely in the Black Hawk war in 1832, and was again taken prisoner by General Dodge. In 1845 he became head chief of the Winnebagoes. He was a fine specimen of the red man, both physically and intellectually; tall, well-proportioned and of dignified bearing, graceful in manners and a fearless warrior. He never became reconciled to the hard fate of his race to be continually dispossessed of their lands by the whites, and was their implacable foe to the end of his life. Waukon - Decorah, signifying White Snake, was another of the noted Winnebago chiefs. He was inclined to keep peace with the whites, as he realized that war upon a powerful government was useless. The village of his band was located on the Upper Iowa river, near the site of the town of Decorah, which bears his name. After his death the citizens of that village gave his remains a final resting place in the public square. In 1829 the Winnebagoes numbered 5,800. In 1836 the small-pox had destroyed one-fourth of their people. In 1855 they had become reduced to 275. When the Winnebagoes were first seen, by the French, they were of good stature, strong, athletic and dignified, with straight black hair, piercing black eyes, and superior mental capacity. But after generations of contact with the whites they had degenerated rapidly, having acquired a strong appetite for intoxicating liquors. They were not a quarrelsome people, and made war only to avenge wrongs inflicted upon members of their own tribe.

### THE POTTAWATTAMIES.

This tribe belonged to the Algonquin race, and was first seen by French missionaries near the northern limits of the Michigan peninsula. They were allies of the French in the war with England. They moved west and settled in Iowa. In 1825 they were parties to a treaty negotiated by Gov. William Clark to settle disputed boundaries among the tribes occupying Iowa. In 1829 they ceded to the United States a portion of their lands in Wisconsin and northern Illinois. In 1833 they ceded to the United States all of the remainder of their Michigan lands for 500,000 acres in southwestern Iowa, and in 1835 they moved to their new lands. An agency was established in what is now Mills county, at Traders' Point. At this place Col. Peter Sarpy, a French trader from St. Louis, for many years carried on trade with the Indians of that region. Another agency was established at Council Bluffs. One of the Pottawattamie villages was on the Nishnabatona river near Lewis, the old county seat of Cass county. Its Indian name was Mi-au-miee (Young Miami), after one of their chiefs, and here was located their largest burial ground. On the 5th of June, 1846, a treaty was made with the Pot-tawattamies by which they exchanged their Iowa lands for a reservation thirty miles square in the limits of Kansas, to which they removed. The French called these Indians Pouks and by that name they were designated on the early maps. The word Pottawattamie means "makers of fire." Their relations with the Ottawas and Chippeways were very intimate, as the language of the three tribes was substantially the same. In the transactions of important business their chiefs assembled around one council fire.

### THE DAKOTAS.

This nation occupied the upper Mississippi val-ley as early as in the sixteenth century. Their wanderings extended northward to latitude 55° in the Rocky mountains to the Red river of the north, southward along the headwaters of the Minnesota and east to the shores of Green Bay. In the Rocky mountains they were found as far south as the head-waters of the Arkansas, and down to the Red river of Louisiana and eastward to the Mississippi. The Sioux Indians belong to the great Dakota nation and were first known to the French in 1640. Dur-ing the wars between the French and some Indian

*Ma-Taw-E-Qua, a chief of the Sac and Fox tribes.*

tribes the Sioux were forced southward into the limits of northern Iowa, about the Okoboji and Spirit lakes. The branch of the Dakotas known as Sioux, was divided into five bands, called the Tetons, Yanktons, Sissetons, Mendawakantons and Wahpakootas. When Lewis and Clark explored the Missouri valley in 1804, the Yankton Sioux occupied the country along the Upper Des Moines and Little Sioux valleys, and about the group of lakes in northern Iowa and southern Minnesota. They had villages along the shores of Okoboji and Spirit lakes. Their name for the latter was Min-ne-Me-coe-he-Waukon, or lake of the Spirits. The Little Sioux river was called by the Indians Ea-ne-ah-wad-e-pon, signifying Stone river. It was so named from the fact that in the southern part of

Cherokee county is an immense red granite boulder projecting above the surface 20 feet, being about 60 feet long and 40 feet wide. It was called by the early settlers of that region, Pilot Rock. In 1805, Lieutenant Pike estimated the number of Sioux Indians at about 21,000. One of their most noted chiefs of the nineteenth century was Wa-ne-ta, of the Yanktons. He was instrumental in organizing a union of all the Sioux tribes, and became the chief of the Sioux confederacy after leading them successfully in battle against the Iowas and Chippeways. In 1830 the Sioux ceded to the United States a strip of land 20 miles north of the line of 1825, from the Des Moines river to the Mississippi, receiving in exchange a tract about Lake Pepin. In 1841 a party of Sioux surprised a camp of twenty-four Delaware Indians, hunting along the Raccoon river. The Delawares made a heroic fight against overwhelming numbers, killing twenty-six of their enemies. Their chief, Neo-wa-ge, alone killed four Sioux warriors. But one of the number escaped the massacre to carry the tidings to their friends, the Sacs and Foxes, who were camped on the east bank of the Des Moines river, near where the state house now stands Pash-e-pa-ho, the chief. who was then 80 years old, mounted his horse, and selecting 500 of his bravest warriors, started in pursuit of the Sioux. Following the trail for more than 100 miles from where the Delawares were slain, the Sioux were overtaken. Led by the old chief, the Sacs and Foxes raised a fierce war cry and charged upon the Sioux camp. The battle was one of the

bloodiest ever fought on Iowa soil. The struggle was hand to hand, the Sioux fighting for life and the assailants to avenge the slaughter of their friends. The defeat of the Sioux was overwhelming; more than 300 of their warriors were left dead on the field as the remnant of the shattered band fled from their infuriated foes. The Sacs and Foxes lost but seven killed. In 1852 a band of Musquakies from Tama county attacked a camp of Sioux near Clear Lake and killed sixteen of them.

A band of Sioux, under Si-dom-i-na-do-ta, had two battles with the Pottawattamies in northwestern Iowa. One was fought near Twin Lakes in Calhoun county, and the other on the South Lizard in Webster county, in both of which the Sioux were the victors. The Sioux were the fiercest and most treacherous of all the Iowa Indians. It was a band of Sioux which massacred nearly the entire settlement at Okoboji and Spirit lakes, and slaughtered and drove the colony from Springfield in 1857. It was an uprising of the Sioux in Minnesota in 1862 that slaughtered more than 1,000 men, women and children.

The barbarities perpetrated in that horrible massacre upon defenseless women and children have never been surpassed in the annals of Indian outrages.

The Indian tribes here mentioned are the principal ones that have occupied portions of Iowa since it became known to the whites. The only remnant remaining among us now is the colony of Musquakies on their lands in Tama county.

---

## CHAPTER III.

*First White Settlers in Iowa—Julien Dubuque, 1788—Dubuque Lead Mines—Dubuque's Colony—Auguste Chouteau Purchase—Litigation Over Titles—Final Decision in 1855—Louis Honore Tesson, 1799–1803—Exploring Expeditions—Lewis and Clark, 1804—Zebulon Pike, 1805—Johnson, LeMoliere, 1808–1820—Fort Madison; Dr. Samuel Muir, Dr. Isaac Galland—First Form of Government in Iowa.*

In 1785 Julien Dubuque, a mineralogist, emigrated to the province of Louisiana and settled at Prairie du Chien. He soon began to trade among the Fox Indians on the west shore of the Mississippi, near the site of McGregor. He acquired great influence with the Indians and on the 22d of September, 1788, he secured from them a grant or permit to work the lead mines on a large tract of land, claimed by him to extend seven leagues up along the river and nine miles back into the country. It was located north of the Little Maquoketa to the Tete des Morts on the Iowa side of the Mississippi river. The Fox chiefs granted him the exclusive privilege of working the lead mines in the limits of the land leased. He was a shrewd, intelligent man, at this time about 26 years of age. He took with him ten Canadians, as laborers, and

they all settled near the Indian village of Kettle Chief, at the mouth of Catfish creek. Here they built cabins, married Indian wives, and made the first white settlement within the limits of Iowa. They cultivated some land, built a horse mill, erected a smelting furnace and began mining. Dubuque also became an extensive trader among the Indians. He kept goods which pleased them and which he exchanged for furs, mineral and whatever would bring money. The Sac and Fox Indians had several villages along the Mississippi river, on either side, between Prairie du Chien and the mouth of Rock river, the largest of which were at Rock Island, Dubuque, and at the mouth of Turkey river.

Dubuque was called by the Indians, Little Cloud, and was a great favorite of Kettle Chief, the leader of the Fox village and band. The village of Kettle chief stood about two miles below the present site of the city of Dubuque, at the mouth of Catfish creek.

Dubuque managed to acquire great influence among the Indians, both the Foxes and Winnebagoes, who lived on the east side of the Mississippi river, and settled many of their quarrels and controversies. He gradually extended his trade, buying such goods as would please the Indians, in his trips to St. Louis, which he exchanged with them for labor in his mines. His Canadian companions were overseers of his mines, smelters, clerks in his store, teamsters and woodchoppers, while the hard labor in the mines was performed by Indian women and the old men of the tribe. Twice a year, Dubuque with some of his white companions took trips in boats, loaded with ore, furs and buffalo hides, to St. Louis. He was one of the most extensive traders at that frontier town, and his arrival with his merchandise was always a notable event in the village. But, for some reason, he did not prosper in his extensive business enterprises and as the years went by became involved in debt.

In October, 1804, Dubuque sold to August Chouteau, a wealthy trader of St. Louis, seven-sixteenths

*Autograph of Julien Dubuque.*

of his large tract of land including the mines, with a provision that at his death all of the remainder of his interest in the lands and mines should go to Chouteau. In this deal Dubuque raised a large amount of money to pay on his debts and secured Chouteau's powerful aid in developing his mines. Although Dubuque had no title to the land from the Fox Indians, and only a permit to mine for lead on it, obtained from a council of chiefs in 1788, yet he intended to hold the valuable tract as his own. His influence with the Indians was so great that he did not anticipate any trouble from them in appropriating the land as his own. With this view he began to negotiate with Governor Carondelet of Louisiana territory, for a title from the Spanish government for the lands, which he called the "Mines of Spain." On the 10th of November, 1796, Governor Carondelet made the grant to Dubuque, of the land petitioned for. These mines had been discovered in 1780 by an Indian woman, the wife of Peosta, a Fox warrior, and in the lease or contract made by the Fox Indians with Dubuque they "agreed to sell to him all the coast and contents of the lead mines

discovered by the wife of Peosta, so that no white man or Indian shall make any claim to it without the consent of Sieur Julien Dubuque." The quantity of land sold by Dubuque to Auguste Chouteau in 1804 was 72,324 arpens, for which he received $10,848. For twenty years this first white colony ever planted on Iowa soil, lived in peace and friendship with the Indians and worked the lead mines. The yield of the mines was from 20,000 to 40,000 pounds of lead per year. But suddenly all was changed. Dubuque was taken sick and died on the 24th day of March, 1810. His death produced great consternation among his white companions and his Indian friends. The latter treated his remains with the most distinguished honor and his funeral was conducted with extraordinary pomp. The chiefs and orators extolled his virtues with great eloquence. He was buried on a high bluff overlooking portions of three states. The Indians kept a fire burning at his grave for several years, day and night. Chouteau sold the Dubuque land and mines to Pierre Chouteau, John P. Cabanni and William Russell, but the Indians refused to recognize the sale, claiming that their grant or lease to Dubuque expired at his death. Soon after they drove Dubuque's white companions off and took possession of the property. Thus came to an end the first white colony established on Iowa soil. But in 1832 the Spanish claimants took possession of the houses and lands, and again began to work the mines, but were soon after forcibly ejected by United States troops. The Chouteau heirs brought suit to secure the lands and for many years the title was in litigation, after Dubuque had become a flourishing city and the land of very great value. But finally in March, 1853, the long-continued litigation was ended by a decision of the United States supreme court, which held the Chouteau claim to title to be invalid.

In March, 1799, another attempt was made to establish a settlement within the limits of Iowa. On the 30th of that month Louis Honore Tesson obtained permission from the lieutenant-governor of Upper Louisiana to make a settlement within the Sac and Fox possessions. He selected lands about where the town of Montrose now stands, in Lee county. He erected cabins, cultivated lands and planted an orchard in that vicinity. But in 1803 it was sold under execution to Thomas F. Reddick. His title was confirmed by act of congress July 1, 1836. Bazil Giard had secured a grant of lands in Clayton county, near where McGregor now stands, to the amount of 6,808 arpens, from the Spanish government and made some settlement upon it. After long litigation it was finally patented to his heirs July 2, 1844.

Spanish rule in the vast territory of Louisiana was now nearing its end. Napoleon Bonaparte had become the master of Spain and it was compelled to cede Louisiana to the French on the 1st of October, 1801. But soon after, Napoleon, fearing its conquest by Great Britain, sold it to the United States on the 30th of April, 1803, for $15,000,000. The vast territory thus acquired by President Jefferson has since been made into the states of Louisiana, Arkansas, Missouri, Iowa, Minnesota, North and South Dakota, Nebraska, Kansas, Colorado, Montana, the Indian territory and Oklahoma. On the 26th of March congress passed an act organizing the territory of Orleans, which embraced what afterwards became the state of Louisiana. The remainder of the purchase was made the district of Louisiana, and was placed under the jurisdiction of Indiana territory. This district embraced Iowa. In March, 1805, Louisiana was organized into a territory, with James Wilkinson as governor. The white population at this time did not exceed 4,000, and St. Louis was the capital of the vast new territory.

away to a range of hills broken into sharp points and deep ravines. They describe the mouth of the Platte river as six hundred yards wide and the water not more than six feet in depth, and not navigable for boats larger than Indian canoes. On the 22d of July the party camped on the Iowa shore ten miles above the mouth of the Platte to hold a council with the Indians. They realized that their own safety and the success of the expedition depended upon the establishment of friendly relations with powerful tribes of Indians through whose country they were passing. Here they met the Otoe and Pawnee tribes and established friendship with them. On the 3d of August they met Ayauways (Iowas), represented by six of their chiefs, and had a friendly conference, distributing presents for the tribe. Captains Lewis and Clark

*Showing the frame-work of a wickiup.*

EXPLORING THE LOUISIANA PURCHASE.

Soon after the acquisition of Louisiana, the president of the United States had an expedition organized to explore the valleys of the Missouri river and some of its great tributaries. The command was given to Capt. Merriwether Lewis and Capt. William Clark. Several large boats were built and equipped and manned by forty-three men. It started from St. Louis on the 14th of May, 1804, and began to ascend the Missouri river, of which very little was known. The river was high, the current swift, and the progress very slow. At night they camped on shore. On the 8th of July they reached the Nodaway, and as they passed up along the western shore of Iowa they found the country open prairie with wide bottom lands covered with a dense mat of tall grass, stretching miles

named the place where this conference was held Council Bluffs. On the 7th of August they camped near the mouth of the river named by the French *Petite Rivere de Sioux* (the Little Sioux). On the 18th they landed on the west shore at a point opposite the southwest corner of what is now Woodbury county and held a council with a band of Missouri Indians, with whom they established friendly relations. While camped here one of the party, Seargent Charles Floyd, was taken very sick and died the next day. His body was conveyed to a high bluff on the Iowa side and buried. He was the first white man known to have been buried on Iowa soil. A river which the party passed, emptying into the Missouri from the east, a mile north, was named by them Floyd river, in memory of their young companion buried in the bluff near by. No large bodies of forest are mentioned until they reached the mouth

3

of the Big Sioux. It was on the 21st of August when the expedition passed the bluffs where Sioux City was to grow up fifty years later. And here they left the shores of Iowa and turned their course towards the great unexplored region extending westward to the Pacific ocean.

### PIKE'S EXPLORING EXPEDITION.

The year after the departure of Lewis and Clark, another expedition was sent to explore the upper Mississippi river region. Its commander was Zebulon Pike, a brilliant young officer but 24 years of age.

On the 9th of August, 1805, Lieutenant Pike started from St. Louis with twenty men in a keel boat seventy-five feet in length. They carried provisions for a four months' voyage, and expected to explore the Mississippi river and valley as far up as they could sail. By the 20th of August they had reached the mouth of the *Riviere des Moines*, as Pike writes it He writes: " We have arrived at the foot of the Rapids des Moines, which are immediately above the confluence of the river of that name with the Mississippi We were met here by William. Ewing, an agent of the United States, residing in the Sac village here to instruct the Indians in agriculture." Lieutenant Pike here met the Sac Indians in council and explained to them the friendly object of the expedition. Lieutenant Pike gives interesting descriptions of the country through which they passed at the points where the Iowa rivers empty into the Mississippi, and the Indian villages they passed by. He stopped at the Dubuque lead mines and held a conference with the proprietor, but could not get much information from him. On the 4th of September Lieutenant Pike landed near where McGregor now stands, and held a council with some of the Winnebago Indians. Before leaving this place Pike selected a site for a military post three miles from the mouth of the Wisconsin river, on a high bluff called "Pilot Gris." He writes: "On the west side of the Mississippi are three log houses on a small stream called Giard river." These houses were where North McGregor now stands. On the 9th of September the expedition reached the mouth of Upper Iowa river, which is near the northern limits of Iowa.

An agent of the American Fur company, Col. J. W. Johnson, had established a trading post at the Flint hills, near where Burlington now stands, in 1808. His first shipment of merchandise was received in August of that year from a factory at Bellefountain and was valued at $14,715. These goods were exchanged with the Indians for furs and skins. On the 28th of March, 1809, Colonel Johnson reports that he had traded for 710 beaver skins, 1,353 muskrat skins, 3,585 raccoon skins, 28,021 pounds of deer skins, bear and other skins to the value of $426 and beeswax and tallow valued at $141, in all worth $10,477. In 1812 the trading house was destroyed by fire. In 1820 Le Moliere, another French trader, had established a trading post six miles above the mouth of the Des Moines river, on the Iowa side of the Mississippi river.

In 1808 Col. Zachary Taylor was sent to build some forts along the upper Mississippi river. He built one on the Iowa side, about ten miles above the Des Moines rapids, and named it Fort Madison. This was in direct violation of a treaty with the Indians. The Indians made bitter complaint and some time after, under the lead of Black Hawk, they made an attempt to capture and destroy it. On the 4th of June, 1812, the Territory of Orleans was admitted as a state under the name of Louisiana, and the remainder of the vast territory, including Iowa, was organized into Missouri territory.

After the death of Dubuque the first white man known to have made a home in the limits of Iowa was Chevalier Marias, a scion of the French nobility and an adherent of Louis XVI. When the French revolution swept over his country, and the lives of the nobility were in danger, Marias fled to America and for twenty-two years was a wanderer in the wilds of the far west. In 1812 he married the daughter of the head chief of the Iowa Indians, established a trading post at the mouth of Buck creek, in the limits of Clayton county, and lived there many years, carrying on a large trade with the Indians.

During the period in which the various explorations had been made along the rivers bordering on the east and west boundaries of Iowa, this region had passed nominally under the jurisdiction of various territories. When Missouri was admitted into the Union as a state, on the 4th of March, 1821, all of that portion of Missouri territory north of its northern boundary was left without civil government until 1834.

The first steamboat that ascended the Mississippi river to the limits of Iowa was the General Pike. It came up in August, 1817, and was commanded by Capt. Jacob Reed.

In June, 1819, Maj. S. H. Long was sent with an expedition to explore the valleys of the river in the far northwest. The trip to Council Bluffs was made on the steamer Western Engineer, which was one of the first steamboat trips made up the Missouri. He reached the mouth of the Platte on the 16th of September, and found no settlements on the Iowa side of the Missouri. Indian and fur traders had often traveled over portions of western Iowa, but had established no settlements up to this time.

Peter A. Sarpy, a French trader, was for a long time engaged in trade with the Indians at a place called Traders' Point, on the Iowa side of the Missouri river, near the south line of Pottawattamie county, as early as 1824. Mr. Hart, another French trader, in 1824 explored the western rivers and established a trading post within the present limits of Council Bluffs. Quite a settlement of trappers and traders gathered in the vicinity. Francis Guttar, a French trader, built a cabin there in 1827,

crossed the river and built a cabin where Keokuk now stands. He had married a beautiful girl of the Sac Indian tribe, and their home was on the Iowa farm where this cabin stood. Some years later an order was issued by the war department command-

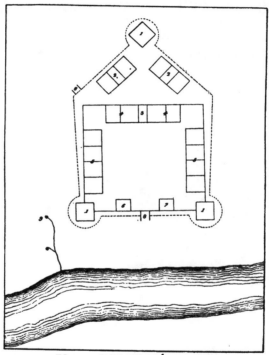

*Plan of Ft. Madison, 1808.*

1. Block Houses.  4 Officers Quarters.  7 Surgeons Office
2 Factory        5 Barracks           8 Gates
3 Passage-way    6 Guard-house        9 Spring

*Old Fort Madison.*

and for a long time carried on a profitable trade with the white and Indian trappers and hunters. In 1820 Dr. Samuel C. Muir, a surgeon in the United States service, was stationed with a command at Fort Edward (now Warsaw, Ill.). He

ing officers of the army to abandon their Indian wives at the various posts on the frontier. Dr. Muir, who was a native of Scotland, and a graduate of the Edinburgh university, refused to desert his wife, and resigned his commission. He made a beautiful but modest home on his Iowa farm and was devotedly attached to his wife and children. In 1832 he was stricken with the cholera and died suddenly, leaving his widow with five children. Unscrupulous parties trumped up claims against the dead surgeon, and after long and expensive litigation dispossessed his family of their home and they were turned out entirely destitute.

In 1821 Isaac R. Campbell explored the southern portion of the territory embraced in Iowa, and afterwards settled near the foot of the Des Moines rapids in Lee county, where he opened a farm and kept a public house. In writing his recollections

building and the orchard he had planted were all that remained of his settlement. In 1828 Moses Stillwell with his family came to Puch-e-shu-tuck, a name given by the Indians to the point at the mouth of the river where Dr. Muir had made his home. In the spring of 1829, Dr. Isaac Galland* came with his family and settled on the west shore of the Mississippi, opposite the upper chain of rocks in the lower rapids, where Nashville has since been built. This place was called by the Indians, Ah-wip-e-tuck. Dr. Galland labored long and hard to found a city here, but his reward never came; the city was built at Puch-e-shu-tuck and was

*First schoolhouse in Iowa.*

of that part of Iowa at that early day, he says: "The only indications of a white settlement at the time of my first visit at the rapids was a cabin built by Dr. Samuel C. Muir, on the site of the present city of Keokuk. The next cabin built by a white man in that vicinity was about six miles above, where a French trader, Le Moliere, had established a post. Another Frenchman, M. Blonden, had a cabin a mile farther up the river. At the head of the rapids the Indian chief Wapello, with a band of his tribe, had a village. This was near where Louis Honore Tesson, a French trader, had established a post and secured a grant of land in 1799 from the governor of Louisiana. The ruins of his

named after the old Sac chief, Keokuk. But the point is notable in Iowa history as the birth place of the first white child in the limits of Iowa. Elenor Galland, the doctor's daughter, was born here in 1830. The first school in Iowa was one established at this place by Berryman Jennings in 1830. As we passed up the river we saw the ruins of old Fort Madison, about 10 miles above the rapids near a sand bluff, which rose up nearly perpendicular from the waters' edge. On the second day after our keel boat reached Shoe-o-con, or Flint Hills, an Indian village of the Foxes stood at the mouth of Flint creek. Its chief was Ti-me-a. In 1825 I took a trip

*Father of Washington Galland. See biography.

with an ox team and an Indian guide up the river. We passed Wapello's village and crossed the Des Moines river on a raft. We ascended the high lands, Grave Yard Bluff (now Buena Vista). We followed the divide, passing a lone tree standing on the bluff, which was a land mark for the Indians. In the fall of 1825, I settled at Quash-qua-me village, where my father-in law, Capt. James White, had purchased the old trading house and a tract of land adjacent, which was an old Spanish grant made to Monsieur Julien, on which he lived in 1805. Captain White made his first trip to this point in the steamer Mandan, which was the first that came to the foot of the rapids."

In 1830 a trading post was established on the Iowa river, in the limits of Johnson county. John Gilbert was the agent in charge and was, probably, the first white man to make a home in that part of the state. The post was near Poweshiek's Indian village. Goods were brought up the river in keel boats, from St. Louis, and exchanged for furs and skins of wild animals, with the Indians and white hunters and trappers. In 1831 Col. George Davenport explored the Cedar river in a canoe above the mouth of Rock creek, where he established a trading post and carried on a profitable trade with the Indians up to 1835.

In 1831 Mr. Campbell moved down to Puch-e-shu-tuck. Here the American Fur company had erected, on the river bank, a row of hewed log buildings for their traffic with the Indians, and the collection and storing of furs and skins and the goods used in their purchase. Several white men had settled here and married Indian wives. The place was known by them as "Farmers' Trading Post." In 1834 a meeting of half-breeds was held at this place to prepare a petition to congress praying for the passage of a law authorizing them to sell their lands known as the half-breed reservation. There were nine families living in that vicinity and after the adjournment of the meeting, these citizens held a conference at John Gaines' saloon, to consider the plan of building a city at that place. After the project had been agreed to and the plans fixed up, John Gaines proposed that the city of the future should be named Keokuk, which was finally agreed to. Although no title could yet be acquired to land in the limits of the future state of Iowa at this time, still pioneers kept going over and obtaining permission of the Indians to stay among them. In June, 1829, James Langworthy, a young man from Vermont, who had purchased an interest in the Galena lead mines, crossed over the Mississippi river to try to get an interest in the old Dubuque mines. Securing Indian guides, he explored the country from the mouth of the Maquoketa to the Turkey river, in search of the old lead mines formerly worked. He managed to secure the permission of the Indians to work the old mines. The next year, with his brother Lucius H. Langworthy, and a company of miners, he moved over the river and began work. A village of the Sac and Fox Indians still stood at the mouth of Catfish creek, where Dubuque and his men had formerly lived, but was now nearly depopulated. Its former occupants had been killed by the hostile Sioux several years before. There were about seventy cabins unoccupied when the whites from the Galena settlement began to cross over and take possession of the abandoned "Mines of Spain." Some of the reckless miners thought to intimidate the Indians by burning these cabins, so that no Indians could occupy them again They held a public meeting and elected a so-called legislature, consisting of James L. Langworthy, H. F. Lander, James McPheters, Samuel Scales, and E. M. Wren, who were instructed to prepare a code of laws for the settlement. These pioneer law-makers gathered about an old cottonwood log for a table and elected Mr. Langworthy clerk to keep their records. The following is a copy of the code adopted: "Having been chosen to draft laws by which we, as miners, will be governed, and having duly considered the subject, we unanimously agree that we will be governed by the regulations on the east side of the Mississippi river, with the following exceptions:

ARTICLE I. That each and every man shall hold 200 yards square of ground by working said ground one day in six.

ART. II. We further agree that there shall be chosen by a majority of the miners present a person who shall hold this article, and who shall grant letters of arbitration on application having been made, and said letters of arbitration shall be obligatory on the party so applying.

The regulations referred to on the east side of the river were the laws established by the superintendent of the United States lead mines at Fever river (Galena).

Under their code, the settlers proceeded to elect Dr. Jerote their first governor, and it is known that their laws were as rigidly enforced as have been more formal acts of later years. This first government ever established on the soil of Iowa, was respected by all, and preserved order, protected property and life in the absence of any legal form of government.

## CHAPTER IV.

*Iowa in Early Times—Settlers Driven out by the Military Authorities -- Indian Treaties — The Black Hawk Purchase—Founding of Dubuque—The Flint Hills, or Burlington—Fort Madison.*

At this time there were probably not more than 100 white people within the limits of the future great state of Iowa. But for many years the fame of its beautiful valleys, groves, rivers, and vast, fertile prairies had reached the eastern states and territories.

It was known to be reserved from settlement and in sole possession of the Indians, and was their ideal home and hunting ground. Thousands of people were waiting impatiently for the removal of the red men from such a fair land. When the time came for the Indians to go farther west, the white-top emigrant wagons turned their course towards the land of promise. The home-seekers swarmed over the ferries, explored the prairies, groves and valleys for choice locations. Minerals, water powers, good timber and town sites were eagerly sought for. Who, of early times, can ever forget the visions of beauty spread out before the eye as Iowa in its virgin wildness was first seen in spring-time by the emigrants in search of homes? How we gazed with rapture from the summit of the river bluffs out over the vast, green prairie landscape. The great, rolling meadows of upland and valley seemed to have been cleared of forests, stumps and stones, by some former generation, and to lie waiting for us to come and choose a beautiful farm ready for the plow and scythe; not an obstruction in the way of immediate cultivation; not a road, or bridge, or house, or barn, or a human being in sight in any direction. Winding along through the vast plains were long, varying lines of trees, marking the meanderings of a beautiful creek or river in the far distance. The delicious breeze that never ceases wafts to the senses the pure perfume of grass, flowers and trees.

But the autumn scene was far different. The frosts had withered the grass and all is changed to sombre brown. The air is clear, pure, frosty and invigorating. As night comes on a bright glow of red lights up the distant horizon, from which dense smoke ascends. Higher and higher the fiery glow shoots upward and volumes of black smoke slowly rise up in darkening clouds. A long, varying line of circling fire spreads out for a great distance, and the steady roar of advancing flames is heard. Higher and higher the fiery forks shoot upward, and rolling above them dense black volumes of smoke as the heavy winds fan the awful and swiftly advancing lines of fire into a fiercer glow. On, on,

it comes with the mighty roar of a tornado, the fearful heat scorches the very air. Death follows in its terrible march, and no living thing in its path can survive its scorching, shriveling breath. Houses, barns, stacks, and wild animals melt down before its resistless march. As it sweeps by like a race horse and recedes in the distance the whole plain over which it swept is one black, barren waste, a picture of desolation.

When winter came upon the sparsely scattered settlements of the early pioneers there was often suffering and danger. There were no fenced roads, no comfortable barns for domestic animals, few and very far between were the towns. The settler who had to venture out on the great, bleak, trackless prairie on a journey to a distant mill or market, encountered perils of no trifling degree. The terrible blizzards which sometimes came in those days often found some traveler far from home or friendly shelter. The snow soon hid every sign of a road or path, and as the wind came down from the northwest hundreds of miles with nothing to check its fury, the fine, icy particles of snow drove into face of man and team with a pitiless force that was hard to endure. Many of the pioneer settlers were caught out on the great prairies from time to time in these terrible storms, far from help or shelter, and perished. These scenes of beauty, grandeur, desolation and death, so common to the early settlers in Iowa, have passed away with the buffalo, elk, deer and Indians, which everywhere disappear before advancing civilization. They linger only in story and memory of the pioneer times on the great wild prairies, and in the generations to come will only be preserved in tradition. But no sketch of early times in Iowa would convey a true picture of pioneer life from which these scenes were omitted.

Before the Indian title was extinguished in any portion of Iowa, as we have seen, people began to cross the river and settle among the Indians. This was in direct violation of our treaty obligations, and the government was called upon to expel them. Col. Zachary Taylor, commanding the military post at Prairie du Chien, sent Lieutenant Abercrombie with a company of soldiers over to drive the settlers at the Dubuque mines back to the east side of the river. A detachment was left at the mines to protect the Indians in possession of their lands and mines. Down at the Flint Hills, Samuel

S. White and other squatters who had entered upon the Indian lands and built cabins, were driven out and their cabins burned by the military company sent there.

At the close of the Black Hawk war a treaty was made with the Sac and Fox Indians on the Iowa side, opposite Rock Island. General Scott, commanding Fort Armstrong, and Governor Reynolds, of Illinois, were the commissioners for the United States, while Keokuk, Pashapaho and thirty minor chiefs and warriors represented the Sac and Fox Indians. Under the pressure of military power and recent defeat, the Indians were compelled to cede

treaty was ratified on the 13th of February, 1833, and on the first of June following, the Indians surrendered possession and removed to their new reservation. The new territory thus opened for settlement had not yet been named Iowa, but was called the "Black Hawk Purchase," although Black Hawk had no voice in the treaty by which his people were dispossessed of their lands. When the troops were withdrawn from the "Mines of Spain," in June, 1833, the Langworthy brothers crossed the river again and took possession of their claims and resumed work in the mines. Settlers flocked in and a frontier village began to grow up.

*The troops under Gen. Smith landed on Rock Island in May, 1816, and established a fort which they named after the Secretary of War—Fort Armstrong.*

to the United States a large section of country west of the Mississippi river, 50 miles wide, and extending from the north line of Missouri to the mouth of the Upper Iowa river. The United States agreed to pay for this tract $20,000 annually to the Indians, and $50,000 to Davenport and Farnam, a claim they had against the Indians. Six thousand bushels of corn, fifty barrels of flour, thirty barrels of pork, thirty-five beef cattle and twelve bushels of salt were also appropriated for the support of Indian women and children whose husbands and fathers had been killed in the Black Hawk war just ended. It was estimated that this magnificent tract of land cost the United States nine cents an acre. This

A school was opened early in the fall in a log house built by James L. Langworthy and other settlers. George Cabbage was the teacher and his school term extended through the winter of 1833–4 with an average attendance of about thirty-five pupils. All obstructions to settlement now being removed before the close of the year, there was a population of 500 in the vicinity of the mines. A pioneer among these early inhabitants of this first Iowa village gives the following picture of the frontier town the previous year:

"The valley resounded to the woodman's axe; the sturdy oaks fell before them on every side. The branches were used for fuel, and of the trunks were built rude log cabins without doors or windows. Three openings served for the entrance of light and the settlers, and the egress of smoke. The winter of that year shut us in from all communication with the outside world, with a short supply of provisions, and not a woman in the entire settlement. There was plenty of whisky, and the demon intemperance stalked everywhere during the long winter evenings and the short bleak days. The cholera claimed many victims, and the sick lay down and died with no gentle hand to nurse them, no medical aid to relieve, and no kindred or friends to mourn their untimely fate. We had no mails, no government, and were subject to no restraints of law or society. Drinking and gambling were universal amusements, and criminals were only amenable to the penalties inflicted by Judge Lynch, from whose summary decrees there was no appeal. In the spring of 1834, a transient steamer came up from St. Louis, bringing provisions, goods, groceries and newspapers. A few women came, also, to join their husbands, and from that time on we began to exhibit some elements of civilization." It is related by Eliphalet Price that the first American flag raised by a citizen of Iowa was made by a slave woman and run up in Dubuque by Nicholas Carroll, immediately after 12 o'clock on the morning of the 4th of July, 1834. The same authority says the first church in Iowa was built in Dubuque in the fall of 1834. It was a log structure, and Mr. Johnson, a devout Methodist raised the money by subscription among the citizens, and the church was used by preachers of various denominations for several years. The first Catholic church in Iowa was built of stone, in Dubuque in 1835, through the efforts of a French priest, Father Mazzuchelli. The first settler to cross the Mississippi and open a farm in the vicinity of Rock Island, was Capt. Benjamin W. Clark, a native of Virginia. He had emigrated to western Illinois before the Black Hawk war, and in 1833, when the lands west of the Mississippi were opened for settlement, Captain Clark took a claim and began to cultivate it. He soon discovered coal and opened some mines; he planted an orchard and established a ferry across the river, the first between Burlington and Dubuque. In 1835 he built a large public house and the next year laid out the town of Buffalo and built a sawmill near the mouth of Duck creek. His son, David H. Clark, was the first white child born in that portion of the Black Hawk purchase lying between Dubuque and Burlington, on the 21st day of April, 1834. For several years Buffalo did a flourishing business, and had a fair prospect of becoming an important city in the future. But two rivals soon sprung up in Rockingham and Davenport, and the latter was destined to become the large city of that region. Rockingham was laid out in 1836, by A. H. Davenport, Col. John Sullivan and H. W. Higgins. It was several miles up the river from Buffalo and opposite

the mouth of Rock river. The original claim upon which Davenport was first laid out was made by R. H. Spencer and A. H. McCloud Soon after Antoine Le Claire purchased it for $100. In 1835 it became the property of eight persons, who proceeded to lay out a town named in honor of Col. George Davenport. A long and bitter contest arose between the rival towns of Rockingham and Davenport, and finally the latter won the county seat, which proved a death blow to Rockingham, which eventually disappeared from the map of Iowa as a town.

In 1829 the American Fur company had a trading post where Burlington now stands, at which

*BERRYMAN JENNINGS,*
*Who taught the first school established in Iowa.*

traffic in skins and furs was carried on by the Indians. They had log buildings erected for the accommodation of their agent, his men and goods. In the summer of that year Simpson S. White and Amzi Doolittle were employed by the company to build additions to their buildings. While thus employed they prospected around that region and determined to take claims as soon as settlements could be made in the Indian country. There was no prospect then that the Indians would sell their lands soon, but these men determined to pick out their claims and occupy them when they could. The land they selected was where the river front of Burlington now stands. It began at a ravine near the upper end of the bottom lands and extended down the river banks about a mile. A treaty was made with the Indians September 21, 1832, by which the eastern portion of Iowa was acquired, to take effect June 1, 1833. As soon as the pioneers heard of this treaty, Simpson S. White, Amzi Doolittle and Morton H. McCarven crossed over the river and took possession of the claims they had staked out three years before. They proceeded at once to build a cabin on Mr. White's claim and employed men on the east shore to build a flatboat to be used in establishing a ferry across the river. They had no doubt that a city would spring up there. They procured a license from the authorities of Hancock county, Illinois, to establish a ferry. In February, 1833, Mr. White moved his family over the river into his rude cabin, and his was the first white family that lived on the ground where Burlington of the future was to grow up. But as the time had not yet expired in which the Indians had a right to hold the land, complaint was made, and the commander of the fort at Rock Island sent Lieut. Jefferson Davis with fifteen soldiers, who drove the settlers off across the river. Several settlers had come over and made claims in

the vicinity and all were driven off and their cabins and fences burned by the soldiers. But they were determined to return as soon as the Indians left the country. In the summer of 1833, Morton H. McCarven and Simpson S. White crossed the river with their families and occupied their claims where Burlington now stands. In the fall they established a ferry across the river to enable emigrants to come over. They were the first settlers of Burlington. That fall W. R. Ross brought a stock of goods over and opened a store in the place. In November, 1833, the original town was laid out and platted by Benjamin Tucker and W. R. Ross for the proprietors of the ground. John Gray, a friend of the proprietors and a Vermonter, suggested that they name the town after Burlington, in Vermont, and it was done.

Next to Dubuque, Fort Madison was one of the first places in the limits of Iowa occupied by the whites. The fort buildings were destroyed by fire in 1813. In 1832 Zachariah Hawkins, Berryman Jennings and several other young men crossed the river and made claims in the vicinity of the old fort. Their claims were purchased the next year by John H. and Nathaniel Knapp, who proceeded in 1835, to lay off a town plat.

---

## CHAPTER V.

*Boone's Exploring Party—Iowa District—Iowa Named—Half-breed Lands—Wisconsin Territory—First Iowa Newspaper, 1836—Iowa Territory Organized—First Governor and Legislature—Capital Located—Iowa City in 1839—Governor Chambers.*

In 1834 there was stationed at old Fort Des Moines (now Montrose), a military post on the west bank of the Mississippi river, three companies of the First United States dragoons, under Lieut.-Col. Stephen W. Kearney. As but little was known of the country in the interior it was decided to send a party to explore in the direction of the valley of the Des Moines river. Capt. Nathan Boone, a son of the famous Daniel Boone of Kentucky, was placed in command of the party sent out. They were well mounted, and on the 6th day of June, 1835, they started out, following a dividing ridge between the Skunk and Des Moines rivers. Their route took them through the counties of Lee, Henry, Jefferson, Keokuk, Mahaska, Jasper, Polk, Boone and Hamilton. For a week they rode over the beautiful wild prairie country, finally striking the Des Moines valley in what is now Boone county. Following up the valley, on the 22d day of June they came to a river flowing from the northeast into the Des Moines. It was named Boone river, after the commander of the expedition. They followed the divide between the Boone and Iowa rivers for some distance. They found a beautiful prairie country, quite level, with occasionally a grove of timber.

They spent nearly two months traveling over what was afterwards the counties of Humboldt, Wright, Hancock, Cerro Gordo, Worth, Franklin and Hardin. Up to the last of July they had seen very few Indians. On the 30th they were in camp on the east fork of the Des Moines river. They were suddenly attacked by a large party of Sioux warriors. They were in the heart of the Sioux country, and that fierce tribe determined to resist their march through their possessions. Captain Boone made a successful defense until darkness put an end to the battle. Knowing that his little command was far beyond the reach of reinforcements, Captain Boone ordered a retreat, and during the night placed many miles between his company and the enemy. By the 8th of August they reached the Raccoon river where it enters the Des Moines, and established a camp on the ground where the city of Des Moines now stands. From here they explored northwest and southwest. They followed the Des Moines valley down to where Ottumwa stands, where they found an Indian village under the chief, Appanoose, having a population of about 350. The Indians here had large cornfields under cultivation.

One of the officers of Boone's command was Lieut. Albert M. Lea, who was a civil engineer and an accomplished draughtsman. He made a map of the country they had explored. He also wrote a lengthy description of the country examined, and, in 1836 published a book entitled "Notes on Wisconsin Territory, the Iowa district." This was the first publication ever made, descriptive of the Iowa country. And Albert M. Lea thus gave the name to the region which became the state of Iowa. We make the following extract from the closing sentence of the little volume: "Taking this district all in all, for convenience of navigation, water, fuel and timber, richness of soil, beauty of landscape, and climate, it surpasses any portion of the United States with which I am acquainted."

The town of Iowa, on the Mississippi river near the mouth of the Pine, was regarded at this time by Lieutenant Lea "as the most promising city of the future state, and likely to become its capital." It was about ten miles up the river from Muscatine, at the mouth of Pine creek. In 1834, Benjamin Nye and a Mr. Farnam had established a trading post at that place on "Grindstone Bluff," where for several years a large trade was carried on with the Indians. But the prospective capital of Iowa is now a farm.

In a convention which met at Burlington soon after the publication of Albert M. Lea's little book, to urge a division of Wisconsin territory, the country west of the Mississippi river was called the IOWA DISTRICT. The name of the *Dubuque Visitor* was soon after changed to the *Iowa News*. In the summer of 1837, James Clark, of Burlington, gave his paper the name *Iowa Territorial Gazette*. William L. Tool, who was a delegate to the Burlington convention above named, says that it was decided there to give the proposed new territory the name IOWA, after other names had been proposed and discussed.

### THE HALF-BREED LANDS.

Many of the early Indian traders and trappers who made their homes near the mouth of the Des Moines river, married Indian wives, and their children generally adopted the habits of their Indian mothers as they grew up. When the treaty of 1824 was made by William Clark with the Sac and Fox Indians, the following stipulation was made: "The small tract of land lying between the Mississippi and Des Moines rivers is intended for the use of the half-breeds belonging to the Sac and Fox nation, they holding it by the same title and in the same manner that other Indian titles are held." This reservation embraced about 113,000 acres of good land lying in the southeast corner of Iowa, in the county of Lee.

In June, 1834, congress authorized the half-breeds to individually pre-empt and acquire title to and sell these lands. A company was organized to buy and sell these half-breed lands. The tract had been divided into 101 pieces and the company purchased forty-one of these tracts. There was no way to determine who of the half-breeds were entitled to these lands, and the parties purchasing could not know whether the persons selling could give good titles. The Wisconsin legislature passed an act requiring all persons claiming title to file their claims with the clerk of the county of Lee, within one year, showing the nature of their claims. Commissioners were appointed to take evidence. The lands not sold by the half-breeds were to be sold and the money paid over to such half-breeds as could establish their claims to it. The commissioners brought suit against the owners of the lands for compensation for their services, got judgment, and 119,000 acres of the land was sold to pay their bills for services. Hugh T. Reid got a deed for that amount of lands. Settlers had gone on them and made improvements and a long litigation took place over the titles. After various conflicting decisions the case was at last taken to the United States supreme court, where Reid's title was set aside as invalid, and the long conflict over the titles was settled. In June, 1834, congress passed an act extending the jurisdiction of the territory of Michigan over the country embraced in Wisconsin, Iowa, Minnesota and Dakota.

In September of that year the legislature of Michigan divided the Iowa district into two counties by running a line due west from the lower end of Rock Island to the Missouri river. The territory north of the line was named Dubuque county, while that south of it was called Des Moines county.

A court was organized in each county, terms of which were to be held at Dubuque and Burlington. The first court in the limits of Iowa was held at Burlington in April, 1835. The judges appointed by the governor of Michigan for these courts were Isaac Leffler, of Des Moines county, and John King, of Dubuque county. On the first Monday of October, 1835, George W. Jones, who lived in the limits of the present state of Wisconsin, was elected the delegate to represent Michigan territory in congress. He secured the passage of a bill to create the new territory of Wisconsin, which embraced Iowa and Minnesota in its limits. General Henry Dodge, an officer in the regular army, was appointed governor and John S. Homer secretary of the new territory. Governor Dodge order a census to be taken in September, 1836, and it was found that the counties of Dubuque and Des Moines, which included all of the Black Hawk Purchase, had a population of 10,531, which gave them six members of the council and thirteen members of the house of representatives in the territorial legislature, which convened at Belmont on the 25th of October, 1836. Peter H. Engle, of Dubuque, was elected speaker of the house, and Henry T. Baird president of the council. An act was passed authorizing the establishment of the Miners' bank at Dubuque with a capital of $200,000. Des Moines county was divided into seven counties, named Des Moines, Lee, Van Buren, Henry, Louisa, Musquetine and

11th of May, 1836, by John King. The printer who set the first type on the Dubuque *Visitor* (as the paper was named) was Andrew Keesecker. It was during the year 1836 that the second newspaper was started in the limits of Iowa by Dr. Isaac Galland,

Cook. The permanent capitol of the new territory was located at Madison and until a suitable building could be erected, the temporary capitol was fixed at Burlington, on the west side of the Mississippi river. The first newspaper in the limits of Iowa was established at "Dubuque Lead Mines," on the

at Montrose, named the *Western Advertiser*. After a vain effort to build a city at Montrose, the paper was moved to Fort Madison and purchased by James G. Edwards, who converted it into an organ of the whig party, changing its name to the Fort Madison *Patriot*. The first number of the

*Patriot* printed a bill which had been introduced into congress by Hon. George W. Jones for a division of Wisconsin territory, and the creation of a new territory west of the Mississippi river, to be named Iowa.

On the 6th of November, 1837, a convention was held at Burlington, composed of delegates from that part of the territory of Wisconsin lying west of the Mississippi river, to memorialize congress to organize a separate territory of that portion lying west of the river. It was largely attended, and drafted a memorial which was forwarded to congress, giving good reasons why the request should be granted.

The Wisconsin territorial legislature, which met in Burlington this year, divided Dubuque county into Dubuque, Clayton, Jackson, Scott,

*ROBERT LUCAS,*
*First Territorial Governor of Iowa.*

Clinton, Linn, Johnson, Jones, Benton, and Delaware counties. In the fall of 1837 a treaty was negotiated with the Sac and Fox Indians, by which 1,250,000 acres of land lying west of and adjoining the Black Hawk purchase was ceded to the United States and opened to settlement. The opening of this vast tract of new land to settlers attracted a large immigration, and in May, 1838, when a new census was taken, the territory west of the Mississippi river was found to have a population of 22,859.

In June, 1838, the bill providing for the creation of Iowa territory having passed both branches of congress and been approved by the president, became a law, to take effect on the 4th of July. President Van Buren proceeded to appoint the following officers for the new territory of Iowa:

Governor, Robert Lucas, formerly governor of Ohio; secretary, William B. Conway; marshal, Francis Gehon; United States attorney, Cyrus S. Jacobs; judges, Charles Mason, Joseph Williams and Thomas S. Wilson. Governor Lucas selected for his private secretary a young college graduate, Theodore S. Parvin,* of Ohio.

The governor named Burlington as the capital of the new territory. A territorial legislature was elected, which met at Burlington on the 12th of November, 1838, and proceeded to enact a code of laws for the territory. Its acts filled a volume of nearly 500 pages. An unpleasant controversy arose during the session between the legislature and the governor which resulted in an attempt of that body to secure his removal from office, but it was not successful. A controversy arose between Missouri and Iowa, as to the boundary line between them, which resulted in the calling out of the territorial militia to protect some of its officials. It was several years before the disputed boundary was finally settled. Commissioners chosen by the legislature to locate the capital of the territory selected a point on the Iowa river in Johnson county, two miles northwest of the town of Napoleon, which was platted and named Iowa City. There was no road leading to the newly-located capital and Lyman Dillon was employed to run a a furrow with a breaking plow from Iowa City to a settlement on the Mississippi river to guide travelers to the new city. Soon a well-beaten road was made beside the furrow guide and plenty of emigrant wagons came by way of the new road to the growing city of rude log cabins. During September, 1839, Governor Lucas and two daughters, piloted by General Fletcher, of Muscatine, all on horseback, rode out to see the new capital. While there the governor purchased a claim near the prospective city, which in after years became his home.

No mail route had yet been established to the new capital; letters and papers were brought from Muscatine by anyone who happened to go there on business. There was no mill nearer than the Mississippi river, and many of the first settlers in Iowa City ground their corn for bread in coffee mills. The first pioneers who located in the new town are described by a writer at that time as "mostly young men without families, who had left the paternal roof in the older states in search of homes on the frontier, to work their own way in life The young pioneer is not encumbered with much baggage; a gun, a knife, a bake-pan, a tin cup, some cornmeal and bacon, all packed on his back, he explores the country on foot. He selects a claim, builds a rude log cabin, cooks his coarse food, and freely shares his scanty supply with any traveler who comes along. When absent, his cabin door is left unfastened, and some cooked food left in sight for any

* See personal biography.

weary, hungry pioneer who may chance to come in to rest. When several settlers have taken claims in one vicinity, the first act toward civil government, is to meet at one of the cabins and form a claim association for the mutual protection of their homes. They select officers, record the names of members, and the number of each member's claim. They pledge themselves to stand by each other in holding possession of their respective homes until they can be purchased from the government."

In 1840 the census showed an increase in population of Iowa territory to 43,112. After the election of General Harrison as president, the territorial officers in Iowa were removed and their places filled by whigs. John Chambers, of Kentucky, was appointed governor to succeed Lucas, and O. W. H. Stull was appointed secretary. On the 20th of June, 1841, the steamer Ripple ascended the Iowa river to the new capital. The first grist mill in this part of the territory was erected on Clear creek by David and Joshua Switzer this year, which took the place of the coffee mills in making cornmeal and wheat flour. *The Iowa Standard*, a weekly whig paper, was started at the capital by William Crum, June 10, 1841, and the *Iowa Capital Reporter*, a democratic paper, was established on the 4th of December of the same year.

By the terms of the treaty negotiated by Governor Chambers, at Agency City, on the 11th of October, 1842, the Sac and Fox Indians ceded to the United States the last of their lands in Iowa, but they were to occupy them until October 11, 1845. It was feared that hostilities might arise between these Indians and the Sioux and Pottawattamies on the north and west, who still held lands in that portion of the territory.

It was, therefore, determined to establish a military post at the junction of the Raccoon and Des Moines rivers, garrisoned with a sufficient force to preserve peace among the Indians and protect the settlers. Capt. James Allen was sent with a company of the First U S. Dragoons and a company of infantry to build and occupy a fort at that point. He embarked his command on the little steamboat "Ione" which ascended the Des Moines river and on the 9th of May, 1842, landed at the mouth of the Raccoon river. The "Ione" was the first steamboat that ascended the Des Moines river to the point where the future capital of Iowa was to be located. Another trip brought the remainder of

the little army of occupation. The tents were pitched along the river banks while the men proceeded to fell the trees and build twenty log barracks. Lieutenant Greer was in command of the dragoons, and the infantry was under command of Lieutenant King. The Indian agent was Major Beach, whose interpreter was Josiah Smart. There were several Indian traders and mechanics with the army, most of whom remained as citizens after the fort was vacated. No white settlers were permitted

*GOVERNOR CHAMBERS.*
*Second Territorial Governor of Iowa.*

to take claims until October, 1845. A government reservation one mile square, was established around the fort, which was maintained until after the post was abandoned in 1846. Fifteen mounds, the work of a pre-historic race, were scattered over the site where the city of Des Moines now stands. In 1843, a military road was laid out from Toole's Point (now Monroe) to the fort, crossing Four Mile creek near where the Rock Island railroad now crosses it, as most of the supplies for the garrison were transported from Keokuk by wagon.

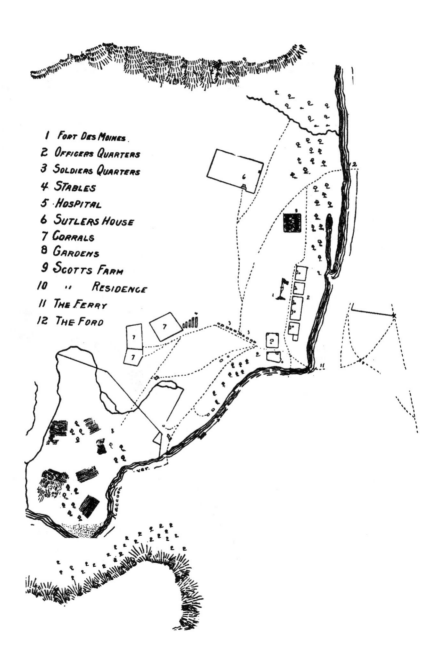

1 FORT DES MOINES
2 OFFICERS QUARTERS
3 SOLDIERS QUARTERS
4 STABLES
5 HOSPITAL
6 SUTLERS HOUSE
7 CORRALS
8 GARDENS
9 SCOTTS FARM
10 " RESIDENCE
11 THE FERRY
12 THE FORD

## CHAPTER VI.

*Constitutional Convention, 1844–1846—First Governor of the State—Monroe City—California Emigration in 1849-50—New Counties—The Wet Season of 1851—Fort Dodge Established—First Railroad—Political Revolution—Prohibition—Railroad Land Grants—New Constitution, 1857—Hard Winter.*

The winter of 1842-3 was one of unusual severity, the hardest known since the first settlement in Iowa. Snow began to fall early in November and continued at frequent intervals until late in March. The cold was intense, with terrific winds which piled the snow in huge drifts. The settlers were poorly prepared for such weather; their cabins were cold and little shelter had been provided for their live stock. Great suffering ensued, provisions became nearly exhausted, and cattle perished by the thousands. Deer, prairie chickens and quail were nearly exterminated; half-starved wolves prowled about the settlements devouring the pigs, sheep and poultry. Bank failures had left the people without money, business of every kind was prostrated, and the collection of debts became almost impossible. Money commanded 25 per cent interest, and there was little to be had on any terms.

In 1844, the legislature submitted to a vote of the people a proposition to call a convention to frame a constitution for admission of Iowa as a state. It was approved, and a convention was elected which framed a constitution. It was submitted to a vote of the people for adoption, but, owing to dissatisfaction over the proposed western boundary, it was rejected. In 1846, another constitution was framed, which was adopted by a popular vote, and, on the 28th of December, Iowa became a state in the Union. In 1845, Governor Chambers was removed from office by President Polk, and James Clark appointed. In September, 1846, Governor Clark issued a proclamation for the election of state officers and members of the first state legislature. Ansel Briggs, democrat, was elected and became the first governor of the new state of Iowa. In June, 1846, a treaty had been made with the Pottawattamie Indians, who occupied a large portion of western Iowa, by which they ceded it to the United States, to be vacated in 1847. In 1845, the Mormons had been driven out of Illinois, and large numbers of them crossed over into Iowa, and, going on to the Missouri river, founded a town on Indian creek, where Council Bluffs now stands. It was named Kanesville.

A large grant of lands was made by congress to the state of Iowa, in 1846, for the purpose of improving the navigation of the Des Moines river, and for many years work was carried on in the construc-

tion of dams and locks to afford slack water navigation for light draft steamers. After a long time and the expenditure of a large portion of the proceeds of the sale of the lands, it became evident that the project was impracticable, and the balance of the land was transferred to the Des Moines Valley Railroad company, to aid in the construction of a railroad up the Des Moines valley.

*Third Territorial Governor.*

The first state legislature fixed the salaries of the state officers as follows: Governor, $1,000; auditor, $600; secretary, $500; treasurer, $400; supreme judges, $1,000 each.

The state was entitled to two representatives in congress, and it was divided into two congressional districts. The first legislature failed to elect United States senators, and consequently the state was not represented in the senate until 1848. Commissioners had been chosen by the legislature of 1847 to locate a permanent capital for the state.

They purchased a large tract of wild prairie in Jasper county, which then had a population of but 560, and was remote from any river, grove or line of public conveyance. It was a wild, bleak prairie, and in time would make a good farm, but possessed no natural advantages for a town. They platted a town site and named it "Monroe City;" but the legislature refused to approve of such an absurd location for the capital and it was abandoned. The census of 1847 showed a population in the new state of 116,454. In 1848 the gold discoveries in California began to attract a great emigration to that country, and in 1849 thousands of gold seekers passed through Iowa on their long journey over the plains. Companies were formed in Iowa and other western states, to make the long, hard, overland trip by wagon to the Pacific coast. Most of them fitted up heavy wagons for transporting the men, tools, and provisions for the journey, and provided ox teams of from three to six yoke of oxen to a wagon. It was a slow, tedious trip, taking the whole season, and passing through a country infested by fierce tribes of hostile Indians. But by going in large caravans all well armed, most of them got safely through. But a small proportion of those who left their fertile Iowa farms bettered their condition, and many perished from exposure and hardships.

The legislature of 1850 created and named forty-nine new counties. The commissioners appointed to revise and codify the laws of the state finished their work in 1851, and the work when printed was known as the code of 1851. There was published in 1850, a complete list of the school teachers of the state then employed in the public schools, showing the name, age, and birthplace of each teacher, and the county in which the teacher was employed. This is probably the only published record of the pioneer teachers of Iowa ever made In looking over the record, we find many who afterwards became prominent citizens as lawmakers, judges, editors and educators.

### THE WET SEASON OF 1851.

The year 1851 will long be remembered for the floods which came in Iowa, and the great damage which resulted to the crops from them. The heavy rains began early in May, and continued well into the summer. Rain fell in torrents from day to day and week to week, soaking the ground so that the flat lands, river and creek bottoms could not be cultivated in many parts of the state. The roads became almost impassable; the sloughs, quagmires, and much of the tilled land vast areas of mud and water. The Mississippi river overflowed its banks, and its Iowa tributaries spread out into vast floods. Where early crops had been put in, much of them was drowned or washed out by the long continued rains. People living along the river bottoms were

driven from their homes by the floods; fences were carried away, stock drowned, and stacks destroyed. Great ditches were plowed through farms by the swift currents, and bridges by the hundred were swept away.

Towns along the rivers were inundated and huge masses of driftwood and great beds of sand were lodged among the houses and spread out among the streets and lots. When the rains ceased in July hot, dry weather came on, baking the saturated soil and parching such vegetation as survived the floods, so that crops were almost a failure throughout the state. Cholera broke out along the Mississippi and Des Moines valleys and the ravages of that terrible plague added to the misery and despair of the afflicted people. The frightful disease struck down hundreds in apparent robust health, often proving fatal in a few hours. In some places famine added to the horrors of floods and pestilence, as the crops were entirely destroyed, and many sold their farms for a trifle and left the state. Those who remained and raised crops found a good market for any surplus in the crowds of emigrants who were crossing the state on their way to the California gold fields.

Early in 1849, Colonel Mason, of the Sixth United States Infantry, was sent to select a site on the Upper Des Moines for a military post. The Sioux Indians in that part of the state had been committing depredations and a fort was to be erected for a military company for the protection of the settlers in that section. Colonel Mason selected a site on the high table land opposite the mouth of the Lizard creek on the east bank of the Des Moines river. Early in the spring of 1850, Maj. Samuel Woods, with a detachment of the Sixth Infantry, was sent to the new post, which had been named Fort Clark. Soon after the name was changed to Fort Dodge, by order of the war department. The command of Colonel Woods had started from Fort Buckner on the Iowa river on the last day of July, with a wagon train, to transport provision, tools and camp equipments. There was no road and they had to bridge many streams and sloughs on the way. They reached the Des Moines about the middle of August and pitched their tents on the plat where the city of Fort Dodge now stands. They proceeded to cut trees and build twelve substantial log buildings, which were completed before winter. During the first year the troops occupied Fort Dodge the government expended about $80,000 in buildings and other improvements. The fort was vacated on the 3d of October, 1853, when the troops were sent 150 miles northwest to establish another post on the frontier.

In 1854, the California immigration had subsided and the tide was turning strongly into Iowa. The Chicago and Rock Island railroad had reached the Mississippi river at a point opposite Davenport, on the 22d of February. For the first time Iowa was within reach of the eastern world by a direct line of railroad, and the era of its prosperity was at hand. Soon the railroad would push westward and open up our great prairies to settlement, by transporting lumber and fuel to encourage settlement and afford markets for their products. The census of 1852 had shown a population of 229,929, and at the beginning of 1854 it had increased to 324,401. Immigration was now flowing in with great rapidity, as people for the first time seemed willing to settle on the great prairies away from the rivers and timber. All hopes were now turned towards railroad building as the one thing needed to open up the vast fertile inland prairies to markets and rapid settlement. Water navigation on our inland rivers had proved a failure and the hope now was in railroads. Millions of acres of public lands were unoccupied and there was a general feeling that some of them should be granted to aid in securing railroads into the interior and western portions of the state.

In anticipation of the completion of the railroad from Chicago to Rock Island, a company had been formed in Davenport in 1853, composed of citizens of eastern cities and Iowa men, to secure its extension at an eary day on through our state. It was called the Mississippi & Missouri Railroad company and had an authorized capital of $6,-000,000. The first board of directors was J. E. Sheffield, Henry Farnam, J. M. Wilson, N. B. Judd, Ebenezer Cook, John P. Cook, Hiram Price and James Grant. Breaking ground for this first railroad in Iowa was celebrated by an immense gathering of people. A long procession was formed, conducted by A. C. Fulton, chief marshal, to the corner of Fifth and Rock Island streets, where the railroad was to begin on the Iowa side. Stands had been erected for speaking. John P. Cook was the first speaker, who portrayed the privations of the pioneers who had long been shut in from the outside world, and spoke in glowing terms of the bright future with its railroad soon to cross the great river and connect Iowa with the east. Soon it would push on over the great prairies and bring to Davenport the products of the opening farms of western Iowa.

Other eloquent speakers foretold the great advantages to come from the railroad. When the time came for breaking ground, Antoine Le Claire, the founder of the city, pulled off his coat, seized a spade and wheelbarrow, and amid loud cheers and music from the band, this half-breed old pioneer who weighed 300 pounds, began the grading of the first railroad in Iowa. The building of the road was pushed with vigor, under John E. Henry, master of construction, Peter A. Dey, B. B. Brayton, and S. B. Reed, civil engineers. Scott county took $50,000 of stock, Davenport $75,000 and private citizens subscribed $100,000. John A. Dix, of New York, was elected president of the company; Wm. B. Ogden, of Chicago, vice-president, and John E. Henry, secretary. The grading went on during 1854, and the iron came on to Rock Island. The first locomotive was brought over the Mississippi river on a flat boat in September, and was named the "Le Claire." Soon after the "Iowa," another locomotive, was carried over in the same way, and when winter formed a solid ice bridge, the third locomotive, "John A. Dix," was brought over. Some construction cars were also brought over and the work progressed slowly, as there was an immense bluff to be cut through, and it was August 25, 1855, when the first excursion train run out to Walcott, 12 miles west of Davenport. On the 1st of January, 1856, the road was completed to Iowa City,

*First Governor of the State.*

and it was then predicted by Mr. Farnam, its moving spirit, that it would reach Council Bluffs in three years. But hard times and the great war intervened and it did not reach Des Moines until long years after that time. The first railroad bridge across the Mississippi was built from Rock Island to Davenport. It was begun September 1, 1854, and completed so that the first railroad train that ever crossed the Mississippi came over on the 27th day of April, 1856.

In 1854, a political revolution began in Iowa. Up to this time the state had been ruled in every branch of its government by the democratic party. But the efforts of the national democratic administration to open the new territories of the west to slavery had aroused a bitter antagonism on the part of thousands of freedom-loving people of the north. The whigs of Iowa nominated for governor James W. Grimes, who was strongly opposed to the spread of slavery into the new territories, and he received the support of the anti-slavery voters generally throughout the state. The result of a very warm contest was the election of Grimes by a majority of 2,120. James Thorington, the free soil candidate for congress, was elected in the Second district over ex-Governor Hempstead, democrat, by a majority of 1,562. The legislature also, early in 1855, elected James Harlan, free soil, to the United States senate, to succeed A. C. Dodge, democrat. In all of these important elections the principal issue was the question whether slavery should be permitted to extend into the western territories. Iowa, which had heretofore, in all general elections for state officers or president, given its support to democrats, now refused to follow that party in the support of slavery extension. Many democrats left their old party on this issue, and soon after helped to organize a new party opposed to the spread of slavery into free territory. Hiram Price, of Scott county, was the most notable leader of these free soil democrats at this time. The legislature, in 1855, also inaugurated the prohibitory liquor law, which had for its object the suppression of the sale of intoxicating liquor to be used as a beverage, and the entire and absolute abolition of drinking saloons. The legislature also provided for the removal of the capital of the state from Iowa City to Des Moines. An act was also passed providing for an election to determine whether a convention should be chosen to revise the constitution of the state. The prohibitory liquor law was submitted to a vote of the people for adoption or rejection, and was approved by a majority of 2,910. With some modifications and amendments, this law remained on the statute books for more than forty years, until nullified by a mulct law.

The conflict between the political parties over the extension of slavery continued to grow more intense, until in 1856 a new party was organized

*Second Governor of the State.  Elected from Dubuque in 1850.*

having for its chief purpose opposition to the extension of slavery. On the 22d of February, 1856, a convention was held at Iowa City, at which the republican party of Iowa was organized, which for more than forty years controlled the state, enacted and administered its laws. The efforts which had been made for many years to secure a grant of lands to aid in the building of railroads in Iowa were at last successful. James Thorington, the republican member of congress from the Second district, had worked untiringly for this object, and, finally, with the co-operation of our senators, had secured a grant of public lands to aid in the building of three lines of railroad over the state, from Lyons, Davenport and Burlington to points on the Missouri.

The grants embraced every alternate section of government land six miles in width on each side of the proposed lines of railroad. The legislature in extra session accepted these grants, and appropriated the lands under certain restrictions to the Iowa Central Air line, the Mississippi and Missouri, and the Burlington and Missouri Railroad companies. The election held to determine whether the constitution of the state should be revised gave a majority for the convention of 18,628. At the presidential election in 1856, Iowa, for the first time, gave its vote against the democrats, and for John C. Fremont, republican, by a plurality of 7,774. The convention chosen to revise the constitution assembled at Iowa City on the 19th of January, 1857, and proceeded with its work. The principal important changes were as follows:

*First.*—Providing that the general elections should be held on the second Tuesday in October.

*Second.*—That the biennial sessions of the legislature should begin on the second Monday in January.

*Third.*—That it should require the votes of a majority of the members elected in each branch of the general assembly to pass a bill.

*Fourth.*—The office of lieutenant-governor was created, and he should be president of the senate.

Upper Row—Francis A. Springer, President; Sheldon G. Winchester, Alpheus Scott, James A. Young, Thos. Seely, Daniel H. Soloman.
Middle Row—William A. Warren, John Edwards, William Patterson, David P. Palmer, Geo. W. Ellis, Squire Ayers.
Lower Row—Daniel W. Price, Jas. C. Traer, Jas. F. Wilson, Geo. Gillaspy, Jonathan C. Hall, Harvey J. Scott.

Upper Row—Aylett R. Cotton, Jeremiah Hollingsworth, David Bunker, Rufus L. B. Clark, John T. Clark, Amos Harris.
Middle Row—Timothy Day, Albert H. Marvin, Lewis Todhunter, Hiram D. Gibson, Edward Johnstone, Moses W. Robinson.
Lower Row—Wm. Penn Clarke, John A. Parvin, Hosea W. Gray, J. H. Emerson, John H. Peters, A. H Marvin.

MEMBERS OF CONSTITUTIONAL CONVENTION OF 1857.

*Fifth.*—The supreme judges shall be elected by the people.

*Sixth.* — Banks may be established under laws enacted by the general assembly, provided such banking laws must be approved by the people at a special election.

*Seventh.* — The limit of the debt of the state was changed from $100,000 to $250,000. In case of invasion, insurrection or defense in time of war, this limit may be exceeded.

*First capitol of Wisconsin Territory, then including Iowa, at Belmont, now a farm in Lafayette county, Wisconsin. Gov. Henry Dodge was appointed Governor, and convened the first legislature there in 1836. The next session, 1837-8, and the extra session of June, 1838, were held at Burlington.*

*Eighth.*—The number of senators in the general assembly of the state is fixed at fifty, and the number of representatives is fixed at one hundred.

*Ninth.*—A state board of education was provided for to legislate for the public schools.

*Tenth.*—The permanent capital of the state was fixed at Des Moines, and the State university was permanently located at Iowa City.

*Eleventh.*—A proposition to be submitted to the people to strike the word "white" from the article on suffrage, the effect of which would be to permit negroes to vote if the proposition should be adopted.

The census taken for 1856 gave the population of the state 517,875, showing an increase in two years of 193,474.

The past two years had been a period of great prosperity to the people of Iowa. Settlements were spreading out over the great prairies in every direction at a rate unprecedented. Crops had been large and prices of farm products high. Breaking teams by the thousands were turning over the prairie sod and converting the great wild plains into productive farms. Groves, orchards and hedges were being planted and improved farm machinery was taking the place of the toilsome and slow hand labor.

## THE HARD WINTERS.

The winter of 1855-6 was one of great severity. The weather had been mild up to the first week in January. But soon after deep snows began to fall and fierce winds came, bringing intense cold. Very few barns or good sheds had been provided for domestic animals. Cattle had generally been kept in the shelter of hay and straw stacks and run in the stalk fields, and had wintered very well. The majority of farms of the early settlers had groves of native timber which afforded shelter from the bleak winds of winter, for their cabins and live stock. But the terrible storms, deep snows and severe cold of the winter of 1855-6 was so long continued that thousands of cattle perished. Many persons were caught out in the fearful blizzards far from shelter and were frozen to death. The next winter, that of 1856-7, was very cold with deep snows, covered with crust, which proved fatal to most of the deer in Iowa. Breaking through the crust in the deep drifts they became exhausted and were slaughtered by the hundreds by men and dogs, until they became nearly exterminated.

*A. J. Kynett, Chaplain; Francis Thompson; W. Blair Lord, Reporter; H. M. Parkhurst, Reporter; S. C. Trowbridge, Sergeant-At-Arms; Thos. J. Saunders, Secretary; Ellsworth N. Bates, Assistant Secretary.*

*MEMBERS OF CONSTITUTIONAL CONVENTION OF 1857.*

## Chapter VII.

*The Lott Massacres—Inkpadutah—Northwest Settlements—Indian Outrages on the Little Sioux Settlers at the Lakes in Dickinson County—Massacre of the Settlers in 1857.*

### SPIRIT LAKE.

Long before the first white settlements were made in Iowa the beautiful group of lakes near the headwaters of the Des Moines and Little Sioux rivers had been favorite hunting and camping resorts for the Sioux Indians. In 1680, Louis Hennepin, in his explorations of the Upper Mississippi valley in Minnesota, encountered the Yankton Sioux Indians. In 1700, La Sueur explored a portion of country about the Blue Earth river and found Sioux Indians occupying all of that region and southward into what is now northern Iowa. Their name for Spirit Lake was Minne-Waukon, which signifies "Spirit water."

The Sioux were very reluctant to give up the region about the lakes to the whites, as they were required to do by the treaty of 1851. As early as 1848, when Mr. Marsh, a government surveyor, was running the correction line near Fort Dodge, his party encountered a band of Sioux Indians under Si-dom-i-na-do-tah, a Sioux chief, and was compelled to turn back and leave the country. In 1849 some adventurers went up the Des Moines valley and made claims near the mouth of Boone river. The Indians soon discovered the invaders, destroyed their cabins and drove them out of the country. This and other troubles led to the establishment of Fort Dodge and stationing a military company there. Sidominadotah was the chief of a band of Sisseton Sioux; his name signified "Two Fingers." His band numbered about 500 when first known by the whites, and he had led them in several battles with the Pottawattamies in northwestern Iowa. One was fought near Twin Lakes in Calhoun county. The last battle was on the Lizard, in the present limits of Webster county. The Sioux chief, who was a brave and skillful commander, had concealed his warriors in the woods and brush on a high bluff. The enemy was led into ambush where they encountered a terrible fire from the Sioux. The Pottawattamies made a stubborn fight, but, outnumbered and surprised, they were defeated with great slaughter, and the survivors who reached their own country were so few that their tribe made no more raids into the Sioux country.

In 1847 a desperado, named Henry Lott, went up the Des Moines river and built a cabin near the mouth of the Boone, which became a rendezvous for horse-thieves and outlaws. Horses were stolen from the settlements in the valley below and from the Indians, secreted on Lott's premises, taken from there to eastern settlements and sold. In 1848 some of Lott's gang stole a number of ponies from the Sioux Indians who were hunting along the river. Sidominadotah and six of his party tracked the ponies to Lott's settlement and found them concealed in the woods. They were recovered and Lott and his gang were ordered to leave the settlement within five days. Lott refused to go, and at the expiration of the time the Sioux chief ordered his cabin to be burned and his cattle to be killed. Lott became alarmed, abandoned his wife and small children, and with a step-son fled down the river. Upon reaching the Pea settlement he spread the report that his family had been massacred by the Sioux. The settlers at once organized a party to punish the Indians. Che-mause, or "Johnny Green," a Fox chief, was at Elk Rapids, sixteen miles below, with several hundred of his band. He furnished twenty-six warriors for the expedition, which was placed under his command and piloted by Lott. When they reached his claim the Sioux were gone and Lott's wife and children were there without food. A young son of Lott had followed his father when he fled, but after wandering for twenty miles along the river had perished with cold. Lott remained on his claim where his wife died during the year, Lott reported from abuse by the Indians and from exposure in his absence. Lott swore terrible vengeance upon the Sioux chief, but made no haste to execute it. In the fall of 1853, Lott and a son passed through Fort Dodge with an ox team and a wagon loaded with provisions, goods and three barrels of whisky. He went up to Humboldt county and built a rude cabin on the banks of a creek, which still bears his name. There he opened trade with the Indians in goods and whisky. In the month of January, 1854, Lott learned that his old enemy, Sidominadotah, with his family, was camped on a creek, which has since been named Bloody Run. Taking his son one day, both well armed, Lott started out on his fearful mission to the camp of the Sioux chief. Finding that he was not recognized, Lott made professions of warm friendship for the Indians. He told the chief that there was a large herd of elk on the river bottom and induced him to go off after them. Lott and his son then started away as if going back to their cabin, but as soon as the old chief was out of sight, they turned back, and hiding in the tall grass watched until he returned from the hunt. Riding along on his pony, unsuspicious of danger, they opened fire upon him, and he fell to the ground dead. They took his gun and pony, and stripping off his clothing they disguised themselves as Indians and concealed themselves again and waited for night. When darkness came on, they skulked back to the dead chief's tepees and gave the war cry, and as the terrified women and children ran out they were murdered one by one. The wretches then plundered the camp of everything of value and left the mutilated bodies of the women and children to be devoured by wolves. The victims were the aged mother, the wife and children of Sidominadotah and two orphans living with him. One little girl

chief to some of the settlers. He spread the report that they had been driven from his claim by the Indians. Lott continued his flight down the river, leaving one of his boys at T. S. White's, six miles below Fort Dodge, and his two little girls at Doctor Hull's, in Boone county. Major Williams and several of the Indians followed rapidly on the trail of the murderers, but Lott and his guilty son having several days start of them, soon struck off west over the great unsettled prairie and escaped. It was afterwards learned that they crossed the Missouri river above Council Bluffs, and struck out on the great plains. Several years after it was learned from a letter written by Lott's son to an acquaintance in Boone county, that after settling in California, Lott met a deserved fate at the hands of a vigilance committee for one of his numerous crimes.

*Old building first used for a capitol at Iowa City.*

escaped in the darkness, hiding in the grass, and one little boy terribly wounded and left for dead, eventually recovered, and from these was learned the particulars of the horrible massacre. The murderers returned to their cabin, packed everything of value in their wagon and fled down the river, after setting fire to their own cabin, to throw suspicion on the Indians as the perpetrators of their horrid crimes.

Ink-pa-du-tah, a brother of the murdered chief, with another band of Sioux, was camped a few miles away, and in a few days he discovered the mangled bodies of his mother, brother, and family, partly devoured by wolves. Inkpadutah and Major Williams, of Fort Dodge, investigated the affair thoroughly, tracked the murderers down the river to the mouth of the Boone, where Lott sold the pony, furs, gun, and other property of the murdered

Inkpadutah brooded sullenly over the fate of his brother and family, seeming to believe that some of the white settlers besides Lott were parties to the massacre and aided him to escape. The Sioux were greatly incensed upon learning that the head of their murdered chief had been taken to Homer and nailed up on the side of a house, and they threatened to be revenged upon the whites. Inkpadutah never renewed his friendship with the whites after the Lott massacre, but looked upon them as treacherous enemies. There can be no doubt that he determined to bide his time and watch for an opportunity to retaliate, as he did in 1857 upon the innocent people who had settled at the lakes.

During the seasons of 1855-6, adventurous pioneers had prospected the valley of the Little Sioux, and made claims at various places along the river, built rude cabins, and settled there with their families at Correctionville, Pilot Rock, Peterson and Gillett's Grove. An Irish colony had settled at Medium lake on the west branch of the Des Moines river in Palo Alto county, and a Mr. Granger had built a cabin in Emmet county near the Minnesota line. A small party had ventured farther up the river and made a settlement called Springfield (now Jackson). Asa C. and Ambrose A. Call, brothers, had taken claims and lived on the east branch of the Des Moines river near where Algona now stands, as early as 1854. Settlements had been made about Okoboji and Spirit lakes in Dickinson county in 1856, numbering about fifty persons. Most of the Indians had by this time removed from northwestern Iowa, but parties of Sioux frequently returned to hunt and fish along the rivers and lakes. Inkpadutah, who often came with his band, had recently professed friendship for the people in these frontier settlements, but those who knew of the Lott massacre and understood the Indian character, were apprehensive that some day he would take terrible vengeance on the whites for the murder of his relatives by Lott.

The winter of 1856-7 was one of great severity. Frequent storms had swept over the great prairies of northwestern Iowa, covering them with a depth of snow that made travel very difficult and dangerous. They continued late into March, filling the ravines with drifts so deep that communication between the scattered settlements was almost impossible for weeks and months. The provisions of the settlers had become greatly reduced during the long snow blockade, and parties had been sent to distant eastern settlements for supplies.

Inkpadutah now saw the time for which he had been waiting more than three years had come when he could safely take vengeance upon the whites for the slaughter of his mother, brother and their families. It mattered not to him that these settlers where wholly innocent of any act, knowledge or sympathy with the brutal murders; they were of the hatred white race to which Lott belonged and their lives must atone for his horrid crimes. Inkpadutah, with members of his band, had, during the summer of 1856, visited most of the frontier settlements and carefully noted their isolation and helplessness in case of sudden attack. When the deep snows of the long winter had shut them off from aid, Inkpadutah carefully laid his plans.

In February, 1857, the Sioux chief selected thirty of his fiercest warriors, and accompanied by their squaws to allay suspicion of danger on part of the settlers, they started out on their relentless mission. They followed up the Little Sioux valley, separating into small parties; a detachment was sent to each cabin as they took their way up the valley. Their first act at each place was to seize the guns and ammunition of the settlers, thus rendering resistance impossible, then

they took the provisions and cattle. Then the horrid work began. The women and girls were next seized, while loaded guns were pointed at their husbands, fathers and brothers, as the brutal savages dragged the defenseless, terrified women to their camps. There they were subjected to the most horrid abuse, then left to wade through the deep snow to their desolated homes.

Resistance on the part of the widely separated settlers would have brought certain death to all. At Gillett's Grove, ten armed savages forced their way into a cabin occupied by two families, seized the women and girls, perpetrating the most brutal outrages upon them. They then destroyed the furniture, beds and dishes, killed the cattle and

*JAMES W. GRIMES.*
*Third Governor of the State.*

hogs, carried off the horses, and even robbed the women of clothing and every article about the house. At midnight, the terrified families fled through the deep snow, thinly clad, wandering about for thirty-six hours, until they reached Abner Bell's, their nearest neighbor, utterly worn out and nearly perished with cold. From cabin to cabin the Indians proceeded, everywhere repeating the horrible outrages upon the defenseless people. Up to this time no one had been killed. As soon as the Indians went on towards the lakes, Abner Bell, Mr. Weaver and Mr. Wilcox made their way through the deep snow to Fort Dodge, seventy miles distant. Their story of the Indian outrages created intense excitement, and all realized that the frontier settlers were in imminent danger. But several days had elapsed, no one knew where the Indians had gone, and the snow was so deep there was no hope that they could be overtaken by the time a military company could be organized to pursue them.

The pioneers who first erected a cabin in the beautiful grove on the shores of Lake Okoboji were Rowland Gardner and Harvey Luce, his son-in-law. They had recently emigrated from the state of New York. Crossing the great prairies in a covered wagon drawn by oxen, they found no settlement west of Algona. They traveled in a northwesterly direction until the evening of July 16, 1856, when they camped in a fine grove on the shore of West Okoboji. They were charmed with the beauty of the lakes, woods and prairie, and decided to make

little children, Albert, 4 years old, and the baby, Amanda, a year old. A short time after their arrival four young men from Red Wing, Minn., came and camped on the narrow strip of land separating East and West Okoboji lakes. They were Dr. I. H. Harriott, Bertell Snyder, William and Carl Granger. They were the first white men to paddle a canoe on these lakes. They were so enchanted with the beauty of the country that each took a claim near the lakes, and together they built a cabin on a peninsula since named Smith's Point.

The next settlers were from Delaware county, Iowa, James Mattock and his wife, Mary, with

*Council Bluffs' old log house. First building erected in Pottawattamie county. Erected in 1832 by a detachment of regular troops stationed to keep peace among the Indians.*

their home here. Not a sign of human habitation or smoke of camp-fire was to be seen in any direction from the highest point in the vicinity. Elk and deer were grazing on the prairies; waterfowl were coming and going from lake to lake; great flocks of prairie chickens were seen; squirrels and song birds were heard in the beautiful woods on every side. The emigrants pitched their tent and selected a site for their cabin on the southeast side of West Okoboji, near the rocky projection since known as Pillsbury Point. The families consisted of Rowland Gardner, his wife Frances, little Rowland, 6 years old; Abbie, 14; Eliza, 16; Mary, the oldest daughter, married to Harvey Luce, and their two

their children, Alice, Daniel, Agnes, Jacob and Jackson. They built a cabin between the lakes opposite Granger, on the south. Robert Mathieson and a son lived with them. Some weeks later Joel Howe, his wife Millie, with six children, Lydia, Jonathan, Sardis, Alfred, Jacob and Philetus, settled on the east shore of East Okoboji. Lydia had married Alvin Noble and they had a boy, John, two years old. This family, with Joseph M. Thatcher, his wife, Elizabeth, with an infant daughter, Dora, lived in a cabin they had built a mile north of Howe's. A trapper, Morris Markham, boarded with Noble and Thatcher. These people were all from Hampton, in Franklin county. Six miles northwest on the west shore of Spirit Lake, William Marble and his young wife, Margaret, recently married in Linn county, had taken a claim and built a cabin. This made a settlement among the lakes in the winter of 1856-7 of six families, separated by distances of from one-half to six miles, among the beautiful groves in which were living sixteen men, eight women and fourteen children. This little colony, coming to the lakes in the summer of 1856, had not been able to raise crops sufficient to furnish food for the winter. Early in February their supply was getting low and they had to send parties a long distance for flour, meal and meat. It was a perilous trip through the deep snows, over the bleak, trackless prairies, where the fierce blizzards of that cold winter swept with

The four young men made a large hand-sled and on it took some of the provisions, and started for the lakes. After a hard struggle through the drifts, amid blinding storms, Luce and his three companions reached the Gardner cabin on the evening of March 6th. Jonathan Howe was a son of Joel Howe, Clark was from Waterloo and Ryan was from Hampton. Jonathan Howe and Ryan went on that night to the Howe settlement. On the second day after the arrival of the young men at the lakes the weather became mild and pleasant and Mr. Gardner determined to go to Fort Dodge for provisions. As the family sat down to an early breakfast the cabin door was opened and fourteen fierce Sioux Indians walked in, led by Inkpadutah. At first they professed friendship and called for food.

*The massacre at the Gardner cabin. From an oil painting by Mrs. Abbie Gardner Sharp.*

resistless fury. The ravines in many places were drifted full of snow and difficult to cross. But supplies must be obtained, and Joseph M. Thatcher and Harvey Luce volunteered to undertake the perilous trip to Waterloo with an ox team and sled, at the risk of their lives. After a slow and dangerous journey over the unsettled, trackless prairies, working their way through immense drifts, they reached Waterloo, loaded their sled and started on the return. Finally, reaching a cabin ten miles below the Irish colony, on the Des Moines river, their oxen became exhausted and could go no further. It was decided that Thatcher should remain here with the team several days until they could proceed with the load, while Luce should go on home. Here he found Jonathan Howe, Enoch Ryan and Robert Clark on their way to the lakes.

When they had eaten all in the house they undertook to seize the guns and ammunition, but Luce and Clark resisted them, and a most unequal struggle began. At this moment Dr. Harriott and Carl Snyder came in, and seeing five determined men, the savages quieted down and again seemed friendly. But Mr. Gardner was not deceived; he realized that the entire settlement was in great danger and quietly urged the young men to slip away and notify all of the settlers to come immediately to his house with their arms, as his cabin was the largest and strongest for defense. But Harriott and Snyder thought there was no danger, and after waiting awhile started off towards their cabin. The Indians hung around until near noon when they started towards the Mattock house driving Gardner's cattle and shooting them on the way. Gardner, Luce and Clark now realized the great danger and made a heroic effort to warn their neighbors of their peril. Mr. Gardner remained to protect his family while Luce and Clark hurried off to give the alarm.

Soon after 2 o'clock, the rapid fire of guns was heard in the direction of the Mattock house, and the frantic screams of terrified women warned the Gardner family that the terrible massacre had begun. Mr. Gardner hastily barricaded his doors and prepared to defend his family to the last, but his terrified wife, realizing how hopeless the contest must be, begged of her husband not to fire upon the Indians. She had hope that the many acts of kindness bestowed upon them in times past would save her family from slaughter. Mr. Gardner yielded to his wife's intreaties, but all in vain, for

*Interior of the Gardner cabin.*

the savages soon forced an entrance into the cabin and shot Mr. Gardner dead. Then turning upon his helpless family they beat out the brains of the women and children. The only one spared was Abbie, the daughter of fourteen. The terrified child when seized by them begged the bloody savages to kill her, too, as she could not endure the thought of the worse fate she was to be saved for. But heedless of her entreaties, with the dying moans of her mother, sister and the little children sounding in her ears, they dragged her away.

At the Mattock house a brave resistance was made. When the attack began, Dr. Harriott and Bert Snyder seized their guns and hastened to the assistance of their neighbors. But outnumbered as they were, five to one, by the Sioux warriors, there was no chance for successful defense. The five men fought with the desperation of despair to protect the women and children and their own lives. But one by one they fell before the rifles and clubs of the well armed savages. Not one survived to tell the story of the brave but hopeless struggle of the settlers at this place. When the last man had fallen the Indians turned upon the

frantic and defenseless women and children and slaughtered them without mercy. When Abbie Gardner was dragged to this spot, the mangled bodies of five men, two women and several children were lying in the blood-stained snow, while the shrieks of other children roasting in the flames of the burning house, made up a picture of horrors too hideous to be described. A careful examination of this vicinity later by the party who buried the dead, throws some light on the struggle here. It appeared that Dr. Harriott and Bert Snyder, from their cabin, had heard the guns and the shrieks of the women and children when the attack began at Mattock's. Regardless of their own safety, the brave young men seized their rifles and hastened to the defense of their neighbors. At the first fire, Dr. Harriott laid out one of the Sioux, then rushing into the thickest of the fight the two brave young men shattered their empty guns over the heads of the savages in a hand to hand fight. But the contest was too unequal; five men against twenty or more Sioux warriors were soon killed. How many of the Indians were killed or wounded in the desperate conflict can never be known, as the Indians always carefully conceal their losses from the enemy. Abbie Gardner believed that none were killed and but one wounded. But Major Williams, the veteran commander of the relief expedition, is of a different opinion from the careful investigations of the burial party made a short time after the massacre. He was intimately acquainted with the customs of the Sioux Indians and their cunning concealment of their losses in battle. In his report to Governor Grimes, made on the 12th of April, immediately after the return of the burial party to Fort Dodge, Major Williams writes:

"The number of Indians killed or wounded must have been from fifteen to twenty. From the number seen to fall, and judging from the bloody clothes and pools of blood left in their encampments, the struggle at the lakes must have been severe, particularly at the house of Squire Mattock. Eleven bodies were found at this house, together with several broken guns. They appear to have fought here hand to hand."

Abbie Gardner's recollections of the massacre were written more than twenty-five years after her escape from captivity, and she was but 14 years old at the time of the tragedy, and it is not strange that such a discrepancy between her estimate of Indian losses and that of Major Williams should occur. It is not likely the wily Sioux would permit their helpless captive to know the extent of their losses. Luce and Clark, who started from the Gardner house to warn the settlers of the danger, went south of East Okoboji towards Mr. Howe's. They were stealthily followed by a party of Sioux, and shot down and scalped near the outlet. This closed the first day's horrid work on the 8th of March, 1857.

That night the Indians celebrated the butchery of twenty men, women and children with blackened faces, keeping time in their war dances to the beating of drums, and circling round with unearthly yells among the mutilated bodies of their victims over the blood-stained snow until exhausted by their horrid orgies. Crouched in an Indian tepee, Abbie Gardner, the only survivor of the first day's massacre, prostrated by the horrors of the awful fate of her family and neighbors, this tender young girl endured such anguish as seldom comes to a human being to bear. While the bloody massacre had been going on, the neighbors of the victims living on the east side of the lakes had no warning of their impending danger and the awful fate awaiting them. Luce and Clark, who had started out to warn them, were lying dead on the way.

entered the cabin. Thus Noble and Ryan were deceived and had no thought of danger, when the Indians suddenly turned their guns upon them and fired before they could reach their own arms. Both were instantly killed, and the savages snatched the two children from their mothers' arms and, swinging them by their feet against a tree near the door, crushed their heads. They then plundered the house, killed the hogs and cattle, and then returned and seized Mrs. Noble and Mrs. Thatcher, who were crushed with anguish and despair, and dragged them along back toward the Howe cabin. Here they stopped to plunder the house, and Mrs. Noble saw with unspeakable anguish the mutilated bodies of her mother, sister and brothers. As she sunk down prostrated with horrors, she discovered her brother Jacob, though

*The killing of Mrs. Thatcher. From an oil painting by Mrs. Abbie Gardner Sharp.*

Early in the morning of the 9th, Joel Howe started to make his way through the deep snow to Mr. Gardner's to borrow some flour. He was met by the Indians on their way to his house to continue their horrid butchery. They shot him down and severed his head from his body, then hurried on to his cabin. Mrs. Howe, her son Jonathan, his sister Sardis and her three younger brothers were in the house all unsuspicious of danger. Suddenly the door was burst open, a wild rush of yelling Indians with gleaming tomahawks and scalping knives were upon them; and a few moments later, amid shrieks of terror, all of the little household were gasping in dying agony. Going on to the Thatcher cabin, the savages found Alvin Noble, his wife and child, Mr. Ryan, Mrs. Thatcher and her child. Seeing two stalwart young men at home, the cowardly Indians professed friendship as they

terribly wounded, was still alive. When the Indians went off to kill the cattle, Mrs. Noble tried to get her brother into the house, hoping he might be found and saved; but, before they left, the Indians saw he was still alive and killed him in the presence of his sister.

The Indians remained about the lakes until the 13th, while Wm. Marble and his young wife, in their home on the west shore of Spirit Lake, knew nothing of the terrible fate that had overtaken every family of their neighbors. They were several miles from any house, and as the snow was very deep Mr. Marble had not ventured away from home and had heard nothing to alarm him. On the morning of the 13th, soon after breakfast, as Mrs. Marble relates, looking out of their cabin window, a band of painted and armed Indians was seen approaching. They came into the house professing friendship. One of them wanted to exchange his rifle for a very fine one belonging to Mr. Marble who, fearing to offend them, consented to trade. The Indians then proposed shooting at a mark; and Mr. Marble stepped forward to put up the target when the treacherous Sioux shot him in the back. Mrs. Marble, who had been anxiously watching them from the window in fear for her husband's safety, sprang out with piercing screams as he fell, and threw her arms around her murdered husband, in the agony of despair. He was dead, and she was alone in the hands of the brutal, merciless savages. They flung her one side and searched the body of their victim, taking from it a belt containing $1,000 in gold. This was the little fortune the young couple had brought with them to improve and stock the beautiful farm they had chosen on the shore of the lake for their future home. It was a terrible ending of all their hopes and plans. The Indians then plundered the house, took Mrs. Marble's gold watch, clothing and all of her household treasures, placed her on a pony and started off. In one brief hour the young wife had lost husband, home, liberty and everything but life, and was dragged away into captivity to endure a living agony, too horrible to contemplate. The Indians returned to the main body and here Mrs Marble found three other captive women as wretched, hopeless and despairing as herself. These four helpless young women now learned from each other the entire destruction of the settlement, and that not a man was left alive to carry the terrible tidings of the massacre and their enslavement to the nearest settlement. With visions of the merciless slaughter of fathers, mothers, sisters, brothers, husbands and children, ever before their eyes, with moans of the dying ever in their ears, and the torturing memory ever in their minds, death would have been to them a merciful relief. But they were reserved for the further tortures that fiendish brutality of savages could still inflict upon their helpless victims. Before breaking camp the Indians proceeded to leave a record of their now completed massacre up to this time. Peeling the bark from a large tree, on the white surface they pictured in signs the scenes of their late atrocities. This ghastly record was visible for many years, and was seen by many of the early settlers.

Carl Granger's body was found near their cabin where he had been shot down, as it is supposed he was returning from a hunt after his two companions had been slain at the Mattock cabin. His brother, William, had gone back to his home in Minnesota and thus escaped. Eliza Gardner had gone to Springfield to spend the winter; while J. M.

Thatcher fortunately had not yet returned from his trip to the settlements for provisions; while Morris Markham was absent in search of cattle. Thus four members of the colony were saved by absence, while three unfortunate visitors, who arrived two days before the massacre, were among the victims.

Inkpadutah had bided his time and this was his awful vengeance for the massacre of his relatives by Henry Lott and son more than three years before.

Not a person was left in the entire colony to carry the news of the massacre to other settlements. But it so happened that the massacre was discovered on the 9th, the day upon which the Howe, Noble and Thatcher families were slaughtered. Morris Markham was returning from his trip to the Des Moines river on that day, and reached the Gardner cabin about midnight, cold, hungry and nearly exhausted.

It was very dark and a cold wind was blowing from the north. He was surprised to find the door open and the Gardner cabin deserted. Upon looking around he found the dead bodies of the family, some in the house and others lying in the snow. Horror stricken by the evidences of some terrible tragedy, he cautiously went on through the dark forest towards the Mattock house. When near, he discovered the Indian camp, and at once concluded that the savage Sioux had come in his absence and murdered his neighbors. He could see the smoldering ruins of the Mattock cabin and the mutilated bodies of more of the settlers lying around in the snow. Almost overcome with the horrors around him he turned back towards the Howe settlement, hoping it had escaped the massacre. But upon reaching Howe's cabin he again came upon the ghastly forms of women and children lying in the snow. Almost paralyzed by the horrid sights he turned towards his own home at the Noble cabin, hoping against hope that it might have escaped. But there before him lay the mangled forms of Noble, Ryan and the children. Markham had waded through the snow for thirty miles since morning, without rest or food. His feet were frozen and he was now completely exhausted and overcome by the horrors around him. He crawled into a deep ravine, not far away, where he started a fire with some matches he fortunately had, and where, without shelter or food, he sat the remainder of the night, not daring to lie down lest he might fall asleep and be found and murdered by the Indians. Before daylight he started for the nearest settlement at Springfield, eighteen miles distant. He reached that place completely worn out and spread the news of the terrible fate of the Okoboji colony.

## CHAPTER VIII.

*The Heroic Defense at Springfield—Several Massacred—Twenty Escape—Their Terrible Sufferings and Final Rescue—The Relief Expedition of Major Williams—Bury the Dead—Caught in a Great Blizzard— Great Suffering and Two Perish.*

Most fortunate it was for the Springfield settlement that Markham's strength held out to enable him to warn them of the danger, or they would surely have shared the fate of their neighbors. After a hurried consultation the people determined to gather all of the families at the houses of Mr. Thomas and Mr. Wheeler for defense and protection. Two messengers were sent to Fort Ridgely for aid. For seventeen days the people at Springfield were kept in fearful suspense, hourly expecting the appearance of the Indians. There were twenty-one men, women and children at the Thomas house when the attack began. The Indians were greatly surprised to find the people prepared to give them a warm reception. The cowardly savages dressed one of their number in citizen's clothes, who approached the Thomas house in a friendly manner and called some of the people out on a cunning pretext. The remainder of the band were concealed behind trees in the forest surrounding the house. As soon as the people came out the Indians opened fire upon them, mortally wounding Willie Thomas, a little boy eight years old, and severely wounding Mr. Thomas, David Carver and Miss Drusella Swanger. There were now but three men left in the house unhurt, Morris Markham, Jareb Palmer and John Bradshaw. Hastily barricading the door, the three men, bravely assisted by Mrs. Thomas, Louisa Church, Eliza Gardner and Miss Swanger, prepared for a vigorous defense. All of the wounded had got back into the house except little Willie Thomas, who had fallen outside and was overlooked in the excitement until the doors had been barricaded. It was then too late to rescue him without endangering the lives of all. His father was severely wounded, and his mother begged piteously to be permitted to open the door and bring him in. It was almost certain that if the door was opened the Indians would make a rush upon them and all would be lost, and the poor little boy had to be left to his fate. The Indians dodged from tree to tree, gradually getting nearer the house, while keeping up a rapid fire upon the besieged settlers, but were careful to keep in shelter of the large trees and the log stable. Eliza Gardner and Miss Swanger cast bullets while Mrs. Church took the place of a wounded man at a port hole, so that all the guns should be kept busy. Watching a tree behind which a huge Sioux war-

rior was steadily firing at the cabin, Mrs. Church gave him a load of buckshot as he was aiming his rifle at the house. He fell back howling into the blood-stained snow.

So the fight went on until dark; the vigorous fire from the house checked the Indians from making an assault upon it. After dark all was still, but the besieged settlers kept a sharp lookout. Another party of Indians was prowling about the settlement in search of victims and plundering the deserted cabins.

William and George Wood, who kept a store, had always been on friendly terms with the Sioux, frequently doing considerable trading with them. When Markham brought news of the massacre at the lakes, they refused to believe it, and declined to unite with their neighbors for common defense. They said if the Indians came, they would not be molested. When they appeared, the Woods' were at their store, and the Indians who had often traded with them went there and bought a keg of powder and a quantity of lead and caps for their rifles. This ammunition was used in the siege of the Thomas house, and the slaughter of the Stewart family. But the Woods brothers suffered a terrible penalty for their criminal recklessness and folly. A few days later the treacherous Sioux returned to the store, shot the proprietors with some of the ammunition lately purchased of them, plundered the store of its goods, and piling brush over the bodies of the two brothers, set it on fire.

Joshua Stewart was another of the settlers who had confidence in the friendship of the Indians, and staid with his family at their house. An Indian who had always been friendly with them came to the house and enticed Mr. Stewart out, where he was shot down by other Indians concealed near by. His wife and two children were then butchered; the oldest boy managed to hide from them and escaped. After dark he made his way to the Thomas house, and was taken in. Soon after the firing on the Thomas house ceased, Mr. Shelgley, a neighbor, was seen going by and taken in also. The fact that these two persons had reached the house in safety, led to the hope that the Indians had abandoned the siege. A consultation was now held by the inmates of the house as to what had better be done. The three wounded persons were suffering and needed medical aid. Nothing had been heard from the messengers sent for aid to Fort Ridgely. It was feared the Indians would fire the house, thus drive them out and massacre the entire party. Whether they should stay and fight, or try to escape in the darkness; there was little hope in either direction. But at last they determined to send a man out to learn whether the Indians had gone, and if they had, it was decided to try to escape by flight. Who would venture out and explore the surroundings? It was a perilous undertaking, and all hesitated. But brave Morris Markham volunteered to make the venture. Carefully examining his rifle he stepped out into the darkness with his rifle cocked, and noiselessly disappeared. Markham moved cautiously through the snow from tree to tree listening for the Indians. Slowly and

hastily loaded into the sled with some blankets and provisions. They started out in the darkness on a most perilous journey, the brave women following on foot, all guarded by the men well armed.

The only coward in the settlement was Dr. E. N. Strong. In October, he went with his family from Fort Dodge to Mr. Gardner's at the lakes, on his way to settle at Springfield. His wife persuaded Eliza Gardner to go with them to Springfield and spend the winter, and thus she escaped the fate of the other members of her father's family. When the news of the massacre at the lakes was carried by Markham to Springfield, Dr. Strong took his wife and child and Eliza to the Thomas house for safety. On the morning before the attack, Dr. Strong had been called to Mr. Wheeler's to attend

*The Spirit Lake Massacre Monument.*

silently he made a wide circuit of the premises, expecting at any moment to hear the crack of a rifle shot or a sudden rush of the Indians for the door. Half an hour passed, while his companions in the house waited with intense anxiety; but not a sound reached them from outside. A terrible fear came over them that he had been tomahawked by the stealthy foe, before he could give an alarm. At last they heard footsteps approaching, and hastily barricaded the door; after another moment of intense waiting with their loaded guns at the portholes, they heard the well-known voice of Markham. He informed them that the Indians had disappeared, and he had found a yoke of oxen which had escaped the general slaughter, and he had hitched them to a sled. The small children and the wounded were

two men who had lost their legs by freezing. While there, all through the day he heard the guns at the Thomas house, where the fight was going on, and where his wife and child were. He was so terrified that he never ventured out of the house during the day. When the firing ceased and he had seen the Indians retreating, he made no effort to learn the fate of his family and neighbors, but the next morning he persuaded Mrs. Smith, who was at Wheeler's, to go over to the Thomas house and learn the fate of the settlers gathered there. When the brave Mrs. Smith returned with the report that it was deserted and that a boy was lying dead in the yard, Dr. Strong left his crippled patients, the three women and their little children, and fled from the settlement without further effort to learn the fate of his wife and child. There was now left at the Wheeler house but one able-bodied man, J. B. Skinner, and his wife, Mrs. William Nelson and her child, Mrs. Smith and her crippled husband, whose leg had recently been amputated; Mr. Henderson, who had lost both legs, and Mr. Sheigley's little boy. To remain now until the Indians returned seemed certain death for all. They had no team and no way to carry the disabled men. Hard as it was, they had to abandon Smith and Henderson, and started through the deep snow to try to escape before the return of the savages. In their haste and terror, Mr. Sheigley's little boy was left behind. On the second day out, they fortunately fell in with the Markham party. Mr. Sheigley, learning that his little boy had been abandoned in the flight, started back alone to rescue him. Late in the afternoon the fugitives came in sight of a grove on the Des Moines river where George Granger lived. In the distance they saw a man running towards the grove, and in his wild flight he pulled off his boots and threw them away to increase his speed. In his terror he probably mistook the escaping party for Indians. He was recognized as Dr. Strong making his way down the river after having, two days before, abandoned his wife and child to save himself alone.

The party remained two nights at the Granger cabin waiting the return of Mr. Sheigley, who was unable to find his boy. He was afterwards found safe with some neighbors. The next day the fugitives, accompanied by Mr. Granger, went on towards Fort Dodge with a short supply of food and clothing, while the wounded were suffering greatly for medical attendance. At night all had to sleep in the snow without shelter from the chilling winds, their shoes and clothing wet with melting snow and wading streams and sloughs. Miss Swanger gave up her place on the overloaded sled to the tired children, and with a painful bullet wound in her shoulder, walked on through the deep snow. The sufferings of the entire party were enough to exhaust the strongest men, as they dragged themselves along through deep drifts, plunging into the icy floods that filled the ravines, weakened by hunger and shivering in water-soaked clothing. On Monday, the 30th of March, it had been three days since they left the shelter of the Granger cabin; a cold wind was blowing from the north and it was feared that the wounded, the women and children could not survive another night on the open prairie, so deplorable was their condition. Towards noon they sighted a party approaching which they had no doubt were the pursuing Indians. It was felt by all that escape was impossible. But Morris Markham and John Bradshaw were not men to tamely submit to be massacred without resistance, and no thought of seeking their own safety by deserting the women, children and wounded in their care ever entered their heads. A hurried consulta-

tion was held and it was decided to divide the guns among the men who were not disabled.

Brave John Bradshaw volunteered to advance alone upon the Indians with five loaded rifles and pick off at long range as many of the Sioux as he could. Markham took command of the well men as they surrounded the helpless ones of their company, determined to defend them to the last. Bradshaw advanced with his loaded guns, laid them on the ground beside him, lying down to protect himself from the fire of the enemy, took good aim with his trusty rifle at the figure in advance. Every eye of the fugitives was upon him as they sternly awaited the hopeless conflict. Suddenly loud shouts and signals from the advancing party proclaimed them friends! It was the advance guard of the Major Williams relief expedition, coming to their assistance. In order to protect themselves from the cold north wind they had drawn shawls and blankets about their heads thus giving them the appearance of Indians. Language cannot describe the emotions of the poor, suffering fugitives as the sudden transition from hopeless terror and despair, to the presence of friends and safety, came upon them. As they came nearer, J. S. Church, of the rescue party, joyfully recognized among the rescued his wife and children, whom he had feared were among the victims of the massacre. Another of the party, J. M. Thatcher, learned from Markham the butchery of his child and the worse fate of his young wife, probably dragged into a captivity more horrible than death. Everything possible was now done by the relief party for the comfort of sufferers. Dr. Bissell dressed the wounds of the injured and all rested in safety now for the first time since their flight began. An escort was sent the next day, which conducted them safely to the Irish colony. Mrs. Smith now turned back with the soldiers who were on their way to Okoboji to bury the dead, to find and rescue her crippled husband, who had been left at the Wheeler house. She reached there in safety and found Mr. Smith and Henderson where they were left, as the Indians had gone from the settlements without returning to molest them.

### THE RELIEF EXPEDITION.

The first news of the massacre at the lakes was taken to Fort Dodge by O. C. Howe, R. U. Wheelock and B. F. Parmenter, of Jasper county, who had taken claims in that vicinity the fall before. They started for the lakes early in March and reached the Thatcher cabin about midnight of the 15th. No one could be aroused to let them in, but upon opening the door the lifeless bodies of Noble and Ryan were found. Horror stricken by the sight, they went over to Howe's cabin and there found the mutilated bodies of seven women and children. They now realized that the Indians had probably exterminated the entire colony, and hastened back to Fort Dodge. They reached there on the 22d and the terrible news aroused the wildest excitement. Prompt measures were taken to send a relief expedition at once. Major Williams issued a call for volunteers and in three days more than 100 young men had responded. They were organized into three companies. Company A, of Fort Dodge, was commanded by C. B. Richards, captain; Company B, of Fort Dodge and vicinity, Capt. John F. Duncombe; Company C, of Webster City and vicinity, was commanded by Capt. J. C. Johnson. So intense was the excitement and so strong the desire to overtake and punish the Sioux, that the little army started off in haste without suitable equipments for a long winter march over an unsettled open prairie country. The winter, which had been the severest on record, was still unbroken, although it was near the last of March. But few tents could be procured, and the blankets, clothing and provisions that were hastily collected were insufficient for such an expedition. Major Williams, the commander, was 62 years of age, although still a vigorous man. He had been commissioned by Governor Grimes two years before to act upon his own judgment in any troubles with the Indians. The news of the Indian outrages on the Little Sioux a short time before had prepared the major to expect serious trouble and he acted with great promptness. Howe, Parmenter and Wheelock joined the expedition at Fort Dodge; J. M. Thatcher at the Irish colony, Morris Markham, John Bradshaw and Jareb Palmer turned back with it after conducting the Springfield fugitives to safety. A hard crust on the snow rendered the march slow and difficult, as it was not strong enough to bear up the teams, and the men often broke through. At the close of the second day they camped at Dakota, but eighteen miles from Fort Dodge. From this place on the snow became deeper and the obstructions, hardships and sufferings increased. In many places the ravines they had to cross were filled with snow to a depth of from ten to twenty feet, into which the teams sank helpless and exhausted. Then long ropes were hitched to the floundering horses and they were dragged through, one at a time, by the men. Then the loaded wagons were drawn through in a similar manner. Sometimes it required the entire brigade to drag one loaded wagon through the immense drifts into which it had sunk down. Often the men had to wade two abreast, in long lines, up to their waists in snow to break a road for the teams and wagons.

On the third night the expedition had to camp out in the snow on the unsheltered prairie, without fuel for fires, with a bleak wind sweeping down on the exhausted men. They made a supper on crackers and raw pork, chained the oxen to the wagons, which were arranged close together to break the wind, while the men crowded together on their beds of snow to rest and sleep. The next day was a renewal of the hardships, until night, when they reached McKnight's grove, where they found fuel to cook their food and cabins to sleep in. On the morning of the 28th, after roll call, Major Williams made a brief address to his men, alluding to the hardships encountered and the complaints of some of the faint-hearted men. He told them plainly that greater sufferings were ahead of them, and if any lacked the courage or endurance to encounter them, now was the time to say so and

*APPANOOSE.*

return to their homes. Nine men stepped out and turned their faces homeward, leaving the command with weakened ranks to encounter the dangers yet to come. No record has been kept of the names of the men who here turned back. On the 29th the expedition reached the Irish colony, where they found Dr. Strong fleeing from danger, too badly frightened to turn back with the command to learn the fate of his wife and child. But J. M. Thatcher was waiting for company to go with him to learn the fate of his wife, and gladly enlisted. Here some of the worn-out teams were exchanged for fresh animals, and several young men joined the command, bringing the total number up to 125 men. Major

Williams now knew that they might soon encounter the Indians, and determined to send out some scouts in advance, to make an investigation. The men selected for the advance guard were C. C. Carpenter, J. M. Thatcher, Frank R. Mason, W. L. Church, W. K. Laughlin, A. N. Hathaway, William Defore and A. H. Johnson, under command of Lieut. J. N. Maxwell. They started on the morning of March 30th, and carried corn bread to last three days. They went in a northward direction and traveled about twelve miles by noon. Upon reaching an elevation one of the men shouted "Indians!" Far in the distance could be seen a party slowly advancing. Lieutenant Maxwell quickly formed his men in line for the attack and followed a high ridge to keep the other party in

Mr. Carver, also severely wounded in the fight at Springfield; Mrs. Dr. Strong and child, who had been deserted by her craven husband. In the haste of their flight they had taken but few provisions and scanty clothing. The women had worn out their shoes and their dresses were worn into fringe about their ankles; the children were crying with cold and hunger, and the wounded were in a deplorable condition for want of surgical aid. Their food was entirely gone; they had no means of making fire; their clothing and blankets were wet and freezing, and in their exhausted condition it is hardly possible that many of them could have survived another night's exposure from the fearful storm then coming on. The refugees were so overcome by the sudden transition from deadly peril

*Iowa's first brick house. Erected at Burlington in 1836.*

sight, who seemed to be preparing for battle. Approaching nearer, William L. Church, who was in advance, suddenly dropped his gun and sprang forward, exclaiming, "My God! there's my wife and babies!"

☐ Governor Carpenter, years afterwards, thus described the scene which followed:

"They had surrounded the ox sled in an attitude of defense, as they supposed us to be Indians, and had resolved if overpowered never to fall into the hands of the savages alive. Upon discovering that we were friends, such a heart-rending scene I never before witnessed, as the relatives and friends of the refugees had supposed they were dead. In the party were Mrs. W. L. Church and her children; her sister, Drusella Swanger, shot through the shoulder; Mr. Thomas, who had lost an arm;

and impending death that seemed to confront them, changed in an instant to relief in their desperate extremity, that they sunk down in the snow, crying and laughing alternately as their deliverers gathered around them. If nothing more had been accomplished by the relief expedition, every member felt that the salvation of eighteen perishing refugees from almost certain death from exposure and starvation had richly repaid them for all the hardships encountered."

On the 31st the expedition pushed on northward, finding frequent indications of Indians, until it reached the Granger house on the west branch of the Des Moines river, near the Minnesota line. Here Major Williams learned that a company of soldiers from Fort Ridgely had been sent to Springfield for the protection of the settlers, and that the

5

Indians had hastily fled to the westward. Learning that the dead at the lakes were still unburied, Major Williams called for volunteers to go to the lakes and bury the mutilated remains of the massacred settlers. Capt. J. C. Johnson, Lieut. J. N. Maxwell and Privates W. E. Burkholder, J. M. Thatcher, O. C. Howe, B. F. Parmenter, R. U. Wheelock, R. A. Smith, W. K. Laughlin, Henry Carse, W. N. Ford, J. H. Dailey, George P. Smith, O. C. Spencer, S. Van Cleve, C. Stebbins, Jesse Addington, R. McCormack, W. R. Wilson, James Murray, A. E. Burtch, E. D. Kellogg and John Dalley promptly stepped forward and volunteered to perform that sad and perilous duty. On the morning of the 2d of April the command separated, the main body to return to the Irish colony, while the volunteers, under Captain Johnson, started for the lakes. They reached East Okoboji about 2 o'clock, guided by Thatcher to his own cabin, where a horrible sight confronted him. His home was in ruins, and lying in the yard were the dead bodies of his friends, Noble and Ryan, as they had fallen three weeks before, when surprised and shot down by the treacherous Sioux. Inside of the cabin nothing was left but the ghastly forms of the two little ones who had been snatched from the arms of their terrified mothers, Mrs. Thatcher and Mrs. Noble, and killed by the brutal savages. The fate of the two young mothers, who had been carried off by the Sioux, was then unknown. From cabin to cabin, all through the settlement, the company went, burying the dead until all were laid beneath the snow-covered sod, twenty-nine in number. The bodies of Howe, Luce and Clark, who were killed south of the lakes and some distance from any house, were not found by this burial party. Mr. Marble's body had been buried by the soldiers from Fort Ridgely. Not a living person was found in the entire settlement. The body of young Dr. Harriott was found near Mattock's cabin with his rigid hand still grasping his broken rifle, the barrel empty, where he had fallen in a hand-to-hand struggle with the Indians, while bravely fighting in defense of the women and children of his neighbors.

Their sad mission ended, and unable to learn anything of the fate of Mrs. Thatcher, Mrs. Noble, Mrs. Marble or Abbie Gardner, on the 4th of April the burial party started homeward, their provisions entirely consumed. The weather had turned warm and the melting snow filled the sloughs and creeks with water, in many places waist deep, through which the men had often to wade. About 4 o'clock the wind, which had been blowing warm from the south, suddenly changed to the northwest, and in half an hour a howling blizzard was sweeping down upon the party. Their wet clothing was soon frozen stiff. Some of the men had pulled off their boots to wade the sloughs, while others had cut holes in theirs to let the water run out. Many had their boots frozen before they could put them on

and were compelled to walk along through the snow and freezing water in their stockings, which were soon worn out. As night came on, the piercing wind nearly chilled them to death. They dared not lie down to rest, for it was only by violent exercise that they were able to keep warmth and life in their stiffening limbs and bodies. They got separated into two parties as they marched along in the driving storm, one led by Captain Johnson, the other by Lieutenant Maxwell, as darkness came upon them, and finally they feared to get lost if they went on all night, so they tramped back and forth in the blinding blizzard until morning in a desperate struggle to keep life in their benumbed bodies. Often the weaker men would fall down exhausted in the drifting snow and stronger comrades would raise them up and lead them along.

"In the morning," says Lieutenant Maxwell, "I saw Johnson and Burkholder some distance from us going in a southerly direction, while we were traveling east. They were following the directions of an old trapper, and we soon lost sight of them. Henry Carse became unconscious during the day and sank down in the snow, blood running from his mouth. We carried him to the river timber where a fire was finally made by saturating a damp wad with powder and shooting it into the weeds. Carse was now entirely helpless, and when we cut the rags from his feet, the frozen flesh came off with them."

As soon as the fire was well started, Maxwell and Laughlin, who were the strongest of the party, determined to cross the river and go to the Irish colony for help. They reached the settlement and promptly sent assistance to their comrades, who were brought in badly frozen.

Major Williams gives the following account of all that was known of the sad fate of Capt. J. C. Johnson and Wm. E. Burkholder. "G. P. Smith was the last man who saw them. He fell in with them after they separated from the main party, and traveled some time with them. They were very much exhausted from wading ponds and sloughs, their clothing was frozen and covered with ice and their feet were badly frozen. Unable to walk farther, they finally sank down in the snow and Smith helped them to pull off their frozen boots. They tore up a part of their blankets and wrapped the pieces about their feet, which were very painful. Smith urged them to get up and make another effort to reach the Des Moines river timber, which was in sight. But they had become so chilled through and exhausted by that terrible night's tramp and their frozen limbs that they were unable to rise, and said they could go no farther. After doing everything in his power to get them on their feet for one more effort, Smith at last found he must leave them to save his own life. It was a sad parting, and after going some distance Smith looked back and saw them still on their knees in the snow, apparently unable to arise. It is not likely they ever moved from the spot where Smith last saw them, but finally overcome with cold they sank down side by side and perished. Eleven years after, their skeletons were found near where they were last seen, and identified by the guns and powder flasks lying beside them.

The main body of the expedition, which had returned to the Irish colony, experienced no trouble, until near night of the second day's march. They had a short supply of food and were put upon half rations. The water in the river was very high and the melting snow was filling the sloughs and creeks. When the command reached Cylender creek, late in the afternoon of April 4th, they found it had overflowed its banks and spread out in the valley a mile in width, in places, and twelve feet deep in

vain search for a better place to cross. When help and material for a raft came, so strong and cold was the wind, and so swift the current filled with floating ice, that all our efforts to build a raft failed. It was now dark and still growing colder, and the roar of the blinding storm was so great that we could no longer hold communication with our companions on the other side. We were benumbed with cold, utterly exhausted and three miles from the nearest cabin. We were powerless to aid our comrades and could only now save ourselves. It was a terrible walk in the face of the terrific blizzard, our clothes frozen, our feet freezing and our strength gone. After wandering in the storm until 9 o'clock we fortunately found the cabin. Here we passed a night that will never be obliterated from my memory. We gathered about the fire, vainly trying to

*One of Iowa's first frame structures. Erected at Bellevue in 1837. Home of Brown's banditti.*

the channel, with a swift current. All efforts to find a place where it could be crossed failed. The wind had now suddenly changed to the northwest and it was growing very cold. Captains Richards and Duncombe now saw serious work before them, and sent Major Williams and Mr. Dawson (both of whom were old men), back to the settlement, while they sought for some way to get the men over the flooded stream. An effort was made to convert a wagon box into a boat in which to cross, with a long rope to establish a ferry. Four men undertook to cross in it, but it was swamped on the farther shore and the rope lost, but four men had got across. A messenger was now sent by them to the nearest house for help and material for a raft. Captain Richards says: "The wind was now blowing a terrific gale and the cold was intense, so that our wet clothing was frozen stiff upon us as we traveled up and down the banks of the swollen current in a

dry our frozen clothing. We had no blankets, the piercing wind was driving through every crevice of the cabin, and we walked the floor in the most intense anxiety over the fate of our companions left on the banks of the creek, exposed to the fury of the blizzard without shelter, food or fire. All through the long night we kept looking out on the wild storm in hopes it would cease, but the cold ever grew more intense, the wind howled more fiercely, and no one could sleep. We knew that Carpenter, Stratton, Stevens and Wright were men endowed with courage equal to any emergency, and trusted they would find some way to keep the men from perishing. Still the harrowing fear would come over us that in the morning we should find all frozen to death. Terrible visions of their fate tortured us through the long hours of the night, and with the first dawn of day Duncombe, Smith, Mason and I were wading through the drifts towards Cylender creek. The mercury was now 28 degrees below zero and the blizzard still at its wildest fury. Mason gave out and sank down in the drifts. I got him back to the cabin and soon overtook the others. Strong ice was forming on the creek from the shore, and we hurried over it to the main channel, where the current was so swift the ice was too weak to bear us up. We could go no farther, could not see across for the drifting snow, and could hear no sound on the other side in answer to our loud shouts. Our faces and hands were now freezing and we had to return to the cabin and wait until the ice should be strong enough to support us. Towards night we made another vain effort to cross and had to return to the cabin oppressed with the conviction that not one of our companions could survive until morning. But soon after dark three of them came to the cabin and reported all safe."

Governor Carpenter tells how they managed to save themselves from freezing:

"We took the covers from the wagons and some tent canvas, and stretching them over the wheels made a rude shelter. We then put all of the blankets together on the snow and crowded in, lying down close together in our wet and frozen clothing, where we remained from Saturday evening until Monday morning, with nothing to eat until we reached the Shippey cabin Monday noon. We had waited until the ice was frozen over Cylender creek hard enough to bear up our teams and loaded wagons. I have since marched with armies from Cairo to Atlanta, and up to Richmond, sometimes traveling continuously for three or four days

and nights, with only a brief halt occasionally to give the exhausted soldiers a chance to boil a cup of coffee. Under burning suns, through rain, sleet and snow, we endured great suffering; but never in all the weary years could our sufferings be compared with that of the two terrible days and nights we endured on the banks of Cylender creek."

Lieutenant Mason says:

"How we survived those fearful nights I do not know, with the mercury down to 34 degrees below zero the last night. The poor boys were slowly freezing and many of them were insane; I think all of us were more or less insane the last night. The tongues of many of them were hanging out and the blood oozing out of the mouth or nose as we got up the last morning."

The command now broke up into small parties and scattered out over the country. In no other way could they find food from the scanty supply the few settlers had who lived along the river. The sufferings of some of the parties reached the last degree of endurance as they traveled homeward. But for help from the settlers, who divided the last they had, many must have perished. But all finally reached their homes except Johnson and Burkholder, though many were badly frozen.

Capt. John F. Duncombe, thirty years afterwards, truly wrote:

"For severe hardships, continuous toil, constant exposure, bodily and mental suffering, I do not believe it has ever been surpassed by men who have risked their lives to rescue their fellow men from peril and death."

---

## CHAPTER IX.

*Four Young Women Captives—Barbarous Treatment by the Indians—Two of Them Murdered—Rescue of the Others.*

### FATE OF THE CAPTIVE WOMEN.

While the events recorded in the last chapter were transpiring, four young women, dragged from their homes by the merciless butchers of their families, were cowering in the Indian camps. Soon after their defeat at the Thomas cabin the Sioux returned loaded with plunder from the settlement at Springfield and moved westward. The squaws, ponies, and captive women were heavily loaded down with packages and driven along by the cruel warriors like beasts of burden. Mrs. Thatcher was sick with a burning fever and barely able to walk, but the merciless savages fastened a large load upon her back which she staggered under, through the deep snow, and waded the icy streams, sometimes waist deep. When the Indians

went into camp the four young women, who were exhausted by the day's march, were driven like slaves to gather and cut up wood for the fires, and do all kinds of camp drudgery, until they often sank down exhausted. When Mrs. Thatcher could go no longer she was lashed to the back of a pony and carried along. But she bore her sufferings with great fortitude in the knowledge that her husband had escaped the massacre and would do all in his power for her rescue. On the third day the Indians discovered that they were pursued by a company of soldiers. The warriors prepared for battle while the squaws hastily tore down the tents and hid among the willows. One Indian was left with the captive women, with orders to *kill them when the attack began!* An Indian sentinel in a tree watched the soldiers and signalled their movements to the Sioux warriors. After an hour and·a·half of intense excitement on the part of the Indians and captives, it became known that the soldiers had turned back and abandoned the pursuit. This was a detachment of twenty-four soldiers under Lieutenant Murray, which had been sent out by Capt. Barnard E. Bee, from Springfield, in pursuit of the Indians. Captain Bee had arrived from Fort Ridgely and secured two half-breed guides for Lieutenant Murray. They reached the grove at 3 P. M., at which the Indians had camped the night before. Lieutenant Murray, upon examination of the camp ground, believed he was close to the

*JAMES HARLAN IN 1841.*

Indians, but his treacherous guides assured him the trail was three days old and that further pursuit was hopeless. Thus deceived, Murray turned back when actually in sight of the Indian sentinel, who was watching his movements. The Sioux were in ambush in superior numbers and well armed, so that the result of a battle would have been doubtful, but would have caused the instant death of the captive women. But the Indians were thoroughly alarmed and fled for two days and nights without stopping. The poor captives suffered greatly in this hurried retreat. Kept on the constant march, wading through deep snows and swollen streams, cold, hungry and worn out, it is a wonder that they survived. Before they reached the Big Sioux river the horses taken from the murdered settlers had starved to death, their bodies were cut up for food, and the loads they had

carried were transferred to the backs of the squaws and the white captives.

Six weeks of the most intense suffering and horrors unspeakable had now been endured by the four young women in the hands of the savages when they reached the river. As they were preparing to cross, an Indian came up to Mrs. Thatcher, who was carrying a heavy load, and took the pack from her shoulders and ordered her to go onto the driftwood bridge in the Sioux river. She saw from his manner that some harm was intended. She turned to her companions and tenderly bade them "goodbye," saying, "If any of you escape to reach home, tell my dear husband that I wanted to live for his sake." The savage then drove her along before him, and when about half way across he seized Mrs. Thatcher and hurled her into the river. With wonderful strength and courage, she swam in the icy current until she reached and clung to a fallen tree on the shore. Some more of the merciless savages came along and beat the poor woman off with clubs, and with tent poles pushed her out into the swift current again. But again the brave woman swam for the opposite shore, where the cruel wretches beat her back into the rapids. As she was carried along by the current, the brutal savages ran along the shore throwing stones and clubs at the exhausted, drowning woman, until one of the warriors raised his rifle and shot her as she clung to some driftwood.

The annals of Indian barbarity nowhere record a more inhuman crime than this wanton murder of Mrs. Thatcher, without the least pretense of provocation, after her heroic endurance of suffering and horrors the recital of which is impossible. She was but 19 years of age, a lovely girl in the bloom of youth, who had come with her husband to make a home on the beautiful, wooded shore of Okoboji. Mrs. Noble and Mrs. Thatcher had been intimate friends in their girlhood days. They had married cousins, and together had moved to the distant frontier with bright anticipations of long and happy lives in each other's society. Now, as Mrs. Noble closed her eyes to shut out the horrors of the dying struggles of her dearest friend, and thought of her murdered husband, child, father, mother, brother and sister, she felt that death would be a welcome relief for a load of misery she could not endure. That night she begged Mrs. Marble and Abbie to go with her and end their sufferings beneath the dark waters of the river where her last friend had perished. From that day Mrs. Noble's despair led her to hope for speedy death as the only release from the horrors that every night brought to the helpless captives.

When news of the massacre at the lakes and the captivity of four white women reached the Indian agency on Yellow Medicine river, the agent, Charles E. Flandreau, S. R. Riggs and Dr. Thomas Williamson, missionaries, began to devise plans for the rescue of the captives. Two friendly Indians had visited the Sioux camp and there seen the white women, and at once opened negotiations for their purchase. They finally succeeded in buying Mrs. Marble. On the morning of May 6th Mrs. Marble learned that she had been sold by Inkpadutah to two strange Indians. She told Abbie and Mrs. Noble, and had a hope that she was to be taken to a white settlement. As she bade her companions a sorrowful "good-bye," Mrs. Marble assured them that if she should reach a white set-

*Fourth Governor of the State.*

tlement she would do all in her power for their rescue. Mrs. Marble was taken to the agency at Yellow Medicine, where after several weeks she was ransomed by Mr. Riggs and Dr. Williamson, who paid the Indians $1,000 for her release. This money had been raised by Major Flandreau. Mrs. Marble at once proceeded to do all in her power for the rescue of her companions. Major Flandreau undertook the work in their behalf and secured an appropriation of $10,000 by the Minnesota legislature, to be used by the governor to secure the rescue of the captives. Large rewards were offered to friendly Indians who would secure their release, and volunteers came forward at once. Major Flandreau procured an outfit, and on the 23d of

May they started out with instructions to purchase the white women at any price. Four companies of soldiers were ordered at once to be marched from Fort Ridgely as near Inkpadutah's camp as was prudent, to fall upon the Sioux as soon as the captives were secured, and exterminate the perpetrators of the massacre if possible. But just as the troops were ready to start, orders came for them to join General Johnston's Utah expedition, and Inkpadutah and his band were permitted to go unpunished.

While these events were transpiring the two captive women were being taken farther into the wilds of Dakota, and became hopeless of rescue. One evening after the two women had gone to their tent, Roaring Cloud, son of the chief, came in and ordered Mrs. Noble to come with him to his tepee. She indignantly refused to go. He seized her and attempted to drag her along but she resisted with all her strength. She determined then and there to end her wretched existence if need be, before she would again submit to the horrors from which there seemed no other escape. She alone of the helpless captives had always resisted the brutal savages until her strength was exhausted and she was finally overpowered. Since the murder of her friend, Mrs. Thatcher, she had felt her wretched life a burden too great to be endured, and could see no release from its horrors but in death. This night she nerved herself to end it in one stern struggle. Wild with rage at her heroic resistance, the young savage dragged Mrs. Noble out of the tent, seized a club and beat her head again and again in all the strength of his fury, leaving her mangled form by the door of the tent. For half an hour her dying moans reached the ears of the terrified girl Abbie, who was cowering in a corner, now left entirely alone with the brutal savages. The next morning Indians took the scalp of the murdered woman with her long braids of hair hanging to it, and otherwise mutilated her body, then left it to be devoured by the wolves. Abbie now abandoned all hope, expecting any day to share the fate of her last companion. But powerful friends were at work for her rescue, urged on by Mrs. Marble. Major Flandreau had procured Indian goods in great abundance to tempt them, and had selected three of the most trusty of the race to proceed with all possible haste to overtake Inkpadutah's band. John Other Day led the party and on the 30th of May they reached the vicinity of the Sioux camp, secreting their team and wagon. They entered the village and soon learned there was but one white woman now left. After three days' negotiations they succeeded in purchasing Miss Gardner. They took her to St. Paul and delivered her to Governor Medary and received $1,200 for their faithful services in rescuing the last of the surviving captives. The two women who were rescued never recovered from the brutal treatment they endured while in captivity. While their lives were spared, their bodily and mental sufferings could only end with death. Abbie never saw Mrs. Marble after her release from captivity, but found Mr. Thatcher and conveyed to him the last message of his young wife, and the full particulars of her cruel fate. At Hampton she found her sister Eliza who made her escape with the refugees from Springfield after their successful defense against the Indians. In 1885, Abbie Gardner Sharp wrote, and had published, a book containing a full history of the massacre at the lakes, the captivity and sufferings of

in Indian captivity, none have surpassed the sufferings of Elizabeth Thatcher, Lydia Noble, Abigail Gardner and Margaret A. Marble.

A son of the Indian chief Sidominadotah (who was murdered with his family by Henry Lott, the desperado,) saved the lives of the family of John B. Skinner, who had settled at the lakes. Mr. Skinner had often befriended this boy, Josh, who was badly wounded by Lott when his father and family were massacred. He recovered, and at times found a home at Skinner's. When his uncle, Ink-

*Che-Ten-Maga, Rescuer of Abbie Gardner.*

the enslaved women and the defense at Springfield, from which many of the facts in this sketch were obtained.

Of all the narratives of Indian massacres and barbarities that for more than 200 years have marked the settlement of our country, there are no pages in the bloody record more thrilling or pathetic than those recording the horror attending the extermination of the first colony planted on the beautiful shores of Okoboji and Spirit lakes in 1857. Of all the horrors endured by white women

padutah, planned his terrible massacre of the Okoboji settlement, Josh learned his intentions and warned Mr. Skinner of danger, and was so persistent and earnest in his entreaties that Mr. Skinner moved his family back to Liberty, and so escaped the massacre. Whether Mr. Skinner notified his neighbors of the impending danger, is not known. Josh also warned Mr. Carter, of Emmet county, of the danger, and spent a part of that winter in Kossuth county. Josh was seen and recognized by Mrs. J. B. Thomas as one of the leaders in the attack upon their house at Springfield. He was undoubtedly engaged in the massacre at the lakes. In 1862 Josh was one of the most active in the terrible Minnesota massacres with a band at Lake Shetech, which nearly exterminated that settlement. Thus we can trace back to Henry Lott's massacre of Sidominadotah and his family, the inspiring motive which led the surviving relatives of the murdered chief to visit upon the innocent pioneers of Okoboji and Springfield a most terrible vengeance. Forty-one innocent men, women and children were the direct victims who perished for Lott's crimes, while the sufferings of the captives, relatives, and members of the relief expedition, make up a fearful record of misery seldom, if ever, surpassed.

It can never be known how many of Inkpadu-

tah's band were killed. But we know that Roaring Cloud, who murdered Mrs. Noble, was riddled by bullets from Lieutenant Murray's soldiers; and the friendly Sioux claimed to have killed three more of the fiends. It is probable that a few were killed by Dr. Harriott, Snyder and Mattock, and Mrs. Church shot one at the Thomas house siege. As Inkpadutah's band was among the most ferocious of the butchers in the Minnesota massacres in 1862, it is not unlikely that some of them were among the Indians killed by the soldiers, or among the thirty who were hung at Mankato. Inkpadutah himself escaped all punishment for unparalleled barbarities, and was last seen among the Sioux who fled to the far west before General Sibley's army in 1863.

---

## CHAPTER X.

*Horse Thieves—Regulators of 1857—Lynching of Page, Conklin, Clute, Warren, Soper, Gleason, and Roberts—A Reign of Terror—Brave McCollough ends it.*

From 1840 to 1857 a region of country extending from the Big Woods in Jackson county through the eastern parts of Jones and Cedar and the western portions of Clinton and Scott counties, had been infested with suspicious characters who were believed to be connected with a gang of horse thieves, robbers and counterfeiters. Many crimes had been committed in that region and it seemed to be impossible to convict and punish those arrested and believed to be guilty. Those suspected generally lived in the sparsely settled sections where brush and timber enabled them to conceal their movements and secrete the stolen property, and hide from officers sent to arrest them. In 1856 and 1857 a large number of horses had been stolen from farmers in that section of the state, causing much distress. Most of the farmers were poor men struggling to make new homes on the wild prairies and support their families while bringing the new land under cultivation. Common horses cost from $200 to $300 for a team, and the loss of a horse or a team in those days of general poverty meant deep distress, and often left the farmer without means to cultivate his land or save his crops. The hardships thus brought upon many hard working people became so serious that the neighbors at last determined to organize for their own protection. Frequent arrests had been made, but the employment of the best lawyers and the assistance of confederates as witnesses and jurymen had generally enabled the guilty parties to escape conviction and punishment. This emboldened the thieves to continue their depredations and exasperated the settlers to organize associations and band together to hunt down and punish the lawless men who were

robbing them. The people who thus organized became known as "regulators" or "vigilance committees," and eventually a large majority of the farmers in that section infested with thieves, became members of these organizations. The little country village of Big Rock, near the corners of Scott, Clinton and Cedar counties, was for some time the headquarters of the regulators. Here many meetings were held and plans laid for the detection and summary punishment of the thieves. No records were kept of their proceedings and no member of the organizations has ever been known to divulge the full proceedings of their meetings, or the names of their officers or members. Hence it is exceedingly difficult to give anything like a complete and reliable history of their doings.

Alonzo Page was a young married man who lived in a log house near the east line of Cedar county, about two miles southeast of the present town of Lowden on the North-Western railroad. His house was built in the scattering timber called the "barrens," and he had a small farm under cultivation about it. He was an intelligent and industrious young man, and frequently worked out among his neighbors during haying and harvest. He had in some way incurred the enmity of a man named Corry, living over on Rock creek. Soon after the organization of the regulators, Corry joined them and circulated a report that Alonzo Page was connected with a gang of horse thieves. Believing the report, in June, 1857, some of the regulators rode over to the Page cabin and notified him that he must leave the country. When informed of the charge against him, Page solemnly protested his innocence and refused to be driven from his home. But he was told that he must go by a certain time or suffer the consequences. He consulted some of his neighbors, after the regulators had gone, and they advised him to pay no attention to the notice or threats. One night, sometime after, Mr. Page heard the tramp of horses and the voices of several men about his cabin. Looking out of the window he saw a large body of horsemen apparently surrounding his cabin. Soon heavy raps came on the door and a demand that he should open it. He inquired what was wanted and got no satisfactory reply. Mrs. Page, who was in bed very sick, became greatly alarmed for the safety of her husband. There was no way to notify his neighbors or procure their assistance. The heavy pounding on the door continued with threats that it would be broken down unless it was opened. Mr. Page went to the window and told the mob that his wife was very sick and that he could not permit her to be terrified by strange men com-

Mr. Corry, who instigated the raid on the house. The regulators were led to believe that Mr. Page was connected with the horse thieves and they expected to be able to drive him out of the country; but conscious of his own innocence he refused to be driven from his home and died in its defense.

The next victim was Peter Conklin, who had committed many crimes in Johnson county and vicinity, and was believed to be a prominent member of the gang of horse thieves. A band of regulators was scouring the country near Yankee run, in Cedar county, on the 27th of June and came upon Conklin in the woods, on horseback. He fled, was pursued, overtaken, shot down and instantly killed. There is little doubt that he was a desperado of a very dangerous character.

Charles Clute, a carpenter, living on a farm nine miles northeast of Tipton, fell under suspicion and suffered persecution, if not death, at the hands

*The sod house of the pioneer.*

ing into the house. He now realized his danger in view of the threats that had been made at the former visit of the regulators, and prepared to make the best defense he could, for he felt sure his life would not be safe if he went out in the dark among the mob. He barricaded the door as well as he could and loaded his double-barrel gun with buckshot, determined to make the best defense in his power. The door was soon broken down by the regulators, and Page stood at the opening, gun in hand, to defend his home and wife the best he could. But as soon as he appeared in sight a rifle ball pierced his body and he fell in the doorway mortally wounded. The regulators then hastily retreated, leaving the dying man and his frantic, sick wife to their fate. It was not believed that the regulators engaged in this tragic affair went to the house intending to murder Mr. Page, and several of them declared that the fatal shot was fired by

of the regulators. He married the daughter of Mrs. J. D. Denson, a widow, and for several years attended to her business. They kept a hotel and had a large farm. The widow finally married J. A. Warner and the two men worked harmoniously together at farming, building and hotel-keeping. One day in the winter of 1856, a peddler named Johnson, stopped at the Denson house, and, being blockaded by a snowstorm, remained several days. Some months later, Johnson came there again with a good team and left it to be sold by Mr. Clute. Some time after Johnson was arrested and taken to Wisconsin, charged with horse stealing. As Mr. Clute had sold the horses for Johnson, some of his neighbors caused his arrest, charging that he was an accomplice of Johnson's. But no evidence appeared against him and he was released. One night a gang of men came to the house, called him out, seized and bound him, conveyed him into the woods and gave him a terrible whipping. He was then released and returned home. Late in the summer Mr. Clute was again arrested, charged with selling stolen horses for Johnson, but no evidence could be found to sustain the charge and he was released. After the organization of the regulators in 1857, Mr. Clute's old enemies moved against him again. As he and Warner were building a house in Scott county, the regulators seized them one day and took them across the Wapsipinicon river off into the woods, near the residence of Bennett Warren, and gave them a trial for harboring horse

were stolen, and there is little doubt that he was entirely innocent of all charges made against him. It was believed, by his friends, that he never got out of Scott county, but met his death at the hands of the regulators. On the other hand, many believed that Mr. Clute had become convinced that his life was in danger from the regulators, and that his only safety was in going to some distant state, and that he did so. But this does not explain the facts that his family never heard from him and were unable to find any trace of him in all the years that have passed since.

*Water's lead furnace, near Dubuque, constructed in 1834. The first hearth lead furnace in Iowa and the second in America.*

thieves, but again no evidence could be found to sustain the charge. But the regulators decreed that they must leave the country. They were compelled to witness the hanging of old Mr. Warren and then taken to Big Rock and kept at Goddard's tavern over night. Terrified by the tragedy they had seen enacted the day before, they were intimidated into promising to leave the country. In a few days Mr. Clute disappeared and was never afterwards seen or heard of by his family.

When Johnson was brought to trial, it was proved that Mr. Clute was in no way implicated with him, and had no knowledge that the horses

## LYNCHING OF BENNETT WARREN.

In 1857 there was living in Clinton county, about four miles northeast of Wheatland, near the Wapsipinicon river, a farmer named Bennett Warren. He was about 60 years of age and an old settler in that region. He kept a sort of public house, entertaining travelers. Some in that vicinity suspected that he was in some way connected with the gang of horse thieves that was believed to infest that region. It was reported that strangers were frequently seen at his house who were believed to belong to the gang. The regulators were determined to make a terrible example of any person found guilty of stealing horses or harboring horse thieves. On the 24th of June several hundred of the regulators had assembled and taken Mr. Clute and Mr. Warner from Scott county over into Clinton, to try them upon charges made against them. Not finding any evidence against them, the regulators went to Warren's house, seized him and organized a court of their own to try him on charges of being connected with horse thieves. They selected a jury from their own number of twelve men, and went through the forms of a trial. R. H. Randall, a well known, respectable and intelligent farmer of Clinton county, presided over all of their deliberations. Mr. Warren had no voice in the selection of the jury, was given no time or opportunity to prepare a defense or to procure counsel to aid or advise him. Witnesses were brought forward to convict him, but no chance was given him to bring witnesses in his own behalf. It is not strange, that after such a trial, the jury found him guilty of all charges brought against him. The chairman then called upon all who were in favor of administering punishment to step to one side of the road, and all voted for punishment. Then came a vote on the nature of the punishment. There were two propositions made—one to whip him, the other to *hang him*. The vote was taken the same way as before. The accounts now disagree as to what followed. The history of Clinton county says:

"At first the majority was largely for the milder punishment. Those who favored the extreme measure said: 'What satisfaction will there be in whipping an old, gray-haired man? What good will come of it? We are here to protect our property and deter others from these crimes.' As the arguments progressed one by one, in knots of two and three, the people passed over the road so fateful to the doomed man, who was a silent witness to these proceedings, until a clear majority stood for the death sentence. A rope was then placed around Warren's neck, and he was asked if he had anything to say. His only response was: 'I am an old man, and you cannot cheat me out of many years.' The rope was then thrown over a limb, men seized it, and amid silence that was awe-inspiring, the signal was given, and Bennett Warren was ushered into eternity."

The body, cold in death, was then taken down by the executioners, carried to the house and left with his agonized wife and terror-stricken children, who were helpless witnesses of the fearful, merciless tragedy.

R. H. Randall, who presided at the trial, lived on Rock Creek where, for half a century, he has been known as a citizen of the highest standing, gives the following account of the tragedy: "When the jury found Warren guilty, the question arose, what shall be done with him? Many motions were made and voted down, when some one moved that he be

hung. When the vote was to be taken on this motion I requested all who were in favor of hanging to walk over to the east side of the road, and all opposed to go to the west side. Only a few went to the west side. I was astonished and did not indorse the decision. I got up on a wagon and began to tell my reasons for opposing the vote as best I could, for about ten minutes, and was making many changes of votes when a man came to me and said, 'Randall, if you don't stop that you will be shot inside of five minutes.' I replied, 'one murder is enough,' and ran out of sight."

This statement of the judge who presided at the trial shows most conclusively that some members of that band of regulators were bloodthirsty and determined to take Mr. Warren's life if they had to murder a member of their own company to bring it about.

## LYNCHING OF GLEASON AND SOPER.

In 1857, Edward Soper was a young man living three miles southeast of Tipton, and Alonzo Gleason was staying at various places in that vicinity, having no regular occupation. In the spring of that year these two young men, in company with three other bad characters, started out to steal a valuable horse belonging to Charles Pennygrot, who lived two miles from Lowden. They succeeded in getting the horse and with another they had stolen from near Solon, they started for Illinois to dispose of the property. By traveling nights for a long distance and then avoiding public roads, they got away without detection, crossed the Mississippi river, and went on to the Illinois river. Here they sold the horses and returned to Cedar county to resume their stealing. But the citizens had found strong evidence of their guilt and caused their arrest by the sheriff. They were taken to the old court house at Tipton on the 2d of July and confined in the court room on the ground floor, guarded by the sheriff, John Byerly, and twenty men. In the meantime the regulators had been notified, and about midnight a large body of them rode into the village and surrounded the court house. They were well organized, forced the doors, and after a brief struggle overpowered the guard and seized the prisoners. They conveyed them to the farm of Martin Henry, south of Lowden, near where the valuable horse had been stolen. Here the regulators came in from every direction, until more than two hundred had assembled. They proceeded to organize a court, select a jury and then began the trial of the prisoners, who watched the proceedings in fear and trembling, remembering the fate of Page and Warren. They saw no hope of escape as the trial proceeded, and felt they were doomed. After the evidence was presented the jury brought in a verdict of guilty. Then the two men, in the hope that their lives might be spared if the horses were recovered, made a full confession and told where the last horses taken could be found. But there was no mercy for them in the determined faces of the regulators. They now had horse thieves of whose guilt there was no doubt, and sentence of death was pronounced against them by almost a unanimous vote. Very little time was given them, and ropes were soon placed around their necks and thrown over the limb of an oak tree, while they stood in a wagon beneath. Soper was completely prostrated, crying and begging piteously for mercy. Gleason was firm, cool and reckless to the last. Two men held Soper on his feet, fierce men pulled on the ropes, the wagon

leaders of the regulators. But witnesses and jurors were threatened with death if they should convict any of the members. When court convened in Tipton, hundreds of armed men came in from the country with stern determination to prevent the arrest or trial of any who had taken part in the lynchings.

Citizens who condemned and denounced the crimes perpetrated by the regulators were visited by them, and warned that they must cease their talk, or they would be driven from the country, and for a time there was a reign of terror in that part of the state. Those who approved of the lynching, together with the large number who had taken

*Mormon hand-cart train passing through Iowa in 1856.  Drawn from memory.*

was driven from under them, and two more victims were counted by the regulators.

The law-abiding people were horror-stricken over these deliberate and cold-blooded lynchings, in which killing was the penalty not only for stealing, but for being *suspected*, where in some cases there was little doubt of the innocence of the parties charged, as in the cases of Page and Clute. Where were these horrors to end? Stealing was bad enough, but murder was infinitely worse. Who would be safe if law could be defied with impunity? Any innocent person might be sacrificed by an enemy, as in case of Page.

A determined effort was made by Judge Tuthill to procure the indictment and arrest of the known

part in them, were a vast majority of the people, and it soon became apparent that they would tolerate no punishment of the regulators.

The last victim was a farmer of Jones county named Hiram Roberts. He had long been suspected of being connected with the horse thieves, as he frequently was seen in Cedar county among the suspected parties. On the last of October in 1857, Roberts rode over to James W. Hamlin's, four miles northwest of Tipton. The regulators hearing of his presence, quietly notified a large number of the members, who, at a fixed time, gathered at Hamlin's and captured Roberts. He was taken into Jones county and placed in a barn belonging to George Saum, and left in charge of several men, who had been engaged in his capture. The regulators in large numbers retired to a grove near by to consult as to what should be done with the prisoner. After awhile it became evident that another victim was to be sacrificed, and one young man who was strongly opposed to these murders by mobs, refused to be a party to the impending tragedy, and went to the barn to get his horse to ride home. Upon opening the door he was horrified to see Roberts suspended by the neck from a beam overhead by a rope, writhing in the agonies of strangulation. It was soon learned that the men left to guard Roberts, while waiting for the return of the main body, had tried, condemned, sentenced and executed the helpless prisoner.

Six of the prominent actors in the tragedy were arrested and bound over to appear at the next term

influence was making a strong impression in the community, and the regulators feared that the growing opposition to their lawless acts might result finally in their punishment. Some of them decided to proceed to intimidate the most prominent advocates of law and order.

Canada McCollough, a near neighbor of Alonzo Page, the first victim of the regulators, was a substantial farmer and one of the most highly esteemed citizens of Cedar county. He was confident that Page was entirely innocent of the accusations which cost him his life. He was outspoken in his denunciation of that cruel murder, and tried to have the guilty parties punished. The regulators waited upon him and warned him that he must keep quiet or leave the country.

McCollough was a fearless old pioneer, skilled

*Overland wagon.*

of court at Anamosa. In the meantime the regulators held meetings and resolved to protect the accused members at all hazards. Witnesses disappeared; friends of the arrested were on the grand jury, and as the prisoners appeared at court, surrounded by several hundred armed regulators, no indictments were found and the perpetrators of the crime escaped punishment, as had all of their confederates in former efforts to enforce law. While public opinion was largely in sympathy with the regulators, there was a numerous minority of the best citizens who were firmly opposed to their defiance and disregard for law, and the summary lynching of persons suspected of crimes without giving them an opportunity to make a defense. It was believed that several innocent men had fallen victims to the lawless proceedings, and that no citizen was safe when law was openly defied. Their

in the use of the rifle, and a man who would defend his rights and speak his mind on all occasions. He lived in a good log house, owned a large farm and could neither be driven nor intimidated. He quietly set about preparing for defense. He had two good rifles and borrowed another of a neighbor and made portholes on the side of his house the outside door was on; and continued to express his opinion of the murderers of his neighbor. One day he saw approaching his house from the east, a large band of horsemen, all armed. He recognized among them several well-known regulators. His rifles were loaded and he stepped to the front door with one in his hand as the band halted in the road near by. He recognized the leader, a man living near Big Rock, who rode forward near the gate. McCollough ordered him to halt, and demanded to know what his gang wanted. The leader informed him that they had come to notify him that he could not be allowed to denounce them any longer, and that he must leave the country or take the consequences. McCollough told them calmly that he should defend his home to the last, that he had a right to express his opinions and should do so. That he was a law-abiding citizen, guilty of no crime, and that they knew it. He continued, "you know Mr. G. that I am a good shot; I have three good rifles here and plenty of ammunition. My family can load them as fast as I can shoot. You may be able to kill me as you did Lon Page, but I shall kill some of you first, and I shall not surrender." Suddenly stepping back in the house, he raised his rifle, took deadly aim at the leader and said, "I will give you one minute to get out of my yard and if you attempt to raise your gun you are a dead man! You know I never miss my mark." The leader knew the man who had the drop on him, and saw he meant what he said. He hesitated a moment, turned and rode back to his men. McCollough hastily stepped back, closed and barricaded the door and then his rifle was seen pointing from a porthole at the crowd. They consulted a while and then attempted to get him to promise that he would keep still in the future. But he stood firm for his rights as an American citizen and would make no concessions. His fearlessness convinced them that he had friends in the house who would stand by him, as they saw the muzzles of several rifles pointed from the portholes. The band now began to realize that they had determined men to deal with who could not be intimidated. They knew also that there was a large number of law-abiding citizens whom they had sought to intimidate who had recently been consulting together for mutual defense and protection, and that if they got into a conflict with them it was very likely that Governor Grimes would order out the militia and arrest and severely punish them for their past transgressions. So they finally told Mr. McCollough that they would leave him now and give him time to consider the matter, and if they heard of any more denunciation from him that he must leave the country. They then rode away and never disturbed him again.

While the terrible deeds of the regulators must be condemned, the region in which they operated was entirely freed from further depredations of horse thieves from that time on. The gangs which had so long infested that part of the state were entirely broken up and thoroughly terrified by the fearful fate that had overtaken those suspected who had fallen into the hands of the regulators. And the regulators came to realize that their lawless combination and acts would not longer be tolerated. All efforts to bring them to trial failed, and not a member of them was ever convicted or in any way punished for participating in the lynching of the seven men who became their victims.

*The old state capitol at Iowa City, 1844-57.*

## CHAPTER XI.

*The Underground Railroad—John Brown in Iowa—His Springdale Friends and Recruits—The Fight at Harper's Ferry—The Iowa Men Who Fought There—Escape of Barclay Coppoc—The Ride for Life—The Virginia Governor Foiled—Death of Barclay Coppoc.*

Soon after the enactment of the fugitive slave law with its barbarous penalties, many humane people, who could not resist the impulse to aid slaves escaping from bondage, organized a line of stations across the state by which they could co-operate in affording shelter, assistance and transportation to fleeing fugitives. Beginning at Tabor in Fremont county, near the state line, the abolitionists had stations, known only to trusted friends, extending by way of Des Moines, Grinnell, Iowa City, Springdale to Davenport. There were many other stations on branches south of the main line, all of which were on what was called the "underground railroad." When escaping slaves reached any station on these lines, they were secreted until night and then conveyed by covered wagon to the next station. Food, lodging, clothing, money and transportation was freely furnished to the escaping slaves. A train generally consisted of a lumber wagon, covered with canvas, drawn by a good team of horses, driven by a cool, courageous man, well armed. The colored passengers were concealed beneath the cover, and traveling was mostly in the shelter of night. Arriving at the next station, the slaves were concealed and kindly cared for until the next night, when they were conveyed on their journey by the keeper of this station to the next. The trains were run with such secrecy that their coming and going was very seldom discovered by the slave catchers in pursuit of their human chattels. Hundreds of slaves from Missouri found their way to freedom across the prairies of Iowa from 1850 to 1860 by various lines of the "underground railroad." The men and women who, from feelings of humanity and without other compensation, kept the stations well knew the risk of ruinous fines and imprisonment they were taking, but, with the true John Brown spirit that moved them to aid men, women and children to freedom, they never shrunk from danger.

After the long time that has elapsed it is impossible to give much information as to these perilous journeys, the dodging and outwitting of slave catchers, United States marshals and their deputies, the contests before the courts for freedom or enslavement, as most of the conductors have passed away. But here is one incident, related by Gov. James W. Grimes, in a letter to his wife, written from Burlington, June 24, 1855: "Exciting times here; Dr.

James was captured on the Illinois side of the river with a fugitive slave in his carriage. Bowie knives and revolvers were drawn on them by the Missourians in pursuit, and he and the negro were forced back to town. A process was afterwards obtained and the negro was thrown into jail, where he is to remain to await his trial Tuesday. There is great excitement in the city, and several personal collisions have grown out of it. How it will end no one knows. I shall certainly furnish no aid to the man-stealers, and it has been determined that the negro shall have able counsel, and resort to all legal means for release, before any other is tried. I am sorry that I am governor of the state, for, although I can, and shall, prevent the state authorities and officers from interfering in aid of the marshal, yet, if not in office, I am inclined to think I should be a law-breaker. It is a very nice question with me, whether I should act, being governor, just as I would if I were a private individual. I intend to stand at my post at all events and act just as I shall think duty may require under the circumstances.

"June 27th. The negro is free, and is on his way to Canada. There was a great crowd in town. I sent on Monday to Davids, Yellow Springs and Huron, and told my friends and friends of the slave to be present at the trial. They were here *en masse*. Marion hall was filled, and guards were stationed at the door to prevent any more people entering, and also around the house. Rorer and Crocker appeared for the negro. When the decision was made, such a shout went up as was never heard in that hall before, and then it was caught up by the people outside of the building, and the whole town reverberated. A thousand men followed Dr. James to the river, and rent the air with their cheers as the boat was unlashed from her moorings and started with the poor fellow on his road to freedom. Judge Lowe was brought up from Keokuk Monday night, and a writ of *habeas corpus* was ready to be served if the decision had been adverse to us. Writs were sued out against the negro stealers for kidnaping, assault, etc., but unfortunately they escaped before service could be made upon them. I am satisfied that the negro could never have been taken into slavery from Burlington. Our friends, Col. Fitz Henry Warren and W. F. Cowles, showed that there was some marrow in their spinal columns." This letter of Governor Grimes' shows the spirit prevailing in Iowa at this time over the cruel and inhuman fugitive slave law, and the determination of a majority of the Iowa people to aid slaves on their way to freedom.

Among well-known Iowa men who were always ready to help the colored travelers on the lines of the "underground railroad," can be mentioned Rev. John Todd, Jas. C. Jordan, John Teesdale, Isaac Brandt, Thomas Mitchell, J. B. Grinnell, John R. Price, H. G. Cummings, William Penn Clark, Jesse Bowen, S. C. Trowbridge, Dr. H. G. Gill, John H. Painter and James Townsend.

When Kansas was invaded in 1855-6 by armed hordes of Missouri ruffians, for the purpose of forcing slavery into that territory, many citizens of Iowa moved there to help make it a free state. For several years Kansas became the battleground of the contending forces. John Brown, who went to Kansas in the fall of 1855, expected a bloody conflict over slavery, and went there to take part in it. He passed through Iowa in September of that

*John Brown prior to the Kansas raid.*

year with a son and son-in-law, and joined four sons who were already living in that territory. He at once began to organize the free state men in military companies to resist the "border ruffian" invaders from Missouri, and soon became a famous leader among the free state men. At the battle of Black Jack his little army, in which five of his sons were serving, after a hard fight compelled the surrender of a band of invaders twice as large as his own little army. This was the first bloody conflict for the overthrow of slavery, yet few besides John Brown at that time realized its mighty significance. His mission was the overthrow of slavery, and never during the few remaining years of his life did he for a moment waver from his inflexible purpose. Every energy of this remarkable man was henceforth concentrated upon the great work that he

religiously believed that he was ordained to accomplish. Many young men from Iowa enlisted under John Brown and participated in his warfare against slavery, and several of them joined him in his Harper's Ferry raid a few years later. Brown made five trips through Iowa while engaged in the Kansas conflict, learned the location of many of the stations on the "underground railroad," and became acquainted with a large number of Iowa men who were in active sympathy with the free state cause, and were always ready to assist slaves on their road to freedom. Hundreds, perhaps thousands, of slaves traveled safely over the various lines of "underground railroad" through Iowa from 1850 to 1860. Richard J. Hinton, who was actively engaged in the Kansas war, was one of the young men who in 1856 marched from Iowa City to Lawrence, Kan., to reinforce the free state men. At Iowa City they took 1,500 muskets from the armory. The key had been left on Governor Grimes' desk, and Hinton *borrowed* it to open the door of the armory. When they reached the Kansas line the Rev. Pardee Butler took charge of the muskets and safely conveyed them to the free state commanders. Mr. Butler was a well known Christian minister, who lived several years at Posten's Grove, in Cedar county, Iowa, and had moved to Kansas in 1854. He was an active free state leader and had been seized by a band of border ruffians at Atchison and placed upon a raft made of three logs and set adrift on the Missouri river. They painted his face black and warned him never to return or they would kill him. But Pardee Butler was not a man to be intimidated, and, managing to land some miles below, he returned to his home, armed himself, and defied the ruffians. He never ceased his work in the good cause until Kansas became a free state.

George B. Gill, Barclay Coppoc, Jeremiah G. Anderson and Charles P. Moffett, all young men from Iowa, took an active part in the Kansas war to save it from slavery. Some of them served under John Brown in Kansas, and afterwards enlisted in his Harper's Ferry expedition. West Branch in 1856 was a little country village in a Quaker settlement in the southwest corner of Cedar county, Iowa. At that time a Quaker, James Townsend, kept a public house there called the "Traveler's Rest." In October, 1856, John Brown on his way east from Kansas, on horseback, stopped at Townsend's over night. He informed the landlord that he was the John Brown, of Kansas, who had a large reward offered for his capture by Missouri slaveholders. Townsend gave him a warm

*John Brown, Jr.*
*Reproduced from an old and almost obscure photo*

welcome and told him of the large Quaker settlement at Springdale, four miles east. Brown knew that the Quakers were all opposed to slavery and made many friends among them.

From this time forward until his last visit to Iowa in 1859, John Brown made Springdale his favorite stopping place. James Townsend became one of his warmest friends. John Brown had long contemplated striking a blow at slavery in the mountain region of Virginia, and in 1857 he began to mature his plans. He believed that a small body of determined men could make a safe lodgment in the mountains and liberate slaves who would join them. His plan was to arm the escaped slaves with pikes, drill and organize them under experienced officers chosen from the young men who had distinguished themselves in the Kansas war. He expected thousands of slaves to flock to his standard when his purpose and presence became known to them, and in this way he expected to be able to raise a large army of liberators. In August,

6

1857, he engaged Hugh Forbes, who had served under Garibaldi in Europe, to open a school of military instruction at Tabor, Iowa, for the purpose of drilling men for his expedition. Tabor was largely settled by anti-slavery people and was an important town on the line of march for the free state men who passed through Iowa on their way to assist in the Kansas struggle. Brown and Forbes did not agree, and Forbes was dismissed and Brown went to Kansas to enlist some of his old followers. There he was joined by John E. Cook, Luke F. Parsons, Richard Realf, A. D. Stevens, C. W. Moffett, J. H. Kagi and Richard Richardson, who accompanied him back to Tabor, where they were joined by C. P. Tidd and W. H. Leeman, who had served under Brown in Kansas. Owen Brown was now with them and soon after they all left for Springdale. Here Brown decided to open a school of military instruction under Aaron D. Stevens, who had served in the regular army. William Maxson, who was not a Quaker, but lived on a farm near the village, boarded the men, and it was in his meadow that the drilling was carried on. Springdale was a quiet country village, remote from any public line of travel. It was a peaceful community of thrifty, prosperous farmers, nearly all Quakers and abolitionists. John Brown and the young men of his party were a remarkable group. Many of them were eloquent public speakers, some were poets, and others scholars and accomplished writers.

During the winter of 1857-8 these heroes of the Kansas war, who had for years endured the hardships and survived the dangers of that fierce struggle, found warm admirers and sympathizing friends among the refined and intelligent people of that rural village. They often assembled at the hospitable homes and spent the long winter evenings in recounting the exciting events of the war, their perils, escapes and battles. The horrors of slavery were discussed, and the young men who had dealt sturdy blows against that national crime in Kansas and Missouri, found themselves exalted into heroes by the liberty loving people of Springdale. While the Quakers were by tradition and principle opposed to war, so warm were their sympathies for the oppressed that they found a way to hold in the highest esteem and admiration these fearless young men who had risked their lives and struck sturdy blows for freedom in Kansas. The fame of John Brown, as one of the most daring leaders of the free state men in the territory, had reached every part of the country, and the people of Springdale saw in him a remarkable man, whose life would be freely given to the emancipation of slaves. Brown made his home with John H. Painter, and won the enduring friendship of William Maxson, Dr. H. G. Gill, Griffith Lewis, Moses Varney and other good citizens of Springdale and vicinity, that winter. He gradually made known, to some of these friends, his

plans for the future, and the purpose for which he
was drilling his men. Not one of these trusted
friends looked with favor upon the desperate enterprise, and all tried to dissuade him from undertaking such a hazardous, and as seemed to them, such
a hopeless raid. They saw clearly that it could not
succeed, as the whole power of the federal government would be quickly arrayed against it, and that it
must end in death or imprisonment of all who
engaged in it. But nothing could shake the stern
resolve of the fearless old emancipator. He as
firmly believed that he could strike a blow that
would lead to the overthrow of slavery. His faith
was so firm in ultimate success that several youn5

*Owen Brown, the last survivor of the raid on Harper's Ferry.*

men from Springdale and vicinity enlisted in his
band, among whom were George B. Gill, Edwin
and Barclay Coppoc and Steward Taylor. Before
Brown went east he had a confidential talk with
Dr. H. G. Gill, in which he gave his plans as follows: Doctor Gill says, "that he had not then
decided to attack the armory at Harper's Ferry, but
intended to take fifty or a hundred men in the
mountains near the ferry and remain there until he
could collect quite a number of slaves, and take
such conveyances as were needed and transport the
slaves into Canada. After the excitement had
abated he would make a strike in some other slave
state and continue to make such raids until slavery
ceased to exist. I did my best to convince him
that he would probably be killed. He said for him-

self he was willing to give his life for the slaves.
He repeatedly told me that he believed he was an
instrument in the hands of God, through which
slavery would be abolished. I said to him 'you
and your handful of men cannot cope with the whole
south.' His reply was 'I tell you, doctor, it will be
the beginning of the end of slavery.'" As improb-
able as it seemed to all but John Brown and his
devoted little band, he and they were not mistaken;
the sacrifice at Harper's Ferry was the beginning
of the end of American slavery. Therefore every
incident relating to this most desperate enterprise
becomes of absorbing historical interest and its
inception and execution are so intimately associated with Iowa, and Iowa men, that it demands
large space in our state's history. When Brown
went east and consulted his intimate friends there,
such as Gerret Smith, Wendell Phillips and F. B.
Sanborn, all remonstrated with him against such a
hopeless undertaking. His reply to all was that he
believed himself to be the instrument ordained to
destroy slavery, and that every member of his little
band was willing to risk his life in the attempt.

Brown, who had gone east during the winter to
raise money for his enterprise, returned to Springdale on the 27th of April, and ordered his band to
move east at once. It was a sorrowful leave taking
between the good people of Springdale, and the
young men who were going away on the most perilous enterprise that sane men ever enlisted in.
Warm friendships had grown up and all realized
that it was more than likely a last farewell, as it
proved to be to all. But it was more than a year
and a half before the blow was struck, so many obstacles intervened. In the meantime Brown returned to Kansas, and in company with Tidd,
Stevens, Kagi, J. G. Anderson, Albert Hazlett,
George B. Gill and others, in December, 1858,
crossed over into Missouri to liberate some slaves
who were to be sold and families separated. They
took twelve slaves, wagons, horses, cattle and other
property which Brown claimed the slaves were
entitled to for years of unpaid labor. One of the
slaveholders who resisted was killed. Brown and
his party reached Tabor on the 5th of January, 1859,
and remained there until the 11th, but the citizens
of that place who had been heretofore friendly to
him, did not approve of this raid, and in a public
meeting denounced him for his recent action.

A large reward had been offered by the governor of Missouri for the capture of Brown, but no
one ventured to attempt his arrest, and on the 11th
they started on across Iowa, finding shelter and aid
at the various stations on the "underground railroad." On the 18th the party reached Des Moines,
and on the 20th they met a cordial reception at
Grinnell; and on the 25th they passed through
Iowa City, reaching Springdale in the evening.
The postmaster at Iowa City was anxious to earn a
large reward and tried to raise a posse to cap-

ture John Brown and his escaped slaves: but the courage of the slave catchers oozed out when they learned that Brown and his men were well armed and ready for a fight. William Penn Clark and other friends of Brown at Iowa City procured a box-car, and in it conveyed the slaves over the Rock Island railroad to Chicago, while the old leader and his Kansas boys took seats in the passenger car on the sharp lookout for danger. At Davenport Laurel Summers, United States marshal, with a strong posse was watching the wagon road and ferry boat for the party, but never suspected that they were safely resting in the box-car that was attached to the passenger train that was then crossing the bridge for the Illinois side. John Brown had left Iowa for the last time. In July following John

Brown did not reach him. On the 16th of October, 1859, when the roll was called at the Kennedy farm, twenty-two men were present, thirteen of whom had proven their valor on the battlefields of Kansas. It is not my purpose to give a history of his last campaign, but chiefly to show that Iowa furnished more actors in the last great tragedy leading to the martyrdom of John Brown and most of his youthful followers than any other state. It was in Iowa that he had established his chain of stations on the "underground railroad" leading from the Missouri slave plantations to freedom. Among his co-workers for emancipation were Rev. John Todd, James C. Jordon, John Teesdale, Isaac Brandt, J. B. Grinnell, William Penn Clark, Jesse Bowen, S. C. Trowbridge, Dr. H. G. Gill, William Maxson,

*The home in which John Brown wintered his men in Springdale, Iowa.*

Brown, his sons, Owen and Oliver, and John E. Cook were near Harper's Ferry making their arrangements for the attack. They were living under assumed names on the Maryland side of the Potomac at the Kennedy farm, which they had leased. John H. Painter, at Springdale, had shipped 196 Sharpe's rifles and some revolvers to him at the farm, and pikes had been procured for the slaves to use. Of the Iowa men, Jeremiah G. Anderson, Steward Taylor, Edwin and Barclay Coppoc were with him, while Moffett and Gill had been notified to come on. But suspicion having been aroused by the gathering of so many strangers at the Kennedy farm, Brown decided to strike the blow at once before arrests could be made. This was eight days in advance of the time first set, and consequently many who were on the way to join

John H. Painter, James Townsend and Moses Varney, all well-known Iowa men. It was at Springdale that his men were drilled for the desperate assault upon slavery. Of the twenty-six volunteers who enlisted in this "forlorn hope," Edwin Coppoc, Barclay Coppoc, Steward Taylor, Jeremiah G. Anderson, George B. Gill and Charles W. Moffet, were Iowa men. It was in Iowa that the rifles and revolvers were collected and secreted for arming the volunteers who were expected to join the expedition at Harper's Ferry. It was from West Liberty, Iowa, that they were shipped as "carpenter's tools" by John H. Painter to a fictitious consignee near Harper's Ferry. It was from Iowa that the mysterious letter of warning was written to the secretary of war two months before the attack. It was an Iowa governor that saved from the Virginia gallows the Iowa boy who escaped capture and slaughter in the bloody conflict.

When the true story of the tragic affair came, we learned that twenty men captured Harper's Ferry, and seventeen of them held it for two days and three nights against Virginia citizens and militia, from 1,000 to 2,000 strong. One by one the members of the heroic little band fell. Not a man flinched. When the third night came, John Brown, Edwin Coppoc, Shields Green, Jeremiah G. Anderson, Watson Brown and Dauphin A. Thompson were the only survivors cooped in the engine house. Ten had been killed and several more severely wounded; still Brown sternly refused to surrender. It required a reinforcement of 100 United States marines, commanded by Robert E. Lee, and an

*Wm Maxson, in whose home John Brown wintered his men at Springdale before the raid.*

assault led by J. E. B. Stuart to enable the army to capture or slay the six unyielding emancipators. Of the Iowa members of the little army, Steward Taylor was killed at the engine house; Jeremiah G. Anderson was pierced through by bayonets in the last assault; Edwin Coppoc, who fought to the end, was disarmed and captured unhurt. Owen Brown, Barclay Coppoc and F. J. Merriam had been left on the Maryland side to guard the arms there stored, while John E. Cook and C. P. Tidd were sent over Tuesday morning to take some prisoners to the schoolhouse. More than 1,000 armed men were now between them and the spot where their leader and six survivors were making their last desperate fight. To join them was impossible.

Anderson and Hazlett escaped across the river in the gathering darkness, the latter only to be captured and hung. The men on the Maryland side would not abandon their companions as long as

there was a ray of hope. Led by Owen Brown they approached as near as possible to the Ferry, and saw more than 1,000 armed men between them and their comrades. Their rescue was hopeless.

Volumes have been written in this country and Europe on John Brown, the liberator and martyr, who gave his life without a murmur to free the slaves. The noblest men and women of his generation have given tributes to his unselfish life and his fidelity to duty as he saw it—a fidelity which led him to the scaffold. His name will live in history for all time. But little is known of his twenty-two followers who, in the early morning of their lives, actuated by the same spirit of self-sacrifice, enlisted in his "forlorn hope" and bravely marched to heroic deeds and almost certain death. In the world's history no more desperate and apparently hopeless undertaking has ever been entered upon by sane men. The chances for success were not one in a thousand; and yet these young men were so imbued with their leader's abhorrence of slavery, a fierce and fearless determination to devote their lives to its destruction, that they stopped not to count the cost or to coolly consider the chances for success. They had such confidence in the wisdom, courage and invincibility of their leader that, where he commanded, they marched without a murmur; where he would lead, they hesitated not to follow.

Not one of them could have been actuated by selfish motives. There was no hope of reward even in case of success. There was no pay for time or services, promised or expected. There was no honor to be won; there was no glory to be achieved.

It is well that the people of the state should know more of these Iowa men than is generally known, as the time is not distant when their names and deeds will occupy a prominent place in our history.

Steward Taylor was born at Uxbridge, Canada, October 29, 1836. He came to Iowa when but 17 years old, and learned the wagonmaker's trade at West Liberty. · Here he became acquainted with George B. Gill, who took him to Springdale in the winter of 1858, and at John H. Painter's house they met John Brown. Young Taylor was greatly impressed with the fervor of the old "hero of Ossawattomie," and listened eagerly to his recitals of the horrors of American slavery. He made the acquaintance, also, of the brilliant young men who were drilling under Stevens at the Maxson farm, for the Harper's Ferry campaign, and soon after enlisted with them. When the Chatham convention was held, he went to Canada to attend it. While waiting for the leader to complete his plans for the invasion, Taylor found work at his trade in Illinois. He waited impatiently for many months for notice to join the expedition. He raised what money was due him, and at once started for the rendezvous at Chambersburg, Pa., paying his own expenses. He was now 22 years of age, and is described as of medium height, rather heavy in build, strong and capable of great endurance. His complexion was dark, his hair reddish-brown, his eyes dark brown, large and full. He was smooth-faced and boyish looking. He was a con-

*Edwin Coppoc.*          *Barclay Coppoc.*

stant student, always carrying books with him. He was a stenographer, and he played the violin. He was quiet but persistent in his purposes, faithful, courageous and loyal When John Brown issued his eleven orders, just before the night attack, No. 6 required Capt. Watson Brown and Steward Taylor to "hold the covered bridge over the Potomac, and arrest anyone attempting to cross, using pikes, if resistance is offered, instead of Sharpe's rifles." Taylor was cool and fearless throughout the terrible conflict. He escorted one of Brown's prisoners to his home, to let his family know of his safety, and brought him back through crowds of armed, excited, desperate, drunken men. Later on in the day, while bravely fighting near the engine house, he received a mortal wound. He fell in the thickest of the fight, and suffered great agony for three hours, when death came to his relief. The day before the attack he remarked to his comrades that he felt he would be one of the first killed.

Jeremiah G. Anderson was the grandson of an officer of the American revolution. His father, John Anderson, left the slave state of Virginia soon after his marriage, and settled in Putman county, Indiana, where Jeremiah was born on the 17th of April, 1833. After his father's death, his mother moved with her family to Des Moines, Iowa. Jeremiah was well educated. He was sent by his mother to a Presbyterian academy at Kossuth, in 1854, to prepare for the ministry. Hon. James W. McDill, afterwards judge and United States senator, was one of his instructors. Judge McDill said "he was an eccentric young man, quiet and very studious." But he had no taste for the orthodox

ministry. In an essay he declared his belief in universal salvation, and soon after became a spiritualist. In 1857, Jeremiah went to Kansas and took a claim on the Little Osage. He joined Colonel Montgomery's army, and fought with him to make Kansas a free state. He afterwards served under John Brown, and was with him in one of his successful incursions for the liberation of Missouri slaves. He again joined his old commander in New York, where he was organizing the Harper's Ferry campaign, and was one of his most trusted and faithful friends. When Colonel Lee's marines broke through the barricade and charged on its six defenders, Anderson was pierced with three bayonets as his smoking rifle fell from his grasp. Mortally wounded, he was dragged out by his captors and thrown down on the stone flagging and left to the mercy of the brutal crowd. He lingered there in great agony for three hours, subjected to the most fiendish tortures. A gang of Virginia "chivalry" now mustered courage to approach the disarmed and dying man, kicking his face with their heavy boots, then opening his eyes they spit tobacco juice into them, while others forced their filthy quids into his mouth amid laughter, jeers and horrid oaths. When death finally ended his sufferings, two village doctors came along and

*Mother Coppoc, of Springdale.*

crowded his mutilated body into a salt barrel, stamping it down with their feet. They carted their prey off toward their office, and that was the last seen of Jeremiah G. Anderson, the close friend of John Brown, and one of the bravest Iowa soldiers who ever marched to the field of death.

Edwin Coppoc was born near Salem, Ohio, June 30, 1835. His father died when he was a child. He lived many years with his grandfather, going to district school and working on a farm. He is described as a studious, industrious boy of cheerful disposition. His eyes and hair were brown, and his skin fair. His head was large and well formed; he was fond of athletic sports, and was a genial companion. As a young man he was intelligent, active, brave, loyal, and the soul of honor. He had winning manners, was amiable, generous and kind. Anne Brown says of Edwin: " He was a rare young fellow, fearing nothing, yet possessed of great social traits, and no better comrade have I ever met." His mother was a woman of unusual intelligence and force of character. She strongly opposed the determination of her sons to enlist in the desperate enterprise. She had married again, and her sons were living with her at Springdale, when John Brown and his men came there to prepare for the Virginia invasion. Her boys eagerly listened to the story of the wrongs and cruelties inflicted upon the helpless slaves, as eloquently told by John Brown, and longed to help them to freedom. Edwin and his younger brother, Barclay, at last determined to join the brilliant young men who were drilling at the Maxson farm that winter, and follow wherever the old liberator should strike the next blow for emancipation. On the 15th of July, 1859, a letter came from John Brown request-

*Letter written by John Brown in the Charlestown jail a few days prior to his execution.*

Charlestown, Jefferson Co, Va, 16th Nov, 1859.

My Dear Wife

I write you in answer to a most kind letter of Nov 13th from dear Mrs Spring. I owe her ten thousand thanks for her kindness to you particularly + more especially than for what she has done, + is doing in a more direct way for me personally. Although I feel grateful for every expression of kindness or sympathy towards me, yet nothing can so effectually minister to my comfort as acts of kindness done to relieve the wants, or mitigate the sufferings of my poor distressed family. May God Allmighty, + their own consciousness; be their Eternal rewarders. I am exceedingly rejoiced to have you make the acquaintance, + to surround yourself, of such choice friends as I have long known some of those to be, with whom you are staying (by reputation) I am most glad to have you meet with one of a family (or I would rather say of two families) most beloved + never to be forgotten by me. I mean dear gentle Sarah Wattles. Many a time has she, her Father, Mother, Brother, Sisters, Uncle, + Aunt (like Angels of mercy) ministered to the wants of myself; + of my poor sons; both in sickness + in health. Only last year; I lay sick for a quite a number of Wattles with and was cared for by all; as though I had been a most affectionate Brother, or Father. Ill he met I ask God to bless, + reward them forever. "I was a stranger, + they took me in." It may possibly be that Sarah would like to copy this letter; + send it to her home: If so by all means let her do so. I would write them; if I had the power. Now let me say a word about the effort to educate our Daughters. I am no longer able to provide means to help towards that object; + it therefore becomes me not to dictate in the matter. I shall gratefully submit the direction of the whole thing to those generous where to my, undertake in their behalf, while I give ever a little expression of my own choice respecting it. You my Wife perfectly well know that I have always expressed a decided preference for a very plain but perfectly practical education for both Sons and Daughters. I do not mean an education so very miserable as that you & I received in early life; nor as some of our children have enjoyed: when I say plain but practical. I mean enough of the learning of the schools to enable them to transact the common business of life comfortably; & respectably; together with that thorough training to good business habits which best prepares both men & women (to be useful though poor:) & to meet the stern realities of life with a good grace. You well know that I always claimed that the music of the Broom, wash tub, needle, Spindle, Loom, Axe, Spade, Hoe, Flail &c should first be learned at all events: & that of the Piano &c afterwards. I put them in that order; as most conducive to health of body, & mind; & for the obvious reason; that after a life of some experience; & of much observation: I have found ten women; as well as ten men; who have made their mark in life Right: whose early training was of that plain practical kind; to one who had a more popular, & fashionable early training. But enough of that.

Now in regard to your coming here: If you feel sure that you can endure the trials, & the shocks; which will be unavoidable (if you come): I should be most glad to see you once more. But when I think of your being insulted on the road; & perhaps while here; & of only seeing your wretchedness made complete: I shrink from it. Your composure; & fortitude of mind may be quite equal to it all; but I am in dreadful doubt of it. If you do come: defer your journey till about the 27th or 28th of this month. The scenes you will have to pass through on coming here; will be any thing but those you now pass with tender, kind hearted, friends; & kind faces to meet you every where. Do consider the matter well before you make the plunge.

I think I had better say no more on this most painful subject. My health improves a little; my mind is very tranquil; I may say joyous: & I continue to receive every kind attention that I have any possible need of. I wish you to send copies of all my letters to all our poor children. What I write to one; must answer for all; till I have more strength. I get numerous kind letters from friends in almost all directions; to encourage me to "be of good cheer:" & I still have as I trust "the peace of God to rule in my heart." May God for Christ's sake ever make his face to shine on you all    Your Affectionate Husband
                                        John Brown

ing them to come on to Chambersburg, Pa. On the 25th they bade their mother good-by, and started ostensibly for Ohio. But their mother was not deceived; she knew too well their destination, and expected never to see them again.

Order No. 9, made out by Captain Brown the day of the attack, details "Lieut. Albert Hazlett and Edwin Coppoc to hold the armory opposite the engine house after it is taken, remaining there until morning, when further orders will be given." The fight began early in the forenoon, and Brown was so hotly engaged that his usual good judgment failed him, and he did not realize their great peril until his little band was hemmed in on all sides by overwhelming numbers, and retreat to the mountains was impossible. His detachments, widely separated, stood at their posts with a courage never surpassed in the annals of warfare. One by one they fell before the volleys pouring in upon them from every side. We hear of Edwin Coppoc standing at his post at the armory gates, while balls rained around him like hailstones. Soon after he joined Brown at the engine house and the siege began. Watson and Oliver, sons of the leader, were mortally wounded, but the heroic Watson fought on to the last. John Brown, his son Watson, Jerry Anderson, Edwin Coppoc, Dauphin A. Thompson, Steward Taylor and Shields Green were now the only survivors left on the Virginia side. Escape was impossible, and they determined to die fighting, knowing that no mercy would be shown them as prisoners. Col. Robert E. Lee, who was now in command of their assailants, sent a message to Brown demanding his surrender.

"No!" said Brown, "we prefer to die here."

Firing began again on both sides, while Lee formed a column for assault.

When the shock of the final charge came, Brown, Anderson and Thompson went down beneath the savage thrusts of sabres and bayonets. Edwin Coppoc fired the last shot, and he and Green alone were left unhurt to surrender. The fight was ended. Ten of the little band were slain. Brown and Stevens were desperately wounded, and, with Coppoc, Green and Copeland, were prisoners. William Thompson and W. H. Leeman, who had before surrendered, were butchered in cold blood by the Virginia "chivalry." Harper's Ferry had been held forty-eight hours by seventeen men, against the assaults of from 500 to 1,500 armed citizens and militia from Maryland and Virginia.

Nowhere in modern warfare is there recorded such an unequal contest of similar duration. Of the immortal seventeen, three were Iowa boys under twenty-four years of age. On the 22d of November, Edwin Coppoc wrote home an account of the battle, from which I give a few extracts:

"Eleven of our little band are now sleeping in their bloody garments with the cold earth above them. Braver men never lived; truer men to their plighted word never banded together. * * * As our comrades fell, we could not minister to their wants as they deserved, for we were surrounded by troops firing volley after volley, and we had to keep up a brisk fire in return to keep them from charging upon us. Watson Brown was wounded on Monday, at the same time Stevens was, while carrying a flag of truce; but he got back to the engine house. He fought as bravely as any man. When the fight was over he got worse. He and Green and myself were put in the watch-house. Watson kept getting worse until Wednesday morning, and begged hard for a bed but could not get one. I pulled off my

*Captain Avid, John Brown's captor and jailor.*

coat and put it under him and placed his head in my lap, and in that position he died. * * * Whatever may be our fate, rest assured we shall not shame our dead companions by a shrinking fear. They lived and died like brave men; we, I trust, shall do the same."

On the 19th, Edwin Coppoc, Green and Copeland were taken to Charleston jail, which was guarded by state militia with two cannon trained on it. Edwin's trial began on the afternoon of November 1st and ended next day with his conviction. He was sentenced to be hung on the 16th of December. He bore himself bravely through the ordeal and calmly awaited his doom. He and Cook were confined in the same cell and were very warm friends. Great sympathy was felt for Edwin Coppoc, and it was not confined to his Ohio and Iowa friends.

Even Governor Wise could not refrain from expressing his admiration for his noble bearing through all the trying scenes of the battle, the surrender, the trial and conviction. He asked no favors, made no complaints, but calmly accepted the consequences of his heroic effort to free the slaves. He faced his awful doom without a murmur. His grandfather and uncle from Salem, Ohio, and Thomas Gwynn, of Cedar county, Iowa, went down to Virginia to appeal to Governor Wise for a commutation of his sentence to imprisonment, and to his credit let it be known that the governor made such a recommendation to the legislature, as in cases of treason he had not the power to interfere. A committee of that body recommended the commutation, but the Virginia legislature demanded his death. Shields Green, the faithful negro, managed to secrete an old knife when captured, which he now gave to Coppoc. Edwin contrived to notch the blade into a rude saw. With this he and Cook sawed the shackles from their limbs and, digging a hole through the brick wall of their cell the night before execution, they made a bold strike for freedom. But the guards discovered them as they crept out and they were returned to their cell.

The few remaining hours of their lives were spent in writing farewell letters to their friends.

The morning of their last day dawned upon Cook and Coppoc. They were as calm and brave in death as they had been all through the two days of fierce battle. Their comrades, Green and Copeland, were executed at 10:30 A. M., December 16th, and at half-past twelve Cook and Coppoc were taken from their cells. They were permitted to bid Hazlett and Stevens good-bye, on their way to the scaffold. When the black caps were drawn over their heads, they clasped each other's hands in a last farewell and calmly met their doom. Edwin's body was taken by his friends to his boyhood home at Salem, and there laid to rest among his kindred.

Barclay Coppoc, Edwin's younger brother, was born January 4, 1839. He was somewhat taller than Edwin, of slender build, brown hair, bold, large eyes and a determined expression. He was threatened with consumption from boyhood. When nineteen years of age he joined a party going to Kansas. Emigrant life improved his health and he enjoyed the stirring events of the free state conflict with the Missouri invaders. Here he met Aaron D. Stevens, Richard Realf and John Brown, and enlisted in some of their expeditions. When his old leader came to Springdale, a year later, Barclay was ready to again take up arms against slavery under his former commander. As we have seen, he was not in the desperate fight at Harper's Ferry, from the fact that he was sent with Owen Brown's party to guard their arms on the Maryland side. After all was lost and they escaped to the mountains, Owen Brown was by common consent made their leader. A large reward was offered by Governor Wise for their arrest and delivery to the jail of Jefferson county. The country was soon alive with armed men hunting for the fugitives. Governor Wise described Barclay Coppoc as follows:

"He is about twenty years of age; is about five feet seven and a half inches in height, with hazel eyes and brown hair, wears a light mustache, and has a consumptive look."

Each member of the party was as minutely described. Cook was so well known at Harper's Ferry that a perfect description was given of him, and a reward of $1,000 was offered for his capture. As they passed near Chambersburg, in the mountains, Cook could not resist the temptation to venture into that town in the darkness of night to see his young wife and say good-bye before going on to Canada. His companions protested most earnestly, but he started on, after appointing a place to meet them before morning. They waited at the meeting place long and anxiously, but never saw him again.

The story of the fearful sufferings of these men, as they wandered for thirty-six days through the wilds of the Maryland and Pennsylvania mountains, would fill a volume. Subsisting on unground field corn, occasional fruit, a raw chicken now and then, without shelter or fire, huddling together when sleeping amid chilling rains, sleet and snow, with feet lacerated by sharp rocks and thorns, always nearly perishing from hunger, human suffering reached its limit. They were pursued by human and brute bloodhounds—the first eager for blood money, and the latter thirsting for their life blood. Merriam soon gave out. He was left on a railroad track, and entered an obscure station, and, at great risk, took a train and escaped. After reaching northern Pennsylvania, starving and utterly exhausted, the others at last ventured to seek shelter at a farmhouse. Weeks had elapsed since they had escaped, and not a word had reached them of the fate of their comrades. A paper was lying on the table. Tidd took it up and began to read. His face paled as he read on. Owen and Barclay were watching him intently. With a forced calmness, Tidd then began to read aloud the story of the trial and death sentence of John Brown and Edwin Coppoc, and the capture of Cook and Hazlett. Tears rolled down Barclay's cheeks as the fate of his brother, the old captain and the gallant Cook was read; but not a word dared they utter. After leaving them, it seems that Cook had suddenly come to a clearing in the woods before dark, and found himself face to face with three woodchoppers. Two of them were stalwart brothers named Logan, professional slave catchers. They had seen the description of Cook, and knew of the $1,000 reward. They recognized and seized him at once, and, binding his arms, they delivered him over to the Virginia officers, and pocketed the reward.

One of the Logans joined the rebel army two

years later and was killed by a Union bullet. The
other lived many years, always suffering remorse
for their infamous sale of the gallant Cook to the
Virginia hangman. He was finally crushed to
death beneath the wheels of a railroad train.

The three famished men traveled on, after a
night's rest for the first time in a month under a
roof, and after a few days more felt reasonably safe
to travel by daylight. Coppoc soon after took the
cars for Iowa which he safely reached, worn almost
to a skeleton by starvation and exposure. He
appeared suddenly in his old home on the 17th of
December and met a warm and tearful welcome.
His brother Edwin and his comrade Cook had died
on a Virginia scaffold the day before. Barclay was
so near death from his terrible sufferings, that his
Springdale friends determined to defend him in his
own home from surrender to the Virginia hangman. Armed and drilled, the guard kept nightly

calmly listening to the violent language of this
individual, who was swinging his arms wildly in
his wrath. The governor quietly suggested to the
stranger that "he had supposed he did not want
his business made public."

The rude reply was: "I don't care a d—n who
knows it now, since you have refused to honor the
requisition."

The pompous man then proceeded to argue the
case with the governor, and we soon learned that
he was an agent from Virginia bearing a requisition from Governor Letcher* for the surrender of
Barclay Coppoc.

In reply to a remark by the agent, that Coppoc
might escape before he could get the defect in the
requisition cured, the governor, looking signifi-
cantly at us, replied, "There is a law under which
you can arrest Coppoc and hold him until the requisition is granted," and the governor reached for

*John Brown's sons at home in later years in Southern California.*

watch over him for many weeks. F. C. Galbraith,
of Springdale, thus describes the plans of his
defenders:

"Springdale is in arms and prepared at a half-
hour's notice to give his pursuers a reception of 200
shots. There are three of our number who always
know his whereabouts, and nobody else knows anything of him. He is never seen at night where he
was during the day, and there are men on watch at
Davenport, Muscatine, Iowa City, West Liberty
and Tipton. It is intended to baffle them in every
possible way without bloodshed."

On the 23d day of January, 1860, in company
with the late Gen. Ed Wright (both of us being
members of the legislature then in session), I went
into the executive rooms on business with Governor Kirkwood. We found in conference with
the governor a pompous-looking man, who seemed
to be greatly excited. Governor Kirkwood was

the code. We waited to hear no more, but saying
to the governor that we would call again when he
was not engaged, and giving him a look that was a
response to his own, we walked out.

We felt there was not a moment to lose if we
would save Coppoc from the Virginia gallows. We
hastily communicated with J. W. Cattell, J. B.
Grinnell, David Hunt, Amos Hoag and other well
known anti-slavery members of the legislature. It
was instantly decided that a special messenger
must be sent to warn Coppoc and his friends of the
danger. A purse was hastily made up, and Isaac
Brandt was delegated to find a man of nerve, who
could endure a horseback ride in midwinter of 165
miles without sleep or rest. He soon produced a
small, wiry young man, who was an experienced
horseman and as tireless as a cow-boy. His name

---

*Governor Wise's term expired January 1, 1860, and he
was succeeded by Governor Letcher.

was Williams. A fast horse was procured, while Williams equipped himself for a ride for life. Credentials were hastily prepared, to be presented by our messenger to the agents of the "underground railroad" on the route, to enable him to procure fresh horses at each point without delay. A note was written to a trusted friend at Springdale, of which the following is a copy:

DES MOINES, January 23, 1860.

JOHN H. PAINTER—There is an application for young Coppoc from the governor of Virginia, and the governor here will be compelled to surrender him. If he is in your neighborhood, tell him to make his escape from the United States.                            YOUR FRIEND.

It was not prudent to sign a name to the note, but it bore its stamp of genuineness in the well known handwriting of Senator Cattell, with which Painter was familiar. In less than two hours from the time we left the executive rooms the sharp,

before hung John Brown, Edwin Coppoc, John E. Cook, Shields Green and John Copeland. If our messenger could reach Springdale before Mr. Camp could get to Iowa City and procure a posse to make the arrest, a bloody conflict would be prevented, and Coppoc could reach a place of safety.

On the morning of the 25th, Mr. Williams alighted from his last foaming horse at John H. Painter's, and Barclay Coppoc was saved.

When Mr. Camp reached Iowa City, he heard of the armed guard of Coppoc's friends at Springdale, and remembering that John Brown, with seventeen young men of the same stamp, had held Harper's Ferry two days and three nights against 1,000 armed Virginians, he had no consuming desire to lead an officer's squad against the Sharpe's rifles of Coppoc's defenders. He slunk away to Muscatine to wait for legal requisition papers.

The day after our messenger started, it became

*John Brown's sons and cabin in California.*

rapid strokes of the shoes of a fast horse on the frozen ground resounded on the old stage road out by the "Prairie Queen" and on to Four Mile Ridge. The rider was enveloped in a huge buffalo overcoat and fur cap, while a small leather saddle valise carried his baggage and refreshments to fortify against a piercing east wind which he faced. His instructions were to reach Springdale as soon as horse flesh and human endurance could make it, and then rest, sleep and return at his leisure.

We confidently expected that Mr. Camp, the Virginian, would take the first stage east, which traveled day and night with frequent change of horses, and arrest Coppoc before his friends could be rallied. We knew there was a drilled band of seventy-five determined young men in and about Springdale who were well armed, and had declared that Barclay Coppoc should never be surrendered to the Virginia governor who had a few weeks

known that Governor Kirkwood's legal learning had enabled him to detect some fatal flaws in Governor Letcher's requisition papers, and that he had refused to surrender Coppoc. M. V. Bennett (a bitter democratic partisan member of the lower house of the legislature from Marion county) presented resolutions of inquiry, some time after the affair became public, as follows:

WHEREAS, A requisition was made on the governor of Iowa, by the governor of Virginia, for Barclay Coppoc, an alleged participant in the difficulties at Harper's Ferry, Va., as a fugitive from justice, and

WHEREAS, The governor of Iowa has refused to deliver up said Coppoc under said requisition, alleging technical defects therein; therefore, be it

*Resolved*, That the governor of Iowa be requested to lay before this house a copy of the requisition directed to him by the governor of Virginia, and all matters connected therewith; also to inform this house whether he possesses any knowledge in regard to a rumor that a special messenger was dispatched to inform Coppoc of his danger;

and if so, by what authority said messenger was dispatched to inform Coppoc of his danger.

On motion of W. H. F. Gurley, of Scott county, the resolutions were somewhat changed and passed. In response to them Governor Kirkwood sent all the papers in the case to the house, with a special message, which is excellent reading even now after thirty-six years have elapsed.

Briefly, the reasons Kirkwood gave for refusing to order Coppoc's arrest were:

*First.*—No indictment had been found against him.

*Second.*—The affidavit was made before an alleged notary public but was not authenticated by a notary's seal.

*Third.*—The affidavit did not show that Coppoc was in Virginia aiding and abetting John Brown.

*Fourth.*—It did not legally charge him with commission of any crime.

The governor says:

"It is a high prerogative of official power in any case, to seize a citizen of the state, and send him upon an *ex parte* statement without any preliminary examination, and without confronting him with a single witness, to a distant state for trial. It is a prerogative so high that the law tolerates its exercise only on certain fixed conditions, and *I shall not exercise that power to the peril of any citizen of Iowa, upon demand of the state of Virginia,* or any other state, unless these conditions are complied with.

"The fact that an agent of Virginia was here with a requisition for Coppoc became publicly known, solely through the acts of that agent himself. After I had communicated my determination to him, not to grant the warrant, he sat in my office conversing with me on the subject. During our conversation, other persons came in, and to my surprise he continued the conversation in their presence. I said to him that 'I supposed he did not wish his business made known to the public.' He replied that as the warrant had been refused he did not care who knew it. In this manner the fact that a requisition had been made for Coppoc became known in this place. The insinuation that I had anything to do, directly or indirectly, with sending information to Coppoc that a requisition had been made for him, is simply and unqualifiedly untrue; nor have I any means of knowing whether such information was sent by others, or if so, by whom sent, other than common rumor. Permit me to say in conclusion, that one of the most important duties of the official position I hold is to see that no citizen of Iowa is carried beyond her border and subjected to the ignominy of imprisonment, and the perils of trial for crimes in another state, otherwise than by due process of law. That duty I shall perform.          SAMUEL J. KIRKWOOD."

These ringing words of the fearless old war governor stand out in bold contrast to the cringing attitude of Governor Packer of Pennsylvania, who hastened to send two of Coppoc's companions (Cook and Hazlett), back to the Virginia gallows, without even an investigation of the legality of the papers.

Governor Letcher was in a great rage when the Iowa governor's refusal reached him, but he understood that nothing short of a rigid compliance with all requirements of law would enable him to wrest another victim for execution from Iowa. He had the grand jury summoned, and procured Coppoc's indictment. Here is one of the counts in the famous document:

*Thirteenth Judicial circuit of Virginia, Jefferson county:*

The jurors of the commonwealth of Virginia, in and for the body of the county of Jefferson, duly empaneled and attending upon said court, upon their oaths present, that Barclay Coppoc, being a free person, on the 16th and 17th days of October, in the year 1859, and on divers other days before and after that time, in the county of Jefferson and commonwealth of Virginia aforesaid, and within the jurisdiction of this court, not having the fear of God before his eyes, but being moved and seduced by the instigations of the devil, did maliciously, wilfully and feloniously conspire with certain John Brown, Edwin Coppoc, John E. Cook, Shields Green, John Copeland, Aaron D. Stevens and other persons to the jurors unknown, to induce certain slaves of said county and commonwealth aforesaid, to-wit,—slaves called Henry, Levi, Ben, Jerry, Phil, George and Bill, the slaves of John H. Allstadt,—and each of said slaves respectively to rebel and make insurrection against their said masters, and against the authority of the constitution and laws of the commonwealth of Virginia, to the evil example of all others in like case offending, and against the form of the statute in that case provided, and against the peace and dignity of the commonwealth of Virginia.

Endorsed—"A true bill," February 3, 1860.

                                        J. A. LEWIS,
                                            *Foreman.*

It was the 10th day of February before Governor Letcher's legal requisition reached Des Moines. Then Governor Kirkwood was compelled to issue his warrant for the arrest—but Coppoc was not to be found. His friends got news of the new requisition promptly. That night, with his staunch friend, Thaddeus Maxson, Barclay was conveyed in a sleigh to Mechanicsville, accompanied by a well armed guard. Coppoc and Maxson took the night train on the Northwestern road for Chicago, where they stayed several days with a trusted family of colored friends. They went on to Canada and remained until the Virginia officer left for his home. Learning that his late companions, Owen Brown and F. J. Merriam, were staying in Ashtabula county, Ohio, Barclay and his friend Maxson joined them, and the little party stayed several weeks at the town of Dorset. They were always well armed and ready to defend themselves day or night.

The young man who so narrowly escaped death

the second time, was not to be intimidated by dangers. Barclay Coppoc never ceased his war upon slavery. Early in the summer of 1860 he went to Kansas and aided some Missouri slaves to freedom. When the civil war began, he hastened to join the Union army, and was commissioned a lieutenant in the Fourth Kansas Volunteers, commanded by the gallant Colonel Montgomery, of Kansas war fame. Lieutenant Coppoc was sent to his old home in Iowa to secure recruits who wanted to serve under him. On his return with them he met his death on

the 30th day of August, 1861, from the burning of a railroad bridge by Missouri guerrillas, precipitating the train he was on eighty feet into the Platte river. A large number were killed and wounded. Lieutenant Coppoc's body was taken to Leavenworth, and buried in Pilot Knob cemetery. On a fine soldiers' monument erected at Tipton, near his old home, by the patriotic people of Cedar county, to the memory of its citizen soldiers who gave their lives for their country in the rebellion, is inscribed the name of Barclay Coppoc.

CHAPTER XII.

*Financial Depression of 1857—Wild-cat Banks—Iowa State Banks—Great Tornado of 1860—Camanche Destroyed—War of the Rebellion Coming—The War Session of the General Assembly—The First Iowa Regiment.*

A building having been erected by the citizens of Des Moines for a temporary state house, in the fall of 1857 the state officers moved the records and furniture from Iowa City, and the capital of the state was established at Des Moines. Under the new constitution provision had been made for the election of a lieutenant-governor, and at the October election of 1857 Oran Faville, the republican candidate, was elected to that office, and became the first lieutenant-governor of Iowa.

The year 1857 closed with great financial depression throughout the country. Most of the banks had suspended specie payment and the redemption of their bills, and a very large number of them had failed. There were no banks in Iowa permitted to issue bills for currency, and it was impossible to get good money in sufficient amount to buy the farm produce or carry on the ordinary business. In order to meet the emergency two banks were established by Iowa men in Nebraska, one called the Bank of Nebraska and the other the Bank of Florence. These banks issued paper currency, which was brought into Iowa and put into circulation by the Iowa banking houses which owned the Nebraska banks. So long as Iowa people would receive these bills as money, a very large amount of business was done with them in the absence of a supply of better currency.

A firm of Davenport merchants and produce dealers procured fine plates and had printed in the form and style of bank bills their promises to pay, and put them in circulation in exchange for farm produce, and for a time did an immense business. But, in competition with such currency, gold and silver and good bank bills were retired from circulation and hoarded until none was to be procured except at a large premium. Taxes had to be paid in gold and silver, as it was the only legal money in Iowa. Under such conditions the Seventh General Assembly convened on the 11th of January,

1858, the first session under the new constitution, which authorized the establishment of banks in Iowa. An excellent banking law was enacted, providing for a system of state banks and branches, which had to be submitted to a vote of the electors for approval. The laws were made to harmonize as far as possible, and a commission appointed to revise the general laws and report at the next session. Governor Grimes was elected to succeed General Jones in the United States senate, and, for the first time in its history, Iowa had not a democrat in congress. The people at an election adopted the banking system enacted by the legislature, and Iowa soon after had as good banks and as sound currency as any state in the Union.

THE GREAT TORNADO OF 1860.

The greatest tornado that ever swept over Iowa was formed from a hailstorm that was first seen on the great prairies of Calhoun and Webster counties on Sunday, June 3, 1860, at about half past 3 o'clock. The day had been very sultry, with the exception of an occasional slight breeze which would spring up from some direction and in a few moments would die away. The next breeze would come from an entirely different direction, and after blowing for a brief time disappear. As the day advanced the heat became more intense, and not a breath of air was stirring. It was noticed that the cattle and horses in the pastures were uneasy, and kept walking around throwing their heads up in the air as though disturbed by some unusual apprehension. They would follow along the fences, seeking a place to get out. The birds gathered in the groves and shade trees about the houses. The dogs were seen sniffing the air, as though someone or something unusual was approaching. I was living on a high, sightly prairie elevation from which we could see several groves at great distances to the west and southwest. The air seemed to be unusually clear, and I could see the trees near Tipton, a distance of seventeen miles, that day, something that had very seldom been known. At about 5 o'clock, we noticed in the west, just above the horizon, banks of light-colored clouds, appearing in a long, irregular line from far in the north to away off in the south. Very slowly they arose, and in half an hour we could see below them the darkest, blue-black, continuous cloud, reaching the whole distance from north to south, that I remember to have seen. Soon after, a very light haze, of a bluish-green tint, began to be visible in the atmosphere. At this time the air seemed most profoundly still and oppressive. The uneasiness of all domestic animals increased. Those running at large upon the great prairie ranges were seen to be approaching the settlements with a startled, fright-

tions I had read of their appearance. The cloud had now been in sight about three quarters of an hour, and the vivid flashing of the lightning and steady roar of the thunder were continuous, without any perceptible cessation.

The wind had come up in gusts from the east, then south and again suddenly veering to the north, then as suddenly dying away into a dead calm. The cloud was now rising rapidly and trailing below it seemed to be an immense waterspout, the lower end of which appeared to be dragging on the ground. We could hear a steady roar, very heavy, but not loud, like an immense freight train going over a long bridge. Looking off about three miles towards a grove in the path of the black, trailing waterspout as it passed through the timber, high up in the air great trees, torn and shattered, could be plainly seen thrown by the force of the whirl-

*First capitol—Des Moines, 1858—before it was rebuilt.*

ened appearance. As the long line of clouds slowly arose, the lower portion, where it seemed to touch the earth, became of inky blackness. We could now barely hear the long continued rumble of thunder, and for some time sharp tongues of lightning had been visible. The atmosphere, the haze and the rising bank of clouds had a wierd, unnatural appearance, and the oppressiveness of the lifeless heat became almost unendurable. It was now noticed for the first time that the light-colored upper clouds, which resembled the dense smoke of a great prairie fire, were rapidly moving from the north and south toward the center of the storm cloud, and as they met they boiled like foaming water and descended in a rapid movement to the black cloud below. We were all now intently watching this strange movement, something we had never before seen. It flashed over me in a moment, *this is a tornado!* as I remembered descrip-

wind outside of its vortex and falling towards the earth. My family had been sent into the cellar, which was made of large rocks upon which rested our balloon-frame house. I stood close to the outside doorway, ready to spring in if the fearful, black, swaying trail should come towards the house. It appeared to be going about half a mile north of us. The sight, while grand and fearful, was too fascinating to be lost unless the danger came nearer. The roar was now awful, and a terrific wind was blowing directly towards the swaying, twisting, dragging, black trail, which seemed to be sweeping down into the ground. It was now coming directly towards the log house of my nearest neighbors on the north, and I saw them run out and down a steep bluff of Rock creek and cling to the willows. Suddenly the black trail raised up in the air, and I could see falling to the ground tree tops, rails, boards, posts, and every conceivable broken fragment of wrecked buildings. As the storm swept by no more could be seen of that devouring, whirling, irresistible, black trailing demon of air, water, and electricity that had wrought such destruction. We learned the next day that the whirlwind part of the storm did not strike the earth again until it had gone about seven miles, when it united with another branch coming from the northwest, when they tore on in a broad path for twenty-eight miles,

OLD BRICK CAPITOL, DES MOINES.

*Old capitol, Des Moines, after it was rebuilt. Destroyed by fire in 1892.*

sweeping everything from the face of the earth to the Mississippi river. Night came on and we could learn nothing of the terrible damage wrought until the next day, when the news came of the destruction of the town of Camanche.

It was nearly a week before the full particulars of the fearful ruin brought by this greatest of northern tornadoes could be gathered up. It first assumed the whirlwind form in Hardin county, and the first loss of life came near New Providence. Twelve houses were destroyed in that village but most of the people were at a meeting some distance away and the loss of life was small. Seven miles south of Eldora Michael Devine's brick house was destroyed, four persons killed, and five terribly injured. Schoolhouses, barns, sheds, stacks, fences, were blown for miles across the prairies. Mangled bodies of horses, cattle and hogs were strewn in every direction. Corn and wheat was literally torn up by the roots and everything above ground was destroyed. The tornado crossed the Iowa river at Sanderson's mill, swept a clean path through the woods and passed on through the north of Marshall county. The number of persons killed in Hardin county was seven; wounded, twenty-seven; houses destroyed, thirty-seven; estimated loss, $75,000. It swept down through Linn county, destroying farm houses, barns, orchards and groves, horses and cattle. Eighteen persons were killed, thirty-five wounded severely, eighteen houses destroyed, and the property loss estimated at $150,-000. A branch of the main line of the tornado, which passed over a portion of Jones county, killed nine persons, wounded thirty, destroyed thirteen

houses and did damage to the amount of $30,000. In Cedar county three persons were killed, thirteen wounded, eight houses destroyed and a property loss of $15,000. In Clinton county, after the two storms united, the destruction was awful. In many places the path of the tornado was from 80 to 160 rods in width and this track was left a desert waste. Scores of people were killed and mangled, and beautiful homes utterly swept out of existence. The full fury of the united tornadoes struck the village of Camanche at about 7 o'clock in the evening. One who visited the place the next morning gives the following description of the ruin: "Amid the devastation that met the eye and is utterly indescribable, wherever a few boards hung together, were gathered the survivors, some slumbering, others sitting in despair, mourning the loved and lost; some nursing the wounded, while many lay dead side by side in rough boxes in a building. The tornado had swept through the town a quarter of a mile wide, literally prostrating everything before it. The town was not a *mass* of ruins, but it looked as though the houses and their contents were literally *scattered*. There were fragments of what had been houses everywhere. All that was left of Camanche was a few houses, and all of these injured. No houses were left in the direct track of the tornado, and those at the edges were riddled as if by cannon shot. In many cases broken timbers had been hurled through houses, carrying death and destruction. Eleven store buildings, fronting on the river, were piled in ruins, and much of them, with their contents, was swept into the river. There is not a business house in the town left uninjured, and nearly every one was totally de-

*Old capitol, Des Moines, after the fire (afterwards torn down).*

stroyed and their contents ruined. The scene was appalling and cannot be described.

"Of the 350 houses in the town not 50 are left standing, and with scarcely an exception, those left are more or less injured. It is doubtful whether any attempt will be made to rebuild the town."

In Albany, on the Illinois side of the river, scores of houses were destroyed and many people killed. From Albany the tornado swept on over Illinois, sometimes rising high up in the air and again swooping down to the earth, and sweeping everything before it, killing twenty-six persons and severely injuring more than fifty. It crossed Lake Michigan and finally disappeared, after having traversed a distance of more than 450 miles. Forty-three persons were killed in Camanche and eighty severely injured. Two hundred and three buildings were totally destroyed, and 113 more badly wrecked. Eight hundred and sixty homeless people were in the streets of Camanche on the morning after the tornado passed through that town. The total number of persons killed in the entire track of the tornado was 146, and many more died of their injuries, bringing the total fatalities to near 200. The destruction of property was over $700,000. When it is remembered that in 1860 the larger part of the country over which the tornado passed was very sparsely settled, the magnitude of this greatest cyclone that ever visited the northern latitudes, can be realized. It traveled at the rate of about sixty-six miles an hour, and the velocity of its rotary motion was estimated to be not less than 300 miles an hour, or equal to a cannon ball fired by a full charge. The fact that all of the bark was entirely stripped from many live trees, shows the wonderful power of the tornado.

### WAR OF THE REBELLION.

The great contest over the extension of slavery in the territories, which had agitated the country for many years, was by the success of the republican party in the election of Abraham Lincoln in November, 1860, substantially settled against the further extension of slavery in the United States. The south clearly saw that this meant a change of policy that would deprive slave holders of the control of the national government in a few years permanently, by the admission of free states, and that there was no hope that the south could ever again reverse this decision. That meant logically the beginning of the destruction of slavery in the United States. They must submit to such a result in the not distant future or separate from the union and found an independent nation to preserve the institution. Before President Lincoln was inaugurated the movement began by which the southern confederacy was organized. Seizure of forts, arms and public property followed. The loyal states were called upon for volunteers to suppress the rebellion. Samuel J. Kirkwood had been elected governor.

When the war of the rebellion began on the 12th of April, 1861, by the confederate army under General Beauregard firing on Fort Sumter in Charleston harbor, Iowa was poorly prepared for war. Our state had very few drilled soldiers ready to march to the defense of the union. Peace had prevailed so long that little attention had been given by our lawmakers to military organization. When on the 15th of April President Lincoln issued a proclamation calling upon the loyal states for 75,000 volunteers, one regiment only was required from Iowa. On the 17th of April Governor Kirkwood issued his proclamation calling upon the militia of the different counties to organize into companies, with a view to entering the military service of the United States; that one regiment of ten companies of not less than seventy-eight each was required by the 20th of May.

The call for volunteers aroused great enthusiasm in the state, and young men responded in sufficient numbers to have organized several regiments. Of the companies accepted for the First Iowa Volunteer infantry, two were from the county of Dubuque, two from Muscatine, two from Des Moines, and one each from Scott, Linn, Henry and Johnson. As the companies left their homes for the general rendezvous at Keokuk, the friends and neighbors of the citizen soldiers so suddenly called upon to march to the seat of war, assembled and tendered them every mark of honor and admiration for their patriotism, in their power to bestow. Ladies met and helped to provide suitable clothing, uniforms and other equipments. Fine flags were presented with speeches; public dinners and patriotic toasts were tendered; and when the companies departed they were escorted to the trains and steamers by vast crowds of cheering men and sympathizing women. At Keokuk the men were drilled five hours a day; company officers were chosen by ballot, and on the 11th of May the field officers appointed — John F. Bates, colonel; William H. Merritt, lieutenant-colonel, and Asbury B. Porter, major. On the 14th the First Iowa infantry was mustered into the United States service by Lieut. Alexander Chambers of the regular army. On the 3d of May the president had issued a call for 200,000 more volunteers, and the country began to realize that a terrible civil war was upon it, the end of which no one could foresee. The first call for soldiers was for only three months' service, as it was thought by many that the rebellion might be suppressed in that time. But it soon became evident that the south was going to put forth every energy to establish an independent confederacy, and the last call for volunteers was for three years' service.

Governor Kirkwood, finding that a large amount of money must be used in the raising and equipment of volunteers, had called an extra session of the legislature to meet on the 15th of May. But before the legislature could provide money, heavy expenses had been incurred. Governor Kirkwood, Ezekiel Clark, Hiram Price, J. K. Graves and W. T. Smith, in this emergency, raised the money required by their own exertions to pay the Iowa soldiers and supply their necessities, until they could be otherwise provided for.

When the general assembly met in extra session, a large majority of the members felt that in this time of national peril, party spirit should be put aside, and all loyal citizens should unite in an earnest support of the national government. The republicans had a clear majority in each branch of the legislature, but at the opening session of the house they voluntarily divided the offices with the democrats. John Edwards, republican, was chosen speaker, and William Thompson, a prominent democrat and an ex-member of congress, was elected chief clerk by a unanimous vote.

Governor Kirkwood's message stated briefly the action he had taken to raise and equip our state's quota of soldiers called for by the president. The two important objects for which the legislature had

resources of the state of Iowa, both in men and money, are hereby irrevocably pledged to any amount and extent which the federal government may demand, to suppress treason, subdue rebellion, enforce the laws, protect the lives and property of all loyal citizens, and maintain inviolate the constitution and sovereignty of the nation.

*Resolved*, That the governor and secretary of state be and they are hereby authorized to forward a certified copy of these resolutions to the president of the United States.

The resolutions were adopted by a unanimous vote of the house, and on the next day they also passed the senate and were immediately forwarded to President Lincoln. Iowa was one of the first states to thus officially pledge its resources in men

*Samuel J. Kirkwood (Fifth Governor of Iowa) and wife, in 1852.*

been convened, the governor stated, were to provide for the protection of our state against invasion, and to promptly supply the general government all aid required in the suppression of the rebellion.

R. D. Kellogg, the democratic member from Decatur county, promptly offered the following resolution in the house, after the reading of the governor's message:

WHEREAS, The president of the United States has appealed to all loyal citizens to aid the efforts to maintain the honor, integrity and existence of the national union, and suppress treason and rebellion against the federal government; therefore, be it

*Resolved*, By the house of representatives (the senate concurring) that the faith, credit and

and money to the president to preserve the national integrity.

The war session of the legislature lasted but fourteen days, but during that brief period it framed and enacted the following important laws:

An act providing for the organization of the militia of the state.

To provide for raising two regiments of infantry, one battalion of artillery, five companies of cavalry and one regiment of mounted riflemen for the protection of the southern border from invasion, and the northwestern counties from the Sioux Indians.

An act authorizing the governor to purchase arms, ammunition, clothing and other supplies for Iowa troops.

An act providing for raising a "War and Defense Fund '' by the issue and sale of state bonds to the amount of $800,000.

An act providing for the payment of volunteer soldiers of the state until they were mustered into the United States service.

An act authorizing the counties of the state to provide aid for families of volunteers who entered the service.

An act forbidding the commencement of civil suits at law against any volunteer soldier during his term of enlistment.

Ex-Gov. Nathaniel B. Baker* was, in July, appointed adjutant-general and at once proceeded to place that department in efficient working order. Hiram Price was appointed paymaster-general and immediately visited the three Iowa regiments in the field and paid them up to the time they entered the United States service.

The First Iowa regiment was sent to Missouri to reinforce the union army under General Lyon, which in the face of a greatly superior rebel army was trying to hold that state in the union. With an army of less than 6,000, near Springfield, on the 9th of August, he found it confronted ·by a rebel army of more than 20,000 under General McCulloch, which was occupying a strong position on Wilson's creek.

General Lyon had to choose between a battle and retreat. He decided to fight and try to surprise the enemy. He started his little army in the evening, and by 2 o'clock in the morning was within striking distance of the énemy. Here they halted and rested until it was light enough to see the position of the rebel army, when the artillery at once opened fire. Soon the engagement became general; a charge was made on our lines where General Lyon was commanding in person, which, after a severe conflict was repulsed with heavy loss. General Sigel, who had been sent to attack the

*N. B. Baker was governor of New Hampshire in 1854. He came to Iowa in 1856, settling at Clinton. In 1859 he was elected to the Iowa legislature as a democrat. At the extra session of May, 1861, he was the leader of the war democrats in the house, giving a warm support to all war measures.

rebel army in the rear, after a brave fight was overwhelmed by superior numbers, losing five pieces of artillery. Charge after charge was made upon our lines where General Lyon was commanding, and for three hours the roar of artillery and the rattle of musketry was almost continuous. The little union army held its ground firmly, and repeatedly charged upon the enemy. The Iowa First was in the thickest of the fight, and among the bravest of the brave. Sheltering themselves on the brow of a hill, as they awaited a charge from overwhelming numbers, they held their fire until the rebels were within sixty feet of their line, when they poured into the ranks of the advancing foe a fire that routed them with fearful slaughter. Their loss was also heavy, but they held their position. General Lyon now ordered a bayonet charge and led it in person, the Iowa First and a Kansas regiment leading the way. A terrific fire assailed them as the enemy slowly retired delivering a galling fire which mortally wounded the heroic Lyon. The command now devolved on General Sturgis. A part of the Iowa regiment now went to the support of Captain Totten's battery, where they did gallant service. All through the battle the Iowa soldiers stood up to the work like veterans, and the regiment sustained a loss in killed, wounded and missing, of 155 men.

While the battle of Wilson's Creek cannot be counted a decided union victory, it holds a place similar to Bunker Hill. It was the first important battle in the west, the first in which Iowa soldiers fought, and it demonstrated the unflinching courage and excellent fighting qualities of western soldiers. Coming soon after the humiliating defeat and wild flight of the union army at Bull Run, the battle of Wilson's Creek redeemed the reputation of the northern army.

The term of service of the Iowa First had expired several days before the battle was fought, but they nobly staid and won imperishable glory in the desperate conflict where the gallant Lyon laid down his life for his country. They gave the northern people renewed hope of ultimate success, so sorely needed at this time.

## CHAPTER XIII.

*The Second Iowa Infantry — The Third, Fourth, Fifth, Sixth, Seventh, Eighth, Ninth, Tenth, and Eleventh Iowa Regiments.*

The Second Regiment of Iowa volunteers was organized in May, and was the first from the state to enter the service for three years. Samuel R. Curtis was its first colonel, James M. Tuttle first lieutenant-colonel, and M. M. Crocker its first major, all of whom were promoted to generals during the war.

This regiment took a prominent part in the battle of Fort Donelson, which resulted in the first great victory for the union cause in the war. Curtis had been promoted to brigadier-general and J. M. Tuttle to colonel of the Second regiment. The army under General Grant, about 15,000 strong, had moved on to invest Fort Donelson February 12, 1862. The confederate general, A. S. Johnston, was in command of that department, and had sent an army of about 18,000 under Generals Floyd, Pillow and Buckner to garrison the forts on the Cumberland and Tennessee rivers and resist Grant's march southward. Commodore Foote with several gunboats co-operated with Grant in the attack upon Fort Donelson. Before the battle opened Grant had collected heavy reinforcements. On the 14th the fort was nearly surrounded and the gunboats opened a heavy fire upon it. But the heavy guns from the fort soon disabled two of the vessels, and the fleet dropped down stream with a large loss of men. Early on the morning of the 15th General Pillow led a strong force against McClernand, who commanded the right wing of the union army, and after four hours of hard fighting drove him back with heavy loss. But reinforcements coming to his aid the enemy was driven back behind the defenses. General Grant now ordered General Smith to assault the works on the left. Col. J. G. Lauman, of the Seventh Iowa, commanded the brigade, composed of the Second, Seventh, and Fourteenth Iowa regiments, with the Twenty-fifth and Fifty-second Indiana, and this made up the storming party. Colonel Tuttle led the Second in the advance. The rebel works were 500 yards distant on a hill, obstructed with abatis. At 2 o'clock the line moved to the assault and met with a terrific fire of artillery and infantry. Not a man faltered; on they moved, as the ranks were thinned by the deadly missiles which smote them like hail, but they carried the outer works which they held, sleeping upon their arms as night came on. The confederates now saw that the fort was doomed, and during the night Pillow and Floyd fled with some of their troops on a steamer up the river. In the morning General Buckner surrendered the fort, his army of 13,000 men, sixty-five cannon, 20,000 stand of arms, and a vast quantity of stores. The Twelfth Iowa also took an active part in the battle, making four Iowa regiments which shared in the glory of the greatest union victory of the war up to that time. General Halleck sent the following dispatch to Adjutant-General Baker: "The Second Iowa infantry proved themselves the bravest of the brave; they had the honor of leading the column which entered Fort Donelson." Corp. V. P. Twombly, of Company F, the color-bearer, planted the flag on the captured fort.

Of the 630 officers and privates who led this heroic charge, forty-one were slain and 157 wounded. The great victory at Fort Donelson revived the hopes of the union cause everywhere, and was received with great rejoicing throughout the north. It wiped out the stigma at Bull Run and again showed the valor of western soldiers. The Second Iowa went from Donelson to Pittsburg Landing, and on the 6th and 7th of April did gallant service in the great battle of Shiloh, where it lost more than seventy men. The next battle in which this regiment took part was at Corinth on the 3d and 4th of October. Colonel Tuttle had been promoted brigadier-general; James Baker, colonel; N. W. Mills, lieutenant-colonel, and James B. Weaver, major. The Second did gallant service in this desperate battle and lost nearly one-third of its number engaged. Among the mortally wounded were its colonel, James Baker, and Lieut.-Col. N. W. Mills, who fell while leading in the thickest of the fight. On the 13th of October, James B. Weaver was promoted to colonel and took command of the regiment, and it became a part of General Sherman's army, that made the great march to the sea, always doing excellent service on that famous campaign.

### THE THIRD INFANTRY.

This regiment numbered about 970 men when mustered into the service at Keokuk on the 10th of June, 1861. The field officers were Nelson G. Williams, colonel; John Scott, lieutenant-colonel, and Wm. M. Stone, major. The regiment left for the seat of war on the 29th, landing at Hannibal, Mo. It did service for several months in eastern

Missouri, sometimes divided and again united. On the 17th of September Lieutenant-Colonel Scott, with about 500 of the Third Iowa, seventy home guards and a squad of artillery with a six-pound gun, attacked a rebel army of about 4,000, under General Atchison, near Blue Mills Landing. The rebels were concealed in a dense woods and their numbers unknown. There was a short, sharp fight when Scott's little army was driven back by overwhelming numbers and with heavy loss, amounting to 118 men. In March the regiment joined Grant's army at Pittsburg Landing and fought bravely at Shiloh on the 6th and 7th of April. Colonel Williams was disabled, Major Stone was taken prisoner, and the loss in killed, wounded and captured was very heavy. In October, under Lieut.-Col. M. M. Trumbull, the Third fought bravely at the battle of the Hatchie. Colonel Williams resigned in November, 1862; Scott had resigned in June, and Trumbull resigned in November, and Aaron Brown

*Brevet Second Lieut. U. S. Grant. From a portrait taken in St. Louis in March, 1844.*

now became colonel; James Tullis, lieutenant-colonel, and Geo. W. Crosley, major. The regiment did good service under General Grant at the siege and capture of Vicksburg. It was in the battle before Jackson, July 12th, fought bravely and suffered heavy loss. The regiment was divided in 1864, and a portion of it, under Tullis, joined the Red River expedition under General Banks.

The two parts of the regiment were never reunited again and in the battle of Atlanta the last battalion of the gallant regiment fought itself out of existence. In its last desperate conflict on that bloody field Colonel Abernethy, its commander, was slain; Captain Griffith, the brave old color-bearer in many battles, fell mortally wounded, while the handful of undaunted men gathered around the flag, amid a shower of shot and shell, fighting madly in its defense. As the little remnant of the gallant old regiment was overwhelmed by numbers, before surrendering they tore the old flag in a dozen pieces, concealed them in their clothing, so that it was never captured by the enemy. Thus, amid the thunder of artillery, the screeching of shells, the rattle of musketry and the wild shouts of men in their death struggle, the last remnant of the Third Iowa passed out of existence.

### THE FOURTH IOWA INFANTRY.

This regiment was raised and organized in the summer of 1861, and entered the service in August. The first field officers were Grenville M. Dodge, colonel; John Galligan, lieutenant-colonel; William R. English, major. Its first active service was in General Curtis' army of the southwest in Missouri, and its first fight near Springfield, on the 12th of February, 1862. Soon after, General Curtis marched in pursuit of the rebel army under General Price, towards the Boston mountains. Here Price was strongly reinforced by Generals McCulloch, Van Dorn and McIntosh, who united their commands to fight Curtis. Moving his army to Pea Ridge, General Curtis took a strong position and awaited the attack of the combined confederate forces, 20,000 strong, a force largely superior to his own. General Sigel was at Bentonsville, ten miles southwest of General Curtis' center. Van Dorn, who now commanded the confederate army, sent a strong force to capture Sigel's command, which had already started to join Curtis. But, sending his train in advance, Sigel made such a strong fight with artillery and infantry during the retreat that he brought his command off with small loss, and joined Curtis on the battlefield. During the night Van Dorn moved to the flank and rear of the union army, taking a strong position and rendering Curtis' defenses of the day before useless. The battle opened at 10 o'clock and raged with great fury for hours. Colonel Dodge commanded a brigade, and the Fourth was under Lieutenant-Colonel Galligan in this battle, and fought bravely during the two days of desperate conflict. At one time it made a brilliant bayonet charge on the advancing enemy. Several Iowa regiments were engaged in this battle, all rendering gallant service. The battle of the second day was even more fierce and desperate than on the first. The confederates, knowing their superiority of numbers, were determined to crush and destroy the union army. But General Sigel wheeled battery after battery into position, until he had thirty cannon pouring shot and shell into the ranks of the advancing foe. With the batteries slowly advancing, supported by long lines of infantry, no charge of the enemy could face the iron hail that thinned their ranks, and at last human endurance ended in flight as regiments went to pieces and the retreat became general. Among the confederate killed were two famous generals, McCulloch and McIntosh, while Generals Price and Slack were severely wounded.

Iowa occupied a proud position in this battle and brilliant union victory. The commander of the union army, Curtis, was an Iowa officer. Two brigades which did brilliant service were commanded by Iowa colonels, Vandever and Dodge, and two batteries in the thickest of the fight, Hayden's and David's, were from Iowa, while the Iowa

*Gen. G. M. Dodge.*

cavalry, under Trimble and Bussey, did fine service. The Fourth Iowa lost in killed, wounded and captured nearly half of the number engaged. J. A. Williamson was promoted to colonel, and Captain Burton to lieutenant-colonel.

The next important battle in which the Fourth was engaged was under General Sherman in his disastrous assault on Vicksburg on the 29th of December, 1862. This regiment made a desperate charge upon the works and carried the first line of defenses, but not being supported had to abandon them with heavy loss. Of the 480 who went into the fight 112 fell. The regiment was in the battle of Arkansas Post, after which it joined Grant's army in the campaign against Vicksburg. After the capture of that stronghold it was in the campaign against Chattanooga, and took part in the battle of Lookout Mountain and shared in the glory of that brilliant victory. On the 1st day of January, 1864, their term of service having expired, the members of the regiment re-enlisted and received a furlough to visit their homes. The general assembly was in session when the veteran Fourth reached Des Moines, March 9th, and it adjourned and gave the soldiers a reception worthy of the glorious deeds they had performed. Early in May they returned to service and joined Sherman's army in the march through Georgia. It took an active part in the battles of that brilliant campaign up through the Carolinas and at its close marched to Washington, was sent from there to Louisville, Ky., where it was mustered out in July, 1865, numbering then twenty-three officers and 457 men.

## THE FIFTH IOWA VOLUNTEERS.

This regiment was made up largely of companies raised in the counties of Cedar, Jasper, Louisa, Marshall, Buchanan, Keokuk, Benton, Van Buren, Jackson and Allamakee. The first field officers were William H. Worthington, colonel; Charles L. Mathies, lieutenant-colonel; and William S. Robertson, major. It entered the United States service at Burlington on the 17th of July, 1861, with 918 men. It was sent to Lexington, Mo., on the 14th of August. The regiment was attached to General Pope's army, and on the 22d of May, 1862, its commander, Colonel Worthington, was killed by a picket of our army, while visiting during the night the grand guard of the division, as general officer of the day. He was succeeded by Colonel Mathies, who commanded the regiment at the battle of Iuka, which was fought on the 19th of September, 1862.

General Sterling Price, with a confederate army, had seized Iuka, at which place Colonel Murphy had been left with a Wisconsin regiment to guard a large supply of stores collected for Grant's army. Upon learning that General Price was at Iuka, General Grant sent General Ord with 6,000 men to attack Price. General Rosecrans, with 9,000 men, was ordered to co-operate with Ord from the south. The Fifth Iowa was in the advance column sent against Iuka on the 18th. General Price came out and attacked Rosecrans in the woods and hills as he was advancing upon Iuka, and the battle opened. The hills were too steep to form a strong line of

*Gen. J. A. Williamson.*

infantry and several batteries were planted in good positions to open on the confederates. The Fifth Iowa was brought up to help protect these batteries which were pouring a hot fire into the enemy's ranks. The Tenth and Sixteenth Iowa regiments were warmly engaged, and from 5 o'clock until darkness put an end to the conflict, it was waged with great fury on both sides. The Ohio battery, which was doing great execution, was taken and retaken several times by desperate charges. The horses were all killed, most of the gunners killed or wounded, during the fierce struggles for possession of the guns, until most of them were disabled. When darkness put an end to the contest the union

*Maj.-Gen. W. S. Rosecrans.*

army held its ground and during the night Price's army retreated to Iuka to unite with Van Dorn's. The union army marched into Iuka on the 20th. The losses on each side exceeded a thousand. The Fifth and Sixteenth Iowa regiments won the highest honors of the day and were especially commended in General Rosecrans' report. The loss of the Fifth was 220. On the 1st of October the regiment returned to Corinth and was in the battle of the 4th, where it guarded the Eleventh Ohio battery. In 1863, the Fifth was in Grant's Vicksburg campaign and shared in the series of battles and victories which made up the wonderful achievements of that most glorious campaign of the war. It was also in Grant's army which fought the great battles about Chattanooga, and met with heavy losses. On the 8th of August, 1864, the small remnant of the Fifth infantry was consolidated with the Fifth Iowa cavalry, after more than three years of honorable service.

### THE SIXTH IOWA INFANTRY.

This regiment was organized in June and July, 1861, and was made up of companies raised chiefly in the counties of Linn, Lucas, Wayne, Clarke, Monroe, Hardin, Franklin, Appanoose, Johnson, Lee and Henry. It consisted of about 900 men, and its first field officers were John A. McDowell, colonel; Markoe Cummins, lieutenant-colonel; John M. Corse, major. It entered the service in August, and was sent to reinforce General Fremont's army. In 1862, it was sent to Pittsburg Landing, and saw

its first battle on the bloody field of Shiloh. The regiment held a position on the extreme right of the army, and fought with great bravery, holding its position until all of its supports were driven back, when it retired in good order. Colonel McDowell was in command of a brigade, and the regiment was led by Capt. John Williams until he was wounded, when Capt. M. M. Walden took command. Lieutenant-Colonel Cummins was under arrest, and Major Corse was on Pope's staff. The loss of the regiment was heavy. In 1863, Colonel McDowell resigned and J. M. Corse was promoted to colonel of the regiment. At the siege of Jackson, the Sixth Iowa did good service, and received the special commendation of General Smith. Colonel Corse was promoted to brigadier-general and placed in command of the Fourth brigade, in which the Sixth Iowa was now placed. The Sixth was in the battle of Missionary Ridge, and lost sixty-nine men; it was now commanded by Lieut.-Col. J. A. Miller. In May, 1864, this regiment joined Sherman's army in its march to the sea. It fought bravely at the battles of Resaca, Dallas, Big Shanty, Kenesaw Mountain, Atlanta and Jonesboro. Colonel Miller was wounded at Dallas, and the command devolved on Major Ennis, who was mortally wounded before Atlanta. Capt. W. H. Chine now took command of the regiment and led it through the desperate battle. Its losses in the campaign were 159, and its numbers were now reduced to 120 men fit for duty. It fought bravely to the end of the campaign, and at the close marched to Richmond, and was at Washington in the grand review, where but 284 out of the 900 who entered the serv-

*General Howard.*

ice responded to the roll call. Its losses in battles amounted in the aggregate to 115 killed, 375 wounded and sixty-seven captured.

### THE SEVENTH IOWA INFANTRY.

The companies composing this regiment came from many counties throughout the state, and a majority of them were mustered into service soon after the disastrous battle of Bull Run, in July, 1861. It now became evident that the war must last several years. Missouri, on our southern border, was to be held into the union by military force, and General Fremont was raising a large army for that purpose. The Seventh regiment was sent to the front in great haste, before its arms, clothing or equipments had been furnished. It numbered 902 men, and its field officers were Jacob G. Lauman, colonel; Augustus Wentz, lieutenant-colonel; E. W. Rice, major. General Grant was in command of a district in southeastern Missouri, with headquarters at Cairo, in November, and the Seventh Iowa was sent to his army. But little was known of Grant at this time, but the country soon learned that his idea of the way to crush out the rebellion was to fight the enemy wherever found. There was a rebel camp at Belmont, in Missouri opposite Columbus, in Kentucky, protected by heavy guns of the latter place. On the 7th of November Grant embarked two brigades on four steamers, to strike the enemy at Belmont. The Seventh Iowa was in the second brigade, which landed two miles above Belmont. The confederates had been reinforced by General Pillow with three regiments. Grant's little army made a vigorous attack and after a severe fight drove the confederates and captured their camp. Generals Polk and Cheatham now hurried over from Columbus with five regiments and assailed Grant's little army on the flank and rear, hoping to capture it. But Grant's army cut their way through greatly superior numbers, captured two cannon, and after several hours' hard fighting reached the boats and embarked. The Seventh Iowa, in this, their first battle, fought like veterans. General Grant says, " it behaved with great gallantry and suffered more severely than any other of the troops." Colonel Lauman was severely wounded, Lieutenant-Colonel Wentz was killed, and Major Rice was wounded. The total loss of the regiment in killed, wounded and missing was 227. This was Grant's first battle as well as the first for the gallant Iowa Seventh. Captain Parrott was promoted to Lieutenant-Colonel in place of Wentz, killed, who had been a brave soldier in the First Iowa. The Seventh shared in the glory of Grant's great victory at Fort Donelson, where it bore a conspicuous part. At the battle of Shiloh the Seventh was in Tuttle's Iowa brigade and did excellent service and won fresh honors. Lauman commanded a brigade and Lieutenant-Colonel Parrott led the Seventh at Shiloh. At the two days' battle of Corinth on the 3d and 4th of October, the Seventh maintained its high reputation in the thickest of that desperate conflict, losing nearly one-third of its number. In January, 1864, three-fourths of the members of the regiment re-enlisted and were granted a month's furlough to visit their homes. Two hundred new

recruits joined the regiment upon its return to duty to take part in the Atlanta campaign. It participated in many of the battles of that famous march to the sea, and was one of the best fighting regiments in Sherman's fine army. It was among those which went to Richmond and on to Washington, participating in the grand review at the national capital. At Louisville it was mustered out with as high honors as were won by any regiment in the war.

### THE EIGHTH IOWA INFANTRY.

This regiment was made up of companies raised in the counties of Clinton, Scott, Linn, Benton, Washington, Marion, Keokuk, Iowa, Mahaska, Monroe, and Louisa. It was organized at Davenport in September, 1861, and its first field officers were Frederick Steele, of the regular army, colonel; James L. Geddes, lieutenant-colonel, and John C. Ferguson, major. It numbered about 900 when it embarked for St. Louis and joined General Fremont's army. In its march through southwestern Missouri it lost many men from exhaustion and sickness. In February, 1862, Colonel Steele was promoted to brigadier-general, Geddes to colonel of the Eighth, Ferguson to lieutenant-colonel, and Capt. Joseph Andrews, major. On the 12th of March the regiment was sent to reinforce Grant's army at Pittsburg Landing. In the battle of Shiloh the Eighth regiment was in Sweeney's brigade, and when the battle began it was on the extreme left of General Smith's division, joining the right of Prentiss. Here it fought desperately for ten hours on that terrible Sunday, repelling charge after charge in supporting a battery. When finally assailed on three sides it slowly retreated, but was soon after surrounded by the advancing confederates and forced to surrender. It was one of the last to leave the field and left nearly 200 of its brave men among the killed and wounded. The regiment was reorganized at St. Louis early in 1863, and was in Grant's Vicksburg campaign, was in the assault of the 22d, and fought at Jackson. Lieutenant-Colonel Ferguson died of sickness during the siege of Vicksburg. It was at Memphis in August, 1864, and helped to defend that city against the attack by General Forrest. In March, 1865, the Eighth was in the campaign against Mobile. On the 8th of April Colonel Geddes led the assault on the Spanish Fort, in which he commanded a brigade. The rebels were driven from their works, leaving many guns and prisoners in our hands. The Eighth Iowa alone captured several hundred of the enemy. This was the last important battle of the war, and in that campaign Iowa furnished the following regiments: The Eighth, Twelfth, Nineteenth, Twentieth, Twenty-first, Twenty-third, Twenty-seventh, Twenty-ninth, Thirty-second, Thirty-third, Thirty-fourth, and Thirty-fifth.

## THE NINTH IOWA INFANTRY.

On the day after the defeat of the union army at Bull Run, in July, 1861, Hon. William Vandever, representative in congress for the Second Iowa district, went to the secretary of war and tendered a regiment of volunteers to be raised by himself. His offer was at once accepted, and in September the Ninth regiment was ready to enter the service. William Vandever was commissioned colonel, F. J. Herron, lieutenant-colonel, and William H. Coyle, major. The companies were raised chiefly in the counties of Jackson, Jones, Buchanan, Clayton, Fayette, Bremer, Black Hawk, Winneshiek, Howard, Linn, Chickasaw and Dubuque.

The regiment was taken to St. Louis and placed in camp of instruction, where it remained until October, when it was sent to guard the southwestern branch of the Pacific railroad. In January, 1862, the Ninth joined General Curtis' army in pursuit of General Price. At Sugar Creek it was first under fire, making a brilliant charge on the enemy. Colonel Vandever was placed in command of a brigade composed of the Ninth Iowa, Twenty-fifth Missouri, Third Illinois cavalry and Third Iowa battery. In the battle of Pea Ridge, which soon took place, the Ninth, under Lieutenant-Colonel Herron, did gallant service and sustained heavy loss. Herron was taken prisoner after being wounded, Major Coyle was wounded, and the loss to the regiment was nearly 200. General Curtis, in his report, says "The Fourth and Ninth Iowa won imperishable honors." The Ninth was, soon after the battle, marched to Helena, Ark., where it remained for five months and became one of the best drilled regiments in the volunteer service. Its next active service was under General Sherman at the battle of Chickasaw Bayou. It took part in the battle of Arkansas Post. For a long time it was with Steele's division, encamped on the low ground opposite Vicksburg, where the army suffered severely from sickness which was more fatal than battlefields. Capt. David Carskaddon was now promoted to Colonel, and soon after the regiment joined Grant's grand campaign against Vicksburg. During the siege its losses were 121 men. It was with Sherman in the battle before Jackson, and in the brilliant campaign of Chattanooga, and the battle of Lookout Mountain it did excellent service. At the beginning of the next year about 300 of its soldiers re-enlisted as veterans and returned home on furlough, where they met a royal reception. On the 1st of May we find the regiment marching with Sherman through Georgia and participating in many of the battles of that glorious campaign. The command of the regiment soon after devolved on Maj. Alonzo Abernethy, as Major Granger had died at Nashville, and Carskaddon had resigned. On the 26th of January, 1865, the regiment began its march northward, and on the 19th of May went into camp in sight of the national capital, and was in the grand review of the 26th. On the 24th of July this veteran regiment reached Clinton, Iowa, and was there disbanded. It had marched more than 4,000 miles, been transported by rail and steamer 6,000 more, and participated in twenty-three battles, and numbered, when mustered out, 594 men.

## THE TENTH IOWA INFANTRY.

The Tenth was composed of companies chiefly enlisted in the counties of Polk, Warren, Boone, Tama, Washington, Poweshiek, Greene, Jasper and Madison, and numbered 913 men. It was mustered into the service on the 7th of September, 1861, at Iowa City, with the following field officers: Colonel, Nicholas Perczel; lieutenant-colonel, William E. Small; major, John C. Bennett. They were conveyed by steamer to Cape Girardeau, Mo., where they remained drilling the first winter. On the 13th of December, Colonel Perczel was ordered to march his regiment to Charleston and capture a body of rebels. The night was rainy and very dark. As he marched through a dense forest, his command was surprised by the enemy in ambush and fired upon. After a sharp fight, the foe gave way and the command proceeded to Charleston. The loss in this fight was eight killed and sixteen wounded. The regiment was with General Pope's army at the siege and capture of New Madrid, in March, and Island No. 10, but met with no loss. During the summer, the Tenth was stationed at Corinth, where its losses from disease were large. It was with Rosecrans at the battle of Iuka, and fought bravely, and in the two days' battle at Corinth it did gallant service. Major McCalla commanded the regiment, and Capt. Jackson Orr acted as major at the battle of Corinth, as Colonel Perczel was in command of a brigade. The loss at Corinth was about forty. The Tenth was in the campaign of General Grant which resulted in the capture of Vicksburg and the entire confederate army under General Pemberton. At the battle of Champion Hill, the Tenth bore a conspicuous part in that bloody conflict. The brigade of which it formed a part was thrown in to check the rebel advance when Hovey's division was overwhelmed by superior numbers. The brigade did its work nobly, but at a fearful sacrifice, losing half of its number. The Tenth lost nearly 50 per cent of those engaged. In the assault on Vicksburg, May 22d, the Tenth made two heroic charges. In the campaign of Chattanooga, the Tenth was in several severe battles, always displaying its usual gallantry. P. P. Henderson had been promoted to colonel upon the resignation of Perczel, and Major McCalla was made lieutenant-colonel in place of Small, resigned, with Robert Lusby as major. In February, 1864, the regiment re-enlisted as veter-

*The Iowa Soldiers' and Sailors' Monument. Erected at the state capital, Des Moines.*

ans, and was in Sherman's campaign through Georgia, fighting bravely in many of the battles. At its close, the Tenth went to Washington, was in the great review, and was sent from there to Louisville and thence to Little Rock, where it was mustered out on the 15th of August, 1865, numbering a little more than 300 men. It disbanded at Davenport on the last day of August. Of the 1,200 men who had belonged to this regiment during its four years of service, but one-fourth of its number were left.

### THE ELEVENTH IOWA INFANTRY.

The companies which made up this regiment were enlisted chiefly in the counties of Muscatine, Louisa, Cedar, Henry, Linn, Marshal, Keokuk, Washington and Van Buren. Muscatine furnished four companies. The field officers were Abraham M. Hare, colonel; William Hall, lieutenant-colonel; John C. Abercrombie, major. The Eleventh was the first regiment which received uniforms from the government before leaving the state. It numbered over 900 men and their first sad duty was to escort the body of Lieutenant-Colonel Wentz, killed at Belmont, to his grave at Davenport. The regiment was sent to St. Louis on the 16th of November and on the 8th of December moved to Jefferson City. In March, 1862, it was sent to Grant's army at Pittsburg Landing, and in April was in the great battle of Shiloh. Colonel Hare commanded a brigade, and the Eleventh regiment was led by Lieutenant-Colonel Hall in this, its first conflict with the enemy. It bore itself bravely through the terrible slaughter of the first day, losing more than 200 of its number in killed and wounded. Soon after the battle Colonel Hare resigned and William Hall was promoted to the position. The regiment was in the battle of Corinth where its loss was light. It was in the Vicksburg campaign, and afterwards in the Lousiana expedition to Monroe, which caused a great amount of sickness and suffering and accomplished nothing. In February, 1864, the regiment joined General Sherman's army and was in the Meridian expedition. Soon after it became a veteran regiment and the men were granted a furlough to visit their homes. Upon its return to service the Iowa brigade started with Sherman on the famous march and fought bravely at Kenesaw Mountain. It was engaged in many of the battles which followed in that campaign, and its losses from June to September were 218. In the battle before Atlanta, Maj. Charles Foster received a severe wound from which he died on his way home. Captain Neal was killed in the same battle. The regiment was present at the surrender of Gen. J. E. Johnston's army, and went from there to Washington and participated in the great review. It was disbanded at Davenport, July 19, 1865.

---

## CHAPTER XIV.

*Twelfth Iowa Infantry—The Thirteenth, Fourteenth, Fifteenth, Sixteenth, Seventeenth, Eighteenth, Nineteenth, Twentieth and Twenty-First Iowa Infantry Regiments.*

### THE TWELFTH IOWA VOLUNTEERS.

This regiment was composed of companies raised during the summer and fall of 1861, principally from the counties of Hardin, Allamakee, Fayette, Linn, Black Hawk, Delaware, Winneshiek, Dubuque and Jackson. The last company was sworn in on the 25th of November. J. J. Woods was commissioned colonel; J. P. Coulter, lieutenant-colonel, and S. D. Brodtbeck, major. It was moved to Benton Barracks near St. Louis, where, during the month of December it lost seventy-five of its number from sickness. In February it joined Grant's army, where it participated in the capture of General Buckner's army and Fort Donelson. It was in the battle of Shiloh and fought bravely all through that terrible Sunday, and had to surrender to overwhelming numbers just before sundown. Colonel Woods was severely wounded and the loss in battle by the regiment before surrender was very heavy. The prisoners were sent south. In May about half of them were paroled and sent to Benton Barracks, the rest suffered the hardships of rebel prisons until the 20th of November, when they were paroled. In April, 1863, the regiment was reorganized and sent to Rolla, Mo. Lieutenant-Colonel Coulter had resigned and Major Edgington was promoted to his place and Capt J. H. Stibbs was appointed major. The Twelfth was now placed in the Third Brigade of the third division of the Fifteenth Army Corps, and joined in the Vicksburg campaign. After that campaign the regiment now commanded by Major Stibbs was on duty at various points in the south and participated in the Meridian expedition under Sherman. In January, 1864, most of the men re-enlisted and the Twelfth became a veteran regiment, and they were granted furloughs to visit their homes.

In May the regiment was sent to Memphis, and in July fought bravely in the vicinity of Tupelo in repelling an attack upon the army trains, losing heavily in killed and wounded.

In June it made a brilliant defense of a post at White River, beating off General Marmaduke's attack with heavy loss.

In October the regiment was with Gen. A. J. Smith's army in pursuit of Price, in Missouri, and endured hard marching and hard fare.

In December the Twelfth was with General Thomas in the siege of Nashville and fought with its usual valor, and joined in the pursuit of Hood's army. It was in the Mobile expedition and participated in the siege and capture of that city, and remained in the service until 1866.

## THE THIRTEENTH IOWA VOLUNTEERS.

The companies making up this regiment were raised in the counties of Linn, Jasper, Lucas, Keokuk, Scott, Polk, Benton, Marshall and Washington, with numerous enlistments from Jefferson and Iowa. M. M. Crocker was colonel; M. M. Price, lieutenant-colonel; and John Shane, major, and it was mustered into service in November, 1861, with 989 men. Its first service was at Jefferson City, where it spent the winter in drilling. In March it was ordered to join Grant's army at Pittsburg Landing, and fought bravely at the battle of Shiloh a few days after its arrival. In this terrible battle the regiment was first under fire and sternly resisted the rebel advance for ten hours on the first day. Its loss in killed and wounded was heavy, reaching 172. Lieutenant-Colonel Price resigned a week after the battle and Major Shane was promoted to his place and Captain Van Hosen became major.

The regiment next fought at Corinth, where its losses were light. Colonel Crocker had been placed in command of the Iowa brigade and early in 1863 Van Hosen resigned and James Wilson succeeded him as major. Upon the promotion of Crocker to brigadier-general, Shane became colonel, Wilson, lieutenant-colonel and W. A. Walker major of the regiment.

During the Vicksburg campaign the Thirteenth was on active duty under Sherman, but sustained slight losses. In March, 1864, it was with Sherman in his Meridian campaign and soon after became a veteran regiment and the men had a furlough to visit their homes.

Upon their return to duty the regiment was sent to Sherman, who was preparing for his march to the sea. They were in the battle of Atlanta, on July 21st, and did gallant service, losing 113 men. On the next day the regiment was engaged in the thickest of the fight and lost more men than the day before. Among the killed was Major Walker, and Capt. Thos. P. Marshall was promoted to the vacancy.

In January, 1865, the regiment was at Pocotaligo, where James Wilson was promoted to colonel; J. C. Kennedy, lieutenant-colonel. On the march through South Carolina, Colonel Kennedy's regiment was the first to enter Columbia and hoist the stars and stripes on the capitol of the state which led in the rebellion. The regiment was in the battle of Bentonville, and after the surrender of General Johnston marched through Richmond to Alexandria, where, in sight of Washington, it went into camp. On the 28th and 29th of July, 1865, it was disbanded in Davenport.

Its first colonel, the gallant Crocker, had become a major-general, and was compelled from failing health to go to New Mexico in 1864, but in August, 1865, he died of consumption.

## THE FOURTEENTH IOWA INFANTRY.

This regiment had but seven companies with it during the first year of service, as the first three companies raised were sent to Fort Randall, on the western frontier, and never joined the regiment. The members of the Fourteenth were largely enlisted in the counties of Henry, Des Moines, Lee, Van Buren, Jasper, Tama, Jones, Linn, Dubuque and Johnson. Its field officers were William T. Shaw, colonel; E. W. Lucas, lieutenant-colonel; and Hiram Leonard, major; and it numbered 600 men when organized on the 6th of November, 1861. Its first active service was at the battle of Fort Donelson. It was in Lauman's brigade, which forced its way into the enemy's works, and shared in the highest honors of that great victory. Its loss was twenty-one men. It was sent to Pittsburg Landing in March, and fought at Shiloh in the brigade commanded by Colonel Tuttle. At the end of ten hours' hard fighting it was surrounded and compelled to surrender. The men were held prisoners until the 19th of November, when they were released on exchange, and during the winter the regiment was reorganized, two new companies and many recruits being added to it. Capt. J. H. Newbold was commissioned lieutenant-colonel, and Edgar A. Warner, major, with Colonel Shaw again in command. On the 10th of April, 1863, it left St. Louis for Cairo, where another company was added to it. In January, 1864, it was sent to Vicksburg and assigned to the second brigade of the third division of the Sixteenth army corps, with Colonel Shaw in command of the brigade and Lieutenant-Colonel Newbold at the head of the regiment. It was in Sherman's Meridian campaign, after which it was with General Banks on the disastrous Red River expedition. On the 13th of March the brigade, led by Colonel Shaw, was with Gen. A. J. Smith in the attack upon Fort De Russey, which was stormed and taken with ten cannon and a large quantity of small arms and stores.

The details of General Banks' blunders and disasters on this expedition need not be repeated, but after his defeat at Mansfield, Colonel Shaw's brigade fought bravely at Pleasant Hill and helped to save the army from destruction. The Fourteenth fought with great bravery, losing its colonel, the gallant Newbold, who was killed on the field. Several other brave officers and many men were among the losses of the regiment in this battle. Banks continued his retreat, followed by the confederate army, which harassed it at every step. At the various battles, as the retreat continued, the Fourteenth was frequently engaged and lost thirty-five men. In September the regiment was with General Ewing in a battle at Pilot Knob, in which it lost eighteen men. The regiment was mustered out at Davenport on the 16th of November, 1864. Colonel Shaw, who was a superior officer and had commanded with marked ability on many battlefields, was dismissed from the service on the 8th of October, 1864, for having written a letter to a friend at home, severely criticising the incompetency and drunkenness of some of the generals in the Red river campaign, which led to its disgraceful failure. This letter was published in a newspaper, and General Banks at once proceeded to have the able and fearless commander of the Iron brigade dismissed from the service. This petty act of revenge did not injure the gallant officer, who helped to save Bank's army from destruction at Pleasant Hill, in Iowa where his brave deeds were known so well.

### THE FIFTEENTH IOWA INFANTRY.

This regiment was organized at Keokuk in the winter of 1861-2. The companies composing the Fifteenth Iowa were raised chiefly in the counties of Linn, Clinton, Polk, Mahaska, Wapello, Van Buren, Lee, Fremont, Mills, Marion, Warren, Pottawattamie, Harrison, and Clarke, and mustered into service on the 14th of March, 1862. The first field officers were Hugh T. Reid, colonel; William Dewey, lieutenant-colonel; W. W. Belknap, major. Its first service was at the bloody battle of Shiloh, where it went into the fight the day it landed. Colonel Reid and Major Belknap were wounded and the total loss of the regiment was 188. At the battle of Corinth the Fifteenth was under command of Lieutenant-Colonel Belknap, Colonel Reid being sick, and Dewey transferred to command of the Twenty-third. The regiment fought bravely and lost eighty-five men in the battle. It was in Grant's campaign against Vicksburg, taking part in several of the battles without loss. Belknap was now promoted to colonel; J. W. Hedrick, lieutenant-colonel, and George Pomutz, major. The Fifteenth was in General Sherman's Meridian expedition and afterwards in his march and battles through Georgia. At Kenesaw Mountain and before Atlanta it did good service and sustained heavy loss. At the battle of the 22d Colonel Belknap captured the confederate colonel, Lamply, seizing

him by the collar. Thirteen Iowa regiments fought in this battle and the Iowa brigade contributed largely to the victory. Colonel Belknap was soon after promoted to brigadier-general, and Major Pomutz took command of the Fifteenth. The regiment continued with Sherman to the end of the famous campaign, and was mustered out at Louisville, Ky., on the 24th of July, 1865.

### THE SIXTEENTH IOWA INFANTRY.

This regiment was made up of companies recruited in the counties of Scott, Clinton, Dubuque, Clayton, Muscatine, Hamilton, Boone and others. Capt. Alexander Chambers, of the regular army, was commissioned colonel; A. H. Sanders, lieutenant-colonel; William Purcell, major. Its last company was mustered into service on the 24th of March, 1862, and on the 6th of April the regiment was in the battle of Shiloh. It had had little time to drill, but fought bravely in that terrible conflict. Colonel Chambers was wounded and the regiment lost heavily. When the Iowa brigade was formed, soon after the battle, the Sixteenth was assigned to it, and continued in it to the end, sharing in its glorious record. It took part in the defense of Bolivar, in September, and at the battle of Iuka every man of it covered himself with glory. Colonel Chambers was here very severely wounded and taken prisoner. General Rosecrans, in his report, says: "The Sixteenth Iowa, amid the roar of battle, the rush of artillery horses, the charges of a rebel brigade, and a storm of grape, canister and musketry, stood like a rock holding the center." The loss of the regiment was sixty-five, and among the killed was the gallant young adjutant, George Lawrence. Two weeks later the Sixteenth, led by Lieut.-Col. A. H. Sanders, fought at Corinth, where its commander was severely wounded. In January, 1863, Colonel Chambers again took command of the regiment. Just before the Third brigade started on the Vicksburg campaign, Major Strong, inspector-general of the Seventeenth army corps, visited and inspected Crocker's command, and said of it: "I have never seen a brigade that can compete with this. Take the brigade together, I never saw such a splendid body of men. The officers and soldiers of the Third brigade, commanded by Colonel Crocker, are an honor to the army of the Tennessee, to their state and country, to their friends at home, and I know, from their record in the field, that they must be a terror to the foe." What higher praise could be given to the Eleventh, Thirteenth, Fifteenth and Sixteenth Iowa regiments than this from an old army inspector? Soon after, General Crocker took command of the Seventh division, and Colonel Chambers of the Third brigade, leaving Colonel Sanders in command of the Sixteenth regiment during the Vicksburg campaign. One of the med-

*The Navy, as personified on the Iowa Soldiers' and Sailors' Monument.*

als of honor was awarded to Color Bearer Samuel Duffin, of Company K, Sixteenth Iowa, as one of the three bravest soldiers in the Vicksburg campaign. He was from Davenport, was promoted to lieutenant and killed at Kenesaw Mountain, June 27, 1864.

Before accompanying General Sherman on his grand march to the sea, the regiment re-enlisted, went home on furlough, and early in June joined the army in Georgia. In the great battle before Atlanta, on the 22d, the Sixteenth fought with heroic courage but was finally surrounded and compelled to surrender after having inflicted very heavy loss on the enemy. The officers of the regiment were confined at Macon, Charleston and finally at Columbia, while the men were sent to Andersonville and suffered every horror that human barbarity could inflict. The survivors of this "hell upon earth" were finally exchanged on the 22d of September, while the officers were imprisoned much longer. There was a remnant of the regiment, of about 100, that was not included in the surrender, which fought through the campaign in Sherman's army. It was mustered out at Davenport at the close of the war, under command of Lieut.-Col. J. T. Herbert, who had enlisted in the regiment as a private from Davenport in 1862.

THE SEVENTEENTH IOWA VOLUNTEERS.

The companies making up this regiment were raised chiefly in the counties of Lee, Van Buren, Des Moines, Wapello, Decatur, Polk, Jefferson, Washington, Appanoose, Marion, Dallas and Warren. It was mustered into the service on the 16th of April, 1862, with 935 men. Its first field officers were John W. Rankin, colonel; David B. Hillis, lieutenant-colonel and Samuel M. Wise, major. It was sent to join General Halleck's army at Corinth, in May, and joined in the pursuit of the confederate army. At the battle of Iuka the regiment was engaged and thrown into confusion, for which it was censured by General Rosecrans, as many believe, unjustly. Colonel Rankin resigned on the 3d of September.

On the 3d and 4th of October was fought the battle of Corinth, in which the Seventeenth took an active part, and fought with great bravery. Smarting under the unjust censure cast upon them at Iuka, the men went into this battle with a determination to wipe out the stigma, which they did most effectually. At a crisis of the battle, when the rebels had forced their way into Corinth, the Seventeenth made a splendid charge upon the advancing column and after a sharp conflict drove it back in confusion.

After the victory was won, General Sullivan, commanding the brigade in which the Seventeenth Iowa served, wrote to Governor Kirkwood as follows: "I have the honor to present to you the colors of the Fortieth Mississippi regiment, captured by the Seventeenth Iowa on the battlefield of Corinth, in a gallant charge on the advancing columns of the enemy, which the Seventeenth alone met, broke and pursued. I have never led braver men into action than the soldiers of the Seventeenth proved themselves in the desperate and bloody battle of Corinth." The colors were captured by Corporal John King, of Company G, from Marion county.

General Rosecrans, in a general order, said: "The Seventeenth Iowa infantry by its gallantry on the battlefield of Corinth, charging the enemy and capturing the flag of the Fortieth Mississippi, has amply atoned for its misfortune at Iuka, and stands among the honored regiments of this army. Long may they wear with unceasing brightness the honors they have won."

The loss of the regiment on the field of Corinth was twenty-five. Ingersoll says: "The Seventeenth inflicted as much damage upon the enemy as any regiment at Corinth, and received less damage in return." Lieutenant-Colonel Hillis was now promoted to colonel of the regiment, and Capt. Clark R. Wever to lieutenant-colonel. For several months the Seventeenth was employed in Tennessee and Mississippi, joining General McPherson's army in February, 1863. It shared in the hard marches, severe battles and glorious victories of Grant's Vicksburg campaign. At Jackson and Champion Hill it fought bravely and lost heavily. Colonel Hillis had resigned in May and Lieutenant-Colonel Wever was now colonel, Major Archer, lieutenant-colonel, and Capt. John F. Walden, of Company F, was major of the regiment.

The Seventeenth participated in the Chatanooga campaign and fought bravely at Lookout Mountain, where it lost fifty-seven men. In April, 1864, the regiment re-enlisted as veterans to the number of 479. In July, the regiment occupied Tilton. Two companies were captured near Dalton after exhausting their ammunition in a brave defense. On the 13th of October the garrison at Tilton was assailed by overwhelming numbers. Lieutenant-Colonel Archer made a heroic defense until his blockhouse was rendered untenable by artillery, when he was forced to surrender. Colonel Wever was in command of a brigade at Resaca when he was attacked by Hood's army. He had but about seven hundred men and four pieces of light artillery. He defended the post with great energy all day, and at night was reinforced by 500 cavalry. Colonel Wever spent the night strengthening his position, and early in the morning the attack was renewed; but further reinforcements came, and General Hood finally retreated as General Sherman's army came in sight. Colonel Wever received warm commendations from Sherman and Howard for his brave and successful defense. When the Seventeenth was captured at Tilton, Captain Horner and some forty men of the regiment only remained in the service, and were disbanded in August, 1865.

## THE EIGHTEENTH IOWA INFANTRY.

This regiment was made up of companies raised largely in the counties of Lucas, Clarke, Monroe, Keokuk, Iowa, Mahaska, Muscatine, Louisa, Linn, Wapello, Appanoose, Marion, Warren, Polk, Fayette, Benton, Clinton and Washington. It was mustered into the service early in August, 1862, with John Edwards, colonel; Thos. F. Cook, lieutenant-colonel, and Hugh J. Campbell, major, and numbered 875 men. It was sent to southwest Missouri and joined General Schofield's army at Springfield. Here it did garrison duty for a long time, and in January, 1863, took part in the defense of that city against the Confederate army, under General Marmaduke. This general, with an army of over 4,000 men, well supplied with artillery, moved against Springfield which was then held by General Brown with Missouri militia, some invalid soldiers in hospital and the Eighteenth Iowa Volunteers, in all, about 1,500 men. There were some unfinished forts about the city, but not in condition to aid much in the defense. When the battle opened on the morning of January 8th, five companies of the Eighteenth regiment were absent on outpost duty. The Missouri militia did excellent service, charging on the right and center of the advancing army. Captain Landis' battery supported by three companies of the Eighteenth Iowa, advanced on the enemy, but a charge in overwhelming numbers captured his guns, and the rebel army continued to advance. General Brown was severely wounded and the command devolved on Colonel Crabb. When the militia were driven back by superior numbers at about 4 o'clock, the five companies of the Eighteenth came in from their outpost and, under command of Lieutenant-Colonel Cook, charged on the rebel center, compelling it to give way. When night came on we still held the city and in the morning of the 9th our troops were ready to renew the battle, but the enemy had retreated with a loss of more than 200 men. Our loss was about the same. The Eighteenth remained at Springfield a long time after this battle, holding southwest Missouri from General Shelby's rebel army and driving it out of the state. In October the Eighteenth was stationed at Fort Smith. In March, 1864, it joined General Thayer and marched to unite with General Steele's army moving towards Shreveport, La., to co-operate with General Banks. But when that general was defeated at Mansfield Steele marched towards Camden, and at Moscow was attacked by a rebel army. Colonel Edwards commanded a brigade and had quite a lively fight in which the Eighteenth lost a few men. In guarding a forage train near Poison Springs, the Eighteenth and First Kansas had a severe battle in which the Iowa regiment fought bravely and lost seventy-seven men. The regiment was mustered out late in the summer of 1865.

## THE NINETEENTH IOWA INFANTRY.

This regiment was raised under the call of President Lincoln, issued July 2, 1862, after the failure of McClellan's campaign against Richmond. The companies were raised principally in the counties of Lee, Jefferson, Washington, Louisa, Van Buren and Henry. The regiment numbered 982 and its field officers were Benjamin Crabb, colonel; Samuel McFarland, lieutenant-colonel and Daniel Kent, major. It was sent to Rolla, Mo., in September and some time later became a part of the Third division of the army of the frontier, under command of General Blunt.

In the battle of Prairie Grove, the Nineteenth did its first fighting and sustained the reputation won by Iowa soldiers on so many bloody fields. Early in December, 1862, General Blunt's army was lying at Cane Hill, Ark., while General Herron, with the Second and Third divisions, was at Twin Springs, more than 100 miles distant. General Marmaduke had united his army with General Hindman's, and the latter now proposed to strike and overwhelm Blunt's army before Herron could come to his assistance. General Herron received a dispatch from Blunt December 13th, to hurry to his help and in a few hours his divisions were on the road, and he sent his cavalry in advance to Blunt. He marched his infantry 110 miles over mountain roads in three days, and on the 7th was within fifteen miles of Cane Hill. In the meantime General Hindman with a superior force, had placed his army between Blunt and Herron. As Herron advanced, Hindman opened a fierce attack upon his regiments sent to aid Blunt, and drove them back in confusion. General Herron formed his line of battle and opened on the enemy a heavy artillery fire from his batteries well placed. The Twentieth Wisconsin and Nineteenth Iowa were ordered to charge a rebel battery. They moved across the open field in a splendid charge, with fixed bayonets, up a steep hill, drove the supports and captured the guns. McFarland was leading the Nineteenth in as brave a charge as was ever made when a bullet pierced his heart and he fell dead from his horse. The two regiments were overwhelmed by superior numbers and driven back with heavy loss. The rebels in turn charged on our batteries with great bravery and were met with a fire that hurled them back in confusion. General Blunt, in the distance, heard the heavy artillery fire and at once set his army in rapid motion for the battle field, marching the last five miles in half an hour. He fell upon the enemy's left with great fury. Fifty cannon were now pouring shot and shell into the ranks of the rebels, while infantry was charging upon other parts of their line. Night put an end to the conflict, and under cover of darkness the confederate army retreated towards Van Buren, with a loss of not less than 2,000. The loss of the union army was 1,148. The Nineteenth Iowa lost 198 men and some of its bravest officers.

The First Iowa cavalry and the Twentieth Iowa infantry also did good service in this battle. Major Kent was promoted to fill the vacancy occasioned by the death of the gallant McFarland and Capt. John Bruce became major. The regiment remained on duty in that part of the country for many months. In June, 1863, it joined Grant's army in the Vicksburg campaign, sharing in its hard marches, battles and glorious victories. In September a portion of the regiment and the Twenty-sixth Indiana, under the command of Lieutenant-Colonel Leake, of the Twentieth Iowa, was on duty near Morganza, La., when they were attacked by greatly superior numbers and after a vigorous resistance were compelled to surrender. Two-thirds of the regiment had been left at other points and the organization therefore remained intact. Long afterwards the prisoners were exchanged and joined their old regiment at New Orleans. Its last service was in the campaign which captured Mobile, and at that city it was mustered out in July, 1865, proceeding to Davenport, where it was disbanded.

### THE TWENTIETH IOWA INFANTRY.

This regiment was raised under the call of July 2, 1862, for 300,000 more men. It was made up of five companies from Scott and five from Linn, and went into camp at Clinton, where, on the 25th of August, its organization was completed. It numbered 902 men, and its field officers were William McE. Dye, colonel; J. B. Leake, lieutenant-colonel; William G. Thompson, major.

Early in September the regiment was sent to Rolla, Mo., where it was placed in a brigade with the Thirty-seventh Illinois, First Iowa cavalry and a section of the First Missouri light artillery, under Colonel Dye. Through the months of October and November this brigade did hard marching in Missouri and Arkansas, and the members of the Twentieth suffered greatly from sickness and deaths. On the 4th of December the regiment started on a long, hard march to the battlefield of Prairie Grove, and reached it in time to participate in the battle of the 7th. The Twentieth did excellent service on that field, and lost forty-seven men killed and wounded. The defeat of the confederate army drove the rebel forces out of that section of the country for a long time. In May, 1863, the regiment was sent to reinforce the army operating around Vicksburg. Here it remained doing siege duty until the surrender of that stronghold and General Pemberton's army. It was soon after sent to reinforce General Banks' army in Louisiana. Lieutenant-Colonel Leake was captured with his command by a largely superior force of the enemy on the 29th of September, 1863, at Sterling Farm,

and the command of the Twentieth regiment devolved on Major Thompson. It was soon after sent to Texas, where it remained until September, 1864, when it was sent to New Orleans. Major Thompson had resigned in May, and the regiment had been under the command of Capt. M. L. Thompson, of Company C. In September Lieutenant-Colonel Leake having been exchanged, rejoined the regiment. The regiment was soon after sent to Brownsville, Ark., where it did duty until the 8th of January, 1865. In February it joined the army in the Mobile expedition, and remained in that region until July 8th, when it was mustered out of the service with 464 men.

### THE TWENTY-FIRST IOWA INFANTRY.

This regiment was organized in August, 1862, and numbered 976 men. The companies were recruited chiefly in the counties of Dubuque, Black Hawk, Worth, Clayton and Delaware. Its field officers were Samuel Merrill, colonel; C. W. Dunlap, lieutenant-colonel; and S. G. Van Anda, major. The regiment was mustered into service at Clinton, and in September was sent to Rolla, Mo., and in October was placed in a brigade with the Thirty-third Missouri and the Ninety-ninth Illinois, with some cavalry and artillery, under command of Gen. Fitz Henry Warren, of Iowa. In January, 1863, a force of 1,000 men with artillery was sent to reinforce the garrison at Springfield, under command of Colonel Merrill. On the morning of the 11th it encountered General Marmaduke's army near Hartsville, retreating from Springfield. A sharp engagement took place, lasting several hours, when Merrill retreated, having exhausted his ammunition, with a loss of but seventy-eight men. The enemy had not less than 2,500 men in this battle and gained no advantage, and lost several good officers. The Twenty-first regiment was commanded by Lieutenant-Colonel Dunlap and fought bravely, losing twenty-one men. Among the wounded was Colonel Dunlap. In February the regiment made a very hard march from Houston to Iron Mountain, in which it suffered greatly from cold, hunger and insufficient clothing, many of the men being without shoes. In March the regiment was sent down the river to Milliken's Bend, and soon after joined McClernand's corps for the Vicksburg campaign. At the battle of Port Gibson, April 30, 1863, the Twenty-first Iowa was in the advance, four companies supporting the First Iowa battery, Captain Griffith, and had a lively fight with the enemy on that day. In the severe battle which came on the next day the Twenty-first fought well in Colonel Stone's brigade with the Twenty-second and Twenty-third and lost quite a number of men, Lieutenant-Colonel Dunlap being again wounded. At the battle of Black River Bridge on the 17th, the Twenty-first made a fine charge and fought with

J. B. Sample, First Lieutenant Co. D. Seventh Infantry; Major and Assistant Adjutant General of Volunteers and Brevet Brigadier-General.
Samuel Duffin, Second Lieutenant Co. K, Sixteenth Infantry.
James Hartman, Sergeant Co. F, Second Cavalry.
Charles H. Smith, Second Lieutenant Co. C, Fourth Cavalry.

George A. Stone Colonel Twenty-fifth Infantry and Brevet Brigadier-General.
Noah W. Mills. Lieut.-Colonel Second Iowa Infantry; commissioned Colonel but not mustered.
J. L. Geddes, Colonel Eighth Infantry, Brevet Brigadier-General.
Joseph B. Reed, Captain Second Iowa Battery.

*Portrait Medallions on the Iowa Soldiers' and Sailors' Monument.*

great courage. Colonel Merrill in command, was severely wounded. Its loss was about eighty in killed and wounded. In the assault on Vicksburg, May 22d, the Twenty-first was prominently engaged and Lieutenant-Colonel Dunlap was among the slain and Major Van Anda was wounded; the total loss of the regiment was 113. After the surrender of Vicksburg it was sent with the army that pur-

sued Johnston and lost fifteen men at Jackson. In August the regiment was sent to Texas, now under command of Captain Crooke, who had been promoted to major. After many changes of place the regiment was finally sent to join the expedition against Mobile and took an active part in the campaign, after which it was mustered out of the service.

---

## CHAPTER XV.

*The Twenty-second, Twenty-third, Twenty-fourth, Twenty-fifth, Twenty-sixth, Twenty-seventh, Twenty-eighth, Twenty-ninth, Thirtieth and Thirty-first Iowa Infantry Regiments.*

### THE TWENTY-SECOND IOWA INFANTRY.

Seven companies of this regiment were raised in Johnson county, one in Jasper, one in Monroe and one in Wapello. It was mustered into service at Iowa City on the 9th of September, 1862. Its first field officers were Wm. M. Stone, colonel; John A. Garrett, lieutenant-colonel; Harvey Graham, major. The regiment was first sent to Rolla, Mo., where it did garrison duty for about four months. In March, 1863, it was sent to Grant's army to take part in the Vicksburg campaign, and was in the First brigade of the Fourteenth division of the Thirteenth army corps, under General McClernand.

At the battle of Port Gibson, Colonel Stone commanded the brigade, and Major Atherton led the Twenty-second regiment, which lost twenty men. At the battles of Champion Hill and Black River Bridge the loss of the Twenty-second was light. Having driven Pemberton's army behind the fortifications of Vicksburg, General Grant determined to assault the works on the 22d of May. Early in the morning the artillery from the fleet and all of the guns in position in the rear opened on the enemy's works and kept up a heavy fire until 10 o'clock. Then the bugles sounded the charge and the assaulting columns moved forward with fixed bayonets. They were met by a terrible fire of musketry all along the lines. Still the troops pressed on and fell before the deadly fire by hundreds. It was impossible to face the terrible volleys which smote the advancing columns. They sought such shelter as they could find and returned the fire, but could not dislodge the enemy.

The Twenty-second led the charge made by the brigade under General Lawler, and a few men, led by Sergeant Griffith scaled the enemy's defenses, entered the fort and captured some prisoners. But most of them were killed or captured; Sergeant Griffith and David Trine alone escaped. Lieutenant-Colonel Graham and several men were captured in the ditch, and the assault was ended.

The loss of the regiment was 164. There were sixteen Iowa regiments engaged in this battle, the Fourth, Fifth, Eighth, Ninth, Tenth, Twelfth, Seventeenth, Twenty-first, Twenty-second, Twenty-fourth, Twenty-fifth, Twenty-sixth, Twenty-eighth, Thirtieth, Thirty-first and Thirty-fifth, and the First and Second Iowa batteries.

Before the end of the siege, which followed the assault, Iowa had thirty regiments in Grant's army, which won this greatest victory of the war.

In this campaign the confederacy lost, in killed and wounded, 10,000 men, and in prisoners, 37,000, fifteen general officers, arms and munitions for an army of 60,000, and an immense amount of property, with the strongest fortified city in the limits of the confederacy, opening the navigation of the greatest river of the continent.

No soldiers in this great campaign surpassed those of Iowa. The First Iowa brigade led the advance at Port Gibson; the Seventeenth surpassed all others at Jackson; the Twenty-fourth and Twenty-eighth won immortal honors at Champion Hill; the Twenty-first and Twenty-third covered themselves with glory at Black River Bridge, while the Twenty-second alone, at the assault on Vicksburg, entered the confederate defenses. Colonel Stone resigned soon after the surrender of Vicksburg, having been nominated for governor by the Iowa republicans. The Twenty-second regiment was sent to Texas in November, where it was employed several months, Lieutenant-Colonel Graham having been promoted to colonel, Major White promoted to lieutenant-colonel, and Captain Gearkee, major. In July, 1864, it was transferred to Virginia, and in August became a part of General Sheridan's army and took part in the battle of Winchester. It made a most gallant fight in that great battle and did its full share in winning a glorious victory. Its losses were heavy and among them were several of its bravest officers; 109 were killed, wounded and captured. At the battles of Fisher's Hill and Cedar Creek the

Twenty-second was engaged and met with losses. These were its last battles, and on the 3d of August, 1865, it was disbanded at Davenport, after having traveled more than 13,000 miles and served in nearly all of the southern states.

### THE TWENTY-THIRD IOWA INFANTRY.

This regiment was raised chiefly in the counties of Polk, Dallas, Story, Wayne, Pottawattamie, Montgomery, Page, Jasper, Madison, Marshall, and Cass counties. It contained 960 men, and was organized with the following field officers: Colonel, William Dewey; lieutenant-colonel, William H. Kinsman; major, Samuel L. Glasgow. It went into camp at Des Moines, and was mustered into service on the 19th of September, 1862. Its first campaign was in Missouri, where it did guard and garrison duty for several months, making some long and toilsome marches. Colonel Dewey died at Patterson on the 30th of November, and was succeeded by Kinsman, who was promoted to colonel; Major Glasgow was promoted to lieutenant-colonel, and Capt. Charles J. Clark, of Company B, was made major. Early in 1863 the regiment was sent down the Mississippi and became a part of Grant's army in the Vicksburg campaign. Its first battle was at Port Gibson, where, under Lieutenant-Colonel Glasgow, it did excellent service, losing thirty-three men. In the battle of Black River Bridge, May 17th, in the brigade commanded by General Lawler, the Twenty-third, led by Colonel Kinsman, made a brilliant charge on the enemy's works, which were captured with a heavy loss. Among the slain was the gallant Colonel Kinsman, who fell at the head of his regiment, pierced through with two musket balls. General Grant pronounced the charge a brilliant and daring one.

On the 6th and 7th of June the Twenty-third, with some negro regiments, had a severe battle with a superior force of the enemy at Milliken's Bend, and, after a fierce contest, defeated the rebels with heavy loss. It was the first battle in which the colored troops had taken a prominent part, and they proved good soldiers. The regiment, now under the command of Colonel Glasgow, who had been again promoted after the death of Colonel Kinsman, lost twenty-three killed and thirty-four wounded out of 110 men engaged in the battle of Milliken's Bend. About the middle of August, the regiment was transferred to the department of the Gulf, and for nearly a year was on duty in Louisiana and Texas. In the spring of 1864, it was sent to New Orleans to reinforce General Banks' army after his disastrous Red river campaign. For some time it was employed in Arkansas. Early in 1865, it was sent to take part in the Mobile expedition, now being under command of Lieut.-Col. Charles J. Clark, as Colonel Glasgow was commanding a brigade. It fought

bravely in the assault on the Spanish Fort, where it again met its old antagonist, the Twenty-third Alabama, which it had first encountered at Port Gibson. In June, the regiment was again sent to Texas. On the 23d of July, 1865, it was mustered out of service with 417 men.

### THE TWENTY-FOURTH IOWA INFANTRY.

The Twenty-Fourth was made up of companies raised chiefly in Jackson, Clinton, Cedar, Linn, Johnson, Jones, Tama and Iowa counties. It went into camp at Muscatine in September, 1862, and on the 18th was mustered into the United States service, numbering 950 men. Its field officers were Eber C. Byam, colonel; John Q. Wilds, lieutenant-colonel; Ed Wright, major. On the 19th of October the regiment was sent to Helena, Ark. From here it was sent on various expeditions into Mississippi and Arkansas, doing some hard marching and suffering from sickness. Lieutenant-Colonel Wilds was in command of the regiment a large portion of the time as Colonel Byam resigned June 30th, 1863. The Twenty-Fourth was attached to General Grant's army early in 1863 and was in his campaign against Vicksburg. It was actively engaged in the battle of Port Gibson, in General Hovey's division. At the great battle of Champion Hill no regiment in the union army surpassed the Twenty-Fourth for desperate fighting. A rebel battery of five guns on a commanding position was doing fearful execution on Hovey's division, as it advanced on Champion Hill. The Twenty-fourth alone charged upon it under a terrific fire of grape and canister, drove the gunners from their pieces and overwhelmed the infantry supports, carrying everything before them. But no other regiment coming to its support, it was assailed by overwhelming numbers and finally driven back. The loss of the regiment in this heroic charge was 195, including several gallant officers. The regiment participated in the hardships and dangers of the siege of Vicksburg and was in the campaign against Jackson. It was afterwards transferred to the Army of the Gulf and was in General Banks' disastrous Red river campaign. At the battle of Sabine Cross Roads the Twenty-fourth fought bravely, but nothing the army could do was sufficient to counteract the incompetency of the commanding general, Banks, who led it only to defeat and retreat. In July, 1864, the regiment went by river, gulf and ocean to Alexandria, Va., from there to Harper's Ferry, and joined Sheridan's army in the Shenandoah valley. At the battle of Winchester the Twenty-Fourth was hotly engaged and lost seventy-four men. It also took part in the battles of Fisher's Hill and Cedar Creek, which followed, fighting with its accustomed vigor and bravery and losing many good men. Among the mortally wounded at Cedar Creek was the gallant Colonel Wilds. In

January, 1865, this fighting regiment which had seen service in some of the greatest campaigns of the war, was again sent south by ocean steamer and did duty in Georgia and North Carolina. It was finally, at the close of the war, mustered out at Savannah, transported back to Iowa and disbanded in August. Few Iowa regiments traversed as many miles of the enemy's country or fought in as many battles as the Twenty-Fourth.

### THE TWENTY-FIFTH IOWA INFANTRY.

The companies composing this regiment were made up as follows: Four in Henry, three in Des Moines, two in Washington and one in Louisa. It was organized in September, 1862, with field officers, George A. Stone, colonel; Fabian Brydolph, lieutenant-colonel, and Calvin Taylor, major. It numbered 995 men, and was mustered into the service on the 27th of September, at Mount Pleasant. It was thoroughly drilled before entering the field, and its first service was at Helena, Ark. It was in General Sherman's expedition against Vicksburg in December, and in January, 1863, it was in the battle of Arkansas Post, where it lost sixty men. It was in Grant's campaign against Vicksburg, but did not participate in many of the battles which preceded the siege of that stronghold. It was in the movements against Jackson, and later was sent to reinforce the army at Chattanooga. It took part in this campaign, and at the battle of Ringgold lost twenty-nine men. Colonel Stone was soon after placed in command of a brigade, and Lieutenant-Colonel Palmer succeeded to the command of the regiment. In General Sherman's march to the sea the Twenty-fifth was placed in the Iowa brigade of the Fifteenth corps. This brigade was made up of the Fourth, Ninth, Twenty-fifth and Thirty-first regiments of Iowa infantry, under command of Col. James A. Williamson, of Iowa. This brigade fought at Resaca, Lovejoy Station, Dallas, Kenesaw Mountain, Atlanta, Ezra Church, Jonesboro, and all through that great campaign, with distinguished bravery, the Twenty-fifth losing sixty-seven men in battle. It reached Savannah on the 21st of December, 1864. Here Colonel Stone took command of the Iowa brigade again, and Lieutenant-Colonel Palmer of the regiment. Colonel Stone's command on the morning of the 17th of February forced a passage over the river after a sharp fight, and entered Columbia, the capital of South Carolina, and planted the stars and stripes on the dome of the state house. The city surrendered through its mayor, and forty pieces of artillery were among the arms captured. On the 20th of March the Twenty-fifth had a hard fight at the battle of Bentonville, and lost twenty-seven men. This was its last battle, and it marched with the army to Goldsboro, Raleigh, and after the surrender of Johnston, it went by way of Richmond to

Washington. In June the regiment returned to Iowa, and was disbanded at Davenport.

### THE TWENTY-SIXTH IOWA INFANTRY.

This was largely a Clinton county regiment, and was organized at Clinton, in September, 1862. It had about 900 men, and its field officers were Milo Smith, colonel; Samuel G. Magell, lieutenant-colonel; Samuel Clark, major. In October, it was sent to Helena, Ark., and from there to the vicinity of Vicksburg. It was at the battle of Chickasaw Bayou, but met with no loss. In January, 1863, it was in the expedition sent to capture Arkansas Post. The fleet under Admiral Porter co-operated with the army in this battle, which began on the 10th. Fort Hindman was a strong position, and made a vigorous defense. General McClernand ordered an assault, and, after a desperate fight, the fort was captured, with 5,000 prisoners and seventeen pieces of artillery. The Twenty-sixth here made a splendid fight, and suffered as severely as any regiment engaged in the battle. Colonel Smith was among the wounded, while the loss of the regiment was 120. It was soon after moved down the river near Vicksburg, where the men worked on the canal that was designed to change the channel of the river. In May, the Twenty-sixth was sent with the army to capture Jackson, and afterwards took part in the siege of Vicksburg, and was engaged in the assault of the 22d, where it lost many men. After the close of the Vicksburg campaign, the Twenty-sixth, after considerable service at various places, was sent to take part in the expedition operating about Chattanooga, and was in the battles of Lookout Mountain and Missionary Ridge. The loss was not heavy, but included some good officers wounded. After service in parts of Alabama, the regiment joined Sherman's army in its campaign against Johnston, where it belonged to the Fifteenth corps. From this time on the history of the Twenty-sixth is intimately associated with the hard marches and successful battles of that brilliant campaign. At Resaca, Dallas, Kenesaw and the siege of Atlanta, at Jonesboro and Lovejoy the Clinton county regiment did valiant service, and its dead lie buried all along the line of the great march to the sea. In December, 1864, it was in camp at Savannah, and in January it marched with the army through the Carolinas. It was at the capture of Columbia, and at the battle of Bentonville its last fight was made. It marched to Goldsboro, Raleigh, and on to the national capital, and was mustered out at the close of the war, covered with honors.

### THE TWENTY-SEVENTH IOWA INFANTRY

The companies for this regiment were mostly recruited in northern Iowa and came largely from Allamakee, Clayton, Chickasaw, Delaware,

*The Artillery, as personified on the Iowa Soldiers' and Sailors' Monument.*

Buchanan, Mitchell and Floyd counties. They went into camp at Dubuque late in August, 1862, where they were drilled for about two months, and on the 3d of October were mustered into the United States service, about 1,000 strong. Its field officers were colonel, James I. Gilbert; lieutenant-colonel, Jed Lake; major, Geo. W. Howard. Soon after it was ordered to report to General Pope, commanding the Department of the Northwest, where the Sioux Indians had begun a war of extermination against the inhabitants of western Minnesota. They were perpetrating the most horrid massacres of modern times on defenseless men, women and children in that region. The Twenty-seventh was first sent to Fort Snelling, but the Indian war having ended it was soon after sent down the river to Cairo, and from there to Memphis to join General Sherman's army. The regiment served in Mississippi for several months, making hard marches and suffering heavy losses from hardships, exposure and consequent sickness. It was employed in guarding railroads, protecting lines of communication and similar duties until in August, 1863, when it joined General Steele's army in the campaign against Little Rock. The regiment lost during the year 1863, mostly from sickness, more than 180 men. In January, 1864, it was with General Sherman in his Meridian expedition, after which it was sent to take part in General Banks' Red river campaign. In the battle of Pleasant Hill the Twenty-seventh was in Colonel Shaw's brigade, which made a most heroic fight that day, and by its valor and sacrifices saved the army from greater disasters, and covered its retreat that night and the next day to Grand Ecore. The regiment met with heavy loss in its brave fight, and during the retreat was of the rear guard protecting the army from the pursuing enemy. At the battle of Yellow Bayou the Twenty-seventh was actively engaged and lost seventeen men. Colonel Gilbert commanded a brigade for some time after this campaign, in which was his regiment, and several times had combats with the enemy, being in the battles of Tupelo and Old Town Creek. In September and October the regiment was in a campaign in Missouri against General Price, marching 700 miles in forty-seven days. In November it was sent to reinforce General Thomas near Nashville and was in the two days' battle which resulted in the defeat of Hood's army with heavy loss. Colonel Gilbert commanded a brigade in this battle and Lieut.-Col. Jed Lake led the Twenty-seventh. They joined in the pursuit of the defeated army as far as Pulaski. Soon after the regiment was sent to join the expedition now organizing for the capture of Mobile. Major Howard led the regiment in an assault on the rebel works, while Colonel Gilbert commanded a brigade. After its capture they moved to Montgomery, and went into camp at the old capitol, where they remained until the close of the war. The regiment

returned to Iowa early in August, 1865, where it disbanded on the 8th.

## THE TWENTY-EIGHTH IOWA INFANTRY.

The Twenty-eighth was made up of companies raised in the counties of Benton, Iowa, Tama, Poweshiek, Johnson and Jasper, in August and September, 1862. At the time it went into camp at Iowa City it numbered 956 men. The field officers were, colonel, William E. Miller; lieutenant-colonel, John Connell; major, H. B. Lynch. Early in November it embarked for Helena, Ark., where it remained most of the time until January 11, 1863, when it joined General Gorman's expedition up the White river. The weather was very severe, and the men suffered greatly from exposure and sickness, resulting in many deaths. Returning to Helena, the regiment went into rude winter quarters, where disease ravaged the camps and death and misery reigned everywhere. With clothing worn out, clad in rags, living in rude huts, without pay, or any of the ordinary comforts of life, it was a winter of wretchedness and despair never forgotten. On the 14th of February General Washburn left Helena with a large force to remove the obstructions from Yazoo Pass. Great trees had been felled across the river, and the men worked here in the swamps and water, dragging with cables the obstructions from the pass. Soon after the return to camp Colonel Miller resigned, and was succeeded by Colonel Connell, and Capt. B. W. Wilson was promoted to lieutenant-colonel. On the 11th of April the Twenty-eighth, then brigaded with the Twenty-fourth Iowa, and other regiments started on the Vicksburg campaign. It was first under fire at the battle of Port Gibson, and fought bravely, losing seventeen men. At the battle of Champion Hill, on the 16th, the officers and men fought like veterans. General Hovey says: "Of the Twenty-fourth and Twenty-eighth Iowa—in what language shall I speak? Scarcely more than six months in the service, and yet no troops ever showed more bravery or fought with more valor." The Twenty-eighth in this battle lost 100 men in killed and wounded. It was in the siege of Vicksburg, and after its surrender was sent to assist in the Jackson campaign. Major Lynch resigned and was succeeded by Capt. John Meyer.

In September the regiment was sent to western Louisiana and was with General Franklin's army on its march to Opelousas in November.

In March it was sent to join General Banks in the disastrous Red river expedition. It fought well at Sabine Cross Roads, where Colonel Connell was severely wounded and taken prisoner; in the absence of higher officers Capt. Thos. Dillin took command. When the army, in its retreat, reached Grand Ecore, Lieutenant-Colonel Wilson joined his regiment, bringing a number of recruits.

In June the regiment was lying at Carrollton where Colonel Connell, who had been exchanged, rejoined his command, having lost an arm at the time of his capture. In July, 1864, the regiment embarked for Alexandria, Va., which place it reached on the 2d of August. Soon after it was sent with the Twenty-second and Twenty-fourth Iowa to join Sheridan's army in the Shenandoah Valley.

At the battle of Winchester it was heavily engaged and lost ninety men. On the 22d it was in the battle of Fisher's Hill, where it captured a battery with small loss.

At the battle of Cedar Creek the Twenty-eighth did valiant service. Overborne, in the early part of the day by the furious onset of the enemy, the regiment made a vigorous resistance and Lieutenant-Colonel Wilson was borne from the field severely wounded. Major Meyer took command and soon, the tide of battle turning; the confederates were driven with heavy loss, the Iowa regiments joining in the pursuit. The Twenty-eighth lost nearly a hundred men in killed, wounded and prisoners.

In January, 1865, it was sent to Savannah and joined Schofield, and remained in Georgia until late in June, when it was mustered out of the service, numbering about 500. It reached Davenport in August, where it was disbanded.

THE TWENTY-NINTH IOWA INFANTRY.

The companies making up this regiment were recruited on the Missouri slope, from the counties of Pottawattamie, Mills, Harrison, Adams, Fremont, Taylor, Ringgold, Union and Guthrie. The regiment numbered 900 men and was mustered into the service in December, 1862, with the following field officers: Colonel, Thomas H. Benton; lieutenant-colonel, R. F. Patterson; major, C. B. Shoemaker. It was sent to join General Curtis' army in Missouri, in December, and from there was transferred to Helena, Ark., and went with General Gorman's fruitless expedition up the White river. Upon its return it was attacked by measles and there were over 400 men on the sick list. In August the regiment was in General Steele's campaign against Little Rock, and fought bravely in the battle which preceded the capture of that city, losing thirty-one men.

In March, 1864, Steele's army moved southwest with a wagon train of 400 teams which strung out four miles long, guarded by the Twenty-ninth Iowa. On the 2d of April General Shelby's rebel brigade of cavalry made a dash upon it. A lively fight ensued and the result was doubtful when General Rice came up with reinforcements. For miles the fight continued as the long train moved on, but finally the rebels made a fierce charge which was repelled with heavy loss and the train came into

camp without the loss of a wagon. The Twenty-ninth lost twenty-seven men during the day. At Jenkin's Ferry the regiment fought for six hours and made a brilliant bayonet charge, losing altogether fifty-nine men. The army returned to Little Rock, where General Steele was soon after relieved of the command. Early in 1865 preparations were made for the Mobile campaign in which the Twenty-ninth took part, fighting with its usual vigor. The regiment was sent to Brazos Santiago, Texas, in June and in July returned to New Orleans where it was discharged from the service in August. It returned to Iowa, landing at Davenport on the 19th of August, 1865, numbering 765 men, including parts of the Nineteenth, Twentieth and Twenty-third which had been attached to it.

THE THIRTIETH IOWA INFANTRY.

This regiment was organized from companies raised in the counties of Lee, Davis, Jefferson, Van Buren, Washington and Des Moines, late in the summer of 1862. It was mustered into service on the 23d of September and went into camp at Keokuk, with Col. Charles H. Abbott, Lieut.-Col. W. M. G. Torrence, and Maj. Lauren Dewey as its first field officers. It was sent to Helena, where it suffered from sickness for a long time. The regiment was a part of General Thayer's brigade and joined General Sherman's army before Vicksburg. It was in the battle of Chickasaw Bayou, December 28th and 29th, but suffered very slight loss. In the campaign against Arkansas Post, the Thirtieth Iowa participated and did good service, under command of Lieutenant-Colonel Torrence, losing forty-five men. In April the regiment joined Grant's army in the Vicksburg campaign and in the assaults of the 19th and 22d of May. In this last bloody battle Colonel Abbott was slain while leading his regiment in a charge on the confederate works. He was an able officer and highly esteemed by the army, and his death was a sad blow to the regiment he commanded. Major Millikin was mortally wounded in the same battle and died the next day. Lieutenant-Colonel Torrence was promoted to command of the regiment and Aurelius Roberts, of Company C, was promoted to lieutenant-colonel and Robert D. Creamer, of Company G, became major. The regiment joined the army sent against Jackson, and after its capture was sent with Osterhaus' division to repair and guard the Memphis and Charleston railroad. On the 21st of October the Thirtieth, with the advance guard of the army, had a severe battle with the enemy near Cherokee, where Colonel Torrence was killed in the thickest of the fight, while bravely leading his men into action. Soon after the regiment was sent to reinforce the army operating about Chattanooga. In the great battle which followed, the Thirtieth took an active part in the assault and capture of the rebel strongholds of Lookout Mountain and Missionary Ridge. In the battle of Ringgold, on the 27th of November the Thirtieth did excellent service and lost many good men. In the Atlanta campaign which followed, the Thirtieth was in many battles and always sustained its high reputation for valor. At the close of that victorious campaign it marched on to Washington and participated in the last grand review at the close of the war. On the 6th of June it started for Iowa, landing at Davenport, where it was honorably discharged.

### THE THIRTY-FIRST IOWA INFANTRY.

This regiment was composed of companies raised in Linn, Black Hawk, Jones, Jackson, and Cedar counties. It had 970 men and its field officers were: Colonel, William Smyth: lieutenant-colonel, J. W. Jenkins; major, Ezekiel Cutler. It went into camp at Davenport in October, and early in November sailed for Helena, Ark. It soon after joined Sherman's army operating against Vicksburg, and was in the battle of Chickasaw Bayou. In January, 1863, it was in the expedition which was sent against Arkansas Post, and took part in the battle at that place. It was in the battle of Raymond May 12th, and was in the army that captured Jackson. In the siege and capture of Vicksburg it rendered good service, fighting bravely in the assault of May 22d, where Lieutenant-Colonel Jenkins was wounded. After the fall of Vicksburg it was in the army sent to Chattanooga and participated in the battles of Lookout Mountain, Missonary Ridge, and Ringgold, losing many men. In

May, 1864, the regiment marched to northern Georgia and made a part of the grand army, 100,000 strong, under General Sherman, then marching towards the sea. Gen. J. E. Johnston was in command of the confederate army of about 50,000 gathered to resist the invasion.

Johnston's army had taken a position near Dalton on a spur of the mountains. At Resaca, fifteen miles south, the hostile armies came into collision on the 12th of May. The battle raged fiercely for several days, as one after another of the strong positions were carried by the union army. Lieutenant-Colonel Jenkins was again wounded in these battles. On the 28th a severe battle was fought at Dallas and several other sharp engagements followed. But the union army continued to advance, and Atlanta was finally taken. On the 15th of November Sherman's army again started on its march to the sea. In the battles which had taken place the Thirty-first had lost many men, always doing good service. Colonel Smyth resigned in December and was succeeded by Lieutenant-Colonel Jenkins, who was an excellent officer. In the march through the Carolinas the Thirty-first was engaged in several fights with the enemy and did good service at the battle of Bentonville. It reached Washington in May and was at the grand review of the 24th. It was disbanded at Davenport, where it received a great ovation from the citizens. From nearly 1,000 men who marched with it to the war, but 370 remained when it was mustered out. Disease, hardships, and battles had thus reduced its numbers.

---

## CHAPTER XVI.

*The Thirty-second, Thirty-third, Thirty-fourth, Thirty-fifth, Thirty-sixth, Thirty-seventh, Thirty-Eighth, Thirty-Ninth, Fortieth, Forty-fourth, Forty-fifth and Forty-sixth Iowa Infantry Regiments.*

### THE THIRTY-SECOND IOWA INFANTRY.

This regiment was made up of companies recruited in Hardin, Hamilton, Cerro Gordo, Black Hawk, Boone, Butler, Floyd, Franklin, Webster, Story and Marshall counties. It went into camp at Dubuque, where in October, 1862, it was mustered into the service, numbering 920 men. Its first field officers were: Colonel, John Scott; lieutenant-colonel, E. H. Mix; major, G. A. Eberhart. In November it was sent to St. Louis, where it was soon after divided, six companies under Colonel Scott being sent to New Madrid, and four companies under Major Eberhart stopped at Cape Girardeau. In April, 1863, the post at Cape Girardeau, under General McNiel, was attacked by General Marmaduke, and after a vigorous defense of four hours the confederate army retired. Major

Eberhart's command did good service in the battle. In August it accompanied a detachment up the White river, where it had a fight with the rebels and lost six men.

The detachment was employed in various duties until January, 1864, when it was sent to Gen. A. J. Smith's army. at Vicksburg. In the meantime, Colonel Scott with the other companies of the regiment was stationed at New Madrid doing garrison duty.

In December General Davis, in command at Columbus, Ky., ordered Colonel Scott to destroy the gun carriages and ammunition and spike the guns and evacuate New Madrid and proceed to Fort Pillow. Colonel Scott obeyed the order, destroyed all the public property and took his command by steamer to Fort Pillow. Soon after he was placed under arrest for so doing, but upon trial

*The Cavalry, as personified on the Iowa Soldiers' and Sailors' Monument.*

he was honorably acquitted. In June, 1863, the command was sent to Columbus, where the companies of the regiment were separated and employed in various duties. In January, 1864, six companies were sent to Vicksburg and assigned to a brigade commanded by Colonel Shaw, where soon after the entire regiment was reunited.

In the disastrous Red river campaign, the Thirty-second Iowa bore a conspicuous and honorable part. In the assault on Fort De Russey, this regiment made a brilliant charge and sustained some loss. On the 9th of April, was fought the battle of Pleasant Hill, where a portion of Banks' army made a firm stand against the confederate army, which had defeated the advance corps the day before at Mansfield or Sabine Cross Roads. General Banks had retreated fifteen miles after his bloody defeat, and being now reinforced by General Smith's command, he determined to make a stand at Pleasant Hill. Colonel Shaw's brigade held the center of the position and made a heroic fight with his four regiments, one of which was the Thirty-second. A terrific battle ensued, lasting until dark. This regiment made a most determined fight, and was at one time entirely surrounded by the enemy, but bravely cut its way through and faced the enemy again. It suffered fearful losses, among which were its gallant Lieutenant-Colonel Mix, who was slain. The total loss was 210 killed, wounded and missing. In the retreat down the Red river, the army was closely followed and continually harassed by the victorious enemy. At Bayou de Glaize the Iowa regiments under Colonel Shaw saved the army from further disasters by a heroic stand. At the battle of Nashville the Thirty second did good service and lost twenty-five men. It was also in the campaign against Mobile, after which it remained some months in Alabama. Colonel Scott resigned soon after the Red river campaign, and was succeeded by Lieutenant-Colonel Eberhart, with Capt. Jonathan Hutchison major. Returning to Iowa, the Thirty-second was mustered out covered with honors nobly won.

### THE THIRTY-THIRD IOWA INFANTRY.

This regiment was raised largely through the influence and exertions of Samuel A. Rice, late attorney-general of the state. Four companies were recruited in Mahaska county, three in Keokuk and three in Marion.

They went into camp in August, 1862, at Oskaloosa, and on the first of October were mustered into the service.

The field officers were Samuel A. Rice, colonel; Cyrus H. Mackay, lieutenant-colonel and Hiram D. Gibson, major.

The regiment left for the seat of war in November; went to St. Louis, from there to Columbus, Ky. In January, 1863, it was sent to Helena, Ark.,

where, in June, Colonel Rice took command of a brigade, and from that date Lieutenant-Colonel Mackay commanded the regiment.

At the battle of Helena, where 15,000 confederates under General Holmes attacked the city, the Thirty-third was first brought into action. It was in an exposed position, made an excellent fight in support of two batteries, and captured a large number of prisoners. Colonel Rice commanded the brigade to which it was attached.

In April the brigade was with General Steele in his expedition toward the Red river, and had several engagements with the enemy. Upon his retreat, the battle of Jenkins' Ferry was fought, on the 29th, and it was here that General Rice received a wound in his foot which proved fatal. In this battle the Thirty-third lost 129 men. Colonel Mackay was severely wounded and the command of the regiment devolved on Captain Boydston. Major Gibson, who had resigned, was captured at Mark's Mills. The regiment went to Little Rock in November, where it remained until February, 1865, when it joined the expedition against Mobile, taking an active part in that brilliant campaign. Soon after it returned to Iowa and was mustered out.

### THE THIRTY-FOURTH IOWA INFANTRY.

The four counties of Lucas, Decatur, Wayne and Warren furnished the ten companies that made up this regiment. It had 934 men and went into camp at Burlington in September, 1862.

The field officers were George W. Clark, colonel; Warren S. Dungan, lieutenant-colonel; R. D. Kellogg, major.

It was sent to Helena, Ark., in November, where the smallpox broke out in their camp.

Its first service was with General Sherman's disastrous campaign against Vicksburg and the battle of Chickasaw Bayou. It afterwards shared in the brilliant campaign against Arkansas Post. After the capture of the post and garrison, Colonel Clark was sent with his regiment and five companies of an Illinois regiment to convey the 5,000 prisoners to Chicago. The 6,000 men were crowded into three steamboats and they suffered almost beyond human endurance for the two weeks it took to reach St. Louis. The smallpox broke out among them and the misery they endured is beyond description.

When his command returned to Benton barracks in February, it was completely prostrated by the horrors the men had passed through, and many were discharged. From St. Louis the regiment was sent to Pilot Knob, Lieutenant-Colonel Dungan in command, as Colonel Clark was in command of a brigade. Soon after the regiment joined General Grant's army, then besieging Vicksburg, and was sent under General Herron in an expedition to Yazoo City. It was afterwards sent down to Port Hudson, and finally on to near the mouth of the Rio Grande in Texas. It was in the battle at Fort Esperanza, in which that post was blown up and evacuated. The regiment remained in this vicinity for five months, when it was transferred to New Orleans and sent up to Alexandria to reinforce General Banks' defeated and retreating army. In July the regiment was sent to join in the expedition against Mobile, and participated in that successful campaign. After the capture of Mobile the Thirty-fourth was sent to New Orleans, and in November was in camp at the mouth of White river. Soon after the Thirty-fourth and Thirty-eighth regiments were consolidated, numbering now 950 men. In January the regiment was sent to Florida, and from there it joined the army in the siege of Mobile. After the capture of that city it was sent to Galveston, Texas. It was mustered out of the service on the 15th of August at Houston, and reached Davenport, where it was discharged, on the 29th. Since entering the service the regiment had traveled more than 15,000 miles, and faced the enemy in many hard battles.

### THE THIRTY-FIFTH IOWA VOLUNTEERS.

Muscatine county contributed eight companies and Cedar county two for this regiment, which went into camp on Muscatine Island late in the summer of 1862. The regiment numbered 957 men when mustered into the United States' service on the 18th of September. Its field officers were Sylvester G. Hill, colonel; James H Rothrock, lieutenant-colonel; and Henry O'Connor, major. Its first service was in western Kentucky, during the winter of 1862-3. In April the regiment joined the army of General Grant in the Vicksburg campaign, and took part in the capture of Jackson. In June Major O'Connor resigned, and in August Lieutenant-Colonel Rothrock retired from the service. They were succeeded by William B. Keeler, promoted to lieutenant-colonel from captain of Company A, and Abraham John, captain of Company B, promoted to major. It was on duty in western Tennessee for several months. In March, 1864, it joined General Banks' army, and participated in the hard marches, battles and retreat of that campaign.

On the 22d of March, the regiment, under command of Lieutenant-Colonel Keeler, made a march with another regiment to Henderson's Hill, surprised and captured a body of 350 confederates with four pieces of artillery, horses and other property. At the battle of Pleasant Hill the Thirty-fifth did good service, and lost many good officers and men. At the battle of Yellow Bayou it made a gallant fight, losing forty men. Its total loss in this disastrous campaign was more than 100. In June, at the battle of Lake Chicot, the regiment made a

brave fight, in which Major John was mortally wounded. From September to the middle of November, the regiment was in the army sent to drive General Price out of Missouri and Arkansas. At the battle of Nashville, in December, the Thirty-fifth was under the command of Major Dill, who had been promoted from captain of Company C, Colonel Hill commanding a brigade. This brigade, in which was his own regiment, made a brilliant charge on the enemy's batteries, which it captured, but the gallant colonel was killed in the conflict. The last battle in which the Thirty-fifth was engaged was in the campaign against Mobile. Soon after it was sent to Selma, and late in July it started for home. On the 10th of August it was mustered out at Davenport, and soon after disbanded at Muscatine, after nearly three years' honorable service.

### THE THIRTY-SIXTH IOWA INFANTRY.

This regiment was made up of companies raised in the counties of Monroe, Wapello and Appanoose. When it went into camp at Keokuk late in the summer of 1862 it numbered 930 men. But soon after smallpox and measles broke out and the men suffered terribly for several months; many died and others were discharged for disability, reducing the regiment about 100. Its field officers were: Charles W. Kittredge, colonel; Francis M. Drake, lieutenant-colonel; Thomas C. Woodward, major. On the 19th of November it was sent to St. Louis, and in December to Helena. In February, 1864, when the regiment embarked for the Yazoo Pass, its number had been reduced by sickness to about 630. In that fruitless expedition the regiment suffered greatly from sickness and buried many of its brave boys in the swamps along the way. It was in the battle of Helena and in August went with the Arkansas expedition under General Steele and spent a portion of the winter in camp at Little Rock. The regiment was with General Steele in his march to Camden and had a fight with the enemy at Little Missouri in April. A detachment of about 1,000 men under Lieutenant-Colonel Drake was sent to guard a train of 300 wagons sent to bring army supplies. On the 25th of April it was attacked by a superior force of the enemy near Mark's Mill. After a severe battle, in which Lieutenant-Colonel Drake was severely wounded, the command was compelled to surrender. The Thirty-sixth fought bravely under Major Hamilton, but the force against them was too large and the regiment surrendered with the others. They were taken to Tyler, Texas, where they were imprisoned. In July Major Hamilton, Captains Miller and Lambert escaped and reached Little Rock; both of the captains died from sufferings in prison and privations endured in their escape. At the battle of Jenkins' Ferry a portion of the Thirty-sixth, which had escaped capture, fought bravely under Lieutenant Huston. At Little Rock a number of recruits joined the fragment of the regiment, and it now numbered about 250 men, under Colonel Kittredge, who had command of the post. In April 1865, the survivors of those captured at Mark's Mill were released and joined the regiment at St. Charles. It soon after was moved to Duvall's Bluff, and on the 24th of August was honorably discharged.

### THE GRAY-BEARD REGIMENT.

This regiment, which was number Thirty-seven of Iowa infantry, was made up exclusively of men over 45 years of age, and who were consequently exempt from military duty.

Secretary Stanton, of the war department, had, at the request of men over age who wished to enter the service, authorized the organization of such a regiment to do garrison duty. The various companies making up the regiment went into camp at Muscatine, and were mustered into the service about the middle of December, 1862. Its field officers were George W. Kincaid, colonel; George R. West, lieutenant-colonel and Lyman Allen, major. Every congressional district in the state was represented in the ranks of the regiment. They were farmers, mechanics and business men, most of whom had sons or near relations already in the army. Many of them were over 50 years old, but when they marched through the streets of St. Louis in January, 1863, General Curtis, who had seen the volunteers of two wars, declared that he had never seen a finer looking body of men. For two and a half years these men performed garrison and guard duty, thereby relieving younger men for field service and thus contributing valuable aid to their country. The last general officer under whom they served thus wrote of their services, on the 13th of May, 1865:

"*General L. Thomas, Adjutant-General U. S. Army:*

"The Thirty-seventh Iowa Volunteer infantry, called the 'Gray-Beards,' now on duty at this post, consists exclusively of old men—none under 45, many over 60 years of age. After the men of this regiment had devoted their sons and grandsons, numbering 1,300 men, to the service of their country, their patriotism induced them to enlist for garrison duty, thus enabling the government to send the young men to the front. Officers and men would cheerfully remain in the service as long as they are wanted, though they are very badly needed at home to save the next harvest, most of them being farmers. They have received the commendation of their former post commanders. At this post they have performed very heavy duties, which would have been difficult for an even number of young men. The high patriotism displayed by these men in devoting a few years of their old age

to their country's service is unparalleled in history, and commands the respect of every true republican. I therefore recommend that the Thirty-seventh Iowa Volunteer infantry may be mustered out of the service immediately, with honors and acknowledgments of their services, due to the noble spirit with which they gave so glorious an example to the youths of their country.

"Very respectfully,

"J. WILLICH,

"*Brigadier-General.*"

General Willich's request was granted, and the Gray-Beard regiment was mustered out, being the first of the three years men to be discharged from the service. The Thirty-seventh was disbanded on the day of the grand review at Washington. A large number of the men had died from exposure and the hard duties of camp life.

### THE THIRTY EIGHTH IOWA INFANTRY.

This regiment was made up of companies raised in the counties of Howard, Chickasaw, Bremer, Winneshiek and Fayette. It went into camp near Dubuque in August, 1862, and numbered about 900 when it was mustered into the service on the 4th of November. The field officers were David H. Hughes, colonel; Joseph O. Hodnutt, lieutenant-colonel, and Charles Chadwick, major. In December it embarked for St. Louis, and soon after was sent to hold New Madrid, where it stayed until June, 1863. From there it was sent to General Grant's army before Vicksburg, and took part in the siege. Later it was sent to Port Hudson, where it suffered fearfully from disease; at one time there were but eight officers and twenty privates fit for duty. Among those who died here from disease were Colonel Hughes, Captain Tinkham and Lieutenant Stevens, all excellent officers. The regiment was at this time almost a wreck, and went into convalescent camp at Carrollton, La.

In October, the regiment was sent to Texas, and in July, 1864, returned to New Orleans, and from there joined the expedition against Mobile. After the capture of that city, it returned to New Orleans, and in January, 1865, the Thirty-eighth was consolidated with the Thirty-fourth, and Lieutenant-Colonel Hodnutt was honorably discharged. The regiment, as a distinct organization, now ceased to exist, a large number of its survivors forming a portion of the Thirty-fourth. Its history was a sad one, as its colonel and 300 of its officers and men had in two years perished from disease, and 100 more were discharged as invalids. There were many long, weary weeks when it had not enough well members to care for the sick or bury the dead. It was composed of as good and brave men as any that Iowa sent into the service, but the deadly malaria of southern swamps nearly destroyed it, and the fortunes of war kept it from

*Victory, as personifi-d on the Iowa Soldiers' and Sailors' Monument.*
*(Photographed in the workshop.)*

participating in the great campaigns and victories of the war, while its sacrifices were not surpassed by any.

### THE THIRTY-NINTH IOWA INFANTRY.

The companies of this regiment were chiefly raised in the counties of Polk, Dallas, Madison, Clarke, Greene, Des Moines, and Decatur. It went into camp at Davenport in October, 1862, and was mustered into the service in November with 802 men. Its field officers were: H. J. B. Cummings, colonel; James Redfield, lieutenant-colonel; Joseph M. Griffiths, major. It went south on the 13th of December, stopping at Jackson, Tenn., and marched from there to Trenton. It was in the battle of Parker's Cross Roads, under Colonel Dunham, in which Lieutenant-Colonel Redfield distinguished himself for energy and bravery. He was severely wounded in rallying his men. The loss of the regiment was thirty-seven. Soon after 100 of its members were captured and suffered ten months in a rebel prison. In January, 1863, the regiment joined General Dodge at Corinth, and was assigned to the Third brigade of his division, and served under Dodge for nearly two years. It took part in Colonel Straight's raid in Alabama. Soon after Company H was surrounded and captured. It joined Sherman's army in the Atlanta campaign, and in the defense of Allatoona it made a most heroic fight. General Corse was ordered by Sherman to hold Allatoona Pass to the last extremity. He had 2,000 men, including the Thirty-ninth Iowa. General French, with a large confederate army, attacked the place on the morning of the 15th of October, and a desperate battle ensued. Hour after hour the battle raged with the greatest fury, not surpassed by any conflict during the war. At 2 o'clock the confederates made a most determined charge on all sides, but they met such a storm of grape, canister, and rifle balls as no troops could stand, and were driven back in confusion, with heavy loss. In this heroic defense of Allatoona no regiment fought more gallantly than the Thirty-ninth Iowa, commanded by Lieutenant-Colonel Redfield. This brave officer was wounded in his foot early in the battle, but he dragged himself along the lines, cheering and directing his men. He was again severely wounded but would not relinquish his command, but seated on the ground issued his orders and encouraged his regiment to stand firm, until a fatal bullet pierced the heart of one of the bravest officers that Iowa sent to the war. His regiment lost 165 men in this battle. The Thirty-ninth marched on with Sherman's army to Savannah, and on through the Carolinas to Alexandria, Va., in sight of the national capital. In the final great review this regiment, with banner torn by shot and shell, marched in Gen. E. W. Rice's brigade before the vast concourse of people gathered to do honor

to the war-worn veterans. Soon after it was sent home to Clinton, where it was disbanded.

### THE FORTIETH IOWA INFANTRY.

This regiment was composed of companies raised in the counties of Marion, Poweshiek, Mahaska, Jasper, Keokuk and Benton. It was called by some the "copperhead regiment," because a large number of anti-war democrats were among it, men and officers, but the truth is, a majority of its members were republicans. It went into camp at Iowa City, in September, October and November, 1862, being a long time filling up the ranks. Its field officers were John A. Garrett, colonel; Samuel F. Cooper, lieutenant-colonel and Sherman G. Smith, major, and it numbered about 900 men. In December the regiment was sent to Columbus, Ky., where it remained during the winter, and

*James Wheeler Mackenzie, who waved the answer back to Sherman at Allatoona Pass.*

in March it moved to Paducah, where it stayed three months. For several months it was on the Yazoo and at Helena, and in July was with General Steele in his expedition against Little Rock. In March, 1864, General Steele's army moved from Little Rock towards Camden, and on its retreat the battle of Jenkins' Ferry was fought on the 30th of March. The Fortieth did good service in this battle and lost forty-five men. The retreat after the battle was through mud and storms, and without food. Men and horses sunk down in the swamps exhausted by fatigue and hunger, and a more woe-begone army has seldom been seen. In February, 1865, the regiment was under General Bussey in the Fort Smith district, and later was at Fort Gibson, where Colonel Garrett was in command of the district of Kansas and Indian Territory. On the 2d of August it was mustered out of the service and returned home.

Of all the captains who went into the service when the regiment was organized, but one remained in command to the end—Capt. E. W. Ridden, of Company F, all the others having resigned or been discharged.

Attempts had been made to organize the Forty-first, Forty-second and Forty-third regiments of infantry, but were unsuccessful. In the summer of 1864 the governors of the western states proposed to the general government to send to the field a number of regiments enlisted for a short term to relieve the older regiments doing garrison duty and stationed on the western frontier. The proposition was accepted and Governor Stone, of Iowa, issued a proclamation calling on the people of the state for volunteers for 100 days. In response 3,900 men volunteered and were organized into the Forty-fourth, Forty-fifth Forty-sixth and Forty-seventh regiments and the Forty-eighth battalion of infantry.

The Forty-fourth was organized of companies raised in the counties of Dubuque, Muscatine, Linn, Butler, Clinton, Marshall, Boone, Polk, Dallas and Scott. The field officers were S. H. Henderson, colonel; Henry Egbert, lieutenant-colonel; Josiah Hopkins, major. It was mustered into service in June, 1864, at Davenport, and had 867 men.

The Forty-fifth was raised largely in the counties of Henry, Washington, Van Buren, Lee, Davis and Des Moines, and numbered 912 men. It was mustered in at Keokuk, May 25, 1864, with A. H Bereman, colonel; Samuel A. Moore, lieutenant-colonel; and James B. Hope, major.

The Forty-sixth was enlisted chiefly in the counties of Dubuque, Poweshiek, Dallas, Guthrie, Fayette, Taylor, Linn, Delaware, Winneshiek, Appanoose, Monroe, Wayne, Clarke, Cedar and Lucas, and numbered 892 men. Its field officers were David B. Henderson, colonel; L. D. Durbin, lieutenant-colonel; and George L. Torbert, major; and it was mustered into service in June, 1864.

The Forty-seventh was made up from companies raised largely in the counties of Marion, Appanoose, Benton, Wapello, Buchanan, Madison, Madison, Johnson, Keokuk and Mahaska, and numbered 884 men. Its field officers were James P. Sanford, colonel; John Williams, lieutenant-colonel; and George J. North, major. It was mustered into service in June, 1864.

The Forty-eighth battalion numbered 346 men, raised mostly in the counties of Warren, Jasper, Decatur and Des Moines, and were mustered into the service at Davenport, in July, 1864, with O. H. P. Scott, colonel.

The Forty-fourth, Forty-fifth and Forty-sixth regiments were sent to Tennessee, to guard railroads and perform garrison duty, while the Forty-seventh was sent to Helena, where it suffered greatly from sickness. The Forty-eighth battalion guarded rebel prisoners on Rock Island.

The services of the hundred-days-men were acknowledged in a proclamation issued by President Lincoln in October, and thanks were tendered to the states which furnished them.

---

## CHAPTER XVII.

*First Iowa Cavalry, Second, Third, Fourth, Fifth, Sixth, Seventh, Eighth and Ninth Iowa Cavalry Regiments—Iowa Artillery—Frontier Defense—The Tally War—Capital Removed to Des Moines—Negro Suffrage—Agricultural College—Railroad Building.*

### THE FIRST IOWA CAVALRY.

Colonel Fitz Henry Warren, one of the most distinguished citizens of Iowa, commanded the First regiment of cavalry raised in Iowa for the war of 1861. The men making up this regiment were enlisted from all parts of the state in the summer of 1862. Charles E. Moss was the first lieutenant-colonel and E. W. Chamberlain, James O. Gower and Wm. B. Torrence were the first majors. The regiment went into camp at Burlington, where it remained until October, when it was ordered to St. Louis. The different battalions of the regiment were employed in Missouri through the winter in the field, patrolling a large portion of the state, protecting union settlements from guerrillas and doing hard riding on various duties. In July, 1863, Major Gower with his battalion whipped Quantrill

near Pleasant Hill, killing a large number of the outlaws. On the 7th of August the regiment was brought together for the first time since it left camp at Burlington. Soon after Colonel Warren was promoted to brigadier-general and took final leave of his regiment to enter upon his new duties, and Lieutenant-Colonel Gower succeeded to its command. On the 6th of December, two battalions of the regiment, under Colonel Gower, joined General Blunt and took part in the battle of Prairie Grove. In the pursuit after the battle the First Iowa cavalry was in the lead and came up with two regiments of the enemy's cavalry near Van Buren. A lively fight ensued and a large amount of stores, wagons, four steamboats and all the camp equipage was captured from the retreating army. In General Steele's campaign against Little Rock, the First Iowa cavalry had a sharp fight with the enemy at

Bayou Metaine, in which it made a brilliant charge, losing thirty-seven men. In the capture of the city the First cavalry was under fire a good portion of the day and lost several men. Among the wounded was Major Caldwell. Colonel Gower resigned in August on account of ill health and Lieutenant-Colonel Anderson succeeded him, Major Caldwell was made lieutenant colonel and Captain McQueen was promoted to major. The regiment continued to serve (having re-enlisted) with distinction until the close of the war and was one of the last to be mustered out of the service. Few regiments have left a more worthy record of duty well and faithfully done.

### THE SECOND IOWA CAVALRY.

The companies composing this regiment were raised chiefly in the counties of Scott, Jackson, Clayton, Lee, Muscatine, Washington, Marshall, Polk, Hardin, Hamilton, Hancock, Johnson, Iowa, Cedar, Delaware and Jones. They went into camp at Davenport late in the summer of 1861, and remained there drilling for nearly three months. It was a fine regiment of excellent men, and became well equipped for service before it left camp, 1,050 strong. Its first colonel was Capt. W. L. Elliott, of the Third U. S. cavalry, an accomplished officer of the regular army. Edward Hatch was lieutenant-colonel, and the majors were William P. Hepburn, Datus E. Coon and Hiram W. Love. On the 7th of December the regiment went south, stopping at St Louis, and soon after moving down the river to Bird's Point, and from there it joined General Pope before New Madrid and participated in his campaign and victory. It was with Halleck in his cautious advance upon Corinth. At Farmington it had a fight with the enemy, and made a brilliant charge to save a force of infantry under General Paine, which had been attacked by greatly superior numbers. It lost fifty men in the charge. Soon after Colonel Elliott, with the Second Iowa and Second Michigan cavalry, made a brilliant raid to Booneville, where they destroyed a large amount of arms, supplies and other rebel property with slight loss to his force. For this brilliant raid, Colonel Elliott was promoted to brigadier-general, and was succeeded by Colonel Hatch in command of the regiment. At the battle of Boone-ville, on the 1st of July, fought by Col. Phil. Sheridan, the Second Iowa cavalry took a prominent part. Sheridan had but one brigade, consisting of the Second Iowa and the Second Michigan cavalry. This small force was attacked by General Chalmers with nearly 5,000 men. Sheridan dismounted the Michigan regiment, fell back to a swamp and sent the Second Iowa to assail the flanks of the advancing enemy. When they became hotly engaged, he sent 100 of the Second cavalry through the woods to the rear of the enemy with orders to charge

upon them. The order was obeyed, and the rebels, being attacked at the same time in front and rear, supposed that heavy reinforcements had come to Sheridan, and they fled in confusion. This victory made Sheridan brigadier-general. The Second Iowa lost twenty-two men in this brilliant engagement, in which it bore a conspicuous part.

During the fall the regiment was active in the battles of Iuka, Corinth, and Grant's expedition into central Mississippi. Early in December it was at the battle of Coffeyville and did good service. In Grierson's raid, the march against Forrest, at Moscow and the Meridian expedition, the Second cavalry did good service. It was at the battle of Nashville and many other minor engagements, and in October, 1865, was mustered out of the service. Few, if any, regiments in the war of the rebellion performed more valuable service or won more honor for gallant deeds than the Second Iowa cavalry.

### THE THIRD IOWA CAVALRY.

This regiment was raised largely by the personal exertions of Cyrus Bussey, a member of the state senate, from Davis county. General Fremont, in command of the department of the Missouri, in 1861, requested Bussey to raise a regiment of cavalry, and he at once issued a call for volunteers. On the 28th of August 1,000 mounted men had responded and assembled at Keokuk. The field officers were, colonel, Cyrus Bussey; lieutenant-colonel, Henry H. Trimble; majors, Carlton H. Perry, Henry C. Caldwell and Wm. C. Drake, and the regiment numbered 1,096 men. The companies were recruited largely in the counties of Lee, Davis, Van Buren, Marion, Appanoose, Jefferson, Wapello and Wayne. It left the state for St. Louis on the 4th of November and on the 12th of December Major Caldwell was sent with the second battalion to Jefferson City, and did not unite his command with the regiment again for nearly two years. During that time he was employed against the rebels in central and southern Missouri, having several sharp engagements with them at various times and places.

Lieutenant-Colonel Trimble, having been severely wounded at Pea Ridge, resigned in September, 1862, and Major Caldwell was promoted to the vacant place. The remainder of the regiment, under Colonel Bussey, joined General Curtis' army in February. It had a conspicuous part in the battle of Pea Ridge, where it lost forty-nine men, killed, wounded and missing. Major Drake had been sent with two companies to Salem. Soon after he marched against a rebel force at West Plains, killed, wounded and captured sixty of them. He had several other fights with the enemy in that vicinity. The Third was in the hard campaign through Arkansas to Helena, and had several engagements with the enemy, meeting with some losses. In November Major Drake died and John W. Noble, adjutant, was promoted to fill the vacancy. Colonel Bussey was now in command of the Second brigade, which included his own regiment, Major Noble in command of a battalion, and Major Scott in command of the Third cavalry. In June the Second battalion was sent to join Grant's army in the Vicksburg campaign, and was with Sherman in his march against Jackson. On the turned to St. Louis in November, 1864. A part of the regiment was in the brilliant Grierson campaign, and soon after the regiment was united at Louisville. On the 22d of March, in the Wilson raid through Alabama, nearly 7,000 prisoners and 240 pieces of artillery were captured in this brilliant campaign, in which the Third cavalry took a prominent part, and lost forty men. On the 9th of August, 1865, the regiment was mustered out, and reached Davenport on the 21st.

*Scenes in and about Corinth.*

1st of January, 1864, more than 600 men of the Third cavalry re-enlisted as veterans, and on the 6th received a furlough of thirty days to visit their homes. About this time Colonel Bussey was promoted to brigadier-general, H. C. Caldwell was promoted to colonel, and J. W. Noble to lieutenant-colonel. In the disastrous Guntown expedition, under General Sturgis, the Third Iowa cavalry lost sixty-seven men. The regiment was now under command of John W. Noble, promoted to colonel; George Duffield, lieutenant-colonel. It was in the campaign against Tupelo, and made a brilliant charge on the enemy at Old Town, losing nineteen men in the campaign. It was in Winslow's brigade in several brilliant engagements in Missouri, and re-

### THE FOURTH IOWA CAVALRY.

This regiment was raised chiefly in the counties of Henry, Fremont, Delaware, Buchanan, Poweshiek, Wapello, Mahaska, Lee, Chickasaw, Bremer, Mitchell, Madison and Jefferson. They were mustered into the service in November, 1861, and numbered 1,036. The field officers were: Colonel, Asbury B. Porter; lieutenant-colonel, Thomas Drummond; majors, Simeon D. Swan, Joseph E. Jewett and George A. Stone. In February, 1862, the regiment was ordered to St. Louis and was sent from there to southwestern Missouri. In April it joined General Curtis' army and afterwards went to Helena, where it remained until April, 1863.

9

In October Major Rector, with fifty men of the regiment, was defeated and captured with fourteen of his men. In May the regiment joined Grant's army in the Vicksburg campaign and did good service in the capture of the city. Colonel Porter resigned and Major Winslow was commissioned in his place. The Fourth was engaged in several raids in the enemy's country and had some sharp fights with slight loss. It was in the Meridian campaign and had frequent skirmishes with the rebels. In March, 1864, the veterans of the regiment who had re-enlisted went home on furlough. The regiment received enough recruits to bring its number up to 1,354 in May, 1864.

In June General Sturgis led an army of 12,000 men against the rebel army under Forrest. Colonel Winslow commanded a brigade of cavalry composed of the Third and Fourth Iowa and the Tenth Missouri. Through the utter incompetency of General Sturgis, his army was beaten at Guntown, his wagon train and artillery captured and his disorganized infantry driven in a vast mob of fleeing men back to Memphis. Colonel Winslow commanded the rear guard in the disastrous flight and with his cavalry made a gallant resistance and saved the army from total destruction. Sturgis' loss of men was about 4,000, most of whom were captured. The Fourth also participated in the battle of Tupelo, where Gen. A. J. Smith, with 12,000 men, defeated General Forrest with 14,000. In September Winslow's brigade of cavalry joined in General Smith's pursuit of General Price's army in Missouri and fought bravely in several battles, in one of which Colonel Winslow was severely wounded. In this campaign the Fourth Iowa had marched more than 2,000 miles and worn out two sets of horses.

Colonel Winslow was promoted to brigadier-general and Lieutenant Colonel Peters was in command of the Fourth cavalry. The regiment was with General Wilson in his campaign through Alabama and April, 1865, in which the Fourth fought in several battles and captured more than 900 prisoners. In August, 1865, this regiment, after its brilliant career, was mustered out and discharged at Davenport.

### THE FIFTH IOWA CAVALRY.

This regiment was made up of cavalry companies enlisted in Iowa, Nebraska, Minnesota and Missouri, but as Iowa furnished the most men it was called the Fifth Iowa cavalry. The organization was completed in February, 1862. Its field officers were: Colonel, William W. Lowe, of the regular army; lieutenant-colonel, M. T. Patrick, of Omaha, Neb.; Carl S. De Bernstein, of Dubuque, William Kelsey, of Omaha, and Alfred B. Brackett, of St. Paul, were the majors. The regiment was ordered to Fort Henry in February. On the 3d of May a detachment of 150 men was sent to Lockridge's Mill where it was attacked by Colonel Clayborne with 3,000 men, and cut to pieces; the commander, Major Bernstein, was mortally wounded. On the 25th of August the regiment had a sharp fight at Fort Donelson, in which Lieutenant Summers was mortally wounded. For a long time the Fifth was scouting and performing various services in Tennessee. In January, 1864, most of the regiment having re-enlisted, they were granted a furlough and visited their homes. In July the regiment was in the great raid made by General Rousseau, in which they marched over four hundred miles in the enemy's country. The Fifth lost fourteen men in this expedition among whom was Captain Curl, killed. In another raid under General McCook, which resulted disastrously, the Fifth lost 120 men. The regiment was now reduced to about 100 effective men, but continued under Major Young, to do good service. In September two companies of the First cavalry were united with the Fifth, and about this time Lieutenant-Colonel Patrick resigned. On the 28th of October a brigade commanded by Colonel Capron, in which was the Iowa Fifth, was surrounded by a large rebel force. The colonel disappeared and Major Young, of the Iowa regiment, took command and by a most daring charge his brigade cut its way through and rode safely into camp. It was next in the battle of Nashville and later in General Wilson's great raid through Alabama and Georgia. Major Young had been promoted to colonel and commanded the Fifth in that brilliant campaign, which fought bravely in several conflicts with the enemy. In August, 1865, it was mustered out of the service covered with honors nobly won.

### THE SIXTH IOWA CAVALRY.

This regiment was raised in October and November, 1862, and was made up of men enlisted in various portions of the state. Some of the companies went into camp at Davenport late in 1862, and others were not mustered in until March, 1863. It numbered over 1,100 men. The field officers were David S. Wilson, colonel; Samuel M. Pollock, lieutenant-colonel, and Thomas M. Shepherd, E. P. Ten Broeck and A. E. House, majors. It marched to Sioux City in March and April, and crossed over into Dakota territory to serve against the Indians. In June, they marched with General Sully's army on a campaign up the Missouri river to the mouth of the Little Cheyenne river, near which the battle of White Stone Hill was fought. The Sixth cavalry took an active part in it, losing twenty-two men. The Indians were driven from the field, 156 captured, and probably as many more killed and wounded. The march continued up through the bad lands, where several skirmishes took place with the retreating Indians, and the Yellowstone river was reached on the 12th of August. Colonel

Wilson resigned in June, 1864, and Lieutenant-Colonel Pollock was promoted to the command of the regiment, which remained in the Indian country until September, 1865, when it returned to Sioux City, and was mustered out on the 17th of October.

THE SEVENTH IOWA CAVALRY.

This regiment was made up largely of companies raised for other organizations, and was not fully organized until July, 1863. Its field officers were: Colonel, Samuel W. Summers; lieutenant-colonel, John Pattee; majors, H. H. Heath, George W. O'Brien, and John S. Wood. The regiment was sent to Omaha, where it remained until July, 1864, but many of its companies were scattered at posts on the western frontier. In Dakota, Nebraska, Colorado, and Kansas they marched and were in several skirmishes at times with the Indians. At Julesburg, in Colorado, Company F, under Captain O'Brien, fought a band of Indians, killing fifty-five of them and losing thirteen men. Colonel Heath fought and defeated the Indians in a battle near Alkali late in the fall, and for a long time had command at Fort Kearney. The Seventh cavalry was not sent south during the war.

THE EIGHTH IOWA CAVALRY.

This regiment was raised by Col. J. B. Dorr, of Dubuque, by special authority from the secretary of war, in the summer of 1863. The companies were recruited largely in the counties of Fremont, Page, Jefferson, Wapello, Van Buren, Clarke, Ringgold, Henry, Appanoose, Dubuque, Jackson, Marshall, Clayton, Johnson, Cedar, Muscatine, and Polk. The regiment numbered 1,234 men and was mustered into the service at Davenport in September, 1863. The field officers were: Colonel, J. B. Dorr; lieutenant-colonel, H. G. Barner; majors, John J. Brown, James D. Thompson, and Alvo J. Price. In October the regiment was ordered to Chattanooga to guard lines of railroad and suppress the guerrillas. During the winter it captured nearly 500 of the members of small rebel bands, and afforded security to union men in eastern Tennessee. On the 28th of July Colonel Dorr, with a part of the Eighth, joined General McCook's expedition to Lovejoy. In a battle near the Chattahoochee, on the 29th, the Eighth cavalry bore a prominent part, and lost about thirty men. The next day the command was assailed by General Roddy's army on its way to Atlanta. A sharp conflict ensued and Colonel Dorr and his regiment, after a fierce fight, were taken prisoners near Newnan, Ga. The remainder of the regiment was under command of Major Price for a time, but upon his resignation in September, Captain Cummins succeeded him. Colonel Dorr was exchanged in November and resumed command, and was with the army at the battle of Franklin. The Eighth took part in the battle of Nashville, and joined in the pursuit of Hood's army, and soon after stopped at Waterloo. About the middle of January, 1865, it joined General Wilson's army in its great raid. The Eighth remained at Macon, Ga., about three months, where the gallant Colonel Dorr died from a congestive chill on the 28th of May, 1865. Lieutenant-Colonel Barner was promoted to colonel and took command of the regiment, and in July it was mustered out.

THE NINTH IOWA CAVALRY.

This was the last Iowa regiment raised under the call for three years troops. It was organized at Davenport in November, 1863, and had nearly 1,200 men. The field officers were, colonel, M. M. Trumbull; lieutenant-colonel, J. P. Knight; majors, Edgar T. Ensign, William Haddock and Willis Drummond. The services of this regiment were in Arkansas, scouting, garrison and guard duties,

19, 1866, when it was mustered out at Little Rock, Ark. During its term of service it marched more than 2,000 miles. It lost from sickness 164 men; by drowning, two, and from wounds, fifteen.

*Approval*
*Wm. T. Shaw*
*Comd'g Post*

where it lost many men from disease, but none killed in battle. Detachments had some skirmishes with guerrilla bands but the regiment was not engaged in any battles. It served until February

Company A, of the Eleventh Pennsylvania cavalry, was made up of Iowa men. It was raised for Col. Josiah Harlan's independent cavalry, which afterwards became the Eleventh Pennsylvania.

The majority of its men were enlisted from Webster county and it numbered eighty-three men. It was mustered into the service October 29, 1861, and was commanded by T. A. Stratton, captain. This company served in the army of the Potomac.

The Sixtieth regiment of colored troops was largely made up of Iowa men. Six companies of this regiment went into camp at Keokuk and were mustered into the service of the United States on the 13th of October, 1863. The field officers were,

parts of the state and was mustered into the service in August, 1861, with 116 men. The captains were Charles H. Fletcher, Junius A. Jones and Henry H. Griffith. This battery was for a long time commanded by Captain Griffith, and did good service in several battles from Pea Ridge to Atlanta.

The Second battery was organized in July and August, 1861, most of its members being from the counties of Dallas, Polk, Harrison, Fremont and Pottawattamie. It was mustered into the service

*Gen. John M. Corse, the Hero of Allatoona.*

colonel, John D. Hudson, of St. Louis; lieutenant-colonel, Milton F. Collins, of Keokuk; major, John L. Murphy, of Keokuk. For one year and one-half this regiment served on guard and garrison duty at various places in the Mississippi valley with fidelity.

### IOWA ARTILLERY.

Iowa furnished four batteries of artillery for the war. The First battery was made up from various

at Council Bluffs, in August, 1861, with Nelson T. Spoor as captain. It did excellent service in the campaigns of Vicksburg, Atlanta and Nashville.

The Third battery of light artillery was recruited chiefly from the counties of Dubuque, Black Hawk, Butler, Delaware, Floyd and Grundy. It numbered 140 men, and was commanded by M. M. Hayden. It greatly distinguished itself at the battle of Pea Ridge, where it rendered brilliant service. It was in several other battles and campaigns.

The Fourth battery of light artillery was recruited in July, August and September, 1863, with 152 men. The men were chiefly from. the counties of Mills, Mahaska, Fremont, Henry and Scott. Philip H. Goode was the commander, and it was mustered into service at Davenport November 23, 1863. Its services were mostly in Louisiana.

During the war, Iowa sent into the field 78,659 soldiers. Of these 3,263 were killed or died of wounds, 8,409 died of disease and 9,777 were discharged for disability. Of Iowa soldiers who entered the service, four became major-generals, twenty-one brigadier-generals, five brevet major-generals and seventeen brevet brigadier-generals.

While the governor and the people of Iowa were putting forth every effort to raise and equip regiments for the field, our southern border was threatened with invasion from Missouri rebel bands and troops had to be raised for protection and defense. John R. Morelege raised a regiment for this service, of which he was made colonel. In August, 1862, the Sioux Indians taking advantage of the fact that most of the military forces in the country were in the south, and the northwestern frontier in a defenseless condition, assembled their warriors and began a savage war of extermination in Minnesota and threatened northwestern Iowa. They had never been punished for the massacre of 1857 and seemed to feel a contempt for a government that would tamely submit to such a massacre of its citizens and permit the perpetrators to retire unharmed. They had since invaded northwestern Iowa, in June, 1861, and killed two members of the frontier guards and driven off stock within a few miles of Sioux City. Colonel Hubbard, by authority of the war department, raised a regiment of cavalry for defense against the Indians. About the middle of August, the Sioux in great force fell upon the frontier settlers of Minnesota and in the course of a few weeks massacred more than 1,000 men, women and children and drove 5,000 more from their homes. Houses were pillaged and burned, stock killed and driven off and more than 250 women and children dragged off into captivity. Of the perpetrators of this horrible massacre 425 were captured and brought to trial, of which 321 were convicted and 303 were sentenced to death. But only thirty-nine were executed, as the President ordered them to be simply imprisoned and they were eventually released. Some of them were kept in jail at Davenport a while and then turned loose to engage in other massacres which followed later. This massacre surpassed in the number slain and the horrible atrocities perpetrated upon women and children, and amount of property destroyed, any that ever occurred in American history, and was entirely unprovoked. The Iowa frontier was so well protected by military forces that had been organized and maintained since the massacre of 1857, that our citizens escaped this

terrible slaughter. The Iowa legislature, in extra session on the 9th of September, while the Sioux were still at their terrible work, authorized the raising of 500 mounted men and such other force as might be necessary to protect the frontier. Five companies of fifty men each were soon after raised and organized into the Northern Border brigade, commanded by Lieutenant-Colonel Sawyer. Stockades were built at Iowa Lake, Estherville, Peterson, Cherokee and Correctionville. So complete were the preparations that no Indians ventured

*First Colonel Eighth Iowa; afterwards Brigadier-General.*

over the Iowa line, and in the spring following the Sioux were driven into the Yellowstone valley.

### THE TALLY WAR.

During the war there was a class of people in the northern states who were in sympathy with the rebellion, and who never ceased to do all in their power to aid their "southern brethren" in their war upon the government, short of fighting for the cause. They were called "copperheads." In Keokuk county, one George C. Tally was a leader among them. He was a Baptist minister and an orator of some power. He was open and bold in his denunciation of the war against secession, and preached treason to the government. A great democratic mass meeting was held on the 1st of August, 1863, near the English river, at which Tally was the chief speaker. Several hundred were present, most of whom brought arms concealed under straw in their wagons. Wild threats were made to clean out the town of South English, a republican stronghold. The people there, learning of these threats, armed themselves for defense. As Tally passed through the village on his way to the meeting, he displayed a butternut badge as an open advertisement of his disloyalty. Some of the friends of union soldiers who had been killed in battle with the rebels tried to tear this badge of treason off of Tally's clothes, but failed. After the meeting, Tally's crowd started in a procession to go through the town, Tally standing up in a wagon defiantly displaying his disloyal badge in the most offensive manner. The republicans had been holding a meeting in the town, and a large crowd was in the street through which Tally's procession was trying to force its way. An altercation began, and soon firearms were used. More than a hundred shots were fired in rapid succession. Tally was standing in a wagon at the head of the procession, with a long bowie knife in one hand and a revolver in the other. As soon as the first shot was heard, he began to fire at the crowd. As the third shot left his revolver, he fell dead in the wagon, pierced by three bullets. News of the killing of their leader was spread rapidly through the adjoining country, and threats of vengeance were made by enraged friends of Tally. Great crowds began to gather, and alarm was felt lest bloody work should begin.

Messengers were sent to Governor Kirkwood at Iowa City, who promptly ordered arms and ammunition to be sent to the scene of the impending conflict. He immediately gave orders for several companies of infantry and a squad of artillery to report at the place of danger, and at once started for South English. Tally's friends gathered in large numbers on the banks of the Skunk river, about two miles from Sigourney and began to organize into military companies and choose officers, and forming a brigade, began to drill. About sundown the governor, with three of his aids, reached Sigourney, where a great crowd was assembled. He addressed them from the steps of the court house and gave all to understand that he should suppress all disturbances with a firm hand. That night there arrived on the ground, nine companies of infantry and one of artillery. The Tally forces were estimated at nearly two thousand men, but when they saw the governor on the ground with his well armed military companies, their courage

failed and they slipped away during the night. The next day all was quiet and peace was restored. Twelve men were arrested for killing Tally, who waived examination and gave bonds to appear at the next term of court. The governor's prompt action prevented a bloody conflict.

When the capital of the state was removed from Iowa City to Des Moines, in 1857, the old state house became the property of the State university. A building had been erected by the citizens of Des Moines for the use of the state, until such time as the legislature should make an appropriation for a permanent state house. In 1870 the general assembly made an appropriation for the beginning

*Gen. Ed. Wright.*

of such a state house. The act provided for a board of nine commissioners, including the governor of state, who should have control of the work. This board proceeded to put in a foundation for a plan they had adopted, under the supervision of one of their number. But the stone used proved to be defective and had to be taken out at a loss to the state of over $50,000. The next general assembly abolished the large board of commissioners as unwieldly and elected John G. Foote, M. L. Fisher, Peter A. Dey and R. S. Finkbine, the governor to be *ex-officio* president of the board. The plan of the building was made by Cochrane & Piquenard, architects. Gen. Ed. Wright was chosen secretary of the board, R. S. Finkbine was superintendent and J. G. Foote superintendent of finance. In 1884, the building was so far constructed that the general assembly held its session in it. The state library and executive rooms were also occupied. The length of the building north and south, including porticos, is 363 feet; width east and west, 246 feet. The height to top of the dome is 275 feet. The entire cost of the state house July 1, 1885, was $2,615,170, and the cost of furnishing up to that time $82,789.

From the close of the war the history of Iowa has been devoid of exciting events. The state has been making steady growth in population and wealth from year to year. Many enterprises which were suspended during the war were soon after resumed. At the republican state convention, held at Des Moines in June, 1865, an exciting controversy arose over negro suffrage in Iowa. Edward Russell, a delegate from Scott county, offered an amendment to the platform reported by the committee on resolutions which aroused a warm discussion. The amendment was as follows: "Therefore we are in favor of amending the constitution of our state by striking the word *white* from the article on suffrage." The object of the amendment was to pledge the republican party to remove the last remnant of race discrimination from the laws of Iowa. Some of the timid delegates were alarmed and afraid such a declaration would bring defeat to the ticket, and they made earnest efforts to persuade Mr. Russell to withdraw the amendment. There was a conservative element in the party opposed to negro suffrage; it was uncertain how strong this element was, and whether they would refuse to vote the republican ticket nominated on a platform so radical.

But Mr. Russell, aided by Hiram Price, ably and vigorously defended the proposed amendment on the broad ground that it was right and that the republican party was strong enough to do right and should not seek to shirk the responsibility. Hiram Price, in a strong and eloquent appeal to the convention, said: "The colored men north and south were loyal to the government in the days of its greatest peril. There was not a rebel or traitor among them. Now when slavery has been forever banished from the country, they ask the privilege of citizenship. Why should the freedom-loving people of Iowa longer deny them this right? Not one reason can be given that has not been used to bolster up slavery for the past hundred years." After a warm discussion the amendment was adopted by a vote of 513 to 242. In the campaign which followed, negro suffrage was the chief issue and was advocated by the republican candidates for governor and lieutenant-governor, who were elected by majorities of 16,375 and 20,526 respectively. The next legislature took the preliminary steps to so amend the constitution. The amendment was submitted to a vote of the people and was adopted by a majority of 24,265.

During the years 1866-7-8-9, a second geological survey of the state was made, under the direction of Dr. Charles A. White, with O. H. St. John,

assistant. Much valuable work was done in examination of the coal measures, rock and soils. The report was published in two volumes in 1870.

In 1868 the building for the State Agricultural college having been partially completed, a portion of it was fitted up and the school was opened in the fall of that year, continuing through the winter. On the 17th of March, 1869, the college was formally opened with addresses by the president, A. S. Welch, the president of the board of trustees, the governor of the state, and others, in the presence of a large assembly from various parts of the state. A grant of the public lands had been made by congress in 1862, for the support of agricultural colleges

*A. S. WELCH.*
*First President Iowa Agricultural College.*

and Iowa had selected its portion of these lands, amounting to over 200,000 acres, within its own limits. This was the foundation for a fine endowment fund for the support of the college. In 1864 an attempt was made by the friends of the State university to consolidate the two schools and divert the land grant to the support of the university, but the attempt was not successful and the entire grant was appropriated to the agricultural college.

The Iowa Central Air Line railroad, which received a land grant in 1856, failed to comply with the conditions of the grant, and the land was regranted in March, 1860, to the Cedar Rapids & Missouri River Railroad company. The old line was to run from Lyons, on the Mississippi river, by way of Tipton to Iowa City, and received a large amount of county aid, but was never built. The new company started their road from Clinton, two miles below Lyons, and built by way of Cedar Rapids to Council Bluffs and also to Blair, on the Missouri river. This road reached Boone in the fall of 1865 and Council Bluffs in the fall of 1867. Although the Rock Island road was the first to enter Iowa, it was two years longer building to the Missouri river than the Cedar Rapids & Missouri. The Burlington & Missouri Railroad company was ten years building its line from the Mississippi river to Albia, in Monroe county, but it reached the Missouri river in 1868. The Dubuque & Sioux City Railroad company, which also had a land grant, built to Iowa Falls, a distance of 143 miles, where it stopped until 1867. In 1869 it reached Fort Dodge, and in about two years more was completed to Sioux City. The land grant to this line embraced more than 1,000,000 acres of fertile land which, if sold at $8 per acre, would have paid the entire cost of building and equipping the road from Dubuque to Sioux City. The lands granted to the Rock Island road were sold at an average price of more than $8 per acre, and the Burlington land grant brought that company over $12 an acre. In 1864 congress made a grant of lands to aid in building a railroad from McGregor westward. After various changes of companies, this road was built to Algona in 1870 and to Sheldon in 1878. The total number of acres of land granted by congress to Iowa railroads was 4,069,942.

## CHAPTER XVIII.

*Cardiff Giant Deception—Senator Grimes on Impeachment—Soldiers' Reunion—Grasshopper Scourge—Great Railroad Disaster—The Grange Movement—Kate Shelly's Noble Deed—Tornado of 1882—Removal of Auditor Brown.*

### THE GREAT CARDIFF GIANT DECEPTION.

One of the most successful frauds of modern times was conceived in the year 1868, and perpetrated in connection with the great gypsum fields near Fort Dodge, which made that town famous over the civilized world.

In the month of October, 1869, strange stories were whispered about the streets of the city of Syracuse, N. Y. It was reported that a petrified human body had been found on the farm of a Mr. Newell, near the village of Cardiff, some thirteen miles from that city. Upon investigation made by a reporter of the Syracuse *Journal*, who hurried to the spot where the discovery was said to have been made, the following facts were learned:

William Newell, the owner of a small farm lying a mile west of Cardiff, a small country village, had begun to dig a well for stock water near his barn. The spot selected was the low swampy margin of Onondaga creek. Two well diggers began excavation on the morning of October 16th, and when about three feet below the surface their spades struck what seemed to be a rock. Upon trying to unearth the bowlder, a huge foot was discovered, and upon digging further an enormous leg was found, and then an immense human body. Mr. Newell, who had been directing the work from the start, had cautioned the men to be very careful when their spades first struck a hard substance. He now took one of the spades and uncovered the body until it was found to be an immense stone giant buried in the earth. He directed the further digging until an excavation had been made about fifteen feet long, disclosing the full stature of a petrified man. The news of the wonderful discovery on the Newell farm spread rapidly among the neighbors, and soon an excited crowd of villagers gathered around the grave of the great unknown, and gazed with awe-stricken faces upon the colossal form of the "petrified giant," as Newell called it. The excitement increased hourly, and before Sunday night, more than 1,000 curious people had gathered at the Newell farm from the surrounding country to see the wonderful discovery. The news had reached Syracuse and glowing accounts of the mysterious giant had been published in the daily papers under displayed head lines. Every livery team and hundreds of private rigs were conveying hundreds of people from the city to the scene of the wonderful discovery. Large offers were made to Mr. Newell by some of the visitors for the giant, but he refused to sell.

Early on Monday morning it appeared to dawn upon Mr. Newell's mind that he had struck a huge bonanza in his shallow stock well. He procured a large tent and erected it over the resting place of the giant, enlarged the excavation around the body, the water was pumped out, guards were stationed around it, and Newell began to collect half a dollar from each of the hundreds of visitors coming to see the wonder. No one was permitted to touch the reclining giant as he held his silent reception lying prostrate in his ancient grave with closed eyes, majestic form, in calm, awful repose acquired by centuries of unbroken slumbers, while earth's tragedies and pleasures had rolled unceasingly by. Ten thousand dollars offered by a little city syndicate on Tuesday morning to the small farmer for his petrified giant, awakened him to a realization of the sudden fortune that had come to him like the discovery of a gold mine. But he steadily refused all offers and continued to take in half dollars at a rate that almost bewildered him. A cousin of Newell now appeared upon the ground, named George Hull, who took charge of the exhibition. Accounts of the wonderful discovery had been telegraphed to all parts of the country and the great newspapers sent special reporters to Cardiff to investigate and write up every phase of the great discovery. Scientists became interested and began to make examinations and put forth their learned opinions upon antiquity of the colossal figure so strangely deposited. Up to this time no one seems to have doubted that it was a petrified giant. But some of the geologists who had examined it pronounced it a statue carved from rock. But the owner, from the day of its discovery, refused to permit anyone to go very near it, or make any tests as to the material in the body or statue. Prof. James Hall, the noted New York geologist, who made the geological survey of Iowa in 1855, wrote a lengthy account of his examination and his theory as to what it was. He says: "It is certainly a great curiosity, and, as it now presents itself, the *most remarkable archæological discovery ever made in this country.* It is clearly a statue cut by human hands, and in no way connected with petrification or with calcareous deposits from springs, nor is it a cast or model of any kind, but an original. The importance of the object lies in its relations to the race or people of the past, formerly inhabiting that part of the country. The statue is of a far higher order and of an entirely different character from the smaller works of rude sculpture found in Mexico and Central America, or the Mississippi valley. In regard to the question of the antiquity of its origin we are compelled to rely upon the geological and chemical evidence. *That the statue has lain for a long time where it now lies there can be no doubt.* The entire length of the left side and back of the statue is eroded to the depth of an inch or more from the solution and removal of the surface by water coming in along the stratum upon which it lies imbedded. Such process and removal of the gypsum, a mineral of slow solubility in the waters of that region, must have required a long period of years. Any theory of the recent burial of the statue in this place is disproved by the fact of the extensive solution and removal of the surface by the water coming in along the gravel bed from the southwest. The most extensive erosion has taken place upon the left side and beneath the back upon that side, corresponding to the direction whence the water came. You will see, therefore, upon any theory of inhumation, you must have time for this process of the gradual dissolving of the stone. So long as the alluvial deposit was going on,

this portion was covered by water, and there would be no current along the gravel bed, and this movement of the water would only take place after the drainage of the stream or lake to a lower level. Therefore, so long as the alluvial deposit was going on, and the water remained above that level, there would be no current and consequently no erosion. This statement answers the inquiry as to what are some of the evidences of its antiquity."

Thus one of the most eminent living geologists proved the great antiquity of the giant, and also proved that it could not have been buried where found in recent ages.

Dr. Amos Westcott wrote to the *Scientific American* an elaborate article, in which he says: "It would be far easier to suppose this a veritable petrifaction of one of the giants who lived in those days than to suppose it a statue. There is not a chisel mark upon the entire image, nor of any other implement employed by the human hand. The style of model, its perfection, its peculiar smooth surface—all defy the artist. Not a single individual has ever examined it who was not impressed with the feeling and belief that it is the most extraordinary and gigantic wonder ever presented to the eye of man. Be it what it may, it presents a most perfect human form of colossal size, defying the present state of science, whether geology or archæology. Its origin, we have to confess, is as deep a mystery as when first brought to light."

An Onondaga squaw who came to see the giant said that her tribe believed that it was the petrified body of a gigantic Indian prophet who lived many generations ago, and foretold the coming of the "pale faces." He warned his people of the coming encroachments of the white men, and of their extermination of his people. He told them he should die and be buried out of sight, but that their remote descendants should see him again.

The mystery surrounding the whole affair seemed only to deepen with investigation. The scores of learned men who came to look upon the wonder differed widely as to what it was, its antiquity and probable origin, but all agreed that it was the most remarkable discovery ever unearthed in America. People came by hundreds and thousands from all over the country, paid the admission fee, looked upon the giant and went away in awe and wonder. Col. J. W. Wood, of Chicago, who had large experience in the show business, was employed to take charge of the exhibit and he greatly enlarged the tent, issued a pamphlet giving a history of the finding of the giant and the opinions of learned men. P. T. Barnum sent an agent to purchase the wonderful giant who was drawing such crowds. But a syndicate was formed which offered a larger sum—said to be $40,000—and the great showman did not get him.

Here the scene changes. A thousand miles westward, on the upper Des Moines river, was the picturesque village of Fort Dodge. In its vicinity are extensive deposits of gypsum. In the year 1867, one H. B. Martin stopped several days at the St. Charles hotel, and spent some time among the gypsum beds. He seemed to be deeply interested in the beautiful variegated stone which had been used in the construction of some of the finest residences in the village. He disappeared and was forgotten. On the 6th day of June, 1868, he returned, accompanied by a large, well dressed, intelligent looking man. They registered at the St. Charles as George Hull, Binghamton, N. Y., and H. B. Martin, Boston, Mass. They took frequent strolls among the gypsum quarries and finally leased an acre on Gypsum creek, south of Fort Dodge, and employed Mike Foley, an experienced quarryman, to get out an immense block of gypsum for them. It was four feet wide, two feet thick and

GEN. SAMUEL A. RICE,
Colonel of the Thirty-third Iowa Infantry.

twelve feet long. After many tribulations, breaking down wagons and miring down in wet places, they reached Boone, the nearest railroad station, on the 27th of July. The next day the block of gypsum was shipped east over the North-Western railroad. This was the last seen of Hull and Martin by the Fort Dodge people.

When, in November, 1869, the papers were filled with accounts of the wonderful "petrified Onondaga giant," that had been resurrected near Syracuse, N. Y., and the whole civilized world was wondering what race of remote antiquity he had belonged to, and scientists were puzzled over the mystery, a New York paper stated that Professor Boynton had pronounced it a statue carved from crystalline gypsum, but of a different color and appearance from the New York gypsum. Galusha Parsons, an eminent Fort Dodge lawyer, saw this report, and on his return from New York stopped off at Syracuse to take a look at the giant. He

wrote back to the editor of the *North West:* "I believe it is made of that great block of gypsum those fellows got at Fort Dodge a year ago, and shipped east." The editor and a few others at once began to investigate. Syracuse papers were sent for, letters were written to friends in that city, and it was learned that George Hull was one of the exhibitors of the "petrified giant." A description of the New York Hull corresponded in every particular with the George Hull who, with Martin, got out the Fort Dodge gypsum block fifteen months before. The clue was followed up with energy, and in the course of several weeks a chain of evidence was secured so complete that it reached without a missing link from Gypsum creek, Iowa, to the grave of the wonderful giant on the Newell farm near Cardiff, N. Y. Quietly, but with great celerity, the evidence was put in type at the *North West* office at Fort Dodge, and a pamphlet was issued that was destined to expose in all its details the most ingenious and successful fraud ever perpetrated in America, and wreck the great fortune then in sight for Hull, Newell and Martin. * * * * Going back where thousands were flocking to see the "petrified giant," it had been moved to Syracuse by the syndicate which now owned it, where fine accommodations had been prepared for its exhibition. It was now valued at $100,000, and the daily revenue coming from its exhibition justified that valuation. Preparations were being made to remove it to Albany and place it on exhibition at the state geological rooms. Early one morning a newsdealer offered a counter attraction on his stand in a large package of forty-page pamphlets, illustrated with portraits of the "stone giant," his inventors, his sculptor, his burial and resurrection. Its title page bore this inscription:

THE CARDIFF GIANT HUMBUG—THE GREATEST DECEPTION OF THE AGE.

The pamphlets sold like hot cakes. Intense excitement followed. The proprietors were soon seen reading the exposition of a fraud that must ruin them. One of them rushed to the news stand, bought the pamphlets and burned them. In a few days another lot was on the ground, and as soon as discovered these were bought and burned. But many had escaped them and got out among the people, and suppression was impossible. The owners of the giant must now fight for their vanishing fortune. They issued a statement denying every word of the exposition, and ridiculed the entire "yarn," as they termed it. But the newspapers, keen on the scent of a great sensation, got hold of some of the pamphlets and saw at once that the evidence was complete and conclusive as to the great fraud, and gave summaries of the exposition and evidence.

In the meantime P. T. Barnum went to the Chicago sculptor who made the giant, and whose name was given in the Fort Dodge pamphlet, and got a plaster cast made, which was a good duplicate of the original. He put it on exhibition in his museum in New York as the original "Cardiff giant." The proprietors of the genuine original hastily shipped it to New York, and the war of the giants was on. They applied to Judge Barnard for an injunction to restrain Barnum from exhibiting his cast, but the court declined to protect one fraud from the encroachments of another. Hull, Martin, and Newell now came forward and made solemn denials of all the charges and evidence in the Fort Dodge exposition, and certificates of character were procured and published. But it was all in vain. The public saw that the chain of evidence was continuous and conclusive.

The following is a brief summary of the facts as set forth in the Fort Dodge exposition: George Hull and H. B. Martin came to the St. Charles hotel and registered their names on the 6th of July, 1868. They remained there until the 14th, getting out the block of gypsum described by Mike Foley, who did the work for them. On the 27th of July they shipped the block from Boone, in car No. 447, to E. Burkhardt at Chicago. Hull followed it to Chicago, stopped at the Garden City hotel, where he was often seen by Fort Dodge men who knew him, until September 22d. The block was traced from the car to a building on the west side, where a sculptor named Otto worked on it until the giant was completed. Hull served as the model. It was securely boxed and shipped as *finished marble*, its weight now reduced to 3,720 pounds. It was directed to George Olds, Union, N. Y. This is a station on the New York & Erie railroad, ten miles west of Binghamton. It arrived there October 13th, and was delivered to a man who gave his name as George Olds, on the 4th of November. It was taken away in a wagon drawn by four horses, and they stayed the first night at the house of Mr. Luce, a few miles north of Union. From there the route of the four-horse team was followed up by way of Homer to Newell's farm. At Homer one of the men was recognized as George Hull by men who knew him well. When questioned as to what was in the large iron-bound box, Hull always replied, "castings" or "machinery." The team was seen by five persons on the evening of November 9th, within a mile of Newell's house, going in that direction. Some of the men were found who helped to lower the giant into his grave, which was ready for him on Newell's farm. The night was dark and rainy, but the four-horse team was seen and recognized by a Mr. Cummins, starting on its return before daylight on the morning of November 10th. Hull had left the four-horse team at Tully, got a livery team and drove to Cardiff on the night of November 9th, and walked from there to Newell's late in

the evening, where the four-horse team had already arrived. Hull again appeared at the Tully hotel before daylight in the morning of the 10th, wet through and covered with mud. He disappeared soon after breakfast, and was seen no more in that vicinity for nearly a year, or until a few days after Newell had discovered the wonderful petrified giant in his new stock well. Martin, who joined Hull at Newell's, proved to be a blacksmith from Marshalltown, Iowa. These three men turned out to be the owners of the "Cardiff giant."

All efforts made by the owners and exhibitors to refute the chain of evidence which appeared in the Fort Dodge pamphlet, proved futile, for the names and residence of all witnesses, dates of shipment, shipping bills, copy of hotel registers, affidavits of the quarrymen were published in full, and every step of progress in the most ingenious and successful deception of modern times, was given with an accuracy that left no doubt. A piece of the very ledge of gypsum from which the giant was manufactured, was taken out of Gypsum creek at Fort Dodge, showing the erosion of the water (which so completely deceived Professor Hall), and sent to Syracuse to be compared with the "petrified man," and the mass of evidence could no longer be disputed. It has never been made known how much Hull, Martin and Newell realized out of their enterprise, but it must have been a large sum, for they sold out to a syndicate before the exposition came.

The genius that could conceive such an original scheme; the executive ability that could successfully carry out all of its difficult details, would have achieved success in legitimate business. The shrewdness that led them to select a block lying in the bed of a creek, where for ages erosion of water had left its marks; the instructions to the sculptor to leave these marks untouched; completely deceiving the eminent geologists into pronouncing the statue of great antiquity, has never been surpassed.

Years afterwards Hull and Martin made full confessions of their part in the enterprise, confirming the truth of the evidence as published in the Fort Dodge pamphlet, and the last lingering doubt was removed.

The gypsum quarries at Fort Dodge, have since been developed by local enterprise and capital and the manufacture of stucco has become an important and profitable enterprise. One of the mills has in its name perpetuated the memory of the "Cardiff giant," which gave world-wide notoriety to Fort Dodge gypsum in early days.

When the attempt was made to impeach President Andrew Johnson, by congress, party feeling ran very high; and although he had been elected by the republicans, they had become so hostile to his policy that a vast majority of them favored his removal from office. Senator James W. Grimes, of Iowa, who by virtue of his position as a member of the Senate, was called upon to try the president on the charges preferred against him by the house of representatives, could not agree with his party that the president was guilty, and so voted. He gave his reasons for his vote, in which he declared that, "in his opinion, the president was not guilty of an impeachable offense by reason of anything alleged in either of the articles preferred against him at the bar of the senate by the house of representatives." So intense was the feeling that the republican press and people of Iowa denounced their senator in the most violent, intemperate and abusive language. Calumny and vituperation exhausted themselves upon his name. He bore the reproach with a heroic spirit, and gave a fine example of unshaken faith and loyalty in a national crisis.

COL. SAMUEL MERRILL,
*Seventh Governor of Iowa—1868 1872.*

He never for a moment regretted the stand he had taken. He said a year later: "I shall always thank God that He gave me the courage to stand firm in the midst of clamor, and by my vote, not only save the republican party, but prevent such a precedent being established as would in the end have converted ours into a sort of South American republic, in which there would be a revolution whenever there happened to be an adverse majority in congress to the president for the time being." Although at the time Iowa republicans were ready to persecute and repudiate their great senator, a few years later when passion had subsided, the whole country realized and acknowledged that Grimes was right.

In the summer of 1870, a great reunion of Iowa soldiers, engaged in the late war, was planned by Adjutant-General Baker. The time fixed was the 31st of August. Free transportation was secured and General Sherman, and General Belknap, then secretary of war, came from Washington to greet the Iowa soldiers. It lasted two days, and more than 20,000 Iowa soldiers gathered at the capital of the state. It had been five years since they were mustered out of the service, and this meeting again for the last time of thousands of comrades who had marched, camped and fought together in so many hard campaigns, was an event never to be forgotten. No such reunion had occurred since the grand review at Washington, in 1865, at the close of the war. Most of the surviving notable Iowa officers were present and participated in the exercises, and looked once more upon members of their old commands. It was the first and last great reunion of Iowa soldiers, an event ever to be remembered.

In 1872, northwestern Iowa was visited by an immense swarm of grasshoppers, which destroyed the crops over a vast area of country. Great destitution prevailed in some fifteen counties where the devastation had been most extensive. As winter approached, thousands of new settlers found themselves and families on the verge of starvation. When the situation became known to the state at large, the generous people in more favored regions began to contribute out of their abundant crops. General Baker secured from the railroad companies reduced rates of transportation, and volunteered to superintend the collection and distribution of the vast amount of provisions and seed grain for the destitute. In this way an immense amount of aid was judiciously given to meet the unusual exigency, and widespread destitution was relieved.

### THE GREAT RAILROAD HORROR OF 1877.

A small creek rises not far from Altoona, and empties into Four Mile creek about three miles east of Des Moines. Its ordinary stage is but a quiet little brook, but in times of great rains it becomes a raging torrent, sweeping out large bridges, fences, and overflowing the valley. The Rock Island railroad follows this valley several miles, and crosses Little Four Mile several times on bridges of considerable height and length. On the night of August 29, 1877, a terrific storm came up, and the rain fell for several hours, almost like a cloudburst. It was the heaviest fall of rain ever known in central Iowa. Every little run became a wild torrent, and the larger creeks spread out like rivers. Bridges were swept away and deep gullies plowed into the ground. The night express train from Chicago, due in Des Moines at 3:40 A. M., consisted of Barnum's advertising car, next to the engine and tender, followed by the baggage and express, then the smoker, two passenger cars and the sleeper—six in all. They passed through Altoona on time, and two miles beyond entered the valley of Little Four Mile, running on fast time. A few minutes later the entire train, with the exception of the sleeper, was lying in the bottom of the raging flood of the creek, a mass of splintered ruins, with the crushed and mangled bodies of more than fifty men, women, and children mingled in the horrid pile. The bridge had washed out, and in the darkness and raging storm the train had gone down in twelve feet of water. The chasm was but little wider than the length of a car, and there, piled on top of the engine, were the splintered remains of five cars. Barnum's car was utterly demolished, and the seven men in it were instantly killed. The engineer was lying dead in his buried engine. The three passenger cars were telescoped together down in the chasm, while the sleeper stood uninjured on the track at its brink. Twenty crushed dead bodies were taken out of the wreck by the people who escaped unhurt, and the citizens who gathered in from the vicinity. Thirty-eight more mangled, crushed, and bleeding living people were rescued from the wreck, some of whom died in fearful agony. So wedged into each other were the telescoped cars that it was five hours before all of the wounded and imprisoned victims were released.

While the state had always treated the railroad companies very liberally, its laws had from the time of the beginning of railroad building affirmed the right of the legislature to control the roads. The first act of railroad legislation, in 1855, re-granting lands to certain roads declared "that railroad companies accepting the provisions of this act, shall at all times be subject to such rules and regulations as may from time to time be enacted and provided for by the general assembly of Iowa." From time to time thereafter, as lands were re-granted, a similar provision was incorporated in the various acts.

In 1871 an organization among farmers, known as the Patrons of Husbandry, began to extend its granges throughout the west. Its objects were to provide for the co-operation of farmers in various ways by which their interests, as a class, might be advanced. One of the abuses which they sought to reform was the regulation or limitation, by law, of freight charges, by railroad companies. In 1871 this movement became so strong in Minnesota and Illinois as to control the legislatures of those states and they passed laws fixing maximum charges for transportation of freight and passengers. In 1873 the Grange movement controlled the legislature of Iowa, and a similar act was passed. The law which went into effect July 4, 1874, in no case compelled the railroads to carry freight at a lower rate than they had voluntarily carried it in the past. The average rates fixed by law were actually higher than the rates at which the railroads had previously carried a large portion of corresponding freight. But the law prevented the roads from charging exorbitant rates at points where there was no competition to keep prices reasonable. The railroad companies made a powerful fight against such legislation and carried cases to the highest courts

to test the constitutionality of the laws. The supreme court of the state and of the United States sustained the laws. These laws remained in force until 1878, when they were repealed and a railroad commission was provided for by act of the legislature. This act did not give the commissioners sufficient power to correct abuses, and after a long and fierce struggle in 1867, the people secured the election of a legislature that gave the railroad commission enlarged power, sufficient to correct most of the evils within the limits of the state.

### KATE SHELLY'S HEROIC DEED.

It was a wild night on the 6th of July, 1881; the rain was coming down like a cloudburst; the fierce wind howled among the swaying tree tops; sharp flashes of lightning and startling claps of thunder shook the houses. It was in the valley and gorges of the east bank of the Des Moines river, where the wild torrents of Honey creek, swollen by the heavy rains, was rushing with a mighty roar towards the river. A bridge on the line of the Northwestern railroad, a few miles west of Boone, spanned this creek. The flood had undermined the abutment and an engine sent out from Boone to inspect the track before the arrival of the eastward bound passenger train, went down through the wrecked bridge in the water, now twenty feet deep. Two men on the engine perished, and two others escaped by clinging to tree tops. The Shelly cabin was near by, where Mrs. Shelly and her sixteen-year-old daughter, Kate, lived. They heard the wild cry of the men as the engine carried them into the torrent below when the bridge went down in the flood. The women heard the cry above the roar of the storm and Kate at once determined to go to the aid of those in peril. She took a miner's lamp and fixed a lantern and started out in the wild storm, towards the railroad bridge, from which the cry of distress seemed to come. Her course was around a bluff for nearly half a mile, through brush and over fallen trees, which tore her clothing and scratched her face and neck. The ground was slippery and pools of water filled every depression. Wet and chilled, torn and bleeding, the brave girl kept on until she reached the roaring torrent where the bridge and engine went down. There, clinging to a tree top, was the engineer, who told her of the disaster and death of his companions. She could do nothing to help him, but knowing that the passenger train would soon be due from the west, she urged the engineer to hold on until she could go to Moingona, a mile distant, and cross the river, to warn the coming train and get help to rescue the men clinging to the trees. When she came to the railroad bridge across the Des Moines river, her light gave out and she could only feel the way over the long bridge which had no floor aside from the cross ties, which were eighteen inches apart. She dare not undertake to walk over these ties in the fierce storm that came with terrific force at that height, against which she could hardly stand. But, crawling on hands and knees, the heroic girl kept on, while the fearful gusts of wind nearly swept her from the bridge many times before she reached the west shore, nearly exhausted, but firm of purpose as ever. Springing to her feet she ran on to the station, gave the alarm and the approaching train was saved from a terrible wreck. An engine was soon started for the wrecked bridge with men and implements to rescue the imperiled survivors, and Kate was taken along as a guide. When they reached the fallen bridge it was necessary to go up the creek until a bridge could be found where they could cross over the swollen torrent to rescue the men on the other side. In all this groping in the dark Kate was the guide, conducting the party down the east bank to where the two men were still clinging to the tree tops, and they were at last rescued, but two others went down to death in the wreck. When all was over, the passenger train saved, and the men rescued, Kate sank down, overcome by the mental strain, the exposure and unparalleled exertions that had carried her through the fearful ordeal, that would have appalled the strongest man. For a long time her recovery was doubtful but a good constitution brought her through. The great railroad company, whose train the heroic girl had saved from an awful fate, by risking her own life, manifested very poor appreciation of her noble deed. It made her a trifling present, and there ended its gratitude. The traveling men presented her with a gold watch as a token of recognition of her brave and humane deed. The state legislature presented to her a gold medal and $200 as a token of the public appreciation of her heroism. For long years Kate was the main support of her widowed mother and younger children, and although her name became known and honored throughout the country, and wherever brave deeds command admiration, her life has been one of hard toil and sacrifices. The sum the Northwestern Railroad company would have paid for a single life among the many that must have been sacrificed but for the heroism of the humble little Irish girl, would have brought comfort and plenty for life to Kate Shelly and the widow's family.

## THE TORNADO OF 1882.

The second great tornado passed over a portion of central Iowa on the early evening of Saturday, June 17, 1882. It was first seen by the citizens of Greene county about 4 o'clock. An eye witness at Angus, in Boone county, writes that "It hung over us for nearly an hour, whirling and increasing in volume as the clouds from the northwest met those from the southeast, joining together and whirling as the huge mass started off southeast. The column,

after traveling rapidly for a few minutes, seemed to put forth a pointer to the earth, and immediately there arose from the column a black, seething mass, and it traveled rapidly towards Ogden. It was a grand and fearful sight. I have seen waterspouts at sea and this looked exactly like them." It seems first to have reached the ground on the west side of the Des Moines river, some six miles northwest of Madrid, where the destruction began, taking houses, barns, and trees, killing people and stock. Passing on through Story county, about six miles south of Ames, and bearing southeast into Jasper, and on to Poweshiek, sometimes raising from the ground for several miles, and again descending to the earth, destroying everything in its path. As the great black mass of clouds swept on in a general easterly course, small whirlwinds seemed to be forming from time to time, some suspended high in the air, and again lowering downward until they swept the earth with irresistible force. Central Iowa seemed to be in a vast cyclone pressure, as it developed terrific storms in Keokuk, Johnson, and Henry counties, all doing more or less damage. The great storm cloud moved at the rate of about forty-five miles an hour on its easterly course, and tornadoes or whirlwinds were continually forming and disappearing. The velocity of the wind in the whirlwinds, or rotary motion, was estimated to be 200 miles an hour. The cyclone conditions continued until June 24th, doing great damage in Buchanan, Palo Alto, Clarke, Sioux, Clay, and other counties.

The greatest destruction was in the college town of Grinnell. The first indications of the impending horror at this place are described as follows: "The peculiar aspect of the sky was very striking towards night. The northern sky was hung with conical, downward pointing clouds, the like of which none of us had ever seen. After sunset the western horizon and sky, half way up to the zenith, was lurid, brilliant and unearthly, an ominous sight, which fascinated while it filled one with ill-defined dread. Almost before the brilliant apparition in the west disappeared the storm broke. It came with an awful roar, like a dozen heavy freight trains passing rapidly over a long bridge. Chimneys, trees, barns, and houses were torn to pieces and were hurled through the air. The total darkness that had suddenly come down was now lighted up by continuous flashes of lightning, and the mighty power of the whirlwind swept everything from the face of the earth. Then came a deluge of water, as though a cloud had burst and emptied a lake upon the earth. In going through the first quarter of the town the waterspout, or whirlwind, performed one of its great loops or quarter circles, in which it appeared to turn about every three miles. It struck Grinnell on its highest land, along the ridge of its best and finest houses, and no pen can picture and no mind comprehend the instant and utter ruin it wrought, and the swath of death and desolation it left in its path, all done in less than three minutes. As the tornado turned this first loop, crashing in pieces every house in its pathway, it killed, mutilated, and so completely covered with mud the bodies, that they could not be recognized until they were washed. It swept houses so completely out of existence that nothing was left of the structures but the cellars. It tore great trees into splinters, and stripped the bark entirely off of others. It passed on with its gyrating motion and loops, crushing two more squares filled with beautiful homes. Then the two fine college buildings went down in shapeless ruins before its irresistible power. It hurled thirty loaded cars from the Central railroad, then rushed away down the valley of Bear creek and hurled a

loss in property of the last, though traversing but about one-third of the distance of the former, was considerably greater, and the loss of life about one-third of that of 1860.

J. L. Brown, auditor of state, was re-elected at the election of 1884, to serve two years from January 1, 1885. When he filed his bond for a second term, Governor Sherman declined to approve it, for the following reason: "That the auditor had not accounted for the funds and property in his hands during his first term, as the law specifically requires." A commission was appointed by the governor to examine into the affairs of the auditor's office, and upon their report, the governor issued an order suspending the auditor from office. The auditor declined to vacate the office, and on the 19th of March, 1885, the auditor

*Iowa Capitol Building, Des Moines—from the west.*

Rock Island train in the ditch, crushing to death two men in its fall. Six miles from Grinnell it swept through the village of Malcom, leaving death and destruction in its path.

Thirty-nine people were killed in Grinnell and thirty others along the line of the tornado and nearly 500, more or less, injured, of whom many died. In Grinnell the property loss was estimated at $400,000, and outside of Grinnell at $500,000; 150 buildings were destroyed in Grinnell.

Governor Sherman issued an appeal to the people of the state for aid for the sufferers, which was most liberally responded to by the people. The line traversed by this tornado was about 150 miles in length, while that of the great tornado of 1860, was about 450. But twenty-two years had given the state such a vast increase in population, that the

was forcibly ejected from the office by the military power of the state, by order of the governor. J. W. Cattell was appointed by the governor on the same day to fill the position. After the expiration of Governor Sherman's term of office and the inauguration of Governor Larrabee, J. L Brown was reinstated. At the session of the legislature of 1886, a committee was appointed to investigate the auditor's office, and upon its report, charges were filed against J. L. Brown, auditor, and upon these charges the house presented articles of impeachment, and the senate proceeded to try the case against Auditor Brown, as a court of impeachment.

On the 13th of April Mr. Brown was again suspended from office pending the trial, and Charles Beardsley was appointed to fill the place. There were thirty articles of impeachment against the auditor. The principal charges were the following:

Article 1 charges that from 1883 to 1885 Brown received fees for copies of official records to the amount of $600, and failed to account for them.

Articles 7, 8, 9 and 10 charge official misconduct in the examination of the Bremer County bank.

Articles 12, 13, 14 and 15 charge that he drew certain warrants for clerk hire without taking vouchers for them.

Articles 16 and 17 charge that Brown resisted the governor's order of suspension, and exercised the duties of auditor after suspension.

Articles 20, 21, 22, 23 and 24 charge official misconduct in relation to his deputy, Stewart, and their examination of banks.

Articles 28, 29 and 30 charge that his examiners of insurance companies were permitted to extort exorbitant fees from several companies.

After a lengthy trial, the senate, on the 13th day of July, voted upon the various articles of impeachment. Every senator was in his seat and voted.

On articles 1, 2, 3, 4, 5 and 6 every senator voted "not guilty." The largest vote for conviction was on article 17, which charged Brown with resisting the governor's order of suspension, and exercising the functions of auditor after he was suspended and before he was reinstated. On these charges fifteen senators voted "guilty" and thirty-five voted "not guilty." It required thirty-three votes to convict.

The auditor was acquitted on every charge by more than two-thirds of the votes of a full senate, and on the next day—July 14th— was reinstated in office.

Several years after, the legislature, by a two-thirds vote, refunded to J. L. Brown the amount he had expended for the employment of attorneys to defend his right to the office from which he was removed or suspended.

---

## CHAPTER XIX.

*The Tornado of 1893—Fifty Years a State—Iowa Governors, Lieutenant-Governors, United States Senators, Representatives in Congress, Supreme Judges, Secretaries, Auditors, Treasurers of State and Attorney-Generals.*

### THE TORNADO OF 1893.

The third great tornado which has visited Iowa since it begun to be settled by white people began near Quimby, in Cherokee county, late in the afternoon of July 6, 1893. It is described by those who first saw it as forming from two black clouds approaching each other, one coming from the southwest, the other from the northwest. The air had been very sultry, and as these clouds came swiftly together a cool breeze sprang up from the east. As the clouds rushed fiercely together, the fatal waterspout form of dense blackness began rapidly to reach down like the huge trunk of an elephant, and the deadly work began. As the people saw the swaying, black trail strike the ground, they realized that a terrible tornado was coming, and most of those at home ran into the cellars or caves. In nearly all cases these proved to be places of safety. Its path was narrow, but in this fatal line of march houses, barns, people and animals were hurled like feathers in a breeze. Nothing but the solid earth could stand before its mighty power. On the serpent-like trail swept, leaving destruction, death and desolation in its path. It passed on in a southeasterly direction into Buena Vista county. Sometimes the destroying trail raised from the ground for several miles, and again it would drop down, sweeping everything off the face of the earth. It went through Storm Lake, raising the water 100 feet in the air, just

missing the town of the same name and on towards Fonda, taking farm buildings and leaving dead and mangled people in its track. Sometimes from three to four of the black trails would be seen hanging from the mass of clouds, one reaching the ground and others suspended in the air, all sending off a fearful roaring sound. It passed south of Fonda and struck Pomeroy at about 6:40 P. M. It passed through the residence part of the town, making complete destruction over a space 1,200 feet in width, and partial destruction for a width of 1,800 feet. Twenty blocks were swept clean of every thing above ground, and 80 per cent of the residences of the town were destroyed. The human victims bore evidence on their persons that the air was filled with swiftly moving splinters, sand, mud, plaster, limbs of trees and other movable objects.

Those who were near the path of destruction but just missed it, described the appearance as it struck the town, as a rolling, whirling, writhing mass of greenish blackness from and through which millions of tongues of electric flame darted and twisted in fearful fantastic shapes. The sight was grand, awful and harrowing to the strongest nerves. The survivors who were just outside of the terrible path, and first looked upon the ground, say that for a few minutes, not a living object was seen. Every live person was stunned. They wondered if there was a living person in the path of destruction. But soon the wail of distress began. The cries of agony, the groans of anguish, and the calls for help.

The rain was falling in torrents and women and children were calling frantically for the members of their families. Darkness soon came down on the scene of awful desolation, where the survivors were busy rescuing the wounded. Out of a population of 1,000 persons but twenty-one families were left with no dead or wounded of their own to care for. A citizen says "the heartaches of the uninjured almost equaled the sufferings of those whose mangled bodies could not much longer contain the breath of life. Men, women and children were tortured in nearly all the cruel modes that the ingenious savage could contrive, for while none were consumed by flames, yet many were scorched and burned by the subtle fluid accompanying the death-dealing tornado. Some had rough stakes thrust into their bodies to the depth of several inches; some had limbs crushed, broken or torn from their bodies, while others were scalped as savagely as though done by an Indian. One woman's scalp was torn back on top of her head, and then a nail had been driven deep into the tender place left open. People were rushing to and fro frantic with grief and anxiety for missing relatives or friends, and many were too overwhelmed for expression in words or cries. The number killed and fatally injured in Pomeroy was forty-nine, and in other places twenty-two, making the total number of deaths from the tornado, seventy-one. One hundred and fifty homes were destroyed and the property loss was estimated to exceed $250,000. Two hundred and thirty-seven people were wounded who survived, many badly crippled for life. Governor Boies issued an appeal to the public for aid for those who lost their homes and property, and the people responded liberally. The amount contributed in money was over $69,000, while food, clothing, lumber and other supplies worth many thousands more were donated by the people. The entire track of the tornado was less than sixty miles in length. In comparing the three great tornadoes that have visited Iowa, we find that all originated in northwestern Iowa, and were first seen forming between 4 and 5 o'clock in the afternoon of June and July days. Their comparative magnitude may be judged from the following items:

Date, 1860; miles traversed, 450; number killed, 194; value of property destroyed, $700,000.

Date, 1882; miles traversed, 150; number killed, 69; value of property destroyed, $900,000.

Date, 1893; miles traversed, 60; number killed, 71; value of property destroyed, $250,000.

It was fifty years on the 28th day of December, 1896, since Iowa became a state in the union. At the time of its admission its population was 102,388. It is now more than 2,000,000. During this fifty years there has been brought under cultivation more than 25,000,000 acres of wild prairie. The farms thus made, in 1895 yielded products to the value of more than $400,000,000. The value of the products of our mines and factories was more than $70,000,000. The assessed value of the entire property of the state has in that time increased from $12,271,000 to $559,650,000, while the actual value has grown to $2,800,000,000, of which the farms are estimated to be worth $1,088,000,000.

Our state has now 8,486 miles of railroad penetrating every one of its ninety-nine counties, leaving no farm in the entire state twenty miles distant from some line of transportation.

The state has formulated an educational system not surpassed by any in the union, under which 530,000 children in our common schools annually receive free instruction, while 268 academies, colleges and universities have been established, which furnish higher education. We have 15,613 schoolhouses, exceeding in value the entire property of the state fifty years ago.

Steady progress in other directions is shown by 5,000 churches, 1,019 newspapers and periodicals and 152 public libraries, which have grown up in the state.

When the war of the rebellion broke out, Iowa sent more than 78,000 of her stalwart young men to swell the ranks of the union army, of which 11,000 perished in that terrible war. Our state furnished officers competent to command armies and military departments. It has given the nation some of its most illustrious statesmen, judges and soldiers.

––––

TERRITORIAL OFFICERS FROM 1838 TO 1846.

––

GOVERNORS.

Robert Lucas; appointed 1838.
John Chambers; appointed 1841.
James Clarke; appointed November, 1845.

SECRETARIES.

William C. Conway; appointed 1838; died in office, November, 1839.
James Clarke; appointed 1839.
O. H. W. Stull; appointed 1841.
Samuel J. Burr; appointed 1843.
Jesse Williams; appointed 1845.

AUDITORS.
(Office created January 7, 1840.)

Jesse Williams; appointed January 14, 1840.
William L. Gilbert; appointed January 23, 1843; reappointed February 27, 1844.
Robert M. Secrest; appointed 1845.

TREASURERS.
(Office created January 24, 1839.)

Thornton Bayless; appointed January 23, 1839.
Morgon Reno; appointed 1840.

DELEGATES IN CONGRESS.

William W. Chapman, from 1838 to 1840.
A. C. Dodge, from 1841 to 1847.

SUPREME COURT.

Charles Mason, chief justice, 1838 to 1846.
Joseph Williams, associate justice, 1838 to 1846.
Thomas S. Wilson, associate justice, 1838 to 1846.

---

STATE OFFICERS FROM 1846 TO 1899.

---

GOVERNORS.

Ansel Briggs, Jackson county; elected October 26, 1846.
Stephen Hempstead, Dubuque county; elected August 5, 1850.
James W. Grimes, Des Moines county; elected August 3, 1854.
Ralph P. Lowe, Lee county; elected October 13, 1857.
Samuel J. Kirkwood, Johnson county; elected October 11, 1859.
Samuel J. Kirkwood, Johnson county; re-elected October 8, 1861.
William M. Stone, Marion county; elected October 13, 1863.
William M. Stone, Marion county; re-elected October 10, 1865.
Samuel Merrill, Clayton county; elected October 8, 1867.
Samuel Merrill, Clayton county; re-elected October 12, 1869.
Cyrus C. Carpenter, Webster county; elected October 10, 1871.
Cyrus C. Carpenter, Webster county; re-elected October 14, 1873.
Samuel J. Kirkwood, Johnson county; elected October 12, 1875; resigned February 1, 1877, having been elected United States senator.
Joshua G. Newbold, Henry county; lieutenant-governor; took oath of office as governor February 1, 1877.
John H. Gear, Des Moines county; elected October 9, 1877.
John H. Gear, Des Moines county; re-elected October 14, 1879.
Buren R. Sherman, Benton county; elected October 11, 1881.
Buren R. Sherman, Benton county; re-elected October 9, 1883.
William Larrabee, Fayette county; elected November 3, 1885.
William Larrabee, Fayette county; re-elected November 8, 1887.
Horace Boies, Black Hawk county; elected November 5, 1889.
Horace Boies, Black Hawk county; re-elected November 3, 1891.
Frank D. Jackson, Polk county; elected November 7, 1893.
Francis M. Drake, Appanoose county; elected November 5, 1895.
Leslie M. Shaw, Crawford county; elected November 2, 1897.

LIEUTENANT-GOVERNORS.

(Office created September 3, 1857, by the new constitution.)

Oran Faville, Mitchell county; elected October 13, 1857.
Nicholas J. Rusch, Scott county; elected October 11, 1859.
John R. Needham, Mahaska county; elected October 8, 1861.
Enoch W. Eastman, Hardin county; elected October 13, 1863.
Benjamin F. Gue, Webster county; elected October 10, 1865.
John Scott, Story county; elected October 8, 1867.
Madison M. Walden, Appanoose county; qualified January 14, 1870; resigned 1871.
Henry C. Bulis, Winneshiek county; appointed by the governor September 13, 1871, and elected to the office October 10, 1871.
Joseph Dysart, Tama county; elected October 14, 1873.
Joshua G. Newbold, Henry county; elected October 12, 1875; became governor February, 1877.
Frank T. Campbell, Jasper county; elected November 9, 1877; re-elected October 14, 1879.
Orlando H. Manning, Carroll county; elected October 11, 1881; re-elected October 9, 1883; resigned October 12, 1885.
John A. T. Hull, Polk county; elected November 3, 1885; re-elected November 8, 1887.
Alfred N. Poyneer, Tama county, elected November 5, 1889.
Samuel L. Bestow, Lucas county; elected November 3, 1891.
Warren S. Dungan, Lucas county; elected November 7, 1893.
Matt Parrott, Black Hawk county; elected November 5, 1895.
J. C. Milliman, Harrison county; elected November 2, 1897.

---

REPRESENTATION IN CONGRESS.

---

XXIX CONGRESS—1846 TO 1847.

*U. S. Senators.*

First General Assembly failed to elect.

*Representatives.*

S. Clinton Hastings, Muscatine.
Shepherd Leffler, Burlington.

XXX CONGRESS—1847 TO 1849.

*U. S. Senators.*

Augustus C. Dodge, Burlington; elected December 7, 1848.

George W. Jones, Dubuque; elected December 7, 1848.

*Representatives.*

William Thompson, Mt. Pleasant, First district.
Shepherd Leffler, Burlington, Second district.

XXXI CONGRESS—1849 TO 1851.

*U. S. Senators.*

George W. Jones, Dubuque.
Augustus C. Dodge, Burlington; re-elected January 10, 1849.

*Representatives.*

First session, William Thompson, Mt. Pleasant, First district; unseated by the house of representatives on a contest, and the election remanded to the people.
Second session, Daniel F. Miller, Ft. Madison, First district; elected September 4, 1850.
Shepherd Leffler, Burlington, Second district.

XXXII CONGRESS—1851 TO 1853.

*U. S. Senators.*

George W. Jones, Dubuque.
Augustus C. Dodge, Burlington.

*Representatives.*

Bernhart Henn, Fairfield, First district.
Lincoln Clark, Dubuque, Second district.

XXXIII CONGRESS—1853 TO 1855.

*U. S. Senators.*

Augustus C. Dodge, Burlington.
George W. Jones, Dubuque; re-elected December 21, 1852.

*Representatives.*

Bernhart Henn, Fairfield, First district.
John P. Cook, Davenport, Second district.

XXXIV CONGRESS—1855 TO 1857.

*U. S. Senators.*

George W. Jones, Dubuque.
James Harlan, Mt. Pleasant; elected January 6, 1855, and January 17, 1857.*

*Representatives.*

Augustus Hall, Keosauqua, First district.
James Thorington, Davenport, Second district.

XXXV CONGRESS—1857 TO 1859.

*U. S. Senators.*

George W. Jones, Dubuque.
James Harlan, Mt. Pleasant.

*Representatives.*

Samuel R. Curtis, Keokuk, First district.
Timothy Davis, Elkader, Second district.

XXXVI CONGRESS—1859 TO 1861.

*U. S. Senators.*

James Harlan, Mt. Pleasant.
James W. Grimes, Burlington; elected January 26, 1858.

*Representatives.*

Samuel R. Curtis, Keokuk, First district.
William Vandever, Dubuque, Second district.

XXXVII CONGRESS—1861 TO 1863.

*U. S. Senators.*

James Harlan, Mt. Pleasant; re-elected January 11, 1860.
James W. Grimes, Burlington.

*Representatives.*

First session, Samuel R. Curtis, Keokuk, First district.†
Second and third sessions, James F. Wilson, Fairfield, First district; elected October 8, 1861.
William Vandever, Dubuque, Second district.

XXXVIII CONGRESS—1863 TO 1865.

*U. S. Senators.*

James Harlan, Mt. Pleasant.
James W. Grimes, Burlington.

*Representatives.*

James F. Wilson, Fairfield, First district.
Hiram Price, Davenport, Second district.
William B. Allison, Dubuque, Third district.
Josiah B. Grinnell, Grinnell, Fourth district.
John A. Kasson, Des Moines, Fifth district.
Asahel W. Hubbard, Sioux City, Sixth district.

XXXIX CONGRESS—1865 TO 1867.

*U. S. Senators.*

James Harlan, Mt. Pleasant.‡
James W. Grimes, Burlington.
Samuel J. Kirkwood, Iowa City; elected January 13, 1866.

*Representatives.*

James F. Wilson, Fairfield, First district.
Hiram Price, Davenport, Second district.
William B. Allison, Dubuque, Third district.
Josiah B. Grinnell, Grinnell, Fourth district.
John A. Kasson, Des Moines, Fifth district.
Asahel W. Hubbard, Sioux City, Sixth district.

XL CONGRESS—1867 TO 1869.

*U. S. Senators.*

James W. Grimes, Burlington.
James Harlan, Mt. Pleasant; elected January 13, 1866.

*Representatives.*

James F. Wilson, Fairfield, First district.
Hiram Price, Davenport, Second district.

*Election declared illegal by the U. S. senate, January 21, 1857; again elected as above.
†Vacated seat by acceptance of commission as brigadier-general, and J. F. Wilson chosen as his successor.
‡Became secretary of the interior May 1, 1865, and resigned his seat in the senate. Samuel J. Kirkwood chosen his successor as above.

William B. Allison, Dubuque, Third district.
William Loughridge, Oskaloosa, Fourth district.
Grenville M. Dodge, Council Bluffs, Fifth district.
Asahel W. Hubbard, Sioux City, Sixth district.

### XLI CONGRESS—1869 TO 1871.

*U. S. Senators.*

James Harlan, Mt. Pleasant.
James B. Howell, Keokuk; elected January 20, 1870, to fill vacancy caused by the resignation of James W. Grimes.

*Representatives.*

George W. McCrary, Keokuk, First district.
William Smyth, Marion, Second district.
William B. Allison, Dubuque, Third district.
William Loughridge, Oskaloosa, Fourth district.
Frank W. Palmer, Des Moines, Fifth district.
Charles Pomeroy, Sixth district.

### XLII CONGRESS—1871 TO 1873.

*U. S. Senators.*

James Harlan, Mt. Pleasant.
George G. Wright, Des Moines; elected January 20, 1870; term commenced March 4, 1871.

*Representatives.*

George W. McCrary, Keokuk, First district.
Aylett R. Cotton, Clinton, Second district.
W. G. Donnan, Independence, Third district.
Madison M. Walden, Centerville, Fourth district.
Frank W. Palmer, Des Moines, Fifth district.
Jackson Orr, Boonsboro, Sixth district.

### XLIII CONGRESS—1873 TO 1875.

*U. S. Senators.*

George G. Wright, Des Moines.
William B. Allison, Dubuque; elected January 16, 1872; term commenced March 4, 1873.

*Representatives.*

George W. McCrary, Keokuk, First district.
Aylett R. Cotton, Clinton, Second district.
William G. Donnan, Independence, Third district.
Henry O. Pratt, Charles City, Fourth district.
James Wilson, Traer, Fifth district.
William Loughridge, Oskaloosa, Sixth district.
John A. Kasson, Des Moines, Seventh district.
James W. McDill, Afton, Eighth district.
Jackson Orr, Boonsboro, Ninth district.

### XLIV CONGRESS—1875 TO 1877.

*U. S. Senators.*

George G. Wright, Des Moines.
William B. Allison, Dubuque.

*Representatives.*

George W. McCrary, Keokuk, First district.
John Q. Tufts, Tipton, Second district.

L. L. Ainsworth, West Union, Third district.
Henry O. Pratt, Charles City, Fourth district.
James Wilson, Traer, Fifth district.
Ezekiel S. Sampson, Sigourney, Sixth district.
John A. Kasson, Des Moines, Seventh district.
James W. McDill, Afton, Eighth district.
Addison Oliver, Onawa, Ninth district.

### XLV CONGRESS—1877 TO 1879.

*U. S. Senators.*

William B. Allison, Dubuque.
Samuel J. Kirkwood, Iowa City; elected January 25, 1876.

*Representatives.*

J. C. Stone, Burlington, First district.
Hiram Price, Davenport, Second district.
T. W. Burdick, Decorah, Third district.
N. C. Deering, Osage, Fourth district.
Rush Clark, Iowa City, Fifth district.
E. S. Sampson, Sigourney, Sixth district.
H. J. B. Cummings, Winterset, Seventh district.
W. F. Sapp, Council Bluffs, Eighth district.
Addison Oliver, Onawa, Ninth district.

### XLVI CONGRESS—1879 TO 1881.

*U. S. Senators.*

William B. Allison, Dubuque; elected January 29, 1878.
Samuel J. Kirkwood, Iowa City.

*Representatives.*

M. A. McCoid, Fairfield, First district.
Hiram Price, Davenport, Second district.
Thomas Updegraff, McGregor, Third district.
N. C. Deering, Osage, Fourth district.
Rush Clark, Iowa City, Fifth district.
J. B. Weaver, Bloomfield, Sixth district.
E. H. Gillette, Des Moines, Seventh district.
William F. Sapp, Council Bluffs, Eighth district.
C. C. Carpenter, Ft. Dodge, Ninth district.

### XLVII CONGRESS—1881 TO 1883.

*U. S. Senators.*

James W. McDill, Afton; appointed by the governor, March 8, 1881, to fill vacancy by resignation of S. J. Kirkwood.
William B. Allison, Dubuque.

*Representatives.*

M. A. McCoid, Fairfield, First district.
S. S. Farwell, Monticello, Second district.
Thomas Updegraff, McGregor, Third district.
N. C. Deering, Osage, Fourth district.
W. G. Thompson, Marion, Fifth district.
M. E. Cutts, Oskaloosa, Sixth district
John A. Kasson, Des Moines, Seventh district.
W. P. Hepburn, Clarinda, Eighth district.
C. C. Carpenter, Ft. Dodge, Ninth district.

XLVIII CONGRESS—1883 TO 1885.

*U. S. Senators.*

William B. Allison, Dubuque.
James F. Wilson, Fairfield; elected January 17, 1882.

*Representatives.*

M. A. McCoid, Fairfield, First district.
J. H. Murphy, Davenport, Second district.
David B. Henderson, Dubuque, Third district.
L. H. Weller, Nashua, Fourth district.
James Wilson, Traer, Fifth district.
M. E. Cutts, Oskaloosa, Sixth district.
John A. Kasson, Des Moines, Seventh district.
William P. Hepburn, Clarinda, Eighth district.
W. H. M. Pusey, Council Bluffs, Ninth district.
A. J. Holmes, Boone, Tenth district.
Isaac S. Struble, Le Mars, Eleventh district.

XLIX CONGRESS—1885 to 1887.

*U. S. Senators.*

William B. Allison, Dubuque, elected January 16, 1884.
James F. Wilson, Fairfield.

*Representatives.*

B. J. Hall, Burlington, First district.
J. H. Murphy, Davenport, Second district.
David B. Henderson, Dubuque, Third district.
William E. Fuller, West Union, Fourth district.
B. F. Frederick, Marshalltown, Fifth district.
J. B. Weaver, Bloomfield, Sixth district.
H. Y. Smith, Des Moines (to fill vacancy), Seventh district.
W. P. Hepburn, Clarinda, Eighth district.
Joseph H. Lyman, Council Bluffs, Ninth district.
A. J. Holmes, Boone, Tenth district.
Isaac S. Struble, Le Mars, Eleventh district.

L CONGRESS—1887 TO 1889.

*U. S. Senators.*

William B. Allison, Dubuque.
James F. Wilson, Fairfield.

*Representatives.*

John H. Gear, Burlington, First district.
Walter I. Hayes, Clinton, Second district.
David B. Henderson, Dubuque, Third district.
William E. Fuller, West Union, Fourth district.
Daniel Kerr, Grundy Center, Fifth district.
James B. Weaver, Bloomfield, Sixth district.
E. H. Conger, Des Moines, Seventh district.
A. R. Anderson, Sidney, Eighth district.
Joseph Lyman, Council Bluffs, Ninth district.
A. J. Holmes, Boone, Tenth district.
Isaac S. Struble, Le Mars, Eleventh district.

* E. R. Hayes elected in 1890, to fill vacancy caused by resignation of E. H. Conger.

LI CONGRESS—1889 TO 1891.

*U. S. Senators.*

William B. Allison, Dubuque.
James F. Wilson, Fairfield; elected January 18, 1888.

*Representatives.*

John H. Gear, Burlington, First district.
Walter I. Hayes, Clinton, Second district.
David B. Henderson, Dubuque, Third district.
J. H. Sweney, Osage, Fourth district.
David Kerr, Grundy Center, Fifth district.
John F. Lacey, Oskaloosa, Sixth district.
Edwin H. Conger, Des Moines; E. R. Hays, Knoxville, Seventh district.*
James P. Flick, Bedford, Eighth district.
Joseph R. Reed, Council Bluffs, Ninth district.
J. P. Dolliver, Fort Dodge, Tenth district.
Isaac S. Struble, LeMars, Eleventh district.

LII CONGRESS—1891 TO 1893.

*U. S. Senators.*

William B. Allison, Dubuque; elected March 4, 1890.
James F. Wilson, Fairfield.

*Representatives.*

J. J. Seerley, Burlington, First district.
Walter I. Hayes, Clinton, Second district.
David B. Henderson, Dubuque, Third district.
W. H. Butler, West Union, Fourth district.
J. T. Hamilton, Cedar Rapids, Fifth district.
F. E. White, Hedrick, Sixth district.
J. A. T. Hull, Des Moines, Seventh district.
James P. Flick, Bedford, Eighth district.
Thomas Bowman, Council Bluffs, Ninth district.
J. P. Dolliver, Fort Dodge, Tenth district.
George D. Perkins, Sioux City, Eleventh district.

LIII CONGRESS—1893 TO 1895.

*U. S. Senators.*

William B. Allison, Dubuque.
James F. Wilson, Fairfield.

*Representatives.*

John H. Gear, Burlington, First district.
Walter I. Hayes, Clinton, Second district.
David B. Henderson, Dubuque, Third district.
Thomas Updegraff, McGregor, Fourth district.
Robert G. Cousins, Tipton, Fifth district.
John F. Lacey, Oskaloosa, Sixth district.
J. A. T. Hull, Des Moines, Seventh district.
W. P. Hepburn, Clarinda, Eighth district.
A. L. Hager, Greenfield, Ninth district.
J. P. Dolliver, Ft. Dodge, Tenth district.
George D. Perkins, Sioux City, Eleventh district.

LIV CONGRESS—1895 TO 1897.

*U. S. Senators.*

William B. Allison, Dubuque.
John H. Gear, Burlington; elected January 16, 1894.

*Representatives.*

Samuel M. Clark, Keokuk, First district.
George M. Curtis, Clinton, Second district.
David B. Henderson, Dubuque, Third district.
Thomas Updegraff, McGregor, Fourth district.
Robert G. Cousins, Tipton, Fifth district.
John F. Lacey, Oskaloosa, Sixth district.
J. A. T. Hull, Des Moines, Seventh district.
W. P. Hepburn, Clarinda, Eighth district.
A. L. Hager, Greenfield, Ninth district.
J. P. Dolliver, Ft. Dodge, Tenth district.
George D. Perkins, Sioux City, Eleventh district.

LV CONGRESS—1897 TO 1899.

*U. S. Senators.*

William B. Allison, Dubuque; elected January, 1896.
John H. Gear, Burlington.

*Representatives.*

Samuel M. Clark, Keokuk, First district.
George M. Curtis, Clinton, Second district.
David B. Henderson, Dubuque, Third district.
Thomas Updegraff, McGregor, Fourth district.
Robert G. Cousins, Tipton, Fifth district.
John F. Lacey, Oskaloosa, Sixth district.
J. A. T. Hull, Des Moines, Seventh district.
W. P. Hepburn, Clarinda, Eighth district.
A. L. Hager, Greenfield, Ninth district.
J. P. Dolliver, Ft. Dodge, Tenth district.
George D. Perkins, Sioux City, Eleventh district.

LVI CONGRESS—1899 TO 1901.

*U. S. Senators.*

William B. Allison, Dubuque.
John H. Gear, Burlington.

*Representatives.*

Thomas Hedge, Burlington, First district.
Joseph R. Lane, Davenport, Second district.
David B. Henderson, Dubuque, Third district.
Gilbert N. Haugen, Northwood, Fourth district.
Robert G. Cousins, Tipton, Fifth district.
John F. Lacey, Oskaloosa, Sixth district.
J. A. T. Hull, Des Moines, Seventh district.
William P. Hepburn, Clarinda, Eighth district.
Smith McPherson, Red Oak, Ninth district.
J. P. Dolliver, Ft. Dodge, Tenth district.
Lot Thomas, Storm Lake, Eleventh district.

---

## SUPREME COURT OF IOWA.

### CHIEF JUSTICES.

Charles Mason, Des Moines county; resigned in June, 1847.
Joseph Williams, Muscatine county; appointed by the governor June, 1847; term expired January 25, 1848, by constitutional limitation.

S. Clinton Hastings, Muscatine county; appointed by the governor January 26, 1848; term expired January 15, 1849.
Joseph Williams, Muscatine county; elected by the general assembly December 7, 1848, and commissioned December 26, 1848, for six years—from January 15, 1849.
George G. Wright, Van Buren county; elected January 5, 1855.
Ralph P. Lowe, Lee county; elected judge October 11, 1859, with Caleb Baldwin and Lacon D. Stockton, and, drawing the shortest term, became chief justice.
Caleb Baldwin, Pottawattamie county; elected as above, and drawing the second shortest term, became chief justice January 1, 1862.
George G. Wright, Van Buren county; January 1, 1864.
Ralph P. Lowe, Lee county; January 1, 1866.
John F. Dillon, Scott county; January 1, 1868.
Chester C. Cole, Polk county; January 1, 1870.
James G. Day, Fremont county; January 1, 1871.
Joseph M. Beck, Lee county; January 1, 1872, and January 1, 1873.
William E. Miller, Johnson county; January 1, 1874, and January 1, 1875.
Chester C. Cole, Polk county; January 1, 1876; resigned January 17, 1876.
William H. Seevers, Mahaska county; February 17, 1876.
James G. Day, Fremont county; January 1, 1877.
James H. Rothrock, Cedar county; January 1, 1878.
Joseph M. Beck, Lee county; January 1, 1879.
Austin Adams, Dubuque county; January 1, 1880, and January 1, 1881.
William H. Seevers, Mahaska county; January 1, 1882.
James G. Day, Fremont county; January 1, 1883.
James H. Rothrock, Linn county; January 1, 1884.
Joseph M. Beck, Lee county; January 1, 1885.
Austin Adams, Dubuque county; January 1, 1886 and 1887.
William H. Seevers, Mahaska county; January 1, 1888.
Joseph R. Reed, Pottawattamie county; January 1, 1889; resigned February 28, 1889.
Josiah Given, Polk county; March 12, 1889.
James H. Rothrock, Linn county; January 1, 1890.
Joseph M. Beck, Lee county; January 1, 1891.
Gifford S. Robinson, Buena Vista county, January 1, 1892.
Charles T. Granger, Allamakee county; January 1, 1894.
Josiah Given, Polk county; January 1, 1895.
James H. Rothrock, Linn county; January 1, 1896.
L. G. Kinne, Tama county; January 1, 1897.
Horace E. Deemer, Montgomery county; January 1, 1898.
Gifford S. Robinson, Woodbury county; January 1, 1899.

## ASSOCIATE JUDGES.

Joseph Williams, Muscatine county; appointed chief justice June, 1847.

Thomas S. Wilson, Dubuque county; resigned in October, 1847.

John F. Kinney, Lee county; appointed by the governor June 12, 1847, and again January 26, 1848; elected by the general assembly and commissioned December 8th; resignation accepted January 20, 1854, to take effect February 15th.

George Green, Dubuque county; appointed by the governor November 1, 1847; and again January 26, 1848; elected by the general assembly December 7, 1848; term of office commenced January 15, 1849; succeeded by W. G. Woodward.

Jonathan C. Hall, Des Moines county; appointed by the governor January 20, 1854, to succeed Kinney, resigned; succeeded by N. W. Isbell.

William G. Woodward, Muscatine county: elected by the general assembly January 5, 1855.

Norman W. Isbell, Linn county; elected by the general assembly January 6, 1855; resigned in 1856.

Lacon D. Stockton, Des Moines county; appointed by the governor May 17, 1856, vice Isbell, resigned; elected by the general assembly January 12, 1857; re-elected, under the present constitution, October 11, 1859; died June 9, 1860

Caleb Baldwin, Pottawattamie county; elected October 11, 1859.

George G. Wright, Van Buren county; appointed by the governor June 19, 1860, vice Stockton, deceased; elected November 6, 1860; re-elected October 10, 1865.

Ralph P. Lowe, Lee county; elected October 11, 1859; re-elected October 8, 1861.

John F. Dillon, Scott county; elected October 13, 1863, vice Baldwin.

Chester C. Cole, Polk county; appointed March 1, 1864, by the governor; elected November 8, 1864; re-elected October 11, 1870; resigned January 13, 1876.

Joseph M. Beck, Lee county; elected October 8, 1867; re-elected October 14, 1873; re-elected October 14, 1879; re-elected November 3, 1885.

Elias H. Williams, Clayton county; appointed by the governor January 19, 1870; resigned September 14, 1870.

James G. Day, Fremont county; appointed by the governor September 1, 1870, to succeed Judge Wright; elected October 11, 1870; re-elected October 10, 1871; re-elected October 9, 1877.

William E Miller, Johnson county; appointed by the governor September 14, 1870, to succeed Judge Williams; elected October 11, 1870.

Austin Adams, Dubuque county; elected October 12, 1875; re-elected October 11, 1881.

James H. Rothrock, Cedar county; appointed by the governor February 24, 1876; elected November 7, 1876, for unexpired term; re-elected November 5, 1878; re-elected November 4, 1884; re-elected November 4, 1890.

William H. Seevers, Mahaska county; appointed February 16, 1876, to fill vacancy caused by resignation of C. C. Cole; elected November 7, 1876, for balance of the unexpired term; elected November 7, 1876, for full term commencing January 1, 1867; re-elected November 7, 1882.

Joseph R. Reed, Pottawattamie county; elected October 9, 1883; resigned February 28, 1889.

Gifford S. Robinson, Buena Vista county; elected November 8, 1887; re-elected November 7, 1893.

Charles T. Granger, Allamakee county; elected November 6, 1888; re-elected November 6, 1894.

Josiah Given, Polk county; appointed March 12, 1889, to fill vacancy caused by resignation of Joseph R. Reed; elected November 5, 1889, for balance of unexpired term; elected November 5, 1899, for full term commencing January 1, 1890; re-elected November 5, 1895.

L. G. Kinne, Tama county; elected November 3, 1891.

Horace E. Deemer, Montgomery county; appointed by the governor May 8, 1894; elected November 6, 1894, for balance of the term ending January 1, 1898; re-elected 1898.

Scott M. Ladd, O'Brien county; elected November 3, 1896.

Charles M. Waterman, Scott county; elected November 2, 1897.

### ATTORNEYS-GENERAL.
(Office created February 9, 1853.)

David C. Cloud, Muscatine county; elected August 1, 1853; re-elected August 7, 1854.

Samuel A. Rice, Mahaska county; elected August 4, 1856; re-elected August 2, 1858.

Charles C. Nourse, Polk county; elected November 6, 1860; re-elected October 14, 1867

Isaac L. Allen, Tama county; elected November 8, 1864; resigned January 11, 1866.

Frederick E. Bissell, Dubuque county; appointed by the governor and qualified January 12, 1866; elected October 9, 1866; died June 12, 1867.

Henry O'Connor, Muscatine county; appointed by the governor June 20 and qualified June 29, 1867; elected October 8, 1867; re-elected November 3, 1868; re-elected October 11, 1870; resigned February, 1872.

Marsena E. Cutts, Mahaska county; appointed by the governor February 23, 1872; elected November 5, 1872; re-elected October 13, 1874.

John F. McJunkin, Washington county; elected November 7, 1876; re-elected October 8, 1878.

Smith McPherson, Montgomery county; elected November 2, 1880; re-elected November 7, 1882.

A. J. Baker, Appanoose county; elected November 4, 1884; re-elected November 2, 1886.

John Y. Stone, Mills county; elected November 6, 1888; re-elected November 4, 1890; re-elected November 8, 1892.

Milton Remley, Johnson county; elected November 6, 1894; re-elected November 3, 1896, and re-elected November, 1898.

### SECRETARIES OF STATE.

Elisha Cutler, Jr., Van Buren county; elected October 26, 1846.

Josiah H. Bonney, Van Buren county; elected August 7, 1848.

George W. McCleary, Johnson county; elected August 5, 1850; re-elected August 2, 1852; re-elected August 7, 1854.

Elijah Sells, Muscatine county; elected August 4, 1856; re-elected October 12, 1858; re-elected November 6, 1860.

James Wright, Delaware county; elected October 14, 1862; re elected November 8, 1864.

Ed Wright, Cedar county; elected October 9, 1866; re-elected November 3, 1868; re-elected October 11, 1870.

Josiah T. Young, Monroe county; elected November 5, 1872; re-elected October 13, 1874; re-elected November 7, 1876.

J. A. T. Hull, Davis county; elected October 8, 1878; re-elected November 2, 1880; re-elected November 7, 1882.

Frank D. Jackson, Butler county; elected November 4, 1884; re-elected November 2, 1886; re-elected November 6, 1888.

W. M. McFarland, Emmet county; elected November 4, 1890; re-elected November 8, 1892; re-elected November 6, 1894.

George L. Dobson, Polk county; elected November 3, 1896; re-elected November, 1898.

### AUDITORS OF STATE.

Joseph T. Fales, Des Moines county; elected October 26, 1846; re-elected August 7, 1848.

William Pattee, Bremer county; elected August 5, 1850; re-elected August 2, 1852.

Andrew J. Stevens, Polk county; elected August 7, 1854; resigned in 1855.

John Pattee, Bremer county; appointed by the governor September 13, 1855; elected August 4, 1856.

Jonathan W. Cattell, Cedar county; elected October 12, 1858; re-elected November 6, 1860; re-elected October, 14, 1862.

John A. Elliott, Mitchell county; elected November 8, 1864; re-elected October 9, 1866; re-elected November 3, 1868.

John Russell, Jones county; elected October 11, 1870; re-elected November 5, 1872.

Buren R. Sherman, Benton county; elected October 13, 1874; re-elected November 7, 1876; re-elected October 8, 1878.

William V. Lucas, Cerro Gordo county; elected November 2, 1880.

John L. Brown, Lucas county; elected October 7, 1882; re-elected November 4, 1884; suspended by the governor March 19, 1885.

Jonathan W. Cattell; appointed March 19, 1885, and served until January 23, 1886.

John L. Brown; reinstated January 23, 1886; suspended April 13, 1886.

Charles Beardsley, appointed April 13, 1886, and served until July 14, 1886.

John L. Brown; reinstated July 14, 1886.

James A. Lyons, Guthrie county; elected November 2, 1886; re-elected November 6, 1888; re-elected November 4, 1890.

C. G. McCarthy, Story county; elected November 8, 1892; re-elected November 6, 1894; re-elected November 3, 1896.

Frank F. Merriam, Delaware county; elected November, 1898.

### TREASURERS OF STATE.

Morgan Reno, Johnson county; elected October 26, 1846; re-elected August 7, 1848.

Israel Kister, Davis county; elected August 5, 1850.

Martin M. Morris, Polk county; elected August 2, 1852; re-elected August 7, 1854; re-elected August 4, 1856.

John W. Jones, Hardin county; elected October 12, 1858; re-elected November 6, 1860.

William H. Holmes, Jones county; elected October 8, 1862; re-elected November 8, 1864.

Samuel E. Rankin, Washington county; elected October 9, 1866; re-elected November 3, 1868; re-elected October 11, 1870.

William Christy, Clarke county; elected November 5, 1872; re-elected October 13, 1874.

George W. Bemis, Buchanan county; elected November, 7, 1876; re-elected October 8, 1878.

Edwin H Conger, Dallas county, elected November 2, 1880; re-elected November 7, 1882.

Voltaire P. Twombly, Van Buren county, elected November 4, 1884; re-elected November 2, 1886; re-elected November 6, 1888.

Byron A. Beeson, Marshall county; elected November 4, 1890; re-elected November 8, 1892.

John Herriott, Guthrie county; elected November, 1894; term commenced January, 1895; re-elected November, 1896, and November, 1898.

THE END.

# PROGRESSIVE MEN OF IOWA.

GUE, BENJAMINE F., was born in Greene county, N. Y., on the 25th day of December, 1828, and is the son of John and Catherine (Gurney) Gue. His father was born in Westchester county, N. Y., and was a descendent of one of the French Huguenots who settled in Ulster county in 1760. On the mother's side the Gurneys were from England, and closely related to Joseph John Gurney, a distinguished member of the British parliament. John Gue, with his wife and children, moved to western New York in 1833, settling in Ontario county, where the subject of this sketch spent his boyhood years on a farm. His father and mother were Quakers and abolitionists, and the first newspaper the children learned to read was William Lloyd Garrison's *Liberator*. Their home was one of the stations on the "underground railroad," where escaping slaves always found shelter and aid. Benjamine F. was the oldest of six children, and when he was 10 years of age the father died, and the mother had a hard struggle for many years to provide for and educate the children. In the spring of 1852 the two older sons came to Iowa and bought a claim on Rock Creek, in Scott county, where they lived in a log cabin, doing their own cooking for a year and a half, until their mother and younger children joined them in the fall of 1853.

Benjamine F. took an active interest in the "free soil" movement against slavery, and in the winter of 1856 was one of the delegates to a state convention which assembled at Iowa City on the 22d of February and organized the republican party of Iowa. In the fall of 1857 he was elected to represent Scott county in the house of the Seventh General Assembly. He was one of the authors of a bill to establish a State Agricultural college, and on the floor of the house fought it through against an adverse report from the committee on ways and means. In 1859 he was re-elected to the house, and at the end of his second term in 1861 he was elected to the senate for four years. During his term in that body he was the author of many laws, the most important of which were the following: Prohibiting the circulation of foreign

bank bills in Iowa; the estray law, still on the statute book; an act requiring a jury fee of $6 to be taxed with the costs in suits in the district court, saving to the taxpayers of the state more than $100,000 annually. But the most important was the law devised by Mr. Gue, Senator Clarkson and Governor Kirkwood, by which the agricultural college land grant of 240,000 acres was reserved for sale at low prices, and

leased for a long term of years at a rental that supported the college and held the lands until good prices were secured for them. By this plan a permanent endowment was secured for the college far larger than that of any other state having the same amount of land.

At the close of his service in the senate in the spring of 1864, Mr. Gue moved to Ft. Dodge and assumed control of the republican paper of that place which he had purchased. In June, 1865, he was nominated for lieutenant-governor by the republican state convention, His chief competitors were Gen. James B. Weaver and Hon. George W. McCrary. He was elected by a majority of more than 4,000 greater than was given to Governor Stone, who was at the head of the ticket. In 1866 Governor Gue was elected president of the board of trustees of the State Agricultural college. During his term the main college building was erected, and he was made chairman of the committee on organization. In that capacity he visited the principal agricultural and scientific colleges of the country, to examine into their methods and work. He was a warm advocate of the admission of girls as students, and in the face of a strong opposition finally prevailed upon the board to admit them.

After giving more than a year to investigation, he made a report to the trustees and presented a plan of organization, which was adopted. He also recommended Prof. A. S. Welch, then United States senator from Florida, for president of our college, and he was elected to that position, where he served eighteen years with distinguished ability.

Governor Gue has always been a staunch friend and vigorous defender of the Iowa State college from the day of its inception, and regards the work he has done in its behalf as by far the most important of his public service. In 1872 he moved to Des Moines and took editorial charge of the *Iowa Homestead.* In December he was appointed by President Grant United States pension agent, serving for eight years, paying out many millions of dollars to the pensioners of Iowa and Nebraska. At the expiration of his second term in 1880, he and his son purchased the *Iowa Homestead,* and built it up into one of the most influential of Iowa papers. For more than thirty years Governor Gue has been among the ablest of Iowa political, industrial and historical writers, contributing to the leading journals, historical publications, and magazines. In 1886 he was one of the founders of the "Pioneer Lawmakers' Association of Iowa," which has gathered and published a vast amount of early Iowa history. For three years, from 1892, he assisted Hon. Charles Aldrich in organizing and systematizing the historical department of Iowa, and reviving and conducting the "Annals of Iowa." For more than fifteen years he has been gathering and preparing material for an elaborate history of Iowa, which is well on towards completion. As a public speaker Governor Gue ranks high, and has long wielded wide influence in the state.

On the 12th of November 1855, he was united in marriage with Miss Elizabeth Parker, who began teaching in the public schools when but 17 years old. She was a daughter of Francis Parker, a Vermonter, who settled in Iowa in 1840. Mrs. Gue died on the 3d day of July, 1888, leaving four children: Horace G., Alice, Gurney C. and Katherine.

Governor Gue was one of the founders of the Iowa Unitarian association, and also of the Unitarian church in Des Moines.

----

DODGE, HENRY, soldier and statesman, was born in Vincennes, Ind., October 12, 1782; died in Burlington, Iowa, June

19, 1867. His father, Israel Dodge, was a revolutionary officer of Connecticut. Henry commanded a mounted company of volunteer riflemen in August and September, 1812; became major of Louisiana militia under General Howard on September 28th; major in McNair's regiment of Missouri militia in April, 1813, and commanded a battalion of Missouri mounted infantry, as lieutenant-colonel, from August till October, 1814. He was colonel of Michigan volunteers from April till July, 1832, during the Black Hawk war, and in the affair with the Indians at Pickatolika, on Wisconsin river, June 15th, totally defeating them. He was commissioned major of United States rangers June 21, 1832, and became the first colonel of the first dragoons March 4, 1833. He was successful in making peace with the frontier Indians in 1834, and in 1835 commanded an important expedition to the Rocky Mountains. General Dodge was unsurpassed as an Indian fighter, and a sword, with the thanks of the nation, was voted him by congress. He resigned from the army July 4, 1836, having been appointed by President Jackson governor of Wisconsin Territory and superintendent of Indian affairs. He held this office till 1841, when he was elected delegate to congress as a democrat, and served two terms. In 1846 he was again made governor of Wisconsin, and after the admission of that state to the union was one of its first United States senators. He was re-elected, and served altogether from June 23, 1848, till March 3, 1857.

----

DODGE, AUGUSTUS C. (United States senator), deceased, is numbered among the honored pioneers of Iowa, and during his life was among the most noted men. He sprang from good old revolutionary stock, and the patriotism of his ancestors found an abiding place in his heart. Henry Dodge and Christina, daughter of James McDonald, were married in 1800, a few miles west of St. Louis. Of their children nine grew to maturity, Augustus C. being the fourth in order of birth. He was born January 2, 1812, at Ste. Genevieve, Mo., then in the territory of Louisiana, the oldest settlement on the west side of the Mississippi river, about sixty miles below St. Louis. In that new and sparsely settled country his boyhood days were passed. His father was a man of note, even at that time, and during the struggle with Great Britain, from 1812 to 1815, was in command of a battalion of militia whose duty it was to keep the Indians at bay. For his services he was appointed brigadier-general of the militia of Missouri Territory. On the return of peace he engaged in mining and smelting and in the manufacture of salt.

The educational facilities of that region were very scant, and the only school Augustus attended for a few months was kept in a log schoolhouse, in which the light came through greased paper; pencils were made from bullets beaten into shape and hammered to a point; pens were made with a Barlow knife, and ink from the boiling of butternut bark or gunpowder. Meanwhile the boy gained strength and self-reliance for the struggle of life in which he was to engage.

In 1827 the family removed to the Fevre river lead mines. Upon arriving at Galena, July 4th, they found the town in a state of alarm from fear of an attack from the Winnebago Indians. Henry Dodge was at once waited upon by citizens and asked to take command of forces for the defense of the mining district. Young Augustus wished to join them, and, when told that he was too young, appealed to his father, who, giving him a small shotgun, advised, "Shoot well, my boy."

Upon the restoration of peace, Henry Dodge located at a point about forty-five miles northeast of Galena, to which was

given the name of Dodge's Grove. When the Black Hawk war broke out in 1832 he was colonel of the militia of Wisconsin Territory, and on the 25th of April was directed by General Atkinson to raise as many mounted men in the mining regions as could be obtained for service against the hostile Indians. In one company then raised Augustus was elected lieutenant of volunteers for home protection, and in the battle of the Wisconsin he conducted himself bravely. On the march, or camping out, he was always cheerful and obliging to the men.

During these years the family divided their time between their residence near Dodgeville and Ste. Genevieve, and Augustus made frequent trips between the two places. In February, 1837, he visited the national capital, where, as a son of a friend of the president, and one who had made a national reputation in the Black Hawk war, and through the attentions of his uncle, Senator Linn, he enjoyed unusual facilities for seeing public men and observing public affairs. Returning home, on March 19, 1837, he was united in marriage with Miss Clara A. Hertich, daughter of Prof. Joseph Hertich. Their union was an exceedingly happy one, and to them were born eight children: William J., Marceline M., Augustus V., Christina, Clara A., Henry J., Charles J. and William W.

In 1838 A. C. Dodge was appointed by President Van Buren register of the United States land office at Burlington, and removed to that city, which was his home the rest of his life. He made an exceedingly popular officer, often going out of his way to help some unfortunate settler in securing the title to his land. The services then rendered were remembered in after years.

January 14, 1839, Mr Dodge was appointed by Governor Lucas as brigadier-general of the Second brigade of the first division of the militia of Iowa Territory. In the fall of that year Missouri laid claim to a portion of Iowa Territory, on its southern border, which was the occasion of great excitement. December 11th General Dodge's brigade was called out. On reaching Van Buren county, General Dodge was sent with two others to the encampment of the Missouri militia, and a friendly conference following, an amicable settlement was arranged, and the troops disbanded.

In the summer of 1840, without thought or effort on his part, General Dodge was nominated delegate to congress. He made a canvass of the territory in company with his whig competitor, Alfred Rich, and was elected by a majority of 585, receiving many whig votes. On the 2d of September he took his seat in congress, and on the 7th of December following he welcomed his father to a seat by his side, as a delegate from the territory of Wisconsin—the first and only instance of a father and son sitting together in the house of representatives since the foundation of the government. He served as delegate until the admission of Iowa into the union, December 28, 1846, a period of six years of laborious service. In the limits of this sketch a record of his service cannot be given, and the reader's attention is called to the life

of General Dodge, by Dr. William Salter, published in 1887.

The First General Assembly of the state of Iowa was not able to agree upon the election of United States senators, but the Second assembly, December 2, 1848, elected General Dodge and George W. Jones. Mr. Dodge drew for the short term, ending March 4, 1849, and was at once re-elected for the term ending March 4, 1855. As seven years before, the son had welcomed the father to a seat by his side in the house of representatives, so now the father, who had entered the senate on the 23d of the previous June as one of the senators from the state of Wisconsin, greeted the arrival of his son in the senate chamber. This was an unprecedented occurrence. It was also noteworthy that Augustus C. Dodge was the first person born west of the Mississippi river to become a senator of the United States. He was congratulated by Mrs. Fremont, wife of General Fremont, who said: "General, I am sure that you will be the best behaved man in the senate, on the ground that a dutiful son will be exceedingly decorous in the immediate presence of his father."

The time in which General Dodge served in the United States senate was an exciting one in the history of the country. He favored the compromise bill of 1850, but voted against Jefferson Davis' proposition to make void the prohibition of slavery that had existed under the Mexican law, and extend the Missouri compromise line of 1820 so as to authorize slavery north of it, and he voted for the admission of California under her constitution prohibiting slavery. Mr. Dodge served as chairman of the committee on public lands, and favored the passage of the homestead bill. In the Kansas-Nebraska struggle of 1854, he followed the lead of Stephen A. Douglas. One of the best speeches delivered in the senate in favor of the organization of Kansas and Nebraska under the Kansas-Nebraska bill, and sneeringly spoken of as "squatter sovereignty," was by him. In answer to Senator Brown, of Mississippi, who said "There are certain menial employments which belong to the negro," he replied: "Sir, I tell the senator from Mississippi, I speak upon the floor of the American senate, in the presence of my father, who will attest to its truth, that I perform and do perform when at home, all of these menial services to which the senator referred in terms so grating to my feelings. As a general thing I saw my own wood, do all my own marketing; I have driven teams, horses, mules, oxen, and considered myself as respectable then as I do now, or as any senator on the floor."

On the 8th of February, 1855, Mr. Dodge resigned his seat in the senate, and on the following day President Pierce nominated him to be minister plenipotentiary to the court of Spain. He was confirmed, and served with great credit to himself and the general government until the summer of 1859, when he returned home and made the race for governor of Iowa on the democratic ticket, but could not overcome the strong republican majority. The following extract is from Salter's life of the general:

"Withdrawn the rest of his life for the most part from official station, Mr. Dodge retained to the end of his life his interest in public affairs, and his unswerving devotion to the democratic party, of which he remained a recognized leader. On several occasions his name was presented as a suitable candidate for the highest offices in the nation, but he himself never aided or abetted any movement to that end. In 1872 he advocated union with the liberal republicans, and the election of Horace Greeley for president. In 1874 he was elected mayor of Burlington by a spontaneous movement of citizens, irrespective of party. In 1875 he served, by appointment of Governor Carpenter, on a commission to investigate alleged abuses in a reform school at Eldora, and aided in introducing a more humane discipline into that institution. An ardent friend of youth, he was a frequent visitor at schools, and gave help and cheer to many in their struggle for an education. He sustained the cause of temperance in vigorous addresses, discountenanced the drinking habit by consistent example, and looked to the invigoration of man's moral sense for the suppression of intemperance—not to prohibitory legislation. At meetings of pioneers and old settlers he was an honored guest, and never wearied in commemorating their exploits and labors.

"He presided over the semi-centennial celebration of the settlement of Iowa on the 1st of June, 1883, at Burlington, and gave surpassing dignity and zest to that occasion. It was a sight that can never be looked upon again, to see that illustrious pioneer of Iowa, at the age of more than three score and ten, pour forth from his capacious, accurate and ready memory treasures of information concerning the beginning of the commonwealth. It seemed as if he were inspired with a religious zeal to snatch from oblivion the memory of our founders for the instruction of after times. A few months later came the fatal sickness and the final hour. He died at Burlington, Iowa, on the 20th of November, 1883, in the bosom of his family, sharing the consolation of religion, his last words being 'Bless the Lord.'"

---

DODGE, HON. WILLIAM WALLACE, of Burlington, Iowa. Throughout the great state of Iowa can be found no name so

thoroughly interwoven with the history of the state as is that of the Dodge family. In making that history they have been most important factors, and have marked with deeds the vanishing traces of swift-rolling time.

The name of Augustus C. Dodge, the father of the subject of this sketch, will ever be revered throughout the Hawkeye state, and the son who has risen to prominence solely by his own merit is in every way qualified to maintain the honor, ability and integrity for which the preceding members of the family have been renowned. Like his father and his grandfather, his career has been characterized by ability, thoroughness and persistence, and, although he has not yet attained his forty-fifth year, his reputation has extended far beyond the boundaries of his native state.

Mr. W. W. Dodge was born in Burlington, Iowa, April 25, 1854. He was elected state senator from the Ninth senatorial district of Iowa for eight years, from 1885 to 1893.

William Wallace Dodge received his literary education at Notre Dame university, Indiana, taking a scientific course and graduating in the class of 1874. He then entered the law department of the State University of Iowa, graduating in June, 1876. He had the honor of being chosen president of class day exercises on that occasion, June 19th, and was awarded the literary prize offered to the graduating class for the best written argument on a given thesis of law. Immediately after taking his degree Mr. Dodge entered upon the practice of his profession in his native city, in company with his brother Charles J., under the firm name of Dodge & Dodge. By his brilliant talent, high moral character and close application to business he has won a prominent position at the bar.

Mr. Dodge is an earnest democrat, and seems to have been born with a natural instinct for politics; in fact it might be said to be hereditary with him.

He began reading and talking politics in his youth, and made his maiden campaign speech while in company with his father at the little town of Franklin, Lee county, Iowa, during the presidential campaign of 1876, since which time he has taken an active part in every local and national campaign, speaking from the stump, serving on committees, presiding at conventions and working at the polls. He was chosen captain of the Cleveland and Hendricks club during the campaign of 1884, served as chairman of a number of democratic county conventions, and as delegate to local and state conventions, and as an alternative delegate for the state at large to the national convention at St. Louis, at which Grover Cleveland was nominated the second time. At the democratic convention held at Des Moines, September 1, 1887, he had, for a young man, the distinguished honor of being chosen temporary chairman of that organization, and performed the duties of his position with dignity and dispatch.

During many years of indefatigable effort in behalf of his party Mr. Dodge never sought, nor would he accept, public office till the fall of 1885, when his friends induced him to accept the nomination for state senator, when, as if to prove the exception to the rule that "a prophet is never without honor save in his own country," he was elected by a majority of 934 over a popular republican candidate who had the advantage of age; political experience and the prestige of a good soldier record. It was charged that while Mr. Dodge possessed superior ability and unquestioned integrity, he was guilty of the heinous crime of being a young man, and was lacking in legislative experience. The first fault, his friends claimed, time would remedy, and the latter he would more quickly overcome by placing him where the necessary opportunity existed. His course in the senate fully justified the most sanguine expectations of his friends and constituents, and, as a result, he was re-elected to the state senate, in 1889, by a majority of 1,876, more than double his former majority. His introduction of important bills, and able management in securing their adoption, soon proved his lack of experience no serious hindrance to his usefulness. His manly course in rejecting the so-called "$216 salary grab," growing out of the impeachment trial of Auditor of State John L. Brown, and his sensible speech opposing it, was consistent with his high sense of honor, and was generally approved by his constituents. He was first to introduce a bill in the Iowa legislature on the subject of child labor, designed to prohibit the employment of children under 15 years of age in factories, mines and workshops. Mr. Dodge had made the subject of that bill and the laws of other states and countries, in regard to the same, a special study. His correspondence in relation to the subject was voluminous and varied, until he was well qualified to be the champion of that worthy cause. June 21, 1890, he was appointed lieutenant-colonel on the staff of Gov. Horace Boies.

Near the close of the session of the Twenty-second General Assembly of Iowa he was appointed one of the two selected from the senate to act on the committee of five appointed to investigate certain charges that had been preferred against the State University of Iowa. The investigation began on May 15, 1889, ended July 20, 1889, and to his credit be it said that he was the most faithful member of the commission, not having lost a day from his labors. This was but additional evidence of his fidelity to public duty.

At the Twenty-third General Assembly

Senator Dodge introduced a bill creating the first Monday in September as a legal holiday, to be known as "Labor Day," which was approved April 5, 1890. He is known throughout the state of Iowa as the "Father of Labor Day."

At the Twenty-fourth General Assembly he was the author of a bill which at that session became a law, being "A bill to protect workingmen in the use of their labels, trade-marks and forms of advertising," now known as "Dodge's Union Label Bill."

Senator Dodge was selected on the part of the senate to deliver the eulogy over the remains of State Senator P. G. Ballingall, who died at Hongkong, China, March 7, 1891. The eulogy was delivered April 14, 1891, in the Coal Palace at Ottumwa, Iowa. Gov. Horace Boies and staff, as also the members of the state senate and house of representatives were present, in addition to a vast concourse of people. He delivered an able and beautiful address over the remains of his dead friend and colleague.

Mr. Dodge is a most indefatigable worker in whatever he undertakes, possessing intellectual faculties of a high order, and, with studious habits, his abilities, both natural and acquired, are such as attract attention and command respect. Nature has happily endowed him with a fine physique, a good voice and a gift of oratory, and, for a number of years past, his has been a familiar figure at state conventions, as also public gatherings, being frequently invited to deliver addresses and responses at banquets. Quick in perception and correct in analysis, his conclusions are logical and convincing.

The scope of Mr. Dodge's capabilities is not confined to his senatorial career. In the legal profession he is recognized as one of the leading lawyers in the state, and his far-reaching thought enables him to cope successfully with the most intricate problems of jurisprudence. He is the possessor of those admirable qualities so essential to every statesman, of being able to deliberate with caution, act with decision, yield with graciousness and oppose with firmness. Tact, sense, and a quick appreciation of the right, are characteristics he possesses in such high degree that they are the elements of his success both at the bar and in the administration of his public trusts, and public ambition is always subordinate to the public welfare.

Already an approving constituency is favoring his name as a future candidate for governor of Iowa, and also for congress, and it is only a question of time when this talented young lawyer will be found following closely upon the footsteps of his illustrious ancestors.

May 18, 1892, Senator Dodge was married, at Mt. Pleasant, Iowa, to Miss Della J. Stubbs, a beautiful, charming and accomplished lady. On June 19, 1893, a son was born to them, who was named William Wallace Dodge, Jr. The senator and his wife are living in the old homestead (of Gen. A. C. Dodge) in Burlington.

ALDRICH, CHARLES, founder and curator of the Iowa State Historical department, and a pioneer newspaper editor of northwestern Iowa, where he founded,

in 1857, the *Hamilton Freeman*, at Webster City, is enjoying, during his lifetime, the appreciation which a grateful people have shown him for the great work he has done for the state. Mr. Aldrich is a native of New York, born October 2, 1828, in Ellington, Chautauqua county, and was the son of Stephen and Eliza Nichols Aldrich. The family was of English origin and first lived in Rhode Island after coming to America. Stephen Aldrich was an amiable, energetic and impulsive man, a blacksmith in early life and afterward a merchant-lumberman and farmer, who came west soon after his

11

son's removal to Iowa, settled on a farm near Webster City, and died there in 1882, his wife having died in 1880. His mother, Charles Aldrich's grandmother, was a woman of great intellectual power and a gifted orator. Such education as could be obtained in the common schools was supplemented by a year in Jamestown academy, at the age of 15.

In June, 1846, he began his long career as a newspaper man and printer, entering the office of Clement & Faxon, publishers of the *Western Literary Messenger*, in Buffalo. Jesse Clement, of that firm, was editor of the *Dubuque Times* during the war, and another companion printer was H. L. Rann, afterward editor of the *Manchester Press*. Having learned the trade, young Aldrich worked as a compositor in the villages of Attica and Warsaw, N. Y., and Warren, Pa. In June, 1850, he established his first paper, *The Cattaraugus Sachem*, a weekly, at Randolph, N. Y. He conducted this paper one year and then established the *Journal*, in Olean, N. Y., and remained in its control for nearly five years, when he removed to the home farm in Little Valley and remained there until he came west in 1857.

When Mr. Aldrich set up his modest little printing outfit in Webster City, Hamilton county, Iowa, and began to proclaim republican principles with that courage and tenacity which have marked his whole life, the village had but 200 inhabitants and the county, with all its patronage, belonged to the democrats. The new editor was not only a vigorous writer, but an organizer as well, and with the fire of enthusiasm burning in him, and the energy and tact to meet pioneer conditions, he soon had a strong following and his office became the political headquarters of the district. The political complexion of the county and district soon changed and *The Freeman* had no insignificant part in bringing it about. It was considered a valuable ally, demonstrating its good judgment by its support of James W. Grimes for senator in 1857. Mr. Aldrich was subsequently, for a short time in 1864, editor of the *Dubuque Times*, and for three years, beginning in 1866, published the *Marshall Times*, now the *Times-Republican*, of Marshalltown. He has since been editorially connected with the *Waterloo Courier*, *Council Bluffs Nonpareil* and the *Chicago Inter-Ocean*.

In 1862, with characteristic devotion to principle, Mr. Aldrich locked up his printing office in Webster City and went into

the union army as adjutant of the Thirty-second Iowa infantry, commanded by Col. John Scott. He was afterward post-adjutant under Col. Wm. T. Shaw, at Columbus, Ky. He returned in 1864. In 1860, 1862, 1866 and 1870 Mr. Aldrich was chief clerk of the Iowa house of representatives. In 1872 he became interested in the river land settlers' troubles, and was a member of a commission created by the legislature to attempt righting the wrongs of the settlers on the Des Moines river lands. Later he was appointed by President Grant as a member of the commission to investigate the matter and recommend some course of action. The relief bill reported by this commission passed the house but failed in the senate. Mr. Aldrich was a member of the United States Geological survey in 1875. His contributions to the literature of this subject attracted wide attention and are of permanent value. In 1881 Mr. Aldrich, who had returned ten years before from Marshall county, was elected to the house from Hamilton county. He originated the custom of printing a house calendar, and previously had been the author of the bill that abolished the county judge system. He has always been a champion of the harmless and useful birds, whose destruction he has tried to prevent in every way. Much of the state legislation on this subject is due to his efforts. He has been a member of the American Ornithologists' union from its foundation.

In founding and establishing the historical department of Iowa Mr. Aldrich has rendered the state a most valuable service. The great building now being erected will stand as a monument to his unselfish devotion and energetic persistence, for without him the historical department would not exist. He began to collect autographs when he was a boy, and as he grew in knowledge of the world and into wider opportunities for obtaining interesting and instructive specimens, he acquired a reputation as a collector, and by the time that he and his wife suggested its presentation to the state, it had become both interesting and valuable. In 1884 the legislature accepted the gift of Mr. and Mrs. Aldrich, which was conditioned upon its being kept in suitable cases, by itself, in the state library, and that they might make additions to it. This was continued until 1892, Mr. Aldrich devoting a large amount of time and much money to making additions to, and caring for, the collection, which was an object of universal interest and instruction. In 1892 the legislature, upon the showing made by Mr. Aldrich, established the historical department, with an annual appropriation of $6,000, and assigned it to rooms in the basement of the state house. Since then its growth has been rapid. It long ago outgrew its cramped quarters and Mr. Aldrich set out to get a building. The legislature was at first slow to provide for the work, but as the people began to see its importance, and to receive benefits from the small beginning, the legislature, in response to popular demand, made an appropriation in 1897 for a small building, to cost $25,000, including grounds. The ground was purchased, but the executive council considered the amount too small to commence building, so it was decided to wait for the next legislature, in 1898, which provided for the present wing, to cost $50,000, and by the sale of another piece of property a better site was secured, plans for a $300,000 building adopted and work commenced in the fall of 1898. The corner stone of the first, or west, wing was laid with imposing ceremonies May 17, 1899. Governor Shaw, James Harlan, John A. Kasson Theodore S. Parvin, A. B. F. Hildreth, Dr. W. M. Salter, Rev. T. M. Lenehan and Mr. Aldrich participated in these exercises. The man to whose efforts all this achievement was due has the rare satisfaction of seeing his work for the people fully appreciated during his lifetime. The educational value of the department is now recognized by everyone, for it is collecting and preserving from destruction and making accessible the historical materials of the state.

Mr. Aldrich took a deep interest in the monument to the victims of the Spirit Lake Indian massacre of 1857, which was built in 1894, by a legislative appropriation. He placed a tablet in the Webster City court house to the memory of the rescue company that went to the relief of the settlement, and he gathered the data and prepared the inscriptions that went on the monument, including the names of all the members of that heroic band of pioneers. Mr. Aldrich was a member of the commission appointed by Governor Jackson to have charge of the erection of the monument.

In July, 1851, Mr. Aldrich was married to Matilda Olivia Williams, in Knowlesville, N. Y. She was born in Dansville, Livingstone county, N. Y., August 8, 1836, and died in Boone, Iowa, on the 18th of

September, 1892. Her grandfather was a revolutionary soldier. She was an ideal companion for her husband. She sympathized with him in all his ambitions, and was his most valued and kindly critic and counsellor. In the love and protection of animal and bird life they were especially united, and their home was always the paradise of numerous pets. Her death was a very hard trial for her husband and he has devoted some of his best efforts to memorials to her. Mr. Aldrich was married a second time, November 12, 1898, to Miss Thirza Louise Briggs, of Webster City, who had been the most intimate friend of his first wife, and their closest companion for many years. They live in Boone, where they have an ideal home.

The historical department publishes a quarterly known as the *Annals of Iowa*, in which is collected important historical papers, liberally illustrated, and short obituaries of the noted men of the state who have passed away during the three months previous. To the editorship of this publication Mr. Aldrich gives his best thought. As a writer he has been successful, because he wrote from conviction and upon thorough information. He is a many-sided and well informed man, versed in science, literature and politics, having had a part in all. He has been a welcome contributor to periodicals, and is the friend and intimate of many distinguished men and women, who have been glad to lend their aid to his work for the state of Iowa. No man has a greater pride in his state than he, and none has done more to demonstrate it.

———

PARVIN, HON. THEODORE S. (Written by Hon. Charles Aldrich.) It is so long since Mr. Parvin came to Iowa that he almost antedates history. The memories of but few of our day go back to the time when he crossed the Mississippi. His career from that early period has been one of distinguished usefulness—in fact, speaking from what I believe to be a just and impartial standpoint, I do not know of another Iowa man whose public career in far-reaching results has been more truly useful.

Judge Parvin was born in Cedarville, Cumberland county, N. J., January 15, 1817, and has therefore just entered upon his 82d year. He was educated at Cincinnati and Woodward colleges, Ohio, but emigrated to Iowa, settling at Burlington in 1838—sixty-one years ago. In August of that year he appeared before the Hon. Thomas S. Wilson of Dubuque, then associate judge of the supreme court of the territory, by whom he was admitted to practice at the bar. As a memorial of those days Mr. Parvin's certificate of admission "to practice in all or any courts of record in the territory aforesaid," is carefully preserved in the 'Aldrich collection" in the Historical Department of Iowa. At the first session of the territorial supreme court of this state, November, 1838, Mr. Parvin was the youngest of twenty attorneys who were admitted to practice. Of this class he is now the sole survivor. During that year Gov. Robert Lucas, whose Andrew Jackson face used to appear on the bills of the old State Bank of Iowa, appointed Mr. Parvin territorial librarian and also private secretary. About this time Mr. Parvin went east to purchase books for the foundation of the territorial library—to the amount of $5,000. Governor Lucas receipted to him for these books, and that receipt, with the governor's quaint signature, is also in the "Aldrich collection," as well as Mr. Parvin's commission as territorial librarian. Mr. Parvin should have been kept in the position of state librarian from that day to this for he has scarcely an equal—I fully believe no superior—as a collector of literary wares, antiquities, materials for history, etc., in the United States. Wisconsin had "a mate to him"—Hon. Lyman C. Draper—who retained the position until three or four years ago, when he was forced to retire by the infirmities of age. Parvin was not retained, for our state adopted the senseless policy of appointing our librarians for short terms and for political reasons, a policy now happily abandoned.

The next position to which Mr. Parvin was appointed was that of district attorney for the middle district of Iowa, in the year 1839. In 1840 he was elected secretary of the territorial council. In 1844 he, with Lieutenant-Governor Eastman and Hon. Shepard Leffler. successfully stumped the middle district of the territory against the adoption of the proposed constitution because the boundaries of the state would cut Iowa off from the Mississippi river. To him and his colleagues the defeat of that measure is due. From 1847 to 1857 he was clerk of the United States district court. From 1848 to 1850 he was county judge. This last was a position in those

days of much power and responsibility, as the county judge in those days had more power than the present board of supervisors. Mr. Parvin held for one term the position of register of the state land office, 1857-8. From 1860 to 1870 he was professor of the natural sciences in the State university, acting also as secretary of the Iowa State Historical society during the years 1864, 1865 and 1866. He edited

"The Annals of Iowa " for many years, and has been a contributor to its pages from the beginning.

Since the introduction of Freemasonry in Iowa, in 1840, Mr. Parvin has been its foremost representative. In 1844 he was chosen grand secretary of the order, a position which he has filled admirably until the present time. He has superintended its publications during all these years, initiated and attended its most distinguishing functions, laying corner stones, delivering lectures and addresses, finally crowning his grand work by the erection of the

Masonic library building at Cedar Rapids, where the headquarters of the fraternity was established in 1885. This building contains the finest Masonic library in the world, a single fact which shows the eminence of Mr. Parvin as a Masonic collector. Aside from its Masonic material it contains the finest general museum in our state.

Many men are mere collectors and nothing else; Parvin, on the contrary, is a man of wide intelligence, possessing extensive and accurate knowledge in many directions. He has written a history of the "Newspaper Press of Iowa," from 1836 to 1846. He is also the author of "Masonry in Iowa," a "History of Templary in the United States," and of "Early Schools and Teachers in Iowa," 1830-60.

The readiest of speakers, there are few men living who have delivered as many addresses, or upon as wide a diversity of subjects, as Masonry, early history, education, politics (in the olden time, long ago), natural history, social science, etc. He has also contributed largely to other collections, as the Davenport Academy of Sciences, the State library, the library of the State university, the State Historical society, and the "Aldrich Collection" at the capitol of the state. Other collectors always find him whole-souled and liberal, with no stint of good words for all earnest workers on collateral lines.

His memory will be perpetuated in all of the institutions named, as long as they shall exist. Recollections of men stand little chance of preservation unless they are "salted down" in print which is gathered into public libraries. Of the men who filled the public eye twenty-five years ago, how few are remembered to-day! They have come and gone like the ephemera of a soft night in June! But in the libraries I have named the reader in future years will find multiplied and most precious gifts from the ever free and generous hand of Theodore S. Parvin. They will also preserve the names and records of hundreds of other men, and not at all unlikely, of many who have looked upon his own work in this direction with coldness and distrust, doing their best possibly to thwart or embarrass him in his earnest and most patriotic efforts. "And if," as Daniel Webster said, speaking of himself, "the mould shall gather upon his memory," there will be plenty of students of Iowa history who will scrape the moss away from the inscription.

All honor, then, to the man who has done so much more than all others to preserve the materials of early Iowa history. His will be one of the very few names of Iowa men which will be imperishable. His good works will live after him to the latest generation, "to the last syllable of recorded time."

———

DODGE, GENERAL GRENVILLE MELLEN, whose name is written permanently in the history of the United States and whose fame is cherished as a precious heritage by the people of Iowa, who claim him as their own, is a resident of Council Bluffs, Iowa;

his business is in New York City. He occupies a position of the highest honor in the estimation of the public and of the business world, for he has achieved extraordinary success as a commander, a leader, not only in time of war but in time of peace. General Dodge is at this time and has been for some years regarded as the greatest of the surviving generals of the civil war. The confidant of Lincoln and Grant, the man they unquestionably trusted, both in matters of judgment and execution, he is a conspicuous figure in the history of the civil war. His long and uninterrupted series of triumphs as a railway builder, have made him not only famous as an engineer and financier, but have given him the comforts which wealth has secured, and which he so richly deserves.

General Dodge was born in Danvers, Mass., April 12, 1831. His father was Sylvanus Dodge, born in Rowly, Mass., in 1801, and died in Council Bluffs, Iowa, December 23, 1871. The first of the Dodge family in America was Richard, born in England, who came over with the Plymouth colony in 1629, with his brother William. General Dodge is of the ninth generation in America. His mother was Julia Theresa Phillips, a native of New England, whose family came from England in the year 1700. She and Sylvanus Dodge were married in 1827, and they had three children: Grenville M., 1831; Nathan Phillips, 1837 and Julia Mary, 1843. Mr. Dodge was a merchant and postmaster of his town at one time. His children enjoyed only limited educational opportunities, assisting in the store and working on farms during the summer time and going to the common schools during the winters With the industry, energy and determination which characterized his subsequent career, Grenville M. Dodge set to work when a young boy to secure an education. He had good health and could stand work, so he prepared himself at the age of 14 to enter the academy at Durham, N. H., and the following year entered the Norwich university of Vermont, from which he was graduated as a civil engineer in the scientific course in 1850. After this he had a short course in Captain Partridge's Military academy in Vermont. In 1851 he went west and began his career as a railway builder, being soon engaged with Peter A. Dey, afterward railway commissioner of Iowa, in building the Chicago & Rock Island railway, and then the Mississippi & Missouri River railroad, from Davenport to Council Bluffs, now united as the Chicago, Rock Island & Pacific railway. During this time he began to form the plans which he afterward carried out for the building of the great Pacific railway, and as he had opportunities from 1853 to 1861, he explored the country west of the Missouri and examined the Rocky mountains from north to south to find the best place to cross with a railway, which he predicted would be built some day not far off. He laid out, in his mind and in letters, the route which was afterward selected. In 1854 he removed to Council Bluffs and engaged in engineering and freighting across the plains. He also helped to organize the banking house of Baldwin & Dodge, which is now the Council

Bluffs Savings bank, of which N. P. Dodge is president. In 1856 he organized the Council Bluffs guards, the nucleus of his future great command, and was made its captain.

In 1855, the parents of the young engineer removed to Dodge county, Neb., settling among the Indians, the farthest west of any white settlers. Three years later they removed to Council Bluffs, where they spent the rest their days.

The war of the rebellion took from General Dodge some of the best years of his life and robbed him of his splendid health, but it gave him an undying fame. His services to the nation have been spoken of with enthusiasm in the official letters of his commanding officers and have been recognized by many marks of honor not ordinarily bestowed. Being sent to Washington by Governor Kirkwood in 1861, to arrange for equipment for Iowa troops, his worth was instantly recognized by the war department, for he secured the arms, ammunition, etc., after the delegation in congress had failed, and he was offered by the war department a commission as captain in the regular army. He declined this to return to his own state, and upon the recommendation of the war department, Governor Kirkwood commissioned him colonel and authorized him to raise a regiment, the Fourth infantry. A surplusage of volunteers was converted into the Second (Dodge's) artillery. Early in the summer of 1861, Colonel Dodge took a part of his command, before it was completed, and made an excursion into Missouri, driving the guerrillas that infested the northwestern part of that state to flight. He also checked the rebel colonel Poindexter's movement and forced him to retreat into the southern part of the state. Colonel Dodge, with his regiment, was first assigned to Rolla, Mo., and he was placed in command of the Fourth brigade. In the celebrated battle of Pea Ridge, this brigade was under fire for three days, March 6, 7 and 8, 1862, and its commanding officer was in the thick of the fight; had three horses shot under him, and was seriously wounded, but stayed in his place till the end of the fight. He lost one-third of his entire command, every field officer being either killed or wounded, for he would not retreat. His cool head, full appreciation of the importance of the situation and his unswerving courage helped to win a great victory. For this he was immediately promoted to the rank of brigadier-general.

After recovering from his wounds, General Dodge was assigned to duty at Columbus, Ky., to rebuild the Mobile & Ohio railroad, which had been destroyed by the rebels, and was much needed to supply the army. Later, in 1862, General Dodge was assigned to the command of the second division of the Army of the Tennessee, in the district of Corinth, where he rendered valuable service. He opened the campaign of 1863 by defeating the rebel forces under Forrest, Roddy, Ferguson and others, and took a principal part in a movement on Granada, Miss., that resulted in capturing fifty-five locomotives and 1,000 cars. On July 5th, the day after the fall of Vicksburg, General Grant was so much pleased with General Dodge that he assigned him to the command of the left wing of the Sixteenth Army corps, with headquarters at Corinth, and later in the month recommended and requested that he be promoted to be major-general. This was approved by General Halleck, and afterward by Gen. W. T. Sherman, and the promotion was made May 22, 1864, in recognition of General Dodge's brilliant work in the opening of the Atlanta campaign. With two divisions of the Sixteenth Army corps he joined General Sherman, at Chattanooga, on May 4, 1864, and was intrusted with the advance of the Army of the Tennessee in its famous movements at the opening of the Atlanta campaign, taking Ship's Gap, at midnight, on May 5th, and Snake Creek Gap, on May 8th, reaching Johnson's rear at Resaca and forcing him to give up his impregnable position at Dalton, Ga. His corps also took part in all the battles up to Atlanta and Jonesborough, Ga. He was successful in many brilliant engagements, and especially distinguished himself in the greatest and most decisive battle of the Atlanta campaign, July 22, 1864. While standing in a trench before Atlanta he was severely wounded in the head, August 19, 1864, and was sent north to recover. On the first of November, following, he was ready for duty and was assigned to the command of the department of the Missouri, December 2d, superseding General Rosecrans. The country there was overrun by guerrillas and the army was in bad condition. General Dodge soon had the army in good shape, quelled the general Indian outbreak which then threatened along the entire frontier, and made vigorous war on the guerrillas. Gen. Jeff Thompson's command, with 8,000 officers and men in Arkansas, surrendered to him.

At the close of the war General Dodge's command was made to include all the Indian country of the west and northwest. For a year after the close of the rebellion, General Dodge was engaged in fighting Indians, and he succeeded in bringing them to peace by his vigorous and uncompromising methods. After completing the Indian campaign General Dodge was, at his earnest request relieved of his command May 1, 1866, and his resignation from the army was accepted May 30, 1866. General Dodge was selected by General Grant at the head of the list of major-generals of volunteers whom he would have retain this rank in the regular army.

In July, 1866, the republicans of the Fifth congressional district of Iowa nominated General Dodge for congress, wholly without his solicitation. He reluctantly accepted one term. He was of great assistance in putting the army on a peace footing, and in the solution of questions pertaining to the internal improvement of the west and the building of the transcontinental railway lines. His fame as an engineer made his counsel heeded. During his term in congress General Dodge had kept up his work as chief engineer of the Union Pacific, a position which he had accepted immediately upon his retirement from the army. The building of that great railway is the chief monument to the greatness of the man, the engineer. He overcame all obstacles, and they were many. At one time the whole project was about to fall when General Dodge appeared in New York, in 1867, and proved that the fears of the financiers, as to the cost, were greatly exaggerated. and the plans were carried forward. Nearly every mile had to be built under military protection, on account of the hostility of Indians, and many of the best men employed in the work were killed. The materials had to be hauled hundreds of miles. Opposition and suspicion were encountered on every hand, but the genius of the engineer and the man of affairs was great enough to conquer all the enemies of the enterprise and satisfy the doubters. He stood by his locations and grades regardless of the criticisms of others and had the satisfaction of seeing his work approved by all the government commissioners appointed to examine it, and by the engineers who examined it to find changes that would better it. No material changes were made. The great undertaking was completed May 10, 1869, at Promontory Point, Utah, 1,186 miles from the starting point on the Missouri river.

General Dodge has built many other railways, among them the following: Texas & Pacific; Missouri, Kansas & Texas; International & Great Northern; New Orleans & Pacific; Des Moines, Northern & Western; Oriental & Mexican Southern (partially); Fort Worth & Denver; Denver, Texas & Fort Worth, and several other lines in which he was more or less interested. From 1874 to 1879 he spent a portion of each year abroad, and was consulted by the builders of the great Russian trans-continental line from St. Petersburg through Siberia to the Pacific ocean, and on other foreign enterprises. He was asked to take charge of a system of internal improvements in China, but the project failed at first on account of the death of Anson Burlingame, former United States minister to China, who had it in charge, and when the Chinese government again asked him to go to China for this purpose, in 1886, he was unable to go.

All the military organizations growing out of the civil war have found in General Dodge a strong supporter. He was one of the first organizers of the Loyal Legion and belongs to the G. A. R. Upon the death of General Sherman he was elected president of the Society of the Army of the Tennessee. He is also vice-president of the Grant Monument association and president of the Grant Birthday association, both of New York. He belongs to the Odd Fellows, to the Union League club of New York, and the United Service club. He is president of the Norwich University association of New York and belongs to many other organizations. He was made chairman of the commission to investigate the conduct of the war with Spain by President McKinley.

Always an earnest republican, General Dodge, was a delegate-at-large from Iowa to the republican national coventions at Philadelphia, Chicago, and Cincinnati, and has taken an active part in every presidential campaign during and since the campaign that resulted in the election of Abraham Lincoln.

---

TRIMBLE HENRY HOFFMAN, of Keokuk, is one of the oldest and best lawyers in Iowa, and a prominent leader of the democratic party. His father, John Trimble, was born in Belmont county, Ohio, in A. D. 1800. He was of German descent,

and was the son of a Virginian who served in the revolution. In 1820 he became a pilot on a pioneer steamboat plying between Pittsburg and Cincinnati. He was married in 1823 to Elizabeth Hoffman, also a native of Ohio, and of German and Scotch descent. She persuaded him to quit boating, for she considered it demoralizing; so they moved into the wilderness of Dearborn county, Ind., and opened a farm.

Here Henry H. was born May 3, 1827. He memorized Noah Webster's spelling book from beginning to end in the little log schoolhouses of Rush and Shelby counties, which were provided with rude furniture and ruder masters, who sat in the

middle of the room holding beech switches long enough to reach the remotest child. At 13 young Trimble became interested in reading, through the influence of James Clark, an Englishman, who organized a small circulating library near by. The boy eagerly read such books as "Grimshaw's History of Greece and Rome," Good's "Book of Nature," and Dickens' works. He was deeply impressed, and was filled with a desire for higher education. At 14 he sold a horse, the gift of his grandfather, and with the money secured six months' schooling at a small academy in Shelbyville. He then worked a year longer on the home farm, studying at every spare moment. At 16 he taught a six months' term of school in Bartholomew county, near Columbus, after which he began the study of law. He read Blackstone and Kent; spent a year in a little college just started at Franklin, Johnson county; and the next year, 1844, entered the State university at Bloomington, Ind., and remained until the close of his first term of the senior year, when he went to Greencastle and entered the senior class of Asbury college, graduating July 27, 1847, at the age of 20, with the degree of master of arts. He paid all his expenses by manual labor, such as cutting cordwood and teaching night schools. After graduation he served a year in the Mexican war, enlisting as a volunteer with the Fifth Indiana infantry. He spent most of the time as a clerk in the quartermaster's department. At the close of the war he took charge of the Shelbyville academy, at the same time studying law under Thomas A. Hendricks, afterwards vice-president, and E. H. Davis. He came to Iowa in November, 1849, and in February, 1850, began practicing law at Bloomfield, Davis county. He was county attorney four years, beginning in 1850, and state senator from 1855 to 1859. In 1861 he was a leading organizer of the Third Iowa cavalry, and as lieutenant-colonel had charge of the regiment during his stay in the service. It bore the reputation of being one of the best drilled regiments in the volunteer service. In 1862, while leading a charge at the battle of Pea Ridge, he was severely wounded, and in October was discharged on account of disabilities resulting from the wound. During the same month he was elected judge of the Second judicial district of Iowa, and served four years. In 1866 he helped organize the St. Louis & Cedar Rapids Railroad company, in 1868 becoming its president. A road, now a part of the Wabash line, was constructed from Coatsville, on the state line between Iowa and Missouri, through Bloomfield to Ottumwa.

Before the war Judge Trimble was in partnership with a brother-in-law, James Baker, colonel of the Second Iowa infantry, who was killed at the battle of Corinth. After the war his partner was S. S. Carruthers, another brother-in-law, from 1867 to 1881, when Judge Trimble removed from Bloomfield to Keokuk.

He has been attorney for some of the leading railroads of Iowa, and since 1882 has been employed by the Chicago, Burlington & Quincy, the St. Louis, Keokuk & Northwestern, and the Chicago, Burlington & Kansas City Railroad companies. The judge is a diligent, thorough student of law, and stands in the front rank of the Iowa bar. He was president of the State Bar association in 1877.

He has organized and is now president of three banks: the Albia State bank, Keosauqua State bank, and the Bloomfield State bank, all of which are prosperous institutions.

Judge Trimble has always been an active democrat but has never asked for office except when he was elected judge of the district court. He, however, received the support of his party once for United States senator, twice for congress, three times for supreme judge, and once for governor. He repudiated the Chicago platform in 1896, and helped organize the national democratic party, being a delegate at large to the national convention at Indianapolis.

The judge was married May 5, 1849, to Miss Emma Carruthers. They have five children, as follows: Palmer, Frank K., Henryette, now Mrs. O. D. May; Hattie, now Mrs. O. S. Stanbro, and Helen Trimble. Frank is now dead.

---

DUNCOMBE, JOHN FRANCIS, of Fort Dodge, is, and has been, for more than forty years, one of the best known citizens of Iowa. He is a direct descendant from the Duncombes of England, several of whom have, in different generations, served their country in parliament and other public positions. Charles Duncombe, from whom the American branch of the family has descended, was a staunch patriot in revolutionary days. Out of his large fortune he contributed more than £60,000 in aid of the struggle of the colonies for independence. He gave his life as well as a large share of his fortune to the patriot cause in the war for national freedom. His son, the grandfather of John F., was a volunteer in the American army in the second war with Great Britain, in 1812. Eli Duncombe, the father of John F., was a farmer in Erie county, Pa., in moderate circumstances. His son was born on the farm October 22, 1831. His education began in a log school house, and when 16 years of age, he was sent to Allegheny college, at Meadville, where he pursued his studies for three years. From there he went to Centre college, at Danville, Ky., where he graduated with high honors, in June, 1852, and, returning to Allegheny college, graduated there the same month. Afterwards, Allegheny college conferred on him the degree of A. M. During his college course Mr. Duncombe taught school during vacations to procure the means to defray his expenses, beginning to teach before he was 17 years of age. After leaving college he studied law at Erie, Pa., was admitted to the bar and entered into practice in 1853. December 29, 1852, he was married to Miss Carrie Perkins, who died November 19, 1854, at Erie, where they had settled. In 1855 Mr. Duncombe borrowed $300 from his father, having surrendered his interest in the paternal estate in consideration of money advanced to meet college expenses, and with that small sum as his entire fortune, boldly struck out for the west to make his way in the world. He pushed on out to the little frontier town of Fort Dodge, Iowa, then (in April, 1855), a village of a few hundred inhabitants, remote from railroads, and surrounded by vast, wild, unbroken prairies. Here he opened a law office in a county that had a population of but little more than 1,000 people, counting men, women and children. The land in all directions still belonged to the government, with the exception of isolated claims along the streams where timber and springs could be found. The pioneers had little money and seldom indulged in the luxury of litigation. The prospect for profitable law business was in the remote future, and chiefly upon such anticipation the sanguine young attorney somehow managed to live in a style that was far from luxurious. He had faith in the development of a region rich in nature's elements of wealth, which the hopeful and vigorous young pioneers were determined to hasten by every energy they were endowed with. It was a long, hard, slow process of evolution, but Mr. Duncombe, and a few others, stuck to the beautiful location, and were powerful factors in working out the transition from poverty, in the bleak wilderness of water-soaked, muskrat populated marshes, to a garden spot of well tilled farms, and a city of thrift, wealth, culture and refinement. Year by year, the old trail of Indians, buffalo, hunters and trappers were gradually effaced by plow, cultivator, wagon and railroad. With youth, energy, sanguine expectations and unflagging courage, the young men who sought homes in the wilds of northwestern Iowa, could not fail. They came of the sturdy race of men and women who had, generations before, subdued the forests, savages and all impediments to civilization in the east, and their inheritance of the sterling qualities of such ancestors was a sure guaranty of success and prosperity as the years passed by. In the early spring of 1857 news came to Fort Dodge of the extermination, by Sioux Indians, of the colony which the year before had settled among the groves that surrounded the beautiful lakes of Okoboji and vicinity, on the extreme northern boundary of the state, in Dickinson county. The winter had been one of unprecedented severity; the whole country was still covered with a heavy blanket of snow, filling ravines and sloughs to a depth of many feet, rendering travel very difficult. The

report that all the colonists were massacred, with the exception of four young women, who were dragged away into captivity more terrible than death, aroused a frenzy of horror that demanded instant pursuit, rescue and punishment. A hundred fearless young men from the neighboring counties hastily assembled at ,Fort Dodge, organized into three companies, choosing for their captains C. B. Richards and John F. Duncombe, of Fort Dodge and J. C. Johnson, of Webster City. The veteran Major Williams, then nearly 60 years of age, took command, and the little battalion, poorly equipped for such a perilous winter march, hastened to the rescue.

Their sufferings and heroic endurance of hardships, almost equal to those of Napoleon's army in the Moscow campaign, are matters of history. Every member of that little army of volunteers proved himself a hero, and won a place among the "bravest of the brave." Captain Johnson and William Burkholder perished on the return march and many others barely survived to reach their homes. The state has commemorated their heroism by a monument placed on the site where the terrible massacre began; Mr. Duncombe being appropriately appointed one of the commissioners to superintend its erection.

In 1858, Mr. Duncombe became one of the editors of the Fort Dodge *Sentinel*, which had been started by A. S. White, in July, 1856. Some years later he was editor and proprietor of the Fort Dodge *Democrat*, but he never relinquished his law practice while connected with journalism. In 1859 he was nominated by the democrats of the Thirty-second district, consisting of twenty-three counties, for state senator, and was elected, serving four years. He has been a member of the house twice, and was, for eighteen years, one of the regents of the State university. He lectured on railroad law in the university for ten years. He was one of the Iowa Columbian commissioners, having charge of the Iowa exhibit at the World's Fair, in 1893. For more than thirty years Mr. Duncombe has been one of the ablest leaders of the democratic party of the state, and has often been on their ticket for presidential elector. He has been the candidate of his party for lieutenant-governor, supreme judge, and representative in congress; but large republican majorities, in state and district, have always defeated him. It has often been remarked that if Mr. Duncombe had been a republican he could easily have obtained any office within the gift of the people, as his ability is unquestioned. But he has been a sincere free-trade democrat all his mature life, and the state of his adoption is one of the republican strongholds of the union. The congressional district in which he lives has never failed to give an immense republican majority since its organization. While giving his chief attention to the practice of law, Mr. Duncombe has been an active promoter of several railroads and other business enterprises. He was one of the incorporators of the Iowa Falls & Sioux City railway, the Mason City & Fort Dodge railroad, the Fort Dodge & Fort Ridgely, now the Minneapolis & St. Louis railroad, and all other lines projected to enter Fort Dodge. He was also one of the first to develop the coal mining interests in that section, and was the builder of the principal hotel in Fort Dodge. For many years he has been engaged largely in coal mining and in the manufacture of stucco and all its products from the extensive gypsum deposits which underlie a large tract of country about Fort Dodge, his sons having charge of the business.

While Mr. Duncombe has given his services largely to the legal business of the Illinois Central Railway company, holding the position of district attorney, having nineteen counties in three states in his jurisdiction, he has had also a large general practice. He has defended in twelve trials for murder and prosecuted in two. When the great legal contest was made over the validity of the prohibitory amendment to the state constitution, Mr. Dun-

combe, with Judge C. C. Nourse and Senator James F. Wilson were appointed by the governor to represent the state in sustaining the legality of the act. He was chairman of the Iowa delegation to the democratic national convention held at Baltimore in 1872, which nominated Horace Greeley for president. In 1892 he was again chosen chairman of the Iowa delegation to the Chicago national convention, but having been selected to present the name of Governor Boies as a candidate for president, he resigned the chairmanship, and presented the Iowa candidate in a speech of great power and eloquence. May 11, 1859, Mr Duncombe was united in marriage with Miss Mary A. Williams, daughter of Major Williams, the founder of Fort Dodge and for many years one of the best known citizens of northwestern Iowa. They have two sons and three daughters living. The family attend the Episcopal church. No citizen of northwestern Iowa has done more to develop its great natural resources than John F. Duncombe; and for more than forty years his time, money, best energies and superb executive ability have been devoted to the building up of his beautiful home city. Of robust build, commanding figure and presence, an eloquent and impressive public speaker, a genial companion and neighbor, a vigorous and resourceful antagonist in legal or political conflicts, he can give and take sturdy blows and harbor no resentment. Some of his warmest friends are life-long political opponents. They respect the manhood of one who is true to his political convictions, and has battled for a generation courageously in a hopeless minority.

---

SHAW, COL. WILLIAM T., is a name well known to all Iowa soldiers who participated in the great war of the rebellion. He was one of the best fighting colonels that went into the army from Iowa. He came of fighting stock. His great uncle was an officer in the revolutionary war, serving on the staff of General Knox. General Washington, November 3, 1783, issued an order certifying that "Captain Samuel Shaw, throughout the war, has greatly distinguished himself in everything which entitles him to the character of an intelligent, active and brave officer. January 5, 1784, Major Shaw took leave of his old commander, General Knox, who, in his own handwriting, issued the following certificate: "This is to certify that Captain Samuel Shaw has borne a commission in the artillery service of the United States of America for upwards of eight years, more than seven of which he has been attached to my staff as adjutant, brigade major and aide-de-camp. In the various and arduous duties of these positions, he has in every instance proved to be an intelligent, active and gallant officer. Given under my hand and seal at West Point, upon the Hudson river, on this 5th day of January, 1784. Knox, major-general."

His paternal grandfather, Francis Shaw, was actively engaged in the public service during the war of the revolution. He negotiated a treaty with the Indians, on St. Johns river, in 1776. He was commissioned by General Washington, in 1777, as major and directed to remove these Indians to their own reservation. In 1780 he was still in the service, and remained to the close of the war.

His father was William N. Shaw, and his mother Nancy D. Stevens Shaw. They lived in Washington county, in the state of Maine, in the town of Steuben, where their son William was born September 22, 1822. In boyhood he attended the district schools and closed his school days with three years in the Wesleyan seminary at Redfield. When 19 years of age he went west and taught school at Greencastle, Ind., and at Harrodsburg, Ky. While here the Mexican war began and young Shaw at once enlisted in the Second Kentucky volunteers, commanded by Col. W. R. McKee. He was an excellent soldier, marched and fought bravely with his regiment in every engagement it had with the enemy, to the close of the war. In the desperate battle of Buena Vista, Shaw was in the thickest of the fight on hillside and ravine, where the brave Colonel McKee was killed. When the war closed he assisted in clearing the southwest border of hostile Indians, who were annoying the settlers. In 1849 he led a company of thirty-six men over the plains by the Santa Fe route, to the newly discovered gold regions of California. He settled, in 1853, at Anamosa, Jones county, bought land in the vicinity and began to improve farms. He superintended the building of the Dubuque Southwestern railroad from Farley to Anamosa, and was in the midst of the work when the great rebellion began. When the Fourteenth Iowa Volunteer infantry was organized, in October, 1861, William T. Shaw was commissioned its colonel, and at once took command. Its first battle was at Fort Donelson, where it did good service. At the great battle of Shiloh the Fourteenth was in the thickest of the fight on the first day, and with the Eighth and Twelfth Iowa fought desperately for hours against greatly superior numbers of the enemy, which, by the most heroic bravery, they held at bay against the fierce assaults that were again and again hurled against them. At last they were cut off from support, surrendered and taken prisoners. After several months in rebel prisons Colonel Shaw and his men of

the Fourteenth were exchanged and returned to the service. In the disastrous Red River campaign, at the battle of Pleasant Hill, Colonel Shaw commanded a brigade, and by his ability, skill, and the most heroic resistance of his command, saved General Banks' army from utter route and capture. In that desperate battle Colonel Shaw's brigade was the first engaged with the enemy, and the last to leave the field. Its losses were over 500 men. For his superb services in this battle, Colonel Shaw merited promotion to the rank of brigadier-general. But his fearless exposure of drunken and incompetent

superiors only brought upon him persecution instead of promotion.

On the 5th of September Maj.-Gen. A. J. Smith sent the following request to the president:

MEMPHIS, TENN.

*To His Excellency, Abraham Lincoln, President of the United States:*

DEAR SIR—I desire to place before you a recommendation for the promotion to the rank of brigadier-general the name of William T. Shaw, Fourteenth Iowa Volunteer infantry (now commanding the Third division, Sixteenth Army corps), who has been a very efficient officer under my command for the last twelve months. He was with me in several engagements and at all times proved himself an efficient and worthy commander. His term of service expires in about sixty days and I should not like to see him leave if it could be avoided.

Your obedient servant,

A. J. SMITH, *Major-General.*

For a time he commanded the Third division of the Sixteenth Army corps, and was finally relieved October 29, 1864. Upon his retirement from the service, Gen. A. J. Smith, in special order No. 132, says of Colonel Shaw: "It is but justice to an energetic, thorough and competent officer to say that for the last fifteen months he has been in this command, commanding a post, brigade and division, and in every position he has performed the incumbent duties faithfully and well, with an ability that few can equal. With courage, patriotism and skill, above question. The service loses an excellent officer when he is mustered out."

When about to leave the division he had so bravely commanded, its officers presented him with an elegant sword in token of their esteem for him personally and the gallant services he had rendered the country. Colonel Shaw returned to his home at Anamosa, and has long been actively engaged in business. In politics he is a republican, and in 1876 was elected to the legislature by that party. He is too blunt and outspoken for a successful politician, denouncing incompetents and hypocrites with unsparing vigor. While a good hater of all frauds and shams, he is strongly attached to his friends and liberal to the deserving unfortunate.

In the annals of Iowa for April and July, 1898, volume 3, page 401, Colonel Shaw has put upon record the history of the battle of Pleasant Hill, in which he participated, together with statements of Judge T. Granger and Quartermaster T. C. McCall, who also participated.

Colonel Shaw was married May 1, 1854, to Helen L. Crane, daughter of Roswel and Paulina Crane, who died on December 25, 1867. He was again married to Retta Harmon, daughter of Joseph W. S. and Zilpha Harmon. After the death of this wife he was again married to Elizabeth C. Higby, nee Crane, February 24, 1870. She was a daughter of Louis A. and Sarah Crane.

His children are Helen Louisa Shaw, born June 8, 1855, and Antonette Nancy Shaw, November 7, 1859.

---

PERKINS, CHARLES ELLIOTT, president of the Chicago, Burlington & Quincy railroad, is a native of Cincinnati, Ohio, born November 24, 1840, and on both the paternal and maternal sides is descended from ancestors who were of old Puritan stock, and were prominently identified

with the early history of the New England colonies. The first of the family to settle in America was Edmund Perkins, who emigrated from England in 1650, and was a member of the Salem colony of Massachusetts, and from him descended a line of ancestors of the Perkins family, who have ever been distinguished, not only in the New England states, but in the western country, in which many of them subsequently made their homes. Our subject takes his middle name from his mother's family, the Elliotts, who were no less distinguished in the early annals of New England. Their first ancestor also landed in

Massachusetts, but the family afterward removed to Connecticut.

Charles E. Perkins was educated in Cincinnati, Ohio, until 16 years of age, when he engaged as clerk in a store, where he learned practical bookkeeping and business methods. After some years' service in that line he came to Burlington, Iowa, in August, 1859, and was given a clerkship in the office of Charles R. Lowell, the assistant treasurer of the Burlington & Missouri railroad, at the munificent salary of $30 a month. He was soon made paymaster under Mr. Lowell, and filled that position until late in the autumn of 1860, when Mr. Lowell, having accepted the position of manager of the Mt. Savage Iron works, at Cumberland, Md., left the Burlington & Missouri River railroad service, and Mr. Perkins, who was only 20 years of age, was promoted to the office of assistant treasurer.

Until January, 1865, Mr. Perkins continued to serve as assistant treasurer, when Hans Thielsen (the superintendent of the road at that time) was called to Nebraska to serve as chief engineer in making a survey of the road to be built from Plattsmouth to Kearney Junction, and Mr. Perkins was made acting superintendent, to fill the vacancy. Some months later, it having been determined to extend the Burlington & Missouri railroad to the Missouri river, and that Mr. Thielsen was to devote his attention to that part of the work, Mr. Perkins was promoted to be superintendent of the road, which at that time extended only from Burlington to Ottumwa, a distance of seventy-five miles. During the period of construction of the road through to the Missouri river he served both as superintendent and vice-president. In the meantime he had been active in promoting the organization of the Burlington & Missouri River Railroad company in Nebraska, of which he was one of the incorporators and a member of the first board of directors, being chosen to that position October 28, 1869. On the 26th day of July, 1871, he was elected a director of the Burlington & Missouri River Railroad company in Iowa; the Nebraska road was opened through to Kearney Junction in the summer of 1872, and November 4th of that year Mr. Perkins was chosen vice-president of that company. Upon the consolidation of the Burlington & Missouri River Railroad company of Iowa with the Chicago, Burlington & Quincy of Illinois, on January 1, 1873, he was deprived of his official connection with the former company through the changed condition of affairs. On the 2d of April, 1875, Mr. Perkins was chosen a member of the board of directors of the Chicago, Burlington & Quincy railroad, then owning and operating the original road in Illinois and the newly acquired extension in Iowa; and on the 2d day of March, 1876, he was elected vice president of the Chicago, Burlington & Quincy company, still retaining the vice-presidency and general management of the road west of the Missouri river. On the 5th day of May he was elected president of the Burlington & Missouri River railroad in Iowa; and on the first day of January, 1880, the Burlington & Missouri River rail-

road in Nebraska became consolidated with the Chicago, Burlington & Quincy railroad, throwing the whole under one corporate management, Mr. Perkins remaining as vice-president until September 29, 1881, when he was chosen president. He has been re-elected at each succeeding election, and is now serving his eighteenth year in that capacity. Mr. Perkins is also officially connected with several other railroad corporations which are connected with the Chicago Burlington and Quincy railroad, and is director and president of the Hannibal & St. Joseph and the Kansas City, St. Joseph & Council Bluffs railroads, the two named being maintained as distinct and separate corporations.

When Mr. Perkins first came to Burlington, nearly thirty years ago, in August, 1859, he was not quite 19 years of age, so that it may be said of him that he began his connection with the important corporation of which he is now the chief executive officer, or rather with a constituent part of it, while but a boy, and that he has earned and won, by superior executive ability, energy and fidelity to the trust reposed in him, an honorable promotion through all the grades of service, from that of a clerk in the treasurer's office to his present prominent and responsible position, as chief executive officer of one of the greatest railway systems of the country.

In September, 1864, at Milton, Mass., near Boston, Charles E. Perkins was united in marriage with Miss Edith Forbes, daughter of Com. R. B. Forbes, of Boston, Mass. Mrs. Perkins was born and educated in Boston. Their family comprises six children — two sons and four daughters. It may be an item of interest to make some mention of the places of abode and the manner of Mr. Perkins' way of living in his early days in Burlington. He first made his home with Mr. Lowell and Leo Carper, both of whom were connected with the railway company. They lived together in what was known as Patterson's hollow, now Agency street, until the fall of 1860, when they removed to Shepard Leffler's farm, now West Burlington. Mr. Lowell had taken a lease of Mr. Leffler's farm and house, which he transferred to Mr. Perkins when he left Burlington for Mt. Savage. The following spring (1861) Mr. Perkins succeeded in getting Mr. Leffler to take the farm off his hands and thus escaped becoming a granger. He then returned to the city, and for a while boarded at the Barrett house, and later with Mrs. Fletcher, on North Hill, in the house now owned and occupied by R. M. Raab. Remaining there until the fall of 1862, Mr. Perkins then rented a house on South Hill, of Mr. Nelson Dills, which he afterwards purchased, and in which he now resides. There were originally sixty acres in the place, but he has sold off several tracts until he now has but twenty acres, which, with the commodious residence, beautiful groves and lawns makes an elegant and pleasant suburban home. At the time of his marriage, in the autumn of 1864, he established his residence on the place now owned by Mrs. Erastus Chamberlain on North Hill, remaining there until the spring of 1867, when he sold to Mr. Chamberlain, and purchased the Dills farm, to which he removed at once. While Mr. Perkins and his family spend some months of each year in Boston, Burlington is their home.

Mr. Perkins is a republican in his political sentiments, but is not in any sense a politician. His important business relations, both private and official, leave him no time, even were he so disposed, to win prominence in the political arena. As a rule large corporations recognize superior ability and integrity of character in their employes, and reward true merit with promotion, and while the motive on the part of the corporation may be purely selfish, the success of the individual officer is none the less creditable. This is well illustrated in the career of Mr. Perkins in Burlington. Beginning before reaching his majority as a clerk at $30 per month, he has steadily risen through all the grades.

---

SHAW, LESLIE MORTIER, governor of Iowa, was born in Lamoille county, Vt., in 1848. He learned when a boy, while fighting stones on a rough, upland farm, that the good things of life are secured only by hard work, and that has been the rule of his life.

He came to Iowa when 21 years of age, resolved that he would never again see his Green Mountain state till he had won some measure of success. He worked on a farm when he first came to Iowa, in Linn county, where he cast his first vote; taught school; attended Cornell college at Mount Vernon, where he graduated in 1874. Part of his school expenses were paid in selling fruit trees, in which he was eminently successful. He sold to the farmers of Crawford county over $4,000 worth of nursery stock,

which he delivered in 1874 and 1875 at Denison, where he located in the practice of law in July of 1876. He had in the meantime graduated from the Iowa College of Law. He went to Denison because he liked the country and the people, and was willing to risk his reputation among those with whom he had had dealings. He was successful in his profession, as he had been in other lines. As his practice increased, an extensive loan business was added, until he became joint proprietor and president of two banks in the county. Of over $2 000,-000 loaned by his firm on farm security for

eastern clients, only one mortgage has been foreclosed.

While Mr. Shaw is one of the best trial lawyers in the state, it has always been his policy to settle his cases whenever it can be done with justice to his client. This policy has probably contributed its share to the harmony among the business interests of his thriving town. During twenty years of Governor Shaw's residence there, no case has ever come to trial between the business men of Denison.

While in Cornell college, Governor Shaw joined the Methodist church, and has ever since been an active worker and a liberal contributor to that church. For about twenty years he was superintendent of the Sunday school at Denison, and for the last few years of his superintendency had an average attendance equal to one-seventh of the entire population of the town. He is practical in religion as in all things, believing that Christianity, to be of use in the world, must be made to fit the ordinary experiences of life.

Mr. Shaw has manifested great interest in educational matters. He has made several donations to Cornell college, Simpson college, and some other institutions of the state. He was the principal contributor to the Denison Academy and Normal school erected in his own town, and has been president of the board of trustees since its inception. He is also a member of the board of trustees of Cornell college.

Though always active in support of the republican party, he was never a seeker for political preferment In the campaign of 1896 he took a prominent part in battling against what he thought to be a most dangerous attack upon the national honor and commercial and industrial interests. As early as February of that year, Hon. William Jennings Bryan, subsequently silver candidate for president, delivered an address in Denison, in support of the doctrines afterwards formulated in the Chicago platform, on which he ran for president. A few days after this speech, Mr. Shaw was requested by the sound money men of his town to reply to Mr. Bryan, which he did. From that time his services were in constant demand; he made over sixty speeches in various parts of the state in favor of a single gold standard. He makes no pretensions to oratory, as most people understand the art, but he is a persuasive, logical, incisive, earnest and effective speaker. He made friends wherever he spoke.

His candidacy for governor was not of his own seeking; his name was brought forward three weeks before the convention, where he was nominated on the fourth ballot in a field of ten candidates, every one of whom was worthy of the highest honors of the state. The campaign of 1897 centered around the gubernatorial contest. He made his campaign on the money issue, and never indulged an unkind utterance against his opponent. He requested the committee in charge of the speaking campaign not to send him into the county of his adversary, preferring to do nothing personally to reduce his opponent's vote at home. He was elected over the fusion nominee, Hon. Fred E. White, by 29,875

majority. The next year he conducted a similar campaign in the interest of the state ticket, and contributed his full share to the republican majority in his state of 63,282, and the election of a solid republican delegation to congress.

The administration of Governor Shaw has been eminently successful, though he has had some serious problems to solve, chief of which has been the preparation of the Iowa troops for the war with Spain, and the protection of the soldiers after they entered the United States army. To these duties the governor gave his best thought, and while reflecting credit upon the state for the high grade of troops furnished, succeeded in securing for them many concessions, and in adding to their comfort in many ways. At his suggestion and request, the legislature, previous to its adjournment, placed $500,000 at his disposal in aid of the government in supplying the troops. From this fund Governor Shaw equipped the regiments to such an extent that they won the admiration of every camp where they went; and he declined no request for supplies or equipment made by any officer or soldier in the four regiments sent forward.

Governor Shaw is now, with but little more than half of his term completed, a national character, on account of his contributions to monetary science, and his other excellent addresses. While declining a large majority of the invitations received to speak outside of the state, he presided and made the principal address at the national monetary convention at Indianapolis, in February, 1898. He addressed the Chamber of Commerce at Rochester, N. Y., at their annual banquet in 1898. He was the guest of honor and principal speaker at the annual banquet of the manufacturers of the state of New York, in February, 1899, where President McKinley had preceded him as the principal speaker the year before.

Governor Shaw has an ideal home at Denison, which is the center of hospitality. Mrs. Shaw was Alice Crawshaw, daughter of James Crawshaw, one of the best known pioneers of eastern Iowa, who came to the state when a territory in 1887. They were married in Camanche, in December, 1877. Three children have been born to them, Enid, who is now a student in Cornell college, Earl and Erma, both in the public schools of Des Moines.

CHRISTIAN, GEORGE MELVILLE, United States marshal for the Southern district of Iowa, for many years a resident of Grinnell, is one of the best known republican leaders in the state. He has had an influential part in shaping the affairs of the republican party of the state for many years.

Mr. Christian is a native of Illinois, born in Chicago June 19, 1847, in the house that stood where the Chicago, Rock Island & Pacific station now stands, at Van Buren and La Salle streets. His parents were David William Christian, who was born in Albany, N. Y., in 1813, and served four years in the Fifty-first Illinois Infantry during the war, and Lucy Anna Patrick, who was a native of Ware, Mass. His father was a cabinet maker and carpenter and his ancestors were Manxmen. His mother's ancestors were English.

Young Christian attended public school in Chicago and later Bryant & Stratton's Commercial college in Davenport, Iowa, in 1866. Having his own way to make in the world he did not attend school after he was 12 years old, except in the Commercial college, and had no other college education. He first came to Iowa in 1865 as a telegraph operator, but did not remain permanently. He finally settled in Grinnell in the spring of 1870, where he continued to reside.

Mr. Christian has had an active business life. He began to earn money when he was a young boy by folding papers for the *Press* and *Tribune* in Chicago, owned by the famous "Long John" Wentworth. His first steady job was acting as messenger boy for Stephen A. Douglas while that famous democrat was president of the United States fair in Chicago in 1860. In 1861 he became a news agent on the Rock Island road from Chicago to Kellogg, then the western terminus of the line. In 1866 he went to work for H. F. Royce, afterward general superintendent of the Rock Island, then engaged in general merchandise and lumber business in Pond Creek, Ill., and as station agent of the Rock Island at that point. He taught Mr. Christian the art of telegraphy, so that he soon became an expert operator and was employed at Tiskilwa and Morris, Ill., and later in Superintendent Kimball's office at Davenport. In 1868 he owned and managed a restaurant at 174 South Clark street, Chicago. Mr. Christian's ability as a telegraph operator and his knowledge of the railroad business secured him a position as station agent on

the Rock Island at Grinnell, in 1870, and after being there a few months he entered into partnership with Hiram Johnson and purchased the Grinnell House, which he conducted until 1877. In the spring of that year he purchased the leading hotel in Grinnell, known as the Chapin House, which he conducted until 1890 and still owns. For three years, from 1885 till 1888, he leased and operated the Hotel Colfax, the large summer resort hotel at the big spring a mile east of the town of Colfax. In 1889, Mr. Christian was appointed assistant superintendent of the railway mail

service by Gen. J. S. Clarkson, who was then first assistant postmaster-general. He held this position for fifteen months and on July 1, 1890, was appointed postoffice inspector by the postmaster-general, John Wanamaker. His record for efficiency in this position was such that he was reappointed year after year notwithstanding changes in administration, and held the place until he resigned, March 1, 1898, and accepted his present appointment at the hands of President McKinley upon the recommendation of the Iowa delegation in congress. During his term as postoffice inspector, Mr. Christian was connected with some of the most famous cases in the department and was regarded as one of the most valuable inspectors in the service.

He has always been a republican and has never voted any other ticket. He was five times alderman, and twice mayor in Grinnell. For a number of years he was chairman of the republican county committee and a member of the republican state committee from the Sixth district serving as chairman of the finance committee. In 1888 he was a delegate to the republican national convention in Chicago and was chairman of the finance committee of the Iowa delegation. He had charge of the organization of the Allison campaign for the presidential nomination in that convention. He has been a delegate to nearly every republican state convention for twelve years.

Mr. Christian was only 14 years of age when the war broke out. He tried several times to enlist, but was refused on account of his age. He is a member of the Masonic fraternity, is a Knight Templar and is a charter member of the Franklyn club at Grinnell. He is a member of the Congregational church.

Mr. Christian was married in 1869 to Miss Margaret M. Rowse, of Davenport, Iowa. They have four children living, viz: Geo. H., born April 9, 1873; Jessie Isabel, born October 27, 1876; Alma, born July 1, 1878, and Margaret, born February 11, 1880.

---

HOWARD, JOSEPH EDWARD. The story of the life of Joseph Edward Howard, of Forest City, is like that of many others of Iowa's progressive citizens in that his advancement from the position of a farmer boy in lowly circumstances to an honored citizen, filling a position of responsibility, has not been without its trials, vexations and arduous toil. The parents of Mr. Howard were natives of Pennsylvania. They removed to Fayette county, Iowa, in 1855, and engaged in farming. This vocation was followed until 1869, at which time they removed to Forest City where they now reside. It was in Fayette county that Mr. J. E. Howard was born, on August 31, 1855. He lived on the farm and attended the common schools until 13 years of age. At 17 he began teaching, which was followed for four years, a part of that time in country districts and part in Forest City. He later entered the law department of the State university, and was admitted to the bar on June 8, 1878. From 1879 to 1883, he followed the practice of law at Forest City, and then accepted the position as traveling collector in Iowa, Nebraska, Dakota and

Minnesota, which position he held for seven years. In 1890, he established a real estate business in Forest City in connection with O. A. Olson, and the firm is now doing a most excellent business.

In 1892, the firm of Howard & Olson organized the banking institution of Howard, Olson & Ulland, at Buffalo Center, with a capital of $25,000, fully paid, and the same is to-day one of the solid financial concerns of that county. During his long residence in Forest City, Mr. Howard has held many offices of trust and honor. In 1893, he was elected mayor, without opposition, and in 1894, a member of the town council, which last named position he has

filled up to the present time. It was during his terms of office that the city put in a first-class electric light plant and system of water works, improvements which, by the way, reflected great credit upon the officers having them in charge. In 1895, he was appointed clerk of the district court of Winnebago county, to fill the vacancy caused by the resignation of Mr. G. S. Gilbertson, who was elected to represent the Forty-first district in the state senate, and that position he held until his successor was elected in 1896, and is now postmaster at Forest City. He still makes Forest City his home and dealing in real estate a prominent part of his business. He has been identified with the history and progress of his county for the past twenty-five years; has contributed generously for the public improvements, and has crowded the avenues of benevolence with good deeds. He was married in 1879 to Miss Elnora Skinner, of Forest City, and seven children have been born to them, all of which are living. He is a prominent Mason and member of the Odd Fellows.

NORRIS, WILLIAM HENRY, of Manchester, is a native of Massachusetts, although he came to Iowa as early as 1861. He has been prominent in political affairs of the state for a number of years, having been elected a delegate to the republican national convention at Chicago in 1884; more recently a member of the Twenty-fourth General Assembly, and in 1890, a member of the state central committee. This position he occupied for four years and during the last two was chairman of the executive committee. In 1894 he was chosen a member of Governor Jackson's staff, with rank of lieutenant-colonel, and served in that capacity during the governor's term of office.

Mr Norris was born at Stoneham, Mass., February 3, 1857, and is of Scotch-Irish descent. His father, Thomas Norris, was a farmer, and in 1861 removed to Delaware county, Iowa, with his family. In 1864 he removed to Linn county. William secured his early training in the public school and completed a course of study at a business college in Davenport. From there he went to Cornell college and finally to the State university, where he graduated from the law department in 1882. Here he was chosen by the faculty as one of ten members, out of a graduating class of about 130, to represent the class in the commencement exercises. One year after graduation he was chosen a member of the examining committee, selected to pass upon the fitness of the members of the class of 1883, for graduation, and in 1892 was again selected by the supreme court of Iowa to act as a member of this committee. While a student at Iowa City he was a member of "Irving Institute," one of the old literary societies of the university. Mr. Norris commenced the practice of law in 1882, locating at Manchester, and soon after formed a partnership with Judge A. S. Blair, with whom he was associated for a number of years. In 1893 Judge Blair was elected district judge and Mr. Norris associated himself

with George W. Dunham. Although actively engaged in the practice of law, he is a director in the First National bank of Manchester, and is interested in many other enterprises. Prior to 1891 Mr. Norris held the office of city solicitor for two terms and that year he was elected mayor of Manchester, which position he resigned when elected to the legislature. While a member of the Twenty-fourth General Assembly he was made chairman of the house committee on appropriations, an unusual honor for a first term member. At this session of the legislature he introduced the Australian ballot bill which was passed and became the law of the state. Mr. Nor-

ris is a prominent Mason, having taken all the York rite degrees, and the Scottish rite up to and including the thirty-second degree, being a member of DeMolay Consistory No. 1, located at Clinton. He is a "Shriner," K. of P. and a member of the I. O. O. F. He has been master of Manchester Lodge No. 165, A. F. and A. M.; H. P. of Olive Branch Chapter No. 48, R. A. M.; E. Com. of Nazareth Commandery No. 33, K. T., and is now grand patron of the Iowa Grand Chapter, O. E. S., and grand captain-general of the Grand Commandery of Iowa Knights Templar.

March 15, 1886, Mr. Norris was married to Martha B. Toogood, of Manchester.

They have three children, Carleton Howard, born July 2, 1887, Laura Marie, born August 16, 1889, and Thomas Toogood, born June 21, 1898. Mrs. Norris has always taken an active interest in club and society affairs. She is a member of the P. E. O. sisterhood and has been president of the local chapter of Manchester. She is now P. W. Matron of Orient Chapter No. 15, Order of the Eastern Star.

---

STEVENSON, SAMUEL KIRKWOOD, was born on a farm in Scott township, Johnson county, Iowa, March 10, 1867. His father, John A. Stevenson, now a retired farmer, is a native of Pennsylvania, who came to Iowa in 1857. He was a member of the board of supervisors of Johnson county for a number of years, has always taken an active interest in public affairs, and is an ardent republican. He is of Scotch-Irish descent, and the family for six generations have been steadfast in their adherence to the Presbyterian church. Several members of the family have been prominent ministers in that church.

William E. Stevenson, uncle of Samuel K., was the first governor of West Virginia. Mr. Stevenson's mother's maiden name was Henrietta Griffiths. She was born in London, Eng., and came to America when 18 years of age.

Samuel K. received his early education in the schools of the rural districts of Johnson county, after which he attended the academy at Iowa City, and graduated from that school in 1889. He then entered the State university, and graduated in the class of 1893 with the degree of Ph. B. He was chosen one of six out of a class of forty-eight to deliver an oration on commencement day. He was president of the Zethagathian Literary society during the fall term of 1892, and was one of the three debaters in the first joint debate between the universities of Iowa and Minnesota, held at Minneapolis, Minn., which debate was won unanimously by Iowa. He was business manager of *Vidette Reporter*, the university paper, during the years 1892-3. and was also the treasurer and one of the organizers of the University Lecture Bureau. He was just completing the law course in the State university when he was elected to the position of superintendent of schools of Johnson county in November, 1893. The high regard in which he was held by the people, and the faith they had in his qualifications for the position, was shown

when they elected him on the republican ticket with a majority of 725, while the head of the ticket was democratic by 700 majority. He was re-elected in November, 1895, and was the only republican elected in the county. During all the time that he held his office, nearly two terms, he devoted a great deal of attention to educational meetings, holding them in every township in the county. They were very largely attended, and resulted in arousing a deep interest in school work on the part of parents and teachers. He organized the Johnson County Teachers' association, which now holds four yearly meetings. He also organized the Johnson County School Officials' association, which is one of the first of its kind in the state, and has a large and enthusiastic membership. He introduced the school library movement in Johnson county, and during the last two years he was in office, ninety-five school libraries were established in that county. He raised the standard of qualification for teachers so that the grade of teachers in Johnson county now stands second to none

in the state. He was the editor of the *Johnson County Teacher*, a monthly school paper published in the interest of education. In the spring of 1897 he organized the Johnson County School of Methods, which was largely attended by the progressive teachers of eastern Iowa because of the high quality of instruction given. At this meeting resolutions were unanimously passed by the teachers and others assembled there, expressing their commendation and appreciation to Superintendent Stevenson for making possible for them this most excellent institute of methods. He has read several papers on educational themes before the State Teachers' association on "School Libraries, How to Establish and Maintain Them," and on "School Exhibitions; are They Beneficial?" He has organized and held school exhibitions at the Johnson county fairs with good results to the school work.

Mr. Stevenson was elected superintendent of the city schools of Iowa City, April 28, 1897, which position he still holds. The position was tendered him without solicitation. He is a member of the board of trustees of the Iowa City public library. He is also secretary of the Johnson County Sunday School union, and superintendent of the First Presbyterian Sunday school of Iowa City. He is a member of the First Presbyterian church, and has been a ruling elder in the church since April, 1895. Superintendent Stevenson was married to Miss Marcia A. Jacobs, of Cedar Rapids, on August 2, 1898.

---

JOICE, PETER MARTIN, at present a resident of Lake Mills, might very properly be termed the young Napoleon of finance in northern Iowa. Although born as late as the breaking out of the civil war he now holds foremost positions of responsibility in half a dozen banks, and is among the chief promoters of several business enterprises of considerable magnitude. His father, E. J. Joice, was born in Bergen, Norway, in 1827. The early years of his life were spent in farming and the manufacturing of cooperage. He came to this country in 1848, and located in Stoughton, Wis., where he ran a cooper shop for thirteen years. He removed to Forest City in 1879, where, for the last twelve years of his life, he was engaged in the lumber business. The mother of Mr. Joice was one of a prominent family in Norway, a brother having been a member of parliament for fourteen years.

Mr. Peter Martin Joice was born in Greene county, Wis., January 4, 1860. Following the regular period in the public schools of his native town he attended the colleges of Albion and Janesville, grad-

uating from the last named institution in 1878. In May, 1879, he engaged in the lumber business with his father, at Forest City, and earned his first money of any consequence during that partnership. In the fall of 1880 he entered the Winnebago

County bank as bookkeeper, and in 1883 was taken in as special partner, and made cashier. In July, 1886, he entered into partnership with Secor, Law & Plummer, bankers of Forest City, under the firm name of P. M. Joice & Company. This firm organized a bank at Lake Mills, and the same was placed in charge of Mr. Joice, by whose intelligent management it has been firmly grounded among the solid financial institutions of that section of the state. Besides owning the greater share of the stock in the bank last mentioned, Mr. Joice is vice-president of the First National bank at Wells, Minn., director in the First National bank at Albert Lea, president of the First National bank of Britt, Iowa, and president First National bank of Buffalo Center, Iowa. Mr. Joice is considered one of the best financiers in his section of the country, and there is no one who stands more ready to help his town than does he. He has served in the capacity of mayor for two terms, has been a member of the city council and school board for six years, and was re-elected to the same positions at the recent elections. He takes a warm interest in matters pertaining to education, and has contributed generously of his time and means toward bringing the schools of his town up to their present high standing. In June, 1896, he was elected a trustee of Cornell college at Mt. Vernon. Religiously, he is a member of the M. E. church, and a trustee of the denomination of that faith in Lake Mills; politically, he is a republican. He was united in marriage on January 2, 1883, to Miss Ida M. Law, and three children, Marie, Wilford and Katherine, have been born to them.

THOMPSON, F. W. The Thompson family, of which the subject of this sketch is a member, no doubt inherited the ability of an illustrious father. Mr. O. P. Thompson, the father, is a wealthy dry goods merchant of Decorah, Iowa. The beginning of his present fortune was made in McGregor. Born in Norway in 1834, he came to this country in 1853, and located in Decorah early in the sixties. He passed through all the panics from war times up to the present, but by keen business judgment, and ability of a high order, succeeded in keeping safely without the whirlpools which carried many great men down. Of the five children that were born to him several have attained distinction in the financial circles of the country. Edward T. is president of the First National bank of St. Thomas, N. D.; Charles J. holds a like position in the Forest City National bank, and T. A. Thompson is junior member of the firm of O. P. Thompson & Sons at St. Thomas. Edward T. is also the present grand chancellor of the Knights of Pythias for the state of South Dakota and has served four years as county treasurer of Pembina county, in the state of North Dakota.

Mr. F. W. Thompson was born at Decorah, Iowa, April 6, 1869. He graduated in the high schools there, and later took a business course under the tutorship of an expert accountant. He was then engaged as a clerk in his father's mercantile establishment, where he remained for four years. It was his early ambition to become a banker, and when an opportunity was presented to enter that business in connection with Thompson Brothers, at Forest City, the same was promptly accepted. This firm, while of the same name,

were in no way related to F. W. Thompson. In October, 1892, the banking institution of Thompson Brothers & Thompson began business, with Mr. F. W. Thompson as cashier. He held, in addition to that office, the position of treasurer of the Chicago and Iowa Western Land and Town Lot company, a corporation of $75,000 capital, and embracing within its assets 2,500 acres of choice land adjoining the town of Thompson, including the town site. Negotiations are about concluded, however, whereby Mr. Thompson will dispose of his interest in this corporation and identify himself with a bank of large capital, of which he

will be the principal officer and manager. He has always been a republican, and has taken a lively interest in the campaigns of his party, but has held no office except that of alderman in his own town. Being unmarried he is socially quite popular, and holds the foremost office in several clubs of considerable social note. He is a past grand officer in the order of Odd Fellows, and venerable consul in Camp 7, of the Modern Woodmen of America. He belongs to no church, but is trustee of the Baptist organization at Thompson. Mr. Thompson is now cashier of the First National bank of Thompson, Iowa, and president of the Citizens State bank of Lakefield, Minn.

LEWIS, HON. LESTER WARREN, of Clarinda, has served in both branches of the general assembly. In both the house and the senate he was chosen to the responsible position of chairman of the committee on appropriations, and it is a matter of history that no state warrants were stamped "unpaid for want of funds" during the following biennial periods. He was identified with all measures for the more economical administration of county and state government, and was particularly active and influential in the passage of the bill for a more strict accounting and examination of banks under state control. He distinguished himself while a member of the house by his determined efforts to secure legislation favorable to the miners and laboring men of the state.

He was born at Maple Park, Ill., August 8, 1860. His father, Seth Lewis, was a lumberman and banker, a successful man who was the soul of honor in all business affairs. His mother, Celina Woodworth Lewis, was educated at the Warrenville academy, a suburban school in Chicago, in the early history of that city. Two brothers, John and James Lewis, came from England during the first settlement of New England, and located at Barnstable, Mass. James Lewis was the great-great-great-grandfather of the senator, whose young son, Lester, belongs to the ninth generation of Lewises in America. The paternal ancestors for almost two centuries back have been farmers, and one or another has occupied the old homestead at Suffield, Conn., where the father of Hon. L. W. Lewis was born. Mr. Lewis' father was one of the pioneer settlers of Illinois, having located at Aurora when that country was very new. The mother was a native of New York. She had three brothers in the union army, one of whom, John M. Woodsworth, was a surgeon on the staff of Gen. John A. Logan, and afterwards became the first supervising surgeon-general of the marine hospitals of the United States.

Young Lewis was educated in the common schools of Marengo, Ill., the Chicago high schools and the Wheaton college, graduating from the latter in 1882. The college was a non-sectarian but Christian institution, strict in discipline, and few sports were indulged in, hard, conscientious study being required of all students. Mathematics and language were the specialties offered by the college, and in these, as well as the other studies in the curriculum, Mr. Lewis excelled throughout the

course. He came to Iowa, July 4, 1882, without a dollar, and went to work in his father's lumber yard in Seymour, Wayne county. In 1883 and 1884 he was teacher of the grammar room of the Seymour schools and at the same time kept the books for his father. The wages thus earned were carefully saved, and in May, 1884, he purchased a second-hand outfit and launched the Seymour *Press*, which he published until January, 1895, none of the time, however, making it his principal occupation. Later he became assistant cashier of the Farmers and Drovers bank, at Seymour and on January 1, 1886, secured

an interest in the bank and was elected its cashier. This position he filled until 1895, when he severed his connection with the bank to become vice-president of the Page County bank, of Clarinda, Iowa, of which Hon. Charles Linderman is president and J. N. Miller, cashier.

In 1887 he was elected to the house of the Twenty-second General Assembly, from Wayne county, and in 1889 was re-elected by a well-pleased constituency; in 1891 the same county, with Lucas county, elected him a member of the senate, and at each election he received an increased majority. He is a member of no society or club, but has been an active worker of the Presbyterian church since his college days. He was married to Miss Nellie E. Hills, September 13, 1882. She graduated from the same college and in the same class with him. They have five children—Eva, Olive, Florence, Lester and Marion Lewis.

___

LANE, CLARK WHITE, is one of Centerville's leading business men, and is a member of the firm of Drake & Lane. His father, John Walker Lane, was born in 1818 in Westmoreland county, Pa. He is a retired farmer, and is now living comfortably at Centerville. The mother of C. W. Lane was Sarah Welty, who was born in Ohio in 1825, and died at Centerville at the age of 42. C. W. Lane was born at Independence, Washington county, Pa., September 16, 1848. He received a common school education, and, as his father was for many years both merchant and farmer, he received early training in both these lines of business, which well fitted him for the affairs of later life. In 1864, at the age of 16, he came with his parents to Iowa, settling in Appanoose county, where for ten years he worked with his father. In 1874 he was given the management of Gen. F. M. Drake's mercantile establishment, and in 1875 he formed a partnership with General Drake and R. F. Lyman, and engaged in general merchandise under the firm name of Drake, Lane & Lyman, at Centerville. In 1878 he purchased Mr. Lyman's interest in the business, and the firm name was changed to Drake & Lane, though General Drake was succeeded in 1885 by his son, F. E. Drake. In July, 1898, C. W. Lane purchased the interest of F. E. Drake, and is now sole owner. Under Mr. Lane's exclusive management, this business has grown from a small beginning to be one of the strongest and largest establishments in southern Iowa. In addition to handling an extensive mercantile stock, he buys and ships large quantities of farm produce, including grain, hay and flour. Mr. Lane also has extensive interests in coal mining property, and probably controls more coal mining stock than any other man in the county. He has strong faith in the future greatness of the Appanoose coal fields, and regards his interest in them as a better investment than government bonds. He has built and now owns several very fine business buildings, one of which he occupies with his extensive stock of general merchandise.

Mr. Lane was married June 23, 1874, to Miss Kate Ella Drake, a daughter of Judge John A. and Harriet J. Drake, and a sister of Gov. F. M. Drake and of J. H. Drake, of Albia, Iowa. Mrs. Lane was a woman possessed of many admirable traits, and was very devoted to her family. She died October 20, 1890, leaving four children—John Clyde, born October 26, 1876; George Hamilton, born December 10, 1878; Clark White, Jr., born June 5, 1883; and Marion, born May 7, 1886. The oldest son, John, is studying law at Drake university; the second, George, is attending the Military academy at Culver City, Ind.; and the third, Clark, is in school at home. The youngest, Marion, died July 22, 1894.

In politics Mr. Lane is a democrat. He has served one term as city alderman, four years as member of the school board, and president one term. He is president of the Centerville Block company, a company with a quarter of a million capital stock. He is a member of the Christian church, and for five years has been superintendent of the Sunday school, which has a member-

ship of over 200. Mr. Lane takes pride in the fact that he never bet on a horse race, never speculated on the board of trade, and never knew how to play a game of cards, pool or billiards.

HEAD, HON. ALBERT, whose name for more than thirty years has been identified with every stride that Greene county and Jefferson have made towards progress and improvement, was born November 25, 1838, in Highland county, Ohio. His father being a farmer, he was reared to this life until he attained his majority. In 1855, with his parents, he came overland from their Ohio home to Poweshiek county, Iowa, where his father again located on a farm. During the winter of 1857 and 1858 Mr. Head taught district school, at the close of which he took up the study of law, reading with the late Hon. M. E. Cutts, with whom he remained until 1859, when he was admitted to practice. At the same time he co-operated with Col. S. F. Cooper in the newspaper business, publishing the Montezuma *Republican*. He continued this but a brief time, however, for in 1861 he assisted in the organization of Company F, Tenth Iowa infantry, and was elected captain. He commanded the company until promoted to assistant adjutant-general in 1863.

During his service he was wounded several times, once at Corinth, Miss., once at Champion Hill, and once at Vicksburg, the latter being a severe injury of the head, which detained him in the hospital from May 22 until September, 1863.

Upon regaining his health he assumed his rank as assistant adjutant-general, serving on the staffs of Generals Mathias, McPherson and Raum, and was with Sherman on his famous march through Georgia to the sea.

Immediately after the close of the war he came to Greene county, locating in Jefferson, where he took up the practice of his profession, and also, in co-operation with Mahlon Head, established the banking firm of Head Brothers. Under this caption the bank was continued until 1893 when it was merged into the Greene County State bank, with Hon. Albert Head as president and the principal stockholder.

While the captain has recently transferred a great deal of the responsibility of his numerous financial and real estate interests to the care of his sons, A. A. and R. C. Head, he is yet a busy man and holds many important positions of honor and trust. Aside from being president of the Greene County State bank, he is president of the Jefferson Land and Loan company, president Bank of Paton, president of Citizens' bank, Grand Junction; vice-president Bank of Pilot Mound, trustee Drake university, of Des Moines, and president of the Greene County Agricultural society. He is also very prominent and takes a deep and active interest in numerous civic societies and holds leading offices in many of the most prominent lodges of the state, among them being treasurer Des Moines Consistory No. 3, Scottish Rite Masons; treasurer M. O. O. L., of United States; is a thirty-third degree Mason; noble grand of Greene Lodge No.

315, and member Jefferson Encampment, I. O. O. F.; member of Capital Lodge No. 110, Masonic Order, Des Moines, and Chapter R. A. M., and Knight Templar, of Jefferson, and El Kahir Temple, Mystic Shrine, Cedar Rapids.

He has been a member of George H. Thomas Post, G. A. R., ever since the institution of that post, and he takes special interest in all the doings

of his friends and comrades who endured with him the hardships and privations of war. His sterling worth as a citizen and business man has long been recognized by his fellow citizens, and many times he has been called to fill high offices in the gift of his constituents.

For eight years he represented Greene county in the house of representatives, having been four times nominated by acclamation by the republican party, and was speaker of the house one term. The valuable services he rendered in this position will long be remembered by his constituents. He was several times mayor of Jefferson and each time proved an admirable executive officer and gave the city a progressive and prosperous administration. He served one year each as president and treasurer of the Iowa State Agricultural society. The captain is a gentleman whose personal deportment never fails to win the admiration of all his associates and his kind-hearted nature strongly testifies the high appreciation in which he holds the confidence that has been reposed in him by his fellow citizens and associates. He is public spirited and enterprising in the extreme and can always be relied upon to give liberally his time, counsel and money to aid any enterprise that will promote the public welfare.

He has a bright and interesting family— four children, three sons and one daughter. His eldest son, M. M. Head, is the capable and efficient cashier of the Greene County

State bank. His only daughter, Estelle, is the wife of C. E. Marquis, the popular assistant cashier of the Greene County bank, and also one of Jefferson's leading grocers.

His second son, A. A., assists him in caring for his real estate interests, while the youngest son, Roscoe C., is a graduate of the law department of the State university and is practicing his profession in Jefferson.

In 1895 the captain erected the Head house, one of the finest hotels in the state, where he resides with his sons. Since his residence in Jefferson he has erected several fine structures, among them "Head's opera house," the city hall and several brick business houses. He is the owner of about 6,000 acres of land in Greene county, in which he is more interested, personally, than in any other branch of his varied business. His 1,000-acre farm near Jefferson receives his personal attention.

---

TOSTEVIN, THOMAS, city engineer of Council Bluffs, is one of the well known pioneers of that region. In the year 1854, he was appointed as government surveyor to survey the claims of "squatters" on the original town site of Council Bluffs and efficiently performed that duty. Mr. Tostevin was born December 21, 1830, on the Island of Guernsey, one of that beautiful group in the English channel known as the Norman Isles. He is a direct descendant of the Normans who located upon and occupied those fertile isles at the time of the Norman conquest of England. His father, John Tostevin, came to America when a young man and lived for several years in Germantown, Penn. He then returned to Guernsey where he married Martha Le Prevost and brought up a family of seven children. About 1834 he returned to the United States with his family and located in New York city. He followed the business of contracting and building and was a faithful member of the Society of Friends. His children were educated in the schools of that society. In 1848, with his wife and two younger children, he removed to Salem, Henry county, Iowa, which was at that time settled principally by Friends. He and his wife returned to New York in 1856, and soon afterward died at the home of a daughter, Mrs. Rachel L. P. Alexander, in Brooklyn, N. Y. They both rest in the old Quaker burying ground now surrounded by Prospect park in that city.

Thomas Tostevin was educated in the

Quaker schools and finished his course at the Friends seminary in Duchess county, N. Y. While there he studied surveying with the purpose of making it his life business in connection with civil engineering. With his parents and younger brother he came to Iowa in 1848, arriving in Burlington on the Fourth of July, while the inhabitants were celebrating the glorious day with the old fashioned vigor and spirit characteristic of early ante-prohibition days. After locating in Iowa, Thomas taught school for several years in Jefferson and Henry counties. In 1850 he acted as "rodman" under General McKane, a

United States engineer from West Point, in the survey of a projected line of railroad from Keokuk to Dubuque to parallel the Mississippi river, and in 1852 acted as rodman under Guy Wells, city engineer of Keokuk.

In 1853, Mr. Tostevin was candidate for surveyor of Henry county on the whig ticket. In 1854 he received a government appointment and moved to Council Bluffs, and in October of that year took a contract in conjunction with J. Hanks, a relative of President Lincoln, to survey eight townships of government land. He was appointed by the legislature of Nebraska, in 1857, as a commissioner to survey a territorial road from Rulo, on the Missouri river, to Fort Kearney. In the same year he laid out the town of Rulo.

Mr. Tostevin was appointed in 1861 to fill a vacancy in the office of county treasurer and recorder of Pottawattamie county, and he was re-elected for three subsequent terms to the same position. He was elected mayor of the city of Council Bluffs, in 1868 and in 1870 was an alderman. He went to Utah in 1870, and for four years was engaged in silver mining. He was deputy United States mineral surveyor in that territory during two years of that time. He returned to Council Bluffs in 1874, and since that time has been for several terms county surveyor of the county and city engineer of the city. He is the inventor and patentee of several useful inventions, the latest being a combined protractor and parallel rule for surveyors and architects.

During the war Mr. Tostevin was appointed captain of artillery in the Iowa militia, but was not sent to the front. He was one of the first organizers of the Union League in that section of the state and was president of that order for three years. He has been a republican since the organization of the party.

He was married October 31, 1852, to Miss Harriet Gibbs, who was born in Schoharie county, N. Y., June 17, 1832. They have had nine children, four of whom are now living, Walter J., born October 31, 1861; Julia L., born July 30, 1863, and now Mrs. E. E. Harvey, of Denver, Col.; Albert T., born November 6, 1865; Ida, born August 8, 1867, and now Mrs. W. H. Wakefield, of Omaha, Neb.

---

POTTER, Hon. LEVI FRANKLIN, banker of Oakland, Pottawattamie county, and one of the leading members of the legislature, was born in Wauwatosa, Milwaukee county, Wis., March 27, 1855. His father, Levi Brigham Potter, who settled in Wisconsin in 1839, was of New England stock, and prominent in municipal and church affairs. His mother, Hitty Wenzel Potter, was a woman of marked ability and of great influence in her community. Ebenezer Potter and Col. Levi Brigham, great grandparents of the subject of this sketch, were veterans of the great struggle for the independence of the colonies.

Levi Franklin Potter completed his education in Ripon and Beloit colleges, and after teaching three years came to Oakland in 1879 and then engaged in mercantile business. In March, 1884, he became partner and cashier in the Citizens bank, now the Citizens State bank, of that town, which position he now occupies. He is a prominent member of the Iowa Banking association, having served as a member of the executive council and on the legislative committee of that body.

Prominent in municipal affairs, he has twice been mayor of Oakland. Always affiliating with the republican party, he was elected by a flattering majority to represent the county in the Twenty-sixth Gen-

eral Assembly, which met in 1896, and in extra session in 1897, to complete the codification of the laws of the state. He was re-elected to the same representation in the Twenty-seventh General Assembly, which met in 1898. Mr. Potter's record as a legislator is one in which his constituency have just pride. During his first session he was chairman of the committee on telegraph, telephone, and express, and member of the committees on ways and means, code revision, banks and banking, municipal corporations, police regulations, and labor. His work on the ways and means committee of that session so attracted the

attention of its chairman, Hon. J. H. Funk, that when Mr. Funk was elected speaker of the Twenty seventh General Assembly one of the first chairmanships he determined was that of ways and means, which went to Mr. Potter. In this session Mr. Potter was also member of the committees on railroads and commerce, banks and banking, telegraph, telephone, and express, municipal corporations, rules, and labor, and a member of the joint committee on retrenchment and reform.

At this session Mr. Potter introduced and secured the passage of several important bills, among which were House file 199, providing shorter forms for assessment rolls and assessors' books, an important act that will save hundreds of dollars every year to each county; House file 165, appropriating $25,000 (in addition to the $10,000 appropriated at the previous session) for the Iowa exhibit at the Trans-Mississippi exposition; House file 101, extending the term of school treasurers from one to two years (a measure the merit of which is appreciated by those who have noticed the efforts of banks for control of school funds); House file 147, providing severe penalties for the adulteration of candy.

At his first session Mr. Potter had charge of, and secured the passage in the house, of the senate bill taxing express companies 1 per cent on the gross amount of business done by them in the state, and in the Twenty-seventh General Assembly he supplemented this work by introducing and securing the passage of House file 234 doubling the taxes so paid by these companies. He was also deeply interested in the encouragement of the beet sugar industry, and the value of his work on these lines ranks him among the pioneers of this important enterprise.

Mr. Potter was married in 1881 to Miss M. J. Wood, and has established a delightful home in Oakland, where he and his wife are important factors in all local matters tending to advance the education, morals, and well being of the community.

---

MILLS, OLIVER, of Lewis, Cass county, has been for nearly fifty years a resident of Iowa, and through his connection with the State Agricultural society, which lasted for about twenty years, became well known to the people of our state. For three successive terms he served as president of the society, and was for many years a director and one who took a leading part in building up the society and making it a success. He, like many others of our prominent citizens, is a native of Ohio, born at Gustavus, Trumbull county, February 1, 1820. This village is situated in northeastern Ohio, about fifty miles east of Cleveland and almost in sight of the beautiful Lake Erie.

Harlow Mills, the father of Oliver, was of pure New England stock and a native of Hartford county, Conn. He was a prosperous farmer and dairyman and married Faith Ann Spencer, also a native of that county, but of German descent. In 1819 they emigrated to what was then the wild west and located in northeastern Ohio. In this beautiful lake region, known then as the western reserve, Oliver was born and grew to manhood. He attended the district schools in that locality, which were then excellent, until he was 14, when he went to Farmington academy to finish his education.

When old enough to start out for himself he engaged in farming and stock raising, in which he was very successful. April 17, 1839, he married Sophia Arnold. Attracted by the fame of the wonderful prairie west of the Mississippi, in 1850 he removed his young family to Lee county, Iowa, and settled at Denmark. Since that date he has been active in building up the industries of the new state and has managed his own business with a sagacity which has enabled him to accumulate a competence.

After residing at Denmark nearly eight years he removed to Lewis, Cass county, in 1857; at that time almost all of the country west of Des Moines was a prairie wilderness. It is now, 1899, a thickly settled and most beautifully improved country. Mr. Mills still resides at Lewis, at the age of 78 years, with mind as bright and clear as ever, with interest unabated in state and nation.

Mr. Mills was originally a whig, but since the organization of the party has been an active and influential republican He has held several minor offices and was a

member of the Fourteenth General Assembly, representing Cass, Montgomery and Adair counties, then forming the Twentieth representative district.

Since the early age of 14, Mr. Mills has been a member of the Congregational church. He has always practiced and advocated the strictest temperance. Mr. Mills has six children: John A., born March 9, 1840; Edward P., born August 25, 1841; N. L., born March 25, 1846; Sophia, born April 21, 1849; George S., born June 1, 1852, and Franklin O., born June 1, 1854. His first wife died in 1876 and April 25, 1877, he married Julia A. Forgy.

NICHOLSON, DELOS FREMONT, cashier of the State bank at Lamoni, is a man of great energy and business sagacity, and entirely through his own efforts has already amassed a very comfortable fortune. His ancestors were of the thrifty New England type, his great-great-grandfather, Joshua Nicholson, having come from England in 1740 to settle in Philadelphia. His grandfather, Joshua Nicholson, was one of the early pioneers of western New York, and died in 1865 at the age of 87. Mr. Nicholson's father, Charles Nicholson, was born in 1819 in Duchess county, N. Y. He was a great lover of books, and dealt in them for over forty years. He was liberal in religion, and a republican in politics. He died in 1883. Mr. Nicholson's mother, Fanny S. Cady, was born in 1828, in Oneida county, N Y. Her parents were also pioneers of that state, her father, Philip Cady, having moved from Vermont to New York, with his family, in 1830.

D. F. Nicholson was born December 11, 1855, in Hector, Schuyler county, N. Y., near the banks of Seneca lake. He spent his youth on a farm, and until he was 15 attended school at the little red schoolhouse on the hill. At 15 he came west with his parents, who settled on a small farm near Sandwich, Ill. Here the opportunities for securing an education were more favorable, and he made good use of them, walking two miles to town during the winter to attend the Sandwich high school, where he made rapid progress. He afterwards attended the Classical seminary at Paw Paw, and then began teaching in the district schools, but soon advanced, teaching a year in the public schools of Paw Paw and a year in the Paw Paw seminary, and then became principal of the Sandwich high school, where he had been a student four years previous. Though successful as a teacher, he resigned in 1880 in order to engage in more remunerative employment, and accepted a position with the D. M. Osborne Machine company, taking charge of a branch agricultural implement house at Salt Lake City. He remained with this company five years, receiving an increase in salary each year, and successfully managing their business throughout Utah, Idaho and Montana. While in Salt Lake City he was appointed territorial treasurer of Utah in 1882 by Governor Murray, but the Mormon legislature did not permit him to accept the office on account of his not being a polygamist. During his residence in the west Mr. Nicholson acted as

reporter and correspondent for several newspapers, and his descriptions of the Rocky Mountain country, which appeared in eastern periodicals, were read with much interest. In 1885 he came to Lamoni, Iowa, and for three years successfully conducted a hardware business. In 1888 he sold out at a good profit, and in company with Robert Winning, a capitalist from St Joseph, Mo., he organized the

first bank of Lamoni, which was soon incorporated as the Lamoni State bank, with Mr Nicholson as cashier and manager. Lamoni was then a village of but 400 inhabitants, but it has grown rapidly, and its population is now about five times that number. During this period he bought and sold many farms, and also a large tract of land adjoining the town which he laid off in half-acre lots. In this way he rapidly increased his income and wealth, until now he owns the controlling interest in the bank, besides hundreds of acres of valuable farming land, and an elegant home in Lamoni.

Mr. Nicholson has always been a republican in politics, and has held numerous local offices. He is a pioneer member of the Odd Fellows lodge at Lamoni, and is also a Modern Woodman. He is secretary of the board of trustees of Graceland college, and has served several years as city alderman. He was brought up a Methodist, but has since become a member of the church of Latter Day Saints.

He was married March 6, 1878, to Miss Minnie Blair, daughter of Elder William and Elizabeth Blair, of Sandwich, Ill. They have four children: Harry Carl, born in 1879, who is now attending Graceland college; Todd Blair, born in 1883; Ray

Kessler, born in 1886, and Gracia, born in 1896.

This ends the first twenty years of Mr. Nicholson's married life, and he is now just in his prime. Commencing as a poor farmer's boy, he educated himself and has reaped the fruits of his labors, being a self-made man in every respect, and has much to expect from the future.

McHENRY, W. A., son of James and Sarah (Allen) McHenry, was born in Almond, N. Y., on the 6th of March, 1841. He is of Scotch-Irish descent. His grandfather, John McHenry was born in Coleraine, County Antrim, Ireland, and came to America in 1730, on the same ship with the father of DeWitt Clinton. He served as major of the First New York battalion in the French war of 1756-7. His son, Henry McHenry, was born at Wallkill Valley, Orange county, N. Y., July, 1752, and served as captain in the Second United States (or Continental army) infantry during the war of the revolution. His son, James McHenry, was born at Fishing Creek, Northumberland county, Pa., in 1788, and in 1797 the family moved to McHenry Valley, Allegany county, N. Y. In the war of 1812 he served as first lieutenant in Captain Van Campen's company of rifles, and died in June, 1841. W. A. McHenry was his youngest son. He lived in the old homestead until he was 14 years of age, when he went to Milton, Wis., with his brother, Vincent McHenry. He received a common school education, and, in 1860, removed to Ogle county, Ill., where he worked on a farm until the commencement of the civil war. Thrilled with patriotic fire he volunteered, September 5, 1861, as a private in Company L, Eighth Illinois cavalry. The regiment was immediately sent to Washington and attached to the army of the Potomac, participating in all the important battles in which that army was engaged until January, 1864, when the regiment was veteranized and transferred to the department at Washington. It was then made their duty to look after Mosby's band of guerrillas, and the regiment gained for itself great distinction in hand to hand encounters with the enemy. During his service Mr. McHenry personally captured eight of the enemy and had many narrow escapes, but escaped without injury. He was mustered out of the service as first sergeant, July 23, 1865. He was previously recommended by Captain

Bradley to fill a vacancy of lieutenant in the company but owing to the close of the war did not receive the commission. At the close of the war he formed a partnership with his brother in the real estate business at Denison, Iowa. Emigration rapidly followed the extension of railroad lines to the Pacific and the firm of McHenry Bros. did a large and profitable business in the selling of land. Banking was added and success attended both enterprises.

In 1877, Mr. W. A. McHenry purchased his brother's interests and conducted the business alone until the W. A. McHenry bank was merged into the First National

bank of Denison, with a capital stock of $100,000. Of this bank Mr. McHenry is president and principal stockholder. In business methods he is conservative, and, during the panic of 1893 he was not obliged to borrow a single dollar. The rapid accumulation of deposits testifies that the people in his vicinity have the utmost confidence in his ability and integrity and the Iowa bankers have honored him by electing him president of their association. During his long experience in the real estate business Mr. McHenry has bought and improved many valuable tracts of land, some of which he still retains. Of late years he has engaged extensively in feeding cattle for market, and on his fine valley farm, of 600 acres, adjoining the city of Denison, he has a large herd of thoroughbred Aberdeen-Angus cattle which have a world-wide celebrity as the "McHenry Park Herd." They carried off the highest honors at the World's Columbian exposition in Chicago, taking twenty-four prizes. He served three years as president of the American Aberdeen-Angus Cattle Breeders' association, and takes great pride in everything pertaining to the improvement and advancement of the "doddies."

Politically, Mr. McHenry is a republican and cast his first vote for Abraham Lincoln. His great business interests, however, prevent him from entering the political arena. He is an enthusiastic member of the G. A. R., and always meets with the "boys" in the state and national encampments. He is a past department commander of Iowa. He is a prominent member of the Baptist church and has for many years been one of the most earnest supporters and generous contributors. While at home on furlough, in 1864, he married Miss Mary L. Sears, of Rockford, Ill. She preceded him to Denison and served as deputy county treasurer and recorder until the close of the war. She is prominently identified with the Woman's Relief Corps of the G. A. R., was elected department president in 1887 and national president in 1890. Mr. and Mrs. McHenry have four children, two sons and two daughters. In 1885 Mr. McHenry built the elegant residence he now occupies, and surrounded by congenial friends and a happy family he enjoys the comforts of a well earned fortune

STEELE, THOMAS H. One of the leading and most active men in the work of developing and the varied interests of Cherokee county, especially in the way of securing eastern money for farmers who desired to improve their land and for individuals lacking capital for the promotion of different enterprises, is Thomas H. Steele, of Steeles' bank at Cherokee. The father, Thomas S. Steele, who was at the head of the firm until his death in 1896, did not give his personal attention to the business at Cherokee. The mother before her marriage was Isabella Fenwick, a niece of Rev. Alexander Bullions, for more than fifty years pastor of the Associate Presbyterian church at Coila, N. Y., and the Rev. Peter Bullions, author of a series of Latin school books. The early paternal ancestors came from Coleraine, Ireland, about 1760, and settled in Salem, Washington county, N. Y. The mother's parents were natives of Scotland, who came to Salem, N. Y., in 1810.

Thomas H. Steele was born at Salem, N. Y., May 2, 1844. He attended the district school, the Cambridge academy, and the Clinton Liberal institute at Clinton, N. Y. He came to Iowa in the fall of 1872, and through the assistance of J. H. Leavitt, of Waterloo, secured employment with Bowman & Burr, bankers, of Waverly. While thus engaged he became convinced of his own ability to undertake a like en-

terprise, and in the spring of 1874 communicated that belief to his father in the east, who at once authorized him to look up a location and promised to join him in the venture. The son decided upon Cherokee, and in the spring of 1874 a banking business was started there under the firm name of T. S. Steele & Son. The county at that time was new, and the pioneers stood in great need of money, so the business of the new firm grew to goodly proportions. More help being required for the transaction of the constantly increasing business, two brothers, D. T. and J. F. Steele, were taken into the firm, and continued the business for some years as T. S. Steele & Sons. Since the death of T.

S. Steele, which occurred August 14, 1896, the bank has been known as Steeles' bank, the firm consisting of T. H., D. T. and J. F. Steele. These men have been of material assistance in promoting the prosperity of the town of Cherokee and the surrounding country, and are regarded as among the most progressive and useful citizens of that community.

Mr. Steele is a republican, but has held no political office except that of member of the school board. He is an elder in the Presbyterian church, but is not a member of any social club or secret society. He was married August 25, 1875, to Miss Evaline M. Washburn. She was born in New York, but came to Iowa while yet young. Her education was secured in the high school of Cedar Falls and the Iowa college at Grinnell. At the time of her marriage she was principal of the Waverly high school. They have had ten children, nine of whom are living. The children are: Eva Belle, Grace S., Winifred, Mary B., Fannie Corey, Susan W., Margaret T., Harrison C. and Richard T., besides a son, Thomas H., Jr., who died in his fourth year.

---

CLARKE, Hon. A. D., was born at Darlington, Canada, September 26, 1842. His father was Jasper Clarke, a farmer of moderate means. His mother's maiden name was Laura Sumner, a daughter of Shuball Sumner, of the town of Jay, Essex county, N. Y. Grandfather Sumner was a volunteer in the revolutionary army and captain of what was called the Silver Grays, of the town of Jay, Essex county, N. Y., in the war of 1812. He was an uncle of the late Charles Sumner, senator from Massachusetts.

Mr. Clarke spent the most of his childhood and early manhood on a farm in Fond du Lac county, Wis. Here he had the advantage of a district school education. He earned his first dollars husking corn at 25 cents per day on the farm of Homer Watters, of Byron, Wis.

When the civil war broke out patriotic young Clarke enlisted in the first call for three months' men. Later he enlisted in the Third Wisconsin Volunteers, Company F, but failed to pass muster, being under the required age at that time.

In 1865 Mr. Clarke moved to Algona, northwestern Iowa. Here he is a successful business man, has borne an influential part for the past thirty-two years in the

development and building up of both town and country.

He began by renting a farm, which he operated three years. Studied law with Marcus Robins, an attorney at Algona, and in four years was admitted to the bar. Circumstances caused him to drift into the real estate business. This business growing rapidly, he gave little attention to the law.

Mr. Clarke has always been a republican. In 1887 he was elected a member of the Iowa legislature, and served one term. In 1893 Governor Boies appointed Mr. Clarke as delegate to the Trans-Mississippi congress, he being one of the two republicans from the state. Governor Drake also, in 1897, appointed him as delegate to the International Gold Mining convention held at Denver, July 7, 1897.

In 1891 Mr. Clarke helped to organize the Algona State bank, and was elected its president, a position he now holds. In 1893 he was one of the organizers of the Iowa Bankers' State bank at Des Moines. As a result of this very active, busy life

Mr. Clarke is one of the wealthy men of northwestern Iowa.

In 1864 he married Mary J. Phelps, of Byron, Wis., a woman with that strength of character and vigor of purpose to accomplish whatever duty seemed necessary, either in business or social life. This, with a quiet womanly dignity and love and devotion to her family, has ever been a powerful factor in her husband's success. As a result of this union five children were born. Mary Edith, Irma D. and Fred S. are now living.

Mr. Clarke is still farming, owning about 5,000 acres of land, with about 2,000 acres in cultivation.

Hope, cheerfulness and charity are among this man's chief characteristics.

---

CARR, EDWARD M., is a native of New York; born June 28, 1850, in Cattaraugus county. John Carr, his father, was born in Ireland and came to this country when quite young. He became a prosperous farmer in New York state, and was a soldier in the Mexican war. He married Anna Keane in New York city, who was a well educated lady, and a sister of Captain Keane, of the British navy.

In 1856 the family removed from New York to Iowa and located on a farm in Buchanan county. At that time the county was very new and there were no school facilities near them, but his mother, who was a ripe scholar, taught him the rudiments of a good education in their Iowa prairie home. Afterwards he attended several winter terms of a district school, and the graded school at Independence, helping his father on the farm summer seasons. This he continued to do until he was 17 years of age, when he began teaching school, giving the very best satisfaction wherever he was employed. In April, 1871, he entered the State university at Iowa City, and three days before attaining his majority graduated from the law department, receiving the degree of bachelor of laws and a certificate of admission to practice before the supreme court. Immediately thereafter he located at Manchester and became a member of the law firm of Griffin, Crosby & Carr. This partnership lasted until 1875, when he aided in establishing the Manchester Democrat. In 1877 Charles E. Bronson and himself became sole owners and editors of the paper. Messrs. Bronson & Carr have been partners since that date in nearly all their business enterprises. A lucrative law practice has enabled the firm to purchase, among other things, a large stock farm near the town, where some good horses and choice herds of Shorthorns and Jerseys are kept. Mr. Carr is a director of the First National bank of Manchester, and is identified with several other business enterprises in the place.

Ever since he commenced the practice of law, Mr. Carr has taken an active interest in politics, and, during that time, has attended, as a delegate or alternate, nearly every national and Iowa state convention held by his party. For nearly a score of years he has served continuously upon political committees, but has never sought or desired a political office for himself, and, with the exception of a few positions

13

which did not interfere with his law and editorial work, he has refused to allow his friends to nominate him for any place Although at all times an uncompromising democrat, his political battles have been waged in such a spirit of fairness that, at

no time, has he forfeited the confidence or respect of those who were opposed to him. Reference to a few instances will show the extent of this feeling. In May, 1879, Governor Gear commissioned him "major and judge advocate of division, Iowa National guard," at that time one of the most prominent positions in the Iowa militia. This appointment came without solicitation, or even knowledge on his part that such a step was contemplated. And, again, about eighteen years ago, the republican judge of his district appointed him a commissioner of insanity, an office which, through successive appointments, he still continues to hold. But it was not until the city election of 1891, in his own town, that he was made the recipient, in a small way, of about as gracious a compliment as is ever passed "over the garden wall" of politics. Manchester has always been a republican stronghold. Twenty years ago the vote of that party was nearly unanimous, and even now its supporters outnumber the democrats nearly two to one. Notwithstanding this, Mr. Carr's neighbors, who know him as a wise adviser and able defender, laid aside their politics long enough to unanimously elect him to the office of city attorney, a position which he continued to hold for three successive terms. This much can be said of Mr. Carr: He has made a success of every business he has undertaken and has given good satisfaction in every position of trust which he has held. Mr. Carr was permanent chairman of the democratic state convention, held in Dubuque in 1896, and secretary of the democratic state committee in the memorable campaign of that year, and, on account of the illness of the chairman, almost the entire burden of the work was thrown upon him.

He was married to Miss Emma Preussner, October 18, 1873. His only son, Hubert Carr, is now 21 years of age, and married to the youngest daughter of Hon. Lore Alford, of Waterloo.

———

HOLMES, SAMUEL, of Hamburg, is a lawyer whose professional as well as individual reputation is now state wide, and well worthy of the proud commonwealth to which he belongs. He was born in West Leigh near Manchester, Eng., January 1, 1839. Both his parents were silk weavers, and in 1841 left England for America and settled on a farm near Hennepin, Ill. In 1852, his father, James Holmes, went overland to California, remaining two years. Upon his return he took his family to La Salle county, Ill., where he cultivated a large farm, twelve miles south of La Salle city. In 1868, his mother, Hannah Mort Holmes, died.

Like many sons of pioneers, Mr. Holmes obtained an education with difficulty. During the winter months he attended the public schools, working on the farm the remainder of the year. He was fond of books and of study, and made the most of the opportunities presented to him. He would go many miles to attend a debating society and was an expert speller. After he was 21 years of age he attended Granville academy and Wheaton college, working at the same time in order to pay for his board, tuition and clothing. After two years at Wheaton he taught school in his home district. He then began to read law in his leisure moments. In 1865, he came to Iowa, and in the following year located permanently at Hamburg, which was then a village of very few houses. For two years he read law in the office of R. K. Crandall, when he entered the law department of the State university and graduated in 1868. He returned to Hamburg and formed a partnership with Mr. Crandall. He was afterwards associated in the firms of Holmes & Simons, Dalby & Holmes, and Holmes & French, all leading law firms of southwestern Iowa. During the past eleven years he has been alone in the practice. Mr. Holmes has one of the largest offices and one of the most complete law libraries in that part of the

state. He has been retained as counsel in many important cases in the district, supreme and United States courts. For twelve years Mr. Holmes held the office of United States commissioner, but resigned the position in order to devote all his time to his profession. He is the author of the well-known book, "Township Laws of Iowa" which has run through two large editions. For ten years he was vice-president and president of the Farmers and Merchants bank, of Hamburg. During recent years he has devoted some of his time to developing one of the largest fruit farms in the state.

Politically, Mr. Holmes was an uncompromising republican until the party took, what he considered to be, a "backward step" in 1894, on the temperance question. He was a prohibitionist in theory, a leader in local and state temperance organizations,

and was one of the chief factors in the re-election of Senator Clark to the state legislature, aiding him in engineering the prohibition law through the senate and house. Fremont being a border county, had the reputation of being a tough place, and "rum-ruled." By vigorous personal effort, Mr. Holmes assisted in changing public sentiment, in banishing the saloons from the county and making Hamburg one of the most temperate and law-abiding, educated and patriotic cities in Iowa. Becoming an active prohibitionist, he was honored in 1896, by the nomination for judge of the supreme court, and in 1897 was nominated for representative from Fremont county, and at the prohibition state convention in

1898, he received the nomination for attorney-general. Mr. Holmes is imbued with the true spirit of the reformer and has always led in educational, moral and temperance reform. Ridicule and threats have no influence with him.

When a young man he was a Congregationalist, but in recent years united with the Presbyterian church. He is a ruling elder in the church to which he belongs. He assisted in organizing and superintending the first permanent Sunday school in Hamburg, and has been an active officer and teacher ever since. He has several times been a member of the board of education and for fifteen years a trustee of Tabor college.

He was married in August, 1864, to Sarah B. Hewitt. They have six children, Abraham Lincoln, William Thomas, Mary Elizabeth, now the wife of Rev. Evore Evans, Jesse George, Samuel Arthur and Sarah Marcia.

Mr. Holmes is a liberal man and no advanced course for human good has ever appealed in vain to him. He has the loving regard of all his fellow citizens. In a comfortable home, his children a credit to him, a handsome competence for his old age, he is enjoying the results of a life well spent in the service of the Master and his fellow-men.

---

MILES, HON. LEWIS, of Corydon, who served several terms in the legislature and has been twice appointed United States district attorney, was born in Marion county, Ohio, June 30, 1845. He came to Wayne county with his parents in April, 1853, and has resided there constantly since. His father, William Miles, was a farmer. He died December 26, 1879. His mother, Emily Welch Miles, died October 11, 1865.

Lewis Miles worked on a farm until 19 years of age, when he commenced the study of law in the office of Gen. S. L. Glasgow. He was admitted to the bar at Corydon, in October, 1872, and commenced active practice in November, 1872, at which time a partnership was formed with Capt. J. N. McClanahan. In October, 1869, when but a few months past 24, he was elected to the state legislature, and despite his youth, was recognized as one of the most influential members of the lower house. In June, 1873, the relation with Captain McClanahan was dissolved, and another formed with W. H. Tedford, now a judge in the Third judicial

district, under the firm name of Tedford & Miles, which continued until February, 1879. His next law associate was J. W. Freeland and the firm of Freeland & Miles enjoyed a prosperous business until 1891, when it was dissolved. Mr. Miles practiced alone until August 1, 1894, when he became associated with C. W. Steele, under the firm name of Miles & Steele, which still continues.

Mr. Miles was married February 20, 1868, to Miss Mary D. Robb, at Corydon. They have an interesting family of four children; William E., born March 9, 1871; Charles B., born February 4, 1874; Winifred, born

March 9, 1876, and Lois, born August 5, 1882.

In 1879 he was a candidate on the republican ticket for the state senate, and was defeated, although running far ahead of ticket. In 1880 he was presidential elector for the Eighth district and voted for Garfield and Arthur. He was the choice of his party for member of the upper branch of the general assembly again in 1883, and was elected by a good majority, serving in the Twentieth and Twenty-first General Assemblies. President Harrison appointed him to the position of United States district attorney for the southern district of Iowa, and during his incumbency of that office, extending over a period of four years, not a single indictment drawn by him or in his office was quashed or declared insufficient. His record as an officer and his distinguished party services secured his reappointment to the district attorneyship when the republicans returned to power in 1896, the Iowa delegation being united in recommending him for the place. He takes an active part in politics, and is in demand as a speaker during every campaign. He made thirty-seven speeches in the McKinley-Bryan campaign. He has been engaged in the active practice of law since 1872, except when broken by his appointment to the United States attorneyship, and has a law library of over 3,000 volumes. He is regarded by the bar of the state and by the leading politicians of all parties as one of the brightest and ablest men in the state.

---

VAN VECHTEN, GILES F. AND CHARLES D., of Cedar Rapids, have made that name known and honored throughout that region. The name of Van Vechten dates back in its origin to the time of Cæsar, and is traceable to the name of an old Roman camping place called Vectum (now Vechten) near Utrecht in Holland. The name of Van Vechten signifies *from the fighting place.*

The first of the family who came to America, was Teunis Dircksen Van Vechten, who came to New Netherlands in the ship "Arms of Norway," with his wife, one child and two servants, and settled on a farm at Greenbush, opposite Albany, N. Y., in 1638. Persons of this name are now found in nearly every state of the union; but the Dutch habit of continuity clings to the greater number, who have remained near the home of their fathers in New York. The family, however scattered or mingled with the blood of other families, has retained a remarkable resemblance in its different members and has furnished its full share of those who, in peace and war, have made a history for this country.

The father of Giles Fonda and Charles Duane Van Vechten, was Gilbert Van Vechten, a farmer, of Lewis county, N. Y. Their mother, Ilona Bent, came from New-England stock, her father having been born in Templeton, Mass. He removed, soon after his marriage, to Lewis county, in northern New York, which was then a dense forest, with only two families anywhere near the place which became his home.

Giles F. was born in Denmark, Lewis county, N. Y., August 5, 1827. He was educated in the district schools and at Denmark academy. In 1854 he moved to Milledgeville, Carroll county, Ill., and engaged in farming and stock raising. In 1865 he and Henry G. Page, of Lanark, Ill., opened the private bank of Van Vechten & Page, in the town of Lanark. He remained there for about ten years, changing the bank meanwhile into the First National bank of Lanark. In 1875 he sold his interest in the bank and other property at Lanark and soon after removed to Minneapolis, Minn. In Novem-

ber, 1876, he came to Cedar Rapids, where he has since resided, and opened the private bank of G. F. Van Vechten. In 1886 the bank was changed to the Cedar Rapids National bank, of which he has since been vice-president.

In 1889 he assisted in organizing the Security Savings bank, of which he has since been president. Mr. Van Vechten is naturally conservative, his ventures have been along the line of safety, and his business career has been in the best sense successful. Passing through several panics, his business methods have always been sufficient defense against disaster, and the financial institutions with which he has been connected have never suffered failure. He has given much of his time to the investment of funds intrusted to him for that purpose, and can truthfully say he has never lost a dollar for his clients. Although naturally a money-maker he cares little for simply accumulating money, but believes that men who occupy positions of trust owe

*Giles F. Van Vechten.*

it to the community in which they live to help others as well as themselves. He would, if he could, give all men and women an opportunity in the world and would guard them against failure.

Politically, Mr. Van Vechten has, as a rule, acted with the republican party, although he was never a partisan. In his later years he has grown more independent in politics and is a believer in the justice of the doctrine known as the "Single Tax."

He was married to Miss Emma Melissa Humphrey on April 14, 1858. They have had no children of their own. They have one adopted daughter, Mary, who is now the wife of Merritt W. Pinckney, a Chicago attorney.

Charles D. Van Vechten was born in Denmark, N. Y., September 4, 1839. At the age of 16 he went to Battle Creek, Mich., where he attended school for one year and then went to the Kalamazoo schools for two years.

When about 22 years old he went into the general merchandise and lumber business at Mattawan, Mich., about twelve miles west of Kalamazoo,

*Charles D. Van Vechten.*

where he remained until 1876. He then removed to Minneapolis, Minn., with his brother, Giles F., and in February, 1877, came to Cedar Rapids, where he has since resided. For about seven years he acted as cashier of his brother's bank. In August, 1884, he was elected secretary of the Cedar Rapids Insurance company. In January, 1885, the stockholders of this company placed it in liquidation on account of losses which occurred prior to Mr. Van Vechten's connection with it, and an arrangement was made by which its risks were gradually reinsured in the Continental of New York. He acted as state agent for the Continental until January, 1888. In February, 1888, he accepted the position of associate general agent in the general agency of northern and western Iowa, for the Northwestern Mutual Life Insurance company, of Milwaukee. Although taking up insurance business rather late in life his success has been entirely satisfactory. Politically, he is independent, although usually acting with the republican party. He is a believer in the "Single Tax," and is warmly interested in other reform movements. The only public office he ever held was that of alderman for the fifth ward of Cedar Rapids.

August 8, 1861, he was married to Ada Amanda Fitch. They have three children: Ralph, born August 29, 1862, and cashier of the Cedar Rapids National bank; Emma, born June 11, 1867, and the wife of Clifford K. Shaffer, of Cedar Rapids; and Carl,

born June 17, 1880, who has recently completed the high school course.

———

GUITTAR, THEODORE, of Council Bluffs, ex-sheriff of Pottawattamie county, and at present deputy oil inspector for the state of Iowa, has had much to do with the history of this state although a native of Missouri. His father, Francis Guittar, was among the first white men to come to western Iowa. He first visited Council Bluffs, in 1825, in a keel boat while in the employ of the American Fur company. He thus traded with the Indians until 1840, at which time he engaged in the business on his own account. In 1852, having accumulated some money through his transactions with the Indians, he put in a stock of merchandise at Council Bluffs, and the same was continued until 1878, when he retired with a competency. He was of French-Canadian stock, but was born at St. Louis, as was his wife, Eugenia Bono.

Theodore Guittar was born December 20, 1842, at St. Louis, Mo. He removed to Council Bluffs with his parents when a

small boy, and it was in the common schools of that place he acquired his education. He clerked in his father's store until 1862, when he responded to the tocsin of war, enlisting in the Second Iowa battery. He served throughout the whole of the great struggle, participating in the battles of Vicksburg, Nashville, Tupelo, Jackson, Raymond, Hurricane Creek, Old Town Creek, Oxford and others of less importance. He is a member of Abraham Lincoln post, No. 29, Grand Army of the Republic, department of Iowa.

The war over, he returned to Council Bluffs and engaged as a clerk until 1868, at which time he went into the grocery business. This he followed until 1870, when he purchased a farm and engaged in fruit raising and agricultural work until 1875, returning at that time to Council Bluffs. Having done effective work for the republican party, of which he was an enthusiastic supporter, he, in 1877, was appointed deputy sheriff of the county, serving as such for two years. In 1878 he was elected constable, and so well did he perform the duties of that office during the three years of his incumbency that he was the logical candidate for sheriff of the county. He was elected by a handsome majority, and was re-elected at the close of his first term. In 1890 he received the appointment of deputy internal revenue collector for the southern district of Iowa, serving for three years, and in 1894 was made deputy oil inspector, which position he is now filling. He was married December 20, 1869, to Elizabeth Beecroft. They have but one child, a daughter, Eugenia I. Guittar.

---

GARDNER, WILLIAM WATSON, is a direct descendant of one of the oldest Puritan families, one that landed in America in the year 1656. His grandfather, Benjamin Gardner, carried a musket through the revolutionary war; a great uncle, William Gardner, was aid-de-camp to General Washington. Governor Gardner, of Massachusetts, was one of this family, who are all descendants from John Gardner, of Hingham, Mass. He received from the crown, in 1856, a grant of land located in that region. William Gardner, the father of William Watson, was born in Plainfield, Mass., July 10, 1803, and July 3, 1828, married Ann Parkhurst. He was a contractor and builder and his early life was spent in Massachusetts and in Ontario county, N. Y. In 1840 he moved to Le Claire, Iowa, and lived until March 6, 1891.

Ann Parkhurst was the daughter of Sterling Parkhurst, of Ontario county, N. Y., who moved with his family in 1837 to what is now known as Le Claire, Iowa. The place was first called Parkhurst-town in honor of his family.

William W. Gardner was born March 20, 1841, at Le Claire, Scott county. He attended the village schools and then spent his early life in teaching. Later he studied medicine and became proficient in the theory of that profession but never practiced, and in 1870 he located at Avoca, in the drug business. In this business the knowledge of medicine has naturally been of great advantage to him. He has acquired a fine reputation as a careful, conscientious and reliable druggist. Having lived in Pottawattamie county for about

twenty-seven years, he has a large acquaintance and is very favorably known throughout that section of the state. Mr. Gardner's father was a whig and he was raised in that faith, but when the party went to pieces in 1856, he became a democrat, and the son has always been associated with that party. He became a Mason as early as 1867 and has been prominent in the affairs of that fraternity. He has taken the Knight Templar degrees and presided as master and high priest for several terms. He served as postmaster during President Cleveland's second term. He was married November 2, 1873, to Frances Maud Smith, and they have had two daughters, one of whom died in infancy and the other, Frances Maud, was born in 1883.

VAN ALLEN, GEORGE C., a prominent business man of Mt. Pleasant, Henry county, was born July 6, 1830, on the north shore of Pillar Point, Jefferson county, N. Y., and was the oldest child of Cornelius Van Allen and Lory Ann Ackerman, his wife.

The family consisted of eleven children, nine of whom are still living. Besides the subject of this sketch they are: Martin, a Chicago real estate man living in Ravenswood; Sarah H. White, of Carthage, N.Y., widow of Gen. D. B. White; Lory Ann Hoover, of Chicago, Ill., widow of George Hoover; Catherine Grinnell, of May Fair, Cook county, Ill., widow of G. G. Grinnell; Mrs C. M. Beckford, of Hampton, Va., widow of Selwyn E. Beckford; Cornelius A., real estate, of Effingham, Ill ; William, surveyor, of Ukiah, Cal., and Florence O. Baulch, wife of J. J. Baulch, of St. Louis, Mo. In 1831 the family moved to a farm of their own near by, overlooking Black River bay. Across the bay could easily be seen Madison barracks, where General Grant was once quartered, and the village of Sackett's Harbor, famous in one of the early battles of the war of 1812, in May, 1813. Upon this farm the boy grew to manhood, attending the country schools, working at the forge and in the ship yards, and at times engaged in hauling heavy timbers out of the forest into the shipyards. Living so many years near the water he grew to love it, for it afforded him pleasure as a boy and helped to earn his living as a man, in the early days before railways took the place of boats. In this vicinity Mr. Van Allen taught in the public schools, and later attended Falley seminary in Fulton, N. Y. From there he went to the Old Wesleyan university in Middletown, Conn., where he was a member of a secret society organized by a few congenial fellows, including William and Andrew Roe, O. W. Powers, Mr. Bailey, and David J. Brewer. The latter, then one of the most modest of young men, is now a judge of the supreme court of the United States. Mr. Van Allen remained there a little less than two years, when he was obliged to return home, carrying with him gentle memories of the kindness of student friends, especially Brooks. Fellows, and Bishop. He had good standing in his classes in school, but the teachers did not deeply influence him, for he was a close student and reached his own conclusions, taking but little on the authority of teachers alone.

After some weeks recuperation at home at Pillar Point, he took what little money he had and started west by way of the great lakes. The trip was a delightful one, and gave him broader ideas of the size of the world than he had ever obtained from books. Detroit and Milwaukee were beautiful cities at that time, but Chicago was a dirty little village, although full of hustling men, broken sidewalks, and muddy streets, with a disordered levee and railway yards. Mr. Van Allen went to Dubuque, expecting to secure employment at surveying, but finding nothing in this line, an old friend, George Rogers, secured him a place in the business office of the Dubuque *Herald* as bookkeeper. The *Herald* was then published by J. B. Dorr, afterward colonel of the Eighth Iowa cavalry. In the spring the young surveyor secured a place with Webb and Higby, surveyors, and afterward with Charles Smith, local engineer of the Dubuque & Pacific railway. In July his brother Martin secured for him a still better position in the land department of the Illinois Central railroad. At

first he traveled for the company in Wisconsin, Minnesota and Iowa. January 1, 1857, he was promoted and sent to Effingham, 200 miles south of Chicago, on the Illinois Central, to sell the company's lands. His sales by the first of October amounted to 13,000 acres. One could hardly see a dozen houses in an hour's ride on the cars, except a few at the scattered stations. During this season of prosperity Mr. Van Allen was married, August 6, 1857, in Scriba, N. Y., to Miss Jennie M. Wright, who had been a classmate in Fulton. She was a cultured lady of domestic tastes, and Mr. Van Allen always regarded the event of their marriage as the beginning of a very happy part of his life.

In October, 1857, the great financial crash came, destroying or badly crippling all the business of the country. Land sales stopped, payments failed, enterprising people who had started out to make new homes fell back to their old domiciles to begin

life anew or die of disappointment. Mr. Van Allen lost about $6,000 in this panic and had to begin over again, falling back on his knowledge of surveying to support his family. In his spare moments he read law, and in the fall of 1859 went to Watertown, N. Y., and spent two years in the office of Judge F. W. Hubbard, then lately from the bench of the New York court of appeals. During the following two years he studied part of the time in the Albany Law school, and at the April, 1861, term of the supreme court he was admitted to the degree of counsellor at law in the state of New York. He soon after returned to Chicago and then to Kenosha, but the war was on and there was no business for him, so he spent a few months in the office of Judge Pettitt. He was elected to the superintendency of the high school in Plover, Wis., that fall, remaining till July, 1862, when he went to Burlington, and engaged in the survey of the Burlington & Missouri River railroad from Ottumwa to Chariton. At the close of the season he located in Mt. Pleasant, where he engaged in compiling records for the examination of titles. Here he has ever since remained, closely confined to one of the most laborious, and by no means least important, branches of the law. He suffered another backset in 1883, when his office was destroyed by fire, at a loss of $2,000. But he soon recovered from the shock and began to re-write his books.

His wife died January 27, 1891, and he was again married, October 26, 1893, to Miss Anna L. Watters. One son, Alfred M. Van Allen, was born October 3, 1869. He was educated in the Iowa Wesleyan university, graduated from the state university law school in June, 1894, and is now engaged in the successful practice of his profession in Mt. Pleasant.

Mr. Van Allen had always been a republican, and a quiet but efficient worker for others when offices were to be filled, but never seeking any office for himself. He was brought up a Methodist, but on removing to Mt. Pleasant united with the Presbyterian church, to which his wife belonged. He is a man who thinks for himself, decides for himself, and acts for himself, and is one of the most public spirited and highly respected men in his community.

---

VAIL, ALEXANDER M., M. D., of Rock Rapids, is a son of Alexander Vail, a hatter during his earlier years in the city of Newark, N. J. Following the election of Buchanan, however, he foresaw the possible destruction of the manufacturing industries of the east, and so, in 1857, removed to Illinois and settled on a farm near Kewanee, where he lived until 1865. He died November 1, 1894, while visiting the doctor, at the advanced age of 90 years. The mother, Sarah Sebring Vail, was a woman whose life was one of great activity in the work of benevolence. She died at the age of 62. King George I of Great Britain granted a tract of land in the Orange mountains in New Jersey to the early ancestors of the Vails, and there several generations of the family passed their lives. Among the descendants of these was Judge Stephen Vail, of Patterson, N. J., who was the father of Alfred Vail, said to be the originator of the Morse system of electric telegraphy. Little is known of the mother's antecedents except that they were natives of Holland.

Alexander M. Vail was born at Greenbrook, Summerset county, N. J., May 9, 1848. His educational advantages were limited; he attended country school during winter and by hard study evenings when engaged as a clerk at an early age. He

started to learn the tinner's trade at 14, but was induced to abandon the idea by his mother, and entered the service of his brother, who owned a clothing store. After four years in that capacity he made a tour of Kansas and Nebraska, but finding no place to his liking returned to Kewanee, Ill. He went to Chicago shortly after the big fire, and from there to Red Oak, Iowa, where he was engaged for a time in clerking, but the company failed and he was thrown out of employment. After working at various places he, in 1877, took up the study of medical electricity and hydropathy.

In the fall of 1879 he went to Chicago and began a regular course in medicine and surgery. While there he assisted Dr. L. G. McIntosh in perfecting the electric battery now known as the McIntosh battery, and by his practical genius aided in bringing out one of the best and most extensively used batteries now in use by physicians. He graduated from the Chicago Medical college in 1882. During his junior year he took second prize, consisting of a medal and a $10 gold piece, in an

oral contest in anatomy, and the next year received a like prize for the best dissection. Following graduation he engaged in practice in Red Oak, in partnership with Dr. F. M. Hiett, where he remained one year; removed to Rock Rapids in 1884 and went into the drug business with Dr. A. McNab, practicing the while; sold out in 1887 and devoted his whole attention to practice. While there he established a reputation in the treatment of diseases of women and children, and his success with tuberculosis by the iodine method, a discovery of his own, has attracted wide attention. In 1886 he assisted in organizing the Medical Association of Northwestern Iowa, and in 1887 was delegated a member of the American Medical association, which then met in Chicago. In 1894 he succeeded in organizing the Lyon County Medical society. He is a member of the National Association of Railway Surgeons, and is local surgeon for the Illinois Central railway. He is a republican and prohibitionist, but regards the latter as a moral rather than a political question. He is a member of the I. O. O. F., and has filled most all the offices in his home lodge; was district deputy grand master for one year. He is highly prominent in the work of the M. W. of A., having assisted in organizing one of the strongest lodges in any small town in the state. He was married to Miss Ida F. Burrough, of Tecumseh, Mich., September 8, 1886. They have no children.

THOMPSON, WALTER H. W. H. Thompson, as he usually subscribes himself, cashier of the Bank of Collins, is a splendid type of the hustling, progressive and successful young Iowan. He is but 31 years of age, yet has for years been at the head of a large mercantile establishment, has served two terms as mayor of his city, and at this time fills a conspicuous place in the financial circles of that section of the commonwealth.

He was born in Jasper county, Iowa, November, 1, 1866. His father, John Thompson, is a man who has made a complete success of agriculture, and though now retired from the management of his farm, is serving as president of the Bank of Collins. The mother's maiden name was Ann E. Angelo, a family name that is mentioned in connection with the early history of the country. Although the younger Mr. Thompson received a common and high school education, he did not have the advantage of a collegiate course. He resided on the farm until he had reached his nineteenth year, at which time his father exchanged stock owned by him in the Wolf Creek Coal company for the general store

of R. H. Hampton & Son, at Collins, and he was placed in charge of the same. With a proper appreciation of the services rendered him, the father gave the young man a one-half interest in the business, he remaining upon the farm and permitting his

son to manage the concern in his own way. Events proved that Walter H. was equal to the task, for in 1890 he purchased the father's interest and conducted the business in his own name in a very profitable manner until 1896. At this time he found a customer in J. M. Hall, so disposed of the store to good advantage. Previous to selling out, he and his father had founded the Bank of Collins, with the father as president and the son as cashier. This institution still continues to flourish, and its stability goes unquestioned in that section of the state.

The junior Mr. Thompson was appointed postmaster at Collins by President Cleveland, and he creditably discharged the duties of the office. He was elected assessor of the incorporated town of Collins in 1892-3, and mayor of the same city on the citizens' ticket in 1896, being re-elected in 1897. He joined the order of Odd Fellows in 1890; has filled the office of noble grand four terms and was appointed D. D. G. M. for the Seventy-seventh district in 1894; is also a member of the A. F. and A. M., having held the office of worshipful master for several successive terms, and is prominent in the Modern Woodmen of America.

He was married to Miss Luna May Crabb in June, 1887, and two children have come to them—Forest G., aged 8, and John B. Thompson, aged 2 years.

GETZ, HIRAM LANDIS, of Marshall-town, ranks among the foremost physicians and surgeons of the state, and has also been prominent in political and educational circles; commissioned by President Cleveland, July, 1894, for a term of four years as postmaster at Marshalltown; was for a number of years a member and twice elected president of the Marshall-town school board; elected president of the department of school administration, National Educational association, 1896. He is of German and Swiss descent, although his ancestors have lived in America many generations. His father, Levi Gross Getz, was a farmer and fancy stock breeder, noted for his integrity and thrift. He died in February, 1896, in Lancaster county, Pa., aged 68 years, having spent the most of his life on the farm which had been owned by the family since 1804. John Getz, the doctor's grandfather, was an extensive land owner, and was also engaged as a school teacher. His wife, Magdalena Gross, was of German descent. Jacob Getz, Sr., the doctor's great-great-grandfather, emigrated from Pfalz, Germany, during the eighteenth century, and settled in eastern Pennsylvania. Maria Long Landis, Dr. Getz's mother, was a resident of Manheim township, Lancaster county, Pa., and is a descendant of Rev. Benjamin Landis, who came to America in 1717, from the vicinity of Manheim, on the Rhine, where his ancestors had been driven from Zurich, Switzerland, about 1660, on account of their religious belief, Hans Landis having been there beheaded in September, 1616. Their denomination was that of Pietus or Mennonites. The Landis family is a very old one, their name having been known to the French and Germans many centuries ago. A large number of their descendants still live in Lancaster county, Pa., and twenty-seven representatives of them were in the civil war.

Dr. H. L. Getz was born November 14, 1850, in East Hempfield township, Lancaster county, Pa. He obtained his early education at the district school and the high school at Manheim, Pa. He also received private instruction in Latin and German. He has been a student all his life. In 1885 he graduated from the Chautauqua Literary and Scientific circle, and in 1890 received the honorary degree of A. M. from Iowa college. He began the study of medicine in 1871, with Dr. John M. Dunlap, of Manheim, Pa., attended four terms at the Jefferson Medical college in Philadelphia, graduating March 11, 1874, with special honors in anatomy, being also secretary of the graduating class. He also attended lectures and clinics at Will's Ophthalmic, Allen's Obstetrical and other hospitals in Philadelphia; was connected with

some of the city's free dispensaries, and was an assistant and student under Dr. R. J. Levis, a noted surgeon. He came to Marshalltown, March 20, 1874, opened an office April 1st, and has been in active practice ever since.

In addition to his regular professional work the doctor has served as medical examiner and surgeon for numerous life and accident companies, and medical director for the Northern Life association, of Marshalltown, Iowa; was for many years the city health officer of Marshalltown, and was the first regularly appointed county physician for Marshall county. He is the present chief surgeon for the Iowa Central Railway company, district surgeon for the Chicago & North-Western Railway company at Marshalltown, local surgeon for the Chicago Great Western Railway company, and surgeon for the Marshall Light, Power and Railway company. He was elected professor of physiology at the Chicago College of Physicians and Surgeons in 1882, but declined the offer owing to property and other interests at Marshalltown. In 1884 he was elected professor of obstetrics, surgical diseases of women and diseases of children in the Iowa College of Physicians and Surgeons, at Des Moines, where he served until 1887, when he resigned in order to give more time to professional duties at home. In 1894 he was elected professor of anatomy and clinical diseases of women in the St. Louis College of Physicians and Surgeons, but did not accept, owing to his receiving the appointment as postmaster, there having been thirteen candidates for the position. He was appointed assistant surgeon of the Iowa National Guard, and commissioned captain June 12, 1887, by Governor Larrabee; commissioned lieutenant-colonel, as a member of his staff, June 14, 1890, by Governor Boies; commissioned past assistant surgeon-general August 19, 1889, rank of colonel of the U. R. K. of P. of Iowa. He has been especially skillful and successful as a surgeon, performing most of the major and special operations known to surgery. He has devised an improved combined trocar canula and aspirating needle; a new uterine repositor; an antiseptic surgical cabinet; Getz's bicycle ambulance and handstretcher, and has designed Getz's physicians' and surgeons' labor saving day book and ledger and Getz's daily conduct record and ledger for penal institutions, which is now used by the state industrial schools. He has been a frequent contributor to many of the principal medical and surgical journals of the United States, among them the *Journal of the American Medical Association*, the *Medical and Surgical Reporter*, the *Medical Record* and the *Iowa State Medical Reporter*, etc., etc. Some of these contributions were translated and published in foreign journals, and he has often read original papers at the state, national and international meetings of the surgical and medical fraternity.

In politics the doctor is independent, having voted with the republican party until 1884, when he identified himself with the democrats. In the presidential campaign of 1896 he was in sympathy with the national democracy. He was appointed a member of the board of trustees of the Iowa industrial schools in 1886 by Governor Larrabee, to fill a vacancy, and in 1887 the legislature elected him for a full term of six years. During Cleveland's first and second admistrations he served as a member and president of the board of pension examiners. Under his management of the Marshalltown postoffice many reforms and improvements were brought about in the office, and it was very generally conceded that the service was the best in the history of the city. The doctor was appointed to fill a vacancy as a member of the board of education of Marshalltown in 1889, and in 1890 was elected for a term of three years, re-elected in 1893 to a third term. In 1896 he was unanimously chosen president of the board and re-elected president in 1897. He was a delegate to the department of school administration at the National Educational association (Buffalo, N. Y.) in 1896, and was there elected the first president of this department.

Dr. Getz is a member of the leading medical and surgical societies of the state and nation; was second vice-president of the State Medical association in 1882, and first vice-president in 1897; and the founder and first president of the Iowa Central (State) Medical association. He was elected vice-president of the International Association of Railway Surgeons in 1897, and a member of the executive board in 1898; October 14, 1898, he was elected

president of the Iowa State Association of Railway Surgeons, at Clinton. He is a member of the following civic societies: Knights Templars, Mystic Shriners, Knights of Pythias, Uniformed Rank, K. P., Odd Fellows, Elks, Princes of Iran, Knights of Korrassan, and was a charter member of the Woodmen's camp organized in Marshalltown. He joined the German Reformed church at Philadelphia, but upon removal to Marshalltown was admitted to the Presbyterian. His views becoming too liberal to be in keeping with the church creed he requested that a withdrawal letter be granted and that his membership be canceled.

Dr. Getz was married May 27, 1874, to Miss Mary E. Worley, daughter of Nathan and Susan Worley. Her paternal grandmother was the first white female child born where the city of Cincinnati now stands. Dr. and Mrs. Getz have two children, N. Worley, born May 12, 1875, graduated from the Marshalltown high school, was a student for three years at Iowa college, general delivery clerk in the Marshalltown postoffice for one year, after which he attended lectures at Jefferson Medical college, Philadelphia, for one year, and in 1897–1898 was a student in the medical department of the University of Berlin, Germany; Igerna M., who was born July 13, 1878, graduated from the Marshalltown high school, later a student at Miss Baldwin's Bryn Mawr, Pennsylvania, and in 1897-1898 was a student of languages in Europe.

———

SAWYER, FRANK PAYSON, who is at the head of one of the most important industries in the west, lives in Muscatine and is the secretary and general manager of the Muscatine Oat Meal company, which manufactures the celebrated "Friends' oats." Mr. Sawyer comes of New England ancestors. His father, Stephen P. Sawyer, was born in Amsbury, Mass., in 1832, but removed to Hamilton, Ont., about 1848, where he lived until 1871. At that time he removed to Muscatine and retired from business in order to use his income for the benefit of his family and to prolong the life and afford comfort to his wife, who had been a confirmed invalid for many years. She died March 18, 1897. Her maiden name was Frances Phœbe Gillett, and she was a native of Newport, N. H.

F. P. Sawyer was born in Hamilton, Ont., November, 30, 1856, and he has lived in Muscatine most of the time since 1872. His early education was acquired in the Canadian public schools, well known for their thorough training and substantial foundations for a thorough education. He graduated from the Muscatine high school and entered the Iowa State university in 1874. During his sophomore year illness compelled him to retire, and a year's change of climate and travel in the east convinced him the only sure foundation and reliance for life was a trade, and that the professions and ordinary mercantile pursuits could not always be relied upon in case of financial upheaval. So he decided to lose no time, left college and learned the marble cutter's trade, which for a time he followed in Des Moines.

lowed in Des Moines. He found this was too arduous an employment and involved too great a risk to his health, so he interested himself in the Muscatine Oat Meal company, and upon request became personally identified with the management. He had been interested in the concern since its organization, and in 1883 was placed in the management of the business. Since he took hold of it, it has grown every year until now it is the second largest oat meal industry in operation in the United States. The factory is of the greatest importance to the city of Muscatine, as it employs over 160 persons in addition to a large number of others indirectly obtaining their income from the business. The company's trade extends all over the world, from South Africa to the European markets, and in all of the large cities of the United States and Canada. Mr. Sawyer takes a broad view of the notable business success which he has achieved and finds his best reward and the most satisfaction in the benefits it has brought to others in furnishing remunerative employment to so many persons. He is naturally gratified at the financial success of the enterprise and other investments that he has made, but says that the pleasure derived from the *use* of such accumulations is that which affords him the most satisfaction and not the mere fact of *possession*. Mr. Sawyer is a director of the Muscatine Savings bank and the First National bank and the Muscatine Water company, and also treasurer of the latter concern. He is a republican but is not a hidebound partisan. He keeps informed on the effects of political changes upon business matters and he always reserves the privilege of voting for the

nominee showing the best business qualifications and recommendations for integrity. Party ties and obligations do not strongly bind him.

Mr. Sawyer is a member of the Presbyterian church and has been secretary of the official board for about a dozen years. He was married November 30, 1882, in Milford, Pa., to Joanna Wells, daughter of H. B. Wells, probably the most prominent and successful business man of Pike county, Pa. They have three children, Henry P., born November 19, 1883; Aura M., born February 17, 1885, and Maud W., born May 4, 1892.

---

DAVENPORT, FRANCIS M., of Carroll, was one of a large family of children born to Joseph Davenport and Rebecca Coverston Davenport, in their home in Ohio, of which state both his parents were natives. His birthplace was Gallia county, Ohio, and his natal day May 1, 1840.

Both of his parents were of large families, nearly all of whom lived to a ripe old age. The family came to Iowa in 1847 and settled in Mahaska county, near Oskaloosa, where his father died in 1884, at the age of 70 years. His mother died in 1892. at the age of 76. Mr. Davenport was a pupil

in the country district schools until he was 19 years of age, when he entered college and completed the classical course in the Iowa Wesleyan university, at Mount Pleasant. He was graduated in 1864, after which he studied law one year in the University of Michigan, at Ann Arbor. Returning to Iowa he spent eight months in the law office of

Seevers & Cutts, of Oskaloosa, and was admitted to the bar October 20, 1869. He then began the practice of his profession in Oskaloosa. The firm with which he studied law was composed of Judge W. H. Seevers, who was subsequently a member of the supreme court of Iowa for thirteen years; and of M. E. Cutts, who for five years was attorney-general of Iowa, and at the time of his death a member of congress.

Mr. Davenport early learned the good lesson of independent self-support and earned by his own efforts all the money he had. He was very successful in his practice in Oskaloosa for a period of eighteen years, retiring from 1887 to 1892. He was city solicitor in Oskaloosa for a term of two years, declining a second term. He is a loyal democrat, and has been chosen at various times to represent his party on their ticket, but democratic victories were few in the county, and although Mr. Davenport always ran ahead of his ticket and was deserving and popular and a strong man in his party, he was not elected to office. The contest of 1880 is well remembered in Mahaska county, where Mr. Davenport was the democratic candidate for circuit judge in the Sixth judicial circuit. He received twenty-two votes more in his home county than the combined vote of the democratic and greenback candidates for president of the United States; and in the county where his opponent lived he ran 157 votes ahead of his ticket. In 1892 he became a resident of Carroll, and resumed his law practice.

In 1896 he was a candidate for county attorney of Carroll county, but was counted out by the judges of election and the board of canvassers. He contested the election and a court of contest, organized under the statutes, tried the case and declared him elected by twenty-seven majority. But on appeal to the higher courts he was defeated upon a technicality, the higher courts refusing to count the ballots.

In 1898 he was chosen one of the democratic candidates for district judge of the Sixteenth judicial district This district is composed of Carroll, Crawford, Calhoun, Greene, Ida and Sac counties. The district having a large republican majority he was again defeated, though he ran far ahead of his ticket, not only in his home county, but in the entire district.

Mr. Davenport is one of the leading lawyers in his part of the state and is so recognized by the legal profession and the public generally. He is one of the referees in bankruptcy under the federal bankruptcy act of 1898, holding his appointment from the federal court for the southern district of Iowa. In his new home, he is

loved and respected, as he was in his former one, as a man of honor and integrity, loyal to his friends and a good citizen.

On May 1, 1870, Mr. Davenport was married at Mount Pleasant, Iowa, to Miss Martha M. Griffith. They have one son, Warren, born August 17, 1874. Mr. Davenport is, and has been for over forty years, a member of the Methodist Episcopal church, and besides being a member of the bar, is not a member of any other organization, fraternal or otherwise.

---

BREWSTER, THOMAS KELSEY, of Oskaloosa, one of the oldest and best established dentists of southeastern Iowa, was

brought up in Ohio, where his ancestors were among the very earliest settlers.

His father, Francis Brewster, was born in Green county, Ohio, November 29, 1795, and was a carpenter by trade. During the later years of his life he owned and operated a farm near Bell Brook, Ohio, where he resided until his death in 1874. He was an abolitionist, and stood for the right in all reforms that required great moral courage and perseverance. At the time of his death he was in comfortable circumstances, and was always held in great respect by the community in which he lived. Dr. Brewster's mother was Sarah Kelsey, who was born in Kentucky, May 5, 1802, and was married to Francis Brewster, August 15, 1822, near Centerville, Ohio. She was an exceptionally brave and patient woman, bearing with fortitude and courage all the many trials of early frontier life. She became the mother of eight children, of whom Thomas was the third. Mrs. Brewster died in 1853 at Bell Brook, Ohio. Both parents joined the Methodist church very early in life.

Dr. Brewster was born June 11, 1828, at Bell Brook, Green county, Ohio. His early life was spent on a farm, working in the fields during summer and attending district school in the winter. In 1840, he attended the high school at Bell Brook. In 1850 and 1851 he studied medicine and dentistry under Dr. A. S. Talbert, at Dayton, Ohio, and in the fall of 1851 entered the Ohio Dental college in Cincinnati, returning home in March, 1852. The same year he located at Dayton, Ohio, where he enjoyed a good practice for twenty-two years. In 1874 he moved to Iowa, locating at Oskaloosa, which he has made his home ever since. During his twenty-three years of residence in this place, he has continued to practice dentistry, and he has certainly been successful.

The doctor enlisted May 14, 1864, in the 100-day service with the One Hundred and Thirty-first Ohio National Guards, at Dayton, and served for five months. His regiment was stationed at Baltimore, Md., and was mustered out September, 1864.

He identified himself with the whig party early in life, and voted with it until 1856, when the republican party was organized. Since that time he has always been a republican. His first ballot was cast in 1852, when he voted for Gen. Winfield Scott, for president. He is a member of Phil Kearney Post No. 40, G. A. R., and formerly belonged to the Independent Order of Odd Fellows. At the age of 12 years he united with the Methodist church, and remained a member until 1874, when he and his wife brought their letters from the Grace M. E. church, of Dayton, Ohio, and united with the First Congregational church of Oskaloosa.

Dr. Brewster was married, April 12, 1858, to Mary E. Snowden, in Green county, Ohio. Three children were born to them, James B., Bertha B., and Kate S.; Bertha died in 1864 and Mrs. Brewster on the 3d of June, 1893.

---

VAN HAVESKERKE, ANDREA was born in the harbor of New York city, August 31, 1854, while his parents were on a two-years' wedding journey, and little thought their child would one day be a prominent American citizen.

His father is Baron Jean Louis Van Haveskerke, viscount of Leland, estate owner and attache at the court of the king of Belgium at Brussels, officer of the Legion of Honor, etc. His family have been titled nobles for 400 years, distinguishing themselves in political and religious wars, under the French and Spanish or Austrian governments, always on the side of the Roman Catholic church. The family has been recognized in French, Austrian and Spanish courts as staunch and incorruptible for the Flemish race. Although of the Catholic faith, they fought unwaveringly against the Spanish-Austrian yoke during the inquisition. His mother was Cecilia De Lafouillade; her ancestors were French noblemen, and were liberal patrons of the arts. As a child, young Haveskerke was taught by a private tutor and afterwards was a pupil of the Royal Atheneum at Antwerp. At the age of 4 years he entered the conservatory of music in Antwerp, where he was taught musical notation and sight-reading by Professor Schermers, and violin playing by Prof.

Victor Bacot. The latter was a pupil of the celebrated violinist, Chas. De Beriot, under whom Mr. Haveskerke was afterwards a pupil.

At the age of 14 he graduated from the conservatory of Brussels, having completed all branches, including composition by Director Fetis, whom he considers the greatest theorist of the age in music. When the Franco-Prussian war broke out, young Haveskerke was attending the Catholic university of Louvain, Belgium. He promptly joined the French army, in company with others of his countrymen, and stood by the cause till after the surrender of Paris and the fall of the commune, attaining the rank of adjutant of the Chasseurs. The result of his devotion to the French cause was banishment from his own country and home. Coming to America, he made use of his unusual musical talent and thorough education. Having had as fine a musical education as Europe affords, and learned German French, Flemish, some Italian, Latin, Spanish, Greek, Hebrew, and Arabian, he was well qualified to support himself. In fact, his youth was spent almost entirely in the company of tutors, for he lived at school and saw his parents but two or three times in a year. After a residence of a year and a half in New York, he came to Independence, Iowa, where he taught music in the convent of the Sisters of Mercy, and organized a cornet band composed of young men who had never played before. He next resided in Columbus Junction, where he also taught music and organized a band. Five years later he came to Pella and took charge of Cox's Light Infantry band, and taught music in Central university. After five years of hard work there, he removed to Newton, his present home, where he has been devoting his energies to educating the people to a higher standard of music. The towns he has worked in show that he has been successful in developing a taste for the music of the masters, and he has been handsomely remembered for his efforts, both by handsome gifts and appreciative newspaper comments. His services to the public have always been freely given, and thus he hopes to lay up treasure in the world to come. Professor Haveskerke is now organist of the Catholic church in Newton, which is famous for its music and orchestral accompaniment, said to be better than any in the larger cities of the state. Since coming to America, the young nobleman has supported himself, and takes pride in doing so. He was married October 24, 1886, to Hattie Snyder, of Columbus Junction. They had two children, one of whom died when 5 days old, and the other at the age of 7 years. Since then they have adopted a 15-months-old child, which is now 3 years old, and is cherished as a true offspring. Professor Haveskerke is a member of the Newton Masonic lodge, No. 59, and Gebal chapter, No. 12. He joined the Congregational church a few years ago, but is not a regular attendant.

HART, EDWARD LORENZO, one of the foremost attorneys of Corydon, was born near the village of Hadley, Lapeer county, Mich., December 3, 1850. He is of English descent on the paternal side, the early

ancestors having come to America at a very remote day and settled at or near Hartford, Conn. Members of the family later removed to Rochester, N. Y., from whence William Hart, the grandfather of this subject, moved with his family to Hadley, Mich. The Harts, as far back as they can be traced, were farmers and mechanics. Ansel Hart, the father of E. L. Hart, settled near the village of Cambria, Wayne county, Iowa, in 1856, where he was postmaster for several years. He died there in 1877. His wife and the mother of Edward L. was Clementina Russell, a mem-

ber of one of the pioneer families of Ionia county, Mich.

E. L. Hart attended the common schools of Wayne county about six months in the year from 1856 to 1862, and became proficient in the studies taught in that early time. He was notably good in orthography, and earned considerable notoriety by "spelling down" all comers at the spelling schools, then very common in the neighborhood. No schools were taught during the two years following the outbreak of the war, and it was decided that he should return to Michigan in order that he might have school advantages. Accordingly, on his fourteenth birthday, he started on foot to Ottumwa, then the terminus of the Chicago, Burlington & Quincy railroad and sixty miles distant, from which point he took the train for his native state. Arriving there he at once entered school, remaining until 1866, at which time he returned to his home in Wayne county, making the journey from Ottumwa on foot. At Cambria the following winter he attended a school which was taught by Theodore Laing, now a prominent lawyer in Concordia, Kan., whose interest in the boy did much to encourage him to further pursue his studies. The fall of 1867 found him in the schools of Garden Grove under the tutorage of Prof. R. A. Harkness, now of Parsons college. Here he remained for four years, excepting the time required to earn money with which to pay his expenses, by teaching. He was but 17 years of age when he began teaching, and that avocation was followed for six years. The last school taught by him was at Corydon. In 1872 he spent six months as clerk and bookkeeper in a dry goods store, and again in 1876 about the same length of time as clerk in a drug store. It was late in 1876 when he took up the study of law by devoting a portion of each day to reading standard law books borrowed from J. B. Evans, now of Princeton, Mo., who later became his preceptor. After having been admitted to the bar in 1877 he opened an office in the town of Allerton, in his home county. In 1878 he formed a partnership with George Albertson, and the same was continued until 1881, when he purchased the interest of that gentleman and continued alone till 1891, at which time he removed to Corydon. The following May a business relation in practice was established with R. C. Poston, and the same is still existing.

When Mr. Hart first came to Wayne county, away back in 1856, the country was new, very new, and but few farm residences broke the monotony of the wide, trackless prairies. His father purchased 240 acres of land at that time, which was during the following years fenced with rails hauled from a point five miles distant. Helping with this and driving four yoke of oxen to a breaking plow furnished the amusement to while away the spare hours of Mr. Hart's youth.

He was reared a republican, and voted with that party until reaching his twenty-sixth year, when, after a careful study of political economy, he was led to repudiate the doctrine of protection and became a radical free trader. However, he has always advocated measures and policies rather than parties. He has taken a more or less active part in the campaigns of his county for the last twenty years. He was married to Miss Ida Matson September 8, 1873. She is a daughter of Thomas A. Matson, formerly of Chariton. They have six children—Edward L., Jesse B., David R., George A., Mary and Charles A.

KENYON, WILLARD GIBBS, one of the prominent citizens of Manchester, is a native of New York. He was born in Jefferson county, near Sackett's Harbor, August 3, 1836. His father, John Kenyon, was a farmer, and was born in Vermont in 1808. He was the youngest of a large family, all of whom moved to Jefferson and Oswego counties, N. Y., and became farm-

ers, when that part of the state was very new. They were industrious, sober and law-abiding citizens and usually lived to a good old age. The mother, Sophronia Jenne, was born in Jefferson county, N. Y., in 1818. Her grandfather came from England to America and her father was a brave soldier in the war of 1812.

Willard's early education was limited because of his having to assist his father with the farm work, but he attended the district school for several winters. In 1857 he started west and May 12th reached Dubuque, Iowa, with only a few shillings in his pocket. He secured work in the wholesale grocery house of Munn, Clough, Merriam & Tucker, who were all from his own state of New York. Later he was in the employ of Smith & Stevens, manufacturers of confectionery, and he remained in Dubuque for nearly three years. Early in the year 1860 he started for Colorado, and while on his way, at a point in Kansas, opposite to the city of St. Joseph, he saw the first railway train which entered that state. It consisted of a construction en-

gine and four flat cars. Arriving in Colorado he worked at prospecting and mining for two years and a half, with many ups and downs, until he secured a claim of 250 feet on the Justice of Williams' lode in Lake Gulch, Gilpin county, Colo. Having contracted rheumatism by working in the mines he returned in December, 1862, to Manchester, Iowa, and opened the first exclusive grocery store in that town. About two years after his return from Colorado he had a chance to sell his claim in Lake Gulch and sent to his attorney a deed of the property for that purpose. The attorney died soon after getting the deed and the administrator of his estate sold Mr. Kenyon's claim for $20,000 and kept the money, he never being able to recover a dollar.

Mr. Kenyon started in life as a democrat but the war of the rebellion made him a republican and he has remained with that party until this day. He has never held any office or allowed his name to go on a ticket as a candidate. He is a Mason of long standing and a member of the Methodist church. He was married December 31, 1862, to Mary Elizabeth Marvin, and they have three children: Annie R., born January 21, 1864; Harry M., born May 22, 1873, and Mary E., born July 18, 1876.

In February, 1896, Mr. Kenyon sold his grocery business to Messrs. Cobb & Cobb, and he is now president of the Manchester Lumber company and takes an active part in the management of the business.

Mr. B. H. Keller and W. G. Kenyon laid the first sidewalk in Manchester. It consisted of two planks, one foot apart, where now stands substantial brick blocks and cement walks.

---

BOWERS, HENRY FRANCIS, of Clinton, was born in the city of Baltimore, Md., August 12, 1837.

His father, Augustus Bowers, or Bauer, as it was originally spelled, was a native of Germany, and before emigrating held the position of lieutenant in the German regular army. He came to America and settled in Baltimore, where he married Emaline Lewis. She was a native of Baltimore and a niece of Dr. Nelson Reed, who, with Dr. Coke, established Methodism in America. Thomas Barton, of Newark, one of the first Baptist divines of this country, was another uncle, and General Wayne, familiarly known for his desperate valor as "Mad Anthony Wayne," was a grand-uncle.

When Henry was a child his father started to return to Germany to settle up the estate of his paternal ancestor, and by the foundering of the ship in which he took passage, was drowned at sea. Henry's early education was obtained at home from the instruction of his mother and aunt. During the time when he should have been attending the public schools they were closed and he was deprived of that privilege which the youth of to-day enjoys so fully. The schools of the entire state of Maryland were closed by an act of the state legislature and remained closed for several years. In April, 1857, the family moved west and located on a farm near

14

De Witt, Clinton county, Iowa. At this period Henry completed his education by candle-light study while others slept. Their farming experience was not satisfactory and they moved to the town of De Witt, where Henry secured employment as carpenter and cabinetmaker.

In 1863 he entered the office of the clerk of the courts of Clinton county as deputy.

He served one term in the clerk's office and two terms as deputy recorder of the county and during this time studied law. Soon after he was elected and served two terms as county recorder. June 20, 1877, he was admitted to practice law in the courts of Iowa, and in 1878 was appointed special aid-de-camp on Governor Gear's staff and served to the end of his term. He was admitted to practice in the supreme court in April, 1879, and in the United States court in April, 1882, and has enjoyed a good practice since. Mr. Bowers' party affiliations have always been with the republican party. Shortly after the convention which organized that party, he had the pleasure of seeing and hearing the candidate for president, Gen. John C. Fremont, in the city of Baltimore, and with his uncle occupied a position on the platform during the meeting.

Mr. Bowers enjoys the distinction of being the founder and the past supreme president of the American Protective Association, commonly known as the "A. P. A." He was led to establish this organization by the closing of the Maryland public schools, which deprived citizens of their rights under the ordinance of 1798, where it is recommended that every American child should have a common school education. It was established for the purpose of maintaining the public schools against the machinations and influence of their enemies and does not oppose any church societies or any man's right to worship God as he sees fit. No organization is antagonized so long as it does not resolve itself into a political faction for the destruction of our public institutions, the abridgement of free speech, a free press and a free ballot.

For twenty-eight years Mr. Bowers has been a member of the Masonic Blue Lodge and for twenty-five years a member of the Consistory and of the Scottish Rite bodies of the thirty-second degree and of the Mystic Shrine. In religious matters he follows the church relations of his mother and is a Methodist.

He was married October 25, 1870, to Emma V. Crawford, of Barnsville, Belmont county, Ohio, and they have three children, Clyde C., born October 21, 1871; Homer H., born May 7, 1876, and Emma V., born July 3, 1878. His wife died October 24, 1878.

STILSON, O. H. A character who has been associated with the growth and progress of the beautiful little city of Corwith ever since that place was founded, is O. H. Stilson, banker and real estate dealer. His father, James M. Stilson, traveled across Iowa in 1851, in company with an old hunter named Rufus Clark, the trapping of beaver and otter and hunting elk being the object of the trip. In the fall of 1852 he returned to Illinois and engaged in farming. In 1855 he was married to Miss Dorlisca R. Stone, of McHenry county, Ill., and in 1856 they removed to Chippewa county, Wis., and entered land from the United States government. In 1888 they removed to Corwith, Iowa, where they now reside. The father entered the union army in 1864, and was honorably discharged at the close of the war.

O. H. Stilson was born on the old homestead near Chippewa Falls, Wis., on February 9, 1857, where he remained until 21 years of age. In the fall of 1878 he came to Iowa, and located in Cerro Gordo county, where he engaged in teaching district school. Shortly thereafter he engaged

with E. L. Stilson in the hardware business at Forest City, at the same time attempting the management of a farm which he had rented. In order to give proper attention to the store he was obliged to hire all the farm work done, and, the season proving a wet one, the crop was drowned out, and the young man found himself wofolly in debt. It was about this time that he heard of the new town of Corwith in Hancock county, on the then new line of the Minneapolis & St. Louis railway, and, after settling up his affairs as best he could, he removed to Corwith, and on September 1, 1880, on $500 borrowed from his father, started a general store there, in partnership with E. L. Stilson, under the firm name of O. H. Stilson & Co. The

subject of this sketch was given entire charge of the business, and it prospered from the start. Within one year the firm was obliged to erect a new store building, and at the end of the following year had more than $5,000 in stock on their shelves. In 1885 they were doing a business which amounted to $40,000 per year. About this time the firm started a private bank, with a capital stock of $10,000, and shortly thereafter sold out the store and confined their business to banking and real estate. In 1895 the bank was reorganized as the First State bank of Corwith, with a capital stock of $60,000, and a new bank building was erected at a cost of $17,000. Thirty thousand dollars of the stock of the institution was retained by Stilson & Co., and the remainder sold mostly to farmers and merchants. E. L. Stilson was made president and O. H. Stilson, vice-president of the new organization. The real estate business is still continued under the firm name of E. L. Stilson & Co., who now own 6,000 acres of northern Iowa land which, ten years ago, was worth $6 to $8 per acre, but is now selling at from $30 to $40 per acre. He was elected president of the First State bank of Corwith in 1897, and still holds the position. He was postmaster at Corwith during President Arthur's administration.

Mr. Stilson belongs to the Masons and Knights of Pythias. In politics he is a republican. He is a member of the Methodist church of Corwith, and is a steward and trustee of the organization of that faith there. He was married to Miss Lydia Olmsted, a Delaware county girl, on October 2, 1881, and they have four children, Lyell, Mabel, Ethel and Hazel.

---

McCLURE, ISAAC N., is a successful merchant and influential business man of Mediapolis, Des Moines county. He was born in Des Moines county within six miles of his present home, February 1, 1844, and is the son of William McClure, a farmer in comfortable circumstances, who settled there on government land in 1839. His parents were both natives of Pennsylvania, who came to Ohio, then to Illinois at a very early day. Mr. McClure was a man of strong convictions and high moral character. They reared a family of eleven children, eight of whom are now living. One of them, William G., is now a Christian missionary in Asia. Mr. McClure died in 1864, while his wife lived to the age of 77. They lie side by side in the Kossuth cemetery and their children "arise and call them blessed." Their son Isaac had a good early training, learning the value of money by working on his own account in the harvest field as a boy, following the cradle at 25 cents a day.

He is of Scotch-Irish descent. His mother, Cynthia Evans McClure, was of Welsh extraction. Isaac attended the country schools until 17 years of age, when the war broke out and he did not attend school any more until the winter of 1864 and 1865, when he paid his own expenses in a private school in Mt. Pleasant. The following winter, 1865, he attended the Yellow Springs academy at Kossuth, and had made such progress that the following fall he secured a teacher's certificate and taught school in the winter. In the summer he worked on a farm and ran a threshing machine in the fall, keeping this up for three years. During his last term of school in the winter of 1869, he secured a two weeks' vacation and went to Lyndon, Ross county,

Ohio, where he was united in marriage to Miss Susan Elizabeth Parrett, a very worthy young lady of that place, daughter of Joseph and Molena Parrett. Mr. McClure says that ever since his wedding day, December 28, 1869, he has been a firm believer in that passage of scripture recorded in Proverbs 18: 22, "Whoso findeth a wife, findeth a good thing." After his marriage, he farmed until the winter of 1873, when he bought a half interest in the general store of A. C. Brown, in Mediapolis, entering actively into the business in February of that year. The firm of Brown & McClure continued in business until February, 1886, when Mr. Brown retired from the firm and Mr. McClure associated with him Mr. J. I. Roberts under the firm name of I. N. McClure & Co. After doing business for five years their large store building burned to the ground, February 3, 1891. About $12,000 out of the $23,500 stock of goods were removed and the balance

was reduced to ashes, but was entirely covered by insurance. After the fire Mr William S. Patterson was associated with the firm under the old name and a fine brick store room 40x110 feet with a large brick warehouse, was built over the ruins of the old store. This firm did business together for three years, when in February, 1894, Mr. Roberts and Mr. Patterson retired from the firm and Austin J. Evans became Mr. McClure's partner, the firm becoming McClure & Evans, which has continued in business until the present time.

During the year of 1891, Mr. McClure became impressed with the need of a bank in Mediapolis, the nearest one being sixteen miles away, and succeeded in convincing others of the need. A corporation was formed under the name of the State bank of Mediapolis with a paid up capital of $25,000, and has been very successful. Mr. McClure is its vice-president and one of its principal stockholders.

He is a staunch republican in politics, and has been an elder in the Presbyterian church for years,

also superintendent of the Sunday school at Mediapolis for eighteen years past with the exception of
three years.

To Mr. and Mrs. McClure have been born three
children, Marcus P., Loue M., and Frank E. Marcus Parrett was born April 9, 1872, and graduated
in the classical course at Parsons college, Fairfield,
Iowa, in June, 1893. He spent the subsequent year
in Washington, D. C., taking a special course, and
there received a second degree coupled with a
diploma bearing President Cleveland's signature.
He taught one year in Vermont in the Green
Mountains, and then being convinced he was called
of God to preach the gospel, in September, 1895, he
entered the McCormack's Theological seminary in
Chicago and completed the course in June, 1898.
Previous to leaving the seminary he received a
unanimous call to become the pastor of the First
Presbyterian church of Kilbourne City, Wis., which
he accepted and entered on the duties of the pastorate. In September, 1897, he was united in marriage to Stella, daughter of Hon. Wm. E. Fuller,
of West Union, Iowa. To them in June, 1898, was
born a son, Donald Fuller McClure. Loue Maggie
was born May 19, 1875. She graduated at Parsons
college in June, 1897. Miss McClure had talent as
an elocutionist and she took the $20 prize in the
oratorical contest in March, 1896. In June, 1898,
she was united in marriage to Rev. Herbert W.
Rherd, pastor of the First Presbyterian church of
Milan, Ill. Franklyn Evans was born November
27, 1877. He graduated in the classical course at
Parsons college, June 13, 1899. He took the first
prize in the oratorical contest in March, 1897, and
in September, 1898, received his grade from Parsons college and entered the senior class of the
Occidental college of Los Angeles, Cal., where he
at once took high rank. He received the first prize
in the college oratorical contest in February, 1899,
and in consequence was the representative of the
college in the inter-collegiate oratorical contest
held at Los Angeles, April 25, 1899. After completing the year at Occidental college, he received his
grade and returned to Parsons college and graduated with his old class, June 13, 1899. He has
announced that the practice of medicine is his
chosen profession.

---

FULLERTON, KERN M., D. D. S., of
Cedar Falls. This bright and successful
young professional man was born in Crawford county, Pa., February 9, 1865. His
great-grandfather on the paternal side
emigrated from the north of Ireland to the
United States. The family originated in
Scotland, but the exact date of the removal
of the first members to Ireland is not
known. In the spelling of the name the
letter "e" has been substituted for that of
"a," as it appeared in the second syllable
of the signatures of the early Fullartons.
At the time of their residence in Ireland
they were termed Protestant Catholics,
that being the name given to those settlers
who came from Scotland and located in
the north of Ireland. Grandfather Fullerton was a very rich man, as riches went in
those days, and his wealth was represented
in most part by broad, fertile acres and
chests of gold and silver. The maternal
grandparents were natives of Germany,
but a branch of the family came, at a very
early period, from Greece.

The early life of this Mr. Fullerton was
spent at the place of his birth near Meadville, Pa., where he attended the district
school. Later he entered the high school
at Cambridge. Upon leaving the home
farm permanently he removed to Ohio and
engaged with a railroad contractor, remaining there for several months; then he
returned to Pennsylvania and was employed in the lumbering districts of Elk
county. In 1887 he came to Iowa, and
soon thereafter entered the dental department of the Iowa State university, from
which he graduated in 1889. During his
college life he was a tireless student, and
the hours that were spent in a chase after
pleasure by many of his associates were by
him devoted to hard and persistent study.
He was foremost among those who organized the S. U. I. Dental society. This organization was composed of the students

of that department, and held weekly meetings where papers on dentistry, prepared
by the students, were read and discussed.

In politics Dr. Fullerton is a democrat, but
is not a radical politician. He is a member
of the Knights of Pythias and B. P. O. E.

In a professional way he belongs to that class to which work for the elevation of his science is a positive pleasure. He is a member of the Eastern Iowa Dental society and the Iowa State Dental society, having served as president of the first named organization. He was elected president of the Iowa State Dental society at its annual meeting held in Des Moines in May, 1897, serving one year. Being keenly alive to the importance of being up to date in his profession, Doctor Fullerton takes a deep interest in all matters that will in any way assist him to that end. His library is well stocked with dental literature, and he keeps up with the spirit of progression in his profession.

STEWART, JAMES ORBISON, of Cedar Rapids, is of Scotch-Irish descent and is a native of Mercer county, Penn., having been born near North Liberty, in that state, October 3, 1837. His father, John Stewart and family, moved to Washington, Iowa, in 1844. His mother's maiden name was Wadell. Her father, who was of Scotch descent, was a soldier in the war of 1812. James was only 7 years old when the family moved to Iowa, and to him at that age it was the event of a lifetime. This was long before the day of railroads and the trip was made by water from Allegheny City, Penn., to Keokuk, Iowa. Wagons and horses were brought along to make the balance of the distance. In 1850 the family moved in the same primitive fashion to Cedar Rapids, which was then but a small village. The country was very sparsely settled and the family endured all the hardships and vicissitudes incident to early pioneer life in the west.

James Stewart's early education was procured in the common schools and in a country printing office. At the age of 16 he entered the office of the *Progressive Era*, the first paper published in Cedar Rapids, earning his first dollar rolling and inking the type for the printing of the Iowa supreme court reports, on a hand press. After about six months' service in that capacity he was regularly apprenticed as the "printer's devil" for four years, receiving the sum of $30 the first year, $50 the second, $75 the third and $100 the fourth year. Out of this princely salary he was supposed to pay his board and clothe himself. He worked at the printing trade until the spring of 1861, when he enlisted as a private soldier in Company K, First Iowa infantry, under the first call for volunteers. He took part in the skirmishes of Mud Springs, Forsythe and the noted battle of Wilson's Creek, Mo., where he received his first "glory mark" and in which the noble General Lyon fell while he was leading the First Iowa. In May, 1862, he re-enlisted, entering the service as first sergeant of Company B,

Twentieth Iowa infantry, and took part in all the marches and battles of the regiment; the more important being Prairie Grove, siege of Vicksburg, Fort Morgan, Blakely and the capture of Mobile, Ala. He was, soon after entering the service, promoted to second lieutenant and later commissioned first lieutenant and then captain, but not

mustered in the two latter owing to the reduced size of the company. About eighteen months of this service he acted as adjutant of the regiment, an honor seldom conferred on a second lieutenant. He also acted for a time as judge advocate of the second division of the Thirteenth army corps, and later as mustering officer on the staff of Gen. C. C. Andrews, and in October, 1865, when mustered out of service, held that position on the staff of Gen. Joseph C. Mower, for the department of Texas

On his return to civil life he again took up the printer's trade and in 1866 bought a half interest in the Waverly *Republican;* selling this later he bought the Clarksville *Star,* which he published for twelve years, building up a state reputation for himself and for the paper as an unswerving advocate of the principles of the republican party, to which he still adheres. Captain Stewart has always been an enthusiastic Grand Army man and has held all the positions in the post from the lowest to the highest, and also appointments on the staffs of the national and department commanders; but his best work has been in quiet aid to indigent comrades and other dependents. In 1884 he re-located in Cedar Rapids and was connected as a writer and otherwise with various newspapers. In

1895 he was appointed deputy clerk of the United States circuit and district courts and United States commissioner for northern district of Iowa, which position he still holds. He takes an active interest in politics, but is not a politician only in the better sense of the term. In all his long and active career he would never allow his name to be presented for an elective office, although often urged to do so, preferring to aid others to taking office himself. He has never held office only these he now holds and four years as assistant postmaster in his home city.

He was married in 1868 to Miss Leah E. Alexander, of New York state. They have one child, Raymond Grant Stewart, who is now a resident of Cedar Rapids, and following in the footsteps of his father as a printer. He was brought up in the faith of the United Presbyterian church and is now a member of that society.

---

WOOD, CHARLES ROLAND, of Corwith, is county attorney of Hancock county, and one of the well-known lawyers of northwestern Iowa. He is the son of Charles Roland Wood, a farmer and a native of New York, who was born in 1818 and died in 1883. His mother was formerly Mary A. Gilbert. She was born in Connecticut in 1821. His parents were residents of Kendall county, Ill., from 1855 until the death of the father. His mother now resides in Iriquois county, Ill., at Onarga, with her youngest daughter, Mrs. Dr. I. F. Palmer.

C. R. Wood was born February 15, 1851, at Governeur, St. Lawrence county, N. Y. He was brought up on a farm, and obtained his earliest schooling in the district school. At the age of 18 he secured a position in a drug store, where he learned pharmacy, and continued in this employment until 1876, when he began the study of law in the office of L. D. Holmes, at Aledo, Ill. After two years thus spent, he passed the examination before the appellate court at Ottawa, Ill., and was admitted to the bar in June, 1878. He soon opened an office at Aledo, remaining there one and one-half years and enjoying a good practice. January 1, 1879, he removed to Rock Island, Ill., and formed a partnership with A. W. Atwood; but the firm was dissolved in March, 1880, and Mr. Wood then located at Williamsburg, Kan., where he practiced his profession about three years; moved to Tebo, Coffey county, Kan., remaining

three years, then moved to Hutchinson, Kan., and from there to Corwith, Iowa. He came to Iowa January 2, 1891, settling at Corwith, his present home. Here he again established himself in the law business, and also purchased a half interest in the Corwith *Crescent*, the only newspaper published in the town, with A. A. Johnson as a partner. They continued to manage the paper together until April 1, 1892, when Mr. Wood became sole owner and editor. His law practice increased so rapidly, however, that he was obliged to dispose of the paper after a short time, and accordingly sold out February 3, 1893, in

order to devote himself entirely to his profession as a lawyer. He has been appointed, and now holds the position of local attorney for the Iowa Central Railroad company.

Mr. Wood has always been a republican in politics. In 1894 he was elected county attorney of Hancock county, and is still holding the office with much credit to himself and his party, having been re-elected in 1896. He belongs to the Masonic order and to the A. O. U. W. In religion Mr. Wood is a Baptist.

Mr. Wood was married July 9, 1879, to Miss Linnie R. Houk, of Aledo, Ill. Three children have been born to them: Charles R., Jr., in 1880; Edgar H., in 1882, and Blanche, in 1884, who died in infancy.

During all of the time he has been engaged in other business, he has never entirely relinquished his law practice, but continued it in connection with his other business.

---

WICHMAN, JOHN E., of Garner, is one of the most prominent lawyers and politicians of Hancock county, and has a wide acquaintance in northern Iowa. His ancestors were Germans, both his parents, Frederick and Eliza (Kemler) Wichman, having been born in the town of Bremerhaven, in the province of Hanover, Germany. They emigrated to this country in 1843 and settled at Galena, Ill., in 1844. The father was a miner and always lived in the humblest circumstances.

J. E. Wichman was born April 16, 1859, at Galena, Ill., where he grew to manhood, obtaining his early education in the public schools of that city. After finishing the public schools he entered the Northwestern German-English college, an institution owned by the German Methodist church, which was then situated at Galena, but has since been removed to Charles City, Iowa. He graduated from the normal department of this school in 1876. While in college he was a member of the Washington Literary society, and of the Teutonic, a German literary society. After graduation he taught school, and in 1881 came to Iowa, settling near Garner, in Hancock county, where he worked on a farm during the summer and taught school during the rest of the year. He commenced the study of law at Garner in the spring of 1882, in the office of A. C. Ripley, remaining with him a year and then pursuing his studies in the office of H. H. Bush, of the same town. He was admitted to the bar in July, 1884, at Charles City, Judge Granger, now of the supreme court, presiding. While studying law Mr. Wichman was obliged to continue working on the farm during the summer in order to provide himself with the means for carrying out his plans. After his admission to the bar he formed a partnership with Henry H. Bush, of Garner, which was continued nearly six years, being dissolved January 1, 1890, since which time Mr. Wichman has been practicing alone. In addition to his law business he has loaned money extensively, and has taken a prominent part in other financial interests of the county. He assisted in the organization of the First National bank of Garner in 1892, when he was elected as a member of its board of directors, in which capacity he still serves. He was also one of the organizers of the State Savings bank at Klemme the same year, and was its first president.

Mr. Wichman has always been a republican in politics, casting his first vote for Garfield. He has taken an active part in local and state politics, serving as chairman and secretary of the county central committee and frequently representing Hancock county in the district and state conventions. He has served two terms as mayor of Garner, two terms as councilman and four terms as recorder. In 1886 he

was elected county attorney, being the first to fill that office in Hancock county under the new law changing from district to county attorneys. He was re-elected in 1888, and during his four years in office was especially active in working for the enforcement of the prohibitory liquor law. In 1895 he was selected by the republicans of his county as their candidate for the office of senator from his district. Mr. Wichman is a member of the Knights of Pythias lodge. He has been chancellor commander of the local organization and has represented them in the grand lodge, both at Sioux City and at Muscatine. He belongs to no church, but is a regular attendant of the Methodist Episcopal.

Mr. Wichman was married November 15, 1888, at Garner, to Miss Mary L. Prescott. They have one child, Lois Della, who was born August 17, 1895.

---

BARHYDT, THEODORE WELLS, has been conspicuous in the history of Burlington for more than forty years, and has had a large part in advancing the prosperity and growth of that city. Mr. Barhydt was born in Newark, N. J., April 10, 1835; he was the son of Nicholas and Phœbe H. Gardner Barhydt. His father was a native of New York and his mother of New Jersey. On both sides, his ancestors were among the first settlers of their respective states. On the paternal side, the Barhydts settled on the Hudson river below Albany in 1665, and the Gardners were among the early settlers of New Jersey, and very prominent citizens of that state. Jerome Barhydt, grandfather of Theodore W., was a revolutionary soldier and a very highly-respected citizen of Schenectady, N. Y. T. W. Barhydt received his education in the private schools and Lyceum academy of Schenectady, and spent his time in school and in working in his father's boot and shoe store until 1855 when he came west, locating at Burlington, where his relatives, Dr. and Mrs. G. W. Snyder, persuaded him to try his fortune. Soon after his arrival, Mr. Barhydt accepted a clerkship in the shoe store of Mr. Sweetser, and, not long afterwards, became one of the principal clerks in the postoffice. In 1859 he opened up a new boot and shoe store, in partnership with Mr. Tizzard, who was postmaster at that time. The partnership continued for one year, when Mr. Barhydt purchased his partner's interest, and, for some years, ran the business alone. In 1866 he took in, as a partner, his brother-in-law, Mr. Henry A. Brown, and, since that time, has not been active in the business himself. In 1870 he assisted in the organization of the Merchants National bank, and has been its president ever since, and is also a director in the German-American Savings bank. He became interested in the building of railroads in Iowa in an early day, and was one of the organizers of the Burlington, Cedar Rapids & Minnesota, now the Burlington, Cedar Rapids & Northern Railway company, and was for several years one of its directors, and also a member of the executive committee. He was also one of the directors of the Burlington & Southwestern railroad. In 1880

he was elected president of the Burlington & Northwestern Railroad company, and has served continually in that position since that time. When the Burlington & Western road was built, in 1881, he was elected president of that corporation, and has been annually re-elected since that time. Mr. Barhydt has large real estate interests in Burlington, and is the owner of the Dolano hotel, and several other business blocks.

He has never been a politician, but has held several offices of public trust. He was one of the citizens through whose influence the Burlington water works were established, and was one of the principal builders and promoters of the first street railway in the city, serving for several years as treasurer of the company. He has been president of the board of trade, a member of the city council, and a director and treasurer of the city water company. Mr. Barhydt has every reason to be gratified with the results of his labor, both financially and intellectually. He has been an extensive traveler and has profited by contact with the distant scenes which he has visited. He has been a man of the world, and at the same time an earnest student of literature and art. As a business man, as a member of society, as a manipulator of public affairs, and as a man who has taken every opportunity of advancing the welfare of his

home city, he has the highest respect of all. The young business man who takes Mr. Barhydt's career for example need fear no disaster from which he may not readily and quickly recover.

He has been prominently connected with the Masonic order since 1862, being a member of the Des Moines Lodge No. 1,

A. F. & A. M., of Iowa Chapter No. 1, R. A. M., St Omar Commandery No. 15, K. T., and of Kaaba Temple of the Mystic Shrine. He is also a member of the Sons of the Revolution, and is one of the board of managers for the state of Iowa. He has lately been elected a member of the Holland society of New York. Politically he has always been affiliated with the democratic party, but his life has always been too much taken up with business pursuits to accept or desire any public office.

His wife was Miss Eleanor Christiancy, of Knickerbocker Dutch origin, and, like himself, of revolutionary stock. They have both been active members of the First Presbyterian church of Burlington since 1863.

———

WYANT, OTIS BLAIR, one of the leading physicians of Tipton, Cedar county, is the son of Isaac Wyant, who came to Iowa in the early fifties, and was one of the pioneers in the settling of Cedar county. Upon a farm in Iowa township he made his home, brought up a family of eight boys and girls, and was one of the leading citizens of the county. In politics he was a democrat, and his son has inherited his father's opinions in that respect. Mr. Wyant was a progressive, wide-awake farmer, as is evidenced by the fact that the first McCormick reaper ever brought west of the Mississippi river, was bought by him for use upon his farm. In the early days all of his trading was done at Davenport and Muscatine, they being then the nearest trading points.

Judith Ann Guild, Dr. Wyant's mother, was a thoroughly energetic and good woman. When her husband died the five younger children were left to her care and guidance. Such was her capability, she was able to manage the farm in a businesslike and successful manner, keep the children together, and give them all a good education.

Otis B. Wyant, the youngest of this family of children, was born in Cedar county, January 6, 1865. Until he was 17 years old he remained at home, attending the country school, and later, the West Liberty high school, working on the farm during his vacations. His medical studies were pursued at the State University of Iowa, and at Rush Medical college, Chicago; from the latter school he graduated, the youngest member of a class of 160, in February, 1886, being then just 21 years of age. So fine was his standing in his class

that he was offered, upon graduation, an assistantship to a prominent specialist of Philadelphia.

Immediately after finishing his medical studies, Dr. Wyant came back to Cedar county, locating at Clarence, where he

built up a large practice in a few months. Here he remained until 1890, when, desiring to study further, he returned to Chicago, where he spent eleven months in the different hospitals and in taking post-graduate courses of study.

In June, 1891, the doctor located in Tipton, where he enjoys a lucrative practice. Constantly being called in consultation, his reputation as a careful, well-informed physician, is rapidly growing.

He was United States examining physician during Cleveland's second administration, where his services were highly satisfactory. All old soldiers were treated with uniform courtesy.

He was one of six men who organized a fraternal beneficiary association, known as the Modern Brotherhood of America, being elected their head physician. This association has grown to a membership of more than 50,000, with more than $7,500,000 in force, thus making the most remarkable record ever known in insurance circles. During the first two years of the existence of this association there were issued more than 15,000 certificates, every loss paid in full from the start, thereby gaining the world's record for any association two years old.

Mr. Wyant is a Knight of Pythias and vice-president of the Hawkeye club of Tipton. He is a member of the Eastern Iowa Union Medical society. His religion is briefly paraphrased as, love, truth and good will toward all.

Dr. Wyant was married on March 4, 1886, to Norma D. Maxson, daughter of Eliza Maxson, of Springdale, who figures prominently in our history of John Brown in this volume.

---

POWERS, JOHN LESLIE. Carroll county and the city of Carroll has a very popular and influential daily and weekly newspaper, known as the *Sentinel*, edited by Messrs. Powers & Colclo.

John L. Powers, the senior editor, was born on a farm near Woodville, Sandusky county, Ohio, March 21, 1863. He is a son of Charles Powers, merchant and farmer, born in Columbia county, N. Y., in 1819, who moved to Perrysburg, Ohio, in 1836, casting his first vote there in 1840 for Martin Van Buren; went to Woodville the same year to engage in mercantile pursuits, adding farming in 1864. He was always a democrat, and was appointed postmaster at Woodville by President Pierce, and held that office until elected to the legislature by the democratic party in 1859. He served in the lower house during the stirring session just preceding the war, and when James A. Garfield, Jacob D. Cox, and others afterwards famous, were in the senate. He went south after the battle of Shiloh to look after the Sandusky county soldier boys who were in that battle, returning north on the hospital boat, where he served as nurse to the wounded soldiers. He removed from Woodville to Perrysburg in 1869, where he died in 1871, leaving some property gained by industry and frugality. His wife, Lydia Ann Banks, was born at St. Johns, Ontario, in 1829, and was also a pioneer of the Black Swamp country. She married Mr. Powers in 1847, and is the mother of eight children, Helen A., George P., Julia N., Charles A., James Freeland, Edward Adorns, John L. and William Howard. All are living but Julia, who died in infancy. Mrs. Powers is now living with her youngest son at Pawtucket, R. I. She is of a long-lived family; her maternal grandmother lived to be 95 years old, and her mother is now living, hale and hearty, at the age of 88. She was born on the same day as Abraham Lincoln, February 12, 1809.

Mr. Powers received a common school education, but he has learned more from following the reading habit and keeping his eyes and ears open as he went through the printing offices in which he was employed. He started to learn the printer's trade March 15, 1875, just before he was 12 years old, in the office of the *Buckeye Granger*, in Perrysburg, Ohio, at $2 a week. Three years there and two in the *Bee* office in Toledo fitted him to travel, so he took to the road and worked in various Ohio offices, among them the Cleveland *Leader*, *Herald* and *Plaindealer*. He held cases on the latter paper when the office was still fresh with the fragrance of the gentle humor of Artemus Ward, who, years before, had delighted with his wit the *Plaindealer's* entire office force, as well as the readers of that paper.

Mr. Powers came to Iowa at the age of 19 to take cases on the Marshalltown *Times - Republican*, afterward being employed in the job department. He returned to Ohio in 1883 and took a position in the mail type room of Nasby's Toledo *Blade*, remaining there only a few months, when he returned to Iowa, and in the winter of 1883–4, with others, founded the *Marshall County News*, of which "Old Grizzly" Chapin was the editor. In the summer of 1884 he sold out, and took a position as foreman on the *Statesman*. He remained there nearly five years, when he went to Carroll and purchased of Mike Miller a

half interest in the Carroll *Sentinel*. This partnership continued until January, 1891, when Mr. Miller sold his interest to C. C. Colclo, and the present firm of Powers & Colclo has since controlled that paper.

Mr. Powers says he was born a democrat and expects to die one. He has generally voted for his party's nominees, but in 1884 voted for that great statesman, James G. Blaine. He has been a delegate to several state conventions of the democratic party, and to various congressional, judicial and other minor conventions. He was appointed postmaster at Carroll by President Cleveland, and took charge of that office in May, 1893, holding it until October, 1897. He is a member of the Masonic and Knights of Pythias lodges, serving in several of the official positions of the latter, and also as secretary of the former during 1898. He was secretary of the Enterprise club, an association of local business men, is vice-president of the Boos Shoulder Brace association, a local manufacturing corporation, and always takes an active part in the promotion of all the interests of his city.

He joined the Presbyterian church when a boy, but now usually attends the Episcopal church, of which his wife is a member.

He was married October 14, 1885, to Miss Luella A. Osman, of Marshalltown. They have four children, Charles Osman, Gretchen, Frederick Dodge, and John Leslie, Jr.

---

HEINSHEIMER, D. L. . The Heinsheimer mercantile company of Glenwood is well known throughout all southwestern Iowa. The head of that firm is the subject of this sketch. He is widely known, not alone on account of his connection therewith, but by reason of the interest he takes in orcharding and the breeding of fine cattle. He is, in truth, a man who has amassed a fortune through close application of his fine business talents to the management of his mercantile business and in wise investments, and that wealth he has used as becomes a good citizen, in advancing the various interests of his community.

He was born in Eppingen, Baden, Germany, March 19, 1847. Although his parents died while he was yet young he was given a good education in the common schools. He came to Iowa and to Glenwood in April, 1861, a poor boy, and through his own efforts has become one of the leading citizens of that section both as to wealth and influence. He began his business career as clerk in a store and saved what he could from his small salary, which was carefully invested as fast as earned. In 1872 he was in position to purchase an interest with his employer, Mr. P. D. Foster, and the business was conducted under the firm name of P. D. Foster & Co. until 1875, at which time he engaged in business alone for three years, then a brother, Albert Heinsheimer, was taken into partnership and the firm was known as D. L. Heinsheimer & Co. until 1894.

He is at this time connected with several banks, and is president of the Mills County National bank at Glenwood, is a large land holder and owns one of the finest orchards in Mills county, in which he takes great pride. He has given much attention to improving and raising the standard of cattle and is the owner of Hugo Countess, the Jersey that made the great record in the breed tests at the World's fair. The Iowa commissioners voted and paid to him $250 for the excellent showing made by this cow.

His varied interests becoming a tax upon his time he, in 1894, concluded to take into business with him another partner, and accordingly in that year was incorporated the D. L. Heinsheimer Company,

of which this subject was made president, E. R. Heinsheimer, secretary, and Albert Heinsheimer, treasurer. E. R. Heinsheimer, the secretary, is a son of the head of the corporation and a young man of fine business ability. This company is still existing.

Mr. Heinsheimer is a republican. He has held local positions of trust since becoming a voter, has served as member of the city council and was elected to the honorable position of mayor. He was a member of the school board for eighteen years, twelve of which he served as its president. He was a delegate to the national republican convention in 1892, and was the Iowa member of the committee on rules and organization. Was elected presidential elector for Iowa in 1896.

He was married to Miss Sarah Pettinger, September 20, 1870. They have been blessed with six children, five of whom are now living. They are named respectively, Carrie (now Mrs. B. Shoninger of Chicago), Edward, Jeannette, Lester and Theresa.

---

COVER, O. ALVIN, M. D., of Seymour, was born in Union county, Ill., Feb. 22, 1862.

His father, Abram Cover, was of German descent and a man of firm character and fixed habits, being recognized for his sterling worth and ability in the community where he resided. He was a soldier in the Mexican war and when the war of the rebellion broke out enlisted in the Sixth Illinois cavalry, and served his country faithfully as lieutenant of his company until receiving his discharge on account of ill health. He died at his old home in 1892. He was engaged in the milling and mercantile business and was a man of some means. At the time of his death and for several years previous, he was a licensed exhorter in the Methodist church, and was always found at his post of duty in religious work. He was married to Sophia Miller. She was a woman of more than ordinary intelligence and ability, and a shining light in the church. She possessed all the qualities of a devoted wife and a kind and loving mother. Nine children were born to them, five boys and four girls, of whom four boys and three girls are living, all residents of Illinois except the subject of this sketch, who is the youngest of the boys.

Dr. Cover received a good common school education at home, and then attended the Frankfort, Ill., high school, after which he went to the Southern Illinois Normal school. After completing his education he taught school for a period of ten years. His record in the class-room and as principal of the Alto Pass high school, gave him a place among the educational leaders of southern Illinois. But he was not satisfied with this. From the age of 18 years his one great desire was to become a physician. To this laudable ambition every energy was bent, and after a long and studious course he now occupies a high place in his profession. In the year 1891 he entered the college of physicians and surgeons in Keokuk, and at the end of one year went to Centerville, and associated himself with Prof. Robert Stephenson, remaining with him until the death of the latter. He then went into the office of Dr. J. L. Sawyers, where he remained five months. He then attended the Baltimore Medical college at Baltimore, Md., where he received the degree of M. D. in March, 1893. He was again professionally connected with Dr. Sawyers for a period of eight months of active practice; still not being satisfied and desiring further

preparation for his life-work, he entered the Jefferson Medical college at Philadelphia, Pa., and received a second diploma in May, 1894. The next month he located in Seymour, Iowa, where he has since remained, enjoying a large and constantly increasing practice. He has a first-class professional standing in the county and state and holds the respect and good will of his co-workers in the cause of relieving suffering humanity, according to the allopathic school of medicine. Dr. Cover has many warm personal friends and is a favorite in social circles. He is a prominent Odd Fellow, having passed through all the chairs; is a master Mason and a member of the Modern Woodmen of America. He is the medical examiner for the New York Life Insurance company, Bankers' Life association, the Modern Woodmen and the New York Mutual Life insurance

The doctor has always been an enthusiastic republican, and during his residence in Illinois participated in several hotly contested campaigns, and served as chairman of the township committee. He was

several times a delegate to congressional and senatorial conventions. The one great aim of his life is to excel in his profession. Hard study and close application have already brought him up to the high rank enjoyed by many of mature years. He is a member of the Des Moines Valley Medical association.

Dr. Cover was married December 28, 1898, to Miss Jessie Llewellyn, of Seymour, Iowa.

---

DAVIDSON, THOMAS M., the founder of the Elkader *Argus*, and a man who has a self-acquired education in the law as well as in the ordinary departments of learning, was born in Licking county, Ohio, December 19, 1838. He comes of poor and obscure parentage, of whom but little is known except that they were of Scotch descent. At the age of 3 years Mr. Davidson was adopted by an uncle, with whom he lived until the breaking out of the war in 1861. His school advantages were very limited, never attending more than three months in the year and having had no opportunity whatever after he had reached the age of 18. He came to Iowa in the fall of 1856 and worked on a farm in the vicinity of Volga City. At the commencement of the civil war he enlisted in the Sixteenth United States infantry and was assigned to Company F, First battalion. He participated in the battle of Shiloh and the Corinth and Stone River campaigns. He was promoted to sergeant and in February, 1864, was sent to regimental headquarters at Ft. Ontario, N. Y., where he superintended the drilling and equipping of recruits, remaining there until the expiration of his term of enlistment. He then returned to Clayton county, Iowa, but as his health was too poor to admit of farm work, and having had no opportunity to accumulate capital with which to go into business he learned the shoemaker's trade and supported his family by working at the bench. Being ambitious for better things, he took up the study of law, which he pursued at night, after his day's work, with no assistance other than the encouragement of a true and devoted wife. His election as constable gave him more opportunity and purpose for the study of law. He was admitted to practice in the state courts in 1877. In 1883 he formed a partnership with Hon. Samuel Murdock, of Elkader, which continued for four years, at which time the relation was dissolved and Mr. Davidson continued alone. In 1890, his health growing worse, he gave up the practice altogether and established the Elkader *Argus*, a republican weekly newspaper. The duties of this enterprise being greater than he could perform alone, at the beginning

of 1896 he sold a half interest to Marvin Cook.

Mr. Davidson cast his first ballot for Abraham Lincoln for president and has ever since been identified with the republican party. In 1886 he received the nomi-

nation for the office of county attorney of Clayton county, and, although the democratic majority in the county was about 1,200, he was defeated by only 700 votes. He was again nominated for the same office in 1896 and during the campaign took the stump and did much toward swinging the county into the republican column by a majority of over 400 and electing himself and three other republican candidates to their respective offices. He is now serving a second term, being re-elected in 1898. He is a member of the I. O. G. T., I. O. O. F., A. F. and A. M., K. of P., and G. A. R., in all of which he has held important offices.

While yet a soldier he was married to Miss Margaret E. Wickham, of Licking county, Ohio. They have reared two children, one of whom, M. Anna, is the wife of Rev. R. C. Lusk, pastor of the Methodist church at Elma, and the other, Wilmer W., is foreman in the *Argus* office. He is reading law also, with a view of some day following the profession of his father. At this writing the health of Mr. Davidson has so far improved that he is again in practice in connection with his newspaper work.

---

ROBERTS, ABEL COMMINS, M. D., is a native of the state of New York, and was born January 15, 1830. His father was a farmer in that state, but removed while Abel was a child to Lenawee county, Mich. to secure a share of the advantages offered by the then unsettled west. In Lenawee county Abel attended the country school and acquired an education which enabled him, as soon as he was old enough, to teach school. His education from this time on was secured entirely by his own unaided efforts. In 1850 he entered the medical department of the Michigan university at Ann Arbor, determined to get a first-class medical education. Being very poor at that time, he had hard work to support himself through the first term and subsisted for many weeks on less than many of the other students spent for tobacco.

In the spring of 1851 he borrowed money enough to pay his passage to California, arriving there sick and destitute. After a year and a half of the hardest kind of life, during which luck came to him, he returned to his studies at Ann Arbor with gold enough to carry him through college, graduating with the degree of M. D. there in 1854. In 1876 he received an *ad eundem* degree of M. D. from the Louisville (Ky.) Medical college.

He married Emily A. Cole, of Ann Arbor, and soon after located at Otsego, Mich., where he remained until removing to Fort Madison in 1589. Mrs. Roberts died May 19, 1898.

In 1862 he was given the position of surgeon at the government hospital at Keokuk and later received the army commission of surgeon, with rank of major of cavalry, to the Twenty-first Missouri volunteers, with whom he served three years, being mustered out in April, 1866. Upon his return to Fort Madison at the close of the war, he continued the practice of medicine. While never making special pretensions as a surgeon, he was noted for his success in this branch of his profession both during his work in the field and in private practice, and once ligated, successfully, the left subclavian artery. While army surgeon he was most of the time in charge of a brigade or division, and though many times operating during and after serious engagements, from twenty-four to forty-eight hours almost continuously, he had the satisfaction of never having a man die on the operating table, though frequently that table was necessarily mother earth, and often the work had to be done by candle light.

He was for two terms a lecturer on theory and practice of medicine at the College of Physicians and Surgeons at Keokuk. He was, while in active prac-

tice, a member of the American Medical association, and a delegate to its meetings. He is also an honorary member of the California Medical society.

The doctor has always been an ardent democrat and has labored faithfully and efficiently for the cause of true democracy. He has the respect and confidence of his community and has been several times honored by election to important offices. In 1869 he was selected for county treasurer and filled that office very satisfactorily for six years. The citizens of Fort Madison elected him mayor of the city in 1873 and he served in that position for several terms. In 1893 he had the honor of being commissioner to the Columbian exposition at Chicago.

He has always been an active promoter of Fort Madison's interests and was the originator of the Chicago, Fort Madison &

Des Moines railway, at that time the Fort Madison & Des Moines railway, and was its first president. He was also one of the hardest workers in securing the Southwestern railway from Fort Madison to Carrollton, Mo., now known as the Chicago, Burlington & Kansas City railroad. In all matters connected with the prosperity of Fort Madison, he has always worked heart and soul and has given much time, cash and energy to promote her interests.

The doctor has not been engaged for a number of years in the active practice of medicine, having surrendered the practice to his oldest son, F. C. Roberts, M. D. He has been for many years the owner and editor of the Fort Madison *Democrat* and is regarded as one of the strongest and most influential editorial writers in the state. He has made several trips abroad and once made a trip around the world. He is an active member of the Masons and is an Odd Fellow. His church connection is Baptist.

Dr. Roberts has three sons, Dr. F. C. Roberts, his successor in practice; Nelson C. Roberts, a newspaper man, who, during Cleveland's last term, was postmaster, and who is now manager of the Fort Madison *Democrat*, and Edward M. Roberts, engaged in dramatic and literary work.

---

RUTH, CHARLES EDWARD, M. D. Among the eminent gentlemen who compose the faculty of the Keokuk Medical college, is Prof. C. E. Ruth, the subject of this biography.

Before recording the history of the life of the professor, it is fitting that something be said of his antecedents. His father, Alexander Ruth, was born in Greene county, Penn., July 18, 1836, and came to Iowa in 1857. It was from this state that he enlisted to fight for "old glory," serving with the gallant Fourteenth Iowa Volunteer Infantry for eighteen months, when he was transferred to the Seventh cavalry, receiving his discharge late in 1864. He was a farmer by occupation, and in 1889 had accumulated sufficient means to enable him to leave the old homestead in Johnson county and enjoy life in the beautiful city of Muscatine, where he now resides. Dr. Ruth's mother, Sarah Jane Funk, was also a native of Pennsylvania, born in 1840. She came to Iowa in 1858, was married in 1860 and died at Muscatine July 21, 1896. The ancestors on both sides for at least four generations were farmers. The founders of the family came to this country prior to the revolution, on the paternal side, from England and Ireland; on the maternal side, from Germany.

Dr. Ruth was born in Johnson county, Iowa, August 17, 1861. After having finished the high school of Iowa City, he entered the medical department of the Iowa State university, from which he graduated March 7, 1883. He located at Atalissa and engaged in practice until January, 1887, when he removed to Muscatine and formed a partnership with Dr. G. O. Morgridge, which relation existed for two years. It was severed by reason of the election of Dr. Ruth to the chair of descriptive and surgical anatomy, in the Keokuk Medical college. He still holds that position and has purchased a one-eighth interest in the college.

In 1893 he was made professor of clinical surgery at St. Joseph's hospital, and since then he has regularly held weekly clinics there as a part of the regular course of the

Keokuk Medical college. Though now engaged in a general practice, his surgical work chiefly occupies his attention. His researches have given the first published record of the resistance of the brain to penetration by probes of given diameters, in exploring that organ for bullets which have traversed its substance, a full account of which appears in the report of the American Medical association, at its meeting in Detroit in 1892. He is the inventor of various surgical instruments and appliances, including bullet forceps, turbinated gouges, scissors for sectioning the second and third divisions of the fifth nerve far

from the surface in the smallest possible space, placental detachers and a metallic rotary adjustable aseptic operating table; also a combined rotary bookcase and desk. He performed the first successful resection of the cæcum for sarcoma in a child 5 years old, in which the Murphy button was used to make an end to end anastomosis of the ileum to colon.

The doctor is a republican prohibitionist. He is a member of Eagle Lodge A. F. and A. M., Sons of Veterans, American Medical association, the Iowa State, being chairman of the section in this society on obstetrics and gynecology for 1898, Military Tract, Tri-State, of which he was elected president in 1898, Des Moines Valley and Southeastern

Iowa Medical societies. He belongs to the Methodist church. He was married October 3, 1883, to Miss Adella Tautlinger, of Lone Tree, Iowa. They have three children— Verl Alton, Una Gertrude and Zana. The doctor's success is due entirely to his own efforts. He earned his first dollar by binding oats for a neighbor after night, after his work for his father was done. With the money thus earned he purchased his first book, Webster's Academic dictionary. He left home at the age of 18 to complete his education with just 11 cents, a present and start in life from his mother and sister, this being all the money they possessed. That money is one of his most treasured keepsakes for he did not part with it.

Dr. Ruth was appointed major brigade surgeon by President McKinley, June 4, 1898, but was compelled to resign July 29, 1898, on account of illness.

---

PRALL, ARTHUR AMIN, M. D., of Dayton, Webster county, is of German descent. His father, Thomas Prall, was a farmer in fair circumstances living in Pennsylvania. He was born February 15, 1836, at Washington, Washington county, Pa., and came to Iowa in 1857, settling in Van Buren county. September 7, 1859, he was married to Rachel Richardson, whose father, Nathan Richardson, was a carpenter and cabinet-maker and worked at that trade for more than fifty years. Her mother, Sarah Richardson, was a very intelligent woman, and in her early life learned from the Indians to use the herbs, roots and barks which they employed to cure the common diseases. Later in life she practiced medicine among neighbors, who came to rely more upon her than the regular physicians. Mrs. Prall's ancestors were of English and Irish descent.

In March, 1860, Thomas Prall and his young wife moved to Johnson county, Iowa, and in September, 1862, he enlisted at Iowa City in Company G, Twenty-second Iowa volunteers. In about a month his regiment was sent to the front and was in several of the important battles of the war, principally under the command of Grant and Sheridan. Returning home on the 6th of August, 1865, he resumed the pursuit of farming in Johnson county, and in 1875 moved to Warren county, where he now owns a fruit and stock farm of 200 acres.

Arthur A. Prall was born at Hickory Grove, near Keosauqua, Van Buren county, July 1, 1860. During his early childhood

and while his father was in the army, Arthur and his mother made their home with her father, Nathan Richardson. Young Arthur attended the common schools of Johnson and Warren counties and the Friends' academy at Ackworth, Warren county. He spent two years at Western college, Toledo, Iowa, and took a three years' course at the Iowa Eclectic Medical college at Des Moines, where he graduated in 1887. Dr. Prall first located at Le Grand, where he had a fair practice for a young physician, but being anxious to do better he moved in 1888 to Pilot Mound, where he practiced very successfully for nine years. Wishing to secure better school advantages for his children, he removed in 1897 to Dayton, Webster county, where he has a good and rapidly growing practice. Being a studious and progressive man, the doctor has discovered a new and successful method of treating hernia, which has effected some permanent cures. He also practices a new system of reducing strangulated hernia, which is certain and effective without resort to knife.

In politics Dr. Prall has always been a republican. He belongs to the Independent Order of Odd Fellows, Modern Woodmen and Knights of Pythias. He was married June 1, 1887, to Della E. Bufkin, of Toledo, Iowa. They have two daughters, Pearl Ethel, born June 13, 1888, and Mae Fern, born May 28, 1890.

The doctor has lately invented and applied for a patent on a steel frame attachment to be placed on buggies, making thereby an excellent storm cab for the use of doctors, preachers and others obliged to be out in all kinds of weather.

---

MARTIN, COL. LARKIN M., is working out a phenomenal career, such as is only possible in a country where individual merit is the avenue of advancement to greatness. He was born near Point Pleasant, Va., December 6, 1853.

During the revolutionary war his great-grandfather, John Martin, lived on the banks of the Yadkin river in North Carolina. The family suffered much from the bands of marauding British, who overran the Carolinas in 1780 and 1781, and towards the close of that century moved to West Virginia. Five years before the son, Simpson Martin, had married Mary Keer, a revolutionary girl who developed into a woman of great strength of character. Both parents were persons of more than ordinary intelligence, each possessing a limited education. The father, Simpson Martin, dying soon after the birth of the youngest child, and the elder sons having gone forth into the world to follow their own pursuits, the chief care of the mother and sisters devolved upon the youngest son, George W. Martin, who was born in 1815. At the time of his father's death he was a lad of 10 or 12 years of age. To the duty of protecting his mother and sisters he gave himself with such earnestness that there was but little time left for study, but so strong was his desire for knowledge that after he had passed his thirtieth year and had himself become the head of a family, midnight often found him poring over his text-books. In 1843 he was married to Louisa Ann Kaufman, the eldest daughter of a family of eleven children. She was of German-Irish descent. Her father, Reuben Kaufman, was reared on a large tobacco plantation near Fredericksburg, Va., the latter being their market place. He was a man upright in all his dealings, and possessed of true German thrift. Her mother, whose maiden name was Julia D'Robine Reynolds, possessed a vivaciousness of temperament which brightened her home, and made it a welcome spot to all comers.

In the fall of 1854, when Larkin M. Martin was but 1 year old, his parents, Mr. and Mrs. George W. Martin, left their native state, came to Iowa, and settled in Marion county. The rigors of the climate pressed heavily upon these new comers, sickness soon came, and before the process of acclimating had been completed, most of the savings with which it had been the purpose to build a new home, were exhausted. The days were dark, but their faith in the future was not shaken. Mr. Martin and his wife were Christians, members of the Baptist church at the time of their marriage, and both died trusting in God. For several years Mr. Martin taught school during the winters and farmed in the summers. Being interested in politics, he was several times nominated for county offices, and polled more votes than any other man on his ticket, but failed of election, because his county was strongly republican. The eldest son, Monroe C. Martin, enlisted in the union army at

15

the age of 18 years; possessing a weak constitution, he soon fell victim to disease and his young life was sacrificed. The death of their eldest son was a severe blow to his parents, from the effects of which the father never fully recovered. In 1876 Mr. Martin and his family left the farm and went to Pella, so that the children might enjoy the edu-

cational advantages of the famous Central university of Pella. Two years later death removed the father. His wife survived until July 20, 1896, when she, too, passed to the life beyond.

From the time he was old enough to work until 1870, Larkin M. Martin helped on his father's farm. He then went to Pella, where he was engaged in the Blade office for one year, when he went to Prairie City and learned telegraphy. In May, 1872, he was appointed agent for the old Des Moines Valley railroad at Comstock, and remained there until October, when he was transferred to Beacon as assistant agent and telegraph operator. He remained in Beacon until November, 1874, and was then transferred to Pella as telegraph operator and clerk, where he remained until July, 1877; he was then transferred to Des Moines as chief clerk in the office of the same company. In October, 1877, the Chicago, Rock Island & Pacific railway company having leased the Keokuk road, he was appointed agent of the Keokuk & Des Moines division of that line, and remained with the Rock Island until October, 1882, when he resigned to accept the position of general agent of the St. Louis, Des Moines & Northern railway company at Boone. This position was given him by Gen. Supt. C. F. Meek, who, having left the service of the Rock Island a short time previous, prevailed upon him to accept service with this line. He remained at Boone until February 1, 1883, when Mr. Meek, having been appointed superintendent of the Wabash railroad, brought him to Des Moines and made him freight and ticket agent for both lines. Here he remained until October, 1887, when, through Mr. Meek's resignation to accept the position of general manager of the Denver, Texas & Fort Worth railroad, he was appointed superintendent and general freight agent of the St. Louis, Des Moines & Northern railway, and also commercial agent for the Wabash, having charge of the freight and passenger business of the latter line in Iowa. In October, 1889, the St. Louis, Des Moines & Northern railway was sold to a company known as the Des Moines & Northern railway, which company retained Colonel Martin, and under his management changed the gauge of the track from a narrow to a standard gauge. In December, 1889, Colonel Martin was appointed general manager of this new company, after having made a very valuable traffic agreement whereby the Des Moines business of the Chicago, Milwaukee & St. Paul system was transacted over his line, thus bringing that great system of roads into Des Moines. He also, by a brave and determined stand, inaugurated the through billing system of joint rates in connection with that line, thus enabling Des Moines jobbers to gain access to all the territory covered by the Milwaukee lines. On May 1, 1894, he was made general manager of the Iowa Central railway company, which position he now fills. Under his management the Iowa Central has gained steadily in earnings, and at the same time the condition of the property has improved in other ways.

Colonel Martin was a delegate to the democratic national convention in Chicago, in 1892, when Governor Boies was a candidate for the nomination for the presidency, and was one of the chief promoters of the governor's candidacy.

In 1896, when the democratic county convention was held in the city of Des Moines, notwithstanding his disagreement with a majority of the delegates present on the financial issue, he was offered a position on the delegation to the state convention at Dubuque. This was refused on account of the delegation having been instructed to work and vote for the free coinage of silver at the ratio of 16 to 1. After this convention Governor Boies was again a candidate for the presidency, and Colonel Martin was importuned to support him on the grounds of personal friendship, and because he had served four years on his staff, but he demurred. The governor was again defeated for the nomination, and immediately following the adjournment of the Coliseum convention, which nominated William Jennings Bryan, Colonel Martin advocated a third ticket and the calling of a state convention. The movement there started by Colonel Martin was put forward by the shrewdness and persistency and power for which he is noted, and it resulted in the creation of the new political party which placed the Palmer and Buckner ticket in the field. In all matters leading up to the national convention of the national democratic party, and in the convention itself, Colonel Martin had a prominent part. Having been chosen as a delegate at large to attend the Indianapolis convention, he was by that body selected as the national committeeman for the state of Iowa, to represent the national democratic party for four years. He was also made chairman of the speakers' bureau, having in charge all national speakers who were engaged in making speeches throughout the country in favor of the sound money national democratic ticket.

Colonel Martin is a Blue Lodge Mason, Royal Arch Mason, Scottish Rite Mason, thirty-second degree Mason, Knight Templar, and a member of the Benevolent and Protective Order of Elks. He was married October 22, 1872, to Sarah Ellen Cox, of Pella. They have three children: George Monroe, Frank Hain, and Louisa Charity Martin. George is at present in the chief engineer's office of the Iowa Central railway, Frank attending college at Amherst, Mass., and Louisa at St. Katherine's Hall, Davenport.

PLACE, THOMAS WHEELOCK, holds the responsible position of master mechanic of the Iowa division of the Illinois Central railway, formerly known as the Dubuque

& Sioux City railroad. He has been with this company since 1856, and in his present capacity since 1861, a testimonial to his worth which few men can improve upon. Railways do not keep men long at the head of a department unless they are of extraordinary value, and Mr. Place is so regarded by the great corporation he serves so well.

He was born at Ackworth, Sullivan county, N. H., January 2, 1833. His father, Ebenezer Place, was a native of New Hampshire, where he was born November 14, 1800. He died there at the age of 36. The mother, whose maiden name was Polly Dickey, was born in 1803, at Ackworth, N. H., and died in 1874, while residing with this subject at Waterloo.

The life of Thomas W. Place, until he reached his 17th year, was spent on the farm, where he attended district school in the winter, and, as is customary with farmers' boys, helped with the crops in summer. In March, 1850, he entered the employ of Park & Woolson, manufacturers of machinery for finishing woolen goods, as machinist apprentice. In 1852 he went to Boston and secured employment as machinist in the Boston locomotive works, and during the following year was engaged in firing a locomotive on the Northern railroad of New Hampshire, now a part of the Boston & Maine system. In January, 1854, he removed to Chicago and entered the service of the Chicago & Aurora railway (now a part of the Chicago, Burlington & Quincy) as machinist. The following April he went to the Illinois Central, where he ran a locomotive until November, 1856, at which time he resigned to accept a similar position with the Dubuque & Sioux City line, then under construction from Dubuque to Dyersville. He held the throttle on the locomotive which drew the first passenger train from Dubuque to Dyersville on the occasion of the opening of that line for business, May 11, 1857. He continued in the employ of the company as engineer until August, 1859, when he was appointed foreman of the repair shops with headquarters at Dubuque. In May, 1860, he was tendered the foremanship of engine repairs by the Chicago & Alton, which he accepted, and removed to Joliet, Ill., to assume the duties of the position. In 1861 he returned to the Dubuque & Sioux City, as master mechanic, and remained in Dubuque until the shops were removed to Waterloo in 1870. That line had, in the meantime, been extended to Sioux City and merged into the Illinois Central system, of which it is still a part. At present he is master mechanic of the Dubuque and Cherokee divisions—the Iowa lines.

In politics Mr. Place is a republican, and as such was elected a member of the city council of Waterloo almost consecutively for the years 1872 to 1880; also a member of the east Waterloo school board 1876 to 1885. He is a member of A. F. & A. M., Dubuque; Halcyon Encampment No. 1, and Harmony Lodge No. 2, I. O. O. F., having filled all the chairs in the last two lodges.

Mr. Place was married, July 24, 1860, to Mary Josephine Myers, daughter of William and Susan Shannon Myers, one of Dubuque's oldest and most-respected families. They were both natives of Missouri,

who came to Dubuque county at a very early day. Mr. Myers died in Dubuque in 1884, and Mrs. Myers in Waterloo, at the residence of her daughter, Mrs. Place, in 1890. The marriage of Mr. Place and Miss Myers took place when the family were living in Julien, Dubuque county. They are the parents of four sons, now grown to manhood and holding positions of responsibility and trust. They are, Augustus Mason, James Williams, Frederick Ebenezer, and Dorrance Myers.

SQUIRE, JAMES W., a leading citizen of Council Bluffs, was born in New York,

February 1, 1847. His father, Daniel Squire, was a boot and shoe merchant in Rockford, Ill. His mother was Mary Keeling Squire. James was educated in the public schools of Rockford and is a graduate of the high school. He earned his first money in the harvest field, but his first self-supporting work was that of a teacher at McGregor, Iowa, where he spent two years.

At the age of 16 years he joined the Sixty-seventh Illinois infantry volunteers and went to war. After an honorable discharge he enlisted in the Forty-fifth Illinois volunteers, which is known as the old "Lead Mine regiment," where he remained until the close of the war.

Mr. Squire removed to Council Bluffs on April 1, 1871, and worked in a real estate office and in the savings bank and in the Pacific National bank for four years. Under the firm name of Squire & Walker, a real estate and abstract office was opened during the year 1875. Mr. Squire afterwards purchased Mr. Walker's interest and took his brother, E. L. Squire, into the firm. Soon after, however, he purchased his brother's interest, and with a force of efficient clerks has ever since continued the same line of business.

He is a member of the Abe Lincoln Post, G. A. R., Council Bluffs. Mr. Squire is an ardent republican, and is the soul of loyalty to any cause he may espouse.

He was married October 15, 1872, to Elizabeth Howard, of West Hartford, Vt. They have four children, two sons and daughters—Wilson J., Louie C., Elizabeth and Florence.

---

FARLEY, JAMES M. The virtues of the Irish people, that race so many members of which were driven from their native soil by the oppressions which sent at one time 450,000 of the flower of its youth to fight in the armies of every country in Europe, are marked in the descendants who have contributed so much to the defense and development of this land of liberty.

James M. Farley, of Whittemore, is of the vigorous and liberty-loving Irish stock which volunteered its services to preserve the republic that was given birth in the bloody ground of Sedan. There were Farleys among those who faced the mobs in the streets of Paris and stood resolutely and fearlessly for the dignity and perpetuation of the infant government, and again in our own country they have left their stamp on the enduring pages of military glory. Michael Farley and Mary Dolan Farley, the parents of this subject, were born and reared on the little green isle, but came to the United States and Wisconsin in an early day. It was there James M. Farley was born May 19, 1844, in Lyons township, Walworth county. His early education was received in the common schools of his native state. He worked on the farm until 1878, when he removed to Iowa and located in the now prosperous little city of Whittemore. At that time the place contained but one dwelling house, two warehouses and the railroad depot. The depot was a two-story building, the

upper part being occupied by the family of the agent, with whom Mr. Farley boarded. For a place to sleep he was obliged to make the best of the accommodations offered by the waiting room. With $1,000, which he had saved from his labors on the farm, he erected a store building and embarked in the hardware business. Although it was his first business venture it proved a quite successful one, and there were added, in time, coal, lumber and live stock. The country has made wonderful progress during the time that Mr. Farley has lived there, and he has kept step with the advancement. The town now has more than 600 people, solid brick business blocks, churches, a model and modern schoolhouse and scores of handsome residences. During the time his section has been undergoing the transformation from a bleak prairie settlement to a well improved and prosperous town, Mr. Farley has, through good management, tireless endeavor and honorable dealings with his patrons, earned for himself a comfortable competence. In politics he is a republican,

as was his father before him. In 1872, however, he supported Horace Greeley, and in the late campaign was on the side of William Jennings Bryan. He represented his district in the Twenty-seventh General Assembly. He is a thirty-second degree Mason, a member of the Knights of Pythias and order of the Modern Woodmen. He is not connected with any religious denomination. He was married in October, 1873, to Miss Tressa J. Dutcher. They have three children, two girls and one boy. Frances E., the oldest, was born in Wisconsin; Mary A. and Guy E. were born in the Hawkeye state.

---

AHLBRECHT, WILLIAM H., conspicuous as one of the progressive men of Tama county, was born at Iowa City, Iowa, January 13, 1854, and has ever since made this state his home. He came from staunch German ancestry, being the son of Henry and Louise Fictor Ahlbrecht, both born in the kingdom of Hanover, Germany, the first in 1806 and the second in 1811.

The father was a linen weaver by trade, and came to the United States in 1832, locating at Wheeling, W. V., where he was married in 1834. Later the couple concluded to go farther west, and accordingly, in 1843, removed to Iowa and settled at Iowa City, which place was their home until the death of the father in 1883. The good old mother is still surviving, and resides upon the homestead which her labors helped to provide. The father was one of those sturdy, industrious and thrifty characters so often found among the early settlers, and left to his children, as a heritage more to be valued than the goodly amount of this world's goods which had been accumulated through strict economy and persistent labor, the example of a pure, honorable and consistent Christian life. The subject of this sketch recalls an incident that occurred after he had been in business for several years, in Tama, Iowa. A prominent citizen of Iowa City called, and after congratulating Mr. Ahlbrecht on his apparent prosperity, said: "Will, if you are half as good a man as your father was, you will be a good citizen." There is no question that the remarkable success of the son is due in a large measure to the excellent moral and business training given him by the father.

This subject attended the common schools of Iowa City, and took besides several terms in the German Lutheran school of that place. He was a diligent student, and at the age of 14 was prepared to enter the freshman class of the State university, but believing that he should have an avocation of some kind, learned the baker's and confectioner's trade. In that respect he was wise, for thereby were early instilled in his mind the principles of business which served him well in later years. Being ambitious to commence life for himself he went to Tama, in February, 1875, and secured a position with John T. Matson. His good judgment, industry and fine ability aided materially in the building up of his employer's business, and so successful was he that that city has continued

to be his home to the present time. Taking an active interest in municipal and educational affairs, he was elected to serve many terms on the city council, and after re-incorporation became an alderman, assisting as such in the shaping of much

important legislation. He has been a member of the school board for many years, a portion of the time acting as its president. In politics, he was independent until five years ago, when he allied himself with the republican party, and has since been one of its strongest supporters. In the spring of 1899, at one of the most closely contested municipal elections ever held in the city, Mr. Ahlbrecht was elected by the republican party to the position of mayor, and is now acting in that capacity. Possessing a keen business judgment he has, by judicious investments in real estate, acquired a snug little fortune, and all in the short space of a few years; for he went to Tama without capital. He now owns two fine store buildings on Main street and several fine residence buildings. He was one of the foremost of those who secured for his town the Mutual Savings and Loan association, was its first president and for eight years its secretary. The association has helped build more than seventy-five structures in the place and has made over 100 loans. It is one of the flourishing concerns of its kind in the state, and much of its success is due to the personal efforts of Mr. Ahlbrecht. He was married to Miss Mary Matson, September 20, 1876. They have three children, Emma, Alda and Edith. Their beautiful home is filled with the best of art and literature, and is a model one in every respect.

---

HOBSON, ALFRED NORMAN. In a study of the lives and character of the men who have been chosen to administer the laws of Iowa, it is pleasant to note the recognition of the younger men at the bar. It is gratifying to find instances where such recognition is based on solid merit combined with modest demeanor, as in the case of Hon A. N. Hobson, of West Union. Judge Hobson is a native of the state of Pennsylvania born in Allegheny City. His father, Hon. Joseph Hobson, moved to Iowa with his family in 1855, settling at Fayette, where he entered upon the practice of law. In 1858 he was elected county clerk and moved his family to West Union. After five continuous terms as clerk, he was elected to a seat in the house of the Thirteenth General Assembly, serving with ability during his term. At the close of it he was appointed assessor of internal revenue, in which position he served until the office was abolished. Mr. Hobson was a man of great force of character and enjoyed the respect and confidence of all who knew him. His wife was Miss Elizabeth Baker, who was an ideal wife and mother, presiding over the home with dignity and tenderness, giving the best of care and counsel to her children. It was under the influence of such a home that Alfred N. Hobson grew to manhood. In boyhood he attended the public schools of the village, afterwards the Upper Iowa university, and later at the State university. He chose law as his profession, and entered upon the study under the direction of his father and later in the office of Hon. L. L. Ainsworth. He spent three years in Dubuque in the office of the United States assessor of internal revenue, gaining a knowledge of the business and a wide acquaintance among the prominent men of Iowa. In 1875 he became associated with Hon. L. L. Ainsworth in the practice of law, which was continued for twenty years, until Mr. Hobson was called to the bench at the beginning of 1895. During this time he devoted his energies to acquiring a thorough practical knowledge of the profession, and won recognition at the bar of the district as a chancery lawyer, unsurpassed in northern Iowa. In 1894 there was a spontaneous movement in the district to elevate him to the bench, and the republicans tendered him the nomination, which he accepted. He was elected and entered upon the duties of the position, for which he was eminently qualified. As a judge, he has been remarkably successful, not only in earning the esteem of the bar and litigants, but in the care and caution exercised in ruling on points of law, in his methods of expediting business in the court room, and in rendering decisions that have been affirmed in the higher judicial tribunals. His judicial

district consists of the counties of Allamakee, Clayton, Winneshiek, Fayette, Howard and Chickasaw. Judge Hobson was re-nominated by acclamation for a second term, and elected practically without opposition.

In 1878 Judge Hobson was married to Miss Mattie Kincaid Ingham, daughter of John B. and Catherine (Neeb) Ingham, of Allegheny City, Pa. They have three children: Joseph I , Ida N., and Florence L. Mrs. Hobson is a lady of intelligence and refinement, and while devoted to her domestic duties, is imbued with the public spirit of the modern woman, and is active in club work, and a favorite in social circles of the community in which they are loved and esteemed.

SIGWORTH, HARRISON W., M. D., of Anamosa, is of German and French descent.

His grandfather, John D. Sigworth, was born in Wurtemburg, Germany, in 1786, and, crossing the ocean in 1804, settled in Lancaster county, Pa. He married Rosana Henlen, who was born at Strassburg, France, in 1789, and came to Lancaster county in 1808. They were married in 1810 and moved to Clarion county, Pa., settling in the woods in company with two other families, but ten miles from any other white settlement.

His father, John H. Sigworth, was born in Lancaster City, Pa., October 17, 1811, and removed with his parents to Clarion county. He built a log house on a tract of timber land, in 1836, and soon after was married to Frances Neely. Her father, Capt. Henry Neely, was born in Westmorland county, Pa., in 1780, married Barbara Fry and moved in 1805 to Clarion county. They settled in the woods, made a fine farm and raised a family of thirteen children. In 1812 Captain Neely raised a company and marched to Lake Erie about the time of Commodore Perry's victory.

Harrison W. Sigworth was born at Fryburg, Pa., February 25, 1837, and received his early education in one of the most primitive of log schoolhouses. In 1854-6 he taught school near his home for $15 to $20 per month, during the winter, and in the summer assisted in clearing the farm. Later he dug coal and limestone and burned lime to put on the land as a fertilizer. In 1856 he attended Coopertown academy, and in 1857 started west in company with Fred W. Byers, who is now surgeon-general of Wisconsin. He started with what he could carry on his back, and $60 in his pocket, and, after walking twenty miles, took the stage for sixty more, and reached Erie, Pa., where he, for the first time, saw a railroad. They went to Freeport, Ill., and from there, finally, to Blue Earth City, Minn., where he pre-empted 160 acres of land. In the summers of 1859 and 1860 he attended the Wisconsin State university. In April, 1861, he commenced the study of medicine with Dr. Naramore, of Orangeville, Ill., and at the same time taught the village school. The next winter he attended Rush Medical college. In June, 1862, Dr. Sigworth enlisted in Company H, Sixty-seventh Illinois infantry. In October, following, he was discharged on account of disability, and left the army on crutches. Returning to Rush Medical college he graduated in February, 1863, and located at Waubeek, Linn county, Iowa.

Dr. Sigworth was married May 18, 1863, to Miss Phebe Bowen, daughter of Senator T. S. Bowen, of Green county, Wisconsin. She had been one of the pupils at the school which he taught for four winters. They had six children: Dwight L., who was born in 1864, and became a doctor, graduating at Rush college in 1887. He was appointed physician to the state penitentiary, at Anamosa, and died August, 1896; D. Bird, born June, 1868, and is now one of the leading druggists of the city; Fred Byers, born November, 1873, is now a student at Rush Medical college; Gladys Love, born April, 1876; Harry W., born May, 1878, graduated from Rush Medical college in May, 1899, and became one of

the firm of Dr. H. W. Sigworth & Son; Miles A., born August, 1883, died in infancy. Gladys is teaching school. Mrs. Sigworth, who died in August, 1890, was a most estimable woman, a member of the Baptist church and of the church societies, Woman's Christian Temperance Union, Woman's Relief Corps and Order of Eastern Star.

The doctor was married May 18, 1892, to Miss Jennie Meade, of Anamosa, who is a native of Courtland county, N. Y., and a daughter of G. W. Meade, one of the oldest settlers of Jones county, who enlisted in Company E, Thirty-first Iowa vol-

unteers and died in the service. She is a member of the Baptist church and its societies; of the Suffrage and Fortnightly clubs; the Woman's Relief Corps and Order of Eastern Star.

Doctor Sigworth moved from Waubeek to Anamosa in April, 1877, and bought the practice of Doctor Blakeslee. In 1878 he formed a partnership with his brother, Dr. M. P. Sigworth, which continued four years. He formed a partnership in April, 1895, with his son, Dwight, which lasted until his death, and in October, 1896, he entered into partnership with Doctor McKay, which still continues. He is, and always has been, a republican. He is a Master Mason and Knight Templar, and has been commander of Fred Steele Post No. 4, G. A. R., noble grand of Anamosa Lodge No. 40, I. O. O. F., is a member of Iowa Union State and United States Medical societies. At an early age he became a member of the St. John's Evangelical Lutheran church, in Pennsylvania, and is now a member of the Anamosa Baptist church and one of its trustees and deacons. It has been the custom with Doctor Sigworth, for some years, to take an outing during the summer months, and this year, accompanied by wife and daughter, they sail from New York for an extended tour of Europe.

---

EDDY, WILLARD, M. D., is a descendant of the family which came from England to this country more than 250 years ago. Both his grandfather, Esek Eddy, and his great-grandfather, Samuel Eddy, were soldiers in the revolutionary war. His father, Erastus Eddy, was a farmer and owned 150 acres of land near Buffalo, N. Y., upon which he lived for over sixty years, and died at the age of 87 years. His mother continued to own this farm until November 21, 1897, when she died at the age of 83 years. Her name was Dorliska Middleditch, and she raised a family of ten children, six boys and four girls. She was a sister of Dr. A. Middleditch, who has lived in Waterloo ever since 1856.

Willard was born in Erie county, N. Y., July 30, 1838, and received a common school education. He then went to the academy at Springville, N. Y., and from there to Genesee seminary near Rochester, N. Y., for four years. In 1860 he went to the University of Michigan and commenced the study of medicine. In March, 1863, he graduated from the medical department of that university and was one of the five that stood highest. All his expenses at seminary and medical college were paid by himself, by his pre-emption of public land in Minnesota, then selling it. In 1863 he came to Iowa and located at Monticello, Jones county, where he practiced medicine for four years. He removed to Waterloo in 1867 and has practiced there ever since that date. Dr. Eddy saved money from the commencement of his practice, and carefully invested his surplus earnings in real estate and real estate *loans*. He has always been very careful and conservative in business affairs, and has made an eminent success both as a physician and a financier. His income is now several

thousand dollars per year above his expenses, and his estate must be worth many thousand dollars. He has never received any property by inheritance. He acquired it all by his professional labors and careful investments.

Dr. Eddy was married in June, 1864, to Miss F. Gertrude Hammond, of Waterloo, Iowa. They had one child, Walter F., who was drowned while skating, Thanksgiving day, 1886, when only 13 years of age. The sudden and tragic death of their only child was a terrible shock to both the parents, and one from which Mrs. Eddy never recovered. Her mind became partially unbalanced and she finally went to travel in Europe, hoping to regain her normal composure of mind. After waiting ten years the doctor was again married June 29, 1896, to Miss Sarah E. Cadwallader, of Waverly, the daughter of Philip Cadwallader. They have a son, born April 29, 1897, a strong, healthy boy, Roger Willard Eddy.

Dr. Eddy's first vote was cast for Abraham Lincoln, and he has voted the republican ticket ever since. He has been a

member of the First Congregational church of Waterloo for thirty years. For many years he has belonged to the Black Hawk County Medical society, Cedar Valley Medical society and the Iowa State Medical society.

WELLS, ARTHUR LEE, a prominent attorney of Corning, Adams county, is a native of the state of New York.

His father, Anson Wells, was born in Madison county, N. Y., in the year 1809, and was a farmer. In 1833 he was married to Caroline M. Young, who was also a native of that county. In 1841 the young couple moved to Cattaraugus county, settled on a new farm in the pine and hemlock forests of that then wild region, and entered upon the slow, laborious work of clearing up the heavily-wooded land. Mrs. Wells was a devoted wife and mother, and early taught her children to adhere to truth and pure lives, and sought to awaken and stimulate in their minds a love of books and a desire for knowledge. She was descended from Scotch and English ancestors, one of whom came to America before the revolutionary war, settling at Martha's Vineyard. One of her brothers, Horace C. Young, was for two terms a member of each house of the New York legislature; another brother, Eugene, was a prominent physician in Illinois; and her youn est brother, William C., was major of the Eighth Wisconsin volunteers in the late war. Mrs. Wells died in 1866.

Arthur L. Wells was born November 7, 1838, in Madison county, N. Y., and was brought up on his father's farm, spending his summer in all the various kinds of labor necessary in farm life. There were forests to clear off, brush to burn, and stumps to work among for many years. During the winter months he attended the country district school. By hard study he acquired sufficient education to become a teacher, and, in the winter of 1857, taught his first school in the country village of Eddyville. He returned to farm work in the summer and taught school again in the two succeeding winters. In the spring of 1860 he entered the preparatory department of Hillsdale college in Michigan. For the next five years he managed, by manual labor of various kinds and teaching school in the winters, to earn enough to pay his way through the whole college course. In June, 1866, he graduated in the classical course with a class of nineteen, with the highest honors. One year his standing was the highest in the college, with an attendance of 350 students. He was a member of the Alpha Kappa Phi Literary society, the leading one of the college. He entered the Albany law school after leaving college, and graduated in the class of 1867. He then came to Iowa, and traveled on foot from the terminus of the railroad at Chariton to Quincy, in Adams county. He taught a department of the public school during the winter, and at the spring term of the district court was admitted to the bar. He was twice elected recorder of the county, and served as treasurer a full term and also to fill a vacancy of a portion of a preceding

term. When the county seat was located at Corning, in 1872, Mr. Wells removed to that place, and was three times chosen its mayor. In 1876 he entered into partnership with Hon. F. M. Davis in the practice of law, and is still a member of the firm.

He is a member of the Masonic fraternity, and has for seventeen years held the office of treasurer of Instruction lodge at Corning. His ancestors on the father and mother's sides were whigs in politics, and afterwards republicans, and Mr. Wells has always been a republican. He has served as chairman of the republican county committee several times, and has been a member of the judicial and congressional committees. He at one time owned a half interest in the *Adams County Gazette*, and for two years was its editor. On the 15th of March, 1871, Mr. Wells was united in marriage with Miss Lucina Register, daughter of Dr. J. H. Register, of Quincy, formerly from Muskingum county, Ohio. They moved to Adams county, Iowa, in 1859. Mrs. Wells is a prominent member and officer of the Eastern Star, being worthy matron of her chapter, Emblem No. 64; is president of the Ladies' Cemetery association; member of the board of trustees of the public library; secretary of the Woman's Foreign Missionary Society of the Presbyterian Church of Iowa, and a member of the Presbyterian church. She is a scholarly woman, active in church, society, literary and charitable work, and a helpful and devoted wife and mother. Two children have been born to them. Carrie died in infancy. Arthur R. was born December 1, 1873; attended the public schools in Corning and several terms at the Corning academy, and finally graduated at Princeton college in the classical course with such standing as entitled him to deliver an oration at commencement exercises. He attended the law department of the State university, and was admitted to the bar upon examination before the supreme court, and in 1896 entered upon practice at Corning. He is rapidly rising to a high standing in his profession.

Mr. Wells acquired a taste for farming in early life, and after coming out onto the Iowa prairies had a strong desire to own a farm. After a time he was able to purchase 160 acres in Adams county, and has since enjoyed the pleasure of planning and carrying on its improvements from year to year. He is an exceptionally close reader and student, finding much of his gratification in literature.

---

TIRRILL, HON. RODNEY W., department commander of Iowa, G. A. R., is a native of New Hampshire. His father, Timothy Tirrill, and his mother, whose maiden name was Mary Drew, were born in the same state, where they grew up and were married. In 1850 they removed to Wisconsin, locating first at Prairie Du Sac, and later at Lodi, where the mother died in 1866 and the father in 1880.

They were plain, substantial people, whose lives were passed in the peaceful avocation of agriculture. He was a man of considerable public note, however, and conspicuous for his acquaintance with the great men of his day, as well as his work for the abolition of slavery. As an illustration of the interest he took in the promulgation of anti-slavery doctrine the instance may be related where he drove forty miles to see Fred Douglass and prevail upon that gentleman to return with him and deliver a lecture in the community where Mr. Tirrill resided. This was shortly after Douglass was freed, and so strong was the sentiment or prejudice against the negro, that no church or public building could be obtained in which to hold the speaking. But Mr. Tirrill was not to be outdone. He threw open the doors of his own home and the lecture was delivered. To the subject of this sketch the distinguished freedman some years ago said, with considerable emotion: "Timothy Tirrill was one of my first benefactors and as good a friend to the colored race as has ever lived."

Hon. Rodney W. Tirrill is the third child of a family of nine. He was born December 22, 1835, in Colebrook, N. H., where he lived until 15 years of age, removing to Wisconsin with his parents at

that time. To a common school education was added a scientific and literary course in the Wisconsin State university, and then, under the direction of his father, be began the study of law. When he was on the point of being admitted to the bar the war broke out and, for the time, changed all his plans for the future. He enlisted in October, 1861, in Company F, Twelfth Iowa infantry, and going immediately to the front, saw his first active service at Ft. Donelson, which was followed by the more serious engagement at Shiloh. He was wounded in the last named battle while his brigade was being taken prisoners. This was about 6 o'clock in the afternoon of the first day, Sunday, and he was left on the battle field until the next Tuesday morning at 3 o'clock, before being removed to the hospital boat. He was then sent to the Mound City, Ill., hospital, where he remained for six weeks, and as the wound in his thigh proved stubborn,

because of neglect when first inflicted, he was given a furlough. The injury proved more serious than was first supposed, and he was accordingly discharged January 3, 1863.

In 1863 Mr. Tirrill was elected superintendent of schools of Delaware county, at which time he settled permanently in Manchester, and, in addition to his duties as superintendent, turned his attention to real estate, insurance, loans and the securing of pensions for soldiers and their heirs. The official position he held for four years, declining a re-election in 1867, on other lines he still follows.

It has been one of the settled rules of Mr. Tirrill, not to sacrifice the fruits of his labors for the uncertainty of political honors, yet it could hardly happen that a man of his talents should not have been called on to fill some positions of public trust. He was a member of the school board of Manchester for twenty-one years, refusing further election, and has in no small measure contributed to the educational interests of the county. While county superintendent, he introduced the first map drawings, and in many other ways rendered signal service.

In the fall of 1879, without solicitation on his part, Mr. Tirrill was nominated by acclamation for the state senate, was elected and served for four years. He declined a re-nomination. Representing a district where the dairying interests had reached considerable proportions, his mind was early drawn to the necessity for the passage of certain measures for the protection of that industry, and one of his first acts was the drafting of a bill requiring that all packages of oleomargarine in the state be branded as such; and he succeeded by his personal efforts and influence in having it enacted into a law, which from all information he has been able to obtain was the first law of the kind ever enacted in any state of the nation. He served on the committees on schools, congressional districts, insurance, suppression of intemperance, fish and game, the relocation of the girls' department of the state reform school, penitentiary and boys' reform school.

He was married December 30, 1860, to Miss Eliza J. Weeks, then of Delaware county, this state, but a native of Massachusetts. She is a lady of fine literary attainments, having matriculated for a two-years' course in the State university at the same time her husband entered upon a course of similar length in the law department of that institution. While he was securing the degree of B. L. she was earning honors in German, French and English literature. Two children were born to them, a son and daughter, L. Claire and John R. W., but both were taken by death in 1878.

Mr. Tirrill is a thirty-second degree Mason, an Odd Fellow and a member of the G. A. R. He was elected department commander for Iowa G. A. R. in 1898.

---

PIERCE, FRANKLIN GILMAN, mayor of the city of Marshalltown, is a young man of wide resources, both native and acquired. He comes of good Puritan ancestry, being a descendant of John Pearce, who settled in Rhode Island in 1632. Another ancestor, John Pierce, served in the revolutionary war. Mr. Pierce's father, William Pierce, a carpenter and builder, of moderate circumstances, was born in 1821, at North Kingston, R. I. He was married in 1865 to Martha Jane Moore, who was born in 1849, at Columbus, Ohio, and whose ancestors, the Moore and Wilson families, are among the oldest in Virginia.

F. G. Pierce is a native of Iowa, having been born at Earlville, in Delaware county, December 7, 1868. When he was three years old he removed with his parents to Marshalltown, where he has lived most of the time since. He began his education in the schools of that city, and graduated

from the high school in June, 1886. He entered the State university in 1888, graduating in June, 1892, with the degree of Ph. B. While attending the university he was a member of the Phi Delta Theta fraternity, and took an active interest in athletics, serving as manager in 1890 and captain in 1891 of the university football eleven. He was also prominent in literary work, being elected editor-in-chief of the *Junior Annual*, published by his class. After his graduation he was engaged in the insurance business at Marshalltown for several years, but in 1895 abandoned this for the more congenial vocation of journal-

ism. He first published the *Marshall County Register*, but in 1896 consolidated with the *Daily Press*, in which he still owns an interest.

Politically, Mr. Pierce has always been a republican. In 1895 he was elected mayor of Marshalltown on a non-partisan ticket. Representing the wishes of the people who desired a reform looking toward greater economy in the city's expenses, he was supported largely by laboring men and elected with a good majority. During his first year in office he had an unfriendly council to contend with, but in 1896 new men were elected who were more in sympathy with him, and he was able to carry out the wishes of his supporters. So well did he accomplish this that he was re-elected in 1897 and again in 1899, and is still serving the interests of the taxpayer. In municipal affairs he has always been in favor of municipal ownership of public franchises and has written a number of articles for different papers dealing with this aspect of city affairs. He was vice-president for Iowa of the League of American Municipalities in 1898.

Mr. Pierce is a member of the Masonic Order, Knights of Pythias, I. O. O. F., Benevolent Elks, Red Men, Modern Woodmen of America, Maccabees, Ben Hur and Court of Honor. He is also a member of the Sons of the American Revolution, and belongs to the Congregational church. He was married June 30, 1897, to Miss Nellie M. Loree, of Marshalltown.

---

STOOKEY, MILLARD FILLMORE, editor of the *Decatur County Journal*, published at Leon, is one of the progressive newspaper men of the state, and a representative man of his section. He was born near Leesburg, Kosciusko county, Ind., April 25, 1849. His father, Levi Jackson Stookey, a farmer by occupation, was born in Fayette county, Ohio, and is of Scotch descent. His grandfather, on his mother's side, fought in the war of 1812. His wife's maiden name was Sarah Jane Clark. She, too, is of Scotch descent. She was born in Miami county, Ohio, and her father, a Pennsylvanian, was a government surveyor, doing a great deal of surveying in Indiana in an early day. She also had a cousin, Rev. Wilson Blaine, who was educated at Oxford, Ohio, and was pastor of a Presbyterian church at Valparaiso, Ind., for many years. Both Father and Mother Stookey are members of the Presbyterian church.

M. F. Stookey came to this state with his parents May 20, 1855, and located near Marion, the county seat of Linn county. He attained a common school education in the public schools of Leesburg, Ind., and Marion, Iowa, and in September, 1866, entered Western college, then located at Western, Linn county, now situated at Toledo, Iowa. He remained there two years. In August, 1869, he entered the office of the *Tama County Republican* at Toledo, when M. B. C. True was editor. He worked at the printing trade nearly two years. He then taught school for several terms in the country, near Marion, when he entered the law office of Thompson & Davis, Marion, and was admitted to

the bar October 30, 1873. In the spring of 1874 he located at Elroy, Wis., and established a newspaper called *The Headlight*. April 5, 1875, he was appointed postmaster at Elroy, and, in the fall of the same year, resigned his position, sold out his business and returned to Linn county, Iowa, where he taught school for several terms. In August, 1877, he located in Leon and commenced the practice of law. The following year he was elected justice of the peace, and, in 1880, was elected clerk of the circuit and district courts, which position he held two terms. In 1887 he was again elected to the same position. In the spring of 1891 he removed to Bethany, Mo., and became the editor of the *Bethany Republican*, which position he held until February 1, 1893, when he purchased a half interest in the *Decatur County Journal* at Leon, Iowa, and returned to that place to take up his duties as editor of that paper, where he has since resided. He has always been a hard-working republican; he has served one term as a member of the state republican committee from the Eighth district,

and two terms as chairman of the republican central committee of Decatur county. He is a member in good standing of Leon Lodge No. 84, I. O. O. F., having joined tha society when 22 years old, in Elroy, Wis.

He was married December 20, 1887, to Miss Jessie Forrey, and to this union there has been born one son, Paul.

RICE, HON. JAMES A. The Hon. James A. Rice, of Oskaloosa, was born in the city where he now resides, September 30, 1855. He is the son of Gen. Samuel A. Rice, who was attorney-general of Iowa from 1856 to 1860. General Rice was mustered into service as colonel of the Thirty-third Iowa Volunteer infantry, October 1, 1862, and on August 4, 1863, was promoted to brigadier-general. He was wounded at the battle of Jenkin's Ferry, Ark., April 30, 1864, from the effects of which he died July 6, 1864, at Oskaloosa. A beautiful monument was erected to his memory by the regiments of his brigade.

The mother of James A. Rice was Louisa M. Alexander, daughter of Rev. James Alexander, D. D., of Virginia, a Presbyterian minister of great prominence, who for more than fifty years preached in Ohio, Pennsylvania and Virginia. He was a trustee of Washington and Jefferson colleges for thirty years, as well as a director of the Western Theological seminary. A large number of the 67 years of her life have been devoted to the rearing of a large family, five of whom are now living. Of late years, she has directed herself to the work of the Woman's Relief corps. She organized the present corps at Oskaloosa, and has been its president for three terms. Samuel A. Rice was of Scotch-Irish descent, a graduate of Union college, New York, and was selected to deliver the address of welcome to Henry Clay on that illustrious patriot's visit to the college.

James A. Rice attended the public schools at Oskaloosa and then completed a classical course at Washington and Jefferson college in Pennsylvania. He graduated from the law department of the Iowa State university in the class of 1877. He was a member of the Zethagathian society, and the Union society at Washington and of the Delta Tau Delta fraternity.

His first dollar was earned in the trial of a case before a justice of the peace in Oskaloosa, since which time he has been engaged in the practice of law in that city. He was elected mayor in March, 1878, and served two terms. During his second term he was largely instrumental in securing for the city its present fine system of water works. He was elected city solicitor in 1881, and, as in the case of the mayoralty, was re-elected at the close of his first term.

While solicitor he tested the right to assess resident agents of foreign loan companies on moneys and credits at the residence of agent, and was successful in maintaining the statute in the supreme court; also tested the powers of corporations to grant long-term franchises with exclusive right to occupy streets, his position being that such powers

were not granted by law, and were void on grounds of public policy. This position was also sustained by the supreme court in the case of the Oskaloosa Gas Light Company v. City of Oskaloosa; also carried to the supreme court the right to assess the property of telephone companies where the office was located, and the case of Iowa Union Telephone

Company v. City of Oskaloosa, settled the mooted question of the law as applied to these assessments. He also tested the power of school boards to purchase maps and charts when there were no funds on hand to pay for same, claiming that any indebtedness incurred under such circumstances was *ultra vires* and could not be collected. In this position also he was sustained by the higher courts. He revised the city ordinances of Oskaloosa in 1885, and the revision is still in force.

He is a republican, but an ardent advocate of bimetallism. He was a delegate to the republican state convention at Cedar Rapids in 1891, and also to the one which nominated Frank D. Jackson in 1895, in which last he served as chairman on the committee on credentials. He was a member of the executive committee from the Sixth district in the republican state league in 1893, and was a delegate from Iowa to the republican national league at Louisville, Ky., the same year. He is a member of the Sons of Veterans and captain of Gen. S. A. Rice Camp. He has served as chief mustering officer of the United States for that organization and as delegate to its national meetings He was married September 10, 1895, to Miss Belle Gray, of

Washington, Iowa, eldest daughter of Capt. J. H. Gray. She is a lady of high culture. She has held the position of national president of the Ladies' Aid society for two terms, and is now president of the King's Daughters, and in October, 1898, was elected state secretary of the international order of this society. They have one son, Samuel Allen Rice. Mr. Rice is an orator of wide reputation. He was chosen to deliver the address on General Grant in Oskaloosa in 1885, the centennial address, "Our Youth the Hope of America;" another on Lincoln before the meeting of Lincoln league of Iowa, held at Washington, Iowa, and many others on patriotic and war subjects in many cities throughout the country.

MILLS, PROF. EARL, who, although but 26 years of age, is superintendent of the Eldon schools with its corps of nine teachers and 500 pupils, was born in Newton, Jasper county, Iowa, December 28, 1871. His father, Levi W. Mills, was a native of Pennsylvania, having been born in Franklin county. He enlisted in Company C, Forty-fifth Pennsylvania Volunteer infantry, and was assigned to the ninth army corps under General Burnside. He was severely wounded at the battle of the Wilderness, but upon his partial recovery returned to his regiment and completed the term of enlistment. The Forty-fifth was sent from Virginia to South Carolina, but returned to participate in the campaigns of the army of the Potomac. Later it was ordered west to operate with the western forces, and saw service at Nashville, Jackson and the many other points that were reddened with the blood of northern men. He received an honorable discharge at the end of three years of gallant service, at which time he returned to his home and joined the family, then about to start for Iowa to locate a permanent home. Some time after his arrival he married Miss Margaret L. Cuthbertson, and to them was born a son, the subject of this sketch, the mother dying while he was not yet 2 years old. The home of the father and son was thereafter with the father's people. The father died July 3, 1894, at the age of 53 years, leaving his son the last of the family in the male line.

Earl Mills attended the public schools at Newton and later the high school, from which he graduated in 1888, then entered upon the profession of teaching. In 1890, he graduated from the Jasper County Normal institute, and then entered the Highland Park Normal college, graduating in 1893, when he resumed his former work as teacher. He served for a time as deputy superintendent of schools of Jasper county, later as principal of the schools at Olin, Jones county, and at the conclusion of his contract at the last named place accepted the superintendency of schools at Eldon, where he is now engaged. To this position Mr. Mills was re-elected by acclamation for the fourth year on April 11, 1899. He holds a teacher's life diploma granted him February 1, 1899, by the state department of public instruction.

As an educator it is safe to say that, considering his age, Professor Mills has no superior in the state. To a thorough education—he holds the degree of B. S., and a state teacher's certificate—is added a native aptness for the work and that subtle quality which governs, interests and advances the pupil under his charge. As an organizer he possesses that skill and tact and knowledge of human nature which prevents friction in any of the departments, and holds alike the friendship and esteem of teachers and pupils. He comes of good old revolutionary stock. Two great-grandfathers on the paternal side were soldiers in the struggle for independence, and an only uncle on the father's side carried a musket in the civil war, having enlisted in the first union regiment raised in his native state. He was never out of government service from 1861 until the close of the war. Five uncles on his mother's side marched to Dixie at the first call, and spent five years fighting in defense of the flag. Professor Mills was married to Miss D. Jessie Lamb, of Olin, Jones county, Iowa, June 17, 1897.

---

HIBBEN, EDWIN HAYDEN, of Marshalltown, is secretary and manager of the Northern Life association, and to his energy and push, combined with business sagacity and rare executive ability, is due most of the success of this well established and thriving insurance company. Colonel Hibben is the grandson of Thomas Hibben, who, for more than forty years carried on a paying business as a retail dry goods merchant at Wilmington, Ohio.

The colonel's father, George Hibben, born at Wilmington, Ohio, in 1818, was also a successful merchant. He moved to Rushville, Ind., in 1837, where he became prominent in many business connections. He was one of the organizers of the East Hill Cemetery association, was elected county clerk, and was president of the branch of the State Bank of Indiana. He removed to Chicago in 1863, and there became a wholesale merchant. He was married April 21, 1842, to Jane Fielding, who was born at Franklin Ohio, October 4, 1821. She was a daughter of William Fielding, who was born in Pennsylvania, May 1, 1796, and who was a direct descendant of Sir Henry Fielding, at one time lord mayor of London. William Fielding served in the war of 1812 and afterwards studied medicine at a school in Cynthianna, Ky., from which he graduated and then practiced extensively in the counties of Logan, Champaign and Miami, in Ohio. He was married to Elizabeth Vail in 1818, at Franklin, Ohio, and settled at Sidney, Ohio, in 1824. Here he organized the First Presbyterian church and Sunday school in Shelby county, and was afterward elected five times to the state legislature, twice as a senator. He was grand master and state lecturer of Masonry, and for forty consecutive years was the presiding officer in the lodge to which he belonged.

Col. E. H. Hibben was born May 14, 1848, at Rushville, Ind. His mother died when he was only 9 years old, and he then went to live with her parents at Sidney, Ohio. Here he received his early schooling, and was given his first lessons in business by clerking in a drug store mornings, evenings and Saturdays. So apt was he in business that at the age of 17 he began life for himself in the wholesale tea, tobacco and cigar trade in Chicago, and for six years conducted the business with success, but in 1871 lost all he had in the great fire. He came to Marshalltown in 1875, and opened a loan and insurance of-

fice. In 1882 he organized the Northern Life association, and under his skillful management it has grown from a small enterprise to be one of the prominent insurance companies of Iowa.

Colonel Hibben is a very enthusiastic worker in civic organizations, and holds membership in nearly every order that has ever been organized. He was twice elected grand chancellor and once supreme representative of the Knights of Pythias, and he organized the first division of the uniformed rank in Iowa, as well as the first section of the endowment rank. He was the first man in Iowa to be commissioned

as an instructor in the secret work, and for thirteen consecutive years he has held the commission of aid-de-camp, with the rank of colonel, on the staff of Maj. James R. Carnahan. His original commission, dated May 1, 1884, is the first ever issued to an Iowa Knight. He is a life member of Hesperia Lodge No. 411, A. F. and A. M., of Chicago, of the consistory of Lyons, Iowa, and of the Mystic Shrine. He served as deputy grand master of the grand lodge of Iowa, I. O. O. F., and is now grand master. He organized R. Howe Taylor Canton No. 26, at Marshalltown. He is sovereign emir of the world of the Princes of Iran, a member of the Benevolent Elks, Red Men and Royal Arcanum.

HALL, PERCY WAVIL, mayor of the city of Sheldon, and one of the prominent young business men of that city, is a young man of unusual energy and business ability, and has the brightest of prospects for a successful future. At present he is one

of the youngest mayors in Iowa. His father, Rev. Roscoe G. Hall, was a Baptist minister and was ranked among the most influential and powerful of the clergy in Illinois, where he spent most of his active life. He died in 1877, aged 42 years. Mr. Hall's mother, formerly Elizabeth Pratt, is the daughter of Doctor Pratt, a prominent physician of Lockport, N. Y. She is still living, at the age of 63 years. Mr. Hall's ancestors, on his father's side, came from England in a very early day and settled in Massachusetts. His grandfather was a farmer; his great-grandfather served in the Maine legislature, and fought in the war of 1812, while his great-great-grandfather was in the revolution.

P. W. Hall was born March 24, 1868, at Greenville, Ill. He graduated from the Ottawa high school in 1887, and, during the same year, came to Iowa and located at Sheldon, his present home. He was first employed as shipping clerk and book-keeper in a flour mill, where he remained two years, and then secured a position as clerk in the Union bank of Sheldon.

Here he gave excellent satisfaction and was promoted to the position of assistant cashier March 1, 1898, he organized the Security Savings bank of Sheldon and has since been its cashier.

In politics Mr Hall is a strong republican. He was chosen city clerk of Sheldon in 1894, and, after serving two years, was elected mayor of the city, which position he is still holding. He adheres in religion to the faith of his parents, and is a member of the Baptist church. He is a member of the Masonic fraternity, and is a very active and enthusiastic worker in that order.

Mr. Hall was married March 24, 1893, to Miss Lucie Wilcox, of Huron, S. D., who is the daughter of a physician. They have had one child, who, however, died in infancy.

———

BROWN, CASSIUS M., of Sigourney, has seen long service as a member of the bar of Keokuk county. He was born November 9, 1845, on a farm near Mt. Vernon, Ohio. His father was a native of Mary-

land, where he was born in 1802. He witnessed the march of the British army after the burning of the capitol at Washington during the war of 1812. Removing to Ohio in 1830, he located on a farm near Mt. Vernon and engaged in farming until 1870, when he came to Iowa, and Keokuk county in 1872, and there passed the remainder of his life, his death occurring in 1890. The mother was a Virginian by birth. Her maiden name was Ann Holland. She died on the farm near Sigourney in 1884 at the ripe age of 70 years. The father was of Welsh descent, while the mother was of German. The subject of our sketch attended the district schools in his neighborhood, the high school at Mt. Vernon and entered the preparatory department of Kenyon college at Gambier, Ohio. He taught several terms of district school, but was not financially able to complete his college course, which was a great disappointment to him. In 1868 he removed to Muscatine, Iowa, where for one year he was associated with his older brother, Thomas Brown, in teaching in the Muscatine academy. His older brother had graduated from Kenyon college in 1861 and had engaged in teaching in Muscatine, Iowa, where he is now successfully engaged in the practice of law.

Before leaving Ohio, Cassius had resolved to study law and had been reading under the direction of W. C. Cooper, the colonel of his regiment. Upon his removal to Iowa, he entered the office of Thomas Hanner, of Muscatine, where he pursued his studies while teaching in the academy and public schools of Muscatine county. He graduated from the law department of the State university in 1871 and at once opened an office in Sigourney, and has remained a member of the bar of Keokuk county since. He was at one time in partnership with Judge Ben McCoy, and from 1878 until 1892 was associated with the late Judge E. S. Sampson.

He was elected state senator in 1882 and served one term, this being the only political office held by him, but he has been an active participant in every campaign. He was candidate from Keokuk county at the judicial convention in June, 1898, for judge of the Sixth judicial district, but failed to secure the nomination. He is and always has been a republican. He enlisted in 1863 in the Ohio National Guards, and in the United States service in 1864, being a private in Company A, One Hundred and Forty-second Ohio infantry. He is a member of Robert F. Lowe post, G. A. R., past noble grand in the I. O. O. F., of which order he has been a member since 1873. He is a member of the Presbyterian church. He was married June 18, 1874, to Miss Flora Sampson, eldest daughter of Judge

16

E. S. Sampson. They have four children, Eunice A., who is a graduate of Sigourney high school, and attended Penn college one year, and now teaching in the public schools of Keokuk county; Roy C., who graduated from the high school of Sigourney and now teaching in the public schools of Keokuk county and pursuing the study of law in his father's office; Millie E., who is attending the high school of Sigourney, and Helen, the baby of the family.

LAFLAR, GORDON WARREN, of Manning, was born near Lewis, Cass county, Iowa, August 10, 1855. His father, Wil-

liam C. Laflar, was born at Mt. Vernon, Ohio, October 19, 1831, and removed with his parents when a boy to Lake county, Ind., where he lived for a number of years. When about 21 he came to Iowa, and August 27, 1854, was married at Des Moines to Margaret Powers. They removed to a farm southwest of Lewis, Cass county, where they resided for many years. In 1878 Mr. Laflar removed to Kansas but returned to Iowa in 1880, and in 1882 located in Manning, where he remained until 1891, when he removed to Hamilton, Wash., residing there until his death, February 17, 1899. Margaret Powers Laflar, the mother of Gordon W., was born at Mabon,

Cape Breton Island, N. S., April 7, 1835, and removed to Lake county, Ind., when a child. There she remained during her early life and until nearly the time of her marriage to Mr. Laflar, when she came to Des Moines. She had two brothers in the war of the rebellion. The eldest, Thomas Powers, died after being in service for two years. The other, James K. Powers, was shot in the right arm at the battle of Shiloh, April 7, 1862, and lost his arm. After returning from the war, J. K. Powers became prominent in political circles and filled many responsible positions in Iowa. He was county clerk of Cass county for six years, from 1868 to 1874. He was appointed, by Gov. C. C. Carpenter, as a member of the state board of immigration. He was elected register of the state land office and served from 1878 to 1882. He was also chief clerk of the house of representatives during the Twenty-first General Assembly.

Gordon W. Laflar received his early education in the public schools of Cass county and remained upon the farm until 1882 when he moved to Manning and engaged in the insurance business. After four years' experience he entered the employ of the law, loan, real estate and insurance firm of Salinger & Brigham, with whom he remained for three years. He then formed a partnership with C. C. Coe and established the *Free Press* newspaper at Manning July 1, 1889. After one year's experience Mr. Coe retired from the firm and in September, 1890, Mr. Laflar sold the office and business to Martin Bros., of Webster City. Soon after this he bought the loan, real estate and insurance business of the firm of Lindsay, Salinger & Company. In March, 1891, he formed a partnership with J. H. Rockfellow, who bought an interest in the business, and the firm became Laflar & Rockfellow. In January, 1893, they purchased a general store at Orillia, Iowa, where Mr. Rockfellow resides.

In politics Mr. Laflar is a republican and has been an active worker for the cause. He was elected mayor of Manning in 1892. He is a member of the A. O. U. W., the I. O. O. F., K. of P., and the Northwestern Legion of Honor. October 13, 1876, he was married to Miss Melessa H. Armstrong. They have had three children: Ida May, Alma Ethel, Artie E. Of these only the son is living.

PALMER, LUKE, SR., was born in Stonington, Conn., October 18, 1808, and is the descendant of Walter Palmer, who came from England in 1629. At the age of 14 he was left fatherless. He went to school until his 19th year, learned the carpenter trade, and in his 25th year went to New Orleans to work at his trade. He shipped a stock of goods to cover expenses, found it paid and shipped more goods. He remained four years, found the climate unhealthy, and in 1837 determined to move. The bank asked 24 per cent exchange for a New York draft, which he declined to pay, so he bought sugar and shipped it to New

York at a profit. Mr. Palmer then spent several months, in 1838, traveling about in the Mississippi valley. He finally bought a stock of goods in St. Louis, and, on January 15, 1839, shipped it up the Mississippi, the river being then open, though closed in the previous November. At Quincy, ice stopped the boats, and teams were hired and the stock brought to Burlington, crossing from Illinois on the ice at considerable risk on January 23, 1839, the legislature being then in session. He opened a general store in Burlington, and remained in business about twelve years.

On January 8, 1851, he married Miss Mary E. Holbrook, a lady who was reared in Connecticut, educated in Hartford and taught school in Connecticut, and, afterwards, a private school in Burlington, Iowa. The union was a happy one until the death of Mrs. Palmer, October 19, 1888, nearly thirty-eight years after the marriage. There were two children, Luke, Jr., a sketch of whose life is subjoined, and Sarah M., who married John S. Cameron, a civil engineer, afterwards secretary of the railroad commission of Iowa, then assistant to general manager of the Chicago, Burlington & Quincy Railway company, later with the Union Pacific railroad, and finally proprietor of an electric railway in Salt Lake city, Utah. Mrs. Cameron died February 24, 1881, leaving two sons, now in Yale, and a daughter, now with her uncle, Luke Palmer, Jr., at Burlington, Iowa.

In 1850 Mr. Palmer closed out his stock of merchandise and turned his attention to the improvement of the real estate which he had accumulated. In 1872 he undertook the erection of an opera house in Burlington, which, when near completion, he lost by fire, June 19, 1873. This was Burlington's largest fire, covering several squares and destroying the county court house and part of the county records. Mr. Palmer cleared away the debris and rebuilt.

Mr. Palmer was elected to the territorial legislature in 1845, but never took his seat, because the territory was admitted as a state pending the meeting of the legislature. He served in the city council as alderman repeatedly, between 1842 and 1861; served upon the board of trustees of the asylum for insane at Mt. Pleasant for fourteen years, from 1862 to 1875 inclusive, and was president of the board for the last four years of the period; served as a school director in Burlington, and was president of the board several years. He subscribed to the stock of all the plank roads and all the railroads built into or out of Burlington. He contributed to the building of the First Congregational church in Burlington, as well as to the present edifice, and gave much of his time, for three years, to the supervision of the work of building. He was for many years president of the board of trustees of this church.

Mr. Palmer was always a toiler, hardworking with hands, as well as with brains, at whatever he undertook, and he followed this practice after he became an octogenarian. He had a remarkably robust frame and great vigor and physical energy, as well as great power of endurance. His chief interests centered in his family. At an early period in his married life he built a fine residence, which he occupied until his death. On June 15, 1892, he was stricken with apoplexy. He lingered nearly three years and died suddenly of a second stroke April 22, 1895, in his 87th year. He is buried in Aspen Grove cemetery.

PALMER, LUKE, JR., was born November 20, 1851, at Burlington, Iowa, and attended the public schools, later Knox academy, and finally graduated at Knox college, Galesburg, Ill., in June, 1872, taking the degree of A. B., and three years later that of A. M.

He spent the following year chiefly in physical labor, though he visited Colorado and spent some time in reading elementary law. In 1873 he entered Harvard law school, passed the examination for the second year, but chose to enter the law office of N. C. Berry, of Boston, and attended lectures at Boston law school, where he graduated in June, 1875, taking degree of LL. B. He returned to Burlington, and was admitted to the bar, practiced three years and determined to go to

Colorado. His father, who had paid the expense of his education, had suffered a heavy fire loss and the young man thought it his duty to make his way alone. With but little money he went to Colorado, and, finding no suitable opening for his profession, owing to his ignorance of mining terms, he turned his attention to making a living by physical labor, chiefly at mining and prospecting, also spending some time in reading mining law. In 1881 he opened a law office in Georgetown, Colo. Soon afterwards he formed a law partnership with Judge Thomas Mitchell. He also arranged to assist Hon. R. S. Morrison in compiling a series of fifteen volumes of Mining Reports, covering the decisions of all the courts of last resort in this country and England. In the preface to this work, the author gives credit to Mr. Palmer "for faithful co-operation in the selection of the cases printed and the preparation of the same for publication." Mr. Palmer also assisted in the preparation of "Morrison's Colorado Digest," published in 1884.

Mr. Palmer was twice elected to the office of county judge of Clear Creek county, Colo., but resigned in the fifth year of service to return to Burlington, where the increasing age of his father and the failing health of his mother made his presence necessary. Soon after entering upon his duties as judge, Mr. Palmer married Miss Emma A. Dunn, of Galesburg, Ill., who had been his classmate in Knox college, and graduated with him. She resigned a position as instructor in the Latin language before her marriage. The union was a happy one until the death of Mrs. Palmer in 1892. There were no children born of this marriage, but it happened that Bessie and Helen Clendenin, the young children of Mrs. Palmer's deceased sister, found a home for several years with Mr. and Mrs. Palmer.

Since Mr. Palmer returned to Burlington, he has engaged only to a limited extent in law practice, but has given most of his time to the management of real estate. He, with the assistance of Mr. J. A. Strodel, rearranged the files and reindexed the records of the clerk's office of the district court of Des Moines county in the years 1895 and 1896, under contract with the board of supervisors, and at the instance of the bar of Des Moines county. Mr. Palmer has been treasurer of the board of trustees of the Congregational church since January, 1890. On April 28, 1897, Mr. Palmer and Miss Marian E. Starr, daughter of the late Henry W. Starr, of Burlington, were united in marriage. Mrs. Palmer died February 11, 1898.

---

DUBBERT, BERNHARD, director of the conservatory of music in Upper Iowa university, at Fayette, Ia., is one of the finest musicians in the northwest, and has spent the greater part of his life in studying the art he so much loves.

He is a German, and inherits much of his talent from his father, August Dubbert, who was a skilled musician, and played the pipe organ in the Evangelical church of his native village for many years. He was also a public school teacher of no ordinary ability, and taught for over fifty years, forty-eight of which were spent in the town of Sonneborn, Germany, where he died December 9, 1893. He was born January 24, 1824, in Elbrinxson. Professor Dubbert's mother, Christine Wieneke, was born in the village of Sonneborn, January 17, 1820, and died there June 12, 1889. She was an intelligent, cultivated woman, and took an active part in the education of her five sons, all of whom grew up to be useful, public spirited men.

Prof. Bernhard Dubbert is the youngest of these five sons, and was born December 19, 1861, in Sonneborn, the little town where his parents spent most of their lives. This village is situated in northern Germany, in the little principality of Lippe Detmold, which is a part of the province of Westphalia, or as the Germans call it, Westfahlen. Here, at the foot of the mountains known as the Teutoburger Wald, and near the banks of the beautiful Wesser river, he attended the school taught so well by his father; and until he was 15 years old he had no other instructor. While very young

he exhibited a marked degree of ability in music.

Under his father's enthusiastic supervision, young Bernhard rapidly progressed in music, as well as in his other studies. In 1877, at the age of 16, he came to America, where a brother and cousin had preceded him in 1871. For several years he worked on a farm in Grant county, Wis., improving what few opportunities he had to attend school. During this period, his love for music never grew less intense, and many a spare moment was spent in practice and study. In 1884 he left the farm and for two years gave lessons on the piano and organ at Fennimore, a town in the county where he had been working. He came to Iowa, in 1886, locating at Laurens, Pocahontas county, near where his brother had purchased a half section of land. Here he continued as a music teacher with the greatest success, and also dealt extensively in musical instruments. He gained a high reputation as one of the most thorough instructors and musicians in northwestern Iowa, where he was widely known. He

spared no time nor opportunity to make visits to Chicago for further study and hearing some of the greatest musical works performed, and also such leading pianists of the world as Dr. Hans Von Bülow, I. Paderewski, Eugene D'Albert and others.

In short, the subject of this sketch is termed a musical enthusiast. In December, 1894, he was offered a position as director of the conservatory of music at Upper Iowa university at Fayette, which he accepted and has since remained there. By faithful, conscientious, enthusiastic work, he has not only won the admiration of those about him, but has succeeded in building up the musical department and creating such an interest in it that the attendance is now nearly twice what it was before he came to Fayette.

Professor Dubbert was married August 18, 1893, to Miss Minnie E. West, of Lake Park, Iowa, whom he met as a teacher in Sutherland, O'Brien county. She, too, is a musician, and has a voice of rare sweetness. She was a pupil of the professor's for some time previous to their marriage. They have two children, Ruth Christine, who was born at Laurens, June 15, 1894, and a little son, Rudolph August, born September 13, 1897, at Fayette, Iowa.

SCHUELER, ADALBERT, of Keokuk, is one of the most noted musical instructors and musical composers of the state. He is of German stock, having been born in Freiburg, in the grand duchy of Baden, Germany, December 16, 1846.

His father was a manufacturer of thermometers, barometers, and all kinds of glass vessels for the measurement of liquids. His mother, whose maiden name was Anna Wissert, was twice married. Her first husband was named Sutter, a relative to the Sutter who first discovered gold in California. To this union there were two daughters. Her second marriage resulted in four sons, of whom A. Schueler is the oldest but one. Both parents were born in Baden, Germany, where their ancestors lived for generations before them. They are distinctly a family of musicians. The boys, excepting the eldest, were singers in the cathedral choir of Freiburg, where the alto part is sung exclusively by boys, until the time of changing voice. A younger brother, Otto, became a solo violinist of considerable note. He came to Keokuk in 1869, lived there till 1873, and later became the leader of the orchestra and Liederkranz society in Louisville, Ky., where he died in 1885.

In his youth Adalbert Schueler attended the public schools for eight years, then entered upon the study of the higher branches and the languages. At 16 he entered a teacher's seminary, having decided to become a pedagogue. He completed the four years' course, which included, as does the course of every German normal school, a fine education in music. Here he received instruction on the violin, piano, and organ, as well as in singing, harmony, and rudimentary composition. In April, 1865, he received his diploma as teacher, and was installed as such soon thereafter. This position he held until 1867, at which time he came to America, locating at Keokuk. He was engaged in giving private lessons in music there for three years, holding at the same time the position of teacher of German in

the public schools, also serving as organist of the First Baptist church. During the following three years every dollar possible was saved from his earnings for the gratification of an early ambition to become a thorough teacher of music.

In the summer of 1870 he went to Germany, entering the conservatory of music at Leipsic in

the fall of that year. Here he studied under Professors Wenzel, Coccius, Herrmann, Paul, Papperitz, Richter, Jadassohn, and Reinecke, organ, piano, singing, harmony, thorough bass, fugue, counterpoint, instrumentation, and composition. Besides being a student at the conservatory he attended lectures at the university on anatomy of the hand, physiology of the throat, music in Greece, music in the middle ages, literature and philosophy and logic under Czermak, Merkel, Dr. Paul, Baumgartner, and Drobisch. After four years of diligent study he returned to Keokuk, taking out at that time naturalization papers and becoming a citizen of the United States. He has since resided in Keokuk, where he has followed the vocation of musical instructor. He was organist for nearly two years of the Westminster Presbyterian church, and filled a like position for eighteen years with the Unitarian denomination. In his work as private teacher he has been very successful. The standard of music in Keokuk is a high one, for which much credit must also be given to Mr. Charles Reps, who came to that city about ten years prior to the time of Mr. Schueler. Both have done good work in a period extending over forty years. During the last twenty years Mr. Schueler has produced compositions of all kinds—for voice, piano, violin, violincello, trios, quartettes, and overtures and operas. His latest composition is a song, "The Rose of Iowa," composed since the wild rose has been declared the floral emblem of the state.

Although taking a great interest in politics, the professor is not a partisan, and votes for whom he considers the best man. He has no preference among religious sects, being a humanitarian, if that kind of religion is in need of a name. He was married in Germany in 1876 to Miss Edeline Preuss, of Hanover, Prussia, who attended the conservatory with him at Leipsic. They have two children living. Irma, the eldest, is preparing herself for the vocation of solo violinist. She has spent five years in Germany, and for the last three years has been staying with her parents, giving concerts and pursuing her studies with her father. She had studied with Isaye in Brussels, and is now studying in Belgium under Ovide Musin. The other child, Preuss, is 17 years of age and is attending the high school at his home, keeping up his studies on the violin the while. The Schueler concerts are well known, and the lovers of good music delight to gather under the hospitable roof of the professor, where a musical treat is always in store for them, since the family itself forms a complete little orchestra. Mr. Schueler with his family moved to New York city in the fall of 1898. The family will spend the summer of 1899 in Keokuk.

---

HARVEY, CHARLES B., of Marion, Iowa, well known in that region as secretary of the Y. M. C. A., is a native of Illinois. His father, John F. Harvey. is a farmer living near Aledo, Ill., and was a brave soldier in the war of the rebellion. He enlisted in Company G, Thirtieth Illinois infantry, and was in the third division of the seventeenth army corps. He never missed an engagement that his company was in; was never wounded and was never in the hospital. After serving three years and eleven months he was mustered out as a sergeant. John F. Harvey's father, Beauchamp Harvey, came to Illinois at an early date, and was of English descent. He was a very active member of the Christian church.

Esther J. McClure, the mother of Charles B., was a daughter of Capt. John McClure, and was born near Attica, Ind., and when a little girl came west to Illinois with her father's family. Most of that country was then unsettled prairie and they came in wagons. Her father was captain of Company G, Thirtieth Illinois Veteran volunteers, and was in the service about three years.

Charles B. Harvey was born near Keiths-

burg, on July 9, 1870. He was rather sickly when a child and attended school irregularly. In 1888 he attended the city high school and in 1889 the academy. He then began to prepare for commercial life and entered the Iowa Commercial college at Davenport. It was there he first came in contact with the Young Men's Christian association, although he had previously joined the Presbyterian church, to which his parents belonged. He found a higher standard of spiritual life among the young men who made up that association than he had found in the country church. Before a year had passed he felt a desire to take

up the Y. M. C. A. work for young men, but no way seemed open at the time.

In 1891 he began work as bookkeeper for the Alpha nursery, at Alpha, Ill. November, 1893, he commenced work for an uncle, Charles McClure, in his grocery store at Keithsburg. While there he found an opportunity to go into Y. M. C. A. work and in October, 1894, became assistant secretary at Davenport, Iowa. From here he went to Chicago to the "Secretarial Training School" of the Y. M. C. A. and in June, 1896, came to Marion as secretary.

He closed his work in Marion, December 31, 1897, resigning to accept a call to Sabbath school missionary work in northwestern Minnesota, with headquarters at Fergus Falls.

He was married December 29, 1897, to Miss Fannie Grace Veach, of Keithsburg, Ill., at the Methodist parsonage, by Rev. W. H. Witter, Keithsburg, Ill. Miss Veach was an active member of the Methodist church, teacher in the Sabbath school and a leading member of the Epworth League. She was also a member of the choir for about eight years, and now aids her husband in his work by the power of song. They have one son, Louis Warden, born January 21, 1899.

---

SNYDER, EDWARD ALLEN, of Cedar Falls, postmaster of Cedar Falls and editor of the *Cedar Falls Semi-Weekly Gazette*, is a landmark in the history of Iowa newspaperdom. The high moral tone and progressive spirit of this paper, which has been under his direction for more than a quarter of a century, speak volumes for his worth as an editor and citizen. Its beneficial impress is universally acknowledged, not only at Cedar Falls, but throughout all that section of the state. As a man of true principles in every relation of life, as a brave soldier of long and honorable record, as a citizen who could be counted upon for more than his part of every good work, as an editor of ability and pure record, as a Christian man, true to his profession, his life is a record of noble deeds and purity, of moral character truly worthy of emulation.

He was born at Cambria, Pa., September 7, 1838. At the age of 16 he was valedictorian at New Columbus academy. He attended Wyoming seminary at Kingston, Pa.; Dickenson seminary at Williamsport, and Dixon college at Dixon, Ill. He was proficient in his studies, always standing well in his classes. During the years of his school work, he spent two years as an apprentice in the printing business, a part of the time doing the foreman's work on the *Williamsport Independent*. He came west to Dixon, Ill., in 1858; taught and attended school for two years, then returned to Pennsylvania, spending the winter of 1860-1 as principal of one of the schools at Hollidaysburg. He delivered an address while there upon "Success in Life" before a large audience, which received much commendation.

He was an enthusiastic supporter of the war, and the following July, at his old home, made an address in advocacy of that belief. He returned to his late home, Dixon, and enlisted in September, 1861; became post adjutant of the Dement Phalanx until January, 1862, when they were ordered to Springfield, consolidated with a Freeport regiment under Col. John A. Davis—the Forty-sixth Illinois volunteers, and took part in the siege of Ft. Donelson, where great exposure was endured. He was in both days' fighting at Shiloh; took part in the siege of Corinth and battle of Hatchee river; was subsequently commissioned from a private over the non-commissioned officers of the company as second lieutenant, the commission having conspicuously upon it these words: "Promoted for meritorious service at Ft. Donelson and Shiloh."

He was later detailed for service as an officer of the United States signal corps, and at Vicksburg sent the first messages Generals Grant and Sherman made use of in the west, by opening communication late during the first night of the investment, for General Sherman, with Admiral Porter's fleet seven miles up the Mississippi river. He served in Mississippi and Tennessee and was mustered out at Nashville in the winter of 1864-5. He has been commander of the G. A. R. post at Cedar Falls and a delegate to the national G. A. R. encampment.

He first commenced business after the war as a surveyor at Dixon, but shortly removed to Clinton, Iowa, where he made a profitable trade of a tract of timber land purchased by him, located in Wiscon-

sin, and in the spring of 1866 erected a store building and stocked it with groceries, under the firm name of Snyder Brothers & Santee. In the early part of 1867 he moved to Cedar Falls, where he has since resided. He and his brother, C. W. Snyder, purchased the *Cedar Falls Gazette* in 1888. He was associate editor until 1869, since which time he has been editor. He was elected county surveyor in 1870, and held that position for four years. For the past eighteen years he has devoted his entire time to the editorial work of the paper, and it has become one of the substantial newspapers of the state. It is now published as a semi-weekly. He has been a republican ever since the birth of the party; was in the Chicago convention at the time Lincoln was nominated; cast his first ballot for him, and has voted for every republican president since that time. In 1899 he was appointed by President McKinley to be postmaster of Cedar Falls. He has been an earnest temperance worker; conducted, in a large measure, the prohibitory amendment campaign in Black Hawk county in 1882, and made many addresses. In later years was untiring in the enforcement of the law. The freedom of Cedar Falls from the iniquitous saloon and the enviable reputation of that city as to morals is admitted as being largely due to his fearless prosecution and earnest work with law and pen.

He has been active in church and Sabbath school work for forty years; a teacher and class leader for over thirty years. In 1887 was elected as a lay delegate, with Hon. J. P. Farley, of Dubuque, as his colleague, by the Upper Iowa conference, M. E. church, to the general conference which sat in New York during May, 1888, and served on important committees. He is a member of several fraternal orders; a Master Mason and Knight Templar.

He was married September 25, 1867, at Cedar Falls to Miss Mary A. Cameron. Two children have been born to them, the oldest dying at the age of 7 years. The younger is married, and a sweet grandchild gladdens the home of the parents and grandparents. They have a fine residence on the most sightly spot in that beautiful city of Cedar Falls, and there Mr. and Mrs. Snyder faithfully ministered to the comfort of her parents, one of whom was helpless from paralysis for more than eleven years. Since their death, the same dutiful care is being given to the venerable father, aged 90 years, of this subject, and stepmother.

---

PUGH, ROBERT WOOD, born August 29, 1858, near Muscatine, Iowa. His father, Jonathan G. Pugh, was born at Mansfield, Ohio, January 12, 1825, and served as a soldier in the war with Mexico, and in 1849, with his brother, Dr. J. W. Pugh, went to California, where they were quite successful and after a few months returned with a good supply of gold dust. The next season the two returned by team on the overland route to California. J. W. settled there and became a prominent and influential man in the community. He was elected to the legislature of that state and chosen speaker of the house. Jonathan G. returned to Ohio and in 1854 he made a trip to Iowa and entered a large tract of government land in Poweshiek and Mahaska counties and later removed to Iowa. November 25, 1857, he was married at Muscatine, Iowa, to Miss Harriet V. Baker, who was a school teacher, and the daughter of Isaac and Clarinda Baker, of Bainbridge, Ohio. They settled on a farm near Muscatine, Iowa, and Mr. Pugh became largely engaged in the stock business.

Robert Wood is their oldest son. His education began at home under his mother's instruction and was later continued in the country schools. His success in life has been largely due to the excellent instruction, advice, and care she bestowed upon him in boyhood. In 1876 the family removed to their farm near Deep River, in Poweshiek county. R. W. soon afterward attended a normal institute and secured a certificate to teach. After teaching a few terms he took a course of instruction at the Southern Iowa normal, at Bloomfield. For several years he worked on the farm in summer and taught school in the winter. In the years 1880 and 1881 he taught school in Kansas. Returning to Iowa, he continued teaching. In 1882 he went to school at the Iowa City academy and afterwards returned to teaching. He was a close student and an excellent teacher. In 1885 he was professor of penmanship and bookkeeping in the Iowa City academy for two terms. In 1884 he decided to study law, and, procuring some books, gave his leisure hours to reading law. In September,

1885, he entered the law department of the State university and graduated in June, 1886, with the degree of LL. B. In 1886 he entered upon the practice of his profession at Williamsburg, Iowa, where he has remained to the present time.

He has served as mayor of the town, secretary of the school board, and trustee of the First Presbyterian church.

In 1896 he served as one of the committee appointed by the supreme court to examine the students of the class of 1896 at the State University of Iowa for admission to the bar.

He was married at Williamsburg, Iowa, December 24, 1888, to Miss Mary H. Long, a school teacher, and a daughter of James and Catharine T. Long. They have four children, Helen, Robert E., John and Mary L. The Longs were early settlers of Iowa county, and came from Columbus, Ohio.

Mr. Pugh is an able lawyer, has a large practice, and a wide reputation as a commercial lawyer. He is a member of the Iowa State Bar association, which he helped to organize. He is also a member of the Commercial Law League of America. He is an active republican and a good campaign speaker. In the campaign of 1896 he was a member of the county central committee and in the fall of 1898 was elected county attorney of Iowa county. Mr. Pugh is a genial man, always ready to accommodate a friend, and modest and unassuming in his manners.

---

BARTOW, GEORGE L., of Sigourney, was born on a farm in Jefferson county, Iowa, in 1860, where he lived until he was 18 years old. His father's name was George P. Bartow, a native of Ohio, coming to this state in 1851, where he grew to manhood. He was married in 1856 to Susan Baker, a native of Ohio, who came to Iowa with her parents in 1853 and settled on a farm in Jefferson county. She is still living in the town of Richland, Iowa.

After receiving an academic education, Mr. Bartow took up the study of medicine, graduating from Scuder's Eclectic school of medicine in Cincinnati, Ohio, which profession he followed until his death, October 28, 1888. He was in good financial circumstances at the time of his death, owning 500 acres of land in Jefferson county, and considerable town property. George began his education as most boys do on a farm, working in the summer and attending school in the winter. In 1883 he entered the Pleasant Plain academy, graduating from that institution in 1886 after completing a three-years' course. After leaving the academy he taught school for fourteen terms, being principal of the Richland and Martinsburg schools. In

1887 he was appointed postmaster of the town of Richland by President Arthur, holding the office for one year. He was appointed railway postal clerk on the Cedar Rapids & Kansas City railway postal route by President Cleveland, which posi-

tion he held until the first of January, 1890. He then resigned from the mail service to become county superintendent of schools of Keokuk county, to which office he had been elected at the previous election. This position he held four years, being re-elected in 1892. After leaving this office he again entered school work, being principal of the Thornburg schools for some time. He then became editor and proprietor of the Sigourney *Review*, the official paper of Keokuk county. He was married to Miss Belle Pfaff, of Sigourney, April 10, 1890. She was one of the primary teachers in the Sigourney schools. They have two children, Vora S., born July 20, 1892. and Vera A., born January 22, 1894. He is a member of the Independent Order of Odd Fellows and a member of the Methodist church.

Mr. Bartow was admitted to the bar May 12, 1897, and is now a member of the law firm of Gambell & Bartow, Sigourney, Mr. Gambell being county attorney of Keokuk county.

---

SENNEFF, JOHN ALBERT, of Manilla, is the son of Joel F. Senneff, a farmer of Carroll county, Ill. His father was from Pennsylvania, and was one of the early settlers of Illinois, and acquired a comfortable property. John's mother was Ellen Boyts before her marriage, and her parents came from Pennsylvania also, and were among the early settlers in Carroll county, Ill. John was born April 1, 1876,

and his boyhood days were spent on his father's farm, where he acquired habits of industry and economy. His early education was begun in the public schools of that period, and continued at Morrison during the winters of 1893-4. When the time came to choose an occupation he decided to fit himself for the legal profession, and in 1895 entered the law department of the college at Valparaiso, Ind. Here he pursued his studies industriously for two years, graduating in June, 1897, with the degree of LL. B. He was a member of the Crescent Literary society, and recognized as one of its most able orators. He taught school for some time before entering the law school, earning money to pay his expenses. In January, 1898, he came to Iowa to enter upon the practice of his profession in company with his former classmate, A. L. Freelove. They located in Britt, Hancock county, and began to build up a good practice. In politics he is a republican, and in college debates supported his belief with reasons and arguments for his faith. He is a member of the Christian church and of the or-

der of Modern Woodmen of America and of the law alumni of N. I. L. S.

FREELOVE, ARTHUR LOYD, is the son of Madison B. and Mary Gounclery Freelove. The father was a native of Rutland, Vt. He was of Scotch-Irish descent, and his early life was spent in Troy, Pa. For several years he lived at Great Lakes. The greater part of his life was spent in farming and dealing in real estate, at which he accumulated a comfortable property, but misfortune swept it away in later years. He died in 1897. His wife, Mary Gounclery, was a native of New York. Her father was of English and her mother of German descent. They settled in Iowa in 1858. Arthur was born at Arcadia, in Carroll county, November 24, 1873. He attended the common schools in boyhood, and graduated from the high school at Manning in 1891. The principal, Sarah L. Garrett, was an excellent instructor, and directed the aims of her students towards right living, the acquisition of knowledge, and the desire to lead useful lives. After

leaving the high school Arthur L. taught in the public schools for three years, and served as a clerk in Manning for one year. When a boy he was industrious, working at anything that would help to get the means to pay his way in acquiring a good education. He finally determined to make law his occupation, and in order to become well equipped for the profession he entered the Northern Indiana Law School at Valparaiso, from which he graduated in June, 1897, and soon afterwards was admitted to practice in the supreme and federal courts of the state of Indiana. Early in 1898 he entered into partnership with a former classmate, John A. Senneff, and the young lawyers located in Britt, Hancock county, to begin their professional work, succeeding to the practice of L. D. Womeldorf. In politics Mr. Freelove is a republican, and is a member of the Christian church. He belongs to the order of Modern Woodmen of America and to the alumni of N. I. L. S. Mr. Freelove was married January 11, 1899, to Miss Alma Franke, of Manning, Iowa.

FORBES, JAMES MADISON, a leading attorney and politician of Jefferson, is of English, Scotch and German descent. His great-great-grandfather, Alexander Forbes, was born in Scotland about 1755, but came to America while quite young, settling in Pennsylvania. John Forbes, James' grandfather, was born in Pennsylvania in 1790. In 1824 he married Elizabeth Jaimeson, who was born in Pennsylvania in 1800 Her mother's name was Nancy Magee. James' father was Andrew Forbes, who was born near Middleton, Washington county, Pa., March 8, 1825, and died August 16, 1898. Early in life he moved to Steubenville, Ohio, and in 1852 came to Illinois on a steamboat, via the Ohio, Mississippi and Illinois rivers. He was married June 22, 1854, soon after his arrival in Bloomington, to Christy Ann McMillan, who was born in Guernsey county, Ohio, November 12, 1829. Her father, James McMillan, was a mechanic, and was for many years engaged in steamboating down the Ohio and Mississippi rivers, buying and selling flour. Her mother, Hannah Atkinson, was born in New Jersey in 1801, and was a daughter of John Atkinson, an English Quaker, and Sarah Pullinger, of German descent, born about 1770. Sarah's father was a German blacksmith, who was of great service to the colonists during the revolution.

J. M. Forbes was born September 26, 1860, near Bloomington, Ill., and was one of six children, all of whom are living. He attended district school until he was 17 years old, when he entered the Illinois

Wesleyan university at Bloomington. He remained there only one year, and in 1880 began teaching. He received his first certificate from Prof. William Hawley Smith, the author of "The Evolution of Dodd." He attended the Northern Indiana Normal school at Valparaiso, Ind., from 1884 to 1885, and in the same year removed to Jefferson, Iowa, where he again engaged in teaching. In 1887 he began the study of law in the office of A. M. Head, remaining there six months when he continued his studies in the office of Russell & Toliver. He entered upon the senior law course of Drake university at Des Moines in the fall of 1888, and graduated in June 1889, with

the degree LL. B. He began the active practice of the law at Jefferson in 1891. He has made a specialty of commercial law and of real estate, of which he is a clever holder in Jefferson. Aside from his suburban residence he owns a number of tenant properties and a quarter section of land within the corporate limits of the city.

Mr. Forbes has always been a conservative republican. In 1894 he was secretary of the county central committee of Greene county, and in 1895 was elected chairman. In 1896 he was president of the McKinley Sound Money club of that place. For a number of years he has been a member of the Jefferson board of education. He is a member of I. O. O. F. Lodge No. 315, and in 1895 was one of a committee of three selected by the Jefferson Improvement company who visited the grand lodge at Marshalltown and aided in securing the location of the I. O. O. F. orphans' home at Jefferson. He belongs to the Methodist church.

Mr. Forbes was married October 31, 1889, to Miss Ida A. Williams, daughter of Mr. and Mrs. N. M. Williams, old settlers of Jefferson. Mrs. Williams died of peritonitis the 6th of December, 1897, at the age of 67 years. Mr. and Mrs. Forbes have no children.

---

SAUNDERS, CHARLES GEORGE, the gentleman whose name heads this sketch, is a man who by hard study, natural business ability, energy and willingness to work, has won for himself a place among the most successful lawyers of the state.

His parents, George W. and Mary E. (Walker) Saunders, were born in England, the father coming to this country at the age of 14 and the mother at the age of 5 years. They with their parents settled in Oneida county, N. Y., and were married at Westmoreland, in that county, April 21, 1860, and here Charles G. was born April 10, 1861. After his marriage, George W. Saunders followed the occupation of a farmer until the spring of 1868, when he removed to Iowa City, Iowa, and entered the employ of the Chicago, Rock Island & Pacific Railway company as the foreman of a large gang of construction men. Having a family of five sons and two daughters and not wishing to rear his boys in town and about a railroad, he resigned his position and moved upon a farm near Stuart. In the fall of 1875 he removed to Vail, Crawford county, and in the fall of 1879, bought a half-section of land near the town of Manilla. To this tract he made additions and at the time of his death, which occurred May 19, 1896, he was regarded as one of the leading citizens, most prominent and wealthy farmers of his county. He was a member of the Methodist church and lived a consistent and charitable Christian life and died universally mourned in the community where he lived. Mrs. Saunders, a devout Christian woman, whose chief object in life was to hold the love of her husband and children, now resides in Manilla.

Charles G. attended the village school at Westmoreland, N. Y., one year before his parents came west, and after that attended the ordinary country schools for some time. From a mere child he was consumed with a desire for books and before he was ten years old had read Harriet Beecher Stowe's work, "Dred, a Tale of the Dismal Swamp," Greeley's "American Conflict" and several other works of a similar character. While his parents were residents of Vail, he had access to the carefully selected private library of Mr. James P. Fitch, and there obtained a stock of information that has always been of great benefit to him. He attended the public schools of Vail from two to three months during the winters of 1878, 1879 and 1880, riding on horseback a distance of three to four and one-half miles. During the winter of 1880-81, he took care of a team of horses and taught country school three miles away. When he received his order for $35, his first month's wages, he felt richer, he says, than he ever can again. That winter he saved $100 and the next winter taught again and saved another $100. The next spring, 1882, he was 21 years of age and September 15th, of that year, he entered Drake university, at Des Moines. He had $350 and one suit of clothes. He remained in that school four years, partly working his way through and graduating in the classical course, June 15t , 1886. During his senior year he was editor of "The Delphic," the organ of the university and was one of the active members of the Philomathean society while in school. In his sophomore year he was chosen by the faculty as chairman of the oratorical delegation that went to the state oratorical contest, and acted in the same capacity the following year. After leaving school, and in the summer of 1886, he commenced to read law with Judge C. C. Nourse, of Des Moines, and in the fall of that year became principal of one of the schools in south Des Moines, but kept up his law work, reading nights and Saturdays. He taught school nine months, and in September, 1887, entered the law department of the State university and graduated in June, 1888. The committee appointed by the supreme court to examine the class, said he passed the best examination of any member of the class. He entered upon the practice of law in Council Bluffs in October, 1888. In December of the same year he entered

the law office of Stone & Sims, a firm composed of Jacob Sims and John Y. Stone, one of the leading firms in the city. In August, 1890, he formed a partnership with Jacob Sims. The firm dissolved in 1892, since which time he has been alone. In November, 1894, he was elected county attorney of Pottawattamie county, and was re-elected in 1896, running several hundred votes ahead of his ticket both times. In 1898 he was tendered the nomination for a third term, but declined. He has been very successful as a prosecutor and has lost very few cases. He is the attorney for the Burlington & Missouri Railway company and represents several other very important interests.

Mr. Saunders has been a very enthusiastic republican all his life, and an active campaigner. He has the reputation of being one of the best public speakers and orators in the western part of the state, having been very active in convention work and having presided over several county conventions and also over the congressional convention in that district, in 1894. February 1, 1896, he was appointed by Governor Drake as a member of his personal staff with the rank of lieutenant-colonel. He also received the appointment of judge advocate general from Governor Shaw. He has twice been elected a trustee of Drake university by the alumni of that school.

Mr. Saunders is a prominent member of the Odd Fellows lodge, is a Knight of Pythias and chancellor commander of the local lodge, a Mason and a very active member of the Modern Woodmen of America. He has been delegate to the head camps of that order for several years, serving as state consul and a member of the board of auditors of the Modern Woodmen of America. He is an active member of the Methodist church. Mr. Saunders was united in marriage to Miss Flora Newkirk, at Delta, Iowa, July 2, 1890. The marriage was the result of an acquaintance formed when both were students at Drake university. They have two daughters, Vera, born September 25, 1891, and Marian, born September 24, 1894.

---

LEWIS, JUDGE W. R., of Montezuma, is a man of very genial and affable manners, and one of the leading lawyers of the state. He is of Welsh and German descent, and was born in Muskingum county. Ohio, October 12, 1835. In 1849 he removed with his parents to Coshocton county, Ohio. In 1856 he went to central Illinois, remaining in Peoria, Marshall and Stark counties for about one year, teaching in the winter and working at the carpenter trade during the summer. In April, 1857, he removed to Poweshiek county, Iowa, which has since been, and is now, his home. Utilizing the evenings and time not employed otherwise, he had substantially fitted himself for admission to the bar before coming to Montezuma, but chose not to be admitted until he thought it possible to make the practice of law his only business.

He worked at his trade and taught school until 1861, when he was elected superintendent of county schools. He resigned in 1862 to take the position of clerk of courts.

In 1865 he was married to Miss Mary E. Cutts, a sister of the brilliant lawyer and congressman, M. E. Cutts, of Oskaloosa. Their married life was a singularly happy and devoted one until her death, which oc-

curred in 1893. They had no children. He was admitted to the bar in December, 1866. In 1867–8 he was a member of the board of supervisors, and was elected judge of the circuit court in 1880. He held this office six years and until the court was abol-

ished. In the scramble which followed Judge Lewis was not renominated, but his work on the bench had been so satisfactory, and he was such a general favorite with all with whom he had come in contact, that in response to the almost unanimous wish of his constituents, he permitted his name to be used as an independent candidate, and was elected by a sweeping majority. There was a prevailing belief that his defeat in the convention was due to unfair means, and this contributed to his success. He retired from the bench in 1890 and resumed the practice of law in Montezuma.

He is a man of great legal ability, and while on the bench was a warm friend of the young practitioner. He never permitted a young lawyer to sacrifice his client's interests if a word or suggestion from the court could help him. His decisions were rarely reversed. No district or circuit judge has a better record in the supreme court than Judge Lewis. So unerring were his views, especially in equity cases, that the attorneys in his court learned it was next to useless to appeal, as he was nearly always sustained. He was slow in deciding, but his work never had to be done a second time. As special counsel for the county in the famous cases against the Rowes and against the bondsmen of the defaulting treasurer, he earned new laurels.

In the fall of 1897 Judge Lewis was nominated by acclamation for the state senate by the Twelfth senatorial district, composed of Poweshiek and Keokuk counties, and was elected.

---

MARSH, OSCAR HAMDON, of Glenwood, is the superintendent of the public schools of Mills county. He is one of the scholarly men of Iowa and has devoted himself with enthusiasm to his chosen work of instructing the young. Mr. Marsh was born near Williamsport, Penn., July 23, 1864, and is of notable ancestry on both father and mother's side.

His father was of English extraction, his ancestors coming to America in 1750, settling near Munice, Lycoming county, Penn. They were of patriotic mould and many of them took arms in defense of liberty during the war with Great Britain. They were also concerned in the military movements of the Wyoming Valley and New York against the Indians. One branch of the family located at Lewisburg, Penn., and one of them invented and manufactured the once famous "Marsh Harvester." His grandfather located near Williamsport, Penn., where he was a man of wealth and prominence. During the civil war many of family took part in the battles in which the army of the Potomac was engaged, and two cousins met their death by starvation in Andersonville prison. On his mother's side, the family were of German descent, and early in the colonial period settled in Snyder county, Penn. His mother was a granddaughter of the famous Simon Snyder, who was for several terms a state senator and later the governor of Pennsylvania. His mother's father, Elijah Couldren, was a merchant of Selin's Grove, and did a prosperous business in the days of packet transportation. He had two children, Mr. Marsh's mother and a son who served throughout the civil war.

Mr. Marsh's father, George W. Marsh, is a resident of Selin's Grove, Penn., and is engaged in fruit raising and farming. He was educated at Susquehanna university at Selin's Grove. He taught school while a young man and was recognized as one of the ablest educators in the state.

Mr. Marsh began his education in the district schools. His father's interest in his education induced him to study and read a great deal at home, and at the age of 15 he was far advanced for his years and was sent to the preparatory department of Susquehanna university, where he remained four years. In this school he took the full classical course and was a proficient

Latin, Greek and German scholar. He also became a diligent student of history and literature. He was an active member of the Philosophian Literary society, and was editor of its literary journal for four consecutive terms. He was chosen several times to represent the society in public exercises, and was its president two terms. He graduated from Susquehanna university with honors in 1882. The following year he entered the junior class of Pennsylvania college, at Gettysburg, where he ranked high in his class. He here took a classical course and paid special attention to history and literature. He was a prominent mem-

ber of the Phrenakosmian literary society. He was also a member of Beta chapter of the Phi Delta Theta society. He graduated in June, 1894, taking the degree of A. B. and one year later the degree of A. M. In August, 1887, Mr. Marsh came to Iowa as principal of the Oakland schools. He had previously taught in Winfield, Union county, Penn., for two years, employing his spare time in reading law in the office of Charles P. Ulrich of Selin's Grove. In 1886 he was admitted to the bar, but after a successful year of practice he returned to his first loved work, that of instructor and educator. He remained as principal of Oakland schools four years and his efforts were well appreciated by patrons. Following this work he had charge of the Henderson schools two years and the Emerson schools three years, meeting with fine success in both places. For ten years Mr. Marsh has been considered one of the best educators in the west in normal institute work and his services have been constantly in demand. His special subjects are history and literature. He has written a text-book entitled "Aids and Methods in United States History," to be published this year. He holds state certificates and life diplomas from Pennsylvania and Iowa, and was made a member of the educational council at the Iowa State Teachers' association in 1898. In Mills county Professor Marsh is regarded as efficient and of superior ability. He is a popular man both in and out of school work and makes a host of friends wherever he goes.

Mr. Marsh is a democrat and was nominated in Pottawattamie county for auditor in 1893. He was a delegate to the state democratic convention which nominated Governor Boies the second time. He was also a delegate to the state democratic convention in 1892. He was a member of the county central committee of Pottawattamie county and was assessor of Oakland two years. His present office was tendered him by the democrats of Mills county in 1897. They gave him the largest democratic majority since the organization of the county.

Mr. Marsh earned his first money as a field hand in the harvest time. He is a Lutheran in religious belief. He is a member of the Iowa State Teachers' association, also a Past Chancellor in the Knights of Pythias order and was a delegate to the grand lodge in 1894.

He was married September 4, 1888, to Miss Stella G. Bebee, of Corry, Penn.

---

BLOODGOOD, FREEMAN H., B. S., county superintendent of schools of Fayette county, lives in West Union, and was born in Linn county, Iowa, in 1867. He has the reputation of being an active and progressive educational man who has kept up with the times. He attended a graded rural school in Linn county until he was 13 years old, when his parents moved to Huron, S. D., and he went to school there until 1885, working on a farm between times, thus getting physical strength as well as mental culture. In 1885 he entered Upper Iowa University, from which he graduated in 1890 with a creditable record.

He was a member of the Zethegathian Literary society, and gained a high reputation for oratory. He represented the college in the state contest in 1890. Immediately upon his graduation he was elected to the principalship of the Fayette public schools, which he filled satisfactorily for two years, and then resigned to enter Harvard university for post graduate work. He returned to Fayette in the fall of 1893, and was elected county superintendent as a republican. December 19, 1893, Mr. Bloodgood was married to Miss Ethel Hulbert, a charming and accomplished lady, one of his classmates in college and a resident of

Fayette. They have since lived in West Union. Mr. Bloodgood is now serving his third term as county superintendent.

He believes in encouraging teachers to cherish the ambition to be professional educators instead of making teaching a mere makeshift. The schools of Fayette county have been given a close supervision and have been much improved by this energetic young man. He has demonstrated the result of his work at the State Teachers' association in Des Moines, where Fayette county for three consecutive years, beginning in 1895, won a prize for the greatest number of miles traveled by teachers in attending the association.

In December, 1898, he was chosen president of the Iowa State Teachers' association at Des Moines, and has unanimously been chosen as city superintendent of the Vinton schools for the year beginning September, 1899.

He is universally recognized among educational workers as a man of ideas, who has something to say and knows how to say it. He takes a leading part in the several educational associations to which he belongs, and was elected president of the Northeastern Teachers' association in 1895, and president of the Iowa County Superintendents' association in Des Moines in 1897. Oratorical ability and the genius for teaching combined cause him to be in general demand as a lecturer and institute instructor. In these capacities Mr. Bloodgood has been employed in various counties in the state, and also in cities outside the state. His success in educational work and the other qualities which make a popular man have often suggested the fact that he is available for the office of state superintendent of public instruction.

TURNER, GEORGE A., of Marshalltown, represented his county in the state

senate in the Twenty-fourth and Twenty-fifth General Assemblies. He is now a resident of the city of Marshalltown,

where he is engaged in the real estate and loan business, but for many years he was a successful and progressive farmer. While in the senate he was chairman of the important committee on insurance.

Senator Turner was born in Canton, Ill., March 28, 1843, and his parents were of Yankee ancestors, coming from Vermont and New York. His father, Samuel Turner, was a farmer in moderate circumstances, and was one of the pioneers of Illinois. His wife was Miss Sallie Brookins, a native of New York. Their son was educated in the public schools, including the graded school of Canton. Mr. Turner came to Marshall county April 2, 1867, and settled on a piece of new land in the northwestern part of the county. He owns the same farm now, and his success may be imagined from the fact that it has grown to a fine estate of 1,100 acres, near Bromley. Mr. Turner has been successful in business since boyhood, when he was taught the essential principles of business. He earned his first dollar in Canton, raising onions. He has been for fifteen years a director in the Marshalltown State bank, and is largely interested in public enterprises in Marshalltown. He has always been a republican, and for nine years was a member of the board of supervisors of Marshall county. During this time the magnificent new court house and jail were built, and he says he is more proud of his part in this than anything else of a public nature that he has done. He is at present a member of the school board of Marshalltown. He is a Mason and Knight Templar, and a member of the Christian church and of the Grand Army of the Republic. He enlisted three times as a volunteer during the civil war; first for three months, but never saw very active service. He was first lieutenant and quartermaster of the Fifty-first Illinois infantry.

Mr. Turner was married September 15, 1870, to Miss Maggie Garber, of Marshall county. They have two children, Ella F., born 1876, and Frank E., born 1883. Mrs. Turner died October 12, 1898.

IRISH, HARRY RUSSELL, of Forest City, is one of the leading physicians of Winnebago county. He is the son of David Irish, who was a native of Vermont and a farmer in moderate circumstances. He removed to Dane county, Wis., in an early day, and from there to Kellogg, Jasper county, Iowa, in 1867, where he died in

1885 at the age of 61. Dr. Irish's mother, Harriet Brownell, was also a native of Vermont, and died in October, 1894, at the age

of 68 years. The ancestors of David Irish were Quakers of Norman descent, who came to America about 1630 to escape religious persecution in England. The ancestors of Dr. Irish's mother were of Anglo-Saxon and Dutch descent. They came to America long before the revolution, and took an active part in that war.

Dr. H. R. Irish was born October 1, 1860, and removed with his parents to Kellogg, Jasper county, Iowa, at the age of 6 years. Here he made his home until 1883, when he located at Forest City. His preliminary education was obtained in the common country schools, and he also completed a course at Hazel Dell academy at Newton. He entered the medical department of the State university in 1881, and graduated March 7, 1883, and during the same month located in Forest City, where he has been in active practice ever since, enjoying a liberal patronage. He has the satisfaction of knowing that he has worked his own way to his present rank, having earned the money to secure his training by working on a farm. For four years and a half Dr. Irish served as one of the examining surgeons for the United States pension department at Mason City. He is a member of the Iowa State Medical society and

of the Austin, Flint, and Winnebago county medical societies.

In politics Dr. Irish is a democrat. He served one term as mayor of Forest City, beginning in March, 1893, and is at present a member of the board of education. He holds no church membership.

The doctor was married April 8, 1887, to Alice S. Peirce, at Cedar Falls, Iowa. They have two children, Leita, who was born June 5, 1889, and Thomas J., born February 4, 1897.

———

CASADY, JEFFERSON P., for many years a resident of Council Bluffs, was one of a family of brothers who are thoroughly identified with the history of Iowa, the others being Hon. P M. Casady and Weir Casady, of Des Moines, and the late Hon. S. H. Casady, of Sioux City, and J. N. Casady, of Council Bluffs. Each and all of these have been potent factors in the development of the state.

J. P. Casady was born in Connersville, Ind., September 1, 1828. Of Scotch-Irish ancestry, the conquering traits of that race were well reproduced in him. Like so many of the notable men of America, he was raised upon a farm, attended the public schools until 18 years of age, afterwards pursuing an academic course. Having little taste for farm life he chose the profession of law for his field of labor. He was most fortunate in receiving his law training from Hon. Samuel W. Parker, one of a coterie of great lawyers who made the bar of Indiana. In 1852 Judge Casady moved to Des Moines and was there admitted to the bar. In the following year he took up his residence in Council Bluffs, and, in partnership with Hon. Hadley D. Johnson, opened a law and land office. His fine talents, united to his conservatism and prudence soon won for him wide recognition and in 1858 he was elected to the office of county judge, an office that he filled with marked ability, conducting his private business at the same time. In 1861 he was elected a director of the Council Bluffs and St. Joe Railway company, and afterwards became president of the road.

Politically, Judge Casady was a democrat, in the broad and Jeffersonian sense of the word. In 1868 he was elected to the state senate, serving four years. He was frequently a delegate to state conventions, and, in 1880, to the national convention. In 1872 he was nominated for auditor of state, and, although not elected to the of-

17

fice, ran far ahead of his ticket, polling many votes from the opposition. He was not an office-seeker and when he accepted office it was always at a personal sacrifice.

Judge Casady was widely known for his public spirit and this was well shown in his skill, diplomacy and untiring efforts that finally secured the appropriation for the school for the deaf and dumb, at Council Bluffs. No one in his county was ever more favorably known than he was, and his influence was always for good. As a citizen he was universally loved and respected. In his friendships he was most loyal and unswerving. Many young men of the west owe their start in life and much of their success to the kindness and interest of Judge Casady. He was an Odd Fellow and a charter member of Council Bluffs Lodge No. 49. On June 16, 1856 he was married to Miss Hannah Joiner. They had five children; Lawrence, born July 15, 1860, died October 16, 1863; Jefferson J., born June 18, 1863, died October 27, 1864; Thomas E., born in 1868, is at present a practicing lawyer in Council Bluffs; Ida, born September 20, 1865; Albert W., born November 5, 1870, employed in the office of Deere, Wells & Co.; Mrs. Casady died May 6, 1882. They were members of the First Presbyterian church. Judge Casady died April 27, 1892.

CASADY, THOMAS E., a native resident of Council Bluffs, is one of the brightest of the younger members of the bar. He was born April 27, 1868. His father, Judge Jefferson P. Casady, was a man widely known for his abilities as a lawyer and his nobility as a man and citizen of Iowa. His mother, Mrs. Hannah Joiner Casady, was of Scotch-Irish ancestry, as was his father, and the sturdy and estimable traits that belong essentially to his ancestry are fully developed in the son. In his boyhood Thomas E. Casady attended the public schools of Council Bluffs. In 1884 he entered Parsons college at Fairfield, and was graduated in 1888 with the degree of bachelor of science. While a student at Parsons college he was elected president of the Iowa Collegiate association, and as such presided at the oratorical contest and annual meeting of the association held in Des Moines in February, 1887. In 1890 he received the degree of master of science from his alma mater; and the year following was honored by being elected a member of the board of trustees, serving six years. In 1888 he entered the law department of the University of Iowa, remaining

until the serious illness of his father required his presence in Council Bluffs, where he completed his study with Finley Burke. He was admitted to the bar in the following year. In January, 1891, he formed a partnership with Mr. Burke, which continued about four years, since which time he has practiced alone. Mr. Casady is a staunch democrat, and has always been one. He was appointed assistant United States district attorney for the southern district, but as the duties of his office consumed too much time he resigned. In 1898 Mr. Casady was nominated by the democrats of his county for the office of county attorney, and although he ran over 500 votes ahead of his ticket he was defeated, as was the whole ticket. The republican majority in the county ranged from 1,200 to 1,500, while the majority against him was only between 500 and 600. Mr. Casady good-naturedly says: "Spain did it."

He was married November 12, 1895, to Miss Agnes Wickfield Barnard, of Moline, Ill., daughter of H. A. Barnard, a pioneer in the manufacturing industries of Moline, and now president of the Barnard & Leas Manufacturing company of that city. Few, if any, of the lawyers in western Iowa have had better educational training than Mr. Casady, or taken deeper interest in scholastic matters. He is a man of high personal character and integrity, and enjoys the confidence of the people both on the score of ability and responsibility. He is possessed of a logical mind, studious habits, courteous bearing, and ability to talk well to the point, good judgment and common sense, and a fixed pride and determination to succeed.

The name Casady is closely interwoven in the legal history of the state, and the subject of this sketch is well worthy to perpetuate the history so creditably begun by his elders.

---

CASADY, JR., JAMES N., a successful young business man of Council Bluffs, belongs to the family of Casadys so well known throughout Iowa for their success in business, and the high standing they have maintained as progressive and upright citizens. Mr. Casady is a native product, having been born in the city of his present residence, June 10, 1869. His father was long a resident of the state and came from Indiana in 1850. His mother's maiden name was Ellen M. Joiner. Mr. Casady attended the public schools of his native city, followed by a four years' course in the Allen academy, located at 1832-6 Michigan avenue, Chicago; he graduated

from this institution in 1887. His father established a real estate and loan business in Council Bluffs in 1853, and built up the largest loan agency in the city, and other extensive interests by close attention to details. This large and increasing business was succeeded to by James N., Jr., and is now being successfully carried on by him. He deals largely in farm and city property; cares for property of nonresidents; pays taxes and negotiates loans, and is resident agent of a large number of well known insurance companies, such as Continental of New York, Scottish Union and National of Edinburgh, Scotland, and Sun Fire Office of London, Eng.; London Guar-

antee and Accident company, limited, London, Eng. Financial correspondent of several large eastern institutions, also resident assistant secretary of the National Surety company of New York, having power to execute all bonds in his office, known as the Casady building. In politics Mr. Casady is a democrat; is nephew of the Hon. P. M. Casady, of Des Moines, president of the Des Moines Savings bank of that city; was married to Miss Mamie Cavanagh of Omaha, Neb., the only daughter of P. J. Cavanagh, Esq., October 12, 1893. They have two children, Geraldine, born November 29, 1894, and Joiner, born July 24, 1897.

SECOR, EUGENE, of Forest City, is descended on his father's side from a family of French Huguenot refugees, who came to America in 1689 and settled in New York. The name is spelled in the letters of denization S-y-c-a-r-d, but has gradually evolved into the present name, Secor. His ancestors on both sides were participants in the revolutionary struggle. British soldiers were the terror of the country where they lived. They were all loyal to the American cause, and this subject is a "Son of the American Revolution" by virtue thereof. The father of Mr. Secor was an enthusiastic horticulturist of his time. He was also justice of the peace for many years, and among the attorneys who practiced in his court was Chauncey M. Depew. His mother was Sarah Caroline Knapp, whose mother was a Lee prominent among the leading families in Yorktown.

Mr. Eugene Secor was born May 13, 1841, near Peekskill, N. Y. He never attended any except the New York country school, until 21 years of age. The family consisted of eleven children, and, being in only moderate circumstances, much of their time was required in clearing their land of stones and trees. Without educational advantages himself his father wanted the children to be more fortunate, and made them so by providing a good library, containing the best works in literature of that day. In the spring of 1862 Mr. Secor came to Iowa. It may be asked why he did not go south. There were many reasons, for he was not disloyal. He never shirked a duty to his country and later did enlist in the 100 day service, but for some reason the company was never called out. It must be understood that he lived at the time more than a hundred miles from railroad or telegraph. In 1864 he entered Cornell college, but in the fall of the same year was called home to look after his brother's business as county treasurer, he having gone to the front in the service of Uncle Sam. That ended his school life. His practical business education was in the county offices of Winnebago county, where he was deputy treasurer two years, deputy clerk for one year, clerk for six years, deputy auditor one year and auditor four years.

In 1880 he entered into partnership with his brother, David Secor, and John Law, under the style Secor Brothers & Law, to carry on a real estate business, but through the retiring of Mr. Law in 1893, whose place was taken by Willard Secor, the firm

is now known as Secor Brothers & Co. In 1882 the firm of Secor Brothers & Law erected the brick block in which the First National bank of Forest City is now located, and established the City bank, with B. A. Plummer added to the banking firm. In 1893 the bank was nationalized. Mr. Secor is one of its directors and its vice-president. He is also a member of the banking firm of P. M. Joice & Co., of Lake Mills, and has connections with four similar enterprises in Minnesota. Another concern in which he is a director and stockholder is the Forest City Electric Light and Power company.

Although nurtured in the lap of democracy, of the pro-slavery type, Mr. Secor is and always has been a republican. His early training was received during Seymour's reign in New York and Buchanan's weakness in Washington. He has been a delegate to nearly every state convention for the past fifteen years, and was a Tenth district delegate to the National Republican convention held at Minneapolis in 1892, and supported Harrison. He has been identified for many years with the State Horticultural society, was its president two years, and is at this time a director thereof and manager of one of its experiment stations. He

was sole judge at the World's fair and at the Omaha exposition in the department of the apiary. He is a prominent beekeeper, and not uncommonly has a ton of honey in a season. He has been president of the National Beekeepers' society, and is at present its treasurer and general manager. The Twenty-second General Assembly elected him as a trustee of the Agricultural college, which position he held for six years. He has been for many years, and still is, a trustee of Cornell college and one of its executive committee. Was one of two lay delegates from the Northwest Iowa conference to the general conference of the M. E. church in 1892. He was the first mayor of Forest City, and re-elected to the same office three times. Was on the council for many years following. Has been a member of the board of education for many years, and is now its president. He organized the Winnebago County Agricultural society, and was its president for two years.

Mr. Secor has contributed to the papers and magazines, both literary and technical, for many years. He wrote by request, a resume of the apiarian industry in the United States and its representation at the Chicago fair, for publication in the permanent records of the World's Columbian exposition.

SECOR, ELLSWORTH E., cashier and resident manager of the Buffalo Center State bank at Buffalo Center, and a nephew of Eugene Secor, of Forest City, whose sketch appears elsewhere in this work, is one of the most prominent and progressive young business men in northern Iowa.

He was born January 2, 1864, at Forest City, Iowa. His father is the Hon. David Secor, now president of the Faribault County bank, of Winnebago City, Minn., also president of the bank of Amboy, Amboy, Minn., the Delevan bank, Delevan, Minn. He is also director of the First National bank, of Forest City, Iowa, his former home. He was a representative from his district in the house of representatives in the Iowa legislature for two terms during the years 1872-1874, and was twice elected register of the Iowa state land office. He was one of the early settlers of Winnebago county, coming there in 1858. He was county treasurer two terms during the sixties, occupying that position during the war, but hiring a substitute for his office, he joined the union army and was in Sherman's march to the sea. Mrs. Secor's maiden name was Samantha Van Curen. She died when Ellsworth E. was but 7 years old. Mr. Secor, in early life attended the public schools of Forest City, and in 1881 entered the Iowa Agricultural college at Ames, but before completing the freshman year was taken sick and did not complete his course. His father was identified with the building of the Chicago, Iowa & Dakota railway, known as the "Slippery Elm" road, so the ambitious young man concluded to fit himself for future life in the railway service. He put in four years as freight brakeman, mostly on the Winona & St. Peter division of the Chicago & Northwestern railway, and later on the What Cheer branch of the same railway, out of Belle Plaine. Near that place, in the winter of 1886-87, he nearly lost his life one frosty morning just before daylight, by stumbling between the tender and the first car, striking on the draw bar and cutting through his heavy clothing and through the flesh of one leg, to the bone. He realized his perilous position and managed somehow to climb to the top of the car, where he fainted, but was brought to his senses by the cold air; this experience caused him to change his occupation.

His father was preparing to remove to Minnesota and wanted him to go to Forest City, and, in a measure, take his place in the firm of Secor Brothers & Law. This he accordingly did, leaving Belle Plaine, his former headquarters, January 25, 1887,

to take charge of the conveyance and abstract work of his father's firm, remaining with them until July, 1892, when he took charge of the Iowa Investment company's business at Buffalo Center. The company soon began to do an exchange and banking business, Mr. Secor occupying the responsible position of secretary and resident manager of the company's business. The banking feature of the business grew so rapidly that a separate institution for that purpose was organized, and the Buffalo Center Savings bank was launched forth January 16, 1893, with Mr. Secor as its cashier. In February, 1894, the two institutions were merged into one, and thus the Buffalo Center State bank was organized and commenced business February 12, 1894, with a capital of $25,000. It is still the principal bank of the town with the following named officers: G. S. Gilbertson, president; C. J. Thompson, vice-president, and E. E. Secor, cashier. The bank has built up a fine business, has a surplus fund of $8,000, pays 15 per cent dividends to its stockholders and has deposits amount-

ing to over $55,000. On January 1, 1899,
Mr. Secor, in connection with H. G. Gardner, G. S. Gilbertson, C. J. Thompson, F.
W. Thompson, and F. L. Kelley, all prominent bankers of northern Iowa, formed a
limited partnership, and are now operating
a bank at Titonka, Kossuth county, under
the firm name and style of Secor & Gardner, of which Mr. Secor is president. Mr.
Secor has always been a staunch republican, filled the office of city clerk of Forest
City; was the first mayor of Buffalo Center,
refusing re-election, but in 1896, he was
chosen by the citizens' caucus and elected
without any opponent. Re-elected in 1897
and resigned mayorship July 1, 1897, on
appointment by President McKinley as
postmaster at Buffalo Center. He was also
nominated as a candidate for school director and received every vote cast, and
re-elected in 1898. He is a member of
Truth Lodge No. 213, A. F. & A. M. at
Forest City; Camp No. 2659 Modern Woodmen of America; Bison Lodge No. 379, and
Buffalo Center Lodge No. 596, I. O. O. F.,
all of Buffalo Center. He was married
April 27, 1887, to Emma J. Harmon, of
Jewell, Hamilton county, Iowa, at Webster
City. They have four children, Ethel
Jozella, born March 24, 1888, Russell Harold, born September 20, 1889, Beryl Joy,
born June 8, 1894, and Raymond, born No-
vember 22, 1898.

GIBSON, JOHN. No more active or
successful business man can be found anywhere in Iowa than John Gibson. His
home is at Creston, but his extensive business interests in Des Moines keep him in
that city a great deal of the time.

Mr. Gibson was born in Wellsville,
Columbiana county, Ohio, October 2, 1849,
and is the son of Josiah Gibson, D. D., now
deceased. Josiah Gibson was a Methodist
minister, and a native of West Virginia.
His first pastorate was in the Pittsburg
conference, after which he was transferred
to the Rock River conference in 1854, and
in which conference he was presiding elder
for eight years. In 1870 he was transferred
to the southern Illinois conference, where
he served ten years. In 1880 he retired
from the ministry and came to the home of
his son, John Gibson, where he died in
1887. The mother, Elvira A. Ebbert Gibson, was a native of Pennsylvania, and
was married to Josiah Gibson in 1845. She,
too, died at the home of her son in 1894.

John Gibson is of Scotch descent, his

grandfather, John Gibson, having come
from Scotland to America in 1798. Mr.
Gibson's education was completed in the
public schools, and one year in the academy
of Elgin, Ill. His first money was made by
selling war books and pictures in Illinois
in 1864. He located in Creston, Iowa, in
May, 1878, having driven across the country
from Pueblo, Colo. His wife and two
sons were with him and they were seven
weeks making the journey. Mr. Gibson
practiced law at Creston until 1882, when
he gave up the active practice of law to
devote his time to other business. He
then engaged in stock and bond selling and

in loaning money for eastern parties. He
was one of the incorporators of the Iowa
State Savings bank at Creston in 1884, and
has been president of that institution most
of the time since its organization. In 1891
he became vice-president of the Iowa Central Building and Loan association, and has
held that office ever since. In 1890 the
Gibson Investment company was organized,
and he has been its treasurer since that
time. The company has very large real
estate interests in Creston. He was one of
the incorporators of the Anchor Mutual
Fire Insurance company and has been
treasurer of that company for the past
three years. He also organized the Nebraska Central Building and Loan associa-

tion, of Lincoln, Neb., in 1898, of which he is the president. In politics Mr. Gibson has always been a republican. In 1897 he was elected to the lower house of the legislature, from Union county, in a very close contest, the county being always classed as doubtful, and served with the ability which has characterized all his business life. He takes a great deal of interest in educational matters, and has been one of the directors of the independent school district of Creston for the past eight years. He is a member of the Methodist church. He was married June 30, 1870, to Miss Tillie J. Martin, of Alma, Ill. They have three children living — Josiah, born April 28, 1873, graduated at Cornell college, Mt. Vernon, Iowa, in 1895; John M., born July 24, 1875, is now living at home, and Jane, born August 8, 1877, is the wife of Frank Phillips, of Creston.

Mr. Gibson is a very busy man and a successful financier. He is also very genial, and a man who makes hosts of friends wherever he goes.

---

PUTMAN, TILFORD LYNN, the leading physician of Shenandoah, is one of Iowa's thoroughly competent and up-to-date surgeons, and he possesses one of the finest medical libraries and set of surgical instruments and apparatus in the state.

He is the son of Green Marion Putman, a farmer of moderate circumstances, who was always popular in the community where he lived, for his generous and sociable disposition. He was one of fourteen children, and was the son of Elija Putman and Elizabeth Duff. Elija Putman was a native of Kentucky, but in an early day located in Fulton county, Ill., and in 1845 removed to Davis county, Iowa. G. M. Putman was born April 12, 1835, and died September 12, 1896, aged 61 years. Dr. Putman's mother was formerly Elizabeth Kelsey, an unusually bright woman, of a quiet, religious nature. She was the daughter of Joseph Kelsey and Rebecca Stevens, who removed from Greencastle, Ind., to Princeton, Mercer county, Mo., where the father died in 1867, aged 65 years, and the mother in 1870, at the age of 66. Mrs. Putman died February 1, 1899, of heart disease.

Dr. T. L. Putman was born on February 8, 1859, at Princeton, Mercer county, Mo. He was reared on a farm and obtained his early education at the district school, which he was permitted to attend during the winter, and then continued his studies the rest of the year alone, poring over his books at night by the light of a tallow candle, and reviewing them in his mind the following day while at work in the field. The school he attended was one of the best of its kind, and after completing it and attending

the teachers' institute he was able to secure a teacher's certificate, and for two years taught a district school in Iowa, which was followed by two years of similar work in Illinois, where he received the highest salary paid any country teacher in Fulton county. In 1883 he entered Rush Medical department of Lake Forest university, graduating February 17, 1885, with great credit to himself, being one of six out of a class of 163 to be placed upon the honor list. A month after graduation, on March 19, 1885, he located in Iowa, at Riverton, where for six years he conducted a drug store and practiced medicine, removing to

his present location in 1891. Since leaving college he has three times graduated in surgery, and in September, 1885, passed the state examinations and became a registered pharmacist. Since entering the medical profession Dr. Putman has always enjoyed a good practice, and is now very well established. He has been especially successful in the line of surgery, possessing a steady nerve, having been well trained under the direction of the intrepid Dr. Moses Gunn. He is now special surgeon for a number of accident insurance companies, and is medical examiner for all the leading life insurance companies of the United States at Shenandoah. He is also physician and lecturer to the Western Normal college at that place.

Dr. Putman has always been a staunch republican and a firm believer in the principles of that party, but has never accepted office. He is a member of the Iowa State Medical society, the Southwestern Iowa Medical society and American Medical association. He has been a member of the Methodist church since 1884, and is a prominent worker in that organization, having charge at present of a large class of young ladies in the Sunday school.

The doctor was married March 25, 1886, to Miss Jessie D. McKean, of Columbus, Neb., formerly of East Palestine, Ohio. They have one child, a boy, Jesse Lynn, who was born December 16, 1886, who is a bright, happy lad and a favorite in school and society. The doctor's wife is a lady of culture and moves in the highest social circle. The doctor is possessed of a happy social disposition, kind, gentle and loved by all his patients, and has the esteem and favor of the foremost men of his profession in the state.

---

HUBINGER, JOHN C., manufacturer, millionaire and public benefactor, is one of the most remarkable men of this country; a Napoleon in business affairs, a man of destiny, through his own indomitable will, tireless energy and brilliant genius he has built up a magnificent structure on a financial foundation as solid as the rock of Gibraltar.

Mr. Hubinger was born in New Orleans, La., forty-six years ago, and is the son of John F. Hubinger, who was born in Bavaria, in 1828, and still survives, as well as his mother, who is a native of France.

It will thus be seen that Mr. Hubinger, having been born in Louisiana, is a Creole, a term peculiar to the state, and having the same significance as Buckeye to those born in Ohio, or Nutmegs to those who first saw the light of day in Connecticut.

At the age of 4 his family moved north and at Falmouth, Ky., young Hubinger received in the public schools the first and only educational training he ever received from any school system; this experience covered about four years of study, and he applied himself so closely that he got a fair foundation, which he has since built on by private study and observation, until to-day he can be considered a well informed man outside of business matters, in which he excels.

His career has been an eventful one, full of exciting incidents, and it is a remarkable

fact that he was 30 years of age before he amassed his first thousand dollars, having innumerable ups and downs in life, but never despairing and always aggressive.

It would require a volume the size of this to recount a history of his life from the time he started out to earn a living up to the present time when he controls millions of business interests, and is at the zenith of his usefulness. We will not attempt anything more than a passing notice of such facts as will interest his friends.

Of an inventive turn, he secured several patents which he sold to more or less advantage, and tried innumerable schemes at one time or another, succeeding at times and losing at others his little capital, through the boldness of his methods.

The idea of Elastic starch came to him years ago, when he acted as agent for a starch concern, and he had it constantly in mind, eventually arriving at the secret which he holds alone to day, and which has made Elastic starch the most popular in the market.

In connection with his two brothers he founded the Elastic Starch company, at

New Haven, Conn., under the name of The J. C. Hubinger Bros.' Co., and at a later period opened another factory at Keokuk, Iowa, where he subsequently amassed a large fortune and became known

as one of the most enterprising and public spirited citizens in the state.

In the west his interests are colossal, as well as the ventures which he has made successful; among his holdings being large tracts of real estate, improved and unimproved, in different parts of the western country.

He is owner of the Keokuk street railway system, the electric light plant and system, the Mississippi Valley Telephone company, capitalized at $2,225,000. This takes in a large number of cities in that section, and is the most dangerous and largest competitor of the Bell Telephone company in America, having over 10,000 telephone subscribers.

A man of rare executive ability, he finds time to personally direct the policy of all the enterprises in which he is interested, and at the same time to evolve many more brilliant schemes of a local nature, all of which are put through in a practical and successful way.

The magnitude of his transactions almost surpass belief; in the starch business they dispose of about 25,000,000 packages each year, the legitimate profits from which are enormous, and in other ways he handles not less than $3,000,000 annually.

His liberality is the marvel of the country in which he is known, and at his palatial home, overlooking the historic Mississippi river, he and his charming wife dispense a boundless hospitality to those fortunate enough to be their guests. All the luxuries and benefits that wealth can procure are there supplied, and an atmosphere of culture and refinement pervades the entire establishment.

Mr. Hubinger's family consists of himself, wife and four children, and while fond of promoting large enterprises, he is still fonder of the home circle and there spends all of his time that is not taken up by business cares.

---

FRICK, MAXWELL W., of Rockwell City, was born October 27, 1859, in a log house on the prairie near the present site of Booneville, in Dallas county. He is the son of John A. Frick, who came to Iowa from Westmoreland county, Pa., in 1856 and settled in Dallas county. He was a farmer during all his active life, in comfortable circumstances, though not wealthy. He is now retired. The mother is a native of Pennsylvania, being born near Connellsville, where she grew up and was married.

Her maiden name was Eliza M. Work. She is of Scotch-Irish descent, with a mixture of Welsh and English blood, and her ancestors served with distinction in the revolutionary war. The father is of German

origin, his people being of that sturdy and prosperous class known as Pennsylvania Dutch.

The early education of Maxwell W. Frick was acquired in the district school, but before reaching the age when pupils are usually placed in school he was fairly started on the way through home teaching. Evincing a remarkable precociousness he soon led the classes in the few departments of learning in the district school, and to give him the opportunity to advance, not offered in the home district, he was sent to the high school at Adel. Before he had graduated he entered the schools of Des Moines. He there became proficient in stenography, but concluded to fit himself for admission to the bar. Following a period of private study he entered the law school in Des Moines, then being conducted by Judge Miller, where he remained until it suspended, then entered the office of M. H. Baugh, a very able, though financially unfortunate, lawyer of Adel. He purchased an interest in the practice *sub rosa*, with the understanding that as soon as he should be admitted to the bar his name was to appear in the firm. Applying himself closely, he passed the examination before the circuit court of Dallas county, February 3, 1881, under Judge Calvert, with marked honors.

After his admission to the bar he became the junior member of the firm of Baugh & Frick, as had been previously arranged; but he disposed of his interests there and the following summer he followed the rush to Rockwell City, then a promising new town on a proposed line of railroad. He located in practice there, and made arrangements with Harlan & Rude, real estate dealers at Perry, to conduct for them a branch office. Although the town was then experiencing the effects of a boom, business did not prove very remunerative for a time, but the young man kept up courage and remained, a course for which he is now very glad.

He was married to Miss Kate M. Marsh, of Adel, November 3, 1881. A few months subsequent to that event his existing real estate business relations were dissolved and another partnership formed under the style of Harlan & Company, consisting of W. H. Harlan, now a mail carrier in Des Moines, and himself. This was continued until 1882, when it was dissolved, since which time Mr. Frick has been in business alone. About this time, he and his wife, having learned of the C. L. S. C., took up the course of reading, pursued it together, and both graduated. He gives particular attention to commercial and real estate law and does a large general practice. In 1886 he added to his business a farm loan department and began a greater prosperity. His practice and brokerage business so increased that in 1891 he found it necessary to employ a stenographer and collector, and the three are kept busy. For several years he has been the attorney for R. G. Dun & Company, for Calhoun county.

In politics he is a republican, but his time is so completely employed in the conduct of his business that he finds little time for other work. He has served as justice of the peace and town assessor. He is a member of the Knights of Pythias and A. O. U. W., being past master of the last named. He has been president of the Westminster Christian Endeavor Union, of the Ft Dodge Presbytery, and is a ruling elder in the Presbyterian church. He was a member of the general assembly of that church which met at Detroit in 1891 and tried Dr. Charles A. Briggs for heresy, and of the one which met at Winona, Ind., in 1897. His election to both these assemblies was not only unsolicited but unknown to him, each a spontaneous tribute of his fellow Presbyterians. He is active in church work, and largely through his efforts the denomination of his faith at Rockwell City has been freed from debt.

His reputation for business capacity caused his selection, in the spring of 1897, as a trustee of Buena Vista college, a promising institution of learning located at Storm Lake, Iowa. It is the testimony of his associates in this work, that in the short time he has been connected with it he has proven the wisdom of his selection.

On the night of August 11 and 12, 1898, he met the greatest trial of his life. His wife died suddenly of apoplexy, after an illness of but little more than two hours, succeeding a day of unusual enjoyment.

GRIFFIN, DR. FRANCIS, one of the prominent citizens of Mapleton, was born in Boston, Mass., July 2, 1847. His father, Frank Griffin, married Mary Nelson, who came to Boston in 1840 from Ireland. Her death occurred in 1853, and his father married again and removed with his family to Port Byron, Rock Island county, Ill. Dr. Griffin attended common schools in Boston, and on coming west worked for farmers in summer and in winter went to the district

school until 1864, when he enlisted in the war, enrolling in Company G, One Hundred and Twelfth Illinois Volunteer infantry. He served until the close of the war and took part in the Atlanta campaign, and afterwards in the battles of Atlanta, Franklin, Nashville and Wilmington. In 1865 he was transferred to the Sixty-fifth Illinois infantry and commissioned sergeant. In July, 1865, he was discharged at Greensborough, N. C. When transferred there were enough in the transfer to form a company, and Company F, Sixty-fifth Illinois infantry, was formed. He is now a member of G. A. R. Hoskins Post, No. 87. In 1865 he attended high school, and commenced the study of medicine at Hampton, Ill. In

1868 and 1869 he attended Rush Medical college, and soon took up his residence in Wheatland, Clinton county, Iowa. Here he was employed in the drug business until 1878, when he removed to Mapleton and bought a drug stock, conducted a store, and at the same time engaged in the practice of medicine. Mapleton was a town of about 200 people when he settled there. It has now a population of 1,200; its people prosperous and with every promise of becoming one of Iowa's leading towns. Dr. Griffin was one of the organizers of the Monona County State bank, of Mapleton, and has been a director since its organization.

Dr. Griffin was married to Caroline E. Grover, February 2, 1870.

---

STOUT, JAMES E., as sheriff of Polk county, holds one of the most important offices in the state, probably the most important county office. He has more business than a dozen ordinary sheriffs and has to employ a small army of men to assist him. The courts of Polk county, or, more properly speaking, the litigation in the city of Des Moines, almost never takes a rest. They are at it nearly all the year around, four courts, making an enormous amount of work and responsibility for the sheriff. But Mr. Stout has been a thoroughly efficient officer, so much so that he was nominated without any opposition for a second term, in July, 1897, by the republicans. He is thorough and conscientious in this office as he was during the time he was chairman of the republican county committee of Polk county.

James E. Stout was born in Trumbull county, Ohio, September 21, 1849. His parents were Jasper and Mary Urmson Stout, both natives of England. The father was born at Northumberland and the mother at Lancashire. They came to the United States in early youth and here were married and reared a family of five children, of whom James was the only son. The oldest sister, Mary A., is the wife of James Taylor, who resides at Youngstown, Ohio; Sidney Jane is the wife of William Madge, of Greenville, Pa.; Esther is the wife of Alonzo Hunter, of Sharon, Pa., where Miss Abbie R. Stout, the other sister, also resides.

The father followed the coal business all his life, as did the son until the time of his election to the office of sheriff of Polk county. The life of Sheriff Stout was passed in Mercer and Lawrence counties, Pa., until 1871,

when he came to Iowa and remained one winter in Webster county. The following spring he returned to the Keystone state, and on October 9, 1871, was married to Miss Margaret L. Hitechew, of Allegheny City, daughter of John and Margaret Hitechew. To this union have been born four children. Mary L., now the wife of Carl Smith, was born in Mercer county, Pa., June 8, 1873; William, who died February 2, 1880, was born in Greene county, Iowa, May 17, 1878; John D., was born in Greene county, March 14, 1880, and Jasper at the same place May 9, 1885.

Mr. Stout commenced work in the mines

at the age of 7 and his education was acquired in night school after he had reached the age when he realized the importance of more book learning than was possessed by those around him. In 1876 he again came to Iowa, settling in Greene county, and a short time thereafter engaged in the coal business in partnership with Isaac Jones and Joseph Markham. They prospered beyond their most sanguine expectations, but, flushed with success, ventured heavily in mining operations and one day found them without a dollar. June 1, 1886, he was appointed state mine inspector by Governor Larrabee and the duties of the office required that he remove to Des Moines. He was reappointed in

1888, but resigned the following year to accept the position of superintendent of the Christy coal mines, adjacent to Des Moines, which place he held until called to the shrievalty in 1895. He has always been a republican and one of the active kind. The only other political office he has held, however, was that of justice of the peace in Greene county, in which capacity he served for three years. He is a member of the I. O. O. F., the Modern Woodmen, Knights of Pythias, Red Men and American Mechanics, in all of which he is highly popular. As a conscientious official, a good citizen, an accommodating neighbor and a modest gentleman he is known by the residents of Des Moines and Polk county.

---

WERNLI, JACOB, who served Plymouth county as superintendent of schools for eight years, has long been known as one of the foremost educators of Iowa. He has been a resident of the state ever since 1875, and during all this time has been identified with the public schools, and has gained a wide reputation among teachers, particularly as an institute instructor and conductor He is a native of Switzerland by birth, and his ancestors were also of that nationality. His father, Jacob Wernli, was a thrifty farmer of comfortable means, who died at the age of 82. Professor Wernli's mother was Salomea Dieteker, whose father was prominent in public life, having served as treasurer and in other official positions. She died at the age of 85 years.

Prof. J. Wernli was born July 13, 1828, at Thalheim, in the county of Brugg, Canton of Aargon, Switzerland, where his early years were passed. He entered the graded school at the age of 6 years and continued to attend until he was 16. He was fortunate in having excellent teachers, who greatly encouraged his studious habits and taste for learning. He was an extensive reader, the books at his period of life being chosen for him mostly by his minister. Not content with a common school education, young Wernli spent all the leisure which was afforded him from hard labor on the farm in pursuing studies to fit himself for college. His parents were unable to give him the advantages of a university training, but through the influence of his teacher and minister he succeeded in gaining admittance to the State Normal school, being one of thirty-five to pass the entrance examinations out of seventy-five

examined. Beginning January 25, 1847, he continued at this institution for three years, receiving practical instruction under some of the foremost educators of Switzerland, all of the Pestalozzian school. Upon his graduation in 1860 he received a patent for all the schools in the canton and a certificate of qualification in twenty-two branches, with marks of excellence in agriculture, horticulture, mathematics and language. He taught his first school, a mixed but graded one of ninety four pupils in the village of Bonisvogl, on Lake Hallvogl. Here he gave such satisfaction that he was soon called to a higher school. But longing for larger opportunities in a new country, he came to America, and in May, 1855, secured work as a common laborer at $1 a day in Oshkosh, Wis. Here, through economy and small investments he soon acquired a capital of $500, and in October, 1856, he moved to Waupaca county, where he bought eighty acres of land and commenced farming. In 1858 he again began teaching at $20 a month, and two years later was elected county superintendent of

Waupaca county, and after serving two terms. was called, in 1864, to be principal of the second ward school in Milwaukee. In 1866 he was elected principal of the Plattville State normal, and in 1868 of the Northwestern German-English school at

Galena, Ill. In 1875 he came to Le Mars and became principal of the public schools, conducting at the same time a book and stationery store. In 1877 he began devoting almost his entire attention to institute work, in which he has been particularly successful, having conducted over 150 institutes in many counties of Iowa. He established the Northwestern Normal school at Le Mars in 1887, which, under his direction, proved to be one of the best private normals in the state. In 1889 he was elected county superintendent of Plymouth county, and so earnest were his efforts in the behalf of the public schools that he was re-elected three times, serving in all four terms.

In politics Professor Wernli has been a republican since the breaking out of the civil war. For many years he has been a Knight Templar, and he is a member of the German Methodist church.

He was married in 1853 in Switzerland, to Miss Anna Marie Steiner, who died December 17. 1866. Professor Wernli was again married at Milwaukee, to Miss Christene Kehres, a native of Germany.

---

BURKART, CHARLES J. A pioneer in newspaperdom is Mr. Burkart, and for so many years was he connected with the *Statesman*, of Marshalltown, that to speak of the one is to allude to the other. Of his ancestors little can be said. His father and mother came to the United States from Switzerland in 1845, and lived a quiet and contented life without seeking to achieve any great financial success.

Charles J. Burkart was born in Galena, Ill., December 22, 1852. His parents removed to Savanna, Ill., in 1853, where he was given the advantages offered by the common schools. When 13 years of age the family went back to Galena, and Charles entered the schools there, where he remained for one year. In 1865 he learned the printer's trade in the Galena *Gazette* office, and he has followed the business of publishing and printing during all the years since that time. It will thus be seen that nearly all his education has been obtained by a series of years of practical experience in the world's greatest educational workshop, and without aid from any person whomsoever. In June, 1868, he went to Marshalltown, where he worked at his trade in the different offices of the city until 1876, when, in partnership with Mr. U. S. Mitchell, he founded the *Statesman*.

Mr. Mitchell brought with him a small outfit of printing material, and with only a few hundred dollars of capital, and that borrowed, he began the difficult task of establishing a democratic paper in the then banner republican county of Iowa. Mr. Burk-

art says that in those days dollars were as scarce as democrats, and the last-named article no more numerous than hen's teeth. In 1876 Mr. Mitchell sold out his interest to Mr. Cook Sanford, and in October, 1879, the entire plant was disposed of to Byron Webster. In the spring of 1880, however, Mr. Burkart again became a half owner in the paper, and the firm of Webster & Burkart continued its publication until November, 1894, when Mr. Burkart became the sole owner. It will be seen that with the exception of four or five months Mr. Burkart had the business management of the paper from the time it was founded, and through his tireless efforts it became the official paper of the county with a large influence and circulation. In January, 1897, the *Statesman* was consolidated with the *Daily Press*, under the name of the *Statesman-Press*, making one of the strongest combinations in central Iowa. In January, 1898, after twenty-two years' connection with the *Statesman*, he disposed of his interests in the *Statesman-Press* and retired from the newspaper business, to devote his time to the Southwestern Mutual Life association, Marshalltown, of which he has been the vice-president since its organization in 1882.

McNUTT, SAMUEL, one of the pioneers of Iowa, who has had a large part in shaping its history, is a resident of Muscatine, where he is passing his advancing years in quiet comfort, engaged in literary study and correspondence. He has contributed to the preservation of Iowa history by a number of writings. Mr. McNutt was born November 21, 1825, in the north of Ireland, twenty miles west of Londonderry, and is the son of Samuel McNutt and Hannah Stewart McNutt. The family is of Scotch origin and descended from a somewhat noted ancestry. While he was yet a child the family came to America, and after a brief stay in Philadelphia settled in New Castle county, Del., near the village of Newark. His mother was now a widow with seven children, of whom Samuel was the oldest. For forty years she devoted her life and energies to the education and interests of her children, three boys and four girls, and had the happiness to see them all honorably settled in life. Her second son, Robert, became an eminent physician in Louisiana, but as he was a union man, he barely escaped to the north with his life, losing all his property in Louisiana. Governor Kirkwood appointed him assistant surgeon of the Thirty-eighth Iowa infantry. The third son, James, also joined the union army, being attached to the medical department of the regular army, and for more than a year had medical charge of Fort Jackson and Fort St. Phillip, below New Orleans. Mrs. McNutt died in Iowa, December 24, 1874, at the age of 85 years. Samuel passed his boyhood working on the little farm in Delaware. Books were few and his early training was largely from the Catechism, Psalms of David, Proverbs of Solomon, Scotch Martyrs and Weems' Life of Washington. He contributed some poems to the *Temperance Star*, of Wilmington, Del., which attracted the attention of Dr. J. S. Bell, of Newark, one of the professors in Delaware college, who assisted the young man to secure an education. During his college days he contributed to *Peterson's Magazine, Neal's Gazette, Godey's Lady's Book,*

*Saturday Courier* and other publications, and his writings had a wide circulation.

Leaving college he engaged in teaching and at the same time studied law under the direction of Hon. Daniel M. Bates, then secretary of state of Delaware. In 1851 he went to Milwaukee, was admitted to the bar and started to practice there, but being offered a professorship in a collegiate institute in Hernando, Miss., he went there for two years. In 1854 he came north and located in Muscatine county, Iowa. In 1856 he was principal of the First ward public school and in that year he and D. F. Wells, who was principal of the Third ward school, edited the first educational magazine in Iowa, called the *Voice of Iowa*, published by Dr. Enos, of Cedar Rapids. At the close of the year he bought a half interest in the *Muscatine Enquirer*,

and became its editor. Subsequently he was associate editor of the *Dubuque Herald*, under the management of Joseph B. Dorr, and remained in that capacity until 1860, when the paper was sold to Mahoney & Co. Mr. McNutt had been a democrat in politics and a friend and supporter of Stephen A. Douglas, but when the southern states began to secede and the war was threatening, he came out strongly in favor of the constitution and the administration of Abraham Lincoln, and supported it by every means. The *Herald* being opposed to the administration, Mr. McNutt, at the request of democratic friends, started the *Daily Evening Union*, to counteract the influence of the *Herald.* Publication of this paper was discontinued in about a year with a heavy financial loss, and Mr. McNutt became one of the editors of the *Dubuque Times.* In the fall of 1862, intending to go into the army, he removed his family to his farm in Muscatine county, where he has since resided. In 1863, while recruiting for the Eighth Iowa cavalry, he was nominated and elected by the republicans of Muscatine county for representative to the Tenth General Assembly, and was afterwards twice re-elected. At the close of his third term in the house he was elected without opposition to the senate. He had a good record in the legislature, and was one of the pioneers in the introduction of bills for the control of railroad corporations. It was he who secured passage through the house of the Gue bill, to drive out of Iowa the "wild cat" currency then in circulation. He was the chairman of the committee which investigated the Fort Madison penitentiary in 1872, and wrote the report which prevented the state from paying a bogus claim of prison labor contractors for $47,000, and recommended a new penitentiary where rock could be quarried. This resulted in the location and erection of the new penitentiary at Anamosa. In 1872 he was a candidate for the republican nomination for state treasurer, and had a large following. He was prominent in the Grange movement, and is author of the monster petition signed by 70,000 Iowa farmers, asking for legislation to regulate railroad charges. President Harrison appointed Mr. McNutt, on August 13, 1890, to be United States Consul at Maracaybo, Venezuela, but a brief residence in that climate convinced him that it was not suitable to him and he resigned and returned to Iowa. He was city judge in 1894 and 1895. For twenty years he was an officer of the Muscatine County Agricultural society, and is a member of the Scotch-Irish Society of America. He belongs to the Presbyterian church but entertains very liberal views of religion and humanity. He joined the Washingtonians when a boy; in 1851, the Odd Fellows; in 1861, the Union League, and in 1872, the Patrons of Husbandry.

Mr. McNutt was married April 14, 1857, to Miss Anna E. Lucas, of Portsmouth, Ohio, niece of Robert Lucas, ex-governor of Ohio. In August, 1889, while his wife was on a visit to their son William, in Nebraska, she was taken sick and died there. Their living children are: William L., a farmer in Ord, Neb.; Robert S., a practicing dentist in Muscatine, and Samuel B., a practicing dentist in Des Moines.

WOOD, IRVING CHARLES, physician of Logan, is a gentleman of high attainments in his profession, earned by a life of energetic study and close application. His stability and energy is primarily an inheritance from Welsh-Irish and English stock, which, supplemented by a natural ability of his own, has placed him in the front rank of his profession. His father, Rufus S. Wood, a retired farmer in moderate circumstances, is, on his father's side, of Irish descent, and on his mother's, of Welsh— some of her ancestors coming to Boston in 1692. Rufus S. Wood's grandfather was a graduate of Yale and served as a surgeon in the war of the revolution. Doctor Wood's ancestors on his mother's side were of English descent. His mother's maiden

name was Susan M. Mann. Doctor Wood was born in Franklin, N. Y., March 9, 1857. He attended the high school until he was 13 years of age, and then entered the Delaware Literary institute, where his progress was so rapid that at the age of 14 he was able to pass the regent's examination, which admitted him to any college in the state. He graduated in civil engineering from the above named institution in 1875. Following his graduation he taught three terms of school and then began the study of medicine. He first entered the medical department of the University of the

City of New York, and afterwards became a student in the Jefferson Medical college in Philadelphia, from which he received the degree of M. D., in 1880. He was secretary of the graduating class. He remained in Philadelphia one year after his graduation, adding to his store of medical knowledge and further fitting himself for his work by taking special courses in gynecology, ophthalmology and operative surgery. He was also assistant surgeon in the medical and surgical department of the Pennsylvania hospital.

In the spring of 1881 he sought a new field for practice and chose the west, coming to Woodbine, Iowa, arriving with a cash capital of $36. He spent two years at this place, and then removed in 1888 to Logan, where he still resides. He has a large practice and occupies many positions of trust. In 1884 he was chosen one of the commissioners of insanity, a place which he still holds. He is and has been since 1886, company surgeon for the Chicago & North-Western railway, and is medical examiner for over thirty life insurance companies.

Doctor Wood has applied himself closely to the practice of his profession, and has built up one of the largest practices of western Iowa. In connection with his practice he also owns one-half interest in the largest drug store in Logan. He is a firm believer in the value of real estate as a safe and remunerative investment, and owns several well improved farms, these being purchased with the proceeds received from his practice. His residence in Logan is one of the most modern and well appointed in Harrison county.

Doctor Wood is the present mayor of Logan, being elected to that office in 1897 and 1898 on the citizens' ticket, and received two-thirds of all the votes cast. He is a member of the Iowa State Medical society, Iowa Association of Railway surgeons and Pan-American congress. He belongs to the Knights of Pythias, Modern Woodmen of America, Knights Templar and is a noble of the Mystic Shrine. In religious belief he is liberal in his views, and is not a member of any church organization. Doctor Wood was married May 12, 1886, to Miss Florence Bolter, only daughter of Senator L. R. Bolter, a sketch of whose life appears elsewhere in this work. They have no children.

---

WOODWARD, JOHN C. AND WINFIELD W., the well-known architects, of Council Bluffs, were born February 16, 1864, and September 8, 1866, respectively, at Mt. Vernon, Knox county, Ohio. Both have shown remarkable ability in their profession, and are among the youngest men of prominence in their profession in the United States. They evinced a phenomenal aptitude for drawing early in life, John C. having been awarded first prize for the best freehand sketch from nature, offered by the *Youth's Companion*, which competition was open to the world. As their whole attention has been given to the development of those talents, it is only natural that they should have achieved

success. Thrown upon their own resources early in life, they succeeded in securing positions in the leading architects' offices, where they studied the profession in all its branches. While John C. excels in the use of the pencil, the other brother is the better business man, so that in partnership they easily succeed. At the time the government architect's office in Omaha was discontinued, the senior member of this firm was thrown out of employment, and it also happened that the younger brother was not engaged at that time, so they submitted plans and estimates for the erection of a schoolhouse in Council Bluffs. To be competent to do the work is one thing, but to secure the contract is another matter entirely, and as the Woodward boys had no office at that time, and were youthful in appearance, it looked as though the older and well-established firms in that line of business stood a much better show of getting the contract. They pressed their claim with such force and in such a pleasing business way, however, that the board decided to let the job to them, and adopted their plans, a decision it has never

*John C. Woodward.*

had to regret. This contract completed, they decided to open an office in Council Bluffs, and though strongly opposed by resident architects they have built up a remarkable business, and scores of private residences and public buildings stand throughout this state, and other states, to witness their skill in modern architecture.

*Winfield Woodward.*

They came from old revolutionary stock. Their grandfather, Mr. Asa Woodward, was born at Rutland, Vt., and enlisted in the revolutionary war at Burlington, Vt., at the age of 17 years, serving all through the war, and drew a pension from the United States government to the time of his death, August 30, 1837, at Homer, Licking county, Ohio. The mother, Mrs. Caroline Woodward, was born at Newark, N. J., August 26, 1834, her maiden name being Scribner and her mother's maiden name being Jelliff. Her forefather owned the land where the city of Baltimore is now built, and the family were distant relatives of General Sturgis.

During the revolutionary war General Washington used to visit them, holding councils of war at their house. The late Hon. Judge Charles H. Scribner, district judge and law partner of the late ex-congressman, Hon. Frank Hurd, of Toledo, Ohio, is an uncle of J. C. and W. Woodward. Their father, Maj. Fayette Woodward, was born at Homer, Licking county, Ohio, April 20, 1827; crossed the plains to California in 1849, walking nearly all the

18

way there, and kept a diary of his trip, which writing is very distinct now. Returning to Ohio from California, he married Miss Caroline Scribner. Had five children, four boys and one girl. Two boys died; the rest living. The first born, Lucius Gillman Woodward, born at Homer, Licking county, December 1, 1852, died March 26, 1854.

Ella Dale Woodward, born at Appleton, Licking county, Ohio, June 17, 1855; Everett Scribner Woodward, born at Appleton, Licking county, Ohio, November 26, 1857, died at Essex, Page county, Iowa, March 2, 1880.

Maj. Fayette Woodward was a prominent druggist at Mt. Vernon, Ohio, removed thence to Westerville, Ohio, engaged in the same business there, thence to Essex, Page county, Iowa, November 10, 1879. Coming west, he engaged in farming, hoping to restore to health his son, Everett Scribner Woodward, who was an artist and druggist of ability. J. C. and W. Woodward locating at Council Bluffs, Iowa, and the daughter, Mrs. S. A. Callins, in Omaha, induced him to remove from Essex, Iowa, to Council Bluffs.

---

HAMMOND, HIRAM, of Le Grand, Marshall county, has lived in Iowa forty-five years, during most of which time he has been engaged in the milling business. He was born near Smithfield, Jefferson county, Ohio, February 20, 1832, and came to Iowa in the spring of 1854. His father, Benjamin Hammond, was a farmer, and so were his ancestors. His mother was Margaret Naylor Hammond. They were plain people, content with the good living which the Ohio farm afforded them, and they remained upon it from 1808 until 1864. Benjamin Hammond never held an office or sought prominence in any way. Hiram had the experience common to the farmer boys of that time, working on the farm during the summer and attending the district school in the winter time. For eleven months, during the years 1851 and 1852, he attended a seminary in Mt. Pleasant, Ohio, where he acquired the rudiments of higher mathematics—philosophy, chemistry, etc. He taught two terms of district school in Ohio and one in Iowa. Arriving in Marshall county in the spring of 1854 with but little means, he managed to get hold of a piece of land, breaking plow and five yoke of cattle. He entered at once upon the work of subduing the virgin soil of his adopted state, and his success has been continuous from that time, though his business training was altogether that of the practical man looking after his own affairs. He had no apprenticeship. In 1863 he sold the farm and bought a half interest in the Le Grand flour mills, where he has continued to manufacture a high grade of the "staff of life" for a large trade. Mr. Hammond's partner for two years was Isocher Scholfield, who sold his interest to his brother, Thomas Scholfield, and he afterwards sold his interest to W. G. Benedict. At this time extensive repairs were made on the mill; two farms contiguous thereto were purchased, and cattle and hogs raised and fed

on a large scale, with good results. An unfortunate investment in Montana mining property resulted disastrously to the firm, and the land was sold to pay up the losses. In 1887 Mr. Hammond purchased Mr. Benedict's interest and sold it to his son, L. A. Hammond, and the father and son are now carrying on the business.

Although he has held no office higher than that of county supervisor, Mr. Hammond began to vote the republican ticket when John C. Fremont was the nominee for president in 1856, and has steadfastly clung to the republican party since that time. He served on the school board when the present comfortable, graded school

building was erected in Le Grand. He is a stockholder in the Friends' Academy Building association, and has been one of the board of managers of this school, which was established in 1872, up to the present time. He is a stockholder in Penn college, in Oskaloosa, and was for some eight or ten years a director. He gave all of his children a full course in the academy, and three of them graduated from Penn college. He belongs to the Friends' church and lives up to the teachings of that sturdy faith. Mr. Hammond was married in 1856 to Anna Foglesong, of Ohio. Two sons and four daughters came to this union, all of whom are living; five of them married, with families. The elder son, Lewis A., born July 16, 1859, is associated with his father in business. The younger son, Charles L., born March 31, 1867, is pastor of the Congregational church in Gilman, Iowa. The oldest daughter, Margaret, born August 24, 1857, married H. H. Salisbury, a machinist, and is pleasantly located in Pasadena, Cal.; the second daughter, M. Elizabeth, born April 23, 1861, married the Rev. R. H. Hartley, pastor of the Presbyterian church in La Porte, Ind.; the third daughter, Adaline, born February 12, 1863, married S. M. Hadley, professor of mathematics in Penn college, in Oskaloosa; the youngest daughter, Nettie, born June 5, 1865, is unmarried and lives at home with her parents.

LINCOLN, GEORGE ALLEN, for three terms mayor of Cedar Rapids, is a familiar figure in republican state conventions and has occupied a prominent position in the councils of the republican party in Iowa for many years   He was born in Chicopee, Mass., January 31, 1848, and was the son of George D. and Mary E. Lincoln. With his parents he went to Madison, Wis., in 1858, and when the war broke out he enlisted in the Third Wisconsin light artillery, December 22, 1863, and served as a private in the army of the Tennessee until discharged July 3, 1865. Soon after the close of the war he came to Cedar Rapids, March 25, 1867, and engaged in the clothing business which he followed until 1878, and retired with a competency to go into the real estate business. He organized the first volunteer fire department in 1869 and was chief engineer from 1870 to 1876. He has always been identified with the State Firemen's association and was president in 1892 and 1893. His connection with the city government of Cedar Rapids began in 1874, when he was elected alderman of the Third ward. In 1878 he was recorder and assessor of the city. He was elected mayor in

March, 1895, and was twice re-elected, serving until March, 1898. Mr. Lincoln was always elected as a republican and has been actively identified with all the movements of the party in Iowa since 1867. During all that time he has hardly ever missed being a delegate to the county and state conventions every year. He served as a member of the republican state central committee from the Fifth district during the years 1890 and 1891. In 1891 he was appointed postmaster of Cedar Rapids, and served four years, and at the present time he is chairman of the republican county central committee of Linn county. Although a strong anti-prohibitionist, he did not leave the party during the prohibitionist fight, believing that the time would come when the party would not make that a test of party fealty and would remove the issue from politics. Mr. Lincoln has had a great part in the development of the enterprising and rapidly growing city of Cedar Rapids. He has been identified with all its improvements and has contributed liberally to promote public enterprises. During his administration as mayor, large public improvements were made, including

paving, sewering, the new union passenger station, and the Chicago, Milwaukee & St. Paul station. It is largely on account of his influence and activity that the republican state convention was twice located in Cedar Rapids. Mr. Lincoln was married in Cedar Rapids, February 17, 1869, to Fannie Atwell, and they have one daughter, Bertha, born February 10, 1875.

Of Mr. Lincoln it can be said without the least exaggeration that he is one of the most popular men in the state. He has friends and intimate acquaintances in every county, so that when he goes to a state convention he can always find friends and acquaintances glad to oblige him, and he is in his turn very eager to serve a friend.

MOORHEAD, DR. JAMES, is a native of the state of Ohio. He is the son of Joseph Moorhead, who was born in Holmes county, Ohio, January 15, 1828, and was married to Miss Clara A. Heller, of Chemung county, N. Y., March 1, 1849. She was the daughter of Moses and Hannah Baker Heller. In 1855 Joseph Moorhead came with his family to Linn county, where he purchased

a farm and settled on it, living a few years in a log house. He worked on the farm in the summer and taught public school in the winter for several years. He was an influential citizen, serving in various township and county offices. He served six years as trustee of the state reform school at Eldora. In 1881 he moved to Marion, having been elected county auditor, serving in that position six years. James was born near Millersburg, Ohio, April 1, 1850. On the paternal side his ancestors were from Scotland, and from Germany on the maternal side. His father and mother both having been school-teachers, his early instruction was carefully directed. He first went to school to his father, who taught in a rough, log schoolhouse two miles from their home. His boyhood, when not in school, was spent upon the farm, assisting his father in the various kinds of labor required of a farmer's son in those early days. When 18 years of age James taught school in the district where he had obtained his education, and continued teaching each winter for eight years. He was a student at Cornell college for three years. In 1876 he entered into partnership with Dr. Terry, at Ely, in the drug business. He was postmaster at Ely for ten years. He took a two-years' course in pharmacy and graduated from the National Institute of Pharmacy at Chicago in 1887. He moved to Cedar Rapids and opened a first-class drug store, having a large prescription business. During all the years he was employed in the drug business, Mr. Moorhead had been a studious reader of medical books and publications, and finally decided to take a medical course of instruction, and entered the State university. There he attended medical lectures, and graduated from the homeopathic department in 1893, beginning practice at Cedar Rapids, associated with Dr. W. A. Hubbard. He afterwards took a post graduate course in the Chicago Homeopathic college in 1895. In 1893 he bought the office and practice of Dr. G. S. Muirhead, at Marion, and entered upon the practice of medicine there. He has established an extensive business, and, by his skill and knowledge, won the confidence of the community. He is local surgeon of the Chicago, Milwaukee & St. Paul Railway company, and also of the Bankers' Accident Insurance company. In 1894 he entered into partnership with Dr. Muirhead, who had returned to Marion. In politics Dr. Moorhead has always been an active republican; has held many township and school offices, and often served as delegate to republican state conventions. He is a member of the following

secret societies: Knights of Pythias, Royal Arch Masons, Ancient Order of United Workmen, Improved Red Men, and other lodges. He is captain of Marion Company No. 23, U. R., K. of P.; past chancellor of Mariola Lodge No. 8, K. of P.; high priest of Marion Chapter No. 10, R. A. M.; pas patron of Marion Chapter No. 188, O. E. S.; past great sachem of Iowa, I. O. R. M. He is a member of the American Institute of Homeopathy, the Hahnemann Medical Society of Iowa, and of the Central Iowa Medical association. He is medical examiner of the Knights of Honor, A. O. U. W., and Pacific Mutual Life Insurance company, and others. He has always been an active worker and member of the Methodist Episcopal church and its auxiliaries. On December 24, 1871, he was united in marriage with Miss Eliza J. Stream, youngest daughter of Elias and Mary A. Waters Stream, who were natives of Virginia. Eliza was born in Licking county, Ohio, October 14, 1851. She came to Iowa with her parents, who settled in Linn county, in 1855. Three children have been born to them—two boys, who died in infancy, and Clara A., born October 31, 1874. She graduated from the Cedar Rapids high school in 1893 and from Cornell college in 1897, receiving the degree of B. A.

---

McKEEVER, A. J., of Sheldon, O'Brien county, is a product of Ireland, the little green isle that has furnished so large a quota of the men who have been foremost in preserving and developing this great land of the free. His parents, Michael and Rose (O'Kane) McKeever, were farmers, and despite the despicable system of landlordism prevailing in Ireland, were in moderate financial circumstances when they came to the United States in 1860. The youth of Mr. A. J. McKeever was spent on a farm in Dubuque county, where his parents resided until 1884, when he removed to O'Brien county. In 1888 he engaged in the grocery business at Sheldon, in partnership with Mr. Theodore Geiger, and after one year's prosperous business Mr. McKeever bought out the interest of his partner and continued the business alone. In his youth he learned well the lessons of prudence, frugality and industry, so valuable to men everywhere in business, and these qualities enabled him to increase his stock and extend his business until now he owns and occupies the handsomest business block in that city. He is the embodiment of a first-class business man; strictly honorable in his dealings, courteous to all, and genial and companionable to a

high degree. He makes a friend of everyone with whom he comes in contact. Coming direct to Iowa from Ireland in 1860, he begun with pioneer life, and has lived to see the wild prairie upon which he first came for a home transformed into a grand agricultural paradise, all settled up with good citizens and industrious farmers, and has accumulated for himself a goodly portion of this world's wealth to make himself comfortable in old age. Religiously, like the greater share of his nationality, he is a Catholic, and is faithful in his labors for, and self sacrificing in his devotion to, his church. In politics he is a democrat, but one of that kind who has the greatest consideration for the views of those opposed to him.

NICOL, DR. JOHN HARVEY, practicing physician of Villisca, came to Iowa with his parents when but a child, and located in Morning Sun about 1853. His father, Josiah Nicol, was a farmer and stock raiser and buyer on a large scale. He carried on a large stock business in Louisa county for more than twenty years, but in 1873 suffered severe losses in shipping stock, and since then has been an active commission merchant in the stock yards at Kansas City. His mother, whose maiden name was Margaret Wilson, daughter of John Wilson, who served his country in the war of 1812, was born in Ireland, and died in Morning Sun in 1878, at the age of 96. Both of Dr. Nicol's parents were born and reared in Ohio and were married there, and moved from Preble county, Ohio, to Louisa county, Iowa, where they brought up a family of eight children, one daughter and seven sons. John H. Nicol was born in Preble county, Ohio, April 3, 1849. He attended school on the opening day when the first schoolhouse in his district in Louisa county was ready for use. The only furniture in the room consisted of two slab benches. In 1873 he completed the course in the academy at Grand View, Iowa, ranking at the top in a class of sixteen. He represented his literary society with honor and success in two annual contests. Having a desire to study medicine, he began to teach school as soon as he had completed his academic course, and whenever he was not otherwise employed he

put in his time studying medicine in the office of Dr. J. W. Holliday, now of Burlington. His father's failure at this time threw him upon his own resources, but by industry and economy he still continued the study of his profession, and with the assistance of some good friends he attended his first course of lectures at the Keokuk Medical college, in the winter of 1874 and 1875. Dr. Holliday and W. M. Braniger, both now prominent citizens of Burlington, are gratefully remembered by the doctor for the confidence they placed in him by extending a helping hand at this time. He began practicing at Lacona, in April, 1875, and remained there until August, 1877, returning to Keokuk from time to time, and graduating in February, 1878, when he resumed his practice in Lacona. He soon gained an extensive practice and was the leading physician in that locality. He is a member of the district, state and American medical societies, and keeps up with the latest discoveries in his profession. In 1892 Dr. Nicol moved to Indianola, and a year later to Villisca, where he has earned a position as one of the most progressive medical men in southwestern Iowa, and is a member of the Southwestern Iowa Medical society, and the Missouri Valley Medical society.

Casting his first vote for General Grant for president, Dr. Nicol has always voted the straight republican ticket, and has taken an active part in its local and state conventions. He belongs to the A. O. U. W., and K. of P., and is a member of the board of education of Villisca.

Dr. Nicol was married February 21, 1878, to Miss Anna E. Lytle, of Ligonier, Penn. They have no children. He is a member of the M. E. church, and has always been active in the Sunday school, and has taken an interest in the musical affairs of the church.

---

PATRICK, JAMES PERKINS, a veteran of the late war, is one of the leading wholesale merchants of Des Moines. He is of Irish descent, his ancestors having come from County Tyrone in Ireland during the seventeenth century, settling at Quinton, N. J. His great-grandfather, Samuel Patrick, with his brother, Abner, served as privates in the revolution under Capt. William Smith, of Salem. Samuel was wounded in an action occurring at Quinton Bridge, March 18, 1778, and both were taken prisoner and lay for two years on board a British prison ship in New York harbor. Mr. Patrick's father, Samuel Patrick, a farmer, was born near Youngstown, Ohio, in 1809, his parents having

moved there from New Jersey the previous year. Here he grew to manhood, and was married in 1833 to Amanda Brown, whose parents were southerners, but who believed slavery to be wrong. Her father, in 1821, disposed of his property in New Orleans, and came with his family to Cincinnati, where he freed all his slaves, and then settled in Bellefontaine, Ohio, where he remained until his death in 1838. He served in the war of 1812. Mr. Patrick's father died in 1878 in Cass county, Mich.

J. P. Patrick was born at Bellefontaine, Ohio, October 27, 1836. He was brought up on a farm and secured his early educa-

tion at the district school. In 1846, when he was 10 years old, he moved with his parents to Cass county, Mich. He came to Iowa in 1857, soon after attaining his majority, and settled in Fayette county, where he put in many hours of hard work to secure funds for acquiring a higher education. In 1860 he entered Upper Iowa university, but left school after a year to join the army, enlisting in Company F of the Third Iowa infantry. He served as a private until 1862, when he was promoted to the rank of sergeant. He was with his company during all its marches and engagements from 1861 to 1863, including the battle of Shiloh. He received a severe wound in the hip from a canister while on board the steamer "Crescent City," in the vicinity of Vicksburg. He was taken to the hospital at Memphis, Tenn., and upon his recovery several months later was commissioned lieutenant of Battery F, Second United States Colored Light artillery, in which position he served until the close of the war, participating in many skirmishes and engagements in western Tennessee and northern Mississippi, the principal battle being at Guntown, Miss.

Upon his return from the war in 1866, Lieutenant Patrick began business as a general merchant at West Union, but after three years sold out and moved to McGregor, where he assisted in organizing a wholesale and retail hardware establishment, under the firm name of Drake, Dayton & Patrick. He did a good business here for twenty-three years, and in 1892 removed to Des Moines, and in partnership with Henry Luthe, established the wholesale hardware house of Patrick & Luthe Co., with which he is still connected, doing a large business with firms all over the state.

Mr. Patrick has always voted the straight republican ticket, but has not been an officeholder, further than serving as mayor of McGregor and as a member of the city council of Des Moines. He is not a member of any church, but his family attend the Congregational.

He was married March 8, 1870, to Miss Louisa M. St. John. Their family now consists of two children, Elizabeth B., born in 1874, and Charles C., born in 1879. Mr. Patrick takes just pride in the fact that in his thirty-two years of business experience in Iowa he has always paid 100 cents on the dollar, and has never been sued for debt.

---

ANSON, HENRY. At Marshalltown, where he is revered and respected, resides Mr. Henry Anson, founder of Marshalltown, and who, though now at an advanced age, is one of its most active and influential citizens. He was born in Ontario county, N. Y., April 19, 1826. His parents removed to Erie county, Ohio, in 1833, and it was there, in 1846, he married Miss Janet Rice, sister of Hon. Wells S. Rice. In 1851 Mr. Anson started for the west, in true pioneer style, arriving in Bureau, Ill., in May of that year. It was there he left his family behind and came over into Iowa on horseback in search of a location, and finally chose Marshall county because of

its central location within the state. It was his belief at that time that the capitol of the state would some day be located within the border lines of that county. On his way he passed the fort being erected by the few early settlers, who were then in a panic because of a threatened outbreak of the Sioux Indians, and when he had reached a divide, which was bounded on the north by the Iowa river and on the south and east by Linn creek, he became enraptured with the scene presented, and concluded to make his future home there. The pre-emption cabin which he then erected was located a little west of what is

now the corner of First and Main streets, of Marshalltown. He at once took steps for the survey of a town site, which he will be pardoned for believing would ultimately be the future capital of Iowa. The first persons to arrive at the new Eldorado were Mr. Anson's mother and two sisters and Horace Anson, a brother. These people erected the second house in the new city. In 1853 settlers began to arrive in great numbers, but lumber was hard to get, and to overcome that difficulty Mr. Anson had a sawmill brought out from Ohio, and the same proved of incalculable benefit to the newcomers. In 1851 commissioners were appointed to locate the county seat of Marshall county, and then began a fight which lasted many years and was only won through the energy and generous contributions of money of Mr. Anson. His many shrewd moves to defeat injunctions by the court during that time would fill a volume. At the present time he is at the head of an immense brick factory, building and real estate business, and has associated with him in business his son Sturgis. Adrian C. Anson, the famous baseball player, is the only other living child. Mrs. Anson, the wife of our subject, died more than thirty years ago.

Mr. Anson always claims that if the same amount of effort and expense dispensed in the county seat fight, which lasted seven years, could have been applied to securing the location of the capital of the state at that time, it could have easily been done. His own contributions in that line were enormous, embracing nearly one-half mile square of the choicest of the city property, including the old court house site, together with a large part of the material for the building. The present court house block was later also contributed to the county by Mr. Anson, he requiring the erection of a building worth not less than $100,000.

In the spring of 1856 there was consumed by fire two immense lumbering mills he had constructed for making lumber, lath and shingles from native timber, that being the only material for building purposes before the advent of railways. Insurance in those days in the west was unknown, and accordingly the loss was entire, and growth of the city delayed until new mills could be erected. The flouring mills of the city at the river were secured by Mr. Anson donating the site, together with forty acres of land and $500 in cash for the improvements, to G. M. Woodbury. Add to this the grounds donated for railroad depots and other expenses of securing the roads, together with attorney's fees and other expenses of seven years' county seat war, and the modern "tenderfoot" may form some idea of the efforts necessary in founding and starting the city of Marshalltown. Mr. Anson has built an enduring monument for his name in the affections of the people of his chosen home.

CRAPO, PHILIP M., a prominent, wealthy, and philanthropic citizen of Burlington, was born in Freetown, near New Bedford, Mass., June 30, 1844. He traces his ancestry through more than two centuries.

The founder of the family in America was Mr. Pierre, or Peter, Crapo. About 1675, when a mere lad, he was cast ashore with his brother upon the New England coast by the wrecking of a French vessel, of which his brother was commander. The elder brother returned to France. Peter remained with the Massachusetts colonists, and when he arrived at manhood married a granddaughter of Peregrine White. His wife's grandfather enjoyed the distinction of being the first white child born in the Plymouth colony. Philip M. Crapo's father, Philip, was born October 12, 1798, and was married in 1823 to Hannah Crapo. Their son enjoyed the benefits of an excellent school system and was prepared for college. His college plans were interrupted by his enlistment as a private soldier in the Third Massachusetts infantry. He served in the eastern department with headquarters at Newberne, N. C. After the war Mr. Crapo went to Michigan, where he engaged as a civil engineer in the construction of what is now the Flint and Pere Marquette railroad. He afterwards engaged in the state offices at Detroit in the preparation of the military history of Michigan. While a resident of Detroit Mr. Crapo occupied a prominent social position, being a member of many social, literary, and military organizations. In April, 1868, he came to Iowa and took charge of the business of the Connecticut Mutual Life Insurance company in the southern half of the state. Subsequently his territory was enlarged and he was made the general agent for the company for Iowa and

Nebraska, to which he devoted his attention for thirteen years. In 1882 he was appointed financial correspondent of the company, which position he has filled continuously since that date. He has served the company successfully and satisfactorily for more than thirty-one years.

While Mr. Crapo has always been an active republican, he has never been an office seeker. He was chairman of the republican congressional committee in his district in the campaigns of 1886 and 1888, and in 1885 was county chairman for Des Moines county. He accepted the nomination for state senator in that year, and, though he ran very much ahead of his party ticket, he could not overcome the democratic majority in the county. In 1889 his friends supported him loyally in the republican state convention for the nomination for governor.

Mr. Crapo has devoted much of his time and has been a liberal contributor to the advancement of public interests. He has been energetic in his endeavors to bring railroad competition to Burlington. In 1887 he organized a company and secured a charter from congress to build a combination bridge across the Mississippi at Burlington, but after completing arrangements for its use, and after the taxpayers had expressed their willingness to vote a large tax to aid the project, a majority of the members of the bridge company declined to assume the responsibility and the bridge has never been built. Mr. Crapo was chiefly influential in securing the establishment of the Soldiers' home, located at Marshalltown, and delivered the address on behalf of the old soldiers at its dedication. He has been active in securing appropriations for the home ever since it was established. With the same energy and devotion he worked for the appropriation for the building of the soldiers' monument in Des Moines, and the passage of the bill was much due to his efforts. When the Burlington Subscription library, a stock company, proposed to donate its valuable collection of books to the city, Mr. Crapo guaranteed the debt so the city council could accept the gift. Heading the list with a generous subscription, he speedily collected the balance, paid the debt, and Burlington's free public library was established. He has continued to take a deep interest in the library and is one of its trustees. As a member of the purchasing committee he has selected nearly all the books that have been purchased for the last fourteen years, something more than 12,000 in number. He has recently made it possible for the city to erect the new public library building by contributing about one-half of the cost thereof. As chairman of the building committee he had almost exclusive charge of the erection of the beautiful and commodious library building, which has no equal in Iowa. During his long and active business career in Burlington, Mr. Crapo has filled many positions of trust, in all of which he has been a zealous and faithful worker, serving without compensation for any services rendered the public. He has been president of the Burlington & Illinois Bridge company, president of the Burlington Board of Trade, president of the Commercial club of Burlington, president of the Burlington & Henderson County Ferry company, trustee of the city for the ferry franchise, trustee of the public library, trustee of the Congregational church, and park commissioner. His name was given to the national guard camp at Burlington in 1888, and it has been adopted as the camp name for the local organization of the Sons of Veterans. Mr. Crapo took an active part in starting the movement for paving the principal streets of Burlington with brick, and his efforts in behalf of the improvement of the Mississippi river were acknowledged by his appointment on the committee to prepare a memorial to congress by not less than five of the great conventions called to consider the question of the improvement of waterways. He was chiefly instrumental in securing a public park for the city

of Burlington. In consideration of his services the city council complimented him by naming the new pleasure ground "Crapo Park."

Another important service which Mr. Crapo rendered to his city and state was the contribution of service and money which he made to the semi-centennial celebration of the admission of Iowa as a state, which was held in Burlington in 1896. Mr. Crapo was president of the board of commissioners appointed by Governor Drake and was actively in charge.

In fact this successful business man has been prominent in all matters affecting the growth and prosperity of city and state, and especially in everything calculated to promote education and contribute to the health and happiness of the people. He was married September 6, 1870, to Ruth A. Ray. They have had seven children: Edith Ray, born August 13, 1871; Philip Ashley, born July 17, 1873; Chester Frederick, born July 25, 1876; Clifford Maxwell, born September 6, 1878; Ruth Kelsall, born September 2, 1880; Lucy Howland, born April 7, 1883, and William Mitchell, born July 24, 1886. The oldest son, Philip Ashley, was a graduate of Phillips Exeter academy and the Harvard Law school. He had recently begun the practice of law in New York city when the Spanish-American war began. He left his business and came to Iowa to enlist in Company F, Fiftieth Iowa infantry. He died in the service, of typhoid fever, at Jacksonville, Fla., September, 1898.

---

BRECKENRIDGE, ALLENDER INSIGN, well known in the business circles of Waterloo, is the son of Josiah Carey Breckenridge, who was a shareholder, director and superintendent of the Meriden Cutlery works, of Meriden, Conn. That immense plant owed its success to the wisdom and energy of Mr. Breckenridge. He was a man of attractive manners, genial, generous and beloved by all his employes Shortly after completing a handsome residence in Meriden his life was suddenly cut short by an affection of the heart. The maiden name of the mother, who now resides with her youngest son in Meriden, was Frances Augusta Bradley. She is a woman of scholarly attainments and great literary ability, and now, at the age of 70, frequently contributes articles to journals and magazines. A tradition concerning the derivation of the name Breckenridge, from the Scotch bracken or common brake, which grows abundantly on the ridge where the family was first known, has been handed down from generation to generation. The name has been changed, however, by the substitution of the letter "e" for that of "a" in the first syllable. The earliest member of the family of whom we have any knowledge is Jacobus Brackenridge, who came to this country and settled on the Ellon tract, in the forks of the Chicopee river, now Palmer, Mass. There he reared a large family in comfort and respectability. He was a good man, abhorring deceit, and through his teachings and example his children grew up to be religious, honorable men and women. The descendants from this family are many, embracing six generations, now scattered throughout the United States. They are

proud of the family name, and the love of kin is one of their most marked characteristics. As a whole they are independent, intelligent, moral and modest. No prominent political positions have been held by them, but

"They do the greatest good who live hidden lives,"

and to that class it appears to be their desire to belong. Someone has said, "There is scarcely a college in the United States that has not educated a Breckenridge," a record of which they are most proud.

A. I. Breckenridge was born at Meriden, Conn., August 12, 1845. He attended the public schools until 18 years of age, then spent two years in the Episcopal academy,

at Cheshire, Conn. This was followed by a course in Trinity college, at Hartford, Conn., after which the young man started out in the world for himself, first taking a position in New York city, in the store and sample rooms of the Meriden Cutlery company; coming to Iowa in 1873 he located at Waterloo and engaged in the coal business, in partnership with George Bancroft. Later he formed a co-partnership with A. J. White, and opened an insurance office. In 1877 he entered the employ of the Illinois Central as timekeeper, but his health failed and he was compelled to go south. After a time he returned to Waterloo and re-engaged in the insurance business in partnership with J. K. Sweeny. In 1894 Mr. Sweeny sold his interest to G. C. Kennedy, since which time the firm of Breckenridge & Kennedy has enjoyed a constantly increasing business. In 1892 Mr. Breckenridge was elected secretary of the Perpetual Building and Loan association, the duties of which he has accurately and faithfully discharged, and to which he now gives his entire time. He is a member of the Columbia club, a social organization of considerable note. Himself and his two oldest sons are members of Ascalon Commandery No. 25, Knights Templar. They enjoy the peculiar distinction of having taken the Royal Arch Mason and Commandery degrees together, there being but one other instance in the history of the United States where father and two sons formed a team for chapter degrees, and, so far as known, no other where they took the Commandery degrees together. His name is among the signers of the original articles of incorporation of Christ Church parish. He was elected secretary of the vestry soon after, which office he still holds, and is lay reader in the church and superintendent of the Sunday school.

August 23, 1871, he was married to Mary Wheelock, the adopted daughter of Walter and Sarah Wheelock, of Brooklyn, N. Y. They have seven children living, Allender Robert, Walter Wheelock, Marietta Sarah, Frances Augusta, William Carey, Frederick Keyes and Harriet Mildred, having lost one daughter, Florence Evelyn, who died in 1887.

BENNETT, HENRY, a well known insurance inspector and rate maker of Cedar Rapids, has been in business in Iowa for about thirty years. He came to the state with his parents in 1855. They settled in

Iowa City, remaining there about two years, when they moved to Cedar Rapids, which has since been Mr. Bennett's home, with the exception of a temporary absence of two years. He is the son of Henry Bennett and Angeline Fife Bennett, and was born in Pittsburg, Pa., October 29, 1850. His father, who came to America when a small boy, was born in York, Eng., in 1827. He followed the merchant tailoring business for more than fifty years, having only recently retired. Mrs. Bennett was, as her name indicates, of Scotch-Irish descent and was born near Pittsburg, Pa., in 1830. Their son attended the pub-

lic schools in Iowa City and afterward graduated from the Cedar Rapids high school in 1867. He began his business career as an office boy in the law office of Greene & Belt. Judge George Greene was the judge of the state supreme court and compiled Greene's Iowa reports. During the war, although young Bennett was not old enough to join the army, he worked on a farm during the summers of 1862-3-4-5. Early in the year 1868 he entered the law and insurance office of West & Eastman, where he studied law and looked after the details of fire insurance and afterward became a member of the firm. The insurance business increased so as to require all his time and attention and he

never began the practice of law or applied for admission to the bar. Soon after, he acquired the insurance business of the firm and conducted it until 1881, when he formed a partnership with A. R. West, continuing in law and insurance for two years, when he sold to his partner and his son, and accepted the position of compact manager, fixing rates and supervising business for nearly all the fire insurance companies transacting business in Iowa. He resigned this position January 1, 1895, and accepted the state agency of the Fire Association of Pennsylvania, which he resigned in June, 1896, to establish an independent rating, fire map and inspection bureau. The legislature had passed a law prohibiting any combination of insurance companies in regard to rates. It became necessary to have some standard to follow and some inspection of business, so Mr. Bennett, enjoying the confidence of the insurance managers of the state in a high degree, established this independent bureau which has no connection with any board, compact or alliance, and is in no sense a combination. Through its agency all risks taken in the state are inspected, advisory tariffs of equitable, uniform and discriminating rates are published and information is furnished to subscribers relating to hazards, faults of management and condition of risks, at a low rate of expense. The system has worked satisfactorily and has accomplished its desired purpose. There are but four similar bureaus in the United States.

Mr. Bennett has affiliated with the democratic party since 1872, but has never held any office. He was junior deacon, secretary and junior warden of Crescent Lodge No. 25, A. F. and A. M., for a number of years, and was high priest of Trowel Chapter No. 49, R. A. M., and was a member of Apollo Commandery No. 26; he was first lieutenant commander of the Grand Consistory Iowa, under the jurisdiction of the Supreme Council of the United States, their territories and dependencies, Scottish Rite Masons. He belongs to St. Paul's M. E. church, in Cedar Rapids. Mr. Bennett was married April 26, 1883, to Ella Janet Evans. They have four children, Helen E., born May 16, 1884; Max, born November 24, 1886; Mary, born July 1, 1891, and Alice, born May 22, 1898.

Mr. Bennett is thus seen to be one of the pioneers of Cedar Rapids, having witnessed its growth from a riverside hamlet to one of the best cities in the state.

BAKER, LUTHER ELIJAH, state manager and general organizer for Endowment rank, Des Moines, Iowa, is one of the best known men in the state. He is a worthy type of a self-made man, and has, through his individual exertions, his business ability and steadfastness of purpose, reached a position of prominence.

A native of Virginia, Mr. Baker was born on the 1st day of January, 1865, being a son of William H. and Sarah (Pulse) Baker. The family was of German and Scotch ancestry, but for many generations had resided in the Old Dominion, and was ably represented in that struggle which resulted in the supremacy of the American arms and the establishment of the grandest republic on the face of the globe. Soon after the civil war the parents of our subject removed to Logan county, Ohio, thence to Bloomington, Ill., and in 1871 to Wilton, Iowa. In 1872 they removed to Tama county, and the father followed contracting and building for a time, being a mason by trade, but later engaged in farming. In early life his advantages for securing an

education were limited, but being a student by nature, and possessed of a retentive memory, he stored his mind with valuable information and became exceedingly well posted. He was an earnest Christian, and after reaching the age of 50 years was or-

dained as a minister of the Methodist Episcopal church. His death occurred at the age of 52 years. His widow still survives and is now living in Melbourne, Iowa.

Early in life Luther E. Baker manifested those traits of character that have led to his success—strong determination, firm purpose and untiring energy. He resolved to secure an education. He had no means with which to pay his tuition, but nevertheless he was enrolled among the students of Western college, in 1882, continuing until the close of the term, in 1885, and he did all kinds of work, no matter how humble, if honest, in order to meet the necessary expenses with which to complete his education. He served as the first principal of the schools in Vining, Iowa, where he taught seven terms, resigning at the expiration of that period to pursue the study of law. It became necessary, however, for him to seek some remunerative employment, and he accepted a position with a wholesale house as manager of a branch store at Webster City. In 1886 he became bookkeeper for the Mutual Benefit association, of Toledo, and made his services so valuable to the company that in 1891 he was chosen secretary and manager of the same. He has grown up with the association, is thoroughly familiar with the business, both in principle and detail, and every book in the office contains some of his work.

The abilities of Mr. Baker are by no means confined to one line of endeavor. He is secretary of the Commercial Telephone company; a stockholder and director in the Toledo Savings bank, of Toledo; a stockholder in the Hoover Cow Milker company, of Hubbard Iowa; and owns 6,242 shares in the Mineral Farm and Deep River Milling and Mining company, of Aspen, Col. He also has two fine farms in Tama county, a well improved farm of 400 acres in Emmet county, and is owner and manager of the Baker Opera house.

Mr. Baker enlisted in the First regiment, Iowa National Guards, and within three years has been promoted to the rank of captain, transferred to the Fourth regiment, made brigade inspector of small-arms practice and elected and commissioned major of the regiment. He was the first secretary of the Iowa National Guard organization, and is at present chairman of the legislative committee. He is also a member of the United States Military Service institute, of New York, and is secretary of the Toledo Enterprise association.

In politics Mr. Baker is a staunch republican. He was elected president of the Republican League club, of the Fifth Congressional district, August 28, 1896, without opposition. Socially he is an enthusiastic Mason, and has attained the thirty-second degree in that order, member of Lodge No. 290, Benevolent and Protective Order of Elks, and the D. O. K. K. He is also past grand vice-chancellor of the Knights of Pythias fraternity in Iowa, and in 1895 declined the nomination for grand chancellor of the state. However, the 25,000 Knights of Iowa singled him out as the ideal grand chancellor, so

August 13, 1896, he was given this, the highest honor they could bestow, and complimented with a unanimous election, a thing never before known in the domain of Iowa. He is now chief of staff of the Uniform rank of Knights of Pythias in Iowa.

Mr. Baker was married on February 12, 1890, to Miss Ida M. Springer, daughter of Dr. J. N. Springer. Mrs. Baker is an educated, refined and agreeable lady, thoroughly domestic and companionable.

September 1, 1897, he engaged with the board of control of the Endowment rank as state manager and general organizer, with office in Des Moines. This is a very strong institution, representing $100,000,000, and nearly three-fourths of a million surplus; also made chairman of the committee to select permanent location for the Grand Lodge Knights of Pythias.

---

DENMEAD, DAVID THATCHER, a quiet man of business, thoroughly conversant with banking, a shrewd financier whose methods are always confined to legitimate channels, and a citizen in whom the utmost confidence is imposed by the people of Marshalltown, is the one to whose life this sketch cannot do full justice. David Thatcher Denmead, son of Thomas and Caroline Denmead, was born in Baltimore, Md., December 4, 1849; from which city his

parents removed during his childhood. After a short residence in Martinsburg, Alexandria and Wheeling, Va., they settled in Steubenville, Ohio, where Mr. Denmead passed the greater part of his early life, attending the public schools. He was

then sent to Gambier, Ohio, to complete his education, but preferring a different course of study, finished his school work at the Ohio Military academy near Cincinnati.

After leaving school he was employed as clerk in the office of the Pittsburg, Chicago & St. Louis Railroad company. He afterwards engaged in general merchandising and coal mining in Tuscarawas county, Ohio, and in those ventures was highly successful. He came to Iowa in April, 1876, and located at Marshalltown, engaging in the lumber and coal business. Later, he became interested in the wholesale grocery firm of Letts, Fletcher & Company, a concern which did an immense business in the western and middle section of the state. In January, 1886, he sold his interest in the company and purchased a large block of stock in the City bank, which has since become the City National bank. Mr. Denmead is now president of the institution. It is one of the sound financial concerns of central Iowa, with a paid up capital of $100,000. He married Miss Gertrude Alice Williams, only daughter of the late Hon. James L. Williams, April 30, 1879. They have three children named James L., Harry K. and Dwight H.

---

DEWITT, CHARLES HERMAN, a well-known physician of Glenwood, is a son of James A. Dewitt, a Methodist minister, who, after serving three years as a private in the civil war, removed to Michigan from New York, and there engaged in farming until his death in 1876. The family was a family of ministers—three of Dr. Dewitt's father's brothers being of that calling. One uncle —H. G. Dewitt, D. D.—was a prominent evangelist, holding revivals in many of the important cities of the United States. His mother, Phoebe Streator-Dewitt, was a native of New York state, her parents being farmers in Cayuga county. Her father served as a soldier in the Mexican war. She was noted for her charitable works and as a lady of culture and a devoted Christian. Her family were strictly farmers, and being successful financially, each one of the boys received a farm to begin life with. Mr. Dewitt's father's family consisted of four children.

Doctor Dewitt was born in Auburn, N. Y., January 2, 1859. He was educated in the common schools of Michigan and Iowa and began teaching when only 16 years of age. For four years he alternately taught and attended school, using the money earned from teaching to assist him in his laudable efforts to secure an education. In March, 1883, he graduated from the medical department of the University of Illinois, at Chicago, and immediately located at

Lucas, Iowa, where he began general practice. He remained at Lucas until 1890, when he removed to Glenwood, where he has since lived. The doctor has had hospital training at Cook county hospital and taken post graduate courses in the cities of Chicago and New York. He devotes special attention to gynecology and surgery, in the practice of which he has become very successful. He is at present chairman of the board of the United States pension examiners at Glenwood, and was formerly surgeon for the Whitebreast Coal and Mining company. He is a member of the Southwestern Iowa Medical society, Iowa State Medical society and American Medical association. He is a member of the Masonic fraternity, Royal Arch chapter, and Knight Templar commandery, and also a member of the Knights of Pythias and A. O. U. W. lodges. Doctor Dewitt has always been a republican, and cast his first vote for James A. Garfield. He has never held or sought any political office and prefers to devote his time and energies to his profession, in which he has attained

a high position as a practitioner. He was married to Miss Eleanor S. Shields, of Henry, Ill., November 9, 1884. They have one child, a son, born June 30, 1886. They have an ideal home in Glenwood, and the doctor attributes much of his success to his wife and home surroundings.

———

SMITH, DR. GEORGE ALFRED, of Clinton, is one of Iowa's best physicians, and is especially expert as a medical examiner. Due to his careful inspection as medical director of the Economic Life association, of Clinton, the mortality record of that company, from its organization to the present time, 1898, has been kept down to 1.14 in 1,000, the best showing any company has yet made. Dr. Smith is a son of Col. John Henry Smith, who was born in Albany county, N. Y., in 1827, and whose ancestors were Germans from the valley of the Rhine. He learned the machinist's trade and was a locomotive engineer on the line now belonging to the Chicago & North-Western Railway company, at the time when it terminated at Dixon, Ill. He was married March 13, 1851, to Miss Emily Perry Cooley, born at Hartford, Conn., in 1834. Her father, Thomas Cooley, a prominent politician, was for many years keeper of the United States arsenal there. He was the son of James Cooley, of Springfield, Mass., who traced his descent from King James of England. Her mother, Ann Kennedy, was of Irish descent, and numerous members of the family were among the early settlers of Connecticut, and their progeny still reside there. Mrs. Smith died in May, 1892. Colonel Smith came to Iowa in the spring of 1852, and settled on a farm in Center township, Clinton county, where he made his home until 1860, when he moved his family to Lyons, where he was at the front, and in 1865 to the town of Camanche, where he still resides. He belonged to the first board of supervisors in Clinton county, and was a member of the convention that organized the republican party in 1856. In 1860 he recruited Company A, Sixteenth Regiment Iowa Volunteer infantry, and entered the army as its captain, serving with distinction through the entire war. He was promoted successively to major and lieutenant-colonel and was mustered out as commander of the regiment. He was captured at the battle of Atlanta, and was for a long time confined in numerous rebel prisons, but finally escaped from one at Columbia, S. C., and in company with eight others reached the union fleet after many hardships. He took an active part in many engagements and was awarded a silver medal by act of congress for bravery in the siege of Vicks-

burg. He was mustered out June 22, 1865, after taking part in the grand review at Washington, at the close of the war.

He was elected to the state senate in 1865, and served one term, being succeeded by Dr. A. B. Ireland. He has held numerous important positions in the United States revenue department, and it was largely through his efforts that the great frauds in the Camanche distillery were brought to light and the property confiscated by the government in 1873. He is still an active man, though over 72 years old.

Dr. George A. Smith was born July 6, 1854, on a farm in Center township, Clinton county, Iowa, and received his earliest instruction from his mother, who taught him at home. He afterwards attended district schools, and the graded schools of Lyons and Camanche. At the age of 16 he was apprenticed to a carpenter and builder, and worked at his trade more or less for four years. At 19 he began teaching, which he continued until 1879. He also clerked in a drug store three years, and in 1877 was a student in the Clinton Business college. He entered the medical department of the State university in 1879, graduating with his class in March,

1881. He located at Camanche, where for four years he practiced his profession and carried on a drug business. In the summer of 1885 he moved to Clinton, and the following January his drug store burned. Since then he devoted himself entirely to his profession, which he carried on alone, except a year when he was in partnership with Dr. A. H. Smith, now deceased. He has built up a splendid practice, and has held many important professional offices. He was for two terms health officer of the city, and was a member and the secretary of the Clinton county board of United States examining surgeons for pensions under Harrison's administration. He was also secretary and afterwards president of the Clinton County Medical society. He is now surgeon for the great lumbering firms of C. Lamb & Sons, W. J. Young & Company, and the Curtis Brothers' Sash, Door and Blind factory. Besides being medical director of the Economic Life association, of Clinton, he is also medical examiner for numerous life insurance companies and fraternal organizations. He was a member of the board of state medical examiners for the commencement of the medical department of the State university in 1893, and was chairman of the section of practice of medicine in the annual meeting of the State Medical society in 1897. He has contributed a number of articles on medicine and surgery to various publications, and is associate in charge of the department of medicine of the *Iowa Medical Journal.*

When the Spanish-American war was declared he tendered his services to the government as a surgeon, and early in June, 1898, he was appointed and commissioned a brigade surgeon by the president. He was assigned to the Tenth Army Corps, but owing to peace negotiations this corps was not organized, and he was placed in the hospital service at Chickamauga Park, Ga. He soon advanced to the command of the Second division, Third Army Corps field hospital, and continued in this command until it was closed. He was soon after taken sick and returning home was honorably discharged from the service September 31, 1898.

Dr. Smith has always been an enthusiastic, active republican, and has done much for the good of the party in the state, as well as in his own county and district. He began as a drummer boy in the campaign of Grant against Seymour, and has taken part in every election since. He has been a delegate to every county convention for the past twenty years, and to every state convention for the past ten years. He was district alternate from the Second district to the republican national convention in 1896, and as chairman of the Clinton county central committee that year, succeeded, by a splendid organization, in carrying his county for McKinley by a majority of nearly 1,000, though it had previously gone democratic for nearly twenty years.

Dr. Smith is a member of numerous civic organizations. He is a Mason, an Odd Fellow, a Forrester, a member of Mystic Workers of the World, the Benevolent and Protective Order of Elks, and of the Knights and Ladies of the Golden Precept. He belongs to no church, and believes more in deeds than in creeds.

The doctor was married October 4, 1882, at Camanche, Iowa, to Miss M. Nettie Ireland, youngest daughter of Dr. A. B. Ireland, deceased. They have two children, Mabel, born August 8, 1884; and Homer, born July 7, 1890.

DODGE, NATHAN PHILLIPS, of Council
Bluffs, was born in Peabody, Essex county,
Mass., August 20, 1837. He is descended
from Richard Dodge, who came from
Somerset England, in 1838 with the Puritan colonists and settled in Massachusetts.
Some half dozen of these colonists had
settled on the west side of the Essex river,
just across from Salem, and in time this
settlement became known as Beverly.

Sylvanus Dodge, the father of Nathan
P., was born at the beginning of this
century in Rowley, Mass. When in middle
life he took an interest in politics, and, during President Polk's administration, he
was appointed postmaster of South Danvers, now Peabody, Mass., which position
he held until he went west in 1855. During his residence in Douglas county, Neb.,
from 1855 to 1860, he was a justice of
the peace and subsequently one of the
county board of commissioners. He then
removed to Council Bluffs, Iowa, and at
the time of his death, in 1871, he was register of the United States land office for
that district. Sylvanus Dodge was a hard-
working man from his boyhood, always
keenly interested in public affairs, and
known for his honesty and general integrity of character. The wife of Sylvanus
Dodge was Julia T. Phillips, born in 1802
on a farm adjoining the Dodges in Rowley.
Phillips has long been a name familiar in
the historic annals of New England, and
Mrs. Dodge was a splendid type of the
New England woman who brought to our
western country the strength and fortitude
of the Puritans. When past the meridian
of life she bravely surrendered the scenes
and friends of her childhood and followed
her husband and sons to the west, passing
the remaining thirty years of her life in
Nebraska and Iowa, where she died in 1888
at the advanced age of 87 years. She
always took an interest in what was going
on in the world; and, in her early days
when our country was ringing with the
eloquence of the great anti-slavery agita-
tors, she would walk miles after a hard
day of household labor to hear such men as
Wendell Phillips, Garrison and Douglas.
The hardships endured by Mr. and Mrs.
Dodge in assisting their sons to hold their
claims, continually molested by claim
jumpers and hostile Indians, cannot be told
in a few lines. Later, when her son, Grenville, was winning a name and fame in
the civil war, the mother at home was
active in the work of gathering hospital
stores for the army, as president of the local

relief society in Council Bluffs. Nathan
P. Dodge was the younger son. He received a common school education in New
England, and then at the solicitation of his
older brother, Grenville, he started west
when 16 years of age to join this brother,
who was a civil engineer, making the first
surveys for the Rock Island railroad across
Iowa.

Leaving home in the spring of 1854
he came directly to Iowa City, where he
expected to meet his brother, but on his
arrival he found a letter telling him that
he had gone east. Weary and homesick,
with not a place to lay his head, the boy
pioneer spent his first night in Iowa in an

office chair. In the morning he reported
to Peter A. Dey, who had charge of the
surveys, and, after a two-days' drive, he
was initiated into camp life at Rock Creek,
seven miles west of Grinnell. The party,
of which he now became a member, spent
the summer of 1854 locating the line between Iowa City and Des Moines. In the
fall he returned east to help his father
close up his affairs, and the following
March found the father and son crossing
Iowa in an open wagon on their way to
Council Bluffs. Here they crossed the
Missouri into Nebraska and traveled
twenty-three miles northwest from Omaha
to the Elkhorn valley, where they found

the oldest son, Grenville, awaiting them. Nathan Dodge staked out a claim adjoining his father's, which he owns to-day. Their cabins marked the western limits of civilization until you reached the Pacific coast, or the Mormon settlement in Utah. Within sight of their door was the Pawnee village, within whose smoking tepees lived 2,000 or 3,000 Indians, who were loth to give up their hunting grounds to the whites. Their depredations forced one after another of the neighboring families to desert their claims and growing crops and seek shelter in Omaha and Council Bluffs. By July only one family remained besides the Dodges. They were favored with growing crops and a garden grown from New England seeds, so they determined to fight it out to the end rather than sacrifice their farms to the redskins. But the latter grew bolder as the settlers decreased in numbers and they began killing the whites in a settlement five miles north; so, on the first of August, the Dodges, with their household goods packed in two wagons, returned to Omaha, then a village of one year's growth. Here Nathan and his father sought shelter in an unfinished cabin, where they made a temporary home for the winter, and here they welcomed the mother and sister on their arrival from Massachusetts. Grenville M. Dodge returned to Council Bluffs, where he formed a partnership with John T. Baldwin and opened a banking and land office.

Under the protection of state militia sent out by Governor Izard to protect the frontier, Nathan Dodge returned and harvested the crops on the Elkhorn farm and hauled them to Omaha. In the spring of '56 he accepted a position in the land and banking office of Baldwin & Dodge in Council Bluffs. Emigrants for California, Utah and Oregon gathered in Council Bluffs by the thousands and laid in their supplies for the long journey across the plains. These supplies came from St. Louis by steamboat.

The year 1856 was one of great activity in the Missouri valley; the entry of lands in western Iowa and the opening of the neighboring territory of Nebraska brought many emigrants to this region. Council Bluffs and Omaha received large accessions to their population, new towns were laid out and lots sold at fabulous prices compared with their actual value. The channels of business were filled with a wild cat currency, issued by banks throughout the western states, Iowa excepted, and this inflated speculation resulted in a general panic the following year, 1857. Young Dodge was so fortunate as to pass through this panic of speculation, followed so closely by one of depression, at an age when its lessons were clearly impressed upon his

19

mind and had an influence in shaping his own business career. The original firm of Baldwin & Dodge withdrew from the banking and land business and Nathan P. Dodge became their successor in 1860, with a large business. In 1863 Caleb Baldwin, then chief justice of Iowa, resigned his office, retiring from the bench to become the partner of Mr. Dodge in the banking and land business, the firm again becoming Baldwin & Dodge, but formed by the brothers of the original firm. In 1868 Judge Baldwin returned to the practice of law, while Nathan Dodge continued the banking business alone until 1870, when he turned it over to the Council Bluffs Savings bank, of which corporation he has ever since been president. The land business has been continued under the name of N. P. Dodge & Company.

Mr. Dodge attributes what measure of success he has had in business life to hard work, close attention to details, and keeping free from obligations. Both his business affairs and personal inclination have influenced him from entering public life, but he has always stood ready to join with others in public enterprises which promised to advance the interests of his city. Apart from his business and the education of his children, his greatest interest has been in benevolent and church work. A member of the Congregational church, he has been a liberal contributor to church and charitable work at home and abroad. He often represents his church at national councils, and in 1891 was a delegate to the international council held in England.

He was married to Susanna C. Lockwood in 1864, the daughter of Isaac Lockwood, of St. Louis. Five children were born to them, four of whom are now living, two sons and two daughters. These have been educated in New England, the sons going through Harvard and studying law at the Harvard law school, the daughters graduating from Smith's college at Northampton, Mass. Three of them—two sons and a daughter—have chosen law as their profession, Miss Dodge being one of the first six women to be admitted to the New York bar after graduating from the law school of the University of New York with honors.

---

PERKINS, GEORGE D., was born in Holly, Orleans county, N. Y., February 29, 1840. He learned the printer's trade at Baraboo, Wis. In 1860 he associated himself with his brother and started the *Gazette,* at Cedar Falls, Iowa. On the 12th day of August, 1862, he enlisted as a private soldier in the Thirty-first Iowa infantry. He was mustered out of the service at Jefferson Barracks, Mo., on the 12th day of January, 1863. In 1869 he left Chicago, Ill., where he had been connected with the service of the Northern Associated Press, and settled in Sioux City, Iowa, where he has since lived, and during that time has been editor of the *Sioux City Journal,* the best newspaper property of Iowa. He was a member of the Iowa senate in 1874-76; was immigration commissioner under Governor Gear; was United States marshal for the

Northern District of Iowa, under President Arthur; was elected to the Fifty-second Congress as a republican, and re-elected to the Fifty-third, Fifty-fourth and Fifty-fifth Congresses.

Mr. Perkins is one of the strong and great men of the state and nation, and it is a matter of regret that he requests so brief a sketch.

LARRABEE, WILLIAM, chairman of the state board of control of state institutions, twice governor of Iowa, and for eighteen years a member of the state senate, has carved an everlasting success out of the raw materials offered by the state he chose to work in.

He was the son of Capt. Adam A. Larrabee, a noted Connecticut soldier and farmer, who graduated from the United States Military academy at West Point in 1811, and served with distinction in the war of 1812. In the campaign of the St. Lawrence river, he took part in the attack on La Colle Mills, as a first-lieutenant of artillery, and was shot through the lungs, the bullet being taken from its lodgment place against his shoulder blade. That historic piece of lead may now be seen in the state historical department at Des Moines, where it is preserved as a relic. For his heroic conduct in this battle, Lieutenant Larrabee was shortly promoted

to be captain, but resigned in 1815 and two years later was married to Hannah Gallup Lester, by whom he had nine children. William, the seventh child, was born January 20, 1832, in Ledyard, Conn. Captain Larrabee was born March 14, 1787, and died October 25, 1869. His wife was born June 8, 1798, and died March 15, 1837. Her father, Nathan Lester, was a revolutionary hero, who was born July 25, 1742, and died October 10, 1813. His wife, Governor Larrabee's grandmother, lived until August 16, 1840. Captain Larrabee's father was also a revolutionary soldier and after the war was a lawyer. After he was discharged from the army, Captain Larrabee returned to farming and was engaged in business. He accumulated a comfortable fortune and was prominent in politics, serving as a member of the legislature, railway commissioner for the state of Connecticut, presidential elector for William Henry Harrison in 1840, and in other positions of trust.

William Larrabee, having received a common school education in Connecticut, and spending two months in a private academy, receiving the elements of a business training from his father, came to Iowa in 1853. He taught school in Hardin, Allamakee county, for a time and then worked on a farm for three years. In 1856 he went into the milling business in Clermont and continued until 1873, when he sold his milling interests and spent three months in Europe. This was his first real vacation. During his younger years Mr. Larrabee worked early and late, often putting in twenty hours a day for months at a time. That was the way he achieved success, and it is the recipe he gives to young men who would succeed—work, work, work. He devoted himself with all his might of body and mind—and both were strong and healthy—to the accomplishment of the business in hand, whatever it might be, and he has followed this rule through life, in his public life no less than in his private business. Mr. Larrabee engaged in banking and farming and has continued in the enlargement of his interests in Iowa banks and Iowa farms since that time. He owns bank stock in several banks in the northern part of the state and is probably the owner of more land than any other man in the state. He regards Iowa farms as about the best and surest way to invest money to secure reasonable and certain dividends.

Mr. Larrabee was appointed, with Senator Doolittle, of Wisconsin, and ex-Governor Dillingham, of Connecticut, to be one of the arbitrators to appraise the property of the Green Bay and Mississippi Canal company, preparatory to its transfer to the United States government. The property was taken by the government on the appraisement of this board.

In 1868 Mr. Larrabee was elected to the state senate and was four times thereafter renominated by acclamation, without opposition, and re-elected in a district which

began to send democrats in his place as soon as he retired. During his long service in the senate, he was chairman of the committee on ways and means most of the time. Here he had the widest opportunity for the exercise of his extraordinary business talents, and was enabled to be of great service to the state. He impressed his views upon the legislation of the state, especially in this line, for a longer period than any other man in the state. In the fall of 1885, Senator Larrabee resigned to accept the republican nomination for governor of Iowa. He was elected, receiving 175,504 votes against 168,502 for Charles C. Whiting, democratic and fusion nominee. Two years later he was re-elected, receiving, 169,686 votes against 153,526 for T. J. Anderson, the democratic and fusion nominee. Governor Larrabee's administration was a highly successful one. Being thoroughly informed about state affairs, he knew what was needed, and he gave to the supervision of the state institutions the closest personal attention. He ascertained by personal investigation just what they were doing, and inaugurated many reforms. The governor exercised a large

influence in politics in the state for a long term of years and is yet counted as one of the potent factors of Iowa republicanism. He began to vote the republican ticket in 1856, when John C. Fremont was the first presidential nominee of the party, and has voted for every republican presidential nominee.

In all of his success, his wife has borne a share, and often a large one. She was Miss Ann M. Appelman, and they were married September 12, 1861, in Clermont. She is almost as well known in the state as is her husband, for her ability to meet all demands, to grasp large affairs, to share in her husband's responsibilities, and withal, to make an attractive, wholesome home, have won for her friends and admirers in the people of Iowa. They have had seven children, all living but one. They are: Charles, born June 13, 1862, now in Armstrong, Iowa, looking after his father's lands; Augusta, born May 21, 1864, married August 20, 1896, to Victor B. Dolliver, and died in Minneapolis, March 14, 1897; Julia, born January 3, 1867, married August 18, 1891, to Don L. Love, and lives in Lincoln, Neb.; Anna, born March 9, 1869, who lives at home; William, Jr., born December 11, 1870, who graduated from the collegiate and law departments of the State University of Iowa and served as captain and commissary during the Spanish-American war, having volunteered as a private and afterward been promoted; Frederick, born November 3, 1873, now in Columbia Law school, New York city, and a graduate of the collegiate and law department of the State University of Iowa, and Helen, born November 30, 1876, now a student in the State university. The Larrabees have a delightful home in the edge of Clermont, where their friends are always welcome. The governor does not belong to any church, but he has been a trustee of the local Presbyterian church for thirty years, and has supported that and the Methodist church. Mrs. Larrabee is, and has been for many years, the superintendent of the Union Sunday school in Clermont, and the family gave the church a fine pipe organ.

When the legislature passed the board of control law in 1898, it was admitted, even by its friends, that its success depended very largely upon the character of men appointed to the board. Governor Larrabee was by common consent selected as the best man for chairman of the board, if he would consent to serve, which he finally did, upon the urgent solicitation of Governor Shaw. This work is most congenial to him and he has again found an opportunity to be of great service to the state. The new law, under the administration of Governor Larrabee and his two able associates, Judge Kinne and John Cownie, is working with excellent satisfaction and beneficent results.

---

BALDWIN, JOHN NEHEMIAH, one of the most distinguished sons of Iowa, born in the city of his present residence, lives in Council Bluffs, and is a lawyer of national reputation. His father, Hon. Caleb Baldwin, was formerly chief justice of the supreme court of the state of Iowa, and was one of the ablest lawyers in the west. His wife, John N. Baldwin's mother, was Miss Jane Barr, prior to her marriage with Caleb Baldwin, in 1848. Their son, John N., was born in Council Bluffs, July 9, 1857. He received a thorough education in the schools of Council Bluffs, and when only a boy entered the law department of the State university, and graduated with high honors in 1877, at the age of 20 years. The next

year he was married, December 18th, to Miss Lilla G. Holcomb. They have two children, Genevieve H., born September 20, 1879, and John N., Jr., born March 18, 1888. Mr. Baldwin has won distinction as a lawyer and political speaker. He is one

of the most successful corporation lawyers west of Chicago, and to his firm of Wright & Baldwin are intrusted the interests of a large majority of the corporations operating in Council Bluffs, and many others. The firm's practice is confined to cases involving large amounts or important law questions, and includes the United States supreme court.

The political arena has always held a charm for Mr. Baldwin, but he has never allowed himself to be a candidate for any office. He has used his splendid ability to advance the interests of others, his friends and the republican party. He was temporary chairman of the republican state convention, in Des Moines, July, 1894, and delivered a speech that fulfilled all the high expectations his friends had entertained. It was one that will long be remembered for its beauty of language, strength of ideas and force. Mr. Baldwin was selected by the friends of Senator Allison to present his name to the republican national convention, in St. Louis, in June, 1896, and again he delivered a memorable speech that attracted national attention. In the presidential campaign that followed, Mr. Baldwin spoke under the direction of the republican national committee, visiting several states. Yet a young man, a career of great usefulness and renown is opening for this brilliant lawyer.

---

WYMAN, MAJOR WILLIE CUTTER, a well known and successful business man of Ottumwa, comes of an old New England family. On both sides of his father's and mother's families he is descended from the earliest settlers of Massachusetts, the members of the old Bay state colony. The Wyman family came to America from England in 1634. Some of them were officers in the English army and were among those who organized the Ancient and Honorable Artillery company of Boston in 1638, the organizers being chiefly officers who were members of the Honorable Artillery company of London before they came to this country either to settle or as officers in the English army. For generations members of the Wyman family have belonged to this company, and Major Wyman holds a commission in it. His father was Edward Wyman, Jr., a Boston merchant and capitalist, and his mother's maiden name was Mary Anna Doyle, of Salem, Mass., where the subject of this sketch was born.

He received a liberal education, attending the Boston Latin school, a military academy, and other New England educational institutions of the best class. He was appointed a captain's clerk in the United States navy in 1870, and later promoted to acting admiral's secretary (rank

lieutenant in the navy), and served in the North Atlantic, West Indian and European fleets, resigning in 1874. He came to Iowa the same year and located in Ottumwa, and two years later engaged in business with Mr. J. Prugh, the firm consisting of Mr. Prugh and himself, and known as J. Prugh & Co. Upon the death of Mr. Prugh some years later Mr. Wyman continued the business. They are importers and wholesale dealers in crockery, china, etc., and the concern is one of the heaviest of its kind in the state.

Major Wyman has always been a republican, as his father and grandfather on both sides were before him. He has been quite active and influential in the politics of his state. His military ancestry and training led him to take an interest in the Iowa National guard, with which he has been actively associated for fifteen years or more. He is now serving his sixth term as military secretary to the governor, which is longer than any other man in the United States ever held this position. He had previously served as first lieutenant,

acting regimental adjutant, and quarter-master, and as brigade quartermaster. He is one of the best known and most popular military men in the state. Major Wyman is a thirty-second degree Mason and Knight Templar and Knight of Pythias, besides belonging to other orders. He is a member of the Society of the Sons of the American Revolution and is either a member of, or eligible to membership in, nearly all the colonial societies. His people held various military and civil positions. One of his ancestors on his mother's side was assistant governor of the Massachusetts Bay colony, under Governor Winthrop. He belongs to the Episcopal church. Mr. Wyman was married in 1876 to Alice Prugh, a daughter of his late partner. They have one son, William Charles Wyman, born in 1882.

———

BLANCHARD, LUCIAN C., by merit and ability has won a high place in the ranks of Iowa's foremost men. His father, Caleb Blanchard, was a native of Rhode Island, whose grandfather was in the revolutionary war. Caleb Blanchard moved to New York when that state was new, settled on a farm in Lewis county, and became prominent in local affairs, serving as justice of the peace and supervisor for many years. He married Penelope Aldrich, a native of Vermont, whose family settled there long before the revolution.

Lucian was born in the town of Diana, Lewis county, N. Y., April 15, 1839. When he was only 5 years old his father died, and he grew up without many of the advantages which others enjoyed. After securing as much education as possible in the rather primitive common schools of that period, he was not satisfied, but determined to go up higher, and went to the Carthage academy, at Carthage, Jefferson county, N. Y. Here he remained some time, and in 1858 came west, and attended the Rock River seminary at Mt. Morris, Ill., for two years. During the time of his studies at the seminaries he taught school several terms, and in 1860 he crossed the plains to Pike's Peak. Returning in the fall to Iowa, he taught school in Jasper county and studied law at Newton.

When the rebellion began, he enlisted as a private in Company K, Twenty-eighth regiment, Iowa volunteers, and was in the battles of Port Gibson, Champion Hill and the siege of Vicksburg. In the fall of 1863 he was taken seriously sick, and on that account was discharged from the service, and came very near dying before he reached the home of his sister at Mt. Morris, Ill. Remaining in Illinois until August, 1864, he regained health sufficiently to enter the University of Michigan, from which he graduated in the law department in 1866.

Mr. Blanchard commenced the practice of law at Montezuma, Iowa, in June, 1866. In 1867 he was appointed county judge of Poweshiek county, and the same fall was elected to that office, but resigned in 1868, and was that year nominated by the republican party and elected circuit judge of the Sixth Judicial district. He was re-elected

in 1872, judge of the enlarged district comprising the counties of Jasper, Poweshiek, Marion, Mahaska, Keokuk, Washington and Jefferson, and in 1876 was re-elected to the same position, and served in all twelve years on the bench.

January 13, 1870, Judge Blanchard was married to Sarah Kilburn, daughter of F. A. Kilburn, a merchant of Montezuma. They had two children: Rose, now the wife of Dr. B. O. Jerrel, of Oskaloosa, and Claude. The judge removed from Montezuma to Oskaloosa in 1874, and in 1878 his wife died. On retiring from the bench in 1880, he commenced the practice of law at Oskaloosa, where he has since enjoyed a fine practice. In 1891, Judge Blanchard

was a candidate for the nomination of supreme judge before the republican convention at Cedar Rapids, but after a spirited contest was defeated by Hon. S. M. Weaver. He was in 1890 elected senior vice-commander of the G. A. R., for the department of Iowa. In 1893 he was elected to represent Mahaska county in the legislature, and in 1895 was elected senator. The judge is a member of the Masonic order, and in 1879 was grand orator of the grand lodge of Iowa, and was grand treasurer of the same body in 1880. With the assistance of the late Judge Wilson, he prepared during 1880, the "Masonic Digest," which was published by the grand lodge.

In June, 1886, Judge Blanchard was married to Jozella Williams, daughter of Hon. Micajah T. Williams and niece of the late Judge Wm. H. Seevers. During that year they made a tour abroad, visiting many of the countries in Europe. Mrs. Blanchard died at Oskaloosa, April 22, 1897. Judge Blanchard is at present vice-president of the State Bar association.

BIRCHARD, ABNER THEODORE, of Marshalltown, Iowa, was born near Montrose, Susquehanna county, Pa., on the 24th day of August, 1834.

His father, Plinny Birchard, was a native of Massachusetts, and came to Susquehanna county, Pa., with his parents when a boy, at a time when the country was an unbroken forest. The trip was made with what was called a spike team—a yoke of oxen and one horse ahead. He was reared and spent his days in that county, hemmed in from outside strife and trouble, and led the quiet and uneventful life of a farmer and neighborhood miller. He died in 1851 at the age of 59. His mother's maiden name was Martha Griffis, daughter of a revolutionary soldier and pensioner, living at Unidilla, Otsego county, N. Y. Abner T. received his education at the country schools of Susquehanna county, Pa., where the teacher received the munificent sum of $1.25 per week and boarded around. This kind of education was continued summer and winter, till he was twelve years old, when the school term was cut in the middle, when thereafter he only attended three months in the winter. This continued until he was sixteen years of age, when he was indentured three years to learn the cabinet-maker's trade. This indenture included six months' schooling at a private academy, to finish his education, and provided for an annual salary of $25, $40 and $70.

Mr. Birchard came to Iowa in 1856, when railroads were a rare convenience, the only one in Iowa then being the Rock Island, terminating at Iowa City. He came to Iowa City by rail, thence to Oskaloosa by stage, having worked at Hampton, Ill., as carpenter, for sufficient money to pay fare to Oskaloosa. Here he hired out as an itinerant tin peddler during the summer, and in the fall he had the good fortune to be employed as manager of a general store to be opened up at Dakota City, Humboldt county. Thence he made his way through a wilderness of prairie to his new position. The county was not then organized and included a great area of northwestern Iowa. Here he remained during the winter of 1856-57. During this winter the last session of the legislature was held at Iowa City, which was in continuous session till July.

The excitement incident to the Spirit Lake Indian massacre drove the settlers from the country, and so he moved his store to Boonesborough, Boone county, where he located and was joined by his family. He was married to Orpha Celia Smith, of Dimmock, Susquehanna county, Pa., July 24, 1854. His wife died at Boonesborough, Iowa, July, 1860. During the year 1861,

he assisted in the survey and location of the Chicago & North-Western railroad from Marshalltown to the Des Moines river. In August, 1862, he enlisted in the Thirty-second Iowa Infantry volunteers, and on October 7th of the same year he was mustered into the United States service, with Company I, and was immediately made quartermaster sergeant and served in that capacity with the regiment until October 7, 1864, just two years, when he entered the general hospital at Jefferson Barracks, Mo., as a patient. Upon becoming convalescent he was sent home on a furlough, returning to the hospital on December 7th, and was at once assigned to duty as a clerk in the headquarters office

where he remained until May, 1865, when he was mustered out of the service by reason of the termination of the war, having occupied all the various clerkships in the office; and the last few months, that of chief clerk. After mustering out, he took the position of chief clerk with Capt. T. C. McCall, A. Q. M., remaining until October, 1865, closing up the business in the quartermaster's department at New Madrid and Kansas City, Mo.

Returning home to Boonesborough, he entered the service of the American Express company, as messenger,—Boone to Omaha,—and in August, 1866, as agent at Jefferson, Greene county, having formed a partnership at that place with Dr. W. S. McBride in the drug business.

In December was married to Mrs. Margaret Steele Lytle Birchard. In May, 1867, he removed to Missouri Valley, Harrison county, establishing a drug business. Closing out the business at both points in October, 1870, he removed to Marshalltown, continuing the partnership in the same business until the fall of 1872, and continued the business till spring of 1886, about two years of this time being in partnership with C. J. Lander. In 1883 he became a stockholder in the Marshall Canning company, and in 1891 acquired all the stock and has since continued the business. In 1886 he established a milling business in Norfolk, Neb., under the firm name of Birchard, Bridge & Co., which was continued until September, 1897. He has always been a republican. Has held the position of school director for several years at Boonesborough, Missouri Valley and Marshalltown, postmaster at Missouri Valley, member of city council at Marshalltown, member of board of commissioners of Iowa Soldiers' home, treasurer and president of same, and acting commandant.

---

PERRIN, HON. WM. B. Senator Wm. B. Perrin is one of those public men who has passed through the lower branch of the general assembly to a place in the upper and more dignified body—the senate. He was a member of the house from Chickasaw county in the Seventeenth and Eighteenth General Assemblies, and at this writing is representing the counties of Floyd and Chickasaw in the senate. He is the son of Porter and Lucy Kinney Perrin, rural people in good circumstances. His grandparents were natives of Connecticut. Zachariah Perrin and family came from Hebron, Conn., and settled in the forest upon territory that was afterwards within the town of Berlin, Vt. This was in 1789. The father of this subject was the first male white child born in the town. The premises settled upon by the grandfather are still in the possession of the family and owned by a brother of Senator Perrin. The grandparents on the maternal side settled in Plainfield, Vt. Grandfather Jonathan Kinney was a Baptist minister, not in good standing with his denomination, however, because he did not believe in nor practice close communion. The home he established over 100 years ago still remains in the Kinney family.

Senator Wm. B. Perrin was born at Berlin, Washington county, Vt., January 19, 1839. His education commenced in the district school, was continued in Barre academy. In 1861 he entered Dartmouth college and graduated therefrom in 1866, his course having been interrupted by military service. He took a course of lectures at the Albany Law school in the fall and winter of 1866 and spring of 1867, then

came to Iowa and became a student in the law office of Tracy & Newman at Burlington. In August, 1868, he located at Nashua, Iowa, where he has since been engaged in practice. His first dollar was earned in teaching school. He has served

as justice of the peace, county supervisor, secretary of the school board, school director and president of the school board, member of the council, and mayor.

He has a good record as a soldier. He enlisted in the First Rhode Island cavalry, Company B, Seventh squadron, composed mainly of college students. They saw service in the Shenandoah Valley, about Harper's Ferry and at Antietam. He afterwards enlisted in the Third Vermont Light battery, and was in the campaign from the Wilderness to Petersburg, and until Lee's surrender. He is unmarried. In politics he is a republican, having cast his first vote for Lincoln, but in his duties as a public servant he places the good of the whole people above devotion to party. As a legislator he has gained many friends and no enemies, for his conduct is always courteous, and his ability is recognized by every member of the senate. He has a keen sense of humor and a droll, inimitable way of expressing himself, so that he never lacks for a reply.

BLYTHE, SMITH GREEN, of Nora Springs, is one of the leading physicians of Floyd county. He is the son of Rev. Joseph William Blythe, a minister in the Presbyterian church, who was born in Kentucky in 1808, and graduated from Transylvania university in Kentucky, and from Princeton Theological seminary. He preached in Pittsburg, Pa.; Monroe, Mich.; Cranbury, N. J., and several important towns in Indiana. He was for several years fiscal agent for Hanover college in Indiana, and during the civil war was chaplain in the United States hospitals at Evansville and Madison. After the war he was pastor of the church at Lexington, Ind., where he died in 1875, aged 67. Dr. Blythe's mother was Ellen Henrietta Green, a daughter of Caleb Smith Green, a farmer of Lawrenceville, N. J, and a sister of Henry W. Green, once chief justice of New Jersey. She was a woman of rare attainments and of a strong character. She died at Cranbury, N. J., in 1852, aged 38. The ancestors of Dr. Blythe were from several different nations, including England, Scotland, Wales and Holland. His grandfather, James Blythe, was president of Transylvania university, and later of Hanover college.

Dr. S. G. Blythe was born November 6, 1841, at Cranbury, Middlesex county, N. J. He first attended the district school there, and later, until he was 14, was one of the pupils at a parochial school connected with his father's church. When he was 14, he moved with his parents to Vincennes, Ind., and entered the Indiana university, and in 1857 became a member of the sophomore

class in Lafayette college, at Easton, Pa., from which he graduated in 1860, at the age of 19. While in school he was a member of the Washington Literary society and of the Zeta Psi fraternity. Soon after graduating he entered the army as a private in Company D, of the First New Jersey regiment of infantry. The quota of the state was filled by the mustering in of the militia, so that the volunteers were held in reserve for another call, when, May 18, 1861, without having gone out of the service, they re-enlisted for three years. In this organization Dr. Blythe was appointed commissary sergeant of the regiment, and served as such through the battle of Bull Run and the reorganization of the army of the Potomac at Alexandria, under McClellan. In a competitive examination held March 24, 1862, he rose to the rank of second lieutenant of Company A, First New Jersey infantry, and became first lieutenant of Company F, same regiment, October 7, 1862, and captain of Company F, November 29, 1862, and held this position during the remainder of the war,

being mustered out June 23, 1864, for disability from wounds. He belongs to the G. A. R. and was a charter member and first commander of Gardner Post at Nora Springs.

Dr. Blythe began the practice of medicine in 1867, at Vinton, Iowa, removing to Rudd, Iowa, in 1869 and to Nora Springs in 1873, where he has remained ever since, enjoying a good practice. He belongs to the following secret orders: Knights of Pythias, A. O. U. W., Modern Woodmen, and Tribe of Ben Hur. In politics he has always been a republican. He has held numerous local offices, and in 1880 was district elector for the fourth district. He is now serving his fourth term as mayor of Nora Springs. He does not belong to any church, but his family attends the Congregational.

The doctor was married July 8, 1863, to Miss Emily Gill Sharpe, daughter of Judge William R. Sharpe, of Belvidere, N. J. They have had ten children, four of whom are now living: Margaret Emily, born in 1866, now the wife of Rev. Thomas J. Woodcock, of Lead, S. D.; Hannah Longstreet, born in 1872, now the wife of Prof. F. F. J. Exner, of Wilton College, Iowa; Redford Vancleve, born in 1876, and Winfred Vanderen, born in 1884.

HEATH, HENRY ROBBINS, has been a resident of Des Moines for more than forty years, and during all that time has occupied an active and important place in the business life of the city and state. He was born in Tyringham, Berkshire county, Mass., April 6, 1830. He was the son of Cyrus and Clarissa Cheney Heath; both descended from old New England families. Three brothers came from England early in the seventeenth century; one settled in New Hampshire, one near Boston, and one in Connecticut. Mr. Heath is descended from William Heath, who settled in Connecticut, and, with his brother, served in the revolutionary war.

William married at the age of 19 and moved " to the wilds of Massachusetts," where he took up land and lived and died. Cyrus Heath, the father of Henry R., was his youngest son, and died in 1874, aged about 73 years. Henry R. Heath received the usual common school education of those days, and a practical education in the form of the carpenter's trade. He was employed seven years in the manufacture of sash, doors and blinds. He was married May 1, 1850, to Edith A. Underwood, daughter of Wm. O. Underwood, of Tyringham, Mass. They have three sons, Chas. H., born December 29, 1858; Albert G., born October 12, 1866, and James C., born June 25, 1871. One daughter, Frances Ella, died in 1871, aged 21 years.

Charles and Albert are associated with their father in the milling business in Ft. Dodge and James C. is in the brokerage business in Des Moines. They are all married and have families. In April, 1856, at the age of 25, Mr. Heath came to Des Moines and went into the contracting business. Many of the early buildings in the

city of Des Moines are of his work. In 1860 he became interested, in company with many other young men, in the gold discoveries in Colorado, and took a trip to Pike's Peak. After six months' prospecting in Colorado he concluded to return to Des Moines, where he had a sure business.

For several years he was employed as foreman of a planing mill, and in 1869 he purchased a planing mill, which he successfully operated for ten years in the manufacture of sash, doors and blinds.

In 1879 he converted the planing mill into an oatmeal mill. This business was most satisfactory. The output was very large, often reaching 200 barrels of meal a

day, and it found a ready market in the United States and in Europe. In 1882 he added an elevator to the plant and began to deal heavily in grain. This property was destroyed by fire October 4, 1890, and the same year he established a large oatmeal mill in Ft. Dodge, in which his sons are associated with him. Its capacity is 500 barrels a day. The sons live in Ft. Dodge, but he still retains his residence in Des Moines. During the civil war Mr. Heath was in the quartermaster's department at Memphis, and was master mechanic of the district of west Tennessee.

He is a member of the Masonic Lodge, the Temple Commandery, Corinthian Chapter, Kaaba Temple Mystic Shriners, United Workmen, Legion of Honor and other civic organizations. He is largely interested in other business enterprises in Des Moines and is one of the wealthy men of the city, who has built up his fortune by persistent and honorable industry and good management. He enjoys a fine reputation as a reliable and responsible business man, whose word is always to be relied upon. In politics, Mr. Heath first voted for Franklin Pierce. He has since voted for John C. Fremont, Abraham Lincoln, U. S. Grant and Horace Greeley, and is thoroughly independent in his political actions. He believes in expansion and George Dewey.

SINGMASTER, SAMUEL, was born in Berks county, Pa., in the year 1807. His parents were German farmers who came to America in their youth. Samuel received very little schooling and such learning as he acquired came to him by experience and observation during a busy lifetime. When a boy he was placed as an apprentice to learn the tanning business. He served for three years in the city of Philadelphia, and at the end of that time was hired by his master at a salary of $72 per year.

In 1831 he formed a partnership with his brother and they operated a tannery of their own until 1838, when a disastrous fire destroyed their business and he abandoned it for the pursuit of farming. In 1840 he went to Millerstown, Perry county, Pa., and began buying and selling cattle and sheep. In those days, when transportation facilities were very meager, he purchased his stock in Ohio and drove it long distances to the Philadelphia market, riding on horseback and carrying his money in a belt strapped about his body. He came westward to Iowa in 1848, located a claim in Keokuk county, returned to Pennsylvania the next year and brought a family out with him to hold the claim, and then brought his own family in 1845. The spot which he called home then is his home to-day. Mr. Singmaster immediately launched into the stock business, buying calves at 50 cents a head and selling the steers as four-year-olds at $10 a head. He kept the heifer calves and in a few years had a large herd. The cattle business prospered and in 1875, in company with his sons, he began the importing of horses from France. Their first importation consisted of six head of Percherons. F rom that time on they made sixteen importations, one a year, the largest in a single

*The Singmasters.*

year numbering 140 head. The son, William, did the importing from France, England and Germany. At present the inventory of the Singmaster stock—that which is owned by father and sons—is 500 head of registered male and female, and an increase of 150 colts a year, Percheron, Shire, Clydesdale and coachers; 100 head of grades; 600 head of cattle, mostly fat ones.

Mr. Singmaster has conducted this large business for fifty years. During the late years he has had the assistance of his sons, who have remained at home and shared the burdens of the rapidly increasing business. In addition to the stock business he has carried on quite a business in money loaning at his home, Valley, Iowa, and has never

foreclosed a mortgage or met with any losses in that line.

He has been a republican in politics all his life. His religion is of the Lutheran faith. He was married in 1832 to Mary Seischalts, and to them were born eight children: Charles F., born 1834; Sarah Ann, Eliza, Thomas, James, Henry, William and Marietta. Two sons and two daughters are now living. Upon the shoulders of the two sons, Charles F. and Thomas, have fallen the entire management and conduct of the large business. It must indeed be a source of pride and gratification to him to know that the results of his life of toil, hardship and privation have fallen into such safe keeping. C. F.'s sons live and work together the same as their grandfather's family did.

Since the above was written, Samuel Singmaster has gone to his reward, and in the *Western Agriculturist* we find the following notice:

A grand pioneer is lost to the west in the death of Uncle Samuel Singmaster, at the ripe old age of 92 years. He died April 18, 1899. He was born in 1807 in Pennsylvania, where he learned the tanner's trade and worked for $72 a year for two years; then went to farming and dealing in stock, and in 1843 he came west and lived in a log cabin for several years. Thus began the pioneer life that has become famous, as Singmaster & Sons, all over America and France, as the largest draft horse breeders in America, the pioneer draft horse breeders in Iowa.

He had the foresight to see the great future for the American draft horse. In 1875 his two sons, Charles and William, made their first importation of four draft horses under his advice, he furnishing the money, and in 1876 they imported six horses and rapidly increased to 100 and 140 head a year until the death of William Singmaster in 1891, who spent much time in France selecting the horses, since which time Charles Singmaster and his sons Owen and Charles, Jr., have conducted this extensive business, numbering now over 600 recorded draft horses. Samuel Singmaster and his sons owned about 10,000 acres of land and conducted three banks besides the large horse business.

He was generous, kind and hospitable; loved and appreciated by all his family and neighbors. He was a friend to all who came to him in trouble for advice and assistance. The great benefit to the state and to the nation in the large draft horse business cannot be estimated, that Samuel Singmaster established and his sons so successfully conducted under his advice and instructions.

The importation and the breeding of so many pure bred draft horses has added millions of dollars to the wealth of the west, and his son Charles and his sons continue the business of Singmaster & Sons, to perpetuate the good work established in the p oneer days of Samuel Singmaster. The world is always better with the good work of such men.

PALMER, DAVID J., member of the state board of railroad commissioners, was born in Washington county, Penn., November 15, 1839, and came with his parents to Iowa in 1856, settling in Washington county, which is still his home. They began on eighty acres of raw prairie and passed through all the struggles incident to pioneer life. The family had previously lived for some time in Carroll county, in eastern Ohio, where they located in 1842. Here young Dave attended the country district and subscription schools, which were conducted in log schoolhouses in those days. For about a year and a half before the war young Palmer attended the United Presbyterian college in Washington, Iowa. He taught school for a few terms, but has chiefly followed farming, in which he has been highly successful. Colonel Palmer's parents were Samuel R. Palmer, a farmer, with rather limited means who had been a wagon maker by trade, and Margaret Munce. Samuel R. Palmer was born in County Armagh, Ireland, in 1811, and came to America with his parents at the age

of 18, settling in Washington county, Penn. His wife was born in Washington county, Penn., in 1812. Her father was a native of Ireland and died at the age of 99. Colonel Palmer enlisted August 10, 1861, as a private in Company C, Eighth Iowa infantry. He

was promoted and mustered into the United States service August 31, 1861, as third corporal. At the battle of Shiloh, Tenn., April 6, 1862, he was severely wounded in the left shoulder, and was discharged by the order of the secretary of war September 9, 1862, to accept a position as captain of Company A, Twenty-fifth Iowa infantry. They were mustered into the United States service September 27, 1862. He was slightly wounded in the left foot at Arkansas Post, January 11, 1863, and was promoted to lieutenant-colonel of the Twenty-fifth Iowa June 9, 1863. At the battle of Taylor's Ridge, near Ringgold, Ga., November 27, 1863, he was wounded in the left leg, though he remained in the service until the close of the war, and was mustered out in Washington, D. C., June 6, 1865. He was in the battle of Shiloh, Chickasaw Bayou, Arkansas Post, the charge upon and siege of Vicksburg, the second attack on Jackson, Miss., also Canton, Miss., campaign from Memphis to Chattanooga, Cane Creek, Tuscumbia, Cherokee Station, Lookout Mountain, Mission Ridge, Taylor's Ridge, campaign to Atlanta, including Dalton, Snake Creek Gap, Pumpkin Vine Creek, Resaca, Dallas, Altoona Hills, New Hope Church, Kenesaw Mountain, Marietta, and final attack and capture of Atlanta, East Point, Jonesboro, Sherman's march to the sea, engagement near Macon, Ga., attack and capture of Savannah, campaign through the Carolinas, resulting in capture of Columbia, Bentonsville, Goldsboro, and occupancy of Raleigh, N. C., final march through Petersburg, Richmond, and on to Washington, D. C. Very few soldiers have passed through the number of battles and seen the service that Colonel Palmer saw, and come out with as little permanent injury as he has suffered. His record as a soldier is held up as a model by his companions in arms. He is a member of the G. A. R., and was commander of I. G. White Post, No. 108, of Washington. The soldier ties are very strong with him, and he and his old comrades are always found standing together.

Colonel Palmer has always been a republican and has done his share of party work in every campaign. He is an eloquent and very vigorous speaker, and, when his feelings are aroused, is capable of most effective and inspiring oratory, as he has often shown while a member of the state senate. He has served as road supervisor and auditor of Washington county, and presidential elector, First district, 1884, and a member of the senate from the Tenth district, composed of Henry and Washington counties, elected in 1891 and serving two terms. He resigned the office of senator April 1, 1898, to accept the appointment tendered him by Governor Shaw to be member of the board of railroad commissioners to fill a vacancy caused by the death of C. L. Davidson. He received the unanimous nomination from the republican state convention that year and was elected by a handsome majority in November. His standing at home is shown by the protest which the democratic paper in his town made against the methods used by the opposing candidate to injure Colonel Palmer. This paper, the Washington *Democrat*, declared that " because men differ in politics is no reason why they should not be decent. Colonel Palmer is a rank partisan, and the *Democrat* owes him nothing. He not so much as takes the *Democrat*, but we believe in fair play, and say what you will against him, he is a whole-souled, big-hearted, public-spirited citizen, and when a man is in trouble Colonel Palmer never asks whether he is a democrat or a republican, or a Hottentot; he helps him out." Colonel Palmer is a member of the Grant club, of Des Moines, and belongs to the United Presbyterian church. He was married October 25, 1866, to Miss Letitia H. Young. They have no children.

KINNE, LA VEGA G., of Des Moines, member of the state board of control of state institutions, and for six years judge of the supreme court of Iowa, was born in Syracuse, N. Y., November 5, 1846. His father was Aesop Kinne, a farmer in moderate circumstances, who was married to Lydia Beebe. Their son, La Vega, began his education in the common schools of Syracuse and graduated from the high school. Afterward he took a full law course in the University of Michigan, where he was a member of the Webster society, the leading one of the law department. He also pursued certain studies in the literary department of the university while he was taking his law course. He graduated from the law department in 1868 with the degree of LL. B. He then took an examination and was admitted to the bar in Ottawa, Ill., in the same year. He practiced law in Mendota, Ill., until he moved to Iowa, which was in September, 1869. He located in Toledo and practiced his profession in that place until he was

elected to the bench. He was a member of the firm of Applegate & Kinne from 1869 to 1876, when the firm was dissolved and he continued alone until the fall of that year, when he formed a partnership with Hon. G. R. Struble, who was afterward

speaker of the Iowa house. The firm soon after became Struble, Kinne & Stiger and was among the strongest law firms in Iowa, all its members having attained distinction in their profession and in politics. This partnership existed until Mr. Kinne became district judge in 1887. During his residence in Toledo he was mayor for three terms and held the offices of city attorney and president of the school board.

Judge Kinne has been a democrat since 1870 and was the nominee of his party for governor in 1881 and in 1883, leading the speaking campaign both times. He was also the nominee of the democratic party for United States senator, and for district attorney and circuit judge at different times. For many years he served as secretary and later as chairman of the democratic state central committee, and was a delegate to the national convention in 1876. Again in 1884 he was a delegate-at-large to the national convention of his party. In 1886 he was elected district judge in the Seventeenth district, a normally republican district, but resigned January 1, 1887; was

nominated again that fall and elected to
fill his own vacancy. He was re-elected
without opposition in 1890 and in the fall
of 1891, was elected supreme judge on the
democratic ticket, receiving 1,000 majority
in his old district, which had given him
only seven majority in 1886. In 1897 he
was renominated, but the republican majority was too large to be overcome, though
a movement was started by republicans
to re-elect him as a non-partisan judge.
In 1894 Judge Kinne was appointed as
one of the commissioners from this state
upon uniform legislation in the several
states; in 1896 he was president of the
Iowa State Bar association. The judge is
now a member of the American Bar association and has served on important committees. He has for many years been a
lecturer upon the law of domestic relations
and taxation in the Iowa State university,
and a lecturer on the law of corporations
in the Iowa College of Law in Des Moines.
He has always been much interested in
efforts to improve the methods and procedure in the courts and has read two
papers before the State Bar association on
this subject. He is the author of ''Kinne's
Pleadings and Practice,'' a standard work
in Iowa. Judge Kinne is a member of the
Knights of Pythias and one of the most industrious members of the Prairie club of
Des Moines, a men's literary club of high
standing.

Judge Kinne was married to Mary
Abrams, of Penn, Ill., in 1869. They have
two daughters, Lillian, born in 1870, and
Hettie, born in 1873. The family has a fine
home in West Des Moines.

Judge Kinne's record on the bench and
at the bar has given him a high rank with
the legal profession in Iowa, and the value
of his judgment is recognized thoroughout
the state. In 1898 he was appointed by
Governor Shaw as the democratic member
of the state board of control. A first-class
lawyer and conservative, reliable man was
wanted, and the choice of Judge Kinne to
fill these requirements was universally approved. With large experience in life, a
modest, self-made man, he has brought to
the board of control, safe counsel and important service. His term expires April
1, 1902.

---

MOSHER, LEMUEL LEIGH, county attorney from January 1, 1895, to January 1,
1899, one of the leading lawyers of Warren
county, living at Indianola, has won high

professional standing by attending to the
work before him conscientiously.

He was born June 9, 1853, in Morrow
county, Ohio. His father, Stephen Mosher,
was a farmer in moderate circumstances,
and is now retired from active business on
account of age and infirmities. He came
to Iowa in June, 1856, and settled in the
southern part of Warren county. He is a
member of the Friends' church. The
mother's maiden name was Mary Farring-
ton. Her parents were of Quaker parentage and residents of Ohio. There were
several ministers in the families of both
Mr. and Mrs. Mosher, but the most of the
members of their families were quiet, unassuming pioneers.

L. L. Mosher obtained his early education in the most primitive schools of early

Iowa, but they were characterized by the
sturdy influence of those days and evidently made a lasting impression upon the
character of young Mosher, as he has ever
been thoroughly disgusted with the shams
and false pretenses of modern society. In
after years he attended the academy of
Friends, at Ackworth, Iowa, for two years.
He afterwards attended the school at Florence, N. J., a suburb of Philadelphia, on
the Jersey side of the Delaware river. He
then entered the law department of Simpson college, in Des Moines, and graduated

from that institution June 8, 1880. Mr. Mosher attained his present position as an attorney by no marked flashes of advancement, but the growth of his practice has been marked by steady and continued development. He has now quite a reputation as a criminal lawyer, and has been employed in all the criminal cases tried in his county for years. He was prosecuting attorney in the case of the State of Iowa v. T. P. Edgerton, indicted and tried for murder. He secured a verdict of murder in the second degree, being a verdict for the highest degree of killing sustained in any like case in Iowa, namely, the killing of another who was in the act of procuring and carrying away the property of the assailant.

In politics he has always been an ardent republican, and has held the office of mayor of his city, justice of the peace, and was elected prosecuting attorney for his county in 1894 and again in 1896. He is a member of the Odd Fellows, having filled all the offices in a subordinate lodge and been in attendance at the grand lodge a number of times. He is also a Knight Templar, thirty-second degree Mason, a member of the order of the Knights of Phythias and the Modern Woodmen of America.

Mr. Mosher has been twice married, the first time to Elizabeth Jones, who died, leaving three children, Edward Everett, born August 1, 1879; Maggie M., born April 30, 1881, and Arthur A., born July 27, 1884. He was married again in 1888, to Maud Young, at Beaver, Pa. They have five children living, Lemuel Leigh, born February, 19, 1890; Wendell W., born December 12, 1891, Donovan D., born December 12, 1895; Edith E., born March 2, 1897, and Hugh H., born March 14, 1899. Mr. Mosher is an active member of the Methodist church.

MOFFIT, JOHN T., of Tipton, lawyer and man of affairs, is a son of Hon. Alex Moffit who was a member of the Sixteenth General Assembly of Iowa. The father was born in 1829, in the county of Tyrone, Ireland, and came with his father to America and settled in Cedar county in 1840, where he has since resided. He is a farmer and lives on his farm and personally directs the management.

The mother's maiden name was Martha J. Poteet, who was born near Dayton, Ohio, in 1840, and came to Iowa in 1857.

John T. Moffit was born on his father's farm, near Mechanicsville, Cedar county, Iowa, July 8, 1862. He attended the common schools of that county from 1868 until 1876, after which he spent three years in the Mechanicsville high school. In September, 1879, he entered the preparatory department of Cornell college, at Mt. Vernon, took the classical course, and on June 16, 1884, graduated with the degree of A. B. He was manager of the college base ball team for two years and held various offices in the Adelphian Literary society.

He then entered the University of Michigan, at Ann Arbor, and July 1, 1886, graduated from the law department with the degree of LL. B.

In June, 1887, Cornell college conferred upon him the degree of A. M. In 1885 he enlisted as a private in the Iowa National Guard and rose successively to orderly-sergeant and second lieutenant in 1889, captain in 1890, and major in 1894.

Governor Shaw issued his call for volunteers for the Spanish-American war on April 25, 1898. On this day Lieutenant-Colonel Moffit had been in his office attend-

ing to business as usual and was called from his bed about midnight by a message directing him to report at Des Moines forthwith to be enrolled.

The next morning, after having travelled across half the state, found him reporting to the adjutant-general for duty, at 9:30 A. M.

He was enrolled as major of the Fiftieth Iowa on April 26; mustered into the United States service on May 18th, and on August 20th was promoted to lieutenant-colonel of the Fiftieth Iowa Volunteer infantry.

This regiment was the first to leave Iowa for the south. He was regularly mustered out, with his regiment, on November 20, 1898.

After his college days were over he formed a law partnership with Charles E. Wheeler, under the firm name of Wheeler & Moffit, and commenced business November 1, 1887, at Tipton, Iowa. September 1, 1894, Judge J. H. Preston resigned his seat on the district bench and became associated with the firm of Wheeler & Moffit under the firm name of Preston, Wheeler & Moffit, and immediately the new firm opened an office in Cedar Rapids, to be conducted in connection with the one at Tipton. Mr. Wheeler withdrew September 1, 1897, and the firm is now Preston & Moffit. Judge Preston has charge of the business in Cedar Rapids and resides there, while Mr. Moffit looks after the practice in Tipton. They have been connected with all the important litigation of Cedar county and are regarded as a strong firm.

Lieutenant-Colonel Moffit has always been a republican. He was a delegate from Iowa to the republican national convention which met at Minneapolis in 1892, being but 29 years of age at that time. He was one of the youngest members of that body, certainly the youngest of the Iowa delegation. He takes an active interest in politics, but has never sought office. In the spring of 1896, Tipton was organized into a city of the second class and he was elected its first mayor under the new order, although against his wish. He was president of the Republican club of Cedar county in 1888, and held a similar office in the McKinley club of Tipton in 1896. He was married to Miss Winifred E. Hecht, daughter of Fred and Margaret E. Hecht, at Clarence, Iowa, September 28, 1892. Has one daughter, Margaret Eleanor, born May 6, 1897.

---

WORK, W. A., of Ottumwa, Iowa, is the senior member of the law firm of Work & Lewis, and is an enthusiast in his devotion to the law, his chosen profession. Mr. Work turns neither to the right nor left in

search for honors or preferment that will not come to him as a devoted laborer in the profession which he has chosen as his life work, and which he loves so well. Mr. Work was born on the 25th day of December, 1844, on a farm in Jefferson county,

Iowa. His father, Joseph Work, was a native of Clark county, Ind., and came to Jefferson county, Iowa, in 1843. The same year, before leaving Indiana, he was married to Miss Eleanor Huckleberry. They moved to Van Buren county, Iowa, near Birmingham in 1845, where young W. A. was reared on a farm and became inured to all the hardships, labor and privations incident to pioneer life. His father represented Van Buren county in the state legislature in 1872.

The subject of this sketch was educated in the old schoolhouse of pioneer days, where he attended a winter and a summer term till he was old enough to work in the field, when he was limited to a winter term for several years. In these schools everything learned was not from books. The wide expanse of prairie fringed with forests, over which they roamed, gave the boy a breadth of character not attained in the limited environments of the city.

Such was young Work in the latter fifties, when he entered the then well known academy at Birmingham. In 1862, he was admitted to the college course of Iowa Wesleyan university, at Mt. Pleasant. He completed one year's work there and in 1863, enlisted in the United States navy, and was assigned to the United States gunboat, Benton, flagship of Admiral Porter's lower Mississippi squadron.

He served during a part of 1863 and 1864, when many of the great engagements on the Mississippi river occurred. Island No. 10; Memphis, Vicksburg and New Orleans had fallen when he quit the service, and commerce was restored to the great river. When his term of service closed, he returned to the Iowa Wesleyan and finished the college course in 1867. After graduating he taught school at Keosauqua for a year, but in the meantime took up the study of law with Hon. Robert Sloan of the Keosauqua bar, and when Judge Sloan was elected to the circuit judgeship he succeeded to his practice. Eight years later he associated himself with Judge Alexander Brown, under the firm name of Work & Brown, and in 1882, Judge Sloan, after leaving the bench, became a member of the firm. In 1883 Mr. Work came to Ottumwa and opened an office, but still continues his association with the old firm at Keosauqua, and regularly attends both the courts of Van Buren and Wapello counties. He has been successfully engaged in some of the most important litigated cases in southeastern Iowa. As a trial lawyer, either to the court or before a jury, Mr. Work has few equals. His mind is naturally analytical and logical, and whether discussing a point of law or presenting an analysis of the evidence of a case, he is strong and convincing.

In 1895 Mr Work became associated with John W. Lewis, and the firm ranks among the first in the Ottumwa bar. Mr. Work is a republican in politics and is a strong supporter of his party, but he is in no sense a politician, devoting his attention to his chosen profession, seeking no honors but those that strictly belong to it. Mr. Work and Miss Hinda H. Marlow were united in marriage at Keosauqua in 1869. Mrs. Work is a daughter of Benjamin P. Marlow, and a native of Van Buren county, Iowa. They have born to them six children, three sons and three daughters. They have a beautiful home of unfailing hospitality on the corner of Court and Fifth streets, in Ottumwa. He is a member of the M. E. Church.

WHEELER, HIAL AUGUSTUS, M. D. Among the many members of the medical profession to whom the management of the Iowa State university may point with pardonable pride is Prof. H. A. Wheeler, for five years dean of the faculty of the Sioux City Medical college, and at present filling the chair of medicine, clinical medicine and neurology in that widely known institution. He is the son of Silas and Jane F. Wheeler, both of English and Scotch parentage, who are now living in La Grange, Ill. There were three children besides Hial A. He was born at Barton, Vt., June 20, 1854, where his early educa-

tion was acquired in the common schools. At the age of 16 he was placed in the Free-will Baptist seminary at Lindon Center, where he remained one year, then worked for a time as clerk in manufacturing establishments in Boston and New York. In 1873 he returned home and assisted his father, who was engaged in the livery and stage business, until September 9th, at which time he started for the west. Stopping for a time in La Salle county, Ill., he followed the vocation of school-teacher, and in the spring of 1875 came on to Monona county, Iowa, in a covered wagon, where he engaged in farming and teaching for two years, while he continued the study of medicine under local physicians. He entered the medical department of the Iowa State university in 1878, graduated therefrom in 1881, practiced at Riverside until June, 1883, then removed to Onawa, where, for eleven years, he devoted himself to his profession. During this time he purchased a large professional library, and the hours not required by his practice were spent very largely in study. The office of county physician was tendered him, and he filled the same for five years, but was obliged to give it up by reason of the demands made on his time in other directions. From September 1, 1887, to January 1, 1891, he was senior member of the drug firm of Wheeler & Egli. In 1890 he compiled and published "Abstracts of Pharmacology," a work prepared for the use of physicians, pharmacists, and students of medicine and pharmacy, preparing for examination in colleges and before state boards of examiners. Many thousand copies of the work have been sold throughout the middle and western states. In 1887 he conceived the idea of a college of medicine for the northwest, and at once started the movement which resulted, in 1890, in the establishment of the Sioux City Medical college. He was the prime mover, one of the original incorporators, and served as dean of the faculty during the first five years of its existence. Although his time is taken up with a large practice in Sioux City, he still maintains an active connection with the institution, and now fills a chair of the highest importance in the school.

The doctor is a member of the Missouri Valley Medical society, and has acquired a reputation as lecturer upon subjects pertaining to his profession. He was married to Miss Mary C. Ingham, a native of Texas, September 27, 1876, and they have four children: J. Rush, born in Iowa City, April 28, 1879; E. Ruel, born at Morse, Iowa, March 6, 1881; A Ray, born at Onawa, April 16, 1885, and Jessie J., born at Onawa, June 20, 1886. Both the doctor and his wife are members of the Congregational church. He is a staunch republican, though not active in politics.

---

McCLAIN, EMLIN, chancellor of the law department of the State University of Iowa, a distinguished legal authority, author of many standard works, and best known in Iowa as the annotator of the code, both old and new, is now a resident of Iowa City, where he has been connected

with the law department of the State university since 1881. He was born in Salem, Ohio, November 25, 1851. Both his parents were born in Pennsylvania, of Quaker antecedents. His father, William McClain, was of Scotch-Irish descent and was prin-

cipal and proprietor of Salem institute in Ohio. He removed to Tipton, Cedar county, Iowa, in 1855, where he had charge of the public schools of the town. For a time he operated a farm in that county and afterward owned and conducted the Iowa City Commercial college, and in connection with it founded the Iowa City academy. A few months before his death, in 1877, he opened a commercial college in Des Moines. Emlin McClain lived on the farm until he was about 13 years old and his early education was obtained almost entirely at home, concluding with one year at an academy in Wilton. In 1866, at the early age of 15, he entered the State university and graduated in the philosophical course in 1871, taking the classical degree in 1872 and graduating from the law department in 1873. During his college course he was a member of the Zetagathian literary society and one of its presidents. He was also a member of the Beta Theta Pi fraternity, and was one of the commencement speakers of his collegiate and law classes. Upon the completion of his law course he went at once as a clerk in the law office of Gatch, Wright & Runnells, in Des Moines. He was private secretary of United States Senator Geo. G. Wright, and clerk of the senate committee on claims during the two sessions of the Forty-fourth Congress, 1875–77. For the next four years, until 1881, he practiced law in Des Moines and during that time prepared McClain's Annotated Statutes of Iowa, which was published in 1880 and immediately became the standard code, regarded as an absolute necessity by every lawyer in Iowa. In 1881 he was appointed a professor in the law department of the State university, and removed to Iowa City; he was made vice chancellor in 1887 and chancellor in 1890.

Since 1881 he has devoted himself entirely to teaching law and writing law books. His principal works are: "Outlines of Criminal Law and Procedure," 1884; "Synopsis of Elementary Law and Law of Personal Property," 1884; "Digest of Iowa Reports," in two volumes, 1887, with third volume, 1898; "McClain's Annotated Code and Statutes of Iowa," in two volumes, 1888, with supplement, 1892; "Criminal Law," in two volumes, 1897; "Cases on the Law of Carriers," 1893, second edition, 1896. Besides these he has published numerous articles in the Western Jurist, The American Law Review, Harvard Law Review, Central Law Journal, The Green Bag, Iowa Normal Monthly and the Iowa Historical Record. He has been an active member of the American Bar association since 1889; he has been chairman of its committee on classification of the law and member of its committee on legal education, and in 1896 was chairman of the section on legal education. He presided at the organization of the Iowa Bar association in 1895 and has since been chairman of its committee on legal education. In 1894 Chancellor McClain was appointed one of the commissioners of Iowa to act with commissioners from other states to recommend uniform laws, and acted with such commissioners in preparing a negotiable instruments act which was adopted by the commission in 1896 and has become a law in New York, Connecticut, Colorado, Florida and other states of the union, and will probably be the basis of the future commercial law in the United States. In 1894 he was selected by the senate as one of the code commissioners to report to the general assembly of Iowa a revised code. Their work was presented to the Twenty-sixth General Assembly and formed the basis of the revised code which was adopted at the special session of the legislature in 1897. Under the special authority of the general assembly Chancellor McClain was selected to prepare the annotations for the new code which was published by the state, October 1, 1897.

Chancellor McClain was married February 19, 1879, to Ellen Griffiths, daughter of the late Capt. Henry H. Griffiths, of Des Moines, who was one of the early settlers of Des Moines, and during the rebellion was captain of the First Iowa battery. They have three children: Donald, born April 15, 1880; Henry Griffiths, born De-

cember 18, 1881, and Gwendolyn, born June 4, 1894. The chancellor has received the honorary degree of A. M., 1882, from the State University of Iowa, and LL. D., 1891, from the same institution and from Findlay college, Ohio. Upon the organization of the University Chapter Phi Beta Kappa fraternity, he was one of those selected from the previous classes on the ground of scholarship, to be charter members. He is an honorary member of the law fraternity, Phi Delta Phi, the university chapter of which bears his name. His political connection has always been with the republican party. His father was an original and ardent republican, having been identified in sympathy and action with the abolitionists. Chancellor McClain is president of the board of trustees of the Congregational church of Iowa City, though not a member of the church.

---

HALEY, FELIX EMMET, secretary and treasurer of the Iowa State Traveling Men's association, is a resident of Des Moines, where, as a business man, he is well and

favorably known. Mr. Haley was born in Iowa, at Mt. Pleasant, May 31, 1862, and is the son of Timothy and Mary Haley. They are prosperous farmers, now living in Henry county; well provided for by the industry and thrift of a prudent and active life. They have not sought any public notoriety, but have attended to their own affairs and brought up a respectable and successful family of children. Mrs. Haley is known as a good mother and wife, and what more need be said? They were born in Ireland, and all their ancestors lived in the Emerald Isle. Their son, F. E. Haley, received his early education in the public schools and in Howe's academy in Mt. Pleasant. But some of the best lessons of his boyhood were those of industry and economy, which were taught him on his father's farm. He began early in his youth to support himself and learn to depend upon his own efforts. After leaving school in 1883 he was at once elected principal of the public schools of New London, Iowa, and in this capacity he was uniformly successful. Four years of his life were spent in this work. In the fall of 1886 he became associated with the *Iowa State Register*. In this line of work he at once achieved success as traveling representative for the paper, and built up a large and valuable acquaintance all over the state. He increased the business of the paper and did well for himself at the same time. While employed as a traveling man he became interested in the Iowa State Traveling Men's association, which was first organized partly for social intercourse and partly for a mutual accident insurance association. He devoted himself with all his accustomed energy to building up this association, and secured several hundred new members for it. In 1890 he was elected secretary and treasurer and very shortly gave up his work on the road to put all his time into the development and management of the association, which had, in the fall of 1891, grown to a large and substantial membership. Mr. Haley has been re-elected each year since that time and has rarely had any opposition. Under his administration the organization has grown and developed into one of the largest and strongest accident insurance associations in the United States, paying out annually something like $100,000 in benefits and death losses. Their membership has steadily increased, although the restrictions have been multiplied until now no one but an actual traveling man, who has been selling goods on the road by sample for more than one year, can become a member. It now has, in 1899, 10,500 members. The members fully appreciating the value of Mr. Haley's services, and being nearly all business men themselves, consider that it is only a plain business matter in which they are all interested to retain the services of Mr. Haley as chief administrative officer.

Mr. Haley was married in Burlington, Iowa, January 29, 1895, to Miss Katherine A. Norton. They have a family of two children, Mary and Katherine, both bright, interesting girls. Mr. Haley has been successful in business ventures. He is conservative in his dealings, both in the management of the corporation he represents as its chief officer and in his personal business transactions. Besides being energetic and aggressive, he is particularly courteous, and no young business man in Des Moines stands higher in the estimation of the general public than the subject of this sketch. Whatever degree of success he may achieve, to his own personal efforts, strength of character and honesty of purpose can the credit be given. His highest ambition is to faithfully perform every duty and to live the life of a good and upright citizen.

———

MOWRY, WELCOME, member of the state board of railroad commissioners, makes his home on his 700 acre farm in Tama county, where he has lived since 1867. His parents were George A. and Nancy Jack Mowry, and he was born in Putnam county, Ill., April 3, 1842. His father was born in Rhode Island and his mother in Maryland. They were both members of the Society of Friends and Mr. Mowry often preached for them. They came to Bureau county, Ill., in 1841, and later went to Putnam county to educate their children, and then returned to Bureau county, where Mr. Mowry died in 1889. Their son, Welcome, was educated in the common schools and attended Dover academy. At the age of 17 he began supporting himself, working on a farm at $10 per month. In the spring of 1861 he made his first effort to enlist in the union army at Wyanett, Ill., and went with his company to Springfield, but as the quota of Illinois on the first call had been filled, he returned home after about a month. In August of that year he enlisted under C. S. Merriman and went with his company to Fort Leavenworth, which became Company D of the Seventh Kansas Volunteer cavalry. They spent the first winter in Missouri keeping down the guerrillas, and in the spring of 1862 went to Tennessee, spending the next two and a half years in Tennessee, Mississippi and Alabama. They participated in the battles of Corinth, Coffeyville, Tupelo, and the soldier of whom we write was under fire, in addition to the above, at Iuka, Coldwater, Abbeyville, Holly Springs, Oxford, Water Valley and Jackson, Tenn., and at Rippey, Miss. While following Price through Mississippi, he with four others was sent to reconnoiter Price's position. It was a perilous undertaking in the night, wading streams and taking all hazards. They ran onto the enemy's camp guard and then fell back. The enemy, not knowing the size of the force opposing them, soon evacuated the town. This is probably the only instance where five men started a whole army. "He was frequently on duty

as scout or courier in hazardous enterprises," says one of his commanders, "where his unflinching bravery, quick intelligence, sound judgment were signally displayed, winning for him the praise of commanding officers. He was our ideal of a soldier." Being honorably discharged at St. Louis, September 27, 1864, he returned home and went to school for a short time, but re-enlisted February 13, 1865, in Company F, One Hundred Fifty-first Illinois Volunteer infantry, and on account of previous service was made drill sergeant, and in a competitive drill was placed in command of the headquarters guard of General Judea, which he held under Generals Judea and H. F. Sickles, until the close of his enlistment. He was discharged

the last time in February, 1866, and returned at once to Wyanett, Ill., and resumed peaceful pursuits. He was married September 5, 1866, to Miss Lucina Sapp, daughter of Hezekiah and Mary J. Bosket Sapp, who were both natives of Delaware. They have three children, Lorena C., born December 18, 1868, Burdette F., born April 22, 1870, and Alzad B., born October 10, 1873. In the following spring the young couple started in a covered wagon for Iowa, and settled in Oneida township, Tama county, on the same farm where they now reside. He commenced with eighty acres, and now has 700 acres of Iowa's most productive soil. Although the land is gently rolling he has laid over four miles of tiling under it.

Colonel Mowry has always been an active republican, casting his first vote for Abraham Lincoln in 1864, and has never missed an election since he came to Iowa. He was justice of the peace for ten years. In 1873 he was placed on the republican ticket for supervisor but the anti-monopoly movement was then at its height and he was defeated by thirty-seven votes in the county. In 1875 he began taking part in speaking campaigns and in every year since then he has stumped either the county, the district or the state In 1883 he was elected to represent his county in the legislature, and took an active part in the business of the session. Believing that laws were too often changed he spent more time in defeating what he considered bad measures, than he did in securing the enactment of new laws. He, however, secured the passage of the measure to reduce the penalty on delinquent taxes to 1 per cent a month. He took the ground that if the state did not allow an individual to collect more than 6 per cent interest, the state should be satisfied with 12. He received special credit from the farmers for the defeat of the bill to abolish independent and subdistricts in the country, making no change in the school laws applying to cities and towns. This bill was championed by State Superintendent Akers and Senator L. R. Bolter, and supported by the representatives of the cities. In 1892, when the Fifth congressional district was democratic, Colonel Mowry was urged to become a candidate for congress, but was defeated in the convention by R. G. Cousins, the present member. Colonel Mowry immediately took the stump for his successful rival and worked for Mr. Cousins until he was elected. In 1896, without being a candidate, Colonel Mowry was unanimously selected republican candidate for presidential elector in the Fifth district, and made twenty-five speeches thoroughly over the state in that campaign. He was elected by the largest vote of any elector, except Major Conger, elector at large. Colonel Mowry's long service to the republican party and his eminent business qualifications were recognized by the party in 1898, when he was nominated for railroad commissioner by the republican state convention in Dubuque. He received on the first ballot 242½ more votes than his strongest competitor and more than 100 majority over all. He was elected by 62,883 plurality. He is now filling the office with the good sense and industry that have brought him such a large measure of success in all that he has undertaken in life.

ALLEN, MILTON HENRY, of Sheldon, is one of the best-known and most widely employed lawyers of O'Brien county, as well as of northern Iowa generally. He has been brought up in a law office, as it were, for his father, Charles T. Allen, is also a prominent lawyer. He is one of the very early settlers of northeastern Iowa, having come to Winneshiek county from Henry county, Ill., in 1856. He served during the war as captain of Company K, Thirty-fourth Iowa Infantry volunteers. Mr. Allen's mother was formerly Carrie Smith, a native of New York state.

Milt. H. Allen, as he is commonly called, was born February 11, 1859, at Decorah. His earliest instruction was received in the public schools of that town, and was continued at Spencer, in Clay county, whither he moved with his parents in 1871. Five years later the family moved to O'Brien county, settling at Sheldon, where Mr. Allen began reading law in 1877 in the office of Barrett & Allen, the members of the firm being O. M. Barrett, afterwards state senator, and C. T. Allen, the father of Milton. He was chiefly occupied by his studies for the next few years, though at one time he stopped to accept a position as brakeman on the old Sioux City & St. Paul railway. He was admitted to the bar in the

district court of O'Brien county, May 9, 1881, and immediately began practicing in his home town. He removed to Sanborn in 1884, and, after enjoying a good business there for nine years, returned to Sheldon, November, 1, 1893, where he still resides. One of the most important cases he has tried was in February, 1891, on a question of *habeas corpus*, in which he succeeded in releasing John Telford from the penitentiary at Sioux Falls, S. D., where he had served two of a fifteen-years' sentence for robbery. The point raised was the uncertainty of the statute under which the sentence was pronounced. Since that time Mr. Allen has been employed in nearly all the important cases in O'Brien and adjoining counties, making a specialty of railroad, corporation and criminal law. He has been the local attorney for the Chicago, Milwaukee & St. Paul Railroad company since 1889 and of the Chicago, St. Paul, Minneapolis & Omaha since 1895.

In politics Mr. Allen was a democrat all his life until 1896, when he bolted the Chicago free silver platform and joined the republican forces, making campaign speeches all over northwestern Iowa for McKinley and sound money. He is a member of the Benevolent and Protective Order of Elks, belonging to the Sioux Falls Lodge No. 262. He is not a member of any church

----

ANDERSON, EDWIN, a prominent merchant and druggist of Ruthven, is a native of Sweden, having been born in that country March 24, 1857. His parents were Andrew and Matilda Johnson Anderson, natives of Sweden. Their ancestors were all soldiers and sailors.

Edwin attended the common schools in his native country up to the age of 12 years, when he came to the United States with his parents. They located at Ft. Dodge, Iowa, in 1870, where Edwin attended school in the winter and worked on a farm in the summer for the first two years. After this, he went to work for one of the leading doctors in Ft. Dodge, as hostler, also taking care of his office, and at the same time studying medicine with him. He remained in this service several years and afterwards clerked for several firms in different lines of business until 1885. He was strictly temperate and never idle, and saved his salary, so that he had accumulated enough to start in business for himself. This he accordingly did at Ruthven, in

1885. He is a registered pharmacist, having passed examination before the board of pharmacy in 1881. He is now conducting one of the largest book, notions and fancy goods and drug stores in northwestern Iowa.

In politics he has always been a democrat, and in 1898 was a candidate on this ticket in the Tenth district for congress, cutting down the plurality of his opponent, Mr. Dolliver, by 3,552, and in doing this made the largest gain of any candidate. He is an Odd Fellow, Mason and Shriner.

He was married January 1, 1882, to Ada V. Hendrickson, of Fulton county, Ohio.

CONLEY, JOSEPH BERNARD, is one of the craft of honest millers whose "mill goes round" at the beautiful little city of Lake Mills. The parents of Mr. Conley were natives of Vermont, but removed to Wisconsin in 1850, where they engaged in farming. They reared a family of eleven children, five sons and six daughters, which, together with the few opportunities for enriching one's self afforded by the early times in Wisconsin, prevented any great accumulation of this world's goods. There were no railroads in the neighborhood where they resided, and they were compelled to haul their farm products to

Milwaukee by ox team, and as that city was eighty miles away they would receive scarcely enough from their produce to pay the expenses of the trip. In 1881 they removed to Chicago, where the father engaged in the grocery business with moderate success. The earlier ancestors of Mr. Conley were natives of Ireland and were people of considerable importance, some being closely related to Marshal MacDonald, of France.

Mr. Joseph Bernard Conley was born in Clinton, Rock county, Wis., in 1852. His common school education was supplemented by a course in the Sharon academy, where he received the education which has been so useful to him throughout his life. After some years of teaching and farm work in Wisconsin, in 1877 he came to Iowa, and was employed for several years in drilling wells throughout the state. He located in Lake Mills. In 1881 he secured the interest of S. D. Wadsworth in an old buhr flouring mill, the business of which was conducted under the name of Conley, Smith & Company, until the year 1883, at

which time the interest of Smith & Company was purchased by Mr. Winslow, after which the firm was known as Winslow & Conley. The property was greatly enlarged and improved by these gentlemen, and in 1895 an electric light plant was

added which now furnishes illumination
for public and private use. In March,
1897, Mr. Conley bought the interest of
Mr. Winslow and has since operated the
business alone.

Mr. Conley was a republican until Mr.
Cleveland received his nomination, since
which time he has been identified with the
democratic party. He has been mayor of
the city of Lake Mills two terms, and has
served several years as member of the city
council of that place. He is a devout member of the Catholic church. In 1881 he
was married to Miss Sarah B. Kenny, of
Delavan, Wis. They have two children:
Vere, aged 12, and Wilfred, aged 10. The
home life of Mr. Conley is a most happy
and congenial one. He has ample means
to provide the necessities as well as the
luxuries of life, in which they indulge to a
reasonable and consistent extent.

WINNINGER, JOSEPH URBAN, is one
of the leading business men of the city
of Waterloo, and has worked his way up to
his present prominent position entirely

by his own efforts, having worked at the
trade of a tailor ever since he was 14 years
old. Both his father, John Winninger,
and mother, Marie, were natives of Alsace.

J. U. Winninger was born May 25, 1863,
near Muehlhausen, in the province of
Alsace. He attended the common schools
until he was 14 years old, receiving the
thorough discipline and instruction so
characteristic of the educational system
of that country. Living so near the
boundary of France, the French and German languages were both taught in the
schools which he attended. At 14 he left
school, and was apprenticed to learn the
trade of a tailor. This occupation he has
followed ever since. In the summer of
1882, when he was 19 years old he came to
America, and, after spending two months
in New York city, he came to Waterloo, in
October. Upon his arrival in New York,
he had only $6, but, with the little he
earned in that city, and with the help of a
friend in Waterloo who loaned him $15, he
was enabled to reach his destination. He
immediately secured work in Waterloo, and
within two weeks he was square with the
world and began to accumulate money for
himself. After about four years spent
in strict attention to business, he was able
through thrift and economy to start in
business for himself. He first located at
Manchester, and, after two prosperous
years there, went to San Jose, Cal., where
he secured a position as cutter in a large
tailoring establishment. He soon launched
out for himself again, however; this time at
Woodland, Cal. For six years he did a flourishing business, and in September, 1895, returned to Waterloo and opened a tailoring establishment of his own. He has increased
the scope of his business from year to year
until he now commands a very wide patronage

Mr. Winninger has always been a republican in politics, having voted with that
party ever since he became naturalized.
But he has never had time to take any
active part in politics. He is a member of
the Masonic and Knights of Pythias
lodges.

Mr. Winninger was married January 5,
1891, to Louisa Ewald, at Waterloo. They
have one daughter, Gladys, born in 1895,
and Mr. Winninger has a daughter, Marguerite, aged 12, by a former marriage.

NELSON, N. I. Mr. Nelson is engaged
in the general merchandise and wholesale
grocery business at Lake Mills, being a
member of the well-known Scar-Nelson
Merchandise company. He is descended
on his father's side from the old Vikings.
His mother's grandfather was of Teuton
descent, but his own grandfather was born

in Norway, and served in the war of 1812 for his native country. Iver Nelson, the father of N. I. Nelson, landed in New York on the 1st day of July, 1851, having crossed the Atlantic in a sail boat. He was more than three months in making the voyage.

From New York he went by water to Milwaukee, and with an ox team drove overland to Stoughten, Wis. He assisted in the construction of the first railroad leading west of Chicago. In 1853 he settled in Winneshiek county, this state, where he was married, in 1856, after which he removed to Mitchell county and engaged in farming. At the present time he resides in St. Ansgar, and is among the wealthiest citizens of that place. His mother, Ingelberg Rosby Nelson, came from Quebec to Winneshiek county July 4, 1856, where she was married to the father of our subject.

Mr. N. I. Nelson was born June 1, 1857, at Calmar, Winneshiek county. He was given a good common school education and in addition took two courses at the St. Ansgar seminary and a commercial course at the Decorah college, from which he graduated in the spring of 1882. He worked upon a farm, however, until he had accumulated $1,000. In June, 1882, he entered the hardware store of Johnson & Annis, at Osage, as clerk at $20 per month. Shortly thereafter his salary was raised to

$35 per month, and in less than one year to $50 per month. That position he held until the spring of 1886, when he removed to Lake Mills and formed a partnership with Mr. O. Scar in the general merchandise business under the style of Scar & Nelson. This firm is still in existence, operating three stores, with extensive cold storage facilities, and also a canning factory. The last named enterprise is known as the Lake Mills Canning company, and is an institution that has proved of inestimable value to the farmers of that section. Mr. Nelson, in addition to the concerns mentioned, is largely interested in the Arlington Hotel company. He is an energetic business man, and by honorable dealing, economy and good business judgment, will, if he lives, become as well off in this world's goods as is his father. He has always voted the republican ticket, but has never held office except such as have been forced upon him. He has served as mayor of his town, and was for six years member of the city council. He is a member of the United Lutheran church, the Masonic order and the A. O. U. W. June 2, 1883, he was married to Miss Anna C. Sorbon, of Rock Creek. They have two children, Eda E. and Irving A., 9 and 5 years of age, respectively.

SCAR, OLE, of Lake Mills, is a good type of thrifty, intelligent class of citizens which Norway has contributed to this country. Beginning life with no other capital than energy, perseverance and good sense, he has succeeded in acquiring a very comfortable fortune, and in being classed among the most prosperous merchants of the state. He was born August 11, 1845, at Bang, Norway. His early educational advantages were somewhat limited, but by the aid of self-instruction, he fitted himself for business, so that at the age of 12 he secured a position as clerk in a store, where he remained about five years. But feeling the need of a more complete and thorough education, he petitioned for admittance to the Sargeant Military school, at Christiania, where he was accepted, and in 1866 graduated with first honors, as sergeant. Not satisfied, however with the future which a military life offered, he secured his discharge and permission to emigrate to America, the requests not being granted until after three successive petitions.

Mr. Scar sailed for this country in

July, 1868, when not quite 23 years old, and first settled in Black Earth, Wis. Here he secured work at once as clerk in a store, and after remaining a year concluded to go farther west and accordingly located at West Mitchell, in

Mitchell county, Iowa. His funds being limited, he was unable to start in business for himself, so he was again employed as clerk. While here he became acquainted with William Larson, a business man of Osage, who was so well pleased with young Scar that he offered him a position as manager of a branch store at Lake Mills. He conducted the business so successfully at this place that Mr. Larson soon sold out his stock at Osage and established himself at Lake Mills, where the two men prospered well until the mill burned in 1871. This misfortune caused a check on all trade, as the mill had been the life of what was then a small trading post. The dullness of business made Mr. Scar restless, and in 1871 he went to California to try the gold fields. He was quite successful at first, but soon feeling that luck was not with him there, he concluded to go to Puget Sound, where it was expected that the Northern railway would terminate. He settled at Olympia, Wash., where he entered eighty acres of land in hopes of striking the terminus. The railroad project finally failed, but Mr.

Scar proved up on his land, which he still owns, and in 1874 returned to Iowa. He formed a partnership with his former employer, Mr. Larson, and after a few years bought him out, but the connection was again resumed, and finally dissolved in 1880. Soon after this Mr. Scar purchased the business of S. D. Wadsworth & Co., which he conducted alone until 1883, when he entered into partnership with his brother-in-law, N. I. Nelson, and in 1893 the firm was incorporated under the name of the Scar-Nelson Mercantile Co., and has been very successful, enjoying a wide patronage. Mr. Scar has also dealt considerably in real estate. Mr. Scar is a bachelor.

———

CONDIT, WILLIAM DAVIDSON, is one of the most active and enterprising men in the state, and as secretary of the Duplex Typewriter company has done much for the city of Des Moines by helping to develop one of its most important industries, the manufacture of the Duplex and Jewett

typewriters. Mr. Condit was born June 19, 1847, on a farm near New Castle, Pa., and is the son of Jabez Condit and Ruth A. Scott, his wife. Jabez Condit was a farmer; he sold his farm and started west in 1852, but by an accident enroute he was crippled for life and stopped in Iberia, Ohio, to send his children to the Presbyterian school in that village. He resumed his journey westward in the spring of 1861, settled in Washington county, Iowa, and resided in Iowa until his death at Holstein, September 23, 1896, in his 85th year. He was of Welsh descent. His ancestors were good citizens and generally large property holders. They came to America and settled in New Jersey long before the revolutionary war, and were well represented in that struggle for freedom and in the war of 1812. In civil life they were found in the Presbyterian ministry, in the professions, in business, teaching and farming. Several were members of the state legislature. One was a representative and senator in the United States congress for thirty years in succession, and another was a trustee of Princeton university for forty years.

Mrs. Condit was of Scotch-Irish descent; a very intelligent woman, and a teacher for several years before marriage. She died September 12, 1878, in her 68th year. Her father, Francis Scott, died when she was a little girl, from exposure in the war of 1812.

Both of Mr. W. D. Condit's parents were Presbyterians, and of strong Christian character. They had five children, as follows: Cyrus, now a resident of Boston; Ezekiel C., of Denver, Col ; W. D., of Des Moines; Mrs. Carrie Judiesch, of Holstein, Iowa; and Mrs. Lizzie Mallory, of Denver. The older two sons served during the civil war in the Nineteenth Iowa infantry, and Cyrus was severely wounded in the battle of Prairie Grove, Ark. William D. attended the primary department of Iberia college and the common schools of Washington county, Iowa. He had the usual experience of teaching country schools in the winter and working the farm in the summer, and later was principal of city schools for six years. He also taught vocal music. In 1875 he engaged in the book business, and two years later located in Burlington, where he was successful, but sold out in 1882 and removed to Des Moines. Here he continued the same business for eleven years under the firm name of W. D. Condit & Company, with Mr. John R. Nelson as partner during much of the time. In May, 1893, he became interested in the manufacture of the Duplex and Jewett typewriters; became one of the large stockholders, and, as secretary of the company, had special charge of the sales department. This enterprise has become one of the largest in the state in the value of its product and amount of wages paid employes, and is constantly and rapidly growing.

His first business venture was at the age of 17, when he succeeded in a single year in paying off the $600 mortgage on his father's farm, supported the family, attended the stock, and had a handsome profit besides.

In politics Mr. Condit has always been a republican and a prohibitionist. He has been an elder in the Presbyterian church for twenty-seven years, and is now a ruling elder in the Central Presbyterian church of Des Moines. He was married November 3, 1870, to Miss Rhoda M. Glasgow, daughter of William Madison Glasgow, of Washington county. They have five children: Lola May, born December 26, 1872; William Glasgow and Anna, born March 30, 1876; Frederick, born May 22, 1882; and Bessie, born June 8, 1884.

GEIGER, Hon. WILLIAM G. W., of Tipton, is well known throughout the state as a lawyer and politician. He possesses a fine judicial mind and great mental and physical activity. He is a native

of Cedar county, born on the old homestead entered by his father, in time to be old enough to just remember the return of the boys in blue from the war of the rebellion. It was there the long winter evenings were spent in study;

there was laid the foundation for a classical education, and there were acquired the habits of industry, which have enabled him to become a man of affairs. In September, 1874, he entered college at Carthage, Ill., where he took the classical course, graduating in the spring of 1879, at the age of 22 years. At that time he received the degree of bachelor of arts, and three years later the honorary degree of master of arts. He was a member of Cicero Literary society during his college days, and as such earned considerable distinction. He commenced the study of law in the office of Wolf & Landt at Tipton in the fall of 1879, and was admitted to the bar the following year, after which he read law in the office of Blake & Hormel, at Cedar Rapids. In the fall of 1881 he opened an office in Tipton and laid the foundation for a successful professional and business career. His first fee in the practice of his profession was earned in defending one charged with a felony. He secured the discharge of his client on preliminary hearing. He now enjoys a practice that is second to none in his native county. In his fifteen years of practice he has covered all lines of court work and has had entrusted to his care many extensive and complicated cases wherein the responsibility was great, in all of which he has performed his duties to the satisfaction of all concerned. He has the confidence of the courts before which he is in almost constant practice, and is held in the highest esteem by his brothers in the profession.

Mr. Geiger is a democrat and says he expects to affiliate with that party as long as its principles come nearest to his convictions, but only so long. He places party second to individual conviction. He has never held office nor sought political preferment, believing it the best policy to keep out of politics as far as possible until such a time as one has become independent as he cares to be financially. However, in 1888, when Cedar county was in the republican column, he was nominated for county attorney on the democratic ticket, and through loyalty to party permitted his name to go before the people. Although defeated, he reduced the republican majority to fourteen, running far ahead of his ticket. This splendid endorsement led to his nomination for judge of the Eighteenth judicial district in 1890, and again in 1896, to fill the vacancy caused by the death of Judge William P. Wolf, but he was defeated in both instances by reason

of the political complexion of that section. Mr. Geiger has been a diligent reader all his life and has traveled extensively. His father's home was well supplied with good books and the family custom of reading aloud stimulated the taste for profitable reading. Mr. Geiger feels grateful to his parents for the correct ideas they gave him in his boyhood, and especially for teaching him habits of industry.

Jacob Geiger, father of William, was a native of Germany. He came to this country when 8 years of age, and was given a college education, after which he learned the trade of currier and tanner. He located in Cedar county in 1853, and died there in 1894, owning the same old farm he had entered, though it had grown to 520 acres. He was a candidate for congress on the greenback ticket against Hiram Price. The mother's maiden name was Elizabeth Lichtenwalter. She was born near Taneytown, Md.; came to Iowa in 1852, and here met and married Jacob Geiger. Of this marriage there are seven children living: Mrs. Anna E. Cravens, of Lake City, Minn.; W. G. W. Geiger, the subject of this sketch; Judge A. C T. Geiger, of Oberlin, Kan.; Mrs. H. Ruth Emahizer, of Oberlin, Kan.; Mrs. M. Alice Spielman, of Fairfield, Iowa; Etta I. Geiger and Jacob L. Geiger, who are now with their mother at Long Beach, Cal.

Mr. Geiger made a trip in 1896 to Mexico to learn more of the Aztecs, the Toltecs and the Montezumas by personal research and to study the silver question. He traveled about 4,000 miles in that strange republic. Mr. Geiger has tried to make the most of his surroundings and circumstances, and by hard work and close application avoid the jarring and discordant sounds of the closing doors of lost opportunities.

He has been across the continent by two different routes, camped through the Yellowstone National Park, in northwest Wyoming, with its hot springs, geysers, beautiful lakes, gorgeous canon and magnificent scenery; visited the Grand Canon of the Colorado river in Arizona, been around the lakes on the north and to the Gulf on the south of our country; loves the quiet scenery of the little Alleghanies and the rugged, wonderful views of the towering Rockies. Mr. Geiger takes great delight in the beauties of nature, loves the flowers, and finds much pleasure in music. He weaves past experiences together to aid in the judgments of the present. He likes to look back along the "River of Time" and see the achievements of the centuries as well as to reflect upon the ruined hopes and wrecked fortunes that strew its shores.

He was married April 7, 1885, to Miss Flora H. Manier, daughter of W. H. Manier, a lawyer of Carthage, Ill. She was his classmate in college and graduated in the classical course with him. But death came and the husband is left with four little daughters, Maud Marguerite, Laura Helen, Sarah Gertrude and Flora Miriam, now with their grandparents at Carthage. Mr. Geiger is a member of the Odd Fellows, Knights of Pythias and Modern Woodmen of America fraternal societies, and is also a member of the Lutheran church. In 1895 he was a delegate to the general synod of that church in Hagerstown, Md.

He built at Tipton, in the summer of 1897, a substantial and pretty office building with granite front for his own use.

BOWEN. E. E., now county attorney for Dubuque county, who was born and raised in Dubuque, has the advantages of that city to thank for the high position in his chosen profession his own energies have given him. Mr. Bowen is the son of

the late John Bowen, and was born in West Dubuque June 17, 1869. In the practice of his profession he has been very successful, and is recognized as one of the leaders among the members of the Dubuque bar. His able conduct of cases before the courts has won for him the encomiums of the judges and the respect and esteem of his brother attorneys. Mr. Bowen was educated in the Dubuque public and parochial schools. He studied at St. Joseph's college and completed the business course at Bayless' college. He studied law with Powers, Lacy & Brown, and Alphonse Matthews and Judge M. C. Matthews and graduated from the law department of the State University of Iowa on the 5th of June, 1892. On being admitted to the bar he started to practice for himself and was signally successful from the start and soon built up a business that made him independent. Two years ago he entered into partnership with T. J. Fitzpatrick, and the firm of Bowen & Fitzpatrick is looked upon as one of the most successful and honorable in Dubuque county, which now has a

population of 70,000. He was elected to the office of county attorney on the 8th of November, 1898.

---

ARCHER, JAMES, one of the substantial business men of Cherokee, Iowa, was born at Dundee, Scotland, on the 1st of June, 1829. His father, William K. Archer, was a merchant in that city, in good financial circumstances. His mother, before marriage, was Miss Anna Finn. Her father was a liberal politician of Dundee. In 1842 the family emigrated to America and pushed out to the great wild prairie country of northern Illinois, settling in Winnebago county. While a boy in Scotland, James had attended school at a private academy in Dundee, but when they got out onto the western prairies, the only instruction within reach was at the pioneer district schools, which were kept generally only through the cold weather. On the 26th of October, 1861, when James was 32 years of age, he was united in marriage with Miss Arminda Stephens, at Leona, in Winnebago

county, and in 1864 they moved to Iowa, settling on a farm in Fayette county, then moved to Waverly, Iowa, in 1867, and engaged in the lumber business. In 1870 they moved farther west, locating in the new town of Cherokee, where Mr. Archer established the first lumber yard, and connected with his business grain buying. As the county settled up and the town grew into a large village, and the Illinois Central railroad was constructed through it, Cherokee became one of the best business points in northwestern Iowa, between Ft. Dodge and Sioux City. Mr. Archer extended his business as the population increased and by fair dealing and enterprise has built up an extensive trade in the surrounding country, dealing largely in lumber, sash, blinds, window screens, doors and all kinds of building materials, supplying coal and buying grain. Politically Mr. Archer is a republican, having come in at the organization, casting his first vote in November, 1856, for Gen. John C. Fremont, the first republican candidate for president. Mr. Archer has served on the board of county supervisors, as a member of the city council, and for nine years on the school board, and always takes a deep interest in public affairs in his own town, county and state. Mr. and Mrs. Archer have had four children: George H., Frank B., Guy S. and Elmo S., three of whom are living, Frank B. having died in infancy.

---

WARREN, DR. JOHN NELSON, of Sioux City, is a native Iowan and a well-known physician of northwestern Iowa. He is the son of Monroe Warren, a blacksmith, who came to Iowa in the spring of 1844, first locating in Davenport, but soon afterwards removing to De Witt, Clinton county, where he has since resided. He was married July 4, 1845, to Betsy Ann Saliss, who came to Iowa with her parents from Albany, N. Y., in 1844.

Dr. Warren was born at De Witt, Iowa, April 30, 1846, and has resided in the state the principal part of his life. He attended the public schools of De Witt and the Mt. Carroll, Ill., seminary, from which he graduated in 1863. Following this he entered Cornell college for a collegiate course, but in April, 1864, he enlisted in the Forty-fourth Iowa Volunteer infantry as a private and served until September, 1864, when he was mustered out at Davenport. After being mustered out he took a course in Bryant & Stratton's Commercial college, of Chicago, and, after returning home, was clerk in the county clerk's office for one year, when he accepted a similar position in the county recorder's office. While in the recorder's office he commenced work on

the first set of abstract books of farm lands of Clinton county, doing the work for Mr. Dennis Whitney, now of Clinton. In the fall of 1868 he commenced reading medicine under the late Dr. Asa Morgan, of De Witt. In 1869–70 he attended a first course in medicine in the medical department in the University of Michigan and then entered the Miami Medical college at Cincinnati, Ohio, from which he graduated in March, 1871. Following his graduation he received the appointment as assistant physician in the hospital for the insane at Athens, Ohio, which position he held for a period of one and a half years, resigning in order

to return to his home, where he opened an office In March, 1878, he located at Storm Lake, and was in general practice there until October, 1889, at which time, having received the appointment as chief surgeon for the Sioux City & Northern railroad, he moved to Sioux City. Since this he has devoted most of his time to surgical practice, and, in order to better qualify himself for such work, he attended, in the fall of 1883, the Post Graduate Medical college, of New York city, and also took a course of private instructions in abdominal and gynecological surgery under the late Professor Dawson, of New York city.

Dr. Warren has been a life-long republican, but has never aspired to any public office. He is a member of the International Association of Railway Surgeons, State Association of Railway Surgeons, an association which he himself organized, the first meeting being held at Sioux City, October, 1894. He was elected president at that time, and has been chairman of the judiciary committee since retiring as president of the association in 1895. He is a member of the American Medical association, Sioux City Medical association, Sioux Valley Medical association, being secretary of the latter since its organization at Sioux Falls, S. D., in June, 1893. He is a member of the Surgical Society of the Chicago, Milwaukee & St. Paul Railway company, and is chief surgeon of the Sioux City & Northern railway, Sioux City, O'Neill & Western railway, and local surgeon for the Chicago, Milwaukee & St. Paul railway, and is also professor of practice of surgery and clinical surgery in Sioux City College of Medicine.

Dr. Warren was married June 27, 1877, to Mary V. M. Hubbard at Lindon, Ill. They have three children: Alexis M., born 1879; Renita Madge, born 1883; and Nelson Jay, born 1885.

---

PRYCE, SAMUEL DAVID, a patriot of the late civil war and one of the most influential citizens of Iowa City, Johnson county, was born in Ebensburg, Cambria county, Penn., September 11, 1841. His father, Samuel D. Pryce, was born in the same county, of Welsh parents, who emigrated into the mountain regions of Pennsylvania in the latter part of the eighteenth century, and his mother, Elizabeth Jones Pryce, was a native of Wales coming to this country when she was eighteen years old. The son received a limited education in the common schools under the stern discipline of the grim and irascible Yankee school-teacher, in the period just prior to the war. His father was in fair circumstances, but was compelled to yield to the stringency of the times following the panic of 1857, and the old homestead was sold under foreclosure, and the family consisting of parents and four children, broken up. Sam D. went to Pittsburg, where he expected to enter a law office, but concluded to try his fortune in the west. He worked his way down the Ohio river to Cairo, and from that point north on the river to Burlington, and walked from there to Iowa City, arriving in the early spring utterly destitute of means. He worked

for his board several weeks, then taught school a few terms, returning to Iowa City in the spring of 1862, intending to matriculate in the State university, but yielding to his patriotic impulse, enlisted as a private in a company being recruited by Capt. Harvey Graham, which was assigned to the Eighteenth regiment, then in rendezvous at Clinton.

This company was afterwards transferred to the Twenty-second at Camp Pope in Iowa City, and became part of one of the fighting regiments of the war, having campaigned in nearly every southern state from Virginia to Texas, making a complete circuit of the confederacy. The Twenty-second first served with General Curtis in southwest Mis-

souri during the winter of 1862-3. It was then transferred to Vicksburg and was the first regiment landed at Bruinsburg, below Grand Gulf, under the shelter of the gunboats that had run the city. It was the first regiment (with the Twenty-first Iowa) that engaged the enemy on the midnight march to Port Gibson. It participated in the battles of Champion Hills, Black River, and led the assault on Vicksburg on the 22d of May, 1863, losing in killed and wounded 164 out of a little more than 200 engaged. Incidents in this charge are reported the most daring in the history of the war on either side. General Grant, in his report to the secretary of war, said: "The Twenty-second Iowa was the only regiment that succeeded in entering the enemy's works on the entire line of investment."

Mr Pryce participated in all the battles and campaigns in which his regiment was engaged, and never missed a day's service. He was for a long time regimental adjutant, and was promoted to the captaincy of his company; served on the staff of

General Molineux of New York as inspector-general, and the last year as assistant adjutant-general of the Second brigade, second division, Nineteenth army corps, and was one of the youngest officers of this rank in the volunteer service. With thirteen officers of other regiments and Sergeant Major George Remley of the Twenty-second, who was killed in this battle, he is mentioned in general orders, now published in the official register, for conspicuous bravery at the battle of Winchester. He was one of the first officers to meet General Sheridan on the Winchester road on the retreat at Cedar Creek and saw him rally the scattered remnants and heard the magic words that turned defeat into victory. He was sent in command of a scouting party to reconnoitre Fisher's hill with ten picked men, and spent the entire night, at times, inside of the enemy's lines, returning before daylight the next morning, and made his report in person to Generals Sheridan, Custer and the other famous generals of this campaign. The charge was made in a few hours and the position taken. He wrote the reports of the regiment for the adjutant general·of the state, and a history of the regiment which was published in pamphlet form in the name of the regimental bugler. Ingersoll, in his history of "Iowa and the Rebellion," refers to Adjutant Pryce's generous praise of officers of his regiment in his reports to Adjutant-General Baker, and says "It is for me to say, on the authority of eye witnesses, that in this great battle where not a single man faltered, no one acquitted himself more handsomely than he did himself."

At the close of the war, Mr. Pryce was elected county superintendent, but resigned to accept a position in Chicago, where he remained two years. He returned to Iowa City and engaged in mercantile business in the firm of Donaldson, Pryce & Lee; and from 1868 to 1872 served on the staff of Governor Merrill with the rank of lieutenant-colonel of cavalry. In 1874 he purchased an interest in the Iowa City *Republican* and was associated with Col. J. H. C. Wilson in the editorial management. Pryce & Wilson established the Iowa City *Daily Republican* June 6, 1876. He was at this time chairman of the county central committee, and succeeded in the election of the entire republican ticket, the first and last time in the history of the county. After his retirement from the *Republican*, he was for several years president of the Republican Publishing company, and at the same time president of the Iowa City Cutlery company, which employed seventy-five men and was destroyed by fire in 1880. From 1876 to 1886 he was the senior member of the firm of Pryce & Schell in the hardware and machinery business. In 1881 he was nominated by the republican party for representative in the legislature, but declined on account of business. He was a delegate to the first national encampment, which met at Indianapolis for the organization of the Grand Army of the Republic, and with General Vandever, of Dubuque, represented the state. He was a member of the committee on constitution and by-laws, and with Colonel Lester, of Wisconsin, was the joint author of the laws for the future government of the order. He has also done much toward the good roads movement in Iowa.

He was one of the leading contributors to the press of the state against discriminations in favor of living persons on the Iowa soldiers' monument, and said if there were any distinctions to be made, they should be made in favor of the dead

heroes, who met the supreme test of patriotism on the battle field.

Mr. Pryce is a member of the Iowa City Lodge, No 4, A. F., Royal Arch Chapter, Palestine Commandery of Knights Templars, Knights of Pythias, and Kirkwood Post, Grand Army of the Republic.

CHRISTY, IRA SHERIDAN, expert violinist and one of the leading musicians of the state, resides at Keokuk and was born at Williamstown, Lewis county, Mo., March 1, 1866. He is the son of H. D. Christy, a farmer in easy circumstances, who came from a musical family and was a fine singer. Mr. Christy's mother, whose

maiden name was Shoptaugh, was not a natural musician although an accomplished pianiste. Our subject learned the first rudiments of music from his mother. Still, she did not like violin music and compelled him to leave the house in the summer and go to the most distant room in the winter to practice. When he was 12 years old his oldest brother gave him a toy violin for a Christmas present and taught him to play a few simple tunes upon it. His brother took quite an interest in his progress and soon made him a better instrument out of a gourd, which he prized very highly. With this same brother he played for small parties until he had earned enough to buy a $10 violin. In 1880 he borrowed a so-called self-instructor for the violin, which he studied carefully for about a year. With the money he earned playing the violin he next made arrangements to take his first violin lessons of a German musician, who came every week to teach his sister piano music. He only took a few lessons and was compelled to stop for want of money. He had no more lessons in music until he was 23 years of age. His father, while he seemed proud of his son's musical accomplishments, would not give a cent towards his musical education, but offered instead to send him to college if he would give up music as a profession. This, as might be expected, he refused. He was allowed to go to school three months in the year but did not take as much interest in that as in his musical studies, and at 16 years of age quit school altogether. He took up the study of harmony in 1883 alone, and also purchased his first good violin method, "David's Violin School," for which he paid $5, and was reprimanded very severely by his father for so doing. He, however, studied this work together with others all his leisure time for four years. In 1887, at the age of 21 years, he left home and located in Keokuk, leading the orchestra at the opera house and teaching violin for a season. The next season we find him in Des Moines leading the orchestra composed of members of the now well-known "Iowa State Band." He also led the orchestra at the old Capital City opera house and played in L. S. Gerberich's Symphony orchestra. He traveled then for about two years with Peyton's Comedy Company No. 2, as leader of the orchestra. When he attempted violin solo work he received the most flattering press notices, but was still sadly in need of better schooling. Finally, by a written request, signed by all the members of his company, his mother was induced to furnish him with the necessary financial aid to continue his musical education under some of the best teachers. He then, in February, 1891, took violin lessons of S. E. Jacobson for two years, during which time he received harmony under Adolph Koehling, followed by additional exercises to Richter's manual of harmony under Walter Petzett; then counterpoint under Louis Falk; and after that a few violin lessons from Bernhard Listemann. At the same time he taught violin music in Chicago, making a specialty of the rapid and modern school art. He returned to Keokuk in 1894 to resume work with his

former pupils. Since that time he has been engaged especially in advancing the methods of violin teaching, having written and published in 1895, "The Analysis of Violin Playing," which has been highly recommended and well received by leading violin teachers and players. At present he is compiling a "Synthetical Violin School," which, it is hoped, will be equally well received. During last season (97-98) he had charge of the violin department of the Ottumwa Conservatory. He was married in Chicago September 7, 1892, to Lucy P. Bozeman. They have no children. A Keokuk paper says: The "Analysis" has the unqualified praise of America's greatest violin teachers and is said to be epoch-making in the best sense. Mr. Christy is destined to be, if he is not already, one of America's greatest violin school reformers. Since his return from Chicago his influence in establishing the modern school of violin playing in Keokuk, is very apparent as the progress of those fortunate enough to become his pupils will testify.

MORRISON, JOSEPH BLACKER, of Fort Madison, is the president and treasurer of

the Morrison Manufacturing company, the largest establishment west of the Mississippi river for the making of agricultural implements. He has been brought up in

21

the business, for his father, Samuel D. Morrison, a native of New York, was one of the pioneer plow-makers in the state, coming from Ohio to Iowa in 1847. The remote ancestors of the Morrisons were Scotch, but the family has been in this country for many generations. One member of the family, Rev. Dr. Morrison, a noted Presbyterian missionary in Africa, was the originator of the week of prayer, observed so widely, now the first week in January. Captain Morrison's mother, was Maria Blacker, whose ancestors were German and Irish, but they came to America early enough to take part in the revolutionary war.

J. B. Morrison was born August 31, 1842, in Ross county, Ohio, and at the age of 5 years came with his parents to Iowa. His education was obtained in the public and private schools, and at the age of 16 he commenced business as a clerk in a hardware store at Fort Madison. Here he remained two years, and at the breaking out of the civil war entered the volunteer service as a private in Company D, of the Seventh Iowa infantry. This regiment was one of the most active in the army, serving in the battles of Belmont, Ft. Henry, Fort Donelson, Corinth, Shiloh, and Iuka, besides many other skirmishes and all the engagements of Sherman's famous march to the sea. In their first battle, that of Belmont, over one-third of these boys were killed and wounded, and young Morrison was then given the rank of first sergeant. For leading his company in the charge upon Fort Donelson, he was promoted to the rank of second lieutenant. He was wounded at the battle of Corinth, and soon afterward became a first lieutenant and a member of Gen. E. W. Rice's staff, and for his gallantry in leading a charge at Lay's Ferry, where Rice's brigade forced a crossing of the Ostaunola river, near Marietta, was made captain of his company. At Dallas, Ga., a determined charge was made on Rice's brigade, which would have met defeat had it not been for Captain Morrison's quick observation and action, in warning the commanding colonel to advance 100 feet farther to the crest of the hill. The captain's act resulted in a repulse of the rebel charge and was highly complimented in general orders, and later, by a special act of congress he was breveted major and lieutenant-colonel for his meritorious conduct in the war, special mention of this service at Dallas, Ga., being made. After several other important

engagements, Captain Morrison resigned his commission September 17, 1864, and returned home, having served three months over his term of enlistment.

In company with his brother, D. A. Morrison, and his father, he began business September, 1865, in the manufacture of plows. In 1879 the father retired, and the firm was known as Morrison Bros., until 1883, when it was incorporated as the Morrison Mfg. Co. In 1892 Colonel Morrison bought out his brother's interest, and is now associated with his two sons in the ownership of a large manufacturing business, which extends all over the west and south. The large brick factory is complete and well equipped with improved machinery for the manufacture of plows and similar farm implements. Colonel Morrison is always prominent in the public enterprises of his community, having been an organizer in nearly every stock company in Fort Madison, including the Fort Madison Town and Land company, Street Railway company, First National bank, Fort Madison Savings bank, and the Fort Madison Paper mill, of all of which he was president. When the Sante Fe Railway company built the Chicago line, crossing the Mississippi at Fort Madison, Colonel Morrison was made a director of the bridge company, and was entrusted with $100,000 to purchase real estate, for which he was required to give no security. With this money the land adjoining Fort Madison was bought, and the Fort Madison Town and Land company, with a capital of one-half million dollars was formed, and which caused a rise of $1,500,000 in the value of real estate, and a boom to the town which more than doubled the population.

In politics, Colonel Morrison is a republican; in religion a Catholic. He is past commander of the G. A. R., and a member of the Iowa Commandery of the Loyal Legion. He was married May 3, 1868, to Miss Toma Espy, and eleven children have been born to them, ten of whom are now living, as follows: Vincent Espy Morrison, Wm. Iverson, Genevieve, Mabel, Marie, Helen, Lucille, Joseph B., Jr., Dennis A., and Virginia.

The two oldest sons are graduates of Notre Dame university, and the daughters finished their education with Madames of the Sacred Heart academy, Chicago, and by extensive travel at home and abroad.

The business of the Morrison Mfg. Co. now absorbs the attention of Colonel Morrison and his two sons; Vincent E., who is superintendent and W. I., who is secretary of the company. Branch houses and wholesale depots are kept in all the principal distributing points west and south and some foreign trade is developing. The company are also wholesale dealers in buggies and carriages, and are taking steps to establish a carriage factory to be run in connection with the plow works.

WILLIAMS, GEORGE TOWNSEND, mayor of Ida Grove, Iowa, editor and proprietor of the *Ida Grove Pioneer*, an all-at-home, eight-column newspaper, was born in Nauvoo, Ill., in 1854, moving across the country in an ox wagon from there to Tabor, Fremont county, Iowa, with his uncle and his mother, and was raised on a farm. Circumstances were such that his parents were unable to send him to school except during the winter terms. He never attended a high school or college a day in his life. In the spring of 1872 he received an injury in his right hip, which threatened to render him a cripple for life and he was compelled to abandon farm work. He came to Ida county and taught a term of school in the little village of Ida Grove, it being the second term the village ever had. There were eleven pupils in attendance and the price he received was $30 per month. Realizing that his education was not sufficient to make a specialty of teaching, and desiring to learn a trade, he accepted W. P. Evans' proposition to go into the *Pioneer* office, although he had been offered the school for the winter term. In October, 1872, he was employed in the office as the "devil" on a salary of $2 per month for one year. The second year he received $15 per month, and at the end of which time he purchased a one-half interest in the office, and secured A. B. Chaffee, of Storm Lake, as his partner, Mr. Evans, at that time, was holding the office of postmaster, and confined himself to that and the real estate business. The office was sold to Williams and Chaffee for $700, Mr. Williams turning in his two years' wages, of which he had not drawn a cent, toward his part of the purchase price, and giving his notes for the balance.

The *Pioneer* is now owned, controlled and edited by George T. Williams, where he gives employment to seven hands. Six persons connected with the office have families to support, and in all nineteen persons receive their support directly from the *Pioneer*. The *Pioneer* gives employment to more persons than any other firm or establishment in Ida Grove. Mr. Williams owns and enjoys the luxuries of a pleasant home, besides owning the Williams opera house and the Williams park, a beautiful fourteen-acre tract of land, almost in the center of the city. During the last six or seven years he has been traveling over the United States as a special correspondent, which has taken him to every state in the union, and in every town in Iowa, and to every county in all the middle and southern states, and he has probably traveled over the American continent more than any other one Iowan.

All the money he has thus earned he has brought back and invested in Ida Grove. He erected the first dwelling, the first brick building, set out the first trees in Ida Grove, shipped the first power printing press into Ida county, and established the First National bank that was ever commissioned to do business in Ida county. He is now one of the most enterprising men of his city, and in short he is a fine sample of those so-called self-made men. He has been successful in all his undertakings and victorious in all his battles—among the latter being fourteen libel suits. The first dollar he earned for himself was from the sale of three bushels of popcorn, which he planted, hoed, gathered and marketed during some spare moments obtained from the regular routine of farm work. On June 17, 1897, he celebrated the twenty-fifth anniversary of the existence of his paper and his connection therewith, and the exercises, novel indeed, consisted of a literary program and a public meeting in his opera house where fully 1,500 people were present. Following this he issued a 20,000 souvenir edition, beautifully printed, with over 200 illustrations, and one of the best editions of the kind ever issued in this or any other state. Mr. Williams has always been a republican and has represented his county twelve times in the state conventions and assisted in the nomination of Governors Larrabee, Sherman, Gear and Jackson.

Mr. Williams was married in March, 1878, at Ida Grove, to Miss Sarah H. Rankin, an estimable lady who still presides over their beautiful home, but as yet no children have added to their joys. The mother of the subject of this sketch is Mrs. M. T. Spees, of Marion, Kan., who is an active and hearty old lady, having just passed the three score and ten mile post.

---

VanEATON, G. L. Of the men who have made a success in mercantile pursuits without the advantages bestowed by

a college education, none are more conspicuous than G. L. VanEaton, of Little

Rock. His father was a Hollander and his mother a Quaker, and from that strong combination he inherited the qualities which have won for him such signal success in the avenues of trade. Born in Boone county, Ind., he attended the inferior schools of those pioneer days, and enlisted in the civil war before he was 18 years of age, so that his educational advantages were very limited indeed. During his early life he never suffered himself to remain idle, although for a considerable time he was obliged to work for the mere pittance of $6 per month. When the war for the preservation of the union was necessary, he was among the first to offer his services in defense of the stars and stripes, and was accepted September 1, 1861, at Berlin, Wis. He participated in the battles of Shiloh, Corinth, Iuka, the second fight at Corinth, and was on the march with Grant to Vicksburg. The term of his first enlistment having expired, he re-enlisted at Vicksburg in the fall of 1863, and immediately thereafter secured a furlough for thirty days. Following a brief visit at his home, he went to Cairo, and thence up the Ohio and Tennessee rivers to Clifton, where he joined the forces of General Blair and marched to Big Shanty. He was then transferred to the Seventeenth corps, in which he served until mustered out of the service July 12, 1865. In 1872 Mr. VanEaton came to Iowa and took up a homestead in Osceola county, and the land has never passed out of his ownership. Aside from the time spent in military service, his whole life, up to 1885, was spent upon the farm. During that year he purchased a one-half interest in the lumber, wood, coal and grain business of Mr. L. Shell, at Little Rock, and the partnership then formed continues to the present time with profit and satisfaction to both parties.

In politics Mr. VanEaton is a republican, and although he has held positions off and on for many years, they have, in every case, been without remuneration. In township, county and state conventions, he has been a familiar figure in the past, and is considered a "wheel horse" for his party. He is a member of the G. A. R., is junior past commander of L. B. Ireland Post, of Sibley, Iowa. He is a past grand officer in the Odd Fellows, also, and was a representative to the grand lodge at its meetings in Burlington and Marshalltown. October 10, 1865, he was united in marriage to Miss Lizzy Fridd. They have two children, Jennie and Mertie VanEaton. In religion he is liberal in his views, and is not a member of any church.

---

RAWSON, CHARLES ELBERT. The name of C. E. Rawson is a familiar one in every quarter of the middle west, where life insurance is in demand. He stands pre-eminent as an organizer and promoter, and for complete knowledge of every detail of that most important business, he has no superior if, indeed, an equal in the state. With no professional training to start with, nor capital other than was earned with his own hands, and almost alone through his keen sagacity, profound wisdom and remarkable energy, he has placed himself at the head of a great and prosperous insurance company—the Des Moines Life association, of which it may be said it is entirely a creation of his own brain, a result of his individual effort, aided by his accomplished wife. The success that has been achieved by Mr. Rawson is frequently accredited to the heroes of fiction, but infrequently observed in real life. And it is not alone in a business way that his career must be highly pleasing to him, for socially he and his family are among those held in popular esteem in the capital city of Iowa. Their home, "The Oaks," on Arlington avenue, with its modern conveniences, fine old trees and spacious grounds, is one of the handsomest in the city. But it is not alone the beauty of architecture and drives and lawns that are pleasing to the eye of Des Moines people—it is the genial hospitality which is so lavishly dispensed within. No person has ever been beneath that roof but will gladly testify to this, and few there are of Des Moines' best people who have not been accorded that pleasure.

Mr. Rawson was born at Batavia, Kane county, Ill., March 5, 1849. His father, Harvey M. Rawson, was a farmer in fair circumstances, who settled in Clinton county, this state, in 1852. He is a direct descendant of Edward Rawson secretary of the Massachusetts colony, who came from England in 1836, and established the first family of the name on American soil. The mother, whose maiden name was Mary A. Daniels, was a native of New York, but removed to Michigan in an early day.

Mr. Rawson's early education was acquired through a course of private instruction at the old home near Maquoketa, Iowa, and later in the district schools of that county. It was in that early day he earned

his first dollar, building fires in the country schoolhouse. His youthful days were spent amidst the pleasures and labors of the farm, and not until 1873 did he start upon the work in which he has attained such signal success. It was in that year he entered the service of the State Insurance company of Des Moines as a farm solicitor. Later he was given a recording agency and still later a special agency. His success was phenomenal and his progress in the way of knowledge of the business rapid. In 1889 he was made general manager of the Des Moines Life association, and at once reorganized it on what is now known as the "Rawson System." Of this asso-

ciation little need be here said. It is one of the foremost organizations of its kind in the land, and has extended its business into every hamlet and township of the great middle states. In 1896 he was elected president of the National Insurance Convention of Mutual Life and Underwriters.

Politically he is a staunch republican, and is one of the influential members of the widely-known Grant club of Des Moines. He is a member of the Congregational church.

Mr. Rawson is an active influence in the upbuilding of Des Moines, always ready to put his shoulder to the wheel in all worthy public enterprises.

MACY, SHERMAN RILEY. professor of chemistry in Highland Park college and in the Iowa College of Physicians and Surgeons, Des Moines. He is also chemist to the state board. of health, having been re-elected recently to that important office. Professor Macy has won a great reputation among the pharmacists, physicians and chemists of the country, and stands in the foremost rank in his profession. His ancestors came originally from the north of Ireland and settled in Massachusetts, but during the persecution of the Quakers they fled to Nantucket Island, off the coast of Rhode Island, where they engaged in ship building. Professor Macy's great-

grandfather moved to Indiana early in the century, and here Riley Macy, the professor's grandfather, grew to manhood. The Macys, like so many other Quakers, were abolitionists, and the hotel which they conducted was called Tucket and was one of the important stations of the "underground railway " during slavery days. Riley Macy moved to Iowa in 1842, locating in Davis county, where as a prominent farmer and the first justice of the county, he was a leader in legal business matters. He died at the age of 33, leaving a wife and five children, four of whom were boys. Years afterward, when the civil war broke out, three of these young men

went to the front, and two were killed in battle. The one who returned home was Allen, the father of Professor Macy. He was born in 1842, and is now living on a farm in Warren county. He has a valuable farm and also owns property in Des Moines, where he resided at one time. He is a man of much ability, well known for his integrity and for the earnest expressions of his opinions. Professor Macy's mother was formerly Nancy A. McBride. She was born in 1842 and died in 1892.

S. R. Macy was born August 3, 1865, on a farm in Perry township, Davis county, Iowa. He received his earliest instruction at the district school and from his father, who directed and encouraged his son's inherited taste for scientific study. In the spring of 1884 he graduated from the Bloomfield high school, and the following summer was spent largely in travel for the benefit of his health, which improved greatly, and in the fall he entered the college at Bloomfield, where he pursued a general scientific course and did much special work in chemistry. In 1885 he engaged in the drug business with his father and Horace Mendenhall, and after several years of practical experience entered the pharmaceutical department of Northwestern university at Chicago. In the university he was privileged to do special work under the personal direction of Dr. J. H. Long, one of the most highly educated chemists in this country. He graduated in June, 1890, with honors, and in the fall of that year accepted the position of dean of the pharmacy and chemistry departments of Highland Park college. He held this position with gratifying success for five years, when he resigned and went to Chicago to accept a position in the faculty of Northwestern university. He served as an instructor for a year, at the same time pursuing a post-graduate course. He returned to Des Moines in 1896 and resumed his position at Highland Park college, and was also appointed to the other positions which he holds at the present time. Professor Macy has made a specialty of analytical chemistry, and is frequently called to make difficult examinations and analyses.

Within recent years he has been identified with a number of important cases of murder by poisoning, as expert chemist. Among the most important of these trials were the Betsy Smith case of Des Moines, the Doolin case of Webster City, and the Sallhausen case of Clinton. Professor

Macy has been employed also to make examinations of water, food stuffs, oils, etc., but his chief delight is in toxicology, for he greatly delights in working out the details of a poison case.

Professor Macy is a republican in politics. He is a member of the I. O. O. F., of the American Chemical society and of the Methodist church. He was married July 14, 1891, to Josie E. Ethell, of Bloomfield, who was a classmate in the public schools at that place. He lives in a very pleasant home in Highland Park, Des Moines, but a short distance from the college in which his interest is centered.

---

SPENCER, ROBERT H., of Algona, ex-member of the general assembly of Iowa and at present treasurer of his county, was born at Thornville, Perry county, Ohio, September 20, 1840. His father, Eli A. Spencer, was born near Somerset, Ohio, May 27, 1817. The early life of the father was spent on a farm and later he was engaged in the mercantile business. When he had received a good common school education he entered upon the study of law and after his admission to the bar soon became one of the leading members of the legal profession in his section of the state. The principal portion of his time, from 1852 to 1858, was devoted to the building of the Sciota & Hocking Valley railroad, in which venture all his private means were invested. The line of road extended from Portsmouth on the Ohio river, north, to connect at Newark with the road running to Sandusky on Lake Erie. He was president of the road for a period of two years. The financial crash of 1857 caused suspension of work on the construction of the road, and it was never wholly completed. The portion that had been built was finally merged into the Baltimore & Ohio system. In politics he was an ardent whig until the division of that party, when he was among the first to join the republican party at its organization. He was a delegate to the first republican state convention in Ohio, which was held in Columbus in July, 1855, and nominated Salmon P. Chase for governor. In the fall of the same year he was elected, on the republican ticket, state senator from the district comprising the counties of Muskingum and Perry, both hitherto strongly democratic, and served until January, 1858. In the spring of 1858 he removed to Wisconsin, locating at Madison, where he resumed the practice of

law, but devoted a portion of his time to the cultivation of a farm, previously purchased near the city, he being especially fond of agricultural pursuits. He soon became prominent in the state, and on January 1, 1864, was appointed assistant secretary of state, in which position he served until 1870. In the meantime he compiled and published a digest of the laws of the state. At the conclusion of his term of service he retired to his farm, though continuing the practice of his profession to some extent. In 1883 he sold his farm and removed to Rice Lake in the northern part of the state, and there died of apoplexy

June 2, 1887, in the 71st year of his age. He was married, in 1839, to Ann M. Chilcote, who was born at Huntingdon, Pa., in 1818. She is the eldest of a family of ten children, seven of whom are now living. She is still hale and hearty, although 78 years old.

The family of which Robert H. Spencer is a member consists of four sons, all of whom are living, the youngest being now in his 52d year. Three served in the late war. One has held positions in the treasury department and United States senate, at one time the chief clerk of that body. The early youth of Robert was spent on his father's farms in Ohio and Wisconsin until 1861 when he enlisted as a private in the

Tenth Wisconsin infantry. He was promoted to lieutenant and captain and assigned to the army of the Ohio, under Buell, and later transferred to the army of the Cumberland, under Rosecrans and Thomas. He was captured toward the close of the battle of Chickamauga, and imprisoned in the holes of rebel torture at Richmond, Danville, Macon and Charleston. He escaped in October, 1864, and re-enlisted as lieutenant-colonel of the Forty-seventh Wisconsin infantry, in which he served until the end of the war, and was mustered out as brevet-colonel of volunteers. He was made the first commander of the Fourth district Wisconsin G. A. R., at its organization. The war over, he returned to Wisconsin and engaged in the mercantile business at Sheboygan Falls. He removed to Algona, Iowa, October, 1870. In 1872 he was appointed postmaster, and held the office until 1885. He was a member of the general assembly during 1885–1886. In 1893 he was further honored by election to the office of treasurer of his county, and at the close of his first term was re-elected. He is a member of the Masonic, Knights of Pythias, Woodmen, and G. A. R., orders. He was married in 1866 to Josephine L. Rowley, of Sun Prairie, Wis. They have one daughter. A son died in infancy.

STUART, WILLIAM, who is extensively engaged in the land business in the new town of Armstrong, Emmet county, has had an active life which has been crowned with success, especially in a business way. He was born in the County Antrim, Ireland, near the town of Carrigallen. His father was Alexander Stuart and his mother was Margaret Ellis Stuart. He was of Scotch and she was of English descent. They were farmers, and emigrated to Canada, settling near Mitchell, Ontario, where their son William received his early education. Later he was sent to school in West Mokton, Ontario. In 1879 William Stuart located in Grundy Center, Iowa, where he was engaged in the blacksmithing trade for several years. After he had accumulated about $700 he went into partnership with a brother in Fulton, Ill., which he sold out in 1884 and engaged in the agricultural implement business for eight years, part of the time with E. H. Dodd as a partner. He then sold his interest in this business, and left Grundy Center, and formed a partnership with B. F. Robinson to start a bank in the pros-

pective town of Armstrong, Emmet county. They organized the Armstrong bank in 1892, with William Stuart as president and B. F. Robinson, cashier, erecting a substantial building of their own. Three years later he sold his interest in the bank to John Dows and has since been dealing extensively in land. Mr. Stuart has served as mayor of Grundy Center, and chairman of the republican county committee and is at present a member of the committee, and is a member of the county board of supervisors. He has always been a republican. He belongs to all the Masonic lodges, the Blue Lodge, and Chapter and Commandery, Mystic

Shrine and Eastern Star. He is a member of the Methodist church. On the 26th of December, 1882, Mr. Stuart was married to Jennie Dunn. They have three children: Grace, Alta and Hazel.

Mr. Stuart is one of the substantial business men of northwestern Iowa, who has had a large part in the building up of the state and developing the country. In doing so he has achieved for himself a large measure of success, showing what the free institutions of America will do for a man who is willing to do for himself. He has, moreover, gained the confidence of the people among whom he lives to an unusual degree.

LETTS, FRANK CRAWFORD, president of the Letts, Fletcher company, wholesale grocers of Marshalltown, is well known all over the state for his conspicuous success in life. He was born in Magnolia, Ill., April 28, 1858. He was the son of N. H. Letts and Herma Cowen Letts, natives of Ohio, who went to Illinois in their childhood. The Letts family settled near La Salle and the Cowen family in Putnam county, near Magnolia. The Letts family were farmers and owned, and still own, large tracts of land in Illinois. The Cowen family has been quite prominent in the history of Illinois. The Dents and Hamiltons were of her family. Ex-Governor Hamilton was a first cousin of Mrs. Letts. The latter was born in 1825 and Mr. Letts in 1823. They are both living in Yates Center, Kan. When Frank C. was 5 years old the family moved to Louisa county and settled near the town of Letts, which was named for a brother of N. H. Letts. Frank C. attended the country school until he was 13, when the farm was sold, and the family went to Afton and bought and conducted a hotel for several years. At this time Frank went to Wenona, Ill., and spent some time with his grand parents, attending high school. He afterwards attended public school in Afton, and took a business course at A. D. Wilt's Business college in Dayton, Ohio. He had his first business experience working for P. Allen mornings and evenings, before and after school, in his general merchandise store in Afton, but his business instincts were better illustrated by an incident which occurred on the farm.

When he was about 7 years old, several little pigs were left motherless, and his father told him if he could raise them he might have half the proceeds. He was successful, and when the pigs grew up and were sold he realized about $35. This he reinvested, and before leaving the farm, at the age of 13 years, he had about $300. After leaving Afton, at the age of 17 years, young Letts went to Chicago and accepted a position in the wholesale dry goods house of A. T. Stewart & Co. He worked hard and within a year had been rapidly promoted. Before he was 19 years old he attracted the attention of A. C. Jordan, of the firm of W. A Jordan & Company, of Ottumwa, a customer of the house, who asked him how he would like to go into business for himself in Iowa, and offered to furnish the capital. This seemed a very promising opportunity, and Mr. Letts advised with Jas. H. Walker, then the manager of the house, later himself the head of the great dry goods house of J. H. Walker & Company. The firm disliked to lose Mr. Letts, but said that it looked like a good opportunity. Mr. Jordan selected Marshalltown as the place to begin; furnished about $30,000 capital, and left Mr. Letts entirely in charge of the business. The business was very successful. About six months later W. I. Bates & Company, one of the

largest concerns in the town, failed and Mr. Jordan bought the stock from the mortgagee and consolidated the business. That was in the fall and winter of 1877 and 1878, and there being fewer railroads and small towns around Marshalltown than now, the country trade was immense, the retail sales sometimes amounting to $1,200 on Saturdays. The profits were better than they are now, and inside of a year the young partner had quite a sum to his credit. Mr. Letts speaks very highly of Mr. Jordan, who started him in business. Later he and Mr. Walker, both Mr. Letts' early friends when he was a poor boy, met with reverses and lost their property.

In the summer of 1879 Mr. Letts sold his interest in the dry goods business to Mr. Jordan and joined the Hon. Delano T. Smith in the breeding of Shorthorn cattle. In a year he had the business thoroughly mastered, and owned it all. He visited

all the sales and bought cattle of good family and individual merit, and took them home and fed them up so they presented a better appearance and brought higher prices. He was highly successful in the Shorthorn business. Later he was interested in the Ketchum Wagon company, and was its secretary. In 1883 he closed out all his other interests and went into the wholesale grocery business in Marshalltown. The firm was Lacy, Letts & Gray, but Mr. Lacy and Mr. Gray concluded there was too much hard work and too little profit in the business and they withdrew, selling to Mr. T. J. Fletcher and Mr. D. T. Denmead, bankers of Marshalltown. The firm was changed to Letts, Fletcher & Company. In 1886 a stock company was formed and Mr. Letts was elected president and treasurer, which offices he now holds. Mr. Denmead and Mr. Fletcher have since retired. The officers of the company, besides Mr. Letts, are H. L. Spencer, Oskaloosa, vice-president; A. P. Spencer, Oskaloosa, secretary; and the directors are the three officers named, and

H. E. Sloan and W. S Robbins. In 1894 the firm started another house in Mason City and incorporated the Letts, Spencer, Smith company, of which Mr. Letts is president. In May, 1898, they bought one of the oldest wholesale grocery establishments on the Missouri river, the Turner-Frazer Mercantile company, of St. Joseph, and formed a stock company called the Letts, Spencer Grocery company, with $200,000 paid-up capital. Mr. Letts is president of that company. For several years he was secretary of the Iowa-Nebraska Wholesale Grocers' association, and resigned the position during 1898 because of lack of time. He is a director in the City National bank, of Marshalltown.

Mr. Letts has borne a prominent and influential part in the politics of the state and has always been an enthusiastic republican. His activity in politics has been directed towards helping others, and he has never been a candidate for any office, although in 1895 he was widely mentioned for the republican nomination for governor. He served on the military staff of Governor Jackson, Governor Drake and Governor Shaw. In the year when Robert G. Cousins was first nominated for congress, and during Mr. Letts' absence from home, some of his friends started a movement to secure him the congressional nomination. When he reached home he put a stop to this and called attention to Mr. Cousins, for whose nomination he put forth his best efforts. He has always been an ardent supporter of Mr. Cousins, and is proud to say that he always will be.

Mr. Letts is a Knight Templar and Shriner, but has been too busy to hold office in either organization. He is not a member of any church, but usually attends services at the Presbyterian church. Mr. Letts was married April 28, 1879, to Mary J. Smith, daughter of Hon. Delano T. Smith, in Marshalltown. She died in August, 1892. To this marriage were born two children: Fred C., born November 27, 1884, and Herma Leoni, born April 14, 1888. Mr. Letts was again married November 11, 1897, in Washington, D. C., to Miss Cora Perkins, daughter of the late United States Senator Perkins, of Kansas.

Few men in business have found the time to make as large an acquaintance and accumulate as many friends in all parts of Iowa, and particularly among the young men. He was for several years treasurer of the republican state league, and should he ever appear in the political arena as a candidate, would have a great many active supporters in every part of the state.

---

PRICE, BENJAMIN, a well-known citizen of Iowa City, is descended from Welsh ancestors who came to America soon after the founding of the colony of Maryland by Lord Baltimore, and settled in that part of the country which is now Calvert county. Robert Y. Price, the father of Benjamin, was born in Calvert county, Md., in 1814, and when only 2 years old his family removed to Belmont county, Ohio, where he resided during his life and followed the occupation of farming. The mother of Benjamin Price was of Welsh and Saxon descent and was born in Arklow, Wicklow county, Ireland. Her ancestors were among those who removed to, or were colonized in, Ireland during the dictatorship of Cromwell.

Benjamin was born near Barnesville, Ohio, February 28, 1844, and attended the country school during such time as farm work was not pressing, until he was 12 years old. After this his help was needed to carry on the farm up to the time he was 16, when he attended the village academy for a while. He also taught school for several terms and attended the Southwestern Normal school at Lebanon, Ohio.

In the early spring of 1865 he came to Iowa, hoping to find an opening for busi-

ness where enterprise, energy and courage might supply the lack of money, and located at West Branch, Cedar county. He soon secured a clerkship in the general store of Mr. Joseph Steere and was for over two years in his employ as clerk at West Branch, and manager of his store at Springdale. During that time he had taken up the study of dentistry and after leaving the store went to Iowa City and completed a course of study in the office of Dr. N. H. Tulloss, and commenced practice on January 1, 1868, at Wilton Junction.

Finding the business small at Wilton he remained but a short time, and then removed to Garnett, Anderson county, Kan. Not being satisfied with that location he returned in 1869 to West Branch, Iowa, and in 1870 formed a partnership with Dr. Savage in the drug business. In 1871 he sold out his interest in the drug store and formed a partnership with his former instructor, Dr. Tulloss, of Iowa City, which lasted until the doctor's death in 1882.

October 12, 1869, Dr. Price was married to Priscilla Milnes, of Springdale, Iowa. They have five children: Stella H., Anna Mildred, Louis R., George M. and Ralph. Mrs. Price was born in Derbyshire, England, and with her father's family came to Iowa in 1856.

Dr. Price has always taken a great interest in educational matters; has been a member of the school board of Iowa City for six years and twice president of the board. During these years he has, with the assistance of his colleagues, succeeded in getting a high school and two new ward schools built. They have enlarged the course of study in all the grades; raised the standard of qualifications for teachers, and insisted on more thorough and comprehensive work by them, until they have placed the schools of Iowa City on as high a plane as the best in the state.

---

IVES, CHARLES JOHN, of Cedar Rapids, president of the Burlington, Cedar Rapids & Northern railroad, was born in Wallingford, Rutland county, Vt., October 4, 1831, and is descended from honored New England ancestry, connected with the history of that section of the country almost from the beginning. The founder of the family in America sailed from England, on the Truelove, and landed at Boston, Mass., on the 19th of September, 1635. Our subject is numbered among his direct lineal descendants. His son, Joseph Ives, married Esther Benedict, and became the father of Nathaniel Ives, whose wife bore the maiden name of Mehitable Andrews. Their son, Lent Ives, was the grandfather of our subject, and married Mary Mighell. The father of our subject, John Ives, was born in Wallingford, Vt., and by occupation was a farmer and merchant. In 1847 he came to the west, locating in Lee county, Iowa; he died at the age of 63 years. His wife, who descended from New England ancestors, bore the maiden name of Lucretia Johnson. Mr. Ives, whose name introduces this sketch, may well be called a self-educated man, for his school privileges were somewhat limited, and in the school of experience he has learned more valuable lessons than the common institutions of learning ever afforded him. He attended the public schools of his native county, and for a short time was a student in the academy at Poultney, Vt.

This ended his school life, but an observing eye and retentive memory and sound judgment have made him a well-informed man.

Till 1847 he worked on his father's farm, in Vermont. Then in Lee county, Iowa, for several years, on a farm which his father had purchased and upon which the family had settled. He then delved in

the mining regions for several years, near Pike's Peak, Colo. He does not seem to have gathered much wealth, however, and on the 1st of October, 1862, he became connected with railroading as a clerk of the Burlington & Missouri River railroad, at Mount Pleasant, Iowa. On the 15th of January, 1864, he was appointed clerk in the local office in Burlington, Iowa, and from January, 1867, until July, 1870, was clerk in the general freight office in that city.

Since the latter date he has been continuously connected with what is now the Burlington, Cedar Rapids & Northern railroad, but at the time when he allied his interest with it, it was called the Burlington,

Cedar Rapids & Minnesota road. During the first year he was general freight agent of the first division, and from 1871 until October 15, 1874, served as general passenger and ticket agent. On the 15th of October his duties were further increased by an appointment as general freight agent, and he served in that capacity, as well as others, until October 28, 1875, when he was made acting superintendent and general freight, passenger and ticket agent. From November 26, 1875, until November 28, 1879, he was superintendent and general freight, passenger and ticket agent; and from the latter date until June 14, 1884, he was general superintendent. He was then president and general superintendent until June, 1893, and since that time he has been president of the road. His advancement has been steady and continuous. The growth of the road with which he has been connected so long, has been largely accomplished through his progressive efforts. When he became connected with the Burlington & Missouri River railroad, its western terminus was at Ottumwa, Iowa; now the state is crossed and recrossed by a perfect net-work of railroads, facilitating commerce, introducing all the improvements known to the east, and advancing the state with a rapidity that is known only to western districts. The road of which Mr. Ives is now president was only forty miles in length when he first became identified with it. Now its aggregate length is 1,150 miles, and it justly ranks among the most important business institutions of Iowa. He rode upon the first train of steam cars that made a trip in this state. His own progress has been proportionate to that of the road, and the farm boy of forty years ago is to-day at the head of a concern whose importance in the world of commerce cannot be estimated. While promoting in all possible ways the interests of the railroad company, Mr. Ives has also aided materially in the prosperity of Cedar Rapids, by his connection with various enterprises there. He was for some time president of the Cedar Rapids Electric Light company, but resigned that position in January, 1893, owing to the press of other duties. His capital has been judiciously invested and he has become the possessor of a handsome property. He is purely a business man, practical, energetic and capable, with a mind to plan and a will to execute.

In 1854 Mr. Ives was united in marriage with Miss Ellen M. Dale, of Wallingford, Vt., and six children were born to them. A son and daughter are living with and near him. The mother died April 16, 1895. Personally Mr. Ives is courteous and affable, a gentleman in the truest and best sense of that term; and while his career excites the admiration, it also commands the respect of all.

———

CONNIFF, ROBERT E., president of the state board of health, is a resident of Sioux City, Iowa, where he is well known as one

of the leading physicians of the state. He was born at Houston, Minn., in 1858, and came to Iowa in 1869. He graduated from the State University of Iowa in 1884, where he completed his professional studies in a most creditable manner, after which he located at Sioux City, where he has since been engaged in the active practice of medicine. He has developed an increasing love for his profession, and his one aim in life is to reach the top. He does not aspire to mix extensively in politics, nor does he seek political preferment, although he was appointed by Governor Boies a member of the state board of health, a political appointment, and has held that position under three republican governors up to the present time. As a member of the board of health he has been a constant and efficient worker in the field of preventive medicine and sanitation. He is a member of a number of medical societies, among others, the American Medical association, the Iowa State Medical society, American Public Health association.

---

POWELL, DR. FRANCIS MARION, is the well known superintendent of the Iowa Institution for Feeble-Minded Children, at Glenwood, a position he has held with increasing usefulness, to the appreciation of the people, for more than fifteen years. The right sort of training was given young Powell, amid the trying surroundings of a pioneer life, to fit him as an important factor in state building, in the development of Iowa's possibilities.

Born in Morgan county, Ohio, November 12, 1848, the second child in a family of seven, his parents William and Melissa (Williams) Powell, removed in 1857, to Badax, now Vernon county, Wis. The father was a pioneer teacher and minister, and came of Welsh stock; the mother was of English ancestry. Ten years of life in a new country gave the young man a training that has served him well in after life, inculcating in him habits of industry, frugality, economy, honesty, and a perseverance which have carried him to success.

He attended the primitive schools in log cabins in winter time and by his own efforts earned means to attend select schools, working for board and tuition, finally becoming a teacher himself, his purpose being to study medicine. With his own earnings he returned to Ohio and attended the Ohio Wesleyan university, at Delaware. After this he taught school for a time, keeping the medical profession constantly in view, and at length graduated from the Starling Medical college, Columbus, Ohio, in February, 1875, with class honors. The next month, poor in purse, but rich in mental, physical and moral endowments, the young physician settled in Hastings, Iowa, where he at once achieved success, which application and merit secures. In the fall of 1881, he removed with his family to Glenwood to secure better advantages for the children. The following spring he was appointed superintendent of the Institution for Feeble-Minded Children, located there. At that time the institution cared for less than 200 inmates, being yet in its infancy. It has developed under his management, until now the population is over 700 inmates,

or pupils. No criticism has ever been made of Dr. Powell's work; instead it has been highly praised, and he has become a recognized authority on the care and management of persons affected with mental weakness. Having a warm, sympathetic nature, and being ably assisted by his faithful wife as matron, Dr. Powell has been singularly successful in the development of the unfortunates placed under his care. The business of the institution has been well looked after, too, and the appropriations of the legislature were made to go as far as possible. The institution suffered a severe loss from fire by lightning

in August, 1896, and the skill and resources of the superintendent were heavily taxed in this trying emergency, and he was not found wanting.

But Dr. Powell is not a one-sided man, for he has earned distinction as a horticulturist, outside his profession. He is serving his second term as president of the State Horticultural society, and has been a regular attendant upon horticultural meetings in the state for many years. He was one of the first to realize the possibilities of the wonderful apple belt of southwestern Iowa and to take advantage of the opportunity. He has been a hard working horticulturist ever since he settled in that part of the state. and has won distinction in the business. He owns two orchards of 3,000 and 6,000 trees, near Glenwood, and numerous smaller ones, besides having started and sold several fruit farms. Through his energy in this direction, the state owns one of the most valuable orchards in Iowa. Dr. Powell was active in organizing the Mills County Fruit carnival at Glenwood, in 1895, which has now become an annual feature of the great apple harvest in southwestern Iowa. He has always been a republican, but has held no elective office besides being a member of the school board. He is a member of the State Medical society, and an active member of the National Conference of Charities and Corrections. Dr. Powell was married in 1870, to Louisa M. Newton, and they have four children: Ida M., Velura, Orrin W., and Fred M. The oldest daughter, Ida M., is married to Elmer E. Black and lives in Chicago.

PATTERSON, JOHN W., was born on his father's farm in Perry township, Ashland county, Ohio, June 3, 1847. His father, William Patterson, lives with two unmarried

daughters at Waterloo, Ind. His father was also a merchant for many years after leaving the farm. His wife was Elizabeth Shaeffer, whose father served his country in the war of the American revolution.

While a boy John W. helped his father on the farm, attending the public school in the winter months until he was 17 years old. In September, 1862, at the age of 15, he answered the call of Governor Todd, of Ohio, for the minute men of the state to go to the defense of Cincinnati, then being threatened by the confederates. Every man furnished his own arms and ammunition. The troops thus assembled, after serving in the intrenchments and fortifications of the city for ten days, were honorably discharged, and are known in Ohio's history of the war as "The Squirrel Hunters." He was too young to enter the army at the beginning of the war of the rebellion, but when he reached the age of 17, in 1864, he enlisted in the One Hundred and Seventy-sixth Ohio Volunteer infantry, commanded by Col. E. C. Mason. The regiment was assigned to the army of the Cumberland, which was then at Nashville, Tenn. He was in the great battle of the 15th and 16th of December, 1864, in which General Thomas won a great victory over the rebel army, under General Hood. Mr. Patterson acted as quartermaster of the regiment during the larger part of his term of service. After being mustered out, Mr. Patterson secured a position as a clerk in a grocery. He came to Iowa in the fall of 1881 and engaged in the retail dry goods business in Marion, Linn county. For many years he has been a commercial traveler. His first vote was cast for Abraham Lincoln for president in 1864, and he has always been an active republican since. He has been a member of a campaign glee club in nearly every political campaign since the close of the war. He has often been a delegate to county, congressional and state conventions of the republican party, and has served as chairman of Linn county republican central committee for four years. He was assistant sergeant-at-arms at the St. Louis republican national convention which nominated McKinley for president. He is a member of the Masonic order, a Shriner, and a member of the Knights of Pythias, and of Post No. 204 of the Grand Army of the Republic at Marion. January 5, 1898, Mr. Patterson was appointed collector of internal revenue for the Third district of Iowa, and entered upon his duties February 7, 1898.

January 12, 1870, he was married to Miss Ella Howell, of Danby, N. Y. They have had five children, three of whom are living: Ida H., Clarence H., and Walter J.

PATRICK, Oscar Rudd, of Glenwood, is a member of the firm of Winkler & Patrick, and is a bright young lawyer with the best of prospects before him for a busy professional life. His ancestors were strict Scotch Presbyterians. His grandfather, Alexander Patrick, came from Scotland in 1827 and established a woolen factory in South Granville, N. Y. His father, Robert Patrick, was born in Glasgow, Scotland, October 12, 1823, and when 4 years old came to America with his parents. He farmed successfully for many years, but is now retired and lives at Emerson, Iowa. He is in comfortable circumstances, owning a 240-acre farm a mile from the town. Mr. Patrick's mother was Mary McDonald, who was born September 4, 1825, and died February, 1894. Her ancestors were also from Scotland, and came to this country as members of the Scotch Highland troops. They were filled with a spirit of liberty, and deserted his majesty's service to join the American revolutionists.

O. R. Patrick was born October 13, 1864, near Blue Island, Cook county, Ill., but soon afterward his parents moved to Iroquois county. Here he attended district school, and his education was continued in the graded schools of Emerson, Mills county, Iowa. He was always a bright pupil, and the first money he ever earned was received in the shape of a prize awarded him for excellence in spelling, when he was only 7 years old. During his last year in the public school his ambition for a university training was aroused by George W. Goodsoe, a graduate of Dartmouth college, who was then principal of the schools at Emerson. Mr. Patrick entered the preparatory department of Parsons college at Fairfield, March, 23, 1886, graduating the following June. The next September he began regular college work, and in June, 1890, graduated from the classical course. While in college he took particular delight in the study of literature, history and mathematics, and excelled in composition and oratory. During his junior year he won first place in the home oratorical contest, and this victory entitled him to represent the college at the state oratorical contest, which occurred in March, 1889, at Cornell college, Mount Vernon. Here he succeeded in again winning first honors, though he had the best orators from all the leading colleges of the state with whom to compete. While at school he was a member of the Orio Literary society, and was prominent in all college activities.

The first year after graduation was spent in Emerson, Iowa. In November, 1891, he was elected county superintendent of schools in Mills county, and held this office until January 1, 1896. Though devoted to his educational work he managed to find time for the study of law while holding this position. He entered the office of Hon. Shirley Gilliland, at Glenwood, in 1892, and by earnest study under this able and generous man he was prepared for the state examinations and was admitted to the bar in the supreme court of Iowa, January, 1896, at Des Moines. Since then he has practiced law at Glenwood in partnership

with A. H. Winkler, a real estate man of wide experience, who has greatly aided Mr. Patrick in getting a start in the profession. In addition to legal business the firm loans money, deals in real estate and does some insuring.

Born in the north in war time, Mr. Patrick was taught very young to admire Lincoln and other great republican leaders, and he has always stood by the party which they served so well. The superintendency is the only office which he has held. He is an Odd Fellow and a Free Mason. In religion he is a Presbyterian, but at present holds his membership with the Congregational church, there being no denomination of his choice in Glenwood.

He belonged to the state militia under Governor Jackson's administration, and assisted in expelling Kelly's army, acting as first lieutenant of Company .G, Third regiment of the I. N. G.

Mr. Patrick was married June 25, 1893, to Miss Bertha E. Tubbs, the youngest daughter of Judge L. W. Tubbs, of Emerson, and to her counsel and cheer he attributes a large part of his success. They have no children.

———

RICKEL, HENRY, of Cedar Rapids, was born in Richland county, Ohio, August 16, 1835. His father, Samuel Rickel, was of

German descent and was born in Bedford county, Penn. Several members of his family were in the revolutionary war, and an uncle was killed at the battle of Brandywine. His more remote ancestors came from Frankfort-on-Main, where many of the same name are now living. He was a cabinet maker, and in 1829 removed to Richland county, Ohio. He married Barbara Smith, who was of German and English descent, and whose father, Henry F. Smith, was a soldier in the war of 1812. Samuel Rickel and his family moved in 1839 to Springfield, Ill.; from there to Galena, and in 1849 to Clayton county, Iowa.

Henry Rickel's education was commenced in a log schoolhouse in Illinois, and completed in the schools of West Union, Iowa. He learned the cabinet-making trade and worked at that until about 21 years old. After that he engaged in the book and stationery business at McGregor and at West Union, Iowa, under the firm name of Rickel & Huffman, until 1860, when he commenced the study of law with Hon. L. L. Ainsworth, of West Union. In September, 1862, he assisted in raising Company C, of the Sixth Iowa cavalry, and served with that regiment until June, 1864, when he was compelled by ill health to resign. Captain Ainsworth commanded the company and Mr. Rickel was second lieutenant. The regiment was engaged in frontier service, under Gen. Alfred Sully. Before enlisting he assisted in raising five other companies in Fayette county.

In 1866 Mr. Rickel formed a law partnership with Hon. William McClintock, of West Union, which continued for a number of years. He was also connected in the law business with Hon. William E. Fuller and D. W. Clements, of the same place. Later he was a partner of Hon. W. V. Allen, now United States senator from Nebraska. In 1878 he removed to Cedar Rapids, and became a member of the firm of Rickel, West & Eastman. For the past twelve years he has been a member of the firm of Rickel & Crocker.

Politically, Henry Rickel is a republican and his first vote was cast for John C. Fremont, but from 1863 to 1874 he voted with the democratic party. He then voted for Hayes for president, and since that time has usually voted the republican ticket. He was for several years mayor of the city of West Union, and was a member of the house of representatives from Fayette county during the session of the Seventeenth General Assembly.

He was married October 14, 1857, to Susan Brown, of West Union, who was born in Yates county, N. Y. They have had two children, Willie, who died at the age of 11 years, and Lillian M., who is the wife of Alfred H. Newman, of Cedar Rapids. Mr. Rickel is a member of the Methodist church, and belongs to the Odd Fellows. For many years he has been active in promoting temperance reform in Iowa, and took a leading part in the enactment and enforcement of the prohibitory law, delivering many lectures in northern Iowa.

JOHNSTON, WILLIAM F., of Toledo, is one of the most prominent citizens of central Iowa, and is considered the wealthiest man in Tama county. He was born April 20, 1833, at Mt. Pleasant, Pa., and was the oldest of eleven children. The blood of several nations flows in his veins, for his father, U. S. Johnston, a carpenter, was of Scotch-Irish descent, while his mother, Mary Keister, was a Pennsylvania German. His education was obtained in the common schools of the village where he lived, and at Mt. Pleasant college, where he studied one year. He worked at his father's trade a few years, and was also employed as a salesman in his native town. He came to Iowa in 1856, and at Iowa City secured work as a carpenter, and later as clerk in the store of Gower, Mygatt & Galley. He had the good sense and judgment at this early day to appreciate the value of Iowa land, and seized an opportunity to bid off 900 acres at a judicial sale. He had no money, but all that he needed was loaned him without security by his employer and eastern friends. This investment was the beginning of a long series of successful ventures, which have marked him as a man of rare business sagacity, amounting almost to genius. Mr. Johnston removed in 1858 to Toledo, where, in company with Henry Galley, now of Des Moines, he opened the "People's Store," which soon became by far the largest and most prosperous mercantile establishment in Tama county. He sold out his interest in the store after about twenty years, his other lines of business having grown to such large proportions as to demand his entire attention; for during all this period he had been buying and selling land, at one time owning fifty good farms in Tama county alone, besides large tracts of land in northwestern Iowa, Minnesota and other states.

He has been connected with almost every large business enterprise of the community, for not only are his extensive means desirable for the establishment of commercial institutions or ventures, but his long experience and rare good judgment are widely sought and consulted. Through his influence and persevering efforts, more than to any other cause, the building of the Toledo & Northwestern railroad in 1880 is to be attributed. The construction of this line was really the making of the towns of Toledo and Tama. In connection with this work Mr. Johnston and Hon. Leander Clark, also of Toledo,

purchased the ground and laid out the towns of Gladbrook and Garwin.

Mr. Johnston has been a republican ever since the organization of the party. He has always been prominent in the politics of his county, but has never been an office seeker. He has, however, been frequently called to positions where there was a demand for sound judgment, especially in financial matters. Thus, he has served as a member of the board of supervisors and as a trustee and mayor of Toledo. Mr. Johnston has long been a member of the Methodist church and a trustee of Cornell college since 1871, serving as president of

the board since 1876. He has contributed many thousands of dollars to the support of this institution, but has not confined his gifts to schools of his own denomination. He aids liberally in the maintenance of Western college, and ever since its location at Toledo in 1880 has served as a member of the executive committee, having ever since taken a close interest in its success and management.

Mr. Johnston was married September 21, 1858, to Maria J. Newcomer, of Mt. Pleasant, Pa., his native town. They have but one child, a daughter, Anna B., who was born at Toledo, Iowa, and who lives at home with her parents. The Johnston home is an elegant and spacious

22

one, and many are the friends who can testify to the genial warmth of hospitality which they have felt while being entertained at "Oak Hill."

---

FLETCHER, CHARLES W., ex-mayor of Sioux City, and president and manager of the large manufacturing establishment of Fletcher & Hutchins company at that place, was born at Pittsburg, N. H., June 30, 1837. His father was a pioneer farmer of northern New Hampshire, well educated, industrious and fairly successful in the accumulation of wealth. The mother was a daughter of Judge Cummings, of Canaan,

Vt., and the effects of early culture were shown throughout her whole life. Grandfather Ebenezer Fletcher settled at Charlestown, N. H., and there followed the avocation of carpenter; Great-grandfather Peter Fletcher was a soldier in the revolutionary war, and Great-great-grandfather Ephraim Fletcher served in the French war until captured by the Indians, after which he was never heard from.

The early education of Charles W. Fletcher was acquired in a rude country schoolhouse, roughly seated and in which few text-books were used. From that time until the outbreak of the civil war he was engaged as trapper, bookkeeper, traveling agent, railroad agent and merchant, respectively. In April, 1861, he enlisted in the Second New Hampshire infantry, serving as fourth sergeant. He was disabled at the first battle of Bull Run and upon his partial recovery was sent to Lancaster, N. H., to do duty in the recruiting service. After peace had been declared he came to Iowa and located at Charles City, and engaged in the general merchandise business for five years, then lumber for ten years, then boots and shoes until 1882, at which time he located in Sioux City and assisted in the establishment of the concern of which he is now the president. The Fletcher & Hutchins company conducted their business at first under the firm name of Andrews & Fletcher, and employed about twelve hands. Some years ago the company was reorganized and incorporated and a new plant erected with a capacity sufficient for the employment of eighty men. The establishment receives the personal attention of the president and manager in its every detail. As manufacturers of bank counters and fine store fixtures, stair work, church decorations in fine woods, mouldings and all the commoner stock used by lumber dealers they have a reputation extending throughout the west.

Mr. Fletcher is an Abraham Lincoln republican. His convictions have continued to grow stronger since the time when he cast his first vote for "Father Abraham" and his courage has kept pace with that growth. He declares his views upon all proper occasions and leaves nothing undone to promote the interests of his party. The only political positions held by him have been ones of sacrifice rather than remuneration. At the expense of his personal interests he served for three terms as mayor of Charles City and for one term as mayor of Sioux City. He is a ruling elder in the First Presbyterian church and a member of the Grand Army of the Republic. In all movements of a charitable character he is foremost and his purse is not kept open for the notoriety of such a course, but because of a kindly and generous nature, to whom the doing of good deeds is in itself a satisfaction and a pleasure. He was married at Prairie du Sac, Wis., August 18, 1864, to Miss Carrie E. Moore. They have two children. Jessie M., who is the wife of L. L. Redding, of Brooklyn, N. Y., and Ralph M., bookkeeper in the establishment of Fletcher & Hutchins company.

WINSLOW, HORACE S., of Newton, ex-judge of the Sixth judicial district, is a native of Vermont, having been born in Pittsford, Rutland county, July 18, 1837. He is a direct descendant, eight generations removed, from the band of Pilgrim fathers who landed on the Massachusetts coast from the Mayflower. His father, Elhanan Spencer Winslow, was a farmer in modest circumstances, managing, however, to give his large family of children a fairly good education. His mother, Elmina Winslow, nee Kingsley, was a native of Connecticut and a descendant of the Robinson family of that state.

Young Winslow attended the common schools of his neighborhood, and the academy of his native town and afterwards the seminary at Brandon, Vt. From here he went to the State and National Law school at Poughkeepsie, N. Y., graduating from the Ohio State and Union Law college at Poland, Ohio. He was less than 19 years of age at the time of his graduation. The laws of Ohio required that an applicant for admission to the bar should be 21 years of age, and his diploma under those laws, entitled him to admission to the bar. His face was as smooth as a girl's and he looked even younger than he was. The situation worried him and at last he laid his troubles before Professor Leggett, afterwards General Leggett, who taking out a pencil, wrote the figures "21" on a piece of paper, and handed it back to the boy saying, "Put it in your shoe, and if anyone asks you about your age, tell them you are over 21." The boy received his diploma July 1, 1856, and was afterwards duly admitted to the practice. At the graduation exercises. he was given a place in the commencement law trial, the place of honor.

Immediately after graduation, Winslow started for Newton, reaching there July 5, 1856, with only five cents in his pocket. On the first day of September thereafter, he opened a law office and hung out his shingle as a practitioner. In the spring of 1857, he formed a partnership with Thomas H. Miller, which continued until the fall of 1862, Mr. Miller enlisting as a volunteer in the war of the rebellion. In 1863 he formed a partnership with Hon. S. N. Lindley, which continued until January 1, 1869, Judge Lindley at that time having been appointed judge of the second circuit of the Sixth district. In 1870, Col. J. W. Wilson became his partner and this business arrangement continued until Mr. Wil-

son's health gave way and he was compelled to give up all professional work.

During his many years of professional life, he has occupied a prominent position at the bar and it has fallen to his lot to have charge of a greater number of cases of importance than usually comes to the city practitioner.

He was elected district attorney in 1862 and served in that capacity for four years. In 1868 he was elected judge of the second circuit of the Sixth district, resigning however, at the end of one year's service. In 1874 he was elected judge of the Sixth district, leaving the bench, after four years'

service, with the reputation of disposing of more business in a given time, and doing it well, than any other judge in the state. He was one of the code commissioners to revise and codify the laws, receiving his appointment from the supreme court in 1894. Politically, he is and always has been a republican.

He is a member of Newton Lodge No. 59, A. F. and A. M., of Gebal Chapter No. 12, R. A. M., of Oriental Commandery, No. 22, Knights Templars and a charter member of Newton Chapter No. 100, O. E. S. In 1877 he was elected grand high priest of the Grand Chapter of Royal Arch Masons of Iowa, and served in that office two years. In 1880 he was elected grand commander of the Grand Commandery, Knights Templars, of Iowa, and was in charge of the Iowa knights at the Grand Encampment of the United States, held in Chicago, in 1880, at which 1,500 Iowa people were in attendance and encamped on the lake shore. He is an Odd Fellow and has served as the presiding officer of his local lodge; being unable, however, to give it proper attention, he some years ago took a clearance card from the order.

Judge Winslow was married to Sarah E. Dunkle, at Pittsford, Vt., November 7, 1858. They have two children, Kate E., now the wife of J. F. Cavill, who is now, December, 1898, steward of the Iowa State college at Ames, and Jessie L., residing at home. He is a member of the Congregational church.

---

ORMSBY, COL. EDWIN S., of Emmetsburg, is the pioneer banker of Palo Alto

county. He also has the distinction of being the first national bank president in the county. His parents were born in Massachusetts. The father, Lysander Ormsby, is still living in Deerfield, Mich., and is 82 years of age. The ancestors on both the paternal and maternal sides were prominent New England families and each branch was represented in the Lake Erie

or Toledo war. A great-grandfather, Nathaniel Ormsby, was killed in the revolutionary war. They emigrated to Michigan about 1840, and there, on a farm in Monroe county, Edwin S. was born April 17, 1842. His early education was acquired in a little log schoolhouse that stood in the timber near his home. When he had reached his eighteenth year he responded to the call for troops to defend the integrity of the nation, and on September 21, 1861, was made a "high private in the rear ranks" of the Eighth Michigan Volunteer infantry. Having served out the term of enlistment he was, in 1863, discharged, but he immediately proceeded to raise a company and in 1863 again took the field, this time with the First Michigan Engineer corps, receiving his discharge October 1, 1865. He then engaged in insurance for a time, then conducted a general merchandise business, but finally disposed of the last named to enter upon a study of the law. Since that time he has been engaged constantly in banking, law and real estate, a portion of the time in Michigan, but since 1872 in Emmetsburg. He is a strong advocate of republicanism. His father assisted in the organization of that party and the son regards it as representing those principles which, if put in practice, will result in the greatest good to the whole people. He was the mayor of Emmetsburg at the time of incorporation and had much to do with the readjustment of assessments made necessary thereby. Because of the interest he at all times manifests in school affairs, he has been called upon to serve on the board of education, acting at times as its president. He is at present one of the trustees of Cornell college. Colonel Ormsby has been one of the recognized leaders of the republican party in Iowa for many years, and has been mentioned for the governorship and other offices. He is actively identified with the Republican League, and was a delegate from Iowa to the national convention in Detroit in July, 1897. He has recently added to his business a new bank, known as the Farmers Savings bank, of which he is president. For thirty years he has been active in the work of the Methodist Episcopal church. He is a high order Mason and member of the society of the Sons of the American Revolution. He was married July 4, 1862, to Miss Mary A. Bateman, an accomplished and most estimable lady. They have had three children, only one of whom is living. She is the wife of George

J. Consigny, of Emmetsburg. The grand-children are Venita Ormsby, and Reginald Ormsby Consigny.

---

ROSENBERGER, ABSALOM, A. B., LL. B., president of Penn college, Oskaloosa, has, by persistent hard work, made a place for himself in life where he is able to help others, and that is his highest aim. Through a busy life he has held out the hand of strong and helpful friendship to those he has been associated with. A natural leader and teacher, with keen sympathy, well grounded principles and an even temper, he has made a lasting impression for good upon the young people who came to him for instruction. He has filled them with an ambition to go farther, giving them what only a few teachers are ever able to do, the desire to know more, the inspiration to dig and find the treasures of human knowl-edge. The serious training of his youth started young Rosenberger into the right path and furnished the foundation, strong and enduring, upon which the superstruc-ure of a well-proportioned and useful life is built. Born December 26, 1849, in a log cabin near Thorntown, Ind., he did not have much of an educational start in his boy-hood, for the nearest school was in a log schoolhouse in a dense forest five miles from Thorntown, where the privileges were very meagre. But the boy went to the little school, attended the meetings of the Mortonian Literary society and debat-ing club, and there became filled with the desire to get an education. His parents were of the kind to encourage this ambition. His father was James Henry Rosenberger, a farmer by occupation and a man of lim-ited circumstances. He was for many years a devout elder in the Friends' church, to which the son has always remained true. His mother was Elizabeth Mills Rosen-berger, a quiet, pious woman, whose fam-ily came from England and helped William Penn in founding Pennsylvania. She was much attached to her home. The father's family came from Germany. The mother died when Absalom was 13 years old and the father when he was 16, leaving him to support himself. In 1872, Mr. Rosenberger entered Earlham college, in Richmond, Ind., graduating from the classical course in 1876. He was one of the editors of the college paper for three years, and served as assistant proctor for two years. With him attending college was serious business, for he earned his own way and maintained a

manly independence that left him with few debts to pay at the end of the four years' course. It is said of him by Dr. Joseph Moore, president of the college at that time, that "He furnishes another proof that the youth in college whose first and highest work is to build up a character is pretty sure, later in life, to build some-thing else." Now well fitted for teaching, Mr. Rosenberger entered the work of edu-cation and spent ten years as an academic teacher, most of the time in Union high school, a Friends' institution in Westfield, Ind., and it was in that field that he did some of his best work. He was fresh from

his own struggle for an education and he keenly sympathized with every boy and girl who was trying to make something of himself. He inspired them with some of his own ambition, and by patience and for-bearance and respect for the opinion of his students, and an absence of dogmatism and pedantry, exerted a powerful and last-ing influence upon their lives. He helped them in every possible way, to help them-selves, finding them places where they could earn their board, when necessary.

In 1885, Mr. Rosenberger went to Ann Arbor, Mich., and took the law course in the University of Michigan, graduating in 1887, and at once entered upon the practice of his profession at Wichita, Kan., where he remained three years, returning to the teaching profession in 1890 as president of Penn college, the place he now fills with so much credit. While in the university in Ann Arbor, Mr. Rosenberger enjoyed the privilege of being in the classes of President Angell in international law and history of diplomacy, constitutional law and history, under Judge Thomas M. Cooley, and economics under Dr. Adams. His previous training and mental equipment made him a prominent figure in the class, and he was persuaded to act as class historian, a duty requiring much labor, which the class felt sure he would perform. He was known as a plodder and one of the faculty has said of him that "He soon won the good will of his fellows by his candor and cordiality, by his culture and character." For five years Mr. Rosenberger was a member of the board of trustees of Earlham college, and has twice been appointed a representative from the Iowa yearly meeting of Friends to the quinquennial conferences of Friends of America held in the city of Indianapolis in 1892 and 1897. He was a delegate from Iowa to the national arbitration convention held in Washington, D. C., in April, 1896. President Rosenberger is a member of the republican party. He was married September 5, 1877, to Miss Martha Ellen Kendall, of Thorntown, Ind. They have five children, Homer G., born January 17, 1880; Ethel C., born July 8, 1882; Lucile, born March 10, 1885; Frank Kendall, born September 18, 1890, and Helen, born June 23, 1895.

---

BROOKS, Dr. James M., is a popular physician who has resided in Newell for nearly twenty years, during all but two years of the time having been engaged in the practice of his profession with unvarying success. He was born in Harrisonville, Meigs county, Ohio, September 13, 1857. His parents were natives of England; his father was a prosperous farmer and all-round money-maker. The mother's maiden name was Catherine Berkley and she was a descendant of Governor Berkley of colonial fame. He attended the public school in the village where he was born and afterwards the high school in Carthage, Ill. Having a taste for business and desiring to become proficient in those studies which enter into practical business life, he entered one of the principal business colleges in Chicago and took a course there.

Before entering upon his business career, however, he concluded that a professional calling would be better suited to him, so he entered the College of Physicians and Surgeons in Chicago and was graduated March 13, 1883. Two days later he was married to Miss Lyde J. Davis, of Abingdon, Ill., and together they returned to Newell, Iowa, where Dr. Brooks had, for two years previous to this time, made his home. His residence and practice in this town have been so satisfactory to himself and to the people there that he has had no occasion to change his location. He has prospered financially and in a professional

way has achieved all that he could ask. He started in with but very little capital beyond a well trained mind and a sound body and thorough professional preparation, and what he has been able to do has grown out of his own natural ability. Three children have been born to Dr. and Mrs. Brooks, viz.: Lettie, born December 29, 1883; Bessie, born June 4, 1886, and Julian, born October 14, 1894. On the 13th of March, 1896, the dark messenger entered the home and took away the wife and mother, who had been such an important element in the happiness and well being of that home. February 8, 1898, Dr. Brooks was again married to Miss Mollie E. Redfield, of Newell.

ELLSWORTH, EUGENE STAFFORD, is a grandson of Stukley Stafford Ellsworth, of New York, who is a native of Otsego county and became prominent in the commercial and political history of that state. Orlando Ellsworth, the father of Eugene, and his mother, Almira Shaw, were reared in Otsego county, and married there before coming west to Milwaukee county, Wis., in 1836. There he occupied a prominent position and served in the legislature of 1857 and 1858. At the outbreak of the civil war he raised a company of volunteers and was chosen captain. The company was assigned to the Twenty-fourth regiment of Wisconsin volunteers and was known as Company K. The regiment was ordered to the front in September, 1862, as a part of the Army of the Tennessee, and Eugene S. Ellsworth, then a lad of 13, went with them as a drummer boy. He remained with his company until the hardships of the campaign broke down his health and he was sent to the hospital. After the close of his military service Captain Ellsworth removed to Iowa Falls, Ia., and remained there until his death in 1872.

Eugene attended school in Milwaukee county until he went to the front with his father's company. In 1863 he went to Iowa Falls and engaged in hauling lumber, supplies and goods of all kinds from the nearest railroad points, then Cedar Falls and Marshalltown, some fifty miles distant. In 1866 he took a course of study at Baylies Commercial college in Dubuque, and in 1870 went into the real estate business, and although the country was new, he soon built up a fine business. In those early days he also did a large amount of loaning on Iowa farms for eastern investors and still continues this branch of the business, which has grown to colossal proportions. In twenty-six years of business, amounting to millions of dollars, he has not met with any loss. In 1884 Mr. L. E. Jones, who for several years had been his confidential clerk, became a partner in the business, which is still carried on by the firm of Ellsworth & Jones. They have offices in Iowa Falls, Chicago and Boston.

Mr. Ellsworth has always entertained great faith in the future of the state of Iowa, which is well demonstrated by his investments in Iowa real estate to the amount of many thousands of acres of highly improved farming lands. These farms are carried on under his own direction with the aid of managers, and require many men to handle and market their pro-

ducts. In 1896 Mr. Ellsworth was chosen president of the First National bank of Iowa Falls. For several years he was a director in the lines of the Burlington, Cedar Rapids & Northern railway, and for some years served as secretary and treasurer of the Town Lot company, organized for the purpose of establishing towns on the line of that road. He had the management of the business of this company, by which some thirty of the best towns in Iowa were brought into existence.

Politically, Mr. Ellsworth is a republican and has served as mayor of Iowa Falls.

He has always taken a strong interest in educational matters and Ellsworth college at Iowa Falls, established in 1890, was named for him. It is well known as one of the most flourishing institutions in the state. He joined the Masonic fraternity in 1878 and has taken all the degrees up to and including the thirty-second. In 1887 he was eminent commander of St. Elmo Commandery No. 48, Knights Templars. He also belongs to the A. O. U. W., and the order of the Mystic Shrine.

In September, 1872, he was married to Miss Hattie A. Northrop, of Otisville, Franklin county, Iowa, and they have two children: Ernest Orlando, a graduate of Shattuck Military school, and Caroline Parsons, who is now at Vassar college.

MELENDY, PETER, of Cedar Falls, has been for more than a third of a century one of the most widely known of the public men of Iowa.

His father was James Melendy, who was a native of Amherst, N. H., where he was born October 15, 1791. He was a breeder of fine stock and a manufacturer of fanning mills. He was a whig in politics, but with strong anti-slavery views, and was active in working for the abolition of slavery. He served his country as a gallant soldier in the war with Great Britain, in 1812; was long an elder in the Presbyterian church. In 1822 he married Miss Susan Smith, who was a native of Delaware, and with her parents moved to Cincinnati, Ohio, in the fall of 1818. Her father was Rev. John Smith, a Baptist clergyman. The first ancestors of the Melendy family, of which any record exists, was a

Spaniard, Pedro Melendze, who was appointed governor of a colony in Florida, in 1565. After a life's vicissitudes too lengthy for narration here, he finally found a home in Scotland, and from him the Melendys have descended. William and Mrs. Standish Melendy fled from Scotland, in 1675, on account of religious persecution and, settling in Massachusetts, became the founders of the Melendy family in America. Thomas, the grandfather, and William, the great-grandfather of Peter Melendy, served as soldiers in the war of the revolution. His father, James Melendy, moved to Cincinnati, Ohio, in 1814, where he married Miss Susan Smith in 1822. Their son Peter was born February 9, 1823, and when 5 years of age accompanied his father to the old homestead at Amherst, N. H., and went to school one year in the same schoolhouse where his father had attended when a boy. Upon his return home he attended private schools and academies until 1837, when he entered Woodward

college, where he remained about three years. In 1840 he went into his father's factory and learned to manufacture fanning mills, and assisted in carrying on his father's farms, where breeding of fine stock was a business. October 20, 1846, he married Miss Martha F. Coddington, daughter of Hon. William Coddington, of Cincinnati, Ohio. Three years later he purchased a farm near Cincinnati, and moved onto it, and in 1855 he had so improved it that it took the prize offered for the best managed farm in the state. In 1855 he helped to organize the Iowa Fine Stock Breeding company, with a large capital. The company entered 10,000 acres of land in Butler county, Iowa, near Bear Grove. In 1856 Mr. Melendy came to Cedar Falls, Iowa, and purchased 1,080 acres of choice land in the same county, and placed upon it some of his best fine stock from his Ohio farm. In 1857 he moved onto the farm. But being remote from good schools, church and society, a year later he moved, with his family, back to Cedar Falls for a permanent home. In 1859 Mr. Melendy and W. M. McCoy took a contract to construct the roadbed for a railroad from Cedar Falls to Waverly, Iowa; they expended a large amount of money in the work, but by the failure of the company before the road was completed they lost heavily. In 1860 in company with A. D. Barnum, Mr. Melendy helped to establish the first implement, grain and produce warehouse in the Cedar valley, which grew into a large business. In 1862 Mr. Melendy was appointed by Governor Kirkwood, commissioner for the state, to select 240,000 acres of land, lately granted by congress to Iowa, for the endowment of the State Agricultural college. There were at that time nearly 6,000,000 acres of government land in the limits of Iowa, from which to select, and, after careful investigation, with excellent judgment, Mr. Melendy made the selections which have brought to the State college an ample income. In 1863 and 1864 Mr. Melendy was also, by appointment of Governor Kirkwood, made the agent of Iowa at Washington for proving up the swamp lands of the various counties. In 1864 he was chosen secretary and superintendent of the State Agricultural college. He was appointed by President Lincoln, in 1865, United States marshal for Iowa. When President Johnson abandoned the party that elected him, and sought to build up a new personal party, he removed Mr. Melendy and nearly all of the Iowa federal officials who refused to ally themselves with the Johnson party. Mr. Melendy was one of the projectors and early officers of the Iowa Central Railroad company. In 1871 President Grant reappointed Mr. Melendy to his old position of United States marshal, from which he had been removed by Andrew Johnson, in 1865, which position he held for four years, performing its responsible duties with fidelity and ability. After the breaking out of the rebellion, Mr. Melendy was very active in raising troops to defend the union. In September, 1861, he was commissioned by Governor Kirkwood, to enlist volunteers for the Thirteenth Iowa infantry. He procured nearly men enough to make two companies for that regiment. He served for some time as quartermaster for the troops stationed at Cedar Falls, from time to time, as the war progressed, and assisted in organizing the militia of Black Hawk county by direction of Adjutant-General Baker. Gov. S. J. Kirkwood, in a letter to him under date of December 10, 1890, said this: "I take great pleasure in saying that Mr. Peter Melendy, in war times, rendered me and our state very valuable service in raising, organizing and placing in the field many of our soldiers, in whom we all took such pride, and in caring for their welfare when within his reach, in doing the work to which he was assigned." In 1865 he was instrumental in securing the location of the Soldiers' Orphans' home at Cedar Falls, of which he was a member of the board of trustees. He was one of ten citizens of that town to purchase forty acres of land upon which the home was located, and which is now occupied by the State Normal school. In 1864 Mr. Melendy was one of the delegates from Iowa to the national republican convention which renominated Abraham Lincoln for president, and was one of the committee sent to Washington to notify the president of the action of the convention. That was a mission of which Mr. Melendy has always felt proud. He was in Washington and witnessed the second inauguration of the great president who was so soon to fill a martyr's grave. In 1867 Mr. Melendy was named among the men from whom the next governor of Iowa, was likely to be chosen, but he declined to be a candidate. He was chairman of the republican state central committee, and under his direction of the the campaign, Iowa gave an overwhelming majority for General Grant for president in 1868. He was a delegate at large from Iowa to the Chicago national convention which had placed Grant and Colfax in nomination that year. Mr. Melendy was for many years a director of the State Agricultural society, and served as vice-president, treasurer and marshal, and was for five years its president, serving a longer period than any president before or since. He was a member of the board of trustees of the Iowa Agricultural college for fourteen years, doing invaluable service in organizing and building up that great State college. He was, in 1866, appointed to serve with the president of the board of trustees, Lieut.-Gov. B. F. Gue, to visit other industrial colleges of the country, formulate and report a plan for the organization of our college, and finally to select suitable persons to constitute the faculty. They served three years on this important mission, and their action met the unanimous approval of the trustees, both in the plan of organization proposed, and the choice of Hon. A. S. Welch, for president, and of other members of the faculty.

Mr. Melendy has taken a deep interest in horticulture, and was for many years a member of the State Horticultural society. He has served many years as agricultural editor of the Cedar Falls papers, and was for a long time a regular writer for the *Ohio Farmer.* He became associated, in 1873, with A. D. Barnum and D. C. Overman, in railroad building. They constructed the Burlington, Cedar Rapids & Northern railway from Waterloo to Cedar Falls, and also built a large elevator at Cedar Falls. In 1877 Mr. Melendy was associated with parties in building fifteen miles of railroad on a line from Chicago towards Muscatine. In 1879 he received the appointment of agent for the quartermaster's department of the United States, for the adjudication of claims arising out of the war. His field was in Tennessee, where he served until 1886. It would take a volume to record the important work done by Mr. Melendy during his more than forty years of busy life in Iowa. Endowed with good health, unbounded energy, fine ability, and broad liberality, he has for almost half a century been one of the conspicuous public men of the state. In all his varied occupations and public positions he has won warm and abiding friends, and the sincere respect of the people who know him best.

His first wife died at Cedar Falls, August 6, 1867, at the age of 38, leaving two children,

Charles B., born May 15, 1848, and Luetta Isabella, born January 19, 1852. In 1868, Mr. Melendy married Mrs. Mary A. McFarland, daughter of ex-Senator T. W. Woolson, at Mt Pleasant. She is a sister of Judge John S. Woolson, of the United States district court.

Mr. Melendy has been an active and prominent member of the Presbyterian church all of his mature life. Now in the evening of a long, busy and useful career, his old neighbors keep him in the mayor's office of the city he has served so well, in various ways, for almost half a century.

EDMUNDSON, MR. JAMES DEPEW is a native of Iowa. He was born on the 23d day of November, 1838, on a farm near the city of Burlington, and has spent the whole of his life in his native state.

His father, William Edmundson, was a native of Kentucky, and was of Scotch-Irish descent, his ancestors having settled in Virginia early in the eighteenth century. He was one of the early pioneers, having settled in the territory of Iowa in 1836, and lived in the state until his death, in 1862. He was one of the organizing officers of Mahaska county, and a member of the First General Assembly of the state.

His mother, Priscilla Depew, was a native of Virginia, and was a member of a Huguenot family of that name, which was driven from France at the time of the revocation of the Edict of Nantes by Louis XIV, and which settled in America soon afterwards.

When Mr. Edmundson was about 6 years of age, his mother having died, his father and other members of the family removed to Oskaloosa, where he first attended private schools, afterwards attending the normal school located in that city, and finishing his school days at an academy in Newton, Iowa. Soon after leaving school he returned to Oskaloosa and entered the law office of the Hon William H. Seevers, afterwards and for many years a judge of the supreme court of the state, as a law student, and was admitted to the bar in 1860, by the late ex-Gov. William M. Stone, then presiding judge of the district. In the meantime, and while a law student, he was elected a page of the Eighth General Assembly of the state, where he gained his first knowledge of public affairs, and formed the acquaintance of many leading men, which proved of great benefit to him in after years.

Soon after his admission to the bar he removed to Glenwood and associated himself, under the firm name of Hale & Edmundson, with his old friend and schoolmate, the Hon. William Hale, afterwards governor of Wyoming territory, in the practice of law and the transaction of a general real estate business. He remained here until the spring of 1866, when he removed to Council Bluffs and formed a partnership with the Hon. D. C. Bloomer, under the firm name of Bloomer & Edmundson. The firm conducted a real estate business in connection with the practice of law, until the spring of 1870, when it was dissolved by mutual consent.

Mr. Edmundson, then discontinued the practice of his profession and devoted his time and attention exclusively to the purchase and sale of real estate. In this business he covered a wide field, having correspondents by the hundreds in all parts of the country. For about twenty years thereafter he was thus actively employed, and these were the years of his greatest business activity.

He never dealt largely in city property, but early began making investments in farm lands in Pottawattamie and other counties of western Iowa. In these operations he was remarkably successful, and still owns large tracts of land throughout the western part of the state, which have become very valuable.

As the years went by he began to turn his attention to new modes of investment, and in 1877, was influential in the organization of the Savings, Loan and Building association, of Council Bluffs, one of the most useful and prosperous associations of this kind in the country.

About the same time he became quite largely interested in banking, and in 1882 united with other citizens of Council Bluffs in the organization of the Citizens bank, the title of which was afterwards changed to that of the Citizens State bank of Council Bluffs, and became its largest stockholder and first president, which position he held until January, 1899, when the Citizens State bank was consolidated with the First National bank of Council Bluffs, Iowa, the new organization retaining the title of the First National bank, and Mr. Edmundson continuing to hold the position of president.

He is also a large stockholder and director in the State Savings bank, of Council Bluffs, and the Sioux Valley State bank, of Correctionville, Iowa, and a stockholder in the Atlantic National bank, of Atlantic, Iowa, and the Bankers National bank of Chicago, besides being interested as a stockholder in the Pioneer Implement company and the Empkie-Shugart Hardware company, both of Council Bluffs. He does not, however, give to any of these corporations his personal attention, preferring to take life more quietly, and, while looking after the management of his ample fortune, to employ himself in pursuits more congenial to his tastes.

Mr. Edmundson is an independent thinker, and looks carefully into the current questions of the day. He is a great reader, and has gathered about him a handsome library, in which he spends much of his time.

He is not a great lover of fiction, although quite familiar with the leading writers in that department of literature, but rather gives his attention to historical works, and those dealing with abstruse questions of modern research.

Being a lover of books, it was quite natural that he should and did take an active interest in the establishment of a free public library in Council Bluffs, of which he has for many years been an active and efficient trustee.

Mr. Edmundson's first presidential vote was given for Abraham Lincoln, and he has adhered steadily to the republican faith through all subsequent years, and has always taken a warm interest in the political action of his party, giving freely of his means to advance its success, often attending political conventions, and in various ways aiding in the election of its candidates. He has, however, never sought office, having been too closely engaged, until recent years, in the care of his business; leaving to others the honors and emoluments of official life.

In addition to his other holdings, he is now one of the stockholders in and a director of the New Nonpareil company, publishers of the *Daily Nonpareil*, the leading republican newspaper in western Iowa.

For the last fifteen or twenty years Mr. Edmundson has been quite a traveler, and has visited every state and territory in the union, including Alaska, and has also traveled extensively in Europe.

In his journeyings through Europe he has traveled to the extreme north and looked at the midnight sun from the North Cape, the northernmost point of Norway, and has, with one or two exceptions, visited every other country in Europe.

Mr. Edmundson has given a great deal of attention to ethical questions, but has never united with any religious denomination. He gives freely, however, toward their support, and usually attends the Congregational church, having been the treasurer of that organization in Council Bluffs, for seventeen years, resigning that position only about two years ago. He related to the writer the remarkable fact that during the whole period of his holding that office he only failed a few times, perhaps not more than half a dozen in all, to pay the pastor in charge his regular salary when it became due. Such examples of remarkable promptness in religious corporations are believed to be exceedingly rare.

Mr. Edmundson has no children. His first wife was Miss Jennie Hart, daughter of Dr. H. W. Hart, a prominent physician of Council Bluffs. She was a woman of excellent attainments, both in mind and person. They were married in May, 1871, and Mrs. Edmundson passed away in February, 1890. A noble monument erected to her memory by Mr. Edmundson, stands in Walnut Hill cemetery.

He was again married on the 1st day of January, 1894, to Mrs. Laura Barclay Kirby, and spent the most of the following year, with his wife, in Europe.

The above leading incidents of Mr. Edmundson's life show him to be, emphatically a self-made man. Like many other western boys, he started out to make a place for himself in the busy world, and he has nobly succeeded.

He has accumulated an ample competence, and has gained the esteem and confidence of the people among whom he has spent more than half of his life. And all this he has accomplished by careful attention to business, by strict honesty and fair dealing in all his transactions, and by the exercise of prudence and a rare good judgment, which never fails him.

He is genial and pleasant in his manners, an interesting conversationalist, and a friend who will never fail in the hour of severest trial.

THOMPSON, COL. JAMES KNOX POLK, of Rock Rapids, Iowa, was born near Carey, Ohio, August 21, 1845.

His father, Matthew Thompson, who was a soldier of the war of 1812, was born at Head Elk, Cecil county, Md., January 8, 1781. His paternal grandfather, Isaac Thompson, and paternal grandmother, Sarah Bell, were native of Belfort, Ireland, where they were married and where their first son, Thomas Cruse Thompson, was born. Both the Thompson and Bell families were related to the famous Lord Thomas Cruse, who was compelled to flee the country for his participation in the revolution of 1798. He sought an asylum in the United States, where he died soon after. His mother, Martha Spaulding Thompson, was a daughter of Abel Spaulding, who served with distinction in the revolutionary war, and through her is a direct descendant of Aquila Chase, who settled in Newberry, Mass., in 1640, and is therefore closely related to Bishop Philander Chase (1775-1852) and Salmon P. Chase (1808-1873), chief justice of the supreme court of the United States.

He first attended school in a log schoolhouse in Ohio, where everything was of the rudest and most primitive character. His education was carefully superintended by his mother, who was a prominent educator of her time, to whom he went to school for several years. He came to Iowa in November, 1857, and settled in Clayton county, then a sparsely populated frontier county. The trip from Ohio was made in a covered wagon and consumed more than forty days. In the year 1869 he commenced the study of law under the tutorage of S. T. Woodward, of Elkader, while carrying on his regular farm work, and was admitted to the bar in May, 1873, and soon thereafter removed to his present location. In June of that year he opened the first law office in Lyon county. He was actively engaged in practice until 1893, and was conspicuous in all the prominent cases litigated in that section. His business was not confined to that county alone, but extended to adjoining counties, and his collections covered a radius of more than 100 miles. He was counsel for the board of supervisors during the stirring period of the defalcation of the treasurer of the county, during the settlement of which scenes having the smack of life in the woolly west were enacted. In 1876 he formed a partnership with his brother, T. C. Thompson, and the same was continued until 1880, when it was dissolved by mutual consent. He organized the Lyon County bank in 1877 under the style of J. K. P. Thompson & Co. The bank was reorganized in 1889, and the capital increased to $25,000, with Hon. William Larrabee and others as special partners, and O. P. Miller as general partner. The capital stock was increased from time to time until it reached its present amount, $100,000. Mr. Larrabee retired in 1893, the interest of the other special partners having been previously purchased by the general partners. He enlisted August 18, 1862, as a musi-

cian in Company D, Twenty-first Iowa volunteers, and served throughout the war with as much distinction as comes to the average soldier. He was engaged in the following battles: Hartsville, the running of the blockade at Vicksburg, bombardment of Grand Gulf, Port Gibson, was in the forefront when the pickets were fired upon, Champion Hill, the charge at Black River Bridge, assault and siege of Vicksburg, when he was under fire for forty days and nights. He was severely wounded in the assault on the works of Vicksburg, and was at the time within a few feet of his commander, General McClernand. After the surrender of the city, he was sent to Jefferson barracks hospital, and rejoined his regiment at Matagorda Bay the February following. He also participated in the Mobile campaign, was in the siege and assault of Ft. Blakely and Spanish Fort, the surrender of Mobile and the capture of Kirby Smith, having taken part in seven hard-fought battles, and participated in the most noted campaign of this or any other age.

He is a charter member of Dunlap Post No. 147, Department of Iowa, G. A. R., which he was instrumental in having named after his lieutenant-colonel, who was killed while gallantly leading his command on the works of Vicksburg. He is past commander of his post, and past commander Department of Iowa, G. A. R., having served in that capacity during the years of 1895-6. He also served on the staff of Commander-in-chief Vezy, and as aid of several commanders of Iowa. He was appointed lieutenant-colonel in the Iowa national guard on the staff of Governor Larrabee, again on that of Governor Jackson, and promoted to the rank of colonel by Governor Drake in February, 1896, which rank he now holds.

His father was an old-line democrat, but the son did not embrace the faith of the father. He cast his first vote for a republican, and has several times managed with consummate skill the campaigns of his county as chairman of the central committee. He was elected recorder of the county in 1875, and held the office for one term, although he had been in actual charge of the office since 1873, and was at one time in charge of all the county offices. He was nominated for the office of representative by the republicans of the Seventieth district, and was defeated by Hon. William Barrett, the democratic nominee, by only a few votes. There were only thirty-three votes cast against him in his own county. He is a member of all the Masonic orders, past eminent commander, a member of the Knights of Pythias, and a Son of the American Revolution. In nearly all of these orders he holds high official positions. He is a member of the Congregational church and a trustee of Iowa college. He was instrumental in establishing the Vicksburg National Military park, and has been a member of the provisional board of directors of the organization from the beginning.

He was married to Miss Celestia A. Fobes, at Elkader, Iowa, November 18, 1869, who is also of revolutionary ancestry; her great grandfather served with great valor in the revolutionary war. They have three children, two daughters and one son: Lily Foster Thompson Parker, Leta May Thompson and Hoyt Fobes Thompson. They are all graduates of the Rock Rapids high school. The older daughter was a student at Cornell college. The second daughter graduated from Iowa college, where the son is now a student. He will soon enter Princeton.

Colonel Thompson has been closely identified with the development of northwestern Iowa. and especially with Lyon county, having become a resident thereof a few months after its organization, and has borne a conspicuous part in its settlement. He bore evidence of his faith in its future by large investments in her rich soil, and by tenaciously clinging thereto. The result more than justified his faith.

----

WILL, FREDERICK J., of Eagle Grove, Iowa, is a true representative of the active and progressive medical profession of the state. He is not only a well-known and successful physician and surgeon, but well known throughout the political circles of the state, having always been an active worker in the ranks of the republican party.

He is an Iowa man, having been born in Story county, Iowa, June 11, 1859. His father, James S. Will, is a native of New-market, Va. The doctor's mother was Miss Kate Berlin, also of Virginia. Her brother, George W. Berlin, was one of the original signers of the articles of secession of Virginia.

In 1873 Dr. Will entered the Agricultural college at Ames, Iowa, where he was a student until 1876, when he was appointed a cadet midshipman in the United States navy. He spent three years in the Naval academy at Annapolis, Md. Resigning his position at the end of the three years, he

returned to Iowa and began the study of medicine, graduating from the medical department of the Iowa State university in 1883, when he began the practice of medicine at Jewell Junction. He afterwards located in Eagle Grove in 1885, where he has been ever since.

The doctor is a self-educated man. He was a successful teacher and thus acquired the means to complete his education. He is prominent in several of the fraternal orders, being a member of the Masons, Odd Fellows, Knights of Pythias, and Modern Woodmen. In June, 1897, Dr. Will was elected head physician of the Modern

Woodmen at the state camp held in Dubuque. The competition was strong, but the doctor had the most friends. He is the district surgeon of the Chicago & Northwestern railway; is a member of the American Medical association, National Association of Railway Surgeons, Iowa State Association of Railway Surgeons, and of the Iowa State Medical association.

He was an alternate delegate from the Third district to the republican national convention at St. Louis in 1896, and was an earnest supporter of William B. Allison for president.

Dr. Will has two brothers, Arthur Lee Will, a successful business man located at Salina, Kan., and Harry Clayton Will, a graduate of the Chicago Medical college, and now practicing in Chicago.

Dr. Will is a man who holds the high esteem of all who know him, and is one of the most influential men of his town and county.

DINGLEY, FRANK, SR., of Algona, was born in Chautauqua county, N. Y., in the year 1829. He is the son of Warren Dingley, a sailor during his early and middle life. He first went to sea from Boston harbor, at the age of 12 years, as a cabin boy of the ship "Three Brothers," of which his father was part owner and commander. Before he became of age he made a voyage around the world. He later became sailing master of the "Walk-in-the-Water," the first steamboat that plowed the lakes. General Lafayette, during his last visit to the United States, took passage with him from Buffalo, and through the upper lakes. While thus employed he purchased a tract of land from the Holland Land company in Chautauqua county, N. Y. and there reared his family of eight children. The maiden name of the present Mr. Dingley's mother was Anne Patterson. She was of Scotch descent, and removed with her parents to western New York when but 12 years of age. She acquired an education, which at that early time fitted her for the avocation of teacher, and for several years prior to her marriage, in 1821, taught in the village and district schools in Chautauqua county. The ancestors on the paternal side were English, and the coat of arms is still in the possession of Mr. Dingley. Ex-Gov. Nelson Dingley, of Maine, now a member of congress, and famous as the author of the Dingley tariff bill, and the late Dr. Amasa Dingley, of New York, are among the more notable members of this family. On the maternal side may be mentioned ex-Governor Patterson, of New York. In a work prepared by him that branch is traced back to the time of the settlement of the colony at Massachusetts bay, and indirectly to the settlement at Flatbush, Ireland, by the Scotch, centuries ago.

Frank Dingley, Sr., was the youngest of three brothers in a family of eight children, and remained on the farm with his parents until 21 years of age. Among the companions of his early school days, in the little red schoolhouse of Chautauqua county, were General Schofield, late commander of the United States army, his brother, Rev.

James Schofield, Col. George Camp and Hon. H. C Waite, all of whom became noted in after life. He came to Dubuque, Iowa, in 1854, then to Jamestown, a mining camp in Grant county, Wis., where he engaged in lead mining. In this he was not successful, and the following spring went to work on his uncle's farm, having leased it in company with his cousin, George Patterson, and, having a good contract, together with a bountiful crop and good prices, their agricultural operations were very profitable. In the spring of 1857 he went on the road for the Eagle Reaper company, and in that, too, he was highly

successful, so that at the end of one year he was able to open a general store at Georgetown, Wis. Here he remained for a year, when the hard times which still linger in the minds of the older citizens came on, and the business was disposed of. Going thence to Alabama he soon became convinced that the south was no place for a northern man, and his stay there was of short duration. He was married at Old Windham, Conn., in August, 1859, to Miss Harriet C. Williams, a native of Willimantic. They have had three children, two of whom are now living. Shortly after the marriage they returned to Wisconsin, where they remained for five years, then removed to his early home in New York. In the spring of 1879 he again came west, locating this time at Masonville, Delaware county, Iowa, where he engaged in the general merchandise business. On the death of his eldest son he disposed of his interest there and returned to Wisconsin, but after two years became dissatisfied and removed to Algona, his present residence, and has since formed a partnership with his son-in-law, J. L. Donohoe, in the real estate, loan and insurance business. After extended travel all over the United States he is firmly grounded in the belief that of all that is good Iowa furnishes the best. His son, Frank W., is a successful druggist in Algona.

---

LAW, ROBERT, manager of the Burlington & Northwestern and Burlington & West-

ern Railway companies, is a resident of Burlington, and has grown up in the railroad business, which he has followed since the age of 12 years. His father, Robert Law, was a steamboat captain on Lake Erie, and was drowned in a gale at the age of 25, while in charge of the steamer Wave. The family lived in Hamilton, Canada. John Law, his grandfather, was also a seafaring man, who came from England to Canada in his old age and settled on a farm, where he remained until his death. His wife's maiden name was Deborah Elliott. Their son, Robert Law, was married to Eliza M. McNalage. She was born in Port Hope, Canada West, and married at the age of 17. Their son Robert was born in Port Hope,

Canada, May 26, 1850. After the death of her husband, when Robert was only 8 months old, she moved to New York, where she remained for several years, going from there to western Nebraska, where she now resides. Her mother's maiden name was Jane Baxter, born in London, England, and married Mr. McNalage, who was associated with his uncle in a silk store in London.

Robert Law began his education in the public schools of New York, and earned his livelihood during the summer on a farm, when a small boy. When he was 12 years old he entered the service of the Atlantic & Great Western Railroad company, now a part of the Erie system, remaining with that company in the track department four years, until the winter of 1866, when he accepted service with the track department of the Union Pacific, and was afterwards advanced to division roadmaster, general roadmaster, division superintendent, and finally to general superintendent. He resigned the latter position at Cheyenne, Wyo., in the fall of 1882 to take charge of the Burlington lines in Missouri, headquarters Keokuk, Iowa, where he remained four years, afterwards accepting service with the Northern Pacific at Livingston, Mont., as division superintendent, and was later promoted to the position of assistant general manager, headquarters at Helena, Mont. He subsequently became manager of the Montana Union, with headquarters in Butte. A few years later he took the management of the Chicago Railway Transfer association, which he held for several years, until its dissolution in December, 1893, when he immediately returned to the Burlington system as manager of the Burlington & Northwestern and Burlington & Western lines.

Mr. Law ranks with the leading railroad managers of the west, possessing energy, acumen, knowledge of human nature in combination with fine executive and general business ability. He is a staunch republican, never having voted any other ticket; belongs to the Masonic order, and is a member of the Episcopal church. Mr. Law married during the summer of 1873 Miss Rozette C. Michael, and to that union there have come four children. The two eldest, Robert and Morell, completed their college education in the University of Chicago. The third, Leonore, is a student of Mrs. Loring's Private school, 2535 Prairie avenue, Chicago, and the youngest, George, is with his parents in Burlington.

MUSSER, RICHARD, of Muscatine, one of the pioneer lumbermen of Iowa, was a native of Lancaster county, Pa., and was born in Adamstown on the 15th day of November, 1819. His parents were Peter and Elizabeth (Adams) Musser, who were also natives of Pennsylvania. The father was born in Berks county and was of Swiss origin, while the mother was born in Lancaster county and was of Scotch-English descent. He received a common school education, and began his business career as a merchant's clerk, and on attaining manhood engaged in the tanning and leather business in Pine Grove, Schuylkill county, until October, 1854, when he emigrated to Iowa. The first year Mr. Musser spent at Iowa City, and in 1855 located at Muscatine, where he formed a partnership with his brother and Mr. Edward Hoch in the lumber business, the firm being known as Hoch & Musser. The partnership was for a term of three years and at the expiration of that time Mr. Hoch retired, and the business was continued under the firm name of R. Musser & Co. Various changes in the firm occurred, until the incorporation of the Musser Lumber company in 1871.

In 1849, at Pine Grove, Schuylkill county, Pa., the marriage of Mr. Richard Musser and Miss Sarah Filbert, daughter of Peter Filbert of that place, was celebrated. In less than a year after her marriage, Mrs. Musser died, and about five years later Mr. Musser, who was then in business in Muscatine, Iowa, returned to Pine Grove, Pa., and on March 15, 1855, was united in marriage to Miss Sarah Elizabeth Berger. Nine children were born of this union, of whom those now living are William, residing in Iowa City; Suzanne, Kathryn, Grace, Gertrude and Linda, living in Muscatine.

In early life Mr. Musser was a whig in political sentiment, but on the dissolution of the old party he joined the infant republican party, which has since become historic in the annals of the nation.

He took a warm interest in the cause of education, and served nine years as a member of the Muscatine school board. He was a member of the city council and served two terms as mayor of the city, first in 1874 and again in 1878. He has been prominently identified with the leading manufacturing industry of Muscatine for forty years, and by his energy and enterprise has been instrumental in building up one of the most important lumber corporations on the middle Mississippi. He was also identified with the extensive sash, door and blind factory, carried on by the Muscatine Manufacturing company in Muscatine and Kansas City, the Muscatine waterworks and other companies. The people of Muscatine need no printed eulogy of Richard Musser and his achievements to herald his praises to the present generation; his works speak for themselves. But when this generation shall have passed away and the history of the people, who, by their enterprise and public spirit improved and developed the natural resources of this state, is to be read by posterity, it will

only be proper that the records should show that the subject of this sketch was always foremost in encouraging and sustaining all public improvements calculated to benefit the city or county at large; that he was active and influential in organizing various manufacturing companies that furnished employment to all classes of labor and which, in their operation, added wealth and importance to the city; that he was just and honorable in all his relations to society, both public and private, and that the general good and welfare of the community were considered as well as the prospect of personal gain. His death occurred on the 2d of October, 1896, and the little city of Muscatine has never witnessed a more genuine expression of widespread sorrow than that which accompanied the obsequies of Richard Musser. "It would be a brighter world were there more of his type left."

HUSSEY, JOHN MARION, president of the Western Normal college at Shenandoah, is one of Iowa's best known school men; a practical educator; wide awake to the demands of the age. He is the son of Henry H. Hussey, a farmer and stock-raiser of comfortable means, who is a native of North Carolina, but who moved to Ohio and later to Illinois, finally settling

in Missouri in 1859, where he still resides. He served actively during the civil war for nearly four years. Professor Hussey's mother, formerly Miss Emilia E. Darnell, is a native of Indiana, and is of Irish descent. The Hussey family was one of the very first to settle in Massachusetts, Christopher Hussey having come over in the "Mayflower." Many of his descendants were Quakers, the poet Whittier being among them. Another distinguished member of the family tree was Daniel Webster, who descended from a niece of Christopher Hussey.

J. M. Hussey was born September 22, 1863, at Mount Pleasant, Mo., and was reared on a farm until he was 17 years old. The first school he attended was held in a frontier log structure, very crudely equipped, both as to teachers and furniture. The most helpful teaching during these early years was that given him by his mother. At 17 he entered college in a denominational school of high rank, but upon determining to make teaching his profession, he entered and completed normal and scientific courses in two of the best normal schools of Missouri. Later he completed a thorough teacher's professional course in one of these normal schools. While in school he was twice chosen on the anniversary program; was president of all his classes; won valedictorian honors on the basis of rank in two of them, and now holds two life state teacher's certificates, three undergraduate diplomas, and two others conferring the degrees, M. S. and Pe. B. After the completion of a thorough business and professional course he began clerking in a hardware store and for the next few years was employed as postoffice clerk, bank clerk and bookkeeper, country school-teacher, and instructor in a high school. In 1886 he accepted a position as city superintendent of the schools of King City, Mo., and later of Ord, Neb., and still later of Aurora, Neb., where he remained until 1892, when he purchased a half interest in the normal college at Fremont, Neb. In December, 1892, he sold his interest in this institution in order to accept the presidency of the Western Normal college at Shenandoah, and under his business-like and careful management, his professional skill and enthusiasm, the school has greatly improved and grown, and is now one of the largest and best known institutions in the west, having an enrollment of over 1,200 students annually. Professor Hussey is especially well fitted for the work he is now doing, having been educated in normal schools, and having had thorough training in business, and as a teacher in all grades of work, from the country school to the college. He is in much demand as a popular and educational lecturer and institute instructor, and has taught in or conducted more than twenty different teachers' institutes.

The professor has been a life-long republican, though he has taken no active part in politics since embarking in the work of an educator. He belongs to the Masonic order, having received its highest degrees; to Omaha temple of the Mystic Shrine, and to the Modern Woodmen of America. He is a member of the Presbyterian church, and an elder in that organization.

He was married December 23, 1890, to Miss Icy May Carson, a daughter of John H. Carson, a merchant of Ord, Neb. Mrs. Hussey is a lady of rare accomplishments and talents, fitting her for the exercise of her high duties to the students of the institution over which her husband presides. They have one child, a son, John Wendell, who was born February 8, 1896.

WHITAKER, ROMAINE ADRIAN, treasurer of the Cutler Hardware company, of Waterloo, has been in active business in Iowa since 1853, now about forty-five years, and still continues, though nearly 70 years old. He is a genuine Yankee, the ancestors of both his parents having been among the earliest settlers of the New England colonies. His father's ancestors settled at Haverhill, Mass., prior to 1650. William Whitaker, his great grandfather, rendered valuable services to the colonies during the French and Indian wars, and fought in the revolution. Clemence, the son of William, and grandfather of Romaine, was one of the early settlers of Oneida county, N. Y., where he cleared up a farm in the comparative wilderness of that country in 1801. He was married to Alice Hall, and their oldest son, Jerome, was born May 25, 1806, in South Trenton, Oneida county, N. Y. He was married August 27, 1827, to Lydia N. Demming, who was born October 19, 1807, at Holland Patent, N. Y. Their oldest son was Romaine A., the subject of this sketch. Jerome Whitaker died at Waterloo, Iowa, December 25, 1886, and his wife at Carthage, N. Y., November 12, 1875.

R. A. Whitaker was born August 26, 1828, at Holland Patent, N. Y. He lived on a farm until he was of age, receiving his education at the district school and at Lowville academy. He taught school a few years, and in 1853 came to Iowa, locating at Waterloo in 1856, purchasing an interest in a sawmill, which he operated for two years. He began work January 1, 1860, as a clerk in the office of the county treasurer and recorder, and in 1867 was elected to the office of treasurer of Black Hawk county, and held the position for eight years. He formed a partnership in 1876 under the firm name of Whitaker & Edgington, dealers in agricultural implements, which he continued for two years. In February, 1878, he was elected grand recorder of the Ancient Order of United Workmen, and held the place for fifteen

23

years, resigning in 1893 to become one of the Cutler Hardware company, and is still a member of this firm, serving as its treasurer.

Prior to the civil war Mr. Whitaker was democratic in politics, but for the last thirty-five years has been an ardent republican. Besides the offices already mentioned, he was first mayor of Waterloo, holding the office five consecutive terms. He was also a member of the school board for eighteen years, serving as its president for several years. He was secretary of the Black Hawk County Agricultural society for twenty-one years. He is a member of the

Masonic fraternity, and has served as presiding officer in the lodges at Waterloo for a number of years, and as one of the grand officers of the Grand Royal Arch Chapter of Iowa. He was a member of the board of custodians of the grand chapter for ten years. He is a member of the Episcopal church.

Mr. Whitaker was married September 17, 1856, at Great Bend, N. Y., to Mary E. Clark, who was born at Evans Mills, N. Y., April 17, 1832, and died at Waterloo, August 24, 1893. They had three children, one daughter and two sons, but both of the boys died in infancy. The daughter, Ardelle Genevieve, was born June 29,

1858. She was married to G. A. Goodell, October 12, 1881, and died March 24, 1893, leaving two children, who live with their father at Cedar Rapids.

Mr. Whitaker has had much to do with the growth and prosperity of Waterloo during his long residence there, and is held in the highest esteem for his liberality and public spirit, and his generous, charitable disposition. He is a walking encyclopedia of the history of Black Hawk county and Waterloo, possessing a remarkable memory, which has been assisted by keeping a diary, in which he has made daily records of passing events ever since the days of his early youth.

---

WRIGHT, DAVID SANDS, professor of mathematics in the State Normal school at

Cedar Falls, has the honor of being the first person to conduct a recitation in that institution, and to his strong personal influence much of the growth and success of the school are attributed. He has now been connected with this school for over twenty years, and has been giving the best years of his life in furthering the cause of better and more thorough preparation for teachers, and is a firm believer in the mission of the Normal school. He was born December 7, 1847, at New Petersburg,

Highland county, Ohio. His father was Joseph Wright, a prominent and able minister in the Friends church, and his mother was Lydia Cowgill. He was educated in the public schools of Highland county, Ohio, at New Vienna, Ohio, high school. He also received private instruction under Dr. McKibben, an eminent scholar and mathematician at Hillsboro, Ohio; but on the whole, he has been largely self-educated. He received the honorary degree of A. M., from Penn college, Oskaloosa, Iowa, in 1887.

Professor Wright began teaching in the county schools of Highland county, Ohio, in 1866. He came to Iowa in 1872, locating at the town of Salem, where he was elected principal of Whittier college. In this capacity he served four years, and in 1876, when the State Normal school was opened, he was given the chair of English language and literature. In 1880 he was transferred to the chair of mathematics in the same institution, which position he still holds. The professor is widely known throughout educational circles in Iowa, in many capacities. He has conducted teachers' institutes in all parts of the state, and has been a lecturer on a great variety of subjects, the one best known being "The Coming Woman," which he has delivered many times. For the past twenty-two years he has been an active member of the State Teachers' association, and has frequently read papers before that body, and has served upon numerous important committees in the association. For three years he was a member of the executive committee, one year of which he acted as its chairman. He is now a member of the educational council of the state association. He is an extensive contributor to educational magazines. Prominent among the articles from his pen may be mentioned the series of papers entitled "The Scroggs Family," "Frank Davis," "A. Jackson Smyth," and "The Jug Town Academy." He has also written and published a number of hand-books for teachers, which have had an extensive sale. The most important of these are "A Drill-book in English Grammar," "Teachers' Hand-book of Arithmetic," "Geometrical Exercises," and "A Geometry Note Book."

Professor Wright is a member of the Friends church, and is also a minister in the same. He was married June 24, 1880, to Miss Eliza Rawstern, of Greencastle, Jasper county, Iowa. They have four children,—a son and three daughters.

WILSON, ISRAEL P., D. D. S., M. D., of Burlington, is of Scotch-Irish and English descent. Jonathan Wilson, his father, was a Quaker farmer of Scotch-Irish ancestry, and a native of Ohio. He located in 1852 at Springdale, Cedar county, Iowa. Dr. Wilson's mother, Mercy Kinsey, was a descendant of John Kinsey, a Quaker from London, England, who was one of the commissioners for the settlement of West Jersey. He arrived at New Castle on the Delaware in the ship "Kent," June 16, 1677. The first settlement made by the immigrants from this vessel was at what is now known as Burlington, N. J. A son of John Kinsey became chief justice of Pennsylvania. Mercy Kinsey's mother's name was Loyd, and she was a descendant of Thomas Loyd, first governor of Pennsylvania, who came over from England with William Penn.

Israel P. Wilson was born April 12, 1837, at Mt. Pleasant, Jefferson county, Ohio. He received a common school education and then went for one year to the Union school at Tipton, Iowa, and later took a special course at Hopedale college in Ohio. He taught school for three years in Iowa and two years in Ohio. He studied dentistry with Dr. N. H. Tulloss, of Iowa City, then attended St Louis Medical college one year. He afterwards attended Missouri Dental college, at St. Louis, and graduated March 8, 1869, receiving the degree of D. D. S. Locating at Burlington, Iowa, he has continued in practice there since that time. He received the degree of M. D. from the Keokuk Medical college For nearly thirty years Dr. Wilson has been an active member of the Iowa State Dental society and has been elected at different times president and secretary of that organization. He is a member of the American Dental association, has frequently read papers before that body and is at the present time chairman of the section on histology. He is also a member of the International Medical congress and was one of the essayists at the World's Dental congress in 1893. Dr. Wilson was chairman of the committee of three appointed by the Iowa State Dental society, on legislation, which secured the passage of the present law regulating the practice of dentistry in Iowa. He was also one of a committee appointed by the same society which went before the board of regents of the State university and secured the establishment of the dental department of that institution. For over fifteen years he

was lecturer on dental surgery in the medical department of the State university and for six years professor of regional anatomy and dental histology in the dental department. For more than a quarter of a century he has been a regular contributor to dental literature through the columns of the dental journals.

The doctor has for many years been an earnest Knight Templar and is now high priest of Iowa Chapter No. 1, Royal Arch Masons. He has been married three times; first, November 25, 1861, to Miss Mary A. Ewing, of Smithfield, Jefferson county, Ohio. They had one child, Mary Ann, now

Mrs. J. W. Todd, of Minneapolis, Minn. Mrs. Wilson died March 10, 1863. The second marriage occurred May 15, 1866, to Miss Harriet E. Shepherd, daughter of Capt. Solomon Shepherd, of Iowa City. She died August 26, 1873, leaving three sons, Lorenzo Shepherd Wilson, M. D., D. D. S., now practicing dentistry at Burlington; Jay Willis, now in business in New Zealand, and Horace Plummer Wilson, Ph. B., M. D., now practicing medicine at Ottumwa. He was married again October 4, 1876, to Miss Lavinia Shepherd, a graduate of the State university and a sister of his second wife. They have four children, Alfred Luman, Chester Lloyd, Lavina Hortense and Helen.

Dr. Wilson has always been a staunch republican. He was brought up in the Quaker church but for the past twenty-five years has been a Methodist, and at various times superintendent of the Sunday School.

He was for three years a member of the board of education of Burlington, being also vice-president of the board.

---

WITHROW, WINFIELD SCOTT, one of the judges of the Twentieth district, composed of the counties of Des Moines, Henry and Louisa, and living at Mt. Pleasant, is one of the best known and most prominent

men of southeastern Iowa. He is a native of the state, having been born at Salem, Henry county, September 28, 1855. His father was the Hon. A. J. Withrow, who was a member of the Iowa general assembly in 1860. At the expiration of his term he joined the Twenty-fifth Iowa infantry as first lieutenant of Company C. He resigned in 1864, having contracted a disease from the effects of which he died June 6, 1867. His mother, Libertatia A. Arnold, was a native of Ohio, coming to Iowa in 1854. She died September 24, 1896. Judge Withrow obtained his early education in the public schools of Henry county, and in Whittier college, a Quaker institution in

Salem. Being thrown upon his own resources at an early age by the death of his father, he learned the printer's trade, working at the case for several years, and attending school while not thus engaged. He then spent some time in teaching school until he had secured the means with which to take a law course at the State university, graduating from the law department of that institution in 1880. After being admitted to the bar, he returned to Salem and commenced the practice of law, joining with it the management of the Salem Weekly News. At this time he was elected mayor of Salem, and was re-elected for two additional terms. In 1885 he was nominated by the republicans of Henry county for the legislature and was elected. The nomination came to him unasked. He declined a renomination, choosing rather to give his whole time to his profession. In 1887 he removed to Mt. Pleasant, forming a law partnership with Judge W. J. Jeffries, which continued up to the death of the latter. In 1894 he associated himself in practice with W. F. Kopp under the firm name of Withrow & Kopp. January 1, 1895, Judge W. I. Babb connected himself with the firm, the partnership then becoming Babb, Withrow & Kopp. Mr. Kopp retired the same year and the firm of Babb & Withrow continued until the appointment of Mr. Withrow as judge. This appointment was made by Governor Drake, after the Twentieth judicial district was created by the general assembly, and after Mr. Withrow had been nominated by the republicans of the district as their candidate for judge. His work upon the bench after his appointment was endorsed by the voters of his district, in his election by a large majority for the full term of four years. Judge Withrow's business and professional career, both in Salem and Mt. Pleasant has been very successful and during his practice he was connected with practically all of the important litigation in Henry county. He is a staunch republican and was a delegate in the national convention in 1892, from the First congressional district. He is a trustee of the Iowa Wesleyan university, and a member of the executive committee of the board, and was for four years president of the board of education in Mt. Pleasant.

He was married June 17, 1885, to Anna A. Webb, daughter of Rev. W. W. Webb, of Mankato, Minn. They have had four children: Webb and Arthur, deceased, and Dorothy and Miriam, now living.

SWENEY, JOSEPH HENRY, son of Hugh
Sweney and Esther A. Sweney, was born
October 2, 1845, on farm in Warren county,
Pa. There were four brothers and three
sisters in the family. Two brothers are
engaged in banking in Osage, the other,
Dr. C. F., is a practicing physician in St.
Paul, Minn. Mr. Sweney obtained his
earliest education in the public schools in
Pennsylvania. In 1855 he came with the
rest of the family to Iowa, settling in Burr
Oak township, Mitchell county, the father
having visited Iowa in 1847 and again in
1854, when he entered and bought some 400
acres of land. Here was the family home.
J. H. worked on the farm and attended
school at home and at Mitchell until at the
age of 16 years he entered the military
service in 1862, as a member of Company
K, Twenty-seventh regiment, Iowa infantry, under his former teacher, now
Judge C. T. Granger. In this company he
served as private, corporal and sergeant
during three years, the entire term of the
regiment, and took part in its numerous
engagements and campaigns. The fighting
of his regiment ended with the capture of
Fort Blakely, the last of the defenses of
Mobile, on the evening of April 9, 1865,
several hours after Lee's surrender at
Appomattox. Since then he has always
taken much interest in military affairs. He
entered the Iowa National Guard in 1877,
in its early days, as a lieutenant in Company B, Sixth regiment, and served successively as captain, lieutenant-colonel, and
was colonel of the regiment for four years,
resigning that place to accept a commission
as inspector-general, with rank of brigadier-
general. The latter he resigned in the
spring of 1889, after being elected to congress. In 1892, having served in Iowa
organizations for fifteen years, he was
placed on the retired list of the I. N. G.
with rank of brigadier-general.

After returning from the war he resumed and continued his school work and
studies, and graduated with honors from
the law department of the State University
of Iowa. He was one of the organizers of
the banking house of Sweney Brothers at
Osage in 1874, and took an active part in
its management for several years. In 1881
he engaged in the active practice of law in
Osage. He has always been a republican.
In 1888 he was elected by that party to the
state senate of the Twentieth General Assembly, from the Forty-first district, composed of Mitchell, Howard and Worth
counties. He made so good an impression

that he was elected president *pro tem* of the
senate of the Twenty-first General Assembly in 1886 by unanimous vote. He
served on the judiciary committee and
on the committee on mines and mining. He
was re-elected in 1887 from Mitchell, Worth
and Winnebago counties, and during the
Twenty-second General Assembly occupied the responsible position of chairman
of committee on railways, and under his
able leadership and management our present railroad law was enacted. In 1888 he
was elected from the Fourth Iowa district

to the lower house of the Fifty-first Congress, where he served on the committees
of education, railways and canals and interstate commerce, and helped to enact the
famous McKinley bill. After retirement
he resumed his law practice and attention
to his extensive farming interests.

Mr. Sweney is a member of the First
Congregational church of Osage, and has
for several years been president of the
board of trustees in that organization. For
twenty-two years he has been a member of
the board of trustees of the Cedar Valley
seminary at Osage, and served several
years as president of the board. He is
director and president of the Osage Building and Loan association. He belongs to
the G. A. R., is a Knight Templar and a
Shriner.

WILSON, ANDREW GORDON, president of Lenox college, at Hopkinton, comes of Scotch-Irish lineage, on both his father's and mother's side. Rev. James L. Wilson, his father, one of the pioneer Presbyterian ministers of Iowa, was born in York county, Pa., January 20, 1824. He attended Muskingum college, Ohio, and graduated at Jefferson college, Pennsylvania, in the class of 1851; he also graduated at the Theological seminary at Allegheny in 1854. He preached for two years in Indiana and for twenty-nine years in different parts of Iowa, mostly in Jones and Linn counties. He was promi-

nently identified with pioneer church and educational work in the northeastern part of the state. In the spring of 1855, he was married to Ellen Gordon, also a native of York county, and educated at the Ladies' seminary at Washington, Pa. The following year they made their home in the then far-western state of Iowa, buying a farm at Scotch Grove, Jones county. Mr. Wilson had the year before, with the aid of the government surveyor, taken up two farms, one in Sac and one in Harrison county.

At Scotch Grove, April 5, 1861, Andrew G. Wilson was born, and his life has largely been spent in educational work in the state of his birth. The country schools furnished the first rudiments of his educa-

tion and at the age of 14 he entered Lenox college. From there he went to Wooster university, Ohio, where he graduated with the class of 1884, being one of the honor men. After graduation he spent two years in post-graduate work at Wooster.

President Wilson was, during his college work, especially interested in the literary societies of both Lenox and Wooster. While at Lenox he was one of the founders of the Clay Literary society, which is still in a flourishing condition, and at Wooster was of member of the Irving society, and one of the founders of the Webster Debating club. At Lenox he gave evidence of marked ability in mathematics and oratory, winning cash prizes in both these branches.

With the exception of one term as county surveyor, President Wilson has devoted his entire time to teaching and literary work. His first teaching was done in the country and town schools, but in 1884 he was elected professor of natural science in Lenox college, and continued in that position until elected president of the same in 1897. Although a widely read and thoroughly educated man, his especial studies have been in the line of geology, and he is well known among scientific men by his articles on that subject in the *American Geologist*.

President Wilson has always kept thoroughly abreast of the times in regard to his profession, having attended five sessions of the National Educational association, and been for four years a member of the American Association for the Advancement of Science.

In 1894 he helped to organize, and was elected president of, the Armour Irrigating company, which has its headquarters at Armour, S. D., and which is extensively engaged in farming, stock-raising and fish culture.

His first vote was cast for the Iowa prohibitory amendment and he has always voted the republican ticket.

In 1890 he was united in marriage to Miss Elizabeth McKean of the class of 1889, of Lenox college. She is a daughter of Capt. F. C. McKean, of the Ninth Iowa infantry. Her uncle, Rev. J. W. McKean, was president of Lenox college in 1863, when it was closed and he went as captain of a company, organized from the students of the school, to fight for his country in the war of the rebellion. He was afterwards made chaplain and died in the hospital at Memphis.

President Wilson has been a member of the Presbyterian church since his 20th year and for six years an elder in the same.

WELCH, JOHN ROBERT, cashier of the First State bank at Mapleton, was born June 23, 1855, in the town of Fowler, St. Lawrence county, N. Y. His father, George P. Welch, born in 1824 in Hammond, N. Y., was a Methodist minister and a man of more than ordinary ability as a speaker and scholar. He was of English ancestry, his father coming to America in 1816. His mother was of American stock. Her maiden name was Marian Lawton. She was a native of Utica, N. Y. In 1866 the family moved to Dodge county, Wis., Mr. Welch's father dying in the following year. In the spring of 1869 the family came to Iowa, stopping at Sac City, and afterwards located near Newell, Buena Vista county. The trip from Wisconsin was made in a covered wagon. When in his teens Mr. Welch began his business career by driving three pairs of oxen on a breaking plow at $8 a month, sleeping in a covered wagon and boarding himself. After that he worked on a farm, served as apprentice in a livery stable and hotel, and by dint of economy saved $120. With this money he purchased a pair of oxen and put in the summers of 1870 and 1871 working his cattle and going to school winters. In the spring of 1871 he bought another pair of oxen on time and began breaking prairie at the rate of $4 and $5 per acre. Although only 16 years old at the time, he broke ninety acres during the summer, sleeping in a covered wagon and boarding himself, alone from Monday morning until Saturday night. With his money he made payments on eighty acres of land south of Newell, where he attended school the following winter. Soon after this he accepted an offer of $10 a month and board, in a store. And in 1876 the partnership of Blair & Welch was formed, taking charge of the general store of F. W. Runkle. Business prospered from the start. But in one year the store was burglarized and set on fire and both members of the firm lost every cent they had. A friend in need, H. E. Harris, of the banking firm of Parker & Harris, then offered Mr. Welch a half interest in a general store, with his note in payment. The partnership of Norton & Welch was then formed and Mr. Welch took charge of the general store, while his

partner attended to the grain and stock part of the business. They built and operated the first creamery in the county. In seven years Mr. Welch retired from the firm with $15,000 as his share of profits. He then entered business in Storm Lake, doing a larger business in a general store.

In the fall of 1887 he started a store in Fonda, Iowa. This did not prove to be a successful venture and in the spring of 1888 he removed to Sioux City and engaged in the book and stationery business, afterwards removing to Oto, Iowa, where he started the Oto Exchange bank. The following year he started the Anthon Exchange bank, which in 1890 became the

Anthon State bank. Mr. Welch continued as cashier of this bank until 1894 when he bought a large interest in the First State bank of Mapleton, of which he is at present cashier. He is also vice-president of the Anthon State bank and chairman of the examining board.

Mr. Welch has always been a loyal republican, and although not an office seeker, has a strong influence in politics in his town and county. He is a Mason, member of Columbian Commandery No. 18, of Sioux City, a Shriner, member of El Kahir Temple of Cedar Rapids, and an Odd Fellow.

He was married in February, 1885, to

Louise B. Hanson, of Dubuque. Two children have been born to them: Marion C., born March 11, 1887, and Fred H., born February 6, 1888.

---

SMITH, WILLIAM M., of Mount Vernon, is a native of Ohio. He was born in Penn township, Morgan county, May 29, 1848. His father, James Smith, was born in Belmont county, Ohio, March 16, 1826, and with his parents, Thomas and Nancy Smith, moved to Morgan county, Ohio, when a mere boy. James Smith's grandfather, Samuel Smith, was one of the early settlers

of Ohio, and removed from his native state, Virginia, before Ohio had been admitted to the union. He located in Columbiana county and married Sarah Bishop.

James Smith was married to Ruth King April 27, 1847. Mrs. Smith was a native of Morgan county, Ohio, and a daughter of Joseph and Mary Morris King. Three children were born to them: William M., Caroline N. and Charles T., all living. Mr. and Mrs. James Smith were members of the Society of Friends. They resided in Pennsville until 1865, and in September of that year removed to Iowa, and into Mount Vernon in 1873, where they now reside. Mr. Smith has held the office of mayor of Mount Vernon for four terms.

William M. Smith's childhood was spent in Pennsville, and he received his education in the common schools of that place. In his fifteenth year, he enlisted as a volunteer for three years' service in the union army. Owing to his extreme youth, he met with much opposition from his parents to joining the army. He enlisted at Marietta, Ohio, in Company E, Seventy-eighth O. V. I., in February, joined his regiment at Vicksburg, Miss., in March, 1864, and stood his first picket guard at Black River Bridge. In April he came up the Mississippi river to Cairo, Ill., and there met the regiment returning from veteran furlough. They waited there but a short time and then went by transport up the Ohio river to Paducah, Ky., and thence up the Tennessee river to Clifton, Tenn. At Clifton they disembarked and started on the march for Huntsville, Ala., then started to join Sherman and met his command at Big Shanty, Ga.

He was engaged with his regiment in all the principal battles from that time, including Kenesaw Mountain and that of Atlanta, which was fought July 22, 1864.

In this battle he received two gunshot wounds and lay upon the battlefield many hours before being cared for, and after he was found he was compelled to remain two days in the rear before his wounds could be dressed. He was taken, in a wagon, to Marietta and placed in the old military academy, where General Sherman once taught military tactics, at that time used as a hospital. After a few days he was removed to Rome, Ga., where he remained in the field hospital until the latter part of September.

Unable to walk and almost destitute of clothing, he started home on furlough, arriving at his destination about October 1st: his wounds and subsequent suffering unfitted him for further service in the field, consequently he was honorably discharged at Louisville, Ky., in June, 1865. He still carries an ounce ball in his left hip.

Mr. Smith came west with his parents in the fall of 1865, and stopped that winter near Springville, Linn county, Iowa. In March, 1866, the family moved to Tama City, Tama county, and Mr. Smith made that his home for six years. He then returned to Ohio and in September, 1872, engaged with Drs. Jennings and Kessler, West Milton, Ohio (Miami county), to manage their drug store, until they sold out the following spring. He was afterwards engaged as a traveling salesman for E. F. Rinehart, wholesale and manufacturing druggist of Troy, Ohio. He traveled for this house five years, selling goods in Ohio, Indiana and Michigan. In 1878 he pursued the same business for Dr. Cary, of Zanesville, Ohio, traveling in Iowa, Wisconsin, Indiana and Michigan, until the fall of 1879, when he purchased stock in the Rinehart Medicine company and remained with that company until 1883, when he disposed of his interest and came to Mount Vernon. In 1884 he entered into partnership with Dr. James Carson, opening a bank, which he has managed ever since that time. The business has been steadily successful, and February 1, 1893, Col. H. H. Rood purchased one-third interest. The bank was conducted under this management until February 1, 1897, when Dr. Carson sold his interest to W. C. Stuckslager, of Lisbon, and retired from the banking business. At this time the capital was increased to $50,000. During the period of the bank's existence, so conservative has been the management of Mr. Smith as cashier, that not a dollar of its loans and investments has been lost.

He also owns and manages a farm adjoining the city, on which he has a fine registered herd of Aberdeen Angus cattle of the best families.

Mr. Smith has been a life-long republican. He is a member of Mount Vernon Lodge No. 112, A. F. and A. M., Ashler Chapter No. 122, R. A. M., and W. C. Dimmitt Post No. 400, G. A. R.

He was married to Miss Clara A. Brackett, September 9, 1884. Mrs. Smith is a native of Putnam township, was reared in Mount Vernon, and is a daughter of William and Elizabeth Sherman Brackett She is a graduate of Cornell Conservatory of Music, and was for some time a teacher in that institution.

They have had two children: William Edgar, born January 19, 1891, who died in his third year, and Ruth Elizabeth, born December 29, 1893.

----

WALKER, WILLIAM, a prominent merchant of Exira, Audubon county, is a grandson of one of the English soldiers, who came over with Lord Cornwallis during the revolutionary war to help subdue the colonies. Joseph Walker, the father of William, was born in England, and was also a soldier. After being discharged from the army he emigrated to Canada, where he married. In 1833 he moved to Ohio and later to Michigan, where he resided until his death. Catherine Nugent Walker, the mother of William, was born in northern Ireland; left an orphan at an early age, and brought to America by an aunt. She brought up a family of ten children, all of whom are living, and still resides on the old homestead in Michigan. At the age of 89 she is active, energetic and mentally young.

William was born March 2, 1834, in Huron county, Ohio. In 1855 he came to Iowa and located in Audubon county, where he has always remained. When he came to Iowa he bought 200 acres of Audubon

county land at $1.25 per acre. This land he still owns, and has added to it 1,800 acres of fine farming land, which is highly improved and stocked. Besides this he conducts a large general store in the town of Exira.

General Fremont was the first candidate for president who received Mr. Walker's vote and he has never voted any other than a republican ticket. Audubon county is usually democratic, but in 1888 Mr. Walker was nominated by the republicans for representative, and was elected. He was re-elected in 1890, which indicates that the

people of his county, regardless of politics, have a very favorable opinion of his integrity and ability. For twenty years Mr. Walker has been a Mason, and is of the Knight Templar degree. In 1858 he married Nancy J. Bowen, who was a native of Ohio, and moved to Audubon county at an early date. She lived a busy and useful life, performing faithfully the duties of wife and mother. She died very suddenly of heart disease in 1895. They had nine children, seven of whom are now living: J. E., born January 16, 1859; Laura A., born October 16, 1866; U. S., born January 26, 1868; Lula M., born March 10, 1870; Olive M., born July 26, 1872; Eva J., born March 20, 1875; Jay G., born August 31, 1877.

ROBINSON, LYMAN BARTLETT, at Oakland, Iowa, is a lawyer of recognized ability, who holds the respect and esteem of all who know him. He was born in Broome county, N. Y., July 6, 1852. His mother was an Osborne, whose ancestors were among the early settlers of that state.

His father, Russell Robinson, was a native of Massachusetts, and of Puritan stock. He was a farmer for some years in New York, but moved to Illinois in 1853, going there with a small colony of New York people. He remained there in the village of Bristol, until the spring of 1865, when he came to Iowa, settling on a farm

near Belle Plaine. Thus it will be seen that Mr. Robinson lived in three states before he was 18 years of age. Up to this period his education was obtained at the village of Bristol, in the public school. This school is described as being exceptionally good, and during the period that young Robinson attended there, the teachers were men and women of high character and attainments. Such teachers do not really know how much they impart to their pupils, of helpful strength and moral character. The facts are, that in the early school day period, the boy and girl absorbs and assimilates more from their surroundings than they get in any other way.

Again, they are largely engaged in imitating those with whom they are associated, and this doubly applies to their instructor. In this regard Mr. Robinson's education was good and of a high order, when he removed with his father's family to Iowa in 1865. From 1865 to 1874 he lived on the farm near Belle Plaine, receiving only such advantages as came to a country boy in those days in Iowa. In 1874 he entered the Agricultural college at Ames, from which institution he graduated in 1877. During this time he taught school every winter vacation, and came out with such standing as to make him one of the class speakers when he graduated. After graduation, he entered the law office of Johnson & Scrimgeour at Belle Plaine, and was admitted to the bar in 1879. He came to his present location in 1880, with a stock in trade, consisting of a thorough education, a clear analytical mind, a good ancestral influence and early environment. He is and always has been a republican, and he has been active in the support of the doctrines of the party, although not a politician. He was married in 1879 to Miss Lucy A. Lamb, of Bridgewater, Vt. Their children are Melvin, Harold and Rodney Potter.

Mr. Robinson is one of the trustees of his *alma mater*, the State Agricultural college, and in that capacity renders valuable service to the state and to the cause of industrial education.

---

JAMISON, JAMES HARVEY, of Osceola, Clarke county, is an Iowan in every sense of the word, for he was born in Clarke county, March 11, 1859, and has worked for the upbuilding of the state since he has grown to manhood. His father, Robert Jamison, was born in Logan county, Ky., in 1816. He went from there to Indiana and came to Iowa in 1847 and to Clarke county in 1850 where he entered the first quarter section of government land ever entered in that county. He still lives there, owning 400 acres of land and is rated at about $30,000. He is of Scotch-Irish descent. The mother, Christena Kyte Jamison, is of German descent. She was born in Indiana in 1818 and married Robert Jamison in 1845, and is still living with him on the farm in Clarke county.

James H. received his first education in the district school and afterwards attended the academy at Garden Grove, Iowa, under the instruction of Prof. R. A. Harkness, now of Parsons college at Fairfield. He also graduated in the commercial course at Valparaiso college in 1881, and took the scientific course in 1882–83. He taught school during the years 1886–87 and commenced the study of law with McIntyre Bros., in Osceola, in 1888. He was admitted to the bar at the May term of the supreme court in 1890, and at once formed a partnership with McIntyre Bros. under the firm name of McIntyre Bros. & Jamison, of which he is still a member. Mr. Jamison has always been an active member in the republican party, and in the fall of 1891 received the republican nomination

for state senator from the Eleventh senatorial district, consisting of the counties of Clarke and Warren. He was elected and served in the Twenty-fifth and Twenty-sixth General Assemblies and proved himself an earnest and willing worker, the elements necessary for an efficient senator. He was the originator of much beneficial legislation, being the author of the senate bill establishing a code commission for the revision of the code, and was also author of a resolution for woman suffrage in the Twenty-fifth General Assembly, and took active part in a great deal of other important legislation. It may be said of Mr. Jamison that he is one of the brightest and most successful young lawyers in all

southern Iowa, and has won for himself a reputation for honesty and sincerity of purpose and untiring zeal in the practice of his profession, which are sure to some day bring him to the topmost round of the ladder of fortune. He has never married.

---

HUBBARD, NATHANIEL MEAD, one of the most distinguished of western railway lawyers, was born in Oswego, N. Y., September 24, 1829, and was the son of a Methodist preacher and farmer with a New England ancestry reaching back to 1624. The boyhood days of Judge Hubbard were not spent in idleness, for he battled with adverse conditions and conquered them in his determination to obtain an education and attain that station in life which his intellectual powers qualified him to fill. His father was Ansel Hubbard, who descended from George Hubbard, of Middletown, Conn., who was born in England in 1601 and settled in America in 1624. Ansel Hubbard was married to Mary Mead, the daughter of Nathaniel Mead, of New Jersey, and Mary Buryl, a daughter of the first chancellor of New Jersey. When Nathaniel was 7 years of age the family removed to Troopsburg, Steuben county, N. Y., and lived there until the death of Ansel Hubbard.

An elder sister was the first tutor of Nathaniel Hubbard, when he was a hard-worked boy on the farm. By the aid of a pine knot in the evenings, after his regular work was done, he began his earnest efforts to educate himself. After he had progressed far enough, he taught school and carried on his studies out of school hours. After he was 20 years old, he went to Alfred university, a Seventh Day Baptist college in Alfred, N. Y., which has, for more than half a century, welcomed the poor but earnest student. From this institution young Hubbard was graduated in 1853. He studied law in Hornellsville, N. Y., and came west next year, locating in Marion, Iowa, April 14, 1854. Just before he left New York he was married to Mary Wise. Mr. Hubbard continued the practice of law in Marion until the civil war broke out, when he early entered the service of his country and served about three years.

Though he never boasts of his army record, Judge Hubbard has seen much more service than the average soldier and is far more deserving of military distinction than many who have more to say about

what they have done. He simply did his
duty, and is satisfied with that. He raised
a company in Linn county and entered the
service as its captain, August 25, 1862. He
served as captain of Company F, Twentieth
Iowa Volunteer infantry, in General Herron's division of the army of the frontier,
until March, 1863, when he was promoted
to be provost marshal and judge advocate
of the army of the frontier, on the staff of
General Herron. He was transferred to
the Thirteenth Army corps, Major-General Ord commanding, June 2, 1863, and
went to Brownsville, Texas, as judge
advocate and provost marshal of the

Thirteenth Army corps. He resigned
for disability and his resignation was accepted April 20, 1865. He was breveted
major for faithful and meritorious services,
March 16, 1867. Judge Hubbard is a member of the Loyal Legion and is president of
the Society of the Army of the Frontier.
Some of the most inspiring patriotic addresses ever given in the state have come
from his pen, among them a tribute to the
flag, which has been recommended by the
state superintendent of public instruction
for use in the public schools.

Mr. Hubbard was appointed district
judge, November 15, 1865, to fill a vacancy,
and served one year, when he was suc-

ceeded by James H. Rothrock. Judge
Hubbard left the bench to enter the legal
department of the Chicago & Northwestern
Railway company, and has been in that
company's service ever since, most of the
time as its Iowa attorney. He removed to
Cedar Rapids in 1870, and lives there now.
No man has acquired more complete knowledge of the state of Iowa than Judge Hubbard. It has been a part of his duty to
know and measure the importance of all
the elements and influences that could af-
fect the great property he represents in
this state, and the errors of judgment he
has made in law or in the discharge of other
duties, have been very few indeed. His
keen and far-seeing insight into the motives
and purposes of men have been of the
greatest value to the important interests
intrusted to his care. He has been more
than successful. In the important litigation in which the Northwestern has been
sometimes engaged, Judge Hubbard's plan
of conducting it, when differing from that
of other distinguished lawyers, has on
several occasions proved to be the correct
one, notably in the long and short haul
cases several years ago.

Along with his professional duties,
which have not been confined to railway
business alone, Judge Hubbard has found
time to contribute of his time and brain to
political discussions and addresses on current topics, as well as some literary work
of a high order. Whatever appears with
his name attached is eagerly read in Iowa
because the people have learned that they
will find it full of ideas, presented with
telling force and in clear cut, direct language. He has always been in demand as
a speaker on national holidays and other
public occasions. Having always been an
earnest republican, Judge Hubbard has
taken a more or less active part in every
campaign, since he has lived in Iowa, and
in 1896 made a good many strong sound
money speeches.

Of his first marriage were born twin
daughters, Jessie and Jennie, in 1856.
Jessie was married in 1878 to George K.
Barton, of Cedar Rapids, and died in 1894.
Jennie was married in 1877 to John W.
Nye, and died in 1882, leaving two children,
Hubbard Nye and Mary Nye. Judge Hub-
bard's first wife, Mary Wise Hubbard, died
in 1857, and in 1859 he was married to
Katherine Hervey, daughter of James K.
and Mary W. Hervey, in Marion, Iowa. Of
this marriage was born, February 14, 1860,
Nathaniel M. Hubbard, Jr.

HUBBARD, NATHANIEL MEAD, JR., son of Judge N. M. Hubbard, of Cedar Rapids, was born in Marion, Iowa, February 14, 1860. His ancestry is spoken of in the sketch of his father, in this work. One of his mother's ancestors, Rev. James Kieth, was pastor of the first church in Bridgewater and settled in Massachusetts in 1632.

In his boyhood and youth Mr. Hubbard enjoyed the excellent educational advantages of Cedar Rapids, and in 1877 entered the United States Naval academy at Annapolis and was graduated in 1882. After graduation he served three years abroad, first on the United States ship Yantic, in the North Atlantic squadron, and then on the United States ship Juniata, in European and Asiatic waters. He resigned from the navy in 1885, attended Columbia Law school and was admitted to practice law in Iowa in 1887. He was then admitted to his father's law firm, Hubbard, Clark & Dawley, composed of the two Hubbards, Col. Charles A. Clark and Frank F. Dawley. Colonel Clark retired from the firm a few years later, and it was known as Hubbard, Dawley & Hubbard, and now, by the admission of Charles E. Wheeler, as Hubbard, Dawley & Wheeler. Mr. Hubbard was one of the organizers of the Royal Union Mutual Life Insurance company, of Iowa, and has been a director and the general attorney of that company since its organization.

In 1889 Mr. Hubbard went to Omaha and became the attorney for the Chicago, St. Paul, Minneapolis & Omaha Railway company, in Nebraska. He returned to Cedar Rapids in 1894 and has resided there since. The firm is one of the best known in the west, being engaged in important litigation besides its railway business, and enjoying a large consulting clientage. N. M. Hubbard, Jr., has long taken a considerable and growing share in the important work of the firm, relieving his father of many responsibilities and duties and performing them all with credit to the name he bears. Having inherited his father's peculiar ability and great energy, with a resourceful and well trained mind, he has already an established position at the bar as one of the most successful in Iowa.

When Spain declared war on the United States, Mr. Hubbard remembered his duty to the navy, which had given him such valuable training, and he immediately re-entered the service, May 5, 1898, with the commission of an ensign. He was pro-

moted to be lieutenant, July 17, 1898, and was honorably discharged November 19, 1898. During the war he served all the time in the fleet before Santiago, having been attached to the United States ship Justin, and United States battleship Oregon, and took part in the bombardment and blockade of Santiago. At the close of the war, Lieutenant Hubbard was second in command of the double-turreted monitor Miantonomoh, and remained with her until she was taken to the League Island navy yard, Philadelphia, for repairs, and put out of commission. He belongs to the Loyal

Legion, the Naval and Military Order of the Spanish-American war, the Association of United States Naval Graduates, the United States Naval institute, and the Army and Navy club, of Washington, D. C.

Mr. Hubbard was married December 24, 1889, to Miss Harriet Howard, daughter of the late Hiram Howard, of Faribault, Minn.

———

PRAY, GILBERT BALDWIN, lawyer and politician, was born at Michigan City, Ind., April 27, 1847. His father, William S. Pray, settled in Webster City, Hamilton county, Iowa, in the autumn of 1856. His mother's maiden name was Margaret Ellen Baldwin.

The emigrant ancestor of the Pray family settled in Braintree, Mass., about the year 1645.

The elder Mr. Pray was a shipbuilder and general mechanic. He was a man of fine mental power, self-educated, an omnivorous reader, whose memory retained what he read. As an evidence of his wide information and great reasoning powers, it may be stated that from only desultory reading in the general newspapers, he had come to a full comprehension of the theory and teachings of Charles Darwin, though he had never seen a copy of that author's great epoch-making book. Said he: "No thinking man can have anything to do with our common animals without seeing half-human traits in them every day of his life." He died several years ago. His wife, the mother of our subject, is a woman of will and determination, but yet distinguished for her great kindness towards the weakest thing that lives and can suffer pain. Old settlers well remember how she always protected to the extent of her ability, "our feathered friends," the birds, and how it awoke her just indignation to see them wantonly molested or destroyed.

Gilbert B. Pray possesses many of the characteristics of both his parents. He is well read, a lover and buyer of good books, and the daily and hourly rule of his life is kindness to all. Little children love him and instinctively rush to his arms. The born cynic can never understand such a man—but the little ones are the best judges after all.

Educated in and not beyond the common schools of Webster City, thirty to forty years ago, Gilbert Pray, at the age of 17, entered as a student the law office of the late Hon. Daniel D. Chase, where he remained three years. He was admitted to the bar in 1868 and practiced his profession in Webster City until 1880. During the next year he traveled awhile in Colorado on account of his health, but returning to Webster City, was engaged a short time in the newspaper business. In 1882 he was chosen clerk of the supreme court of the state. To this place he was three times elected, holding the office twelve years. It is only simple justice to say that he proved himself a most popular and thoroughly acceptable incumbent of this high and responsible position

This also proved for Mr. Pray an introduction to a deservedly high place in the councils of the republican party of the state. Since 1882 no man in Iowa has been more influential in shaping its policy or in marshalling its forces for hotly-contested battles. Mr. Pray has organized victory. He has twice been chairman of the republican state central committee, including the great deadlock contest in 1890, when he had charge of Mr. Allison's senatorial campaign, which ended triumphantly after a doubtful contest of seven weeks. This was on all hands regarded as one of the most notable achievements in the political history of Iowa. He has also served continuously as member or officer of the republican state central committee since 1889.

Mr. Pray was appointed by President McKinley in August, 1897, to the surveyor-generalship of Alaska, but declined its acceptance. He was then tendered the position of special agent in the Indian bureau. which place he accepted and entered upon the discharge of its duties.

Mr. Pray enlisted in Company F, Sixteenth Iowa infantry, in 1864, and participated in the battle of Nashville and the later campaigns of Sherman's army. The musket which he carried is deposited in the historical department at Des Moines. He was a charter member of Winfield Scott Post No. 66, G. A. R., Webster City, Iowa, and was its first adjutant.

In 1886, in association with ex-Gov. F. D. Jackson, Sidney Foster and other gentlemen, he organized and chartered the Royal Union Mutual Life Insurance company, at Des Moines, of which he has since been the treasurer.

Gilbert B. Pray and Marie B. Beauchime were married October 4, 1868. Their children's names are: Carlton B. Pray, born May 16, 1870; Harry B. Pray, born August 14, 1872; Dr. Gilbert Le Roy Pray, born December 8, 1875; and Miss Cora L. Pray, born November 14, 1877.

THOMPSON, FRANCIS MARION, of Rock Rapids, is a brother of J. K. P. Thompson, whose sketch is included in this work, so his ancestry need not be repeated. He was born in Carey, Ohio, October 11, 1842, attended school with his brother, and came with his parents from Ohio to Clayton county, Iowa, in 1857. He was taught music by his mother, and at the age of 15 could read music better than print. Later he was under the instruction of George F. Root, of Chicago. From his 15th year he devoted much of his time to singing and did evangelistic singing after he was converted and admitted to the church. He was prominent in church and Sunday school work until he, with his brother, enlisted in the Twenty-first Iowa Volunteer infantry, August 15, 1862, preferring this to going to college. The regiment was commanded by Col. Samuel Merrill, and was in many engagements, among them those of Hartsville, Mo., Milligan's Bend, Vicksburg campaign, bombardment of Grand Gulf, Port Gibson, where General Grant highly complimented the regiment on being the first in and the last out of the fight, Champion Hill, Big Black River Bridge, and other engagements. In the last named fight Mr. Thompson was one of those who carried Colonel Merrill off the field when he was wounded. He was never hit but once and that was by a spent ball which struck his toe and did him no harm. The regiment afterward went through the Texas campaign and Mobile campaign, and up the Red river and was present at the surrender of Gen. Kirby Smith. While in camp at Dauphin Island at the mouth of Mobile Bay he was afflicted with trouble with his eyes, which became rapidly worse and resulted in almost total blindness. In the fall of 1865 his old colonel interested himself in the soldier boy who had helped to carry him off the battlefield, and sent him to Chicago, where he was for eleven months under the treatment of a celebrated oculist. His right eye was taken out and his left eye partially saved, so that he saw with the use of an artificial pupil, using a very strong glass. During the time he was entirely blind the government gave him a pension of $8 a month, which increased from time to time until in 1893 he was receiving $72 a month, but Hoke Smith, then secretary of the interior, had this pension reduced to $30 a month.

In 1875 Mr. Thompson went to Rock Rapids and the next year opened the first agricultural implement establishment in the town. He soon traded

for a farm near town, but the grasshoppers destroyed everything and he returned to town and went into the drug business with George C. Wood. He objected to selling whisky, so his partner sold out to J. M. Webb, and for the same reason Mr. Webb sold out to Mr. Thompson. The business was a very successful one. The strain on his eyesight compelled him to retire from this business and in 1887 he took his family to California. Returning to Iowa he, with others, organized the Doon Savings bank. In the spring of 1896 he and his brother, J. F. Thompson, together with others, bought a 1,000-acre tract of land near Sacramento, Cal., and were interested in building the Sacramento, Fair Oaks & Orange Vale electric railway. The Thompson family are republicans and F. M. cast his first vote for Abraham Lincoln in 1864. He is past commander of Dunlap Post No. 147, G. A. R., in Rock Rapids, the post having been named after the lieutenant-colonel of his regiment,

who was killed in the charge at Vicksburg, May 22, 1863. He is a past aid-de-camp on the department commander's staff and past assistant inspector-general on the staff of the commander-in-chief. He is a past master of Border Lodge No 406, A. F. & A. M., past high priest of Lyon Chapter, Royal Arch Masons, and past excellent grand master of Third Vail Grand Chapter of Iowa, Royal Arch Masons.

He was married October 3, 1872, to Nettie Wiltse, daughter of Dr. A. Wiltse, of Strawberry Point, Iowa. They have had three children, Ella E., born June 5, 1878, who is especially interested in music and is a graduate of the Rock Rapids high school, and is now a student of Cedar Rapids Business college; Genie M., born

August 11, 1880; Gertie V., born November 21, 1883. The family are all members of the Methodist church.

---

PATTERSON, MICHAEL FRAMPTON, M. D. One of the leading specialists in diseases of the eye and ear is Dr. M. F. Patterson, of Des Moines. His father, Samuel Patterson, was a fruit box manufacturer. He was a native of Maryland, where he was born in 1828. Grandfather Robert Patterson was born and reared in the north of Ireland, and was of Scotch-Irish descent. He came to the United States in 1816 and settled in Maryland, where he married a Pennsylvania German girl named Anna Stahl. John Patterson was the author of "Conflicts in Nature and Life," and "Political Economy." A third work, "A History of Religion," was unfinished at the time of his death. The mother's maiden name was Martha Frampton, and she was born in Darke county, Ohio. She is still living. Grandfather Hugh Frampton was born in Pennsylvania, of English parents. His wife, Mary Coppas Frampton, was a native of North Carolina, whose parents were slaveholders, but freed their negroes long before the war.

Dr. M. F. Patterson was born at Horatio, Ohio, January 19, 1857. He inherited a liking for books, and evinced a remarkable aptitude for learning at an early age. He graduated from the high school of Berlin Heights, Ohio, before he was 18 years old. When he had made up his mind to prepare for the profession of medicine, he entered the medical department of Western Reserve university at Cleveland, Ohio, where he graduated March 2, 1881; he took a course in eye and ear diseases at the New York Post Graduate college, during the winter of 1888-9, and during the summer of 1893 supplemented his expert knowledge of the eye and ear with a course in the Chicago Polyclinic. During the summer of 1894, and the following winter, his time was devoted to study and practice in the Chicago eye and ear hospitals, during the afternoons, and to work in the Rush laboratory in the forenoons. In the winter of 1894-5 he was appointed a junior ear surgeon in the Illinois Eye and Ear infirmary, but could not retain a position on the staff, because it was his intention to leave the city. He came to Iowa in 1882 and located first at Fonda. That place was his home during most of the years up to 1895, at which time he removed to Des Moines. He was first

engaged in the drug business, with general practice, but in 1889 devoted himself to the eye and ear almost wholly until now he is a successful specialist in his line, holding the chair of otology and rhino-laryngology in the College of Physicans and Surgeons, Des Moines.

He is a member of the American Medical association, Iowa State Medical society, Des Moines Valley Medical association, the Polk County Medical society, and Southwestern Iowa Medical society. Fraternally he is a member of all the Masonic bodies, both York and Scottish Rites. He is a member of the famous Grant club, the lead-

ing republican organization of Des Moines, occupying a fine club house. He was married to Miss Cora E. Wood, of Fonda, December 6, 1883. She is the daughter of A. B. P. and Cordelia K. Wood. Mr. Wood was an attorney of considerable note, and at the time of his death, in 1887, was the owner of several sections of land in Pocahontas county. Dr. and Mrs. Patterson have two children: Alpheas W., born July 28, 1885, and Cordelia, born May 23, 1887.

---

JORDAN, RICHARD FRANCIS, is a leading citizen, successful lawyer and influential democrat of Boone county. He was born in Queensburg township, Warren county, N. Y., not far from Glen's Falls, March 19, 1856. His parents were John and Ann Connelley Jordan. The father was a farmer in easy circumstances, who retired from active life in 1889. Both Father and Mother Jordan were natives of Ireland, coming to this country in early youth. It is understood in the family that his people originally came from Holland, as soldiers under William of Orange in one of his campaigns in Ireland, and that they settled in the city of Waterford, Ireland, and eventually became as children to the manor born. Mr. and Mrs. Jordan were married at Glen's Falls, N. Y., January 25, 1855. They lived in Dixon, Ill., from 1856 to 1866, and in April of the latter year drove overland from that place to Boone county, Iowa, where they purchased a farm in Colfax township, which continued to be the family home until 1889. Richard attended the city schools of Dixon, Ill., until he was 10 years of age, and after that attended the country district schools of Boone county until he was 17 years of age. In March, 1874, he entered the State Agricultural college at Ames in the regular course as freshman, and continued there until November, 1877, when he graduated with the degree of bachelor of science. He stood second in the markings of his class and was selected as one of the ten to participate in the graduating exercises. While in college he was a member of the Bachelors' Debating society, and in general took an active interest in all college class matters while there. During his vacations and for a short time after graduating he taught country schools. In August, 1878, he entered the Iowa Law school at Des Moines, which was a department of the Simpson Centenary college. There he completed the course in the study of law, receiving the degree of bachelor of law, and was admitted to practice in the supreme court of Iowa, June 9, 1879. During the time he was in law school he also read law in the office of Miller & Godfrey, in Des Moines. He has always been a student, keeping abreast of the times, keeping himself posted in all the new changes in the laws of our country and in the decisions of the supreme court. He has been successful and has advanced in his profession by simply sticking to his work, giving his best efforts to his profession and treating all with whom he deals in a fair and honorable manner—a firm believer in the old proverb: "Honesty is the best policy."

24

In 1879, he formed a partnership with M. K. Ramsey, which was dissolved in 1882; he then formed a partnership with G. W. Crooks, which continued until the first of January, 1891, when another partnership was formed with O. M. Brockett, which continued until October, 1896. Mr. Jordan has had active work in his profession ever since he entered it, and in the last ten years has been interested on one side or the other of all the important cases which have arisen in Boone county.

On obtaining his majority, he affiliated himself with the democratic party and has been a democrat ever since. He was a

delegate from the Tenth congressional district to the democratic national convention in 1896. He has never held any public office other than that of member of the school board for three years, city solicitor for nine years and member of the library board of his city at the present time. He was at one time the candidate for senator from his district, but was defeated on account of the strength of the republican party.

Mr. Jordan was married May 23, 1882, at Des Moines, to Martha H. Lynch. They have three children: John W., Frank and Helen. He belongs to no secret society or club.

FLINDT, WILLIAM. Among the representative business men of Spencer, none are more worthy of mention in a work of this character than William Flindt, who was born at Winona, Minn., May 16, 1863. His father, Claus H. Flindt, was a native of Sleswick-Holstein, Germany. He came to this country when a young man and soon after married Anna Walburge Sipple, who was a native of Prussia. They settled on a farm in Freeborn county, Minn., where, by industry and frugality, they managed to amass a competency sufficient to enable them to retire from active life, and they now reside at Albert Lea, Minn., where Mr. Flindt assisted in

the organization of the First National bank of that place and has always been one of the active directors of that flourishing institution. William lived with his parents on the farm until he was 18 years old, when he attended, for one year, the Albert Lea high school, working for his board and working at odd jobs between times to pay his way. After leaving school he worked for a time in a grocery store at $25 per month, and soon after engaged with S. Strauss, a leading clothier of Albert Lea, where he worked for five years and thoroughly learned the business. He came to Iowa September 1, 1887, locating at Spencer, where he opened up a clothing store

in partnership with his former employer, S. Strauss, under the firm name of Flindt & Strauss, the business being conducted by Mr. Flindt, Mr. Strauss retaining his residence in Albert Lea, Minn., where he was still engaged in business. In 1891 they established a branch store in Hartley, Iowa, which they sold a year later. In 1894 they established a branch store at Oelwein, Iowa, under the firm name of Flindt, Strauss & Oleson, which they still own. In 1891 Mr. Flindt established a merchant tailoring business in connection with his clothing store at Spencer, but sold the same to L. Carlson one year later. In 1896 he bought the interest of his partner, Mr. Strauss, in the Spencer business, and has since conducted it alone. He has been remarkably successful in business and although he is still a young man, has acquired a considerable amount of this world's goods.

Several years ago he became a stockholder in the First National bank of Spencer, and was afterwards elected a director of that institution. When the control of the bank passed into other hands in January, 1897, he resigned his position as director and associated himself with others in the organization of the Citizens State bank of Spencer, of which institution he is a large stockholder and director. He is also treasurer and director of the Spencer Building and Loan association, and treasurer and director of the Iowa Mercantile Fire Insurance association, in the organization of which he rendered considerable assistance in 1895. He has always been a zealous republican and has always taken a great interest in politics, but has never been a candidate for, or held, any public office, except for a time a member of the city council of Spencer. He is a member of the Masonic Order, holding membership in the Blue Lodge, Chapter, Knights Templars and Eastern Star. He is also a member of the subordinate Knights of Pythias lodge and Uniform Rank. He has held a number of offices in this organization, among them that of chancellor commander. He does not belong to any church, but usually attends the Congregational.

He was married January 14, 1891, to Miss Emma M. Brundin, at Albert Lea, Minn. They have three children, Lillian M., Charlotta Coline, and William Frederick, Jr. Mr. Flindt is an energetic, wide-awake, progressive business man, public spirited and active in all the affairs of his community. He takes a great interest in everything intended to build up the material and moral institutions of the city, contributes liberally to all worthy objects, and is a good example of a thorough and successful business man.

SEEDS, EDWARD P., former associate justice of the supreme court of New Mexico, and professor of law in the State University of Iowa, was born in Wilmington, Del., on August 1, 1855.

His father, William H. Seeds, was of a family that had been identified with the history and development of Wilmington, Del., for nearly a century. Commencing life as a carpenter, William H. Seeds availed himself of the opportunities then afforded by the new west, and early removed to Manchester, Iowa. Here, after a few years, he accumulated means and engaged in the banking business, in which he continued to be interested until his death. Sarah T. Paxson, whom he married, came of a good, old Quaker family, of eastern Pennsylvania. An uncle of hers was one of the executors of Stephen Girard's will, and a cousin, Edward M. Paxson, was for a score of years chief justice of Pennsylvania.

Edward P. Seeds was educated in the public schools of Manchester and at the State University of Iowa, graduating from the law department of the University in June, 1877. His early tastes may be judged by the fact that, when about 15 years old, he worked out poll tax on the public road for two days in order to secure money to buy a copy of "Mill's Logic," which his father had refused to buy him. After graduating he began his practice of law with Calvin Yoran, of Manchester, remaining with him for three years, and afterwards practicing alone for two years. Then he went into the railway postal service and continued until 1885, when Mr. Cleveland displaced him and appointed a democrat. Mr. Seeds then returned to the practice of law, at Manchester, and was soon after elected city solicitor, which position he held until he resigned, during his second term, to become state senator for Delaware and Buchanan counties in the Twenty-second and Twenty-third General Assemblies. He resigned this position in August, 1890, to become associate justice of the supreme court of New Mexico, a position to which he was appointed by President Harrison, upon the recommendation of Senator Allison and Col. D. B. Henderson. He was judge of the First judicial district, with headquarters and residence at Santa Fe, the capital, and served for the full four-years' term. Before the termination of his official

term, Mr. Cleveland again became president, and an unsuccessful attempt was made by some of the judge's opponents to have him removed. In 1890 and 1891, during his judicial term in the supreme court, some election cases which came before Judge Seeds attracted wide attention and produced considerable excitement locally. The democratic county commissioner of Santa Fe and Taoso counties undertook to control the result of the election for territorial legislators by refusing to canvass the vote, in a strong republican precinct, upon a technicality. The commissioners were summoned before Justice Seeds to show cause why they should not count the whole vote. After hearing the case the court ordered the commissioners to canvass the whole vote, and, upon their refusal to do so, committed them to

jail for contempt. They had no sooner been imprisoned than, upon an order signed by three justices of the peace, sitting as a court, they were liberated by the sheriff, under alleged authority given by a territorial statute. This was a seeming conflict of authority between local and federal courts, and was finally appealed to the United States supreme court, which sustained the decree of Justice Seeds.

At the expiration of his term, Judge Seeds returned to Manchester, where his family had preceded him, with the intention of visiting for a while and then returning to the west. The unexpected death of his father, shortly afterward, caused a change in his plans and he remained in Manchester. In 1895 he was elected professor of law in the State university.

On December 6, 1877, Judge Seeds was married to Miss Willa Holmes. She is a native of Kingston, N. Y., and the families of both her father and mother are known and honored in New York and the New England states. They have two children: Sarah Ethel, born October 23, 1878, who is now at Oberlin college in Ohio, and Bertha Willa, born May 24, 1882.

---

GARDNER, Dr. IRA KILBOURN, of New Hampton, is a highly educated physician,

a graduate of the medical department of Michigan university in 1870, and a postgraduate of the Chicago Polyclinic Medical school in 1890. He was born in Kilworth, Canada, February 8, 1846. His father, Abel S. Gardner, was a miller until he reached middle age and then took up the occupation of farming. His paternal ancestors came to America with the early colonists and were in the revolution. His mother, Mary M. Parker, was born in Switzerland, and came to this country with her parents when only 4 years old.

Young Ira passed through the common schools and when old enough entered the Michigan State Normal school, at Ypsilanti, where he made an excellent record as a faithful and industrious student. After completing his medical course at Michigan university in 1870, Dr. Gardner located first at Lawler, Chickasaw county, Iowa. Here he enjoyed a good practice and acquired the varied experience which is necessary to develop the perceptive faculties and ripen the judgment of young practitioners. In 1877 he was ready for a larger field of usefulness and removed to New Hampton.

Since engaging in the practice of his chosen profession he has gladdened the hearts of many in that vicinity by the exercise of his rare skill as a physician and surgeon, and he possesses the confidence of the entire surrounding community. He enjoys a large practice, and he is a pleasant, intelligent and capable gentleman, as well as an educated and conscientious practitioner. He has a fine library and a full equipment of surgical instruments and appliances.

Two years ago Dr. Gardner completed the finest residence in the city, built of brown stone, brick and frame and furnished throughout with all the latest conveniences, such as electric lights, steam heat, toilet and bath rooms, electric bells, etc. Dr. Gardner has his office, reception and examination rooms, also library and laboratory, at his residence, at the corner of Chestnut Avenue and Court street, all fitted up in an elegant and convenient manner.

In 1871 Dr. Gardner was married to Miss Maggie Gardner, and they have one child, Nellie E.

The doctor has been a constant and consistent republican since attaining his majority, but has always refused to become a candidate for any but minor local offices. He is a Knight of Pythias and a member of numerous medical societies: The International Medical congress, American Medical association, Iowa State Medical society, Austin Flint Medical society, North Iowa Medical society, and Wapsie Valley Medical association. Dr. Gardner is now, and has been for many years, local surgeon for the Chicago, Milwaukee & St. Paul Railway company. The doctor has also been a member of the board of education for the past six years, being its president the last four years.

SMITH, LEWIS H., of Algona, Iowa, was born at West Cambridge, now Belmont, Mass., March 21, 1835. His father, Edward Smith, was a mason and contractor, and afterwards a farmer at the same place, where he married Abigail Wyman Richardson, daughter of Richard Richardson, of Ashby, Mass., the man who constructed the old turnpike road from Cambridge to Concord, Mass. Young Smith was educated in the common school in West Cambridge, in the usual branches, including mathematics and surveying, and the Latin and French languages. He did not enter college, but became a clerk in a wholesale cigar store, for his uncle, one year, 1851. He came west in May, 1853, and was employed as a rodman in the engineering corps on the Chicago & Rock Island railroad, at Tiskilwa, and Sheffield, Ill. He went to Iowa in December, 1853, on the old Mississippi & Missouri, now the Chicago, Rock Island & Pacific railroad, working as a rodman, and afterward as leveller and transit man on the same road, between Davenport and Grinnell, and on a branch line from Muscatine to Cedar Rapids. He worked on all these lines until the fall of 1854. He taught school at Snook's Grove, between what are now Victor and Brooklyn, during the winter of 1855, in the Manatt settlement. He then went to Kossuth county via Des Moines and Ft. Dodge, being engaged in the United States surveys under Gov. C. C. Carpenter. He entered the county July 4, 1855; one month later he was elected the first county surveyor, and in the summer of 1856 surveyed and platted the town site of Algona.

In April, 1857, he volunteered to go with A. L. Seeley, Jacob Cummins, Peter Reibhoff, William Campbell, Mr. Tuttle and his son Columbus, under the leadership of Capt. W. H. Ingham, from Algona to the head of the east fork of the Des Moines river, to learn whether Mr. Tuttle's family were killed by the Indians. They found and drove out of the country, two bands of Indians. In May, 1857, he was elected captain of the first military company raised in the county, but he never saw service in that capacity. He put up the first notary's sign, the first store sign, and in connection with Captain Ingham, the first bank sign in the county. He brought to the county the first sewing machine and the first piano, put up the first frame building in Algona, and burned the first kerosene oil in the county, and received for services the first county warrant issued in the county. He also received the first warrant issued for Emmet county, for locating the county seat of Emmet county at Estherville, under a commission from the governor.

In August, 1857, he was elected judge of Kossuth county, only three votes being cast against him, and was at that time probably the youngest county judge in the state. In 1856 he was appointed

county judge to succeed Luther Rist, who resigned, and at the general election, 1867, was elected county judge, and served till the office was abolished.

He served as enrolling and reading clerk under Hon. Chas. Aldrich, at the legislative session of 1860 (when the code was revised) and at the extra session of 1861 (the first war session). He was deputy county treasurer under L. L. Treat in 1860 and 1861, and read law and was admitted to the bar, being the first admission in the county, by Judge A. H. Hubbard, in 1860. In 1859 he was a commissioner with Judge Pease, and Judge Hutchison, of Humboldt counties, to settle all accounts between Humboldt and Webster counties. In 1862 he was appointed quartermaster of the Northern Border brigade, a force of five companies of cavalry raised by the state, and commanded by Lieut.-Col. J. A. Sawyer, for defense of the border against the Indians, after the Indian massacre in 1862, in Minnesota, continuing in the service till January, 1864. In 1864, with J. E. Blackford

and E. N. Weaver, he operated a saw mill in connection with other business. In 1865 he was again elected surveyor of Kossuth county, but did not qualify, owing to other business. In 1865 and winter of 1866 was engaged as engineer of the Sawyers' wagon road, from the mouth of the Niobrara river to Virginia City, Mont. This road, 1,000 miles in length, was for nearly the whole distance through an unexplored country, teeming with hostile Indians, and but for the bravery and indomitable energy of Colonel Sawyers, the party would never have gotten through.

Like many other government wagon roads, the pushing out of the Northern Pacific railroad, in 1866 and 1867, rendered it useless. In July, 1866, he was appointed postmaster at Algona, but resigned in 1867, on account of other business. In the spring of 1866, in company with his brother, John G. Smith (since a member of the legislature of Iowa, and now a member of the board of super-. visors of this county), he commenced selling merchandise at Algona. In 1868, Francis C. Rist, a brother-in-law and a pioneer of 1855, entered the firm. In January, 1870, Mr. Smith sold out his interest, and entered the banking business in company with Capt. Wm. H. Ingham, as president, and Lewis H. Smith, as cashier, which has been continued to this time with the largest line of depositors and business of any bank in the county. He has always been a republican in politics, was a member of the state republican central committee in 1858-59-60, and was secretary of state conventions in those years. He was made a Mason in 1867, in Prudence Lodge No. 205, and was master of the lodge three years; also a companion in Prudence Chapter No 70. He is also a Knight Templar in Esdraelon Commandery No. 52, of Estherville, Iowa. He does not belong to any church, but attends the Congregational church, where his wife is a regular member. He was trustee of Algona college from its inception in 1870 to its dissolution. Commencing in 1878, he was a member of the board of trustees of the Insane Hospital at Independence, serving twelve years, being president of the board eight years.

He was married in August, 1857, to Abbie M. Rist, daughter of Hon. Luther Rist, formerly of Whitenville, Mass., and a pioneer of Kossuth county of 1866. She died in 1866, leaving four children, Mary A., Nellie E., Fannie S., and Edward L., the last named being now dead.

He was married the second time in 1872, to Eugenia Rist, widow of Francis C. Rist, who was a son of Luther Rist, above named, and a pioneer of 1855. She had at that time three children, Charles W., Hiram E. and Dick, who are still living. The children by the last marriage are Mabel F., Ruby E., and Hortense M., all of whom are now living.

WEEKS, ELBERT WRIGHT, a lawyer and successful republican politician, of Guthrie Center, is a familiar figure in republican conventions, state and national, and has been an important factor in the politics of his state. Possibly this may be accounted for in part by the fact that he was born in Ohio. That event, which gave to the world a man of worth and to many, a royal, true friend, occurred in Lake county, Ohio, October 7, 1850. His parents were Henry Weeks, a farmer, born on Long Island, and Sarah A. Wright, his wife, a native of Canada. In 1856 the family removed to Green township, Iowa county, Iowa, and settled on a farm. The son, Elbert, had about the same experiences as other farmers' boys, doing his share of the farm work during the busy seasons and going to school when he could be spared. He was an industrious boy, picking up a

dollar whenever he could by extra work for neighbors, making rails or doing whatever offered. Largely by his own efforts he attended the State university and graduated from the law department in June, 1873, locating for the practice of his profession in Guthrie Center, May, 1876. Mr. Weeks has always been active in politics. He is naturally adapted to it, for he knows how to make friends and to hold them. Always ready to help others, it is to be expected that he would be selected for political honors, as he has been several times. He was a delegate to the republican national convention in 1884 and an alternate in 1888. He was one of the organizers

of the republican state and national leagues and has been a delegate from Iowa to nearly all the national conventions of the league for ten years. He was assistant secretary of the convention in Milwaukee in 1896. He was elected state secretary of the republican league in 1895 and held the office several years. He has been regarded as a congressional probability in the Ninth district for several years. Mr. Weeks belongs to the Odd Fellows' Encampment, is a Knight Templar in Masonry, and was grand chancellor of the Knights of Pythias of Iowa for 1891 and 1892. He is a member of the Methodist Episcopal church. He was married June 2, 1878, to Miss Lorena

Bower. Two children were born to them: Lena, born January 3, 1880, and Henry, born March 2, 1884. Mrs. Weeks died March 13, 1884, and Mr. Weeks was again married March 17, 1887, to Miss Jennie Biggs. They have two children: Seth, born December 15, 1887, and Wright, Jr., born January 27, 1890. Successful in his profession, with a happy home and a multitude of friends, Mr. Weeks is what people call "comfortably fixed in life."

---

HARRIS, ROBERT HENRY, usually called "Bob Harris," of Missouri Valley, Harrison county, editor of the Missouri Valley daily and weekly *Times,* is the son of Judge D. M. Harris. He was born in Williamsport, Maury county, Tenn., March 23, 1854. His mother's maiden name was Martha Minerva White. In 1854 his parents moved to Audubon county, Iowa, where his father became county judge, and served three terms in the Iowa state legislature. He was a candidate for lieutenant-governor on the democratic ticket in 1866, and afterward a candidate for congress on the democratic ticket from the Ninth congressional district, in both cases being defeated, as the state and district were both largely republican.

"Bob" Harris received a common school education in the district schools of the state. In 1863 his father commenced the publication of the *Guthrie County Ledger,* in the town of Panora, and the subject of this biography commenced at that early age, 9 years, to make himself useful in his father's office, and under the instruction of John McLune, foreman of the *Ledger,* he took his first lesson as a typo. In 1868 his parents moved to Missouri Valley, and his father established the *Harrisonian,* the first paper in this young city, where "Bob" became a leading hand in its publication, working in the office and attending school until 1872, when he went on a tramp, working in many offices throughout the country. During that year Judge Harris, the father, sold his paper, and went to Independence, Kan., and bought of V. B. Bennett, the *Kansas Democrat,* in which "Bob" became a typo and continued with his father, until 1874, when he returned with his parents to Iowa. During that year his father established the *Audubon County Defender,* at Exira, and he assisted in its publication. In 1875 they sold the *Defender* office and located in Atlantic, Cass county, Iowa, and established the *Cap Sheaf,* a weekly paper,

and in 1876 sold the *Cap Sheaf,* and returned to Missouri Valley and bought the *Missouri Valley Times.* They conducted this paper under the firm name of D. M. Harris & Sons until 1894, when "Bob" bought the entire outfit, and became its editor and publisher. It is one of the leading papers of the west. His first and last dollar was made in the profession of printer, having learned the entire business from A to X, to editor and publisher, and never engaged in any other business.

Mr. Harris has always been a democrat, having been born of democratic stock, and having been engaged in publishing a democratic paper from childhood. He is well fitted to fight the battles of the party in a state in which democracy is in the minority, being aggressive and fearless. He has

never held nor has he sought any public office. He has been a Mason from early manhood and also belongs to several other social orders. He was married in Audubon county, Iowa, on September 15, 1874, to Miss Frances Chapman. They have had four children born to them, three of whom are living, viz: Frank, born March 12, 1876, is a musician of note, having studied his profession in Berlin, Germany, for two years; Earl R., born October 5, 1878, who is now local editor of the *Daily Times,* and Della, born December 1, 1884.

SPERING, FRANCIS EDWIN, born in Northampton county, Penn., January 13, 1826; died in Marengo, Iowa, July 25, 1892; was for many years editor of the Marengo *Republican* and was for seventeen years connected with the New York *Herald*, most of the time in the responsible position of day foreman. His father, William E. Spering, was a lawyer of favorable repute in his section of the state, who was honored with numerous public trusts, and was married to Hannah Ewing, who came of a highly respected family and is spoken of as a Christian lady of noble aspirations and rare attainments. They brought up

a family of eight sons and three daughters, of whom Francis was the sixth son. The latter was early thrown upon his own resources, and having energy, ambition and a fixed purpose in life, he succeeded, though he had only a common school education.

At the age of 11 years he began his life as an apprentice in the office of the Northampton *Whig*, a small weekly newspaper published in his home town. At the age of 14 he had mastered his trade and accepted a position on the *Jeffersonian Republican*, in Stroudsburg, Penn. At the close of the Harrison campaign in 1844, with a partner, he took charge of the paper. Although young and inexperienced and having very small capital, they were successful and the partnership continued until the winter of 1848, when young Spering retired and the following spring went to Honsdale, Penn, and took

charge of a democratic paper at that place, where he remained until January, 1849. In May, 1849, he went to New York and entered the composing room of the New York *Herald*. Close attention to his work soon gained the appreciation of his employers and he was made day foreman of the *Herald* composing room at the age of 23 years, occupying a position of great responsibility and trust on one of the greatest daily newsapers in the world. His seventeen years of continuous service on the *Herald* marked an epoch of the most rapid strides of advancement in the history of journalism, embracing the active years of the career of James Gordon Bennett, Sr., including the stirring times before and during the civil war and reaching well down into the period of reconstruction. It was the best kind of schooling for Mr. Spering and he soon developed into a writer of recognized force and ability; but he decided to establish a business of his own, though he might have attained distinction in New York. The west offered wonderful opportunities. Cities were springing up and the wilderness was fast developing into a blaze of activity and improvement. Mr. Spering severed his connection with the *Herald* and started west. In July, 1866, he bought the Montezuma *Republican*, in the thriving county seat of Poweshiek county, which he conducted until the following February, when he removed to Marengo, the county seat of Iowa county, and purchased a half interest in the Marengo *Republican*, having as a partner, H. R. Crenshaw, a popular young soldier, well qualified for the work. The paper soon took rank among the best weekly publications in the state and the partnership was continued until the spring of 1884, when Mr. Spering bought his partner's share and continued the business as editor and proprietor until his death.

Mr. Spering was a whig until the disorganization of that party, when he assisted in organizing the republican party and devoted his masterly talent as a thinker and writer to the service of that party during the rest of his life. He was postmaster at Marengo under the Grant administration and held a number of minor positions of honor and trust in the community. He was a devout member of the Episcopal church and was for many years vestryman at Marengo. During his younger years he was somewhat of a leader in society, but during the latter part of his life he was devoted exclusively to the interests of his business and to the comforts of his home. While he had a warm heart, willing hand and kind disposition, he had a gruff exterior which sometimes made him misunderstood. He was thoroughly devoted to business and when failing health rendered him unable to make his daily visits to his office he failed rapidly.

In 1857 Mr. Spering was married in New York to Mrs. Margaret Williams, a Christian woman of respectibility and refinement, who died in 1862. They had no children. In 1864 he was married to Miss

Phoebe West of Milford, Penn., a cultivated and refined young woman of a highly respected family, who survived him as his widow. To them was born one child, Louise, who died in infancy.

HARRIMAN, HON. W. F. Having represented Franklin county in the Twenty-fourth and Twenty-fifth General Assemblies and being at the present time a member of the senate, Mr. Harriman is known, at least by reputation, by every person who pays any attention to the leading affairs of state. He was born in Warner, N. H., August 16, 1841, and attended the high school in the city of his birth, and the New London Literary and Scientific institution, in his native state. His first money was earned by working sixteen hours a day on the farm, for which he was paid at the rate of $13 per month. By great personal effort he early obtained a certificate and had taught one term when, in 1860, his parents concluded to move to Iowa. The son accompanied them and upon their arrival at Rockford sought and obtained a position as teacher, which vocation was followed for several years. He read law while teaching and working on the farm, and in 1869 was admitted to the bar at Charles City. He immediately opened an office at Cherokee, but as there were few people in the county at that time the practice was very limited and he soon drifted into real estate as a means of making some ready money. It proved much the more profitable and received his whole attention, to the neglect of his law practice. Soon he was the owner of several pieces of property, including a tract of 720 acres immediately west of the town of Cherokee and adjoining the site recently purchased for the new hospital. On this land in 1873 he planted ten acres of trees of various kinds, which was the first artificial grove in the county. They have made such a wonderful growth in the twenty-six years that they may be seen from almost any point within the county, and constitute a landmark that will be regarded with interest in years to come.

In 1876 he disposed of nearly all of the real estate and removed to Hampton, where he again took up the practice of law. He shortly formed a partnership with W. A. Church, a former pupil and graduate of the law department of the Iowa State university, who later sold his interest to the late J. W. Luke, the business being conducted under the firm name of Harriman & Luke until 1888. At that time Mr. Harriman was compelled to retire because of ill health and engage in some pursuit wherein he could have the benefit of pure air and sunshine. He chose farming and stock raising and in that work has been successfully employed to the present time. He has held various offices, viz.: Member of school board in Rockford county; superintendent of schools in Cherokee county; member of town council of Hampton; mayor of Hampton; county attorney by appointment by board of supervisors under former

statute; member of the Twenty-fourth and Twenty-fifth General Assemblies, and was elected to the senate in 1895 to represent Franklin, Cerro Gordo and Hancock counties, and will be re-elected in the present year. In his legislative work he is able, conservative and always loyal to the interests of his constituents. Besides having a place on many of the important committees during each session, he is frequently asked to serve on special committees, always with the greatest satisfaction to all concerned. Members of the senate have often remarked that they could learn more of a subject in a ten-minute speech from Senator Harriman than in an hour of the average speaker, because his ideas are so clearly expressed. He is a member of the Congregational church and belongs to the Masonic and Odd Fellow orders. He was married December 29, 1864, to Miss Ellen E. Mitchell. They have three sons: John W., who is professor of anatomy in the Iowa State university; Wilbert E., filling the chair of pathology, histology and physiology in the Iowa Agricultural college, and Charles B. Harriman, attending the public schools of Hampton.

Mr. Harriman has long served as director and vice-president of the State Agricultural society, and is now its president.

---

HARRIMAN, WILBERT EUGENE, college surgeon and professor of pathology,

histology and physiology, at the Iowa State Agricultural college, is one of those young men who have learned early to appreciate the value and necessity of thorough, systematic training, and by improving every opportunity to secure this training, he has attained success much earlier in life than would otherwise be possible. He is a son of Hon. W. F. Harriman, whose biography is printed herewith. Dr. Harriman's mother was formerly Ellen E. Mitchell, who was born in Illinois, where her parents

were early settlers, but who moved to Wisconsin when she was quite young and afterwards to Iowa.

Dr. Harriman's ancestors on his father's side came from a long line of New Englanders, while his mother's people were of Scotch and German descent. The doctor's great-grandfather, on his mother's side, was an officer in the war of 1812 and his great-great-grandfather was a soldier in the revolutionary war.

Dr. Harriman was born at Cherokee, December 4, 1871, and when 5 years old removed with his parents to Hampton, where he attended school regularly until the time of his graduation from the high school in June, 1890. He entered the Iowa Agricultural college in July, 1890, and selected the scientific course. He was always popular as a student, for he was wide-awake and generous. He was prominent in all the activities of the college, a loyal member of the Welch-Eclectic Literary society, captain of Company E in the college battalion, manager of the baseball team, and during his sophomore year was chosen class president. At the close of his sophomore year, he began the study of medicine in the office of Dr. W. A. Rohlf, of Hampton, continuing this work through the winter vacation of 1891-2, and at the close of his junior year, in November, 1892, he entered the medical department of the State university, and at the close of this year's work had the satisfaction of winning the prize offered for the best examination in histology. Returning to Ames in the spring, he completed his course, graduating in November, 1893. In May, 1894, he passed the examination of the state board of medical examiners, and began the practice of medicine at Gilbert, Story county, where he remained until October, 1894, when he entered Jefferson Medical college at Philadelphia, graduating May 15, 1895. He located at Ames the month following, and on July 16th was elected to the position which he now holds.

Dr. Harriman is the secretary and treasurer of Story county medical society, a member of the Central District of Iowa Medical association, of the State Medical association, of the American medical association and a fellow of the American Academy of Medicine, and is health officer of the city of Ames. He holds a commission from the governor of Iowa as cadet captain. He has never voted anything but the republican ticket. He is a member of no church.

The doctor was married October 4, 1894, to Miss Mary E. Wormley, of Newton, Iowa, with whom he became acquainted while in college at Ames, she having been a member of the class of 1895. They have two children: Loretta Marie, born December 11, 1895, and Walter Franklin, born November 10, 1897. They represent the fifth of five generations now living.

SAYLES, EDWARD RIDELL, of Guthrie Center, a lawyer, was born in Meadville, Pa., August 17, 1852, and is a son of Albert P. Sayles, a native of Ohio, and a dentist, who died at Lyons, Iowa, in 1871, and Susan J. Sayles, a native of Vermont. In 1857 the family moved to Lyons, Iowa, where Edward spent his boyhood attending the public schools. He entered the preparatory course of Iowa college at Grinnell in 1867, receiving the Sargent medal in 1868, and was a member of the Chrestomathian society. His studies were interrupted by the sickness of his father in 1869. In 1873 he resumed his work at Iowa college. He was one of the editors of the *College News Letter* in 1874, first president of the State Oratorical association, organized in 1874, and was a delegate to the Interstate Oratorical association at Indianapolis in 1875. In the fall of 1874 he entered the junior class at the State university, and became a member of Irving institute, but on account of illness in 1875, went to Lyons, where he began reading law with Hon. A. R. Cotton, now of San Francisco. He was admitted to the bar in the district court of Iowa at Clinton, May 22, 1876, and practiced at Lyons, in partnership with Judge Cotton until 1881, when he removed to Guthrie Center and engaged in law and banking. He was for five years cashier of the Citizens bank, and in 1886 resumed the active practice of the law, at which he has continued ever since.

A special feature of his business is a system of abstracts of titles in Guthrie county. He has given much time and study to this kind of work, having been for a long time in charge of a system of abstracts in Clinton county, before he was admitted to the bar, and he is now counsel and president of the Guthrie County Law and Abstract company. His law practice has for ten years past been largely trial work in the district court, and his clientage has included a large proportion of the wholesale merchants doing business in Guthrie county. He is local counsel for R. G.

Dun & Company, Wilber Mercantile agency, the Snow-Church company, the Bartlett agency, and other agencies. His name also appears in most of the leading directories of lawyers, and he is a member of the Commercial Law League of America.

In 1890 and 1891 he was associated in partnership with Hon. F. O. Hinkson, of Stuart, under the firm name of Sayles & Hinkson, and the firm was employed in important litigation in Adair and Guthrie counties. They appeared for the town of Guthrie Center in litigation growing out of its contract for the construction of a water works system, and the case resulted in

favor of the town in the supreme court in 1896.

In politics Mr. Sayles has always been an active republican, and was chairman of the county central committee of Guthrie county in 1888. He has been mayor of the cities of Lyons and of Guthrie Center, these being the only offices which he has held, for he has no political ambitions, preferring to devote all of his energies to the practice of his profession. He is a member of Bower Camp of the Modern Woodmen of America.

He was married on April 14, 1881, to Miss Mary L. Armstrong, of Chicago. They have two children — a daughter, Helen, born August 20, 1882, and a son, Albert, born March 13, 1885.

BENNETT, ALBERT T., is a native of Massachusetts, having been born at Mendon, in that state, October 8, 1855, at which place he resided until May, 1869. The name of his father was Russell Bennett, who died in 1860. His mother's maiden name was Roba M. Farnsworth, a native of northern Vermont. In the summer of 1869 he came with his mother to Carroll county, settling on a farm near the present town of Templeton. His mother continued to reside there until her death in 1889. His early education was obtained in the public schools. From 1874 to 1881 he taught school winters working on his mother's

farm during the summers. In the spring of 1881 he entered the law office of Hon. O. H. Manning, then lieutenant-governor of the state, a talented and successful lawyer and financier, who is now private counsel for a number of Illinois corporations at Chicago. In April, 1882, Mr. Bennett was admitted to the bar, and in June of that year located at Manning, where he has since resided. In addition to his law practice he is engaged in the banking business, being owner and manager of the Bennett bank at Manning. He is an active member of the republican party, and is now serving his fourth term as chairman of the republican central committee of Carroll county. He was married December 20, 1883, to Miss

Clara J. Ayrhart, of Dedham, Iowa. They have one child, Ralph A. Bennett, born May 6, 1886.

———

ADKINS, JOHN VERTNER, the subject of this sketch, like most of those in middle life in our western country, did not come from wealthy parents. On the contrary he was born in a log cabin, near Plymouth, in Schuyler county, Ill. Again, like most of them, he has made for himself a place in the business world that has grown up around him, and all of us, where he can command the best that is going in the way of living and education for his children. He is well situated in business circles, and commands the respect and confidence of his acquaintances. He was born November 15, 1851, as stated above, and now lives at Paullina, Iowa. His father was a native of Connecticut, and consequently a Yankee, as we rate Yankees, but was also a sturdy Scotchman, being descended from ancestors, who came from Scotland in an early day. He was born December 5, 1824, at Litchfield, Conn., and died June 5, 1897, at Newton, Iowa. His mother's maiden name was Lydia Ann Vertner and she was of German descent. Mr. Adkins was educated in the district schools of Illinois and this, with a wide field of reading, constituted the bulk of his educational qualifications, so he cannot boast of a college education. He settled in Iowa in March, 1865, at Prairie City, and worked in a general store for twelve years.

He went to Paullina, O'Brien county, in October, 1883, going into business with his brother in the general merchandise business; sold out in 1886, in the month of July; went into the Bank of Paullina as bookkeeper August 1, 1886, which position he held until July, 1892, when he took the position of cashier, which he now holds. He has always voted the republican ticket but never held any office, or sought one.

He is a member of the Masonic fraternity, being admitted to membership at Prairie City in 1873, Blue Lodge; is also a member of the Hawarden chapter, Crusade Commandery of Cherokee, and El Kahir Shrine of Cedar Rapids. He has never belonged to any church organization, but favors the work being done by all churches.

He was married to Miss A. B. White, daughter of Rev. J. C. White. They have two children, Harry C., aged 18, attending school at Drake university, and Leigh W., aged 11.

PRESTON, BYRON WEBSTER, of Oskaloosa, recently county attorney of Mahaska county, ranks well among the lawyers of central Iowa, and has earned a wide reputation for fearlessness and honesty. His father, Silvester S. Preston, a native of Vermont, was born December 7, 1832; graduated from Harvard college, and for a time read law. He came to Iowa in 1857 and settled on a farm in Jasper county, near Newton. He enlisted in the army at the breaking out of the war, and after its close continued farming in Jasper county four years, when he moved to Marseilles, Ill., and engaged in the mercantile business one year; then established himself in business at Grinnell, where he continued until 1885, since which time he has retired from active business. Mr. Preston's mother, Amelia M. Wilde, was born in New Hampshire, May 18, 1836, and died July 6, 1883. Byron W. Preston is a native of Iowa, and was born February 13, 1858, in Newton, Jasper county. He began his education in the country schools and continued it in the public schools of Grinnell, whither he moved with his parents when he was about 14 years old. He attended, also, the Grinnell academy, and in 1876-7 was a student at Eastman's Business college, in Poughkeepsie, N. Y.

In 1877 he engaged in the mercantile business at Grinnell with his father, under the firm name of S. S. Preston & Son, at the same time conducting a store in Newton. In 1881 he purchased his father's interest, and for two years carried on the business alone. He came to Oskaloosa July 31, 1883, and read law in the office of Judge L. C. Blanchard. He studied day and night, and was admitted to the bar of the Mahaska county circuit court in March, 1884. Soon after his admission to the bar, the law was changed so as to require a two-years' course of study, but, though Mr. Preston had prepared in eight months, he had really done two years' work in that time. He was employed by Judge Blanchard a few months, and they then formed a partnership, which lasted until 1891. In 1890 Mr. Preston was elected county attorney of Mahaska county, serving as such for two terms. During his administration he won the applause of all law-loving people by his fearless prosecution of crime, gaining the reputation among the district judges as being one of the most fearless prosecutors in the state. He prosecuted four murder cases, securing conviction in all of them. Since retiring from

office, in January, 1895, Mr. Preston has practiced alone, and has been retained in many of the most important cases tried in the county, including defense in four murder cases, in all of which his clients were acquitted.

Politically Mr. Preston has always been an enthusiastic republican. He was chairman of the county central committee in 1888–89, and in 1891 was a member of the state central committee. In 1892 he was a candidate for nomination as district judge, but was defeated by Hon. Ben McCoy, who had a small majority over him, Mr. Preston standing second, with five in the field. He

was dissatisfied with the St. Louis platform of 1896, as he is a strong bimetallist, but he remained loyal to his party, nevertheless. He is a member of the Masonic, Elks, Odd Fellows and Woodmen lodges. With the Masons he is a Knight Templar, and as an Odd Fellow he belongs to the encampment. He is not a church member, but his people are Congregationalists and his wife an Episcopalian. He was married October 6, 1880, at Newton to Nellie Blanchard. They have two children: Edith, born May 24, 1882, and a son, Blanchard W., born September 23, 1892.

Mr. Preston is just reaching the period of his greatest usefulness, and is destined to fill still more important places.

FULLER, WILLIAM E., of West Union, former member of congress from the Fourth District of Iowa, is a descendant of the Fullers who were original members of the Plymouth colony that landed from the Mayflower in 1620. Dr. Samuel Fuller was a deacon and physician to the colony. Dr. Levi Fuller, father of William E., has been a leading citizen of Iowa since 1853. His father, Elijah Fuller, was born and lived in Surrey, N. H., and his mother, Matilda Newcomb, was born in Massachusetts. The Fullers were soldiers in the revolutionary war and one of them was shot at the battle of Bennington. Dr.

Fuller has been identified with all the leading events in Fayette county for more than forty years, and has given generously of his means for the building of railroads, churches, universities and other public institutions. He is now president of the board of trustees of the Upper Iowa university at Fayette, and is also president of the board of education in West Union. Since coming to Iowa he has been mostly in the real estate, banking and brokerage business. He was commissioned as a surgeon in an Iowa regiment by Governor Kirkwood, but before entering the field was appointed United States revenue collector for the Third District of Iowa, by President Lincoln, and accepted that office.

He was a member of the Iowa legislature and has done his full share in developing the state.

William E. Fuller, the only son of Dr. Levi and J. E. Tipton Fuller, was born in Center county, Pa., March 30, 1846. After a brief residence in Stephenson county, Ill., the family came to West Union in April, 1853. The son received his literary education in the Upper Iowa university and in the State university. He held a position in the interior department at Washington, resigning in 1867, and in 1869 entered the law department of the State university, where he graduated with honors as the valedictorian, in June, 1870. He immediately commenced the practice of his profession in West Union, continuing it with marked success up to the present time.

Mr. Fuller has been interested in politics from his earliest manhood, always identified with the republican party. He has been chairman of the county committee, member of the district and state committee, and in 1875 was elected to the Sixteenth General Assembly, where he was an active member of the judiciary committee. He declined a renomination. In 1884 he was elected to the Forty-ninth Congress in a district which had been carried at previous elections by the democrats by more than 700 majority. The district was regarded as a forlorn hope from the republican standpoint, but energy and organization, which included fifty speeches by Mr. Fuller, overcame the odds and the democratic candidate, L. H. Weller, was defeated by 241 majority. Mr. Fuller was an industrious and influential member of congress, being a member of the committee on coinage, weights and measures and committee on the revision of the laws, taking an active part in the consideration of the silver question. He was re-elected to congress in 1886 by 1,931 majority, and served on the judiciary committee. He favored free lumber and free sugar in the tariff discussion and made several speeches on the Fitz John Porter, silver, lumber, sugar, interstate commerce and pension bills, and the Nicaragua Canal bill. The laboring people of the country were especially pleased, and commended Mr. Fuller for his watchful care of their interests. He was also attentive to the business of old soldiers at the national capital. Mr. Fuller remained in Washington during the long session of the Fiftieth Congress, the longest in the history of the country, and declined to return to Iowa and canvass for a third term.

Mr. Fuller is in constant demand as a speaker and is often called upon to deliver Fourth of July speeches and to speak on Memorial day and at county fairs. Since his retirement from congress he devotes himself to his professional duties, but has often given his services to his party, on the stump. In 1897 Mr. Fuller's home friends presented his name to the republican state convention as a candidate for governor. There were nine candidates and the contest was a spirited one. Mr. Fuller's candidacy was well received and he had the solid support of his congressional district, which, considering that his name was proposed but a few days before the convention, was very creditable. The favorable impression he made then is likely to be to his advantage in the future.

Mr. Fuller was married in Kossuth, Des Moines county, Iowa, January 1, 1868, to Miss Lou J. Harper, the only child of William and Harriet (Heizer) Harper. She is a native of Des Moines county and was educated in the State university. Her parents were among the early settlers of Des Moines county, where her father has been a prominent resident since 1842, and was a member of the legislature in 1850 and again in 1870. He is now, at the age of 80 years, still active in business and is president of the State bank of Mediapolis. Mr. and Mrs. Fuller have been blessed with a family of nine children, of whom seven are now living, four sons and three daughters. Levi Harper was born December 10, 1868, and is a practicing lawyer in Chicago; he is married and has two children; Harriet May, born May 23, 1871, is married to C. W. Holbrook, a lawyer in Cedar Rapids; Stella, born February 2, 1875, married Rev. M. P. McClure, pastor of the Presbyterian church in Kilbourn City, Wis.; Clara Augusta, born March 6, 1877; William W., born January 28, 1880; Howard T., born September 13, 1884, and Robert E., born December 6, 1888, reside with their parents in West Union. Mr. and Mrs. Fuller are members of the Methodist church and the older children are all identified with some one of the evangelical churches. Mr Fuller is deeply interested in educational affairs, serving on the board of education in West Union for a number of years and also being identified with the management of the Upper Iowa university. He is also a practical farmer and has two fine farms near West Union. His home farm of 370 acres adjoins the town of West Union and is well stocked.

---

WHITE, HENRY BARRE, of Waterloo, better known in newspaper and fraternal circles as H. B. White, was born in Auburn, Ohio, where his early youth was spent. His father's family can be traced back to the Pilgrim fathers, the present Whites being descendants of Peregrine White, whose parents were Mayflower passengers. On the mother's side he descends from Cotton Mather, the famous New England preacher, who labored with great zeal to establish the ascendency of the church in civil affairs, and to put down witchcraft by legal sentences. He was a writer of many books—some 382, not reckoning his illustrations of the sacred scriptures—among which was Magnalia Christi Americana, a

very quaint and curious book, full of learning and piety and not without prejudice. He was a graduate of Harvard, and made D. D. and F. R. S. by the University of Glasgow. With all his faults, he was a man of excellence of character, and his great work in the interests of the poor, for mariners, slaves, criminals and Indians, was remarkable because philanthropy was far more rare in those days than at the present time.

H. B. White came to Iowa in 1856 with his parents, who settled at Garnavillo, then the county seat of Clayton county. At the age of 14 he ran away to become a

soldier, but was overhauled at Benton Barracks, not, however, until he had received a wound from the premature explosion of a new field piece, which kept him six weeks in the hospital. His business training has been a practical one since the day when he took the first job on his own account—cutting hoop poles, at the age of 11. Following a course in the public schools of McGregor, Iowa, and in the Upper Iowa university at Fayette, he clerked, worked on a farm and followed the painter's trade for some sixteen years During all those years, and in the ones that have since passed, he has devoted himself to study, and is now what may properly be termed a self-educated and self-made man. At present he holds the responsible position of grand recorder of the Ancient Order of United Workmen for the state of Iowa, and has much to do in the promotion of the insurance feature of that order. The plan of assessment in use by that organization, and which has proved such a meritorious feature, was formulated by him. He is the editor and manager of the *Iowa Workman*, a monthly paper devoted to the interests of the A. O. U. W. He is also prominent in the Masonic and Odd Fellows orders. In politics he is a sound money democrat. He was married in 1873 to Miss Matilda Luckenbill. They have four children, two girls and two boys. In religious belief they are Presbyterians.

LAYLANDER, ORANGE JUDD, of Cedar Falls, editor of the *Western Teacher*, and for

the past ten years city superintendent of the public schools of Cedar Falls, is one of the leading educators of Iowa, and is a man who possesses rare executive ability and a wonderful capacity for work. He is a son of Andrew Laylander, a farmer of Holmes county, Ohio, who, in addition to his other duties, taught school during the winter for thirty years. His mother, whose maiden name was Amanda Wells, was also one of the first teachers in Holmes county, beginning her work there in the early 40's,

before the free schools were established.

Superintendent Laylander was born March 11, 1858, in Holmes county, Ohio. His early education was obtained at the district school, this being supplemented by a systematic course at home under the direction of his father, covering the ordinary academic course. Speaking of this work, Mr. Laylander says: "This individual drill was worth more to me than all my subsequent training. I had my choice between studying algebra, physics and German at night for two hours, or husking corn by lantern light in the barn. Whatever of studious habits I gained I attribute to this discipline, aided by a district school that taught some things well. I possess no college degree, not even an honorary one, and never try to conceal the fact. I believe that one's worth or worthlessness must be measured in deeds, not degrees." Notwithstanding this opinion, he has done a good deal of college work, for he took the teachers' course in a normal school at Medina, Ohio, and for two years studied social science in the post-graduate department of Wooster university. He thoroughly believes that the best mental growth comes by diligent effort, and that one must never cease to be a student.

Mr. Laylander first came to Iowa in 1876, settling in Poweshiek county, where he had purchased a farm. After working the farm one season he returned to Ohio to resume his studies in the normal school. He came back to Iowa in 1878, rented his farm and accepted a position as principal of the Malcom schools. Here he remained for three years, when he became superintendent of the Brooklyn schools, which position he held for six years. In 1887 he came to Cedar Falls, where he still remains as superintendent of the public schools. Superintendent Laylander is widely known, not only as a teacher, but through his publications, for besides editing the *Iowa Western Teacher*, he has published several text-books, among them a work in orthoëpy and one in geography. He also does a great deal of work as an institute conductor and lecturer and has been elected to various important offices in the State Teachers' association.

He was brought up to have faith in the principles of the republican party, but became a democrat through his belief in free trade. He is a strong anti-monopolist. He was married on July 20, 1880, to Miss Anna Milligan, of Shreve, Ohio. They have no children.

MILLER, HENRY, one of the substantial business men of Calmar, is a native of Germany, and was brought with his parents to America when but 3 years of age. His father, Henry Miller, who was a farmer in the province of Hesse Darmstadt, in Germany, emigrated to this country in 1842, landing at New York. He moved his family in a covered wagon from Newburgh, on the Hudson, out into the heavy timbered country about Pike Pond, now Kenoza Lake, in Sullivan county. There among the hills he cleared off the heavy growth of beech and hemlock woods for a farm. There Henry grew to manhood. There the father lived and prospered. He died at nearly 80 years of age, worth $25,000.

His mother's maiden name was Elizabeth Wehrum. She came from Germany also, after her marriage to Henry Miller, Sr. She was a helpful wife, a kind and affectionate mother, and lived to the age of 86 years. The son Henry was born in the the village of Muchenheim, Germany, March 2, 1839. As his father settled in the dense forests of Sullivan county, New York, before Henry was four years old, where the people were poor and widely separated, there were few schools and very little chance to get an education. He grew up inured to constant hard labor in clearing off the heavy wood, and working among stumps to help support the family. He chopped cord wood and hauled it two and a half miles with oxen, selling it at a dollar a cord to earn the first money he ever had. When 19 years of age he went to learn the blacksmith trade, working a year and a half from 5 o'clock in the morning until 8 or 9 at night, for his board and $3.33 a month, until he was 21 years of age. At the close of his term of service he had $18 in money, to begin his career in the world. He started out on foot to look for work, and after three weeks' search he had spent his last dollar and found work at Port Jarvis at $8 per month. He afterwards went to Goshen, in Orange county, and learned to be a good horseshoer. He soon became a skilled workman and in 1864 earned $45 a month at his trade. In December, 1865, Henry started for the far west, stopping at Calmar, Iowa, where he rented a small building, purchased a few tools and opened a blacksmith shop on his own account. Soon after his brother, who was a wagonmaker, joined him, and they began to repair and make wagons. They

built up a fine business by hard work and good management, and in 1870 took in a partner, put up a good building and began to deal in general agricultural implements. For thirty-two years Mr. Miller, with various partners, has been carrying on a growing business until their sales have reached $35,000 a year and are rapidly increasing.

In politics Mr. Miller has always been a democrat, until 1896, when he left the party, owing to the position it took for free coinage of silver, and he has since voted the republican ticket. He is a member of the German Lutheran church, and has served two terms as mayor of Calmar. In 1867 he was married to Miss Elsie Herklotz. They

had eight children. His wife died in 1879; he afterwards married Eliza Hintermann, by whom he had six children.

Industry, economy, temperate living and honesty have been his watchwords.

Starting with no capital, dependent entirely upon the labor of his hands, Mr. Miller's success in life has come from habits of industry and economy, and a natural ability to manage and build up a thriving business. From the poor boy working for $3.33 a month, he has become a substantial and successful manager of an extensive business, built up by his ability and energy.

25

TORBERT, WILLARD H., the well-known wholesale druggist, of Dubuque, is a native of the state of New York, and his ancestors on both sides have been distinguished practitioners of both medicine and pharmacy.

His grandfather, Samuel Torbert, M. D., was health officer of the port of New York under Gov. Daniel Tompkins. His father, the late Dr. H. G. Torbert, of Camden, was one of New York's most distinguished practitioners. His mother was the daughter of Joshua Ransom, M. D., an illustrious member of the medical fraternity, and her grandfathers on each side, Capt. Elihu Warner, and Lieut. Joshua Ransom, were both distinguished soldiers of the American revolution. Besides those who won distinction in the practice of medicine and with whom the name of Torbert is entwined in

honorable kinship, are others prominent in the history of the country. Among them may be named the McCreas, McNairs, and Lieutenant Burrows of revolutionary fame. In the same direct line descended General Torbert, who distinguished himself in brave and gallant service through many engagements of the civil war. And so on through years, early and late, the family history records traditions of an esteemed and honored race who have figured among stirring scenes and notable events, with which the people of the country are familiar.

Willard H. was born in Camden, Oneida county, N. Y. In preparing for college he attended Falley seminary, at Fulton, N. Y., and later completed his education at Princeton college. His earliest experience as a druggist was in Syracuse, N. Y., after which he engaged in the drug business at Adams, Jefferson county, N. Y. Mr. Torbert made his first acquaintance with Dubuque in 1864, and in 1868 became a resident of that city. In 1868 he purchased an interest in the drug store which had been established by Dr. Timothy Mason in 1836, being the oldest establishment of the kind in Dubuque or in Iowa. Later he became its sole proprietor and soon broadened its trade into one of the largest among western drug houses, while its wholesale business extends over several western states and territories. In 1880 Mr. Torbert was largely instrumental in securing a modification of the state laws regulating the sale of liquor by pharmacists and in securing the repeal of the obnoxious features. This section was so repealed or reconstructed that no further protest or complaint was heard from the pharmacists of the state, who had hitherto been sorely inconvenienced and embarrassed in this branch of their business.

In 1888 Mr. Torbert was elected president of the State Jobbers and Manufacturers' association, and again found an active field for the exercise of his diplomatic acumen. He was a potent factor in securing the enactment of a law regulating rates between railroads and shippers of the state. This measure placed Chicago and Iowa jobbing points on a parity and resulted in untold benefits to the jobbers and manufacturers of Iowa in all branches of their business and trade, and has proven of great value to the railroads themselves. In 1888 Mr. Torbert was elected president of the Iowa State Pharmaceutical association, and in 1889 was unanimously re-elected to a second term, an honor never before extended to any member in the history of the association. At a meeting of the pharmaceutical association at New Orleans and at Louisville, Mr. Torbert was a recognized leader and champion of the interests of the retail druggists of the country. *The Pharmaceutical Era* says: "In selecting him as chairman of the committee to represent the retailers in the tripartite conference in the further and final execution of the Apha plan, it may be confidently stated that the retail druggists have a wise, true and faithful friend at court, as Mr. Torbert never spares time nor effort when the interests of the retail druggists are at stake. If the plan adopted by the tripartite fails of ultimate success, it will not be the failure of his untiring efforts to secure the desired result as chairman of the commercial section of that body." Mr. Torbert is a prominent member in the National Wholesale Druggists' association, also a member of the Iowa Society of Sons of the Revolution. His ability and influence as a member of the Interstate Retail Druggists' league and as the Iowa representative of the state executive committee, has met with deserved and flattering recognition. In all his dealings with his fellow-men in public and private association, his abilities and integrity have been unquestioned. He also possesses many qualities that would eminently fit him for a political career, had he chosen to take advantage of opportunities that from time to time have offered their allurements in that direction. Mr. Torbert is thoroughly familiar with political methods, is an earnest and eloquent public speaker and an engaging conversationalist. He has been mentioned in connection with many distinguished public positions which he would have filled with ability and honor. He has been frequently sought by the republican party, with which he is prominently identified, as a candidate for the highest office within its gift in the state. But he is too thoroughly devoted to his important business interests to forsake them for a political career. He was president of the Dubuque Commercial club and is now president of the Dubuque Jobbers and Manufacturers' union. He was vice-president of the American Pharmaceutical association, the largest society of pharmacists in the world.

He is an earnest worker in whatever direction his sympathies and convictions are enlisted, a genial companion in the social walks of life, upright in his dealings with men and a useful member of the community with which he has been so long and honorably identified. Mr. Torbert was married January 2, 1868, to Mary E. Kirk, a daughter of Rev. R. R. Kirk and Mary Doxtater Kirk. They have one daughter, Mary T., now the wife of Maj. Glen Brown, of Dubuque.

LINDBERG, JOHN AUGUSTUS, president of the Farmers State bank, of Dayton, Iowa, was born in Victoria, Knox county, Ill., December 29, 1850, and is a sample of that American product known as self-made men. His parents were natives of Sweden. His father and his grandfather served as soldiers in the regular army of his native country. On his mother's side there were many who assisted in making the history of that distant northern country. Her uncle, Bishop Landgren, was very prominent in the ministry of northern Sweden. They came to America in October, 1849, having been three months on the voyage, and like most emigrants of that nationality, they made the most of the advantages afforded by their adopted country.

Although the parents of Mr. Lindberg were possessed of the notions of industry and close application to work, for which the people of that tongue are noted, they did not permit their notions in that regard to deprive their children of the opportunities of a good education. Mr. Lindberg was placed in the high school at Boonesborough, and was valedictorian of his class upon graduation. He then entered the Iowa State university, and on June 26, 1871, graduated from the law department

of that institution. From early childhood he was ambitious and while a mere boy began to read law, alternating his pursuit of legal lore with contributions to the papers, and labor on the farm, such as "dropping corn" for his neighbors at 25 cents a day.

Following his graduation he located at Sioux City in connection with T. H. Conniff, and after a period of practice there removed to Dayton and took charge of the *Dayton Review*. This paper he published for ten years, when he was appointed postmaster under Garfield and again under Harrison.

After attaining his majority he was elected justice of the peace, and relates many amusing incidents of his magistracy. His executive ability and integrity being well known he was tendered the position of president of the Farmers State bank, which he accepted, and which office he now holds. It is one of the sound financial institutions of that section of the state.

Mr. Lindberg is a republican and has done a great deal of effective campaign work. At the time of the "late unpleasantness" Mr. Lindberg was too young to take part, being but 13 years old at its close, but praying that it would last a couple of years longer. He is a member of the

Masonic Order and is treasurer of the lodge in Dayton. In his religious belief and affiliation he is a Unitarian. He was married on June 7, 1874, to Amelia Brundien, and two children have resulted from that union: Clarence John and Arthur Channing. The former is on a ranch in Texas and the latter a bookkeeper in the bank. In their model country home, without ostentatious display, Mr. and Mrs. Lindberg enjoy in leisure the company of a host of friends, by whom they are esteemed as model entertainers.

---

LACEY, EDWIN RUTHVEN, of Columbus Junction, rose from bootblack and all-around errand boy to be the cashier of two

of the leading banks of Louisa county, an achievement uncommon, even in this land of great possibilities. He was born at Grandview, in the county where he now resides, October 18, 1858, and has spent most of his time in that county, except one year spent in Sioux Falls, S. D. His early youth did not greatly differ from that of other boys whose parents do not possess the means with which to give their children the best school advantages. He went to common school until he was 12 years old, and picked up small change, with which to satisfy his boyish wants, by blacking

boots and running errands. At the age of 15 he secured a position with the Louisa County National bank of Columbus Junction as errand boy and all-around helper. That humble start led to the position of cashier of the institution, which he now fills. That he evinced an aptitude for the exacting work incident to the banking business and fortified himself in the minds of his employers by close attention to duty, exemplary habits and strictest integrity, goes without saying. Once in a responsible position he had an opportunity to show his ability in handling the affairs of the bank coming under his supervision, and so valuable did he prove in the place, that he was found among the promoters of the Louisa County Savings bank at its organization in 1891. Such confidence in his ability and integrity did the gentlemen have who founded this last named financial institution that he was elected to the position of cashier, so that he now has the distinction of holding responsible positions in two large financial concerns of that section of the state.

His first vote was cast with the republicans and he has ever remained loyal to that party. He is a Blue Lodge Mason, a Chapter Mason, Knight Templar and a Shriner; also a member of the Knights of Pythias. He has held prominent official positions in these orders. He was married to Miss Etta E. Thompson, April 7, 1880. They have two children: Clarence A., born January 3, 1881; Mabel came to rule the household July 23, 1885.

E. B. Lacey, father of Edwin R. Lacey, is now living and is in his 79th year. He was born at Louisville, Ky., October 1, 1820. He came west in 1856 and located at Burlington, but soon thereafter removed to Louisa county, where he has since resided. The war record shows that E. B. Lacey enlisted as a private in Company F, Thirty-fifth Iowa infantry, and was discharged September 3, 1863, on account of ill health and disabilities contracted in the service. He served as sheriff of Louisa county for two terms The mother's maiden name was Sarah C. Wilcox, a woman of most exalted character and many virtues.

Mr. Lacey was elected as one of the alternates from the First congressional district in Iowa to the convention at St. Louis, Mo., at which William McKinley was nominated for president. He is now, and has been for the last five years, a member of the school board at Columbus Junction.

RIGGEN, HON. JOHN A., of What Cheer, Keokuk county, was born in Stark county, Ill., October 29, 1841. His father was a native of Ohio, tracing his Scotch-Irish ancestry to the early settlers of Maryland and Delaware. His mother's name was Bothwell, whose father, a native of Ohio, was of Scotch origin. Her mother was of Irish parentage, and a product of Virginia. Both of these families settled in Knox and Peoria counties, Ill., in the early 30's and projected a generation of people known for their honest and sturdy habits.

Dr. Riggen was not educated in youth but attended a few winter terms in the country schools. What additional knowledge he possesses was obtained from the school of everyday life. He moved with his father to Missouri in 1859, and settled in what proved to be a strong secession community. When the war broke out they unhesitatingly declared their adherence to the cause of the union, and emphasized their sentiments by enlisting in the union army. The father served three years in the First Missouri cavalry, M. S. M., and returned home on account of wounds and disability. The subject of this sketch enlisted June, 1861, joining the Eighteenth Missouri Volunteer infantry at its organization in July following, and was mustered out in July, 1865, serving a period of four years, one month and fifteen days. During this time he was never absent from his regiment except two weeks in the hospital from measles, and two months on veteran furlough and recruiting service. He participated with his regiment in important skirmishes and small engagements in Missouri during the fall and winter of 1861. He was in the battle of Shiloh (where he was wounded), siege and second battle of Corinth, Miss., in 1862, campaigns and skirmishes in West Tennessee, in 1863. The numerous battles in which his regiment was engaged in the Atlanta campaign, and Sherman's march to the sea, the march through the Carolinas, the battle of Bentonsville and on through Virginia to Washington and the grand review in 1865. He is proud of having carried a musket nearly three years, although he was mustered out a first lieutenant, having been promoted from the ranks for "conspicuous bravery and highly meritorious service." After the war he taught school a few months and then began the study of medicine, locating for the practice of his profession, at Johnstown, Bates county, Mo., in 1869, where he maintained an extensive practice for ten years, when he was compelled by failing health to change, coming to Washington county, Iowa, in the spring of 1879, removing to What Cheer, his present home, in 1884. During all this time his practice has only been limited by his physical endurance. He has for eighteen years been division surgeon for the Burlington, Cedar Rapids & Northern railway. He is ex-president of the Keokuk County Medical society, a member of the American Medical association, the Iowa State Medical society, the National Association of Railway Surgeons, and the American Public Health association.

He is a member of most of the secret orders, including Odd Fellows, Knights of Pythias, Mystic Shrine, and all the Masonic bodies up to and including the thirty-second degree. He is also a member of the G. A. R, Sons of Veterans, and the Military Order of the Loyal Legion of the United States. He served seven years as commander of Posts 112 and 144, G. A. R. In 1888 he was elected senior vice-commander of the department of Iowa, G. A. R. and had charge of the Iowa camp at the national encampment at Columbus, Ohio, that year. In 1887 he was the nominee, by acclamation, of the republicans of Keokuk county, for representative, and came within five votes of being elected, although the county was strongly democratic. He has been a member of the city school board, and postmaster under Harrison, resigning in a short time on account of poor health. He was the choice of his county for district delegate to the national republican convention in 1892, and was elected as an alternate from the Sixth district that year. In 1893 he was elected state senator for the Twelfth district. He was nominated by acclamation and elected by a majority of 885, succeeding a democrat. During his term of four years he rendered, in a quiet way, honest and faithful service to his constituents and to the state. He was on

the important committees of ways and means, suppression of intemperance, railroads, corporations, military, mines and mining, labor, highways, elections, public health, and pharmacy.

He was chairman of the legislative committee, to visit the Independence insane asylum 'in 1894, and the Anamosa penitentiary in 1896. From the hour of his election he positively refused to be considered a candidate for re-election, his dislike for the duties of the office and his persistent poor health, making this resolve absolutely necessary. When the war with Spain was declared, he took an active interest in aid of the government, and by his diligent efforts the city in which he resides had the honor of a good representation in the Fiftieth Iowa volunteers. He organized a squad of fifteen, accompanied them to the recruiting station, and by his efforts raised money to pay the expenses of all who were accepted or rejected. He kept in touch with the boys at the front, forwarded them money at Jacksonville, Fla., and when they returned gave his gratuitous professional services to all who were sick. Upon the receipt of the news of the battle of Santiago. he promptly tendered, by telegraph through Congressman Lacy, his immediate and gratuitous service to our wounded. As a number of similar offers had been made, the surgeon-general accepted the services of those who were nearer where they were needed.

Dr. Riggen was married in 1868 at St. Joseph, Mo., to Mrs. Hannah E. Mesley, with whose companionship and love he is still blessed. She is the daughter of the late Mr. John E. Warner, of Syracuse, N. Y. Their only child, Fannie E., is now the wife of Mr. T. C. Legoe, a prominent attorney of What Cheer, Iowa. An adopted daughter, Cora F., married Mr. Joseph C. Rielly, a successful millinery dealer in St. Louis, Mo. Dr. Riggen has a splendid plantation of 2,120 acres in the sunny south, where he spends his winters. He loves Iowa and her people, but his physical condition will not permit him to risk the rigors of a northern winter climate.

---

ELLIOTT, THOMAS KNOX, cashier of the Commercial State bank, of Essex, Page county, was born September 13, 1863, in Warren county, Ill. His father, Thomas Cochran Elliott, was a farmer, and one of the early settlers of Warren county. His mother, Mary Louise Laird, was a native of Ohio. Alexander McCandless Elliott, the grandfather of Thomas K., came from Belfast, Ireland, and settled at an early date in Pennsylvania. From there he removed to Guernsey county, Ohio, and from that point to Warren county, Ill., where he died May 13, 1868. Thomas K. attended country school until after removing to Lenox, Iowa. In the fall of 1880 he returned to Warren county, Ill., and attended Monmouth college three years, in the meantime staying out one year and teaching country school in Adams county, Iowa. While in college he was a member of the Eccretean Literary society, and was the first member of the freshman class to ever have been elected president of this society. He came to Malvern, Iowa, in September, 1884, and accepted a clerkship in the postoffice with O. H. Snyder, postmaster, where he entered his business career, and from a friendship which sprang up with L. Bently, then cashier of the First National bank at Malvern, Iowa, was recommended to B. M. Webster for a position in his bank in 1885. He entered upon the same April 20, 1885, where he has been

continuously since, except one year, July, 1890, to July, 1891, when he went to Lenox, Iowa, and assisted H. Crittenden in opening a bank at that point. Mr. Elliott continued to act as assistant cashier of the Commercial bank at Essex until April, 1895, when he effected a reorganization of the bank, secured a charter as a state bank and became cashier of the new institution. Since taking charge he has so successfully conducted affairs that the business of the bank has almost doubled. Mr. Elliott, in November, 1897, formed a partnership with H. C. Binns. of Red Oak, and his son, C. R. Binns, of Essex, and bought the business of the Farmers Exchange bank, of

Stanton, Iowa, which business is now conducted with H. Binns as president, T. K. Elliott as vice-president, and C. R. Binns as cashier.

Mr. Elliott is a strong republican, but has never held a political office, or even been a candidate for one, but is at present treasurer of the independent school district of Essex, and has been connected with the schools for many years as secretary and treasurer. He belongs to Mountain Lodge 360 A. F. & A. M., Essex, and has held important offices in same; is also a member of Montgomery Chapter No. 51, at Red Oak, and also of the Knights of Pythias lodge, Essex. He is a member of the Presbyterian church, in which he is an elder. Mr. Elliott was married October 25, 1888, to Lillian A. Ralston. They have had two children: Thomas Charles, born October 28, 1889, who died August 7, 1891, and Annis Lillian, born February 1, 1893.

---

METCALF, GEORGE WASHINGTON, editor and publisher of the *Lansing Mirror*, is one of the oldest newspaper men in point of continuous service, in the state. He came to Lansing in 1872 and has been connected with the *Mirror* since that time. He was born in St. Clairsville, Belmont county, Ohio, January 8, 1856. His father, Enoch Metcalf, was born in Chester county, Pa., in 1810; removed to Belmont county, Ohio, at the age of 20 and died there at the age of 59 years. His wife, Abigail Ridgeway, was born in Virginia in 1814, and was brought up a Quaker. She died in Lansing, December 31, 1890, at the age of 76 years. The Metcalf family is of English origin. George W. Metcalf's career as a printer began at the age of 11 years. He had been attending school in Belmont, Ohio, up to that time, when his father noticed an advertisement in the Barnesville, Ohio, *Enterprise*, calling for a boy to learn the printer's trade. Young Metcalf took the place and worked there for about three years. He afterward worked on the *Bellaire Independent* and the *Steubenville Daily News*. He set the first type on that paper, and it was his only experience in a daily newspaper office. Coming to Lansing, Iowa, in 1872, he served as foreman in the office of the *Mirror*, and when his brother, James T. Metcalf, now superintendent of the money order office in Washington, D. C., was appointed superintendent of the census in 1880, he leased the office to George W. Metcalf and E. M. Woodward, now deceased, who was afterward county attorney of Allamakee county. Three years later Mr. Woodward removed to Minnesota and Mr. Metcalf employed Dick Haney to edit the *Mirror*, while he continued to do the mechanical part. Mr. Haney is now judge of the supreme court of South Dakota, and lives at Pierre. In April, 1883, Mr. Metcalf took editorial charge of the paper and has continued in its control ever since, with increasing success. His office has been called "the parlor printing office of Iowa," by old printers and those who have examined many offices. This compliment has been earned by the enforcement of Mr. Metcalf's rule to have

"everything in its place, and a place for everything." In 1885 the *Mirror* was almost destroyed by fire, but by the determined efforts of the editor the paper never lost an issue, although he was compelled to drive thirty-six miles overland to have his press work done. To-day he has a thoroughly equipped printing office, with a circulation of about 1,200, an excellent business for a county paper. Those who have tried it know that such results cannot be accomplished without good management and plenty of push. Mr. Metcalf has accomplished all this alone, for he commenced without capital.

In 1875 Mr. Metcalf was married to Miss Eva Strong. They have four children,

the oldest son, Herbert J., born August 24, 1879, is now editor of the *New Albin Globe*, and is perhaps the youngest editor in the state. George W., born July 4, 1883, is employed on the *Mirror*. A daughter, Edna May, born September 4, 1876, is married and resides in Chicago.

The *Mirror* and its editor have always supported the republican ticket and have done their share towards advancing the interests of the party at all times, loyally supporting its candidates in nation, state and county. He is a member of the Methodist Episcopal church.

BOYD, HUGH, teacher and clergyman of Cornell college, Mount Vernon, Iowa, was born August 6, 1835, in Keene, Coshocton county, Ohio. His father was Daniel Boyd, who was born near Ardara, parish of Inniskeel, County Donegal, Ireland, and his mother was Jane Elliott, of Glenconway, parish of Killibegs, County Donegal, Ireland. They came to this country in 1819 to escape the infamous system of land tenure in their native land. Daniel Boyd's father and mother were Robert Boyd and Jane Ramsey, and his wife was a daughter of John Elliott and Frances Blaine. The preceding generation were Albert Boyd,

Mr. Ramsey and Kate Karrigan, John Elliott and Annie Lee, Moses Blaine and Jennie McKee. When Daniel Boyd first came to America he was a teacher, and afterwards engaged in weaving fine linen and coverlets, and was a retail merchant in Jefferson and Coshocton counties, Ohio. In 1889 he removed to Athens county, Ohio, and opened up a farm out of the native forest, where, for the remainder of his life, he expended his energies to good purpose. He was an active worker in all religious, political, humanitarian and educational movements of his time. He brought up a large family of children, and all of them now living are well established in life. The educational advantages were not many, but the training of the future teacher and preacher was not neglected. There were the weekly papers, the daily reading from the new testament, the earnest and beautiful prayers of the boy's father and mother, and the frequent visits of the pioneer preacher. On these occasions every subject of human interest was discussed between him and the boy's father. The boy was silent and listened. There was a little district school of irregular attendance of two or three months each year, and finally a seminary was opened in a little village five miles away. Here the boy was prepared for college in a surprisingly short time. Often he had to walk the entire distance to the seminary, but he always got there and made the best use of his time. The farm had made him familiar with hard work and he was not afraid of it. He entered the Ohio university and was graduated with the honor of valedictorian in 1859. Some years later he was further honored with the degree of doctor of divinity.

Professor Boyd, after several years of service as a teacher in the public schools of Ohio, and, after having labored several other years as a clergyman in the Methodist Episcopal church, was, in 1871, transferred from the Ohio annual conference to the Upper Iowa annual conference, and appointed professor of Latin in Cornell college. This position he now holds and has adorned with many years of earnest and effective service. He follows no stereotyped method, but has, in great part, made the Latin a living tongue rather than a dead language. His work has received substantial endorsement from Harvard university, from the fact that several students after they had received their early training at Cornell entered Harvard for more advanced work, and the number of courses required of them was lessened as compared with the number of courses required of students coming from other colleges of similar grade. While devoting himself mainly to his duties as teacher, Professor Boyd has been in demand both at home and abroad for addresses, lectures and sermons, in which he has demonstrated himself to be a speaker of commanding force and eloquence. He is often called upon in his own town and no one is received with more kindly interest and generous attention. Aside from his regular duties he is deeply interested in the study of sociology. Besides his membership in other organizations he is a member of the Beta Theta Phi, and belongs to the order of Knights of Pythias, and is a Knight Templar in the Masonic fraternity.

Professor Boyd was married August 20, 1860, to Ida Patterson, daughter of James Patterson and Martha Henry Patterson, of Amesville, Ohio. Two children were born to them: Luella, born October 25, 1863, and Robert Allyn, born July 17, 1866. Mrs Boyd died October 21, 1867. Professor Boyd was married the second time, August 20, 1874, to Mary Ellen Moody, daughter of Gen. Granville Moody and Lucretia Elizabeth Harris Moody, of Ohio. To them were born four children: Granville Moody, born June 12, 1877, died November 3, 1879; Clifford Moody, born October 21, 1879; Lucy Moody, born September 12, 1881; and Elizabeth Moody, born April 17, 1887, and who died April 20, 1887.

UPTON, Hon. C. C., one of Howard county's brightest young men and recently representing the Forty-second district in the upper branch of the general assembly, was born on his father's farm near Cresco, Iowa, July 19, 1859, and therefore has the distinction of being senator from the county wherein he first saw the light. His father, James G. Upton, was engaged during most of his active life as a farmer, but for the last ten years has lived a retired life. He was the first county judge of Howard county, Iowa, having assisted in its organization, and was a prominent figure in all public affairs of those pioneer days. His ancestors came to this country in an early day, the founder of the American family of Uptons having been engaged by Governor Winthrop in 1636. Many of the name are in the New England states, particularly in the vicinity of Boston. A brother and sister are living at Barre, Vt., and one brother resides in Illinois. The last named is Judge C. W. Upton, an able jurist, who has been on the bench of the court of Illinois for twenty-five years and resides at Waukegan. The mother's maiden name was Sarah A. Miles. On her mother's side she was descended from the Prescott family, of which the famous historian was a member.

The literary education of Senator Upton was received in the public schools and by home study; his legal learning at the State University of Iowa, from the legal department of which he graduated in 1889. He worked on the farm until 16 years of age,

then taught school in winter and farmed in summer until 1882. At that time he went to Dakota and pre-empted a homestead, but not liking the country, returned to Cresco, where he farmed for three years and then entered the law office of Barker Bros., as a student. After having been admitted to the bar, in 1889, he went to Pierre, S. D., and remained until May, 1890, at which time W. K. Barker, with whom he had studied, offered him a partnership in his law business at Cresco, which was accepted and continued until February, 1896, when Mr. Barker retired from the firm because of ill health. In 1891 he was elected city

attorney by the voters of Cresco, and the following year he received a similar compliment. In 1892 he was elected county attorney for Howard county, and served so satisfactorily that he was sent to the state senate in 1893. The secret of his success lies in his constant desire to do his duty at all times in a careful and upright manner. He is plain, honest and outspoken on public questions, always uses his best judgment and stands by his convictions in all matters, public or private. He was regarded as the strongest of the younger members of the senate, and, though possessing a due amount of modesty, was evidently there for business and to protect the interests of the section he represented. He had a place on many important committees, of some of which he was chairman. He was married September 14, 1893, to Miss Eva S. Leland, of Cedar Falls, Iowa. They have two children, Gertrude L. and Clark C. Upton.

SISSON, EUGENE ROBERT, one of the most successful real estate dealers and financiers in northwestern Iowa, lives in Storm Lake, where he located for the practice of law in 1886, having purchased the practice of the firm of Robinson & Milchrist, the former being elected to the

supreme court at that time. He is the son of Daniel W. Sisson, former school-teacher in Rising Sun, Ind.; who later became a merchant and engaged in the milling business at Mason, Effingham county, Ill. He was married to Margaret B. Gibson, whose parents died when she was quite young and left her with the care of bringing up three younger brothers. She brought up nine children of her own to maturity, each one making a living, as he was taught, by the hand of honest toil. She was and is one of the most devoted and conscientious of Christian mothers. The Sisson family came from Otsego county, N. Y., and settled in Ohio and Indiana and later in Effingham county, Ill. Five brothers of

Daniel Sisson were in the union army while he cared for their families, and from his mill furnished bread for all the needy who applied. E. R. Sisson was born near Rising Sun, Ind. He attended the public schools and the State Normal school at Normal, Ill., where he fitted himself to become a teacher. He had a natural talent for music and taught band music in St. Elmo and Shawneetown for a time. He studied law two years, in the office of Hon. Carl Roedel in Shawneetown, Ill., and was admitted to the bar in Illinois in November, 1883. For three years he was in partnership with his preceptor, and at the end of that time sought a larger field farther west, locating, as stated, in Storm Lake. He formed a partnership with A. D. Bailie, who was county attorney, and formerly had been his chum and classmate in college. A three years' residence in Storm Lake opened his eyes to the splendid business opportunities offered by the rapidly developing country, and he organized the Northwestern Land company, of which he is manager. He then began a series of important public enterprises, putting on foot the plan for constructing the auditorium and raising funds for the building of a summer hotel and a college. He sold town lots under an arrangement that half the proceeds were to be used for the erection of the hotel and college buildings. In this and in other ways Mr. Sisson has been of great value to the city of Storm Lake. Mr. Sisson has recently opened an additional office at Ft. Dodge, which he operates in connection with his brother-in-law, W. R. Higgins. Of late years he devotes his attention exclusively to locating settlers in northwestern Iowa, and especially in Buena Vista and adjoining counties. These settlers are all ready to give evidence of the realization of every promise made to them. In one season Mr. Sisson's agency sold over 21,000 acres in Buena Vista county alone. It will thus be seen that he has been a very important factor in the settling and development of northwestern Iowa. By the exercise of strict integrity on his part Mr. Sisson's customers have been induced to advertise his business among their friends, and this has been the main element in his success.

While living in Shawneetown, Ill., Mr. Sisson was married to Miss May C. Carroll, the eldest daughter of Charles Carroll, of that place, who was one of the wealthy and honored citizens of southern Illinois. He was the democratic nominee for state treasurer the same year in which T. S. Ridgeway, of the same town, was elected. They have three children, Alice Eugenia, Hayden and Charles Carroll. Mr. Sisson has always voted the republican ticket, although he was a friend to the silver issue while before the people. He feels that the past election was for the purpose of settling the issue and that it should be regarded as settled once for all, in accordance with the expressed will of the people, and that nothing could be more damaging than an uncertain or changeable policy in our finances.

---

CHASSELL, EDWARD D., the editor of the Le Mars *Sentinel*, has acquired a position of very large acquaintance and influence in the state through his connection with the newspaper profession and with politics. He first came into prominence as the editor of the *Osage News* and later as assistant secretary of the Iowa senate. Afterwards he removed to Le Mars and became editor of the *Sentinel*, and was the first republican elected to the legislature from that county from 1888 to 1893. In 1896 Mr. Chassell lacked only a few votes of receiving the republican nomination for secretary of state, being a very strong second in a field of four candidates.

He is a son of William Chassell and a grandson of Rev. David Chassell, D. D., of the Presbyterian church. The latter was a native of Scotland, born in Glasgow, but he passed his youth in Vermont and his later years in central New York. Rev. David Chassell's wife, Anstiss Olin, was a daughter of Judge John H. Olin, of Vermont, who was a descendant of Gideon Olin, a member of the assembly, and a descendant of John Olin, who came from Wales and settled at East Greenwich, R. I., in 1678.

Wm. Chassell was born in Herkimer county, N. Y.; was educated at Fairfield seminary, of which his father was principal, located at Fairfield, N. Y., and came west when a young man. He engaged in mercantile business in Indiana and subsequently removed to Iowa, settling on a prairie farm near Iowa Falls in 1867. He was married in 1857 to Miss Frances A. Jones, a native of Bradford county, Pa. Prior to her marriage she had been a teacher in the public schools and an instructor in St. Mary's Hall, an Episcopal yo n ladies' boarding school in Burlington, N. J. g She was the daughter of Edward W. Jones, Esq., of Bradford county, Pa., whose father and grandfather, Col. Israel Jones and Capt. Israel Jones, were both active revolutionary soldiers and Indian fighters. Colonel Jones served with Washington and was with him during the memorable winter at Valley Forge. Mr. Chassell's great-grandmother, Lois Wadsworth, wife of Col. Israel Jones, was a descendant of Hon. John Wadsworth, who was a member of the colonial assembly when his brother, Capt. Joseph Wadsworth, secreted the colonial charter in the oak tree at Hartford.

The subject of this sketch was born in Holland Patent, Oneida county, N. Y., May 25, 1858, and coming to Iowa with his parents, his boyhood days were much the same as those of other Iowa farmer boys. He went to school in the winter and worked on the farm and studied at home during the summer. He stuck to the Iowa farm with his parents until he was 21 years of age. He graduated from the Iowa State Normal school at the head of his class in 1882, and in 1888 the degree of B. D. was conferred upon him by the institution. He had a successful career as a school-teacher before he went into the newspaper work, beginning at the age of 19 and alternating

between teaching and attending school. He was principal of the schools at Stacyville, Mitchell county, in 1882 and 1883, and in St. Ansgar, of the same county, in 1883-4. In the latter year he became editor of the *Osage News* and was associated with A. C. Ross in its publication until 1889, when he went to Le Mars and acquired an interest in the Le Mars *Semi-Weekly Sentinel*. A large job printing, binding and blank book establishment is connected with this office, and Mr. Chassell has remained at the head of the concern since he went there. All branches of the business have prospered and the *Sentinel* is recognized as one of the most influential county papers in the state. Mr. Chassell has always been a republican and active in the party work. Besides the honors referred to previously he was a presidential elector in 1892 and was secretary of the republican state central committee in 1890. When he was elected to the legislature in 1893, Plymouth county won the Tippecanoe banner, which is awarded to the county showing the greatest republican gain over the previous year. His legislative service was notable for the industry with which he served, not only the interest of his own town and county, but of the state generally. He secured the passage of a bill changing the hour of convening the legislature on the first day of the session, from 2 o'clock in the afternoon to 10 o'clock in the forenoon, which enables the legislature to effect a permanent organization on the first day of the session and obviates the necessity of twice going through the form of electing United States senator, which had previously been done. The change effects a saving of one legislative day at every election of a United States senator. He also took a leading part in securing the passage of the mulct liquor law and of the bill to provide for the location of a fourth hospital for the insane in the northwestern part of the state. He came within one vote of securing the location of the hospital in Le Mars. Masonry has had a strong attraction for Mr. Chassell and he has devoted considerable attention to it. He belongs to the various Masonic organizations, is a Knight Templar, a member of the Chapter and of the Blue Lodge and the Order of the Eastern Star in Le Mars, and is a noble of El Kahir Temple, Ancient Arabic Nobles of the Mystic Shrine. He is also a member of Zeus Lodge, Knights of Pythias.

SMOCK, FINLEY M., of Keota, was born February 18, 1844, in Indiana. His father, Rev. D. V. Smock, was a Presbyterian minister and came to Iowa in 1853, locating at Birmingham, Van Buren county, where he remained until the year 1858, removing thence to Sigourney.

Finley M. enjoyed the benefits of our public school system and at two different periods during his school days was enrolled in excellent private schools. In 1859, at the age of 15, he entered a wagon shop as an apprentice and was mastering this useful branch of mechanics when the call to arms sounded through the land, calling on all loyal citizens to throw down

the implements used in peaceful pursuits, to shoulder a musket in support of our flag and country. Responding to President Lincoln's call, he enlisted in June, 1861, in Company F, Fifth Iowa Infantry volunteers, and served under Capt. E. S. Sampson and Col. C. L. Matthies in that organization for more than three years. He was badly wounded at Champion Hills, Miss., May 16, 1863, through both thighs by a musket ball. In August, 1864, with other members of his company, he was transferred to Company G, Fifth Iowa Cavalry volunteers, under Capt. J. M. Limbocker and Col. W. W. Lowe. He was

with Gen. J. H. Wilson's last cavalry raid of the war in Alabama and Georgia and was mustered out of service in August, 1865. Returning to Iowa, and Keokuk county, he again took his place at the work bench, which pursuit he followed for many years. He was married in 1868 to Mary E. Stranahan, and a few years afterward located in Keota. Here he followed various vocations, and was largely interested in the development of that section of Iowa.

In the fall of 1894, having received the nomination for clerk of the district court of Keokuk county by the republican party, he was successful in the canvass, and was re-elected for a second term. He is now engaged in the real estate business at Keota.

LATHROP, HENRY WARREN, of Iowa City, is a man well known to the students of history of this state. He is the author of the Life of Samuel J. Kirkwood, and is connected with much of the history of Iowa City and the state since he became a citizen of Iowa in 1847. Mr. Lathrop was born in Hawley, Mass., October 28, 1819.

His father was Zephaniah Lathrop, a carpenter and millwright, in moderate circumstances. His mother was Tryphenia Field, a remote relative of Cyrus W. Field. The founder of the family in this country was Rev. John Lathrop, who came in 1634 from England and landed at Plymouth, but settled in Scituate, Mass., afterwards moving to Barnstable. He was educated at Queens college, England, became a preacher in the Established church, from which he seceded and joined the Independents, preaching sometimes in the streets of London, for which he, with about forty others, was arrested and imprisoned under Charles I. He remained in prison two years, but his wife being taken with a fatal sickness, he was permitted to see her, and after her death was given the alternative of returning to prison or leaving the kingdom. He chose the latter. He preached at Barnstable and Scituate. Mr. Otis says of him: "Mr. Lathrop was as distinguished for his worldly wisdom as for his piety. He was a good business man and so were all his sons, six in number. Wherever one of the family pitched his tent that spot became the center of business and land in its vicinity appreciated in value." One of his sons was captain of a company of colonial troops and served in the expedition against the Indian chief, Ninignet.

Of the many preachers and teachers in the family, the most noted was Rev. Joseph Lathrop, of West Springfield (1731-1820). He preached sixty-two consecutive years to one congregation and was a man of unusual talents, good judgment and tact. The most noted educator was Prof. John Hiram Lathrop (1799-1866), who was a professor in Hamilton college, N. Y., and was president successively of three state universities, Indiana, Wisconsin and Missouri. The Lathrops have been a family of original and independent thinkers. It has been said of the Rev. John Lathrop that during his many years preaching he never required one of his members to subscribe to a creed or sign a covenant. Faith in God, a consistent endeavor to keep His commandments, a pure life and a love for the brethren were the terms of admission to his church; with these that member retained his freedom of belief. The present Mr. Lathrop's grandfather served as a minute man in the army near the close of the revolution, and during Washington's first administration held the office of ensign in the Massachusetts militia, his commission being signed by John Hancock, the first signer of the Declaration of Independence, then governor of the state. The Lathrop family moved to Augusta, N. Y., in 1821 and there Henry W. was educated and grew to manhood. He attended the common schools, and an academy at Augusta, spent a year in a classical school near Boston, studied law in the office of John Koon, in Albany, and was admitted to the bar in Iowa City in June, 1847. His certificate of admission, written by himself, was signed by Joseph Williams, T. S. Wilson and John F. Kinney, judges. He came to Iowa City in May, 1847, and has lived there ever since. He spent the first

seven years of his residence in Iowa in teaching in both private and public schools, and was the first county superintendent of schools of Johnson county. He was one of the regents of the State university and was chairman of the committtee that employed the first professors and put the institution in operation in 1854. Closing his school in the spring of 1854 he went into the practice of law, at the same time doing editorial work on the whig paper, the Iowa Republican, and later became one of its publishers, supporting Grimes for governor and Harlan for senator. Two years later he sold the paper to John Teesdale, practicing law until 1860, and then moved onto a 400-acre tract of wild land near the city and converted it into a fruit and stock farm on which, as he says, he "raised boys and girls, hogs, horses and cattle, grapes and apples for thirty consecutive years." He was the first treasurer of the State university, and held the office for seven years. He was mayor

of Iowa City in 1853, and alderman for several terms. In 1889 he became librarian of the State Historical society, and holds that office now, 1897.

He has been a contributor to the Iowa Historical Record and the historical literature of the state for twenty-five years. He is a charter member of the Southeastern Iowa and State Horticultural societies, and has been at different times president and secretary of the former and director and president of the latter. While president of the state society he, with E. H. Calkins, of Burlington, had charge of an apple exhibit at the meeting of the American Pomological society, held at Rochester, N. Y., where a premium was awarded for the exhibit. Mr. Lathrop was an original whig and cast his first vote for "Tippecanoe and Tyler, too," and was president of the Tippecanoe club of Johnson county, organized during the Harrison campaign, and is a member of the famous Tippecanoe club of Des Moines. He was a member of the state convention that organized the republican party in

Iowa City in 1856, and in that convention was a member of the committee, consisting of J. B. Grinnell, Alvin Saunders, J. B. Howell, Wm. H. Stone, Samuel J. Kirkwood, J. A. Palmer and L. A. Thomas, to prepare an address to the people of the state. He has twice been a defeated candidate for the legislature in Johnson county. He was a reporter for newspapers at different times and also correspondent during the legislative and constitutional convention sessions of 1857, for the Chicago *Democratic Press*, the predecessor of the Chicago *Tribune*. He has been a member of the order of Odd Fellows over fifty-one years, and was a member of the Grand Lodge in 1853. He is a charter member of the Iowa Improved Stock Breeders' association, member of the Literary society, and president of the Old Settlers' association for three years. He is a member of no church, but has served as trustee in the Presbyterian society.

Mr. Lathrop was married April 14, 1847, to Mary Welton, of Hamilton, Madison county, N. Y. They have had five children, of whom three are living: Willard Allen, born in 1848, now at Wheeler, S. D.; George Fred, born in 1851, living in Villa Park, Cal., and Edith May Alinnie, born in 1861, married to W. I. Lathrop, living at Sioux Falls, S. D. She is a graduate of the Iowa State university.

EDWARDS, MILLARD FILLMORE, a successful lawyer of Parkersburg, Butler county, brought thorough preparation, natural ability and good health to the practice of his profession. His parents were of German ancestry on his mother's side and Welsh on his father's side, and he was born near the town of Muncy, Lycoming county, Pa., October 22, 1858. His father was William Edwards, a farmer and stock raiser in fair financial circumstances, and his mother's maiden name was Mary Catherine Schmull, sometimes written "Smull" and "Smole." From his early boyhood, Millard F. Edwards enjoyed good educational advantages, first in the public schools of Lycoming county, then in the Lycoming County Normal school and in the Central State Normal school, in Lock Haven, Pa. For some years after this he taught in the schools of Lycoming county, beginning in the country schools and advancing steadily to better positions in the graded schools, until he finished nine years' teaching, as principal of one of the graded schools of that county. Mr. Edwards also took a course in the Commercial college at Williamsport, Pa. He graduated from the Pennsylvania State Normal school in 1882, ranking as one of the best in the class, and being selected to represent his class with

an oration in the commencement exercises. The next year he came to Iowa to enter the law department of the State university, devoting himself to the work of preparing to enter the legal profession with the same industry that had won success as a teacher. Graduating from the law school in 1884, Mr. Edwards returned to Pennsylvania and entered the law office of B. S. Bentley, of Williamsport. Concluding, however, that Iowa offered the best field for his efforts, he decided to locate in this state, coming to Parkersburg in July, 1885, and forming a partnership for the practice of law with Hon. O. B. Courtright, now of

Waterloo. The partnership lasted a little over two years, when Mr. Edwards retired from the firm and has since been engaged in practice alone.

Mr. Edwards has always been a republican and expects to be in the future. He has been honored by his fellow-townsmen by an election to the office of mayor, and has served as secretary of the school board. Aside from these positions, he has devoted his energies to his profession, with good results. He belongs to Royal Lodge No. 218, Knights of Pythias, in Parkersburg, and is a member of the grand lodge of the state. He is a member of the Methodist Episcopal church. Mr. Edwards was married July 21, 1887, to Miss Ida Whiting, of Parkersburg, and two children have come to bless their pleasant home. They are: Helen Catherine, born January 10, 1889, and Mildred Irene, born November 28, 1897.

Since the preparation of this sketch Mr. Edwards has taken up the banner of his party in Butler county, as the republican candidate for state representative, and will in all probability represent that county in the next legislature.

PAULGER, FREDERICK WHEATLEY, cashier of the New Hartford, Iowa, bank, was born at Bucknall Grange, Lincolnshire, England, May 19, 1854. John Paulger, his father, was an Englishman, who came to America with his family in 1869, from Great Grimsby, England. They left Liverpool on the steamship Nestorian in May and landed at Point Levi, across the river from Quebec, Canada, June 7, 1869. From there they came west and after a few days' stay at Rockford, Ill., came to New Hartford, Iowa, and settled on a farm a few miles from town.

Before coming to America young Paulger attended the schools in the city of London and also the Victoria schools in Great Grimsby, where he was a faithful and studious scholar and won several class prizes. After leaving school he worked in a telegraph office as messenger, and also in the steam shipping office of John Sutcliffe at Great Grimsby for about one year before leaving England. After locating at New Hartford he learned telegraphy at the railroad station during the winter of 1872 and was appointed agent and operator for the Illinois Central Railroad company at that point July 4, 1873. This position he retained until 1881. During 1875 he formed a partnership with his father in the coal and grain business, under the firm name of J. Paulger & Son. In August, 1882, this firm bought the lumber and hardware business of J. A. Cousins. In 1883 the father retired from the lumber and hardware business, and Frederick W. formed a partnership with the former proprietor, J. A. Cousins, under the firm name of Paulger & Cousins, which continued until November, 1892, when Mr. Cousins bought the entire business. During the year 1885 Mr. Paulger entered into partnership with W. E. Miner, under the firm name of Miner & Paulger, and started the New Hartford mill, in which he re-

tained his interest until 1888, when it was purchased by his partner. During the year of 1889 Mr. Paulger, with three others, organized the New Hartford bank, of which he became cashier in 1893. He still retains that connection with the bank and its prosperity is largely due to his energetic and conservative management.

Mr. Paulger has always been an active member of the republican party and has been honored by election to several local offices. He was elected mayor of New Hartford in 1892 and in 1894 accepted the position of city treasurer, which he still occupies. He is master of Beaver Lodge, A. F. and A. M., and has held that office

for three consecutive years. He is also a Royal Arch Mason and Knight Templar, being a member of Baldwin commandery of Cedar Falls.

November 10, 1880, Mr. Paulger was married to Ida Guthrie, daughter of Dr. James A. Guthrie, of New Hartford. They have three children: Leo Harry, born March 7, 1882; Mable Frank, born July 20, 1884, and Ruth Genevieve, born July 22, 1889. By a long and successful business career Mr. Paulger has merited, and has won, the confidence and esteem of his fellow citizens, and established a fine reputation for business foresight and ability.

MORGRIDGE, GEORGE OSBORN, of Muscatine, is one of the well-known physicians of eastern Iowa. He is of Puritan ancestry; his great-great-grandfather, John Morgridge, came from England soon after 1700 and settled at Newburyport, Mass., where he was engaged in shipbuilding. His son, Samuel, Dr. Morgridge's great-grandfather, was a man of learning, who also followed shipbuilding until injured by a fall, after which he was a teacher. He married Ruth Siloers, a native of Ireland, and died June 26, 1772. His son, the doctor's grandfather, was born at Amesbury, Mass., August 20, 1760, and died April 19,

1798. Dr. Morgridge's father, Isaac Morgridge, was born September 1, 1798, in Maine. At the age of 15 he came to Marion county, Ohio, where he cut wood and farmed. Two years later he joined the cavalry to serve on the northern frontier in the war of 1812, but before reaching the front peace was declared. He afterwards moved to Iowa, where he died April 8, 1865. Dr. Morgridge's mother, whose maiden name was Anner Thankful Ballentine, was born November 17, 1805, at Schodack on the Hudson, and was married to Isaac Morgridge at Marion, Ohio, September 30, 1828. Previous to her marriage she was a teacher in the public schools of Columbus, Ohio. She was a daughter of

Dr. Ebenezer Ballentine, who was a graduate of Yale college, and was commissioned "Surgeon's Mate" in a Massachusetts regiment during the revolution. His father, Rev. John Ballentine, of Scotch descent, was a native of Boston. He graduated from Harvard in 1735, and was called to the pastorate of the Congregational church at Westfield, Mass., in 1740, where he preached for thirty-five years. He died February 12, 1776, aged 60 years.

Dr. G. O. Morgridge was born January 26, 1840, at Marion, Ohio. The first school he attended was taught in an old abandoned log house, with a drunken cripple for a teacher. He afterwards attended school at Bloomington, Ind. In 1857, at the age of 17, he came to Iowa; crossed the Mississippi at Davenport with but $2.50 in his pocket, walked to Tipton, and there secured work in a brickyard. He was soon afterward engaged for a time at teaching. During the second year of the war he offered himself to his country, and was mustered into the army October 18, 1861, as a private in Company H of the Eleventh regiment of Iowa infantry. He was made first sergeant in March, 1863, and commissioned captain October 16, 1864, commanding his company until the close of the war. He took part in the battle of Shiloh, both battles of Corinth, the siege of Vicksburg, campaign and capture of Atlanta, and Sherman's march to the sea. He marched in the great review in Washington at the close of the war, and was mustered out at Davenport July 24, 1865. He was twice wounded; at Shiloh April 6, 1862, and at Nicko-Jack Creek, Ga., July 4, 1864.

Returning from the war Dr. Morgridge entered the State university, where he studied nearly two years, then entered the office of Dr. J. C. Hughes, Sr., of Keokuk, and in March, 1870, graduated from the College of Physicians and Surgeons, at Keokuk, and from the medical department of the State university in 1874. During the year 1875-6 he completed the course at Bellevue college, New York, and soon afterwards moved to Muscatine, Iowa, where he has made his home ever since, and has enjoyed the liberal patronage which he deserves.

Politically, Dr. Morgridge is a republican. He served twelve years as a member of the Muscatine board of education. He belongs to the Masonic fraternity and to the Congregational church. He was married in November, 1866, to Ruth A.

Casebeer, whose father was a pioneer Methodist preacher and a pronounced abolitionist. Dr. and Mrs. Morgridge have had two children: Henry W., born in 1867, and Myrta E., born in 1870. His son, Henry, graduated in medicine in 1890, was associated with him in business until October 25, 1897, at which date he died aged 30 years. He was a young man of ability and was greatly loved and respected by all.

DICKMAN, JOHN WILLIAM, professor of German and pedagogy in Upper Iowa university at Fayette, is one of the rising young educators of Iowa. He was born in a log house, five miles north of Defiance, Ohio, April 22, 1863, and was brought up on a farm. His father, William Dickman, was born in Ohio also, where he learned the cooper's trade. In 1857 he came to West Union, Iowa, but after remaining five years returned to Ohio, and was married in 1862 to Martha Ann Schott, a native of Germany, who came to America when 3 years of age. Coming to Iowa again in 1865, Mr. Dickman became a farmer, and was very prosperous. He now owns a farm of about 600 acres, in Fayette county, and is worth from $40,000 to $50,000.

J. W. Dickman began attending district school when he was 8 years old, but was never able to go more than about four months each winter, for his services were always in demand on the farm. But he improved his time, and did not leave the country school until he was 18 years old, when he entered the preparatory department of Upper Iowa university at Fayette. From this institution he graduated in 1888, with the degree of Ph. B. While in college he was a leader among students, and was very prominent in social and religious circles. While in his senior year he was elected class president, and in 1886 was chosen by the Y. M. C. A. as a delegate to Mr. Moody's Summer school at Mt. Hermon. He won a prize of $20 in a debating contest, and an honorary prize in a military contest. He was a member of the Philomathean Literary society, and of other college organizations. He helped pay his way through school by doing farm work during vacations, and in his senior year was employed as a tutor in history and mathematics. Immediately after graduation he was chosen by his alma mater as a member of the faculty, his position being that of professor of mathematics and German. Here he remained until June, 1894, when he

26

resigned his position in order to settle up and dispose of his interest in a lumber business at Sumner; for it was the intention of Professor Dickman to take post graduate work in an eastern university after spending one year in Sumner. But during that year he was so urged to accept the position of principal of the Sumner schools that he finally yielded, and his school work, with his business, proved so enjoyable and lucrative that he deemed it best to postpone his post-graduate work. This determination was more fully confirmed by his election June, 1898, to the chair of German and pedagogy in the Upper Iowa university,

and his re-election in June, 1899, to the same position, and also as treasurer of the university and a member of its executive committee.

The professor is a republican, but does not wish to be counted as a blind enthusiast for that party, for he realizes that, though it suits him better than any other, it is still far from being perfect. He belongs to three secret orders: The Knights of Pythias, the Masons, and the Modern Woodmen of America. He is a very active member of the Methodist church in Sumner, at present being president of the board of trustees, superintendent of the Sunday school, and chorister.

He was married August 22, 1889, to Miss

Adella G. Maltbie, preceptress of the Upper Iowa university, and a graduate of Northwestern university, of Evanston, Ill.

EVANS, JAMES McFARLAND, of Salem, is one of the best-known physicians of southeastern Iowa. His ancestors were mostly Scotch and Irish. His father, Abel M. Evans, was the son of Joseph Evans, of Welsh descent, and Sarah McFarland, daughter of Judge William McFarland, whose father, Daniel McFarland, came from Scotland to America about 1750, settling for a time in New England, and then

permanently in Washington county, Pa., where he had much to do with the development of the country. During the revolutionary war he held a commission in the army. He died in 1817, aged 87, leaving a valuable estate, which is still in the possession of his descendant, Abel Evans, the doctor's father, who was born in 1819. He was married March 15, 1838, to Elizabeth Weir, who was born in 1821, and whose father, Adam Weir, was the son of William Weir, who came to this country from Scotland in 1750 and settled in Franklin county, Pa. The Weir family, which belonged to the parish of "Lesmahagow" in Scotland, was at one time very prominent in that country, it being recorded that, in 1695,

two members of the family, James and John Weir, owned a castle and grounds, known as "Glenare," which remained standing until 1857. Others of the family were clergymen, soldiers, and members of parliament. They were quite conspicuous during the war of the covenant in Scotland, which raged during the sixteenth century, bravely contending for liberty of worship.

Dr. J. M. Evans was born September 19, 1841, in Washington county, Pa., and was the younger of two sons, his brother Samuel dying June 30, 1864, from the effects of wounds received in the battle of Cold Harbor, Va. Dr. Evans' mother died when he was but 2 weeks old, and he was brought up by other relatives. His early education was obtained in the common schools of Pennsylvania, which were well up to the average of that day. At 16 he entered Waynesburg college, in Greene county, Pa., but at the end of three years left school without completing the course, in order to enlist in the army. He joined the Eighth regiment of Pennsylvania Reserves, Volunteer infantry, as a private in Company K, May 1, 1861. In the second battle of Bull Run he received a severe wound in the left shoulder and was discharged from service on account of this disability February 13, 1863, at Baltimore, Md. He came to Iowa May 28, 1865, and began the study of medicine with Dr. L. E. Goodell, a broad-minded man and one of the most successful physicians of the state. After a year and a half spent in study under this man's direction, Dr. Evans attended lectures at the Western Medical college in Cleveland, Ohio. He began the practice of medicine at Pilot Grove, Lee county, Iowa, in 1868, removing October 15, 1872, to West Point, in the same county, and on March 2, 1880, he located at Salem, Henry county, his present home. Thus he has practiced for about thirty years over the same field, all these removals having been within a radius of twenty miles. Though he has amassed a comfortable fortune, and owns one of the best medical libraries in the state, the doctor still continues to practice, preferring a life of activity to one of retirement.

Dr. Evans is a member of Salem Lodge No. 17, A. F. & A. M, and is also a member of the G. A. R. In politics he is a republican, and in religion he adheres to the faith of his ancestors, and is a Presbyterian.

The doctor was married December 3, 1868, to Miss Helene Lusk. Their family now includes three daughters: Victorine, born in 1869, now Mrs. C. H. Cook, of Omaha; Winona, born in 1871, and Helen McFarland, born in 1873. His wife died at Salem, Iowa, May 2, 1897. Winona was married in 1897; is now Mrs. Harry Reeves, and lives at Keokuk.

McELROY, EBENEZER ERSKINE, the well known attorney of Ottumwa, is a native of Ohio, and of Scotch-Irish descent. He was born February 16, 1849, near Greenfield, Ohio. His father, Thomas G. McElroy, was a soldier in the war of the rebellion and enlisted in the army when the subject of this sketch was only 14 years old, leaving him with his mother and five younger children to care for themselves on the farm. Before leaving home the father called the children together and told them that as Ebenezer was the oldest he should take his place and they must obey him the same as they would their father. To the 14-year-old boy he said, "There will be many things that will bother you. Questions will come up about whether it is best to break certain fields; whether the wheat has stood the winter so that it will be worth harvesting; whether the stock is fat enough to sell; what kind of crops should be put in certain fields, etc. If such things bother you it would be well for you to talk with your Uncle Hugh, or Mr. Smith about them, but when you hear what they say, I want you to do whatever you think best." Throwing this responsibility upon the boy at an early age probably had much influence on his character and after life, and prepared him for greater responsibilities.

Young McElroy attended country schools until he was fifteen; then studied for two winters in the high school of Greenfield, Ohio, then three years in the South Salem academy, and then finished his course in three years at Cornell university, New York, in June, 1872, receiving the degree of B. S. He then entered the law department of the State University of Iowa, where in June, 1873, he took the degree of LL. B.

Mr. McElroy was married July 2, 1873, to Miss Belle Hamilton, of Greenfield, Ohio, and August 18th they moved to Ottumwa, Iowa, where he has since lived, and has built up an excellent law practice. He formed a partnership with W. E. Chambers, in the law practice in 1875,

which continued until the death of that gentleman in 1890. M. A. Roberts was taken into the firm in 1887, and continued with it until 1895, when he became district judge. His present partner, Mr. George F. Heindel, became associated with the firm in 1894. Their practice is now practically confined to the district and supreme courts of this state, and the United States circuit court for the Southern district of Iowa.

Although taking no active part in politics Mr. McElroy has always been a republican and has served as an alderman of the city of Ottumwa. He has been a member

of the school board of that place for the last fifteen years, and president of the board for the last six years. He is a member of the Iowa State Bar association.

By his first wife Mr. McElroy has five children: Thomas Clifford, now in Cornell university; Carl Erskine, now with the wholesale grocery firm of J. G. Hutchinson & Company; Walter Hamilton, Ralph Theodore and Evalyn, all now in the high school at Ottumwa. After the death of his first wife, he was married, in 1884, to Elizabeth Millner and they have two children, Edna and Edith.

ROBINSON, JOHN BLAIR, a prominent physician and surgeon of Mt. Vernon, has won a high place in the practice of his profession. He was born May 29, 1852, in Knoxville, Marshall county, W. Va., in the same log cabin in which his father was born and brought up, and where his grandparents died. The house which has sheltered three generations of the Robinson family still stands. Dr. Robinson was the son of James Robinson, who was a farmer in good circumstances. He served three years in the union army as a private in Company B, Twelfth West Virginia volunteers. He was accidentally killed on September 9, 1886, his 57th birthday. His

mother, whose maiden name was Sarah Ann Harris, whose ancestors came from Connecticut, was born and still lives in West Virginia. Several of her ancestors served in the revolutionary war. And that they were ardent supporters of the union is attested by the fact that thirty-seven of her, and her husband's relatives offered their lives in the defense of their country during the war of the rebellion. The Terrills, a branch of her family, were instrumental in establishing the first Universalist church in West Virginia, and were uncompromising abolitionists, and noted for opposition to intemperance and capital punishment. The family is of Scotch and

Irish descent, and in America has representives through five to seven generations.

Dr. Robinson was the eldest of thirteen children, and early in life learned the lesson of self-reliance and helpfulness to others. He began when only 7 years of age to perform many kinds of farm work, and thus in advancing years found his field of operations rapidly increasing. In 1858 he began attending a subscription school in a log house. He never saw a free public school until he was 15 years of age. In 1872 he took a five-months' course in the Meadville academy at French Creek, W. Va. He attended the Waynesburg college, Waynesburg, Pa., during the years of 1873-4-5, completing the sophmore year. He taught in the public schools of West Virginia for a period of thirty-two months. In 1876 he began reading medicine in Wheeling, W. Va., under Dr. C. C. Olmstead, who is now a resident of Milwaukee, Wis. In 1877-8 he attended medical lectures in Cincinnati, Ohio, in the Pulte Medical college, and at Hahnemann Medical college, Chicago, graduating from the latter in 1879. The next year he came west to Iowa, locating at Mt. Vernon, where he began the practice of medicine with less than $100 in cash, and was in debt more than $500 to kind friends in the east, which required six years to pay in addition to keeping up his business expenses and supporting his family. By strict attention to business he soon acquired a lucrative practice. In 1883 he formed a partnership with Dr. Joshua Doron in the practice of medicine, and conducted a drug store at Mt. Vernon, which continued until the partnership was mutually dissolved. He did this in order to devote all of his time to the practice of medicine, and his work has been since that time confined to that of a general practitioner. That he has been successful is attested by constantly increasing practice, which has run throughout a course of nineteen years. When the war broke out he was too young to shoulder a musket, but for two or three years he carried the mail on horseback for the soldiers' families in the neighborhood, two or three times a week, from the nearest railroad station, a distance of five miles.

Dr. Robinson has always been a republican, and has frequently served as a delegate to county, congressional and state conventions. He has never been a candidate for any political preferment. He is now, and has been for several years, chairman of the Mt. Vernon school board, and served six consecutive years as a member of the city council. He has for several years held the position of physician to the Mt. Vernon board of health. He is a member of the Iowa Legion of Honor, Modern Woodmen of America, Knights of Pythias, Independent Order of Odd Fellows, and the Modern Brotherhood of America, in all of which he holds, or has held, important offices, and is a member of the grand lodge of Knights of Pythias of Iowa. He is a member of the Methodist Episcopal church, and holds official positions therein. He was married September 28, 1878, at Moundsville, W. Va., to Sarah E. Howe, a daughter of Rev. Wm. R. Howe. They have two children: Nellie Howe, born October 8, 1880, and James Arthur, born December 25, 1883. February 7, 1893, Mrs. Robinson died. He was again married, October 2, 1895, to Anna Coldren Shepler, a daughter of Samuel and Elizabeth Shepler, of Belle Vernon, Pa.

---

REHMANN, J. W., was born on the 14th day of December, 1856, in Schlemmin, Mecklenburg Schwerin, Germany. His early educational training was received in the village school, and was thorough and quite extended. His first higher education was attained in the Luebtheen seminary, where he earned distinction in music and the languages. The ancestry of Mr. Rehmann consists of a long line of peasants, without any great distinction, except that some were physicians to the court of Baden.

At the age of 16 Mr. Rehmann came to America to prepare himself for the ministry in the German Lutheran Synod of Iowa. He continued his college study for a year at Galena, Ill., following which he located in St. Sebald, Clayton county, Iowa. This was in 1873. He there taught district school for one year, at the same time giving private instructions in music. In the fall of 1875 he accepted the professorship of ancient and modern languages in the Cedar Valley seminary at Osage, Iowa. He shortly resigned this position, but remained in Osage where he gave instructions in music until 1890, making in the meantime two European journeys. During his stay abroad he pursued his studies in the languages and literature at the University of Berlin, and in music at the renowned Scharwenka conservatory in 1887–88, visiting, likewise, the educational institutions of Italy, France and England.

In September, 1890, he located at 1336 Sixth street, Des Moines, where he gives private lessons on the piano, in harmony and in the languages. He has also given many lectures on literary and musical topics, besides writing articles for various periodicals on those subjects. Mr. Rehmann has achieved considerable fame as a translator. Of his work in that direction may be mentioned the translation of Prof. Carl Reinecke's work on music, entitled: "What shall we play?" He has been an active member of the Society of Music Teachers of Iowa, having held all the different positions in that organization. He

was its president during the years 1895–96.

On the 13th of August, 1879, the subject of this sketch was united in marriage to Miss Anna M. Gundlach, of Putnam, Iowa, daughter of Christian and Mary Gundlach, who belonged to the first settlers in Fayette county, and were prosperous farmers. Mrs. Mary Gundlach died December 1, 1884, but Mr. Gundlach still enjoys good health at the age of 81 years. Not a single cloud has come to mar the married life of Mr. and Mrs. Rehmann to this day. Five children have been born to them, three daughters, Adelaide, Anna and Elsa; and two sons, John and Theodor.

Having lived in Iowa almost twenty-five years, and having engaged as an active instructor in the lines of higher education for most of that time, Mr. Rehmann is in a position to judge the character of our educational institutions, and he unhesitatingly pronounces them among the very best. To the advancement of everything pertaining to education he is a regular contributor. His religious faith is that of the German Lutheran; politically, he is a republican.

NICHOLS, EDMUND ELON, is a prominent attorney and politician of Perry. He is of English and Welsh descent and his great-grandfather, John Nichols, was a

soldier in the revolutionary war and was wounded in the battle of Concord. His grandfather, Hiram Nichols is yet living at Gouverneur, N. Y., at the age of over 90 years. His father, Orson K. Nichols, within three years after his marriage, enlisted as a volunteer in Company A, Fourteenth New York heavy artillery. He was in the seven battles of Wilderness, Spottsylvania, North Ann Talopatomy, Bethseda Church, Cold Harbor and siege of Petersburg. He was taken prisoner by the confederates at the time of the mine explosion at the siege of Petersburg, and died in Danville prison some time afterwards. Mr. Nichols' mother was Amanda L. Jones Nichols, a native of Vermont. Her

parents moved from Vermont across Lake Champlain and were among the earliest settlers of St. Lawrence county, N. Y. Her father and mother lived to the age of nearly 90 years. Mrs. Nichols remained a widow for a number of years after her husband's death, and then married Cyrus G. Dake, who is a professor in Epworth seminary, Epworth Iowa.

Edmund E. Nichols was born June 4, 1860, at Gouverneur, St. Lawrence county, N. Y. His earliest education was at private schools and at the Gouverneur Wesleyan seminary. At the age of 14 he removed with his mother to Potsdam, N. Y., where he attended the Potsdam State Normal school for four years, taking the classical course. When 19 years of age they removed to Delaware county, Iowa, where he taught school for one year and then tried farming for two years. At the end of that time he entered the law department of the State university at Iowa City, and graduated therefrom in the class of 1883. After graduating he went to Chicago and pursued his studies in the office of Josiah H. Bissell and W. S. Forrest, the eminent criminal lawyer. In 1884 he left the office of Forrest in Chicago and returned to Iowa, where he formed a partnership in the practice of law with T. R. North, of Adel. In Adel he remained until 1888, when he removed to Perry and formed a partnership with Walter W. Cardell, which continued until the spring of 1894. For ten years he has been the attorney for the Chicago, Milwaukee & St. Paul railway for that portion of the state, and was for four years county attorney. His business has consisted almost entirely of the trial of cases and in that department he has been very successful.

Mr. Nichols has always been a republican and there has not been a democrat in his family on either side for two generations. He has been active in local and state campaigns for ten years, and had the unanimous support of his county as a candidate for congress in 1896. As a political orator he has made considerable reputation for a young man. The *Perry Chief* of August 6, 1896, in regard to his speech at the congressional convention, says: "When Mr. Nichols took the platform he was warmly received and from the time the first words were spoken, he had the audience with him, and at times they broke loose with such enthusiasm that it was difficult for him to proceed. His speech was a great effort and completely captivated the convention and its several hundred visitors. At the finish he was given a perfect ovation, and delegates and republicans who had never met him climbed over the seats to congratulate him." Mr. Nichols is a member of the Knights of Pythias, Odd Fellows, Sons of Veterans, Shriners, and other orders.

In 1885 he was married to Dorothy I. Stevens, of Newell, Iowa. They have three children: Lillian, born in 1888; Dorothy, born in 1892, and Josephine, born in 1895.

---

WELLS, LUCIUS, secretary and treasurer of Deere, Wells & Company, an Iowa corporation, is one of the best known business men in the state, and is also prominent and active in the sound money democratic organization in the state. He has always been a democrat, not a seeker after office or other political distinction, but taking such interest in the politics of the country as a patriotic business man should. In explaining his attitude at present he says that he is a democrat from principle, and therefore could not join with the fusion elements in favor of the free and unlimited coinage of silver, which he thinks is not good democratic doctrine. Mr. Wells was born in Hampton, Ill., on the banks of the Mississippi river, February 9, 1845. His father's name was also Lucius Wells, and he was a farmer until he was 50 years old, after which he went into the logging and milling business. His ancestors came from England long before the revolutionary war, and many of them participated in the war. The mother was of Scotch-Irish descent and a great grand-niece of Ethan Allen. Her maiden name was Eunice Mc-Murphy. Mr. Wells emigrated from Vermont, and Mrs. Wells from New York, to southern Illinois, before the day of railroads, or about 1826. They were married at Swaneetown, Ill., and traveled from there to Galena, when there were no towns on the way except Carlisle, Vandalia, Springfield and Peoria. Their records of the journey, show several battles with Indians on the way, and when arriving at Rock river, where Dixon now stands, they were captured by the Indians and held prisoners for several days. They finally settled in Rock Island county, Ill.

Lucius Wells received his early education in the public schools, afterward attending the Lombard university, at Galesburg, one year, leaving at the end of that time to go into business with Deere & Company, the famous plow manufacturers of Moline, Ill. Mr. Wells facetiously remarks that he earned his first money holding the plow by the handles and has been handling the plow ever since, but not as a farmer. He steadily advanced in the firm, until in 1881, the present company was organized, the Council Bluffs house opened as a distributing point for several states, and Mr. Wells took charge of the establishment and has continued in that capacity successfully ever since.

Mr. Wells is a member of the Iroquois club, the leading democratic organization

of Chicago, and of the Omaha club, a social club. In 1892 he was a delegate to the democratic national convention. When the directory of the Trans-Mississippi and International exposition at Omaha was organized, Mr. Wells was made the only active member from Iowa, representing the state in the management of the exposition opening in May, 1898.

He was married in 1868 to Martha A. Wadsworth, whose ancestors for three generations were Germans, who settled in Maryland. They have had three children, Eunice M., born January 21, 1871, and now the wife of A. W. Casady; Marcus F., born September 14, 1873, and died March 14, 1874, and Cherrie, born February 4, 1884.

NICOLL, DAVID, an ex-member of the house of representatives in the Iowa legislature, a minister of the United Presbyterian church, and a farmer in Battle township, Ida county, Iowa, was born in Delaware county, N. Y., February 22, 1841. He was the son of Andrew and Margaret George Nicoll, and was the eighth born of their family of ten children. His father was born in Perthshire, Scotland, in 1797, and grew to manhood and married there. He emigrated to America in 1839 and located on a farm in Delaware county, N. Y., where the rest of his life was spent. His death occurred in March, 1870. His

wife survived him until April, 1890, and died at Clarence, Cedar county, Iowa. All but two of the children are still living. They are: Elizabeth, wife of John Beckwith, deceased; William, married and living in Delaware county, N. Y.; James, deceased; Andrew, married and living in Tarkio, Mo.; Margaret, wife of John G. Russell, living in Delaware county, N. Y.; Ann, wife of Allen Elijah, living in Clarence, Cedar county, Iowa; Christina, widow of John D. Imrie, living in Red Oak, Iowa; David, the subject of this sketch; Jane, wife of William Imrie, of Napa City, Cal., and Jeannette, wife of L. D. Boyd, of Red Oak, Iowa.

David was reared on a farm in his native county, and enjoyed the advantages of the common schools until 1859, when he entered the Andes academy. In September, 1861, he entered Jefferson college, at Cannonsburg, Penn. After completing the sophomore year, he enlisted at Pittsburg, Penn., August 29, 1862, in Knapp's Pennsylvania battery, for a term of three years or during the war. The battery was connected with the Second division, Twelfth army corps, and participated in the battles of Antietam, Chancellorsville and Gettysburg, besides numerous other skirmishes. In September, 1863, the Twelfth army corps was ordered west under General Hooker to join the army of the Cumberland. On the night of October 28, 1863, at Wauhatchie, near Chattanooga, Tenn., Mr. Nicoll received a gunshot wound in the right shoulder, resulting in the permanent and total disability of the right arm. Though disqualified by reason of this wound, for service in the field, he continued in the service of his country in the provost marshal's office in New York city until the close of the war, and received his honorable discharge May 17, 1865.

In September, 1865, he re-entered Jefferson college and remained there until January, 1866, when he went to Illinois and entered Monmouth college, graduating in June, 1867. After leaving college, he attended Theological seminary at Newbury, N. Y., and Monmouth, Ill., graduating from the latter in March, 1869. In September, of the same year, he settled at De Witt, Clinton county, Iowa, as pastor of the United Presbyterian church. He remained there for a period of fifteen years, when on account of impaired health, he resigned his pastorate, moved to Ida county and located on a farm of wild land purchased in 1880, when he donated a site on one corner of his farm, and a church building with a seating capacity of 150 was erected thereon. Since 1884 he has devoted much time and attention to the improvement of his farm, consisting of 320 acres. He has now a good modern house, barn and all other necessary buildings, and is extensively engaged in general farming and stock raising. Mr. Nicoll has always been a republican and is closely identified with all the best interests of the county and township in which he lives. He was twice elected to represent his county in the state legislature, being a member of the Twenty-second and Twenty-fifth General Assemblies. He has also taken a deep interest in educational matters, and has served continually as an officer of the school board of his township ever since he came to the county. He is a member of the G. A. R. and of the A. O. U. W.

January 6, 1870, he was married to Miss Isabella F. Brown, of New York. They have three sons: William E., married and living on the home farm; Thomas Edward and George David, both of whom are students in the electrical engineering department of the State Agricultural college at Ames.

---

ROBERTSON, JAMES CARSON, M. D. One of the leading physicians and member of the board of education at Council Bluffs is Dr. J. C. Robertson, who well deserves a place in this work as one of the progressive men of the state. He is the son of John Denny and Eliza Carson Robertson, the former a native of Pennsylvania, where he was born December 25, 1815, and the latter, born in County Tyrone, Ireland, October 9, 1813. The sire is of Scotch descent. He removed to Iowa in 1842, and in 1844 settled on a farm nine miles westward from Washington, Iowa, where he still resides. Eliza Carson came to America with her parents in 1833, and located in Stark county, Ohio, where, in 1841, she married the father of this subject. She was the mother of seven sons, six of whom grew to manhood. Three sons still survive, but the good mother was called to her reward March 11, 1897.

Dr. Robertson was born June 6, 1845, in the little village of Dutch Creek, Washington county, Iowa. His initial course of educational training was received in a log schoolhouse where a typical old-time school-master was master of the situation, if not of the studies attempted to be taught. He entered the Iowa State university in the spring of 1868, taking the classical course, and in 1870 matriculated in the medical department of the same institution, receiving the degree of M. D. at the end of three years.

He taught school during the time, and in that way earned money with which to defray the expenses of his education. In April, 1873, he commenced the practice of medicine at his old home in Washington county, where he built up a large and lucrative business. Although receiving practically the whole of the patronage of that section he found that the field was a limited one, and not being satisfied to be

forever a "country doctor" concluded to seek a location in city practice. October 1, 1877, he visited Council Bluffs, and became at once satisfied that the place offered the field he desired, so made arrangements immediately to remove to the new location. Events have proved the wisdom of the move, for he has not only a paying and constantly growing practice, but has made a neat sum in real estate investments, the last of which, at least, would have been out of the question in a small country town offering no opportunities whatever for speculation.

He spent the winter of 1882–3, in Bellevue hospital, N. Y., receiving the degree of M. D. November 14, 1883. He also in the same institution took a course in operative surgery under Prof. Joseph D. Bryant, and a private course in physical diagnosis under Prof. Ed. G. Janeway. He has been visiting physician to the W. C. A. hospital and St. Bernard's, being at this time president of staff of the last named; is a member of the American Medical association, Iowa State Medical society, Missouri Valley Medical society and Council Bluffs Medical society. He takes a keen interest in all matters pertaining to education, and is at this time serving as president of the board of education in Council Bluffs. He is a member of the

Masonic, Ancient Order of United Workmen, Woodmen of the World and St. Andrews orders.

The doctor was married in 1875 to Miss Helen S. Houck, of Washington county, Iowa. They have two sons: Andrew A., born April 6, 1878, and Ralph D., born March 19, 1885, who are attending the public schools of their home city. The doctor owns a modern home at 1006 Fifth avenue, and may be considered one of the fixtures of the city of Council Bluffs.

---

THOMPSON, JUDGE WILLIAM GEORGE, of Marion, Linn county, has borne a conspicious part in the affairs of the state

since 1853. He was born in Center township, Butler county, Pa., January 17, 1830. His father was William H. Thompson, a farmer in comfortable circumstances, who died at the age of 73 years. He was a quiet, peaceable man, was six feet five inches in height, weighed 240 pounds and had no surplus flesh. He never had a lawsuit or quarrel. Mr. Thompson's mother's maiden name was Jane McCandless. The grandparents on both sides were Scotch and Scotch-Irish, and emigrated to western Pennsylvania in 1798. Both of Mr. Thompson's parents were born and reared in Center township, Butler county, Pa., and

lived and died there. In forty-five years of married life Mrs. Thompson, mother of William G., was never one night away from home. They were all strict Presbyterians.

William G. received his early education in a log schoolhouse two and a quarter miles from home, where he attended every winter from the age of 7 to 17. He then began to teach school, working on the farm in the summer time. At the age of 19 he entered Weatherspoon institute as a student for two years, continuing to work on the farm during harvest time, and then entered the law office of Wm. Timblin, in Butler, Pa., as a law student, keeping the office open and doing chores for his board in the family of his employer. In two years he fitted himself for admission to the bar, and was given a certificate after thorough examination by a committee, of which Judge Daniel Agnew was chairman, October 15, 1853. A little more than a month later, November 27, young Thompson started for Iowa, not knowing where he would locate. In Davenport he heard about the promising little town of Marion and went there in December without money, books or acquaintances, but with good health and industry and ability. He decided to stay, and has never changed his location. His first dollar was earned in about two weeks after locating by attending to a suit before a justice of the peace, and from that time on he has never lacked a competence. His reputation as a lawyer extends all over the state and he has won considerable renown as a criminal lawyer, having defended in twelve murder trials and lost but two of them. He was in the famous Bever contested will case. Judge Thompson has been a leader in politics, and has always been a republican. He was a delegate to the convention at Iowa City February 22, 1854, which nominated James W. Grimes for governor, and founded the republican party. In 1854 he was elected prosecuting attorney of Linn county, the first republican ever elected in the county. At the expiration of his term he was elected a member of the state senate and was a member of the last senate held in Iowa City and the first one in Des Moines. He was presidential elector-at-large in 1864, and with C. Ben Darwin as the other elector-at-large, stumped the state and cast the vote of the state for Abraham Lincoln, which he says was the proudest act of his life. He was then elected district attorney for the district composed of the counties of Linn, Jones, Cedar, Johnson, Iowa, Benton and Tama, and served six years, declining another term. In 1879 he was appointed chief justice of the territory of Idaho by President Hayes, but declined to accept, but being urged to do so by his friends and members of congress he accepted long enough to hold the term of court then provided for, and in March, 1879, having completed the term, resigned. In November, 1879, he was elected to congress and in 1881 was re-elected. In 1886 he was elected to the lower house of the legislature and served two years. He was one of the committee from the house that prosecuted John L. Brown, auditor of state, before the state senate, sitting as a court of impeachment. In September, 1894, Mr. Thompson was appointed judge of the Eighteenth Judicial district by Governor Jackson, to fill the vacancy caused by the resignation of Judge Preston, and was immediately nominated and elected to that office, which he still holds, and is now re-nominated for second term. Judge Thompson has never been defeated when a candidate for office. His conspicuous ability and vigorous character and innate honesty have attracted people to him.

In 1862 Mr. Thompson was commissioned major of the Twentieth Iowa Volunteer infantry, and was in command of the regiment for over a year. He was severely wounded in the battle of Prairie Grove, Ark., December 7, 1862. He was at the siege and capture of Vicksburg, and then went to Texas and was present at the capture of Fort Aransas Pass. A post was established there and Major Thompson was put in command of the same, and so remained until 1864, when he was honorably discharged from the service. He is a member of the G. A. R. Post of Marion, and is a member of the Loyal Legion. Judge Thompson was married June 12, 1856, to Harriet J. Parsons, now deceased. They had one child, John M. Thompson, born May 24, 1875.

HINCHMAN, JOSEPH V., the leading banker of Glenwood, Mills county, was born May 13, 1831, in Rush county, Ind. He comes of English ancestry on his father's side and English and Irish on his mother's side. The father was James Hinchman, born in Monroe county, Va., in 1800, and settled in Rush county, Ind., in 1822, where he lived until his death, in August, 1882. He was a farmer, who was successful in life, and with his wife brought up thirteen children—ten boys and three girls. His wife was Nancy Nickel, born in 1804 and died March 18, 1897, aged 92 years and 6 months. She had lived and kept house on the same farm seventy-four years. At a family reunion, held at the old family homestead, September 4, 1880, the parents and children were all present, the children all being heads of families; sixty-seven children and grandchildren were present, and neighbors and friends to the number of 400. Joseph V. Hinchman lived on the farm until he was 21 years old, and received a common school education. He had no professional or business training until he went into business for himself. Teaching school at $20 a month, and boarding himself, was his first employment after leaving the farm. He came to Glenwood October 13, 1854, and opened the first drug store in the county, a business which he carried on for twenty-five years, and sold out in 1879. This was his first business venture, and it was started at a time when $1.50 to $2 a day was a very satisfactory profit for the

store. In 1869 he started a private bank in connection with the store, but sold it out in 1871, and helped organize the Mills County National bank, of which he was that year elected president, an office which he held for ten years. In 1882 he sold his interest in the National bank and established the Bank of J. V. Hinchman in Glenwood, of which he is still the proprietor. Here is a case where success has been achieved by steady, hard work and economy, and without any element of speculation. He started with a capital of $1,500, a portion of which was used in entering land in Polk and Mills counties, the remainder employed in

his drug store. This has grown until now Mr. Hinchman is rated at $300,000 above all debts. He never mortgaged a piece of property in his life. While accumulating this fortune he has been generous and has, within the past six years, given away to various churches and colleges $30,000; $25,000 to Des Moines college—the Baptist institution. Mr. Hinchman's has been a purely business life. He has devoted himself with remarkable singleness of purpose to achieving success in a financial way, and by honest dealing, promptness in meeting obligations, economy and industry, and attention to details, small as well as large, he has achieved great success. Like many other strong, successful men, he has no partners and no low-priced clerks or employes. He was a member of the whig party, and has always been a republican. As his generous gift indicates, he belongs to the Baptist church, and has for thirty-three years. Mr. Hinchman was married to Nancy L. Fish in Moundsville, Va., September 27, 1859. They have had only one child, who died in infancy. Mrs. Hinchman was born November 13, 1833, and is still living.

METZGER, GEORGE, postmaster of Davenport, is one of the best known republican politicians in the state. He has

been a familiar figure at republican state conventions for many years, and in Scott county he has been the trusted manager of the republican campaigns for a dozen years or so, during which time the party has made steady gains, and for three years has carried the county. Mr. Metzger was born in Germany, April 19, 1845. Five years later his father, Anthony Metzger, a German revolutionist, came to America to secure his liberty. He was one of the revolutionists of 1848–49, was exiled and fled first to Switzerland, and from there to the United States, in 1850. He was a well-to-do piano and organ manufacturer in Germany. He died in America in 1869. His wife was Elizabeth Mary Stichter, and her ancestors were soldiers under Napoleon Bonaparte, some of them of considerable prominence. She now lives with her son George, in Davenport. The Metzger family were all piano and organ manufacturers for many years in Germany, and the present Mr. Metzger has inherited their musical talent. George Metzger received his education in the public schools of America, but never attended college. He received private tuition in German reading and writing. In the fall of 1869 he took Horace Greeley's advice, and left his home in New York, and came to Scott county, Iowa, where he engaged in the music business, in which he had grown up from childhood. His first earnings, however, were as a private at $13 a month in the union army from 1862 to 1865. He was in the employ of John Hoyt, in his music house, from 1873 until 1894, when he was appointed custodian of public buildings and property, by Governor Jackson, and two years later was reappointed by Governor Drake. His term expired March 31, 1898, and less than a month thereafter, on April 28, 1898, he became postmaster of Davenport by appointment of President McKinley, and now holds that office.

Mr. Metzger has served on the republican county committee in Scott county since 1873, and was chairman of the committee for about ten years, and secretary most of the remainder of the time. He was reared an abolitionist, and soon became an intense republican. He enlisted August 8, 1862, in Company I, One Hundred and Twenty-fifth New York Volunteer regiment, and served until July 7, 1865. He was in the Second Army corps, commanded by Gen. W. S. Hancock, and participated in most of the battles with that corps, in the army of the Potomac, and was severely wounded in the head at Gettysburg, and again at Auburn Church, Va. He was first a private and later a corporal. He is a member and past commander of August Wentz Post No. 1 G. A. R., department of Iowa, and is now serving on the staff of General Gobin, national commander of the G. A. R., as an aid-de-camp. He was a member from Iowa, serving on the resolutions committee at the national encampment, G. A. R., at Cincinnati, in 1898. Mr. Metzger is past chancellor of the Knights of Pythias, and also belongs to the Woodmen of the World. While he believes in the divinity of God, he does not belong to any church.

He was married August 1, 1864, to Sarah E. Coon: They have had nine children, of whom five are living, namely: George L., born July 26, 1866; Sarah E., born March 20, 1869; Robert J., born June 23, 1871; John H., born December 20, 1873; and Mabel M., born March 22, 1882. Mrs. Metzger comes of an old Holland Dutch family that settled on the Hudson river about 200 years ago. She is a descendant of Aneka Jans. Many of her ancestors on both her father's and mother's side fought under Washington in the revolution, and Paulding, one of the captors of Major Andre, was her great uncle. Three of her brothers fought in the war of the rebellion, belonging to the Twelfth New York cavalry, and one of them was starved to death in a rebel prison.

George Metzger has marched in parades and taken part in the campaigns for every republican ticket from Fremont to McKinley, and says that he expects to do so for at least seven or eight more presidents. He is one of those industrious and persistent men who work for their party the year round, and never get tired of it. He has a very large acquaintance all over the state, and enjoys the personal friendship of hundreds of men who appreciate his generous qualities.

---

COTTLE, CASSIUS CLAY, practicing physician in Marshalltown, was born in Glasgow, Iowa, July 22, 1865, and is the son of the late Dr. William Wallace Cottle, of Fairfield, who died in 1880. Dr. W. W. Cottle was born in Belmont county, Ohio, in 1817, and was of English ancestry. He was engaged in the practice of medicine until about 1868, after which he was engaged in business pursuits and was highly successful, chiefly in banking. He was married in February, 1861, to Miss Elizabeth Endersby, a native of Illinois, also of English descent. He was a member of the legislature in 1860–61, and was an influential and useful citizen.

At the age of 5 years Cassius C. Cottle began to attend school and ten years later was ready for the preparatory course of Parsons college in Fairfield, where he entered as freshman in the year 1882. He remained there until the beginning of the senior year, when he went to the Commercial college in Iowa City for six months. He then entered Rush Medical college in Chicago in the winter of 1885, and was graduated in February, 1889. For a year

he was supervisor of the Cook County infirmary. He was a charter member of the Orio Literary society of Parsons college. In his boyhood Dr. Cottle had a liking for mechanics and was fond of working with tools. During vacations he worked at gunsmithing, carpentering and at one time was employed on the survey of the C., K. & N. railroad in Kansas.

He was a charter member of Chapter No. 5 of the Agassiz society of natural history and has been a member ever since. He regards its influence as an important one in directing him to a professional career.

Dr. Cottle located in Marshalltown August 3, 1889, and has been in the successful practice of his profession in that city continuously since that time. He is a member of the American Medical society, Iowa State Medical society, the Austin Flint Medical association and the Central Iowa Medical association. Of the latter he was secretary three years. The doctor has also been interested in real estate in Marshalltown and assisted in laying out an addition and building twenty-eight houses thereon. He cast his first vote for the republican ticket and has remained a straight republican ever since. He was married February 19, 1891, to Hattie May Church, of Marshalltown. They have had three children, Margaret E., born November 22, 1892, died December 9, 1892; Katharine E., born May 4, 1894, and William W., born January 23, 1898.

KILBORN, WILLIAM FRANKLIN. The history of the Kilborn family gives abundant proof that their name, in its varied orthography, is prominent among those whose ancestry can be traced hundreds of years. This name has long been associated with the history of England. It is mentioned in the rolls of Scotland, preserved in the Tower of London and Westminster Abbey, as early as 1336, and is

also mentioned by such noted English writers as Halsted and Brayley, who speak of the Kilborns being "seated" at Kilborn, in Yorkshire, afterwards settling in Cambridgeshire and Essex. "Seated," as used by English historians, signifies that the family heritage was located at the place mentioned. The occasion of the grant of arms to the Kilborn family is unknown, but history states: "This pedigree being authentically proved, is entered in the visitation of London, A. D. 1634.—Hon. St. George Richmond."

The family motto is, "Vincit Veritas." From Thomas Kilbourn, who left Cambridgeshire, England, in 1636 to locate with his family at Wethersfield, Conn., have descended all Americans bearing this name. The Kilbourns are well represented in Canada, Iowa, Wisconsin and Ohio. Payne Kenyon Kilbourn, of Litchfield, Conn., is among the prominent members of the family. He is author of the "History of the Kilbourn Family," a work dedicated to Hon. Byron Kilbourn, president of the Kilbourn Historical and Genealogical society, of Milwaukee, Wis., and for whom Kilbourn City, Wis., is named. Captain Whiting Kilborn, a Canadian settler, had a large family of sons and daughters, of whom Jared and David were noted pioneer preachers of the Methodist church. David Kilborn married Lavina Bowers, daughter of Samuel Bowers, a land owner and manufacturer of Berlin, Ontario. Their second son, William Franklin, was born July 19, 1854, at Washington, Ontario, where his parents lived until he was two years old, when they moved to Plattsville, Ontario, where his father engaged in a successful mercantile and manufacturing business. David Kilborn moved with his family in 1864 upon a farm near Grand Rapids, Mich., where Frank's time was divided between school and farm work. In 1873, at the age of 19, Frank Kilborn came to Cedar Rapids to continue his education. He secured a position in the photograph gallery of his uncle, Wilber F. Kilborn, where his artistic ability, industry and perseverance, with constant study, enabled him to become most proficient. In 1878 he purchased a half interest in the firm of W. F. Kilborn & Co., and became sole owner in 1886. Kilborn's gallery, the oldest in Iowa, has been constantly improved and enlarged until now it is one of the art centers of the west. Through constant application and study under competent instructors, Mr. Kilborn has been eminently successful in his work. His practical turn of mind led him to study chemistry, and his experiments resulted in the manufacture of a paper for photographers' use which was put upon the market in 1891 by the Western Collodion Paper company. This K. K. paper proved very satisfactory, and in 1894 the Eastman Kodak company, of Rochester, N. Y., negotiated for the plant. Messrs. Kilborn & Co. went to New York to establish the plant at Rochester, where Mr. Kilborn had charge of the business for one year, when he returned to Cedar Rapids. He then added a photographic supply department to his business. His chemical experiments during the last two years have resulted in the manufacture of other satisfactory papers. The products of the Kilborn company are fast becoming leading brands. Mr. Kilborn's great success lies in his continual personal supervision of every branch of his work. He is not only one of the leading men in his chosen profession but is also a man of influence in constantly widening circles. Mr. Kilborn was married at Lancaster, Ohio, September 4, 1884, to Miss Mary Carty, daughter of William J. and Ellen Carpenter Carty. Mrs. Kilborn is a lady of culture and refinement and an active worker in the church, social and literary life of Cedar Rapids. Mr. and Mrs Kilborn have two children: Mary Ellen, born July 28, 1885, and Paul Franklin, born June 17, 1897. Kilborn Place, with its spacious lawn, winding walks and drive among forest trees, is one of the most beautiful homes in Cedar Rapids.

MAMMEN, G. H., M. D. Engaged in a lucrative medical practice at Le Mars is Dr. Mammen, a young man whose early life was passed on the farm. His father was born in Germany, in 1840, of plain, honest and poor parents. He received no school advantages worthy of mention, and in 1865, when he had saved enough from his wages on the farm to procure a ticket, came to the United States, landing in New York without money and without friends. After a discouraging search for work, his persistency was rewarded, and for a month he worked as gardener, then came west, locating at Sterling, Ill., where he found employment on a farm. Through the practice of rigid economy he was enabled later to purchase a small tract of land, upon which he built a home. He was married in 1869 to Miss Johanna Margaretta Gesiene Landheer, a young lady who had emigrated from Germany the year before. She died June 10, 1881. The ancestors of both branches of the family were Germans and tradesmen.

Dr. Mammen was born on a farm in Hopkins township, Whiteside county, Ill., March 14, 1872, and is therefore 27 years of age, but notwithstanding his youthfulness he is a professional man of reputation and large practice. When 4 years old he entered the district school, and at 12 removed with his parents to Le Mars, where the process of education was materially retarded by the labor that was required on the farm. In 1886, however, he had the

privilege of attending the German Lutheran school, and so well was the opportunity improved that he finished the following year. Returning to farm work for the purpose of earning money with which to continue his schooling, he was soon enabled to enter the Le Mars Normal school and business college, where he remained one winter. He attended that institution as regularly as his means would permit until 1891, when he graduated. He commenced the study of medicine in 1891 in the office of Dr Richey, and in the fall of that year entered the Iowa State university, where he remained one term, then matriculated in Rush Medical college of Chicago,

from which he graduated May 23, 1894. He at once returned to his home in Le Mars and engaged in practice, with most gratifying success from the start, and is now regarded as among the leading practitioners of that city. He was chosen county physician in 1894, and in 1895 was elected coroner. These offices were given him by republican votes, he being an earnest supporter of that political faith. He is a member of the American Medical association, the Sioux Valley Medical association and the Missouri Valley Medical society, the A. O. U. W., I. O. O. F. and Knights of Pythias. He is medical examiner for the Equitable Life Assurance Society of the United States, American Union of New York, Mutual Reserve Fund Life of New York, Northwestern Life Assurance company of Chicago, Masons' and Odd Fellows' Union Aid association and the orders of A. O. U. W., I. O. O. F., I. W. of A. and Sons of Herman. June 11, 1896, he was married to Miss Emma Louise Ahrensfeld, of Chicago, Ill.

LLOYD, JOHN B., of Lake Mills, is a native of Ohio, having been born in Cincinnati on September 15, 1843. He received his education in the district,

intermediate and high schools of Cincinnati, and at the age of 16 became an apprentice in the trade of pattern making. While thus employed the civil war broke out and he promptly enlisted in Company L, Fourth Ohio Volunteer cavalry. He participated in twenty-two engagements, commencing with the fight at Perryville, Ky.; was in the campaign to Atlanta, and back to Nashville; then the siege of Nashville, after Hood was repulsed; then Selma and Macon, including the side expeditions, and throughout all of the severe fighting done by that division of the army up to June, 1865, when he was discharged. He returned at once to Cincinnati to finish the term of his apprentice-

ship, but a throat trouble, contracted in the army, compelled him to seek different employment. He engaged as bookkeeper for a large commission house, but at the end of one year purchased an interest in the firm of E. H. Cowing Company. Later he engaged in the manufacture of tobacco, then accepted the position of clerk on the steamer "Robert Mitchell," plying between Cincinnati and New Orleans. Tiring of that kind of a life he became bookkeeper for the wholesale candy manufacturing concern of E. Myers & Company, of Cincinnati. He remained with that company five years, then spent a year on the river; then conducted a coal business for a time, and finally became a member of the confectionery company with which he had formerly been connected.

Having secured a large tract of land in Winnebago and Hancock counties, Iowa, Mr. Lloyd concluded to come west and look after his new purchase. It was his intention at first to open up a stock farm, but the firm of Pickering, Hartley & Harwood, of Lake Mills, tendered him a position in their office, which was accepted and held for some eight years. He then bought out the firm, taking in with him as a partner Mr. D. N. Hill, and the business was carried on by these gentlemen until 1895, when Mr. Hill's interest was purchased by Mr. Lloyd. Later Jacob Larson and his son, John R. Larson, were taken into the firm, and it is now one of the leading banking, real estate and loan institutions in that section of the state. Mr. Lloyd is a nephew of Thomas Bebb, governor of the state of Ohio, away back in the 40's. He was married to Miss Mary C. Wade, daughter of Capt. R. M. Wade, who was commander of the gunboat "Corondolet" during the late war, and afterwards had charge of a number of boats on the lower Mississippi. Captain Wade was a grandson of Chief Justice Marshall, of Virginia.

Mr. Lloyd is a man of wide and varied experiences. He has seen the ins and outs of life as few men are privileged to see them, and the bruises against the rough edges have made him considerate, generous and knowing. He has reared a family of three children, two girls and one boy, all married. The son, Richard, is postmaster at Lake Mills.

Mr. Lloyd's success in life is to be largely attributed to his contact with and the advance of Iowa land, and it should serve as a valuable suggestion to young men.

INGHAM, Capt. William H., of Algona, one of the best known pioneer settlers of northwestern Iowa, is a native of the old empire state, came to Iowa nearly fifty years ago, and has been an active force in the development of the state.

His father, Harvey Ingham, was born in Herkimer county, N. Y., in 1795, and was a schoolmate and life-long friend of the eminent anti-slavery leader, Gerrit Smith. He learned the clothier's trade when a boy, and after attaining manhood he erected a woolen mill near the present town of Dodgeville. He acquired other mills and built up an extensive business on East Canada creek, which furnished the water power, and the place was known as Ingham's Mills. He was an active member of the Baptist church, and an ardent abolitionist and temperance worker. He lived to the advanced age of 87 years, having spent his long and useful life in the home he had established in his early manhood at Ingham's Mills. His wife was Sarah Schuyler, who was born in Montgomery county, N. Y., in 1799. She was a woman of most estimable character, a devoted wife and mother, noted for her benevolence and life-long helpfulness and sympathy for the poor and unfortunate. She died in her 82d year, a member of the Baptist church. The Inghams were large and muscular, and a long-lived family; five brothers of Harvey's father attained ages ranging from 90 to 99.

William H. Ingham was born at Ingham's Mills, N. Y., November 27, 1827. The district school furnished him instruction and discipline until he was 10 years old, when he was sent to a private school taught by Elder Beach, a Baptist minister and graduate of Yale university, one of the ablest men of his denomination in that day. Here the youth were immediately drilled in Greek, to gratify the teacher's ambition to have them read his favorite book, the Greek testament. After a course in Little Falls academy, William H., at the age of 17 years, went into business, working in his father's saw mill, flouring mill and woolen mill until he had acquired a good degree of skill in each. In 1846 he entered into partnership with his brother, Warren R., for the manufacture of lime, lumber and wooden ware, and they afterward purchased an oil mill. In 1849 William H., sold his interest and the following spring came to Washington county, Iowa, on a visit to his father's uncle, John Ingham, one of the early settlers of southeastern Iowa. On this trip he passed through Cedar Rapids, and was so much pleased with the enterprising new town that in 1851 he went there to live. Beginning with an engagement to survey and locate lands for the banking house of Greene & Weare, he was soon engaged in a general land business of his own. In November, 1854, he took a trip into Kossuth county, and foreseeing the coming development and prosperity of that beautiful, wild, but fertile country, he decided to make it his home. In January, 1855, he settled on a claim and soon after removed to a new home on section 24, township 96, range 29, in Kossuth county, not far from Algona. In 1865 he moved into the new town of Algona, where he engaged in a general land business and surveying. As the town grew and the demand was felt, he added the selling of exchange and opened the first eastern account from the county, with the since famous New York banker, Austin Corbin, in January, 1867, and drew the first draft for $100, in favor of James L. Paine. In January, 1870, Captain Ingham associated himself with Lewis H.

27

Smith in a general banking business, under the firm name of Ingham & Smith, and in May, 1873, organized the Kossuth County bank, which they still maintain in a prosperous condition, under the name of the Kossuth County State bank, being the first one in the county.

Soon after the massacre of the settlers around Okoboji and Spirit lakes, in the spring of 1857, by the Sioux Indians, under the leadership of Inkpadutah, Mr. Ingham joined a company which was organized by the settlers in his vicinity and marched to Tuttle's lake to protect the settlers on the frontier and quiet their fears of Indian raids. They found and drove off some Sioux Indians who had sheltered Umpashotah, and allayed the alarm of the people in that section. In 1862, after the terrible massacre of the settlers in southern Minnesota and the destruction of New Ulm, by the Sioux Indians, Mr. Ingham and W. B. Carey went to the ruins of the town in order to learn the extent of the outbreak. Upon his return a military

company was organized by authority of Governor Kirkwood, for frontier protection, and Mr. Ingham was commissioned captain. Ed. McKnight, of Humboldt county, was first lieutenant, and Jesse Coverdale was second lieutenant. Other companies were raised, and all were united in the Northern Border brigade, under command of Colonel Sawyer. After protecting the frontier until the summer of 1863, it was relieved from duty by a company under command of Captain Ingham. This volunteer organization of courageous pioneers guarded the settlements until December 29, 1863, when it was relieved by a troop of cavalry from General Sully's army and mustered out by Lieut. L. H. Smith, quartermaster of the Border brigade. Captain Ingham has always been a republican, but has never held an office to which a salary was attached, except that he was postmaster of Kossuth Center for a few years, in an early day. He does not belong to any church, though he has contributed to several; he is a member of the Masonic order.

On the 25th of November, 1857, he was married to Miss Caroline A. Rice, daughter of Thomas A. Rice, of Fairfield, N. Y. They have had eight children, six of whom are living. They are: Harvey, born in 1858, married to Miss Nellie Hepburn, in 1894, and lives in Algona, where he is editor of the *Upper Des Moines*, one of the best known weekly papers in Iowa, and postmaster; Anna C., born in 1860, died in 1895; Mary H., born in 1862, married in 1887, to Clarence M. Doxsee, and lives in Algona; Helen V., born in 1864, married to Charles W. Russell, in 1890, and lives in Omaha, Neb.; Charles S., born in 1866, and died in 1867; George W., born in 1868, and is now a practicing physician in Olympia, Wash., was married April 17, 1895, to Miss Emma Reed; Cornelia, born in 1870, was married November 25, 1897, to William J. McChesney, and lives in Iowa City; and Thomas Frederick, born in 1872, a graduate of the law department of the State University of Iowa, and now a practicing attorney at Spencer, Iowa.

Captain Ingham is now living in the quiet enjoyment of the results of a busy and fruitful life, with his children well settled, good health as his portion and his affairs so arranged that he can and does enjoy life. He is one of the most devoted disciples of Izaak Walton, and one of the most skillful. He knows the inhabitants of American waters, both salt and fresh, and how to lure them from their hiding places. He has caught everything from tarpon to trout

---

HUKILL, ANSON THEODORE, the efficient superintendent of the schools at West Waterloo, is descended from an old Virginia family. His ancestors were pioneers, both in Virginia and later in Ohio. He was born in Belmont county, Ohio, October 4, 1858, but came with his parents to Iowa county, when only 3 years old, so that in training and education he is practically a native of Iowa. His father, Joseph C. Hukill, is a retired farmer in comfortable circumstances, now living at Mt. Pleasant and enjoying the fruits of an industrious and economical life. His mother's maiden name was Mary J. Hall. In the country schools of Iowa county, Anson gained the rudiments of an education

and at the same time a spirit of independence and self-reliance that have been of great assistance to him in the battle of life. At the age of 18 he attended the public schools of Keota, Keokuk county, for a time and prepared himself for teaching country schools, in which he taught during the winter season. In the summer he worked on the farm. He was studious, had a natural aptitude for such work, and was so successful as a teacher that he could about take his choice of the schools of his county. He early determined to make teaching his profession and made plans to fit himself for that work, saving

all his money and employing all his spare time in reading and studying. In the fall of 1882 Mr. Hukill entered the Iowa City academy and spent one year there in preparation for college. He entered the State university at Iowa City in September, 1883, and graduated with honors from that institution in June, 1887, with the degree of bachelor of philosophy. Three years later he received the master's degree from the same institution. During his course at the university he paid his way acting as teacher in the academy from which he formerly graduated. He was a member of the Zetagathean Literary society and was honored by being chosen at different times to fill every office in the society. His college course was finished without financial assistance from any source.

After graduating he became superintendent of the West Branch schools, and retained that position for five years, giving the best of satisfaction in that capacity and making a great success of his work. Removing then to Williamsburg he entered upon the duties of superintendent of schools of that place, which position he held for seven years. He now occupies the more important position of superintendent of the schools of West Waterloo. He holds the highest professional certificate issued, a state diploma, and his work at that point has been eminently successful.

In political matters Professor Hukill has been a republican, but although many times solicited to do so, has never allowed his name to be used as a candidate for any office. He is a prominent Mason, having attained the Royal Arch degree, and a member of the I. O. O. F. He was married July 28, 1887, to Josie Van Meter, of Iowa City. They have one son, Olin V., born August 30, 1890. They are members of the Methodist Episcopal church.

---

SCHROEDER, FRANK NICHOLAS, president of the Schroeder-Kleine Grocery company, of Dubuque, is one of the earliest settlers of the Key city. He came with his parents from Mobile, Ala., to New Orleans and from New Orleans to Dubuque on a steamboat, landing in that city May 17, 1855. He was born in Deikirch in the grand duchy of Luxembourg, Germany, July 16, 1849. His father was Nicholas Schroeder, a carpenter and builder, and his mother's maiden name was Josephine Grasser. Her father, Nicholas Grasser, was a captain in the French army and was with Napoleon's army in Russia when the Russians burned the city of Moscow and left Napoleon's army to starve. He was one of seven survivors who succeeded in returning to France. The rest of the company were killed in battle, or perished with hunger and cold. The Schroeder family early emigrated to America to seek a wider field and better opportunities in life. The son, of whom we speak, earned his first money in his new home carrying papers. He began his business career as a porter in the wholesale grocery house of W. H. Rumpf, in Dubuque, January 19, 1865. He was steadily advanced; became shipping clerk and later house salesman,

and continued with Mr. Rumpf until August 1, 1882. During that month he formed a partnership with J. H. Kleine, under the firm name of Schroeder & Kleine, wholesale grocers. This firm carried on a prosperous business until November 1, 1892, when, with Mr. J. H. Kleine, Mr. Fred Rumpf and Mrs. J. P. Farring, he incorporated the Schroeder-Kleine Grocery company, of which Mr. Schroeder is president. He has always been a member of the democratic party, and in 1897 was chairman of the Dubuque county committee. He was a delegate to the democratic national convention in 1884, and is now county

treasurer of Dubuque county, elected in 1895 and re-elected without opposition in 1897. He belongs to the Pius St. Alphonsus Benevolent society, R. C. M. P. of the state of Iowa, Dubuque Germania society, Dubuque Luxembourger society, Dubuque Business and Traveling Men's association, and the Catholic church. He was married November 7, 1871, to Katherine Beck. They have seven children: William, born May 20, 1874; George W., born June 10, 1876; Anna, born January 17, 1878; John P., born May 12, 1881; Mary, born November 23, 1882; Kate, born May 27, 1885; and Josephine, born August 17, 1891.

CLARK, CHARLES CLAPP, the well known lawyer of Burlington, and county attorney, is a son of J. Warren and Sophia M. Clapp Clark. He was born July·10, 1859, in Huntsburg, Geauga county, Ohio. The original American ancestor on the Clark side was William Clark, who came to Massachusetts about 1630. Roger Clapp, the founder of the mother's family in this country, settled in Massachusetts about the same time, Mr. Clark's father served in the war of the rebellion as a union soldier and died from the effects of that service, in August, 1867. His wife died in November, 1884. The parents had removed to

Iowa City, Iowa, about 1856, and here, in the public schools and in the State university, Charles C. received his education. He took the degree of A. B. in June, 1881, and the degree of A. M. was conferred upon him in June, 1884. After graduation in 1881, he took the position of principal of the Fairfield, Iowa, high school, where he taught two years, and became teacher of mathematics in the high school in Burlington. He resigned that position and entered the State University Law school in 1885, entering in the senior year, having studied during the previous year and summer to make up the junior year work, which he succeeded in doing, as he passed a creditable examination. He graduated in June, 1886,

and in August returned to Burlington and entered into a very desirable law partnership with John J. Seerley, since elected to congress and referred to elsewhere in this work, and the practice and partnership have continued ever since. Unlike his partner, Mr. Clark is a republican, and when Des Moines county became republican in 1896, his party services and professional ability were recognized by an election to the office of county attorney. This was repeated in the fall of 1898. He served as a member of the school board from 1891 to 1897. Mr. Clark belongs to the Masonic fraternity and was junior grand warden of the grand lodge of Iowa, in 1896-97. He was married September 5, 1885, to Ella Lamson, of Fairfield, Iowa. They have one child, Margaret M.

---

WHIPPLE, WILLIAM PERRY, lawyer, orator and scholar, member of the law firm of Gilchrist, Whipple & Montgomery, of Vinton, was born in that town December 26, 1856. His parents settled in Benton county in the year 1854, purchasing their land of the United States government at $1.25 an acre. The father, Cyrenius T. Whipple, is now an extensive land owner there and one of the largest cattle raisers in eastern Iowa. His mother, Nancy Cline Whipple, is a native of Indiana. Both parents are living.

William P. Whipple attended the common schools near Vinton during his boyhood days and entered the State university in 1873, graduating from the collegiate department in June, 1877, and from the law department in 1878. He was a member of the Zethagathian society, and was its representative at the commencement exercises in 1876. He was one of the five selected by the faculty to compete in the junior oratorical contest, securing third place. He was awarded first prize in June, 1878, for the best essay on the subject: "Should the Grand Jury be Abolished?" He began the practice of law in Vinton, August 14, 1878, and the following year was elected city attorney and held the office four consecutive terms. After several years of practice he became associated with Judge George M. Gilchrist. The firm of Gilchrist & Whipple soon became one of the strongest law firms in that part of the state. Mr. Whipple's law firm is now Gilchrist, Whipple & Montgomery, composed of Judge Geo. M. Gilchrist, W. P. Whipple and S. B. Montgomery. They have a branch office in Belle Plaine and enjoy a large and lucrative practice. Mr. Whipple was at different times associated as partner with Cato Sells and Morris Zollinger. Mr. Whipple is president and attorney for the Iowa Paint company, and represents R. G. Dun & Co. and other leading commercial

agencies. The firm is attorney for numerous large corporations. Mr. Whipple's financial and professional success is a demonstration of what energy and ability can accomplish of their own force, as he has been the architect of his own fortune.

Mr. Whipple was married September 7, 1881, to Miss Catherine D. Joyce, who was at that time assistant principal of the Vinton high school. She died April 14, 1886, leaving two sons: Cyrenius and Milo. Mr. Whipple was again married October 18, 1887, to Miss Jennie Keith, a teacher in the primary department of the Vinton schools. His son, Cyrenius, was drowned in the Cedar river below Vinton in June, 1897, and his untimely death called forth universal mourning in the town where he was so well liked. The local papers at the time were filled with tributes to his memory. Mr. Whipple has always been a republican. Though he has not been a candidate for office he has, nevertheless, contributed his full share to the success of his party. He is president of the board of

education, a trustee of the Presbyterian church, and a member of the Odd Fellows fraternity.

———

ITEN, LOUIS, of Clinton, Iowa, was born in Unterageri, Switzerland, Canton Zug., in 1888. His father, John Joseph Iten, was born in 1806 in Unterageri, Switzerland, and was owner of a brickyard in that city. He was also first lieutenant and bodyguard of Louis Philippe of France, in 1830. In 1850 Louis came with his father to America and settled in Milwaukee, Wis. He received his education in the city of his birth, and later finished in America, at Geneseo, Ill.

In 1837 he removed to Davenport, Iowa, where he went into the vinegar business with his uncle, Antonio Iten. In 1853 he formed a partnership with William Smith and continued in business with him until 1867. Since that time he has been engaged in the bakery and cracker business. In 1893 he went to Clinton, Iowa, and erected a cracker factory, conducted under the

firm name of L. Iten & Sons. During the civil war he was a member of the Union League and is a charter member of the A. O. U. W., of Rock Island, Ill. In 1861 he married Theresa Zeiglar, of Rock Island. To this union have been born seven children, six of whom are living: John J., born in 1862; Anna M., born in 1864; Louis C. born in 1865; Lizzie G., born in 1867; Willie F., born in 1869, deceased; Frank J., born in 1873; Sadie M., born in 1876.

CHESHIRE, THOMAS ABBOTT, senator from Polk county, and one of the leading lawyers in the city of Des Moines, is the son of John Wesley Cheshire, of Poweshiek county, who died September 5, 1877. His mother was Grace M. Vestal, a daughter of a clergyman and southern whig, very much opposed to slavery, who emigrated

to Iowa in 1851. Mr. Cheshire and Miss Vestal were married May 15, 1851. He was born in North Carolina and lived there from 1833 until 1853, when he came to Iowa. His family had always been slaveholders. He returned south in 1854, but seeing that the slavery question was bound to provoke a war, he returned to Iowa in 1858, and when the war broke out he volunteered in Company B, Fortieth Iowa infantry, and went back to the south to fight the battles of his country, against his place of birth and many of his kinsmen. He was editor and proprietor of the *Montezuma Republican*.

Thomas A. Cheshire was born April 2, 1854, in a log cabin erected by his father

upon a quarter section of land that he entered in 1853, in Poweshiek county. His first schooling was obtained in a log schoolhouse, about eight miles south of Grinnell, which was of the primitive kind, both as to furniture and books used.

The family removed to Montezuma in 1864, the father having been discharged from service because of disability. Thomas attended Iowa college in Grinnell and the university in Iowa City, but his health did not permit him to finish the course and he entered his father's printing office to learn the trade, helping his father in the editorial work at the same time. In early childhood he had determined to be a lawyer. so he entered the law department of the University of Michigan in 1874, and was graduated in 1876, and at once began the practice of law in Montezuma. His father's death the next year made it necessary for himself and brother to take charge of the paper. They bought it from the estate and conducted it until 1880, when Thomas A. went into partnership with Charles R. Clark, for the practice of law. The next year he sold his interest in the paper to George R. Lee, of Oskaloosa. He continued in his practice until the fall of 1886. He was nominated for county attorney that year, but having come to Des Moines to prepare an argument for the supreme court, he became so much impressed with the advantages of being in Des Moines that he declined the nomination for county attorney, and immediately after election located in Des Moines, entering into partnership with Capt. J. W. Carr. The latter went to Kansas about six months later and Mr. Cheshire practiced alone. Four years later he went into partnership with Cole & McVey. In June, 1893, Judge Cole retired and the firm became McVey & Cheshire, until June, 1896, when it was dissolved. Mr. Cheshire has practiced alone since that time and has been highly successful, especially as an insurance lawyer, and in personal injury cases against manufacturing and railroad corporations, and general civil practice.

For four years, from 1890 until January 1, 1895, Mr. Cheshire was assistant attorney-general, under John Y. Stone, and argued practically all the criminal cases appealed to the supreme court, besides preparing many opinions for the attorney-general. In the summer of 1898 he was nominated by acclamation for senator from Polk county, and was elected by 3,100 plurality. He was re-elected four years later, without opposition in his own party and by a larger majority. During his first session he was chairman of the committee on labor, and was member of committees on judiciary, cities and towns, printing, judicial districts and agriculture, and took a prominent part in changing the laws providing a salary for constables and justices of the peace, instead of fees. The next session he was chairman of the committee on cities and towns, and was second on the committee on judiciary, and served on other important committees. He took an active part in the codification of the laws, and the making of the code of 1897, and as chairman of the committee on cities and towns; gave special attention to the laws in regard to cities and towns, the most intricate part of the codification. He offered an amendment to the revenue bill, providing for the taxation of telegraph, telephone, express and sleeping car companies, which became known as the Cheshire amendment and attracted wide attention. It is similar to the laws of Indiana, Ohio and Kentucky, and provides for the valuation of these properties by taking the market value of stock, the bonded indebtedness being deducted, and also the personal property and real estate taxed locally, and dividing the amount thus obtained by the number of miles regularly operated or run by the company, and fixing this as the value of the property per mile, to be assessed as other property. This would have resulted in largely increasing the taxes of these corporations. The senate failed to agree on the amendment, but it was adopted by the house, and the conference committee reported a compromise measure which embodied some of the features of the amendment, and this brought largely increased revenues to the state from these corporations. Senator Cheshire was chairman of the committee on judiciary in the senate in 1898, and was a member of other important committees. He again offered his revenue measure, but it was swallowed up in other business,—particularly the board of control bill. A substitute bill to tax the cars of fast freight lines, oil companies, coal and refrigerator cars, etc., was reported by the ways and means committee and passed the senate, but it was defeated in the house by the sifting committee.

Mr. Cheshire was married September 18, 1879, to Virginia B. McClellan. One daughter, Virginia, was born to them July 26, 1880. Mrs. Cheshire died August 3,

1880. Mr. Cheshire was married a second time, December 3, 1884, to Harriet L. Hills. They have two children, Henry Hale, born January 1, 1890; and Everett Emmett, born June 23, 1893.

In the practice of his profession and in the discharge of his duties as a legislator, Senator Cheshire has maintained a high degree of honor, and it has never been said that there was anything questionable in his motives. He has kept himself free from all influences that would interfere with the untrammeled exercise of his judgment and has fearlessly and ably stood up for his convictions.

---

BANDY, DR. ROBERT S., of Tipton, is a progressive dentist, a native Hawkeye,

and has enjoyed the best educational advantages the state affords. He was born in Des Moines county, Iowa, November 26, 1863. His father, John Bandy, was among the earliest settlers of this state. He came to the territory of Iowa with his parents in the spring of 1837, at the age of 10 years. He settled in Des Moines county and part of the old home there still remains in the family name. John Bandy was one of the famous California Forty-niners. He crossed the plains in company with other daring and ambitious men in 1849 and remained in California until 1857, returning by way of Panama and New York. He was married in 1860 to Miss Guelmia Stathemn, whose family came to Iowa from Ohio at an early day. They lived in Des Moines county until 1865, when they removed to Minnesota and lived there until 1884, when they returned to Iowa. Mr. Bandy served during the war in the Second Iowa cavalry, commanded by Col. Wm. P. Hepburn.

Robert S. Bandy, having been prepared to enter college, attended at Parsons college in Fairfield until 1888, when he entered the dental department of the State University of Iowa and was graduated from that institution with the class of 1891. He commenced the practice of his profession in Fairfield, but soon after went to Davenport to become associated with Dr W. O. Kulp, then the leading practitioner and educator in the state. In 1893 he located in Tipton, where he has since been engaged in the successful practice of dentistry. Being a studious and progressive professional man, he belongs to the Iowa State Dental association and the Eastern Iowa Dental society.

Dr. Bandy was married in 1893 to Miss Rebecca Thomas, of Iowa City. They have one child, Geneva Kathryn, born June 16, 1896.

CLARK, BENJAMIN BUCKINGHAM, president of the Red Oak National bank, was born in Williston. Vt., July 7, 1848. His parents, Philo Clark, of Williston, and Martha A. Buckingham, of New Milford, Conn., were both of old New England families. Among their ancestors were soldiers of the French and Indian wars and the American revolution, as well as men distinguished in colonial history, among others, Thomas Buckingham, one of the founders of Yale college. Philo Clark was a director, from the time of its organization until his death, in the Merchants Bank of Burlington—one of the oldest banks in Vermont. He was also interested in western lands, and in 1855 entered large tracts of government lands in southwestern Iowa, the most of which is still in the possession of the family.

Benj. B. Clark received his education at Williston academy, which was at one time under the principalship of Rev. Mr. Arthur, whose son, Chester A. Arthur, was once a student there.

In 1869 Mr. Clark came west as far as Burlington, where he was for a short time in the employ of Gilbert, Hodge & Company, lumber dealers. Soon, following the line of railroad as fast as it was completed, he opened lumber yards with Mr. Justus Clark at Afton and Villisca. In the autumn of the same year he established himself finally in Red Oak, where a lumber yard was opened under the firm name of Justus Clark & Company. This firm continued in business until 1883, when the yard was disposed of, and the Red Oak National bank was organized, with Justus Clark as president and B. B. Clark as vice-president. In

1895, after the death of Mr. Justus Clark, B. B. Clark became president.

In politics Mr. Clark is not an extreme partisan, but is inclined to be an independent, and to support the party and candidate of which his judgment at the time approves.

He has been a member of the Congregational church since the early days of the organization of that denomination in Red Oak.

In 1870 Mr. Clark was married to Mary Z. Douglas, of Williston, Vt., and in 1886 to Rosa Shirk, of Peru, Ind. He has two children, a son and a daughter.

HOLBROOK, PARKER KIMBALL, is a well-known banker of Onawa, Monona county, where he was born September 23, 1864. His father, B. D. Holbrook, in partnership with a brother, C. H. Holbrook, established in 1857 the banking business which is now conducted by father and son. B. D. Holbrook was born in Somerset county, Pa., May 22, 1834, and was the son of Henry L. and Mary (Connelley) Holbrook. He was educated in Washington and Jefferson college, Pennsylvania, and came to Iowa in March, 1855. He was one of the founders of the town of Onawa, and has been prominent in the democratic party of Iowa—several times a delegate to democratic national conventions. He has been very successful in business, owning a large amount of real estate besides his interest in the banking house of Holbrook & Brother. He was married May 13, 1862, in Pittsburg, Pa., to Mary F. Oliver, born July 14, 1838, in Donaghmore, Ireland, daughter of Henry W. and Mary Brown Oliver, whose family came to this country in 1842 and settled in Pittsburg, where they have resided ever since. The sons are engaged in the manufacture of iron and steel on a large scale. Mr. and Mrs. Holbrook came directly to Onawa, making the journey from Iowa City west by stage. Nine children were born to them, of whom five are now living, four sons and one daughter; Parker K. is the oldest. Thomas Holbrook, the pioneer of the family in America, sailed from Weymouth, England, March 20, 1655, and settled in Weymouth, Mass., where he lived until 1674. His son, born in England in 1625, died in Braintree, Mass., in 1697. Deacon Peter Holbrook, his son, born in 1665, died in Minden, Mass., in 1712. His son, Joseph Holbrook, born in 1679, died in Billington, Mass., in 1765. Josiah, his son, born in 1714, was a colonial soldier in two French wars, and moved with his family from Massachusetts to New York, settling in Pompey. He was twice married, to Peggy Ives and to Mary Moffitt, and died in 1783. His son, David, born in 1760, served as a soldier during the revolutionary war and was severely wounded at the battle of Bennington. After the revolution he settled in Lafayette, N. Y., where he practiced medicine until his death in 1832. His son, Henry L., was born in 1799. He moved to Somerset, Pa., where he was, for many years, principal of the Somerset academy. In 1865 he removed to Onawa, Monona county, and there con-

tinued to reside until his death in 1874.

Parker K. Holbrook received his education in the public schools, graduating from the Onawa high school in the class of 1880, and prepared for college in St. Joseph's academy and Hiatt's academy, of Iowa City. He entered the State university in the class of 1886, but did not complete the course, leaving in the spring of 1885 to enter upon an active business career. While in the university he was a member of the Irving institute and Sigma Chi fraternity. Upon leaving the university he went to Onawa and took a place in his father's bank, where he has remained ever

since, except the time spent in the bank of Marcellus Holbrook, in Missouri Valley, and in that of Weare & Allison, in Sioux City, for the purpose of securing a business education. He became cashier of Holbrook & Brother's bank April 1, 1889, and September 1, 1894, he purchased the interest of C. H. Holbrook in the banking house, and continued business under the old firm name. Mr. Holbrook has always been a democrat but has not sought office. He was a member of the Iowa delegation to the democratic national convention of 1892, and to the convention of the national democratic party in Indianapolis in 1896. He was unable to support the Chicago platform of 1896, upon which Bryan was a presidential candidate. He was elected regent of the State university in February, 1896, and was made a member of the executive committee of the board of regents in the spring of 1897, and chairman of that committee that fall, which place he still holds. He is also chairman of the building committee and of the library committee, which positions require much work on account of the destruction of the library by fire, and the large amount of building being done under the one-tenth mill levy for this purpose. Mr. Holbrook is a Mason, and a member of the Knights of Pythias, having passed all the chairs in both lodges. He is not a member of any church, but his wife is an Episcopalian. He was married June 7, 1893, to Virginia, daughter of Albert C. and Frances Suydam Robinson, in Green Bay, Wis. They have one son, Weare H., born April 15, 1896.

----

PACKARD, STEPHEN BENNETT, now living in quiet upon his large farm near Marshalltown, has had a notable career, and his name is connected with the history of some of the most troublous times the United States has ever seen.

He is the best known for his connection with the reconstruction days in Louisiana, where he was elected governor in 1876, and afterwards abdicated as a part of the settlement of the presidential deadlock, out of which Hayes was made president. Governor Packard was born in Auburn, Me., April 25, 1839. His parents were Stephen Packard and Roxanna Briggs Packard. Stephen Packard was a son of Nehemiah Packard, who was born in Massachusetts in 1762, and Betsey Packard, born in 1764. Nehemiah Packard, grandfather of S. B., was a son of Samuel Packard, and his wife, a sister of Gen. Benjamin Lincoln, of revolutionary fame. Nehemiah entered the army at the age of 14 years and served as a drummer boy and as drum major with his uncle, Benjamin Lincoln, until the end of the war. The Packard family came from Ipswich, England, in 1638, and settled in Bridgewater, Mass. Samuel Packard was the first of the family in this country. They afterwards moved to Maine, where they attained prominence. The governor's father was born in North Auburn, Me, September 12, 1793, and died there December 25, 1870. He was a mill owner and held several local offices. He served in the militia in the war of 1812. His wife, Roxanna Briggs, came from a wealthy and influential family and had brothers and sisters residing in Auburn. Stephen Packard was a direct descendant of the original Samuel Packard, who came from Ipswich, England in 1638. Young Stephen went to the village school until he was 16 years of age, when he took a course in the Westbrook seminary, and at the age of 20 began the study of law with Hon. C. W. Walton, afterwards one of the justices of the supreme court of Maine. He was president of the Philomathian Adelphi society of the seminary during all the time he was a student there. He taught two terms of school in 1860, previous to beginning the study of law. He left the law office October 15, 1861, and joined the Twelfth Maine regiment of infantry as first lieutenant of Company G. He was promoted to be captain of Company B, and served until the regiment was mustered out in December, 1864. The regiment was assigned to Gen. Benjamin F. Butler's division, which participated in the Louisiana campaign, and in the capture of New Orleans and Port Hudson. In 1864 Captain Packard served as judge advocate in New Orleans under General Reynolds. In July, 1864, the regiment joined Sheridan's army, being a part of the Nineteenth army corps, and served with it until it was discharged. Captain Packard's company was the color company of the regiment during this campaign, and when it was mustered out he was designated to convey the regimental colors to Augusta, Me., and deposit them with the governor of the state, which duty he proudly performed.

While in New Orleans Captain Packard met Miss Emma Frances Steele, a daughter of Captain Peter Steele, an old and respected resident of New Orleans, and they were married in December, 1863, in New Orleans. After he was discharged from military service, Captain Packard went to New Orleans and began the practice of law. In 1867 he was elected delegate to the state constitutional convention, and was made chairman of the board of registration, consisting of seven men, who were charged with the duties of administering the civil affairs of the state from the adjournment in April, 1868, until the inauguration of the new state government in July, 1868. He was appointed register of conveyances for the city of New Orleans and served until April, 1869, when he was appointed United States marshal for the district of Louisiana. At this time Governor Packard was in the height of his power in the state and was recognized as the controlling force in the politics of Louisiana. He was the personal representative of President Grant. As a delegate to the republican national convention in 1876 he voted for the nomination of Blaine only after it did not seem possible to secure a third nomination for President Grant. He was reappointed by President Grant, and in November, 1876, was elected governor of the state. He had made an active and aggressive campaign in the state and was never intimidated or insulted by the southerners, Yankee though he was. He went into the worst districts in the state, where it was supposed that a northern man or republican was hardly safe at all, and yet he was so feared and respected that he was entirely safe. He was inaugurated governor in January, 1877, but in the manipulation of the electoral returns and in the settlement of the famous Hayes-Tilden presidential contest, he was compelled to abdicate, which he did April 25, 1877. A committee appointed by the Hayes administration obtained a quorum of members in the so-called Nicholas legislature by breaking a quorum in the state house legislature, which supported Governor Packard. It was part of the arrangement by which Hayes became president.

Governor Packard was appointed United States consul at Liverpool in July, 1878, and served until July, 1885. Returning from England, he sought a more quiet life and purchased his now famous Strathmore stock farm near Marshalltown, where he now resides with his family. Since living in Iowa he has served as a member of the Iowa Columbian commission, which had charge of the Iowa exhibit at the World's fair, and on the Iowa commission at the Trans-Mississippi exposition at

Omaha. He is a charter member of the Iowa commandery of the military order of the Loyal Legion, and is a member of the Iowa Society of the Sons of the American Revolution.

Governor and Mrs. Packard have six children living, three sons and three daughters, viz.: Ada, born September 4, 1867; Blanche, born January 21, 1869; Stephen Bennett, Jr., born September 19, 1871; Walter Steele, born November 31, 1875; Sidney Steele, born August 7, 1877; Ella, born February 6, 1879.

———

MAGEE, REV. JOHN CALVIN., A. M., D. D., is a prominent member of the Upper Iowa conference of the Methodist Episcopal church, and has served as pastor of some of the strong churches of that body. For six years he was presiding elder, an office which he now holds, residing in Cedar Falls. He was delegate from the Upper Iowa annual conference to the quadrennial general conference, the law-making body of the denomination, which met in Omaha in 1892, being first in the order of election on the delegation.

Dr. Magee is the son of David F. and Abigail Rankin Magee. His father served in the union army as first lieutenant, Company D, Ninth Iowa infantry. His ancestors on both sides of the house were Scotch-Irish. His great-grandfather was a soldier for the colonies in the revolutionary war. His grandfather was a prominent citizen of western Pennsylvania, and lived to the age of 101 years. Dr. Magee was born in Stover's Place, Center county, Penn., October 31, 1845, and was the oldest of eleven children. His parents came to Iowa in 1855, and his boyhood was spent on the farm in that pioneer time. In the debating schools of that period he developed a talent that served him well in later days. Many times during the exciting early days of the war his boyish voice was heard in patriotic appeals in the war meetings. Upon the father's return from the war, the boy, having reached a lawful military age, enlisted and in less than one month, after laying down the ferule of a country schoolteacher, was standing musket in hand on picket guard in Alabama. He served from its veteran organization in the Ninth Iowa infantry, which had at Pea Ridge won the sobriquet of the "Iowa Grey Hounds." He was with the regiment on Sherman's famous Atlanta campaign, and in pursuit of Hood, the march to the sea, through the Carolinas, and on the homeward march,

and on the final grand review at Washington, D. C. He returned to the state with the regiment at "muster out." During his service he was promoted to the rank of a non-commissioned officer. He joined the G. A. R. in its early history; has served several years as a post chaplain, and was the commander of J. W. McKenzie Post No. 81 in Hampton in 1898. He served as department chaplain of Iowa, G. A. R., in 1890 and 1891.

In a very short time after his return from the war he entered the collegiate institute at Hopkinton, in which he had previously been a student. Later he entered

Upper Iowa university at Fayette, from which he was graduated and received the degree, master of arts. For some time he was a student of theology at Garrett Biblical institute in Evanston, Ill. In 1870 he was admitted to the ministerial ranks of the Upper Iowa conference and since that time he has served continuously in his chosen calling. In addition to his ministerial work Dr. Magee has interested himself in educational matters and has served for several years as alumni trustee of his alma mater. Occasional articles from his pen appear in the periodicals of his church, and a few years since the Methodist Episcopal book concern published as one of its general catalogue publications a book entitled "Apostolic Organism," being a discussion from the standpoint of reason, history and scripture of the principles of church government, of which book he is the author. In 1889 Lenox college, a Presbyterian institution in Hopkinton, where he had been a student, conferred upon him the honorary degree of doctor of divinity. Dr. Magee is a type of many progressive men of Iowa, developed by its advancing civilization. He was married in June, 1870, to Miss Jennie A. Cole, of Fayette, an estimable woman of education and refinement. Nine children have been born to them, six of whom are living, one son, Carl C., being the superintendent of city schools in Carroll, Iowa. Dr. Magee delights to call Iowa by that sweetest of names—home. □

HOFFMANN. PHIL., one of the most deservedly popular young newspaper men

in the state, was born and reared in the town in which he now lives and works, the city of Oskaloosa. He was born August 16, 1868, and is the son of Philip Hoffmann, Sr., and Eleanor Addy Hoffmann. He received a good education in the public schools of Oskaloosa, and in Penn college in Oskaloosa, graduating from the high school in 1885. He afterwards spent a year in Penn college. He began his news-

paper career as a correspondent for the Oskaloosa *Messenger* on the Iowa editorial excursion to Oregon in 1885. He was then offered a position on the Oskaloosa *Herald*, where he worked five years, the last three as city editor. In 1892 Mr. Hoffmann, with his brother, Charles W. Hoffmann, the present postmaster at Oskaloosa, went into the steam laundry business, and the Oskaloosa Steam laundry, under their management, became one of the largest in Iowa and was spoken of by leading trade journals as a model plant. They sold the laundry December 1, 1896, and purchased the Oskaloosa *Daily and Weekly Herald*, then owned and edited by Col. Albert W. Swalm, now consul to Uruguay, and his talented wife, Pauline Swalm. The newspaper, under the management of Hoffmann Brothers, has gone steadily on, and in circulation and influence it is among the recognized leading papers of Iowa. It was established in 1850 and has been a power for good, growing in popular favor with increased patronage. While Mr. Hoffmann has been much occupied with business interests he has not neglected the fine literary talents which he possesses and which have been developed in the direction of writing verse. He has earned a creditable reputation in this line. Rolla M. Kendrick, one of the editors of the St. Louis *Globe-Democrat*, recently published a discriminating criticism of Mr. Hoffmann's work, in which he said: "It is a matter for general regret, particularly on the part of his personal friends, that Phil. Hoffmann mounts his Pegasus so seldom. In his nature the muses certainly implanted 'the divine spark;'" but it has been allowed to glow too infrequently. His accomplishments, when he has essayed to enter the field of poetry, have been a source of delight to his readers. Phil. Hoffmann has the poet's nature—gentleness and geniality itself; purity of mind and life; the soul of honor; fertility and strength of imagination. Coupled with these attributes are abundant common sense and a genius for practical affairs. Possibly, it is these latter qualities that have kept him in the routine of a business man's life and out of a Bohemian or a dreamer's career. For ten years Mr. Hoffmann has represented the Des Moines *Register* and other newspapers as correspondent. His poems have chiefly been contributions to Iowa and Chicago newspapers, and to the magazines. Of late years he has written but occasionally, as the inclination comes to him and as he can spare the time from his engrossing business cares.''

Mr. Hoffmann was married May 3, 1893, to Julia Hammond, daughter of Col. J. W. Hammond, cashier and principal owner of the Oskaloosa Savings bank.

---

MARTIN, WESLEY. Aside from the honors which, for quite natural reasons, have been bestowed upon Mr. Martin, Webster City's ex-mayor, ex-treasurer and ex-city attorney, he has the distinction and the glory which attaches to a certificate of honor signed by Abraham Lincoln.

Mr. Martin was born at Navarre, Ohio, on December 19, 1848. He attended the common schools in the city in which he was born and also in those of New Philadelphia. The schools of the latter city were of a very high character, especially while under the principalship of Prof. Joseph Welty. Later he entered Eastman's Business college at Poughkeepsie, but did not graduate. He came to Webster City in 1876, where he began the practice of law, and has resided there continuously since that time. His law education was gained largely in the office of Col. A. R. Mock, of Cambridge, Ill., with whom he studied for a period of three years. In January, 1876, he was admitted to the bar by the supreme court of Illinois.

The war record of Mr. Martin is one of which he may justly feel proud. He enlisted at New Philadelphia, Ohio, on May 2, 1864, in Company D, of the One Hundred and Sixty-first Ohio Volunteer infantry. He was honorably discharged from that organization at the expiration of four months' service, that being the term for which enlistments were made. During this period he was in a number of skirmishes in the Shenandoah and Kanawha valleys. He was in the retreat from Martinsburg to Harper's Ferry, under Siegel, during the summer of 1864, at the time General Early came down the valley, and was also in the rifle pits on Maryland Heights during the time that Early was besieging the garrison at Harper's Ferry and Maryland Heights. November 17, 1864, he enlisted in Company C, Second New York heavy artillery, and was at once sent to the army at Petersburg, Va. He participated in the closing battles of the war around Richmond and Petersburg and was present at the surrender of Lee on the 9th day of April, 1865. He was honorably discharged at New York city by reason of expiration of term of service,

in October, 1865. For services rendered he received a document which is entitled: "The President's Thanks and Certificate of Honorable Service to Musician Wesley Martin," signed by Edwin M. Stanton and Abraham Lincoln.

Mr. Martin is an active republican. He has taken part in a number of political campaigns since coming to Iowa, and has made many speeches under appointment by the state committee. He was nominated for the office of state senator by the republican convention at Eagle Grove in 1885, but declined the nomination for business reasons. He was mayor of Webster

City from March 1, 1882, to March 1, 1883, and has also occupied the position of city treasurer and city attorney of that city. He is a member of the Commercial Law League of America; also a member of the Iowa State Bar association. He not only stands high in Grand Army circles, but is connected with the Masons and other orders. As a lawyer he has a practice extending through the different counties of the state, as well as into the federal courts and the supreme court of the state. He has taken an active part in the important legal controversies in his own and adjoining counties.

He was married on December 24, 1874, to Elizabeth Wonders, at Cambridge, Ill.

DAVIS, FRANCIS MARION, a well-known and successful attorney, residing at Corning, Adams county, was born on a farm in Franklin county, Ohio, August, 13, 1831. His father, Joseph Davis, was a prosperous farmer, living eight miles north of Columbus, Ohio, for a number of years. John Davis, grandfather of Francis M., was a revolutionary soldier, who fought seven years in the war for independence, and was on General Lafayette's staff. He joined the continental army at Valley Forge; fought at Princeton, and in every battle, including the surrender at Yorktown. The gun carried by him at Valley Forge and

Princeton is a highly-prized relic, now owned by Mr. Davis at Corning. His grandmother, Ann Simpson Davis, was a near relative of Hannah Simpson, the mother of General Grant, and Mr. Davis says he well remembers the time when Grant, the cadet at West Point, visited the Davis home, on the farm near Columbus, in 1843, dressed in a roundabout, with stiff leather collar and white gloves. His mother's maiden name was Edith Amanda DeFord. Her mother was a Quakeress, captured by the Indians in the Mohawk valley when a child and taken to Canada about the year 1746. She never knew her own name. She was married to Count Aumile De Ford, one of General Montcalm's

officers, and, after the close of the revolutionary war, they settled in the state of Delaware. Their daughter Edith and Joseph Davis both went west and were married in Franklin county, Ohio, about the year 1824.

Francis M. worked upon a farm, attended the common schools and a private school until 1847' when he entered Blendon college, now Otterbien university, Ohio, and afterwards graduated in the Latin scientific course at the Ohio Wesleyan university at Delaware, Ohio, in 1851. He passed a year in the south, then returned to Ohio and commenced the study of law with Governor Dennison and Mr. Carrington at Columbus, Ohio, and in 1855 settled in Adams county, Iowa, commencing an active business career as surveyor, lawyer and land agent. He had thirty-seven cases on the first court docket of that county.

Mr. Davis was instrumental in organizing the first armed volunteer military company in southern Iowa, called the "Quincy Guards." The company was afterwards known as Company H, Fourth Iowa volunteers, and was offered to and accepted by Governor Kirkwood for service in the war of the rebellion as early as December 10, 1860, Mr. Davis believing from observation and travel in the south that war would surely follow the election of Lincoln to the presidency. Public duties prevented him from going with the company in 1861, but in 1862 he enlisted as a private and was afterwards elected first lieutenant, and promoted to be captain of Company D, Twenty-ninth Iowa. He was afterwards promoted to be first captain of his regiment, and served in the field with staff officers Generals Rice, Pyle, Drake, Bussey, and Colonels Benton, Patterson, Solomon, and others, during the Vicksburg campaign. During the siege of Fort Pemberton, on the Yazoo, Captain Davis received a wound in the right groin, March 26, 1863. This wound was not considered serious at first, but subsequently disabled him for further service, and he was discharged by order of the secretary of war, the order taking effect April 20, 1864, when he retired from the service. Mr. Davis helped organize the first republican caucus in Adams county in February, 1856, and has always been a stalwart republican. He was prosecuting attorney of the county for two years, 1856–58, and was elected a member of the Fourteenth General Assembly of Iowa in 1871, being active in recodifying the code in 1873. He served on the special committee, and wrote the report condemning the foundation of the capitol, which was taken out and rebuilt for the present capitol. He was also on the special committee to devise methods for protecting funds in state and county treasuries from defalcation. He was also the means of getting a law passed limiting the powers of corporations; to authorize suing in local courts on insurance policies in case of loss, and many other laws still in force. His first case in the supreme court was that of *Sands v. Adams County*. The case was won by him and is still a leading case in tax questions, reported in the Eleventh Iowa report.

Mr. Davis has been twice married, and is the father of six children. The eldest, Lillian D., is the wife of Rev. Howard H. Russell, of Delaware, Ohio; Avanelle is the wife of Grover C. Gray, a banker of Montpelier, Idaho; Frederick, died in infancy, 1867; Edith Estelle, Joseph Simpson, and Francis Marion, Jr., all minors, live at home in Corning.

Mr. Davis was a member of the Methodist church from 1857 to 1876, but since that time has been a Congregationalist. Aside from his law practice, he is also quite extensively engaged in farming and stock-raising.

---

CASTER, DR. PAUL, was born in Henry county, Ind., April 30, 1827, and lived there with his parents until he was 14 years of age. About this time occurred the death of his mother, which sad event resulted in young Paul's leaving home and going to Elkhart county, Ind., where he wandered from place to place homeless and friendless. He had a serious impediment in his speech, and some mental peculiarities which prevented him from receiving an education in the usual way and threw him entirely upon his own resources mentally.

In the year 1848 he married Nancy Hatfield, a farmer's daughter. They lived on a farm for three years, when he engaged in the manufacture of chairs, wheels and hubs, in which business he was very successful for two years, when he met with a serious accident; while carrying one end of a heavy log his foot slipped on the ice and he fell, the log falling across his chest. This accident rendered him an invalid for some nine years, and he never entirely recovered from its results. Five children were born to Dr. Paul Caster and his wife: Mary Ann, John Lewis, Samuel, Sarah E., and

Jacob S., now a noted magnetic healer in Burlington, Iowa. Dr. Paul Caster removed to Decatur county, Iowa, in 1855. His wife died in 1863, and in 1864 he married Mrs. Sarah Ferrell, of Decatur county, who still survives him. To them were born four children: Margaret E., George William, Ella and Nettie.

Dr. Paul Caster, from childhood, possessed a wonderful magnetic power to heal. His first patient was a little playmate, who had what had been pronounced a cancer on her breast. One day while playing she became over-heated and suffered greatly. Little Paul felt that he could take away

the pain, and he was successful. The child's parents constituted him her physician until the sore healed. The little girl lived to womanhood, and raised a large family, and this was so early in life that the doctor did not remember his exact age; and his history shows that he continued to heal patients at various times until in 1866 he commenced his public career as a healer in Leon, Decatur county, Iowa. In 1869 he removed to Ottumwa, Iowa, where he remained until his death, April 19, 1881. Dr. Caster commenced the erection of his magnetic infirmary at Ottumwa in 1871 and completed it as it now stands in 1875. In 1877–78 he built his private residence adjoining the infirmary. These buildings were erected at a cost of $78,000, and stand to-day as a monument to the marvelous success attained by only fourteen years of practice in a profession that at that time was looked upon with great disfavor by the majority—especially of western people. Nevertheless he achieved a reputation second to no other magnetic healer known, and which still remains fresh in the minds of not only the people of Iowa, but of many throughout the United States, as he treated patients from almost every state in the union.

Dr. Paul Caster was a firm believer in the deity. He also believed that his strange power was a divine gift and, unlike some of our late healers. he did not believe that it could be taught another, but must come to each one from the same high source. Before his death he became firmly convinced that his son Jacob possessed the same power, and urged him upon his death-bed to take up the work where he was compelled to lay it down, predicting that in so doing alone would lie his future success in life. His son, in 1889, carried out his father's wishes by engaging in the work as a public healer and is carrying it forward in a manner, not only creditable to himself, but also to the reputation of his noted father, Dr. Paul Caster.

---

CASTER, Dr. Jacob S., is a son of the late Dr. Paul Caster, of Ottumwa, and is a native of Decatur county, Iowa. When quite young he became associated with his father in his work in various ways. In 1874 he took charge of the engine in the heating department of his father's large infirmary, which resulted in giving him a taste for machinery that greatly influenced his after life. In 1878 he was made superintendent of the infirmary, which brought him in still closer contact with his father, and probably accounts for much of his subsequent success. He was married March 23, 1880, to Miss Mary E. Biederman, of Ottumwa, and in August of that year resigned his position as superintendent of the infirmary to engage in other business. For a short time he was employed as a machinist in the Chicago, Burlington & Quincy round house at Creston, and in November, 1881, removed to Burlington, Iowa, where he was employed as a machinist by the same company. His father had urged him strongly to use the gift of healing, which he knew he possessed, but the son was prejudiced against it, and felt

compelled to refuse his father's request. It was not until 1887, when out of sympathy for suffering friends, he treated several cases with such wonderful success, that his power became known. He was then sought after constantly by some sufferer, but according to a promise made his father, he received no pay until he came before the world publicly as a magnetic healer. In June, 1889, he received his first public patient. The following November he opened an infirmary, which soon proved too small to accommodate his patients and in June, 1891, he removed to larger quarters, and in November, 1894, to his present location on North Fourth street.

Dr. J. S. Caster has, like his father, had patients from nearly every state in the union and from more than 500 different cities.

He possesses a wonderful power of diagnosis, being able to accurately describe the patient's trouble, sometimes going back twenty years for causes long since forgotten by the sufferer, and this without asking a question.

He does not claim to be able to cure every case that presents itself, but his success has been something almost miraculous, as shown by the joyful testimony of hundreds of patients, including many of the most prominent people of Burlington, as well as of the state, who have been permanently cured or have gained years of comparative health from his treatment, after being pronounced hopelessly incurable. The doctor belongs to a number of secret societies, and originated and carried out a plan for "Secret Society Day" during the semi-centennial celebration in Burlington, in October, 1896, conducting a parade which contained nineteen different secret societies. He belongs to the Masons, Odd Fellows, A. O. U. W. and other orders. The doctor is a strong advocate of the principles of the republican party, and vigorously supports that organization. In 1896 he was elected alderman in a democratic ward, by a large majority.

Dr. and Mrs. Caster have three children living: Charles Edwin, born February 28, 1883; Mabel Rose, born May 25, 1887, and Mary Blanche, born May 7, 1890.

---

HOOPES, WILLIAM HENRY, who originated the system of wholesale gardening on Muscatine island, and developed the wonderful resources of that fertile spot, is a son of Lindley Hoopes, who was married November 22, 1838, in Birmingham, Pa., to Miss Mary Addleman. The family came to Muscatine county from Pennsylvania in 1854. Lindley Hoopes was born in Chester county, Pa., in 1815, and his ancestors came from England with William Penn. They belonged to the Society of Friends, and Israel Hoopes, the first in this country, had sixteen sons. Lindley Hoopes was a builder in Pennsylvania and followed the carpenter's trade for a time after coming to Iowa. He is now engaged in farming and breeding horses, cattle and hogs in Lake township, Muscatine county. They are Methodists and strong temperance people, using their best efforts for the social and moral welfare of the country.

William H. Hoopes was born November 19, 1840, at Warrior's Mark, Huntingdon county, Pa., and was the oldest son in the family of nine children His early education was under the tutorship of Bishop John H. Vincent of Chautauqua fame. He afterwards attended school in Muscatine. When he attained his majority he left the farm and earned his own way through a two years' course in Greenwood academy, in Muscatine. He afterwards engaged in the building business, was principal of the First ward school in Muscatine two years, and for a number of years was in the grocery and pork packing business. In 1874 he commenced the Muscatine Island

28

gardening business, and with various partners has been engaged in that important enterprise ever since. He now has associated with him his two sons. They have 900 acres of land under cultivation there and produce the finest sweet potatoes, melons, cabbages, peas, beans, tomatoes and onions. He also has a vegetable and dairy farm in St. Louis Park, one of the suburbs of Minneapolis. During his farming career he has introduced many labor-saving implements. Among them is one which sets plants of all kinds and saves labor and expense. Outside of his own immediate business Mr. Hoopes has helped

promote the organization of other industries, among them a canning factory, street railway, electric light plant, high bridge over the Mississippi river, and in real estate operations. In public affairs Mr. Hoopes has worked with the republican party on account of its championship of temperance principles, in which he is deeply interested and to which he has given much of his best efforts. He was elected alderman as a republican in a ward usually democratic, and helped to inaugurate some of the most important public improvements in Muscatine, including the building of Riverside Park, which turned an unsightly river front into a beautiful spot. He was one of the most zealous supporters of the prohibitory law and had an important part in the prosecution of those who violated it. He has been prominently identified with the Musserville M. E. church and has been trustee and superintendent of the Sunday school for more than twenty years, making him one of the oldest Sunday school superintendents in the state. He is also an active member of the Y. M. C. A. and the Muscatine Commercial club. He belongs to the Knights of Pythias, Knights of the Maccabees and Woodmen of the World. On the 12th of August, 1869, Mr. Hoopes was married to Phena Thompson, daughter of Philip Thompson, a prominent farmer and stock raiser of Louisa county. Two children were born to them: Frank Everett, born April 29, 1870, and Fred Philip, born November 11, 1872. They assist their father in the management of the farms and the conducting of their large shipping and commission business.

The family has a beautiful home on Beach Grove avenue, a mile and three-quarters below the postoffice, on the west bank of the Mississippi river.

---

ALLEN, MANNING LEONARD, of Tama, is a native Hawkeye, born November 14, 1862, in the country ten miles west of Wapello, Louisa county, Iowa. His parents are Leonard Fletcher Allen, who was born near Saratoga Springs, N. Y., and Harriett Litsey Allen, who was born in Newark, Kendall county, Ill., both of whom now reside at La Moille, Bureau county, Ill., having lived there since 1867. Previously they moved from Louisa county, Iowa, to Little Rock, La Salle county, Ill., where they lived for about three years; from there to Trenton, Ill., or De Pue as it is now called, and thence to La Moille, thirty-two years ago, where they have since resided.

They had seven children — Manning L., Bert L., Hattie, Lowell, Frank, Herman and Jennie, of which Manning is the oldest. He completed the course of study in the La Moille high school in 1880, and clerked in a grocery store until September, 1881, when he entered the College of Physicians and Surgeons, of Joplin, Mo., completing the first year's course of medicine, and in September, 1882, entered the medical department of the State University of Iowa, where he finished his second year's course.

In 1883 he located at Cooper, Greene county, Iowa, and practiced medicine and taught school until the following February,

when he located in Astor, Crawford county, Iowa, and remained there until November, 1886, when, with other business men of the town, he moved to the then new town of Manilla, two and one-half miles northeast of Astor, on the Chicago, Milwaukee & Saint Paul railway. The next year, having a good opportunity to sell out, he did so and came to Garwin, Tama county, Iowa, and remained there until October, 1889, when he removed to Tama, his present home.

In October, 1885, he passed the examination of the state board of pharmacy and received a gold seal certificate, and in 1886

he passed the examination of the state board of medical examiners and received a certificate from them.

In September, 1892, he entered the College of Physicians and Surgeons, of Chicago, graduating from that institution, which is the medical department of the State University of Illinois, April 13, 1893. The same spring he took the post-graduate course of the Post-Graduate Medical and Hospital School of Chicago. His ability and standing as a surgeon and physician are recognized by his appointment as medical examiner for nearly all the best-known life insurance companies in the east, and in Iowa. He is also district surgeon for the Chicago, Milwaukee & Saint Paul Railway company, and surgeon for the Tama & Toledo Electric Railroad company. He enjoys a large, lucrative practice and the respect of the community in which he resides. In April, 1897, he was elected vice-president of the Alumni Association of the College of Physicians and Surgeons of Chicago.

He was married, August 10th, 1882, to Sarah Rebecca Fassett, of La Moille, Ill., who has faithfully shared with him the "ups and downs" of the beginning of a professional life with little or no means, and the success of the same.

They have three children: Frances Rebecca, born June 16, 1883; Raymond Manning, born July 8, 1887, and Leonard Earle, born May 28, 1894.

Dr. and Mrs. Allen are both members of the First Baptist church of Tama.

---

COLE, ELMER J., M. D. Woodbine has the good fortune to have a physician of character and recognized high standing, who tries to treat his patients with both honesty and skill. Being, besides, a close student, he has earned a professional reputation exceeded by very few.

His father, John S. Cole, was a physician before him, and came to Iowa to engage in practice away back in 1855. He was one of the first physicians in western Iowa and practiced at a time when doctors rode horseback and carried saddle bags. There were few bridges in those days. The creeks and rivers had to be forded. There were no regularly laid out roads to guide the doctor to the far-off home of his patient, and many were the difficulties and hardships endured by the pioneers of the profession of medicine that are unknown at the present time. He died in 1881, when the subject of this sketch was 16 years of age. The mother's maiden name was Diana Werley. She is now residing in Woodbine. The venerable Mrs. Cole is known as a great church worker and it is due to her untiring and noble work that the city of Woodbine has one of the strongest church organizations in that part of the state. Hers is the kind of piety that is coupled with benevolence, and many there are to bless her for the bestowal of kindnesses of a material and hunger-satisfying character.

Elmer J. Cole was born on a farm a quarter of a mile north of Woodbine, January 24, 1865. He attended the schools of Woodbine during his childhood days, and

at the age of 18 entered the Agricultural college at Ames. He remained there for three years and during that time was a member of the Greek letter society called Delta Tau Delta; also the literary society known as the Philomathian. He left the school one year before the time of graduation for the purpose of taking a medical course in Rush Medical college, Chicago. He graduated from Rush February 19, 1889, when but 24 years of age. Soon thereafter he opened an office in Woodbine in partnership with Dr. T. M. Edwards. That relation was continued for three years when it was dissolved by mutual

consent, Dr. Cole remaining in the practice. During the eight years that have passed since that time he has built up a substantial business and the same is constantly increasing in volume. The principle to which he has adhered and to which he accredits a great share of his success is honesty in his relation with the patient. It may be said that the golden rule has rarely been more generally applied than in the case of Dr. Cole

Politically he is a democrat and firmly of the opinion that gold and silver should be coined free. However, he has never gone into politics to any great extent. He has held the position of county coroner and received the largest majority known to the history of the county. He served a number of years as a member of the school board and at this time is a member of the city council and a director in the First National bank of Woodbine. He became a member of the Harrison county medical society at its organization and is now filling the position of president; is local examiner for nearly all of the leading life insurance companies and is prominent in the Knights of Pythias. He was married in June, 1891, to Miss Maude Allen. They have three children: Clement, born May 10, 1893; Bernice, born January 8, 1895; and Anita, born September 5, 1897.

---

COOPER, JOHN K., of Council Bluffs, member of the Twenty-fifth General Assembly, and a man who has done much to

advance the educational interests of the state, was born on a farm near Hollandville, Kent county, Del., April 1, 1845. He is the son of Benjamin Abbott Cooper, a farmer and school-teacher, who died at the age of 30 years. He was a man of great promise at the time of his death. The mother's maiden name was Anna Jump. She died when John was 8 years old.

Mr. Cooper's grandmother, on the paternal side, was a niece of George Read,

one of the signers of the Declaration of Independence. John K. attended the country school at such times as there was one to attend. At the time of his boyhood the school system of his native state was not like the perfect one of to-day. The people of each district met every spring and voted on the question: "Tax or no tax," with the frequent result that no tax won. The teacher was usually selected with respect to his muscle, and if he could convince the directors that he could whip any two boys in the school, he was regarded as the proper man for the place. As a result of all this, our subject could barely read and write at the outbreak of the war. The people of his section were divided on the question of secession, and all against the proposition to free the negro. Mr. Cooper's guardian was a southern sympathizer, but the young man was enthusiastic for the cause represented by "old glory." He ran away at 16, and joined a Maryland regiment, serving throughout the whole period of the war. He was not yet 20 years old when peace was declared and immediately upon arriving home he entered school to prepare himself for the vocation of teacher. Two years were spent in Felton seminary, after which he was engaged in teaching the schools of Felton and Hollandville. He came to Iowa in May, 1870, and organized a subscription school in Missouri Valley. The venture did not prove a success financially, and he shortly removed to Fremont county, thence some months later to Pottawattamie county, where he has since resided. He was elected county superintendent of schools in 1879, and re-elected in 1881; was nominated for county treasurer in 1883, but met with defeat. During the next year he was a commission dealer and book-keeper, but gained more largely of experience than in wealth. He was elected a member of the school board of Council Bluffs in 1885, but resigned the following year, and was elected principal of the Bloomer school. Again, in 1887, he was elected county superintendent of schools, re-elected in 1889, and again in 1891. In 1893 he was chosen to represent his county in the lower branch of the general assembly, and therein made a record satisfactory to his people. In 1894 he gave up his public life and became the proprietor of a grocery business, in which he is at present engaged.

As a soldier he was a private in Company D, First E. S. Maryland volunteers.

He participated in the battle of Gettysburg, in Lockwood's brigade, Williams' division, Twelfth Army corps, until they crossed the Potomac, when his regiment was left on the Maryland side to guard the Baltimore & Ohio railroad. He is a member of Union Veteran Legion, Maccabees, Royal Arcanum and A. F. & A. M., and a member of Council Bluffs school board at the present time. He has always been a democrat. June 27, 1882, he was married to Miss Alice Mottaz. They have had two children, one of whom, a daughter Flora, 9 years of age, is living. John K., born August 21, 1884, died August 21, 1885.

---

DEWELL, JAMES S., is at the head of the law firm of Dewell & Garrison, of Missouri Valley. He has been county attorney of Harrison county and mayor of Missouri Valley, and has held many minor positions of trust. He was born in Tipton, Cedar county, Iowa, June 16, 1857. He is a son of Nathaniel Dewell, who was born in Ohio, but moved to Indiana in an early day and to Iowa in 1855, locating at Tipton. He was a farmer by occupation, and accumulated but little until after 1865, when he was very successful, and at the time of his death was in good circumstances. His wife was Winnie Ann McComb. She was a native of Indiana, was married there and died after her removal to Iowa in 1865. The first member of the Dewell family of whom there is any definite history was John Dewell, born in France in 1743. He came to America in 1776, fought in the revolutionary war and died in 1803. He left four sons, Benjamin, John, Thomas and Jesse. Benjamin married Barbara Springer, who did not live long, and he found a second wife in an estimable woman named Mary Deats. He left three sons and two daughters: Solomon, Samuel, Charles, Rachel and Truth. The family was remarkable for the size of its members, none being less than six feet in height nor under 220 pounds in weight. Solomon Dewell was born in 1788. He left seven sons and six daughters, one of whom, Joshua, served through the Mexican war, and died on his return therefrom. Benjamin went overland to California in 1843, served as a soldier during the Mexican war, and was one of those who adopted the Bear flag in the golden state at that time. Charles and John enlisted in the union army at the outbreak of the civil war, and Charles died from wounds received at

Chickamauga. Nathaniel Dewell belonged to this family but was unable to join his brothers in the fight for their country on account of having a hand disabled in youth.

James S. Dewell received his early education in the common schools of Cedar county, then entered the State College of Agriculture and Mechanic Arts at Ames, completing the regular scientific course in November, 1881, after which he graduated from the law department of the Iowa State university. He had received no special business or professional training prior to entering college, and his first earnings were received as a farm hand. He has spent

his entire life within the confines of the state, the greater part of his time since reaching man's estate, at Missouri Valley. He located there immediately upon completing his law course, and formed a partnership with John S. McGavren, who retired in 1890 to accept the position of cashier of the First National bank. Mr. Dewell conducted the business alone until July, 1896, at which time he took in E. S. Garrison, the firm being styled Dewell & Garrison, still existing. Mr. Dewell served for a time as county attorney, but his practice being much more remunerative than the official position, he gave up the office and devoted himself to the former. He has always been a republican, served four years as county chairman of his county, and has been a delegate to the state conventions for the past ten years, with few exceptions. He was a candidate for district judge in 1892, but suffered defeat with the rest of his ticket by reason of fusion of the democratic with the populistic party. In 1897 he was nominated for state senator from the Harrison-Monona-Crawford district, but as the fusion majority in the district was 1,600, he was not elected, though he greatly reduced the adverse majority, running about 500 votes ahead of his ticket in his own county. In 1898 he was elected to represent the Ninth congressional district on the republican state central committee. He is a member of the Masonic, Modern Woodmen and Knights of Pythias orders. He was married in October, 1893, to Miss Emma F. Joy, of Portage, Wis., who for several years had taught school at Missouri Valley and other places in Iowa.

ST. JOHN, HON. R. T. A man of stalwart proportions and soldierly bearing is

Hon. R. T. St. John, member of the house of representatives of the Twenty-sixth General Assembly, representing Mitchell county. He is a man of sterling integrity, and possesses ability of a high order as a

legislator. He was born July 14, 1846, at Elizabeth, Jo Daviess county, Ill., where a part of his childhood was spent. His father, John St. John, was born at East St. Louis, Ill., and was a soldier in the Black Hawk war. He afterward took government land near Freeport, and still later entered the lead mines at Galena. He is now living at Riceville, Iowa, at the advanced age of 83 years. His mother's name before marriage was Nancy Foster. She was born in North Carolina, and descended from one of the first families of Virginia A paternal grandfather was a native of Canada, and traded with the Indians of Illinois in an early day. He later become a fur dealer at St. Louis, and died there at the age of 106 years, having retained his physical strength and mental faculties up to the time of his last brief sickness.

R. T. St. John earned his first dollar by picking lead ore from the rubbish in the Galena mines. He received a very liberal education in the common schools and the Cedar Valley seminary. After coming to Iowa in 1859, he was engaged in farming in Mitchell county. The nearest market for their grain and cattle was McGregor, 100 miles away, and many interesting incidents of marketing trips are told. He enlisted as a soldier at the age of 16, became a member of Company A, Seventh Illinois cavalry, and served valiantly until peace was declared, after which he returned to the farm. Several winters were spent in the pine regions of Wisconsin, where he "roughed it," and though falling behind the times in style of dress and cut of hair, would return to civilization better in health and purse for the experience. He later owned and conducted the Riceville hotel, and handled agricultural implements. At the present time he is the owner of the Oak Park stock farm, located within the city limits of Riceville, Mitchell county, and is actively engaged in breeding fine stock of various kinds. Among other things he has a large pigeon ranch and five artificial ponds, which are fed by springs and stocked with all kinds of game fish, including rainbow and speckled trout.

His election to the office of constable gave him the opportunity to break up several gangs of thieves, and brought him into prominence as excellent material for the sheriff's office, and in the fall of 1881 he was elected sheriff. He was continued in that place for five terms, being elected each time by a large majority. He was elected president of the Iowa Sheriffs' association in 1888. In secret societies his affiliations are with the Knights Templars, Odd Fellows and G. A. R. In Masonry he is a Shriner, in Odd Fellowship a past officer of the highest rank, and in the G. A. R. a past grand commander, having been the first commander of Frank A. Brush Post, at Osage. During the sessions of the Twenty-fifth and Twenty-sixth General Assembles he was a member of various important committees, and chairman of the committee on agriculture. He was prominent in the work of recodifying the laws, and gave particular attention to agriculture, taxation, and compensation of public officers. That his first term was entirely satisfactory to his constituents is evidenced by the fact that he was renominated by acclamation and elected by a majority far in the lead of the state ticket. He was married to Miss Addie E. Sayles, November 4, 1866. They have had three children, two of whom are living: Earl R., 18 years old, is a student in Grinnell college, and Harry D., 10 years of age, is in the Riceville high school.

BALDWIN, WILLIAM WRIGHT, of Burlington, is one of the best-known railroad attorneys of Iowa, having been for many years associated with the Burlington company. His father, Charles Baldwin, also a lawyer of ability, is now living in Keosauqua, at an advanced age, and was one of the very earliest settlers of Van Buren county, coming there in 1840 from Ohio. He is a man of much force of character and the highest integrity. Mr. Baldwin's mother, Rachel Wright, was born in 1816, and came from Indiana to Van Buren county, Iowa, in 1840, and is still living at Keosauqua. The Baldwins are direct descendants of John Baldwin, a leader in the New Haven colony, which came from England in 1638. He settled at Milford, Conn. Members of the family did good service in the revolution, and among many well-known descendants are Abraham Baldwin, a signer of the Declaration of Independence from Georgia, Judge Nathaniel Baldwin, a distinguished jurist of Connecticut, and Hon. John W. Daniel, now United States senator from Georgia. The members of his mother's family, the Wrights, have occupied many prominent positions. Hon. Joseph A. Wright, Mrs. Baldwin's brother, was governor of Indiana, United States

senator, and twice appointed embassador to Germany, where he died at his post in Berlin. Another brother, Hon. George G. Wright, was for many years chief justice of the supreme court of Iowa, and also United States senator.

Hon. W. W. Baldwin was born September 28, 1845, at Keosauqua, Van Buren county. He attended the public schools of that city, and in 1860 and 1861 was a student at Lane's academy, founded by Rev. Daniel Lane, one of the celebrated Andover Band of Congregational ministers. He entered the State university in 1862 from Keosauqua and graduated in 1866. He

helped to found the Zetegathean society, and belonged to the Beta Theta Pi fraternity. He was an active debater, and was thoroughly identified with the life of the university. Upon leaving college, he entered the Iowa Law school, then located in Des Moines, and afterwards established as the law department of the State university. He graduated from the law school in 1867, delivering the salutatory address of the class. While a law student he earned considerable money copying for the printer the opinions of the supreme court, and, upon graduating, had a capital of $75, after paying all bills. He then entered the office of J. C and B. J. Hall at Burlington as a clerk and office boy, and, at the end of a year, accepted an offer to become a partner of the late Judge Harrington, with whom he remained two years, and then formed a partnership with his former employers, J. C. and B. J. Hall. In 1879 he accepted the position of land commissioner for the Chicago, Burlington & Quincy Railway company, and has remained in their service ever since. He is now assistant to the president, and is president of the St. Louis, Keokuk & Northwestern, and other branches of the Burlington system. He was one of the active promoters of the Burlington & Northwestern railway, and has been a member of the board of directors ever since it was organized. Thoroughly public spirited, Mr. Baldwin has always been prominent in aiding local enterprises. He has been president of the Burlington school board for many years, a trustee of the public library, and, from its foundation, president of the Charity Organization society of Burlington. He is also director and secretary of the Opera House company.

While at college, Mr. Baldwin enlisted, in 1864, as a private in Company D, Forty-fourth Iowa infantry, and was discharged September 15, 1864, by the expiration of his term of enlistment. The service of his regiment was in western Tennessee. Mr. Baldwin has always been a democrat, and a firm believer in sound money and a low tariff.

Mr. Baldwin was married in 1870, at Des Moines, to Miss Alice Tuttle. To them four children have been born.

---

HANCHETTE, Dr. JOHN L., of Sioux City, is president of the Hahnemann Medical association of Iowa, and one of the leading homeopathic physicians of the west. He came of a family of physicians, three of his four brothers being physicians. A. P., referred to elsewhere in this work, is at Council Bluffs; W. H. is at Omaha and J. C. is at Salt Lake. The other brother, F. G., is a lawyer in Aurora, Ill. Their one sister is Mrs. Clark Ravlin, of La Porte, Iowa. Dr. John L. is a son of David and Fayette Churchill Hanchette, and was born and brought up on a farm near Kaneville, Ill. He comes of sturdy old New England stock. He remained on the home farm, getting what education he could in the schools of that vicinity till he was 21 years old, when he removed to Parker, S.

D., and farmed on his own account five years, being married in the meantime, before he began to study medicine. He took a course in the University of Chicago, and graduated with high honors from the Chicago Homeopathic Medical college in 1889. He was the valedictorian of his class. Armed with his diploma, good health and courage he went at once to Avoca, where he intended to locate, but within a month he decided that Sioux City offered a better field, as it was then in the height of its financial glory and held out rich promise to the young and energetic. Dr. Hanchette's judgment has been proved unerring by the success that has attended his practice in Sioux City, where he has risen

to a position of comfort and distinction, as his election to the presidency of the state organization of his school of medicine attests. He is also a member of the American Institute of Homeopathy. The republican party represents his political views, and he has always supported it. Dr. Hanchette was married in Parker, S. D., May 20, 1885, to Miss Maria Louise Stevens. They have three children: Anna Fayetta, born July 5, 1886; Ralph, W., born July 16, 1888, and James Harold, born September 29, 1890. The family belongs to the Baptist church.

TEDFORD, JUDGE WILLIAM HAMILL, who at this writing holds a judgeship in the Third judicial district of Iowa, was born in Blount county, east Tennessee, November 8, 1844. He is the son of John and Elizabeth Hamill Tedford, who were of English and Scotch and Scotch descent, respectively. Both great-grandfathers fought on the side of the patriots in the revolutionary war. It was during that struggle that John Tedford and Mary Paxton, the great-grandfather and great-grandmother of Judge Tedford, were married in Rockbridge county, Va. Mary Paxton belonged to that celebrated family of Virginia Paxtons from which sprung Gen. Samuel Houston, of Texas, and other historic characters in the ministry and the profession of law. The grandfather of Judge Tedford was a cousin of General Houston, their mothers being Paxtons. This grandparent served in the war of 1812, under General Jackson, with the rank of captain. After the close of hostilities he removed to east Tennessee, where the judge was born. The family came to Iowa in 1851, and located on a farm, where the education of the young man was secured, the same being such as was afforded by the common schools of that day. At the age of 16 he enlisted in Company F, Eleventh Iowa infantry, and served his country four years, taking part in the battles of Shiloh, Corinth, Vicksburg and Atlanta. He participated in many skirmishes which cannot properly be called battles, although marked by stubborn fighting and considerable loss of life, and was with Sherman on his march to the sea.

When peace had been declared he returned to Iowa, and entered the State university, graduating from the law department thereof at the end of two years with the degree of LL. B. This was in 1869, and in September of the same year he settled at Corydon, Iowa, and commenced the practice of his profession. Within a few years he built up an extensive practice, and had a part in nearly all the important litigation in the county. The firm of Tedford & Miles, of which this subject was a member, in the case of the State of Iowa vs. Kabrich, 39th Iowa, page 277, first took the position in our supreme court that the character of one charged with an offense is not in issue, unless he introduces evidence relative thereto. This point was sustained by the supreme court, making this a leading case.

The judge has always been a republican

and was one of the presidential electors for Iowa in 1884. He was elected one of the judges of the Third judicial district in 1890, and with Judge Towner, his associate, was unanimously renominated in 1894. The democratic party in the district ratified the nomination, and their names were placed on both tickets, so that the election was in fact almost unanimous. They were both again re-elected in 1898. He is very active in the work of his party, and has been called upon to address the people in different parts of the state on many occasions of importance. As an interpreter

of the law he has few equals, and his record in the supreme court is remarkable. In the six years that he has held a seat on the bench he has been affirmed in almost every case.

He is a member of the celebrated Crocker Brigade association, and delivered the biennial address at the reunion of that organization at Ottumwa, September 26, 1894, of which address it was said by the Ottumwa *Courier:* "It was a scholarly and masterful effort. It is unhesitatingly pronounced the finest address ever heard at a Crocker Brigade reunion." The judge is not a member of any church, although reared a Presbyterian. He was married to Miss Emma Thomas, daughter of Capt. W. W. Thomas, of Corydon, June 22, 1875, to which union there has been born one child, a daughter. She is named Eva, born July 9, 1877. The mother and daughter affiliate with the Methodist denomination.

Judge Tedford has one of the handsomest homes in Corydon, and is in good financial circumstances. He is a director in the Wayne County State bank, and a figure in the business as well as legal circles of that section of the state.

WHITNALL, WILLIAM ROLFE. a prominent physician and surgeon of Hastings, was born in Milwaukee, Wis , March 23,

1852. His father William Whitnall, a florist by trade, settled in Milwaukee in 1844. He is a self-educated and thoroughly-informed man, deeply interested in all current topics and the deeper philosophic and scientific questions that underlie them. He is a man who attracts people to him in all grades of society, and has a host of friends wherever he has lived. He is an active worker in the Unitarian church. His mother, Lucy Crosby Rolfe Whitnall, was a native of New Hampshire, and a woman of unusual literary ability and force of character. She was a graduate of Hillsboro seminary. She taught school in Georgia, also in Milwaukee, Wis. She was for many years a valued contributor to the *Chicago Inter Ocean* and local newspapers of southern Wisconsin. Dr. Whitnall's family on his father's side, is traced back to 1600, his ancestors being merchants and farmers. His mother was descended from John Rolfe, one of the heroes of early American history. Dr. Whitnall's early education was received from private instructors, and afterwards at Janesville, Wis., in the public schools. While a student in the high school he devoted much of his time to music and painting. He prepared for Michigan university at Milton college, Wisconsin, and in 1872 took the university work of the freshman year. He then taught school six years in southern Wisconsin, after which he spent a part of two terms in the State normal at Whitewater, Wis. He was a very successful teacher, his specialties being mathematics and the sciences. But, not desiring to make a life work of teaching, he took up the study of medicine with Dr. J. W. St. John, of Janesville. After a year with him he entered the College of Physicians and Surgeons in Chicago, completing his course in 1884. His first location was at Alton, Kan., where he practiced in his profession for two years. In 1886 he returned to Chicago to practice, also to perfect himself in the polyclinics and hospitals of that city. He built up a good practice during his six years' stay in Chicago, but was finally compelled to leave there on account of his wife's health, removing to his present home—Hastings, Mills county, Iowa. Following his father's faith, he is a Unitarian. He has always been a republican. He was coroner of Mills county from 1895 to 1899. At the beginning of McKinley's administration he was appointed examining surgeon of the United States Pension board at Glenwood. He has been an active member of the Knights of Pythias Lodge since 1884. He is an Odd Fellow and organized the Lake View Lodge No. 10, of Chicago. For this lodge he was the representative in the grand lodge for two years. He is also a member of Humanity Lodge No. 378, A. F. & A. M., and Mt. Gerizim No. 59, R. A. M.; also of the Chicago Medical society, and Southwestern Iowa Medical society. He was married in 1885 at Alton, Kan., to Miss Minnie Cox, a woman of rare intelligence and culture, who was educated at Tabor college. They have four children: Rolfe Morse, born at Alton, Kan., in 1886; William Cox, born in Chicago in 1888; Minnie Louise, born in 1892, and Helen Lucy, born at Hastings in 1894.

Dr. Whitnall is well known among his wide circle of friends and acquaintances as a broad-minded, progressive man. His advanced views in surgery, and upon many important questions pertaining to medicine, have attracted wide attention and he has been requested to give them wider publicity through the columns of medical journals. He is a practical electrician and has connected the surrounding country with his residence. Much of the necessary apparatus was manufactured by himself, many of the lines being barbed wire fences.

THOMPSON, JOHN FOSTER. Well versed in the law and in the monetary affairs of the state is Mr. J. F. Thompson, of Forest City. His father was a farmer in northern Iowa, in only moderate circumstances. His mother was a cousin of Salmon P. Chase, a member of Lincoln's cabinet. His grandmother on his father's side was a sister of Sir Thomas Bell, of Belfast, Ireland, who was a leader of one of the Irish rebellions. Mr. J. F. Thompson was born near Carey, Ohio, September 3, 1848. His parents removed to Iowa in 1857, at which time Mr. Thompson was quite young, so his early education was obtained in the county schools of the old-fashioned sort in Clayton county. This, however, was supplemented with a special course in English, Latin and mathematics in the Iowa State university. His legal education was obtained in the law department of the same university, from which he graduated in 1875, and his business education at a branch commercial school of Bryant & Stratton's. After graduating he was appointed deputy register of the state land office, which position he held until 1876, at which time he resigned and removed to Forest City to engage in the practice of law. In 1877 he organized the Winnebago County bank, later made a state bank, of which he is the vice-president. Mr. Thompson is connected one way or another with many other banking institutions besides the one which receives his personal supervision. He is one of the managers of the Citizens bank of Britt, the Buffalo Center State bank and the State bank of Thompson. Together with his brother, he organized the Chicago & Iowa Western Railway company, which built the Forest City division of the Burlington, Cedar Rapids & Northern, and the Chicago & Iowa Western Land and Town Lot company, an organization that

has done much in the way of developing that section of the state.

Mr. Thompson enlisted in Company I, Eighth Iowa cavalry, but was rejected on account of age. In a second trial in the Fourth Iowa battery he was more successful, being made battery bugler. He served in the Gulf department under Generals Canby and Banks. He was severely wounded in the right thigh in an engagement in northwestern Louisiana, and was given an honorable discharge, having served a little more than two years, and not being 17 years old when mustered out. He is a member of the G. A. R., and was

appointed a member of the staff of Department Commander Mills, and inspector-general of Iowa by Department Commander Thompson. He is present commander of Hayden Post. He has always been a republican and prohibitionist, but not a third party prohibitionist; was chairman of the county central committee, and under his administration Winnebago county won the Tippecanoe banner. He was at one time mayor of Forest City, president of its board of education and president of the board of trade. Mr. Thompson had the honor to be one of the two delegates to the National Farmers' congress, appointed by Governor Larrabee and reappointed by Governor Boies. He belongs to the

Masons, Knights Templars, Odd Fellows and Knights of Pythias. Several years ago he united with the Methodist church, but now affiliates with the Congregationalists. He was married December 22, 1875, to Miss Julia A. Clark, oldest daughter of Judge Robert Clark, of Winnebago county, well known in the early 60's. Six children were born to them, three of whom are now living.

FAIRCHILD, DR. DAVID S., who was connected with the Iowa Agricultural college for so many years, is now division

surgeon for the Chicago & Northwestern railway, with headquarters at Clinton. He was born in Fairfield, Vt., September 16, 1847. His ancestors were among the early settlers of Connecticut. A great-great-grandfather, Abraham Fairchild, located in Redding in 1746, where he reared a large family of children. Six sons served in the continental army. From Connecticut they went to New York, then Ohio, and later to Wisconsin. A great-uncle invented the first pin machine, and for many years the Fairchild pin was well known in the market. Dr. Fairchild's father, Eli Fairchild, settled in Fairfield, Vt., in 1844, and engaged in farming. His mother, whose maiden name was Grace D. Sturges,

was born in Fairfield in 1817, and there married Eli Fairchild. Her father was a sea captain, and migrated from Fairfield, Conn., to Fairfield, Vt., in 1802. The Sturges family was among the pioneer families of Fairfield, and has a prominent place in the early history of Connecticut. A great-grandfather on that side was chief justice of the colony at the time of the outbreak of the revolutionary war.

Dr. David S. Fairchild attended the academies of Franklin and Barre, Vt., after which he studied medicine for a time with Dr. J. O. Cramton, of Fairfield, then attended medical lectures at the University of Michigan, during the years 1866, 1867 and 1868. Following his graduation at Albany, N. Y., December, 1868, he located in High Forest, Minn., where for three years he was engaged in a general practice. He located in Ames, Iowa, in 1872. In 1877 he was appointed physician to the Iowa Agricultural college, and in 1879 was elected professor of physiology and comparative anatomy, which position he held until 1893, when he resigned to accept the position of surgeon for the Chicago & Northwestern, covering all the lines of that system in this state. He had served as local surgeon for this road in 1884, and through his satisfactory performance of the work was promoted two years later to district surgeon; in 1897 was appointed special examining surgeon for the Chicago, Milwaukee & St. Paul Railway system; in 1882 he was elected professor of histology and pathology in the Iowa College of Physicians and Surgeons, Des Moines, and in 1885 was transferred to the chair of pathology and diseases of the nervous system; in 1886 he was given the chair of theory and practice, since which time no change has been made. For two years previous to the incorporation of the college as a part of Drake university, he served as its president. The doctor was engaged in general practice for some sixteen years, but for the past eleven years has devoted himself almost exclusively to consultation, giving particular attention to surgery and nervous diseases. He has contributed numerous articles to the medical journals, and his papers have attracted wide attention in the various medical societies. He has always taken a great interest in medical organizations. In 1873 he issued a call to the profession of Story county to meet for the purpose of forming a county medical society, and, at the organization, was elected its president. In 1874 he assisted materially in organizing the Central District Medical society, and in 1886 was made its president. He became a member of the Iowa State Medical society in 1874, was elected second vice-president in 1886, first vice-president in 1894 and president in 1895 He is active in the work of the Western Surgical and Gynecological association, and fills the position of president; is prominent in the American Medical association, the National Association of Railway Surgeons, and the American Academy of Railway Surgeons. He was a delegate to the International Medical congress in 1876; assisted in organizing the Iowa Academy of Sciences, and was chairman of the committee appointed by the State Medical society to prepare a history of medicine in Iowa.

He was a republican until 1884, when, on account of the party's position on the tariff, he affiliated with the democrats. He is a member of the Wapsipinicon club and the Masonic order. He was married May 1, 1870, to Miss W. C. Tattersall, daughter of Hon. W. K. Tattersall, of High Forest, Minn. They have three children. A son, D. S. Fairchild, Jr., M. D., is associated with his father in the practice, and is now major surgeon of the Fifty-first Iowa volunteers, on duty in the Philippine islands, and Misses Gertrude and Margaret are students in the University of Wisconsin.

---

PORTMAN, REGINALD FITZHARDINGE BERKELY, is one of the leading business men in the city of Decorah. He is vice-president of the Citizens Savings bank, and in addition to the duties of this office practices law and deals extensively in real estate. Though a loyal American, Mr. Portman is justly proud of the fact that he has descended from one of the oldest families of the English nobility. One of his ancestors, Sir William Portman, was lord chief justice of England in 1655, his uncle, the late Edward Berkely, Viscount Portman, was lord warden of the Stannaries in Cornwall and Devon, in which are among the most valuable tin mines of England, and was lord lieutenant of Somerset for twenty-four years. The Portmans of to-day own over 300 acres of land in the heart of London, including Portman Square, Bryanston Square and Blandford Square, besides some 37,000 acres in the counties of Somerset, Devon and Dorset. Mr. Portman is a first cousin of the second Viscount Portman and also of Viscount

Peel, late speaker of the house of commons, and is more distantly related to the duke of Somerset His father, Rev. Fitzhardinge Berkely Portman, received his master's degree at Christ Church college, Oxford. He was canon of Wells and a fellow at All Souls college, Oxford. He had three curates and was rector of five parishes: Staple Fitzpaine, Bickenhall, Orchard Portman, Thurlbear and Stoke St. Mary, all in the county of Somerset. He died in 1894, aged 83 years. Mr. Portman's mother was Frances Darnell, daughter of Rev. William N. Darnell, rector of Stanhope, Northumberland, and canon of Durham. She died at the age of 78, in 1889.

R. F. B. Portman was born February 20, 1853, at Staple Fitzpaine, county of Somerset, England, and was educated for the life of a sailor. He entered her majesty's service in 1864 and served as a midshipman, receiving severe injuries in consequence of a fall at sea. After long confinement in the hospitals at Malta and Haslar, he was discharged on account of the injuries he had received. He came to America in 1872, at the age of 19, settling in Iowa at Decorah, his present home. He spent four years in varying lines of business, employing himself successfully as a farmer, manufacturer and mechanic, and in 1876 began practicing law, which he had studied at odd times for several years. He became vice-president of the Citizens Savings bank of Decorah in 1886, the position he now holds. He also does a large business in real estate and loans, and still practices his profession, confining himself mostly to equity and probate cases. In August, 1898, he was appointed United States referee in bankruptcy for the district of Winneshiek county.

In politics Mr. Portman is independent. In religion he is still loyal to the church in which he was brought up, the Episcopal. He belongs to the Masonic order, is past master of Great Lights Lodge No. 181, at Decorah, and past commander of Beauseant Commandery No. 12. He is past grand treasurer of the Grand Commandery, and grand treasurer of the Grand Chapter of Iowa. He has always taken great interest in the public affairs of his locality. In 1876 he organized the volunteer fire department of Decorah, and was its first foreman and chief engineer.

Mr. Portman was married November 6, 1878, to Caroline S. Warren. They have two children, a daughter, Frances C., born in 1880; and a son, John F. B., born in 1885.

STOUT, HENRY LANE, of Dubuque, is the head of "The Knapp, Stout & Co. Company," which has a capital of $4,000,-000, and is one of the largest concerns of its kind in the United States, and probably in the world. Mr. Stout is an illustrous example of that class of men who, by the employment of brain and energy, have risen to a high and honored position. His career illustrates forcibly what can be accomplished by energy, perseverance, steadfastness of purpose and business ability. He was born in Huntington county, N. J., October 23, 1814. His father, William Stout, and his mother, Eleanor Lane Stout,

were both natives of New Jersey. His grandfather was a participant in the early history of the country and fought in the revolutionary war. After its close he was a member of the legislature of New Jersey many years. Their son Henry was reared on the farm, where he acquired the habits of industry and economy which have so largely contributed to his subsequent success. His educational advantages were confined to the public schools. In his 16th year he began life for himself and worked at the builder's trade, in Philadelphia, Pa., until 20 years of age. In 1836 he settled in Dubuque with less than $100 in money, but possessed of good health,

a hopeful heart and a purpose to grow up with the country. For a time he was occupied with building and mining, and in both was moderately successful, though his health was not good during the first ten years of his residence in Dubuque. The country was somewhat unhealthful and physicians advised him to return east, but he refused to do so, being determined to succeed in his original plan, and after becoming acclimated he enjoyed the best of health. In 1853 Mr. Stout invested his capital in the lumber business, purchasing an interest in the firm of Knapp & Taintor, which was then a small business. The name was changed to Knapp, Stout & Company, and Mr. Stout's influence at once made itself felt very strongly. He infused life into the business, and success rewarded the combined efforts of himself and partners. The business soon grew to gigantic proportions. Mr. Stout has been interested in the business over forty-six years, and he and his partners have managed it so successfully that to-day it is one of the largest businesses of its kind in the world, and the oldest under one firm name. In March, 1878, the concern was incorporated as "The Knapp, Stout & Co. Company," with a nominal stock of $2,000,000, which has since been increased to $4,000,-000, although the actual cash value of their holdings is several times larger than that amount. The present officers (July, 1899,) are: H. L. Stout, Dubuque, president; Andrew Taintor, Menomonee, Wis., vice-president; L. S. Taintor, Menomonee, Wis., secretary; John H. Douglas, St. Louis, Mo., treasurer. They have mills and yards at Rice Lake, Wis.; Cedar Falls, Wis.; Dubuque, Iowa; Menomonee, Wis.; Downsville, Wis.; Fort Madison, Iowa, and St. Louis, Mo., and their personal and real property extends from Lake Superior to New Orleans. Their annual output is about 125,000,000 feet. The policy of the company has always been to encourage settlement upon their cut lands, and most liberal terms are made by them to would-be settlers. There are in the employ of Knapp, Stout & Co., at the present time, hundreds of men who have literally grown gray in their service, many of them having been with the company for twenty-five years or more. Faithful service is expected and required and it receives a liberal reward. Besides its large lumbering interests, the company conducts large stores near its mills where large amounts of merchandise are annually sold.

Mr. Stout has always been a great admirer of horse flesh and has always been a lover of trotting horses; partially to gratify this interest and also partially for profit, he and his younger son, Frank D. Stout, entered into the business of breeding and raising the highest grade of trotting stock. Highland stock farm has become very prominent and there some of the finest and most valuable trotting horses in the United States have been bred and raised. In this business, as in all others in which Mr. Stout has become interested, no outlay is considered too great, and no exertion too much to attain eminent success. In 1886, the private citizens of the west were startled, and even horsemen were surprised, when F. D. Stout paid $22,000 for the stallion Nutwood, at that time 16 years old. That they were justified in making this expenditure is proven by the fact that Nutwood became the "king of trotting sires," and proved a remunerative financial investment. He leads all sires of his age in both first and second generations.

Mr. Stout was twice elected mayor of Dubuque and has filled many local offices of honor and trust. He has been a director and stockholder in most of the railroads coming to Dubuque and takes great interest in the development of the enterprises of the city and vicinity. In politics he is a republican, but his business has engrossed all his time and left none for political matters.

On the 23d of October, 1845, Mr. Stout was married to Miss Eveline Demming, a native of New York state. The wedded life of Mr. and Mrs. Stout, which began so auspiciously, was rewarded with happiness and prosperity, and the faithful wife and mother was spared to see her children grow to manhood and womanhood. These are James H. Stout, born in September, 1848; Frank D. Stout, born in March, 1854; Fannie D., born in August, 1858, now Mrs. Fred O'Donnell, and Jennie E., born in December, 1851, now Mrs. A. W. Daugherty. Mrs. Stout died May 12, 1879.

Such is a brief biography of Henry L. Stout. His name is known throughout the entire country; he has climbed the ladder of success step by step until he has reached the topmost round, and now he can look back upon his career and say truthfully that his life has been well spent. His has been self-attained success; no man ever aided him in business, and to-day he can safely be placed among the most successful men of the west.

SMOUSE, DR. DAVID W., enjoys one of the most desirable and lucrative practices in the city of Des Moines. He is a native of Maryland, coming from one of its best families. He was educated at the Rainsbury seminary, graduating at the age of 16. While very desirous of entering upon the study of medicine at once, his father objected because of the hardships necessary to the practice. He was given a stock of general merchandise, which he managed for two years; but as he spent more time over his books than in the store, his father closed out the business and put his son in the Medical college of the University of

Maryland, from which he graduated in 1876. Locating at once at Monroe, Iowa, he remained in active practice until 1880, when he removed to Des Moines. One year later he married Miss Amanda H. Cummings, of Waterloo, Iowa. The doctor, by hard work and perseverance, has attained distinction in his profession. In addition to his city practice he has also a large consultation practice throughout the state, having done work in almost every county in Iowa. He is a member and a regular attendant upon the national, the state, and the local medical societies. Outside of his practice the doctor is recognized as an enterprising business man, having done much to advance the interests of Des Moines. He is a director of two of the banks, president of the Citizens Improvement company, and stockholder in many of the leading business companies of the city.

---

SMITH, SAMUEL FRANCIS, mayor of the city of Davenport, has been a lawyer of wide reputation, and is among the best known bankers in the state. The ancestors of both his parents were of the Puritanic type, coming from England to Massachusetts early in the seventeenth century. He is the son of Rev. Samuel Francis Smith, a noted Baptist clergyman, whose name is

known almost the world over as the author of our national hymn "America." He was born in Boston, December 9, 1808, and died November, 1895, at Newton, Mass. He graduated from Harvard university in 1829, being a classmate of Oliver Wendell Holmes, who refers to him in his poem, "The Boys." Mr. Smith's mother, Mary White Smith, whose name was not changed by her marriage, was born in 1813, and is still living. Her grandfather, Rev. Hezekiah Smith, was for forty years pastor of a Baptist church in Haverhill, Mass., and served as a chaplain in the revolutionary war.

S. F. Smith, Jr., was born September 5, 1836, at Waterville, Me. His education was obtained largely through private instruction from his father, who thus fitted him to enter Harvard, and carried him through the freshman year. Over-work as a student caused his health to fail, and he was obliged to abandon his studies for a time; but he afterwards completed the course by studying alone at odd times. During this time he clerked several years in Boston, serving at different times in a wholesale drug store, the office of a manufacturing company, and a book store. In 1856 he came to Chicago, and after clerking a few months in a store was sent to Davenport, to a branch establishment. Having always desired to become a lawyer, he began the study of law in 1857 in the office of Judge James Grant, at Davenport, and only four years later was taken in as a partner. The firm did a large business in the collection of defaulted city and county bonds, and their income increased with wonderful rapidity. Mr. Smith's portion in 1862, amounted to only $200, while in 1873, the last year of the copartnership, it was over $50,000. The Mark Howard case, ended in 1873 was one of the most notable in which they were engaged. It arose out of bonds of various cities and counties in aid of the Mississippi & Missouri railway, and resulted in securing $1,000,000 for the firm's clients, and their attorney fee was $100,000, probably the largest fee that had then ever been paid in the state.

In the fall of 1873, Mr. Smith's health failed, due to overwork, and to recuperate he went with his family to Europe, remaining nearly three years, visiting the principal cities and points of interest on the continent. Since his return to Davenport in 1876, he has not practiced law, but has been engaged, more or less, in banking. He helped organize the Davenport National bank many years ago, and has been connected with it ever since, much of the time as president or vice-president, retiring from the presidency in January, 1895. He was also one of the organizers of the Union Savings bank, and is now a director and its attorney. From June, 1892, to June, 1893, he was president of the Iowa State Bankers' association, an office which can be held for a period of but one year, and in 1898 was vice-president, for Iowa, of the American Bankers' association.

Mr. Smith has always been a republican, and has held numerous important local offices. He served on the city council for four years, retiring in April, 1893, and during his term of service started the movement which resulted in the paving of Davenport's principal streets, and he served as chairman of the paving and financial committees, under the administration of both parties. In 1897 he was elected mayor of Davenport, being the first republican to fill that office since 1883. In 1896 the democratic majority was 1,035, and in 1897 Mr. Smith's majority was 326. He has always been loyal to the interests of the city, and has taken an active part in many public enterprises. He has been president of the Davenport Business Men's association, and of the Children's Home society of the state, has been a director of the Academy of Science, and now serves in that capacity in the Ladies' Relief association and the Davenport Library association. He has been vice-president of the Iowa Sons of the Revolution ever since its organization, and is now its president, and also holds the position of deputy-governor of the Society of Colonial Wars, for Iowa. He was in early life a Baptist, but transferred his membership to the Congregational church some years after his marriage, his wife belonging to that denomination.

He was married August 17, 1863, to Mary Reed, daughter of Rev. Julius Reed, D. D., of Davenport. They have one child, Anna R., who was born September 15, 1870, and who is still at home with her parents.

———

ALLISON, GEORGE R., of Rockwell City, was born at Oriskany, Oneida county, N. Y., August 3, 1842. His father, Robert Allison, was a noted chemist and druggist, and for thirteen years was connected with the Leeds infirmary in England. He came to this country in 1840 and settled in central New York. Farther down the line on the father's side, the ancestors were prosperous English farmers, and direct descendants of Richard Baxter, an eminent English divine. On the maternal side the family for generations engaged in the manufacture of woolen goods on a large scale. George R. Allison attended the common schools until 16 years of age, when he engaged as clerk in a country store in Oriskany, N. Y. For his services during the first year he received a salary of $8 per month, without board. But as his parents furnished the board and provided the clothing, the lad had nearly the whole of his salary remaining at the end of the year. That he made himself useful, not-

29

withstanding his meager salary, would appear from the fact that he remained with the firm for ten years, and at the time of resigning the position was receiving a much larger salary than is usually paid for like work. His next position was with the Oriskany Knitting Mill company, as bookkeeper, where he remained for one year, and then removed to Illinois, and purchased an interest in a general store in the town of Turner, near Chicago. After four years of prosperous business, the interests in Turner were disposed of, and he engaged in merchandising in Manson, Iowa, where for eleven years

he carried on a business of such proportions as is rarely built up in a small town. In speaking of the incidents in his money-making career which remain lastingly with him, Mr. Allison relates that his first dollar was earned in sawing and splitting four cords of wood for a neighbor. He still insists that it was the longest and highest and broadest pile of wood that was ever piled together.

Mr. Allison has been frequently honored with elective positions of trust and responsibility. He was the first recorder of the incorporated town of Manson, was supervisor of Calhoun county for three years, and subsequently served as county treasurer for six years. At present he is engaged in the real estate, loan and abstract business, having purchased a one-half interest in the Pioneer Abstracting company of that county. In politics he is a republican, and has held the several offices heretofore mentioned, at the hands of that party. He is a Mason; has been warden, secretary and treasurer of his home lodge. In religion he is of the Protestant Episcopal faith. June 9, 1870, he was married to Miss Emma F. Seaman, and from that union there have resulted four children: Emma F., Mary E., Robert S., and Cary J. Allison.

———

McARTHUR, WILLIAM CORSE, is an influential young lawyer and republican

politician of Burlington, the first republican to be elected to the state senate from that county in many years. Senator McArthur was born in the city of his residence and he comes from two historic families. His father, Martin C. McArthur, was one of the pioneers of Iowa, who opened up and developed the express lines of the northwest territory, acquiring a competency, and was for many years one of the leading citizens of Burlington. He was born in New York. The senator's mother, Virginia Corse McArthur, was a native of Illinois and is a sister of Gen. John M. Corse, of Allatoona fame, one of the most

distinguished soldiers Iowa contributed to the war of the rebellion. Her father was prominent in democratic state politics. Mrs. McArthur was deeply interested in religious and charitable work. The Corse family were French Huguenots and settled in Maryland in the Seventeenth century, afterwards going to Virginia and intermarrying with the Marshall family, of which Chief Justice Marshall is the best known. The family was prominent in the revolutionary and civil wars. The McArthur family was of Scotch origin. The parent branch settled near Edinburgh, Scotland. John McArthur, grandfather of the senator, was banished from Scotland on account of being a non-conformist, but through influence at court was pardoned. Being disgusted with that form of government which could deprive him of his natural rights, he came to America, and settled in New York.

Senator McArthur received his early education from his mother and did not enter school until after he was 8 years old. He was first sent to a German school and mastered that language. Subsequently he attended the Institute-college, of Burlington, where he prepared for college and entered the Chicago university in 1878; remaining there one year, he then went to Cornell university, at Ithaca, N. Y., graduating with the class of 1881. He spent the winter of 1881 and 1882 at Columbia Law school, in New York city, and was examined and admitted to the bar in Iowa in July following. He was orator of his class in the senior year of college and is a member of the Zeta Psi Greek letter fraternity. He entered upon the practice of law in Burlington in July, 1882, and has continued successfully in the practice since that time. He has always been an active republican and was connected with the internal revenue service as deputy collector. He served as a colonel on the staffs of Governors Jackson and Drake, and has long been a member of the board of trustees of the Burlington Free Public library. He was elected to the Twenty-sixth General Assembly in 1895, running 581 votes ahead of his ticket. During that session he took a leading part in securing the passage of a bill permitting the manufacture of liquor in the state, as its sale had already been authorized, and the business interests of his district demanded that an article which could be sold might also be manufactured. He introduced and secured the passage of a drainage bill redeeming thousands of acres of low land bordering on the Mississippi river, and a bill preventing city councils from granting or extending franchises to quasi-public corporations, such as water and electric light works, without first submitting the same to a direct vote of the people; also one requiring street car companies to vestibule their cars for the protection of employes during the winter months, and making the liability of such corporations, in personal injury cases, the same as railway companies. He had an influential and prominent part in all the important legislation coming before the legislature during the special session when the new code was made. In 1897 he was elected to the state senate from Des Moines county as the personal representative of United States Senator John H. Gear, and his work in the upper body of the legislature fully bore out the reputation he had earned in the preceding general assembly, as a valuable legislator.

---

HAMILTON, JOHN D. MILLER, one of the best known and most successful lawyers of southeastern Iowa, lives at Fort Madison, and is attorney for the Atchison, Topeka & Santa Fe Railway company, the Chicago, Burlington & Quincy Railway company, and other corporations. He comes of a good old family, his father, John S. Hamilton, having been a member of the legislature of two states, Pennsylvania and Iowa. The senior Hamilton was a lawyer, too, and lived in Pittsburg, where the subject of this sketch was born, July 18, 1851. His mother was Sara Miller, daughter of John D. Miller and Ruth Miller, Mr. Miller being a prominent coal merchant in Pittsburg. The Hamilton family is a historic one, first attaining fame in the north of Ireland, and the south of Scotland during the career of Mary Stuart. The Miller family is of German descent, coming from Strasburg, the capital of Alsace-Lorraine. The Hamiltons moved from Pittsburg to Fort Madison, Iowa, in 1854, and the father was killed by the accidental discharge of a cannon in Fort Madison, while celebrating the election of James Buchanan to the presidency. After his father's death, the young son received a common school education and then entered Knox college, in Galesburg, Ill. After completing the course there he went to St. Louis and graduated from the St. Louis Law school, one of the best in the country. He also studied law in the office of Hon. John Van

Valkenburg, at Fort Madison, and in 1876 was admitted to partnership with Mr. Van Valkenburg, continuing till 1890, when the latter died. Mr. Hamilton has been connected with much of the most important litigation of Lee county, and has continued in practice alone since the death of his partner. In 1878 Mr. Hamilton was elected to the Iowa legistature as a democrat, and he has always acted with that party. He is one of the most conspicuous figures in the party councils of the state. In 1886 he was chairman of the committee on resolutions of the democratic state convention. For four years he was city attorney of Fort

Madison and for six years held the office of mayor. He was a democratic candidate for presidential elector for the First district in 1880. Governor Sherman appointed Mr. Hamilton a member of the commission to locate and build the southwestern hospital for the insane, in 1884. The hospital was located in Clarinda, and Mr. Hamilton has been a trustee ever since, having been repeatedly elected by the legislature. Though he has been an active democrat all his life, Mr. Hamilton has not been an applicant for office. He has preferred to stick to his law practice, and though starting in life without means, he has acquired a fair competence and enjoys a very lucrative practice. Mr. Hamilton is a member of the Odd

Fellows, Knights of Pythias and Masonic lodges, and was grand chancellor of the Knights of Pythias for the state of Iowa, and one of its supreme representatives. During his term as grand chancellor, 1,500 members were added to the order through his efforts. As he is frequently in Chicago on business, Mr. Hamilton is a member of the Union League club. In 1878 he was married to Mary M. Rice, daughter of J. M. and Kate Rice. Two sons have been born to them: Hale R. Hamilton and J. D. M. Hamilton, Jr. The family belongs to the Presbyterian church.

---

PIPER, FRANK TALCOT, of Sheldon, is among the successful men whose lives

have been spent in Iowa journalism. He was born in Maquoketa, Jackson county, Iowa, July 19, 1856, but removed to Green Springs, Ohio, with his parents when but a child. There, when a little boy, he watched the soldiers march away to fight for the union, lamenting the fact the while that he was not old enough to go with them. In 1868 the family returned to Iowa, locating on a homestead near Newell, Buena Vista county. In 1870 he began an apprenticeship in the office of the Newell *Times*, under John T. Long. Later he was employed on the *Sentinel* at Le

Mars; then on the *Times* and *Leader* at Cherokee, and in 1873 located at Sheldon, where he has been engaged ever since in the publication of the *Mail*. The early education of Mr. Piper, like that of many another successful professional man, was limited in its advantages, and had to be secured largely by home study. He attended the common schools a few terms only, but studied with determination, and when, subsequently, he entered McClain's academy at Iowa City, found no trouble in keeping abreast of his class. He remained there but two terms, however, being compelled at the end of that time to go to work to meet the necessities of his purse, and all future schooling was in the broad and engrossing field of journalism. Beginning as an employe in the *Mail* office, on the munificent salary of $2 per week and board—the board consisted of such toothsome dishes as were prepared by his employer, who kept bachelor's hall and did his own cooking, at his homestead a mile or so from the town—he plodded on perseveringly, and ultimately became the editor and proprietor of the paper, which, under his management, has prospered in every way. He has never taken a partner, preferring to bear all the burdens of the business for the pleasure of enjoying the undivided profits thereof.

In politics Mr. Piper is a republican, and was postmaster of Sheldon for four years, under Harrison's administration. He was an alternate from the Eleventh congressional district in the Chicago convention which nominated James G. Blaine for the presidency. He is a Mason, an Odd Fellow and a Knight of Pythias, but belongs to no religious sect.

July 2, 1876, he was married to Miss Eva Bronson, of Sheldon. They have had two children: Arvilla Elizabeth and Roscoe Bronson Piper. The first was taken away by death at the age of 10; the second, who is now about 17 years of age, has taken a preparatory course of two years at Battle Creek, Mich., but is at present in the high school at Sheldon.

In 1895 Mr. Piper was a candidate for the nomination for state senator in the Forty-ninth district, comprising Sioux, O'Brien, Lyon and Osceola counties, but as each county had a candidate the result was a deadlock, which lasted two days. On the 1,635th ballot Mr. Piper withdrew his name and threw his support to Henry Hospers, of Sioux county, resulting in the nomination of that gentleman.

CRAVATH, Samuel Austin, of Grinnell, is a native of Pennsylvania, born at Conneaut, Crawford county, September 27, 1836. His father, James Cravath, was a native of New York, who, after his marriage, settled on a farm in western Pennsylvania, where he died at an early age, leaving three sons. The mother, Emily Davis Cravath, also of New York, was a woman of fine musical attainments, and a singer of considerable local prominence. The name Cravath is of uncertain origin. The Cravaths of this country trace their origin to an ancestor who settled in Boston, Mass., in 1679, and who probably came from near Bristol, Eng. The name has been found in south central Europe as well as in England. Grandmother Bingham Cravath was a daughter of Colonel Bingham, from whom Binghamton, N. Y., was named. He was an officer of the revolutionary war, who lived to be 104 years of age. The immediate ancestors of the family were New England people from northern Connecticut. They moved to western New York, and were all prosperous farmers of good education. The boyhood days of S. A. Cravath were spent on a farm near Oberlin, Ohio, and in a thrifty Yankee community in Gainesville, Wyoming county, N. Y. In 1852 he entered the preparatory department of Oberlin college and continued his studies in connection with that institution until August, 1858, when he graduated, taking the degree of bachelor of arts. On account of his standing as a classical student, he was selected to teach Latin and Greek, in the institution in connection with the pursuit of his other studies. He also spent the three months of winter vacation teaching, either in common schools or schools of higher grade, in order to secure the means to complete his college course. Honors and prizes were not allowed in Oberlin college in those years. Immediately after graduating, he assumed the principalship of Madison seminary, at Madison, Ohio, in which position he remained three years, serving also as one of the county examiners of teachers. During the years 1862 and 1863, he superintended the public schools of Marion, Ohio, studying medicine meanwhile. In the winter of 1863–4, he took a course of lectures in Starling Medical college, at Columbus, Ohio. In the spring of 1864 he completed a course of lectures at the Cincinnati College of Medicine and Surgery, and received the degree of M. D. He began the practice of medi-

cine in the city of Springfield, Ohio, but moved to Mitchell, Mitchell county, Iowa, in October, 1865, and continued in the practice there until 1872. He established the *Mitchell County News*, now called the *Osage News*, in 1869, and edited it for two years, in connection with his practice. Soon after he took charge of the paper, a county convention put in nomination a candidate for county superintendent of schools, who had little qualification for the place. The *News* nominated, and by its support secured the election of, the first woman to hold the office of county superintendent of schools in Iowa, Miss Julia C.

Addington. Finding his double work too great a burden, Dr. Cravath sold the *News* in 1871; but a few months of freedom convinced him that he could not easily lay aside newspaper work, and he decided to return to it in a larger field. January 11, 1872, he bought a half interest in the Grinnell *Herald*, of J. M. Chamberlain, and soon after secured the whole plant. With the exception of a brief partnership with Col. S. F. Cooper, he continued as sole proprietor until 1879, when he sold a half interest to Albert Shaw, now editor of the American monthly *Review of Reviews*. After a partnership of three years, Mr. Shaw received an appointment on the editorial staff of the *Minneapolis Tribune*, and Dr.

Cravath bought back his interest and was sole editor and proprietor until 1890, when he sold a half interest to Hon. W. G. Ray. This partnership continued until August, 1894, when on account of his health, he decided to retire from the business and sold all his interest in the plant to Ronald McDonald, who was for ten years night editor of the *New York Times.* During the twenty-three years of Dr. Cravath's connection with the *Herald,* it grew from a very meagerly furnished country printing office, occupying a single room, to a well equipped establishment with five printing presses and the complete machinery of a publishing house, including a bindery, and occupying both stories of a brick building of its own, built with elevator power and other modern conveniences. In 1878, the *Herald* was changed from a weekly to a semi-weekly paper, and has been issued in that form until the present time. It has always been republican in politics and conservative but positive in its utterances. The whole establishment went up in flames in a fire which consumed the core of Grinnell, June 12, 1889. Within sixty days, it was rebuilt in a better and more substantial manner. During his residence in Grinnell, Dr. Cravath has held several positions of responsibility and trust. He was secretary of the school board for fifteen years, served several years as a director and president of the Grinnell Building, Loan and Savings association; has been one of the directors of the First National bank of Grinnell for more than a decade; also director and second vice-president of the Merchants National bank of Grinnell, president of the Grinnell Savings bank, and one of the trustees of Iowa college.

During the presidency of Benjamin Harrison, he was appointed postmaster of Grinnell, and held the office four years. With these exceptions, and one term as school director, he has kept aloof from public office and candidacy.

S. A. Cravath became a member of the Congregational church when a young man, under the ministry of Charles G. Finney, who was president of the college and pastor of the only church in Oberlin at that time. He was married in Philadelphia, July 11, 1860, to Mary Raley, of Hanoverton, Columbiana county, Ohio, Dr. Albert Barnes officiating. Mary Raley was a Quaker, of Pennsylvania ancestry, who was graduated at Oberlin in 1858, with the degree of A. B. She was later a teacher

of some years' experience. Since her residence in Grinnell she has been, from 1880 to 1895, a deaconess in the Congregational church. The children were Emily, Rose Mary, and James Raley, of whom only the son survives. He graduated from Iowa college in 1892, and occupied the position of electrical editor of the *Street Railway Review* of Chicago for four years. Dr. and Mrs. Cravath also reared a niece of Mrs. Cravath, (Ella B.) who was left motherless in infancy.

FLICKINGER, ALBERT T., the subject of this sketch, was born in Urichsville,

Tuscarawas county, Ohio, August 14, 1846. He is the second of a family of eight children, five boys and three girls. His parents, Eli Flickinger and Margaret McChesney, were both natives of Ohio. In May, 1863, the family moved from Ohio to a farm in Buchanan county, Iowa, where the father died August 5, 1875, and the mother September 19, 1896. Mr. Flickinger, while in Ohio, attended the schools of his native town, and after coming to Iowa, the Lenox Collegiate institute at Hopkinton, in 1866-67; he afterwards worked on the farm during the summer and taught school in winter, until 1871, when he entered the State university at Iowa

City. He graduated from the academic department in 1875 and from the law department in 1876. December 29, 1880, he was married to Miss Ella Spangler, the oldest daughter of Hon. S. T. Spangler, of Buchanan county, Iowa. They have two children, Floyd S., born July 11, 1883, and Reed A., born July 14, 1887.

Soon after his graduation from the Iowa State university, Mr. Flickinger went to Council Bluffs, Iowa, and opened a law office, where he has resided ever since, engaged in the active duties of his profession with his brother, I. N. Flickinger, under the firm name of Flickinger Bros. This firm has a large practice in all the different courts, and enjoys an enviable reputation for integrity and ability.

Mr. Flickinger has always been an active republican, and was a candidate for mayor of Council Bluffs on the republican ticket in 1882. In 1886 he was elected by the legislature as one of the trustees of the Iowa School for the Deaf at Council Bluffs, and in 1892 was re-elected to the same office, his second term expiring May 1, 1898. He was endorsed by his congressional district for governor at the republican state convention held at Cedar Rapids in 1897, receiving 151 votes on second ballot.

---

TITTEMORE, JAMES NELSON, of Marshalltown, was born on a farm near Eureka, Winnebago county, Wis., March 2, 1864. His father, Nelson Tittemore, was a machinist and millwright, and was born in the state of New York. He came of English, Dutch and Holland ancestors, who settled early in the New England states and were mostly farmers. His mother, Margaret Crowley, was born of Irish parentage. When a child her parents settled near Oshkosh, Wis., where she lived about forty years. The father died in 1882.

Mr. Tittemore is unmarried. His mother and two sisters live with him. He has also two sisters married and one brother dead. They have a lovely, hospitable home and are the social center of a large circle of friends. Mr. Tittemore seems to live to brighten the lives and gratify the tastes of his sisters and mother, without a thought of self. His business career has been successful, with promotions following each other in quick succession. His first dollar was earned as telegraph operator at the age of 16. He has been promoted from one to another of the following positions: Telegraph operator and station agent on the Milwaukee, Lake Shore & Western railway in Wisconsin; traveling auditor, Chicago & Northwestern railway; traveling passenger agent, Milwaukee, Lake Shore & Western railway; station agent, Soo Line; chief clerk general freight department, Soo Line; traveling freight agent, Great Northern railway; general freight agent, Sioux City & Northern railway and Pacific short lines; assistant to president of the last named companies; general freight and passenger agent, Des Moines Northern & Western railway, and general freight agent, Iowa Central Railway company; acting general manager of the Iowa Central railway.

Mr. Tittemore aspires to farm life and hopes some day to take a position in this line of work. He is fond of live stock and proud of his farmer ancestry. His father served through the civil war as a private. He was in Andersonville prison several months and was mustered out of service in the summer of 1864. He is a republican and a member of the Catholic church. He is one of Iowa's promising young men, finely educated and polished in manner and speech, although his education in the schoolroom covered only about five years. By personal application and study he stands equal to any who have had the opportunities of the magnificent schools of our commonwealth.

EATON, WILLARD LEE, member of the house from Mitchell county, is a successful lawyer in Osage, and is known all over northern Iowa, and also in Minnesota and Wisconsin, over which territory his practice extends. His father, Arial K. Eaton, was a member of the legislature from 1852 to 1854, while living in Delhi. He was appointed receiver of the Turkey River Land district by President Pierce in 1855, and

moved to Decorah. The next year he went with the land office to Osage, and became one of the proprietors of that town. He was a member of the school board for many years, and died in Osage July 17, 1896, at the end of a long and useful life of 82 years. He was a native of New Hampshire, and was a cousin of Gen. John Eaton, late commissioner of education. In early life he was a school-teacher, but later practiced law, and continued to practice after moving to Osage. Willard Eaton's mother was Sarah Jarnigan Eaton. She married Mr. Eaton in Indiana, and her ancestors came from Virginia. The subject of this sketch was born in Delhi, Delaware county, Iowa,

October 13, 1848. He received his education in the district school in Delhi and Osage, and in the Cedar Valley seminary at Osage, Iowa, of which he was one of the first pupils. He graduated from this institution in 1872. He entered the State University Law school, and graduated in 1872, being selected as one of the commencement orators. He was deputy clerk of courts, of Mitchell county, from 1871 to 1874, and at that time he formed a partnership with John B. Cleland, for the practice of law in Osage. In 1885 Mr. Cleland was made district judge, and Mr. Eaton continued in the practice alone until September 1, 1889, when J. F. Clyde was admitted to partnership, and this continued until January 7, 1897, when Mr. Clyde also went on the bench as district judge. Since then Mr. Eaton has practiced alone. His most celebrated case was the defense of M. E. Billings, accused of the murder of Kingsley, of Waverly.

Mr. Eaton was a democrat until the fall of 1893, when he became convinced that the position of the democratic party was wrong, especially on the question of the tariff and the currency, and since then he has acted with the republicans. He has been mayor of Osage three terms, county attorney one term as a democrat, and was elected in 1897 to the legislature as a republican. He has been for many years a member of the school board, and is now president of the board. He is a member of the Masonic order, and past junior warden, also deputy past grand master. He is a member of the commandery and of El Kahir Temple, Mystic Shriners. Though not a member of the church, Mr. Eaton attends the Methodist Episcopal church in Osage, and is a member of the board of trustees.

He was married September 11, 1874, to Laura R. Annis, a former resident of Westfield, Vt. They have had two children: Ivan Willard, who died September 19, 1884, at the age of 2¼ years, and Allen March Eaton, who was born March 15, 1887.

Mr. Eaton won considerable distinction as a member of the legislature, purely on the strength of his recognized ability as a lawyer and the candor and earnestness with which he met all public questions. He was a member of most of the more important committees in the house, and was chairman of the committee on elections, which at that time was considered one of the very important committees in the house, on the account of several contests and political questions which were referred to that committee. He was chairman of the sifting committee, at the close of the session, the most important of all committee appointments. He formed many strong friendships at this time, and was often pointed out as a man who would be heard from in the future in state politics.

TUBBS, Hon. L. W., of Emerson, has the distinction of having been a member of the first legislature of California after its admission to the union of states. He was born in Binghamton, N. Y., January 4, 1826, and at 12 years of age removed with his parents to the Western Reserve in Ohio. Later he was placed in Oberlin college, but owing to losses sustained by his father in road building, was compelled to give up his college course, in which he was making rapid progress, particularly in the studies of surveying and engineering. He went from school to Sandusky City, where he learned the miller's trade, and at the age of 19 years removed to Michigan. Here he earned the first money he could really call his own, helping to survey a railroad from Detroit to Ypsilanti, now a part of the Michigan Central system. March 1, 1849, he started across the plains with an ox train, of which he was chosen the captain. They were on the road almost six months before Long's Barr, on the Feather river, was reached. Here he tried mining, but made only enough out of it to board and clothe himself. By an extra session of congress, California was admitted to statehood in September, 1850, and he was elected to the legislature from that district. His term ended, he returned to Long's Barr and engaged in the mercantile and mining business, in the first of which he was highly successful. His health failed, and the physician ordered a sea voyage, so he sailed for Honolulu, where he remained about three months, and then went to Chili and remained for some time, finally returning to his home in California to find that his partner had sold out the business and skipped the country. He returned to Flowerfield, Mich., after an absence of four years, and again took up his old trade of milling. Here he was married, October 1, 1853, to Miss Sibyl J. Wheeler, daughter of Hon. William Wheeler, and remained until 1854, when failing health again compelled a change of climate. Iowa was decided upon, and,

though several trips were subsequently made to Michigan, this state has ever since been his home. He has been a resident of Mills county for nearly forty-one years, and all his children but one have been born there. He has six children living, three boys and three girls, the oldest son, W. L., born in Michigan in 1855, being the present sheriff of Mills county.

He was elected probate judge of Mills county in 1858 and held the office until the law was changed — the first republican elected to the position in the county. In May, 1861, he received an order from Governor Kirkwood to raise a company of

mounted minute men, and with the order was the request that no man should be selected or permitted to join who for any reason would not be able to go to war. Within four days fifty-two men were enlisted, and in the election which was insisted upon by Mr Tubbs, that gentleman was unanimously chosen captain. He received his commission June 8, and the organization was kept up to the close of the war. A second communication from the governor in October, 1861, ordered him to recruit a regiment of all the men in the county, exception being made to those enlisted in the mounted force, which was done. An election was called to choose a colonel, and, as before, Mr. Tubbs received all the votes. This last company was never called out, the minute force being ample to keep back the Missouri raiders. Strange to say these men have not yet been mustered out.

In politics he is, and has always been, a republican, as are all his boys. He has been a member of the Masonic order for almost fifty years, and has filled nearly every office in the organization

STANTON, MAJ. CORNELIUS ALBERT, of Centerville, is a soldier and citizen whose virtues it would be almost impossible to

exaggerate in biography. This man comes naturally by his fine traits of patriotism and good citizenship. His father, Nathan Stanton, was a native of Washington county, Ohio, his parents having settled near Marietta at a time when that section of country was an almost unbroken wilderness. He came to Iowa in 1850, and settled in Lee county, removing two years later to Appanoose county. He was an anti-slavery man before the war, a believer in universal human liberty, and the fugitive slave escaping across the Ohio river from his Virginia master always found at Nathan Stanton's door assistance and help on his way toward Canada and freedom.

He became a republican at the organization of that party. The mother was Lydia Conkright before marriage, and a woman of many lovable graces.

Major Stanton was born near Marietta, Ohio, December 28, 1841, and when 10 years of age removed with his parents to Lee county, Iowa, and subsequently to Appanoose county. He enlisted as a private on August 20, 1861, in Company I, Third Iowa cavalry, and during four years of brilliant service was promoted as follows: September 6, 1861, Fifth sergeant; September 20, 1862, second lieutenant; November 1, 1862, captain; September 21, 1864, major. He took part in nearly all the battles in which his regiment was engaged, the more important of which were Pea Ridge, West Plains, Salem, Bayou Cache, Grenada, La Grange, Vicksburg, Jackson, Little Rock, Guntown, Ripley, Tupelo, Tallahatchie, Independence, Big Blue, Mine Creek, Plantersville, Montevallo, Selma and Columbus.

He was severely wounded at La Grange, Ark., May 20, 1863, but continued to serve with his regiment until it was mustered out in August, 1865.

With a view to keeping alive the memories of those days of strife and bloodshed, and for the purpose of perpetuating the sentiment of patriotism he has, since the war, affiliated with nearly all the prominent organizations partaking of a military character. He is past commander of Bashore Post, G. A. R., a member of the Iowa commandery of the Loyal Legion, chief of staff of the Iowa G. A. R., and president of the Third Iowa Cavalry association. In the last-named organization he has been re-elected at each annual reunion since 1887. He cast his first vote for Lincoln for president, while a soldier in the field, and has voted the republican ticket ever since. He was appointed by Governor Larrabee in 1889 a member of the board of regents of the Iowa State university, and was re-elected by the legislature in 1890. At the present time he is a member of the university executive committee. He has served as a member of the board of education in Centerville, and for a time was its president. He is a member of the Presbyterian church, and affiliates with many secret and benevolent societies, among which may be mentioned the Masons and Odd Fellows.

He was married to Miss Emma Houston, May 1, 1878. They have had four children: Edna, Nora, Neil and Anne Stanton.

MACLEAN, PAUL, editor of the *Creston Gazette* and postmaster of Creston, has carved out a permanent place for himself in Iowa newspaperdom and politics. He has been a resident of the state since 1869, when his father's family left the old homestead in Pennsylvania and settled on a large farm near the old town of Columbus City, Louisa county. Paul Maclean was born December 10, 1865, on the old home farm, known as Clover farm, adjoining the village of Springdale, Allegheny county, Pa., about sixteen miles up the Allegheny river from Pittsburg. This farm had been in the possession of the Maclean family for generations, having had but one other owner, to whom it was patented by William Penn, and the instrument executed by William Penn is still in the possession of Matthew Maclean, father of Paul. Matthew Maclean was married in 1860, to Nancy Logan, whose father was famed for being the first white child born west of the Allegheny mountains in Pennsylvania. He was a country merchant, and Charles Dickens was a guest in his home at Logan's Ferry, opposite Springdale, and allusion is made to his visit there in Dickens' American Notes. Paul Maclean's grandfather, on his father's side, was a newspaper man of distinction. He began in his youth, in the office of the *Greensburg Gazette*, of which he was subsequently for several years, the editor. Later, he was editor of the *Pittsburg Gazette*, now the *Commercial Gazette*, which he owned in partnership with his brother. The *Gazette* was the first newspaper established in Pittsburg, and the Macleans made it the first daily. They also conducted an extensive publishing business, devoted mainly to Presbyterian church literature; this is now known as the Presbyterian board of publication. Matthew Maclean, when he removed to Iowa, devoted himself to raising stock, and was very successful. He avoided public office, never wanted one, and announced, when the matter was broached, that he would accept no nomination, and would not serve if elected to office.

Paul Maclean attended the public schools of Columbus City, and took a course in the university in Oberlin, Ohio. At the age of 16 years he began his business education in the office of the *Columbus Nonpareil*, holding the position of "devil" at a salary of $1.25 per week. This was allowed to accumulate for six months, and is still among Mr. Maclean's bills receivable, for the paper, at this time, yielded up the

ghost and left little but debts to mark its existence. Two years later his father bought for Paul an interest in the *Columbus Junction Safeguard*, where he was for a time associated with Mr. Will Colton, and later with his brother-in-law, Mr. J. B. Hungerford, now editor of the *Carroll Herald*. In 1883, Mr. Maclean purchased the *Carroll Herald*, and for several years conducted that paper in conjunction with the late E. R. Hastings. After Mr. Hastings' death, the firm of Maclean & Hungerford was formed, and continued in the management of the *Herald* until 1889, when Mr. Hungerford purchased Mr. Maclean's interest, and

the latter, with his father, purchased the *Atlantic Telegraph* from Hon. Lafayette Young. In the spring of 1892, having sold the *Telegraph*, Mr. Maclean went to Creston and secured control of the *Gazette*, in which his father is also interested.

Mr. Maclean was married in 1892, to Miss Gertrude Young, of Carroll, a neice of Hon. H. W. Macomber of that place, and Judge Macomber, of Omaha. They have one child living, Elizabeth, born May 8, 1895. A son, Malcolm, died in infancy. David A. Maclean, a business man in Indianapolis, and Ralph Maclean, local editor of the *Carroll Herald*, are brothers of Paul. Mary, wife of J. B. Hungerford, and Elizabeth, who lives with her parents in Atlantic, are his sisters. Paul is the elder brother.

In 1896 Mr. Maclean was chosen presidential elector for the Eighth congressional district, and says that he acknowledges no higher honor than that of having voted for William McKinley for president, and Garret A. Hobart for vice-president, in the meeting of the electoral college. He was appointed postmaster of Creston, in March, 1898.

BLOOMER, D. C., LL. D. The public record and private life of Dexter Chamberlain Bloomer, of Council Bluffs, are so filled

with good deeds that they must go into the state's history together. Surely his is a career typical of true Americanism. He was born in Scipio, N. Y., July 4, 1816, of good Quaker stock, which came from England in an early day. Following a literary and classical education, he commenced the study of law, and soon thereafter became active in politics. Because of his knowledge of political science he was made the responsible editor of the *Seneca County Courier*, a whig paper at Seneca Falls, which position he filled for fifteen years. He was admitted to the bar in 1843, and while engaged in practice before the several courts of the state, held many offices of trust and responsibility, among them

that of postmaster during the Taylor-Fillmore administration. His political or public services can be best set forth in the following manner: 1856 to 1897, notary public; 1856 to 1857, alderman of Council Bluffs; 1861 to 1863, member of the Iowa board of education; 1861 to 1873, receiver of public moneys, the commissions he now holds having been signed by Presidents Lincoln, Johnson and Grant; 1859 to 1860 and 1864 to 1874, president of the Council Bluffs school board; 1869 to 1870, mayor of Council Bluffs, and again the same office, 1871 to 1873; 1871 to 1897, director in Council Bluffs Library association, made a a free library in 1882; 1892 to 1897, president of the Free Library association.

He removed to Mt. Vernon, Ohio, in 1853, and assumed the editorship of the *Western Home Visitor*, his wife filling a similar position with the *Lily* of the same city. In 1854 he visited Council Bluffs, and so well pleased was he with the place that the following year found himself and wife aboard a steamboat, bound for the new El Dorado. They disembarked at St. Joseph, and the journey thence was made by stage coach. He immediately established himself in the practice of law and the real estate business, and as the county at that time was strongly democratic, proceeded with other gentlemen to organize the new republican party in western Iowa. The interest which he manifested in political matters and the acute and able manner in which he led the new organization, attracted public attention to him, and caused his party to bestow upon him many trusts. He was frequently presented as a candidate for the office of judge, representative to the legislature, etc., but the opposition was so far in the ascendancy that his election was quite out of the question, although running far ahead of his ticket. His eleven years' service on the board of education was given fitting recognition in the naming in his honor of one of the fine school buildings of the city. During the war he rendered efficient service to the cause of the union, and was president of the Union league.

He was editor of the *Council Bluffs Chronotype* in 1856, and subsequently filled like positions with the *Republican* and *Northwestern Odd Fellow*. He also compiled a history of Pottawattamie county, which was published in the annals of Iowa.

He is a member of the Protestant Episcopal church, of which he has been senior warden for more than thirty years.

He was married to Miss Amelia Jenks, a lady of high attainments and well suited to his domestic and literary tastes. Her first national notoriety was occasioned by her introduction of what was known as the "Bloomer costume," which called the attention of the public to an urgent reform in dress, and has led to important modifications of the old and unhealthful fashion, and secondly, and more lastingly, as a prominent and efficient advocate of the cause of woman. She ranks with Susan B. Anthony, Mrs. Hale, Mrs. Shaw and other co-workers in the cause of reform.

Mr. Bloomer has been as successful in his own business as in the discharge of his public duties. He was in partnership with J. D. Edmundson from 1865 to 1870, and the firm gained an enviable reputation. Since the dissolution of that partnership he has continued in practice and has found time to do much writing, notably a history of Mormonism in Iowa; "The Life and Writings of Amelia Bloomer," etc.

---

HEAD, MAHLON, one of the most influential business men of Jefferson, Greene county, was born on a farm in Highland county, Ohio, July 12, 1835. His father, William M. Head, was also born in that county in 1808, and died in Jefferson in 1893. He came to Iowa in the fall of 1855 and settled in Montezuma. He was a farmer the most of his life, but was treasurer of Poweshiek county for three terms. His wife, whose maiden name was Margaret Ferneau, was also a native of Ohio, born in 1813 and died in Montezuma in 1894. Their remains rest in Jefferson cemetery, in Greene county. Father Head was a firm, conscientious man.

Mahlon Head obtained his education in the common schools of Ohio, attending three or four months of each year and the rest of the time working upon his father's farm. He was 21 years of age when he came to Iowa with his parents. He worked on a farm in Poweshiek county for two years, and since then he has been engaged in the real estate and banking business, except the time he was in the army. He enlisted in Montezuma in August, 1861, as a private in Company F, Tenth Iowa infantry. His first encounter with the confederates was at Bloomfield, Mo. He was in other engagements as follows: New Madrid, Mo.; Island No. 10; at the bombardment of Ft. Pillow; siege of Corinth; battles of Iuka, Corinth, Raymond and

Jackson, Miss.; siege of Vicksburg; again at Jackson and battles of Mission Ridge; Resaca; and through the Atlanta campaign and Sherman's march to the sea. He was promoted to second lieutenant of his company in the spring of 1862, and was acting adjutant after the siege of Vicksburg and until after the battle of Mission Ridge, in which battle he was wounded in the left thigh.

Mr. Head cast his first vote for John C. Fremont for president and has voted the straight republican ticket from that time to this. He was the first mayor of Jefferson and served in that capacity for four years.

He has been the chairman of the board of supervisors of Greene county for six years. He was the first chief engineer of the fire department of Jefferson, serving continuously as such for eight years, when he resigned on account of his health. He is a Thirty-second Degree Mason, a prominent member of the Odd Fellows fraternity and a member of the Methodist church.

Mr. Head is now, July, '99, the nominee of the republican party of his county for representative in the state legislature, and will be elected.

Altogether, Mr. Head is known and regarded as one of the most upright and influential citizens of Greene county, and is respected by all. He was married to Mary

L. Mullikin in the fall of 1866. They have ten children: Florence, Mary M., Dorothy J., Mabel S., John, Mahlon. Va Va, Rena E., Charles D. and Marguerita.

PAUL, DANIEL McFARLAND, one of the well-established and successful men

of Thurman, was born July 26, 1814, in Washington county, Pa. His father, William Paul, was a farmer in that county. His mother's maiden name was Hannah Slack. Both father and son belonged to the whig party until Mr. Paul, in 1856, became a devoted republican, to which political faith he has ever since been true. He was educated in subscription schools until he was 19 years of age. About this time he tried selling goods and succeeded very well. For three years he ran a flat boat on the Ohio river from Rising Sun to New Orleans. He sold out in 1857 and moved to West Point, now Oxford, Mo. Here he engaged in the general merchandise business, continuing till the fall of 1860. On account of the war, Mr. Paul removed to Thurman, Fremont county, then called Plum Hollow. He again engaged in the general merchandise business, continuing in the same until 1874, when he disposed of the business. Mr. Paul was justice of the peace and post-

master in Indiana. He was also postmaster in Oxford and in Plum Hollow, and was the first mayor of Plum Hollow. He is a member of the Odd Fellows fraternity.

He was married January 1, 1835, to Elizabeth Walton. Eleven children were born to them, four of whom are now living: Martha J., born May 21, 1845; Kasiah H., born March 31, 1837; Alice, born October 8, 1847; and Walton M., born April 13, 1861.

His has been a long life of honorable usefulness.

ALDRICH, EDWIN A., of Creston, has made pharmacy a study for many years and has achieved notable success. He began his first work in a drug store in 1866 as a clerk at a salary of $15 a month, and has been continually in the drug business since that time. There is probably not a better versed pharmacist in the state. He was born in Adams, Mass., September 12, 1851. His parents, Edwin J. and Melissa R. Peck Aldrich, came from Adams, Mass., to

Montrose, Iowa, in 1856, and engaged in the mercantile business until the breaking out of the war, when the father enlisted as quartermaster of the Seventeenth Iowa, and was afterwards promoted to brigade quartermaster, and was, at the close of the war, commissary of subsistence, stationed at Camden, Ark. He was breveted major at the close of the war for efficient services rendered. Edwin A. received his early education in the public schools, and finished in Denmark academy, in Denmark, Lee county, Iowa. Later he spent some time in the Chicago College of Pharmacy, after which his first position was in Ormsbee & Hoyt's drug store at Geneva, Ill. After one year he came to Iowa and purchased a drug store at West Liberty, which was run under the firm name of Aldrich & Gibbs. He remained there five years, but business not proving satisfactory he sold out and went to Creston, Union county, Iowa, in 1880, where he engaged as a clerk for Silverthorn & Rugh for three years, when he went to Texas, where the old firm of Aldrich & Gibbs entered into a prosperous business and accumulated considerable money. Owing to the ill health of his wife Mr. Aldrich sold his interest in the business, at the end of three years, and returned to Creston, where he again entered in the drug business on his own account, and has successfully conducted it since that time. He is vice-president of the Creston National bank, and owns an interest in the Keith Furnace company, of Des Moines.

He has always been an enthusiastic republican and a leader in local politics. Mr. Aldrich was brought up an Episcopalian, but was never confirmed. He was married at West Liberty in 1877 to Miss Emma C. Keith. They have five children living and one dead.

DOUGLAS, GEORGE, late of Cedar Rapids, was born in the county of Caithness, Scotland, April 17, 1817. He came to Rochester, N. Y., in 1848, and engaged in canal, railway and bridge construction in western New York, continuing in this work until 1852. In that year he followed the general western movement and moved to Illinois, where he engaged in various railway and bridge building contracts at Dixon, Ill., and vicinity. Here his work lasted until 1855, when he took contracts for building a portion of the railway line now operated by the Illinois Central railway, west of Dubuque, Iowa. From 1855 until 1870 he was actively engaged in railway construction, mostly in Iowa and Nebraska, doing much of the work on the lines now operated by the Illinois Central railway across the state of Iowa, also the present main line of the Chicago & North-Western railway in Iowa, and a considerable portion of the Fremont, Elkhorn &

Missouri Valley railway in eastern Nebraska. Mr. Douglas was associated with Mr. John I. Blair in his projection of the various railway lines in western Iowa, and many miles of the grading, bridging and track laying of the railways promoted by the companies of which Mr. Blair was president, were completed by the firm of Douglas, Brown & Company, of which the subject of this sketch was the senior partner. From 1870 to 1873 Mr. Douglas engaged in his last work in railway construction, completing 155 miles of the International & Great Northern railway in Texas, including the grading, bridging, track laying and depot building complete.

In 1874 he associated himself with Mr. Robert Stuart, now of Chicago, under the firm name of Douglas & Stuart, and engaged in the manufacture of oatmeal and other cereal products, at Cedar Rapids, and continued in active connection with the business until the time of his death, in May, 1884.

The firm of Douglas & Stuart extended its operations materially, and at the time its properties were acquired by the American Cereal company, was the largest producer of goods in the cereal line in the world.

Mr. Douglas married Margaret Boyd at Dixon, Ill., in 1855. She was born in the north of Ireland. Mrs. Douglas and three sons, George Bruce, Walter D., and William Wallace, live in Cedar Rapids at the present time.

---

BICKNELL, ANSON DODGE, lawyer, of Humboldt, is a lineal descendant of one of the oldest families in the United States. Zachary Bicknell, an English naval officer, his wife, Agnes, and their son John, left the county of Somerset, in the southwest of England, in 1635, and braved the dangers of the long and perilous voyage to America, landing at Weymouth, Mass.

They were dissenters from the Established church, and they dared to leave comparative comfort at home and endure extreme hardships, known and unknown, to uphold their faith and escape persecution. None but the sturdiest and best in England were among these earliest settlers, for this was only fifteen years after the landing of the Mayflower and five years after the Puritans had founded Boston. Such was the foundation of the Bicknell family in America. Very few families have been strong enough to maintain their identity as this one has. It is strongest in New England, but is represented in all parts of the country and the Bicknell Family association, with headquarters in Boston, preserves the history and notable achievements of its members.

A. D. Bicknell is of the eighth generation in America. He was born December 30, 1838, in Westmoreland, Oneida county, N. Y. His father, James Bicknell (1795),

was a famous Baptist preacher, who was born and lived all his life in Oneida county, where he preached more than forty years, and went abroad to preach very frequently, especially in the south, where he had great outdoor audiences of 7,000 to 10,000 people. He was a very vigorous man, mentally and physically, and was a good business man as well as preacher. His wife, mother of A. D., was Rebecca Ruth Brooks (1812), also a native of Oneida county. She had a philosophical mind, was quick of observation, devoted to her family and church, and keenly sympathetic. She died in 1862, aged 50, and her husband in 1884, at the age of 88 years. The family was a large one, but the only full brother and sister now living are James Y. Bicknell, of Buffalo, N. Y., and Mrs. Jane E. Bicknell Coats, of St. Paul Park, Minn.

The district schools during Mr. Bicknell's boyhood were somewhat primitive, but he managed to get good out of them and entered Rome academy in Rome, N. Y., where he was prepared in 1860 for the sophomore year in Hamilton college; he did not enter college, however, but went directly into the law office of K. Carroll and J. B. Elwood, where he remained for two years, and in 1862 started for Iowa. The railway stopped at Cedar Falls, and from there he walked, first to Fort Dodge and then to Dakota City, Humboldt county, where he met one of the pioneers of that region, Simon B. Bellows, and went to work for him on his farm, first at a dollar a day and board during harvest and then at $13 a month and board. That was the beginning of his fortune. That winter he taught school five months in Dakota City at $24 a month. In the spring he went to Fort Dodge with $112, so strict had been his economy, guided by a never-forgotten purpose. At Fort Dodge Mr. Bicknell successfully followed the mason's trade.

In the spring of 1864 he and another man bought a forty-acre timber tract near Fort Dodge, on which was a limestone quarry. They built a kiln and the sale of lime was so profitable that Mr. Bicknell was able to return to New York, in December, 1864, where he was married, December 30th, to Miss Sarah Ann Mills, daughter of Allen Mills and Sarah Ann Lee Mills, of Westmoreland, Oneida county. They returned at once to Fort Dodge and went to housekeeping, cheerfully facing together the hardships and struggles of pioneer life. In it all she was a brave and capable helpmeet, and is accorded by her husband a good share of credit for all he has accomplished.

In 1868 Mr. Bicknell sold his interests in Fort Dodge and bought a quarter section of government land in Humboldt county, on the Des Moines river, eight miles west of the town of Humboldt. He farmed with exceptional success until the spring of 1877, when he removed to the town of Humboldt and resumed the practice of law. He long intended to do this, having taken up manual labor for his health, which had been impaired by too severe mental labor, and now he left the farm to give his children better advantages, at a time when he was enjoying great prosperity. He has, however, a first-class law practice, to which he devotes his business attention exclusively. He is the owner of considerable town and country property, and in 1899 added a large stone store building to the business houses of the town.

Mr. Bicknell has always been an active republican, one of the leaders in Humboldt county. He was county superintendent of schools in 1872-3 and raised the standard of teachers. He was a member of the house in the Eighteenth General Assembly, in 1880, and has twice been mayor of Humboldt. He is a member and liberal supporter of the Unitarian church. He is deeply interested in science, particularly astronomy and geology, and is a local authority on these subjects. The family home includes an entire block, which is a beautiful park and a favorite resort for birds In fact birds and parks are specialties with him. He owns the little gem at the end of the business street, River Park, where the town holds all of its out-of door meetings, and where lovers stroll and the weary seek rest and seclusion. But his greatest park lies along the Des Moines river for half a mile on the opposite side of the town. This is a wild tract composed of hills, plains, cliffs and native forest cut up by wild ravines, canyons and brooks, while on one side of it the deep and placid waters of the Des Moines. "Lake Nokomis," furnish first-class boating and fishing in summer and an ideal skating field in winter. All these parks are free to the public for all proper uses.

Mr. and Mrs. Bicknell have four children, all living, viz.: Frank Wade, born March 20, 1866; Clara Rebekah, born December 30, 1870; Charles Mills, born March 22, 1875, and George James, born August 4, 1885.

---

COUTTS, J. H. One of the solid business men of Cedar county, an able financier and a model citizen, is John H. Coutts, of Tipton. He was born in that county, to whose development he has contributed a lifetime of hard work, on July 20, 1850. He is the oldest of seven children born of William and Barbara Banden Coutts. The father was born in Aberdeenshire, Scotland, in 1812. He came to this country in 1832, and lived for a short time in Ashland county, Ohio. In 1887 he came to Cedar county, Iowa, and settled in Red Oak township, where he was married in 1849 to
30

Barbara Banden, also a native of Scotland. He died December 16, 1891.

J. H. Coutts was brought up on a farm, and received a common school education. Although he has been called to fill the highest position of responsibility in his county, he has at no time in his life been a politician or an office seeker, having little or no ambition in that direction. He has devoted himself to business, and, while promoting such enterprises as have proved of inestimable value to the community at large, has accumulated considerable wealth. He was elected county treasurer of Cedar county in 1887 on the democratic ticket,

and was re-elected at the conclusion of his term of office by an increased majority. He then turned his attention to financial enterprises. He became connected with the First National bank, of Tipton; was elected its president, and under the influence of his personality and reputation for integrity, the business of the concern doubled in a short time. He is one of those men who always come to the front in emergencies.

He is a director in the Electric Light company, treasurer of the Eastern Iowa Building and Loan association, and director and treasurer of the Tipton Hotel association, in the organization of which last named concern he was very active.

In 1892 he located a bank at Stanwood, Iowa, which is known as J. H. Coutts' bank, a venture which, like all his others, has proved highly successful. He is progressive, far-sighted in business, honorable to the highest degree, and generous to a fault — qualities which make him respected by everyone in the community where he resides.

In 1896 he took a well-earned vacation, making an extensive European trip, and returned to his large business interests at home with renewed vigor, and with an enlarged acquaintance with his eastern correspondents, and with financial leaders throughout our country.

--

BURCH, GEORGE B., of Dubuque, was born at Lyons, Wayne county, N. Y., on the 22d of March, 1836. His parents were James H. Burch and Ruhama S. Burch, *nee* Dunn, both natives of New York. His early education was obtained at the public schools. His father being in moderate circumstances could give him but little assistance, and at the age of 14 he commenced life for himself by entering the employ of a druggist, as clerk. Later he served in several clerical positions, and in February, 1855, moved to the west, and settled in Portage, Wis., where, in 1859, he formed a partnership in the drug business, under the firm name of Burch & Lewis. In December of the same year he sold his interest in the drug business and removed to Necedah, Wis., in the lumber district, where, for a year, he was employed as bookkeeper. In 1861 he entered the lumber business for himself, by purchasing a small lumber mill in Necedah, and engaged in the manufacture of lumber. He removed to Dubuque in August, 1869, and there established a lumber business in connection with his mills in Necedah. Meanwhile his business in Necedah had steadily increased from year to year, and at one time he was president of two large lumbering companies there, which were later consolidated into one, the Necedah Lumber company, and is still in operation, he being president.

He had gradually become interested in other large enterprises, and in 1881 sold out his lumbering interests in Dubuque, although still retaining his interests in Necedah. In January, 1884, he was elected a director and president of the Second National bank of Dubuque, and has continued

to hold the office ever since. This bank was organized in 1876, with a capital of $100,000, which was increased to $150,000, then to $200,000, then $400,000, and is the largest in the city. Knowing well that competitive railroad lines added to the material prosperity of the city, he became active in building the Dubuque & Northwestern railroad, and was elected president of the company. The road is now part of the Chicago Great Western railroad system. Mr. Burch is still largely interested in it and is closely allied with its management. The Julien house, one of the finest and most commodious hotels ever erected in a city the size of Dubuque, probably owes its

existence to his enterprising and progressive spirit. Besides the offices already mentioned, he is president of the Necedah Lumber company, of Necedah, Wis.; a director and treasurer of the Key City Gas company. He is also vice-president and director of the Dunleith & Dubuque Bridge company.

He was one of the originators of the Finley hospital, and has been a trustee and treasurer since its organization. He has been elected mayor of Dubuque three different times. In 1876 he was the unanimous choice of both parties, and was chosen without opposition; he was re-elected in 1877, and again in 1888, but declined further election. It is conceded that he filled the position with great credit.

He was married on the 27th of February, 1860, to Miss Ellen H. Merrill, daughter of Hon. Samuel D. Merrill, of Vermont. They have six children living.

Mr. Burch has been a resident of Dubuque for over a quarter of a century, and during all that time no man has labored more earnestly, or more steadily, to advance the material prosperity of the city than he has. He has become an acknowledged leader in most of the plans that have been formulated to add to the comfort and wealth of the people.

---

WILLIAMS, ROBERT, is the son of Mr. Wareham Williams, deceased, and Ellen Elizabeth Thacher, now a resident of Norwich, Conn. His father was engaged in the wholesale and retail dry goods business and was prominently identified with other commercial interests at Norwich, Conn., at which place Robert Williams was born, July 11, 1852. He attended school at the Norwich Free academy and then entered Yale university, graduating from that institution in 1873. Desiring to follow the footsteps of his father and perfect himself in commercial pursuits, he in 1874 sought and obtained a clerkship in the Thames National bank of Norwich, Conn., without salary, and he attended to the duties allotted him there under these circumstances until June, 1875, when he secured the position of clearing house clerk in the Continental National bank of New York city, but was soon obliged to give it up on account of his health. In August, 1875, he moved to Cedar Rapids, Iowa, his present home, and entered the service of the Burlington, Cedar Rapids & Minnesota railway company, under Gen. E. F. Winslow, receiver of that company, as clerk for Mr. C. J. Ives, then superintendent of the road. In 1879 he was appointed purchasing agent, the company being reorganized in the meantime as the Burlington, Cedar Rapids & Northern railway company. In 1881 he was made assistant superintendent, and in 1882 promoted to the position of superintendent of the road in charge of the operating department; in 1884 he was elected vice-president of the company, and in 1894 he became its general superintendent, now holding both these positions.

He is in private life of a quiet and retiring disposition, taking much of his social pleasure from the surroundings of his home and in the company of friends with whom he has been intimate for years.

In business matters he is both active and energetic, and pursues all of his duties in that conscientious, earnest manner peculiar to those who have inherited the sturdy traits of a vigorous New England ancestry. He is noted in railway circles for the tenacious way in which he adheres to the principles of fairness and justice in the management of the affairs of the company he has been so closely identified with for the past twenty-three years. As the Burlington, Cedar Rapids & Northern Railway company is recognized and stands in

Iowa, Minnesota and South Dakota, the three states in which its line is located, as the embodiment of fair and reasonable business principles, it can be fairly said that our Mr. Williams bears the same relationship to the company as far as these qualitiations are concerned, as it does to the business interests of the states through which its system extends. He has always been a republican in politics, but cannot be considered a partisan in the strict sense of the word.

He was married in May, 1888, to Miss Mary Foster Bard, of Norwich, Conn. They have one daughter, Ellen Elizabeth, born July 21, 1892.

BROWN, ERNEST C., a practicing physician and surgeon of high standing, now a resident of Madrid, Boone county, is a native of New York state, having been born in Verona, Oneida county, N. Y., August 24, 1867.

His father, Calvin Brown, was one of those highly respectable farmers who, while their holdings are not large, yet from their thrift, probity, and general sterling qualities, take a very high rank. He owned a small farm near Verona, N. Y., on which he lived for nearly fifty years, raised and educated his large family. At the time of his death, in September, 1896, he was one of Oneida county's oldest inhabitants, and his portrait with sketch of life appears in the history of Oneida county and its people as published that year. From the standpoint of ability, he was prepared by nature

for a broader field of action. He gave considerable attention to fruit growing, gaining a state-wide reputation for the excellent varieties of pears, apples and grapes which he produced. He figured prominently in the agricultural and horticultural societies of both county and state. Later he drifted into the dairy business most successfully, and owned at one time what was called the Banner dairy. His wife and the mother of Ernest C., was Mary Jane Morton, daughter of Samuel Morton, of Rome, N. Y., and a descendant of the Mortons so prominent in the history of New England, and in the line of descent from Sir George Morton, who fitted out the Mayflower for its famous voyage, but who, through the intrigue of the British, was arrested and not allowed to sail with the expedition he had formed. The Mortons, however, came to Massachusetts the following year in the ship "Speed-Well." The Browns were also from the

best of old New England stock, coming from Connecticut to New York in 1796, and located on a farm which has ever since remained in the Brown family.

The doctor's ancestry on his mother's side, the Mortons, and his grandmother Brown's side, who was a Talcott, trace well back into the early English history; the Talcotts to the earl of Warwick, and the Mortons to William the conqueror.

Grandfather Brown was a captain in the war of 1812, and Great-grandfather Morton was with Ethan Allen in his revolutionary exploits.

The doctor's early education and home training were looked after by his father, who was always very kind and indulgent, and by his older sisters. After leaving the district school, he attended the Rome Free academy for two winters, working on his father's farm during the summer seasons.

At the age of 21 years, he left the farm and entered Fort Edward Collegiate institute, at Fort Edward, N. Y., pursuing the classical course. Leaving this, he went to Michigan, working for a time for B. F. Johnson & Company, publishers, of Richmond, Va. In the fall of 1890 he entered the Homeopathic Medical college of the Michigan university at Ann Arbor, Mich., and graduated with the degree of M. D. in June, 1893. In August, 1893, came to Iowa and entered at once upon the practice of his profession.

For a few months he was associated with Dr. Martin, the leading Homeopathist of Boone, and in October, 1893, came to Madrid, Iowa, and opened an office for himself, where he has since resided. By his honesty and integrity of character, and his professional ability and skill, he has built up a large and very successful practice. He is health physician for that city and for Garden township. In the spring of 1898 the doctor went east for some postgraduate work in surgical obstetrics and gynecology, and his most marked success has been in obstetrics and diseases of women and children. In politics he is a democrat, going home from Fort Edward, when at school, a distance of over 150 miles to cast his first vote for Grover Cleveland, and David B. Hill, in that memorable New York struggle of 1888. He was the democratic candidate for coroner of Boone county in 1896, running on the Bryan ticket, and though far ahead of his ticket in his home county, he met the same fate as the great champion of free silver. He is a member of the American Institute of Homeopathy, and attended its session at Omaha, in June, 1898; also a member of the Hahnemann Medical association of

Iowa; examining physician for several life insurance companies. In religion he is a Methodist, and is a member of the First Methodist Episcopal church of Madrid, and one of its board of trustees.

KELLY, THOMAS FRANCIS, postmaster of Adair, is the son of M. B. Kelly, who was born in the parish of Balloymoe, Galway, Ireland, March 30, 1834.

His father, Timothy Kelly, who was born in the same parish and county in 1812, came, after his marriage in 1833, to Red Bank, N. J., where he remained for six months, when he returned to Ireland. He died August 15, 1895. The wife of Timothy Kelly, whose maiden name was Catherine

Doud, was born in Galway county, the same year as her husband. In 1894 she visited America, where her children lived. She remained six months, and died shortly after her return to Ireland, on September 20, 1895. Michael Kelly, after his marriage in 1857 to Agnes B. Fane, a native of the same county in Ireland, born May 14, 1838, came to America, direct to Scott county, Iowa, in 1858. Mrs. Kelly assisted her father in the government school, and after their arrival in Scott county worked for the wife of the farmer with whom Mr. Kelly was engaged, earning a salary of $60 a year. She still lives on the old homestead in Scott county. Mr. Kelly received a salary of $100 for two years, when he rented a farm in Sheridan township, which a few years later he purchased, living on the same until his death, which occurred July 7, 1897. Mr. Kelly was well known in Scott and adjoining counties. He bought and dealt in

stock for twenty-five years. He was liberally disposed. His reputation for honesty and fair dealing was above reproach. During the forty years he farmed in Scott county, he was known as one of the hardest working men in the county, and the only vacation he allowed himself was the few months he spent in 1887 visiting his parents in Ireland.

The grandfather of the subject of our sketch, on his mother's side, was Walter Fane, who was born in Killcorn, Ireland, and for twenty-five years prior to his death, which occurred June 16, 1861, he was the government schoolmaster in the parish of Ballymoe. His wife, whose maiden name was Betty Goulden, was born May 14, 1811, in French Park, Ireland. She came to America in 1865 and lived with her daughter, Agnes Kelly, until her death in 1871.

Thomas F. Kelly was born October 16, 1861, in Scott county, Iowa. He attended the district school in his township, his first teacher being Miss Wicks, now the wife of Hon. B. T. Seaman, of Scott county. During the fall and winter of 1881 and 1882 he attended the Wilton academy, at Wilton Junction. Mr. Kelly earned his first dollar, in the winter of 1870, trapping mink and muskrats, on what was then known as the Slopertown big slough, now drained and farmed. During this winter he trapped and sold $27 worth of hides. Most of his trapping was done by moonlight, as he attended school by day, and in the evening had the chores to do at home. He remained at home and worked for his father on the farm until he was 27 years of age, excepting for a few months attending college, and eight months that were spent in the south and west. Following this he rented one of his father's farms in Scott county for two years. Wishing to become owner of a farm of his own, Mr. Kelly went west to Adair, March 1, 1891, where he accomplished his desire, and now owns two well-improved farms in the vicinity of Adair. He is also the owner of considerable property in the town of Adair, which has been acquired through his own industry and economy.

After the death of his wife, December 16, 1893, he rented his farm, and the next spring, in June, 1894, was appointed postmaster of Adair. After the fire, in 1894, which destroyed twenty-two of the thirty-three business places in Adair, he purchased a lot in the center of the business portion of the town and erected a brick building thereon, a part of which he now uses for an office room. Mr. Kelly has given excellent satisfaction as postmaster, and is highly esteemed as a citizen.

He is a charter member of Mount Hope Camp No. 59 Woodmen of the World, and is a member of the Catholic church. He was married March 4, 1888, to Miss Jessie Carter. Three children were born, two of whom died in infancy; Francis Walter, born November 18, 1891, lives with his grandparents in Scott county since the death of his mother.

---

VAN HORNE, GEORGE W., late editor of the Muscatine *News-Tribune,* who, in his more than twenty-five years of active newspaper association, gained for himself the name of being one of the ablest journalists and most eloquent of social and political platform orators in the state, was born in

Chicopee, Mass., October 12, 1833, and died in Muscatine, Iowa, February 8, 1895. After a thorough academic education, he began the study of law. under the guidance of Judge Gillett, of Westfield, Mass., but seeing greater possibilities for his talent in the growing west, he came to Iowa in 1855, entering the office of Cloud & O'Conner, at Muscatine, to complete his studies and learn the Hawkeye mode of procedure. His pleasing address, exceptional command of language and adaptability for his chosen pursuit, quickly won for him deserved recognizance, and upon his admittance to the bar he was taken into partnership by D. C. Cloud, then the first attorney-general of the state. His powers as a public

speaker soon drew him into politics, and in 1860 he was appointed by Lincoln as consul at Marseilles, France. He held this post all through the war, having the distinction of being the youngest man in the foreign diplomatic service of the United States during that critical period. Returning to America in 1866 he accepted the invitation of the republican state central committee of Arkansas to take editorial charge of the new state organ that was being established in Little Rock; but the newspaper plant was destroyed by fire before his arrival, involving a complete loss, and Mr. Van Horne was persuaded to stay in the south in the capacity of registrar of Scott county, Ark., under the reconstruction laws of congress, but he soon resigned his position to return to Massachusetts. Mr. Van Horne, for several years following, turned his attention to various pursuits in New England, returning to Iowa in 1870 and starting the Muscatine *Tribune.* He afterwards bought the Muscatine *Courier* and the Betts Bros. were admitted to a partnership which lasted until Mr. Van Horne withdrew to enter the lecture field. He was afterwards placed in charge of the local editorship of the Muscatine *Journal,* where he remained until 1887, when the Muscatine News Co. was organized and incorporated. Mr. Van Horne was elected secretary and made editor-in-chief of the *Daily News,* which began publication independent in politics. The editor, however, had come to have marked democratic convictions, and soon imbued the paper with his personality. It quickly became the recognized official organ of that party in Muscatine county, and in May, 1889, the Muscatine *Tribune* and *News* were consolidated, with Mr. Van Horne still the editor-in-chief. In 1893 he was again the recipient of political favors, this time from the democratic party, whose cause he had so zealously championed in his editorship, being appointed postmaster at Muscatine by the practically unanimous desire of his local party, his commission issuing May 12, 1893. Mr. Van Horne's genius, as portrayed by his pen, has been said by able critics to have been unexcelled by any associate journalist. A thorough student, he traversed the continent in his stay abroad with eyes open to the observation of the many scenes and places made notable by history and tradition, while his intercourse in life with those notable in society and politics added to his qualities as a "raconteur" and writer. Among other of his literary efforts for paper and lecture field are such as "Storied Scenes of Europe," "Old London Town," "Picturesque France," "Men and Women I Have Seen," "Farmer Whiting Letters," and "Kaleidoscopes of Memory." In the fall of 1892, he became a victim to a malignant form of tumor on his left leg. The surgeons decided that a thigh amputation was the only recourse, and told Mr. Van Horne that in submitting himself to the operation, death was almost inevitable. A week's respite was asked by him to put his worldly affairs in order, and then it was that his journalistic tendencies proved their mastery over the physical man in the preparation of a supposedly farewell editorial, written for his paper and published December 11, 1892, entitled, "Perhaps a Valedictory," which in its graphic word painting displayed so truly the strength of character and noble sentiments of the doomed writer as to be reproduced and commented upon by the press universally throughout the west. He survived the ordeal, however, and lived until the fall of 1894, when he fell a prey to nervous prostration, from which he passed away in the dawn of the following year, mourned by a city and eulogized by the newspapers of the state in a manner rarely accorded to one in the private walks of life. Mr. Van Horne was married September 15, 1858, to Miss Mary Morrow, only daughter of the late Dr. James G. Morrow, one of the founders of Muscatine, and at the time a step-daughter of his former law partner, Mr. Cloud. Of this union there were born four children: Hattie D., born at Muscatine, July 2, 1859; Benny R., born at Chicopee, Mass., July 14, 1861, who died in infancy in France; Lulu C., born at Marseilles, France, May 3, 1865, now the wife of Edward G. Magoon, of Muscatine; and Elworth Stiles, born at Muscatine, June 14, 1874.

---

TEDFORD, JAMES HARVEY, of Mt. Ayr, senior editor of the *Ringgold Record*, is a man who has the reputation of knowing how to make the best use of the English language in his well-known newspaper. He was born in Putnam county, Ind., March 4, 1833, of stock whose genealogy can be traced through the best families of Tennessee. He is wholly self-made, having earned the money with which his education was secured by teaching school. He entered Hanover college at

the age of 17, and graduated therefrom in 1856, with the degree of bachelor of arts. He subsequently attended the United Presbyterian Theological seminary at Xenia, Ohio, for three years, during the time Whitelaw Reid was publishing a paper in that city. On the completion of his education he entered upon the ministry, and for thirty years filled the pulpits of prominent churches in Greenville, Pa.; Tipton, Ind., and Mt. Ayr, Iowa. At the conclusion of his pastorate in the last named city in 1886, he became associate editor and part owner of the *Ringgold Republican*, a paper that had been established

a short time previously. About one year thereafter he, with his partner, purchased the *Ringgold Record*, the oldest paper in the county, having been established in 1865, and the two papers were consolidated.

At the time he first located in Mt. Ayr, in 1879, he was employed as pastor of the United Presbyterian denomination, to which work his time was devoted until entering upon a journalistic career. As a newspaper man he has been a success. Commencing with but limited capital, he now owns, with his son, one of the best newspaper plants in southwestern Iowa.

His political preferences have always been for the republican party. He was clerk for the interstate and foreign commerce committee in the national house in 1895–6, appointed by Congressman W. P. Hepburn, of whom he has ever been a warm supporter and faithful friend in victory and in defeat. He was married in June, 1862, to Miss Elizabeth Rowan, at Argyle, N. Y. They have two children: Howard, who is connected with him in the publishing of the *Record*, and Mary Tedford.

---

TEDFORD, HOWARD. One of the rising newspaper men of Iowa is Howard Tedford, of the *Ringgold Record*. He was born

in Tipton county, Ind., May 30, 1870. His father is the well-known J. H. Tedford, at the head of the firm of Tedford & Son, publishers of the *Record*, one of the leading county papers of southern Iowa. His mother was Elizabeth Rowan, a native of New York, and descendant of the family of patriots of that name who took such a conspicuous part in the war for independence. Howard attended the public schools of Tipton county, Ind., and Ringgold county, Iowa. He entered Monmouth college at Monmouth, Ill., but left college at the end of two years to enter into partnership with his father in the publishing of the *Record*. While at Monmouth he was a member of

the Eccritean society, and at the head of his class in all the branches of study. He came to Iowa first with his parents in 1879, and located in Mt. Ayr, which place has been his home ever since. His first manual labor was performed on the farm, but he early entered the newspaper business, in fact, his common school and college education has been augmented by a thorough printing office training, and thus by theoretical and practical instruction he is fitted for the profession of his father. During his father's absence in Washington he had entire charge of the paper and then, in 1897, exchanged duties with his father in Washington, in order to get the experience of Washington life.

Like his illustrious sire, he is a republican through and through. He is president of the Eighth District Republican league, has been a delegate to several of its national conventions, and occupies a position of influence and usefulness in the league. He was chairman of the republican central committee of his county during the years 1895 and 1896. He is prominent in the order of Knights of Pythias.

---

KELLY, JOHN CHARLES, the well-known editor of the *Sioux City Daily Tribune*, is a native of the "Empire State." He was born in Cortland, N. Y., on the 26th of February, 1852. His mother's maiden name was Mary Kelly, and his father's name was Thomas C. Kelly, but they were of different families and types, although both were natives of Ireland, and well educated in youth. His grandfather on his father's side, was a business man, and on the mother's side a farmer. John C.'s grandmother, on his mother's side, was a Scotch woman. His father's education was completed at the University of Edinburgh, after which he spent some years in travel. Two of his father's brothers held commissions in the British army, but Thomas was educated for civil life, and came to the United States in December, 1849. His wife's people were farmers, in the state of New York, and he engaged in the same occupation soon after he reached America. Upon the opening of the civil war, and in response to President Lincoln's first call for volunteers, Thomas C. tendered his services to his adopted country, and, raising a segment of a company, received a lieutenant's commission. He had become a citizen of the republic as soon as its laws permitted, and took a deep interest in pub-. lic affairs, allying himself with the Douglas wing of the democratic party. When his father entered the union army, John C. was not 10 years old, and, although a mere schoolboy, he undertook to manage his father's large farm, but soon found it too formidable an undertaking for a youth of his years. His education, up to this time, had been such only as the country district schools afforded. But the instruction given by his father at home was found in after life to be of more practical value than that imparted at school. John had a strong desire to get into the union army in some capacity, and went on to Washington in 1862, arriving in the city in time to witness "McClellan's Grand Review," but his youth thwarted this desire. During the war he had but two short terms at school, and after its close he had three months' instruction in a grammar school in Washington. His father was disabled during the war, and the boy found himself the chief support of the family, whose fortunes had been wrecked. He secured employment in stores at the national capital, and spent the late evenings, generally up till midnight, in study. Under this strain he finally broke down. In December, 1869, his father died, and soon after John secured a position in the government printing office, where it was thought his health might be recruited. He made such progress in acquiring a knowledge of the art of printing, stereotyping and electrotyping that, while he had yet a year of the prescribed apprenticeship unserved, he was chosen by Mills & Company, then state printers, at Des Moines, Iowa, to purchase a plant for them, and to come on to the state capital and superintend it. On the 23d of May, 1873, John C. Kelly, then 21 years of age, crossed the Mississippi river, came to Des Moines and entered upon the responsible duties of his new position at a salary of $30 a week. He served more than three years with Mills & Company, and has ever since reckoned the surviving members of the firm among his best friends. While in their employ he divided and numbered the streets of Des Moines on the "Philadelphia plan," it being the first city in Iowa so divided. Mr. Kelly was the pioneer in organizing the first Building association in Iowa. It was established by him at Des Moines, and he became its secretary. Associated with him in the directory were such men as T. S. Wright, Adam Howell and L. Harbach. In

Des Moines Mr. Kelly first met Miss Martha A. Hill, daughter of Col. S. G. Hill, of the Thirty-fifth Iowa infantry, who was killed while leading his regiment at the battle of Nashville. Miss Hill and Mr. Kelly were married at the home of her mother in Muscatine, May 1, 1878. It was a very happy union, and seven children came to make the home an ideal one. Of these, Martha died, while Rose, Mabel, Rachel, John H., Eugene and Gardner are living. Mr. Kelly read law, while living in Des Moines, with Judge William Connor, and also engaged in merchandising, but eventually purchased an interest in the *Daily State Leader*, of

which he became one of the editors. Three years later he disposed of his interest in that paper, and, removing to Sioux City, he purchased the weekly *Tribune* of that place. In 1884 he established the *Sioux City Daily Tribune*, of which he is editor and proprietor. During the same year he established the Sioux City Printing company, which has grown into a large manufacturing establishment, dealing in printers' supplies, and doing auxiliary publishing, of which enterprise he is the principal owner and general manager. In 1893 he was appointed collector of internal revenue by President Cleveland, and also disbursing agent of the treasury department. Mr. Kelly was always a "hard-money" man,

and is an advocate of the single gold
standard. He was a member of the first
free trade or tariff reform club organized
after the war. He has for many years
been a member of the Reform club, of New
York, and a warm advocate of civil service
reform. He was a delegate at large to the
democratic national convention of 1888,
which nominated Cleveland and Thurman.
In 1892 Mr. Kelly supported Goveror Boies,
in the national democratic convention, as a
candidate for president. In 1896 he refused
to support Bryan for president on the
"free coinage" platform, and was a delegate to the national democratic convention
which nominated Palmer and Buckner. He
has served on the committee on resolutions in ten democratic state conventions.
He is not a member of any fraternity or
church, but since his marriage has, with
his wife, attended the Congregational
church. He was for many years president
of the Humane society, of Sioux City.

---

HANLEY, THOMAS B., one of the self-
made and successful men of Tipton, was
born in Cleveland, Ohio, December 11, 1852.
He was one of a family of ten children,
four of whom are dead. One brother, D.
R. Hanley, is a steamboat engineer, who,
with a sister, Mrs. Claus Rolfs, lives in
Davenport; one brother, W. H. Hanley, a
lawyer, and another brother, M. L. Hanley, also a steamboat engineer, live in
Dubuque; another brother, J. A. Hanley,
a lawyer, lives in Davenport. Mr. Hanley's father and mother came to America
from Ireland in the spring of 1852, locating
at Cleveland, Ohio. His father was a
laborer in ordinary circumstances, and with
a family of ten children it was necessary
that they should learn in their early years
to be of use to themselves and to others.
The family removed to Scott county, Iowa,
in 1856.

After leaving the public schools Mr.
Hanley attended the Iowa Agricultural
college for one year and was a member of
the Bachelors' Debating society. He afterwards entered the law department of the
State university, graduating in 1880. His
first work outside of his own home was in
a sawmill. At this time he also taught
school off and on for ten years. After
completing his law studies he located at
Le Claire, Scott county, in 1880, where he
practiced law until 1888, when he removed
to Tipton and formed a partnership with
Hon. William P. Wolf. This partnership

continued until 1894 when Mr. Wolf became judge of the district court. Mr. Hanley continued his practice alone and has
had no partner since. He is a prominent
member of the Knights of Pythias and was
elected grand chancellor of the Knights of
Pythias of Iowa, in 1895. He was unanimously elected representative to the supreme lodge in 1897. He was one of six
men to organize the Modern Brotherhood
of America, a fraternal beneficiary association. He is president of the association.
The organization has been remarkably successful from the start, thus reflecting much
credit upon its originators.

Mr. Hanley was a democrat until 1882,
when he became a republican. He was
mayor of Tipton for two years, and it was
largely through his influence that Tipton
has one of best electric light plants in the
state.

Besides being a Knight of Pythias he is
a Mason, and belongs to the Modern
Brotherhood of America, also Modern
Woodmen of America. He was married
October 7, 1880, to Miss Flora Free, of
Port Byron, Ill. They have one child:
Edna, born August 16, 1882.

Without assistance Mr. Hanley worked
his way up in the world, reaching a goodly
position in society, in his profession and in
the esteem of all who know him.

MARSHALL, Rev. ALEXANDER STEW-
ART, D. D., late pastor of the Presbyterian
church at Marion, had at the time of his
death, February 3, 1896, almost completed
a pastorate of forty years. He was the son
of John and Elizabeth Stewart Marshall,
and was next to the youngest in the family
of five sons and three daughters. He was
born April 29, 1829, on a farm near Dayton,
Armstrong county, Pa., and he received
his education, after the common school
period, in Elder's Ridge academy and
Washington college, graduating from the
latter in 1853. He studied theology at
Western Theological seminary and Princeton Theological seminary, and was licensed
by the Blairsville Presbytery in June, 1855.

In December, 1855, he was united in
marriage to Mary Rob Christy, and removed to Marion the following spring,
preaching his first sermon April 20,
1856, in the old brick school building
torn down four years ago to make room
for the new Prescott building. The congregation April 20, 1856, numbered thirty-
five.

In March, 1882, partly from ill health
and partly from a thought that another
might serve the church more efficiently, he
tendered his resignation, but the church
arose almost in a body to beg him to recon-
sider it, and granted him a three months'
vacation and the means for himself and
wife to spend it as they chose.

A man who can live for forty years in
one community, and have no one speak
slightingly of him when he is gone, is
more than an ordinary man. He was an
extraordinary man.

Among some of the things that were
said of him by L. P. Bardwell, editor of
the *Marion Pilot*, who bore no other relation to him than that of a citizen, are these:
"His kindly greetings were for everybody
he met. Particularly was he a man who
had only good words for all. No unkindly
words were ever spoken in our presence.
Never intolerant in his views, he was nevertheless decidedly firm in his convictions of
what he considered right. We believe his
life was an open book known and read by
all men. His whole soul was in his life
work for the Master, and, as we firmly believe, he fell bearing the cross. In season
and out of season, we have known him to
speak to the weak, discouraged, dejected,
or as some would put it—the fallen
creatures of the earth, always pointing
them to the better way. He was dearly
beloved by the large membership of his

church, and by those called outsiders,
who were regular attendants—by the other
denominations with which he always maintained the most cordial relations, and by
the community at large, who generously
accorded him an honest consistency in all
his convictions "

A writer from Cedar Rapids, in the *Mid-
Continent*, spoke thus concerning him: "He
stood for forty years a witness for Christ
in this community, till his sound Presby-
terianism, his Christian benevolence, his
pastoral influence, and his loyal citizenship,
have left their enduring impress upon the
church, the school, the town in which he

lived, and the whole surrounding community. The people without regard to party
or creed, mourn his death. He was an
earnest expositor of God's word. He was
most mindful of the poor, the sick and the
afflicted. He was the friend of everyone in
need, as well as everyone who craved
counsel and encouragement."

Rev. Dr. Marshall left four children: C.
H. Marshall, division chief clerk for the
Chicago, Milwaukee & St. Paul, at this
point, and a member of the city council;
Miss Lizzie R., the present efficient head of
the Marion high school; Mrs. Rosa Phelps,
of Council Bluffs, and Miss Bertha, a
teacher in Brookline, Mass.

Long will the influence of Dr. Marshall's right living be felt in Marion, and throughout Linn county. When we seek for words to sum up the life of this pure man who lived in the world so long and yet was not of it, we throw aside all weak expressions of our own, and quote the noble lines with which Goldsmith closes his poem, "The Village Preacher:"

As some tall cliff that rears its beauteous form,
Swells from the vale and midway braves the storm,
Tho' round its crest the rolling clouds are spread,
Eternal sunshine settles on its head.

GILLILLAND, SHIRLEY, was born in a log hut on the banks of the Missouri river

in Mills county, Iowa, forty-three years ago, of Scotch-Irish parentage. He grew up on a farm in that neighborhood, with limited school advantages to the age of 17. On the death of his grandmother at that time, who left him $200, he started for Iowa City and entered the old "sub-fresh" department of the university in January, 1874, where he remained through the whole course, sawing wood Saturdays, turning the old *Republican* press nights and working in vacations to help pay expenses. He graduated in 1879 with commencement honors. In 1879-80 he engaged in newspaper work on the Iowa City *Republican*

and *Gate City*. His health failing under the strain of morning daily service, he spent the next three years on the old home place in Mills county, farming in summer and teaching in winter. In 1883–4 he returned to the university and took the law course, graduating among the commencement eight in a class of one hundred and three. In June, 1884, he formed a partnership with Hon. John Y. Stone, at Glenwood, which continued until the latter became attorney-general in 1889. In 1878 he was the annual commencement orator for Irving society. In February, 1879, he was the salutatorian for the annual program of this society. In 1884 was on the debate for annual program of the same. In 1885 he was selected by the faculty of the law department and the supreme court as a member of the examining board of the law class of 1885 as the representative of the class of 1884. In 1894 he was again selected as a member of the examining board, and in 1895 was selected by the supreme court as member of a committee of three to examine applicants for admission before that body. In 1891 he was elected by the board of regents of the university as a member from the Ninth congressional district to fill vacancy occasioned by the resignation of J. J. McConnell. In 1892 he was elected by the legislature to a full term and in 1898 re-elected. On this board he has been frank, direct and fearless, having no patience with red tape or snobbery, and imbued with the one purpose to give the university high rank. In 1892 he was elected county attorney of Mills county, and was twice re-elected, declining to be a candidate in 1898 in order to enter the contest for senator for the Mills-Montgomery district. During his six years as a prosecutor for Mills county he secured the conviction of 118 persons in the district court, collected over $15,000 for the county, and in the whole period not a dollar was paid by the county for assistant counsel. He has been one of the active spirits in bringing Mills county into notice as a fruit region and was the presiding officer at both the apple carnivals. He has been president of the Old Settlers' association, comprising Fremont, Mills and Montgomery counties. In politics, Mr. Gillilland is an ardent republican, and was temporary chairman of the last congressional convention, and in religion he is an earnest Congregationalist, being honored by the Council Bluffs association with election as its delegate to the national association at

Portland, Ore., in 1898. His family consists of a wife, formerly Elsie Moulton, a son, Paul, aged 8, and a daughter, Grace, aged 6.

KUEHNLE, CARL F., one of the best-known young lawyers in the state, is a native Iowan, born in Dubuque April 7, 1861. He is the son of Charles F. Kuehnle, who was born in Germany, and Mary Von Eschen Kuehnle, who was born in Switzerland. He attended the public schools of Dubuque until he was about 10 years of age, when he moved with his parents to Waterloo, Iowa, where he attended the public schools of East Waterloo, graduating from the East Waterloo high school in June, 1878, as valedictorian of the class. Honors thus began to come to him early in life, and more than an ordinary share have been bestowed upon this energetic, young Iowa man. Entering the State University of Iowa immediately after his graduation from the high school, he began to win honors from the first. He won the prize offered by the professor of English literature to the best student of Shakespeare; was one of two successful contestants in the junior oratorical contest; was salutatorian of his class when graduating from the law department, and was a member of the Irving Institute Literary society. He graduated from the collegiate department with the degree of Ph. B., in June, 1881, and from the law department of the same university in June, 1882, with the degree of LL. B. In 1884 he received the degree of A. M. from the same institution. Mr. Kuehnle's professional career began, where it is now in successful progress, in Denison, Iowa. At first he was in the employ of Conner & Shaw, lawyers, commencing in the fall of 1882. January 1, 1885, Mr. Conner, of that firm, became district judge, and the firm was dissolved. Mr. Kuehnle then formed a partnership with the other member of the firm, L. M. Shaw, now governor of Iowa, which still continues under the firm name of Shaw & Kuehnle. In 1887 the firm established a branch office in Charter Oak, Iowa, in charge of P. D. McMahon. In 1888 Mr. Kuehnle became vice-president of the Bank of Manilla, in Manilla, Iowa, a position which he still holds. The Bank of Denison was established by the firm of Shaw & Kuehnle, January 1, 1890, with L. M. Shaw as president; C. F. Kuehnle, vice-president, and C. L. Voss, cashier. Mr. Kuehnle is half owner of the bank, Governor Shaw owning the other half. The firm has done an enormous business in farm loans, their loans being valued in the east at the top of the market, because of the unquestionable character of the securities. The firm has had the best law practice in the county for years, and is one of the strongest in western Iowa. To this result, in both branches of the business, Mr. Kuehnle's great energy and quick perception have contributed a very large share. Mr. Kuehnle is fond of politics, and is well known all over the state as one of the "hustlers" of the republican party. He has repeatedly

been chairman of the republican county committee, of Crawford county; notably, in the presidential campaigns in which Harrison and McKinley were elected; is president of the Tenth district republican league; has been chairman of the senatorial committee of his district, and was vice-president of the republican national league for the state of Iowa in 1893–94. He is now the Iowa member of the executive committee of the national republican league. He was a delegate to the state convention which nominated Mr. Shaw for governor in 1897, and his large state acquaintance was a source of much strength to Mr. Shaw. Mr. Kuehnle is a member of the local lodges of the Masons, Odd Fellows, and Knights of

Pythias; is also a Knight Templar and Mystic Shriner; was grand chancellor of the Knights of Pythias of Iowa for 1893-94, and is now supreme representative from the grand lodge of Iowa to the supreme lodge of the world, Knights of Pythias. He has been president of the Alumni association of the State university, and was one of the founders and promoters, and is now a member of the board of directors of the Denison Normal School association. He was married, October 11, 1889, to Miss Lillie M. Laub, the youngest daughter of Hon. H. C. Laub, of Denison. They have two children: Lydia Belle Kuehnle, born August 10, 1892, and Carl Frederick Kuehnle, born June 22, 1896.

---

HOYT, WILLIAM HENRY, M. D., one of the prominent physicians of Sioux City, was born in Northfield, Vt., April 27, 1862. He is the son of Samuel Norris Hoyt, who superintended for years the wood construction for the Vermont Central railroad, and later had charge of the carpenter department of the Nashua Manufacturing company, at Nashua, N. H. His brothers are natives of the Green Mountain state, living in the vicinity of Peachem Hollow and Hardwick. The mother's maiden name was Mary Jane Ford, a native of Bangor, Me., but subsequently a resident of Hardwick, Vt.

Doctor Hoyt moved to Nashau with his parents in 1867. He at once entered the public schools, continuing in the same until the spring of 1881, when he was honorably graduated, receiving the Noyes' prize medal as one of the leaders in his class in scholarship and deportment for the four years' high school course.

During his boyhood days, the first money earned by his own efforts was while acting as a newsboy for a local paper of large circulation. Thus was started early a wish to be independent, to pave the way for his own future college education, and so in many ways, during his school vacations, he added to his first small earnings. In this he was very successful.

Having conceived at an early date a choice of the medical profession as his future career, he engaged in the drug business, at the completion of his studies in the high school, as a preliminary step to the years of college work necessary to acquire a medical education.

In the fall of 1882 he entered the medical department of the University of the City of New York, graduating with honors in the spring of 1886. He then pursued a valuable and instructive course of surgical and practical medicine by accepting the position of resident physician of the institutions of Westchester county, located near Tarrytown, on the Hudson river.

In 1887 he located in Sioux City, Iowa, through the influence of eastern capitalists, and at once assumed the responsibilities of the active practice of medicine. Becoming well-known and popular through county as well as city, in 1893 he received the nomination for county coroner, and was elected to that office by a remarkable

majority. In 1895 he was made the unanimous choice of the republicans and a second time was easily elected.

Dr. Hoyt, in professional circles, enjoys a high standing, and in the different medical societies and associations is regarded as a valuable member. He still retains his membership with the Granite Lodge, I. O. O. F., of Nashua, N. H.

June 24, 1896, he was married to Dr. Katherine E. Prichard, of Nashua, N. H., a native of Bradford, Vt. She is a graduate of the Women's Medical college of New York city, and engaged in active practice in Nashua, and later in the New England hospital, of Boston. They are both members of the First Congregational church.

PHELPS, Hon. JULIAN, who represented the Cass and Shelby senatorial district in the general assembly, and author of the anti-cigarette law enacted by the legislature, in 1896 and 1897, resides at Atlantic in his beautiful suburban home known as "The Oaks." He was born at South Hero, Grand Island county, Vt., April 4, 1838. His father, William Phelps, was a farmer and the owner of a large tract of valuable land near Milton, Vt. He was one of the prominent men of his town and county, and was especially active in all educational affairs. He died some years ago. The mother was born on Grand Island, in Lake Champlain, and is still living at Milton, Vt., at the age of 82. Her mother's name was Stark, a near relative of General Stark, of revolutionary fame.

Julian Phelps was fitted for college in an academy at South Hero, under the instruction of Rev. O. G. Wheeler, a man of great intellectual attainments and remarkable force of character. He exerted a wonderful influence over his pupils, moral and intellectual. In the fall of 1860 he entered the University of Vermont, and there pursued his studies until early in the spring of 1864, when he enlisted in the union army. The university, like most of the colleges, permitted those students who enlisted during their senior year to graduate with their class. Mr. Phelps was wounded in the battle of Cold Harbor, and was sent to the hospital at Burlington, Vt., where, through skillful treatment, his wound healed rapidly, and he was able to graduate with his class in June, 1864, delivering his oration in uniform and supporting himself on the platform with a cane. He then returned to the front, and served with his regiment to the close of the war, after which he commenced the study of law in the office of Hon. Daniel Roberts, of Burlington, who was associated with Senator Edmunds in much of his law business. He had enlisted in the Eleventh Vermont infantry at Washington, D. C., and was in the battles of Spottsylvania, Cold Harbor, Petersburg, and all others under Grant and Sheridan until Lee's surrender at Appomattox. He is a member of Sam Rice Post, G. A. R., at Atlantic.

In October, 1866, he entered the Albany Law school, and graduated in the summer of the following year. William McKinley, of Ohio, was in the senior class of that institution at the time Mr. Phelps matriculated. After graduation he came to Iowa,

and located at Lewis, in Cass county, where he formed a partnership with Judge Henry Temple. Lewis was then a small town and the county seat, but on the completion of the Rock Island railroad the capital was removed to Atlantic, and the firm of Temple & Phelps followed shortly. The relation existed until the fall of 1887, when Frank O. Temple, son of the senior member, was admitted to partnership, and the style became Temple, Phelps & Temple, and so remained until the death of Judge Temple, a few months thereafter. since which the firm has continued as Phelps & Temple. They were employed with Hon.

Thomas F. Withrow, for B. F. Allen and other plaintiffs, in the noted Atlantic town-site case, involving the title to nearly all of the town of Atlantic, which terminated in their favor at the end of a stubbornly fought legal battle.

He cast his first vote for Lincoln, and has voted the republican ticket since. He was elected to the state senate in November, 1893, from the Eighteenth senatorial district, and at the session of the Twenty-sixth General Assembly introduced and procured the passage of the bill known as the "Bill for an act to prohibit the manufacture and sale of cigarettes." He was among the foremost senators in influence and ability, and was prominent in the more important work of the senate, both in the committee room and on the floor. In 1897 Senator Phelps was appointed by the president to be United States consul at Crefield, Germany, and is now serving his country abroad.

He is a member of the Congregational church. He was married to Miss Mary A. Case in 1869, and she died the following year, leaving an infant son, who died soon after. Mr. Phelps later married a sister of his first wife, Percis M. Case. Two children, a son and a daughter, are now living. The daughter, Anna, is now the wife of F. O. Temple, and the son, Will P. Phelps, is in the law department of the Iowa State university.

---

MARKLEY, HENRY H., ex-postmaster of Cedar Falls, was born in Knox county, Ohio, January 7, 1841. His father, James Markley, was one of the pioneers of Ohio. Born in Bedford, Pa., in 1802, he came with his parents to Knox county, Ohio, in 1807, and in 1866 to Cedar Falls, where he died in 1871. His father was Henry Markley, and when he came to Ohio he bought 1,000 acres of timber land and opened up a farm, where he built and operated a distillery. He died in 1832. His wife was Jane Morrison. Jas. Markley's wife was Catherine Ankeny, to whom he was married in Knox county, Ohio, in 1838. She died March 20, 1899, in Cedar Falls, at the age of 81 years. Henry H. Markley went to school in the log schoolhouse in Ohio and afterward attended the Union Graded school in Fredericktown, and one term in Antioch college. In September, 1861, he entered the law department of the University of Michigan at Ann Arbor, graduating in March, 1863. He was elected and commissioned captain of Company B, Second Regiment Ohio militia, in Knox county, July 4, 1863, and was promoted to lieutenant-colonel of the same regiment September 7, 1863. In October he assisted in raising a company of volunteers for an Ohio regiment, but on account of political influence he did not receive the commission which had been promised him. He then went to California, and April 28, 1864, he enlisted in Company I, Second California Veteran volunteers, of San Francisco. He served as clerk at General Mason's office in San Francisco for a month, then as clerk to the assistant commissioner of musters of the Northern district of California, with headquarters at Fort Humboldt, for three

months, then as company clerk, and finally as commissary sergeant of the regiment, until he was discharged at Fort Yuma, Cal., March 31, 1866. A company had been organized and plans made at this time for laying an overland telegraph line through Siberia and Alaska, and Mr. Markley engaged to assist in the construction of this line. Just as the party was about to start news was received of the successful construction of the Atlantic cable, which rendered the overland telegraph line useless. Mr. Markley then went to British Columbia and engaged in mining and prospecting. He settled in

Walla Walla in 1868 but came to Iowa the next year, arriving in Cedar Falls December 31, 1869.

The next year he went to New York, where he was married, October 11, 1870, in Fulton, to Mary A. Schenck. In March, 1871, they moved to a farm in Butler county, near Parkersburg, where they lived until 1880, when they moved to Cedar Falls and have lived there since. In 1878 Mr. Markley built the first modern creamery and cheese factory in Butler county, and later, in partnership with Thomas Dadswell, erected and operated eight creameries in Butler, Grundy and Hardin counties. This partnership ended in 1893. Since 1884 Mr. Markley has been interested in mining in northern Idaho, and has spent part of his time there. In February, 1895, President Cleveland appointed Mr. Markley postmaster of Cedar Falls. His term expired March 1, 1899. This recognition was earned by his activity and prominence as a democrat, and by his high standing as a business man in the community. He has always affiliated with the democratic party and was elected mayor of Cedar Falls in 1884. He is serving his ninth year as member of the school board and fourth year as president of the board. Mr. Markley belongs to James Brownell Post No. 222, G. A. R., of Cedar Falls, and also to the Iowa Legion of Honor. Mr. and Mrs. Markley have one son living: Fred A., born August 4, 1877. One daughter died in infancy, and another daughter, Kitty S., died May 1, 1897, aged 25 years.

LLOYD, EDWARD S., of Remsen, Plymouth county, a man who leads a busy life in the practice of law, was born at Iowa City, Iowa, June 25, 1859. His father is the well-known Dr. Frederick Lloyd, of Iowa City, where he has been in practice since 1857. He served as surgeon in the Eleventh and Sixteenth Iowa regiments during the war. The mother, before marriage, was Isabella Harriet Wade, and came to America from England when 11 years of age. The father, also, was born in England and emigrated to this country at the age of 10 years. The ancestors on the father's side were for several generations officers in the British army; the mother's—noted clergymen of the Church of England. Henry Hamilton, a member of one branch of her mother's family, was a resident property owner of Dublin, Ireland.

Edward S. Lloyd received his primary education in the private school of F. R. Gaynor, now district judge, of Plymouth county. Then followed matriculation and graduation in the regular order for a period of years, from the Iowa City high school, the Irving institute, and the classical and law departments of the Iowa State university, respectively; the latter June 19, 1883. In the meantime he had worked in various capacities to pay the expense of his schooling. For a time he was clerk in the quartermaster's department of the United States of America, and the following year was with a surveying party in the employ of the Northern Pacific railroad, working in Montana. His first occupation after quitting college was as principal of

the Remsen public schools, in which he served for two years. He then decided to engage in the practice of law, and as the town of Remsen appeared to offer a good field, he at once opened an office. That was in 1886, and at this writing he is still there, enjoying an extensive and constantly growing practice and not at all sorry for having made the venture. The first vote of Mr. Lloyd was cast for James A. Garfield, after which his sympathies and his support went to the democratic party, and he is yet strong in that faith. He has taken an active part in the municipal affairs of Remsen, was instrumental in a large degree in securing its incorporation in 1887,

and has served as city clerk continuously since that time, with the exception of one term. In township matters, too, he is quite prominent, and has acted as clerk at various times; is at present justice of the peace. He is a member of the Roman Catholic church and the Catholic Mutual Protective association. He is active in the A. O. U. W., in which order he has held the positions of recorder, financier, receiver, master workman and past master workman. April 19, 1893, he was married to Miss Lucy A. Kieffer, daughter of J. P. Kieffer, of Remsen. They have three children: Edward George Lucien, Heloise Edith and Harriet Annie.

3¹

HOBART, ALVA C., better known as Senator Hobart, of Cherokee, was born at Royalton, Wis., July 26, 1860. His father C. E. P. Hobart, married Eliza A. Tibbitts, and was formerly an attorney at law, in Wisconsin. He removed to Cherokee, Iowa, in 1870, and engaged in the grain business. He is of English ancestry, being a direct descendant of Edmund Hobart, who came from Hingham, England, in 1634, and settled at Hingham, Mass., where he was a prominent and influential citizen for many years.

Young Hobart attended the public schools of Royalton and Cherokee, and an

academy at Iowa City. During the years 1878 and 1879 he managed his father's farm, near Cherokee, and earned enough money to take him through college. Entering the State university, at Iowa City, he continued his studies for four years, and graduated in June, 1885, taking the degree of Ph. B. He then studied law for one year in the office of Senator A. F. Meservey, of Cherokee, and in 1887 was elected clerk of the district court and served one term. Not wishing to delay his admission to the bar, he was not a candidate for re-election, and was admitted in May, 1889. He immediately opened an office in Cherokee, and in 1890 was elected county attorney and served two terms, or until the close of 1894.

In 1895 he was elected state senator for the Forty-sixth senatorial district, comprising the counties of Cherokee, Ida and Plymouth. The senator's law practice has been successful and satisfactory, and his work has been done alone until June, 1897, when he associated with him, Truxton Goodrell, of Washington, D. C.

The following from a Des Moines daily shows what is thought of Senator Hobart's legislative work: "He is thoroughly unassuming, and if he has any particular fault, it lies in the fact that he under-estimates his own abilities. As a senator he is as plain and unpretentious as he is in his own home. Still, he is an able legislator and wields a large influence in the law-making body of the state. During the extra session he developed much prominence by his advocacy of the famous Temple amendment, which provides that the railway employes who were members of a protective association, organized and controlled by a railroad company, should not thereby forfeit claims for loss of life or limbs while in the employ of the company. This amendment was bitterly opposed by certain railroad corporations, and finally defeated. The joint legislative committee of the railway employes' organizations of the state issued a pamphlet reviewing the result of the proposition involved in the amendment, in which it took occasion to highly compliment Senator Hobart for the manly stand he took in the senate in the interests of the railway men. This pamphlet speaks of him as one "who stood as a beacon light in the interest of the people and public policy," and added that "the railroad men of the state surely ought to know from this, our appreciation of the action of this senator, without an elaborate eulogy." Senator Hobart comes from a town that is largely populated by railroad men, and we are sure they will all remember his good offices in their interests. He was equally as earnest in his opposition to the Berry substitute, which was practically an annulment of the Temple amendment, and made a vigorous speech against it. The vast army of railway men in Iowa should not soon forget Senator Hobart's efforts in their behalf, and the bold and courageous manner in which he defended their interests, when to do so called for the exercise of a vast amount of moral courage. Besides opening and closing the debate in the senate in support of the Temple amendment, he was one of the able supporters of the Cheshire amendment.

In September, 1887, Mr. Hobart was married to Hattie L. Beckwith, and they have three children: Verner, Carroll and Louise. He has always been a republican and has taken a very active part in both state and local campaigns. Is also a member of the Masonic order.

SMALL, WILLIAM EDWARD, of Brooklyn, was born in Portland, Me., September 3, 1822. He is a descendant of Francis Small, who was born in England in 1620, and came to America about 1632 with his father, Edward Small, and their kinsman, Capt. Francis Champernoune. They settled in what is now the state of Maine.

Edward Small, with Captain Champernoune and others, in 1635 founded Piscataqua, which has since been divided into the towns of Kittery, Elliott, South Berwick and Berwick. Captain Champernoune was a member of the famous Devonshire family of that name who were direct descendants of William the conqueror. The Small family is descended from a branch of the Champernounes. In July, 1657, Francis Small, who then lived at Falmouth, Me., bought of the Indian chief, Skittergusett, a large tract of land called Capisic, near the present city of Portland. In 1668 he received of the Indian chief, Sundy, as recompense for the burning of a store by the Indians, a deed to 256,000 acres of land lying between the Great Ossipee, the Saco, the Little Ossipee and the Neihewonock rivers. This land now constitutes the northern part of the county of York, Me. The original deed signed by the Indian chief was recorded in 1773 and confirmed by the courts as valid. It is now in the possession of Lauriston W. Small, of Brooklyn, N. Y. Samuel Small, one of the ancestors of William E., was active during the controversy which led to the revolutionary war, and was at the head of the committee of safety. One of Mr. Small's cousins, Sir John Small, belonged to the branch of the family that remained in England. He was chief justice of India a few years ago. Another cousin belonging to the same branch, Col. John Small, commanded a detachment of the British troops at Bunker Hill.

William Small, the father of William E., was a manufacturer of pianos and served as a soldier in the war of 1812. He married Sarah Barnes Hatch, a daughter of Walter Hatch, of Boston, Mass., and a descendant of William Hatch, of Sandwich, England, who was a merchant, and settled at Scituate, Mass., in 1633. William E. was educated in the common schools of Boston, Portland and Limington, and learned the printer's trade.

He gave this up after three years and went to Bangor, Me., in 1841, where he clerked for two years in the largest mercantile establishment in the city. At the end of that time, when 22 years old, he commenced business for himself by purchasing a tract of timber land and hiring men and teams to cut the timber and haul it to the river where it could be floated to the mills. He next, in partnership with George H. Herrick, purchased what was half a township, or 11,520 acres of timber land. He continued in the land and timber business until 1854, when he came to Davenport, Iowa, and built a planing mill in partnership with John M. Cannon. In the fall of 1856 the firm decided to start a lumber yard at Iowa City, and Mr. Small moved to that place to take charge of that business. In 1859 he was elected president

of the Johnson County Agricultural society, and built the first fair ground and track in the county, which led to the holding of the state fair at that place in 1860 and 1861.

Mr. Small, in July, 1861, joined the Tenth Regiment of Iowa infantry, at Iowa City, with the rank of lieutenant-colonel, and in 1862 was promoted to the rank of colonel. He participated in the battles of Charlestown, Mo., New Madrid, Island No. 10, Farmington, Corinth, and in the campaigns against Vicksburg, via Holly Springs, Yazoo Pass and Grand Gulf to Black River. Here his health failed and he was compelled to retire.

Colonel Small is a member of the G. A. R., and was for several years president of the Brooklyn Veteran Union, since merged into the John J. Drake Post. Politically, Colonel Small was an abolitionist, and when the republican party adopted that principle he acted with them. When, however, it was proposed to enfranchise the blacks, he believed it would prove a curse to both blacks and whites and he opposed that action. Since that time he has affiliated with the democratic party. Colonel Small served two terms as mayor of Brooklyn.

He was married at Bangor, Me., September 25, 1844, to Mary Quincy Chick. They have four children: Frederick A., born at Bangor, Me.; Helen C., born at Bangor, and now the wife of George Neil, of Marshalltown; Fannie P., born at Bangor, and now the wife of John W. Conger, of Los Angeles, Cal.; Sarah L., born at Iowa City, and now the wife of Rev. W. C. Corbyn, of Tower, Minn.

---

VERNON, CARLTON HULLET, for many years one of the modest and unassuming, yet influential and valued citizens of Oskaloosa has just removed his home to Corning, Adams county, June 14, 1899. He is president of the Mahaska County State bank, and has served as member of the city council and director of Oskaloosa schools, in both of which positions he earned the thanks of an appreciative tax-paying public by reason of his wisdom in the management of public affairs and his keen regard for the interests of those upon whom the burden of municipal expense rests. Clean, honorable, straightforward, progressive and generous, his friends, both in public and private life, are many.

His is the story of a boy who rose from the farm to a high place in the financial and political circles of an intelligent and thoroughly business-going community. He was born in Monroe county, Ohio, August 22, 1845, on the old homestead owned by his father, and there lived until he had become a man. He is the son of Jacob Vernon, a conspicuous and highly honored farmer, and Catherine Smith Vernon, who comes of one of the first families of that well-known name in Pennsylvania.

Following the completion of the common school course of Monroe county, he entered the Fairbank academy at Woodsfield. His school days were alternated with work on the farm and trapping fur animals. It was in the trapping business that he earned his first dollar. Later his father gave him an acre of land, or rather the use thereof,

which he planted in tobacco, and so successful was he in the cultivation of the plant that a considerable sum was realized from the sale of the crops.

He came to Iowa in 1869 and located near Oskaloosa on a farm which his father had purchased. When he had reached the proper age he was given a small tract of land by his father, and the same has not only remained in his possession ever since, but has been added to regularly until it is now a large and valuable farm.

He was married to Miss Mary Louisa Jones, November 18, 1872. They have three children: Cora Catherine, Edwin McPherson and Sarah Lena. Mr. Vernon

was reared a democrat, but was converted to republicanism during the Vallandigham gubernatorial campaign in Ohio, since which time he has been an uncompromising advocate of the principles and candidates of the last-named party. In all the affairs of his section he takes an active interest, although not offensive in his manner of supporting those enterprises which he believes to be for the greatest good of the common people. He is a man of genial manner, easy of approach, and impresses one with his strong personality and high character.

Mr. Vernon has for some years been developing a magnificent farm in Adams county, where he now has about 1400 acres in one tract. He has purchased a fine residence in Corning, which will be his future home.

LEWIS, JUDGE CHARLES HENRY. The life of this honorable and honored citizen of Woodbury county as citizen, soldier, jurist and judge, stands a shining example of combined American attributes. He was born October 17, 1839, in Collins Center, Erie county, N. Y. His parents Oren and Elizabeth Nichols Lewis, were natives of Connecticut, descended from English ancestors. When he was but 9 months old the family moved to southern Wisconsin, where they remained for two years, and thence went to Boone county, Ill. They made their home there until 1851, when they came to Iowa, arriving at Independence October 8. Three years later the father moved to Quasqueton, Buchanan county, this state, where he remained until his death, which occurred in 1884. Judge Lewis' early life was spent upon his father's farm, save for a little time when he was employed in the furniture factory operated by the father at Independence. In 1859 he began a close student's life in Cornell college, at Mount Vernon. In 1862 he left the school and enlisted in the army, entering the services as a private soldier in Company H, Twenty-seventh Iowa infantry. For a year he served as a private soldier, was then made sergeant-major of the regiment, and held that position for one year, when he was promoted to first lieutenant, and appointed and commissioned adjutant, which position he filled until the war closed. He served three years and five days, and during all that time was never absent from the regiment, and was off duty but three days, during which time he was on the sick list. The war closing, he returned to his old home in Buchanan county, and soon engaged with his brother, and another in the milling and mercantile business, which he pursued for a little time. He then entered the law department of the State university, and graduated therefrom in the summer of 1869. He at once removed to Cherokee, Iowa, arriving there May 29th of that year, and formed a partnership with his father-in-law, H. C. Kellogg. They were the first lawyers in the county, and their practice was soon extensive and lucrative. Mr. Lewis was county recorder and county superintendent of schools of Cherokee

county, for a time. In 1870 he was nominated district attorney of the Fourth judicial district of Iowa, the district then embracing twenty-two counties in northwestern Iowa. He was elected by a large majority. He served as such until January 1, 1875. So well had Mr. Lewis performed his duties as district attorney, that in the summer of 1874 he was nominated for district judge, and at the fall election, in 1874, he was elected by an overwhelming vote. In the fall of 1878, Judge Lewis was renominated by acclamation to succeed himself, and at the fall election was chosen for another term by an increased

majority. He served two terms more of four years each in that capacity, being re-elected by increasing majorities at each election, showing the appreciation the people had of his talents and his fitness for the office. He has been firm in the enforcement of the law, and has justly earned the reputation of being one of the best judges who ever presided over any court in Iowa In the first trial of John Arensdorf and others accused of the murder of Rev. George C. Haddock, of Sioux City, Judge Lewis presided, and won the favorable opinion of all loyal citizens. He has presided over nearly all the hotly contested legal battles growing out of the temperance legislation and agitation, in so far as the same have had hearing in northwestern Iowa.

The following is taken from the records of the district court of Woodbury county, being a portion of the resolution adopted by the bar association, upon the retirement of Judge Lewis:

*Resolved*, That the bar of Sioux City and Woodbury county tender to Judge Lewis their cordial and affectionate respect, recognizing in him those qualities which make a great judge; that unerring sense of justice which seeks for the right under whatever cloud of technicality; that promptness which takes from the law the reproach of delay; that benevolent spirit which knows how to temper justice with kindness; that firmness which acts and fears not; that impartiality which looks with equal eye upon all men and all causes, measuring them only with the standard of truth.

The judge has been a member of the G. A. R. for many years, and is prominent in the Loyal Legion of Iowa.

———

BURTON, ASA HUNTINGTON, city attorney of Sioux City, is another addition to the long list of successful Iowa men who came from New England stock. His father was Alonzo Hazen Burton, born in Vermont in 1827. In 1846 he came, with his parents, to Denmark, Lee county, Iowa, and located on a farm. He was married to Miss Caroline Louise Ingalls, youngest daughter of Rev. Edmund Ingalls, a Presbyterian minister from western New York, and located near Denmark, Iowa, November 1, 1854, and remained on his farm in that county, until his death, May 14, 1893. They had three children: Edmund Ingalls, born January 25, 1858; Asa Huntington, born August 9, 1861, and Eugene Henry, born August 1, 1863; all now living. They lived very comfortably, in a pleasant country home. The families date back eight generations in America, and on both sides members have attained high rank in public and private life. Asa H. had about the usual life of a farmer's son. He went to school in the district school until he was 11 years old, when he worked on the farm during the busy season, and went to the academy in Denmark in the fall and winter, riding back and forth on horseback between the town and his father's home, where he boarded. When about 18 years of age he commenced teaching, and doing other work around the academy, graduating from that institution, in the classical course, in June, 1883. Having determined to be a lawyer, he commenced studying with that end in

view at once, and in the winter of 1884 entered the law department of the State university, graduating in June, 1885, with the degree of LL. B. After helping his father out with the summer's work on the farm, Mr. Burton located temporarily in the little town of Elliott, Montgomery county, for the practice of law, and here he received his first professional earnings, which he remembers was for drawing some instruments of conveyance. Learning of the fine opening in the rapidly-growing and prosperous Sioux City, the young lawyer remained only six months in Elliott, when he removed to his present residence, where he

has since practiced successfully. He was in partnership with Thomas F. Bevington from May, 1886, to September, 1890, when he purchased Mr. Bevington's interest, and continued alone until he formed a partnership with George Conway, in May, 1893. This lasted one year, when it was dissolved, and Mr. Burton has practiced alone since. In March, 1894, his professional ability was recognized by an election to the office of city attorney of Sioux City, and his work in that position was so satisfactory that he was re-elected in 1896; both times on the republican ticket, for he has always voted with the republican party. Mr. Burton has always been a close student of military tactics, having been teacher and captain of the Denmark Guards, at Denmark academy, and has shown his willingness to respond to the demands of his country by serving almost six years in the Iowa National Guard being a member of Company H, of Sioux City, Fourth regiment. He is a member of Sioux Council No. 1308, Royal Arcanum, Sioux City. He was married September 20, 1888, to Helen S. Turner, only child of Mr. and Mrs. Louis Q. Turner, of Denmark, Iowa. Daughters were born to them, October 26, 1892, named Adelene and Caroline. The latter died when but 2 days old.

---

FOUSE, REV. DEWALT S., D. D., of Lisbon, is a native of Huntingdon county, Penn. He was born near Marklesburg, in that county, November 15, 1840. His father, Dewalt Fouse, was born December 26, 1802, in Blair county, Penn., and was a minister in the Reformed church in the United States. His grandfather was a native of Bavaria, Germany, and came to America in 1784. Dewalt Fouse was married March 25, 1823, to Nancy Shontz, who was born in Huntingdon county. Her father, Christian Shontz, and her mother, Margaret Huber Shontz, were both natives of Lancaster county, Penn., although of Swiss descent.

Young Mr. Fouse received his early education in the common schools of his county and at Marklesburg academy. The young man was naturally studious and made full use of his opportunities for acquiring knowledge. He entered Franklin Marshall college at Lancaster, Penn., in 1859. His college course was interrupted by the rebellion, and September 16, 1861, he enlisted as a private in Company C, Fifty-third Pennsylvania volunteers, commanded by Col. John R. Brooke, now active in the service at Havana, Cuba, as military governor. Mr. Fouse was soon made orderly sergeant, and December 14, 1862, was promoted to first lieutenant of his company. During much of the time he acted as adjutant of the regiment, and when mustered out, October 9, 1864, he was acting assistant adjutant-general of the Fourth brigade, First division, Second army corps. Gen. W. S. Hancock was commander of the corps. Lieutenant Fouse participated in the battles of Fair Oaks, Gains Mills, Peach Orchard, Savage Station, White Oak Swamp, Malvern Hill, Second Bull Run, Antietam, Fredericks-

burg, Chancellorsville, Gettysburg, Mine Run, and in the battles of the Wilderness campaign from the Rapidan river to Petersburg in 1864. Through all the hardships and privations of three years he passed without being seriously affected, but the poisoned air of the swamps brought on malarial fever at last, and his health being shattered and the term of enlistment having expired, he returned home in October, 1864. Six of his brothers were in the army and of these two died in service, one lost an eye, and another has a crippled leg and arm. After resting and recovering his health, Mr. Fouse entered the Theological Seminary of the Reformed church, at

Mercersburg, Penn., from which he graduated in May, 1867. He was soon after sent by the board of home missions of his church to do mission work in Iowa, and settled near Central City, Linn county, in July, 1867. While living there he preached at Boulder, Linn county, and at Brandon, Buchanan county, for several years. In 1872 he moved to Lisbon, where he preached for a number of years, and still resides. In October, 1889, he became general superintendent of the board of home missions of the Reformed church in the United States. This gives him general oversight and supervision of all the home missions of his church in the United States, and requires him to spend much of his time traveling among the churches.

Mr. Fouse was married January 30, 1868, to Sarah A. Geissinger, of Huntingdon county, Penn. They have four children: David Henry, born July 1, 1869, and now a minister in the Reformed church; Samuel G., born February 27, 1871, now a merchant in Lisbon; John D., born June 1, 1873, now a commercial traveler, and Mary Naomi, born April 18, 1879, now attending Cornell college, at Mt. Vernon, Iowa.

---

HUFFAKER, HENRY HARRISON, of Silver City, Mills county, a highly successful farmer and stock raiser, is one of

the most prominent agriculturists in southwestern Iowa. He was born and raised on a farm and from early boyhood was ambitious to follow the independent life of a farmer, and become the owner of broad acres, well stocked and well cultivated.

Mr. Huffaker's father, Israel Huffaker, was the fourth child of John and Priscilla Huffaker, and was born June 9, 1814, in Wayne county, Ky. At the age of 14 years he left his home and, accompanied by his brother Jacob, walked to Morgan county, Ill. Two years later he enlisted in the army for service in the Black Hawk war, serving during the years 1831 and 1832.

After his discharge he returned to Jacksonville and on May 1, 1834, married Ann Maria Kurtz. They resided in Morgan county until 1840, when they removed to Bureau county, Ill., and were engaged in farming until 1854. In that year they removed to Hancock county, where they resided two years, returning to Bureau county in 1856. They lived there for thirty-four years, or until 1890, at which time they removed to Mills county, Iowa, where their son Henry had preceded them a number of years. Israel Huffaker was a zealous Christian man, having, in his early boyhood days, united with the Christian church, remaining a member until 1841, when he united with the Church of Christ, and was ordained as a bishop in 1844; later he was designated as one in the lineage of Levi, and was ever an energetic worker for his Lord and Master. In his occupation of farming he was very successful financially, and accumulated over 2,000 acres of land. He died December 20, 1896.

Henry Huffaker's mother was born near Samuel's Depot, Nelson county, Ky., March 9, 1819, and was the youngest daughter of John and Margaret Kurtz. She was a devoted worker in the Christian church for over half a century, ready at all times to lend a helping hand to the needy and unfortunate. She died August 20, 1895.

H. H. Huffaker was born January 24, 1841, in Bureau county, Ill., near Dover. He attended the district school and Dover academy, completing his education at the Princeton, Ill., high school. In 1868 he came west and settled in Mills county, Iowa, his present home. At that time the country was in its wild state, the settlers being few and far between. His farm at first consisted of about 300 acres, and it was later upon this tract of land that the foundation of Silver City was laid, after securing from the Wabash, St. Louis & Pacific railroad the location of a station there. The embryo town of 1879 has grown until at the present time it numbers about 700 people. Mr. Huffaker has increased his landed possessions until he now owns 1,500 acres which is well improved and well supplied with stock. He does not buy largely of stock but raises nearly all that he feeds, having constantly in pasture from to 200 to 300 head. Mr. Huffaker has held a number of offices of public trust and is a member of several agricultural societies. A share of his ample means is ever ready to be used to advance the cause of education. He is also a liberal giver for the aid of church work and ever willing, like his father, to respond to his Master's will. Was ordained a minister of the gospel January 8, 1872.

He was married to Miss Mary J Post, daughter of Stephen and Jane Post, a native of Pennsylvania, December 11, 1872, in Marion county, Iowa. They have one daughter by adoption, Birdie Almaretta Huffaker.

Father Post was a minister of the gospel fifty-three years before his decease. Both were born in the state of New York.

———

HOLMES, RICHARD, president of the Waterloo State bank, and a resident of Black Hawk county for thirty-six years, is a native of England. He was born near Manchester, under the sovereignty of Queen Victoria, April 20, 1842. His father, James Holmes, was a farmer in good circumstances, and a man of sterling, upright character. His mother, Ann Emerson (Holmes), was a noble woman, whose Christian qualities and tender spirit ever exerted the best of influence over her family of eight children, to whom she was always the devoted mother, instilling into their thoughts and actions, as they grew up around her, all that was good, pure and ennobling.

Richard was the eldest of the children, and from early boyhood was a great aid to his father in helping to care and provide for the family. He thus early learned the principles of industry and economy, which applied to all his undertakings, though active manhood has enabled him to now enjoy the fruits of his labors in comfort. The family came from England in 1854 and landed first at Montreal, after a voyage of eight weeks spent on the Atlantic ocean in a sailing vessel. Three months after arriving at Montreal, they came west and settled in Greene county, Wis. Here Richard assisted his father in erecting a log cabin, and, during the next nine years, was actively engaged in clearing the farm and making a home in the wilds of that state. His education consisted in what he obtained while attending the common schools during the winter months. When Richard was 21 the family decided to come farther west. In company with his father, they walked fifty miles to a railroad, and came to Waterloo, Iowa, where, believing they would have a better opportunity to judge of the quality of the land, and most desirable location for a home, they started

out on foot, and, after a few days' time spent in the search, they located in Lincoln township. Richard's father returned to the family in Wisconsin to remain during the winter and prepare for the journey west in the spring, while he himself obtained employment in a stone quarry, near their new home, and remained there until spring. He then returned to Wisconsin and assisted in moving the family to Black Hawk county, and soon afterwards bought land in Eagle township, where he farmed for a number of years. During the fall and winter of each year he operated a threshing machine, and was very successful financially. Mr. Holmes spent the

winters of 1872-73-74 in England. In 1882 he moved to the town of Waterloo and there engaged in the implement business with James R. Vaughn in 1885, under the firm name of Holmes & Vaughn. This partnership continued for five years, during which time they built up an extensive trade throughout the state. In 1890 he retired from active business life, and was made president of the Waterloo Gasoline Engine company. He is also president of one of the strongest financial institutions in the state — the Waterloo State bank, which was organized in 1893.

Politically Mr. Holmes is a republican, and an advocate of sound money. He is a

member of the Baptist church, and was at
an early age religiously instructed, so that
now one of his greatest sources of strength
is his faith in a Savior, through whom
is gained all happiness and strength.

Mr. Holmes was married September
21, 1876, to Miss Mary Vaughn, daughter
of James Vaughn, a well-to-do farmer of
Black Hawk county.

We have, in Mr. Holmes, an example
of the sturdy business man and upright
citizen, whose honesty of purpose, industry, economy and straightforwardness in
his dealings with his fellowmen has won
for him the honorable though unosten-
tatious position he holds in life.    It is
such citizens as Mr. Holmes who have made
Iowa what she is to-day.

---

JOY, WILLIAM L., has been a resident
attorney of Sioux City since 1857. He
stands out conspicuously as a Woodbury
county pioneer and for many years he has
been the leading lawyer of northwestern
Iowa, where through a legitimate and honorable practice of his profession, together
with prudent investments, he has made a
financial success.  It is said by his friends
to his credit, that he uses the fortune he
has accumulated for the true purposes that
a goodly competency is given to men.   He
is not only an able lawyer, holding the
respect and high esteem of the bar of the
state, and of his neighbors, but is an active,
public-spirited man, representing the best
type of American citizenship.   Having a
kind heart and being a candid man, he has
many friends and admirers.   Mr. Joy is a
New Englander by birth and education.
His birthplace was Townshend, Vt., and
the date August 17, 1830. His parents
were William H. and Hetty Leonard Joy.
His father was a farmer, who also owned
a mill.   His paternal grandfather was a
revolutionary soldier.  William L. remained
at home till he was 20 years old, assisting
his father in his business and fitting himself for college in Leland seminary in his
native town.   In his 21st year he entered
Amherst college and graduated in the class
of 1855. During his college course he
taught several terms of school, being an
instructor in Leland seminary while studying law with Judge Roberts at home.  He
was admitted to the bar early in the spring
of 1857 and started immediately for the
great, growing west to make his fortune.
He reached Sioux City on the 5th of May.
He found there a small village on the

frontier, with no sign of a railway, but full
of energetic young men like himself, with
unbounded hopes for the future and the
courage and industry to do their part in
developing a country of rare promise. Mr.
Joy formed a partnership with N. C. Hudson and the firm of Hudson & Joy was continued until October, 1866.  After practicing alone for two years he took as a partner Craig L. Wright, son of the late George
G. Wright, and for twenty years the firm
of Joy & Wright was the leading law firm
in Woodbury county.   They were the local
attorneys for the Illinois Central Railway
company and the general attorneys for the

Sioux City & Pacific, the Dakota Southern,
the Covington, Columbus & Black Hills
railway companies and the Iowa Falls &
Sioux City Railroad Land company.  Mr.
Joy has always had a large law business,
both in the state and federal courts.  His
son, C. L. Joy, was taken into his father's
firm in 1888, when it was known as Joy,
Hudson & Joy, A. L. Hudson being the
other partner.   Later the firm was Joy,
Hudson, Call & Joy, A. F. Call, of Algona,
having been admitted as a partner.   The
firm at present is W. L. and C. L. Joy.
The younger Mr. Joy has earned a high
standing at the bar.   The senior Mr. Joy
has always been regarded as a strong
pleader before a jury, but is best known

as a court lawyer, and as such has but few equals in the state.

Mr. Joy has always been a staunch republican. He was a member of the lower house in the Eleventh and Twelfth General Assemblies and spent most of his time in Des Moines during the session of the Thirteenth General Assembly, in 1868, looking after legislation for the purpose of securing railways for northwestern Iowa. In this capacity he probably did as much work for his constituents as any member of the legislature, for the legislation he secured has been of inestimable benefit to that part of the state. Having accomplished this work, Mr. Joy has since refused the solicitations of friends to become a candidate for any office, though he served two years as a member of the board of capitol commissioners during the inception of the great enterprise of building the state house. Friends urged him to be a candidate for district or circuit judge, a position he was peculiarly well qualified to fill, but he never encouraged such movements. Mr. Joy has been a prominent lay member of the Baptist church for more than forty-two years. He was married October 18, 1859, to Frances A. Stone, of Westmoreland, N. H. They have two children, the elder, C. L., the lawyer, and Helen F., wife of Giles W. Brown, general manager of the Sioux Milling company, of which Mr. Joy is president. Mr. Joy has always been deeply interested in school matters, and for more than twenty years he gave his valuable time and business experience to the school board of Sioux City, as member and president. To the wise management given the district's affairs by these directors, who included some of the most prominent citizens of the city, is due the excellent condition of the public schools and most of the valuable property owned by the district. Mr. Joy was president of the Sioux National bank, the heaviest in Sioux City, from its organization until January, 1896. He has been a stockholder and otherwise connected with various financial institutions in Sioux City, that have felt the impress of his ability. He is a strong man, physically, mentally and morally, takes an active interest in all public enterprises for the improvement of the city, and it has been fortunate in having such a man among its early settlers.

His has been the work of helping to lay a solid foundation for a great and growing city.

WILKEN, FRANK HENRY, of Fort Madison, is one of the well-known business men and prominent politicians of southeastern Iowa. He is of German parentage, his father, William Wilken, a contractor and builder, having been born in Soegel, Kreis Meppen, Hanover, in 1822, while his mother, Agnes Shuette, was born in Hoerst, Bezirk, Minden, August 7, 1824. He comes of excellent ancestors, many of them having belonged to the learned professions. The mayorship of the city of Grossen Stavern was held by the Wilken family for eight years.

F. H. Wilken was born September 9, 1857, at Fort Madison, Lee county, Iowa.

His education was obtained in the public schools of that city, and in private parochial schools. He began business for himself in February, 1878, several months before he became of age. He at first conducted a small grocery store, and to this he has continued to add year by year, until his business has increased to large proportions, and he now owns a fine stock of general merchandise, and enjoys a splendid patronage.

Politically, Mr. Wilken has always been a democrat. He was a member of the school board from 1886 to 1889, and during his term of office was an earnest worker for the promotion of the best interests of the public schools, securing numerous improvements in the way of better buildings and progressive methods of training. He was elected a member of the city council of Fort Madison in 1888, and re-elected without opposition in 1890, serving as president of the council during all but one year that he held the office. In 1892 he was elected to the Twenty-fourth General Assembly, as a member of the house, and served again during the Twenty-fifth. While in the legislature he took an active part in helping to repeal the prohibitory liquor law, believing that a license system should be allowed where the former law could not be enforced. Mr. Wilken belongs to the Catholic church, and is a member of the German Roman Catholic Benevolent society, serving as president during the years 1895, 1896, 1897, and 1898, having served as state vice-president of the Central Verein in 1895. He also belongs to the Iowa Mutual Protective association, and to the Fort Madison or St. Joseph Benevolent society. He has served for ten years as director of the Fort Madison Building and Loan association, being president thereof in 1898 and 1899.

He was married May 21, 1878, to Anna M. Luebbers, and they have four children: Margaret M., born February 24, 1879; William F , born November 1, 1881; Clara M., born October 24, 1887, and Helen A., born June 27, 1890.

MARSTON, CHARLES SAMUEL, of Mason City, is one of the most promising young physicians of that section of the state. Like so many other successful professional men, he is the son of a farmer, and was brought up in the country. His father, G. W. Marston, still lives on the homestead in Illinois, where his family of seven children grew up. He was a veteran of the civil war, having enlisted in the Fifteenth Illinois infantry on the first call. He fought in several battles, and at the battle of Shiloh received three wounds, and was soon afterwards discharged on account of his disabilities. The Marstons are descendants of an old New England family, the doctor's great-grandfather having been wounded at the battle of Bunker Hill. The family originally lived in Vermont and New York, but migrated to Illinois early in the 40's. The doctor's mother, Sarah Scott, came from Pennsylvania to Illinois when she was a child, and previous to her marriage was a prominent

teacher. She is the daughter of Amos Scott, a retired physician, and on her mother's side is a direct descendant of the McCarty's, who are known in history for the important part they took in the early Indian wars in Pennsylvania. Dr. Charles Marston was born February 6, 1870, near Seward, Winnebago county, Ill., and was the third of seven children, the oldest being Anson, who is now professor of civil engineering at the Iowa State college at Ames. He obtained his general education in the country schools and in the high school at Rockford, Ill., and in the meantime worked on the farm during vacations.

In 1888, at the age of 18, he secured a position as clerk in a drug store at Rockford, where he remained two years, at the same time studying medicine under Dr. R. Sager. He entered Rush Medical college at Chicago in 1890, graduating March 29, 1893. Immediately after his graduation he came to Mason City and began the practice of medicine, in which he was most successful. Dr. Marston is a member of the Baptist church. In politics he is a republican. He was married July 15, 1890, to Miss Evelyn Scott, daughter of Frank B. Scott, deceased (a member of the Second Illinois cavalry in the civil war), and a great-great-granddaughter of General

Chrystiler, who was killed in the revolutionary war. Dr. and Mrs. Marston have two children: Evelyn Frances, who was born August 8, 1893, and Dorris Mardeine, born December 21, 1898.

---

TILTON, JOHN LITTLEFIELD, professor of natural sciences at Simpson college, is a native of New Hampshire, born January 11, 1863, at Nashua, in that state. He is descended from an English family, who came from Tilton Hill, England, in the seventeenth century and settled in New England. Daniel Tilton, born in 1645, was an ensign in King William's war, afterward a member and also speaker of the provincial assembly. Joseph, son of Daniel, was commissioned captain in 1717. Samuel and David, also sons of Daniel, were colonial soldiers in Queen Anne's war. At the battle of Bunker Hill, a lad 14 years of age, named Sinclair, stood with the New Hampshire boys at the rail fence. He left his home in northern New Hampshire when the news from Concord and Lexington first reached his home and served with the American army throughout the war. Others less closely related were also in the revolution.

John Tilton, the professor's father, was born in Sandwich, N. H., July 28, 1828. In 1859 he removed to Nashua, where he was a member of the common council, alderman and representative in the state legislature. As a business man his reputation was of the highest order. His sagacity, promptness and sterling integrity made his word as good as his bond. He was benevolent and open-handed, but his good deeds were always performed in a quiet way and many are able to give testimony to his generous assistance. He married Celia L. Meader in 1853. Her ancestors were from the state of Maine, where they were prominent and highly respected citizens. Professor Tilton has two brothers: Frank H., who is a physician in East Boston, Mass., and Osmon B., who is in the grain business at Nashua.

Professor Tilton's early education was received in the graded schools. He was converted when 13 years of age, in 1876, and joined the Methodist Episcopal church the following year. Like many boys of his age he was indifferent to study during the first half of his high school course, but fortunately, and in due time, he roused himself and at his graduation, in 1881, received a " Noyes prize medal," for scholarship and deportment throughout the high school course. In September, 1881, he entered the Wesleyan university, at Middletown, Conn., for a college course, which he finished with the degree of A. B. in 1885. The following year he served as principal of the public schools at Niantic, Conn. From 1886 to 1888 he was in the service of his alma mater as assistant in natural history, at the same time pursuing a post-graduate course in natural history, which was completed in 1888, when he received his M. A. degree, and was also elected to the chair of natural sciences of Simpson college, of Iowa.

During the summer vacations, he spent his time in the following places: Summer of 1885 in the biological laboratory of Annisquam, Mass.; the summer of 1886 in the zoology department of the Martha's Vineyard Summer institute, and the summer of 1887 as assistant in the latter place. The summer vacation of 1888 was given to the study of quantitative analysis at Harvard university and to special work in electricity at Wesleyan, preparatory to his work at Simpson the following year.

The summer of 1890 he visited Annisquam, Mass., for the purpose of collecting biological material to be used in the laboratory. He took a special course in electrical engineering at Harvard university during the summer of 1893. Parts of the remaining summers have been spent in field work connected with the Iowa state geological survey.

His leave of absence in 1895 was devoted to special courses in geology at Harvard university. These courses were in the following subjects: Fossils, both their biological and stratigraphical relations; petrography, field investigation, and, as an extra subject, physical geography. For this work, together with the theses connected with it, Harvard university conferred upon him the M. A. degree. He holds a membership in the Phi Beta Kappa, in the American Society of Naturalists, and in the Iowa Academy of Sciences.

The following publications will give an idea of the work he has completed, and of the work in which he is still engaged: "The Sixteenth and Seventeenth Annual Reports of the Curators of the Museum of Wesleyan University," Middletown, Conn. Several papers in the proceedings of the "Iowa Academy of Sciences;" "Geological section along Middle river in central Iowa," Iowa Geological Survey, Vol. 3; "On the Southwestern part of Boston Basin," Proceedings of the Boston Society of Natural History, Vol. 36, June, 1895; "Area of Slate near Nashua," Nashua *Daily Press*, October 29, 1896; "The Geology of Warren county," Iowa Geological Survey, Vol. 5.

September 4, 1890, he married Ida M. Hoyt, of Nashua, N. H. His only child, Besse, was born June 15, 1891.

———

HECHT, FREDERICK, of Clarence, is one of the pioneers of Cedar county, having located there in 1855. His father, John Hecht, came from Westenburg, Germany, in 1832, and settled in West Newton, Westmoreland county, Pa. He was a stone mason and contractor. He married Louise Catherine Eisle. They reared a family of four children: John Hecht, of Ida Grove; Henry Hecht, of Tipton; Fred Hecht, of Clarence, and Mrs. H. A. McKelvey, of Chicago. In 1854 Mr. Hecht removed his family to Iowa and went to farming.

Frederick was born in West Newton, Pa., February 13, 1836. When 16 years old he went to Pittsburg and served an apprenticeship of three years with C. Yeager & Company, in the mercantile business. At the end of that period he

came to Tipton, Iowa, and entered the store of Friend & Culbertson as a clerk. He was an active, energetic young man and a good and trustworthy clerk. He was ambitious and had always saved his money, and in 1861 was able to buy a one-third interest in a store belonging to Friend & Culbertson at Clarence. He was manager of this store which was operated under the name of Fred Hecht & Company. So successful was the business that Mr. Hecht was able to buy the interest of Friend & Culbertson, and in 1863 Mr. K. H. Reed came into the firm, which then became Hecht & Reed. They did a large general merchandise and banking business and bought

stock and grain for many years. In 1878 Mr. Reed sold his interest in the business to Mr. Hecht and retired from the firm. In 1885 Mr. Hecht retired from the merchandise business and went into banking exclusively. This was continued with great success for many years, and in 1894 the Clarence Savings bank was organized by Mr. Hecht and he was made vice-president. He is now interested in the large clothing store of which his son, Charles B. Hecht, is manager. He has been a very extensive land owner, having at one time more land than any other one person in the county. He still has 600 acres, 350 of which adjoins the town of Clarence, and is highly improved, with a handsome residence, substantial barns, all supplied by a private system of waterworks. He is largely interested in raising fine stock, having a herd of pure-bred Jersey cattle. Mr. Hecht's long residence in the county and his splendid success in various lines of business have given him a wide acquaintance. In business circles he has always been foremost in all public affairs; he is always for the best interests of his home town. He is a member of the Knights of Pythias, and has always voted the democratic ticket.

Mr. Hecht was married June 8, 1865, to Margaret E. Bossert. They have three children: Winifred E., now Mrs. John T. Moffit, of Tipton; Charles R., and Eleanor L.

WHITNEY, CASSIUS HENRY, of Harlan, county attorney of Shelby county, is a promising young lawyer. His father, Daniel R. Whitney, a farmer of Scotch descent, was born in Ohio July 16, 1822. He was married February 25, 1847, at Rives, Mich., to Isypheny Dow, who was of Dutch descent, and was born November 6, 1827, in Garrard county, Ky. To them ten children were born, and eight are now living — seven sons and a daughter, of whom Cassius H. is the youngest, save one. D. R. Whitney was an early settler in Iowa, coming with his family to Marshalltown in 1857, where he was engaged in freighting, or hauling goods from Iowa City, the nearest railway station, to Marshalltown, Fort Dodge, Webster City, and other pioneer towns. After a few years the family moved onto a farm near Le Grand, in Marshall county.

Here C. H. Whitney was born, June 8, 1865. He was brought up on the farm, and secured his early education at the country school, one of his first teachers being Dr. G. H. Hill, now superintendent of the hospital for the insane at Independence. In March, 1876, he moved with his parents to Shelby county, which was then but sparsely settled. They lived at first in a log house on a rented farm, but soon purchased a farm of 240 acres, which young Cassius helped to break and improve. He entered the Harlan high school in September, 1884, remaining until the following March. In the fall of 1886 he aided in the construction of the Manilla & Sioux City branch of the Chicago, Milwaukee & St. Paul railway, acting in the capacity of "dump boss." In November of

that year he began teaching, and in this he continued alternately with farming until early in the spring of 1888, when he entered Western Normal college at Shenandoah, of which O. H. Longwell was then president. Here he stood well in his classes, as he had done in the high school, and took an active part in the social and literary life of the institution He paid his own way through school, out of the savings of former years, and graduated in July, 1889. During the following year he again taught school, and read law under the direction of his brother, Jesse B., a graduate of the law department of the State university, who was at that

time serving his second term as county attorney. Cassius H. was admitted in September, 1890, to senior standing in the law department of the State university, from which he graduated the following June. He entered into partnership, August 5, 1891, with his brother and former instructor, with whom he is still associated, under the firm name of Whitney Brothers. By close attention to business they have succeeded in building up a good practice, although they are the youngest firm in the city.

Mr. Whitney is a democrat, but is liberal in his political, as in his other, views. In March, 1896, he was elected city solicitor of Harlan, on a non-partisan ticket, receiving about two-thirds of all the votes cast for the office. At the general election that year he was elected county attorney on the fusion ticket, receiving the largest vote of any candidate on the ticket. Mr. Whitney is a member of the American Institute of Civics, and is a Mason, Knight of Pythias, and Modern Woodman. He was married April 5, 1893, to Hattie E. Records, who was born in Delaware, but has been a resident of Iowa since childhood. They have one child, Agnes, born August 27, 1894.

---

CRAIG, JOHN E., one of the prominent lawyers of southeastern Iowa, is of Scotch-

Irish descent. Both lines of his ancestors were from County Down, Ireland, and their descendants settled in Pennsylvania. His father was a farmer, in Washington county of that state, and attained prominence in public affairs as a democratic politician. Alexander K. Craig was in 1890 nominated by his party for representative in congress, and elected. His wife, Sarah F., was a daughter of William McLain, a prominent farmer of Washington county. Their son, John E. Craig, was born at Claysville, Pa., on the 14th of March, 1853.

He was educated in the common schools in his boyhood, and later entered Waynesburg college, attending there one year.

Young Craig earned his first dollar as a laborer in the harvest field. He began to teach country schools when but 16 years of age, continuing for four years during the winter season. He served one year as principal of Lebanon academy, in Allegheny county, Pa. He graduated with honors from Washington and Jefferson college in the class of 1877. He was a member of the Philo and Union literary societies. In May, 1878, he came to Iowa, settling at Keokuk, where he began to read law in the office of his uncle, Hon. John H. Craig.

He was admitted to the bar in 1879, and, after practicing law alone for about a year, he became a member of his uncle's law firm—Craig & Collier. In 1884 Mr. Collier removed to California, when a new partnership was formed, taking in A. J. McCrary, the name of the firm being Craig, McCrary & Craig. At the death of John H. Craig in 1893, the name of the firm became McCrary & Craig. In February, 1895, Governor Jackson appointed Mr. McCrary district judge, and the firm was dissolved; the business of the office has from that time been conducted by John E. Craig alone. In the fall of 1885 Mr. Craig was nominated by the democrats to represent Lee county in the house of representatives of the Twenty-first General Assembly, and was elected. He became a prominent member of the house and served his constituents so well that he was re-elected, serving in the Twenty-second General Assembly during the winter of 1888, and became one of the most influential leaders on the democratic side of the house. For eleven years Mr. Craig served on the Keokuk school board, taking a deep interest in the educational affairs of that city. In 1889 he was elected mayor of Keokuk, and in 1891 was re-elected, serving four years with great efficiency. He was chosen president of the College of Physicians and Surgeons of Keokuk, and became professor of medical jurisprudence of that institution. In 1896 Mr. Craig was elected prosecuting attorney for Lee county, and he is also president of the board of trustees of the public library of Keokuk. He is a public-spirited citizen, taking an active part in all matters relating to city and county affairs. He is an able lawyer and a public speaker, who ranks high in his profession. In religion he is a member of the Westminster Presbyterian church.

EARLE, WILLARD CHAUNCY, of Waukon, is one of Iowa's oldest practicing physicians, as well as a leading business man and politician. He has lived in Waukon between forty and fifty years, ever since 1854, and has probably done more than any other one man to promote the welfare of the city. He is of Puritanic ancestry, tracing his lineage back through seven generations to Ralph Earle, who settled in Massachusetts during the seventeenth century. Dr. Earle's father, Calvin Earle, was born February 1, 1790, in Hubbardstown, Mass., and was a man of great energy and thrift. He was married July 19, 1814, to Betsey Foster, and during the early 20's moved to West Troy, N. Y., and from there to Honesdale, Pa., where he built the first frame house in the town. He returned to Massachusetts in 1840, and came to Waukon, Iowa, in 1858, where he died in October, 1872. His wife died in 1870, aged 72 years.

Dr. W. C. Earle was born October 7, 1833, at Honesdale, Wayne county, Pa. He received a common school education, and attended Westminster, Mass., academy from 1850 to 1852, where he was prepared to enter Brown university, but on account of poor health had to postpone further attendance at school. He was advised by the family physician to go west, and accordingly came to Allamakee county, Iowa, in 1854, at the age of 21. The last part of the journey was made by boat up the Mississippi river. The steamer was so crowded with passengers that many were unable to secure berths, and young Earle, with numerous others, had to sleep on the floor of the cabin. During the last night of the trip his pockets were picked, so that when he arrived at Lansing he had not a cent of money. He was loaned a half dollar by D. W. Adams, and with this paid for a ride in a farmer's wagon to Waukon, where he soon secured work in a sawmill, which he afterwards owned and operated, together with a flouring mill.

Dr. Earle enlisted October, 1861, with the Twelfth Iowa infantry, and was made captain of Company B, which was recruited almost entirely in Allamakee county. He was in the engagements at Ft. Henry, Donelson and Shiloh. At Shiloh he was taken a prisoner, and was held over six months. He was finally released in exchange for rebel prisoners at Jackson, Miss., and his company was one of the very first to enter that city. Here they were in several skirmishes, and then went by forced marches to Champion Hills, and then took part in the siege of Vicksburg, after which they followed the confederate army back to Jackson. Not long after this Captain Earle was detailed by Adjutant-General Thomas to raise on recruit a regiment of colored troops. This he did, knowing at the time that it was sure death to all officers of colored troops captured by the confederates, and was finally mustered out of service as colonel of the Seventieth United States Colored regiment, October, 1865.

After the war he returned to Waukon, and the following winter attended lectures

at Rush Medical college, at Chicago, and later, Jefferson Medical college, at Philadelphia, from which he graduated in 1867, and has practiced at Waukon ever since. He also does an extensive business in general merchandise, and in 1878 built the block in which his store is situated, at a cost of $15,000. He holds much valuable real estate, including several farms, on one of which is situated the Oak Leaf creamery, which he built in 1879. He has been identified with the location of two railroads at Waukon, one in 1854, the P., Ft. W. &. C., for which he helped survey, and the W. & M., in 1877, to which he contributed more liberally than any other man in the community.

32

The doctor was a republican until the nomination of Grover Cleveland in 1884, and since then has been a democrat. He was elected in 1884 to fill the vacancy in the state senate caused by the resignation of William Larrabee, who was then elected governor. He was nominated for congress by the democrats of the Fourth district, but was not elected. This was in 1886.

The doctor was married January 1, 1860, to Miss Ellen A. Hedge, daughter of Dr. I. H. Hedge. They have two children: Minnie, born in 1860, now Mrs. G. C. Hemenway, and Carlton, born in 1866, who is associated with his father in the mercantile business.

---

DAVIS, MAHLON JAMES, M. D., of Lewis, Cass county, is one of those fortunate individuals who, by a peculiar combination of qualities, rapidly accumulates fast friends. His service in the legislature and his activity in politics has given him a state-wide acquaintance, and wherever he has become known the genial doctor is very popular, for he always has a pleasant word for his acquaintances and is always cheerful and never loses his temper. He was born in Juniata county, Pa., October 17, 1837, and was the son of Judah Davis and Charlotte Lease Davis. The family lived on a farm and was in fair circumstances. Mr. Davis was of Welsh descent and his wife of German parentage. They gave their son a good education, in the Airy View academy and Kishacoquilla seminary, both in Pennsylvania. Then he graduated from the medical department of the University of New York, in March, 1862, and in the following July was appointed an acting assistant surgeon in the United States regular army. In the following year he was appointed by the governor of New York assistant surgeon of the Second New York heavy artillery, with which he served until near the close of the war, when he was appointed surgeon of the Two Hundred and Fourth New York Volunteer infantry, but as the war closed before he could be mustered in, he never joined the regiment. From July 6, 1864, until the surrender at Appomattox he served as surgeon-in-chief of the artillery brigade of the Second corps on the staff of General Hazard, chief of artillery of that corps.

When the war closed, Dr. Davis, in 1866, came to Iowa and located in Lewis, his

present residence, where he combined the practice of medicine with the drug business, with notable success in both. For two years, 1873 to 1875, he had a partner, Dr. D. Findley, now of Atlantic. He served as examining surgeon for pensions from 1874 to 1878. In 1880 Dr. Davis retired from the practice of medicine to devote all his attention to the drug business, which he still continues.

Dr. Davis has always been a republican and an active party worker, several years chairman of the republican county committee. He was appointed postmaster of Lewis by President Grant in 1869, and held

the office until 1886. He was elected member of the house of representatives in 1893 and 1895, serving as chairman of the committee on pharmacy in the Twenty-fifth and Twenty-sixth General Assemblies, in 1894 and 1896, and in the extra session of 1897. He was the author of the law prohibiting registered pharmacists from selling malt liquors, and of several other bills in relation to the practice of pharmacy. Besides, he was alive to the general interests of the state and was a working member on many important committees.

The doctor is a member of the Masonic order and was master of Lewis lodge for four years, and for five or six years a delegate to the Grand Lodge of Iowa. He was married December 27, 1864, to Priscilla K. Shuman, in Harrisburg, Pa. They have three sons, the eldest of whom, W. B. Davis, is associated with his father as partner in the drug business. The second son, B. B. Davis is a practicing lawyer in Chicago, and the youngest son, Charles P. Davis, is at this time, 1898, studying law in the University of Michigan, in Ann Arbor. With a comfortable fortune, friends everywhere he goes, and a happy and well-to-do family, Dr. Davis is now enjoying the results of a well-directed period of activity.

———

AINEY, DANIEL WEBSTER, now located on a farm near Lohrville, Calhoun county, started in life as a poor boy, working as a farm hand to get a little start in life, and to get an education. His father, Seth Ainey, was born in Warren county, N. J., of parents who came from Baden, Germany. The son, Daniel, left home at the early age of 13, to work for his schooling, and was placed on his own resources the balance of his life. His ancestors have been for many years prominent in business and politics in Pennsylvania. He was born September 8, 1856, in Susquehanna county, Pa. His mother's name was Harriet (Bennett) Ainey. He first attended country district school, and later a short time at the high school at Montrose, in his native state. His education, however, was very limited when he came to Iowa in 1877, at the age of 21. He stopped the first year in Grundy county, and worked on a farm by the month for a year. He then went to Polk county and entered the Mitchell seminary, where he alternated between attending school and teaching for several years. Such was his determination to secure an education that he did janitor work to supplement his meager earnings in country school teaching, to enable him to pay for his board and tuition. During this period he spent his vacations on the farm of J. M. Chaffee, doing farm work. In the fall of 1881 he entered the Southern Iowa Normal school at Bloomfield, for a course of normal training, to prepare him for higher grade teaching, and also to take a course in elocution. It was but a few weeks, however, till the elocution department was put under his charge, and so remained while he was there. He studied German under Prof. O. H. Longwell during this time. In 1882 he was elected as principal of the schools at Altoona, and

taught one year. In 1883 he was employed to teach higher English, Latin and commercial law, in the Archibald Business college at Minneapolis. His health failed at this period and he was compelled to quit the schoolroom. He accordingly left his work at Minneapolis and returned to Altoona, Iowa, and entered into partnership with J. W. Rider in the hardware business. After two years he sold out and went onto a farm for two years, after which he moved to the Pacific coast, but did not find matters as he had expected from reports, so returned in a few months to Des Moines, and organized the Crescent

Supply company, but soon sold his interest and engaged in the general merchandise business at Altoona. Subsequently he traded his store for land in Calhoun county, and moved there and engaged in farming. In 1896 he sold out, feeling that his health would compel him to retire, but his determination got the better of him and he bought the *Lohrville Enterprise*, but was soon forced to retire on account of failing health. His farm, however, soon came back upon his hands, and he retired thereon in 1897, and is now engaged in stock raising. He is a republican, and has been called upon to fill many minor offices, such as school director, township recorder, justice of the peace, etc. He is continually representing his township and county in county and state conventions, but does not seek or desire a political office. He is a Mason and has occupied several official positions in his local lodge. He belongs to the church organization known as the Disciples of Christ. He was married December 25, 1883, to Kate M. Baker, of Altoona, and four children have been born to them, one of whom is dead.

PENROSE, HON. EMLEN G. Senator Penrose, who represented the Forty-fifth senatorial district in the general assembly,

was born at Chesterfield, Ohio, August 22, 1844. His parents, Thomas and Maria Clenden Penrose, were Quakers, their remote ancestors having come to this country with William Penn. The early youth of Senator Penrose was spent in his native state on the farm, where he received a common school education. He came to Iowa in 1860 and has ever since been a resident of this state. As a young man he worked on the farm, clerked and taught school. During the years from 1864 to 1875 he attended several terms in the Iowa State university. In 1868 he located at Tama City and engaged as clerk in a store, but, having an ambition to fill a wider field,

removed to Grand Junction and, in partnership with C. B. Park, opened a hardware, agricultural implement and grain business, where a large and profitable trade was enjoyed until 1872, at which time he returned to Tama City and put in a complete stock of hardware. While he has ever made it a rule to pay close attention to business, he devotes a portion of his time to the wants and needs of the public, and has been prominent in the management of municipal affairs. He has served several terms on the city council and was mayor both before and after the reincorporation of the place into a city of the second class. Under his administration the city put in a system of waterworks unexcelled by any inland town in the state; erected an electric light plant and built an electric railroad. He is prominent in educational affairs and has been elected repeatedly to the presidency of the school board. For several years he has served as trustee of the Methodist Episcopal church, and has been active in the Masonic, Knights Templars and Knights of Pythias orders.

In politics Mr. Penrose is a republican, starting almost with the birth of the party, casting his first vote for Wm. Stone for governor in 1865, and all the years of his life he has been its earnest friend and staunch supporter. In the fall of 1893 he received the unanimous nomination of his party as a candidate for state senator to represent the district composing the counties of Benton and Tama. The preceding election had given the district to the democrats, but his great popularity and vigorous canvass resulted in his election by a handsome majority, his own city giving him a highly complimentary vote. He was re-elected in 1897. As a legislator he possesses many fine and unusual qualifications. Being a man of excellent judgment in all matters, he moves carefully, yet courageously, when once he has arrived at a final conclusion. He gives a subject due consideration before talking upon it, and then defends his position with great strength and clearness, though always in a manner courteous to those who hold different views. He is a conspicuous figure in the more important committees, and his services as chairman of the railway committee were generally recognized for their thoroughness and care. By his intelligent course he has the esteem of his contemporaries, irrespective of party, who are always ready to join him in facilitating the work he seeks to do, which accounts in a large measure for the considerable legislation he has succeeded in having enacted. He is held in high regard by Governor Drake and was one of the chosen guests who accompanied that official to the sea to participate in the launching of the battleship "Iowa." Honorable to a fine degree, in both his public and private life, generous to a fault and public spirited, he has friends and admirers in all the walks of life. In business matters his word is his bond and it never goes to protest. He was married in 1870 to Miss Jennie C. Stoddard. They have one son, Frank, who assists his father in the conduct of the mercantile business at Tama.

---

HANSSEN, GUSTAVUS ADOLPHUS, of Davenport, is of German ancestry, his

parents being pioneers of his native town, Davenport, where he was born November 22, 1869. His father, Louis Hanssen, is one of the wealthy, retired residents of the old river city in which his sons have risen to do him honor, ranking among the first business men of Davenport. Louis Hanssen's Sons is the firm name, and the store occupies the same spot upon which was built the father's store, early in the 50's. The members of this hardware firm are Louis, Jr.; C. E. and B. C. Hanssen, brothers of the subject of this sketch. His mother's name was Marie Hannemann.

Mr. Hanssen's uncles are successful business men in Hamburg, Germany, one of them, Bernhard Hanssen, being one of the official architects of that European city. The artistic gift of this uncle descended upon the young Gustavus, who early evinced his talent for architectural drawing. He was educated in the public schools, his work in drawing being so creditable that it was sent in the Iowa exhibit to the New Orleans exposition. In the fall of 1885 he was anxious to attend an architectural school, and his parents favored his hope, sending him to the Illinois State university. There he entered the department of the school of architecture, graduating in the class of '90, with second honors. He also took first medal in military and artillery drill.

In the spring of 1891 he took charge of the architectural office of J. W. Taylor, at Middlesborough, Ky. He remained there until October, when he started in business for himself. Since then he has met with marked success, his business improving every year. Many of the finest public buildings, as well as residences, in Davenport are from his plans. He was appointed plumbing inspector in 1893, but, after serving a year, was obliged to resign on account of pressure of business duties.

He is a member of the Unitarian church. He was married in June, 1894, to Lillie May Stibolt. They have one child: Daphne Louise, born in June, 1896.

---

WILCOX, VINTON S., practicing physician of Malcom, was born in Homer, Ohio, October 11, 1848. His parents were natives of Pennsylvania, being brought up at Wilkesbarre. Dr. Wilcox came to Iowa in 1855 and attended the common schools of the state. He afterwards taught for a number of terms, and in 1868 he entered the collegiate department of the Iowa State university. In 1871 he began the study of medicine in the office of Drs. Shrader & Price. During the time that he remained with them, which was for a period of three years, he took a graded course in the medical department of the Iowa State university, under the supervision of Professor Shrader, and graduated March 4, 1874. The following May he removed to Malcom, where he has remained ever since, following the practice of his profession, in which he has been eminently successful, and enjoys the confidence of the people of Malcom and vicinity.

HEINLY, BENJAMIN FRANKLIN, of the well known wholesale firm of B. F. Heinly & Brother, at Creston, Iowa, descended from an ancient German family. His father's great-grandfather, who came from Germany to America, was related to the Ludwigs, that branch of the family from which Emperor William the First was descended. The family settled in Northampton county, Pa., engaged principally in agricultural pursuits and the raising and handling of stock. Joseph Heinly, the father of Benjamin, received his education in the German language, but after moving to Iowa he learned to speak, read

and write the English language. The family that came to Iowa in 1855, and settled on a farm at Sweetland Center, Muscatine county, consisted of six boys and one girl, all of whom were born in Northampton county, Pa. There were four girls born to this union in Iowa, and one girl that died in infancy in Pennsylvania. Benjamin F., was born March 11, 1850, in Northampton county, Pa. Out of that family there are still living three boys and three girls: William Anderson Heinly, who resides at Danville, Ill.; Milton McCarthy Heinly and Laura Georgia Jones, in Muscatine county, Iowa; Ida May Purdy, at Pierce City, Mo.; Ella Savannah Wintermute, at Tacoma, Wash., and George.

The oldest son died while serving his country in the civil war, and another died in Alabama shortly after the war.

Benjamin worked on his father's farm summers, and his early education consisted of about three months in the district school each winter, from the time he was 7 years old until he was 15. He attended a three months' term in the commercial college conducted by a brother, at Vincennes, Ind. This concluded his school education and was of much benefit to him all through his business life. At the age of 16 he started out in life for himself, and in five weeks had earned $90 by work in the harvest field. This was the first money he had earned and appropriated to his own use, and it stimulated his desire to make money for himself and be independent. He went to Louisa county and taught school for six months, and, though he gave good satisfaction, did not like the work. For about two years he conducted a little store near his father's farm in Sweetland Center, then bought a store in Fairport, where he engaged at the same time in other business, but was not satisfied with his opportunities. March 1, 1874, he was married to Miss Isabella Sweet, of Fairport, and the next day started for Creston, where they have since lived. The town then had 1,200 population, and Mr. Heinly went into partnership with I. L. Mackemer, his brother-in-law, in the retail grocery business. The partnership with Mackemer lasted for five years, during which time both added considerably to their stock of worldly goods. Mr. Heinly then purchased his partner's interest, and about six months later his younger brother, T. A. Heinly, was admitted as a partner. The business grew and its owners prospered. In August. 1882, with J. C. Wallace, they started the first wholesale grocery house in Creston, under the firm name of Wallace, Heinly & Brother. With persistent effort many obstacles were overcome, and they did a fairly good business in the jobbing line. After Mr. Wallace had been associated with them for two years, the Heinly brothers purchased his interest and he retired with a good profit on his investment. They then associated with them Mr. H. B. Holcomb, who acquired an interest in the wholesale business which he retained until the death of T. A. Heinly in January, 1890. Mr. Heinly then purchased Mr. Holcomb's interest and continued the business under the firm name of B. F. Heinly & Brother, the brother's widow retaining her interest in the firm.

There has been no change in the firm since 1890. It has held its own through all the trying financial times. Mr. Heinly was one of the incorporators, and is now president of the Anchor Mutual Fire Insurance company. It was organized in Creston in 1889 as the Hotel Owners Fire Insurance company; changed its name a year later, and moved to Des Moines in 1895. It is a strong company.

Since living in Creston Mr. Heinly has served three terms as alderman at different periods. His political affiliations, in the main, have been republican. He loves the grand old party and the humane and brilliant war and reconstruction record it made, but he is a firm believer in the remonetization of silver at the ratio of 16 to 1 by the United States. Mr. Heinly is a member in good standing of the First Congregational church of Creston, superintendent of the Congregational Sunday school, member of the Men's club, the West End Social club, the Masonic order, the Modern Woodmen and the Ancient Order of United Workmen. Mr. and Mrs. Heinly have three sons and a daughter: Earl Casper, born June 23, 1876; Webster Guy, born September 19, 1879; Vinton Sweet, born September 15, 1887; Maurine Louise, born February 6, 1890.

---

DELMEGE, GEORGE J., secretary of the Anchor Mutual Fire Insurance company, of Des Moines, entered upon the insurance business as local fire insurance solicitor in Creston, Iowa, in 1880. Two years later he accepted the state agency for a life insurance company, with headquarters at Fremont, Neb., and he was highly successful as an organizer and underwriter. In 1884 he returned to the field of fire insurance, doing adjusting and special agency work in Iowa. In 1888 a very flattering offer was made him by the Mutual Reserve Fund Life association of New York, which he accepted, and secured the largest personal business ever written by one man in Iowa in the same length of time, for any company doing business on a similar plan. In 1889 Mr. Delmege organized the Anchor Mutual Fire Insurance company, at Creston, Iowa, removing the company to Des Moines in 1895. From the day the Anchor was organized, under the able management and magnetic directive force of Mr. Delmege, it has had phenomenal success. Its record is a part of the insurance history of Iowa. Each year it has made a handsome gain in premiums

written, in assets, in surplus and in cash income, and has maintained the lowest loss ratio known to the business. The Anchor was seven years old July 1, 1896. The record it has made is all the commendation its management needs. Mr. Delmege has demonstrated the fact that he is one of the ablest fire insurance managers in the west.

He was born at Bristol, Ill., of Christopher Delmege and Rebecca H. (Holmes) Delmege, neither of whom is now living. His education was received in the common schools and Simpson college, at Indianola. He came to Iowa in October, 1869, and settled with his parents on a farm in Union

county, where his boyhood days were spent. Being too young to enter the army, he could only participate in those patriotic demonstrations indulged in by the youth during the stirring times of war. Politically, he is a free silver democrat. In 1882 he was a candidate on the democratic ticket for county superintendent of schools of Union county, and was elected by a handsome majority. Fraternally, he is a member of Elks Lodge No. 98, of Des Moines, and the Ancient Order of United Workmen. He is an earnest member of the Christian church. In 1878 he was united in marriage to Miss Clara B. Myers. They have one child.

FERGUSON, JOSEPH P., was born in Montgomery county, Ind., July 26, 1829. His father, Price Ferguson, was a farmer, and of Scotch descent. His mother's ancestors were Germans, and her maiden name was Mary Shank. Both his father and mother died in one day, when Joseph was only 3 weeks old. They fell victims to the mysterious disease, milk sickness, which was so fatal in the pioneer days of Indiana. Soon after their death he was taken to the home of his grandfather, Aaron Ferguson, in Montgomery county, Ohio, where he lived until 12 years old. He was then placed in charge of his only sister,

Elizabeth Ferguson, who lived in Warren county, Ind. During the remainder of his youth he lived with different relatives in Ohio and Indiana, and when a young man went with his uncle, John Ferguson, to Kendall county, Ill., and leased a farm belonging to another uncle by the name of Hiddleson. Soon after commencing work here, he had a severe attack of typhoid fever, which left him much broken in health, and unable to continue farm work that season. He then returned to his sister's home, in Tippecanoe county, Ind., and secured a position as tollgate-keeper on a new plank road just built into the city of Lafayette. The next year he taught school in Warren county, Ind., and in May,

1852, came with his uncle and located in Jones county, Iowa. Here he began breaking prairie during the summer with an ox team and continued it for four seasons, and for several winters taught school in Cedar and Jones counties. In the winter of 1858 Mr. Ferguson taught school in his own dwelling house in Hall township, Jones county. The parents of his pupils hauled wood to the house and then the boys chopped it for him. He accepted for payment for teaching whatever provisions the patrons happened to have. Mr. Ferguson never had the advantage of much schooling; his education was mostly acquired by home study and teaching others. In his first school he had to study hard to keep ahead of some of the smart scholars.

In the summer of 1860, allured by the report of rich gold discoveries near Pike's Peak, he crossed the plains to Colorado. In company with John Weeks he drove a pair of oxen, yoked to a light wagon, and led a cow behind the wagon to insure a supply of milk. While he was making this trip, which yielded more experience than gold, the immortal Abraham Lincoln was nominated for president.

On August 6, 1862, Mr. Ferguson enlisted in Company G, Thirty-first Iowa volunteers, and went with the regiment to Helena, Ark. He was soon promoted to the position of second lieutenant, but his health, which was always delicate, soon failed and he was sent to the hospital at Memphis and afterwards transferred to one at St. Louis. Here he became very sick, and his wife was sent for and took him home. For two years after returning from the army Mr. Ferguson lived on the farm, and then began buying grain and stock, and continued in this business for several years. In 1869 he was appointed postmaster of Clarence, Iowa, by President Grant; held the office for nearly seventeen years, and resigned when Cleveland was elected, although his democratic friends urged him to make application for reappointment, and offered to sign a petition in his favor. When he retired from the postoffice the patrons, regardless of party, presented Mr. Ferguson and his daughter Helen each with a gold watch and chain.

For three terms Mr. Ferguson was elected mayor of Clarence. While attending to his duties as postmaster, he studied law, and on the 25th of February, 1875, was admitted to practice, at the age of

46 years. On March 80, 1856, he was married to Miss Persis Delamater, a native of Lewis county, N. Y., and a most estimable woman. They have seven children: Mary E., Mamie E., now Mrs. Lamos, of Stuart, Iowa; Davie F., who died August 15, 1882, aged 22; Jennie V., now Mrs. Flansburg, of Glidden, Iowa; Helen M., now Mrs. Cook, of Jacksonville, Ill.; Josie P., now Mrs. Lantz, of Sioux City, Iowa; and J. P. W. C. Ferguson.

Mr. Ferguson voted for John C. Fremont for president, and has ever since been a hard worker for the republican party, until the passage of the mulct law and the law allowing the manufacture of liquor. Since then he has acted with the prohibitionists and has been a worker in the temperance cause for many years.

Among the young men who have profited by Mr. Ferguson's experience and advice, and have had the advantage of reading in his law office, are Mr. S. E. Starrig, of Fayette; T. J. Garrison, of Denison; Prof. George D. Skinner, of Clinton; Prof. J. H. Morgan, of Clarence; Prof. Harry Ferguson, of Tama City; N. H. Kent and Fred Orelup.

As this outline indicates, Mr. Ferguson is a man of strong character, and an original thinker. He has always believed that he was called to preach, but resisted the spirit.

———

STONER, CHARLES E., M. D., of Des Moines, is one of the most progressive and successful among the physicians of that city.

His father, Abraham Stoner, was a prosperous farmer from the vicinity of Ashland, Ohio, who moved to this state in the year 1865 and located on a good farm near Fairfield, in Jefferson county. Abraham Stoner was of German descent, his ancestors having been among those attracted in an early day by the wonderful stories of American freedom and prosperity which circulated through the various countries of Europe. They were not only attracted by the bright prospects in America, but they were repelled and alienated from their native land by the tyranny of its despotic government and the imposition of the excessive taxes which were necessary to sustain the great standing armies.

Abraham Stoner married Elmira P. Parsons, and on April 30, 1859, at Ashland, Ohio, Charles E. Stoner was born. Before this son was old enough to attend school,

the family moved to Iowa, and Charles received his elementary education at the district school, held in a log cabin near Fairfield. He afterwards attended the high school at Fairfield, and later Parsons college in that city. At the early age of 18 he commenced the study of medicine in the office of Dr. R. J. Mohr, the well-known surgeon of Fairfield. After two years of diligent study in this office, young Stoner took a course at Rush Medical college in Chicago. He then went to Keokuk, Iowa, and undertook a course of study at the College of Physicians and Surgeons in that city, and graduated there in 1882.

After finishing his medical studies he commenced practice in 1883 at Kossuth, Des Moines county. Here he remained three seasons and then moved to the town of Altoona, near Des Moines, where he staid several years before locating in that city in 1890.

Dr. Stoner occupies the responsible position of medical director to the Central Life Assurance Association of the United States. He also fills the chair of bacteriology at Drake university, and for the past four years has been professor of surgery in the same institution.

In 1884 Dr. Stoner was married to Jeannette Neil, of Fairfield, and they have one child, Carl Barlow Stoner. The doctor is a member of the Polk County Medical society, the Iowa State, and the American Medical societies. He also belongs to the Odd Fellows, and is a Scottish Rite Mason. The responsibilities of the position which Dr. Stoner occupies are such as would test the abilities of any man; but he fills them with credit, and has won the respect and confidence of both the students and his associates.

RATH, JOHN, the well-known banker of Ackley, is a native of Germany, and came to this country when he was 13 years

old with his brother George, who was only one year older than himself. They came by way of Havre, France, in a sailing vessel, which was forty-seven days making the voyage. The boys had only money enough to pay their fare to Galena, Ill., and walked from there to Dubuque, following the telegraph line, as they could not speak English to enquire the way. They arrived in Dubuque in the month of November, 1853, footsore and tired, and were warmly welcomed by their uncle, George Rath, who lived in that city. There was no railroad west of Freeport, Ill., at that time. Their father, Andrew Rath, was a weaver by trade, and their mother's maiden name was Anna Reich.

John remained in Dubuque in the employ of his uncle, who was engaged in the pork packing business, until 1861. During this time he attended a private school for about six months, which was all the English education he received. He had previously attended the common schools of his native town for several years. He was born November 26, 1840, in Breitenau ober amt Sulz, Wurtemberg, Germany. In the spring of 1861 he went to Cedar Falls, and was employed there until August, 1862, when he enlisted for three years in Company B, Thirty-first Iowa infantry, and served until the close of the war. With the First division of the Fifteenth corps, Army of the Tennessee, he took part in the first attack on Vicksburg in December, 1862; battle of Arkansas Post, Ark.; battle of Jackson, Miss.; siege of Vicksburg; battle of Lookout Mountain and Missionary Ridge; all the battles of the Atlanta campaign and Sherman's march to the sea; battle of Savannah, Ga. He was in the first boat that crossed the river at Columbia, S. C., at midnight, by which the army gained a foothold on the Columbia side of the river. This movement resulted in the surrender of the city to Colonel Stone, commander of the Iowa Brigade of the Fifteenth army corps. He was in all the minor engagements up to the surrender of Johnston at Raleigh, N. C., and marched to Washington, D. C. Participated in the grand review in May, 1865, in that city, and was mustered out at Davenport, Iowa, at the close of the war.

When Mr. Rath came to Ackley, after the close of the war, it was a town on paper and contained only one house. The railroad, now the Illinois Central, was not completed to the town until November of that year, 1865. He was employed by Mr. Burns to manage a grain warehouse and lumber yard, and in 1868 bought an interest in the business. In 1870 he bought the other interest and remained sole proprietor until 1880, when his brother, Andrew Rath, became interested with him. During that year Mr. Rath established the banking business which he has carried on very successfully since that date, under the name of the John Rath Exchange bank.

Mr. Rath has always been a republican, for several years was mayor of his town, member of the county board of supervisors for three years, and has held many minor offices. He is an active member of the G. A. R., was commander of the post for two terms and is now aid-de-camp on the staff of Commander-in-Chief General Clarkson. He is a charter member of the Presbyterian church of Ackley, organized in 1867.

October 5, 1865, Mr. Rath was married to Miss Elizabeth Moser, of Dubuque, Iowa. They have had nine children, all but one of whom are living: Carrie M., who died in infancy; William T. S., who is now assistant cashier of the bank; John W., who is married and lives in Waterloo; Amilia M., Elizabeth C., Charles E., Clara E., Walter F., and Howard G.

---

RUEGNITZ, HON. CHARLES, was born at Waren, Mecklenburg-Schwerin, Germany, January 12, 1849. His parents were born near the same place. In 1864, with their ten children, seven sons and three daughters, they came to the United States and direct to Clayton, Clayton county, Iowa. The voyage across the Atlantic, from Hamburg to New York, was made on a sailing ship, and lasted seven weeks. When out at sea four weeks the youngest daughter, one year old, died.

Charles attended the common schools from his 6th to his 14th year, when he went to work as apprentice in his father's cooper shop. During the time, he took advantage of the Mechanics' school, held at night, where he received special training by competent teachers without cost. After coming to the United States, in 1864, he worked at coopering until 1868 in Clayton, at which time he went to Minneapolis and Stillwater, where he followed the same trade. In 1870 he joined a party to go to the gold fields of Montana, but on reaching Omaha gave up the trip, the reports being unfavorable. He remained in that city a short time, when he entered the employment of the Union Pacific railway and worked on the sections at Alkali and Julesburg until fall. He then returned to Omaha and secured employment on the bridge across the Missouri, then in course of construction, where the next few months of his life was spent below the bottom of the river, in the cylinders wherein so many men parted with health, if not life. In 1871 he returned to Clayton county and again engaged in coopering, serving as foreman for Krueger, Werges & Company. In 1874 the Northwestern Hoop company, of Chicago, erected a factory at Clayton, which was provided with all the improved machinery for manufacturing hoops and box straps, and Mr. Ruegnitz was given charge of the concern, which he conducted for

seven years. At the end of that time he engaged in business for himself, which he continued for three years. Although never having had an opportunity to attend school in this country, he was possessed of a good education, self-earned, and to that was added the thorough and more desirable knowledge which is obtained by practical experience. He held the office of township clerk for several years, and was justice of the peace and a member of the school board. In 1884 he was elected county treasurer, which honored position he now fills. If this were not enough to show the high esteem in which he is held,

both as a citizen and a public official, it might be added that in 1892 he received the nomination for state treasurer on the democratic ticket, but was, of course, defeated, owing to the republican party being in the ascendency. He was married in 1872 to Miss Emma Venus, who was born in Clayton county in 1852. Her father, Joseph Venus, a Bavarian by birth, was one of the original thirteen who founded the German Colony Communia in this county in 1847. They have three children, Emma, Fritz and Louis, all of whom have been reared in the Lutheran faith. It must not be omitted that, although always a democrat, Mr. Ruegnitz is an ardent supporter of the gold standard as against the free coinage of silver. He was a charter member of Clayton Lodge 143, A. O. U. W.; of Mystic Camp 319, Modern Woodmen of America, and member and president of the Elkader Turn-Verein and its gesangs (singing) section.

---

SHINN, FRANK, of Carson, is of Quaker ancestry, and was born October 28, 1843, near Jackson, Adams county, Ohio. His grandfather, George Shinn, was a Virginian, and married Elizabeth Woodrow. Both were Quakers, and in the year 1800 emigrated to Highland county, Ohio. Allen

Shinn, the father of Frank, was born in Hillsborough, Ohio, January 14, 1812. When Allen was 15 his father moved with his family to a farm three miles north of Winchester, Adams county, Ohio. Allen T. married Malinda Fenton, who was born July 9, 1812, near Winchester. Her father, John Fenton, was a native of Pennsylvania, and her mother was Sarah Field, a Virginian. Soon after marrying, Allen T. Shinn became a Methodist preacher and joined the Ohio conference. His brother, Moses F. Shinn, was also licensed to preach, and joined the same conference. In 1844 he was sent by the bishop of that church to Iowa as a missionary, and after preaching at Burlington, Keokuk, Keosau-

qua and Mt. Pleasant, was, in 1850, sent to Council Bluffs. He had charge of all the territory in Iowa west of Des Moines, and built the first church in Council Bluffs and also the first Methodist church in Omaha, in 1855. He was not only a preacher but an excellent business man; became quite wealthy and died in Omaha in 1886. Allen T. Shinn was transferred from the Ohio conference to the Kentucky conference, where he preached for four years. He was a strong abolitionist and had trouble with pro-slavery members of his church. He rigidly enforced the rules of the Methodist discipline, prohibiting the selling of slaves, and when any member of his church sold a slave he would arraign him for trial and expel him from the church. The feeling became so intense against him in Kentucky on account of his radical anti-slavery views, that the church deemed it advisable to transfer him to the Iowa conference. He was sent to Marshalltown, arriving there with his family on the 28th day of October, 1856. After preaching there eighteen months his health failed, and his brother, Moses Shinn, asked him to move on a large farm near Macedonia, Iowa. His health continued to decline and he died November 6, 1858. Mrs. Shinn was left with a family of six boys, and remained on the farm near Macedonia. Her father, who was quite wealthy, living in Ohio, insisted upon her coming back where he could provide for her and her children, the father having left his family with but little property. This request she refused to comply with, saying that western Iowa was as rich a country as there was upon the face of the earth, and that she could give her sons no better heritage than to settle them in the rich valley of the Nishnabotana.

In June, 1861, the oldest brother, Asa F. Shinn, enlisted in Company A, First Nebraska Regiment volunteers, he being the first volunteer to enlist in Pottawattamie county. He went into Missouri with his regiment and was taken ill with typhoid fever and died November 14, 1861, and is buried in an unknown grave at Jefferson City. After his death, Frank, being the oldest of the brothers, remained at home with his mother until he was 24 years of age. During that time they were able to purchase a home, and at the time he left his mother's home her property was worth $3,500. In the meantime he had earned money enough to buy eighty acres of wild prairie, which he afterwards improved with his own hands.

Frank's education was obtained in common schools before he was 15 years of age. He began trying lawsuits in justice courts in 1864, and continued to try such cases until 1873, when an old pioneer lawyer at Glenwood, Henry C. Watkins, prevailed upon him to read law, loaning him books which he carried out to the farm home, and, by reading through the winter nights, and rainy days in the summer, was finally able to pass an examination and was admitted to regular practice April 16, 1877. In 1884 Mr. Shinn conceived the idea of enjoining saloons. Having made an effort to enjoin the saloon under the statute at Hastings, the court refused him the right and he at once prepared House File No. 481, Session Laws of the Twentieth General Assembly, a record of which will be found in the house journal of the Twentieth General Assembly, page 295. He tried to get the representatives from Mills and Pottawattamie counties to introduce this bill, and they declined to do so, but Capt. J. A. Lyons, of Guthrie county, consented to, and did, introduce the bill.

In his younger days Mr. Shinn was a democrat, but left the party in 1880 on account of prohibition. He has been an active prohibitionist, having canvassed western Iowa and made thirty-two speeches during the campaign of 1882. He has been an active worker of the republican party since that time and has been on the platform making speeches in the interest of that party every year since. He has never aspired to official positions, but did, at one time, accept the nomination from the republican party and ran for state senator in Pottawattamie county district. The county was then hopelessly democratic. He was defeated but ran ahead of his ticket. Having had a very lucrative practice for the past twenty years, Mr. Shinn has accumulated considerable property. He owns valuable lands in the Nishnabotana valley, besides much other property. When he was 14 years of age he cut his knee with a corn cutter in the field on which now stands part of the city of Marshalltown, and was rendered a cripple for life.

He was married January 25, 1869, to Almyra Schenck, at Council Bluffs. She was the daughter of James A. Schenck, a farmer who resided near Macedonia. There were born to them five children, namely: Addie, born October 28, 1869; Linnie A., born April 16, 1871; James A., born January 18, 1872; Kate, born October 15, 1874, and Myrtle, born October 21, 1880. James

A. and Addie died in the fall of 1882; Kate married C. C. Johnson, a druggist of Carson, and Linnie A. married Ira R. Stitt, an attorney of Carson.

---

TOWNSEND, EDWARD, of Cedar Falls, one of the trustees of the State Normal school, is among the oldest settlers in Black Hawk county, having lived there since 1859. His parents were Elijah Townsend, who began life poor, but through hard work and good management as a farmer acquired a comfortable fortune, and Rosannah Downing Townsend. Both

were English Quakers. The father died in 1860, aged 72 years, and the mother in 1866, aged 72 years.

Edward Townsend was born November 28, 1831, in the town of La Grange, in Duchess county, N. Y. He was brought up on a farm and secured his early education at the district school. He afterwards attended Berkshire academy, Mass., for one year. Circumstances did not permit him to pursue his education any further. In May, 1859, he came to Iowa and settled first at Waterloo. Here he remained for two years, removing in 1861 to Cedar Falls. For a year he was engaged in the banking business, and on August 8, 1862, he enlisted as a private in Company B, of the

Thirty-first Iowa infantry. He was elected second lieutenant, by his company, and was soon afterwards promoted to the rank of first lieutenant. He was in the battles of Chickasaw Bayou, Arkansas Post and several other skirmishes, and in June, 1863, he was compelled to resign his commission on account of disabilities resulting from sickness contracted while in the service. Returning home he resumed his business in the bank and thus continued for eleven years, retiring in 1874. In 1878 he engaged in the lumber and coal business, which he still continues, also dealing in real estate loans.

Mr. Townsend has always been a republican and represented Black Hawk county in the Twenty-second and Twenty-third General Assemblies. He has also held several local and county offices, including membership in the city council, school board and the board of supervisors. He was mayor of his city in 1870-71 and served as a member of the board of commissioners for the erection of the State Soldiers' and Sailors' monument, and has been trustee of the State Normal school since 1894. He was married October 17, 1867, to Sarah A. Seward, who died March 20, 1872, leaving three children, two of whom are living, Katherine S., born in 1868, and Mary L., born in 1870. Mr. Townsend's second wife was Sarah Huntington, of Oswego county, N. Y., whom he married September 26, 1878. They have one child, Edward H., born May 5, 1881.

ROBERTSON, NATHAN ANDA, a prominent banker and business man of Promise City, Iowa, and one whose name justly belongs among the progressive men of Iowa, was born on a farm one mile west of Cincinnati, Iowa, in 1855. His father was Moses C. Robertson, a farmer in comfortable circumstances, who emigrated to Iowa, from Indiana, in 1851, and settled in Appanoose county, near Cincinnati, entering 600 acres of government land, which still belongs in the family. His mother's maiden name was Streepey, and her father, Edward Streepey, also came to Iowa from Indiana, in 1850, and located in Appanoose county. At this time Iowa was one vast prairie, only dotted here and there with a few log cabins. Mr. Robertson's education was received in the district school and in the Cincinnati high school. At the age of 19 he, like a great many other boys, got the gold fever and started west to make his fortune, landing

in Colorado and Nevada among the mines; but he found that a boy or man with small means stood no better show there than elsewhere. He managed, however, to pick up a few dollars, and after one year came back home and concluded that Iowa was good enough for any one with good hands and brains, who was willing to use them. By this time the railroad had reached Cincinnati and Mr. Robertson began buying and shipping stock and grain, following this business for two years until the M., I. & N. railroad pushed on west from Centerville. He then believed Wayne county to be one of the best grain and

stock counties in the state and began to cast about for a new location and decided upon Promise City, locating there in August, 1879, a few days ahead of the railroad. Time proved that his judgment was good. There was plenty of grain and stock to handle and he located buyers at all of the stations west on this road to Humeston, and by careful management succeeded in accumulating considerable money. In 1885 the business of the town had so grown that he concluded to open a small bank as an experiment, scarcely expecting that it would pay. He opened it as the Exchange Bank of Promise City, with a capital of $15,000. This he soon found unable to do the business and the capital was increased to $25,000, and later in 1895 the bank was reorganized and incorporated as the Farmers State Bank of Promise City, with a capital of $25,000 and a surplus of $10,000.

In 1892 Cincinnati, his old home, had grown so that he concluded it would be a good place for a bank, and accordingly in July, 1893, he opened the Farmers and Merchants bank at that place, with himself as president and J. V. Leseney as cashier, with a paid-up capital of $25,000. The secret of his success has been in his push and energy and in unhesitatingly taking advantage of the opportunities that presented themselves to him.

In politics he has always been a republican. He was married in 1875 to Emma Leseney at Cincinnati, Iowa. To them have been born nine children: Raleigh L., Guy C., James Blaine, Nathan Ray, Rex Wayne, Cecil M., Lela J., Addie Mabel and Pansy Independence.

---

LEONARD, JOHN CALVIN, attorney of Cedar Rapids, was born in that city, October 18, 1855. He is the son of Rev. George E. W. Leonard, the pioneer Presbyterian minister of that city, who was known and highly esteemed by all the old settlers. Rev. Mr. Leonard was married March 20, 1854, to Miss Rezilda Crowe, of Columbia county, N. Y., and soon after came west and bought a tract of 120 acres of land which now lies within the city limits of Cedar Rapids and is very valuable. His father was Charles Leonard, a New England farmer of German descent, who located in New Jersey. John C. Leonard is the oldest of seven children; Emma, is the wife of John Stuckslager, a farmer in Sioux county, Iowa; William C., is living in Rock Valley, Sioux county, and is practicing the profession of law; Mary R., a girl of rare intellectual ability, and before whom lay the brightest prospects of a happy future, died in her 22d year, laying down her life with a cheerful resignation to the Divine will; Dora B., now Mrs. A. W. Bowman, residing at Omaha, was a graduate of the high school of Marion; Martha A., now Mrs. Dr. J. M. Aiken, of Omaha, was educated at Coe college; George E. graduated at Ann Arbor Law school and is now practicing in Chicago.

When John C. Leonard was a boy Cedar Rapids was but a country village. His father's farm, now covered by a portion of the city, was one of the most fertile and productive in the township. Upon this farm John worked during the summer, and during the winter months attended school. June 13, 1873, he graduated at the city high school, and during the next two years attended Cornell college at Mt. Vernon. After leaving college he read law for two years with Messrs. Hubbard & Clark, then the attorneys of the Northwestern Railway company, and in 1877 was admitted to the bar and commenced the practice of law at Cedar Rapids. In June, 1879, he was admitted to practice before the supreme court. Mr. Leonard's practice has been

mostly railroad litigation, either for or against the various railway corporations operating in this state. For the last fifteen years he has been attorney for the Burlington, Cedar Rapids & Northern Railway company. He was born and brought up a republican, but takes no part in politics. He is not a member of any society; club or church, but is a man of decidedly independent turn of mind; does not consider himself any better than the average man and not as good as many, but has never drank a glass of intoxicating liquor or used tobacco in any form. He has four children: Mary B., born October 10, 1881; Nathan B., born November 29, 1883; John C., born May 8, 1891, and Thecla C., born August 23, 1892.

McMILLAN, HORACE G., United States district attorney for the northern district of Iowa, and one of the editors and owners of the Cedar Rapids *Republican*, was born in Wayne county, Ohio, May 20, 1854. Three years later his parents moved to Washington county, Iowa, first living at Crawfordsville, and afterwards on a farm four miles northeast of the town of Washington. Mr. McMillan's father was a man of sturdy character and of many attainments; of Scotch blood; and his mother belodged to the American pioneer women, who carried refinement as well as industry into the new states of the west and north-

west. As a boy, the subject of this sketch spent more time on the farm than in the schoolroom. He earned practically his own way to a place, first at the bar, and afterwards in the wider affairs of the state, in the business and politics of which he has been permitted to play a prominent part. His early education was obtained in the country schools of Washington county, and the academies of Grand View and Washington. He studied law with Mc-Junkin & Henderson, of Washington, the senior member of the firm being at that time attorney-general of the state of Iowa. He was admitted to the bar in 1880 by Circuit Judge L. C. Blanchard, of Oskaloosa, and immediately thereafter opened a

law office in Washington. In 1882 he became interested in northwestern Iowa, which was then in process of development, and that same year he located in Rock Rapids, Lyon county. A few days after he left his old home, his father died, and, having endorsed for friends and relatives, left an indebtedness of about $4,000. Upon returning to Washington to attend his father's funeral, young McMillan called upon all the creditors and voluntarily assumed this entire indebtedness. With this burden on his shoulders, and with no money, the young attorney invaded the open country of northwestern Iowa, determined to succeed. Ten years afterwards he returned to Washington for the first time, having paid off every dollar of the family indebtedness. In Rock Rapids he had entered into a law partnership with A. Van Wagenen. This partnership was dissolved in 1891. In 1893 he formed another partnership, this time with J. W. Dunlap, also of Washington county. As a lawyer, Mr. McMillan has been eminently successful. He has been connected with much of the most important litigation of northwestern Iowa, and has been especially prominent in the bond litigation of Lyon county. The county had been fraudulently bonded for $170,000, and the various school districts had been bonded for from $20,000 to $250,-000 each. Mr. McMillan has tried these cases in both the state and United States courts, the supreme court at Washington having decided two of them favorably to him. These services resulted in saving thousands of dollars to the taxpayers of the new county. Mr. McMillan has also been successful in the trial of personal injury and damage cases, especially those growing out of railway accidents. As a boy of 19, he served one year as brakeman on the Chicago, Milwaukee & St. Paul railway. His practice has brought him a large income for many years.

Mr. McMillan is also a business man. He was one of the first to grasp the possibilities of northwestern Iowa, and on his faith in its development made many investments in land, which have turned out even better than he had anticipated. He is to-day the owner of 1,000 acres of land in Iowa, and the adjacent counties of Dakota, and manages the Lakewood stock farm, near Rock Rapids, on which is maintained what is conceded to be one of the finest, if not the finest, herds of Jersey cattle in the state or the west. In 1898 the Cedar Rapids *Daily Republican* was for sale, owing to the death of its former chief owner, Mr. L. S. Merchant. Seeing the excellent opportunity it offered for building up a strong newspaper and a profitable business, Mr. McMillan and Cyrenus Cole, for a number of years associate editor of the *Iowa State Register*, bought the paper. It immediately took rank with the leading dailies of the state, grew in circulation and influence, and is now enjoying a firmly-established prosperity. The change occurred in May, 1898, and Mr. McMillan removed with his family to Cedar Rapids.

Mr. McMillan has, from his boyhood up, taken an active part in politics, being by birth and conviction an unswerving republican. Before leaving Washington county, he served as chairman of the county committee there. In 1886 he was elected county attorney of Lyon county, which office he filled for three terms, although the county was democratic part of the time. In 1892 he was elected a member of the republican state central committee for the Eleventh congressional district. He was re-elected in 1894, and in 1895 was elected chairman of the committee. He was in charge of the campaign in which Gen. Francis M. Drake was elected governor by an almost unprecedented majority, and also had charge of the Iowa campaign for William McKinley and Garret A. Hobart, and his conduct of that campaign won the praise of republicans and gold democrats alike. In 1897 he desired to retire from the state chairmanship, but was again pressed into the service of his party as the manager of the campaign for Leslie M. Shaw for governor. As a campaign manager Mr. McMillan has tenacity of purpose and persistence of effort well combined with judgment and a wise spirit of conciliation. Under him the party has developed no factions, nor has it wavered. At the meeting of the Iowa congressional delegation, in the spring of 1897, Mr. McMillan was recommended to the president for appointment as United States attorney for the northern district of Iowa, an appointment which was made by President McKinley and confirmed by the senate in February, 1898.

In his home life Mr. McMillan has been happy and successful, as well as in business, law and politics. In 1877, before he began to study law, he was married to Miss Alice Van Doren, of Washington county, who has been a helpmeet to him, not only in his home, but in his public life. Six children were born to them, five of

whom are living. They are Glenn V., Viva Alice, Florence, James B., and Horace G., Jr. Mrs. McMillan has taken a deep interest in the political affairs in which her husband has been prominent. She has taken, especially, an interest in educational matters, and was largely instrumental in the founding of the free public library, of Rock Rapids, and feels, with a woman's and a mother's pride, that her best contribution to the world has been her children.

---

DAY, FREDERICK JACKSON, of Council Bluffs, is descended from ancestors on both

sides who fought in both the revolution and the war of the rebellion. Jackson J. Day, his father, was born in 1818 and enlisted as a private in the civil war. His ancestors fought in the war against King Philip, in the Narragansett war and in the revolution. He was a prominent business man and an extensive traveler. He married Caroline A. Minier, who was also descended from ancestors who took part in the revolutionary and civil wars. She was a woman of good education and strong character, and is now living with a daughter in Los Angeles, Cal.

Frederick J. was born October 20, 1859, in Hillsdale county, Mich. Hillsdale

33

county is located in the southern tier of
counties, bordering on Ohio, and is a
beautiful, level and fertile farming country. Hillsdale is the county-seat of Hillsdale county and is situated about midway
between Lake Michigan and Lake Erie,
about seventy miles south of Lansing.
Young Day was educated in the public
schools of Michigan and Iowa. In 1869
the family removed from Michigan to Iowa
and located at Dexter, Dallas county, and
in 1870 removed to Stuart, Guthrie county.
Frederick J. Day removed, in 1881, to
Council Bluffs, where he has since been
actively engaged in the real estate, loan
and insurance business. During his experience in that line of business he has
bought and sold a large amount of farm
and city property, and now owns about 500
acres of farm land and considerable city
property. In 1890 he formed a partnership
with Mr J. P. Hess, under the firm name
of Day & Hess. They have invested over
$1,000,000 of eastern capital in bonds and
mortgages, and represent about the same
amount in value of real estate owned by
others.

Mr. Day is a prominent and active republican and is a member of the city and
county committees, but has never run for
office. He is president of the Pomona
Land and Trust company and treasurer of
the Council Bluffs Mutual Building and
Loan association.

In 1885 he was married to Harriet E.
Rue, daughter of the late John B. Rue.
They are members of the First Presby-
terian church and have two children:
Bessie V., born February 25, 1886, and
Jackson Rue, born May 15, 1890.

---

SMITH, JESSE HITCHCOCK, president
of the Farmers Insurance company, of
Cedar Rapids, is a native of Indiana. His
father was Isaac Smith, a substantial
farmer, living in Elkhart county. His
mother's maiden name was Sarah Thomas.
The son, Jesse, was born on the 27th of
August, 1838, and was brought up on the
farm, working during the summer months,
and attending district school in the winter.
In the summer of 1853 the family moved to
Iowa and again settled on a farm in the
then new state, locating on the fertile
prairie land of Linn county. Here for
many years Jesse assisted his father in
breaking up wild prairie, building fence,
plowing, sowing, planting and reaping,
performing all the varied labor pertaining

to farm life in a new country, before barbed
wire and twine binders had so greatly
lightened the tedious and exhausting labor
of fencing the farms and harvesting the
small grain, then so extensively grown. In
the winter he again attended the district
school, kept in a rude log house meagerly
equipped for educational progress. But
Jesse was studious and prepared himself
to enter the first class organized in Western
college, when that institution was established, not far from his father's home.
Here he got a good education and soon
after studied medicine in Cedar Rapids.
He became a practicing physician in that

city and for fifteen years devoted his time
to that profession, almost exclusively. In
the fall of 1887 Dr. Smith was nominated
by the republicans for senator in the
Twenty-second General Assembly, and
elected for the term of four years, serving
with ability and fidelity. He has always
been an active and ardent republican, casting his first vote for Abraham Lincoln for
president in 1860. He has served four
terms as mayor of Cedar Rapids and for
ten years has been president of St. Luke's
hospital in that city. He owns a stock
farm south of the city, where he has for
many years given attention to stock raising.
But Dr. Smith is more widely known as

president of the Farmers Insurance company, of Cedar Rapids, a position which he has held continuously since the 1st of January, 1869.

---

MILLS, MASON P. (deceased), was born at East Windsor, Conn., January 15, 1843; died at Cedar Rapids, Iowa, July 31, 1896. The life of this soldier, lawyer and citizen was a noble example of the best there is in American citizenship; his death a public calamity. As the public is apt to place a correct estimate upon the character of a man whose career has been a highly prominent one the biographer can do no better than to record in part an editorial which appeared in the Cedar Rapids *Republican* at the time of the death of Mr. Mills:

"As a citizen he was, from the first, active in all things that make for a city. He was public spirited and energetic to a degree attained by few men. He was an alderman for many years, and in this capacity did a great deal to shape legislation. He was a born leader. If there was an enterprise on foot, Mr. Mills was either for or against it with all his might. He had the courage, the strong intelligence, the rare and subtle magnetism which, as public men are analyzed, compose the requisites of the real genius of leadership. As a lawyer he attained a very high rank. He was a worker, a master of the art of accumulation of testimony—a tactician, skillful in cross-examination, a perfect judge of men, and, therefore, one who selected a jury with method and keen analysis of those who presented themselves for acceptance. Many of our foremost business men relied upon him absolutely, and to them the loss will be as a personal bereavement. As a friend, perhaps the word loyal is the best and most expressive adjective descriptive of this phase of his character. It is the fortune of strong characters like Mason P. Mills to be strong in friendship and intense in resentment, to have friends bound to them with hooks of steel, and at the same time have those who swear, Hamilcar-like, to love them not at all. And now, what of him? * * * It does not seem possible that the soul of a man like Mason P. Mills—the force that was in that brain—can have gone out forever. Meeting by the side of his grave this great question which is the dark cloud on the horizon of all of us, we are glad to know that he here found reason for hope."

The father of the deceased died when he was a mere boy and the mother, within a few years, married P. T. Crowell, of Springfield, Mass., a trusted employe of the United States armory at that city. The mother, whose maiden name was Elizabeth Strong, was a lineal descendant of the Grant family of East Windsor. The early education of Mr. Mills was acquired in the common schools. He was a student in the Upper Iowa university at the breaking out of the war, and at the first call for troops went to Washington and enlisted in a squadron of cavalry known as McClellan's Dragoons. This was George B. McClellan's bodyguard. He served in that

capacity under the commanders of the army of the Potomac until the winter of 1863-4, when the squadron of cavalry was ordered to Chicago and made part of the Twelfth Illinois cavalry. There he was made sergeant of the regiment, and afterward promoted to regimental quartermaster and first lieutenant by Governor Yates. He served gallantly at Yorktown, Antietam, Fredericksburg, Chancellorsville, Gettysburg, and in the seven days' fight before Richmond, as well as in the smaller affairs in which the army of the Potomac was engaged up to the year 1864. He was then sent on the Red River expedition, under General Banks.

He was mustered out of the service February 17, 1865, but until July of that year he was in the government employ, having charge of Camp Fry, in Chicago. He was not mustered out as an officer until 1887, when he took advantage of the act of congress permitting volunteer officers to be mustered according to their rank, if they had failed to be so mustered, owing to active operations in the field. He did this in order to become eligible to membership in the Loyal Legion, which he at once joined.

When his country no longer needed his services he commenced the study of law in the office of Ira T. Buell, of Chicago, and was admitted to the bar there in 1866. In 1867 he located at Cedar Rapids and engaged in practice, where he remained until his death. Although not a college-bred man, he was recognized as a thorough scholar. An omnivorous reader, his whole life was a process of self-education. He was a republican in politics and was colonel on the staff of Governor Gear during his last administration. He was a prominent member of the Loyal Legion and served as department commander of the G. A. R. in 1890.

He was married October 14, 1869, to Miss Flora B. Coulter, daughter of Dr. John Parshall Coulter, lieutenant-colonel of the Twelfth Iowa infantry. She is a lady of high attainments and countless personal graces and domestic virtues, so the beauty and happiness of their home life may be imagined. To them were born three children: John, born December 1, 1874; Flora, born May 28, 1877, and Mary, born May 21, 1886.

---

EVANS, MARION LE GRAND, of Emerson, the well-known banker and breeder of Aberdeen-Angus cattle, was born near Decorra, Henderson county, Ill., June 30, 1858. His grandfather, John Evans, Sr., was born in Maryland, April 9, 1794, and was descended from Welsh ancestors. John Evans, Jr., the father of Marion L., was born in Crawford county, Ohio, June 13, 1830, and moved with his parents to Henderson county, Ill., in 1837. Starting in life without financial assistance he has by good judgment and close attention to business accumulated a comfortable fortune, and still resides in Henderson county. He was married April 23, 1857, to Sarah Young Davis, who was born in Ballston, Saratoga county, N. Y., March 13, 1899, and came

with her parents to Henderson county, Ill., in 1836. Her father, Abner Davis, was born in Vermont, September 21, 1794, and served through the war of 1812. In 1836 he settled upon a farm given him by the government in Henderson county, Ill., where he continued to reside until his death, December 10, 1874.

Marion L. Evans received his early education in the country schools and completed an academic course. Later he attended Monmouth college. In the spring of 1879 he moved "out west," as people said, to Iowa, and located on a farm in Mills county. In 1889 Mr. Evans removed to

Emerson, where he built a home and has since resided. Mr. Evans' experience in stock raising began when he was a small boy and when he was 16 he was able to sell all the stock he had raised for $1,200, which was used in paying his school expenses. For many years he has been associated with his father in the live stock business, and they now own 7,300 acres of Iowa land and usually have on hand some 2,000 head of cattle.

Mr. Evans is president of the American Aberdeen-Angus Breeders' association, and has a wide reputation as a careful and successful breeder of black cattle. He is also president of the Farmers bank at Emerson, and a director of the First National bank of Malvern. He is a republican and a member of the A. F. A. M. Chapter, Commandery of Red Oak, and of Tangier Temple at Omaha, Neb.

Mr. Evans was married June 28, 1883, to Hattie M. Tubbs, daughter of Judge L. W. Tubbs. They have five children: Edith L., born April 13, 1884; John L., born November 8, 1885; Frank N., born May 11, 1888; Marion L., Jr., born December 27, 1891, and Volney, born October 4, 1893.

---

JUNKIN, JOSEPH M., represents the counties of Montgomery and Mills in the state senate, and is one of the leading lawyers of western Iowa, living at Red Oak. His lineage is of that stalwart and heroic race, the Puritans (Covenanters), of Scotland. His great-grandfather, Joseph Junkin, had an arm shattered by a musket ball at the battle of Brandywine, September 11, 1777, where he commanded a company of volunteers. His grandfather, Joseph Junkin served in the war of 1812, and his father was a soldier in the civil war. The only known relative of Mr. Junkin who served in the confederacy was Stonewall Jackson, he having married Eleanor Junkin, daughter of Dr. George Junkin, at that time president of Washington college, Virginia. His parents, Joseph and Mary M. Junkin, came from Virginia to Iowa, locating at Fairfield, where Senator Junkin was born in 1854. Later the family removed to Melrose, Monroe county, and from that place, in 1873, Mr. Junkin came to Red Oak, where he has since resided. He attended school at Fairfield, Red Oak and Iowa City. After graduating from the law department of the State university in 1879, he formed a partnership with another young law student, Horace E. Deemer, now judge of the supreme court. The partnership was dissolved in 1896, when Mr. Deemer was elected district judge, and Mr. Junkin has continued the practice alone, enjoying a large and lucrative business. The practice of his profession occupied his attention almost exclusively. Although he took a considerable interest in politics, he never was a candidate for office on his own account, but always on account of some vital issue in which he was deeply interested.

He held a number of minor local offices, but not until 1895, when he was unanimously nominated for state senator, did he consent to accept any office which would take him away from his business. As the

code was to be revised at this session, it seemed an excellent opportunity for a good lawyer to not only make himself felt but to improve himself professionally. Senator Junkin at once took a prominent part in the work of the senate, more than is usually the case with new members. He gave special attention to the work of the judiciary committee, of which he was one of the most industrious members. His work and record in the legislature are marked throughout by a high standard of integrity, and he was never known to lend his support to any proposition that did not commend itself to his approval, or that was

not clearly beneficial to the people, no matter what influence might be exerted in its behalf.

Neither was he afraid, at any time, to denounce that which he believed to be wrong. During the memorable campaign of 1896, Senator Junkin devoted much time and labor in fighting the battles of the party, speaking at many places throughout the state. The convention called for 1899, to select delegates to the senatorial convention, by unanimous vote accorded Mr. Junkin the courtesy of naming the delegates to attend that convention, which will result in his renomination and election to another term in the senate, commencing January, 1900.

Senator Junkin was married in July, 1888, to Miss Olivette E. Chevalier, then principal of the high school at Red Oak. They have two children, Chevalier J., born March, 1891, and Josephine, born March, 1898.

---

MADDEN, P. W.  No state in the union has had a penitentiary warden more universally liked by the unfortunates within prison walls, nor one more popular with the general public than P. W. Madden. He was born in New Castle, Pa., February 4, 1845. His parents were natives

of Pennsylvania, but beyond that fact nothing definite is known of the family history.  He received but a limited education in the public schools, being early required to depend upon his own efforts for a livelihood. His father died when he was 4 years old, and he was therefore compelled to perform manual labor to assist in the support of his widowed mother.  At the age of 10 years he came to Iowa with his mother and settled in Mahaska county, where they resided two years, then removed to Polk county. Here he worked on a farm for several years, placing in the hands of his mother the greater part of his earnings.  It is related that when he first hired to a farmer he was to get $10 for two months' service

hoeing corn.  At the conclusion of the work the farmer paid him with two five-dollar gold pieces.  The lad thought this poor compensation for the amount of labor he had performed, and the more he considered the matter the firmer became his conviction that he had been cheated, never having seen that kind of money, and it required the repeated assurances of his mother to convince him otherwise.

In the spring of 1862, at the age of 17, he enlisted in Company B, Fifteenth United States regulars.  His regiment was sent to Newport barracks, when, after perfecting itself in the drill, it was ordered to the front and assigned to the Fourteenth Army corps, then under command of General Thomas.  The first fight they participated in was the battle of Chickamauga, where the Fourteenth corps held Bragg's army in check after the defeat and retreat of the other corps of the union army.  The Fourteenth performed heroic service on that day, so dark and disastrous for Rosecrans' forces.  The regiment was under Grant at Lookout Mountain, and with the center, under General Woods, scaled that lofty range, hurled shot and shell, and poured death and consternation into the ranks of the rebels.  From Chattanooga it marched with Sherman to Atlanta, and when that city fell, it was ordered back to Nashville.  Besides Franklin and Nashville it participated in the battles of Missionary Ridge, Buzzard's Roost, Big Shanty, Neal Dow Station, Resaca, Kenesaw Mountain, Peach Tree Creek, New Hope Church, Jonesboro and the siege of Atlanta. During his entire service Mr. Madden never missed a roll call.  He was honorably discharged March 4, 1865.  Returning to Iowa he remained in Des Moines for a time, then went to Madison county, where he married.  In 1870 he removed to Clay county, took up a homestead and commenced preparations for a permanent home.  Shortly thereafter the grasshoppers came.  These were years when it tried the nerve, ingenuity and fortitude of the pioneers of northwestern Iowa.  But Mr. Madden was possessed of good staying qualities and remained.  In 1879 he received the nomination for sheriff, but was defeated by eighteen votes.  In 1881 he was again a candidate and was elected by a majority of five.  In 1883 he was re-elected by a majority of 763 votes, and in 1885 by 832.  He was again elected in 1887 and once more in 1889.  In 1891 there was no convention and it was a "free for all" race, with four candidates in the field. He was a winner this time with many votes to spare. These repeated elections attest the esteem in which he is held by the citizens of his home county.

Mr. Madden has served three terms as warden of the state penitentiary at Anamosa. So carefully and economically was that institution conducted by him that at the beginning of 1897 the management was able to operate a plant which furnishes water for the entire institution, and without one cent of additional cost to the state. It came out of savings from the support fund, in addition to $30,000 turned back into the state treasury during his first three years at the head of the institution, and was accomplished without curtailing in any measure the comfort and table supplies of the prisoners. The new improvement is estimated to be worth $20,000 to the state. He has now returned to his home at Spencer.

He is a member of the G. A. R., Odd Fellows and Knights of Pythias, in all of which he is a leading spirit. He was married September 20, 1868, to Miss Abigail Hockett. They have had eight children, all but one of whom are living.

---

LEBECK, CARL LUDWIG, was born in Albersdorf, province of Holstein, Germany, December 16, 1845. His father, Soren Larsen Jensen Lebeck, was a teacher, and taught for over forty-two years in that place. His grandfather and great grandfather were natives of a village in the northern part of Schleswig, called Spandet, and they were farmers. The grandfather's name was Jens Olufsen, and he had a family of eight boys and two girls. Five of the boys became teachers and four of them went to Denmark, but the father of Carl went south to Germany and lived to be 87 years old. He taught for fifty-three years, and during the last thirteen years of his life received a pension of $250 per year. Carl's mother was Hanne Ketelsen. Her father was raised upon a fine farm near Bredstedt, province of Schleswig, which has been in their family for probably 300 years, and is still owned by a cousin of Mr. Lebeck. Carl was one of eleven children, seven boys and four girls. He attended the common school, where his father was a teacher, and at the age of 16 was apprenticed for five years to a merchant to learn the dry goods and grocery business. He worked for four years as

a clerk in different places in Germany, and in 1870 emigrated to America. He came as far west as Illinois, and worked eight months for J. T. Alexander, the "cattle king," on his "Broadland farm" of forty-two sections in Champaign county. In the spring of 1871 he came to Clinton, Iowa, and worked during the season on a farm. In the fall he secured a place in a hardware store in Lyons, and remained in that town until 1874, when he moved to Walnut, Pottawattamie county, and formed a partnership with J. B. Johannsen, and started a general store on a small scale, under the firm name of Lebeck & Johannsen. After four and a half years of successful business he sold his interest to his

partner. Soon afterwards he bought another store in the same business and took in a younger brother, Adolf, as a partner, under the firm name of Lebeck Brothers. They continued in business together for thirteen years, and were very successful. In 1894 Mr. Lebeck bought his younger brother's interest and has since conducted the business alone. Having increased the stock and added another store room, he now has the largest business in town.

Mr. Lebeck has always been a democrat. He is not a member of any of the fraternities. He is a leading member of the

Lutheran church. He was married November 2, 1872, to Minna Steffen, who is a native of Germany. They have had seven children, but the only one living now is Alfred Jens Ludwig, born June 29, 1878, who has attended business college at Cedar Rapids.

HILL, GERSHOM HYDE, A. M., M. D., superintendent of the hospital for the insane at Independence, Iowa, was born in Garnavillo, Clayton county, Iowa, May 8, 1846, and is descended from Peter Hill, who, with his son Roger, came from the

west of England in 1653, and settled in the state of Maine. Dr. Hill's grandfather was once a member of congress from Maine and was noted for his hospitality. James J. Hill, his father, was a member of the famous "Iowa Band of Congregational Home Missionaries," who graduated from Andover, Mass., Theological seminary in 1843. He was a graduate of Bowdoin college and a native of Bath, Me., as was also his wife, Sarah E. Hyde; they were married April 24, 1844, and immediately set out for the west. One of her sisters was the wife of the Rev. Dr. Magoun, of Grinnell, and the other of Rev. Dr. Alden, of Boston. The young minister left his wife in Dubuque, in June, and went up into

Clayton county to spy out the land on which he would locate. Their second son, James Langdon, now a minister in Salem, Mass., was also born in Garnavillo.

In 1849, the family moved to Albany, Ill., just across the Mississippi river from Sabula, where the father continued to preach. Here the mother died in 1852. She was a strong, intellectual, enthusiastic and warm-hearted woman; an earnest, hopeful Christian. In October, 1853, Mr. Hill was married to Sarah Wells Harriman, and took charge of the Congregational church in Savannah, Ill. She was a New Hampshire woman, a graduate of Mt. Holyoke college, in Massachusetts; she proved to be a good step-mother and a capable minister's wife. The family moved to Wapello, Louisa county, in 1856, and to McLeod county, Minn., in 1858, where amid Indians and the extreme rigors and privations of pioneer life, with scanty fare, they lived for a time in a log cabin, and the children acquired part of their education in a log schoolhouse.

They returned to Iowa just before the massacre of 1860, and located in Grinnell, for the purpose of giving the children a college education. Here Gershom became intimately acquainted with the founder of the town, the Hon. J. B. Grinnell, and was employed by him at one time cultivating corn on his land just north of the college grounds. In June, 1861, Gershom took a half dozen refugees from the home of Mr. Grinnell, who was known to keep a station on the "underground railway," and conveyed them by night to Marengo, then the terminus of the Rock Island railroad, from which point they were furnished transportation to Canada by Mr. Grinnell. For this service he was given a Suffolk pig valued at $10. He attended the public schools in Grinnell four winters and in December, 1863, began to teach a country school in Marshall county. In May, 1864, as soon as he was 18 years old, he enlisted in Company B, Forty-sixth Iowa volunteers, and served four months under Col. D. B. Henderson, at Colliersville, Tenn. Returning from the war, Gershom was employed as teamster for a time. In June, 1865, the family moved to Fayette, Iowa, where the father became pastor of the Congregational church, and there died in 1870.

In the fall of 1865 the two Hill brothers entered the preparatory department of Iowa college in Grinnell and, by working in the harvest fields in the summer and teaching school in the winter vacation, they worked their way through college, being classmates throughout, and completed the classical course in 1871.

Gershom at once began to study medicine, first in the medical department of the State University of Iowa and later in the Rush Medical college in Chicago, graduating there in 1874. After several months' practice in Moline, Ill., he was elected first assistant physician of the hospital for the insane in Independence. In October, 1881, Dr. Hill was promoted to the superintendency, which office he continues to hold. The institution was opened in 1873, and when Dr. Hill went there contained but 200 patients, while now it accommodates more than 1,000. Dr. Hill's record in this institution is that of progress in the humane and scientific treatment of the insane. The hospital under his management has gone quietly along without sensational incidents. Its superintendent combines the three qualities so difficult to obtain in one man and yet each is absolutely requisite for this important position: a scientific knowledge, business capacity and executive ability. Dr. Hill has few superiors as an able, conscientious manager, both from a medical and a financial standpoint. The institution over which he presides compares favorably with any of its kind in the United States and he has been highly complimented by the board of control for his admirable methods. He has attended two post-graduate courses in medicine, one in New York, in 1878, and one in Boston, in 1890. He writes for the medical journals and is frequently called upon as an expert on insanity. He belongs to numerous medical societies in Iowa and to the American Medical association, the American Academy of Medicine, the Medico-Legal society of New York and the American Medico-Psychological association. He is president of the board of directors of the Independence Y. M. C. A. and is an elder in the Presbyterian church. He is a life member of the board of trustees of his alma mater in Grinnell and is a lecturer on insanity in the medical department of the State University of Iowa. His father, in 1846, gave the first dollar to found Iowa college, and the brothers, Gershom and James, have together established a prize for excellence in extemporaneous debate and in vocal music.

Dr. Hill was married in 1879 to Louisa B. Ford, in Lynn, Mass. They have one child, Julia, born in 1886. Dr. Hill is an earnest republican.

HERTERT, EMIL BENEDICT MATHIAS, was born at Eich, near Luxemburg, Germany, August 7, 1855. His father, Mathias Hertert, was a tanner by trade, and November 28, 1851, married Catherine Probst. Both were natives of the grand duchy of Luxemburg. Emil's early schooling was received at Weimerskirch, near his birthplace, and in 1866 he entered the college of Beauregard, near Thionville, Alsace. He finished his education at the agricultural college at Ettelbruck, Luxemburg, in 1870. Mr. Hertert came to America in 1872 and located at Luxemburg, Dubuque county, Iowa. He remained in Dubuque and Clayton counties until 1878, when he removed

to Shelby county, where he has since resided. For a number of years he engaged in farming, and in 1884 was appointed deputy auditor of Shelby county, under John W. Herrod, who was then auditor. In 1887 he resigned that position, and with his brother, Lucien R. Hertert, purchased the land, loan and abstract business of Aldenk Riley, which is still under his management and supervision. They have also a branch office at Pierce, Pierce county, Neb., which is conducted by the brother, Lucien R., who resides at that place. The business at both places is carried on under the name of Hertert Bros., and has been remarkably successful and prosperous. Since he became a voter, Mr. Hertert has been affiliated with the democratic party. He is a member of the school board at Harlan, and has been a member of the city council for eight years. In November, 1897, he was a candidate upon the fusion ticket for treasurer of Shelby county, and was elected. He was married at Dubuque, December 16, 1878, to Mary Muller, who was born in Niederauven, Luxemburg. They have had seven children: Charles N., born January 2, 1880; Lucien R., born October 22, 1881; John P., born June 25, 1885; Victor C., born January 24, 1888; Amelia M., born September 21, 1889; and Mary C., born August 23, 1891; Anna M. died December 11, 1889.

---

MITCHELL, WILLIAM EDWIN. Judge J. L. Mitchell, well known to all Iowans by reason of his distinction in legal circles and his gallant services as captain of Company E, in the Twenty-ninth Iowa, once had a nephew to whose young mind the judge was the acme of perfection, the ideal man. When the young man had reached the age at which a profession was to be chosen, he very naturally thought the profession of his uncle good enough for him, so began the study of law. That young man is now one of the leading lawyers of the state, having at one time been presented by a great political party for the position of supreme judge. William E. Mitchell, of Sidney, was the young man thus inspired. He was born April 23, 1860, in Hendricks county, Ind. To a high school education was added a course in Tabor college, during the years 1880-1. Late in the year 1881 he entered the Freshman class at Greencastle, Ind., and there took a classical course in the De Pauw university, from which he graduated in 1885. He also graduated from the law department of the same school in 1888. While there he was a member of the Phi Delta Theta Greek Letter society, and had the distinction of winning the Kinnear-Monette medal, in debate.

His parents were poor people and came to Iowa in 1868, in the hope of bettering their condition. They located on a farm near Sidney, and, as might be expected, the boy was required to labor hard to assist in building up the new home. He was thus engaged until reaching his 20th year, at which time he was placed in college. Upon returning from school in 1885, he was elected to the office of county superintendent of schools of Fremont county, on the democratic ticket. In May, 1888, he was admitted to the bar by the supreme court of the state, since which time he has devoted himself to practice. He is regarded as among the best jury lawyers in western Iowa, if not in the entire state, and has a law library excelled by but few in the profession. He has a large practice in the supreme court of Iowa, and the federal court at Council Bluffs.

He was married December 18, 1889, to Miss Matilda Engelke, a daughter of W. A. Engelke, a prosperous farmer living near Sidney. The union has been blessed with three children: Edwin, Erskine and Mary Mitchell.

Mr. Mitchell is a democrat, and as such has figured, and is now figuring, prominently in the high circles of that party. He received the nomination for supreme judge at the hands of the state convention held in Des Moines in 1894, and was defeated by Judge Deemer, the state that year giving the republican ticket an overwhelming plurality. He takes great interest in the party success, and is a familiar figure in congressional, state and national conventions. He is pronounced in his commendation of the course of Grover Cleveland, especially on the currency question. He was chosen a delegate at large from Iowa, to the national convention of national democrats at Indianapolis, Ind., September 2 and 3, 1896, which placed the Palmer and Buckner ticket in the field, and during that campaign stumped the state against Bryan and his platform. His first political speech was made for General Hancock, during the campaign of 1880, and every democratic candidate since that time has received his support except Bryan, whose free silver ideas and the Chicago platform he could not endorse. He united with the Presbyterian church when 15 years old, and is still a member of that church. He is superintendent of the Sunday school of his home town, in which he takes great pride and interest, and all benevolent causes receive liberal contributions at his hand. He has a beautiful home on the best street in Sidney, where he is surrounded by his family and his books, and with these he is indeed one of the happiest of men.

---

HALL, LINCOLN GRANT, of Coggon, is of Scotch descent and is a distant relative of ex-President Harrison. His father, William Hall, is a prosperous farmer, who moved to Iowa in 1869, from near Lima, Allen county, Ohio, and located in Linn county. William Hall enlisted as a soldier in the civil war and was second lieutenant of Company B, One Hundred and Fifty-first Ohio volunteers. William Hall's father, Jacob R. Hall, served as a private in the war of 1812, under General Harrison, who was his cousin. Jacob R. Hall was a "Campbellite" minister, a merchant and a farmer in Allen county, Ohio.

L. G. Hall's mother was Mary E. Manner, and she was a cousin of Col. A. V. Rice, of Ottawa, Ohio. In her youth she attended a school taught by Samuel J. Kirkwood, war governor of Iowa, in Richland county, Ohio. On October 15, 1863, Lincoln G. Hall was born. He went to the country school in Jackson township, Linn county, known as the Old South Prairie school, and taught by Mrs. Elizabeth Blodgette, at present well known as a prominent member of the Woman's Relief corps. In 1881 and 1882 he attended the Marion high school and in 1883 and 1884, Coe college at Cedar Rapids. He then went to Chicago and took a course in the Chicago College of Pharmacy. In March, 1885, he entered the employ of J. H. Davis, of Paris, Iowa, who was in the general merchandise business. Here he re-

mained for over two years and had the advantage of a thorough training in practical and successful business. In October, 1887, he formed a partnership with Dr. A. S. Cunningham in the drug business at Nugent's Grove, which is now known as Coggon. In 1888 Mr. Hall's father purchased the doctor's interest in the business, which was continued under the firm name of L. G. Hall & Co. for one year, when he became sole proprietor.

On November 23, 1887, Mr. Hall was married to Inez E. Fleming. They have two daughters, Hazel W. and Muriel M. Mr. Hall and his wife joined the Jackson

Congregational church in 1890 and in 1897 transferred their membership to the Zion Presbyterian church at Coggon.

As an active republican Mr. Hall's efficient services in the cause have been recognized by his selection as chairman of the township central committee for three years. He has also been for several years a member of the county central committee. For three years, from 1892 to 1895 he was a member of the council of Coggon.

He was made a member of Level Lodge No. 284, A. F. and A. M., at Central City, in 1885, exalted to Royal Arch degree in Marion Chapter No. 10, Marion, in 1891; dubbed sir knight of Apollo Commandery, Knights Templars No. 26, at Cedar Rapids, in 1891, and was made a noble of the Mystic

Shrine in El Kahir Temple A. A. O. N. M. S., at Cedar Rapids, in 1891. He was a member of D. Hedges Camp No. 68, Sons of Veterans, at Central City, for three years, from 1885 to 1888; was captain of the company during his connection with the order, and for faithful service was presented with an elegant sword by the members of above named camp. Served one year as aid-de-camp on the staff of Gen. Walter S. Payne.

COLE, ROSSETTER GLEASON, director of the musical department at Iowa college, Grinnell, and vice-president of the National

Association of Music Teachers, is among the best teachers and composers of music in the west, and has spared no effort or expense to perfect himself in the art. His father, Henry Walcott Cole, also a musician, was born July 7, 1820, in Sherburne, Chenango county, N. Y. He was a son of Amos Cole (1759–1852), a farmer; a grandson of Thomas Cole (1735–1827); great grandson of John Cole, Jr., born in 1705, who married a sister of Benjamin Franklin; and great-great-grandson of John Cole, Sr., who was born in England in 1670. The family is noted for its longevity. Thomas died at the age of 92, and his wife a few weeks later, aged 90, they having been married over seventy years. Amos

lived one year longer than his father, dying at the extreme age of 93. In 1850 Henry W. Cole came to Ohio, settling at Iberia, Morrow county, where he owned a large warehouse, and for several years taught theoretical and instrumental music in Iberia college. He located on a farm in Oakland county, Mich., in 1863, where he died April 6, 1872. He was a man of high culture, and contributed extensively to the county and state press, and was a vigorous opponent of slavery. In 1850 he married Mary Charlotte Osgood Gleason, who was born September 26, 1826, in Georgetown, Madison county, N. Y. She was a daughter of Rossetter Gleason, a teacher and one of the early prominent educators of Madison county. He was an able mathematician, and served for many years as county surveyor. Her mother, Mary Whitney Locke, was a direct descendant of John Locke, the English philosopher, and two sisters of her mother's father married Gen. Israel Putnam and Eli Whitney, inventor of the cotton gin.

Prof. Rossetter G. Cole was born February 5, 1866, at Clyde, Oakland county, Mich., and was the youngest of six children. He was only 6 years old when his father died, and two years later his mother moved from the farm to Ann Arbor, determined to give her children the best educational advantages, in spite of limited means. By courage, thrift and energy, she succeeded in putting all her children through the high school and her four sons through the university. Rossetter did not attend school until he was 9 years old, receiving his earliest instruction from his mother, whose skillful supervision laid the foundation for his good habits of study. He graduated from the Latin course of the Ann Arbor high school in 1884, and in the following fall entered the University of Michigan, graduating in 1888 with the degree of bachelor of philosophy. While in college, he was an enthusiastic member of the Phi Kappa Psi fraternity.

From his earliest years Professor Cole had a great love for music. He grew up in an atmosphere of it, for his brothers and sisters all played and sang well. He learned these things himself very young, and at the age of 6 composed several instrumental pieces. A fragment of one, "A Storm at Sea," still exists. Nothing was done, however, to develop this creative instinct until during his high school course, when he took lessons in harmony under Francis L. York, and in 1884 began the study of the pipe organ with the same gentleman. While attending the university he helped organize, and was for four years director of, the university glee club, which gained a splendid reputation throughout the west and northwest.

While taking all the required work for the degree of bachelor of philosophy, he laid a broad foundation for his studies in the different branches of theoretical music and composition by electing all the courses offered under Prof. Calvin B. Cady, then professor of music in the university. For his graduating thesis he composed a logical cantata, "The Passing of Summer," which was given the honor of a public performance on the evening before commencement, with full orchestra, solos and a large chorus, the first instance of the kind in the university's history.

The year after graduating Professor Cole taught branches of English in the Ann Arbor high school, and in 1889 accepted a position as instructor in Latin and German in the Aurora, Illinois, high school. In 1890 he went to Berlin, where for two years he studied music under such masters as Heinrich van Eycken, Gustav Kogel and Wilhelm Middelschulte, now of Chicago. At the suggestion of van Eycken he took the examination for admission to the Royal Master School of Composition, the highest school of its kind in Germany, and a part of the Royal Academy of Arts. Though the number of students at any one time is limited to twenty-four, he gained entrance over many competitors, being the sixth American ever admitted. The scholarship thus won entitled him to three years of free instruction under the greatest masters, but at the end of his second year in Berlin under Max Bruch, he had to return home on account of short funds. He obtained the position of musical director at Ripon college, in Wisconsin, where he remained two years, in 1894 accepting his present position. He has done much to build up the department of music at Iowa college and it now includes six teachers and about 130 students. In addition, he has organized and conducted a college glee club of eighteen voices and an orchestra of thirty pieces. These organizations have won much applause in their annual tours.

In 1894 Professor Cole became a member of the New York Manuscript society, an organization of composers, aiming toward the advancement of American music, in whose public concerts his compositions are frequently heard. For two years he has been honorary corresponding secretary from Iowa. At the St. Louis meeting of the music teachers' national association, in July, 1895, he read a paper on "The Relation of Music to Education," and at the New York meeting in June, 1897, a paper of his was read on "The Best College Treatment of Harmony." He was chosen vice-president of the association for Iowa in February, 1897. He has contributed to various periodicals, and his many musical compositions have been accepted by leading publishers In 1893 he was commissioned by Mr. William L. Tomlins to write five children's songs for the Worlds' fair children's chorus of 1,200 voices. In December, 1897, he was elected to active membership in the Manuscript society of Chicago.

The following is a list of his published works up to January 1, 1898:

Persian Serenade (Brainards' Sons), 1888.

Two Novellettes for piano, in G flat and A minor. Opus 1 (Clayton F. Summy), 1895.

Four Songs: "Is My Lover on the Sea," "Love is a Bird," "Outre Mer," and "The Wreath You Wove." Opus 2 (Clayton F. Summy), 1895.

Polly, My Sweetheart (Clayton F. Summy), 1895.

Three compositions for piano: Preludium, Intermezzo and Meditation. Opus 3 (Arthur P. Schmidt), 1895.

Marche Celeste for Organ. Opus 6, in Volume IV of "Vox Organi" (J. B. Millet Co.), 1896.

Barcarolle for Piano. Opus 4 (Pianist Pub. Co.), 1897.

Adante Religioso for Organ. Op. 10 (Pianist Pub. Co.), 1897.

Eight Children's Songs. Op. 7 (Novello, Ewer & Co.), 1897.

Four Songs: "Longing," "Auf Wiedersehen," "A Kiss and a Tear," and "When Love is in her Eyes." Op. 12 (Ditson Co.), 1897.

Saviour, Like a Shepherd Lead Us, for contralto (Ditson Co.), 1897.

Among his larger unpublished works are a sonata for piano and violin, has been performed several times in New York city, Chicago and Detroit, a romanza for violin, a passacaglia for two pianos, festival march for two pianos, a suite for orchestra, besides many compositions for piano, voice and organ.

The professor was married August 6, 1896, at Ann Arbor, to Miss Fannie Louise Gwinner, who had been associated with him in musical work in Ripon college and later in Iowa college. She is a gifted musician, and has gained much praise as the translator of Marx's "Introduction to the Interpretation of Beethoven."

FORSYTH, ROBERT. The story of the life of Robert Forsyth, of Mystic, reads like a novel. He was born in the far-away land of Scotland, town of Kilmarnock, June 2, 1832. His father was a hand loom weaver, a poor man, and the father of ten children, of whom Robert was the youngest. His parents later removed to Dundee, Forfarshire, on the river Tay, at that time a town of considerable importance, and to-day the second manufacturing city in Scotland. Despite poverty, however, he was given a good common school education, and at the age of 14 was placed with Dr. John Gray, a surgeon of some note, who

had quite an active practice and was conducting a drug store, where he clerked and studied medicine for three years. His salary was thirty-seven and one-half cents per week and two hours per night five nights in the week for three years at night school. Although the hours were long and the pay meager, he had a kind employer and careful teacher, to whose training he now looks back with thankfulness. But the young man became dissatisfied with his lot, and determined to follow the sea. He was opposed in this by his parents and his preceptor, but their expostulations were of no avail, and to sea he went. He was shortly thereafter convinced that he had made a mistake; for the opportunity

to get ahead in a financial way was not presented, and while he regained his health and had the pleasure of visiting all parts of the world, he found himself as poor at the end of eight years as he was at the beginning.

He was married in Dundee, August 16, 1857, and at that time concluded to quit the sea and make a home in America. He left his wife with her parents, and without a cent in his pocket, shipped on board a vessel bound for Quebec, coal laden. The ship was six weeks in making the passage, but finally reached the dock in Quebec, Canada, and the following day Mr. Forsyth made his way to Montreal, where he joined the crew of the old propeller, St. Lawrence, and remained with her till the lakes froze up. The boat was taken out of commission at Kingston, and there he remained all winter, and the next spring shipped aboard a small vessel, where he remained until June, 1858, at which time he came to Rock Island, Ill. He expected to find here a land of milk and honey, but at that time the country afforded nothing but discouragement to persons without any means whatever. The land was all right, but the milk and honey were hard to get. It was two years before he could send enough money to procure passage for his wife to this country. Before her arrival he found work in a coal mine, and was thus engaged for about eight years. When he had saved a little money at this work he was persuaded to invest it in a mining property, and through the perfidy of his partners came out of the transaction penniless. He managed some way to get to What Cheer, and for a few years it was the same old struggle with poverty. But he was destined to have a streak of good luck; he purchased coal lands there, mostly on time, and when the Burlington, Cedar Rapids & Northern railroad reached the town he immediately leased his land to a coal company and sold part at a handsome figure. He wisely concluded to get into the drug business, and not take more chances in speculation, so bought one-half interest in one of the leading drug stores in What Cheer, and placed his eldest son to learn the business, and later started two others in the same business in the towns of Mystic and Jerome.

He is a Mason, Odd Fellow and a member of the Presbyterian church. He is the father of nine children, five boys and four girls, all living and seven owning homes of their own. The children are: James

Craig, Donald William and David Butter, born in Mercer county, Ill.; Isabella J. and Robert J., born in Poweshiek county, Iowa; Mary Elizabeth, born in Mahaska county, Iowa; Jessie Elizabeth and Dougald Richardson, born in Keokuk county, Iowa. He is a republican, and regards his political belief as next to his religious faith. He has instilled into his boys the doctrines of the party which, he believes, represents progress and prosperity, and as a very natural consequence they are all republicans of the staunchest sort.

---

STRAHAN, JAMES MILLER, a well-known banker of Malvern, was born in Putnam county, Ind., November 17, 1829. His father, James Strahan, and his mother, Elizabeth Ramsey Strahan, were of Scotch-Irish descent. They started in life with little besides industry for capital, working at farming. The father died when James was a small boy. In August, 1836, the family moved to Henderson county, Ill., where James worked on a farm and at any kind of labor at which he could help to make a living. When the great gold discoveries were made in California in 1848, young Strahan at once set to work to raise the means to try his fortune at gold mining. In the spring of 1850 he found a chance to make the long, slow, overland journey to the gold regions. He followed mining for three years and accumulated enough of the metal to return to Illinois and buy a drove of cattle, which he drove across the plains and mountain ranges to the Sacramento valley, arriving there in 1854. In the spring of 1855 he returned to the states, stopping for a time in Marion county, Iowa. In the winter he returned to his old home in Henderson county, Ill., and January 3, 1856, was united in marriage to Miss Frances C. Davis. They settled in Marion county on a farm, where they remained many years. Mr. Strahan was a successful farmer, buying, feeding and selling stock. In 1870 they moved to Mills county, near Malvern, where Mr. Strahan, in company with John Evans, bought large tracts of land, improving and selling farms, and dealing in and feeding cattle and other stock. In 1873 Mr. Strahan, with others, laid out that part of Malvern known as Strahan's addition. In 1875 he was one of the men who established the First National bank of Malvern, of which he was elected president,

dent, and still holds that position. He is also president of the private banking house of Strahan & Christy in the same town. He is also president of the First National bank of Wayne, Neb. In 1879 he narrowly escaped death in a terrible railroad accident. He was shipping, with others, eighteen cars of stock to St. Louis, and with six other men was in the caboose as the train was crossing the Missouri river on the high bridge at St. Charles. Hearing a frightful noise, Mr. Strahan sprang to the door and saw that a span of 300 feet of the great bridge had fallen, as the engine and one car had gone over. With great presence of mind he jumped for the ties when the car was within twenty feet of the

terrible abyss. An instant later the car went down carrying his six companions into the river. But one of them escaped instant death.

Five children were born to Mr. and Mrs. Strahan, two sons and three daughters. The oldest son, Frank, is vice-president of the First National bank of Wayne, Neb., and the other, Otis, is assistant cashier of the First National bank of Malvern. August 30, 1885, Mrs. Strahan, who had been in poor health for several years, died. In 1889 Mr. Strahan was married to Mrs. Mary Wheeler Gailford. Both are members of the First Baptist church of Malvern. Mr. Strahan's daughters, Lucia, Ella and Rossetta, are married and settled at Wayne, Neb.

GARFIELD, GEORGE SELWYN, a prominent lawyer of northwestern Iowa, lives at Humboldt, where he located in September, 1880, with seven books, $15 worth of furniture, and no money. Mr. Garfield was the son of Benjamin Franklin Garfield, who was, in early manhood, a schoolteacher in New England, and afterward a lawyer in Kane county, Ill., where George was born June 11, 1856. His parents were natives of Vermont, and returned there in the infancy of their child. His boyhood was spent in Windsor county, Vt., and Sullivan county, N. H., until he was 20 years old. Both father and mother were

of Puritan New England lineage, tracing back to the English emigrants who landed at Plymouth about 1640. Mr. Garfield's father was a veteran of the Mexican war and also served in the Eighth Illinois cavalry in the civil war. He was one of the California "forty-niners," and spent several years in the gold mines in that state, although he never accumulated much of the precious metal. Until he was 15 years of age, the only school that George S. Garfield attended was the rural district school, and that for only about three months in the year. Having lost both his parents before he was sixteen, he struggled along, working on farms in the summer and occasionally teaching a dis-

trict school in the winter, until he was 20 years old. His meager earnings meanwhile were spent pursuing a course of study in the State Normal school at Randolph, Vt., where he graduated. In 1876 Mr. Garfield came to Winneshiek county, Iowa; stopped with relatives and spent two years teaching school, and reading law during vacations and winter evenings. For one year he was principal of the public school at Concord, Pa. Afterwards he returned to Iowa and entered the law department of the State university, graduating with the degree of LL. B. in 1880. With a class-mate, Charles A. Edwards, also a New Englander, and a young man of unusual talent, he located at Humboldt for the practice of law. Failing health compelled Mr. Edwards to retire to his former home in New Hampshire, where he soon after died. Mr Garfield continued the business, and with steady application to the study of his profession, combined with the sacred regard for his promises and his business standing, he has built up an excellent practice and established himself firmly with the people of the county. There is no man in that vicinity who enjoys a higher reputation for truth and veracity and courageous devotion to principle than does Mr. Garfield. He has made honesty pay. He has been steadily allied with the republican party, although seeking no political prominence or preference, except in 1894, when he was a candidate for district judge. He has devoted his time and attention to the duties of his profession rather than the political field, and has no taste or tact for prevailing political methods or the workings of any machine. He has now served his eighth year as president of the school board of Humboldt, during which time he was active in the movement for a new schoolhouse, and served upon the committee to select plans and build the edifice, which is one of the best in that part of the state. He has no membership in any secret society. Mr. Garfield is an active member of the Unitarian church and served for ten years as a member of the board of trustees and secretary of the Unity church in Humboldt, which is one of the strongest societies in the state. He has written a history of that church for the State Historical society, and it is on file in the historical department in the state house. In 1891 he was president of the Iowa association of Unitarian and other independent churches.

Mr. Garfield was married July 1, 1884,

to Mary E. White, a daughter of Greenlief B. White, the leading merchant of Humboldt. Two sons, Clement White Garfield, born March 18, 1891, and Theodore Greenlief Garfield, born November 12, 1894, have come to them. Both Mr. and Mrs. Garfield have marked literary ability and have taken a leading part in the literary clubs in this little "Athens of Iowa," as it is often called.

DAYTON, HON. HENRY, senior partner of the law firm of Dayton & Dayton, Waukon, Iowa, was born September 30, 1836, on his father's farm in Saratoga county, N. Y., near Hadley postoffice. His parents were Telem and Lucinda (Fletcher) Dayton. His ancestry is clearly English. In English history the name is preserved by the "Mannor of Deighton," as early as A. D. 1273. The Deightons or Dightons, came to America about 1639. The spelling of the name, as at present, is a product of early days, as in very early history the "gh" is dropped and later the present spelling seems to have been adopted generally. "Deighton Kirk" is one of the oldest church buildings in England. The ancestral name graces such positions in England as lieutenant-general of India; burgess of Hertfordshire; keeper of the great seal of England, and many other prominent positions. David Dayton, the grandfather of our subject, was a son of Henry Dayton, of Long Island, where he was born March 9, 1766. During his early manhood he moved to Saratoga county, N. Y., near Hadley postoffice, where he established a home, and married Cloe Skiff December 29, 1789. They had born to them on this farm, eleven children, of which Telem, the father of Henry, was the fifth, and was born August 21, 1797. Telem lived on the old homestead till he was 50 years of age, and then moved two miles farther up the Hudson river and continued farming. He married Lucinda Fletcher, a daughter of Peter and Sarah (Piper) Fletcher, January 10, 1821. She was born in Alstead, N. H., March 13, 1794. The Fletcher family is one of the oldest in America, and came to Concord, Mass., in 1630, where Peter died in 1677, being a very wealthy and influential man. Telem was a democrat, and most of the family continued in that political faith. Henry Dayton received his first schooling in his native country. When 19 years of age he entered Fort Edward (N. Y.) Collegiate institute, and continued till a

34

scientific course was completed. Six months at the New York Conference seminary, soon after, completed his schooling. He taught his first school at Creek Center, N. Y., when 20 years old. He came to Allamakee county in 1857, and taught school at Hardin that winter. In the spring he went to Batesville, Ark., and read law for three years with Byres & Company. Returned to Iowa in 1861 and read law with W. V. Burdick, at Decorah, and was admitted to practice in Howard county the same November. For eight years Mr. Dayton taught school at Hardin, Lansing and Decorah, and acted as deputy

surveyor to H. O. Dayton, surveyor of Allamakee county.

The present firm of Dayton & Dayton was formed in 1873, in Waukon, of which John F. Dayton was junior member. Mr. Dayton was married at Waukon, Iowa, May 26, 1874, to Mary M. Wilcox, daughter of Cortes and Rebecca (Palmer) Wilcox. The children born to this union are, Harry Lewis, born January 15, 1875, and Ruby Laura, born February 11, 1878. Harry is practicing law, and Ruby is attending school at Mt. Vernon. Mr. Dayton is a democrat and has been greatly honored politically by his party. He was two years county surveyor; for eight years the board of supervisors appointed him as its attorney When the office was made elective he was elected county attorney, and held the office for six years. He was elected to represent his district in the Fourteenth and Fifteenth General Assemblies, and no one in those two bodies did more honest and conscientious work.

DAYTON, JOHN FRANKLIN, was born at Hadley, Saratoga county, N. Y., on the 10th day of January, 1849. His parents were Dr. Simon N. and Lydia (Houghton) Dayton. His ancestors were of old New

England stock, a detailed statement of the Dayton family being given in the biography of Henry Dayton, in this work.

Nathaniel Houghton, one of his great-grandfathers on the maternal side, was a native of Massachusetts, and removing to Vermont, became a captain in the continental service, and was a member of the victorious army of General Gates. William Mitchell, his other maternal grandfather, was an officer in the invading army of Burgoyne, and taken captive in the surrender at Saratoga; taught school in the vicinity, married, and became a citizen of the United States.

The parents of Mr. Dayton removed to Saratoga Springs in 1850, where his father

was engaged in the practice of medicine until 1858, when the family removed to Rockford, Ill. Mr. Dayton attended the public schools of Rockford, graduating therefrom in 1867, and taught school while preparing for college. He attended Beloit college for two years, and in 1871 began the study of law in the offices of Messrs. Brown & Taylor, of Rockford. In 1873 he came to Waukon, Iowa, and was admitted to practice, and formed with Henry Dayton the firm of Dayton & Dayton, which has since been continued.

October 13, 1875, he married Miss Laura Hewitt, of Rockford, Ill.

Mr. Dayton was elected as the first mayor of Waukon, Iowa, upon its incorporation, and served three terms in that capacity. He was the representative of Allamakee county in the Twenty-second, Twenty-third and Twenty-fourth General Assemblies, and took an active part in the legislation of the Twenty-second with reference to corporate control. He was the chairman of the committee upon railroads and commerce in the Twenty-third General Assembly, and the nominee of the democratic party for the speakership of the Twenty-fourth. He was also the candidate of the democratic party for the office of district judge of the Thirteenth judicial district, in the election of 1894, but was defeated by the great republican vote of that year. In 1897 his name was presented to the democratic state convention by the delegates of the Fourth congressional district, as their choice for the nomination for governor, and he received a large vote in the convention.

In addition to the active practice of his profession, Mr. Dayton carries on one of the largest nurseries and fruit farms in the northwest; he is particularly interested in the growth of small fruits, which are shipped to many distant points in Iowa, Minnesota and Dakota. He keeps constantly in his employ a large force of assistants, and in the time of berry-picking a small army of pickers is marshaled, making the enterprise of great value to the community. Mr. Dayton makes a special study of new varieties of fruits, and experiments largely with all recent introductions, with the purpose to select those kinds which are particularly valuable for cultivation in Iowa and in the northwest, and deals largely in the plants and trees which he finds adapted to our trying climate. This experiment station is entirely his private enterprise, and is conducted without state or government aid, and promises to be of great advantage to the citizens of the community.

MAXWELL DR. THOMAS JEFFERSON, professor of surgery and surgical clinics in the Keokuk Medical college, is one of the oldest practitioners and earliest settlers of Iowa. He was born in New Athens, Harrison county, Ohio, March 6, 1837, and came with his parents to Iowa in the spring of 1844. His father, John Maxwell, was a native of West Virginia, and came to Ohio in 1804, where he was married to Jane Orr, daughter of Robert Orr, who came to America in 1795 from County Tyrone, Ireland. John Maxwell was a wheelwright, and in 1842 sought a home still farther toward the frontier. He visited the territory of Iowa, and was present at Agency City when the treaty was concluded with the Sacs and Foxes for the purchase of the western part of the territory. Black Hawk's two sons, and Chief Keokuk, with 2,900 Indians, were present. The territory pleased Mr. Maxwell so much that he made immediate arrangements to move thither, and on the last day of April, 1844, with his wife, five daughters and one son, Thomas J., traveled by water to Burlington, where they landed May 14th, and proceeded across the prairie by team to Crawfordsville, Washington county, then a village of six houses. The country was then in all its virgin beauty, and herds of deer were seen feeding on the prairie along the way. The boy of the family had two or three terms of school in a log schoolhouse in Ohio, and afterwards in the district school in Iowa, and at the age of 17 he attended an academy in Crawfordsville. Afterwards he taught school and found it an even better discipline, out of which he learned more than he did when he went to school himself. He was not without experience on the farm, and his first earnings were from working twelve to fourteen hours a day dropping corn at 25 cents a day. For a time he clerked in a general merchandise store in Crawfordsville, where hogs and produce were bartered for goods, the hogs being sold by the farmers at $1.50 per cwt., and paid for in wildcat money that was gotten rid of as soon as possible.

In the spring of 1858 young Maxwell began the study of medicine with Dr. J. D. Miles. He entered the medical department of the State university, then located in Keokuk, and took two courses of sixteen

weeks each, graduating February 22, 1861. Nearly all of his class of thirty-two at once went into the army, being about equally divided between the north and the south. Dr. Maxwell was commissioned assistant surgeon of the Third Iowa cavalry, January 7, 1863, and was present at the surrender of Vicksburg, where he was in charge of a general hospital for cavalry in that vicinity, having at one time 369 patients under his care. The regiment having been divided, (part under Col. H. C. Colwell, part under Colonel Bussey), was reunited in Little Rock, Ark., and was in the campaign around Memphis, Tenn.,

and Louisville, Ky., from there to Eastport, and assisted in the capture of Selma, Ala., having several engagements with Gen. N. B. Forrest. Dr. Maxwell was left in care of the wounded of both union and confederates, quite a number having been captured at Planter's Station. Gen. N. B. Forrest, after having been driven from Selma, came to the hospital and took possession. Dr. Maxwell was therefore a prisoner for a few hours in the hands of that noted rebel general. He took part in the assault and capture of Columbus, Ga., April 16, 1865. Surgeon Maxwell was transferred to the One Hundred and Thirty-eighth United States Colored troops, as surgeon, at Atlanta and was mustered out

January 7, 1866. He resumed the practice of his profession in Washington, Iowa, but he removed that summer to Olena, Henderson county, Ill., where he practiced until 1878. He removed with his family to Keokuk in the spring of 1882, and three years later was elected to a position in the faculty in the College of Physicians and Surgeons. In the spring of 1890 he and other members of the faculty of that college organized the Keokuk Medical college, in which he occupied the chair of surgery and surgical clinics. He is a member of numerous medical societies in Iowa and Illinois, and in the nation, and is an elder in the United Presbyterian church.

Dr. Maxwell has always been a republican, and is a member of the G. A. R., and a member of the Loyal Legion. He was married in Crawfordsville, Iowa, October 30, 1866, to Elizabeth S. Riley, a native of Richmond, Jefferson county, Ohio. They have been blessed with six children, of whom three are living: Ralph S., born August 16, 1867, died April 16, 1868; Nellie G., born May 18, 1869, died August 16, 1872; John R., born July 16, 1871, now a practicing physician in Keokuk; Mabel Clare, born September 9, 1873, died in New Mexico September 13, 1893; Maud B., born December 22, 1876; and Helen J., born September 27, 1879.

———

McDONALD, WILLIAM JOSEPH, principal of the Minden schools, is, as his name might lead one to suspect, of pure Irish descent. His father, who is a prosperous farmer of Buchanan county, came from Ireland in his early youth to Boston, Mass., where he obtained an education at night school, while working hard during the day to make a living. Unlike many young men he saved his wages, and in 1860 came to Iowa and bought eighty acres of land in Buchanan county. By hard work and saving habits he has now become the owner of a fine and well improved farm, and is regarded as a successful and substantial farmer. He was married in Chicago to Mary McCarthy, also of Irish parentage.

William was born on his father's farm near the village of Brandon, Buchanan county, November 26, 1871. His early education was rather limited; as, after reaching the age of 10 years, he was, like too many other farmer boys, compelled to remain out of school to work on the farm. He seemed to take little interest in securing an education until about the age of 18; after this he became interested in securing an education and made very rapid progress. After receiving his diploma in the common schools in 1891, he entered Tilford academy at Vinton, Iowa, with a firm resolve to complete the three years' course, but with less than $50 in money with which to do it. By teaching two terms and keeping up the regular school work at the same time, selling books through vacation and doing any work that would bring in a few dollars, he managed to complete his course in the academy in 1894 and came out free of debt. During his course Mr. McDonald

was an active member of the Philologion literary society and one of the strongest debaters in the school. Before graduating in 1894 he was elected assistant principal of the high school at Dysart, and served there one year very satisfactorily, being unanimously re-elected, at an advance in salary, for another year. But he received a better offer and went to Minden to take charge of the schools there, where he has given satisfaction to pupils and patrons, and been re-elected. For the past two years his spare moments have been devoted to the study of law, which he intends to take up as a life work. Although Mr. McDonald has taken no active part as yet in politics, he is a democrat. He is a member of the Catholic church and is unmarried.

Mr. McDonald has served several years in the Iowa National Guard, having been a member of Company G, located at Vinton.

RYAN, HON. DAVID, of Des Moines, served three terms as district judge in the Sixth judicial district. His father, Lewis S. Ryan, who died in Jasper county in 1860, was early in his life connected with a line of steamers on the Hudson river, plying between New York and Troy. "Bound out" when but a boy, he was compelled to work without remuneration until he had attained his majority, but from such an unpromising beginning in life we soon find him an indispensable employe of a rich navigation company on a good salary, and, later, the proprietor of a prosperous business in the city of New York. His inclinations were toward farm life, however, and he soon quit the city and purchased a farm in the neighborhood where he had been born and raised. A pleasing part of his history is that the old people to whom he had been "bound" spent their last days with him, for they were much attached to him, as was he to them. He was married twice. The first wife bore him one son, and the second, seven sons and four daughters. Judge Ryan was born of the second wife, whose maiden name was Barbara McKeachie, in Hebron, N. Y., on March 15, 1840. His parents moved to Iowa in 1857, and located on a farm in Jasper county. In early life they united with the Presbyterian church, in which faith they lived and died. The judge's early education was obtained in the district school. Like most country boys he was compelled to assist in the labors of the farm during the summer, and obtained his schooling during the winter months. During 1857, the farm, together with the work incident to "settling," required the united efforts of the family, and not much time was allowed for study, but the following year he was placed in the Wettenburgh Manual Labor college, of Jasper county, an institution which long ago passed out of existence. In 1859 he entered as a freshman in Central University of Iowa, where he continued his studies till the war broke out, when he enlisted. At the close of the war he returned and graduated in 1866. He then entered the Iowa Law school, from which he also graduated with degree, and immediately

entered upon the practice of his chosen profession, and was exactly twenty years so engaged when he was elected judge of the Sixth judicial district of Iowa. Mr. Ryan was married on July 23, 1869, to Miss H. M. Hurd, of Hebron, N. Y. They had been schoolmates together before he left for the west. To them were born three children, all of whom were educated at the Agricultural college at Ames, and the Iowa State university. The two sons, John B. and William L., graduated from the law department of the last named institution, with the class of '96, and on July 1st of that year formed a co-partnership with

Judge Wm. Phillips, and entered on the practice of law at Des Moines, under the firm name of Phillips, Ryan & Ryan. The judge himself is now a member of the firm under the same firm name. On June 30, 1896, the only daughter, Edith B., was united in marriage to Prof. E. E. Faville, a former student of the Agricultural college at Ames, but now located in Nova Scotia, where he has charge of the agricultural department of a college. Judge Ryan has a brilliant war record. He enlisted at Knoxville, Iowa, in a company then being raised, which became Company E of the Eighth regiment, Iowa infantry. On organization of the regiment he was promoted to first lieutenant, and a further promotion was declined at the request of the men of his company that he remain with them. He served with his command in every engagement until 1865. At Shiloh his regiment held a conspicuous place in the "Hornets' Nest" until late in the day, when they were taken prisoners. He was confined in the prisons of Montgomery and Macon and was given his share of the hospitalities accorded to northern soldiers by the management of Libby prison. But at last an exchange was effected and the regiment was again reorganized, and soon thereafter was sent to take part in the siege of Vicksburg. He served with his regiment in the capacity of captain, having received promotion, until September, 1864, when, by special order, he was assigned to the command of the Second regiment of enrolled militia of Tennessee, in which he took rank as colonel. He served as colonel of this regiment until May 15, 1865, when, having been mustered out at Memphis, Tenn., he returned to his home in Jasper county. In the fall of that year he was elected a member of the Eleventh General Assembly, and represented his county in that body.

---

TYNER GEORGE W., late of Salem, was one of the early settlers of Henry county, and a successful farmer and business man, holding the responsible position at the time of his death, in 1896, of president of the Bank of Salem. He was a native of Indiana, where his parents were among the early pioneers. His father, Elijah Tyner, was born March 21, 1799, on Little river, Abbeyville district, S. C., and was the second son of Rev. William Tyner, a Baptist minister, who removed with his family to Kentucky in 1803, and three years later to the territory of Indiana, locating near where Brookville has since been built. He removed later to Decatur county, where he died. Elijah Tyner took a claim in Hancock county, Ind., at a time when the only roads were Indian trails, although he was not more than fifteen or twenty miles from Indianapolis. Here he kept a small stock of merchandise in a log cabin, and was a merchant all his life, a large part of which was spent on his original claim. At the time of his death, he was a man of wealth, owning over 1,000 acres of land in central Indiana, all in one piece. He was married three times, and George W. was the oldest of the third wife's seven children.

G. W. Tyner was born December 3, 1832, in Hancock county, Ind., near Morristown. Here he grew to manhood, and at the age of 22 came to McDonough county, Ill., where he commenced farming and stock raising. The next year he removed to Iowa, and was married October 17, 1855, to Mary Frances Bartlett, with whom he had become acquainted in Illinois. They settled immediately upon the farm in Henry county, which was their home for nearly forty years. After the death of his wife, in 1892, Mr. Tyner no longer cared to remain on the farm, and therefore moved to town and made his home with his sons in

Salem. Eight children were born to Mr. and Mrs. Tyner: William and John, who died in childhood; Elijah, who resides on the old homestead; Sarah C., wife of Dr. A. J. Rogers, of Hillsboro, Iowa; Melvin, a lawyer, at Pasadena, Cal.; Oliver, assistant cashier of the Bank of Salem; James, a clothier of that city; and Elbert, a farmer living near there.

Politically, Mr. Tyner was a republican, but was never an office seeker, having held only local offices. His interests were rather in his home and business than in quest of public honors. For a number of years he was treasurer of the Hillsboro and Salem District Fair association, which owed much of its success to his tireless efforts. During the winter of 1895, a few months before his death, he united with the Congregational church of Salem.

Mr. Tyner's death occurred August 19, 1896, after a tedious illness which he had endured with great patience. At the time of his death it was said of him: "He was a man whom we all loved and admired. In his dealings with his fellow men he was honest, and strived to keep the golden rule; as a neighbor, none could excel him; as a business man, he was a skillful manager, shrewd investor and a splendid financier. As a citizen, he was modest and retiring, leading a life of the utmost simplicity, abhorring anything affected. His greatest pleasures in life were to do acts of kindness for his family"

FELLOWS, HOMER HARRISON, of Wesley, a member of the law firm of Bonar & Fellows, of Wesley and Algona, is one of the self-made men who have had so large an influence in the making of Iowa a proud and substantial commonwealth. He was born April 27, 1864, in a log cabin on the bank of the Des Moines river, in Van Buren county. His father, W. M. V. B. Fellows, was one of the leading and influential farmers of the county. His mother's maiden name was Matilda A. Peterson. His father's family comprised eleven children, eight sons and three daughters, all living, honorable, industrious and successful in their various vocations. Mr. Fellows' ancestry in America dates back to the days of the Pilgrim fathers, the first, William Fellows, coming from England soon after the landing of the Mayflower. In the line of ancestry have been many men of eminence, intellectual, highly moral and patriotic citizens.

Mr. Fellows' early school days were spent in the district schools of Van Buren county. He attended the Keosauqua high school and longed for a college education. But his father denied financial aid, preferring to have his boys remain on the farm, for which work he considered a higher education unnecessary. When he was 19 years of age, the ambitious boy took the ordering of his life into his own hands and left home with the determination to have a college education. He began teaching in Mt. Zion, as principal of the school, at $40 per month, and in 1884 was able to enter the preparatory department of Iowa Wesleyan university at Mt. Pleasant. By his own efforts entirely, earning money by

teaching and by working on a farm in summer, he graduated in 1890 with the degree of A. B., and taking first rank in his class. The next year he became superintendent of Sac City schools, where he remained two years. He then entered the law department of the State university, from which he graduated in 1894 with the degree of LL. B., receiving from his alma mater the same year the degree of A. M. In the fall of 1894 the partnership of Bonar & Fellows was formed. Jesse L. Bonar was born in 1865 at Moundsville, Va., and was reared on a farm near Creston. He is a graduate of the collegiate department

of the State university with the degree of A. B., and was a classmate of Mr. Fellows in his law course. Their first location was at Algona in January, 1895. Soon after they established an office in Wesley, which is managed by Mr. Fellows, while Mr. Bonar has charge of the Algona office. They have been highly successful in business, their practice constantly growing and their reputation as a firm well and favorably established. In school both were members of McClain's Chapter of Phi Delta Phi, legal fraternity, and took high rank in their class. Mr. Fellows is a republican and was a candidate for the office of county attorney in 1897, and Mr. Bonar is a democrat, chairman of the democratic county committee of Kossuth county, which party he led to victory that fall. Mr. Fellows is a member of the Methodist church.

---

DEUR, CLEMENT HENRY, of Missouri Valley, has lived in Iowa the greater part of his life, and is now a leading lumber merchant and grain dealer of Harrison county. His father, Joseph Deur, was born in France February 22, 1830. He was a descendant of an old French family, his people coming from the vicinity of the fort of Belfort, near the Swiss frontier. His

father died when young Joseph was less than a year old, and his mother ten years later. At this early age he had to begin earning his living. He secured work in a screw factory in the village of Moulvilliard, and by the time he was 20 he had saved enough, through strict economy, to bring him to America. He located at Syracuse, N. Y., in 1850, with only $7 in cash, but he had plenty of courage and ambition, and soon made his way. He was married in 1855 to Janette Mohatt, a native of New York, but of French parentage. In 1860 they came to Iowa and settled on a farm in Pottawattamie county, which was their home for twenty-five years. In 1885 they

retired from the farm and moved to Missouri Valley, where they still reside. Joseph Deur served during the civil war as a private in the Thirteenth Iowa infantry.

C. H. Deur was born October 18, 1856, in Onondaga county, N. Y., but when he was 4 years old removed to Iowa with his parents, coming by way of St. Louis and Omaha on the Mississippi and Missouri rivers, the home they selected in Pottawattamie county being 200 miles from a railroad. The rudiments of his education were obtained by attendance at a little log schoolhouse five months in the year. He afterwards attended the Missouri Valley high school one term. He received much practical discipline on the farm, for he was trained to hard work at an early age, often hiring out to neighbors at 50 cents a day. In the spring of 1877, shortly before he became of age, his father secured him a position with L. M. Kellogg & Company, of Missouri Valley, dealers in lumber, coal, grain and lime. He began at a salary of $15 a month and board, which, within two years, was increased to $30. On May 1, 1880, his employer, Mr. Kellogg, gave him a half interest in the firm's business, and they have been associated together ever since. Mr. Deur now has principal charge of the business, and his excellent management is rewarded by a liberal patronage. In addition to his lumber and grain business, he is interested in several other enterprises. He is a director of the First National bank; secretary and principal stockholder of the electric light company; a shareholder in the Missouri Valley Land company. He is an extensive owner of real estate, and is interested in fruit growing, having recently set out over forty acres of apple trees on one of his several farms. He is public spirited, and always loyal to his home town. He has belonged to the volunteer fire department of the city since 1879.

Mr. Deur was a faithful member of the democratic party until the campaign of 1896, when he left its ranks on account of the silver platform adopted, and voted for William McKinley for president. He has not been an office seeker, but served four years on the city council, and was a delegate to the state convention at Des Moines in 1896. He belongs to the Roman Catholic church.

Mr. Deur was married January 21, 1885, to Miss Fannie Kellogg, a daughter of his partner. Four children have been born to them: Lorenzo Joseph, born December 22, 1886; Joanna Janette, born April 13, 1891; Mary Josephine, born December 6, 1893, and Clementine, born March 10, 1896. All are living except Joanna, who died August 17, 1893.

---

READ, WILLIAM LEWIS, is one of the superior attorneys of the particularly strong Polk county bar. He was born in Harrison county, Ohio, May 15, 1851. His father, Ambrose Read, was a farmer all his life, first in Ohio, where he was born February 22, 1822, and afterwards in Iowa, where he died in the city of Des Moines in 1884. He came to Iowa in the fall of 1861, locating on a farm in Scott county. There he resided until 1867, when he moved to Polk county, near Altoona, where he spent the greater part of his after life, engaged in agricultural pursuits. He was a man of more than ordinary ability, a man of thought, who looked into all questions for himself and in his own way. He may not have always been right, but he was always honest. In fact his moral faculties were highly developed, and dominated all his actions and mental processes. In religion, as in everything, he was fearless, and as a result clashed with the conventional dogmas and creeds of his day, especially in the strict construction placed upon them in those early iron-clad days of orthodoxy. He was a liberal thinker, and therefore may be classed as a liberalist in religion. He was a writer as well as a thinker, and very frequently gave to the public his thoughts in newspaper articles. Politically he was a republican, and during the days of slavery and nullification, and finally rebellion, he was deeply imbued with the belief of the righteousness of the doctrines of his party, upon the great questions of freedom and national unity. When, however, these subjects were settled, his liberal disposition asserted itself, and led him into the Greeley movement. From that time forward he was a liberalist in politics, adhering to Peter Cooper and other great liberal leaders.

W. L., as he is known in Des Moines, inherited his liberality, his keen sense of honor and strong mental faculties. From his mother, however, his inheritance was just as rich. Mary Ann Lewis represented, in both name and blood, the two notable families of Virginia, Morgan and Lewis, so well known in colonial days. These two families were very famous as rugged pioneers, patriots and Indian fighters.

Mr. Read attended the village school at Hopedale, Ohio, till he was 10 years old, came to Scott county, Iowa, in 1861, and went to country school, winter terms only, till 1867, when he came to Polk county, and during the years of 1867–68, attended high school in East Des Moines. During the years 1868–69–70 he attended school at Atalissa, Muscatine county, living with his uncle, during that time. In 1870–71 he attended high school at Davenport. During all this time he earned his expenses by work upon the farm, and by

teaching. In 1873 he entered the academical department of the State university, changed to the law department in 1874, and graduated from that department in 1875. He then located in Des Moines. An enviable success has crowned his efforts. He has the respect and confidence of the courts, and of the attorneys. In worldly goods he is well situated, with a lucrative practice, and ability for many years of hard work as a future endowment. He has for many years acted with the democratic party, and many times has had to decline the honor of nomination for office which the party would force upon him. He is a member of the Unitarian church, and the Masonic, Knights of Pythias and Elks organizations.

As a man he is courteous, popular and at all times a gentleman. He was married to Miss Juliet E. McMurray, of Des Moines, in 1882. Two children have been born to them: Ralph L., 16 years old, and Helen, 14 years old. In polished manners, gentlemanly conduct and the natural gift of making the world seem bright to those around him, W. L. Read has no superior in the city of Des Moines.

---

SCHMIDT, HARRY. Among all the arts none have advanced more during the last quarter of a century than that of photography. So perfect is the work of to-day,

so highly proficient must be the operator, that the photographer who is behind the times stands no show whatever in competition with the man who is up to date. The subject of this sketch is of the last named class. He began at the bottom and through close study of the best authorities possessed himself of a perfect theoretical knowledge of his art. To this was added the knowledge which comes of years of actual experience in the operating room, and the result is that he stands at the very head of the list of Iowa's noted artists.

Harry Schmidt was born April 24, 1865, in the city of New York. Here he attended

private German schools and later the public schools. At the age of 14 he entered a photograph gallery on the munificent salary of one dollar per week, where he remained for three years, then started west in search of more remunerative work. Arriving in Council Bluffs on March 10, 1883, he visited the different art studios in search of employment, but met with severe disappointment. Not wholly discouraged, he started in business for himself, on a small scale, of course, for his means were very limited. The people of that city were not slow to appreciate his work, however, and the business continued to prosper until now he has secured the reward which his conscientious efforts and close application to business deserve.

He is the son of Daniel Schmidt, who came to America when a boy, and earned name and fortune as a large contractor. He owns real estate interests in the city of New York, from the income of which he was enabled to retire and live comfortably in his remaining days. He is a native of Germany, as was his wife, whose maiden name was Anna Marie Saltsman.

Harry Schmidt was married in Council Bluffs, Iowa, November 30, 1895, to Miss Lillian M. Shepard, eldest daughter of Mr. and Mrs. S. S. Shepard, of the same city. They have one child: Helen Marie Schmidt.

---

BRUNSON, ASAHEL A., of the firm of Hoxie & Brunson, real estate and collection agents, of Algona, is a native of Vermont, having been born at North Hero, Grand Isle county, May 29, 1839. His father, Lewis Brunson, was of Scotch descent and his mother, Ruth Hazen, came of Irish ancestry, so that, in the subject of our sketch, the sturdy characteristics of the Scotch-Irish combination are well exemplified.

Brought up on a farm, there were implanted the habits of industry, which have served him well throughout a busy and successful life. At the breaking out of the civil war, he was just in the prime of a vigorous, young manhood, and promptly answered his country's call by enlisting in Company H, One Hundred and Sixth New York infantry, at Lawrenceville, St. Lawrence county, N. Y., in August, 1862. It is difficult for those of a later generation to realize that the great armies that fought the terrible battles of that epoch-making war were composed of just such young men—boys from 18 to 25; from the farms, from the workshops, from the schools and colleges they came; young, strong, courageous, bringing the most precious possession on earth, life itself, to lay upon the altar of their country.

This young man, just turned 23 years of age, faced death upon eleven hard-fought fields; those of Martinsburg, North Anna River, South Anna River, Manassas Gap, Mine Run, Wilderness, Spottsylvania Court House, Cold Harbor, Petersburgh, Manopia Junction, and Winchester, besides participating in many skirmishes. He served in the ranks, and as orderly sergeant until July 1, 1864, at Cold Harbor, when he was appointed first lieutenant, and took command of Company I, One Hundred and Sixth New York. His military career ended in February, 1865, when he was discharged on account of wounds received in action, September 19, 1864, at the battle of Winchester. He at once came to Iowa, settling first in Clayton county.

The following year, January 13, 1866, he was united in marriage to Miss Eudora Benjamin, and to them two children have been born, Willis J. and Glenford A. Brunson. Both are living and both are married.

In 1870 they removed to Kossuth county, where they have since made their home. The first two years he lived, as did many of the pioneers of our beautiful prairie state, in a sod house, teaching school winters and improving his homestead summers. In 1874 he was elected superintendent of the county schools, which office he held for four years. At the expiration of his second term as superintendent, he was appointed mail agent on the Chicago, Milwaukee & St. Paul railroad, in which place he remained until 1882, when he formed a partnership with T. L. Crose, to engage in the grocery business. In 1888 Mr. Brunson was elected clerk of the district court, serving two terms.

In 1892 he entered upon the real estate business, in which he is still engaged.

Mr. Brunson is a republican in politics, a Mason, a member of the James C. Taylor Post, G. A. R., and of the Modern Woodmen camp of Algona.

---

THOMAS, ZADOK WILLIS, a well-known lawyer and real estate man of Fort Dodge, is the son of Quaker parents, and inherits from them many of the staunch qualities that go to the making of a successful and honorable career. He was born in Columbiana county, Ohio, May 18, 1856, the native state also of his father and mother and grandparents, the latter having been pioneer settlers. His ancestors were of English and Welsh extraction, and several generations preceded him in America. Mr. Thomas came with his parents to Oskaloosa in the spring of 1865. His education was obtained in the public schools of Oskaloosa, and in a four-years' course at Penn college. Following his college course came a period of work as a teacher in the schools of Mahaska county for four years. He had early chosen for his life-work the profession of law, and as a first step to real estate business and probate law, he

studied abstracting in the office of Capt. C. P. Searle for one year. This was followed by a year's work in the law office of Maj. John F. Lacey, and in the fall of 1883 Mr. Thomas entered the law department of the State university. He was graduated from this school in the spring of 1884. Fort Dodge was chosen by him as a location for business, and a home, and here he began, in the fall of 1884, his successful career as a business man, engaging in his chosen work of real estate, abstract, loan and law business.

Mr. Thomas has well earned his reputation, among the citizens of Fort Dodge, as a man of ability and possessed of all the good qualities that give a man recognition among his fellows. In politics Mr. Thomas is a republican. His aspirations for official positions have not been great, believing as he does that the basis of true political worth should first be proved by one's works and worth as a resident citizen before aspiring to places of trust and power. Deeply interested in the welfare of young men who have, like himself, their own fortunes to make, his advice is to lay good foundations and then take advantage of every opportunity that presents itself.

Although a Quaker by birth, Mr. Thomas is a Methodist by adoption.

He was married in 1885 to Miss Alice Busby, a teacher of marked ability, and daughter of a prominent farmer in Mahaska county. Mr. and Mrs. Thomas have three children: Dana Ernest, born August 5, 1886; Lauren Hubert, born July 24, 1891, and Mildred Irene, born April 10, 1898.

---

VALENTINE, WILLIAM, was born May 6, 1843, at West Point, Tippecanoe county, Ind. His father, J. W. Valentine, was a farmer in easy circumstances, who was born in 1804 at Scotch Plains, N. J. He moved to Ohio when it was a very new country, where, on the 29th of February, 1829, he was married to Miss Rebecca Kinkennon. She was the daughter of James Kinkennon, a minister of the gospel, and a man of fine intellectual powers, having also an extensive knowledge of both law and medicine. J. W. Valentine and his family moved to Tippecanoe county, Ind., in 1836, where they lived until September, 1856, when Mr. Valentine died. Here the son, William, spent his boyhood days on his father's farm, acquiring such education only as the public schools afforded. In April, 1863, he came to Iowa, stopping with his brother who was keeping a hotel at Fontanelle, Adair county. At this time Adair county was very sparsely settled, most of the country being a vast stretch of wild prairie, upon which game was plentiful. He began farming in 1864, his sister keeping house for him. The next spring he purchased a four-mule team and ran a freight wagon between Omaha and Denver. The business was attended with danger from Indians, who sometimes swooped down on the trains, killing the drivers and running off the stock and other property. It was no uncommon sight to find dead bodies of Indians along the route where they had been killed by the freighters in defense of their lives and property. He

afterwards lived on a farm until 1874, when he moved into Atlantic, Cass county, Iowa. In 1876 he moved to Casey, Guthrie county, and there engaged in the lumber business. In 1888 he took in a nephew as partner and they opened a hardware and agricultural implement establishment in connection with the lumber business. In 1895 they built a fine brick building for the accommodation of their rapidly growing business, making one of the best establishments in western Iowa. In 1897 they purchased an implement house in Adair, Adair county, and are carrying on both establishments.

November 17, 1866, Mr. Valentine was united in marriage with Miss Naomi I. Taylor, daughter of Judge N. S. Taylor, of Fontanelle. Eight children have been born to them: Margaret N., born September 3, 1867; Hettie R., born May 30, 1870, died October 16, 1879; Mabel G., born September 10, 1872; John W., born July 23, 1875; Effie M., born December 14, 1877; Irene A., born June 7, 1880; Lucile E., born January 25, 1883, and Ethel C., born September 6, 1885. Mr. Valentine is not a member of any church, but with his family attends the Presbyterian. He is a republican, and belongs to the Masonic Fraternity, Blue Lodge, Casey Chapter, at Fontanelle.

SEEVERS, GEORGE W., of Oskaloosa, general counsel of the Iowa Central Railway company, came to Iowa when a boy, in 1853, and settled on a farm. He is the son of Robert and Ellen Bryan Seevers. He was born September 23, 1846, in

Coshocton county, Ohio. He received his education in the public and private schools of the state and in the University of Michigan, from which he graduated in 1865. His first business partnership was with Col. P. Gad Bryan in Indianola, Iowa, in the year 1868. In 1888 he removed to Oskaloosa and formed a partnership with Judge William H. Seevers after the latter had retired from the supreme bench. The partnership continued until the judge's death in 1894. George W. Seevers continued in the general practice until 1897, when he was appointed general counsel of the Iowa Central Railway company, which position he still holds. He acquired his position in his profession by constant, hard work, and by declining to be led away from it by side attractions. He determined to make the practice of law exclusively and solely his life work, and with a rich, natural, intelligent endowment his habits of industry have brought him distinguished success. He is an earnest republican and a close student of politics in the higher sense, but has never held an office, and

declares that he will not so long as he practices law. Mr. Seevers is regarded as one of the ablest lawyers in the state, and his practice demonstrates that this is the public estimate of his ability. He was married in February, 1868, to Mary L. Bryan. They have five children, four sons and one daughter.

EDGERS, EBEN BARTON, was born on his grandfather's farm near Brockville, Ontario, August 11, 1868, where his boyhood days were spent. He attended the schools of that place for several years, and afterwards went to the Newberry school. He took a course in the high school at Smith's Falls and finally graduated in the dental department of the University of Maryland, at Baltimore, in the class of 1892. When a boy Mr. Edgers had a hard struggle, having to earn his living and work his way through college without aid. As he began to acquire some knowledge of dentistry in the course of his studies, he utilized it during vacations by

practice. In this way he earned the means to defray his college expenses when the term began again, thus managing to finish the course and acquire a thorough knowledge of the profession he was to follow. Soon after graduating he opened his first office at Lyndonville, in Vermont, where he had previously studied in a dental office. He next moved to Tecumseh, Mich., and engaged in the practice of his profession.

He came to Iowa in April, 1893, and located at Waterloo. He associated himself with Dr. A. N. Ferris in the practice of dentistry, the partnership continuing until February, 1895, when Dr. Edgers opened an office for himself on the east side of the river. He is a member of the State society, the Northern Iowa Dental society, and the Black Hawk Dental society.

Dr. Edgers has literary tastes, and is one of the active members of the Fortnightly club of Waterloo, which is the leading literary club of that city. He is past chancellor of Helmet Lodge No. 89 of the Knights of Pythias of Waterloo. He is a member of the Congregational church and in politics votes the republican ticket. He was married June 16, 1895, to Miss Cora Belle Newton, daughter of George and Jane Newton.

---

FRANCIS, BRUCE, superintendent of the Montezuma public schools, is of German descent. Washington Francis, his father, came to Iowa when a boy, in the early 50's, from Darke county, Ohio. He spent several years in the Colorado mining regions, and also engaged in teaming on the plains. Returning to Iowa during the rebellion, he married Catherine Newman, and began the improvement of the farm in Madison county, where he still lives. Catherine Newman Francis removed with her parents from Indiana to Guthrie county, Iowa, when very young. Later, when the family moved to Nevada, she remained with an uncle, and in 1863 was married to Washington Francis.

Bruce Francis was born in Madison county, near Dexter, February 20, 1865. He attended the district school regularly until 12 years old, and afterwards worked on the farm during the busy season, and went to school in the winter until he was 19. At that time his teachers were usually mature men or women who were paid extra wages by subscription, and the schools were crowded during the winter with young men and women past school age. One morning while on his way to school he was met by a neighbor who jokingly asked him to go to Winterset. He accepted the invitation without any hesitation, and, upon arriving there, and finding a teachers' examination going on, he decided to remain

and take part; when he returned his eighteen miles on foot he was the proud possessor of a teacher's certificate.

He was not successful that season in securing a school, but the next summer a neighbor, being disappointed in securing a teacher, tendered him the place, which he retained for five terms. After spending some time at the Dexter Normal school he decided to attend the State Normal school, and entering, in 1888, he was permitted to graduate with the third year class in 1890, having taught in the meantime one term in the village of Hudson. After completing the course, he taught one year at Sheffield,

and the next year was elected principal of the Dexter schools. At the end of three years' work at Dexter he was granted a teacher's life diploma by the state board of examiners. Desiring to make further preparation, the following year he entered the State university, and was graduated after one year's study there in June, 1896. Mr. Francis married Miss Ella Flater, a graduate of the State Normal school, in 1892. They have three children: Dorothy, Helen and Harold. Mr. Francis made his own way through school, and his experiences have given him the greatest faith in the possibilities of young men of determination.

EATON, SENATOR WILLIAM, of Sidney, Fremont county, Iowa, was born October 9, 1849, near Denmark, in Lee county, Iowa. He is one of the many bright examples furnished in American history, of men who have by sheer force of character and dominating will power, risen above their surroundings and advantages. He descended from Plymouth Rock, his ancestors being the Eatons who landed with the Pilgrim fathers on that heroic spot, in 1620. William Eaton's father was Ansel Eaton, a native of Massachusetts, who as early as 1838 came to Iowa and settled in the colony in Lee county, near the old town of Denmark. Here he lived on a farm until the spring of 1852, when he went to California, where he died in September, 1853, and William, at the tender age of 4 years, was left to the care of a widowed mother, in very poor circumstances financially. His mother's maiden name was Elizabeth S. Rice, born at Templeton, Mass., in 1827. She came with her husband to Lee county in 1838, and died in Henry county in 1891. Like most of the old pioneer mothers, she was self-sacrificing for her children and always willing to do more than her duty, and carry more than her share of the burdens of those early days.

William attended the country schools of the period and afterwards studied at Denmark academy. He worked for his mother, however, until he was 21 years old, and only obtained such education as he could secure during winter terms of school. After he came of age, he attended academy, boarding with his mother and walking morning and evening the distance to Denmark, three miles. This was continued till he had finished a scientific course, graduating in June, 1872. In the meantime he was compelled to teach school a part of almost every year to meet academy and college expenses. In the same way he continued with his legal education, until he graduated from the State university at Iowa City, in June, 1874.

He located at Sidney, in Fremont county, Iowa, in the October following. Without friend or acquaintance, money or experience in his profession, he set out upon the battle of life. On such a foundation of self-dependence and self-reliance, it is not surprising that Mr. Eaton has been successful. He has been one of the leading lawyers of southwestern Iowa for twenty years. He has prospered financially, too, the American measure of success. He is a staunch republican and

has been active in republican work and counsels for many years. He was appointed by Governor Gear in the fall of 1880 to the office of district attorney of the Fifteenth judicial district of Iowa, to fill vacancy caused by the resignation of Maj. A. R. Anderson. He was county attorney for Fremont county four years, 1887 to 1890. Elected state senator of Seventh district (Page and Fremont counties) in the fall of 1893 and re-elected in the fall of 1897. As a member of the state senate, Mr. Eaton, as in all other relations, was found to be fully equal to the occasion and demands of the time. He is strong and

fearless in his work and opinions, and above all is honest and patriotic. He has served on good committees and was rarely absent from their meetings, and never shirked a duty or responsibility. His record as a legislator is that of a conservative, fair-minded man, earnestly desiring the best legislative action. Senator Eaton's work has thus far been characterized by independence and sagacity. He endorsed only those policies that commended themselves to his better judgment, regardless of the influence or "pull" of friends or politicians.

He is a consistent member of the Methodist Episcopal church. On August 4, 1874, he was married to Annie E. Grundy, of

Christian county, Ill., from which union there was born to them a son and a daughter, Elmer E., and Lillian Eaton.

HALL, ELMER ELSWORTH, is a native of the state of Iowa, having been born at Nashua, Chickasaw county, February 6, 1865. His father, Jacob D. Hall, was a native of the state of New York and one of the early settlers of this state, having moved to Nashua in 1856 and built the first frame house in the town. He was a carpenter and worked at his trade for a number of years, and with the savings of his labor

purchased and improved a small farm, on which he lived until 1878, when he moved to Dickinson county and purchased a half section farm near Milford, which he still owns. He retired a few years since and now lives in Milford. He married Anna M. Brooks.

Young Hall attended the country schools quite regularly until he was 10 years old, but after that time could attend only the winter terms, having to work on the farm during the remainder of the year. When about 21 he attended the village school one winter, and worked for his board, after which he commenced teaching country schools, but being ambitious, he was not satisfied with the salary, so quit teaching

and sought his fortune at railroading in North Dakota, when the St. Paul, Minneapolis & Manitoba railroad was being built west. He returned to this state in the fall of 1887, when he was offered, and accepted, a position as bookkeeper in the Commercial Savings bank of Milford at a small salary, but by close attention to business his salary was increased and he was advanced and elected assistant cashier in 1889. He held this position until May, 1891, when he was tendered the position of cashier of the Security State bank of Hartley, which he accepted. During the "panic" year of 1893 he reorganized the bank into the First National bank of Hartley, of which he is now the cashier and manager. It has a large and growing business. He is also vice-president and director of the Milford Savings bank and owns a number of farms in the vicinity of Hartley.

Mr. Hall was married to Miss Ella Inman, of Milford, October 12, 1892. They have one child, Carl Inman Hall. He has four brothers, two of whom are bank cashiers. Mr. Hall is a republican, first, last and all the time, and a leader in his party, but has held no important public office. He is a member of the Masonic Lodge at Hartley, of the Royal Arch at Sanborn and the Knights Templars at Cherokee.

CARDELL, WALTER W., was born in Poweshiek county, Iowa, December 16, 1860. His father was the Hon. Wilbur F. Cardell, member of the general assembly in 1873-74 from Guthrie county. His mother's maiden name was Jennie E. Baily. The Baily family were among the first settlers of Poweshiek county, locating there in 1855.

Mr. Cardell laid the foundation for his literary education while a student at Iowa college, located at Grinnell, and in the class of '82 was graduated from the Iowa university law department. Shortly thereafter he located in Perry, where he has practiced continually since, and hence has an extended business acquaintance over the central portion of the state. He is a successful lawyer, and has the business confidence of a large clientage. He practices in both the state and federal courts.

Like many another brilliant lawyer Mr. Cardell's first money was made by teaching school. He has been throughout his life an uncompromising republican, and at the Dallas county republican primaries in June, 1896, he was nominated without opposition for the office of county attorney. He has never aspired to public office, being content in his devotion to his professional interests and a firm believer in the cardinal principles that the office should seek the man, and it was without solicitation, and in truth without consultation, that he was

named as worthy of political preference by his party. Socially Mr. Cardell is very popular. His genial disposition and hospitality are known far outside the little city in which he lives. December 10, 1890, he was married to Miss Lola Manatt, of Brooklyn. As a result of that union they have one child—a boy.

The ancestors of Mr. Cardell can be traced back many centuries, and comprise not a few of the most brilliant and interesting characters of early times. Leaving England at a time when the colonies were yet young, the Cardells and the Bailys linked their fortunes with those struggling patriots, and throughout the final conflict, in which independence was won, played a conspicuous and daring part.

He is prominent in lodge circles, being especially active in the Knights of Pythias.

CROSSON, FRANCIS EMERY, county superintendent of schools of Taylor county, has by more than twenty years uninter-

35

rupted devotion to educational work, achieved a position of prominence and honor in his profession in the state, and especially in southwestern Iowa. He was born near Abingdon, Knox county, Illinois, December 20, 1857. His father, W. H. Crosson, was born in Clinton county, Ohio, and was a farmer in moderate circumstances. While yet a young man he came west and settled in Knox county, Illinois, where, in 1856, he was married to Acenith Vinsonhaler. She was a native of Highland county, Ohio, and was brought to Knox county, Illinois, by her parents when she was a young child. Mr. Crosson enlisted in the First Illinois cavalry in 1861 and was in active service until captured by General Price, in Lexington, and was paroled. After the war he followed farming in Illinois until 1873, when he removed with his family to Taylor county, Iowa, and lived there until his death, in 1894.

The public schools of Knox county, Illinois, and Taylor county, Iowa, with one year's work in the Bedford high school, prepared young Crosson for Oskaloosa college, where he spent one year, and

later attended Drake university, in Des Moines, one year. He was a member of the Athenian society in both these colleges, and took the class honors in oratory in Oskaloosa college. Mr. Crosson began to teach school in 1876, obtaining his first certificate from J. B. Owens. By this means he earned his way through college, and laid the foundation for his future professional success. With the exception of time spent in college, and one year in newspaper work, he has been engaged in school work since that time. In 1896 he was nominated for county superintendent by the republicans over four other candidates, and elected by a handsome majority. Two years later he was renominated without opposition and elected over the fusion candidate, running ahead of the state ticket. He has always been a republican, and an active one, and his election to the office was a recognition of his ability as an educator and his worth as a republican and good citizen. He has made a national reputation in the county superintendent's office, being always spoken of as an efficient and painstaking officer. He belongs to the Masonic and Pythian fraternities, and is a member of the First Christian church in Bedford. Mr. Crosson was married February 2, 1886, to Alice J. Daugherty. They have three children: Phillip, born April 14, 1887; Mary, born January 20, 1892, and Ellen, born September 15, 1894.

———

DE WOLF, MERTON E., of Laurens, one of the young men who, by their own efforts, have achieved notable business success in northwestern Iowa, was born in Cambria, Hillsdale county, Mich., July 23, 1867, and came to Iowa in 1889. His father, S. P. De Wolf, was in very moderate circumstances, and was unable to give his son the liberal education which he and his wife, whose maiden name was Martha J. Frink, would have liked. Mrs. De Wolf was a very intelligent woman of good impulses, who encouraged her son to educate himself. He came of good family on his father's side, too, for his paternal great-grandfather was a Frenchman, who came to America and served as a captain during the revolutionary war. Attending the public schools in Cambria village till he was 14 years old, an uncle invited him to his home in Hillsdale, where he attended the high school. He completed the freshman year in Hillsdale college, and always won the highest marks in mathematics. During the time he attended high school and college he worked on a farm and walked two miles to school. He earned his own way by teaching school and working on the farm.

In 1889 Mr. De Wolf came to Iowa, believing that the state offered the best opportunities for young men dependent upon their own resources. He went first to Rock Valley, where he fell to work at anything he could do. For four months he was employed as a grain buyer and then went to Hull as bookkeeper in the State bank. Seven months later he was made assistant cashier of the State bank of Rock Valley, where he remained for eighteen months. From there he was called to Marathon to be cashier of the

Marathon Savings bank. At the end of three and a half years he retired from the bank and in partnership with A. J. Wilson, president of the bank, removed to Laurens and engaged in the grain business. The firm now operates two elevators, one in Laurens and one in Havelock, and is erecting four new elevators on the new extension of the Chicago, Milwaukee & St. Paul, between Fonda and Spencer.

Mr. De Wolf has attained political prominence by his activity as a republican, having been engaged in campaign speaking for a number of years, beginning with the campaign of 1896. In 1897 he was nominated and elected to represent the

counties of Pocahontas and Humboldt in the lower house of the legislature, where he made a consistent record for independence of thought and action, and it was said of him that he always had the courage to array himself on the side he believed to be right, regardless of what influences such action might offend. In short, he was an honest member and was not afraid to live up to his principles. As this volume goes to press (July, 1899) he is among the leading candidates for speaker of the house in the Twenty-eighth General Assembly, as a second term is conceded to him.

In 1891 Mr. De Wolf was married in Hillsdale, Mich., to Elizabeth Prentice, a high school classmate. They have three children living: Maris, born July 27, 1892; Hester, born November 9, 1893, and Mabel, born August 27, 1895. Prentice Wilson, another son, died March 2, 1899, aged 14 months. Mr. De Wolf is a member of the Masonic fraternity and customarily attends the Methodist church.

HAMILTON, WILLIAM EDGAR, editor and publisher of the Odebolt *Chronicle*, is one of the well known figures in Iowa journalism. He is a grandson of William Hamilton, who served in the war of 1812 as colonel of a Pennsylvania regiment, and was afterward a brigadier-general of the militia, in the same state, for many years. The Hamiltons were natives of Scotland, and afterwards lived in the north of Ireland, whence they came to America just before the revolutionary war, and settled in Cumberland county, Pa. Gen. William Hamilton was one of the pioneers of Mercer county, Pa., and one of the prominent figures of western Pennsylvania in his day. He was the father of nine children, John Hamilton, the father of the subject of this sketch, being the second child born to him. John Hamilton was born in Mercer county, Pa., in 1816, and died in Sharon, Pa., in 1872. He learned the trade of a plasterer in early life, and afterwards farmed and worked at his trade alternately. He was register and recorder of Mercer county from 1854 to 1857, and was a man of more than ordinary ability and information. Ann Powell Stroud was the maiden name of John Hamilton's wife. She was born in Montgomery county, Pa., in 1827, and was the daughter of William Stroud, who was of Quaker descent. She is still living in Sharon. March 13, 1857, William E. Hamilton was born in Mercer, Pa. When he was seven years old his parents moved to a farm near Mercer, and the boy's first schooling was in the country school near his home. At the age of 12 he received better advantages in the city schools of Sharon, to which place the family then moved. For three years he was happily busy with his books, hoping, as does every bright ambitious boy, that he might be able to finish his school work and add thereto a college course. But when he reached his sixteenth year he experienced a great loss in the death of his father, and college hopes and plans were, perforce, given up. He went bravely to work, however, to take care of himself, and his first situation was in a stove and

tinware store, where he was employed for three months, in the summer of 1872, at a dollar a day, pretty good wages, in those days, for an inexperienced lad. In the fall of the same year he entered the employ of the Atlantic Iron works, in Sharon, as invoice clerk, and that he was a valued and trusted employe may be inferred from the fact that he remained with the same firm for eight years, being paymaster during the last four.

In the fall of 1880, Mr. Hamilton concluded to try his fortune in the west, and came to Iowa, locating first at Bloomfield, where he worked for two years on the

*Davis County Republican*, as local editor. In 1883 he went to Odebolt and found employment in the law and abstract office of W. A. Helsell, with whom he remained for four years. Desiring to again engage in the newspaper business he started, in 1887, the Odebolt *Chronicle*, which he has owned and edited since that date. In 1893 Mr. Hamilton compiled a guide to the World's fair called "The Time Saver," which was probably the most popular guide in use. He spent six months in Chicago and sold 150,000 copies of his little book, clearing a handsome profit. Mr. Hamilton's father was a war democrat and he was reared in the Douglas faith. In the campaign of 1880 he became convinced that the protective policy was the true one for American interests, and since that time he has been an ardent supporter of republican principles. He belongs to the Masonic and Knights of Pythias lodges, and is also a Woodman of the World and a Modern Woodman. He belongs to no church but is Unitarian in belief. January 18, 1894, he was married to Mrs. Mabel C. Coy, of Odebolt. He was recently appointed supervisor of census for the Eleventh congressional district of Iowa, the only office, elective or appointive, for which he ever applied.

———

GORRELL, Hon. J. R. Dr. Gorrell, who was a member of the state senate

from Jasper county in 1897, is his own biographer. Although the silken skein of humor runs through and through the doctor's story, the intent that much shall be read between the lines is quite evident:

In the beginning, I was born. The incident happened so long ago that I have quite forgotten it, but I have the fullest confidence in the statements of my mother, who has openly admitted being present on the occasion. My mother always had a good memory of some things, of which I am one.

I was always an object of special interest to my mother, because of my capacity for everything in reach. To tell the truth, I was a born sucker. As I was quite young at this time this frailty ought to be excusable, especially as I was at a disadvantage in beginning business for myself among entire strangers, who talked in a strange language.

Ohio has the honor of being my birthplace—the state that boasts the motherhood of other great men, also. When I was yet an infant I persuaded my parents to remove with me to a Hoosier wilderness, far from the maddening crowd, as it were. With 'possums for my playmates I grew up a genius, strong as Hercules and as handsome as Apollo. My picture is ample evidence of this, but even my face utterly fails to do me justice.

My extraordinary advantages of environment and exceptional beauty of form and feature determined my parents to prepare me for a ministerial career. I was accordingly sent to the Presbyterian college at Fort Wayne, where I soon absorbed the entire curriculum, which consisted of Doddridge's Rise and Progress of Religion in the Soul, Baxter's Saints' Rest and the Presbyterian Confession of Faith—all books of rare interest and unequaled humor.

Soon realizing the temptations of a theological career and my inability to resist the same, I determined to pursue the study of medicine. I graduated from the medical department of the University of Buffalo in 1859, good Dean Rochester kindly admitting that my class record was incompatible with my early associations in the Hoosier jungles.

From the spring of 1863 to the close of the "late unpleasantness," I was giving special attention to the One Hundred and Twenty-ninth Indiana regiment, as surgeon, my efforts resulting in the death or total disability of thirty-four per cent of the entire regiment. I happened to remain among the sixty-six per cent of the living.

After looking round for a congenial location for practice I settled in Jasper county, Iowa, where the good people have since kindly permitted me to remain. In 1892 I was sent to the national convention of republicans at Minneapolis to do what I could for Blaine and silver. My efforts in this direction resulted later in the election of Grover Cleveland. The next year I was sent to the state senate, the single gold standard contingent since petitioning in vain for my resignation.

My ancestral pedigree is traced with difficulty through the long vistas of the primeval past. I am the only one of the genus and species that ever became pre-eminent. If my name means anything to the paleontologist, it means that my ancestors must have cracked cocoanuts in the wilds of Borneo. Even the pronunciation of my name reveals a strong guttural sound and an orthographical resemblance to the names of the present denizens of that birthplace of genus who saunter around among their grinning neighbors dressed in a bobtail and a sickly smile.

I have the hereditary honor, through my mother, of being a lineal descendant of the Scottish hero, Sir William Wallace. As Sir William has been a long time dead, he is illy able to resent the above implied reflection of a common ancestry. The Tam O'Shanter inn, where the genial Robert Burns used to drink Scotch toddy and see serpents, is still a family heirloom and hereditament.

Everything that ever happened worth mentioning has occurred since I was born. My birth must have occurred under a lucky star. Taking into consideration the wonderful happenings and the date of their occurrence, it is evident that I must have lived for about sixty summers—as the old maid would say. Of course I could not be expected to remember all that has occurred. There was a set-back by a blunder of legislation in 1873, from which we have not yet recovered. It was done without my knowledge or consent. It continues against my will and in spite of my protest.

At one time in my life, I felt like leaving a monument to my memory, and I wrote a book. To be sure it would be published I paid for it myself. Its success has been indeed monumental. It made an awful pile, and still makes an awful pile. Good people, to console me, have said many lovely things about the book. They have said that it was a thrilling and dramatic war novel and one that would not make the world any worse for its having been printed, even should it chance to be read. Several have voluntarily told me that they read it entire without any disastrous results. It contains some opinions for which I am responsible, some truths for which the war was responsible, and some pathos for which the facts were responsible. All are tied together by a thread of my own weaving that would seem homespun to the critic looking for flaws, but old comrades seem to like it. I would not think of taking advantage of this opportunity of advertising it or I would tell you to send me fifty cents for a sample copy of "Sins Absolved." You will never get your sins absolved any cheaper.

Taking it all in all, I am proud of the record the world has made since I have assisted in its direction. It has become, for the first time, a decent place in which to live. Slavery has been forever abolished and material development has reached its climax. Electricity has been harnessed and space vanquished. Distance has been overcome and the human voice has been borne by unknown force to distant lands. Human action has been photographed and reproduced like a miniature puppet show. Photographs have been conveyed by wire. Gigantic telescopes have readily brought us to a realization of the stars. The spectroscope has demonstrated that some of the remote nebulæ are now being evolved into solar systems. Scientific men, generally, have accepted the hypothesis that the only difference between heat, light and electricity, consists in the length of the waves in the ether of space and that the sun is the great central dynamo of our solar system. Solid bodies have been penetrated by rays of wondrous light, and human ills, once hidden from the view, have been exposed to searching eyes. Chemistry has unlocked forces, analyzed elements, formed new compounds, traced new effects and made the science of medicine something more than the plaything of the ignorant and the slave of the superficial. The microscope has at last revealed the causes of disease. The measly microbe is no longer concealed and his comings and goings are mapped and platted for the information of the race.

Just to what extent I have been responsible for all this, I will leave the indulgent reader to determine, confident in the belief that impartial history will give even the devil his due.

---

OLSON, O. A., a prosperous clothing merchant of Forest City, was born in Winneshiek county, Iowa, November 11, 1860, the son of John S. and Anna Nelson Olson. They were farmers at that time, but for twenty-five years have been engaged in the mercantile business. Mr. J. S. Olson was a soldier in the union army, serving in Company K, Thirty-eighth Iowa. He and his wife were born in Norway and came to this country in 1850 and

1852. The family moved to Forest City in the year 1870, and the children received a common school education there. While yet a boy O. A. was put to work in his father's store and his first savings were the nickels he earned by running errands.

When he was 22 years old, in January, 1883, his father gave him a working interest in the store and the firm name was J. S. Olson & Son. The father sold his interest in the store to his son April 8, 1890, and two years later the latter sold the business and went into the real estate business with J. E. Howard, which partnership was dissolved in the summer of 1895. In September of that year the present business, Olson Bros. & Co., was started, Mr. Olson's brother, W. A. Olson, being a member of the firm. Mr. Olson, who has always been a republican, was elected mayor of Forest City in March, 1888, and in the great presidential campaign of 1896 he was chairman of the republican county committee. He belongs to the Forest City Commercial club, the Masonic Lodge, Bethel Chapter No. 26, of Garner, St. Elmo Commander ₹, Iowa Falls, El Kahir Temple, Cedar Rapids, Iowa, and to the Odd Fellows, Knights of Pythias and the Elks lodge, the latter in Mason City. He was married September 8, 1885, to Annette Carlburg, of Neenah, Wis. They have one son, Sylvan Leander, born

June 27, 1886. Mrs. Olson died July 10, 1889, after a long, lingering illness, of consumption.

——

McGAVREN, JAMES KIRKLAND, recently postmaster of Missouri Valley, and an ex-member of the house of representatives from Harrison county, was born in Hardin county, Ohio, December 19, 1846. His father, Robert McGavren, was of Scotch-Irish descent, and a native of Pennsylvania. He was a farmer and a physician, and a very successful one. The mother's maiden name was Elizabeth Kirkland. She was born in Ohio, and was of English and Scotch descent.

James K. was brought to Iowa with his parents in 1850, when he was but 4 years old. They settled in Pottawattamie county, and in 1858 moved to Harrison county, where Mr. McGavren was educated in the public schools. He afterwards studied law, and was admitted to practice in April, 1869. He practiced law in Missouri Valley that summer, and in the fall removed to

Seward, Neb., being one of the first settlers of that town. He remained there three and one-half years and then returned to Missouri Valley and opened up a real estate and loan office. He was elected mayor of that city in 1877, and again in

1878 and 1879, but resigned in 1879. He was appointed a member of the board of supervisors of his county in 1879, and re-elected in 1882. In 1883 he was elected county auditor, and was re-elected to that office in 1885. In 1889 the people of his county showed their appreciation of his ability in the management of public affairs by electing him their representative in the legislature, where he served satisfactorily in the Twenty-third General Assembly. He was appointed postmaster of Missouri Valley, April 30, 1894, serving the term of four years.

Politically Mr. McGavren has always been a democrat. He is a prominent member of the Odd Fellows, Iowa Legion of Honor, Modern Woodmen, Woodmen of the World, and the Maccabees. He has been twice married; the first time to Elmira Henry, a native of Ohio. She died April 20, 1874, leaving one child, Elizabeth, now the wife of R. L. Linsley, of Missouri Valley. On January 27, 1876, he was married to Cynthia Deweese. She died October 31, 1889. By this marriage there were seven children, only two of whom are now living. Lawrence died at the age of 19 years, Lucille at 7 years of age, Hugh at 9 months of age, and the twins died in infancy. Lottie and Bruce are now living.

———

HARSHBARGER, HENRY CLAY, of Woodbine, was born March 5, 1840, at Rockport, Spencer county, Ind. His parents were among the pioneers of Iowa, and, when the boy was but 7 years old they came to Mahaska county, to the village of Fremont to locate. Mr. Harshbarger's boyhood was spent among the hardships and privations of early settlers. School facilities were poor and limited, and his life, up to 21, was passed upon the farm, with a few months of schooling during the winters. In 1856 he became a resident of Harrison county, where he still resides. In August, 1861, he enlisted in Company I, First Regiment Nebraska infantry. This was General Thayer's regiment. He went immediately south, and was in Fremont's march to Springfield, Mo., in the fall of '61. He was also in the battles of Ft. Henry, Ft. Donelson, Shiloh, Corinth, Cape Girardeau, Chalk Bluffs, and numerous skirmishes. At the end of three years he re-enlisted in the same regiment and was sent to the Platte valley to keep the overland stage route open. November 24, 1865, he was discharged for disability, at Ft.

Kearney, Neb. Upon his return home he engaged in farming for a year, but his health was so broken down by soldier life that he was obliged to discontinue the work. During 1867 and 1868, he served as county recorder of Harrison county, and was later elected county judge, and served a year as county auditor. He then engaged in mercantile pursuits at Woodbine for three years. Farming again attracted him and he returned to it once more, and still makes it his chief occupation. He owns a fine place of 560 acres near Woodbine, where his home is The raising of stock is the principal work to which he devotes himself. He also has a real estate office in

Woodbine, where he is justice of the peace, member of the school board and mayor of the town, all of which goes to prove his popularity and standing as a citizen of his town.

In politics Mr. Harshbarger is a republican. He is, and has been for five years, chairman of the republican county central committee. He is a member of the Methodist church. He has been married three times. His first wife was Miss Emily Mundy. They were married December 14, 1865. She died January 26, 1871. He was married again September 17, 1871, to Miss Nettie B. Edgerton. Her death occurred

April 5, 1891. In 1892 he married his present wife, Miss Lillian L. Welton. Of the first marriage there were three children: Virginia, born June 8, 1867; John E., born September 6, 1868; Charles C., born January 13, 1871. Of the second there were seven: Hope, December 24, 1872; Miller M., June 1, 1875; Harry S., September 11, 1880; Jesse J., March 22, 1883; Mary M., March 3, 1884; Edwin L., December 15, 1887; Henry C., March 28, 1891. Of the last marriage there are two children: Estella, born December 6, 1892, and Kate, January 6, 1897.

---

TSCHIRGI, MATTHEW, JR., of Dubuque, is the son of Matthew Tschirgi, for years prominent in the brewing business, now retired. The father was born in St. Gallen, Switzerland, and emigrated to the United States when 18 years of age. He was interested in the erection of the first brewery built in Iowa, known as Heeb's brewery, at Dubuque, and, being himself a practical brewer, as was his father before him, made the first brew in the new establishment. Although now past 73, he is still active and vigorous, and takes a keen interest in the business affairs of his children. One son, Arnold, he has established in the brewing business at Sheridan, Wyo., and George and Frank are fitted out with extensive improved ranches near that city. Two daughters, Catherine and Louise, are the wives of Francis Jaeger and J. Traut, respectively, prominent business men of Dubuque. John W. is employed in the Dubuque Malting company's brewery, an establishment which has more than $300,000 invested in its plant. The very latest improved and most expensive electrical, steam and refrigerator machinery is employed, and, of course, the person in charge must not only possess a scientific knowledge of the art of brewing, but must be familiar with every detail in the management of the immense concern. It is such a position of trust and responsibility that Mr. John W. Tschirgi is at present filling. The father has lived to see the great advancement which has marked the brewing business since the time when he ground the grain in a coffee mill and distributed the product of his brew to customers in person by wheelbarrow, and he has also watched, with no less pleasure, the phenomenal development of his adopted city and state in all other lines of manufacture and trade. The mother, whose maiden

name was Catherine Zollicoffer, was the eldest daughter of the late George Zollicoffer, a pioneer settler of Dubuque, well known and highly respected.

Matthew Tschirgi, Jr., was born in Dubuque, Iowa, November 28, 1850. When he had finished the common schools he entered the Michigan university, at Ann Arbor, and graduated therefrom as a civil engineer, in 1872. He began active work in his profession in Dubuque that same year, and was prominent in the surveying of the railroad from that city to Burlington. In 1873 he established a permanent office in Dubuque, and among other things

published a map of the city. He was elected county surveyor in 1875, and appointed city engineer in 1877, holding the last named position continuously until 1891, with the exception of the years 1888–9. His practice includes civil and sanitary engineering, plans for waterworks and sewer systems and bridge construction. Among the many engineering structures which he has designed may be mentioned the stone arch highway bridge at Elkader, Iowa; was engineer of the company which built the bridge spanning the Mississippi river at Dubuque, both of which stand as monuments to his engineering skill. Since 1893 he has acted as president and manager of the Dubuque Construction company. In politics he is a republican, in religion a Methodist. He is a member of the Knights of Pythias. He was married in 1880 to Miss Helene L. Schaad. They have four children: Martha Bernice, Harold Magnus, Charles Corrance, and Arthur Mason.

---

MARSH, CHARLES FRANKLIN, of Mt. Pleasant, is among the best known physicians and army surgeons of southeastern Iowa. He is a son of the late Dr. William Stockman Marsh, who was born January 23, 1817, on Nantucket Island, Mass., and died at Mt. Pleasant, March 1, 1896. He had followed his profession all his life, and he prescribed for patients within a few days of his death. The eldest son of a poorly paid itinerant minister, he had to help support the family, and hence his early educational advantages were quite limited. But with a determined purpose he spent his evenings in study, thus mastering the rudiments of the art. He afterwards studied with his brother-in-law, Dr. Freeman Knowles, later one of the professors of the medical department of the State university. He also attended lectures at the old McDowell college in St. Louis, and in 1854 graduated in medicine at Keokuk. He was married February 9, 1841, to Abigail Simpson Knowles, daughter of Capt. Amasa Knowles, at Hampden, Me. The Knowles family were early settlers at Plymouth, Mass., and trace their ancestors back to the days of Queen Elizabeth. Immediately after his marriage Dr. Marsh started west with his wife, stopping first at Macomb, Ill., and in 1842 located at Lowell, Henry county, Iowa, removing in 1845 to West Point, Lee county, and in 1855 to Mt. Pleasant, where he remained until his death, in 1896. Mrs. Marsh died in 1892. Dr. William Marsh was commissioned surgeon of the Twenty-fifth Iowa infantry, September 16, 1862, but was forced by broken health to resign February 7, 1863. While serving at Young's Point, La., he became so prostrated that he was obliged to crawl on his hands and knees while attending the sick and wounded.

Dr. C. F. Marsh was born January 6, 1842, at Macomb, Ill., and was the oldest of five children. He comes from a long line of New England ancestors. His great-grandfather, John Marsh, was a government agent to the Penobscot Indians, and his grandfather, William Marsh, was connected with the East Maine Methodist conference for over forty years. His grandmother, Susan Spooner Stockman, was born May 22, 1793. She was married to William Marsh, May 21, 1815, and died May 26, 1861. Her parents were Jacob and Susan (Spooner) Stockman. Her grandfather, Charles Spooner, was the son of Wing Spooner, who served as a captain of the militia during the revolution. This family descended from William Spooner, who came to the Plymouth settlement early in 1637 from Leyden, Holland, but originally from England.

Dr. Marsh began his education in the private school of P. P. Root, at West Point, Iowa, and in 1860 graduated from

the Iowa Wesleyan university with the degree of B. S. He immediately began the study of medicine in the State university, the medical department being then located at Keokuk. He was made assistant physician of Estes House hospital, at Keokuk, Iowa, just after the battle of Pittsburg Landing, in 1862, when but 20 years old, and was appointed hospital steward of the Twenty-fifth Iowa infantry in September, 1862. The following February he was promoted to the position of assistant surgeon of the regiment. He served as a surgeon during the entire remainder of the war, helping to establish a general hospital at Vicksburg, in conjunction with Surgeon Alexander Shaw, of the

Fourth Iowa, under orders of General Grant; also at Rome, Ga., with Surgeon G. F. French, superintendent of hospitals for the army of the Tennessee, and again at Atlanta. He was appointed surgeon of of the Twenty-fifth Iowa, November 15, 1864, and was the youngest officer with the rank of full surgeon in Sherman's army. He was with the army at Young's Point, La., Vicksburg and Chattanooga; at the battles of Lookout Mountain, Mission Ridge and Ringgold, at Woodville and Huntsville, Ala., Rome, Ga., Atlanta and Savannah, and accompanied his regiment on the famous march to the sea, and went with the army to Washington.

The doctor has followed his profession with gratifying success since the close of the war, making Mt. Pleasant his home most of the time. He graduated in 1869 from the medical department of the Michigan university, at Ann Arbor. He is a member of the Iowa State Medical society, the Des Moines Valley Medical association, and that of Pensacola, Fla. He was a delegate to the National Medical association in 1893, and a member of the board of surgeons for examination of pensioners at Mt. Pleasant, in 1874-5-6, and at various times since, including President Harrison's administration. He was for years a member of the board of insane commissioners for Henry county, and physical examiner for various life insurance companies.

Dr. Marsh has always been a republican, casting his first vote for Abraham Lincoln, in 1864. He is a member of the G. A. R., and the K. A. E. O., and a member of the Methodist Episcopal church. He was married May 12, 1870, to Mrs. Louise Mather Crawford, at Chicago. They have three children: Frank C., born March 16, 1871; Frederick William, September 10, 1873, and Laura Helen, December 4, 1875.

---

LAUB, HENRY CLAY, the well-known pioneer of Denison, is a native of the Keystone state, born in York, Pa., April 18, 1824. His father, William Laub, was born at Reading, Pa., and was at one time county treasurer of Adams county, of which the famous town of Gettysburg is the county seat. Henry Laub, a brother of William, was a midshipman in the navy under the command of the gallant Commodore Perry, and was killed in one of the naval battles on Lake Erie. When young Henry was less than a year old his parents

moved to Gettysburg and he lived in that town for about twelve years, attending school for about three months of each year when he became old enough. When about 12 years old his father died and Henry was from that time obliged to work very hard to assist in supporting the family. For several years he worked in the country and had very little chance to attend school. At the age of 19 he became a shoemaker and traveled from house to house working at his trade. All this time the young man was eagerly grasping every opportunity for the development of his mind, and often the cold gray of early morning, before time

for commencing work, would find him busily engaged with book and pencil. His evenings were always thus employed, indeed sometimes the active mind would be engaged in the pursuit of knowledge by the uncertain light of a tallow dip, until far into the night, when others, less eager to learn, were calm in the enjoyment of "nature's sweet restorer." This same habit of perseverance has characterized Mr. Laub's whole existence.

He was married February 14, 1848, to Miss Lydia Baer, of Frederick county, Md. In 1851 Mr. Laub and his wife came west and stopped at Muscatine, Iowa, where he secured a position as teacher in the public schools and also held the position of city clerk. After leaving Muscatine he spent a year in Cedar Rapids, and in 1855 went to Crawford county and settled on a farm near Denison and began breaking up virgin sod preparatory to tilling the soil. In about 1856 he became interested in the city of Denison, then in the embryo, and, desiring to widen the scope of his activity, erected, on the corner of what is now Main and Broadway streets, the first store building of Crawford county, and the first building of any kind in Denison,—a miniature affair 14x18, well stocked with goods hauled overland from Cedar Rapids. Mr. Laub is, in very truth, justly entitled to be designated "the father of the town." All went well in the new enterprise until the stock was exhausted and then an unexpected difficulty presented itself. The country was wild and sparsely settled, consequently the few customers who patronized Mr. Laub were as short of money as they were desperately in need of provisions. Mr. Laub was too kind-hearted to let them suffer, and with that magnanimity predominant in his nature, dealt out provisions with a generous hand until all were gone. Then, lacking the wherewith to purchase more, and finding it impossible to make collections, there was no alternative but to shut up shop; so, locking the door behind him, the proprietor passed out and returned to the farm, concluding for the time his career as a merchant. In 1858 he returned to Denison, having traded his farm for a store and hotel. Mr. Laub was a member of the first board of supervisors for the county, and by reason of special qualifications, served twelve successive years as county superintendent. He was also the second sheriff of that county; and for one term was county surveyor. To show their appreciation of this gentleman's services, the people of Crawford county elected him to the honorable position of representative, where he, for a term, rendered very satisfactory service. Later he made the senatorial canvass, but it was at a time when the liquor traffic influenced the issue, and, owing to his pronounced prohibitory proclivities, he suffered defeat.

During the war he served as government recruiting officer for this district, and also erected a stockade and fortress at Cherokee to protect the citizens from Indian ravages. He organized Company D, celebrated in history as the Northwestern Iowa brigade, of which he was first lieutenant and quartermaster.

Mr. Laub was for many years the lead-ing merchant of Denison, and in 1874 he took his clerks into partnership and himself retired from active management of the business. The new management was not satisfactory and in 1876 the firm had become insolvent, in debt to the amount of $78,000. With this great burden resting upon him Mr. Laub resumed management of the business and, having the confidence of the creditors, secured an extension of three years, at the end of which time he had paid every cent of the debt.

Politically, Mr. Laub has always acted with the republican party. He is a member of the Masonic order, Odd Fellows and Good Templar fraternities, and for the past forty two years has been connected with the Methodist Episcopal church, of which he has been one of the most active members and liberal supporters. Mr. and Mrs. Laub have eight children: William H., born June 24, 1855, who is engaged in the livery business at Denison; Eli C., born November 30, 1859, who is a merchant at Correctionville; Alice M., born August 25, 1849, now the wife of J. D. Ainsworth, and is editing Mr. Ainsworth's paper, *The Onawa Gazette;* Mettie E., born April 9, 1851, who is the wife of Hon. J. B. Romans, one of the leading merchants of Denison; Julia Catherine, born January 20, 1857, now the wife of W. T. Perkins, a lawyer of Bismarck, S. D.; Anna L., born March 31, 1862, now the wife of George Bartholomew, Chicago, Ill.; Lydia Bell, born November 27, 1864, who died at the age of 20 years, and Lillie M., born November 2, 1866, wife of C. F. Kuehnle, lawyer and banker of Denison.

---

JOHNSON, JULIUS LAWRENCE, cashier of the Northwestern bank at Ireton, is a young man whose business ability, both inherited and cultivated, will some day make him rank among the prominent business men of the state. He has already won a place which many a young man of his years has given up ever reaching. He has been trained to business from earliest years, for his father, Gilbert Johnson, was a successful lumber merchant, who had prospered in his line of business. The father died twenty-five years since. His mother was formerly Gertrude Klein, who is still living.

J. L. Johnson was born August 31, 1868, at Decorah, Iowa, where most of his early life was spent. His education was secured at the public schools, and was supplemented at an early period by lessons in actual business practice. After finishing the course in the public school he successfully managed a brickyard, a farm and a flouring mill. He removed to Ireton, his present location, in 1891, and was made cashier of the Northwestern bank at the time of its organization, in 1894, with G. W. Pitts as president. This position he still holds, and the bank, though of such recent origin, is doing a splendid business.

In politics, Mr. Johnson has always been a republican. He was married April 10, 1895, to Miss Alice P. Ross. They have two sons: Lyle Gilbert and Earl Drexel.

JOHNSTON, RUFUS SHERMAN, of Columbus City, has had a varied and successful career as farmer, merchant, banker and stock raiser. He was born in Louisa county, Iowa, October 4, 1864. His father, James Harvey Johnston, was a farmer and stock dealer of wide reputation, and at the time of his death, in 1890, owned hundreds of Louisa county's richest acres. He was one of the original stockholders in the Louisa County National bank, and held the office of director for many years previous to his death. He devoted himself to farming and stock raising almost exclusively, caring little for political preferment. He was born in Tennessee, as was his wife, Esther Orr Johnston. Both were of Scotch-Irish descent, and their ancestors were among the best families of that grand, old state. Although living in a slave state, the Johnstons and Orrs never owned a black man, for they were opposed to human slavery. James Harvey Johnston came to Iowa first in 1851, but was not favorably impressed with the country, and shortly returned to his native state. He resided in Washington county during his stay, and, on his return to Tennessee, drove the entire distance with a team. In 1856 his mind turned again into the beautiful prairies of the Hawkeye state, and, returning, he purchased land one mile west of Columbus City, which, with additions, still remains the property of the family.

R. S. Johnston attended the Columbus City public schools until the courses of study there were completed, then entered the Eastern Iowa Normal school, finishing the normal course in 1886. His time, when not in school, until 1891, was spent on the farm, and it was there his first money was earned. Although having been fortunate by birth, he was not reared in idleness, but

was early taught the importance of self-reliance and industry. He was elected a director of the Louisa County National bank in 1890, and has filled that responsible position to the present time. On the organization of the Louisa County Savings bank, he was elected director and vice-president, and so largely did his wise counsel contribute to the prosperity of these concerns that, in 1896, he was made president of the first named institution. His time was not wholly devoted to banking, however. In 1890 he engaged in the hardware, furniture and farm implement business, under the style of Amwyl & Johnston,

and the same was continued with success for five years. But the many enterprises with which he was connected drew so heavily upon his time that he was compelled to dispose of some of them, so decided to quit the store and spend more time on his stock farms.

He affiliates with the republican party, takes a lively interest in county and state politics, and is frequently chosen a delegate to county and state conventions. He represented the First district in the republican state convention of 1896, which sent delegates to the national convention at St. Louis, and was one of the committee on permanent organization.

He was married March 6, 1890, to Miss Loui Colton. They have two daughters: Helen, born February 6, 1891, and Edith, born June 13, 1894.

LEITH, DR. ALEXANDER R., of Wilton Junction, is a native of Iowa, although

of Scotch descent. His father, John P. Leith, left Leith, Scotland, in 1839 and settled in Cedar county, Iowa, when our state was an almost trackless prairie. He was a plain, outspoken and honest Scotchman, who soon won the respect and confidence of his neighbors. To other sterling qualities he added the thrift of a typical Scot, and soon secured a comfortable pioneer home, and married Maria Boydston, daughter of John Boydston, who was also a pioneer of Cedar county. They had ten children, five of whom died in childhood; the others were Mary M., John P., Margaret, George E., and Alexander R., the subject of this sketch, who was born in Sugar Creek township, Cedar county, on June 28, 1856. After studying in the public schools until 14 years old, he attended Wilton college for three years, taught school for several years, and attended Eastern Iowa Normal school. He then went to the State university and took a medical course, graduating in March,

1882. Soon after graduation, Dr. Leith located at Wilton Junction, where he has practiced since. He is a member of the Iowa State Medical society, Muscatine County Medical society, and local surgeon for the Chicago, Rock Island & Pacific railway. In politics he is a republican, and is president of the school board, mayor of Wilton, elected April 28, 1898, and president of Union bank.

In 1880 he married Louisa J. Parks. They have had two children: George G., aged 13 years, and Walter, who died at the age of 6 years.

RICHARDSON, NAPOLEON B., of Coggon, Linn county, is a prosperous banker of that town. His father, Aaron Richardson, came to Iowa in 1855, settling on a farm in Delaware county. His wife's maiden name was Maria E. Belding. Their son, Napoleon, was born July 6, 1857, in a small log house containing but one room, on the farm in Union township, and spent

his boyhood there. His early education was begun in the common schools and as he grew up he took a course in Lenox college in Hopkinton, and graduated from Baylies Business college in Dubuque in September, 1877. From boyhood he had been industrious and economical, saving his earnings. His first business venture was in a creamery which he carried on from June, 1881, with success. He developed fine business ability and so invested his earnings as to bring a good interest. In 1892 he took a subordinate position in a bank for the purpose of getting a thorough knowledge of the business. He worked as a clerk for about a year, developing a capacity for successful banking, so that before the year had expired he was promoted to cashier of the bank, a position which he continues to hold. March 21, 1883, he was married to Miss Flora J. McBride. Three children have been born to them, of which the oldest, Winifred, died in infancy. Florence M. was born July 25, 1891, and Anna, October 18, 1897.

Mr. Richardson has always been a republican and is not a member of any church. He has been successful in business and enjoys the confidence of the community in which he lives.

---

FURNAS, ELWOOD, was born February 22, 1840, in Montgomery county, Ohio. His father, Benjamin Furnas, was a noted advocate of temperance, whose death occurred in Louisa county, Iowa, in 1879. His great-great-grandfather, John Furnas, was born near Standing Stone Meeting House in England, and came to this country in 1763, settling in North Carolina. Among the more noted of his descendants may be mentioned ex-Gov. Robert Furnas, of Nebraska, Sarah Furnas Wells, M. D., author of "Ten Years' Travel Around the World," and Rev. W. Furnas, a noted physician, of Newton, Ohio.

Mr. Furnas' early education was one of the old log cabin kind, on the subscription plan. The desk at which he sat was an inverted slab, but Mr. Furnas thinks that the influence its rough surface afforded was for the good, in that it was not conducive to sleep during study hours. A college education was a luxury not so easily reached in Mr. Furnas' boyhood as now, although in many respects the common schools then were nearer to the required conditions of a college education than the common schools of to-day. Class honors were not recorded then, but Mr. Furnas at one time received a prize for his progress in grammar, a thing seldom bestowed upon a scholar in his days.

In 1857, together with his father, he located in Louisa county, upon a farm.

Later, Elwood Furnas and wife removed to Story county for the express purpose of securing a stock farm, and in that vicinity the family has ever since resided. Mr. Furnas is now one of the most prosperous farmers in Story county, and is authority upon all matters pertaining to agriculture. He holds a responsible position on the auditing committee of the Farmers' Fire and Lightning association, of Story county, and is vice-president of the same; is secretary of the Local Alliance, president of the Farmers' Progressive Reading circle, president of the Story County Farmers' institute, president of the National Farmers' alliance, secretary of the State Farm-

ers' Mutual Protective association, and is one of the honorary members of the Commercial Travelers' fair that was opened at Madison Square Garden, New York, December 16, 1896, by that honorable body, and is a valuable contributor to various agricultural periodicals throughout the United States.

The steps of advancement to the many positions of trust and honor held by Mr. Furnas were not attained without physical exertions and great mental research. He is not only a practical farmer, but is a student of political economy as well.

He was married February 10, 1859, to Miss Mary Elizabeth Sunderland, a descendant of Capt. Richard Sunderland, of revolutionary fame, and whose meritorious character is well known by all students of history. Mr. Furnas is a republican, and takes such active part in all campaigns as the duties of the many positions he fills will allow. He has held all the offices in the township in which he resides except school director and assessor. It is his belief that to be a successful farmer requires the strictest and most intelligent application of one's time and best energies, consequently matters political, however important, must be secondary to the avocation which, if properly pursued, yields up in abundance the staff of life.

---

LA FORCE, DR. DANIEL ALEXANDER, of Ottumwa, is a son of Daniel G. and Margaret W. Monroe La Force, of Woodford county, Ky.; was born May 17, 1837, in Lexington, Ind. He is now one of the best known physicians in southern Iowa, enjoying a large practice, and conducting an infirmary, where many patients are cared for. After a preparatory course in the Iowa Wesleyan university, he began to study medicine in 1857, at Ashland, Iowa, under the preceptorship of Drs. James W. La Force and Samuel M. Evans. He attended lectures at the College of Physicians and Surgeons, in Keokuk, graduating therefrom in 1863. In 1882 he took a post graduate course in the Chicago Medical college, now medical department of the Northwestern university. Dr. La Force practiced medicine in Keokuk, Iowa, one year as assistant surgeon to the United States general hospital, 1863; he was commissioned assistant surgeon of the Fifty-sixth Regiment United States Colored troops, 1864, and was promoted to be surgeon of the same, May 8, 1864, serving until September 15, 1866; was surgeon in charge of the United States general hospital at Helena, Ark., 1864–66, and was medical director of the eastern department of Arkansas, 1865–66; was United States pension examining surgeon from 1888 to 1892.

He was located, in the practice of medicine, at Mt. Pleasant, Iowa, 1866–68; at Burlington, 1868–71; at Agency City, 1871–84; and at Ottumwa since that time. Dr. La Force is a member of the American Medical association; of the Iowa State Medical society; of the Des Moines Valley Medical association; and of the Wapello County Medical society, of which latter he

was president in 1890. He is now president of the Hawkeye hospital, at Ottumwa. While he was surgeon in charge of quarantine in St. Louis, in 1866, during the epidemic of cholera, 700 cases were treated, an experience of great interest and scientific value, which is rarely given to a physician in this country. During his residence in Agency City, Dr. La Force was a member of the school board for ten years, and of the city council for eight years. He was mayor of the city of Ottumwa from 1893 to 1897, serving two terms. He is a republican, and was elected to the legislature from Wapello county in 1885, serving in

the house in the Twenty-first General Assembly, and reaching a position of influence and prominence. He is a member of the Masonic fraternity, the Knights Templars and the Mystic Shrine, Loyal Legion and Grand Army of the Republic.

Dr. La Force was married in 1866, to Miss Mahala J. Dudley, of Mt. Pleasant, daughter of Rev. Edward Dudley. Their children are: William Brooks, Ph. B., State University of Iowa, 1890; M. D., Chicago Medical college, 1891, who also took a course of lectures in the Royal University of Vienna, Austria, in 1893, and is now lecturer on pathology and director of microscopical laboratories in Keokuk Medical college; Burdette Dudley, Ph. G., Illinois College of Pharmacy, 1891; M. D.,

Rush Medical college, 1893, and in 1894 took special courses in eye and ear in Moorfield's Eye and Ear hospital, in London, England; Frank E., Ph B., State University of Iowa; and Charles R., student.

---

ADAIR, DR. LYMAN J., is the oldest son of Alfred and Martha P. Adair, who were of Scotch and English ancestry. Dr. Adair was born in Monroe county, N. Y., in 1840. His parents moved to Summit county, Ohio, in the spring of 1841. He grew up on the farm in Summit county, attending the public school during the

winter seasons. In 1858 he was engaged in teaching district school and attending Hiram college, until the spring of 1861, when he enlisted in the Nineteenth Ohio infantry. After being encamped at Cleveland and Zanesville, Ohio, for a short time he went with his regiment into West Virginia. During that campaign he was with his regiment in several skirmishes and battles, until the expiration of his term of three months' service, when he was discharged and went home to Summit county, and was engaged in teaching school till spring, when he re-enlisted in Company H, One Hundred and Fourth Ohio infantry, and went with his regiment to Kentucky, and was with the army that drove the confed-

erate general, Bragg, out of that state, remaining in Kentucky during the following winter and spring. He was with General Burnside on his march over the Cumberland mountains, and the capture of Knoxville, Tenn. His regiment saw hard service incident to the capture of Cumberland Gap, and later in the siege of Knoxville. General Schofield having assumed command of this army it was marched to join General Sherman at Buzzard's Roost, Ga., and took an active part in the long and tedious campaign before and after the capture of Atlanta. General Schofield and his army were then placed under the command of Gen. George H. Thomas, who was sent by General Sherman to confront the rebel general, Hood, who was advancing on a campaign in middle Tennessee. The base of operations for General Thomas' army being at Nashville, Tenn., his army was distributed along the line of railroad down as far as Pulaski, Tenn., to which place the brigade, to which the One Hundred and Fourth belonged, was sent, engaging in all the skirmishes and battles back to and including Nashville. After Hood was defeated and driven out of Tennessee, Schofield's army was sent to the coast of North Carolina. After the capture of Wilmington, the army rejoined Sherman at Goldsboro, and was with Sherman at the final surrender of Gen. Joe Johnston's army at Greensboro. After the close of the war, Dr. Adair was engaged in teaching, and studying medicine, graduating at Rush Medical college in 1870. After graduating he entered upon the practice of medicine at Manchester, Iowa, later on moving to Anamosa, Iowa, where he has been in continuous practice of his profession up to the present time. In October, 1870, he was married to Miss Sarah J. Porter, of Garnavillo, Iowa. Three children have been born to them, two of whom died in childhood. Fred Lyman, the youngest, was born in July, 1877, and graduated from the University of Minnesota with the class of '98.

Mrs. Adair is a daughter of Giles M. Porter, a brother of the late Noah Porter, of Yale college. Dr. Adair was physician of the state penitentiary for nineteen years. He is surgeon for the Chicago, Milwaukee & St. Paul, and the Chicago & Northwestern railroads. He is a member of the American Medical association, and the International Association of Railway Surgeons. He is a member of the Fred Steele Post No. 4 of the G. A. R.

HAMBLETON, ALBERT F. N., a prominent real estate, loan and insurance broker and examiner of titles, living in Oskaloosa, was born in Forest Home, Poweshiek county, Iowa, September 4, 1857. His father, Levi Hambleton, also a real estate and loan broker, and president of the Central Iowa Loan and Trust company, living in Oskaloosa, came to Iowa from Ohio in 1855, and settled in Poweshiek county, where he laid out the village site of Forest Home. He was engaged in the mercantile and stock business for over twenty years, and in the present business in Oskaloosa for the past eighteen years. His father was a strong anti-slavery man, belonging to the Friends' society, and aided actively in conducting the "underground railway" which carried so many slaves to freedom. He married Ann Hanna, an aunt of Marcus A. Hanna, chairman of the republican national committee in the campaign of 1896, and United States senator from Ohio. Our Mr. Hambleton's mother, whose maiden name was Mary H. Hall, is a native of Pennsylvania. Her ancestors were owners of a large tract of land, now that part of the city of Philadelphia known as Hestonville. She is a great-granddaughter of the well-known Judge Heston, of Philadelphia.

Albert F. N., spent his first school days in the district school during the days of slab benches, and when "lickin' and larnin'" were almost inseparable. At the age of 13 years he spent one year in the preparatory department of Iowa college, at Grinnell. A year later, he entered the high school in Oskaloosa, to which place he had removed with his parents. He entered the first freshman class in Penn college in 1873, that institution having been organized that year. On account of financial losses by fire, of his father, he gave up his college education in the sophomore year, and at the age of 17 entered into employment as a bookkeeper in a retail dry goods store in Oskaloosa, where he remained for three years. He invested his savings in a local building and loan association, and at the end of three years he entered a partnership with his brother, in the general merchandise, coal, grain and live stock business at Springville, Iowa. They did a very successful business for a period of seven years, when Albert sold out his interest and returned to Oskaloosa and engaged in the abstract business as examiner of titles, making a study of real estate law. He has been in the abstract, loan,

36

real estate and insurance business in Oskaloosa, from that time up to the present, with the exception of three and one-half years spent in like business in Des Moines, and six months in Chicago during the World's fair, looking after business there. He is at present treasurer of the Central Iowa Loan and Trust company of Oskaloosa, organized in 1878, and a member of the firm of Cowan & Hambleton, abstract, real estate, loan and insurance agents.

Mr. Hambleton has been a republican since becoming a voter, and has been actively connected with the work of his party as committeeman and delegate to

county and state conventions. He was city clerk and secretary of the public schools of Springville for several years. He united with the orthodox branch of the Friends' church, when 12 years of age, and has always been an active member of the church. He is a trustee of the Iowa Annual Meeting of Friends, and clerk of the representative or executive session of that body, and has acted as its railway secretary for three years. He is also a trustee of the Wells' fund, connected with the church, and has for a number of years been one of the board of trustees of Penn college, having acted as treasurer of that institution, and is now one of the endowment trustees. He was president of the

Oskaloosa Y. M. C. A., for a number of years, and secretary of the Mahaska County Sunday School association, of which he is the present treasurer. He is an earnest temperance worker and was very active during the campaign in 1882, in support of the prohibitory constitutional amendment, and was chosen as a member of the directory, and a delegate to the national convention of the American Anti-Saloon league, from Iowa Friends, at their last session.

Mr. Hambleton was married to Miss Josepha Roberts, September 3, 1879. She is a daughter of Dr. Rueben L. Roberts, now deceased, who was for several years United States Indian agent of the Shawnee tribe. They have one child living, Alma R., aged 6 years. A son died in infancy.

---

GRISWOLD, HENRY J., of Winthrop Buchanan county, who represented that county in the legislature for two sessions, was born in Janesville, Wis., November 13, 1858, and is a son of Harvey Griswold, of Fortsville, N. Y., and Mary E. Dillenbeck, of Janesville, Wis. His father died on Christmas day, 1883. The family came to Iowa when Henry was 5 years old and settled on a farm near Winthrop. His boyhood and youth were spent here, where he followed the usual life of a farmer's boy, attending the district school in winter time and working on the farm when his services were needed. At the age of 17, having passed a satisfactory examination, he began to teach school, and followed that vocation for about three years. Then for a short time he was engaged with a mercantile establishment, but this work did not agree with his health and he was obliged to seek outdoor employment. In the spring of 1882 he removed to Plankinton, S. D., and entered a half section of land. He erected the customary settler's "shack" and lived the independent and care-free life of a bachelor on his claim for about two years, greatly to the benefit of his health. During this time he took the census of the county and surveyed and divided the civil townships of the county into school districts and located the school districts in the county. He had previously acted as census enumerator in Iowa for the census of 1880. In the fall of 1883 he returned to Iowa and was married January 24, 1884, to Miss Marie J. Risk, of Winthrop. He at once engaged in the lumber and grain business in Winthrop, and has remained in business in that place ever

since, being now the proprietor of a large mercantile establishment. Mr. Griswold was unanimously nominated to the office of representative for Buchanan county by the republicans in 1893, and in 1895 he had no opposition for a second term. During his service in the legislature Mr. Griswold was chairman of the committee on mines and mining and served on several other equally, or more, important committees.

He was an industrious and unobtrusive member, belonging to the class who advance legitimate legislation without making show about it. He had a large influence in the house because he was considered a

reliable and conservative man who did not take a position on any question without careful consideration of its merits. Upon the organization of the house in 1896 Mr. Griswold was among the three or four men who were considered for the speakership. In the year 1897 he was a member of the state central committee. In his own county Mr. Griswold is known as a public-spirited and reliable business man; an active and influential republican and a true friend. For a number of years he has been a member of the First Congregational church, filling the position of trustee. He belongs to the Masonic order. Mr. and Mrs. Griswold have two children: Grace E., born November 15, 1884, and Dale A., born March 15, 1890.

BOUCHER, DR. FRANCIS HENRY, of Marshalltown, inherits his taste and talent for his medical profession from his father, James Henry Boucher, A. M., M. D., who settled in Iowa City in 1859 and attained high rank in his profession. He was principal of the Polytechnic college in Philadelphia, and when the war broke out was made assistant surgeon of the Thirteenth Iowa infantry. He was promoted to the rank of brigade surgeon, acting as medical director of the army of the Mississippi, and later became medical director of the army of the Tennessee. He was also medical director of the Seventeenth Army corps under Gen. James B. McPherson, of which the famous Crocker's Iowa brigade formed a part. He was commissioned colonel, and appointed by General Grant, who knew him personally and well, to be medical director of the department of Georgia and South Carolina, being the only surgeon from Iowa who attained that rank. When the war closed he became professor of anatomy in the medical department of the State University of Iowa. His early ancestors were French Huguenots, who were driven into Germany, and finally emigrated to America in the eighteenth century. A great-grandfather served for a time in the New York legislature. On his mother's side the family history goes back to the time of the revolutionary war, members of her family taking part with Mad Anthony Wayne in the storming of Stony Point.

Francis H. Boucher was born in Binghamton, N. Y., November 14, 1855. He attended the common schools in Iowa City, and was prepared for the university in McClain's academy. He entered the collegiate department of the Iowa State university, and later the medical department, where he attended lectures during the winter of 1874-75. He then spent two years in the Jefferson Medical college in Philadelphia and received from that college the degree of M. D. in 1877. For the better preparation for active practice, he took a special course in surgery, under Dr. J. Ewing Mears, and had special courses in obstetrics in the Philadelphia Lying-in institute, and in medicine in the wards of Blockley and Pennsylvania hospitals, two famous institutions. In 1893 he received post-graduate instruction in the Chicago polyclinic for post graduates. He began to practice when but 21 years of age in Clarksville, Iowa, and remained there three years, where he was local surgeon for the Bur-

lington, Cedar Rapids & Northern railway, examiner for several insurance companies, and was instrumental in establishing the local board of health, one of the first organized under the state law. He was appointed the first health officer. He is a charter member of the Butler County Medical society, and was at one time its secretary and president. He assisted in the formation of the Clarksville Library association, of which he was elected president. While located in Clarksville he became a member of the Odd Fellows Lodge, serving successively as its secretary and noble grand, and joined Marton Encampment No. 98. He was also here made a master Mason.

In 1880 he removed to Brooklyn, Iowa, where he married Miss S. Marian Judd, daughter of Rev. F. E. Judd, one of the pioneer clergymen of the Episcopal church in the state, and Isabella Page Judd, his wife. Mrs. Boucher is becoming prominent in newspaper circles as a special correspondent. She is a member of the Women's National Press association, and as a musician is noted for her execution of the works of the classical masters. By this union there have been born to Dr and Mrs. Boucher four sons: Forest Francis (deceased), Francis Emerson, Leonidas James, and James Henry. After five years of successful practice in Brooklyn he removed to Marshalltown, where, for nearly fourteen years, he has been engaged in active practice. He gives particular attention to surgery, especially that branch pertaining to the ear, nose and throat, and has invented several useful surgical instruments. He has successfully performed many capital operations in abdominal, thoracic and cranial surgery, as well as the more common capital operations on the extremities. His surgical, electrical and microscopical office outfit, to which he is constantly adding modern instruments, is most complete for any general surgical emergency, and he has one of the largest medical libraries in central Iowa. He is medical examiner for more than twenty life insurance companies and secret orders; he is local surgeon for the Iowa Central Railway company, and is a member of a number of medical societies and associations, among others the American Medical association, and International Association of Railway Surgeons, Iowa State Medical society, before which he has read papers pertaining to his profession. He is also a contributor to the leading medical journals of the country. He is prominent socially as well as professionally, and his time, such as can be spared from the many duties of his profession, is given to the furtherance of the best interests of his home city, of which he is health officer.

HATCH, EZRA KIDDER, the well-known banker of Central City, is a son of Luther Hatch, one of the first residents of Chicago, who located there in 1831, and who kept an Indian trading post at Naperville before the Black Hawk war. Mr. Hatch's ancestors were all of English descent, who came from England and settled in Massachusetts when it was an English colony. From there the families removed to New Hampshire, where they were prominent citizens and took an active interest in public affairs. His grandfathers, on both sides, held local town and county offices, and were members of the New Hampshire legislature.

Ezra was born in Lisle, Du Page county, Ill., February 3, 1841. His father was a farmer during this period, and the son attended the common schools of his neighborhood, and received from them such instruction as they afforded. When he reached the age of 11 his father died, and at the age of 15 his mother married again

and he had henceforth to shift for himself. Soon after this he came to Iowa and worked on a farm in Jones county at $8 per month and board. When farm work was slack in the winter he went to school, and when about 17 he was able to teach school himself. He then went to school at Oberlin, Ohio, for one year and took a business course. He continued working on a farm in summer and teaching school in winter, saving his money and investing it in land, until March, 1865, when he married Lavonia D. Jordan and settled on a farm of 160 acres. In 1868 he sold the farm and stock for a little over $5,000, and went

into the mercantile business at Central City. In 1884 he started the Bank of Central City, with which he is still connected. Mr. Hatch has been closely identified with all enterprises for the good of his town, and is a successful and conservative business man. He is president of the Central City Land and Improvement company, and manager of the stock, grain and lumber business. He has always been a republican, and has held several local offices at various times. He is a prominent Mason, and a member of the Free Will Baptist church.

They have five children: Laura Marilla, born January 4, 1868; Arabella Lavonia, born December 5, 1869; Calista Lydia, born

October 19, 1871; Lester Orin, born October 4, 1878; and Ellen Jordan, born November 16, 1880.

---

JACKSON, HON. ALBERT E. It is not often that a democrat can be elected to the legislature in Iowa, and the instances are very few wherein a candidate of that political faith has been chosen to represent a district which, ordinarily, is republican by a considerable majority, but that compliment was paid to Albert E. Jackson by the voters of Tama county in 1895. He was born in Wabash county, Ind., September 23, 1860. His parents were Andrew and Catherine Quick Jackson, both natives of Indiana. The father was born in Madison county, October 21, 1833. He came to Tama county, Iowa, in 1855, but removed to Missouri three years thereafter; thence to Indiana, and in 1861 returned to Tama county to reside permanently. He drove a mule team the entire distance from Indiana to Tama county, carrying his wife and three children, together with the few household goods in his possession. He reached his destination without a dollar in his pocket. He was successful as a farmer and stock breeder, having been prominently identified with the importation of improved stock since 1870, and is now rated commercially at $100,000. Grandfather Samuel Jackson was a native of North Carolina. Catherine Quick Jackson was born in 1832 and married Andrew Jackson in 1855. She was best known for her benevolence. Albert E. Jackson came to Iowa with his parents in 1861, and attended the common schools adjacent to his father's farm until the winter of 1876, at which time the family located near the city of Tama and he entered the high school there, graduating with class honors in 1879. He then matriculated for a three years' course in the Iowa State university, but was compelled to leave school because of failing health. While there he was a member of the Zetagathian Literary society, and ranked high in his class. After leaving the university he was engaged for a time as cashier of a construction company then building the Sioux City & Pacific railroad in Nebraska. Later he served a term as deputy county recorder of Tama county, after which he was employed with his father in the live stock trade, shipping cattle to supply western ranches. In December, 1885, he went to Colorado, where his father had a

large interest in a horse ranch and importing company, and while there received an appointment in the railway mail service on the run from Tama to Hawarden. In October, 1889, he formed a partnership with his father to engage in the banking business, and opened the Farmers and Merchants bank at Tama, of which concern he is the cashier and manager. He is also a member of the land, loan and investment company of Jackson & Carson; is city treasurer, treasurer of the school district of the city of Tama, and local representative of a number of fire, life and insurance companies and building and loan associa-

tions, and is interested in a couple of newspaper enterprises. He has been a democrat since old enough to vote. He was the candidate of his party for county superintendent of schools in 1885 and was defeated by but sixteen votes, the county at that time being strongly republican. He has been a member of the county central committee for a number of years, and its chairman. In 1895 he was nominated to represent the Fiftieth district in the general assembly, and was elected against a strong republican majority and over a very popular member of that body, who stood for re-election. As a legislator he was especially identified with the committees on banks and banking, school and text-books, private corporations and building and loan associations; on the last named committee being chairman of the sub-committee that formed the present law governing those organizations. He served through the special session for the revision of the code in 1896, and was re-elected to represent his district in 1897, receiving a largely increased majority. He was one of the two members of the minority party who were accorded a committee chairmanship with a clerk at the 1898 session, being chairman of the committee on federal relations, and was selected by the representatives of his party as chairman of the democratic caucus for the session. He is a member of the Masons and Knights of Pythias, and is supreme treasurer of the Ancient Order of the Red Cross, but is not united with any religious sect. He was married to Miss Mabel Bowen, of Marshalltown, daughter of Webster Bowen, a pioneer of Marshall county, December 21, 1886. They have four children: Helen Hunt, Marjorie, Eloise, and Paul Webster Jackson.

---

COLCLO, CROTON CORTICE, one of the editors of the *Carroll Sentinel*, has been for some years an influential democrat in northwestern Iowa, and at one time postmaster of Carroll. He was born November 2, 1852, in Findlay, Ohio. He was the son of J. H. Colclo, a farmer, and his wife, Hannah Jane Cretsinger. They were of the well-to-do middle class and were not known to fame. Their son was educated in the district school and afterwards completed the course in the high school in Carroll, Iowa. The family moved to Winterset, Iowa, in 1854, and in 1856 settled in Carroll county, and has resided there ever since. When they went to Carroll they took up a homestead and went through all the privations of pioneer life in making of it an attractive home. Our Mr. Colclo began to earn money on his own account at an early day by farm work, and he has a distinct recollection of the way he earned his first dollar by following a man who marked out the rows with a single shovel plow, the boy dropping the corn by hand, and it was then covered by a man with a hoe. He taught school in the country, worked on the farm, and worked his way through the Iowa Agricultural college, graduating with the class of '77. He was a member of the Bachelors' Debating society and filled the position of president of that society, which was one of the

leading literary organizations of the college. He was also a member of the Delta Tau Delta Greek Letter society, and was an active working member of this society, and never failed to perform his part therein. Mr. Colclo was elected county superintendent of schools in the year 1881 and served three and a half years, resigning to accept the Carroll postoffice under President Cleveland's first administration. He held this appointment from 1885 to 1888, and resigned it to again accept the county superintendency, which he held for two years, then engaged in the newspaper work by purchasing a half interest in the *Carroll Sentinel*, one of the best weekly papers in

the state. He and his partner, J. L. Powers, proceeded to carry on the daily which had been started by their predecessors, but they found after six years of experience that the town was not large enough to sustain a daily, and it was discontinued. The paper is now a semi-weekly, issued Mondays and Thursdays. Mr. Colclo cast his first vote for Samuel J. Tilden for president, and has been enthusiastic in the support of the democratic party ever since. He was a delegate to the democratic national convention in Chicago in 1896. He is an advocate of bimetallism and supported Bryan. He is still hopeful of the success of the cause.

He is a member of the Masonic Lodge
and the Eastern Star and the Knights of
Pythias. By early training and associations he is a Presbyterian. He was married November 21, 1890, to Mrs. Sadie E.
Snyder.

———

VOGT, LOUIS, at present engaged in
the practice of law at George, Iowa, was
born at Rockton, Ill., January 3, 1870, and
is, therefore, but 29 years of age. As his
name would indicate, he is a German, his
parents both being descendants of honored
members of that sturdy race. When 4

years old he came to Iowa with his parents,
who settled at Shell Rock in Butler county.
Later they removed to Sanborn, O'Brien
county, where the boyhood days of Mr.
Vogt were passed. He commenced business for himself at the age of 11, as bootblack, which was continued, in connection
with his school work, for three years; also
acted as messenger boy and did any and
all odd jobs which he could find to do. By
this means he was enabled to enter the
Northern Iowa Normal school at Algona,
when 16, where he remained one year. He
then secured a position as brakeman on
the railroad, and for two years served in
that dangerous and arduous work. He
later learned the printer's trade, and when

19 years of age, conducted a weekly newspaper at Lake City, Col. His knowledge
of typesetting served him well in later
years, for it was by working spare hours
in a printing office that he paid his way
through one of the leading law schools of
the country. We have reference to the
Northern Indiana School of Law, at Valparaiso, from which he graduated June 3,
1891. During his class days he was a member of the Star Literary society, taking an
active part in the debates and entertain-
ments of that organization. In 1891, he
commenced the practice of law at Clarkes,
Neb., but later went to Silver Creek, Neb.,
and in the fall of 1892 returned to Iowa
and engaged in the newspaper business at
Sanborn, where he established the *Sanborn
Sun*. In 1894, however, he resumed the
practice of law at George, where he has
built up a lucrative practice.

Politically, Mr. Vogt is, and has ever
been, a democrat. He was a candidate for
county attorney of Merrick county, Neb.,
on that ticket in 1892, and ran for the same
office in Lyon county, Iowa, in 1896, but
was defeated in both instances because of
the decided republican strength in those
counties. He was married to Miss Jennie
McKeever, of Sanborn, June 3, 1896.

———

FOWLER, PHILIP LAFFER, president
of the American Mutual Fire Insurance
company of Des Moines, and for five years
secretary of the Iowa State Agricultural
society, was born in Sandyville, Tuscarawas county, Ohio, September 3, 1845.
He is the son of Lorenzo Dow Fowler and
his wife, Joanna Laffer Fowler. Mr.
Fowler was born in Holmes county, Ohio,
November 1, 1814, and Mrs. Fowler was
born in Campbell county, Ky., February
24, 1817. Thomas Fowler, the father of L.
D. Fowler, was in the war of 1812, going
from Baltimore, Md. The family was engaged in farming in Holmes county, Ohio,
for a number of years previous to 1853,
when they moved to Sandyville, and kept
hotel until they moved to Iowa in April,
1854, and entered several hundred of acres
of land in Clarke county, and purchased the
only hotel in the town of Osceola. It consisted of two hewn log houses. He was
building a two-story frame hotel when
he was accidentally killed in the sawmill
that was sawing the joists for the new
building. His ancestors, on the father's
side, came from England. Mrs. Fowler's
father, Peter Laffer, was blown up on a

steamboat making its trial trip on the Ohio river near Marietta, the latter part of the year 1816. Mrs. Fowler's family, on the mother's side, descended from Christopher Taylor, a Quaker, who was connected with William Penn in the early history of Philadelphia.

Philip L. Fowler attended the common schools and was a student in J. H. L. Scott's high school in Osceola. At the close of his school days in June, 1863, he was employed in the office of A. H. Burrows, clerk of the district court of Clarke county, until 1864, when he enlisted in the Forty-sixth Iowa volunteers, under Col. D. B. Henderson, now member of congress from the Third district. After the war he was for several years deputy clerk of courts and then a bookkeeper in the Osceola bank. For some years prior to 1873 he engaged in farming and stock raising, and in that year was elected auditor of Clarke county on the anti-monopoly ticket, supported by the grangers. He held that office four years, then returned to farming and stock raising, making a specialty of roadster horses and Jersey cattle. In 1891 he was elected a director of the Iowa State Agricultural society and in January, 1894, was elected secretary, an office which he held and filled with credit to himself, and profit to the society, for five years. During his administration, the society emerged from a heavy debt incurred mostly by giving a state fair in 1893, the year of the World's Fair. Mr. Fowler is a member of the Odd Fellows and Grand Army lodges. He acted with the democrats from 1873 until 1894, and

since then he has been an active republican, and is a member of the Grant club, of Des Moines. Mr. Fowler is a fine specimen of manhood, physically and mentally, and his mental processes are deliberate, but clear and decisive, so far as his actions are concerned. So when the democratic party erected its 16 to 1 silver idol, P. L. Fowler studied the question quietly, but deeply, and his reason and judgment united in a revolt. There was no noisy protest or outcry, but in a few weeks he was an applicant for membership in the Grant club, the leading republican club of the state. That was all there was to it so far as outward show would indicate, but any one who is curious to know why he changed his political affiliations, will get a frank and very clear reason. He is genial, courteous and social, and has a friend in every intimate acquaintance. He has belonged to the Methodist church since 1855. Mr. Fowler was married March 9, 1871, in Osceola, to Margaret A. McKee, daughter of Prof. W. A. McKee, who has been a teacher for over fifty years, now a resident of Knoxville.

They have six children: Amy J., born December 10, 1875; Laura A., born March 14, 1879; Margaret M., born January 13, 1882; Mary L., born November 11, 1886; Martha, born April 30, 1889; and Philip Lorenzo, born May 17, 1895.

In addition to the presidency of the American Mutual Fire Insurance company, Mr. Fowler is vice-president of the Mutual Windstorm and Mutual Hailstorm Insurance associations, two companies organized in 1898, under the same management.

END OF VOLUME I.

CPSIA information can be obtained
at www.ICGtesting.com
Printed in the USA
BVHW062300051118
532208BV00015B/1163/P